STARTING WITH INGREDIENTS

BAKING

STARTING WITH INGREDIENTS

BAKING

QUINTESSENTIAL RECIPES
FOR THE WAY WE **REALLY** BAKE

ALIZA GREEN

RUNNING PRESS
PHILADELPHIA · LONDON

This book is dedicated to my brother,
Joel Moshe Green,
whose sweet, loving nature was a gift to all
who knew him during his too-short life.

Zikhrono livrakha.
("May his memory be a blessing.")

9 8 7 6 5 4 3 2 1
Digit on the right indicates the number of this printing

Library of Congress Control Number: 2008921272
ISBN 978-0-7624-3158-8

Cover and interior design by Amanda Richmond
Edited by Diana C. von Glahn and Kristen Green Wiewora
Photography by Steve Legato
Food styling by Aliza Green

Special thanks to Sarah O'Brien, Mark Costello, Richard Kelly,
Jon Weed, Donna Gambale, Nathan Perry, and Bouvier Servillas

Typography: Nofret and Agenda

Running Press Book Publishers
2300 Chestnut Street
Philadelphia, PA 19103-4371

Visit us on the web!
www.runningpresscooks.com

CONTENTS

An Introduction
to Baking ...10

Helpful Charts
...38

Alcohols
...47

Almonds
...65

Anise, Fennel,
& Caraway ...81

Apples
...95

Apricots
...113

Bananas &
Plantains ...125

Barley & Malt
...136

Berries:
Blackberries, Blueberries,
Strawberries, &
Raspberries ...149

Brazil Nuts
& Cashews
...171

Buckwheat
...181

Butter & Other
Animal Fats
...191

Candied Fruits
...221

Carrots
...235

Cheese
...243

Chemical
Leaveners ...279

Cherries
...293

Chestnuts
...309

Chocolate
...321

Cinnamon
...343

Coconut
...355

Coffee
...365

Corn &
Cornmeal
...381

Cranberries
...395

Currants &
Gooseberries
...405

Dates ...417

Eggs ...427

Figs ...447

Flowers
...459

Gelatin
...475

Ginger
...485

Hazelnuts
...497

Honey
...511

Lemons
& Citrons
...525

Limes
...541

Maple
...557

Milk, Cream,
& Buttermilk
...569

Oats
...579

Oil for Frying
& Baking

Oranges &
Tangerines
...591

Peaches &
Nectarines
...607

Peanuts
...621

Pears
...633

Pecans
...647

Persimmons
...657

Pine Nuts
...667

Pineapple
...679

Pistachios
...689

Plums & Prunes
...701

Poppy Seeds
...713

Potatoes
...721

Pumpkin
& Squash
...731

Quince
...745

Raisins &
Dried Currants
...755

Rice ...765

Rye ...780

Sesame Seeds
...794

Sugar, Caramel,
& Molasses
...803

Vanilla Beans
...825

Walnuts &
Black Walnuts
...837

Wheat &
Semolina
...849

Yeast
...871

Yogurt
...893

Index
...906

ACKNOWLEDGEMENTS

My thanks go to all the willing tasters of the seemingly endless array of baked goods that I brought to parties, potlucks, and other gatherings, served at home, and distributed to neighbors. So many generous people helped me gather these recipes. I could never have written this ambitious book without the help of many people.

Clare Pelino of Profile Public Relations and ProLiterary Agency worked with me to bring this book to a wide audience. Clare's thoroughness and encouragement through the whole process helped me to make this book a reality while her highly competent staff put together my tour and arranged for media interviews so that people all over the country could learn about this book. Clare, once again, I couldn't have done it without you.

Three skillful and thorough editors worked on this book including Diana von Glahn, who also did a fantastic job of editing the first *Starting with Ingredients*, Julie Stillman, an extremely detail-oriented baking book specialist, and Kristen Wiewora, who took over the formidable task of editing this book without losing a beat. Designer Amanda Richmond made the book both easy to use and pleasing to the eye, and she's great fun to work with. Jon Anderson, Publisher at Running Press, had the vision to see *Starting with Ingredients* as a "great big book" and brought me this exciting baking book project. As a true food lover and highly respected publisher, he made us all believe in this book and in Running Press. Craig Herman, Associate Publisher at Running Press, shared his great skill and experience, love of food, and caring personality to put together the fabulous marketing program for this book. Food photographer extraordinaire Steve Legato, with whom I've worked on seven books, did the superb job that I've come to expect from him, all with his wry sense of humor and easy-going personality.

Betty Kaplan, a highly professional cooking teacher, was my life-saving tester, assistant, and general cheerleader, who never got overwhelmed even on days when we made eight or even ten new dishes. She didn't ever lose her cool on those hot summer days when the air-conditioning kept blowing the fuse. The success of this book and its recipes are very much due to Betty's help.

Maria Teresa Berdondini, of the custom travel agency, Tuscany, by Tuscans, introduced me to Tuscany's top artisanal Italian chocolatiers, and shared her prized Torta Caprese recipe. Maria Teresa knows everyone in Italy in food and travel and is incredibly knowledgeable about my beloved Italian cuisine.

Velia de Angelis, who I met by lucky chance while she was working for the summer at a restaurant on the Amalfi Coast, and now co-proprietor of La Champagneria in Orvieto, spent several days with me in Orvieto showing me how to make some of her best recipes and introducing me to other baker friends. Velia also convinced her friends, the proprietors of Amalfi's superb Pasticceria Pansa, to part with precious recipes.

Aglaia Kremezi, Greek cooking authority and co-proprietor of Kea Artisanal, shared many of her outstanding Greek country recipes and techniques with me when I attended her cooking and culture program held on the island of Kea. I am so lucky that I got the chance to learn about Greek cooking and baking from her.

I had a marvelous though too-short visit in Turkey with another cooking friend, Didem Ornek Ertan, whom I met when she attended one of my cooking classes for the first *Starting with Ingredients*. Didem, her mother-in-law Sadiye Ertan, her sister, Sinem Sagel, and her parents, Senay and Rahmi Ornek, all showed me why Turkish hospitality is legendary while also patiently working with me until I was able to recreate their baking specialties on my own.

AN INTRODUCTION TO BAKING:

INGREDIENTS, MEASURING, EQUIPMENT, AND TECHNIQUES

From my earliest attempts and memorable failures at baking starting about age eleven, I've been fascinated and challenged by taking simple ingredients like flour, butter, sugar, and eggs and transforming them into something completely different like Crispy Lemon–Cinnamon Cookies (page 351), German Butter Cake (page 216), or Milk Chocolate and Almond Malt Cake (page 146). Because I was lucky enough to live and travel in many places during my childhood and teens, I got an early exposure to food and baked goods in their many irresistible forms. I was a risk taker even back then. Once I had the idea of mixing cookie dough with green food coloring. The cookies baked up to such an unappetizing color that I couldn't bring myself to eat them!

I began using my mother's holiday and party recipes for date–nut bars, raisin–walnut rugelach, and New York cheesecake with farmer cheese, sour cream, and crunchy zwieback crust, (see *Starting with Ingredients*). I explored her small but well-chosen cookbook library, including the stalwart *Settlement Cookbook*, first published in 1901, and Elizabeth David's *A Book of Mediterranean Food*, published in 1958. I soon got my own first grown-up cookbook, Craig Claiborne's *An Herb and Spice Cookbook*, published in 1963. I used Claiborne's title for my own small catering company (Herb & Spice Catering) where I continued to bake, making quiches, cookies, tarts, and cakes, like the creamy chocolate Rigo Jancsi (page 333), one of my signature dishes back then, now working from precious books by Julia Child, Dione Lucas, Claudia Roden, and Diana Kennedy.

As a child in Holland, I gorged myself on so many ultra-rich Dutch butter cookies, I can't bear to eat them even today, though I have no problem overdoing it with aromatic Dutch Speculaas cookies (page 789). In my teens, I discovered Tunisian yo-yo deep-fried by a street vendor in Paris and delighted in having as many crusty baguettes with sweet butter and preserves as I could manage to eat at the student hostel. I feasted on flaky baklava dripping with sugary syrup in Athens and pale, puffy meringues (page 000) in Tel Aviv. Just off an endless train trip from Istanbul (a far cry from the luxurious and legendary Orient Express I fantasized about), I couldn't get enough fragrant focaccia (pages 725 and 788), still warm from the oven in Genoa, Italy.

In my early twenties, I navigated the twisted byways of the Old City of Jerusalem in the early hours of the morning to get hot pita breads just out of the oven. I munched on soft rolled up lamb-topped lahmacun in Istanbul and daintily demolished exquisite fresh fruit tarts in Provence. I studied Italian and traveled many times to Italy in my quest to cook authentic Italian food, learning straight from the "horse's mouth," or in this case my own horse-like mouth, about gianduia (page 508), biscotti (pages 305, 489, 503, and 719), taralli (page 584), Torta Rustica (page 861), Sicilian cassata and cannoli (see *Starting with Ingredients*), and carefully constructed pizzas, not neglecting a few side trips to France for equally wonderful pissaladière (see *Starting with Ingredients*), brioches (page 470), financiers (page 215), and profiteroles (page 287). In Quebec, with my limited funds, I splurged on a rare restaurant meal of yellow split pea soup followed by richly indulgent Maple Bread Pudding (page 554).

Unlike many chefs, I've always considered cooking and baking to be intertwined, perhaps because I've enjoyed both cooking and baking from an early age. From my first restaurant job in the seventies at Under the Blue Moon in Philadelphia's gracious Chestnut Hill section, I baked as well as cooked, making homemade baguette breads, dacquoise (page 377), Queen of Sheba cake (from Julia Child), and frozen coffee toffee crunch pie (I wish I had the recipe for that one). At The Garden, the popular country French restaurant with a lovely outdoor garden (and hellishly hot kitchen in the summer), I learned to make patisserie like Tarte Tatin (pages 517, 616 and 753). I worked with the puff pastry that we made from scratch and served up offerings like Exotic Mushroom Puff Pastry Pillows (page 207), Peach Galette (page 618), and Caramel Fruit Tart (page 830). While working as sous-chef at the Barclay Hotel, I rolled out endless batches of homemade all-butter croissant dough, working in one of the uncountable walk-in refrigerators in that Rittenhouse Square dowager, an effort that helped me work out the technique for the similar laminated (layered) dough that I used to make my Danish pastry (page 273).

At Ristorante DiLullo, I always helped with the baking along with my chef work, making big batches of Zuppa Inglese colored red with Alkhermes liqueur (see *Starting with Ingredients*), hazelnut-chocolate Florentine Zuccotto (page 58), along with long, thin (kind of like those stylish Italian women) Garlic-Sesame Grissini (page 885) to serve at the table. For the California-Mediterranean menu at Apropos Bistro, I made wood-oven baked Arugula and Roasted Tomato Pizza (page 888) and White Pizza with Broccoli Rabe (page 266), along with California Walnut-Rosemary Bread (page 844), Buckwheat Cinnamon-Raisin Bread (page 188), and California Apricot Cheesecake (page 118).

At the White Dog Café, I ran the small basement kitchen twenty-four hours a day so we could produce our own breads (like Seeded Multi-Grain Sourdough Bread, page 186), muffins (like Morning Glory Muffins with Carrots, Asian Pears and Ginger, page 240 and Blueberry-Walnut Streusel Muffins, page 164), and homey American-style desserts like Hot Apple-Cranberry Crisp (page 403) and White Peach and Sour Cream Pie (page 615), using succulent, locally grown fruit. As consultant to the Omni Hotel at Independence Park, I made regional specialties like Persimmon and Black Walnut Bread (page 666), Bourbon-Spice Pumpkin Cake (page 742), and Philadelphia Sticky Buns (see *Starting with Ingredients*). I planned the menu for the Dock Street Brewing Company featuring home-made breads (after all, beer is just a liquid form of bread) like Buttermilk-Sourdough White Sandwich Bread (page 726) and Black Olive Herb Bread (page 889).

Not long ago, I spent more than a year working on the concept, menu, kitchen, and recipes for a new kosher restaurant (www.maxanddavids.com) where I could serve no dairy products. I became interested in oil-based (rather than butter-based) baking recipes from the olive oil-growing regions of the Mediterranean. So, whether you keep kosher and want some great *pareve* (neither meat nor dairy) sweet cakes and cookies, have a dairy intolerance, or just want to try some great-tasting baked goods enriched with olive oil, try some of these recipes: Siennese Cavallucci (chewy fruited lozenge-shaped cookies, page 224), Torta Boscaiola (Italian Chestnut Flour and Hazelnut Cake, page 319), Torta Sbrisolona alla Lombarda (Lombardian Crumbly Cake, page 390), Torta di Miele (Italian Jewish Honey Cake, page 000), Kourambiedes with Olive Oil (page 522), Spanish Orange and Olive Oil Cake (page 586), Maltese Kwaresimal Cookies (page 599 and 603), Lemon Poppy Seed Biscotti (page 719), Spanish Sesame-Anise Cookies (page 799), and Sambuca and Candied Orange Tozzetti (page 90).

As a longtime chef, consultant, and now food writer, I have focused on knowing the ingredients I'm using: what they are, where they come from, and how they're used in different parts of the world. I've approached baking the same way: choosing sixty-two ingredients that are important in baking for this book, including the requisite wheat, butter, sugar, eggs, apples, almonds, walnuts, chocolate, and vanilla along with more unexpected ingredients like persimmons, Brazil nuts, chestnuts, red and black currants, poppy seeds, quince, and rye. I've also included chapters about ingredients that we commonly use in baking but may not understand that well, including chemical leaveners (baking soda, baking powder, and strong-smelling baker's ammonia), yeast, and gelatin. It's worthwhile exploring these somewhat mysterious ingredients to understand how they work.

My driving force in writing this book has been my inveterate curiosity: these are all specialties I wanted to decipher—to know how they work, who eats them and when, and to see how far I could push the envelope to make the results lighter, easier to work with, a better batch size, or just

plain tastier. I collected recipes from friends, bakeries, and restaurant pastry chefs, and traveled afar to taste dishes I had only read about. In Turkey, I learned about the many yogurt-based doughs, including Baked Cheese Turnovers: Puaça (page 899), Pide (with Feta Cheese and Egg, page 900 and with Tahini and Grape Molasses, page 901), and the Sesame-Coated Bread Rings: Susamli Simit (page 798) sold by vendors on practically every street corner in Istanbul.

I learned how to work with phyllo pastry (and though I had a lesson from a mistress of hand-stretch phyllo, I realized it's an art that would take many years of practice to perfect). I worked with this versatile dough to make sweet pastries like the lemon-syrup drenched Lemon Galataboureko (page 532), the tender Greek Phyllo Pumpkin Pie: Kolokythopita (page 739), the hazelnut and candied carrot-filled Turkish Carrot Pastry Rolls: Havis (page 241), and the Quince and Cherry Strudel (page 751). I also used phyllo to make savory pastries like the Greek Eggplant and Walnut Phyllo Rolls (page 842) and the Country-Style Greek Greens Pie (page 262).

Almost all the recipes come from the home baking traditions of the world and are easily created by the home cook who hasn't had any special training. In this book, I've drawn from the traditions of Argentina, Aruba, Australia, Austria, Brazil, France (including Alsace, Corsica and Provence), Canada (including Québec), Curaçao, Denmark, Egypt, England, Greece, Honduras, Hungary, India, Ireland, Israel, Italy (including Lombardy, Piedmont, Sardinia, Sicily, Tuscany, and more), Mexico, Morocco, Slovenia, Spain (including Catalonia and Majorca), Sweden, Switzerland, Tunisia, Turkey, and the Ukraine.

I have not neglected America's own rich baking traditions and have included regional favorites like the Lady Baltimore Cake from Charleston, South Carolina (page 452); a Rose-Scented Angel Food Cake first popularized in St. Louis (page 467); a hearty New England Cranberry-Maple-Raisin Pie, using native American cranberries and maple syrup (page 552); an adaptation of the "Indian Pudding" Cake that hearkens back to Colonial New England (page 286); and a New Haven–Style White Clam Pizza, although not baked in the giant coal-burning oven of the original (page 886).

From my home state of Pennsylvania comes a Pennsylvania Dutch Corn Pie (page 886), and two sweet pies made inexpensively with pantry ingredients: the Amish Black Walnut Oatmeal Pie (page 575) and the Amish Peanut Butter Cream Pie (page 626). The fruit-laden Tangerine Kiss-Me Cake (page 602) comes from Florida; the dense, creamy Heirloom Sweet Potato-Praline Pie (page 651) from Oklahoma; the Biscochitos (page 218), super-flaky with fresh-rendered lard, are a Christmas specialty of New Mexico; while the Calas: Rice Fritters (page 773) from New Orleans can be traced back to West African traditions.

I've explored the Ashkenazi Jewish baking traditions of my own heritage in recipes like the Apple Cake (page 105), here made with Fuji apples; the Kasha-Mushroom Knishes (page 183);

Teiglach (page 587), also known as *cicerchiata*—little chickpeas—in Italy; the Onion Poppy Seed Kichels, (page 715) a recipe of my great-grandmother's; and the Black Kugelhopf (page 717) from Alsace. I've learned to make some fascinating offerings derived from Sephardic and Italkeni (Italian-Jewish) traditions, including the cashew-laden Sephardic Stuffed Monkey (page 176) from England by way of Portugal and Brazil; the sponge cake called Pan di Spagna (page 441) from Italy by way of Spain; the flaky Sesame Spinach Borekas (page 796) from Turkey also by way of Spain; the honey and walnut–filled Sfratti di Pitigliano (page 520), a recipe I got by traveling to that Tuscan hill town known as *La Picola Gerusalemme* (Little Jerusalem); and the moist Torta di Miele (Italian Jewish Honey Cake, page 522), chunky with golden raisins and walnuts.

For this book, I've chosen to define "baking recipes" as broadly as possible, so all the more than 350 recipes fall into one of these categories: sweet baked goods like cookies, cakes, muffins, pies, tarts, meringues, and quick breads; or savory baked goods like pizza, breads, crackers, breadsticks, and filled tarts and pies. Some dishes are made from doughs that are cooked by other methods, because in many places, home cooks don't have ovens. They may be deep-fried like the Spanish Honey-Dipped Spiral Pastries: Hojuelas (page 585) and the Sicilian/North African fusion Sesame Honey Cones (page 800). They may be cooked in a wafer iron, once heated over an open fire in one of the earliest methods of baking cook-

ies, as for the Pizzelle "of the Angels" (page 91), originally from Puglia.

The Tunisian Semolina Bread (page 864) is cooked on a stovetop griddle and I've used a grill in place of the tandoor oven that none of us are likely to have to make the Indian Naan Bread and to make the Kea Stuffed Griddle Bread (page 144). The Austrian Apricot Dumplings (page 122) are made from sweet pasta dough stuffed with apricot halves, boiled, drained, and then tossed with brown butter and sugared bread crumbs. The Spanish Baked Quince with Pine Nuts and Dried Fruit (page 754) is one of the few dishes in the book made with no dough at all, just slow-baked fruits and nuts. The Plantain Empanadas with Black Bean and Añejo Cheese Filling (page 129) are made from an unusual dough: just roasted and mashed starchy plantains.

I've also include various basic recipes including all sorts of sweet and savory pastry doughs, various fruit sauces, pastry cream fillings, and homemade liqueurs. Look for recipes for sweet pantry items that, although often purchased, you can make yourself, like Dulce de Leche (page 566), Candied Walnuts (page 847), Homemade Gianduia (page 508), Hazelnut Praline (page 509), Candied Citrus Peel (page 225), and Speculaas Spices (page 353). Savory recipes for Spanish Sofrito (page 882), Tunisian Chakchouka (page 865), Egyptian Dukkah (page 890), Spicy Harissa Sauce (page 866), and Caramelized Sweet Onions (page 860) are called for in other baked goods, but you'll find yourself using them again and again. Because I like to think

I'm frugal at heart (though truthfully I can be quite extravagant at times), I have included several recipes that use leftover bread like the indulgent Québéçoise Maple Bread Pudding (page 554) and the outrageously rich Papiamento Bread Pudding (page 562), along with a Plum Gingersnap Brown Betty (page 708) perfect for using up leftover gingersnaps, whether homemade (Swedish Pepparkakor, page 493) or purchased.

Although the majority of the recipes in this book tend toward the sweeter side of things, I do enjoy savory baking and have included recipes for interesting breads like the aromatic Moroccan Sesame-Anise Bread (page 87), the tender, slightly tangy Sauerkraut Rye Bread (page 784), the hearty, moist Guinness Oatmeal Bread (page 574), the Turkish Seeded Hazelnut Bread (page 502) for hazelnut lovers like me, and the wonderful Turkish Savory Cornbread: Misir Ekmegi (page 388) with feta cheese and olives. A slightly sweet Honduran Coconut Bread: Pan de Coco (page 360); two chestnut breads from Corsica: the quick Chestnut Cornbread (page 318) and the yeast-raised Corsican Chestnut Bread (page 317); the golden-orange Cucuzzara: Durum Wheat Bread with Squash, Tomatoes, Onions, and Peppers (page 736) from Puglia, Italy are other uncommon bread choices.

Look for savory tarts and pies like the rib-sticking Québéçoise Tourtière with Mushrooms (page 210) and the equally hearty Steak, Guinness, and Mushroom Pie (page 213). There are recipes for several quiche-like custard-filled tortes, including the meltingly rich, slightly bitter Radicchio and Fontina Torta (page 260), a French Roquefort, Apple, and Leek Tart (page 103), a Savory Eggplant and Spiced Almond Tart (page 72) made with goat cheese, along with an unusual but absolutely delicious Sardinian Potato Torta: Coccoi Prena (page 728), and the classic Smoked Salmon and Spinach Quiche (page 434).

The enormous variety of empanadas, the handy meal in the hand known from Spain to Argentina, is represented by Chicken-Cheese Empanadas (page 264) and Spanish Tuna Empanadas with Sofrito (page 881). If you'd like to try your hand at focaccia, try the Grape, Gorgonzola, and Walnut Focaccia (page 788) or the Herbed Focaccia with Goat Cheese, Red Onion, and Black Olives (page 725). There are also boiled then baked mini bagel-like snack rings called Taralli (page 584), hard and crunchy Greek Barley Rings (page 140), great for dunking in juicy tomato salad, and wonderful Rye and Rosemary Breadsticks with Lemon (page 783).

So often baking, especially of sweets, revolves around holidays and celebrations. The Sicilian Cuccidati (page 457 and the Swedish Coconut Dream Cookies (page 361) are both made for Christmas. The Syrian Mahmoul (page 466) and the elaborate Moroccan B'stilla of Chicken (page 436) are made in large quantities by legions of (female) relatives for weddings. The Jewish Honey-Poppy Seed Hamantaschen (page 716) are a specialty of the springtime holiday of Purim. The Dutch Speculaas with Rye (page 789) are associated with the feast of "Sint Nicolaas" or Saint

Nicholas, the original Santa Claus, celebrated on the fifth or sixth of December. The Aruban Cashew Cake (page 178) shows up at every local celebration.

The Torta Pasqualina Genovese (page 438) is made to celebrate Easter and the delicate greens of early spring in Liguria, Italy. Eating Hot Cross Buns (page 230) on Good Friday has been an English tradition for hundreds of years. The Greek cookies called Kourambiedes (page 586), here made here with olive oil, are also known as wedding cookies, while the M'hancha: The Serpent (page 695), makes a dramatic centerpiece for a Moroccan celebration feast. The Tahini Cake: Tahinopita (page 802) comes from the Greek tradition of Lent baking, because it is made without any animal products, including butter or eggs, as are the orange and olive oil–based Kwaresimal Cookies (page 603) from the island of Malta.

Because a good friend of mine is gluten intolerant, I became interested in gluten-free baking, using substitutes like potato starch, ground nuts, chestnut flour, and even puréed white beans to provide structure. I ended up with wonderful desserts and baked goods like the Andalusian Bittersweet Chocolate–Sherry Cake (page 55), the Majorcan Lemon–Almond Cake (page 77), the Piedmontese Mocha–Chestnut Torta (page 314), the White Bean, Chestnut, and Apricot Cake alla Povera (page 316), the White Chocolate, Hazelnut, and Espresso Dacquoise (page 377), and the Torta Boscaiola: Italian Chestnut Flour and Hazelnut Cake (page 319).

Through travels to Brazil (with a group of chefs) and to Venezuela (to research my *Field Guide to Seafood*), I learned to make unusual but delicious desserts and baked goods like the Ruby Grapefruit–Orange Brazil Nut Torte (page 174) and the Brazil–Nut and Guava Sandwich Cookies (Docinhos do Pará) (page 175). On one of the many visits I made to Aruba (where I worked on a cookbook project), I learned to make two typical dishes: Aruban Pastechi (meat-filled turnovers, page 760) and Pan Dushi (anise-scented sweet bread, page 891). The Tunisian owners of the restaurant (Apropos American Bistro) where I once cheffed taught me to make the Makroud: Tunisian Semolina Cookies (page 422), while a Moroccan chef I worked with many years ago first taught me how to make the elaborate and exquisite B'stilla of Chicken (page 436).

To research this book, I was lucky enough to travel to Italy, Greece, and Turkey, where I visited markets, bakeries, pastry shops, food shows, and restaurants, and cooked with friends. I picked up some of the most wonderful recipes, including the unusual but moist and delicious 'mpanatigghi Siciliani: small turnovers made from lard dough and filled with veal (!) and chocolate (page 331), which I tasted at an artisanal chocolate fair in Florence and just had to make for myself (better yet would be to visit Sicily . . .). The Brustengolo (page 389) is a specialty of Umbria, which I learned about from antique fruit tree–rescuer, Isabella dalla Ragione.

I picked up a bag of the ultra-crunchy Biscotti Rococò (page 536) at Pasticceria Pansa in Amalfi, which kept me going (with the help of a couple of pit stops for espresso) on the long drive in my rented car from Naples to Spoleto in Umbria. I found the recipe for the Bitter Chocolate-Hazelnut Torta with Pears (page 645) in an Italian women's magazine I happened to pick up on the train. My friend and fellow chef, Velia de Angelis, prepared the Italian Bittersweet Chocolate-Orange Torta (page 331) for me at her friend's small bakery in Orvieto. The Torta Pasqualina Genovese (page 438) came from an all-too-brief visit to the fascinating port city of Genoa, where fresh herbs flavor everything from pasta dough to fillings, savory pies, fish, and sauces (think of pesto alla Genovese). I'm definitely going back there again!

In Greece, I took a week-long cooking course from charming and knowledgeable Greek culinary authority, cooking teacher, and friend, Aglaia Kremezi. She taught me to make recipes like her savory Greek Eggplant and Walnut Phyllo Rolls (page 842); a Country-Style Greek Greens Pie (page 262), filled with all sorts of wild and seasonal greens picked in her lovely garden; a chewy, crunchy Greek Country Barley Bread (page 142) baked in a Dutch oven; the fabulous Kea Stuffed Griddle Breads (page 144), made from the same dough; along with an adaptation of her Greek Cornmeal Raisin Bread (page 762) that I found in her great big picture book, *The Foods of Greece*, and kept making until I got it right.

In Turkey, I learned to make the Lahmacun: Armenian Lamb Flatbread (page 866) that I lived on thirty years ago when I visited Turkey and had little money but a big appetite. I made the canoe-shaped Turkish Pide (page 900), filled with Feta and Eggs with my cooking friend Didem Ertan and her family at a wood-oven fired bakery near her Turkish home in Çesme on the lovely Aegean Coast. While staying with her gracious parents near Izmir, I learned to make Turkish Goat's Milk Rice Pudding: Sutlaç (page 774), a specialty of her mother's made with goat's milk that we picked up from a nearby farm. We made Tahini and Grape Molasses Pide (page 901) baked in the outdoor wood-burning oven that is the pride of her father. With her mother, I learned to make wonderful small Turkish Baked Cheese Turnovers: Puaça (page 898) and delicate Lor Kurabiyesi, ricotta cookies rolled in sesame seeds (page 272). While taking a day-long cooking class in Istanbul, I learned to make sweet and tender Turkish Semolina Sponge Cookies (page 869). The beautiful green Pistachio Bird's Nest Pastries (page 693) I spotted in a bakery window on the Asian side of Istanbul inspired me to recreate them.

Other friends shared recipes with me, including the Torta Caprese: Bittersweet Chocolate-Almond Cake (page 336), adapted from a recipe from travel expert and cooking teacher Maria Teresa Berdondini; and the equally enticing White Chocolate-Lemon Torta Caprese (page 78), a specialty of my friend from Orvieto, Velia de Angelis. Mary Ellen Hatch, a respected professional pastry chef and bread baker in Philadelphia, shared her recipe for the Brown Sugar-Pecan Sweet Dream Cookies (page 821). I adapted the Potica: Slovenian Honey-Walnut Ring (page 845) from a recipe of television producer Lee Butala's mother; the Bienenstich: German Bee-Sting Cake came from the mother of a new German friend (page 523). I adapted Le Bec-Fin's Fruited Walnut Bread (page 843) from a recipe in the book that I co-authored over ten years ago. My longtime Portuguese friend, Maria Mata, generously parted with the recipe for her deep-fried Port-wine flavored Cuscurols (page 588).

The recipe for the lusty Woodfire Grill Duck Confit Pizza (page 859) was given to me by my Atlanta chef friend, Michael Tuohy, although you'll have to travel there to taste it baked in his wood-burning oven at Woodfire Grill. The multi-talented baker, real estate developer, and cookware importer, Taieb Dridi, a native of Tunisia, spent an afternoon teaching me how to make the unusual Semolina Griddle Bread (page 864) so I could make it myself almost as well as him. My invaluable testing assistant and all-around cheerleader, Betty Kaplan, shared her recipe for the colorful Cranberry-Caramel Pecan Tart (page 654), a perfect make-ahead dessert for Thanksgiving dinner or a holiday party. I'm lucky that cooks and bakers who love to eat also love to share their creations as much as I do.

Although the great majority of the recipes in this book come from home baking traditions and are easy to make, I have included some more elaborate desserts that are assembled from several different component recipes, because there are times when you really want to wow your family and/or guests. When you're feeling ambitious, try the fabulous Lemon-Blackberry Bavarese (page 481); the ultra-lemony Babàs al Limoncello Pansa (page 56) from Amalfi, Italy; the eye-catching, dome-shaped Florentine Chocolate-Nut Zuccotto (page 58); the exquisite Torta di Zabaglione (page 480), adapted from Harry's Bar in Venice; the White Chocolate, Hazelnut, and Espresso Dacquoise (page 377), my own adaptation of the original, balancing luscious but sweet white chocolate with toasted hazelnuts and bitter espresso; the colorfully fruity English Summer Fruit Pudding with Lemon and Mint (page 415); or the Frangelico Mousse Cake with Gianduia-Rice Crunch (page 771), an indulgence well worth trying.

I hope you use this book to learn more about the ingredients you're working with, enabling you to save money and buy better, in season when possible, and to understand more about "the way things work" (someone already used that title unfortunately). This book contains hundreds of varied and wonderful recipes appealing to every palate drawn from the home traditions of bakers in many far-flung places for you to discover, along with lots of American favorites, personal creations, and recipes shared with me by many enthusiastic food loving friends.

Please write to me at www.alizagreen.com with your comments (good and bad), questions, and requests.

INGREDIENT STANDARDS

BUTTER

I always use unsalted butter, both because I prefer its sweet flavor and because unsalted butter must be fresher than salted butter, because the salt acts as a preservative. You may substitute part salted butter in many recipes, but be sure to omit any added salt.

For creaming, it's best to have the butter at room temperature. For cutting into pastry doughs, it's best to have the butter cut into bits then chilled in the freezer until firm.

I occasionally call for European-style high-fat butter, like Plugra from America or various imports, but American-style butter can always be substituted. (See page 192 for more about butter.)

CHOCOLATE

Although I do love to use elite chocolates like Valrhona from France, Lindt from Switzerland, and El Rey from Venezuela, I have relied on American-made Guittard and Scharffen Berger along with the good quality and very reasonably priced Belgian chocolate sold in 500-gram blocks under Trader Joe's own name to keep my food budget somewhere within reason. I always use reddish-brown Dutch process cocoa, either Droste or the excellent one made by Valrhona. Both work beautifully. (See page 322 for more about chocolate, pages 323 and 325 for more about cocoa.)

EGGS

I use large eggs for all my recipes. For estimating purposes, figure on 8 whites per cup and 8 yolks per half-cup. Never fear, you can easily substitute if your eggs are a different size: go to the Miscellaneous Equivalents Chart (page 44). I prefer to use natural or organic large brown eggs, because their shells are thicker and more protective, though I have made many of these recipes using ordinary supermarket or convenience store white eggs, because I just kept running out of eggs. (See page 428 for more about eggs.)

I save any extra egg whites in zipper freezer bags. Defrost by placing the sealed bag in a bowl of hot tap water, replacing the water as it cools down and swishing the contents of the bag around occasionally so the whites melt evenly. Avoid using any heat or the microwave, as the whites easily coagulate.

FLOUR

I have prepared all these recipes using unbleached all-purpose flour, working with King Arthur's Flour, Ceresota Flour (Hecker's west of the Mississippi), Whole Foods store brand unbleached all-purpose flour, or General Mills unbleached all-purpose flour. I prefer to avoid bleached flour although I will occasionally use cake flour (always bleached) for very light cakes, such as the Rose-Scented Angel Food Cake. Most times, I substitute a portion of unbleached all-purpose flour with potato starch to lighten the flour in cake making.

Many recipes include a portion of white whole

wheat flour, because it is more nutritious and adds a nice nutty flavor, pleasing slightly grainy texture, and warm color. The best substitute is unbleached all-purpose flour, not common whole wheat flour, which is too strong in flavor. For specialty flours, I have relied mostly on King Arthur, Whole Foods store brand, and Bob's Red Mill flours because they can be easily found or order by mail or internet.

It is best to store all unbleached flours tightly covered and in the freezer, because they tend to get buggy, especially in warm weather. Of course, you probably won't need twenty or more kinds of flour at once as I did for the testing. Place the flour in a microwavable bowl and heat for one or two minutes on low power to take the chill off when making bread. In hot weather, I prefer working with chilled flour to make tender pastry doughs. (See the chapters on barley, buckwheat, oats, rye, and wheat for more about these grain flours.)

MOLASSES

I like to use molasses for the moisture it provides and the extra layer of bittersweet flavor. I recommend two brands: Mother's and Brer Rabbit, which are both quite mild. The blackstrap molasses sold in natural foods stores is too strong to use here. (See the Sugar, Caramel, and Molasses chapter, page 804, for more information.)

NUTS

I store all nuts tightly wrapped and in the freezer, because they get rancid so easily. I recommend buying shelled nuts from Trader Joe's if you have a store in your area, because they carry a large selection and they always seem to be fresh. The various warehouse club stores are also a good bet for nuts in larger quantities, though the selection is more limited. Look for more types around the Christmas holidays, when many Americans do most of their baking. See the individual nut chapters for more about each type of nut.

SALT

I add at least a pinch of fine sea salt to most recipes. I prefer sea salt to table salt, because sea salt has no additives, but table salt or kosher salt can be substituted, keeping in mind that kosher salt is about half as strong as sea salt. Even though you don't really taste the salt, it provides an important underlying function of accenting the flavors and balancing the sweetness. Most older recipes don't include salt, but most modern pastry chefs feel that salt is important even in sweet recipes.

SUGAR

I try to make sure that sugar is refined from cane syrup rather than beet sugar syrup. See the sugar chapter for a more detailed description of the reasons for that. If the type is not indicated on the package, more than likely, it is made with less expensive beet sugar. Packages of beet sugar will tend to be moister, a bit like wet sand, without the free-pouring character of cane sugar.

VANILLA

I use only pure, natural vanilla extract, the scrapings from inside moist, brandy-soaked vanilla beans, or brandy that has had vanilla bean pods soaking in it. (See the Vanilla Beans chapter, page 826 for more information.)

WATER

Water is such an important ingredient, especially for breads. I use filtered water for these recipes; spring water is another good choice. Water in certain areas may be high in minerals, as alkaline, basic, or hard water. Elsewhere, it may be lower in minerals, or soft water that is slightly acidic. Water that is acidic (lower Ph) weakens the gluten network in bread dough, while water that is basic or alkaline strengthens it.

A typical bread dough will contain 40 percent water by weight, about 1 quart of water for every 3 pounds of flour, though very soft bread doughs (like Italian ciabatta) may contain up 45 percent water. Higher protein bread flours will absorb about one-third more water than all-purpose flours, so the percentage of water also depends on the type of flour used. When making bread, because of changes in the flour according to temperature and humidity in the air, and even the age of the flour, it may be necessary to adjust liquid quantities in recipes. For bread dough, more water helps the dough develop larger holes and rise more easily, but it makes the dough more difficult to handle, because it will be sticky.

In making pastry dough, the tendency is to add too much water (or other liquid). Avoid doing this as the more water you add, the more the gluten develops, and therefore, the tougher the dough will be. Add only enough water, combined evenly throughout the pastry, so that the dough forms large, moist clumps that will hold together if you grab a clump in your hand.

HOW I MEASURE

Perhaps because of my years spent in restaurant kitchens–where I had to teach people who had little or no experience how to make breads, pizza dough, ice cream, breakfast pastries, cakes, pies, and desserts–I became accustomed to working by weight and working in even quantities that are easy to double or halve and work well with ingredients the way they are sold. It's always better to use a whole stick of butter, a whole packet of yeast, or a whole can of sweetened condensed milk. So you will see that most of my recipes use quantities like one-half or one-quarter of a pound with liquids in quarter, half, and full cups. In fact, I don't work with thirds at all if I can avoid it, because they can't be halved or doubled as easily.

American home bakers have traditionally resisted working with a scale, although home bakers in most of the rest of the world are accustomed to using this easy, infallible tool. Part of my mission in writing this book is to convince my readers that an inexpensive digital scale is easy to use and that results will be the same, time after time, if you weigh your dry ingredients, especially flour.

Because flour volume changes so much according to the weather temperature and humidity, not to mention differences in measuring, once you start baking by weight, your results will be more consistent and you'll be able to understand proportional relations, so you can see that a pastry dough is often made with three parts flour ($^3/_4$ pound) and two parts butter ($^1/_2$ pound). The key to working with a scale is to always start with zero: place a bowl on the scale and then push tare (the weight of the container) or zero to get it to zero again. Add one type of flour then zero it out again. As long as you always start with zero, your results will be accurate and easy to understand.

Although I believe in using weights, I am admittedly inconsistent and have left the sugar measurements by the cup, because granulated sugar doesn't change in volume and it's quicker to spoon out a cup of sugar. With soft, sticky brown sugars, it is important to pack the sugar into the cup for measuring. With confectioners' sugar, dip the measure into the box and level the top with a knife. I have also listed weight equivalents as an alternative way of measuring.

ABOUT SCALES AND ESCALI

I have been working very happily through all the testing with several scales produced by the Escali Company of Minneapolis (www.escali.com).

The Primo (P115) is a small, economically priced,

and very easy to use scale with two-button operation (and it comes in 11 colors). The battery operated scale has a capacity of 11 pounds or 5 kilos, enough for most home baking. It is accurate to .1 of an ounce or 1 gram and measures in ounces, grams, or pounds and ounces. This is my take-along scale for demos and classes, because it is so light and the bright colors it comes in makes it fun and eye-catching.

The Pana scale is an excellent choice for the baker who wants to measure by weight but needs to know cup measurements for older recipes. This scale has a capacity of 6.6 pounds or 3 kilos and measures in cups and tablespoons, ounces, pounds plus ounces, and grams. It displays ounces in fractions or decimals and accurately measures in $^1/_8$ cup, $^1/_2$ tablespoon, 0.1 oz or 1 gram increments. The scale has been preprogrammed with more than 150 common baking ingredients that are commonly measured in cups and tablespoons, with a laminated ingredient code list (also available on the company's website). I used the equivalents programmed into this scale for all my recipes when converting weights to cup measures.

The M-Series scale is more expensive, but still reasonably priced, and is NSF approved so it can be used in restaurants, catering companies, and bakeries. This spill-proof stainless steel-topped scale is highly reliable in intense work environments. I have been using the M6630, which has a capacity of 66 pounds or 30 kilos and is accurate to 5 grams or .2 ounce. It measures in pounds, ounces, pounds plus ounces, and grams and kilograms.

Equipment Recommendations

CAST-ALUMINUM BUNDT PANS

I have two plain cast-aluminum Bundt pans, which I much prefer to the newer dark nonstick coated pans, which tend to yield cakes with an overly dark crust. My pans are at least 20 years old and show no sign of wear at all. Go to www.nordicware.com to see all their offerings. I use their Original Bundt Pan in the 10-cup size.

CAST-IRON SKILLET

A 9-inch cast-iron skillet is most useful. I prefer Wagner for cast-iron ware, simply because I find their shapes to be more elegant and well-designed. Go to www.wagnerware.com for more information and to order. I sometimes find good, seasoned (though usually slightly rusty) cast-iron skillets at yard sales and flea markets. After using a cast-iron skillet, rinse it out and then immediately wipe it dry. In the beginning, you'll need to rub the pan with a thin coating of oil to protect it. After you've used it awhile, the pan will begin to get seasoned and won't need this step.

CHICAGO METALLIC LOAF AND MUFFINS TINS

For loaf pans and muffin tins, I prefer the heavy-duty ones made by Chicago Metallic in many sizes. These pans never wear out, they don't warp, and are an all-around pleasure to use. I mostly use a standard, medium, or 1-pound loaf pan, 8½ x

4½-inches and prefer one that is light aluminum not dark. This company's 13 x 9-inch baking pans are also excellent. Go to www.cmbakeware.com for a complete listing. Their products are available online from www.amazon.com and from www.chefscatalogue.com.

CULINARY BUTANE TORCH

It's a whole lot easier to brown a meringue topping or glaze a crème brûlée with a culinary butane torch. I used to use a larger propane torch of the type found at hardware stores. Now, I go for the smaller, easier to use and control torch that uses the same can of butane fuel made for the portable burner called a Cassette Feu. Buy the top, which fits on to a standard can from www.surfasonline.com.

DISHER OR ICE CREAM SCOOP

I use several sizes of universal stainless steel dishers, available at many good cookware stores, to quickly scoop even-sized portions of cookie batter. Look for a complete line of beautifully made Vollrath universal dishers at www.surfasonline.com, which lists the size (based on the number of scoops per quart) and the actual contents of each scoop by the ounce. Because I am left-handed, I avoid the type of disher where you must use a tab built for righties to squeeze the scoop. There are knock-off inexpensive scoops for sale that I've found break much too quickly to be worth their lower price.

DISPOSABLE PASTRY BAGS

I have a 100–bag roll of plastic disposable pastry bags that I find quite useful. In Europe, for good reason, it is illegal to use cloth reusable pastry bags, because they are almost impossible to clean thoroughly. You can buy a roll of 100 (12-inch) disposable bags from www.surfasonline.com for about $15.00. An alternative is to use a quart or gallon-sized zipper freezer bag (heavier than the storage bags) and cut out the corner to the correct size.

ENAMELED CAST-IRON DUTCH OVEN

An enameled cast-iron pot, such as a 5½ –quart Le Creuset casserole, is really useful for baking crusty bread. I love the 6-quart Italian Essentials pot made by Copco for Mario Batali. For product information go to at www.italiankitchenstore.com. It is available at www.chefsresource.com for about $100, quite a bit less than the equivalent made by Le Creuset. I found the persimmon color irresistible as I'm a sucker for all things orange (also Batali's signature color, although I'd been wearing orange clogs for years before I saw his). See the recipe for Greek Country Barley Bread on page 142.

FOLEY FOOD MILL

For straining fruit purees, I use a 20-year-old Foley food mill that never seems to wear out. For finer straining, such as removing the seeds from a raspberry puree, I put the purée through a fine metal China cap (of a kind and quality that is hard to find nowadays) or a fine wire sieve.

FOOD PROCESSOR

The larger the capacity, the better. I have both an older commercial R2 model and a smaller home Kitchen Aid food processor. I've seen the R2 for sale on eBay for about $800, which is admittedly a lot of money. With its powerful motor, it will, however, last a lifetime. I find the food processor to be indispensable in baking, for making doughs, grinding nuts, chopping chocolate to fine bits for easier melting, smoothing out pastry creams, mixing fillings like frangipane almond filling, and for chopping praline chunks into small bits.

FRENCH COMPOSITE PLASTIC CUTTERS

I have switched from the old–time tinned cookie cutters, which tend to rust, stainless cutters, which tend to stick, and copper cutters, which are great but high-priced, to the newer Exoglass cutters from France. These strong, sharp, and rigid composite plastic cutters produce even cuts and prevent rust and bacteria growth. They are also heat resistant and dishwasher safe. Buy the cutters from Previn in Philadelphia, a great resource for serious chefs looking for the best in European and American cookware and bakeware (www.previninc.com).

IMMERSION BLENDER

This is a handy tool for smoothing out lumpy pastry cream and pureeing fruits to sauce. Buy the largest one you can find. Mine is a KitchenAid model that also comes with a whisk attachment, useful for beating small amounts of heavy cream or egg whites.

HALF-SHEET PANS

Also known as bun pans, these heavy-duty 18 x 13-inch pans are a standard in my kitchen. They bake evenly, don't warp, have a bigger yield, and hold a standard silicone baking mat. I couldn't bake without them. Buy them at any restaurant supply store or from many online suppliers. Note that some older ovens may not be large enough for this pan. Frustratingly for this baker, my old ovens were too small for this size pan. Luckily, my newer standard American oven is fine, as are most ovens produced today for the home.

KITCHEN-AID MIXER

For mixing, I use my trusty 12-cup KitchenAid mixer, the NSF-approved Pro Model, which has a somewhat more heavy-duty motor. For back-up and for my wonderful assistant, Betty Kaplan, we worked with my 25-year-old Kitchen-Aid K5A mixer, which takes a licking and keeps on ticking. I also invested in an extra bowl, making it much easier and faster for separated egg cake batters. I use the meat grinder attachment to grind the fruit and nut filling for cookies like the Cuccidati (page 457) and for chunky salsas. It is a better choice than the food processor, which tends to chop things into a paste. Instead, the mixture grinds into small, evenly-sized chunks.

KITCHEN SCISSORS

I use my heavy-duty (that word again) red scissors for all sorts of tasks in the kitchen, from cutting parchment paper to fit to trimming off the ends of disposable pastry bags or zipper bags to fit a pastry tip.

KNIFE SHARPENER

Although many professional chefs prefer using an old-fashioned three-sided stone for sharpening, I've found that I'm not particularly skilled at doing this, so I've become a big fan of the knife sharpener made by Chef's Choice. Go to www. chefschoice .com to see their different models. I have the top-of-the-line electric pro model, but then I sharpen a lot of knives. The smaller, electric home model 120 that comes in different colors will probably work fine for you.

MAGIC LINE CAKE PANS

For cake pans, I prefer the removable-bottom spun aluminum pans made by Magic Line rather than springform pans, because there is nothing to break or lose here. I mostly use 9-inch cake pans though there are a few recipes that call for 8- or 10-inch pans. The pans are nice and heavy-duty so they bake cakes evenly and never wear out. They are available from many online retailers, including Amazon and Target.

MICROPLANE ZESTER

This is an indispensable tool for me, because I use aromatic citrus zests in so much of my baking. See page 179 for more information.

NATURAL BRISTLE BRUSHES

It is best to have a few sturdy brushes. While those made with silicone bristles are easier to clean and don't break, they don't work nearly as well as the old-fashioned brushes made with natural bristles. Avoid brushes with nylon bristles, which will melt instantly if they get too hot. I find that a 1½-inch brush size is the most useful.

PARCHMENT AND WAX PAPER

Both these baker's aids are useful in the kitchen, although now that I've been using my Silpat silicone mats, I don't use nearly as much parchment paper. It is useful for baking things like bar cookies that you'll want to cut into individual portions, because you can't cut on the silicone mats. Wax paper is an old stalwart that works for many of the same applications.

RING OR TUBE PAN

Some dense cakes bake up better in a ring or tube pan that is 9 inches in diameter. If you use a standard round pan, the outer portion will get overdone before the inner portion is ready. As always, I recommend buying the heaviest, best-made pan you can find. Cheap pans, especially those with spring clips, will break all too quickly. Because it seems that plain tube pans are not that common anymore, you may substitute a 10-inch Bundt pan, an angel food pan, or a Turk's head mold traditionally used to make Kugelhopf cakes.

ROLLING PIN

Make rolling doughs easier and more effective by choosing a heavy rolling pin. I prefer my well-seasoned straight French wooden rolling pin to the standard American ball-bearing rolling pin with handles on the ends, because I get a better feel of the dough being worked. This is purely a matter of taste. Use whatever works best for you. For an inexpensive 20½-inch French pin similar to the one I use made from hard birch or maple, go to www.fantes.com, which has a large selection of rolling pins with useful explanations of the different types.

ROUL-PAT

To roll out dough, I invested in a 24 x 18-inch Roul-Pat, a large fiberglass-strengthened silicone mat perfect for rolling as absolutely nothing sticks to it. It is the same material in a larger size as the Silpat silicone baking mats so popular among professional pastry chefs and now available in half sheet pan size for home use. The only drawback here is that you can't cut the dough on the mat.

SHARP CHEF'S KNIFE

I use several different knives, all about 8-inches in length, although probably my favorite is made by the Japanese company, Mac Knives (www.macknife.com) and has an 8½-inch blade. It is perfectly balanced, easy to sharpen, and not overly heavy. I find that for smaller women's hands, it's easier to control a knife of this size than a standard 10-inch chef's knife.

A sharp paring knife for paring fruits and vegetables with a 2- to 3-inch blade is most useful.

SILICONE SPATULAS

The rubber spatula is on the short list of indispensable tools invented in America (another is the swivel peeler). Note that rubber spatulas will melt when immersed in hot liquids, while those made from silicone will not. I have at least half a dozen in both the smaller and the larger size, which are perfect for delicate folding and to scrape every last bit of batter out of the bowl (although dedicated bowl-lickers may not be too happy about this).

SILPAT SILICONE MATS

These are the original silicone mats from France that fit a standard half sheet pan. You'll never need to butter and flour a pan again! There are other companies making silicone mats but I haven't liked any of the other ones I've used nearly as much. Buy the half sheet pan size mat from Bed, Bath, and Beyond. Buy one that fits a 15 x 10-inch jelly roll pan at www.surlatable.com. Just be careful never to cut on the mat (as I found out the hard way the first time I used mine).

STAINLESS-STEEL BOWLS

I prefer using stainless steel bowls, again, the heavier the better, and they'll last forever. You can place a stainless steel bowl on top of a pot full of boiling water when making heated egg batters for sponge cakes. You can quickly cool hot fillings over a second bowl filled with ice and water. I have at least a dozen different sizes of bowls, though you can probably make do with three or four. My favorite is an old (at least 30 years) 13-quart rolled edge stainless steel bowl made by Vollrath, which is the perfect size and shape for folding together light cake batters like angel food cake. There are many cheap, light stainless steel bowls now coming in from China and India, which will tend to quickly get dented and warped, so I would avoid them. Go to www.vollrathco.com to see their listing of American-made heavy-duty stainless steel bowls. Buy a good selection of the bowls online from www.surfasonline.com.

THERMAPEN INSTANT-READ THERMOMETER

The Thermapen, a wonderful instant-read thermometer, can be used for custards, caramel, and deep-frying and to test whether bread is done. (See page 880 for more information or go to www.thermoworks.com).

WHISKS

I use whisks for many tasks when baking: whisking together the dry ingredients so they are evenly combined (this works as well as sifting unless you are combining very light cake flour, starches, or cocoa, which tends to form lumps); lightly beating eggs and sugar when making custards and pastry creams, where you don't need to incorporate air but just need to combine them evenly; combining melted and unmelted chocolate bits so the hard bits melt evenly; beating air into sponge cake batter as it is heating over steaming water; and many other tasks. Invest in several different sizes of sturdy, well-made whisks. It is worthwhile to buy one large balloon whisk to incorporate as much air as possible when making sponge cakes.

WIRE COOKING RACKS

It's best to buy several stainless steel wire racks for cooling pans of cookies and cakes. If you get the heavy-duty type, they will last a lifetime. I also use the racks to drain deep-fried foods, placing the rack over a pan to catch the drips. This way I can put the pan containing the drained foods right into a low (200°F) oven to keep warm while I fry up the rest of the batch. Because there is air circulation all around, the fried bits don't get soggy as the bottoms do if they are drained on paper.

COOKWARE INFORMATION FROM FANTE'S KITCHEN WARES SHOP IN PHILADELPHIA

Go to www.fantes.com for lots of great information about cookware. Go to fantes.com/manufacturer.html to get to a useful listing of websites for the huge list of cookware and bakeware manufacturers they represent.

TECHNIQUES FOR THE BAKER

In baking, you are using the same basic techniques over and over again, most of which are pretty simple. Once you master basics like cutting in butter to make a pie pastry, creaming butter and sugar to make a cake batter, or melting chocolate, you'll be able to have great success in making the wonderfully diverse and delicious recipes in this book. Here are some of the most common techniques used in this book with explanations of why they are done.

ALTERNATING LIQUID AND DRY INGREDIENTS

When making a cake, you often alternate adding the dry ingredients (flours, spices, leavener if any, and salt) with a liquid such as buttermilk, milk, or orange juice into a basic creamed mix consisting of butter and sugar beaten together until light with eggs beaten in. Start and end with the dry ingredients and add one-third to one-quarter at a time, alternating with the liquid. The purpose for this is to keep the batter at basically the same consistency, neither too dry, nor too wet so that it stays light and creamy.

BAKING A CAKE UNTIL DONE

For most cakes, bake in the center of the oven at moderate temperature (350°F) until the cake starts to come away from the sides of the pan, which happens when the batter is baked enough to lose its moisture, and a toothpick or skewer stuck in the center comes out clean. The center should be set and matte in texture, not wet, soft, or shiny.

Chocolate cakes will usually be removed from the oven when they're still soft in the center. If baked until completely set in the center, they will come out dry. If the cake has not been baked long enough it will fall in the center.

Cheesecakes are a different story and must be baked until the center is just firm, the batter has lost its soupy texture and has become firmer, and there is no liquidy jiggling when you shake the pan. If the cheesecake bakes any longer after the center has completely set, it will start to puff up from steam produced by the heated batter, creating cracks and a fallen center when it cools down.

BAKING BREAD UNTIL DONE

For most breads, bake at higher temperature (often 400°F) to create a nice, brown crust, until the bread sounds hollow when tapped on the bottom and an instant-read thermometer inserted in the center reads 190° to 205°F. Using a thermometer is the easiest way to tell when bread is done.

BAKING IN A WATER BATH

Baking in a water bath (*bain-marie* in French) makes the oven heat gentler and more even in a moist environment so the outside of the batter doesn't form a hard crust, which is undesirable in cheesecakes, flans, and other custard-based products. To make a water bath, pour the batter into a prepared pan. Cover with foil, pricked to allow steam to escape and place the pan in a second pan filled with hot water or even boiling water. Bake until the center has just set otherwise the product will start to puff up and rise due to the expansion of the water it contains into steam and once it starts to cool down, the batter will fall and crack.

BEATING CREAM CHEESE (FOR CHEESECAKE)

Most cheesecakes in America rely on cream cheese for their main ingredient. Because most cream cheese contains gums to keep it smooth and spreadable, it tends to form small lumps that are difficult to get rid of if it isn't beaten properly. Start with softened cream cheese if at all possible for smoother texture. In the bowl of a standing electric mixer, beat the cream cheese and the sugar until light and fluffy, scraping down the sides of the mixer, scraping the bottom, and scraping off the paddle once or twice to get rid of any lumps. Once the mixture is smooth, beat in the eggs, one at a time, so that the mixture stays smooth. If the mixture still has lumps, put the batter in the food processor and process until smooth or use an immersion blender to smooth it.

BEATING IN WHOLE EGGS AND YOLKS

When beating eggs into batters, it is best to work with room temperature eggs, because they will combine more easily with the other ingredients. Beat in the eggs one at a time, beating well after each addition so they get incorporated with the other ingredients, making a smooth, creamy batter. If, however, the batter separates and begins to look like scrambled eggs, don't worry. Once you add the flour mixture, the batter will almost always come together and get creamy again.

BEATING EGG WHITES

When beating egg whites, you want to get them as light and full of tiny air bubbles as possible. These bubbles will expand in the heat of the oven, making the product rise and lighten. It is important to make sure that the egg whites contain no portion of fatty yolks, which will keep the whites from rising fully. For the same reason, make sure that the bowl of the mixer is completely clean and dry with no trace of oil on it.

Because it is easy to overbeat egg whites on their own until they are dry and lumpy rather than smooth and supple, I always use part of the sugar in a recipe to beat with the egg whites, making a meringue, which is a lot harder to overbeat. In a standing mixer fitted with a whisk attachment, beat the egg whites until they are fluffy and white, then sprinkle in the sugar and continue beating until the whites are firm and glossy. Note than when making an angel food cake, the whites should be beaten only until soft peaks form, otherwise you'll end up with a tough, dry cake.

BEATING EGGS AND SUGAR

Another way of leavening a batter is to beat whole eggs (or eggs plus extra yolks) and sugar in a standing mixer fitted with a whisk attachment until they are thick, light, and lemony-colored,

which usually takes 5 to 6 minutes. Many cookbooks tell you to beat until the mixture forms "a ribbon," which happens when the sugar has been completely dissolved.

BEATING BREAD DOUGH

When making bread doughs, I find that it works best to beat in all the ingredients in my KitchenAid mixer using the paddle attachment so they are well combined. I then switch to the dough hook and continue beating until the dough is smooth and elastic and comes away cleanly from the bowl. Note that for some breads, the dough will still be sticky when it is ready. This is true for breads made with rye and barley flours, those enriched with butter and eggs, and for sweet yeast–raised breads.

BLIND BAKING A PASTRY CRUST

When making a French-style tart and sometimes even an American-style pie, I often blind-bake the crust, which means that I prebake the crust with nothing in it so that when the wet filling is added, the tart doesn't end up with an unpleasant soggy bottom. To do so, preheat the oven, usually to 375°F. Roll out the dough on a lightly floured surface into a large round about ⅛-inch thick. Transfer to a 10- or 11-inch French fluted tart pan with a removable bottom. Lay the pastry into the pan without stretching the dough and giving it some slack, especially where the sides meet the bottom. Press the dough firmly into the ridged sides, making sure the dough is of an even thickness all around. Trim off any overhang flush with the edge.

Chill the pastry crust again for 30 minutes to relax the gluten so the tart crust maintains its shape well. Fit a piece of heavy-duty foil directly onto the dough and up over the edges, then fill it with beans or other pie weights. (I have a large container of mixed dried beans that I have been using over and over for several years, which work just fine. Blind bake (just the pastry crust, no filling) until the dough is cooked through but not yet browned, about 30 minutes, on the bottom shelf of the oven so that the bottom has a chance to cook through. Once the dough is set enough to no longer be wet and gooey, remove the foil and the weights, reduce the oven temperature, usually to 325°F, and bake about 10 minutes longer, or until the dough is evenly and lightly browned. Remove from the oven and cool to room temperature on a wire rack before filling.

CHILLING OVER ICE WATER

When making fillings such as pastry cream or custard sauces, the filling should be cool before using it or mixing it with something else like whipped cream. To do this quickly, transfer the hot mixture to a bowl, preferably stainless steel, and cool it by placing it over a second bowl filled with a mixture of ice and water. Stir often. When the ice melts, replace it with more ice. The more often you do this, the more quickly the mixture will cool.

COOKING A CUSTARD

Eggs yolks on their own thicken at 165°F; once they've been mixed with sugar and/or acidic ingredients like lemon or orange juice, or thickeners like potato starch or flour, they can be cooked to a higher temperature, thickening well without curdling (turning to scrambled eggs). To make a custard, lightly whisk together the yolks with sugar and vanilla or other flavoring to combine. Pour in a little of the scalded milk or cream to temper (gradually raising the temperature of the mixture so that it stays smooth), then whisk in the remaining hot milk or cream.

Place the custard in a medium, heavy-bottomed pot, and heat over low heat, stirring often with a wooden spoon or silicone spatula, especially at the corners, where the mixture tends to stick and overcook. Continue heating and stirring (patiently) until the mixture starts to release steam and the custard thickens visibly. Until you have practiced this a few times, it can be difficult to tell when the custard has thickened enough. The easiest way to tell is to use an instant read thermometer, which should read 165°F. Remove from the heat immediately as the mixture will continue to thicken from carryover heat. If the custard curdles a little, use an immersion blender to smooth it out. If it has completely curdled, there's not much to do but start over.

CREAMING BUTTER AND SUGAR

Creaming butter and sugar is done to add air bubbles to a cake or cookie batter. To do so, place the softened butter and the sugar into the bowl of an electric mixer fitted with the paddle attachment and beat until soft, light, and fluffy, 5 to 6 minutes, and just barely firm enough to hold its shape, scraping down the sides once or twice. Your goal here is to incorporate as much air as possible into the mixture. The tiny, hard cubes of sugar help to cut the butter so it can absorb more air.

CUTTING IN BUTTER (OR OTHER FAT) FOR PASTRY DOUGH

When making pastry or pie dough with butter used for its shortening properties and its excellent flavor, it's important to start with chilled bits of cut-up butter. I place the dry ingredients in the bowl of an electric standing mixer, add the cut up bits of butter, and place the bowl in the freezer to chill, about 30 minutes. I use the flat paddle attachment to beat the mixture into bits that resemble oatmeal, with few, if any, larger bits of butter showing. While the mixer is beating, pour in enough chilled liquid (ice water, milk, or other liquid) so that the dough forms moist clumps.

Don't beat the mixture until it forms a ball, or the dough will tend to be tough, because once you add the liquid, you are starting to develop the gluten (stretchiness) in the dough. While you need a small amount of gluten to be developed to stick the dough together, you're looking for the minimum of structure here. Dump the dough clumps onto a lightly floured work surface and *lightly* knead with the palm of your hand until they form a ball, which should take about 30 seconds.

You can do the same thing in a food processor, if your machine is big enough to hold the batch of dough. In this case, chill the butter and flour in a metal bowl then transfer to the bowl of the food processor.

CUTTING FAN-SHAPED FRUITS

To cut fruits into attractive fan shapes, use firm but ripe fruit (yes, I know how difficult it is to do just that; the best is to use fruit that is at the height of its season). Cut the fruit into fan shapes by cutting thin, even slices from the bottom three-quarters of the way to the stem end. Spread the fruits out from the bottom to form a fan.

CUTTING SLASHES IN BREAD DOUGH

Many breads need to be slashed across the top to allow them to bake more evenly and to create attractive and crusty cuts in the bread. This should be done just after the bread is formed but before it has risen for the last time before baking. The best tool for this purpose is a French baker's *lame*, a single-edged razor, a box cutter, or a single-edged razor, as even the sharpest knife will tend to pull the dough out of shape. Working quickly and confidently, cut several shallow slashes into the bread, usually either on the diagonal or making a tic-tac-toe pattern.

DEEP-FRYING

To deep-fry, it is most important to keep the oil at the proper high temperature (365° to 375°F). The lower temperature works best for me because the oil doesn't tend to burn, though some chefs prefer the higher temperature because it yields a crisper product. Make sure the pot you use is large enough to allow for the bubbling up that occurs when the product is added to the oil. The oil should come up no more than one-third of the way up the sides. A wok is ideal because the oil heats up quickly and because the bowl shape pools a smaller amount of oil to the proper depth for frying. Otherwise, a large pan with high sides such as a chicken fryer (made for deep-frying chicken), a heavy Dutch oven, or a pot that splays out at the top all work well. You may wish to invest in an inexpensive electric deep-fat fryer.

In a completely dry pot, heat enough oil to come about 3-inches deep to 365°F, or until shimmering hot, and the air above the pot feels hot when you hold your hand about 3 inches above the oil. (See page 583 in the Oils chapter for more about specific oils and their smoking points.) After frying, you may carefully strain the used oil through a paper towel laid into a wire sieve that has been placed over a clean and dry bowl, which is easiest to do when the oil is still rather hot and thin in body, as it thickens as it cools. Always combine new oil with some of the used oil when frying again and discard if the oil darkens too much or it burns.

FORMING AND BAKING EMPANADAS AND OTHER STUFFED PASTRIES

On a lightly floured board, roll the dough out about ⅜-inch thick. Cut out into 4- to 6-inch cir- cles, using a small plate as a guide. Spread the filling over half of each circle leaving a clean ½-inch border all around. Brush the edges with beaten egg or water for glue and then fold the dough over to enclose the filling. Seal the edges by crimping with a fork. Cut several small slits in each empanada to allow steam to escape. Arrange on a parchment paper- or silicone mat–lined baking pan and let the empanadas chill at least 30 minutes before baking to set their shape. It is important to keep the filling from even touching the edges, because this will prevent the two layers of dough from adhering to each other and the pastries will open up. This is not such a problem when baking, but if the pastries are to be fried, the filling will leak out and burn in the oil.

If you are baking the empanadas, brush the pastries with egg wash, then prick with a fork to allow steam to escape. Bake until golden and the filling starts to bubble up through the holes. Cool for about 10 minutes and then serve.

MAKING A CRUMB CRUST

Crumb crusts are a great way to use up bits of dried out cookies and nuts. To make a crumb crust, place the cookie, biscotti, or baked pastry bits into the bowl of a food processor along with nuts, sugar and any spices. Process together until fine crumbs are obtained. Pour in melted and cooled butter and process again briefly to combine. You should be able to press the mixture together with your fingers and have it stick together. If the mixture has too much butter, it will be soft and pasty; if there is not enough butter, it will be crumbly and dry.

Firmly press the crumb mixture into the pan. I like to use the palms of my hands to press the mixture even more firmly into the bottom of the pan so it holds together well when baked. Chill the crust for 30 minutes to set the shape. Meanwhile, preheat the oven to 350°F and bake the crust for about 20 minutes or until lightly browned. Sometimes, a crumb crust will tend to puff up or slide down the sides of the pan, usually because it is too wet or too pasty. To remedy this, once you remove the crust from the oven and while it is still hot, use the flat bottom of a metal measuring cup to press down the sides and bottom of the crust.

MAKING A LATTICE TOP CRUST PIE

Make a lattice top, by cutting about 12 (1-inch wide) pastry strips from a chilled dough circle, using either a sharp knife, or a plain or fluted dough roller. Arrange half of the pastry strips on top of the filling about 1 inch apart. Fold alternate pastry strips over themselves back halfway.

Lay a pastry strip crosswise on the center of the tart against the edge of the folded strips and unfold the strips over top. Lay another pastry strip crosswise about 1-inch away, folding back the other half of the strips. Repeat the weaving until lattice covers the filling. (Alternatively, form the lattice on the wax paper, then refrigerate until firm, about 20 minutes. Use a large spatula to transfer the lattice top to the top of the tart.)

MAKING CARAMEL

Caramel is one of the most useful, most complex flavors in baking, but it is also one of the most challenging things to make. It works best if you have a heavy-bottomed copper pot, which will distribute the heat evenly so the caramel darkens evenly. Next best is a heavy-bottomed stainless steel pot, which will be light enough inside so you can clearly see the color of the caramel as it darkens.

There are two basic kinds of caramel, each used for different purposes. The easier kind to make starts with a sugar syrup: sugar and water heated together until clear and syrupy. You then cook the syrup down until the water eventually boils away and the sugar starts to darken. Once the sugar starts to take on color–something which seems to take forever and then is overcooked in an instant– keep a steady eye on it. Allow the sugar to darken just until it is medium, rich brown and starts to get a reddish tint to it. The sugar will also just begin to smoke at this point. Immediately remove from the heat. If you are new at making caramel, it is best to keep a large bowl of ice water on the side. Once the caramel is ready, remove the pot from the heat and immediately plunge the bottom into the ice water (keeping away from the hot steam it will produce) to stop the cooking process.

The second way to make caramel is to melt sugar on its own or perhaps mixed with a little lemon juice, very slowly until it begins to melt and then, almost immediately, begins to darken. It is very important here to use a heavy skillet or pot so the sugar melts evenly without burning in spots. Shake the pot occasionally so the sugar melts evenly, but avoid stirring it as the sugar will crystallize on the spoon. (A wooden spoon is the best choice if you are going to stir it.) To make the caramel, place the sugar in a medium heavy–bottomed pot, preferably copper, so it makes a layer about ½–inch thick, and heat over low until the sugar begins to melt and turns golden, about 8 minutes. As sugar melts, shake the pot carefully (CARAMEL IS EXTREMELY HOT!), so the sugar cooks evenly or stir with a wooden spoon, until the sugar is sugar is medium brown in color with a faint touch of redness.

If your caramel overcooks and starts to burn, there is really nothing to do except start over. Luckily, sugar is pretty inexpensive; unluckily the pot will probably be a challenge to clean. The best thing to do is fill it with water and bring the water to the boil so the burnt caramel melts into the water.

MELTING CHOCOLATE

I find that by far the easiest way to melt chocolate is to chop it into small bits (unless you have purchased the chocolate in small discs). Place the chocolate in a dry, clean microwaveable bowl and melt on low power (10 to 20 percent) in the microwave, 2 minutes at a time, stirring in between, until the chocolate is just barely melted. Allow the remaining chocolate to melt in the carryout heat, stirring once or twice so it melts evenly.

PREPARING GELATIN

Powdered gelatin has to be "bloomed," meaning it has to be soaked in liquid until it has absorbed it and starts to soften before it can be used. To do so, in a small, microwave-safe bowl, combine the liquid (water, lemon juice, or other liquid) and the gelatin, and allow the gelatin to "bloom," or thicken, and absorb all the juice, at room temperature for about 10 minutes. Place the bowl in the microwave, and heat on low for 1 to 2 minutes, or until the gelatin has melted, the liquid is clear, and there are no more granules visible. While it is still hot, pour into the custard, cream, or pastry cream, whisking well so the gelatin is distributed evenly throughout the mixture. Unmixed gelatin will tend to form unpleasant "ropes."

European sheet gelatin is easier to use and yields products with a more delicate, less rubbery consistency. Soak the sheets in cold water for about 10 minutes or until they soften, then drain and mix directly into hot liquid so they dissolve completely.

SEPARATING EGGS

I learned to separate large quantities of eggs by breaking them open using one hand and dumping them into my other hand, allowing the whites to slip through my fingers, leaving the (hopefully) whole yolks behind. It's a lot easier to do this when the eggs aren't ice cold, or else your hands freeze. These days, we're much more conscious of food safety and tend not to do so many things with our hands. In large hotels, including the Barclay Hotel in Philadelphia, where I once worked as a sous-chef, they would fill a giant mixer with whole eggs, beat them until the shells were smashed into bits and then strain the whole mess through the cone-shaped strainer called a China cap! I certainly hope this practice has stopped, because it is a very effective way of getting salmonella present on the outside of the shell into a big batch of eggs.

Unless you're planning to separate dozen and dozens of eggs like I used to, it is easier to separate eggs while they are cold and firm. The yolk sacs in room temperature eggs will tend to break open. If you're new at separating eggs, the safest way to do it is to set up three bowls, one small and two larger. Crack open an egg, allowing the yolk to fall into one half of the shell. Pour the white from the other half of the shell into the small bowl. Transfer the yolk back and forth between the shell halves, allowing the remaining white to fall into the small bowl. Pour the yolk into one of the larger bowls. If the yolk has broken and mixed with the white, pour it into the small bowl and discard it or reserve for another use. This way, if you do break an egg, you'll only lose one but wipe out the bowl before adding any more egg whites. Once you're more comfortable, you can eliminate working with the small bowl and just use the two bowls. If a bit of yolk does get mixed into the white, use an empty shell to scoop it up and discard. If there is just too much yolk mixed in to remove it with a shell half, start again.

SLICING GOOEY CAKES AND COOKIES

When portioning gooey cakes, cheesecakes, and bar cookies, cut with a sharp knife that has been dipped into hot water and wiped dry in between each slice. Take care not to drip water drops onto a chocolate glaze as it will show spots.

SUGAR SYRUP: SIMPLE SYRUP

In a medium, heavy-bottomed pot, bring the water and sugar (usually equal parts) to a boil over medium heat. Continue to boil for 1 to 2 minutes or until the syrup is completely clear.

SUGAR SYRUP: SOFT BALL STAGE

In a medium, heavy-bottomed pot, bring water and sugar to a boil over medium heat. Continue to boil for 1 to 2 minutes or until the syrup is completely clear. Cook until the syrup is thickened and bubbling and it reaches the soft-ball stage, when a spoonful dropped in a small bowl of ice water forms a soft ball, or reaches 238°F on a candy thermometer.

SUGAR SYRUP: FIRM BALL STAGE

In a medium, heavy-bottomed pot, bring water and sugar to the boil over medium heat. Continue to boil for 1 to 2 minutes or until the syrup is completely clear. Cook until the syrup is thickened and bubbling and it reaches the firm ball stage, when a spoonful dropped in a glass of ice water will form a firm, but still malleable ball, or it reaches 250°F on a candy thermometer.

ROLLING OUT TART PASTRY

When working with tart pastry that contains eggs and sugar, making for a sticky cookie–type dough, it is best to roll the pastry out about ⅛-inch thick between two sheets of lightly floured wax paper. Drape, without stretching the dough, into the pan, preferably aluminum for better browning. Trim the edges evenly, then crimp or pinch in and out alternatively to form a decorative fluted edge. Chill the crust for 1 hour in the refrigerator or 30 minutes in the freezer to set the shape.

Alternatively, press the soft pastry directly into the tart or pie pan, pressing well so the dough forms an even layer, especially at the edges where the bottom meets with the sides and the dough tends to thicken.

PROOFING YEAST

Because yeast is a live microorganism, it can also die if it gets too old. Proofing yeast is a way of making sure that the yeast is still alive and active. To proof it, dissolve the yeast in lukewarm liquid (usually water or milk), then add an ingredient for the yeast to feed on, such as honey, sugar, or flour. Allow the mixture to proof at warm room temperature for about 10 minutes, or until bubbling and puffy.

PROTECTING THE EDGES OF A PIE

To prevent the outside of a pie crust from darkening too much, crimp aluminum foil around the outside of a pie, or use a pie shield.

RISING YEAST DOUGH

Transfer the dough to a large oiled bowl; turn around so the dough is oiled all over. Cover with oiled plastic wrap or a damp cloth and allow the dough to rise until doubled in size, about 2 hours, at warm room temperature. In cold weather, set up a pot filled with water, bring to a boil, then reduce to the lowest heat. Cover the pot with a sturdy baking pan and top with a thick layer of folded kitchen towels. Place the covered bowl on top of the towels and allow the dough to rise. Alternatively, place the dough in an electric oven with the light turned on.

ROLLING BREAD STICKS

Divide the dough into small, even portions about ¼ cup each. Roll out on a lightly floured work surface using the palms of your hands to form it into long "cigar" shapes. (You will have more even-looking sticks if you place the dough on a firm surface and roll your hands across the top, moving from the center outward.)

SCORING PHYLLO DOUGH

When making strudel or other large phyllo pastries, it is desirable to score the dough before it is baked to make it easier to cut afterward without shattering the crisp pastry layers. Use the tip of a very sharp knife to score the top phyllo layers into individual portions, traditionally diamond shapes, taking care not to cut into the filling, or it will burst through the cuts.

SHAPING A LOAF OF BREAD

To make a firm, even-shaped loaf of bread, roll the dough out into an even rectangle about ¾-inch thick with the long side facing you. Fold up the dough in three like a letter, so you have a smaller rectangle with the short side facing you. Fold over the top end of the dough so it reaches the center of the rectangle. Fold over the bottom end of the dough so it reaches the center of the rectangle. Now fold over the top end so it covers the bottom end, pinching together the edges at the bottom to make a tight block-shaped loaf. Bake with the seam side down.

SLICING A LAYER CAKE INTO TWO (OR MORE) LAYERS

Cut a very small notch, about ¼-inch deep, out of the side of the cake to use as a guide. Using a long, serrated knife, cut the cake horizontally into two (or more) layers. Fill the cake as directed. Re-assemble the cake, using the cut wedge as a guide to line up the layers in their original position.

SOAKING CAKES AND PASTRIES WITH SUGAR SYRUP

Many Middle Eastern and Mediterranean pastries are sweetened after they are baked by soaking them in sugar syrup. Poke holes in the cake or pastry with a toothpick or skewer and spoon the cold syrup over the hot cake (or the hot syrup over the cold cake).

WHIPPING HEAVY CREAM

The danger in beating cream is that it can separate and turn into butter bits suspended in whey. To avoid this, make sure the cream is well-chilled before beating. In hot weather, super-chill the bowl, the beater, and the cream in the freezer for 20 minutes before beating. Be sure to tightly cover the whipped cream. Because it is so full of air bubbles, it will quickly pick up extraneous refrigerator odors. Whipped cream will keep its light fluffiness only about 2 hours. If it has deflated, just beat until the cream is light and firm again. The higher the butterfat content, the more stiff the cream will beat and the longer it will hold up. You may add up to about one-quarter sour cream to the heavy cream for a tangier flavor before whipping.

PAN SIZES

Pan Size (Inches)	Approximate Volume (Cups)
ROUND PAN	
6 x 2	4
8 x 1½	4
8 x 2	6
8 x 3	10
9 x 1½	6
9 x 2	8
9 x 2½	10
9 x 3	12
10 x 2	11
10 x 2½	12

BUNDT PAN

7½ x 3 (small)	6
10 x 3½ (large)	12

TUBE PAN

8 x 3	9
9 x 3	12

SQUARE CAKE PAN

8 x 8 x 1½	6
8 x 8 x 2	8
9 x 9 x 1½	8
9 x 9 x 2	10
10 x 10 x 2	12

RECTANGULAR CAKE PAN

11 x 7 x 2	6
13 x 9 x 2	14

LOAF PAN

8 x 4 x 2½	4 (¾ pound loaf)
8½ x 4½ x 2¾	6 (1 pound loaf)
9 x 5 x 3	8 (1½ pound loaf)

MUFFIN CUP PAN

1½ to 2 (mini) muffin	⅛ cup batter
2½ (standard) muffin	½ to ⅓ cup batter
3½ (giant) muffin	⅝ cup batter

FRENCH TART PAN

10 x 1	4
10½ x 1½	5

JELLY ROLL/ SHEET PANS

15 x 10 jelly roll pan	5
18 x 13 half sheet pan	10

SUBSTITUTING PANS

Because not many of us have every size baking pan, it is useful to know that you can often substitute one size for another.

To use a Pyrex baking dish instead of a metal baking pan, reduce the baking temperature by 25 degrees.

To substitute a pan that is shallower than the one called for in the recipe, reduce the baking time by about 20 percent.

To substitute a pan that is deeper than the one called for in the recipe, increase the baking time by about 20 percent.

Because every oven is different, has its own hot spots, and because most of our ovens are not perfectly calibrated, it's best to keep a close watch on baked goods, especially if it's the first time you're using the recipe.

FLOUR AND GRAIN EQUIVALENTS

WEIGHT	VOLUME
BARLEY FLOUR	
1/4 lb. barley flour	3/4 cup plus 2 tbsp.
6 oz. barley flour	1 1/4 cups plus 1 tbsp.
1/2 lb. barley flour	1 3/4 cups
1 lb. barley flour	3 1/2 cups
BUCKWHEAT FLOUR	
1/4 lb. buckwheat flour	1 cup minus 1 tbsp.
1/2 lb. buckwheat flour	2 cups minus 2 tbsp.
BREAD FLOUR (UNBLEACHED)	
1/4 lb. bread flour	1 cup
1/2 lb. bread flour	2 cups
1 lb. bread flour	4 cups
CHESTNUT FLOUR	
2 oz. chestnut flour	1/2 cup minus 1/2 tbsp.
1/4 lb. chestnut flour	1 cup minus 1 tbsp.
6 oz. chestnut flour	1 1/2 cups minus 1 1/2 tbsp.
CORNMEAL, STONE-GROUND	
1/4 lb. cornmeal	3/4 cup plus 2 tbsp.
6 oz. cornmeal.	1 1/4 cups plus 1 tbsp.
1/2 lb cornmeal	1 3/4 cups

WEIGHT	VOLUME
10 oz. cornmeal	2 1/4 cups plus 2 tbsp.
3/4 lb. cornmeal	2 1/2 cups plus 2 tbsp.
1 lb. cornmeal	3 1/2 cups
DURUM WHEAT FLOUR	
1/4 lb. durum	3/4 cup plus 2 tbsp.
1/2 lb. durum	1 3/4 cups
1 lb. durum	3 1/2 cups
ALL-PURPOSE FLOUR, UNBLEACHED	
1/4 lb. all-purpose flour	1 cup minus 1 tbsp.
1/2 lb. all-purpose flour	2 cups minus 2 tbsp.
3/4 lb. all-purpose flour	3 cups minus 3 tbsp.
1 lb. all-purpose flour	3 3/4 cups
1 1/4 lb. all-purpose flour	4 3/4 cups minus 1 tbsp.
1 1/2 lb. all-purpose flour	5 3/4 cups minus 2 tbsp.
OAT FLOUR	
1/4 lb. oat flour	1 cup plus 2 tbsp.
1/2 lb. oat flour	2 1/4 cups
1 lb. oat flour	4 1/2 cups
OATMEAL	
3 oz. oatmeal	1/2 cup
6 oz. oatmeal	1 cup

WEIGHT	VOLUME	WEIGHT	VOLUME
POTATO STARCH AND CORNSTARCH		**SEMOLINA, FINE**	
1 oz. starch	¼ cup plus 2 tbsp.	¼ lb. fine semolina	½ cup plus 2½ tbsp.
2 oz. starch	¾ cup	6 oz. fine semolina	1 cup
¼ lb. starch	1¼ cups	¼ lb. fine semolina	1¼ cups plus 1 tbsp.
¾ lb. starch	3¾ cups	1 lb. fine semolina	2½ cups plus 2 tbsp.
RICE FLOUR		1½ lb. fine semolina	4 cups minus 1 tbsp.
2 oz. rice flour	½ cup	**WHITE WHOLE WHEAT FLOUR**	
¼ lb. rice flour	1 cup	¼ lb. white whole wheat flour	1 cup plus 2 tbsp.
RYE FLOUR		6 oz. white whole wheat flour	1½ cups
2 oz. rye flour	½ cup minus 1 tbsp.	½ lb. white whole wheat flour	3 cups
¼ lb. rye flour	1 cup minus 2 tbsp.	1 lb. white whole wheat flour	5¼ cups
6 oz. rye flour	1¼ cups plus 1 tbsp.		
½ lb. rye flour	1¾ cups		

FRUIT AND NUT EQUIVALENTS

WEIGHT	VOLUME
ALMONDS	
1 lb. whole almonds	3 cups
1 lb. whole almonds	3⅓ cups chopped almonds
1 lb. whole almonds	3½ cups ground almonds
1 lb. whole almonds	4 cups slivered almonds
1 lb. sliced almonds	5⅓ cups
APPLES	
1 lb. apples	2 large, 3 medium, or 4 small apples
2½ lb. (enough to fill a 9- to 10-inch pie)	4 to 5 large, 6 to 7 medium, or 8 to 9 small apples
1 lb. sliced apples	2¾ cups
1 lb. diced apples	3 cups
1 large apple	About 2 cups sliced or chopped, 1½ cups finely chopped
1 medium apple	About 1½ cups sliced or chopped, 1 cup finely chopped
1 small apple	About ¾ cup sliced or chopped, ½ cup finely chopped

WEIGHT	VOLUME
APRICOTS, FRESH AND DRIED	
2½ lb. fresh apricots	4 cups
1 lb. fresh apricots	8 to 12 whole apricots
1 lb. fresh apricots	2½ to 3 cups sliced or halved
1 lb. dried apricots	2¾ cups
1 lb. dried apricots	5 cups cooked
6 oz. dried apricots	1 cup dried apricots
6 oz. dried apricots	2 cups cooked apricots
BANANAS	
1 lb. bananas	3 to 4 medium bananas 1¾ cups mashed bananas
CARROTS	
1 lb. bag carrots	1 bunch of fresh carrots with tops
About ¼ lb., 1 cup shredded carrot	1 large carrot
CASHEWS	
1 lb. cashews	3¼ cups
CHERRIES	
1 lb. fresh cherries	2⅓ cups pitted cherries

WEIGHT	VOLUME
CHESTNUTS, FRESH AND DRIED	
1 lb. whole chestnuts	35 to 40 chestnuts
1½ lb. chestnuts in shell	1 lb. shelled chestnuts
1 lb. shelled chestnuts	2½ cups chestnuts
3 oz. dried chestnuts	1 cup fresh chestnuts
COCONUT	
1 medium-sized fresh coconut	3 to 4 cups grated or flaked coconut
1 lb. dried coconut	4 cups dried coconut
CRANBERRIES	
1 (12-ounce) bag fresh cranberries	3 cups whole cranberries, 2½ cups chopped cranberries
DATES	
1 lb. whole dates with pits	2½ cups dates
6 oz. whole pitted dates	1 cup chopped dates
1 lb. whole dates	50 to 60 dates
FIGS, FRESH AND DRIED	
1 lb. fresh figs	12 small, about 9 medium, about 6 large
1 lb. fresh figs	2½ cups chopped
1 lb. canned figs	12 to 16 whole figs
1 lb. dried figs	about 45 whole figs
1 lb. dried figs	3 cups chopped

WEIGHT	VOLUME
HAZELNUTS	
1 lb. hazelnuts	3½ cups
5 oz. hazelnuts	1 cup
¼ lb. ground hazelnuts	About ¾ cup
LEMONS	
1 lemon	3 to 4 tbsp. juice
1 lemon	1 tbsp. grated zest
LIMES	
1 lime	1 to 2 tbsp. juice
1 lime	2 tsp. grated zest
1 lb. Key limes	18 Key limes
1 lb. Key limes	½ cup juice
PECANS	
1 lb. pecans in the shell	3 cups shelled pecans
1 lb. shelled pecans	About 4 cups pecans
1 lb. shelled pecans	About 3¾ cups chopped
PLUMS AND PRUNES	
1 lb. plums	6 to 8 medium whole plums
1 lb. plums	2½ cups sliced plums
1 lb. plums	2 cups cooked plums
1 lb. pitted prunes	2½ cups
1 lb. pitted prunes	4 to 4½ cups cooked prunes

WEIGHT	VOLUME	WEIGHT	VOLUME
RAISINS		**WALNUTS**	
¼ lb. seedless raisins	¾ cup	4½ oz.	1 cup chopped walnuts
5½ oz. seedless raisins	1 cup	3½ oz.	1 cup walnut halves
1 lb. seedless raisins	3 cups	1 lb. shelled walnuts	3¾ cups

MISCELLANEOUS EQUIVALENTS

WEIGHT	VOLUME	WEIGHT	VOLUME
EGGS		**GELATIN**	
1 medium egg	3 tbsp., about 2 tbsp. white and 1 tbsp. yolk	1 sheet gelatin	½ teaspoon powdered gelatin
5 medium eggs	A bit more than ¾ cup	1 envelope (¼ ounce, 1 tbsp.) powdered gelatin	6 sheets leaf gelatin
1 large egg	3¼ tbsp., about 2¼ tbsp. white, and 1 tbsp. yolk		
5 large eggs	1 cup	2 cups of liquid will set 6 sheets of gelatin	
1 extra-large egg	4 tbsp., about 2¾ tbsp. white and 1¼ tbsp. yolk	1 cup liquid will set 1½ teaspoons powdered gelatin	
5 extra-large eggs	1¼ cups	2 cups liquid will set 1 envelope (¼ ounce, 1 tbsp.) powdered gelatin	

WEIGHT	VOLUME	WEIGHT	VOLUME

GRAHAM CRACKERS

WEIGHT	VOLUME
15 graham cracker squares	1 cup graham cracker crumbs

SUGAR

WEIGHT	VOLUME
7 oz. brown sugar	1 cup
1/4 lb. brown sugar	1/2 cup plus 1 tbsp., packed
1 lb. brown sugar	3 cups loosely packed; 2 1/4 cups, packed
2 oz. confectioners' sugar	6 tbsp. minus 1 teaspoon
1/4 lb. confectioners' sugar	3/4 cup minus 1 tbsp.
6 oz. confectioners'	1 1/4 cups minus 1 tbsp.
1 lb. confectioners' sugar	2 3/4 cups
7 oz. granulated sugar	1 cup
1 lb. granulated sugar	2 1/8 cups

YEAST

WEIGHT	VOLUME
1 ounce (1 cake) fresh compressed yeast	1 (1/4-ounce) packet (2 1/2 teaspoons) active dry yeast
1 standard single-use packet active dry yeast	2 1/2 teaspoons
1/4 ounce active dry yeast	2 1/2 teaspoons

To substitute active-dry yeast for instant yeast increase the amount by 25 percent.

To substitute instant yeast for active-dry yeast decrease the amount by 25 percent.

ALCOHOLS

Eau de Vie . . .49

Grappa and Marc . . .49

Distilled Spirits and What They Are Based On . . .50

How Much Alcohol is Left? . . .51

Madeira Wine . . .52

Scotch Whisky . . .52

Sherry and Port . . .53

Rum . . .53

Types of Sherry . . .53

GERMAN APPLE AND RUM-RAISIN
CUSTARD TORTE (RAHMAPFELKUCHEN) . . .54

ANDALUSIAN BITTERSWEET CHOCOLATE-SHERRY
CAKE WITH SHERRY CUSTARD SAUCE . . .55

BABÀS AL LIMONCELLO PANSA . . .56

Pasticceria Pansa in Amalfi . . .57

Locali Storici d'Italia
(Association of Historical Sites in Italy) . . .58

Limoncello . . .58

FLORENTINE CHOCOLATE NUT ZUCCOTTO . . .58

ZALETI: VENETIAN CORNMEAL COOKIES
WITH GRAPPA RAISINS . . .60

RUM-VANILLA CUSTARD SAUCE . . .61

SHERRY CUSTARD SAUCE . . .61

PASTA FROLLA . . .62

ARUBAN PONCHE CREMA LIQUEUR . . .63

Common Flavored Alcohols . . .64

ALCOHOLS

The chef's secret in many a sauce or braise and the baker's secret in many a cake, cream, or tart is often a generous splash of wine, beer, spirits, or liqueur. In baking, kirschwasser, distilled from cherries; framboise, distilled from raspberries; brandy, distilled from grapes; bourbon, distilled from corn; and dark rum, distilled from sugar cane, are most common. Fortified wines like Marsala from Sicily, Madeira from the Portuguese island of Madeira, Port wine also from Portugal, vin santo from Italy and Greece, ouzo from Greece, and framboise from France are also valuable in baking. Alcoholic beverages add flavor to pastry creams, doughs, and fillings, help preserve holiday fruit cakes, and provide extra moisture and warm flavor in cakes. The alcohol may be added directly to the batter as in the Andalusian Bittersweet Chocolate–Sherry Cake (page 55), used for soaking either on its own or, more commonly, mixed with sugar syrup as for the Florentine Chocolate Nut Zuccotto (page 58).

Distilled spirits, like rum and whiskey, are the concentrated essence of lower alcohol wines and beers produced by taking advantage of the fact that different substances boil at different temperatures. The boiling point of alcohol is 173°F, well below that of water at 212°F. This means that as a mixture of water and alcohol is heated, more of the alcohol than the water will end up in the steam or vapor. The vapor can then be cooled and condensed back into a liquid that has a higher alcoholic content than the original wine (fermented fruit juice) or beer (fermented grain liquid). The substances that give wine and beer their aromas are volatile, so that the same process that concentrates alcohol also concentrates aroma and flavor.

There is evidence that 5,000 years ago the Mesopotamians were using a simple heated pot and a lid into which the condensed vapors were collected to obtain the essential oils of aromatic plants (similar to the way rosewater and orange blossom waters are produced today). The Chinese were already distilling alcohol about 2,000 years ago and by the thirteenth century, alcohol was a commercial product there. In Europe, distilled alcohol was first produced around the year 1100 at the medical school in Salerno, Italy, where it was believed to be a valuable medicine. Two hundred years later, a Catalan scholar, Arnaud of Villanova, named this magical elixir *aqua vitae*, or water of life. Today the same term is found in Scandinavia as *aquavit*, France as *eau de vie*, and in Scotland as whisky, an anglicized version of the Gaelic *usquebaugh*, also meaning water is life. Vodka is a diminutive of the Russian word for water and related to the term *eau de vie*.

Freezing is another method of making concentrated alcohol. This method takes advantage of the fact that pure alcohol freezes at –114°F, far below the freezing temperature of water at 32°F. The liquid is chilled until the water it contains freezes while the alcohol-rich unfrozen fluid is then drained off and used. This simple method of freeze distillation was in use in northern Central Asia as early as the seventh century. Early European settlers in North American made applejack this way, which actually retains and concentrates the flavors without the changes caused by heat distillation. However, because of limitations in geography and climate, freeze-distilling did not become widespread.

Alcoholic elixirs were originally sold by apothecaries and monasteries as cordials to stimulate the heart (*cordial* comes from the Latin word for *heart*). By the fifteenth century, brandy was being produced in Germany and in the Armagnac region of southwest France. Gin, distilled from rye with juniper added for flavor and its diuretic effect, was first produced in sixteenth century Holland where it was and still is known as *genever*. Brandy from the Cognac region just north of Bordeaux was first produced about 1620, while rum was first distilled from sugar cane molasses about 1630. Monastery liqueurs like Benedictine and Chartreuse date from about 1650.

EAU DE VIE

This French term refers to clear, unaged, distilled spirits derived solely from crushed whole fruits that are fermented and then double-distilled. To make eau de vie (eaux de vie in the plural), young, ripe fruits are fermented, distilled, and bottled rapidly to preserve the freshness and aroma of the base fruit. Because eaux de vie are distilled from pure fruits, these clear liquors are both more aromatic and more expensive than flavored liqueurs. (Most liqueurs and schnapps are based on clear grain alcohol with flavorings added.) Eaux de vie include kirschwasser based on cherries, poire William from William (Bartlett) pears, mirabelle from yellow plums, framboise from raspberries, quetsche from prune plums, and pêche from peaches.

GRAPPA AND MARC

Grappa and marc are actually eaux de vie distilled from grape pomace, the pulp including skins and some stems and seeds, which is leftover after the juice is extracted for wine-making. Grappa, which means "grape stalk," and the similar French marc were originally inexpensive, rough beverages made by vineyard workers using the leftovers at the end of the wine season. Both grappa and marc range from 30 to 80 percent alcohol. Strolling the steep, hilly byways of the picturesque artisan's town of Asolo at the foot of the Dolomites in Northern Italy, I found small stores selling grappa flavored with wild mountain herbs, spices, and other aromatics including dried wild mushrooms, juniper berries, gentian root, coffee, quince, honey, anise, almonds, and licorice root. Today, marc and especially grappa can be very expensive beverages indeed, often presented in unusually shaped hand-made bottles. *Aguardiente* is the Spanish version, *tester-branntwein* the German (like brandy-wine in English), and *bagaceira* the Portuguese.

DISTILLED SPIRITS AND WHAT THEY ARE BASED ON

SPIRIT:	DISTILLED FROM:
Bourbon	At least 51% corn along with wheat and/or rye, and malted barley
Brandy, Armagnac, and Cognac	Grapes
Brazilian Cachaça	Sugar cane syrup
Calvados and Applejack	Apples
Gin	Grains, malted barley with juniper and other aromatics added
Grappa, Marc	Grape pomace: the skins, seeds, and pulp left after pressing out the juice for wine
Irish whiskey	Grains and malted barley
Mescal	Maguey cactus
Rum	Sugar cane molasses
Scotch malt whisky	Malted barley
Tequila	Agave cactus
Vodka	Grains, potatoes, malted barley, rye

HOW MUCH ALCOHOL IS LEFT?

According to the US Department of Agriculture, the percentage of alcohol
remaining in a dish based on various cooking methods is as follows:

PREPARATION METHOD	PERCENT OF ALCOHOL RETAINED
Alcohol added to boiling liquid and removed from heat, as for sugar syrup (Torta Gianduia, page 506)	85%
Alcohol flamed, as for bananas foster and cherries jubilee (Brown Bread Apple Charlotte, page 108)	75%
Alcohol not heated, stored overnight or longer, as in macerated fruit for fruitcake (Aliza's Wedding Cake, page 227)	70%
Alcohol combined with other ingredients and baked 15 minutes, in cookies and muffins (Danish Rum Raisin Cupcakes, page 764)	40%
Alcohol combined with other ingredients and baked 30 minutes, as for cake batters (Torta di Savoia, page 535; Torta di Zucca, page 741)	35%
Alcohol combined with other ingredients and baked 1 hour, as for cakes (Brandied Prune Pound Cake, page 710)	25%

MADEIRA WINE

Madeira wine is named after the Portuguese island that sits far out into the Atlantic off the coast of Morocco, where it is has been produced since about 1500. The island of Madeira was a natural port of call for ships traveling to America or south around Africa to Asia that would load up on the famed soft, fortified wine made there. By the eighteenth century, people in the British American and West Indian colonies drank Madeira as their only wine. It was used to toast the Declaration of Independence in 1776 and in 1789 for the inauguration of George Washington.

To make Madeira, wine is fortified with brandy, a practice that was originally done to help keep the wine from turning to vinegar on long sea voyages. It is then aged in wood using a complex method and heated either by the sun or by steam pipes, giving the Madeira its characteristic light, fruity, mellow caramel flavor that makes it so good for cooking and baking.

SCOTCH WHISKY

Scotch malt whisky (its proper spelling in Scotland is without the "e" before the "y") derives from *usquebaugh*, a term of Celtic origin meaning *water of life*, similar to eau de vie and the Scandinavian aquavit, and is distilled from just barley and water. The more common and less expensive grain whiskies from Scotland, England, Canada, and America are usually blends and are partly distilled from wheat. To make authentic Scotch whisky, barley is first malted by soaking the grain until it sprouts, thereby converting its starches into sugar. The malted barley is then dried in a kiln that is traditionally heated by peat (partially decayed vegetable matter that forms in wetlands called bogs, moors, or fens), giving it its smoky character. The malted barley is then milled, mixed with hot water and fed into the mash tun, where revolving paddles stir the mixture for several hours, dissolving the sugars. The liquid, called the wort, is drawn off, and the process repeated twice more, increasing the temperature each time. After cooling, the wort is passed into large vessels called wash backs, traditionally made from wood. There, yeast is added and fermentation begins, converting the sugars into alcohol. After two days, the liquid has a low strength of alcohol similar to beer and is now called wash.

Malt whisky is usually distilled twice in copper-pot stills. The first distillation is called the wash still and the second, the spirit still. The still is heated, and as the steam rises up and passes over the neck of the still, it condenses. The collected liquid is then transferred to the second still, where the same process is repeated. The new-made whisky is then poured into oak casks and, by law, left to mature for three years, during which time the compounds present in the wood help flavor the whisky. Each year, the whisky loses two percent of its volume (called the Angels' Share) due to evaporation.

SHERRY AND PORT

Sherry, known in Spanish as *Vino de Jerez* or *Xérès*, is a fortified wine made in and around the town of Jerez, Spain. According to Spanish law, any product using the registered name Sherry, Jerez, or Xérès must come from the triangular area of the province of Cádiz between Jerez, Sanlúcar de Barrameda, and El Puerto de Santa María. However, Sherry is used as a semi-generic in the United States where it must be labeled with a region of origin such as American Sherry or California Sherry. In earlier times, sherry was known as sack.

To make sherry, grapes are fermented and their juice is first fortified with brandy. If the sherry is destined to be *fino* style, a yeast called *flor* is allowed to grow. *Oloroso* style sherry is fortified to a strength where the flor cannot grow. Because the fortification takes place after fermentation, all natural sherries are dry; any sweetness is applied later. Port wine is fortified half way through fermentation, stopping fermentation so not all the sugars are allowed to turn into alcohol and leaving a sweet wine.

RUM

Rum originated in the Caribbean islands about 1600 and quickly became a valuable commodity in a three-way trade, with slaves from Africa being traded for rum from the Caribbean, which was in turn traded for molasses from the American Colonies, which was made from Caribbean sugar. Because it is distilled from a sugar product (molasses), rum marries very well with desserts and sweet baked goods. It ranges in color from clear to dark brown, with dark rums being the most flavorful and best for baking. The most well-known dark rum and my favorite for baking is Myer's, distilled in Jamaica. Today, most of the world's rum comes from Puerto Rico and the Virgin Islands, though Venezuela also produces some excellent aged rums.

TYPES OF SHERRY

FINO (*fine* in Spanish) is the driest and palest of the traditional varieties of sherry. Manzanilla is a variety of fino sherry made around the port of Sanlúcar de Barrameda.

AMONTILLADO is first aged under a cap of flor yeast, then exposed to oxygen, which produces a sherry that is darker than fino but lighter than Oloroso.

OLOROSO (*scented* in Spanish) is aged while exposed to oxygen for a longer time than a fino or amontillado, producing a darker and richer wine.

SWEET SHERRY (*Jerez Dulce* in Spanish) is created when one of the preceding varieties of dry sherry is sweetened with Pedro Ximénez or Moscatel wine.

CREAM SHERRY is a common type of sweet sherry made from Oloroso. Other varieties include pale cream sherry (made from fino) and medium sherry (made from amontillado).

German Apple and Rum–Raisin Custard Torte (Rahmapfelkuchen)

A delicate, buttery cookie crust, which does not need pre-baking, encloses a layer of apples, plump rum-soaked raisins, and dark rum topped with soft custard in this substantial and satisfying Middle European torte— halfway between a tart and a cake. Sweet, peppery mace (the outer lacy covering of the nutmeg) and sprightly lemon zest impart their aromatic essences to the cake. Make it in cold weather when the wind is blowing up and serve it with hot coffee, hot toddy, or a jigger of rum.

YIELD: 12 SERVINGS

$^{1}/_{4}$ cup dark or golden raisins

$^{1}/_{4}$ cup dark rum

$^{3}/_{4}$ pound German Muerbeteig Dough
   (page 444), chilled

$^{1}/_{2}$ cup soft breadcrumbs

1 tablespoon unsalted butter, melted

4 large tart apples, peeled, cored, and sliced

1 tablespoon lemon juice

$^{1}/_{2}$ teaspoon ground mace

$^{3}/_{4}$ cup sugar

1 cup milk

$^{1}/_{2}$ cup heavy cream (or more milk)

3 large eggs

Soak the raisins in the rum for 30 minutes to soften.

Make the crust: Lightly flour the dough and roll it out between two sheets of wax paper to a circle about 13 inches in diameter and about $^{3}/_{8}$-inch thick. Lay the dough into the bottom and 2 inches up the sides of a 10-inch springform or removable-bottom cake pan without stretching the dough and pressing well into the corners so there are no thick spots.

Alternatively, press the dough out by hand into the bottom and 2 inches up the sides of a 10-inch springform or removable-bottom cake pan, making sure that the pastry is even and not too thick, especially at the corners, where the sides meet the top. Chill the crust for 30 minutes to relax the gluten and so the tart crust maintains its shape.

Make the filling: Preheat the oven to 350°F. Toss together the breadcrumbs and melted butter. Spread over the unbaked pastry crust. Combine the apple slices, lemon juice, mace, and $^{1}/_{4}$ cup sugar and spread over the crumbs. Drain the raisins, reserving the soaking liquid, and sprinkle them over the apples. Bake for 30 minutes or until the apples have softened. Maintain the oven heat.

Combine the milk and cream in a microwavable container, preferably a Pyrex measure, and microwave till steaming hot. In a medium bowl, lightly beat together the eggs and the remaining $^{1}/_{2}$ cup sugar. Whisk in the milk mixture and the reserved raisin soaking liquid. Pour three-quarters of this custard over the apples and bake for 30 minutes or until the custard has formed a thick skin. Poke a hole in the center and pour in the remaining custard. Bake for 30 minutes or until the custard has set in the middle. Cool completely on a wire rack and do

not remove the springform sides until the cake is cool.
Store refrigerated for up to 4 days

Andalusian Bittersweet Chocolate–Sherry Cake with Sherry Custard Sauce

In all my seemingly endless testing for this book, I had my fill of sweets after awhile. However, when I made this cake, I kept sneaking back for another sliver until it was all gone (with help from my family). This ultra-tender, dark chocolate sherry-laden cake barely holds together and gets a warm glow from generous lashings of sherry and kirsch. For an elegant dinner party dessert, bake the cake batter in individual cake pans, muffin tins, timbale molds, or soufflé dishes in a water bath, unmold and serve warm (gently reheat in the microwave) with warm custard sauce. Make sure to coat the pan or molds generously with softened butter, then dust with sugar, as the cake has a tendency to stick. This recipe is gluten-free.

YIELD: ONE 10-INCH BUNDT CAKE, SERVES 12

2 tablespoons (1 ounce) unsalted butter, softened, for the pan

2 tablespoons sugar, for the pan

1/4 pound (1 1/4 cups) potato starch, substitute corn, wheat, or rice starch

3 ounces (3/4 cup minus 1 tablespoon) Dutch-process cocoa

1 teaspoon baking powder

1/4 teaspoon fine sea salt

6 ounces bittersweet chocolate, chopped

1/2 pound (2 sticks) unsalted butter, softened

3/4 cup Amontillado sherry

3 tablespoons kirsch

7 large eggs, separated

1 1/4 cups sugar

2 cups Sherry Custard Sauce (page 61)

Preheat the oven to 350°F. Generously butter a 10-inch Bundt pan and sprinkle with the sugar. In a medium bowl, sift together the dry ingredients: starch, cocoa, baking powder, and salt.

Place the chocolate and butter in a medium-sized microwaveable bowl and melt on low power in the microwave, 2 minutes at a time, or until just barely melted. Add the sherry and kirsch, and whisk to combine, making sure all the chocolate has melted. Cool to room temperature.

In the bowl of a standing electric mixer and using the paddle attachment, beat the egg yolks and 1/2 cup of the sugar until the mixture is light and fluffy, 5 to 6 minutes. Transfer the mixture to a large, wide bowl mixing bowl. Wash out the bowl and wipe it dry. Place the egg whites in the clean and greaseless bowl of a standing electric mixer and using the whisk, beat the egg whites until fluffy, then add the remaining 3/4 cup sugar and continue beating until the whites are firm and glossy, 4 to 5 minutes.

Fold the cooled chocolate mixture into the yolk mixture. Sift the starch mixture over the batter and fold together. Fold in the egg whites in three parts so as not to deflate the batter. Pour the batter into the prepared pan, shaking from side to side to even out the batter. Cover with aluminum foil pricked to allow steam to escape and place the pan in a large baking pan filled with hot water.

Bake for 1 hour or until the cake has just set in the center, has started to come away from the sides of the pan, and a toothpick or skewer stuck in the center comes out clean. Remove the foil and cool the cake on a wire rack to room temperature. (The cake will fall.)

Cut into portions using a knife dipped in hot water and dried completely between each cut. Serve with the Sherry Custard Sauce. (If baking individual cakes, bake for 25 to 30 minutes in a water bath.)

Babàs al Limoncello Pansa

My friend and fellow cook and teacher, Velia de Angelis (proprietor of La Champagneria in Orvieto, Italy, page 79), is the friend of the young couple who are the owners of the justly famed Pasticceria Pansa in Amalfi, Italy. When I visited Pansa, I couldn't get over how light and lemony their babàs were: far different than any I'd ever tasted. I begged Velia to ask them for the recipe and generously, the proprietors passed it on to me. The first time I made them, the babàs came out perfectly, as they have in subsequent testing! Serve the babàs as is, soaked in limoncello liqueur, or, as they do at Pansa, gild the lily and split the babàs in half and fill them with the luscious lemon cream. Babàs are meant to be made ahead and, as long as they soak in the syrup, will maintain their moistness for at least one month.

YIELD: 36 BABÀS

Babàs

1 pound (4 cups) unbleached bread flour

³/4 pound (3 cups minus 3 tablespoons) unbleached all-purpose flour

¹/4 cup sugar

1 teaspoon fine sea salt

1 (¹/4-ounce) package (2¹/4 teaspoons) active dry yeast

1 cup lukewarm milk

10 large eggs, at room temperature

10 ounces (2¹/2 sticks) unsalted butter, cut into small bits and softened

Syrup

4 cups water

4 cups sugar

2 cups Limoncello liqueur, purchased or homemade (page 537)

Juice of 2 lemons (6 tablespoons)

Assembly

3 cups Light Lemon Pastry Cream (page 538)

Make the babàs: Prepare 36 (4- to 6-ounce) babà molds, ceramic ramekins, brioche molds, or muffin tins by spraying them with nonstick baker's coating, or rubbing them with softened butter and dusting them with flour, shaking off the excess.

In a medium bowl, whisk together the dry ingredients: bread flour, all-purpose flour, sugar, and salt. In the bowl of a standing electric mixer, combine the yeast, milk, and 1 cup of the flour mixture, and allow to proof for about 20 minutes or until bubbly.

Using the paddle attachment, beat in three-quarters of the remaining flour mixture. Next, beat in the eggs, one at a time, beating until they are completely incorporated. Add the butter and beat until it has been incorporated and no butter bits remain, about 5 minutes. Finally, beat in the remaining flour, continuing to beat until the dough is smooth and elastic, though still soft and sticky, about 5 minutes. Transfer the dough to a lightly oiled bowl and cover with plastic wrap. Allow the dough to rise at moderate room temperature until it doubles in size, about 1 hour. (If the dough gets too warm, the butter will begin to melt out of it.)

Punch down the dough and scoop or spoon evenly sized portions into the molds. Smooth the tops with your fingers dipped in cold water. Allow the molds to rise at warm room temperature until the dough has almost doubled in bulk again, about 1 hour.

Preheat the oven to 350°F. Bake the babàs for 20 minutes or until they are nicely browned and have begun to pull away from the sides of the molds. Remove from the oven and cool to room temperature in the molds on a wire rack.

Make the syrup: In a small pot, bring the water and sugar to the boil over medium heat. Continue to boil for 1 to 2 minutes or until the syrup is completely clear. Remove from the heat and stir in the Limoncello and the lemon juice.

Remove the babàs from the molds and arrange them in a single layer on baking pans or another shallow container with a lip. Prick each babà with a sharp skewer in several places. Pour the syrup slowly over top, making sure all the babàs are coated. Cover and leave the babàs to soak for 1 to 2 days at room temperature, turning them once or twice so that they are impregnated with the syrup.

When ready to serve, drain the babàs, split open with a serrated knife and spoon or pipe 1 to 2 tablespoons of lemon cream filling into each babà.

PASTICCERIA PANSA IN AMALFI

Located in the heart of the historic center of Amalfi, Pasticceria Pansa would be worth a visit even if the pastries, cakes, gelati, cookies, confections, and more weren't out of this world and made every day from the finest fresh, local ingredients. Dating from 1830, Pansa has delighted numerous patrons, including the playwright Henrik Ibsen, the composer Ricard Wagner, and the writer Henry Longfellow. Today, Pansa is owned by Gabriele Pansa, a member of the fifth generation of the same family that has preserved nearly two hundred years of tradition in the best of Amalfi confectionery.

The shop's early twentieth century furnishings and décor have been beautifully preserved, together with the historic façade. When I visited Pansa in the autumn, huge trays of chocolate-dipped candied local citron, orange, and Sorrento lemon rinds caught my eye, and the cookies, cakes, and pastries I tasted were worth every calorie. Pansa's other specialties include fried zeppole di San Giuseppe, S-shaped Neapolitan susamielli, rococò (hard and crunchy sweet cookie rings page 536), mustacciuoli (chocolate-glazed honey spice cookies), and the thinly layered custard-filled

LOCALI STORICI D'ITALIA (ASSOCIATION OF HISTORICAL SITES IN ITALY)

Pansa is a member of this 200 member plus organization of historic restaurants, hotels, cafes, and confectioners' shops called Locali Storici d'Italia, all of which were founded at least seventy years ago and have been pivotal in Italian history. Go to www.localistorici.it for a complete list of members and links to their respective websites.

LIMONCELLO

Limoncello is a lemon-yellow sweet liqueur made in Sorrento in the southern Italian region of Campania, where the legendary fragrant Sorrento Oval lemon grows in trees overlooking the Mediterranean. There, many people make their own Limoncello and it seems as though every restaurant proprietor pours his or her own version in small stemmed glasses after the meal. Limoncello is also produced on the magical island of Capri, just across the Sorrento Peninsula south of Naples. To make Limoncello, the peels of Sorrento lemons are soaked in grain alcohol (190 proof) to dissolve the lemon-yellow essential oils from the rinds.

One part of the liquid is then combined with two parts sugar syrup to make a liqueur that is about 60 proof or 30 percent alcohol. Villa Massa is considered to be one of the top brands available in the United States (www.villamassa.com). You can make your own by following the recipe on page 537.

Florentine Chocolate Nut Zuccotto

This dome-shaped Florentine pudding gets its name from the fact that it resembles the strikingly beautiful dome-shaped cupola that tops Florence's cathedral. The similarly shaped cardinal's skullcap is called a zucchetto, while a squat, ribbed pumpkin-like squash is called a zucca, perhaps nature's inspiration for all three. Use a deep, hemisphere-shaped bowl to achieve a perfect dome. A copper egg white bowl that holds about 3 quarts is perfect; just make sure to line it with plastic wrap before filling. Many online pastry supply companies, including J.B. Prince in New York, sell the molds in stainless steel (www.jbprince.com). The pudding can be prepared up to three days in advance. Save any extra cake trimmings for another use or grind them for cake crumbs.

YIELD: 12 SERVINGS

$1/4$ pound bittersweet chocolate

3 cups heavy cream, chilled

$3/4$ cup confectioners' sugar

1 teaspoon vanilla extract

$1/4$ cup brandy or dark rum

$1/2$ cup toasted and lightly chopped skin-on almonds

$1/2$ cup toasted, skinned, and chopped hazelnuts

$1/2$ pound bittersweet chocolate, finely chopped

2 Chocolate Sponge Cakes (baked in half sheet pans page 339)

$1/2$ cup sugar

$1/4$ cup Cointreau or other orange-flavored liqueur, or more brandy or rum

Confectioners' sugar, for dusting

Place the chocolate in a microwaveable bowl and melt in the microwave at 10 to 20% power for 2 minutes at a time, or until just barely melted. Whisk until smooth and cool to room temperature.

In the chilled bowl of a standing mixer and using the whisk, beat the cream until it just holds soft peaks. Add the confectioners' sugar, vanilla, and 2 tablespoons of the brandy, and continue beating until the cream is stiff but not at all yellow. Fold in the almonds, hazelnuts, and the chopped chocolate. Divide the mixture between two medium mixing bowls. Fold the melted chocolate into the mixture in one of the bowls.

Line a ($2^1/_2$- to 3-quart) deep hemisphere-shaped bowl with plastic wrap, leaving the edges to overhang by about 4 inches. From one of the cakes, cut out a circle a bit smaller then the diameter of the bowl and reserve (you'll have about one-third of the cake leftover for another use). Cut a 2-inch-wide strip lengthwise from the second cake and reserve for another use. Cut the second cake crosswise into six strips and then cut each strip on the diagonal to form two long, thin triangles. Use the triangles to line the mold completely with the points meeting at the center of the base of the mold and filling in any gaps with small pieces of cake cut from the cake trimmings.

In a small pot combine the sugar with $1/2$ cup of water and bring to a boil, stirring until the syrup is completely clear. Remove from the heat and stir in the remaining 2 tablespoons brandy along with the Cointreau. Brush the cake lining the bowl generously with the syrup, reserving the remainder for the top.

Spread the vanilla cream over the cake in the mold into a layer about 2-inches thick to form an unfilled hollow in the center portion. Spoon the chocolate cream mixture into the center. Cover the cream with the cake circle and brush generously with the reserved liqueur mixture. Cover the mold with the overhanging plastic wrap. Place a plate (or the metal bottom of a removable cake or tart pan) just a bit smaller than the diameter of the bowl onto the mold and top with 2 or 3 cans to weight the mold. Chill at least 6 hours and up to 24 hours.

Cut 8 triangular strips of wax paper or parchment paper, about 6 inches by 2 inches tapering to a point at the bottom to make the "ribs" of the dome. Just before serving, remove the weights and the plate from the zuccotto and invert it onto 9-inch cake cardboard or a cake bottom to support it. Transfer to a wire cooking rack placed over wax paper.

Arrange the wax paper pieces over the zuccotto with the pointed ends meeting in the center of the dome and leaving equal spaces in between. Sift the confectioners' sugar generously over the mold. Carefully remove the wax paper strips and cut into serving portions using a hot, wet knife, washed clean between each cut. Store the zuccotto covered and refrigerated up to 3 days.

Zaleti: Venetian Cornmeal Cookies with Grappa Raisins

These oval-shaped cookies from the Veneto get their crunch from the cornmeal typical of the region. Grappa-soaked raisins, pine nuts, and/or candied fruits are added. Called zaleti, zaletti, *or even* zaeti, *the cookies get their name from Venetian dialect and derive from the Italian word* gialetti, *meaning small yellow things, because of the golden cornmeal. The cookies are a typical sweet of the Venetian ghetto and are also found on the island of Corfu, a Venetian colony from 1386 to 1797, where they are flavored with orange blossom water.*

YIELD: 4 ROLLS, EACH MAKES 15 COOKIES, 5 DOZEN TOTAL

$^1/_2$ pound (1$^1/_2$ cups) golden raisins

$^3/_4$ cup grappa or white rum

10 ounces (2$^1/_4$ cups plus 2 tablespoons) stone-ground yellow cornmeal

10 ounces (2$^1/_2$ cups minus 2$^1/_2$ tablespoons) unbleached all-purpose flour

2 teaspoons baking powder

$^1/_2$ teaspoon fine sea salt

6 large egg yolks

1$^1/_4$ cups sugar

$^3/_4$ pound (3 sticks) unsalted butter, melted and cooled

Confectioners' sugar, for dusting

Soak the raisins in the grappa until softened, at least 1 hour, but preferably overnight. Line an 18 x 13-inch half sheet pan (or other large baking pan) with parchment paper or a silicone mat.

In a bowl, whisk together the dry ingredients: cornmeal, flour, baking powder, and salt.

In the bowl of a standing electric mixer and using the paddle attachment, beat the yolks with the sugar until light and fluffy, 5 to 6 minutes. Add the butter and beat together until incorporated and the mixture is creamy, 2 to 3 minutes. Beat in the cornmeal mixture. Finally, fold in the raisins with their soaking liquid. Transfer the dough to a plastic bag and shape into a flattened rectangle. Chill in the refrigerator for 1 hour or in the freezer for 30 minutes until firm but still malleable.

Divide the dough into 4 portions and form each part into "salami" shapes, about 1$^1/_2$ inches in diameter. Chill again until firm, about 30 minutes (or freeze 2 of the rolls to bake at a later date).

Preheat the oven to 350°F.

Using a sharp knife, cut the dough logs on the diagonal into $^3/_4$-inch thick slices. Arrange the slices on the baking pan about 2 inches apart. Using the palm of your hand, press each slice to flatten into an oblong shape.

Bake for 15 minutes, or until lightly colored. Cool completely on a wire rack then dust generously with confectioners' sugar before serving. Store in an airtight container such as a cookie tin or ceramic cookie jar up to 5 days.

Rum–Vanilla Custard Sauce

This is the time to get out that good, heavy-bottomed pot, preferably copper lined with tin or stainless steel, for the most even cooking. Because copper is such a superb conductor of heat and doesn't tend to develop hot spots, a copper pot will make it easier to cook the custard until it thickens fully without curdling. Use half a plump, fragrant vanilla bean here for those beautiful, tiny black specks that show the sauce contains the real thing. For the boldest flavor, I add dark rum, such as Myer's, to the sauce. Chill the sauce and run it in an ice cream machine, following the manufacturer's directions for rich and creamy French-style rum-vanilla ice cream

YIELD: 2 1/2 CUPS

1 cup milk

1 cup light cream

1/2 vanilla bean, split lengthwise,
    or 1 teaspoon vanilla extract

4 large egg yolks

1/2 cup sugar

Pinch flour

2 tablespoons dark rum

Place the milk, cream, and vanilla bean in a medium, nonreactive, heavy-bottomed pot and heat till scalded.

In a medium bowl, beat the yolks with the sugar until well-combined. Sprinkle with the flour and whisk to combine. Pour in a little of the hot milk mixture to temper the mixture. Whisk in the remaining milk mixture.

Transfer to the pot and heat until the sauce visibly thickens and reads 165°F on a thermometer.

Scrape out the insides of the vanilla bean using a small sharp knife and add back into the custard. Discard the vanilla bean (or rinse well and dry and store in a bowl of sugar). Whisk in the rum and then transfer to a metal bowl to cool, stirring often to prevent a skin from forming.

Serve the sauce warm. Chill any remaining sauce and store for up to 1 week refrigerated. To reheat, place the sauce in a microwavable bowl and microwave at low power (10 to 20 percent power) for 1 to 2 minutes at a time, stirring in between so the sauce heats evenly without curdling.

Sherry Custard Sauce

Serve this sherried sauce warm with the Andalusian Bittersweet Chocolate Sherry Cake (page 55). If you have an ice cream machine, try freezing the custard for a sophisticated super-creamy sherry custard gelato and serve it topped with ground espresso. (If the sauce curdles slightly, blend it till smooth with an immersion blender or transfer to jar of a blender and then blend.)

YIELD: 2 3/4 CUPS

1 cup milk

3/4 cup heavy cream

4 large egg yolks

1/2 cup sugar

Pinch all-purpose flour

1/4 cup Amontillado sherry

2 teaspoons vanilla extract

Place the milk and cream in a medium, nonreactive, heavy-bottomed pot and heat till scalded.

In a medium bowl, beat the yolks with the sugar until well-combined. Sprinkle with the flour and whisk to combine. Pour in a little of the hot milk mixture to temper the mixture. Whisk in the remaining milk mixture. Transfer to the pot and heat until the sauce visibly thickens and reads 165°F on a thermometer.

Whisk in the sherry and the vanilla and then transfer to a metal bowl to cool, stirring often to prevent a skin from forming.

Serve the sauce warm or refrigerate up to four days before serving. To reheat, place the sauce in a microwavable bowl and microwave at low power (10 to 20 percent power) for 1 to 2 minutes at a time, stirring in between so the sauce heats evenly without curdling.

FROM FRENCH GASTRONOMIC SCIENTIST HERVÉ THIS:

Adding a pinch of flour to the custard mix can prevent the sauce from curdling, although the reasons for this protection are still a subject of debate.

Pasta Frolla

This rich and fragile dough, fragrant with lemon zest and Sicilian Marsala, is perfect for Italian-style tortas like the Crostata della Nonna: Grandma's Ricotta Pine Nut Tart (page 676) and the Crostata di Riso: Italian Rice Tart (page 776). I also use it for the Spanish Apple Torte (page 105). You may chill the soft and rather sticky dough then roll it out between two sheets of wax paper or press it into the tart pan. Dry sherry or Madeira can be substituted for the Marsala. If you're using sweet Marsala, cut the sugar down to 1 tablespoon.

YIELD: 1 3/4 POUNDS, ENOUGH FOR 2 TARTS

1/2 pound (2 sticks) unsalted butter,
    at room temperature

1/4 cup sugar

6 egg yolks

1/4 cup dry Marsala, substitute dry sherry

Grated zest of 1 lemon (1 tablespoon)

3/4 pound (3 cups minus 3 tablespoons)
    unbleached all-purpose flour

1/2 teaspoon fine sea salt

Place the butter and sugar into the bowl of a standing mixer. Using the paddle attachment, beat until light and creamy, 3 to 4 minutes. Add the egg yolks, Marsala, and lemon zest, and beat until creamy. Add the flour and salt, and beat again briefly, until just combined.

Transfer to a plastic bag and shape into a flattened rectangle. Chill in the refrigerator for 1 hour or in the freezer for 30 minutes until firm but still malleable.

Store in the freezer for up to 3 months.

Aruban Ponche Crema Liqueur

This eggnog-like thick and custardy liqueur from Aruba is also known as "coddle" because it is "coddled," or gently cooked in a water bath. Super-smooth, lusciously rich, and generously laced with rum, ponche crema is traditionally served with tiny spoons in small glasses to Aruban "aunties," who otherwise never touch spirits. Serve the ponche crema as a sauce for bread pudding like the Papiamento Bread Pudding with Ponche Crema from the Aruban restaurant of the same name (page 562). Or serve it in tiny cordial glasses with demitasse spoons or in larger glasses over ice to accompany pound cakes or cookies.

YIELD: 2 QUARTS

8 large egg yolks

1 (14-ounce) can evaporated milk

2 (13-ounce) cans sweetened condensed milk

1 teaspoon freshly grated nutmeg

$\frac{1}{2}$ teaspoon ground cinnamon

Grated zest of 1 lemon (1 tablespoon)

1 (750-ml) bottle gold rum or brandy

2 teaspoons vanilla extract

In a medium bowl, whisk together the egg yolks, evaporated milk, condensed milk, nutmeg, cinnamon, and lemon zest to combine well. Transfer to a medium, nonreactive pot and heat over medium-low heat, stirring often with a wooden spoon or silicone spatula until the mixture thickens visibly and reaches 165°F on a thermometer, about 8 minutes.

Remove from the heat, and stir in the rum and vanilla. Strain the mixture through a fine sieve into a bowl, preferably stainless steel. Chill the mixture by placing it into a second bowl that has been filled with ice and water. Stir occasionally to prevent the formation of a skin.

Transfer the mixture, preferably using a funnel, into one or 2 sterilized, clear decorative bottles. Close tightly and refrigerate for up to 3 months.

COMMON FLAVORED ALCOHOLS

SPIRIT:	FLAVOR:
Amaretto	Almond
Anisette, Ouzo, Raki, Araq	Aniseed
Aquavit, Kümmel	Caraway and cumin seed
Benedictine, Chartreuse, Jaegermeister	Mixed herbs and spices
Cassis	Black currants
Cointreau, Curaçao, Grand Marnier, Triple Sec	Orange and bitter orange
Crème de Cocoa and Vandermeer	Chocolate
Crème de Menthe and Peppermint Schnapps	Peppermint
Frangelico	Hazelnuts
Limoncello	Lemon peel
Midori	Melon
Nocino	Green walnuts
Sambuca	Elderberries
Slivovitz, Quetsch, Mirabelle	Plums
Pernod, Ricard, Absinthe, Ouzo	Anise, star anise plus wormwood in absinthe
Tia Maria and Kahlua	Coffee

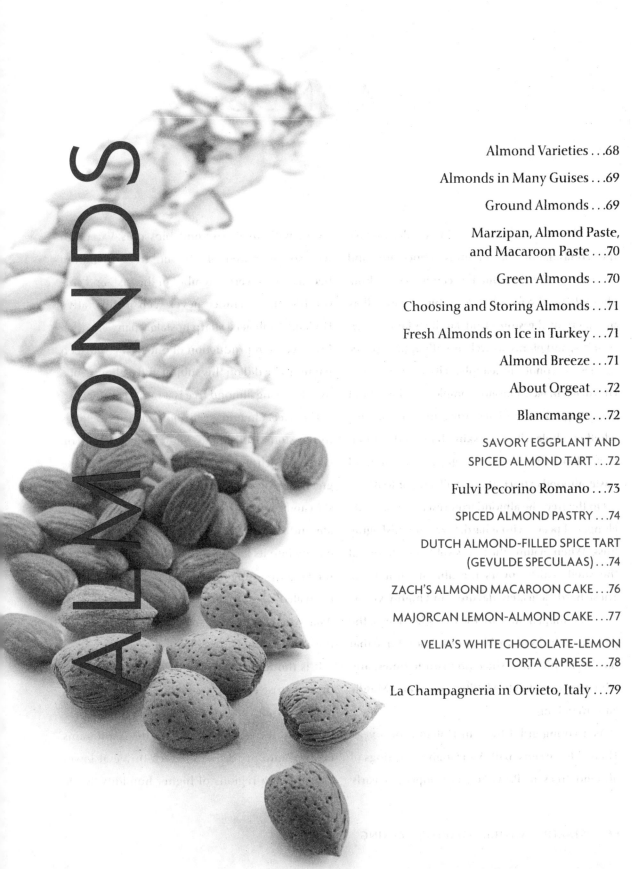

ALMONDS

Almond Varieties . . .68

Almonds in Many Guises . . .69

Ground Almonds . . .69

Marzipan, Almond Paste,
and Macaroon Paste . . .70

Green Almonds . . .70

Choosing and Storing Almonds . . .71

Fresh Almonds on Ice in Turkey . . .71

Almond Breeze . . .71

About Orgeat . . .72

Blancmange . . .72

SAVORY EGGPLANT AND
SPICED ALMOND TART . . .72

Fulvi Pecorino Romano . . .73

SPICED ALMOND PASTRY . . .74

DUTCH ALMOND-FILLED SPICE TART
(GEVULDE SPECULAAS) . . .74

ZACH'S ALMOND MACAROON CAKE . . .76

MAJORCAN LEMON-ALMOND CAKE . . .77

VELIA'S WHITE CHOCOLATE-LEMON
TORTA CAPRESE . . .78

La Champagneria in Orvieto, Italy . . .79

ALMONDS

Almonds give me joy. While I do love the combination of almonds, chocolate, and coconut in the Almond Joy candy bar, I think almonds are also wonderful combined with fellow members of the stone fruit family, like cherries, peaches, and plums, as well as with apples, pears, berries, coconut, pineapple, citrus fruits, and chocolate. In fact, almonds complement just about every ingredient and flavoring used in baking, whether whole with their skins, blanched without their skins, sliced, slivered, ground, as almond paste, almond extract, almond oil, raw, or toasted.

On the tree, the almond fruit resembles a small, elongated peach with a hard, fuzzy greenish-gray husk. When mature, the husks split open to reveal the shell which covers the almond nut itself. These hard, delicately flavored and highly versatile oval-shaped nuts are the inner kernels of the pale green fruits of the beautiful almond tree that has been cultivated since prehistoric times, and which are essential to Mediterranean and Middle Eastern baking.

As a young girl, I lived in Holland for a year. There, I fell in love with Van Gogh's paintings of almond trees in Provence, enveloped in early spring with lovely soft pink blossoms. Van Gogh was so enamored of almond trees in bloom because they were a symbol of the lush and colorful South of France never seen in his native Holland. I still get a sharp nostalgic pang any time I see even a reproduction of one of the fourteen paintings he did on this subject and a glimpse of a live flowering almond tree is a rare treat.

The sweet almond, *Amgydalus communus*, belongs to the stone fruit family along with the apricot, cherry, peach, nectarine, and plum, but its pale green apricot–shaped fruit has tough and leathery skin and can only be eaten when very young. The almond is essentially a fruit tree that puts all its energy into its kernel, rather than its flesh. Part of the larger plum family, the wild ancestors of the cultivated almond came from Western and Central Asia, where trees with small, dry fruits that produce bitter kernels are still found.

It is thought that millions of years ago, when the land rose up to form the mountains that separate Central Asia from China and Mongolia, the trees on the eastern side of the mountains evolved into peach trees, which thrive at lower elevations in regions of higher humidity, while almond trees developed in the drier regions along the fringes of the deserts and lower mountain slopes to the west. Almonds were, and are, prized for their long-keeping qualities and concentrated food energy. In ancient times, nomads mixed ground almonds, chopped dates, bits of pistachios, sesame, and breadcrumbs and rolled the mixture into small balls of "trail mix" to sustain them on long desert journeys.

Almond trees have long been cultivated in the temperate climate of the Mediterranean and do not thrive further north. They have been cultivated in Persia (now Iran) for thousands of years. Today, almonds grow from Afghanistan and Kashmir, India, to as far west as California, where over half of the world's crop is grown. Spain and Italy are the most important producers after the United States.

The almond is one of the first trees to flower in Israel, usually in early February and coinciding with Tu Bishvat, the birthday festival of the trees. In Biblical times, the almond was a symbol of watchfulness and promise because of its early flowering. The almond is described in the book of Genesis as being "among the best of fruits." In the book of Numbers, Levi is chosen from the other tribes of Israel by Aaron's rod, which brought forth almond flowers. According to tradition, Aaron's rod bore sweet almonds on one side and bitter on the other (even now both sweet and bitter almonds can fruit on the same branch). The seven-branched menorah (or candelabra) which stood in the ancient Temple was based on the shape of the almond blossom. In Christian medieval art, the almond is a symbol of divine approval, harking back to the story of Aaron's rod.

Phoenician traders introduced almond trees into cultivation in Spain, and it was being grown in Provence as early as the eighth century BCE. The Greeks cultivated the almond, which they called *amygdalon*, or "tonsil plum". *Amygdalon* is the source of the almond's name in modern European languages from *mandel* in German, to *mandorle* in Italian and *amande* in French. Ancient Romans referred to almonds as "Greek nuts," because they brought the trees from Greece. Italian musicians were inspired by the pleasing oval of the almond in designing the musical instrument that evolved in the eighteenth century into the *mandolino* or mandolin.

Almonds were of great importance in early Arabic and medieval European cooking and confectionary in dishes such as blancmange (in French) or bianco mangiare (in Italian), a light almond-milk pudding, common until Victorian times; almond milk (or orgeat); and marchpane (or marzipan). In Spain and Greece today, religious days of fast mean not only abstaining from meat other than fish but also from the milk of animals and eggs, so orgeat—orange blossom-scented almond milk made by grinding almonds and steeping them in water—was drunk. Today, orgeat syrup goes into milky white cooling drinks and sweet cocktails like the Mai-Tai.

In Greece, ground blanched almonds are used to make a great variety of desserts made without animal products like eggs and butter, called *amygdalota*, which are served during the religious season of Lent. Because of their pure white color and intense sweetness, these sweets also appear at wedding banquets.

Sweet almonds, which come from the common almond tree, were developed by centuries of cultivation and breeding. Bitter almonds, their older ancestor, come from the bitter almond tree, *Amgydalus communus Amara*, and are used in small quantities for flavoring. However, even sweet almond trees sometimes yield bitter almonds, and some sweet almond **cultivars smell faintly of bitter almond. Because they contain poisonous cyanide (which is destroyed by heat), it is illegal to sell bitter almonds in the United States. Fifty unprocessed bitter almonds can be lethal. In Europe, bitter almonds are sold at pharmacies and are added in small quantities to marzipan, amaretti biscuits, and amaretto liqueur for that edge of intense almondy bitterness. In the United States, almond extract, also made from bitter almonds, is substituted for whole bitter almonds.**

ALMOND VARIETIES

In Spain, the plump, rounded, almost coin-shaped Marcona almonds are grown only along the Mediterranean coast from Tarragona south to Málaga. Smooth and juicy with rich, sweet flavor, marconas are usually found in the United States deep-fried in olive oil, sometimes with rosemary, until brown and crunchy, then sprinkled with sea salt. Marcona almond trees bloom early, making them vulnerable to late spring frosts, so they are challenging to grow. But, because they grow inside a hard shell that resists insects, marconas can be grown without the use of pesticides. The Jordan almond is a plump variety of almond from Málaga, Spain, where growing conditions produce unusually large fruits. They are considered to be the finest cultivated almond and are often sold with a hard pastel-colored, candy-coating, also known as Jordan almonds.

Spanish missionaries are credited for bringing the almond to California, now the world's largest producer with over 100 varieties of almonds being grown. In California, the milder nonpareil almond is most common, because its thin shell and smooth kernel makes the nuts easier to process. Mission almonds have a thick shell and dark brownish-red skin with a wrinkled kernel that is wider than that of the nonpareil. They have a stronger flavor and are used in snacks and ice creams, and are often toasted first.

ALMONDS IN MANY GUISES

Almonds are sold in many forms. Young green almonds are the newest (and oldest) form of almonds found in season in early spring across the Mediterranean, and are now starting to be available in the United States from specialty growers, especially in California. They are a true seasonal delicacy that will hopefully become more common in the next few years.

Almonds may be found whole, either skin-on or blanched; slivered (in little sticks); sliced, either blanched or skin-on (my preference for their stronger flavor and more distinctive look); ground; or in almond flavoring. Blanched almonds, or almonds with their skins removed, are valued in baking for their light color, but as with all nuts, toasting enhances their flavor. Delicate and expensive, almond oil is extracted from bitter almonds and used in fine baking to oil pans and molds; the pulpy residue is steeped in water and distilled to make almond extract.

Almonds are further prepared and sold as marzipan, almond paste, almond extract, liqueurs, and almond milk. Store almonds in an airtight container in the freezer to keep them from getting rancid, especially in the summer.

GROUND ALMONDS

Ground almonds help give structure to cakes as an alternative to flour in Austro-Hungarian tortes and French flourless chocolate cakes. Mixed with meringue, almonds add flavor and texture to light, crunchy Dacquoise like the White Chocolate, Hazelnut, and Espresso Dacquoise on page 377 or the similar Japonais cakes in French patisserie. A layer of absorbent *frangipane*, a traditional French mixture of almond paste and pastry cream, spread on the bottom of a fruit tart, prevents the fruit juices from making the pastry soggy as in the Venetian Cornmeal and Cherry Crostata (page 305). Macaroons, Chinese almond cookies, and rich, buttery financiers (page 215) are just a few of the many kinds of cookies based on almonds.

I've found reasonably priced almond meal (made from skin-on almonds) at Trader Joe's and from Bob's Red Mill. In general, though, I prefer to grind my own almonds (ideally mixed with flour or sugar to keep them from getting oily) in the food processor. Once ground, the almonds must be tightly sealed without air to keep them from absorbing unwanted refrigerator or freezer odors. For the finest, most delicate white almond meal, start with blanched (skin-off) almonds.

MARZIPAN, ALMOND PASTE, AND MACAROON PASTE

Marzipan, a smooth, kneaded, stiff sweet paste made by cooking finely ground premium-grade almonds with sugar until the mixture reaches a smooth and creamy consistency, gets its characteristic flavor from bitter almonds and is often flavored with rosewater. Marzipan typically contains more than sixty percent sugar. Believed to have originated in Persia (today Iran), marzipan was probably brought to Europe in the Middle Ages by Arab traders, where it became a specialty of the Baltic region of Germany, particularly in the town of Lubeck. Prized for its moldability, the art of working with marzipan reached a high level in the convents of Sicily, where the sisters made small cakes of "marzapane" formed into miniature fruits, flowers, figures, and vegetables, and painted with food coloring.

Marzipan, rolled into thin sheets and glazed, is traditionally used to cover and decorate wedding cakes and to mold figures. In some places, marzipan is shaped into small figures of animals, such as pigs, to mark the New Year; in Italy, small marzipan fruits are eaten at Christmas. I have a photo of tiny eerily lifelike marzipan babies made in the Greek island of Chios which I visited not long ago.

Almond paste, mostly used for baking, is similar to marzipan but is less sweet (about 50 percent sugar), and is slightly coarser in tex-ture. Look for the sausage-shaped tubes of Odense almond paste from Denmark and small cans of American almond paste in the supermarket baking aisle, especially during the holiday season. Macaroon paste is a blend of ground almonds, sugar, and ground apricot kernels used by many commercial bakeries. Order almond paste and macaroon paste from American Almond at www.lovenbake.com.

GREEN ALMONDS

A traditional springtime treat in Turkey, Greece, the Middle East, southern Italy, France, and Spain, green almonds—the young form of the familiar nut—have recently become available in some American specialty markets in spring. The soft, fuzzy, pale green almond fruits, which resemble apricots, have a jelly-like, soft inside and a distinctive, subtly herbal, slightly bitter flavor. The inner green almond nuts are at their best when the seed case has just begun to plump, the interior is liquid, and there is no hint of a shell. The just-developed, soft, creamy "green" almonds (unripe, not green in color) are shelled and can be sprinkled on fruit salad and fresh berries, either raw or gently fried. Green almonds are in season for a brief three-week period from late April to early May. A few weeks later, the hull and shell toughen, and the inner seed changes from translucent whitish jelly to a crunchy white nut. In season, order from www.greenalmonds.com.

CHOOSING AND STORING ALMONDS

To choose almonds in the shell, shake them. If they rattle, chances are the almond inside has shrunk as it aged. You'll find shelled almonds with skins and blanched almonds with their skins removed. Buy whole almonds and chop or slice them before each use for the freshest flavor. To check for rancidity, slice the almond in half and look for a solid white texture throughout. If it is yellowish or has a honeycomb texture, it is way past its prime and should be discarded. The skin of the almond is edible, but sometimes bitter. Taste first, if it's not too bitter, don't bother removing it as it will add flavor to the recipe.

I find it best to store almonds in the freezer, especially in hot weather to prevent insect infestation and rancidity. An opened can or package of almond paste should be tightly covered to prevent it from drying out, then stored in the refrigerator up to six months. Almonds stored in a hot pantry will deteriorate quickly and tend to get buggy. Once packaged almonds are opened, store in an airtight container or a sealed zipper lock bag with the air squeezed out in a cool, dry, dark place (ideally in the refrigerator) and use within three months, or even better, vacuum-seal them. Toasting almonds before using them in baked goods not only intensifies their flavor but also makes them lighter so they won't sink in the batter.

FRESH ALMONDS ON ICE IN TURKEY

Alaçati is a lovely and lively revitalized old town first settled by Ionian Greeks on the Aegean Coast of Turkey near Çesme. Strolling the streets one evening along with crowds of other window-shoppers, people-watchers, and café-sitters, I just had to try a handful of fresh almonds on ice from the almond vendor. The gentleman had a special cart fitted with blocks of ice on which he kept fresh shelled almonds protected behind glass. These highly perishable, delicately milky nuts must be kept ice cold to keep them fresh. The nuts slipped out of their loose-fitting skins right into my mouth but because they had not been cured or dried, the almonds I didn't get to eat became rancid in one day! *Quel domage.*

Almond Breeze

This unsweetened almond milk from Diamond Almonds is a creamy, mild-tasting, non-dairy beverage made from almonds. I used it very successfully as a natural substitute for milk and cream when making desserts and even creamy gelato without dairy products in the recipes I developed for the upscale kosher restaurant in Elkins Park, Pennsylvania, called Max and David's (www.maxanddavids.com). Almond Breeze, which is certified kosher, is available at Whole Foods markets.

ABOUT ORGEAT

Orgeat, sometimes called "French Orgeat," is a sweetened syrup made from almonds and orange blossom water or rosewater and is often used in mixed drinks. It was originally made from a blend of barley (*orzo* in Italian) and almonds. The syrup is an emulsion of the oils in the almond in water, making it similar in use to milk. The Italian *orzata* and the Spanish *horchata* or *orxata* have the same origin.

Prior to refrigeration, it was difficult to store milk because it would spoil very quickly, so only farmers and their families drank milk regularly. For the most part milk was turned into butter and especially cheese, because it could be stored for a long time and sold as needed. The oils in barley and almond are relatively stable at room temperature and higher temperatures, so they don't spoil very quickly, making them well suited for this milk-like substitute. To prepare it, almonds (and/or barley) are crushed in a mortar while adding water, thereby extracting the oils in the almonds and emulsifying them with the water. After letting the mushy mixture steep, it is filtered through muslin cloth and the resulting milky-looking liquid is used in place of milk.

BLANCMANGE

Blancmange (white dish) is a soft and creamy white pudding made from almond milk, sugar, rice flour, and shredded chicken (usually capon) or fish, and often scented with rosewater. This popular dish of the upper classes throughout Europe was usually eaten during Lent, as far back as medieval times and into Victorian times. Although its origins are obscure, it is believed that blancmange came about with the Arab introduction of rice and almonds to early medieval Europe. However, there seems to be no similar Arab dish at the time. In Turkey, I learned about a traditional chicken breast pudding called Tavuk Göğs, made from shredded chicken breast, rice, milk, sugar, and cinnamon. The dish, which is popular today in Istanbul, must have a similar origin.

Savory Eggplant and Spiced Almond Tart

This recipe dates to a recipe I developed while working as food consultant for a restaurant project that became the candle-lit, romantic Moroccan-style Tangerine in Philadelphia's Old City. While I don't believe any of my recipes have survived the years, I still love to make this sophisticated yet earthy tart with the surprising creaminess of eggplant in the filling. Serve it in smaller portions as an appetizer accompanied by a small salad.

YIELD: 12 APPETIZER SERVINGS;
8 MAIN COURSE SERVINGS

3/4 pound Spiced Almond Pastry (page 74)
1 1/2 pounds eggplant (1 large)
3/4 pound mild goat cheese
1/4 cup shredded pecorino Romano cheese,

preferably Fulvi

3 large eggs

2 egg yolks

2 tablespoons extra-virgin olive oil

2 tablespoons chopped fresh marjoram,
  or 2 teaspoons dried oregano

2 teaspoons crushed garlic

$1/2$ teaspoon Aleppo pepper or
  crushed red pepper flakes

1 teaspoon ground coriander

1 teaspoon ground cumin

Fine sea salt and fresh ground black pepper to taste

$1/4$ cup sliced almonds, skin-on

Bake the crust: Preheat the oven to 375°F. Roll the dough out about $3/8$-inch thick into a 10-inch tart pan with a removable bottom, pressing well into the corners so there are no thick spots. Trim the overhang flush with the edges.

Fit a piece of heavy-duty foil onto the dough and fill with beans or other pie weights. Blind bake (just the pastry crust, no filling) until the dough is cooked through but not yet browned, about 30 minutes, on the bottom shelf of the oven. Remove the foil and the weights, reduce the oven temperature to 325°F and bake for 10 minutes longer, or until the dough is evenly and lightly browned. Remove from the oven and cool to room temperature on a wire rack. Maintain the oven heat.

Make the filling and assemble the tart: Wrap the eggplant in aluminum foil and place in the oven, baking along with the tart crust if desired, about 1 hour or until the flesh is completely soft. Split the eggplant open lengthwise and scoop out the meat, discarding the skin. Drain the meat in a colander for 10 minutes to remove excess liquid and any bitter-tasting juices. Chop finely.

Whisk together the goat cheese, Romano cheese, eggs, yolks, olive oil, marjoram, garlic, hot pepper, coriander, cumin, and salt and pepper until smooth, then combine with the eggplant. Spoon the mixture into the crust and sprinkle with the almonds.

Place the tart on a baking pan to catch any drips and bake for 35 minutes on the bottom shelf of the oven, or until just set in the middle and lightly browned on top. Remove from the oven and cool slightly on a wire rack before cutting into serving portions.

To make ahead, bake one or 2 days before, chill, and cut into serving portions. Arrange the slices on a parchment paper–lined baking pan, cover loosely with aluminum foil, and reheat in a moderate oven about 30 minutes, or until thoroughly heated, removing the foil for the last 5 to 10 minutes of baking.

FULVI PECORINO ROMANO

As is apparent in its name, pecorino Romano cheese originated in the countryside outside of Rome. Today all of these cheeses are actually produced in Sardinia, except Fulvi. To make it, sheep milk from the Lazio region in the hills outside of Rome goes to dairies in the village of Nepi, where, according to the centuries-old method, the cheese is handmade into giant wheels weighing about 65 pounds. The cheese, which is aged for over ten months, is pungent and pleasingly salty, but without the "soapiness" sometimes found in other Romano cheeses. I use Fulvi Romano cheese when I want a sharp accent of pungent flavor and can find it at my local Whole Foods market.

Spiced Almond Pastry

This rich pastry, suffused with North African spices, is crumbly with the almonds that are typical of Moroccan cooking. Use it for savory tarts such as the Savory Eggplant and Spiced Almond Tart (page 72) or to make the crust for a chicken or vegetable pot pie.

YIELD: ABOUT ³⁄₄ POUND, ENOUGH FOR
A 10-INCH TART

6 ounces (1¹⁄₂ cups minus 1¹⁄₂ tablespoons)
   unbleached all-purpose flour
2 ounces (³⁄₄ cup) whole almonds, skin-on
1 teaspoon ground coriander
¹⁄₂ teaspoon ground cumin
¹⁄₄ teaspoon red pepper flakes
¹⁄₂ teaspoon fine sea salt
¹⁄₄ pound (1 stick) unsalted butter, cut in bits and chilled
1 large egg
2 tablespoons buttermilk, substitute yogurt
   or sour cream

Place the flour, almonds, coriander, cumin, red pepper flakes, and salt into the bowl of a food processor and process until the nuts are finely ground. Add the butter and process until the mixture resembles oatmeal. In a small bowl, lightly beat together the egg and buttermilk. Add the buttermilk mixture to the processor bowl and process only long enough for the dough to come together and form large moist clumps. Knead together briefly by hand until the dough forms a ball.

Transfer to a plastic bag and shape into a flattened rectangle. Chill in the refrigerator for 1 hour or in the freezer for 30 minutes until firm but still malleable.

Dutch Almond–Filled Spice Tart (Gevulde Speculaas)

Gevulde means stuffed in Dutch, referring here to a spiced dough stuffed with almond-paste and made into a shallow shortbread-like tart. The dough is sometimes rolled out into a long rectangle, filled with a stick of almond paste and then formed into a thick stick called a banketstaaf (banquet stick). These sticks remind me very much of the Italian Jewish sfratti on page 520. In Holland, sweethearts would form the cookies into banketletter (banquet letter), and present each other with cookies in the shape of their initials. In the past, with the ingeniousness of the poor, people would make mock almond paste from ground haricot (white) beans instead of costly almonds to fill their speculaas. Decorate this tart with fancy cut-outs of excess dough and/or halved blanched almonds. Substitute rosewater instead of the vanilla and almond extracts for a more authentic medieval flavor.

YIELD: 12 TO 16 SERVINGS

Dough

¹⁄₂ pound (2 cups minus 2 tablespoons) unbleached
   all-purpose flour
1 tablespoon Speculaas Spices (page 353), substitute
   apple pie or pumpkin pie spice mix

$^1/_2$ teaspoon baking soda

$^1/_2$ teaspoon fine sea salt

6 ounces (1$^1/_2$ sticks) unsalted butter, softened

5 ounces ($^3/_4$ cup packed) light brown sugar

2 tablespoons milk

2 teaspoons grated orange zest

1 teaspoon grated lemon zest

1 teaspoon vanilla extract

1 teaspoon almond extract

Filling

10 ounces (1$^3/_4$ cups) blanched almonds

$^3/_4$ cup sugar

2 large eggs

1 teaspoon almond extract

1 teaspoon grated lemon zest

Glaze

$^1/_4$ cup confectioners' sugar

1 tablespoon hot water

$^1/_2$ teaspoon almond extract

$^1/_2$ cup blanched almonds, for garnish

Make the dough: In a medium bowl, whisk together the dry ingredients: flour, Speculaas spices, baking soda, and salt.

In the bowl of a standing electric mixer and using the paddle attachment, cream the butter and brown sugar together until light and fluffy, 5 to 6 minutes. Beat in the flour mixture.

In a small bowl, combine the milk, citrus zests, and the extracts, and add to the mixer bowl. Beat only long enough for the dough to form large moist clumps. Knead briefly to combine the mixture into a ball. Transfer to a zipper lock bag and chill for 1 hour in the refrigerator or 30 minutes in the freezer.

Preheat the oven to 350°F. Divide the dough in half, with one portion slightly larger. Press the larger portion of the dough into the bottom and up the sides of a 9-inch tart part or a 9-inch springform cake pan (the dough will only come about 1 inch high up the sides). Roll out the remaining portion of dough between 2 sheets of lightly floured waxed paper to about 10 inches in diameter and keep refrigerated.

Make the filling: Place the almonds into the bowl of a food processor and grind. Add the sugar and process until very fine. Add the eggs, almond extract, and lemon zest, and process briefly until the mixture forms a ball. Spoon the filling into the tart and smooth it out, making sure to avoid covering the top edges of the dough. Turn the second round upside down over the filling and press the edges together firmly. Press any overhanging dough against the edges of the pan to cut it off.

Make the glaze: Combine the confectioners' sugar, hot water, and almond extract, stirring until the sugar has dissolved. Brush over the top of the tart. Press the almonds into the top in a decorative pattern.

Place the tart on a baking pan to prevent drips. Bake for 30 minutes or until the dough in the center is set and the cake has started to puff up. Remove from the oven and cool completely before cutting into portions. Store up to 1 week refrigerated, bringing back to room temperature before serving. This cake can be successfully frozen, tightly wrapped, for up to 2 months.

Zach's Almond Macaroon Cake

This is my son's favorite birthday cake, which he requests year after year. Zach prefers his cake pure and unadorned, but you may dust it with confectioners' sugar, ice it with the White Chocolate Buttercream on page 336, or fill it with a thin layer of high-quality preserves. Serve the cake with hot tea, champagne (for a birthday), or a snifter of cognac. To use this versatile and long-keeping cake in a trifle, bake the cake in a 15 x 10-inch jelly roll pan. To use it as an American layer cake, bake it in an 8-inch round pan; to use it as a European-style torte, bake it in a 9-inch round pan.

YIELD: 1 SHALLOW 9-INCH EUROPEAN STYLE CAKE, 1 TALLER 8-INCH AMERICAN STYLE CAKE, OR 1 SHALLOW JELLY ROLL CAKE

2 ounces ($^1/_2$ cup minus $^1/_2$ tablespoon) unbleached all-purpose flour

2 ounces ($^3/_4$ cup) blanched almonds

1 teaspoon baking powder

$^1/_2$ teaspoon fine sea salt

$^1/_4$ pound (1 stick) unsalted butter, softened

$^1/_2$ pound almond paste

Grated zest of 1 orange (4 teaspoons)

3 ounces (6 tablespoons) dark rum

2 large eggs, separated

$^1/_2$ cup sugar

Preheat the oven to 350°F. Prepare an 8- or 9-inch cake pan by spraying it with nonstick baker's coating, or rub with softened butter and dust with flour, shaking out the excess. (Or, prepare a jelly roll pan by lining with parchment paper or wax paper.) Place the dry ingredients: flour, almonds, baking powder, and salt, in the bowl of a food processor and process to a fine powder.

Place the butter, almond paste, and orange zest in the bowl of a standing electric mixer and using the paddle attachment, beat together until smooth and creamy, 5 to 6 minutes, scraping down the sides once or twice. Beat in the rum and then the egg yolks, one at a time. Transfer the mixture to a wide shallow bowl.

In the clean and greaseless bowl of a standing electric mixer and using the whisk, beat the egg whites until fluffy, then add the sugar and continue beating until the whites are firm and glossy, 4 to 5 minutes. Fold the dry ingredients into the creamed butter mixture, then fold in the egg whites in thirds so the batter doesn't deflate.

Scrape into the prepared pan. Bake 25 minutes for the 9-inch cake, 30 minutes for the 8-inch cake, or 20 minutes for the jelly roll, or until set in the middle and the cake has started to come away from the sides of the pan. Cool on a wire rack before removing from the pan and then decorate as desired. This cake can be successfully frozen, tightly wrapped, for up to 2 months.

Majorcan Lemon–Almond Cake

The cake is believed to have originated in Valldemossa, the town made famous by the lovers Frederic Chopin, the composer, and George Sand, the (female) writer. The couple spent a winter together there in an abandoned Carthusian monastery that today draws many visitors. This flourless Majorcan specialty is usually accompanied by homemade almond ice cream, but purchased almond ice cream will do fine. Majorca, one of the Balearic Islands off the Mediterranean Coast of Spain, is full of lemon and almond trees. I visited there once while on an epic three-week wintertime voyage from Haifa to New York on an old Zim line ship, though I was no more than six years old. I've always wanted to see it again. Serve this cake topped with a drizzle of honey mixed with lemon juice (and a tablespoon or so of brandy), or spoon a dollop of the lemon filling from the Australian Pavlova with Lemon Filling and Tropical Fruits (page 442) over top. This recipe is gluten-free. This recipe can be dairy-free. (Substitute oil).

YIELD: ONE 9-INCH CAKE, SERVES 8 TO 12

¹/₂ pound (1¹/₂ cups) whole blanched almonds

¹/₄ cup potato starch

1 teaspoon ground cinnamon

Pinch of salt

1 tablespoon unsalted butter

¹/₄ cup sliced almonds, skin-on

4 large eggs, separated

¹/₂ cup sugar

¹/₄ cup honey

Grated zest of 2 lemons (2 tablespoons)

Confectioners' sugar, for dusting

Preheat the oven to 350°F. Combine the whole almonds, potato starch, cinnamon, and salt in the bowl of a food processor and process until finely ground.

Rub a 9-inch removable-bottom or springform cake pan with the butter, sprinkle the bottom with the sliced almonds, then dust with a little of the ground almond mixture, shaking off the excess.

In the clean and greaseless bowl of a standing electric mixer and using the whisk, beat the egg whites until fluffy, then add the sugar and continue beating until the whites are firm and glossy, 4 to 5 minutes. Transfer to another bowl.

Using the same mixer bowl (it is not necessary to wash it), combine the yolks and honey. Beat with the whisk until light and thick, about 5 minutes. Fold in the remaining ground almond mixture and the lemon zest. Transfer to a wide, shallow bowl.

Fold the meringue into the almond mixture in thirds so as not to deflate the whites. Spread the batter evenly into the pan and shake the pan back and forth to even the top.

Bake for 35 minutes or until the cake starts to come away from the sides of the pan, the center is set, and a skewer inserted into the center comes out clean. Cool the cake to room temperature on a wire rack, then turn it out onto a serving platter with the bottom up. Dust with confectioners' sugar.

Store the cake wrapped in aluminum foil up to 3 days at room temperature, or wrap well, first in wax paper and then in foil and freeze up to 2 months.

Velia's White Chocolate–Lemon Torta Caprese

In the words of its creator, the irrepressible and highly creative Velia de Angelis, proprietress of La Champagneria, Orvieto (see opposite page), "The batter will be fairly thick. The secret of this cake is that the oven must be not so hot." The perfumed aroma of this cake is a visceral reminder of the inimitable Sorrento lemons of the region. This time made with white chocolate, the cake is another version of the almond-based Torta Caprese from the island of Capri. This recipe is gluten-free.

YIELD: ONE 10-INCH CAKE, SERVES 12 TO 16

3/4 pound (2 1/4 cups) whole almonds, skin-on

1/4 pound (1 1/4 cups) potato starch, substitute corn, wheat, or rice starch

1 teaspoon baking powder

1/2 teaspoon fine sea salt

1/2 pound white chocolate, chopped into small bits

1/2 pound (2 sticks) unsalted butter, softened

1 cup sugar

4 large eggs, separated

Grated zest of 2 lemons (2 tablespoons)

1/4 cup brandy

Preheat the oven to 300°F. Spray a 10-inch removable-bottom or springform cake pan with nonstick baker's coating, or rub with softened butter and dust with starch, shaking out the excess.

Place the dry ingredients: almonds, potato starch, baking powder, and salt in the bowl of a food processor and grind until fine.

Place the chocolate in a microwaveable bowl and melt on lowest power in the microwave, 2 minutes at a time, or until just barely melted. Whisk until smooth and cool to room temperature.

In the bowl of an electric mixer fitted with the paddle attachment, cream the butter and 1/2 cup of the sugar until light and fluffy, 5 to 6 minutes. Beat in the egg yolks, one at a time, and the lemon zest. Fold in the cooled, melted chocolate and the brandy, then fold in the almond mixture.

In the clean and greaseless bowl of a standing electric mixer and using the whisk, beat the egg whites until fluffy, then add the remaining 1/2 cup sugar and continue beating until the whites are firm and glossy, 4 to 5 minutes. Fold the meringue into the chocolate mixture in thirds so as not to deflate the batter.

Pour the batter into the prepared pan, shaking back and forth to smooth the top. Place the cake on a baking pan to catch any drips. Bake for 50 minutes or until the cake is firm in the center and has begun to come away from the sides of the pan. Cool to room temperature on a wire rack before removing from pan. Note that the cake is quite fragile and should be handled with a light touch. Chill the cake in the refrigerator until firm before cutting, but serve at room temperature. Store covered and refrigerated up to one week, or freeze up to 3 months.

LA CHAMPAGNERIA
IN ORVIETO, ITALY

My friend, Velia de Angelis, and her partner, Gianluca Antoniella, have opened a small Champagne bar and caffé called La Champagneria in the charming Medieval walled city of Orvieto, Italy. Centrally located right down the street from the marvelous gold-tiled Orvieto Cathedral, La Champagneria features an up-to-the-minute Italo-chic ambience, outstanding coffee, and well-chosen Champagne and wines by the glass. Hand-made cichetti (Venetian-style small plates) and pastries are prepared by Velia in the tiny kitchen using fresh and organic market ingredients. Gianluca takes care of the wine, champagne, coffee and special events. I visited with them in Orvieto just before their opening, though sadly I had to leave the day of their official opening party. If you get to Orvieto, stop in and let them know Aliza sent you and look for my books in their collection. You can find them online at www.champagneria-orvieto.com.

ANISE, FENNEL, & CARAWAY

Aniseed . . .82

Buying and Storing Anise
and Anise Extract . . .83

Fennel Seed . . .84

Caraway Seed . . .84

Buying and Storing
Caraway Seed . . .85

FENNEL EGG BREAD . . .86

MOROCCAN SESAME-
ANISE BREAD . . .87

CARAWAY SEED BUNDT CAKE . . .88

About Kümmel . . .89

From Mrs. Beeton, A Very
Good Seed–Cake . . .89

A Caraway Feast . . .90

SAMBUCA AND CANDIED
ORANGE TOZZETTI . . .90

PIZZELLE "OF THE ANGELS"
WITH FENNEL POLLEN . . .91

About Fennel Pollen . . .92

About Pizzelle . . .92

Fante's Cookware . . .93

ANISE, FENNEL, & CARAWAY

Whether its a chewy loaf of Jewish rye bread, a French-inspired artisan seeded baguette, wafer-like Italian pizzelle cookies, or hard, crunchy taralli rings from Puglia, they all depend for their very different flavors of native Mediterranean seed spices, like anise, fennel, and caraway. All three are members of the *Apiacea* family that also includes cumin, dill, celery, fennel, chervil, carrots, coriander, and parsley. The seeds have long been used to flavor baked goods, both savory and sweet, though their popularity has diminished in more recent times.

Where other aromatics and spices (like cinnamon, clove, and vanilla) were costly and came from far away in Mexico and the West Indies, India, China, and the East Indies, these seed spices were easy to grow, abundant, and inexpensive. For the same reason, cumin and coriander seed are essential to North African dishes like couscous and tajines. Anise is a key seasoning all over Europe, especially in the Mediterranean region, and in Spanish-influenced Latin America where it goes into sweet pastries, cookies, breads, and cakes. Fennel is especially important in Italy where it was first domesticated and shows up in

savory breads, pies, and biscuits. The use of caraway seeds are more common in Northern and Eastern Europe, in places like Poland, Germany, Russia, and Hungary. Tunisia is an exception, depending on caraway for the biting edge to its national sauce, Harissa (page 866).

ANISEED

Aniseed, *Pimpinella anisum*, is small, plump, oval-shaped, and sage-green to light brown in color. Its frankly sweet flavor is intense with a fresh herbal, slightly bitter zestiness reminiscent of licorice, tarragon, and star anise. This annual plant is native to the eastern Mediterranean region, the Levant, and Egypt, and gets its name from the early Arabic name, *anysum*. Today, aniseed is widely cultivated in temperate regions of North Africa, Europe, Southern Russia, Syria, Turkey, India, Mexico, and Central America. Like cumin, aniseed is a rotation crop, grown with barley, corn, and wheat and has vivid green leaves and clusters of small white flowers. Once the seeds open, the plants are pulled up and dried and the seeds are then threshed by beating.

With its pleasingly sweet, palate-cleansing flavor, aniseed is one of the oldest and most widely used spice plants, found in the kitchen, bakeshop, and apothecary since ancient times. There is evidence that anise was used in Egypt as early as 1500 BCE. Anise was highly regarded in ancient Rome where the seeds were nibbled after meals as a breath freshener and aid to digestion, similar to the way anise and fennel seeds are consumed in India today. (In India, both anise and fennel seed are called *saunf* because of their similarity in appearance and flavor.)

Romans enjoyed anise-spiced cakes after heavy meals and the custom of flavoring cakes with aniseed spread throughout Europe by Roman legions. In 1305, merchants bringing aniseed into London paid a toll levied by King Edward I to help maintain and repair London bridge. One writer of the time warned: "it stirreth up bodily lust," an association that no doubt increased sales.

Aniseed or its extract is widely used to flavor candy, cough drops, and liqueurs including Spanish and Latin American *aguardiente*, Turkish and Middle Eastern *raki* and *araq*, Greek *ouzo*, French *Pernod* and *Ricard*, and Italian *anisette*, though in most cases these days, the unrelated and much less expensive star anise is substituted for all or part of the anise. Aniseed is also combined with licorice root to flavor black licorice candy.

Aniseed is a popular flavor in Mediterranean baked goods in Spain and Italy; especially Southern Italy and Sicily, where it goes into all sorts of sweets, especially pizzelle wafer cookies and biscotti. Anise flavors Mexican and Latin American

recipes that show a Spanish heritage, like the Biscochitos (page 218), and is also found in Spanish cookies and cakes like the Spanish Sesame-Anise Cookies (page 799), Dutch Speculaas (page 789), German spiced cookies like pfeffernusse, North African baked goods like the Moroccan Sesame-Anise Bread in this chapter (page 87), Siennese Cavallucci cookies (page 224), the Anise-Scented Date-Orange Spirals (page 423), the Sweet Fig Focaccia (page 455), the Fig and Pine Nut Bread (page 674), and the Aruban Pan Dushi (page 891).

BUYING AND STORING ANISE AND ANISE EXTRACT

Buy whole aniseed and use as is or grind to a fine powder as needed using a coffee grinder, spice grinder, or mortar and pestle. Once ground, its aromas quickly dissipate. Lightly roast the seeds in a dry pan to make them more aromatic and brittle in texture, so that crushing or grinding them becomes easy. Store whole aniseed in a clean dry jar, preferably in a dark place, and use within one year. Anise extract is also available. I recommend the pure anise extract produced by the Boyajian company (www.boyajianinc.com). Look for anise extract in Italian specialty stores and bakery suppliers, but be sure it is natural, not artificial. Anisette liqueur may be substituted for aniseed in recipes as may the unrelated but similar-tasting Sambuca liqueur (made from elderberries.)

FENNEL SEED

Fennel seeds, *Foeniculum vulgare*, come from the delicate fern-like fennel plant. Intensely perfumed yellow flowers, which are harvested for their delicious pollen, give way to light, bright green, curved seeds (technically these are all fruits and not seeds) with a sweet, slightly earthy licorice-anise flavor. As the seeds dry late in the summer, they lose their bright color. The smaller, brighter colored Lucknow fennel seeds from India are worth seeking out in Indian groceries for their potent, sweet flavor, closer to anise.

Fennel, which may be an annual or biennial plant, gets its name from the Latin *foeniculum*, meaning "little hay," because its aroma is thought to resemble fresh-cut hay. All parts of this versatile plant are edible: roots, stalks, leaves, and flowers, with the spice coming from the dried seeds. Native to the Mediterranean, fennel is an ancient and common plant known to the ancient Greeks, where it was named marathon, after the Battle of Marathon in 490 BCE, in which the Greeks were victorious over the Persians. In Greek mythology, Prometheus used the hollow stalk of a fennel plant to steal fire from the gods. The use of fennel seed was spread throughout Europe by the Romans.

Another form of the plant, known as Florence fennel or sweet anise, is grown for its enlarged bulb and used as a vegetable, especially in Italy and the south of France. Fennel is also grown in India, Asia, Australia, and South America, and has become naturalized in many places, including northern Europe, the United States (especially California), southern Canada, and in much of Asia and Australia.

Although not much used in American cooking and baking, fennel was known as "meeting seed" by the Puritans, who would chew it during their long church services, presumably to keep from nodding off. The seeds flavor liqueurs, including the notorious Absinthe, candies, brandy, ice cream, savory doughs, and breads, especially in southern Italy. Fennel pollen is the most potent form of fennel, but it is expensive because it must be hand-picked from wild fennel. In Italy, aniseed is traditionally reserved for sweets and fennel for savory dishes including breads and biscuits like the taralli from Puglia, Italy. Fennel seed is often found in the mixture herbes de Provence; in Central Europe, fennel often flavors rye bread.

In this book, look for fennel seeds in the Fennel Egg Bread in this chapter (page 86), and in the Taralli: Boiled and Baked "Pretzels" from Puglia (page 584). I use sweetly aromatic fennel pollen in the Pizzelle "of the Angels" (page 91) and chopped fennel stalks for the fillings of both the Country-Style Greek Greens Pie (page 262) and the Torta Pasqualina Genovese (page 438).

CARAWAY SEED

Caraway seeds, *Carum carvi*, are small, hard, dark brown, and crescent-shaped seeds covered with distinct curved longitudinal lines with sharply pointed ends. Their biting, earthy, robust flavor is edged with a slightly bitter, cleansing sharpness that leaves a warm taste in the mouth. Native to North Africa, the Mediterranean, and much of Europe, caraway is used mainly for its seeds, through the leaves and the root are also edible. Caraway is a biennial and resembles cumin in appearance, with which it is often confused, especially in Asia.

Caraway has been found in food dating back to 3000 BCE, making it one of the oldest cultivated spices. The Egyptians buried their dead with caraway to ward off evil spirits. Caraway was used for food and as medicine in ancient Greece and Rome. Julius Caesar's army ate a bread made of boiled caraway root called *chara*. Caraway spread into Northern and Eastern Europe in medieval times. According to legend, caraway had the power to keep things from getting lost or stolen and was used in love potions.

Caraway is most popular in northern, central, and eastern Europe where it is used most commonly in breads but also in cookies and other baked goods. It is cultivated all over Europe, as well as in Turkey, India, and North Africa. Dutch caraway is considered to be of high quality and Holland is one of the largest producers. Caraway is often used to flavor Dutch and German cheeses. Canada, Great Britain, Poland, Germany, Morocco, and the USA also grow caraway. In India, it grows wild in the northern Himalayas and thrives in Kashmir.

Caraway was especially popular in medieval Europe when it was added to breads, seed cakes, and served with roasted apples. In Shakespeare's *Henry the Fourth*, Falstaff is offered "a last years pippin [apple] of mine own grafting, with a dish of caraways." Roasted apples with caraway are still served at Trinity College, Cambridge. In England in Elizabethan times, caraway was popularly used to flavor bread, cakes, and fruit, especially in the seedcakes served with tea.

Caraway shows up in the cuisines of Germany, Austria, Eastern and Northern Europe, and Scandinavia. In baking, caraway seeds are sprinkled on top of Jewish rye bread and ground up to flavor the bread dough itself. It is also used to flavor sweet kümmel liqueur (page 89) in Germany, Scandinavian aquavit, and English gin. It gives Scandinavian, Baltic, Southern German, and Austrian breads, savory strudels, and certain pastries their distinctive flavor. Look for caraway in this chapter in the Caraway Seed Bundt Cake (page 88) and in the Sauerkraut Rye Bread (page 784). A typical flavoring in Tunisia, the seeds also flavor the Chakchouka: Tunisian Vegetable Stew (page 865) and the Spicy Harissa Sauce (page 866) used in other recipes, including the Tunisian Semolina Griddle Bread (page 864).

BUYING AND STORING CARAWAY SEED

Caraway is commonly sold whole. Lightly toast the very hard seeds to make them brittle and easier to grind in a spice grinder, or using a mortar and pestle. Store whole caraway seeds in a cool dry place for up to one year. Store ground caraway in a dry place to prevent it from forming clumps. Once ground, caraway's flavor will start to dissipate after about a month.

Fennel Egg Bread

Akin to Jewish challah and French brioche, the original recipe for this bread came from a reader of the column I wrote for a time for the Philadelphia Daily News *called "Ask the Chef." While she didn't have much detail, my reader clearly remembered the taste and smell of the bread. Here's how it read in my column: "Reader Ann Witkowski sent Ask the Chefs a letter asking if we could recreate her late mother's treasured recipe for Egg Bread with Fennel Seeds. She recalls that 'we could smell the bread from down the street when we came home,' and 'would love to taste the bread again at our house.' The only thing Witkowski had was a card listing ingredients as follows: 5 pounds flour, 2 1/4 cups Crisco, 20 eggs, 1 2/3 packages yeast, 2 cups sugar, and fennel seed.' While the bread I ended up making for this book is much less sweet than her original (and uses butter, not shortening), her letter inspired me.*

YIELD: 2 MEDIUM BREADS

1 pound (4 cups) unbleached bread flour

1/2 pound (2 1/4 cups) white whole wheat flour

1 tablespoon ground fennel seed

1 tablespoon fine sea salt

1 (1/4-ounce) package (2 1/4 teaspoons) active dry yeast

1/4 cup honey

3/4 cup milk

4 large eggs

1/2 pound (2 sticks) unsalted butter, softened

1 large egg lightly beaten with 1 tablespoon milk, for the egg wash

1 tablespoon whole fennel seeds

Spray two medium (1 pound, 8 1/2 x 4 1/2-inch) loaf pans with baker's nonstick coating or rub with butter and dust with flour, shaking off the excess.

In a medium bowl, whisk together the dry ingredients: bread flour, whole wheat flour, ground fennel, and salt.

Dissolve the yeast and honey in the milk in the bowl of a standing electric mixer. Allow the mixture to proof in a warm place for about 10 minutes, or until bubbling and puffy.

Using the paddle attachment, beat in half the flour mixture to make a soft batter. Beat in the eggs, one at a time, beating well after each addition. Beat in the butter, continuing to beat until it has been absorbed completely. (You should not be able to see any lumps.) Beat in the remaining flour mixture. Switch to the dough hook and continue to beat until the dough is smooth and elastic and mostly comes away from the bowl. (It will be rather soft and a bit sticky.) Transfer the dough to a large oiled bowl; turn around so the dough is oiled all over. Cover with plastic wrap or a damp cloth and allow the dough to rise until doubled in size, about 2 hours, at warm room temperature.

Punch down the dough and divide it into 2 portions. Roll each portion into a rectangle about 3/4-inch thick and about 8 inches wide. Roll the dough up tightly and place the rolls into the pans, seam-side down. Brush the tops with the egg wash and sprinkle generously with the fennel seeds. Cover with lightly oiled plastic wrap and allow the breads to rise at warm room temperature until puffy and light, about 1 hour.

Preheat the oven to 350°F. Bake for 30 minutes or until

the breads sound hollow when tapped on the bottom and a thermometer inserted in the center reads 190° to 205°F. Cool the breads completely on a wire rack before slicing. Store in an opened plastic bag at room temperature for up to 3 days or freeze up to 3 months.

Note: When rising bread (or other yeast-leavened doughs), if when you press the dough with your finger and it springs back, the dough needs to rise further; if the dough stays depressed, it is ready.

Moroccan Sesame–Anise Bread

This versatile anise and sesame–scented flat bread was developed for the original menu at Tangerine in Philadelphia, one of super-star restaurateur Steven Starr's many successes. Vary it by rolling out the dough into rounds about the size of pita bread, brushing with olive oil, and grilling, preferably over a natural charcoal fire. Top with Oven-Roasted Plum Tomatoes (page 888) and crumbled feta, with olive tapenade, with grilled merguez (Moroccan spicy lamb sausage) and chopped green olives, or Chakchouka (page 865).

YIELD: 6 (6-INCH) ROUND BREADS

1 ($^{1}/_{4}$-ounce) package (2 $^{1}/_{4}$ teaspoons) active dry yeast

1 $^{1}/_{2}$ cups lukewarm water

2 tablespoons honey

$^{1}/_{2}$ pound (2 cups) unbleached bread flour

$^{1}/_{2}$ cup extra-virgin olive oil

10 ounces (2 cups minus 2 tablespoons) white whole-wheat flour

1 tablespoon aniseed

2 teaspoons fine sea salt

$^{1}/_{4}$ cup white sesame seeds

Semolina or cornmeal, for the baking pans

1 egg lightly beaten with 2 tablespoons water, for the egg wash

Prepare a sponge (soft dough) by combining the yeast, water, honey, and bread flour in the bowl to a standing electric mixer. Allow the mixture to rise at warm room temperature until doubled, about 1 hour.

Using the paddle attachment, beat in the olive oil, whole-wheat flour, aniseed, salt, and 2 tablespoons of the sesame seeds. Continue beating until the dough is smooth and elastic, 5 to 6 minutes. Transfer the dough to a large oiled bowl, cover with plastic wrap, and allow the dough to rise at warm room temperature until doubled.

Punch down the dough, divide it into 6 portions, and form them into smooth rounds. Flatten each round and roll out to about 6 inches in diameter. Arrange the rounds on 2 large baking pans that have been sprinkled with semolina. Use scissors to snip the edges of the breads every inch or so to form a decorative border. Brush each bread round with the egg wash and sprinkle with the remaining 2 tablespoons of sesame seeds.

Allow the breads to rise again at warm room temperature for 30 minutes, or until puffy.

Preheat the oven to 400°F. Bake for 25 minutes, or until the breads are puffed in the center and lightly browned. Remove from the oven and cool before serving. Store in an open plastic bag at room temperature for up to 3 days or wrap well and freeze up to 3 months.

Caraway Seed Bundt Cake

Seed cakes were very popular in England in Victorian times. Although they have fallen out of fashion, perhaps its time to revive the tradition. This moist, long-keeping Bundt cake sprinkled with small, dark dried Zante currants and small, curved caraway seeds gets a good measure of caraway-infused kümmel liqueur and brandy. Serve the cake on its own or with fresh berries, fruit compote, whipped cream, or ice cream.

YIELD: 1 10-INCH CAKE, 12 SERVINGS

1 cup Zante currants

$1/4$ cup kümmel liqueur, substitute brandy

$1/4$ cup brandy

2 tablespoons (1 ounce) unsalted butter,
   softened, for the pan

3 ounces ($3/4$ cup) finely ground almonds
   (or purchased almond meal), for the pan

10 ounces ($2 1/2$ cups minus $2 1/2$ tablespoons)
   unbleached all-purpose flour

2 ounces ($3/4$ cup) potato starch, substitute corn,
   wheat, or rice starch

1 teaspoon fine sea salt

1 teaspoon ground freshly grated nutmeg

1 teaspoon ground mace

$3/4$ pound (3 sticks) unsalted butter, softened

$1 3/4$ cups sugar

Grated zest of 1 lemon (1 tablespoon)

8 egg whites (1 cup), at room temperature

3 tablespoons caraway seeds

Confectioners' sugar, for dusting

Soak the currants in the kümmel and brandy until soft and plump, about 1 hour.

Preheat the oven to 350°F. Rub a 10-inch Bundt or tube pan with 2 tablespoons softened butter and dust with the ground almonds.

Whisk together the dry ingredients: flour, starch, salt, nutmeg, and mace.

In a standing electric mixer fitted with the paddle attachment, cream the butter and $3/4$ cup of the sugar until light and fluffy, 5 to 6 minutes. Add the lemon zest and beat to combine. Add about half the flour mixture and beat just long enough to combine. Transfer the mixture to a wide shallow bowl.

In the clean and greaseless bowl of a standing electric mixer and using the whisk attachment, beat the egg whites until fluffy, then add the remaining 1 cup sugar and continue beating until the whites are firm and glossy, 4 to 5 minutes. Fold the meringue into the batter in thirds so as not to deflate the meringue.

Fold in the caraway seeds and currants with their soaking liquid, then gently fold in the remaining flour, taking care not to over-mix. Spoon the batter into the prepared Bundt pan.

Bake for 50 minutes or until the cake starts to come away from the sides of the pan and a toothpick or skewer stuck in the center comes out clean. Cool in the pan for 20 minutes, then carefully turn the cake out onto a rack to cool completely. Just before serving, dust with the confectioners' sugar. Store covered and at room temperature up to 4 days

ABOUT KÜMMEL

Kümmel, also called kümmel or kimmel, is a sweet, clear liqueur flavored with seed spices: caraway, cumin, and fennel. The word kümmel and its variants originally referred in German, Dutch, and Yiddish to both caraway and cumin. Kümmel was first distilled in Holland during the late sixteenth century by Lucas Bols around the time he began making gin and is still made by the company today. In 1696, Peter the Great, in his quest to build a Russian navy, traveled to Amsterdam to learn about shipbuilding. During the trip, he visited the Bols distillery, where he discovered the spirit and took the recipe back home.

Russia is the largest producer and consumer of kümmel today, although it is also popular in the Baltic States, Scandinavia, Holland, and Germany. Mentzendorff Kümmel has been distilled since 1823 from an old family recipe of the Barons of Allasch near Riga, Lithuania. Today, it is produced at Saumur, France, by Combier, the oldest distillery in the Loire Valley, founded in 1834. For some reason, kümmel is also a favorite drink at British men's clubs and golf clubs where it is known as "putting mixture."

From Mrs. Beeton, A Very Good Seed-Cake

Isabella Mary Mayson, universally known as Mrs. Beeton, the author of *Mrs. Beeton's Book of Household Management*, was the most famous cookbook writer in British history. Her husband, Samuel Orchard Beeton, was a publisher of books and popular magazines, for whom she began writing articles on cooking and household management. The articles were published in 1861 as a single volume. After giving birth to her fourth child in January 1865, Isabella contracted puerperal fever and died a week later at age 28. Below is Mrs. Beeton's original recipe for the seed cake, which I adapted for the cake above.

"1 lb. of butter, 6 eggs, ¾ lb. of sifted sugar, pounded mace and grated nutmeg to taste, 1 lb. of flour, ¾ oz. of caraway seeds, 1 wineglassful of brandy.

Mode. Beat the butter to a cream; dredge in the flour; add the sugar, mace, nutmeg, and caraway seeds, and mix these ingredients well together. Whisk the eggs, stir to them the brandy, and beat the cake again for 10 minutes. Put it into a tin lined with buttered paper, and bake it from 1½ to 2 hours. This cake would be equally nice made with currants, and omitting the caraway seeds.

Time. 1½ to 2 hours. Average cost, 2s. 6d.

Seasonable at any time."

Sambuca and Candied Orange Tozzetti

These hard biscotti cookies, flavored with elderberry-based sambuca liqueur, hail from the region of Lazio (of which Rome is the capital), but they are also baked in homes and pastry shops in nearby Umbria and in Venice, where they are made without the sambuca, a local cordial traditional to Rome. In a variation of classic biscotti, the batter is spread on a baking pan and baked until firm; after a few minutes, the batter is cut into finger-shaped strips, and returned to the oven to dry out into crunchy cookies. If they are kept in an airtight container, the tozzetti keep well for weeks. This recipe is dairy-free.

YIELD: ABOUT 48 COOKIES

1 pound (3³/₄ cups) unbleached all-purpose flour

2 teaspoons baking powder

¹/₂ teaspoon fine sea salt

2 eggs

2 cups sugar

¹/₂ cup grapeseed oil, substitute mild olive oil or vegetable oil

¹/₂ cup fresh orange juice plus grated zest of 1 orange (4 teaspoons)

¹/₄ cup sambuca liqueur, substitute anisette or Pernod

¹/₄ pound (about 1 cup) diced candied orange peel, homemade (page 225) or purchased

¹/₂ pound (1¹/₂ cups) hazelnuts, lightly toasted and skinned

1 egg lightly beaten with 1 tablespoon milk, for egg wash

Preheat the oven to 375°F. Line a 15 x 10-inch jelly roll pan with parchment paper or wax paper.

Whisk together the dry ingredients: flour, baking powder, and salt.

In the bowl of a standing mixer fitted with a whisk attachment, beat the eggs and sugar until light and fluffy, 5 to 6 minutes. Slowly beat in the oil, continuing to beat until the mixture is smooth and creamy. Add the orange juice and zest, and sambuca, and beat briefly, just long enough to combine. Fold in the flour mixture, then fold in the candied orange peel and the hazelnuts.

Spoon the batter into the prepared pan, smoothing the top with a spatula. It should be about ¹/₂-inch thick. Brush with the egg wash for shine.

Bake for 30 minutes, or until firm but not fully cooked. (You may freeze the tozzetti at this point. Defrost to room temperature, then cut into the sticks and rebake.) Remove from the oven, cool to room temperature and then cut into 1 x 3-inch sticks.

Reduce the oven temperature to 325°F. Arrange the

tozzetti in a single layer on one or two baking pans and place back in the oven to toast about 20 minutes, or until lightly browned and crunchy. Cool to room temperature before storing in an airtight container up to 2 weeks.

Pizzelle "of the Angels" with Fennel Pollen

Like so many Italian cookies, these light, crispy wafers are flavored with aniseed or anisette liqueur. Here I have substituted sweet fennel pollen, a favorite of Italian and now American chefs, especially in California where fennel grows wild. The honeyed pollen echoes the sweetness of the anise with an extra delicate, nectar-like perfume. The batter must be cooked in a special pizzelle iron, which resembles a waffle iron, pressing a decorative pattern into the cookies as they bake. Older irons were held by hand over a hot burner; modern irons are electric. Pizzelle are popular during Christmas and Easter and are often found at Italian weddings and other celebrations. Like crêpes, the first one or two pizzelle will likely be rejects, until the iron is fully heated and oiled and the batter consistency is just right. Wait for a day with low humidity to make these cookies so they will stay crisp.

YIELD: 16 TO 18 COOKIES

5 ounces (1$^1\!/_4$ cups minus 4 teaspoons) unbleached all-purpose flour

1 teaspoon baking powder

1 tablespoon fennel pollen, substitute ground anise, which is sweeter than fennel seed

$^1\!/_2$ teaspoon fine sea salt

2 large eggs

$^3\!/_4$ cup sugar

1$^1\!/_4$ pound (1 stick) butter, melted and cooled

Grated zest of 1 lemon (1 tablespoon)

Clarified Butter (page 202) or transfat-free shortening, for greasing the iron

Whisk together dry ingredients: flour, baking powder, fennel pollen, and salt.

In a medium bowl, lightly beat together the eggs and sugar until combined, then beat in the butter and lemon zest. Fold in the flour mixture. Allow the batter to rest for 30 minutes at room temperature to relax the gluten and make it more tender. If necessary, thin the batter with 2 to 3 tablespoons water to make a thick, barely pourable batter.

Meanwhile, preheat the pizzelle iron. Brush the iron on both sides with clarified butter or shortening. Place 1 to 2 teaspoonfuls of batter into the iron, a little bit above the middle. Close the iron; allow the pizzelle to cook (a small amount of batter should seep through the edges of the iron). When steam stops escaping from the iron, open the clasp to check. The cookie should be golden brown.

Remove the cookie from the iron using the tip of a fork to loosen it along the edge. The cookie can be shaped while still warm, by draping it over a rolling pin for a "roof tile." Grease the iron again and add more batter. After the first few pizzelle have cooked, it will probably not be necessary to grease the iron again.

Store the pizzelle in a tightly sealed container, preferably a cookie tin. Pizzelle will keep very well as long as they are kept dry.

Variations: Substitute orange or tangerine zest for lemon zest. Substitute 1 to 2 teaspoons ground cinnamon or 1 teaspoon almond extract for the ground anise. Substitute ¼ cup Dutch-process cocoa (imported type) for ¼ cup flour to make chocolate pizzelle.

ABOUT FENNEL POLLEN

Fennel pollen, also known as spice of the angels or *polline di finocchio selvatico* (wild fennel pollen) in Italian, is the small pollen–laden fennel blossoms gathered by hand from wild fennel plants as they bloom in late summer. Its potent yet ethereal flavor combines licorice-like sweetness, heady cleaning anise, and honey–like fragrance. Wild fennel pollen is sold in Tuscany and in California. One of the secrets of Tuscan cooking, this rather expensive spice can be found in the spice section of Italian supermarkets and specialty markets. Buy American–grown wild fennel pollen online from Sugar Ranch: www.fennelpollen.com; buy imported Italian wild fennel pollen from Chef's Shop: www.chefshop.com.

ABOUT PIZZELLE

Pizzelle (pronounced like "pizza") is a traditional Italian waffle cookie that can be hard and crisp or soft and chewy, depending on the ingredients and method of preparation. Like pizza, the name comes from the Italian word for "round" and "flat" (*pizze*). Pizzelle originated in the Abruzzo region of south-central Italy. Many other cultures have developed pizzelle-type cookies as part of their culture, such a Belgian and French waffle cookies, and Norwegian krumkake. Cialde and brigidini from Tuscany are other Italian wafer cookies. Wafer cookies are known to be among the oldest cookies, as they did not need an oven.

The first pizzelle makers were made of iron. The story goes that Abruzzo's resourceful blacksmiths used old railroad nails and pieces of track to forge the irons, called ferratelle (*ferro* is "iron" in Italian). Because they were used over open fires, the irons had very long handles to keep the wafer-maker from getting burned. Some irons would be custom-made with family crests on them, to be passed down to each generation. The most common pattern on the irons is a floral design on one side and a basket-pattern on the other.

FANTE'S COOKWARE

In Philadelphia, we know "Fante's (truly) has everything!" Every size and shape of cake pan, every decorating tool, every type of European bread baking basket, every small tool, every baking pan, baking paper, and cake boards, and lots of fun stuff you're unlikely to find elsewhere. Looking for a pizzelle mold? Here you'll find at least eight choices, from the original hand-held type to be used over an open flame—preferred by local Italian grandmothers—in several shapes and sizes, to electric irons to make small, medium, large, and oval-shaped cookies with various designs. If you're in Philadelphia, this is a don't miss stop for avid cooks and bakers. If not, order online from www.fantes.com.

Located in the heart of the city's historic Italian Market, the Giovannucci family has been proud owners of this deservedly famous culinary institution since 1981, when Mariella Giovannucci, then General Manager of the store, took over the business from the Fante family. The choc-a-bloc store patched together from several old buildings was founded in 1906 by Domenico Fante and his son, Luigi, with their entire family devoted to the business. Now under the guidance of the Giovannucci family, Fante's has carried on the tradition of the Fante family. Be sure to take a few minutes to peruse the large collection of old cookware and tools hanging on the walls of this idiosyncratic and wonderful store.

APPLES

How to Store Apples . . .98

Best Sweet Apples for Baking . . .98

Best Sweet–Tart Apples for Baking . . .98

Best Tart Apples for Baking . . .98

Apples Not Suited to Baking . . .98

Stark Brothers Nursery and Orchards Company . . .98

Apple Varieties for Baking . . .99

FRENCH ROQUEFORT, APPLE, AND LEEK TART . . .103

Choosing and Storing Roquefort . . .104

FUJI APPLE CAKE . . .105

SPANISH APPLE TORTE . . .105

Baking On the Bottom Shelf When Dough is Raw . . .107

Pastry, Pâte, Pasta, Pastilla, B'stilla, Pâté, (Puff) Paste . . .107

Pie or Pye . . .107

BROWN BREAD APPLE CHARLOTTE WITH RUM-VANILLA CUSTARD SAUCE . . .108

Lowney's Cookbook . . .109

CANDIED WALNUT APPLE PIE . . .109

About Neil Stein . . .111

APPLES

Want to sell your home in a hurry? Bake some apples with butter, sugar, and cinnamon: the aroma wafting through the house will make buyers somehow unable to resist your house. The simple yet magical combination of apples, butter, sugar, and cinnamon turns up in countless recipes in this chapter, including the Apple Torte with Sherry Custard from Spain (page 105), the Brown Bread Baked Apple Charlotte from England (page 108), and the Candied Walnut Apple Pie from Philadelphia (page 109). In Great Britain, apples are coated in toffee candy; in America, they are dipped in caramel and rolled in salted peanuts, or covered with a crackling red "apple-colored" sugar candy shell.

Though we think of apples as "all-American," they are just as common in the French kitchen, especially in the Atlantic province of Normandy, where apple orchards are abundant and apples are used to make tarts, fresh and sparkling hard cider, and Calvados, a brandy distilled entirely from apples. In French cuisine, a dish with the word "Normand" in its name will always include apples. In a custom dating back to at least twelfth century France, apple wedges dipped in honey are eaten during the Jewish New Year holiday of Rosh Hashanah that falls in autumn to symbolize the hope of a sweet new year.

The pleasingly plump, rounded apple, *Malus pumilla*, a fruit of ancient and mythical origins, has sweet, tart, and juicy flesh with soft and friable to hard and crunchy texture. Apples may be dressed in blushing hues of ivory, pink, crimson, scarlet, gold, and green, and may be solid-colored, streaked, speckled, russeted or bi-colored. The smallest are squat, shiny Lady Apples, creamy yellow on the shaded side and deep glossy crimson on the sunny side, in season just in time for winter holiday fruit baskets. The largest are expensive, perfectly formed, light red, golden-accented, grapefruit-sized Fuji's, each one nestled in a cupped holder, prized for gift giving in the Asian community.

Apples originated in Kazakhstan as tiny sour fruits similar to small bitter crabapples that were carried east by traders on the Silk Road. As far back as the second century BCE, people would take cuttings of one apple tree and graft it onto a suitable root stock, because apples don't grow true from seed. Emigrants to America brought along apple pips (or seeds) instead of cuttings, which could not have survived the long voyage. The fruits of these seeds gave rise to entirely new varieties that were diversified by interbreeding with native American crabapples. As a result, American apples became a distinct and diverse group.

These apples spread with the help of Johnny Appleseed, born John Chapman in Massachusetts in 1775. Chapman began upon his career as an orchardist by apprenticing to Mr. Crawford, who had apple orchards. Johnny Appleseed actually planted apple orchards in his travels through large parts of Ohio, Indiana, and Illinois, because apples must be raised from cuttings or scions. He obtained the apple seed for free; cider mills wanted more apple trees planted since that would eventually bring them more business.

By the early 1800s, American nurseries offered about 100 apple varieties; by 1850, more than 500 varieties were being widely cultivated; and by 1872, Charles Downing described close to 1100 apples in his landmark book, *The Fruits and Fruit Trees of America*. Unfortunately, by the late nineteenth and early twentieth centuries, our incredibly rich and diverse apple culture began to decline. The market system shifted overwhelmingly toward apples that could be grown in giant orchards, then packed and shipped cross-country or across the ocean. Variety, flavor, and texture inevitably lost out to appearance and durability.

Today, about 2,500 named varieties of apples are grown in the United States and more than 7,500 worldwide, but alarmingly, only fifteen varieties account for more than ninety percent of our crop. Happily, the all too often mealy and insipid Red Delicious–glossy red "teacher's pet apple" with its famous sheep's nose bottom that once dominated the produce aisles of supermarkets–are being joined by up-and-coming varieties like Braeburn, Cameo, Fuji, Gala, Ginger Gold, Honeycrisp, and Pink Lady. However, Red Delicious alone still account for forty percent of sales in America. The most important apple-growing states are Washington, Michigan, and New York.

Many old lumpy and misshapen apple varieties have been preserved in home orchards by small-scale farmers and in traditional communities such as those of the Amish and Mennonites. There is a growing movement to bring back these heirloom apples through organizations like Slow Food. Search out heirloom apples at local farmers' markets and older orchards to get the unique flavor and complexity of locally grown apples, which have adapted to a specific growing region, or even to the *terroir* (or special quality of the earth and environment) of an individual orchard.

All apples must be picked by hand because they are easily bruised. Apples should be fully ripe for best flavor; if overripe, they will be mealy and soft. There are crabapples (small sour apples), eating (or dessert) apples, cooking (or baking) apples, and cider apples, though most apples in the United States are used for both eating and cooking. According to the United States Apple Association, in 2002, Americans ate almost 16 pounds each of fresh apples and more then 26 pounds each of processed apples (juice, pies, dried, frozen, apple butter, apple jelly, cider, and more). Note that apple seeds contain cyanide, so avoid eating them.

HOW TO STORE APPLES

Apples may be left out for up to two days, but no longer, or they will turn mealy. Store apples in the refrigerator for up to two weeks, making sure to avoid bruising them. Remove any spoiled apples because "one rotten apple spoils the whole barrel." Peeled, cooked apple wedges may be frozen and stored in an airtight container or double plastic zip-top freezer bag.

BEST SWEET APPLES FOR BAKING

Sweet choices for baking are Braeburn, Crispin (Mutsu), Pink Lady, Suncrisp, Rome Beauty, and Empire.

BEST SWEET-TART APPLES FOR BAKING

Jonathan, Fuji, Stayman-Winesap, Jonagold, and Cox's Orange Pippin all provide a good mix of sweetness and tartness.

BEST TART APPLES FOR BAKING

Good tart baking apples include Granny Smith, Idared, Macoun, Newton Pippin, Northern Spy, and Rhode Island Greening.

APPLES NOT SUITED TO BAKING

Stay away from apples that become mushy when cooked. Gala and Cortland tend to become mealy in pie fillings as do Red Delicious and West Coast Golden Delicious. These apples can still work, if mixed with other firm, tart varieties.

STARK BROTHERS NURSERY AND ORCHARDS COMPANY

In 1816, James Stark moved west from Kentucky with a small band of fellow pioneers and settled on the west bank of the Mississippi in Missouri. From the bundle of apple scions he carried along, grew an influential nursery business that still thrives today. Stark Brothers developed both the Red Delicious apple in 1893 and the Golden Delicious in 1914. Botanist and horticulturalist Luther Burbank selected the company to carry on his work and left 750 varieties to the company in his will. Today, Stark Brothers is still known for selecting and propagating the best fruit varieties (www.starkbros.com).

APPLE VARIETIES FOR BAKING

BRAEBURN: The Braeburn comes from New Zealand and was introduced to the market in 1952. It was first found as a chance seedling, probably a cross of a Lady Hamilton and Granny Smith. This juicy, crisp apple has concentrated, rich, sweet-tart, spicy flavor that is notably aromatic. Its firm texture and full-bodied flavor makes it excellent for baking. The Braeburn ranges in color from orange to red on a golden-yellow background. It is available year-round in supermarkets.

CRABAPPLES: Crabapples are native to North America and are green even when ripe. To be considered true crabapples, the fruits must be less than two inches in diameter. Crabapples found in the market are often hybrids, or Asian varieties, and can range in color from yellow to red, or purple when ripe. Crabapples are tasty, though extremely tart, and are excellent for making jellies, glazes for tarts, and applesauce because of their high pectin content. Try mixing crabapples and sweet apples for tarts, pies, and cakes to take advantage of their tangy flavor and crisp texture. Look for cultivated crabapples in fall and winter.

CRISPIN: The Crispin dates from 1930 and is a cross of the Golden Delicious and a Japanese Indo. Originally it had a Japanese name, Mutsu, and was renamed Crispin in 1968. In Michigan, where it is quite popular, this apple is still widely known as Mutsu. The Crispin is a late season variety that

works well as a baking apple. It typically has greenish skin with creamy white, firm-textured, juicy flesh, and moderately sweet flavor. It is in season from September through June.

EMPIRE: The Empire is a cross developed in New York in 1966 that combines the mild tartness of McIntosh with the mild sweetness of a Red Delicious. It is redder and firmer than McIntosh, and stores well. Some claim that Empire's flavor, like fine wine, improves during storage. The Empire is excellent for use in baking and cooking. This apple is a favorite in the United Kingdom, which imports much of its supply from Michigan. Empires are in season from October through July.

FUJI: This immensely flavorful variety was introduced to the United States from Japan in the 1980s. It was first developed in the 1930s at a Japanese research station as a cross of Red Delicious and Ralls-Genet. Now more Fujis are grown in the United States than in Japan, and it gains popularity every year. Fuji apples contain between 15 and 18 percent sugar and have a dense flesh, making them sweeter and crisper than many other apple varieties. The adaptable Fuji's firm, crispy texture and honey-like sweetness is balanced by tartness. It resists darkening when cut and holds its shape well when baked. Fujis picked in late fall's cool weather will have the brightest reddish-pink color and outstanding flavor. Fujis are available year-round though the huge, perfect specimens prized for holiday gift-giving in the

Japanese and Korean communities are to be found mostly in the fall. If I had to choose only one apple, it would be a Fuji. Fujis also have a very long shelf life even without refrigeration. When refrigerated, Fuji apples can last up to 3 to 4 months without deteriorating.

GOLDEN DELICIOUS: The Golden Delicious originated as a chance seedling, perhaps from the Grimes Golden and the French Golden Reinette. It was called Mullin's Yellow Seedling until the rights to propagate these apples were sold to Stark Brothers Nurseries and first marketed as a companion to their Red Delicious in 1914 in Clay County, West Virginia. The large, uniformly shaped Golden Delicious has light yellow skin and mellow, sweet flavor.

Golden Delicious's are the second most popular apple in the United States, after Red Delicious. Goldens hold their shape well when baked, and their flesh stays white longer than other apples when cut, characteristics that make them desirable to bakers. Crisp when picked, this apple is prone to bruising and shriveling and needs careful handling and storage. Goldens from the East Coast are preferable; those from the West Coast and imports tend to be spongy and dull. Goldens are harvested from fall into winter, but because of imports, may be found year-round.

GRANNY SMITH: The Granny Smith originated in Australia and is believed to be descended from French crabapples first cultivated by Australian grandmother Maria Ann Smith in about 1868.

Bright, light green in color with extremely tart, crisp, juicy flesh, the versatile Granny Smith is a reliable, easily found apple for pies and cakes. Grannys hold up well in baking and their tart, though rather unexciting flavor works well when balanced by sugar and spices. The deeper the green, the tarter and firmer the apple, though very green Grannys may be dry and spongy in texture. Granny Smiths may be found year-round. Try mixing them with other sweet or sweet-tart apples for more interesting flavor and texture.

GRAVENSTEIN: This outstanding summer apple has a long heritage in many countries, with names for it appearing in Russian, Italian, German, Danish, and English. I used to pick small, firm, intensely flavored Gravensteins off an espaliered tree in the backyard of my auto mechanic's shop! Now that the shop has turned into an "adult entertainment store," I really miss those apples. First established as an apple variety in the 1600s, the Gravenstein was brought to America in the 1700s, where it is grown commercially, mostly in California. This roundish, irregularly shaped apple has a very short stem. Its skin color varies, but is usually greenish yellow topped with broad red stripes. Noted for their crisp, juicy, aromatic flesh and full of old-fashioned tart-sweet flavor, Gravensteins are excellent for pies. They are in season July through November and are more commonly found on the West Coast.

HONEYCRISP: The increasingly popular Honeycrisp was produced from a 1960 cross of Macoun and Honeygold as part of the University of Minnesota apple-breeding program. The skin of a Honeycrisp has a yellow background covered with mottled red. Its flesh is exceptionally crisp, sweet, and tart in flavor, and juicy in texture. This favorite apple of children is in season July through November and can be successfully stored in the refrigerator for three to four months.

IDA RED: The Ida Red (also spelled Idared) is a cross of the Jonathan with Wagener apples, and was developed at the Idaho Agricultural Experiment Station in 1942. This bright red apple is firm and keeps well. It is widely used for pies and baking because it holds its shape. Although it is grown in greatest volume in the northeast and upper mid-western states, its production is increasing because of demand. This medium to large, bright red apple has creamy white, firm, crisp, and juicy flesh. The sweetly tart, spicy Ida Red is well-suited to baking. It is in season October through June but its flavor actually improves after several months in controlled-atmosphere storage.

JONAGOLD: The Jonagold is, as the name suggests, a cross of Jonathan and Golden Delicious developed in a New York apple-breeding program and introduced to market in 1968. This large, juicy apple has red striping inherited from the Jonathan with large areas of bright yellow from its Golden Delicious forbear. The firm, crackling crisp apple has gleaming white flesh and tangy-sweet, rich,

honeyed flavor and is excellent for pies. It is harvested from September to late October and is a good keeper. It can be kept refrigerated for up to three months.

JONATHAN: The Jonathan apple was a chance seedling that is believed to have originated from an Esopus Spitzenburg seedling in 1826 at the farm of Philip Rick in Woodstock, New York. It got its name from the man who first promoted it, Jonathan Hasbrouck. This crimson apple is crisp, juicy, and sweet, with plenty of refreshing acidity and a spicy tang that blends well with other varieties. A good choice for baking, the Jonathan is in season from November through January. Choose Jonathan apples that are solid and heavy for their size.

MCINTOSH: In 1796, John McIntosh transplanted wild apple saplings from the Mohawk Valley in New York to Dundela, Ontario, not far from the St. Lawrence River, where he established a homestead. Only one of his saplings survived, but it produced fruit of such tangy flavor and fragrance that they became well-known in the region. Years later, his son propagated this single apple tree, which became known as the McIntosh Red. It is thought to be related to the Fameuse apple of the region. The McIntosh has sweet, juicy, pinkish-white flesh and a rather tough skin that is mostly red mixed with green. If you live on the East Coast, McIntoshs make an excellent choice for baking, though they tend to be finicky. The apples must be used in season, generally September, because they get mushy later in the fall and don't keep well. McIntosh apples will collapse when baked whole or in pies, but have excellent flavor. The McIntosh, immortalized though misspelled in the name of the Macintosh computer, is in season September through June.

NORTHERN SPY: "Spies are for Pies!" One of the oldest American varieties, the Northern Spy is the quintessential baking apple on the East Coast, especially in New York State. This venerable apple was discovered south of Rochester, New York, about 1800 as the surviving sprouts of a seedling that had died. A large apple, Spys are often irregular in shape with variable colors, best for baking, not display. The skin is generally greenish-yellow, mottled, and striped with pinkish red and occasionally shows russet (rough brownish) patches. Its yellowish flesh is fine-grained and firm, though quite tender, crisp, and juicy, with good tart balance. Northern Spys keep their shape well, making them well-suited for baking. Though not easy to find, this late-season apple is in season from October through March, and keeps quite well when refrigerated.

PINK LADY®: The Pink Lady is a trademarked cross of the Golden Delicious and the Lady Williams apples, developed in a Western Australia breeding program and introduced to market in 1985. With its fine-grained, firm, white, crisp flesh and tangy, sweet flavor, the Pink Lady is a good candidate for baking. However, its thin skin bruises easily. This

apple starts out green, then turns yellow. When harvested in late October, crisp fall nights bring on the bright pink color that gives the apple its name. It is in season from the fall through the spring.

ROME: The Rome apple is named not for the European city, but rather for its discovery in Rome Township, Ohio, in 1816. This quintessential baking apple is known as the "baker's buddy," or "queen of the bakers." A round colorful apple, it is nearly solid red dotted with white "lenticels," the small spots that allow the apple to "breathe." It has firm, mildly tart, crisp, greenish-white flesh and tough, smooth skin. Baking enhances its sweet flavor and it keeps its shape. Choose Rome apples that are firm with smooth skin and feel solid and heavy for their size. Romes are in season from mid-October through June and are often quite large, a definite advantage when peeling apples for pie or sauce.

STAYMAN-WINESAP: The Stayman-Winesap was developed from the Winesap to obtain larger size, better flavor, and better keeping qualities in 1866 by Dr. J. Stayman of Leavenworth, Kansas, and introduced to market in 1895 by the influential Stark Brothers Nurseries. Medium to large in size, the Stayman has greenish-yellow skin marked with dull red and dark red stripes. Its surface is lightly russeted (rough brownish skin) with heavy gusseting (folding of extra skin) around the stem. The white flesh is tinted greenish-yellow in color and is firm, tender, and fine-grained with distinctive tangy, wine-like flavor that makes it excellent for baking, as long as the apple is firm. Its tendency to cracking has discouraged commercial production. The Stayman Winesap ripens in late October and may be found through June.

YORK (OR YORK IMPERIAL): This apple originated in York, Pennsylvania, in 1830. A medium- sized apple, the York has yellow skin with a pinkish-red blush and is faintly striped with bright red. Its flesh is yellowish in color, crisp, and moderately juicy and has a mildly acidic and sweet taste. A good cooking and baking apple, the York is in season from October through June and is an excellent keeper.

French Roquefort, Apple, and Leek Tart

I developed the recipe for this blue-cheese lover's tart in the early 1990s for the Dock Street Brewing Company and Restaurant, the first brewpub in the state of Pennsylvania. The owner, Jeffrey Ware, successfully fought a case all the way to the Pennsylvania State Supreme Court to be allowed to produce and serve the beer on the same premises. While you can certainly substitute another type of blue cheese here, Roquefort has just the intensity and super-creaminess that marries perfectly with the mild, melting leeks and sweet, tart apples. Serve this tart as a lunch dish or light entrée with amber or dark beer or with hard cider.

YIELD: 12 APPETIZER SERVINGS; 8 MAIN COURSE SERVINGS

$3/4$ pound Savory Spiced Whole Wheat
    Pastry (page 862)

1 medium leek (about $1/2$ pound)

1 tablespoon unsalted butter

2 medium or 1 large apple, preferably Fuji,
    unpeeled and cut into $1/2$-inch dice

4 large eggs

1 cup half-and-half

$1^1/2$ teaspoons finely chopped fresh thyme,
    or $1/2$ teaspoon dried thyme

$1/2$ teaspoon freshly grated nutmeg

Pinch cayenne pepper

Fine sea salt and freshly ground black pepper, to taste

6 ounces (about $3/4$ cup) Roquefort, diced

Make the crust: Roll out the dough on a lightly floured surface into a large round about $3/8$-inch thick. Transfer to a 10-inch tart pan with a removable bottom. Lay into the pan without stretching the dough and press well into the corners so there are no thick spots. Trim any overhang flush with the edge. Chill the dough for 30 minutes to relax the gluten so the tart crust maintains its shape well.

    Preheat the oven to 375°F. Fit a piece of heavy-duty foil onto the dough and up over the edges and fill with beans or other pie weights. Blind bake (just pastry crust, no filling) on the bottom shelf of the oven until the dough is cooked through but not yet browned, about 30 minutes. Remove the foil and the weights, reduce the oven temperature to 325°F, and bake for 10 minutes longer, or until the dough is evenly and lightly browned. Remove from the oven and cool to room temperature on a wire rack before filling.

Make the filling: Reduce the oven temperature to 325°F.

Cut off and discard 3 to 4 inches of dark green tops from the leek. Cut off and discard any dark green outer leaves. Cut off and discard the root end. Split the leek lengthwise into quarters and then cut crosswise into squares. Soak in a large bowl of cold water, swishing around to loosen dirt. Remove the leeks from the water using a skimmer or slotted spoon and then drain, leaving behind any sand. (If the water looks dirty, wash again.)

Heat the butter till sizzling in a medium skillet and then add the leeks and apples. Cook over medium heat until the leeks are brightly colored and the apples softened, about 5 minutes, stirring often. Remove from heat and cool to room temperature.

In a medium bowl, lightly beat together the eggs, half-and-half, and the seasonings: thyme, nutmeg, cayenne pepper, salt and pepper, then transfer to a large Pyrex measure for easy pouring.

Cover the outside of the baked and cooled tart crust with heavy duty foil to prevent leaks (not leeks) and place on a baking pan to catch any drips. Evenly distribute the leek-apple mix over the tart crust. Sprinkle the Roquefort in between the apples and leeks. Pour most of the custard over top, reserving the remainder.

Bake for 30 minutes or until a thick skin forms on the surface. Make a hole in the center of the tart and pour the remaining custard inside to fill as much as possible. Continue baking another 30 minutes or until the custard has just set in the middle, but without allowing the tart to do more than begin to puff in the center. Remove from the oven and cool on a wire rack before cutting.

To make ahead: Bake 1 or 2 days before, chill, and cut into serving portions. Arrange the slices on a parchment paper–lined baking pan, cover loosely with aluminum foil, and reheat in a moderate oven for about 30 minutes, or until thoroughly heated, removing the foil for the last 5 to 10 minutes of baking.

CHOOSING AND STORING ROQUEFORT

Good Roquefort should be crumbly but should hold together well. The cheese should be ivory-colored without any yellow tint. The veins of greenish-blue mold (called the *persillade* or parsley in French) should be abundant and reach right to the edge of the cheese. Because Roquefort has no crust, you can use the entire piece that you buy; though the cheese will be saltier near the edge. Rinse the cheese lightly under cold water to remove excess salt if desired.

Avoid Roquefort with excess moisture leaking from it, which happens when the cheese is rewrapped in plastic over the foil. Because of its worldwide fame, good Roquefort is relatively easy to find. Just about any cheese store will carry the real thing. Though the price can be rather high, you don't need to use much to get the sharp, memorable flavor of genuine Roquefort.

Fuji Apple Cake

I use my favorite Japanese Fuji apples to make my Jewish-style apple cake, because they combine firm yet juicy texture with sweet-tart flavor and they resist browning when cut. What makes this cake Jewish? Because when cakes were served on Shabbat and special holidays, when the meal would generally include meat, they had to be made with oil, rather than butter to keep it pareve (or neutral: neither milk nor meat). This moist apple cake is oil-based and could be made with readily available ingredients. It is also a cake that could be kept for several days and served whenever anyone showed up to serve along with a cup of coffee or tea.

YIELD: 1 LARGE RING CAKE, 12 TO 16 SERVINGS

$^3/_4$ pound (2$^3/_4$ cups plus 1 tablespoon)
   unbleached all-purpose flour

2 teaspoons baking powder

2 teaspoons ground cinnamon

2 teaspoons ground ginger

$^1/_4$ teaspoon ground cloves

$^1/_2$ teaspoon fine sea salt

4 large Fuji apples, peeled, cored, and thinly sliced

Juice and grated zest of 1 orange
   ($^1/_4$ cup juice, 4 teaspoons zest)

4 large eggs

2 cups sugar

1 cup grapeseed oil, substitute canola or vegetable oil

Preheat the oven to 350°F. Prepare a 10-inch ring pan by spraying it with nonstick baker's coating or rub with oil and dust with flour, shaking off the excess.

In a medium bowl, whisk together the dry ingredients: flour, baking powder, cinnamon, ginger, cloves, and salt.

Combine the apples with the orange juice and zest and reserve.

In the bowl of a standing mixer, beat together the eggs and sugar until light and fluffy, 5 to 6 minutes. Slowly beat in the oil and continue beating until the mixture is creamy and thick, like mayonnaise. Add the flour mixture and beat just long enough to combine. Fold together briefly by hand to ensure all the dry ingredients are well mixed.

Spoon half the batter into the prepared pan. Spread half the apples and half of any juices over top. Spoon the remaining batter over top. Spread the remaining apples and any juices on top.

Bake in the middle of the oven for 1 hour, or until the cake starts to come away from the sides of the pan and a skewer or toothpick inserted in the center comes out clean. Cool on a wire rack before unmolding. Turn right side-up with the apple layer on top before cutting into serving portions. Store covered and at room temperature for up to 3 days.

Spanish Apple Torte

Here, Spanish sherry-enhanced pastry cream blankets lightly simmered apples in a rich, crumbly pastry crust and is finished with an appealing shiny apple jelly glaze. I used Ozark Golden apples, purchased from a local farmer. These apples were developed in the Missouri State Agricultural Experiment Station as a mild, early-season type of Golden Delicious that increases in flavor as the season passes. Like Golden Delicious, which would make a good substitute, Ozarks hold their shape very well when baked, but a combination of apples (some soft, some firm) would also work well here. The apples will cook down, so make sure there are enough to mound up in the torte.

YIELD: 8 TO 12 SERVINGS

Pastry and Filling

14 ounces Pasta Frolla (page 62)

1 cup milk

4 large eggs yolks

$^1/_4$ cup sugar

1 ounce ($^1/_4$ cup minus 1 teaspoon) unbleached
   all-purpose flour

$^1/_2$ cup dry sherry

Grated zest of 1 lemon (1 tablespoon)

2 tablespoons (1 ounce) unsalted butter, softened

Topping and Assembly

4 large firm apples, such as Golden Delicious,
   or a combination, peeled, cored, and sliced
   into $^1/_4$ inch-thick wedges

$^1/_4$ cup sugar

1 tablespoon lemon juice

1 teaspoon ground cinnamon

Pinch ground cloves

$^1/_2$ cup apple or apricot jelly, warmed until runny

Make the pastry: Lightly flour the well-chilled dough and roll out about $^3/_8$-inch thick between two sheets of wax paper to a circle about 13 inches in diameter. Lay into the bottom and 2 inches up the sides of a 10-inch removable-bottom or springform cake pan without stretching the dough and pressing well into the corners so there are no thick spots. Chill the dough again for 30 minutes to relax the gluten and so that the tart crust maintains its shape well.

Make the filling: Place the milk in a medium nonreactive pot and heat till scalded.

In a medium bowl, whisk together the egg yolks and sugar until well-combined. Beat in the flour. Slowly pour in the milk.

Transfer the mixture to the pot and bring to a boil over low to moderate heat, whisking constantly to prevent lumps, making sure to get the whisk into the edges where lumps tend to develop. As soon as the mixture boils (a few bubbles should appear on the surface), remove it from the heat. Beat in the sherry, lemon zest, and butter. Transfer the mixture to a bowl, preferably stainless-steel, and cool by placing over a second bowl filled with a mixture of ice and water, stirring often.

Make the topping: Combine the apples, sugar, lemon juice, cinnamon, and cloves in a large nonreactive skillet. Cook over medium heat for 5 minutes, shaking often, until the apples begin to soften. Cool to room temperature.

Preheat the oven to 350°F. Pour the custard into the crust. Spoon the apple mixture evenly over top along with any cooking juices. Wrap the outside of the pan with aluminum foil and place the torte on a baking pan to catch any drips.

Bake for 1 hour on the bottom shelf of the oven until

the pastry is medium brown and the apples are lightly browned. Remove from the oven and cool to room temperature on a wire rack.

Warm the jelly and brush over the apples. Cool until the jelly is set, then cut into serving portions. Store covered and at room temperature for up to 2 days.

BAKING ON THE BOTTOM SHELF WHEN DOUGH IS RAW

When baking a tart with a pastry crust, bake it on the bottom shelf of the oven so the pastry cooks thoroughly. Nothing is more unappetizing and indigestible than soggy, undercooked pastry. Also, when blind-baking (no filling) a pastry crust, be sure to bake it on the bottom shelf so the bottom browns at the same time as the sides.

PASTRY, PÂTE, PASTA, PASTILLA, B'STILLA, PÂTÉ, (PUFF) PASTE

All these seemingly different words share a common root, a group of ancient Greek words referring to small particles and fine textures. *Pasta* is a Latin derivative for flour that has been mixed with water to a paste, which led to the French *pâte* (for dough) and *pâté* (for a mixture of cooked ground meats originally enclosed in pastry for a meat pie). We still call the high-rising layered (or laminated) dough *puff paste* and small, light puffs of dough are made from *choux paste*.

PIE OR PYE

The word *pie* is the equivalent of *pâté* in medieval English and referred originally to any food or mixture of foods enclosed in pastry. It derives from the magpie, a bird that collects all sorts of bits and pieces for its nest. Pies have been around since the time of the ancient Egyptians (about 2000 BCE) and were passed on to the Greeks. Savory vegetable pies are still quite popular in Greece (page 262). From Greece, the pie spread to ancient Rome. Pies spread into Europe along the Roman roads and first appeared in England in the twelfth century. They were usually meat-filled in a sturdy, heavy crust enclosing the filling called the "coffyn." (Does that make us pyes when we're buried?) For a long time, the pastry was too tough to eat and served only to enclose the filling, though now the much-enriched pastry is often the best part. Pies came to America with the first English settlers and in this country are generally filled with fruit, although the Pennsylvania Dutch make corn pies and chicken pies.

Animated pies were popular entertainment at the elaborate banquets in medieval time. The English nursery rhyme "Sing a Song of Sixpence, four and twenty blackbirds baked in a pie," refers to such a fanciful pie. According to the rhyme, "When the pie was opened, the birds began to sing. Wasn't that a dainty dish to set before the King?" More than likely, the birds not only sang, but flew out at the assembled guests.

Rabbits, frogs, turtles, other small animals, were also set into pies to be released when the crust was cut. Sometimes small people (dwarfs) would emerge and walk down the length of the table, reciting poetry, sketching the guests, or doing tricks. The American bachelor's party girl who jumps out of a cake, usually only seen in the movies, seems to have its origins in this English custom.

Brown Bread Apple Charlotte with Rum– Vanilla Custard Sauce

A charlotte is a golden-crusted dessert made by baking a thick apple compote in a mold lined with buttered bread that originated as a thrifty cook's way to use left-over or stale bread. Some historians think it is named after England's Queen Charlotte, who was known as a supporter of apple growers. I use brown bread here to make a heartier dessert, full of rounded flavor. You may mix tart apples, soft apples, quince, or Asian pears for the filling. Although apricot preserves are more tradi-tional, I also like using the excellent quince preserves produced in Turkey; Spanish membrillo (page 175) is another possibility. Ideally, the charlotte should be baked in a special French fez-shaped tinned charlotte pan that holds about 2 quarts, for dramatic presenta-tion and excellent caramelization. Because not many people are lucky enough to have one of these pans (I bought one to make the charlotte for this book), I have adapted the recipe to bake in a cake pan. (Look for the

French molds at www.fantes.com.) Accompany the charlotte with a pitcher of thick, warm Rum-Vanilla Custard Sauce.

YIELD: 12 SERVINGS

1 cup Clarified Butter (page 202)

5 pounds tart, firm apples, peeled, cored, and coarsely shredded or chopped

$1/2$ teaspoon fine sea salt

$1/2$ cup sugar

1 teaspoon ground cinnamon

$1/2$ teaspoon freshly grated nutmeg

1 tablespoon grated orange zest

1 cup apricot or quince preserves

2 teaspoons vanilla extract

$1/4$ cup dark rum

2 tablespoons (1 ounce) butter, softened, for the mold

1 pound loaf day-old wheat sandwich bread, sliced, and crusts removed

3 cups Rum-Vanilla Custard Sauce (page 61)

In a large heavy skillet or Dutch oven, over medium heat, melt $1/4$ cup of the clarified butter. When sizzling, add the apples. Season with salt and cook for several minutes, or until softened. Add the sugar, cinnamon, nutmeg, orange zest, the preserves, and the vanilla. Continue to sauté until the mixture is thick and golden, about 8 minutes.

Remove the pan from the heat, add the rum, and ignite it. Place the pan back over the heat and shake it several times until the flame dies out. Continue to cook the apples for 10 to 15 minutes or until the liquid has been absorbed and the apples are tender, stirring often. Remove from the heat and cool.

Preheat the oven to 375°F. Rub an 8 x 3-inch metal cake pan (or a 2$\frac{1}{4}$-quart French charlotte mold) generously with the softened butter. Cut 6 slices of the bread into thin triangles. Cut 8 slices of bread into 2-inch wide strips. Brush the bread pieces on both sides lightly with remaining clarified butter.

To assemble, arrange the triangles into a circle to cover the bottom of the pan (or mold), with the points meeting in the center. Line the sides with the strips of bread, pressing the bread slightly to adhere. Spoon one-half of the apple mixture into the bottom of the mold. Make a layer of lightly buttered bread scraps in the middle of the mold to help give it structure. Cover with the remaining apple mixture. Top with the remaining bread pieces cut to fit the top and brushed lightly on both sides with butter. Using the back of a spoon, press the mixture into the mold. Drop the pan on the counter from a few inches above to remove any air pockets.

Cover the pan with aluminum foil and place on a baking pan to catch any drips. Bake for 45 minutes or until the sides of the mold are golden brown. Remove the foil during the last 5 minutes of baking. Several times during the cooking process, use the back of a spoon to compact the mixture firmly.

Remove from the oven and allow the charlotte to cool for at least 1 hour or until just warm. Run a knife around the edges of the pan and unmold onto a platter. Slice the charlotte into individual servings and serve with warm Rum-Vanilla Custard Sauce. Store refrigerated up to 1 week. Reheat covered in foil in a 350°F. for 30 minutes.

Candied Walnut Apple Pie

This yummy deep-dish apple pie is a recreation from memory of the chunky, hunky apple pie made famous in Philadelphia by City Councilwoman-at-Large Joan Specter, wife of Senator Arlen Specter. In the 1980s, she was the owner of Joan Specter's Desserts, which supplied over $100 worth of large pies every day to the United States Senate cafeteria. Her bakery was famous locally for its eighties-style, over-the-top candied walnut apple pie, fudge truffle tort, lemon crème chiffon pie, and pumpkin praline mousse cake. Huge numbers of oversized slices of this pie were served at the groundbreaking of Philadelphia restaurateur Neil Stein's restaurant, *The Fish Market*. *The candied walnuts give the pie the surprise of crunchy, caramelized walnuts bits inside and on top, but plain walnuts may be substituted. You'll need a 9 x 2-inch French fluted deep-dish quiche pan, but a 9-inch removable bottom cake pan may be substituted.*

YIELD: 12 GENEROUS SERVINGS

Pie

$^3/_4$ pound Butter Pie Pastry (page 203)

$^3/_4$ cup sugar

2 tablespoons unbleached all-purpose flour

Pinch fine sea salt

1 cup sour cream

4 large eggs

1 teaspoon vanilla extract

1 teaspoon ground cinnamon

2 pounds mixed tart and sweet apples, peeled, cored, and sliced (3 cups)

$^1/_2$ cup Candied Walnuts (page 847)

Streusel

$^1/_2$ cup sugar

2 ounces (scant $^1/_2$ cup) unbleached all-purpose flour

1 teaspoon ground cinnamon

$^1/_4$ pound (1 stick) unsalted butter, cut into bits and chilled

$^1/_2$ cup Candied Walnuts (page 847)

Roll out the pastry about $^3/_8$-inch thick between two sheets of wax paper and drape into a French quiche pan, without stretching the dough and pressing the dough

into flutes. Trim off any overhanging edges, then chill the crust for 1 hour in the refrigerator or 30 minutes in the freezer to set the shape.

Preheat the oven to 425°F.

In a large bowl, stir together the sugar, flour, and salt. Whisk in the sour cream, eggs, vanilla, and cinnamon until smooth. Add the apples, stir to coat with the mixture, then mix in the candied walnuts. Spoon the mixture into the prepared crust and place on a baking pan to catch any drips.

Bake on the bottom shelf of the oven for 15 minutes, then reduce the heat to 350°F and continue baking for 15 minutes more.

Meanwhile, prepare the streusel: Combine the sugar, flour, and cinnamon in the bowl of a food processor. Process to combine, then add the butter and process until a crumbly mix is formed. Remove mixture from the processor and mix in the candied walnuts.

Cover the pie with the streusel, and continue baking to bake for 30 minutes longer, or until the topping is lightly browned, the apples are tender, and the filling is bubbling. Allow the pie to cool on a wire rack to room temperature about 1 hour before cutting into serving portions. Store 2 days at room temperature, up to 1 week refrigerated.

ABOUT NEIL STEIN

Neil Stein, the jet-setting, St. Bart's habitué, and general bad boy of Philadelphia's Restaurant Row, is the man who brought the city the world-class restaurant Striped Bass, who fought the city to allow sidewalk cafés for the small, but madly successful Rouge on Rittenhouse Square, and who jump-started the rebirth of Delaware Avenue with Rock Lobster. According to his childhood friend and ex-partner at Striped Bass, Joey Wolf, Neil is a guy who could "take a leaf on a tree and make Central Park." Now back from serving a prison sentence for nonpayment of taxes, I have no doubt that Stein will soon come up with another high-style, great food, beautiful people project to sharpen the edge of the city and keep it at the forefront of cuisine and style in the nation.

APRICOTS

Choosing Dried Apricots . . .115

Making Dried California Apricots . . .116

Fresh California Apricot Varieties . . .116

Choosing and Storing Apricots . . .117

Substituting Dried, Fresh,
and Canned Apricots . . .117

SLOVENIAN ALMOND-
APRICOT TEA BREAD . . .117

CALIFORNIA APRICOT CHEESECAKE . . .118

FRENCH APRICOT TART SCENTED
WITH CLOVES . . .120

APPLE-APRICOT STRUDEL . . .121

AUSTRIAN APRICOT DUMPLINGS
(WACHAUER APRIKOSENKNODEL) . . .122

APRICOT BRANDY SAUCE . . .123

About Apricot Brandy . . .124

APRICOTS

The delectable and exquisite apricot is more important in the kitchen in its dried form than its fresh, partly because it is so difficult to find good tree-ripened fresh apricots in America, except if you happen to live in California. I couldn't get enough of the fresh apricots (in several varieties) that I bought at a Turkish farmers' market near the Aegean city of Izmir (once known as Smyrna and noted for its sophisticated cuisine). Large, flat, woven baskets were filled to the brim with soft, just-picked apricots covered with velvety fuzz that were as delicious and drippingly juicy as they were fragrant. The farmer-vendors were as proud as new parents with their offspring, each one showing off their best to my camera with a big smile. Because the apricot is so delicate, it's also very finicky, demanding perfect conditions to produce juicy, delectable fruits. This makes these little beauties hard to find in perfect condition outside of local farmers' markets.

A cousin of the peach, the apricot, *Prunus armeniaca*, is smaller and has a hard, smooth, oval pit that falls out easily when the fruit is halved. Like other stone fruits, apricots are sweetest—and most prone to bruising—when they're allowed to ripen on the tree. The small downy-skinned fruit is usually smaller than a peach, warm orange-yellow when ripe, with flesh that tends to be dry, although some varieties are firmer, larger, and juicier.

This richly sweet, aromatic fruit was first cultivated in China over 4,000 years ago. Alexander the Great is said to have brought apricots from their native home in China to Greece in the fourth century BCE, where they flourished. The Romans named the fruit *Preacocium*, meaning "precocious," because it ripens earlier than other stone fruits. Apricots reached Italy as early as 100 BCE, where today they often show up in rustic crostata (baked fruit tarts), and arrived in England in the thirteenth century. The "nectar of the gods," made of the juice and pulp of the apricot, was by legend the drink of choice for Greek and Roman gods.

Franciscan friars brought the apricot from Spain to America in the late 1800s, where they thrived in the gardens of Spanish missions in California, and by 1792, the first major planting of apricots was recorded south of San Francisco. Today, California produces more than ninety-five percent of the apricots in the United States. Over four hundred growers produce apricots in orchards covering 21,000 acres in the San Joaquin Valley and in northern California. Apricots are also a significant crop in British Columbia (Canada), Australia, Italy, the south of France, and Israel. Australian glazed apricots are highly sought after for their plump, satiny–glazed, soft texture, and rich color and flavor.

The petite apricot is appreciated by fruit connoisseurs for delicate flavor, faintly fuzzed skin as smooth as a baby's cheek, and exquisite aroma. But, unless you can pick your own or travel to Turkey as I did, you'll probably have to make do with the slightly underripe, more durable apricots sold in markets. Large quantities of Turkish and American apricots are dried, canned, or used to make jams and jellies.

Pronunciation is pretty much a matter of regional preference. As the saying goes, a rose is a rose is a rose, and this member of the rose family is a particular treat whether its pronounced ape-ri-cot or ap-ri-cot. This luscious fruit of the gods is a delightful addition to baked goods, including tea breads, muffins, cakes, tarts, and pies. In this chapter, dried and plumped apricots form part of the batter for the apricot orange–colored Slovenian Almond–Apricot Tea Bread (page 117). Poached dried California apricots top a California cheesecake that also contains apricot purée in the batter (see page 118), and golden mounds of apricot halves top an elegant French Apricot Tart scented with cloves (page 120). A Hungarian strudel is filled with a not-too-sweet combination of apples and apricots in the Apple–Apricot Strudel (page 121). Fresh or canned apricot halves with a surprise-stuffing of sugar and brandy are enclosed in rich dough and poached for the substantial and so delicious Austrian Apricot Dumplings (page 122).

In other chapters, dried apricots go into the batter for Aliza's Wedding Cake (page 227), Siennese Panforte (page 232), White Bean, Chestnut, and Apricot Cake (page 316), and the Torta di Zucca: Squash Cake with Pine Nuts and Apricots (page 741). Fresh peaches and apricots are combined in the Peach and Apricot Tarte Tatin (page 616) while apricot preserves are mixed with green pistachios meats to fill Pistachio Bird's Nest Pastries (page 693). Apricots are so pectin–rich than strained apricot preserves are brushed on cakes like the Swiss Carrot-Semolina Torte (page 239) and Torta Gianduia (page 506) for an extra layer of flavor and to give the cake a smooth surface suitable for further glazing.

CHOOSING DRIED APRICOTS

Whole dried, light-orange, wrinkle-skinned and pitted Turkish apricots are relatively inexpensive and easy to find, but I much prefer the deeply colored, melting California fruits dried in halves. I've found that the Trader Joe's stores have the best selection and quality (and the lowest prices) for California apricots. Try their slab apricots, which are made from very ripe fruit that have been dried, chopped, flattened, and cut into shape. Because they are processed from such ripe fruit, slab apricots are honey-sweet and soft and giving in texture, with intense apricot flavor. Their soft, luscious Blenheim apricots come from that highly prized variety. Mariani and Sun Maid are good supermarket and warehouse-store brands, but be careful, because if the apricots have sat on the shelf too long, they may be hard, dark, and leathery.

MAKING DRIED CALIFORNIA APRICOTS

It takes about six pounds of fresh apricots to make one pound of dried apricots, which have more concentrated nutrients than any other dried fruit. The fruits are picked at peak ripeness and halved, then arranged on trays, cut side up, and treated with sulphur dioxide (commonly used to keep yellow-colored dried fruits and white wine from darkening). The trays are rotated in the sun for about three days until the fruits are ready for washing and packing. Sweet, tart, and tangy, these dried apricots are superb in color, flavor, and texture, and are extremely versatile in the kitchen. Because they are more expensive, the California type are harder to track down than the imports from Turkey.

FRESH CALIFORNIA APRICOT VARIETIES

The most important apricot varieties in California are the Patterson, Blenheim, Tilton, and Castle-brite. The Patterson is a late-season, firm-medium apricot with good flavor, orange skin, and possibly its most important quality for commercial success: excellent shelf life. The Tilton is a large, firm apricot with tart flavor. The Castlebrite is a medium-sized early apricot with bright orange skin with a red blush, firm flesh, and a tart flavor, unless it is very ripe.

The Blenheim, a medium apricot with intense flavor, is considered the king of apricots and is rarely to be found fresh outside of California. It also makes a superb dried apricot with soft, rich flesh, velvety skin, concentrated flavor, and pectin-rich body, making it well suited for purées, glazes, and tart fillings. Unfortunately, despite the Blenheim's superior flavor, it is rapidly disappearing from California orchards because of its fragility.

Choosing and Storing Apricots

Fresh ripe apricots are a boon when found, because they do not travel well. The majority of the American ripe apricot crop is dried, with less than one-fourth of the harvest coming to the market fresh. Harvest season for apricots in the United States is from June to mid-August depending on variety and location, but dried apricots are available year-round. Most fresh apricots sold to market are picked when not quite mature and still firm to reduce shipping damage. While they will ripen in color, texture, and juiciness after being picked, their flavor and sweetness will remain at the same level as when they were picked and will not improve.

Apricots range in color from yellow to deep orange, often with red or rosy touches. When selecting fresh apricots, look for fruits with no green shoulders (the area surrounding the stem). The small to medium size fruits should yield to gentle pressure when held in the palm of your hand, and the fruit should have a bright, ripe aroma.

If you are not blessed with an apricot tree and vine-ripened fruit, store-bought fresh apricots will continue to ripen if left at room temperature in a paper bag, away from sunlight. Check the ripening progress often as they will quickly deteriorate. These apricots will never achieve the same full sweet flavor as tree-ripened apricots, but will be better than off the shelf. Once ripened, store for no more than a few days in the refrigerator.

SUBSTITUTING DRIED, FRESH, AND CANNED APRICOTS

Dried, soaked, and plumped apricots may be substituted with drained, canned apricots or blanched fresh apricots (dipped in boiling water to remove their skins). To blanch fresh apricots, bring a large pot of water to the boil. Add the apricots, stirring so they heat evenly, and boil for one minute. Immediately scoop from the water and plunge into a large bowl of ice mixed with water, then drain and slip off the skin. Commercial canned apricots often have fuller flavor than fresh apricots from the market because these fruits are tree-ripened and naturally develop more flavor.

Slovenian Almond–Apricot Tea Bread

These easy-to-make and uncommon tea breads are great because they are "quick," meaning they are leavened with baking powder rather than yeast. In the 1930s, American food companies that wanted to sell flour, baking powder, and baking soda flooded the American consumer market with recipes for quick breads. The "breads," which are really more like cakes or muffins, are easy to make and require no special skill or equipment. While banana-nut bread was the first and still one of the most popular, this uncommon brightly colored tangy tea bread makes good use of the apricots that grow abundantly in Slovenia. Situated at the northwestern end of the Balkan Peninsula and surrounded by Italy, Austria, Hungary, and Croatia, Slovenia is one of the youngest European countries, becoming an independent state in 1991.

YIELD: 2 MEDIUM LOAVES

1 cup water

$^1/_2$ cup orange juice

1 cup sugar

$1^1/_2$ cups (6 ounces) diced dried California apricots

$^1/_4$ pound (1 stick) unsalted butter, cut up

$^1/_2$ cup honey

1 teaspoon vanilla extract

Grated zest of 1 tangerine, substitute orange zest
   (4 teaspoons)

4 large eggs

6 ounces ($1^1/_2$ cups minus 1 tablespoon) unbleached
   all-purpose flour

$^1/_4$ pound (1 cup plus 2 tablespoons) white whole
   wheat flour

1 teaspoon fine sea salt

1 teaspoon baking powder

$^1/_2$ teaspoon baking soda

6 ounces (about 1 cup) skin-on almonds,
   toasted and chopped

In a medium saucepan, bring the water, the orange juice, sugar, and apricots to a boil, cover, and simmer for 15 minutes or until very soft and plump and the liq-uid has mostly evaporated. Add the butter, honey, vanilla, and tangerine or orange zest, and stir well until the butter melts, then remove the mixture from the heat. Cool to room temperature, transferring the mixture to a bowl, preferably stainless-steel, and cool by placing over a second bowl filled with a mixture of ice and water, stirring often. Whisk in the eggs.

Preheat the oven to 350°F. Prepare 2 (1-pound, $8^1/_2$ x 4 $^1/_2$-inch) loaf pans by spraying with baker's nonstick coating, or rub with softened butter and dust with flour, shaking out the excess.

Whisk together the dry ingredients: flour, whole wheat flour, salt, baking powder, and baking soda in a large bowl. Fold in the cooled apricot mixture and the almonds.

Spread the batter evenly into the prepared pans. Bake for 45 minutes or until the bread starts to come away from the sides of the pan and a skewer stuck in the center comes out clean. Allow the breads to cool for about 20 minutes on a wire rack before unmolding and cooling to room temperature. Slice and serve or wrap tightly in plastic wrap and then aluminum foil and freeze for up to 3 months.

California Apricot Cheesecake

This apricot-lover's cheesecake is topped with plump, tart, sunset-colored poached apricot halves from California, which contrast beautifully with the rich, creamy filling. I developed the recipe originally in the mid-eighties for the California-Mediterranean menu at Apropos Bistro, on what is now the booming Avenue of the Arts in Philadelphia but was then a mecca for hookers, panhandlers, and the homeless. The zwieback, lightly sweetened twice-baked rusks, often sold in the baby food section of the supermarket because they're good for teething, make an extra-crunchy crumb crust. Start the day before by soaking the apricots so they get a chance to really plump up.

YIELD: ONE 10-INCH CHEESECAKE, SERVES 12 TO 16

Apricots

$1/2$ pound (2 cups) dried California apricots, soaked
    overnight in lukewarm water to cover

1 cup sugar

1 cup water

Crumb Crust

1 box Zwieback, substitute other double-baked rusks,
    biscotti, or plain vanilla cookies

$1/4$ pound (scant 1 cup) walnuts

2 ounces ($1/4$ cup packed) dark brown sugar

1 teaspoon ground cinnamon

$1/4$ pound (1 stick) unsalted butter, melted and cooled

Filling

2 pounds cream cheese, at room temperature

$3/4$ cup sugar

$1/2$ cup heavy cream

4 large eggs

Scrapings of 1 vanilla bean, or
    2 teaspoons vanilla extract

Grated zest of 1 orange (4 teaspoons)

Topping

$1/2$ cup sour cream

2 tablespoons sugar

2 tablespoons apricot brandy, substitute brandy

Make the apricots: Place the apricots, their soaking liquid, the water, and sugar in a medium heavy-bottomed pot and simmer gently until plump and soft, about 15 minutes. Allow the apricots to cool in their poaching liquid. (This can be done several days ahead of time.)

Make the crust: Spray a 10-inch diameter springform pan with nonstick baking coating or rub with butter and dust with flour, shaking off the excess.

Place the zwieback, walnuts, brown sugar, and cinnamon into the bowl of a food processor and process to fine but not pasty, crumbs. Pour in the butter and process 1 minute to combine. Press the mixture into the bottom of the pan and chill for 30 minutes to set the shape.

Preheat the oven to 350°F. Bake the crust for 20 minutes or until lightly browned. Cool and reserve. (If the crust gets puffy when baking, allow it to cool slightly, then use a spoon or spatula to press it down.) Reduce the oven temperature to 300°F.

Make the filling: Using a slotted spoon, remove about $1/2$ cup apricots from the poaching liquid and purée or mash. In the bowl of a standing electric mixer and using the paddle attachment, beat the cream cheese until smooth, scraping down the sides of bowl once or twice with a silicone spatula. Add the sugar, cream, apricot purée, eggs, vanilla bean scrapings, and orange zest and beat again until smooth, again scraping down the sides once or twice to ensure that the mixture is quite smooth.

Wrap the bottom and sides of the springform pan in a single sheet of aluminum foil, preferably heavy-duty. Scrape the batter into the pan. Place it on a second baking pan and pour in enough hot water to come halfway up the sides of the cake.

Bake for about 1 hour, or until the center is just barely set. Check often near the end of baking time to be sure the filling doesn't begin to rise and crack. Remove from the oven and cool to room temperature. Chill 1 hour in the refrigerator or until cold to the touch.

Make the topping and finish the cake: Preheat the oven to 400°F.

In a bowl, whisk together the sour cream, sugar, and apricot brandy and spread evenly over top of cheesecake. Bake for 5 minutes or until the topping has just set.

Drain the remaining apricots, reserving the liquid, and arrange on top of the cheesecake in an attractive pattern. Strain the liquid into a small pot and bring to a boil. Boil for about 5 minutes or until thickened and bubbles appear all over the top. Remove from the heat, cool slightly until thickened, but still pourable, then spoon or brush over top of the apricots. Chill the cheesecake again for about 1 hour or until the topping has set before serving.

Cut into 12 or 16 portions with a hot wet knife, wiped dry in between each cut. Store the cake covered and refrigerated for up to 5 days.

French Apricot Tart Scented with Cloves

This old fashioned apricot tart comes from Tours in Southwest France, where apricots and apricot desserts abound. An underlying hint of clove flavors this country-style apricot custard tart, while yogurt makes a tangy and light filling. Because ground cloves are so potent, I prefer to simmer whole cloves with the apricots and enhance them with just a pinch of the ground spice. The walnut pastry provides a welcome contrast of texture to the creamy filling and tangy topping.

YIELD: 8 TO 10 SERVINGS

$^3/_4$ pound Sweet Walnut Pastry (page 848)

$1^1/_2$ cups sugar

$1^1/_2$ cups water

4 whole cloves, or pinch ground cloves

$2^1/_2$ pounds (8 to 10 small) fresh, firm but ripe apricots, halved and pitted

$^3/_4$ cup whole milk plain yogurt

3 large eggs

2 tablespoons sugar

Pinch of ground cloves

2 ounces ($^1/_2$ stick) unsalted butter, melted and cooled

Make the pastry crust: Roll out the dough into a large round, $^3/_8$-inch thick, on a lightly floured surface. Transfer to a 10- to 11-inch tart pan with a removable bottom and press into the pan without stretching the dough and pressing well into the corners so there are no thick spots. Trim any overhang flush with the edge.

Chill the dough again for 30 minutes to relax the gluten and so that the tart crust maintains its shape well.

Preheat the oven to 375°F. Fit a piece of heavy-duty foil onto the dough and fill with beans or other pie weights. Blind bake (just pastry crust, no filling) until the dough is cooked through but not yet browned, about 30 minutes, on the bottom shelf of the oven. Remove the foil and the weights, reduce the oven temperature to 325°F, and bake for 10 minutes longer, or until the dough is evenly and lightly browned. Remove from the oven and cool to room temperature on a wire rack before filling.

Make the filling: Combine the sugar, water, and whole cloves in a medium pot. Bring the liquid to a boil, then add the apricots. Bring back to a boil, skimming off any foam. Reduce the heat and poach the apricots for 15 minutes, or until tender, but still whole.

Cool in the liquid, and then drain the apricots, reserving the syrup and discarding the whole cloves. Arrange the apricots halves in concentric circles over the pastry crust.

Preheat the oven to 400°F.

Meanwhile beat together the yogurt, eggs, sugar, ground cloves, and butter. Place the baked tart crust on a baking pan to catch any drips and pour the custard mixture over the apricots.

Bake for 15 minutes and then reduce the oven temperature to 350°F and continue to bake until the filling just sets, about 15 minutes.

Meanwhile, strain the apricot poaching liquid into a small pot and bring to a boil. Boil for about 8 minutes or until thick bubbles appear all over the top. Remove from the heat, cool until thickened, but still warm. Remove the tart from the oven, cool for about 20 min-utes, and brush with the apricot glaze. You'll have extra glaze; reserve refrigerated for up to 2 months and use to glaze any fruit tart. Store the tart at room temperature up to 2 days.

Apple–Apricot Strudel

Although it sounds like it would be hard to make, a strudel is one of the easiest desserts to make if you "cheat" and use phyllo leaves. Of course, an authentic strudel would be made from hand-stretched dough pulled out to the size of a tablecloth and thin enough to read the newspaper through. Sweet, juicy apples and tangy, smooth-textured apricots combine here to make a not-too-sweet strudel good for a brunch buffet or to serve warm with tea. Strudel originated in the Austro-Hungarian Empire but is ultimately derived from Ottoman layered phyllo dough pastries (not all histori-ans agree with this). Homemade strudel dough is made from flour with a high gluten content so that it's stretch-able. The strudel, which means "whirlpool" in German, gets its name because it forms a spiral as it is rolled up.

YIELD: 12 SERVINGS

2$\frac{1}{2}$ pounds mixed tart apples, thinly sliced (3 cups)
6 ounces dried California apricots, chopped (1 cup)
3 ounces ($\frac{1}{2}$ cup) golden raisins
$\frac{1}{2}$ pound (1 cup packed plus 2 tablespoons)
    light brown sugar
$\frac{1}{4}$ cup dry breadcrumbs or panko

1 teaspoon ground cinnamon

$^1/_2$ teaspoon ground mace

1 cup Brown Butter, melted and cooled (page 202)

$^3/_4$ pound phyllo dough, if frozen, defrost
   overnight in the refrigerator

Confectioners' sugar, for dusting

Preheat the oven to 375°F.

In a medium bowl, combine the apples, apricots, raisins, brown sugar, breadcrumbs, cinnamon, and mace.

Place a 2-foot long sheet of wax paper on a work surface. Brush lightly with brown butter. Arrange 2 sheets of the phyllo lengthwise and overlapping by about 1 inch onto the wax paper and brush lightly with the butter. Repeat with 10 more sheets, overlapping two sheets for each layer and brushing lightly with brown butter in between each layer.

Spread the fruit mixture along one long side of the rectangle, leaving a 1-inch border at the front edge. Fold up the ends and then roll up the strudel from the long side of the phyllo.

Transfer the strudel to a baking sheet lined with parchment paper or a silicone mat, carefully and gently curving it into a horseshoe-shape. (It helps to have someone else help support the strudel while transferring it.) Brush the outside with brown butter. Cut shallow slits 1$^1/_2$-inches apart across the top of the strudel, leaving the sides intact.

Bake for 45 minutes, or until the strudel is golden brown and flaky. Cool slightly and sprinkle with confectioners' sugar. Using a serrated knife, cut the strudel through the slits into serving portions. Serve warm. Store the strudel covered and at room temperature for up to 2 days.

Austrian Apricot Dumplings (Wachauer Aprikosenknodel)

These fruit-filled dumplings originate in Wachau, the region of Austria along the Danube River where rugged, rocky soils, steep stone terraces, and dramatic landscapes are typical. It is the home of the suddenly stylish white Gruner Veltliner wine. Sweet, poached fruit-filled dumplings, though almost unknown in the United States, except to those with a German, Austrian, or Central European background, are much appreciated in Middle Europe. Here, sugar and brandy-filled apricots are enclosed in an easy-to-roll, stretchy potato pastry, then simmered until tender. The dumplings are then tossed with sugared breadcrumbs toasted in butter for a filling but absolutely yummy dessert. Vary the recipe by filling the dumplings with Italian prune plums instead of apricots, when in season. Once cooked, the dumplings may be wrapped in buttered aluminum foil and reheated in 350°F oven for about 20 minutes.

YIELD: 6 TO 8 SERVINGS

Dumplings and Filling

$^1/_2$ pound (2 cups minus 2 tablespoons) unbleached
   all-purpose flour

$^1/_2$ pound (1 medium) cold cooked baking potato,
   peeled and grated

$^1/_2$ teaspoon fine sea salt

2 ounces ($^1/_2$ stick) unsalted butter, cut into bits

4 large egg yolks

2 tablespoons ice water

$^1\!/_4$ cup apricot brandy, substitute brandy

16 white or brown sugar cubes, preferably large,
    rough-shaped cubes

16 small, firm but ripe apricots, pitted and halved,
    or 3 (15-ounce) cans apricot halves, drained

Topping

$1^1\!/_4$ cups soft white breadcrumbs

$^1\!/_4$ cup sugar

$^1\!/_2$ teaspoon ground cinnamon

2 ounces ($^1\!/_2$ stick) unsalted butter

$^1\!/_2$ cup sour cream

$^1\!/_2$ cup whole milk plain yogurt

Make the dumplings: In the bowl of an electric standing mixer, combine the flour, potato, and salt. Add the butter and beat until the mixture resembles oatmeal. Add the egg yolks and water and beat only long enough for the mixture to come together and form large, moist clumps.

Turn the dough out onto a floured work surface and knead lightly until smooth. Roll the dough out thin enough so you can see through it, or run it through a pasta sheeter to the next-to-the-last setting of thinness.

Cut the dough into 4-inch squares, re-rolling the scraps if desired. Place the brandy in a small bowl. Dip a cube of sugar in the brandy and place it in the center of an apricot half. Cover with a second apricot half, enclosing the sugar cube. Place the filled apricot in the center of a dough square and pinch the edges of the dough together firmly to seal, trimming off any excess. Roll each dumpling between the palms of your hands to make it more evenly rounded and arrange on a parchment or wax paper–lined pan, seam side down.

Repeat with the remaining sugar cubes, apricots, and dough squares.

Meanwhile, bring a large, wide pot of salted water to the boil. Drop the dumplings one by one into the water. Boil gently for about 10 minutes or until puffy and light. Remove with a slotted spoon and drain well on paper or cloth towels.

Make the topping: Meanwhile, in a large skillet, fry the breadcrumbs, sugar, and cinnamon in the butter until nicely browned. Roll the dumplings in the breadcrumbs, reheating them at the same time if necessary.

To serve, whisk together the sour cream and yogurt and serve in a small bowl. Transfer the dumplings to a heated serving dish. Each person can spoon the sour cream mixture on the dumplings as desired.

Apricot Brandy Sauce

This tangy, thick, baby-food-smooth sauce made from apricots complements all sorts of desserts, especially those made with chocolate or nuts. Good-quality California dried apricot halves will yield the brightest, most colorful sauce. An equal quantity of canned apricot halves can be substituted for the soaked dried apricots. The sauce will keep in the refrigerator up to one month, or it can be frozen. Serve the sauce to accompany the White Bean, Chestnut, and Apricot Cake (page 316) or the Italian Bittersweet Chocolate-Orange Torta (page 331).

YIELD: 4 CUPS

¼ pound (¾ cup) California dried apricot halves

2 cups hot water

1 cup orange juice

1 cup sugar

2 whole cloves (optional)

¼ cup apricot brandy or brandy

Make the apricots by soaking them in the hot water to cover until softened and plump, about 1 hour.

Combine the apricots, the soaking liquid, orange juice, sugar, and cloves in a medium, nonreactive, heavy-bottomed pot. Simmer for 20 minutes until quite soft, stirring occasionally so the mixture doesn't stick and burn. Remove from the heat, remove and discard the cloves, and cool to room temperature.

Transfer the mixture to the jar of a blender and blend to a smooth purée or blend right in the pot using an immersion blender. Stir in the brandy.

Store, refrigerated and tightly covered, or freeze up to 3 months, thinning with water as necessary.

ABOUT APRICOT BRANDY

True apricot brandy is distilled entirely from apricot juice and flesh or from a combination of flesh and kernels. Zwack Apricot Brandy-Barack Palinka, from Kecskemét, Hungary, is one brand. Maraska Apricot, from Croatia is an apricot-flavored liqueur as is Marie Brizard Apry, from France, while De Kuyper Apricot Brandy is actually a type of American-style schnapps.

In Germany, Austria, and German-speaking Switzerland, *schnapps* refers to the clear alcoholic beverage distilled from fermented fruits or other ingredients, including cherries, apples, pears, peaches, plums, and apricots, often using the fruit pulp that is a by-product in juice production. True schnapps has no sugar or flavoring added and is equivalent to French eau de vie. In America, schnapps are made from a base of neutral alcohol in which fruits are steeped, rather than being distilled from the fruit itself, a much more expensive proposition. Their alcohol level is usually about 40 proof, about half that of fruit-distilled European schnapps.

BANANAS & PLANTAINS

Sweet or Yellow Bananas . . .127

Plantains . . .127

The Banana Plant . . .128

Where Bananas Grow . . .128

Banana Varieties . . .128

PLANTAIN EMPANADAS WITH BLACK BEAN
AND AÑEJO CHEESE FILLING . . .129

Empanadas . . .130

BABY BANANA CREAM PIE IN
COCONUT-CASHEW CRUST . . .131

BANANA-PECAN ROULADE . . .132

RED BANANA-BROWN BUTTER BARS . . .133

BANANAS
& PLANTAINS

Though I'm a fruit-loving fiend, ever since childhood, I've never enjoyed eating bananas. Though bananas are by far America's favorite fruit, I was turned off at an early age by their penetrating, slightly musty aroma. Don't get me wrong, I enjoy cooking and baking with bananas and my feelings never extended to plantains, the starchy cousin of the banana with many disguises–ranging in color from green to gold to black–that is always cooked. Not many American share my feelings about bananas, which are America's number one fruit at more than twenty-eight pounds of bananas each year per person.

Bananas are a perennial favorite for baking, and for good reason. Though overripe for eating, once the bananas develop a generous sprinkling of spots and a penetrating aroma, they're perfect for baking. And if you have too many ripe bananas and no time, just freeze them in a tightly sealed zipper lock freezer bag with all the air pressed out and use them later.

In this chapter, over–ripe plantains are baked then mashed to form an unexpected, but delicious dough for the Plantain Empanadas with Black Bean and Añejo Cheese Filling (page 129).

Bananas and pecans make a beautiful marriage in the Banana–Pecan Roulade (page 132), which contain a double dose of bananas: in the batter and also in the topping. A La–La Land Baby Banana Cream Pie in Coconut–Cashew Crust (page 131) made with adorable baby bananas is a particular favorite in the City of Angels. The Red Banana–Brown Butter Bars (page 133) are an easy, good tasting bar cookie

The banana, *Musa sapientum*, gets its Latin species name, *sapientum*, from the legend that wise men would sit in the shade of the banana tree and eat its fruit. Antonius Musa was the personal physician to Roman emperor Octavius Augustus, and it was he who was credited for promoting cultivation of the exotic Asian fruit during the years from 63 to 14 BCE, and he for whom the fruit gets its genus name.

Bananas originated in Southeast Asia, where they were called monkey fruit. Alexander the Great's army encountered the supremely phallic-shaped bananas in India where they had been known for several thousand years, and brought tales of the new fruit back home to Greece in the fourth century BCE. The banana reached China about 200 CE, but because it was grown only in the south, it was long considered a rare, exotic fruit in northern China.

During the first millennium CE, the banana also arrived in Africa and traveled east through the Pacific islands. The Arabs spread banana cultivation throughout North Africa before 750 CE, but the fruit was unknown to most Europeans until Portuguese sailors brought them from Guinea in West Africa to the Canary Islands around 1400. Its Guinean name, *banema*, which became *banana* in English, was first found in print in the seventeenth century. The Canaries have remained an important banana–growing area ever since.

A Spanish missionary, Friar Tomas de Berlanga, brought banana roots from the Canaries to the Americas in 1516. The new plant spread so quickly through Latin America that early writers were convinced that it had been known by the Incas. During the nineteenth century, bananas began to be shipped from the Canaries to Europe and from Cuba to the United States, but high shipping costs made the fruits an expensive luxury.

In 1804, the first bananas to enter the United States were shipped from Cuba. At the Philadelphia Centennial Exposition of 1876, bananas were introduced to America as an exotic fruit. They were wrapped in foil and sold for ten cents each. Well over a century later, bananas sell for not much more than that.

With the introduction of refrigerated cargo holds, two American entrepreneurs formed the United Fruit Company in 1899, which had and still has great influence in Central America and the Caribbean countries that became known as the "banana republics" (not a fashion store), because their entire economies revolved around bananas.

SWEET OR YELLOW BANANAS

The yellow sweet banana is a mutant strain of the cooking banana, or plantain, discovered in 1836 by Jamaican Jean Francois Poujot, who found one of the banana trees on his plantation was bearing yellow fruit rather than green or red. Upon tasting the new discovery, he found that it was sweet even when raw. He soon began cultivating this sweet banana variety. Not long after, sweet bananas were being imported from the Caribbean to New Orleans, Boston, and New York, where the rare and exotic fruit was eaten on a plate using a knife and fork, never out of hand.

PLANTAINS

The Latin name for the original starchy banana, or plantain, *Musa paradisiaca*, came about because of an Islamic myth, probably of Indian origin, that the banana (and not the apple) was the fruit of the tree of knowledge in the Garden of Eden (located in Sri Lanka according to the same legend). Furthermore, after The Fall, Adam and Eve covered their naked bodies with generously sized banana leaves, quite a bit more effective that the skimpier fig leaves of Western tradition.

Plantains start out starchy and hard like a vegetable and ripen to become soft and sweet like a fruit. In Spanish, whether green or starchy, the fruits are known as *platanos* (plantains); partially ripe plantains are known as *pintos* (painted); and fully ripened, black-spotted yellow plantains are known as *maduros* (mature or ripe). Sweet plantains may be substituted for common yellow bananas in any recipe.

THE BANANA PLANT

The banana plant is not a true tree, even though it may reach heights of 25 feet with leaves up to eight feet long and two feet wide. Bananas are thought to be one of the first species of plant domesticated by man and are a staple food for many peoples. They provide food, clothing, building materials, and cooking utensils to numerous cultures around the world. Bananas grow in large bunches or "hands," which are formed from the double rows of female flowers on each plant. Each flowering hand produces 200 to 300 individual fruits or "fingers," and weighs about 50 pounds. Under the immense weight of the fruit, the hands bend down towards the ground, making for easier picking.

WHERE BANANAS GROW

No bananas are actually grown in America, although two of the world's largest banana companies are located here: Chiquita and Dole. Fyffes from Ireland, Del Monte from Chile, and Noboa from Ecuador are three of the other top five companies. Most of the bananas raised for export are cultivated in the lowlands of Central and South America. Ecuador, Colombia, Panama, Guatemala, and Costa Rica supply two-thirds of the more than 10 million tons of fruit sold in international markets.

BANANA VARIETIES

BURRO BANANA: This short, stocky banana, also known as the Chunky, comes from Central America and Mexico and is three to five-inches long with squarish edges. When ripened to a golden yellow with scattered black spots, it has a lively, lemony flavor and velvety flesh that is white to yellow in color, and is soft in texture with some firmness toward the center. The Burro may be eaten out of hand or used for baking and is in season year-round from Mexico. Look for it in Latino markets.

CAVENDISH: By far the most common variety in the United States, the Cavendish grows in large bunches of full-sized, sweet, smooth fruit with yellow skin that is slightly ridged on the edges. "Petites" are small versions of the Cavendish that are also known as "institutional" bananas, because they are often included in school lunches. Grayish-yellow or dull-looking Cavendish bananas have probably been exposed to cold temperatures and will not ripen properly. Cavendishes are available year-round almost everywhere. The Guinea Verde is an unprocessed yellow Cavendish used green as a starch, much like plantains.

NIÑO: These mild, sweet, finger-sized baby bananas just over three-inches long originated in the jungles of Colombia where they are called *murapo*. Niños are also known as "lady bananas" in Spanish, no doubt in comparison to the much larger "males." They work well in tarts, where they can be sliced lengthwise and arranged decoratively.

PLANTAIN: Large, firm, four-sided plantains start out starchy and hard like a vegetable and ripen to soft and sweet like a fruit. Fully-ripened plantains may also be substituted for sweet, yellow bananas in any baking recipe where they will be cooked. Plantains are available every day of the year at Latino and Asian markets, though not usually in American supermarkets.

RED BANANA: Red bananas are four- to six-inches long with maroon to deep purple skin and ripe, firm, orange-tinted flesh that can be quite sweet and sticky. These short, rather stout bananas are well suited to caramelizing for desserts because they combine sweetness with firm texture. They also work well in tarts and pies. Look for them in natural foods and Latino markets.

Plantain Empanadas with Black Bean and Añejo Cheese Filling

To make these pan-fried Caribbean-style empanadas (turnovers), ripe plantains are roasted until soft, then puréed to make a unique, easy-to-work-with, and flavorful dough. While the original empanadas from Spain were made with a bread dough, these—made with plantain dough and a hearty vegetarian filling combining black beans, sharp cheese, and chiles— deliciously demonstrate the creativity of New World cooks in adapting old recipes to new ingredients.

YIELD: 8 EMPANADAS

4 plantains (about 2½ pounds), completely
  ripe and unpeeled
1 poblano pepper, substitute 1 jalapeño pepper
1 (15-ounce) can refried black or pinto beans
½ cup thinly sliced scallions
½ pound grated manchego cheese or
  crumbled feta cheese
¼ pound (1 cup grated) Mexican queso añejo or
  Italian romano cheese, grated
2 tablespoons chopped cilantro, optional
1 teaspoon fine sea salt
3 cups canola oil, for frying
1 cup Mexican crema, crème fraîche,
  or sour cream, for serving

Preheat the oven to 350°F.

Cut a lengthwise slit in each plantain and set it on a

baking sheet covered with parchment paper or a silicone baking mat (for easy cleaning). Bake until the flesh is thoroughly soft, about 45 minutes. Remove from the oven and cool to room temperature.

Meanwhile, prepare the stuffing: Blacken the skin of the poblano, either over an open flame or over an electric grill. Remove from the heat, cool, peel, and seed. Finely dice the poblano and mix with the beans, scallions, both cheeses, and the cilantro. (The stuffing can be made up to a day in advance and reserved in the refrigerator.)

Make the dough: Peel the plantains and trim off the tough ends. Combine the plantains and salt in the bowl of a food processor and pulse until a smooth purée is obtained. (Be careful not to overwork the dough, or it will become pasty.) Divide the dough into 8 portions of about 3 tablespoons each. Roll each portion into a ball. Line the bottom of a tortilla press with a small plastic bag and place the ball of dough in the center. Place another plastic bag over the dough and press to form a 3- to 4-inch circle. (If you do not have a tortilla press, place the dough on a sheet of plastic wrap on the counter. Cover with another piece of plastic wrap and flatten into a circle with a rolling pin.)

Place about 2 tablespoons of stuffing on the dough circles and fold over to enclose, pressing the edges to seal and making sure there are no holes. (Patch any holes with a bit of dough wetted with water.) Arrange the empanadas on a wax paper–lined tray and chill for 30 minutes in the refrigerator. (The stuffed empanadas can also be frozen.)

In a wok, a large heavy-duty frying pan, preferably cast-iron, or an electric deep-fryer, heat the oil to 365°F,

or until shimmering hot, and the air above the pot feels hot when you hold your hand about 3 inches above the oil. Gently lay the empanadas into the hot oil and fry until golden, turning so they brown evenly, about 6 minutes. With a slotted spoon, remove from the oil and drain on a wire rack.

Serve hot accompanied by Mexican crema (thickened cream), crème fraîche, or sour cream for dipping.

EMPANADAS

Empanadas, which get their name from the Spanish verb *empanar*, meaning to wrap in bread, are found in innumerable versions in Spain, Portugal, the Caribbean, Latin America, Mexico, and the Philippines. They are thought to have originated with the Moors, who occupied Spain for 800 years, bringing with them stuffed dough dishes similar to Iraq's sambusak. Empanadas often filled with salt cod or chicken made a convenient, portable, and hearty meal for working people in Galicia, Spain. A great number of immigrants to Latin America came from this region of Spain, bringing their taste for empanadas along. The 'mpanatigghi Siciliano (page 331) are a type of empanada from Sicily, filled with chocolate and, surprisingly, ground veal, for moisture. The savory Chicken-Cheese Empanadas with corn (page 264) come from Mexico; the Guava and Cheese Empanadas (page 271) are a sweet-savory treat from South America.

Baby Banana Cream Pie in Coconut–Cashew Crust

Los Angeles is the capital of banana cream pie, where it is ubiquitous on the menus of upscale eateries, diners, and home-style bakeries alike. It seems that the tropical banana and the Southern and Midwestern cream pie came together in the city of angels. The pie may feature a graham cracker crumb crust, a pastry crust, or something more imaginative, like this crunchy tropical coconut-cashew crumb crust. I use the firm, mild-tasting baby or ninōs bananas that are starting to show up more regularly in supermarkets for this pie, although common yellow bananas may be substituted. The adorable "hands" generally have about eighteen bananas in two neat overlapping rows. It takes about three-quarters of a hand to make this pie. The bananas should be barely ripe, completely yellow in color, but without the black specks of a fully-ripened banana, which would darken too easily in the pie.

YIELD: ONE 9-INCH PIE, SERVES 8

Coconut–Cashew Crust

1/4 pound (1 cup) shredded unsweetened dried coconut

6 ounces (1 3/4 cups) cashews

1/2 cup panko breadcrumbs, substitute plain
   dry breadcrumbs

1/4 cup sugar

3 ounces (3/4 stick) unsalted butter, melted and cooled

Filling

4 large egg yolks

1 cup sugar

3 ounces (3/4 cup minus 2 teaspoons) unbleached
   all-purpose flour

1 cup milk

2 ounces (1/2 stick) unsalted butter, cut up

1 teaspoon ground cinnamon

2 teaspoons vanilla extract

2 tablespoons dark rum

14 firm but ripe baby bananas

Juice of 1 lime (2 tablespoons)

1 teaspoon grated lime zest

2 tablespoons confectioners' sugar

1 cup heavy cream, chilled

Make the crust: Combine the coconut, cashews, breadcrumbs, and sugar in the bowl of a food processor, then process until medium-fine. Add the butter and process briefly to combine. Press into a 9-inch-diameter pie pan, preferably metal, and chill for 30 minutes in the freezer or 1 hour in the refrigerator.

Preheat the oven to 350°F. Bake the crust for 35 minutes or until it is dry and lightly but evenly browned. Remove from the oven and, if the crust has puffed up, use the back of a spoon to press the crust firmly into the pan before it cools.

Make the filling: Scald 3/4 cup of the milk. In a medium bowl, beat the egg yolks and sugar briefly together until combined. Beat in the flour and 1/4 cup of cold milk and then slowly add the scalded milk, whisking to combine into a smooth mixture. Transfer the mixture to a medium, heavy-bottomed nonreactive pot and bring to a boil over low to moderate heat, whisking often, especially in the edges where lumps tend to form. As soon as the mixture boils, remove it from the heat, beat in the butter, cinnamon, vanilla, and rum, and transfer to a metal bowl. Chill the mixture, stirring occasionally to prevent the formation of a skin, in the bowl, which has been placed over a second bowl filled with ice and water.

Slice 8 of the bananas and combine with half the lime juice and zest, and the confectioners' sugar. In the bowl of a standing electric mixer and using the whisk, beat the cream until firm but not stiff. (Note: on a hot day, super-chill the bowl, the beater, and the cream in the freezer for 15 minutes before beating.)

Mix about $1/2$ cup of the whipped cream into the custard mixture to lighten it. Fold in the remaining whipped cream, then fold in the sliced bananas. Spread the cream filling evenly into the baked pie crust. Refrigerate the pie for at least 1 hour or up to 24 hours before serving.

Just before serving, slice the remaining bananas lengthwise and combine with the remaining lime juice and zest, and confectioners' sugar. Arrange the banana halves cut side up in an attractive pattern over top. The pie is best eaten the same day it is made. Cover and store 1 day in the refrigerator.

Banana–Pecan Roulade

A roulade is a jelly roll with a French name, filled this time not with jelly, but with cinnamon and allspice–scented cream cheese. The cake batter itself contains lots of mashed bananas: a great way to use up any overripe bananas (if you don't have time now, simply freeze the bananas whole and in their skins to use later), along with the nutty crunch of chopped pecans. Unlike most roulades, the filling and cake batter bake at the same time with the filling spread on the bottom and the batter on top, so it's quite easy to make. I use mild-tasting white whole wheat flour here for an earthier flavor, but all-purpose flour may be substituted. Regular dark whole wheat flour will be too strong here, but may be mixed half and half with all-purpose flour.

YIELD: 10 TO 12 SERVINGS

Filling

$3/4$ pound cream cheese, softened

$3/4$ cup sugar

1 teaspoon ground cinnamon

$1/2$ teaspoon ground allspice

6 large eggs

Cake

6 ounces ($1 1/2$ cups) white whole wheat flour

$1 1/2$ teaspoons baking powder

$1/2$ teaspoon baking soda

$1/2$ teaspoon fine sea salt

6 large eggs, separated

$1 1/2$ cups sugar

1 1/2 cups (3 to 4) mashed ripe bananas

6 ounces (1 3/4 cups) finely chopped pecans

2 teaspoons vanilla extract

Confectioners' sugar, for dusting

Line an 18 x 13-inch half sheet pan (or other large baking pan) with parchment paper, wax paper, or a silicone mat.

Make the filling: In the bowl of a standing electric mixer and using the paddle attachment, beat the cream cheese, sugar, cinnamon, and allspice, scraping down the sides of the bowl once or twice to ensure that the filling is smooth. Beat in the eggs one at a time, beating well between each addition and scraping down the sides of the bowl once or twice. Scrape the sides of the bowl again and whisk the contents of the bowl by hand briefly until completely smooth. Spread the mixture evenly into the bottom of the pan.

Make the cake batter: Preheat the oven to 375°F.

Whisk together the dry ingredients: flour, baking powder, baking soda, and salt.

In the bowl of a standing electric mixer and using the paddle attachment, beat the egg yolks and 3/4 cup of sugar until the mixture is light and fluffy, 5 to 6 minutes. Spoon in the flour mixture, beating until just combined, then stir in the bananas, pecans, and vanilla.

In the clean and greaseless bowl of a standing electric mixer and using the whisk, beat the egg whites until fluffy, then add the remaining 3/4 cup sugar and continue beating until the whites are firm and glossy, 4 to 5 minutes. Fold the meringue into the batter in thirds so as not to deflate the batter. Carefully spoon the batter in small dollops onto the filling and spread out evenly with a silicone spatula.

Bake for 30 minutes or until the cake springs back when lightly touched and starts to come away from the sides of the pan. Immediately loosen the cake from sides of pan and turn out onto a clean kitchen towel sprinkled generously with confectioners' sugar. Peel off the paper or remove the silicone mat.

Starting with the narrow end, roll up the cake using the towel to help roll. (Do not roll the towel into the cake.) Cool the cake completely on a wire rack, sprinkle with confectioners' sugar, then cut on the diagonal into serving portions. Store, covered with plastic wrap or wax paper, for 2 to 3 days in the refrigerator.

Red Banana–Brown Butter Bars

Firm, honey-sweet red bananas top this bar cookie, which is ideal to make for large groups of grown-ups and kids. The base of the bar is made with mild, light-colored white whole wheat flour mixed with mashed ripe red bananas and covered with a layer of sliced red bananas. The cream cheese icing gets its intriguing underlying nuttiness from the brown butter while lime juice and zest make it lively. Try this one for your next bake sale or neighborhood potluck.

YIELD: 32 BARS

Bars

1/2 pound (2 1/4 cups) white whole wheat flour

1 teaspoon baking powder

½ teaspoon baking soda

1 teaspoon ground cinnamon

½ teaspoon fine sea salt

6 ounces (1½ sticks) unsalted butter, softened

7 ounces (1 cup) packed dark brown sugar

4 large eggs

½ cup sour cream

1 pound (2 to 3) ripe red bananas, mashed

1 teaspoon vanilla extract

3 pounds (6 to 8) red bananas, sliced

2 tablespoons sugar

Juice of 1 lime

Icing

½ cup Brown Butter (page 202), melted and cooled

¾ pound (2 cups plus 1 tablespoon)
   confectioners' sugar

½ pound cream cheese, softened

Juice and grated zest of 1 lime (2 tablespoons juice,
   2 teaspoons zest)

32 pecan halves, lightly toasted

Make the bars: Preheat the oven to 375°F. Line a 15 x 10-inch jelly roll pan with parchment-paper or wax paper.

In a medium bowl, whisk together the dry ingredients: the flour, baking powder, baking soda, cinnamon, and salt.

In the bowl of an electric mixer fitted with the paddle attachment, beat the butter and brown sugar until light and fluffy, 5 to 6 minutes. Beat in the eggs, one at a time, then beat in the sour cream, mashed bananas, and vanilla. Fold in the dry ingredients, then spread the batter evenly into the pan.

Combine the sliced bananas with the sugar and lime juice and layer over top of the batter. Bake for 30 minutes or until lightly browned and the cake has begun to come away from the sides of the pan. Cool to room temperature on a wire rack.

Meanwhile, prepare the icing: Combine the brown butter, confectioners' sugar, and cream cheese in the bowl of a food processor and beat until smooth, scraping down the sides once to avoid any lumps. Add the lime juice and zest and process briefly to combine to a smooth cream.

Transfer to a medium bowl and chill the icing for about 30 minutes in the refrigerator or until firm enough to hold its shape. Using an icing spatula, spread the icing evenly over the cake. Lightly score the bars into 32 portions and place a whole pecan in the center of each portion. Chill about 1 hour, or until firm, then cut into portions and serve. Store covered and refrigerated up to 3 days.

BARLEY & MALT

Storing Barley . . .138

Barley Flour in Baking . . .138

Old–Time Barley Sticks . . .138

About Barley Malt . . .139

Malted Milk . . .139

Buying Malted Milk Powder . . .140

GREEK BLACK BARLEY RINGS
(MAVROKOULOURIA) . . .140

Paximadi . . .141

GREEK COUNTRY BARLEY BREAD . . .142

About Mahlab . . .143

KEA STUFFED GRIDDLE BREAD . . .144

Ras el Hanout . . .146

Baharat . . .146

ALMOND AND MILK
CHOCOLATE MALT CAKE . . .146

BARLEY & MALT

Barley, *Hordeum vulgare*, is the oldest cultivated cereal in the Middle East and Europe and may predate the cultivation of rice, dating back as far as 8000 BCE. It is believed to have originated in western Asia or Ethiopia. Barley was, along with emmer wheat, a staple cereal of ancient Egypt, where it was used to make bread and beer. In the Bible, Israel is described as being, "a land of wheat and barley, and vines and fig-trees and pomegranates; a land of olive-trees and honey." In biblical times, barley was the poor-man's staple, eaten as porridge and barley cakes, and fed to cattle and other livestock. Even today, barley is still mostly thought of as a food of the poor.

Barley is a tough and adaptable cereal that thrives where other grains can't grow, surviving and even thriving in cold, dry climates at arctic latitudes and alpine altitudes, even in saline desert oases and tropical climates. Barley is the fourth most important cereal crop in the world after wheat, maize (corn), and rice. However, only about ten percent of barley is used as human food. One-third is used for brewing malt beverages (beer and whiskey) and the remaining majority goes to animal feed in wealthier countries. (With the rising price of barley and other grains, American farmers are having an increasingly difficult time feeding their poultry and livestock.)

For the table, barley is made into syrup, hulled and cooked whole, crushed into grits for porridge and soups, and ground into flour, often to be mixed with wheat flour for lightness. Barley is essential for malting (sprouting) to brew beer, a form of which is distilled into Scotland's renowned malt whisky.

Barley reached Spain about 4500 BCE, and from there spread north into France and Germany, reaching as far as Great Britain about 3000 BCE. Eastward, barley reached India about the same time, and China around 2000 BCE. Barley has been considered a high-energy food since the Roman times, when the gladiators were known as "hordeari" (from *Hordeum*) because they were fed a sprouted barley diet before competing to the death in the Circus. Similarly, in Ethiopia, barley was known as the "king of grains" and children were encouraged to eat lots of it to grow brave and courageous.

Roman soldiers, who readily quaffed barley beer, considered barley bread to be "punishment rations." In Greece, according to respected cookbook author and journalist, Aglaia Kremezi, barley was food for "sailors, travelers, and poor islanders." Barley breads and rusks have now started to gain some of the cachet of authentic, rustic, poor people's food. I couldn't get enough of the superb sunflower seed-coated barley bread sticks from Crete at the high-end seafood restaurant, Milos, in Athens, Greece. The Cretan barley rusks called *dakos* are a specialty of the island and are often crumbled into bread salad.

Across the world and high in the sky, barley has been for centuries a staple food in Tibet, along with yak butter tea. The barley is first parched (dried out using heat), then ground into fine flour called *tsampa*. It is then formed into flat cakes that keep well and are easy to transport. Barley has been grown in the cold climate of Korea for three thousand years. *Mugicha*, an infusion of roasted barley, is enjoyed in Japan; similarly, in Korea, roasted barley kernels are used to make barley tea, served hot or cold. My local Korean market has bags and bags of roasted barley kernels meant for tea and it is also sold premade in clear plastic containers as iced tea for the summer months.

In the Orkney and Shetland Islands, north of Scotland in the North Sea, barley has been milled into flour ever since invading Norse or Danes brought it with them in the eighth century. In Scandinavia, where older types of wheat didn't grow in its cold climate, barley has been grown for food since about 2000 BCE. There it was made into flatbread in Sweden and eaten as porridge and grits elsewhere.

While Columbus brought barley with him to the New World on his second journey in 1494, barley cultivation began with English colonists, who brought it with them on their voyages. Spanish missionaries did the same in the South and Western parts of the country.

In America today, we especially enjoy barley in malted milk and "malt shoppe" shakes, and those malted milk ball candies that come in giant boxes at the movies. Malt powder flavors malted waffles and pancake batters; an ice cream sundae generously dusted with malt powder is known as a Dusty Road Sundae. Try the Almond Milk and Chocolate Malt Cake (page 146) in this chapter—my super-critical kids loved it. ("Mom, when are you going to make something normal?") The delicately chewy Iced Malted Milk Cookies (page 285) also recall those favorite flavors.

It took a week-long cooking course in Greece for me to learn how delicious barley could be in breads. For another side of malt, try the Greek Country Barley Bread (page 142), a recipe I learned from Aglaia Kremezi in her cooking school home on the island of Kea, and the killer Stuffed Griddle Breads made from the same dough (page 144). The traditional hard, almost brittle Greek Black Barley Rings (page 140) are unexpectedly delicious, though made without the addition of any wheat flour, especially when served with soup or salad for dunking.

Barley can be divided by the number of kernel rows in the head: two row and six row. Two-row barley is the oldest form and most like wild barley. It has a lower protein content than six-row barley and thus a lower enzyme content. Two-row barley is traditionally used in brewing English ale style beers; two-row malted summer barley is traditional used for brewing German beers. Six-row barley is common in some American lager style beers.

Covered barley has its hulls still attached and is inedible in this form. When the fibrous outer hull is removed, the product is called hulled barley. At this stage, the grain still maintains its nutritious bran and germ and is still considered a whole grain. In a process called "pearling" the barley is polished to remove the tough inedible outer hull, producing pearl barley, which is less chewy but also less nutritious, though much more easily digestible. Both hulled and pearl barley are processed into barley flour, or into oatmeal-like flakes, which may then be malted (sprouted) and used in the production of alcoholic beverages or used in baking. Pearl barley makes a good substitute for wheat berries.

STORING BARLEY

Store uncooked barley products (pearl barley, hulled barley, barley flour, barley flakes, barley grits) in an airtight container in a cool place, preferably in the refrigerator or freezer up to 6 months.

BARLEY FLOUR IN BAKING

In baking, barley is often mixed with wheat flour to provide lightness. Barley flour adds a subtle nutty flavor and plenty of fiber to baked goods. While barley flour does contain gluten, the protein that makes baked goods rise, it is not in adequate enough quantities to rise on its own, so barley flour is best combined with higher gluten bread flour or all-purpose flour. As a rule of thumb, substitute barley flour for about one-quarter of the total flour in yeast breads and up to half the total amount for quick breads, muffins, and cookies, although these will be on the heavy side if the maximum amount is used.

OLD-TIME BARLEY STICKS

Colorful twisted sticks of barley sugar candy sticks were originally made in the seventeenth century by boiling down expensive and rare cane sugar with barley water (water in which pearl barley had been cooked), cream of tartar, and water, and were said to soothe a sore throat, or at least distract a miserable child with a sweet treat. By the eighteenth century, an artisanal candy tradition developed using imaginatively shaped metal molds to make barley sugar clear toys. These hard candy toys and pops became a popular Victorian Christmas treat, especially in Great Britain and the American Northeast. Today, the so-called barley candy found in "country stores" is often made without the essential ingredient: barley water. For the real thing, go to www.timberlakecandies.com, which will have the biggest selection in the winter holiday season.

ABOUT BARLEY MALT

Malting is a process applied to cereal grains, in which the grains are sprouted then quickly dried. Malting was traditionally done in a specially built malthouse, typically a long, single-story building with a floor that slopes slightly from one end of the building to the other. Malting grains develops the enzymes that are required to modify the grain's starches into sugars, principally maltose. Barley is the most common grain used for malting, because of its high diastatic power, or enzyme content.

Malt can be diastatic or non-diastatic. Non-diastatic malt is simply used as a sweetener and is available in Asian, particularly Korean, markets. Diastatic malt is high in enzymes and helps break down the starch in dough to yield sugars on which the yeast can feed. It has long been a secret ingredient of professional bread makers in Europe, particularly for long rising sourdough and levain breads. It replaces the sugar or honey needed to feed the yeast and brown the crust.

Because diastatic malt is full of enzymes and vitamins, it also increases the nutritional value of the bread. The action of the enzymes on the yeast and flour improves the flavor and appearance of the bread, creating a finer texture, and helps the bread stay fresh. Typically, flour mills add about one-tenth of a percent of malted barley flour; more than this can result in slack, sticky dough, and will not improve the bread.

The sugar derived from the malted barley, which is heavy in maltose (or malt sugar) is called baker's malt or malt syrup. Malt syrup is dark brown, thick, and sticky, with a strong flavor comparable to molasses and is about half as sweet as white sugar. Whiskey or beer can also be called malt as in single-malt Scotch or malt liquor. Strong malt vinegar is also produced, which accompanies fish and chips in Great Britain and in Canada.

Malted Milk

Malted milk was first marketed by the Horlick brothers, who founded the Horlick's in Chicago in 1873. Today, Horlick's manufactures malted milk powder used in a hot milk drink said to promote sleep when drunk at bedtime in the United Kingdom, India, and Jamaica, with India by far the biggest market. Originally manufactured as an infant food, malted milk became better known in the United States in malted milkshakes or "malts" and is basically unknown here as a hot drink.

In 1922, Ivar "Pop" Coulson invented the malted milkshake at Walgreen's Drugstore in Chicago. Until then, the drink was made with milk, malt powder, and chocolate syrup. One day, Pop decided to mix in some ice cream and soon customers were standing three and four deep around the soda fountain to buy the "double–rich chocolate malted milk." Priced at twenty cents, the chocolate malted came with a glassine bag containing two complimentary vanilla cookies.

BUYING MALTED MILK POWDER

It seems that malted milk powder has gone out of fashion in America. When I tried to buy it at my local fully-stocked supermarket, I was told that they no longer carry it. Perhaps this isn't true in other parts of the country. Carnation does manu-facture malted milk powder, but I ended up ordering the powder from an online importer of English products: www.EnglishTeaStore.com. It seems a bit crazy that this product, which was invented in the United States more than 100 years ago, has to be shipped to me in America from England!

Greek Black Barley Rings (Mavrokoulouria)

These ultra-crunchy barley rings, though not as hard as some, are a version of the paximadi, *one of Greece's renowned breads that dates back to antiquity. Traditional in Crete and the Southern Cyclades, the rings are the epitome of rural breads, nourishing and lasting through the winter months. Nutty in flavor, they stay crunchy even when soaked in liquid and are well-suited to use for Greek-style bread salad. They are marvelous crumbled in soup and used for dunking in hot coffee or tea. This recipe is dairy-free.*

YIELD: 12 RINGS

2 ($1/4$-ounce) packages (4 $1/2$ teaspoons) active dry yeast
1 tablespoon honey
1 pound (3 $1/2$ cups) stone-ground barley flour,
   plus more for the work surface
1 $1/2$ cups lukewarm water
$1/4$ cup extra-virgin olive oil,
     plus extra for coating the dough
1 teaspoon fine sea salt

Line two 18 x 13-inch half sheet pans (or other large bak-ing pans) with parchment paper or silicone baking mats.

Mix together the yeast, honey, $1/2$ cup of the barley flour, and $1/2$ cup of the water in the bowl of a standing electric mixer. Cover with a cloth and set aside at warm room temperature until puffy and bubbly, about 30 minutes.

Using the paddle attachment, beat in the remaining water, the oil, salt, and remaining barley flour. Switch to the dough hook and continue beating until the mixture forms a sticky but elastic ball. Transfer the dough to a floured work surface and knead by hand until smooth and elastic, about 5 minutes.

Coat the dough with oil, transfer to a bowl, cover with a cloth, and set it aside to rise at warm room temperature until light and a bit spongy, but not yet doubled in bulk, about 2 hours.

Divide the dough into 12 pieces. With your hands, press each piece out to form a flat oval about 12 inches long, 6 inches wide, and $1/4$-inch thick. Fold in the long sides of each oval so they overlap, forming a thick roll. Then pull the roll around, with the side seam on the inside, to form a ring. Squeeze the ends together and press any cracks closed, moistening the dough first with a little water. Transfer the rings to the baking pans. Cover lightly with a damp cloth and let them rest at warm room temperature until they get a little spongy again, about 30 minutes.

Preheat the oven to 400°F.

Brush the rings with water and bake for 30 minutes, or until they just start to brown. Remove from the oven and allow the rings to cool completely on the baking sheet.

When the rings have cooled completely, reduce the oven temperature to 200°F. Bake the rings until dry all the way through, about 7 hours or overnight. Store in an airtight container for up to 3 months.

PAXIMADI

Paximadi dates from the Byzantine Empire, which formed a bridge between the foods of the ancient world and those of modern Greece and Turkey. In 470 CE, when the future emperor Justin II was a penniless young man, he walked from his home in Dalmatia to the capital of Byzantium, Constantinople, with nothing but the army-issued barley biscuits called *paximadion* to keep him alive. An ancient Greek and Roman food, the hard, toothbreakingly crunchy biscuits have many modern descendants including Arabic bashmat, Turkish beksemad, Serbo-Croat peksimet, Romanian pesmet, and modern Greek paximadi. In modern times, the barley flour is often mixed with wheat for lightness. The hard barley rusks accompany handmade Greek yogurt, so rich that the top layer separates into thick yellow cream, drizzled with thyme-blossom honey in a traditional Greek breakfast I enjoyed every morning while traveling in Greece.

Greek Country Barley Bread

This dense and pleasingly nutty barley, semolina, and wheat bread is still baked in the outdoor wood-burning ovens that are so common in the countryside villages around Greece. It is seasoned with a special combination of Greek bread spices, which includes ground coriander seed, mahlab seed (see opposite page), and the pine-like, slightly bitter, and resinous crushed mastic "tears" (see page 519, About Mastic). Of course, other spices can be substituted, but these particular flavors give the bread an authentic Greek country character. I learned to make this bread from Greek journalist and cookbook author, Aglaia Kremezi (page 17). Always looking for creative ways to bake and cook, Aglaia shapes and rises this bread on a sheet of parchment paper, which she then transfers (still on the paper) into a pre-heated oven-proof casserole, thereby recreating a hearth oven and resulting in a well-browned bread with a hard, crunchy crust. She uses thin rounds of the same dough to make the Kea Stuffed Griddle Breads (page 144). You may use the entire batch of dough to make one large loaf, baking it about 10 minutes longer, or you can make a smaller loaf and use the leftover dough to make the stuffed breads, as directed below.

YIELD: 1 (2-POUND) ROUND LOAF, PLUS 6 (3-OUNCE) ROUNDS FOR STUFFED GRIDDLE BREADS

$3/4$ pound (3 cups) unbleached bread flour

$1/2$ pound ($1^1/4$ cups plus 1 tablespoon) fine semolina

6 ounces ($1^1/2$ cups) white whole wheat flour

6 ounces ($1^1/2$ cups) barley flour

2 teaspoons ground coriander seed

1 teaspoon ground mahlab seed, or more coriander seed

1 teaspoon crushed mastic, optional

1 tablespoon fine sea salt

$1/2$ teaspoon ground white pepper

1 ($1/4$-ounce) package ($2^1/4$ teaspoon) active dry yeast

$2^1/2$ cups lukewarm water, preferably spring water

1 tablespoon honey

Line an 18 x 13-inch half sheet pan (or other large baking pan) with parchment paper. In a medium bowl, whisk together the dry ingredients: bread flour, semolina, whole wheat flour, barley flour, coriander seed, mahlab, mastic, salt, and pepper.

Combine the yeast, 1 cup of the lukewarm water, and the honey in the bowl of a standing electric mixer, and allow the yeast to dissolve. Stir in about 1 cup of the flour mixture and allow the mixture to proof at warm room temperature for about 30 minutes, or until bubbling and puffy.

Using the paddle attachment, beat in the remaining $1^1/2$ cups water and the remaining flour mixture, and continue beating for 2 to 3 minutes to combine well. Turn off the mixer and allow the dough to rest for 15 minutes to relax the gluten and develop the flavor. Switch to the dough hook and beat for 5 minutes longer, turning the dough over once or twice with a spatula. It should be relatively smooth and elastic, though rather soft and sticky, and should start to come away from the sides of the bowl. Transfer the dough to a large oiled bowl and turn the dough so it is oiled all over. Cover with oiled plastic wrap and allow the dough to rise at warm room temperature until it doubles in size, about 4 hours. Note that when the dough has risen to about 1 1/2 times its original size, you may refrigerate it in the bowl and leave it overnight or up to 24 hours. The dough will continue to rise slowly. Bring to room temperature the next day, letting it stand 2 to 3 hours before continuing with the recipe.

Turn the dough out onto a lightly floured work surface and divide into 2 sections, one weighing about 2 pounds and the remainder about 18 ounces. You will be reserving the remainder for later use with the Kea Stuffed Griddle Breads. Divide the 18 ounces of dough into small portions (about 3 ounces each) and roll out on a floured work surface to rounds (6 to 8 inches in diameter). Sprinkle each round with flour, separate with parchment paper, place in a plastic zipper lock bag, and store refrigerated up to 2 days or freeze up to 3 months. Defrost and bring to room temperature before using for the Kea Stuffed Griddle Breads (page 144). Alternatively make 2 smaller breads, each about 1 1/2 pounds.

Form the 2 pounds of dough into a round, then place it with the smooth side up onto a sheet of parchment paper. Using a French baker's lame, a single-edged razor, or a box cutter, lightly score the top criss-cross or in diamond shapes. Sprinkle the dough with water from a plant mister, cover with oiled plastic wrap, and allow to rise another hour at warm room temperature.

Preheat the oven to 450°F. Place a heavy ovenproof (about 4-quart) casserole with a lid, such as a Dutch oven or a Le Creuset or other enameled cast-iron casserole in the oven to preheat for about 15 minutes.

When the dough has almost doubled in bulk, place it—paper and all—into the casserole. Spray the dough

again with water, cover, and bake for 15 minutes; spray again and continue baking, spraying with water every 15 minutes, for a total baking time of 45 minutes, or until the bread is nicely browned and a thermometer inserted in the center reads 190° to 205°F.

Remove the bread from the casserole and cool completely on a wire rack before serving. Store in an opened plastic bag at room temperature for up to 2 days, or freeze up to 3 months.

ABOUT MAHLAB

Inside St. Lucy's cherries, *Prunus mahaleb*, are the small oval-shaped beige kernels called mahlab, which are about the size of a large peppercorn but elliptical in shape. Mahlab has an aroma reminiscent of cherry, almond, flowers, and rosewater, with a nutty yet surprisingly bitter aftertaste. Native to southern Europe, the small tree grows wild in the Mediterranean region across to Turkey. Mahlab was first used for perfumes and medicine, and it later became a popular culinary spice, especially for flavoring breads.

Mahlab is used in Middle Eastern and Eastern Mediterranean cooking to give an intriguing bitter cherry flavor to sweet pastries, cookies, confectionery, and nabulsi cheese (a white brined cheese from Jordan). In Greece, the kernels go into tsoureki, a brioche-like braided sweet bread that is eaten only at Easter time, and into the Crusty Barley Bread above. Iran is the most important grower of mahlab, followed by Turkey and Syria.

Kea Stuffed Griddle Bread

On a day that reached over well over 100°F in summer, I watched while the more intrepid (or at least younger and less sweaty) students at Aglaia Kremezi's Kea Artisanale cooking school, on the Greek Cycladic island of the same name, grilled and filled these delicious hot griddle breads in a matter of minutes. While I'm not lucky enough to have a built-in outdoor charcoal grill and wood-burning oven in my house as does Aglaia, I have had great success making these on an electric grill and on a portable kettle grill. Using natural charcoal does give the breads an extra dimension of flavor. If your friends enjoy cooking, light up the grill and allow them to grill and fill their own bread turnovers, hopefully on a day with a bit of a breeze. Notice the quick and easy way of grating fresh tomatoes on a box grater. When I cooked in Turkey, the women used the exact same method. Try either (or both) of the stuffings for the griddle breads.

YIELD: 8 TO 10 INDIVIDUAL GRIDDLE BREADS

Tomato and Feta Topping

2 pounds ripe beefsteak tomatoes, cut in half
 "through the equator"
$1/2$ cup extra-virgin olive oil
1 medium red onion, finely diced (about 1 cup)
1 tablespoon tomato paste, preferably Greek or Italian
1 cup sweet white wine such as Mavrodaphne from
 Greece, substitute sweet Marsala from Sicily or sweet
 sherry from Spain
1 teaspoon Turkish Maras pepper, Aleppo pepper,
 or $1/4$ teaspoon crushed red pepper flakes

1 stick cinnamon
2 bay leaves
1 sprig rosemary
Salt to taste
$1/4$ pound feta cheese, crumbled (about 1 cup)

Using the large-holed side of a box grater, grate the tomato halves with the flesh side toward the grater until only the skins are left. Discard the skins or bag and freeze them for later, to add to soup stock.

In a medium heavy-bottomed pot, heat the oil, add the onions, and cook until softened but not browned. Stir in the tomato paste and cook, stirring to combine, until the mixture is glossy, about 3 minutes. Add the wine and cook for 2 minutes more to combine the flavors. Add the grated tomatoes, Maras pepper, cinnamon stick, bay leaves, rosemary, and salt, and bring to a boil.

Reduce the heat and simmer for 20 minutes or until the sauce thickens enough for the oil to separate out on the surface. Remove from the heat and discard the cinnamon stick, bay leaves, and rosemary sprig. (Any extra sauce can be cooled and kept refrigerated for up to 5 days or frozen up to 3 months.)

Eggplant and Beef Topping

1 medium eggplant (about 1 pound)
$11/2$ teaspoons fine sea salt, plus more to taste
$1/2$ cup extra-virgin olive oil
1 pound ripe beefsteak tomatoes, cut in half
 "through the equator"
2 medium red onions, finely diced (about 2 cups)
1 green bell pepper, finely diced

1 red bell pepper, finely diced

1 tablespoon tomato paste, preferably Greek or Italian

Freshly ground black pepper, to taste

2 teaspoons Turkish Maras pepper or Aleppo pepper,
  or $\frac{1}{2}$ teaspoon red pepper flakes

1 pound ground lean beef

1 teaspoon ras el hanout or baharat (see page 146), or
  $\frac{1}{2}$ teaspoon ground allspice

$\frac{1}{2}$ cup chopped flat parsley

$\frac{1}{2}$ cup pine nuts, lightly toasted

Half-peel the eggplant in strips, leaving alternating strips of skin and skinless eggplant, then cut into small cubes. Toss the eggplant with the salt and leave to drain for 1 hour in a colander. Rinse the eggplant under cold water to remove the salt and pat dry with paper towels. Heat $\frac{1}{4}$ cup of the oil in a large heavy skillet and brown the eggplant over moderate to high heat until soft. Drain in a colander to remove any excess oil.

Using the large-holed side of a box grater, grate the tomato halves with the flesh side toward the grater until only the skins are left. Discard the skins or bag and freeze them for later, to add to soup stock.

Heat the remaining $\frac{1}{4}$ cup olive oil in a large skillet, add the onions and bell peppers, and sauté, stirring often, until the vegetables are softened but not browned. Stir in the tomato paste and cook, stirring to combine until glossy, about 3 minutes. Add the black pepper, Maras pepper, and beef, and cook, stirring until the meat is no longer red. Add the tomatoes, eggplant, and ras el hanout, and stir to combine well.

Continue cooking, stirring often, until most of the juices have evaporated, 8 to 10 minutes. Remove from the heat and stir in the parsley and pine nuts. Season with salt as needed, noting that the filling should be well-seasoned.

Assembly

$\frac{1}{4}$ cup extra-virgin olive oil

2 teaspoons Turkish Maras pepper, Aleppo pepper
  flakes, or 1 teaspoon red pepper flakes

8 (3-ounce) rounds Greek Country Barley Bread dough
  (page 142)

Tomato and Feta Topping and/or Eggplant
  and Beef Topping

$\frac{1}{4}$ pound feta cheese, crumbled (about 1 cup)

2 teaspoons finely chopped rosemary and/or thyme

Semolina or cornmeal for sprinkling

Preheat a charcoal, electric, or gas grill. Whisk together the olive oil and the pepper flakes and reserve for brushing.

Arrange the bread rounds on a large wax paper–lined baking pan. Brush the surface of the rounds lightly with the olive oil mixture. Place on the grill one by one and grill for 2 to 3 minutes or until nicely browned. Turn over, brush again with olive oil, and grill for 1 to 2 minutes, just until the dough is cooked. Remove from the grill.

Spread about 3 tablespoons of the Tomato and Feta topping, about 2 tablespoons of the crumbled feta, and sprinkle with a pinch of chopped rosemary and/or spread about 3 tablespoons of the Eggplant and Beef Topping on one side of a griddle bread. Fold over to make a half moon shape and serve immediately, or keep warm while preparing the remaining griddle breads. Serve while still hot.

RAS EL HANOUT

Ras el hanout, which means "head of the market" in Arabic, is a complex mélange of as many as one hundred spices, and is basic to the cooking of the Maghreb (Morocco, Tunisia, Libya, and Algeria). Purchase ras el hanout from specialty spice purveyors; each variation will taste different, but will likely include some or all of the following: allspice berries, black peppercorns, mace blades, cardamom seeds, nutmeg, saffron threads, ginger root, cinnamon sticks, turmeric, ginger, and rose petals.

Some exotic ingredients such as chufa (a North African tuber also known as tiger nut), grains of paradise (a numbingly peppery spice related to cardamom), orris root (the powdered dried root of a type of iris), cubeb (a relation of black pepper), and belladonna (which is toxic in large quantities) may be added. Notoriously, at one time hashish and the insect known as Spanish fly (which causes dangerous but effective inflammation of the genitals) were also added.

BAHARAT

Baharat means "spices" in Arabic and derives from the Arabic word for black pepper, which the mixture always includes. While in the Grand Bazaar in Istanbul, I bought a decorative tin baharat holder attached to a chain and decorated with lacquer and semiprecious stones used by the nomads of

Turkmenistan to transport their particular baharat mix. Hot spices like Aleppo pepper from Syria and Maras pepper from Turkey; sweet aromatic spices like allspice, cloves, cinnamon, nutmeg, and cardamom; warm seed spices like cumin, fennel, and coriander; and fragrant herbs like savory and mint are carefully balanced to make this mellow spice mix. In North Africa, baharat may be as simple as a combination of equal amounts ground cinnamon, rose petals, and black pepper.

Almond Milk and Chocolate Malt Cake

The combination of almond flavoring, malted milk powder, and dark cocoa make a delectable layer cake, fit for a child's or grown-up's birthday. The almond milk now sold in many supermarkets and natural foods stores will be a wonderful addition to your repertoire of ingredients. With its creamy texture and mild, adaptable, slightly sweet almond flavor, the almond milk, reinforced by almond extract, lends its delicate flavor to the cake, though half-and-half may be substituted. Look for either the plain or unsweetened vanilla almond milk to use here. A finish of toasted, sliced almonds patted onto the sides adds a bit of crunch and visually emphasizes the almonds. The cake itself freezes very well. Defrost and then ice before serving.

YIELD: 12 TO 16 SERVINGS

Cake

$^1/_2$ pound (2 cups minus 2 tablespoons) unbleached
all-purpose flour

$^1/_4$ pound (1 cup) malted milk powder

2 ounces ($^1/_2$ cup minus 1 tablespoon)
Dutch-process cocoa

2 teaspoons baking powder

$^1/_2$ teaspoon fine sea salt

$^1/_4$ pound (1 stick) unsalted butter, softened

$1^1/_2$ cups light brown sugar, firmly packed

4 large eggs

$1^3/_4$ cups almond milk

1 teaspoon almond extract

Frosting

$^1/_4$ cup almond milk

3 ounces ($^3/_4$ cup) malted milk powder

$^1/_2$ pound (2 sticks) unsalted butter, softened

2 ounces ($^1/_4$ cup minus 1 tablespoon)
Dutch-process cocoa, sifted

2 large egg yolks

$^1/_2$ pound ($1^3/_4$ cups plus $^1/_2$ tablespoon)
confectioners' sugar

1 teaspoon almond extract

$^1/_2$ cup sliced almonds, skin-on,
lightly toasted, for garnish

Make the cake: Preheat the oven to 350°F. Prepare a 10-inch springform or removable bottom pan by spraying it with nonstick baker's coating or rubbing it with softened butter and dusting with flour, shaking off the excess.

Sift the dry ingredients: flour, malted milk powder, cocoa, baking powder, and salt into a bowl, or sift them through a fine wire sieve to break up any lumps.

In the bowl of an electric mixer fitted with the paddle attachment, cream the butter and sugar until light and fluffy, 5 to 6 minutes, scraping down the sides once or twice. Beat in the eggs one at a time, beating well after each addition.

Combine the almond milk and almond extract. Fold the flour mixture into the butter mixture alternating with the almond milk mixture and beginning and ending with the flour.

Pour the batter evenly into the pan, shaking it back and forth to even the top. Bake for 40 minutes, or until the cake starts to come away from the sides of the pan and a skewer stuck in the center comes out clean. Cool completely in pan on a wire rack before removing. Place the cake on a cardboard cake round or leave on the cake bottom for support. (The cake may be wrapped and frozen for up to 3 months at this point. Defrost before icing.)

Make the frosting and assemble the cake: In a medium bowl, whisk together the almond milk and malted milk powder. Allow the mixture to stand for 15 minutes to dissolve the powder.

In the bowl of a standing mixer and using the paddle attachment, beat together the butter and the cocoa until light and fluffy, about 5 minutes. Beat in the egg yolks, one at a time, beating until the mixture is smooth, about 2 minutes. Add the confectioners' sugar, the malted milk mixture, and the almond extract and beat on high speed until the icing is light and fluffy, 3 to 4 minutes.

To ice the cake, cut a very small notch, about $^1/_4$-inch deep, out of the side of the cake to use as a guide.

Using a long, serrated knife, cut the cake horizontally into two layers.

Using a thin icing spatula, spread about one-quarter of the frosting onto the cut side of one layer. Re-assemble the cake, using the cut wedge as a guide to line up the layers in their original position. Spread a thin layer of frosting over the top and sides of the cake to catch the crumbs. Chill the cake in the refrigerator for 30 minutes to set the icing.

Spread a second layer of icing smoothly over the cake. Holding the cake in one hand over a baking tray to catch any stray nuts, pat the almonds onto the sides of the cake using your other hand, picking up and patting on again any nuts that fall off. Chill the cake again for 30 minutes or until the frosting is set, then cut into serving portions, using a sharp knife dipped in hot water and wiped dry in between each cut.

Store the cake covered and refrigerated up to 5 days.

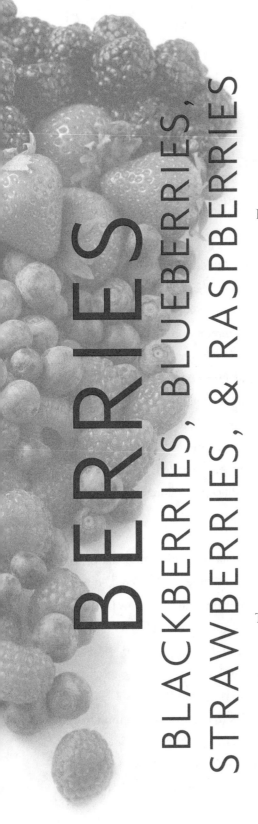

BERRIES

BLACKBERRIES, BLUEBERRIES, STRAWBERRIES, & RASPBERRIES

Blueberries, Wild Blueberries, and Huckleberries . . .151

Other Names for Low–Bush Blueberries . . .153

Bears Love Blueberries . . .153

Choosing and Storing Blueberries . . .153

Freezing Blueberries . . .154

Frozen Blueberries in Baking . . .154

Why Do Blueberries Make Batter Turn Green? . . .154

Blackberries . . .154

Choosing and Storing Blackberries . . .155

Blackberries and Their Hybrid Cousins . . .155

Strawberries . . .156

Choosing and Storing Strawberries . . .157

Washing and Trimming Strawberries . . .157

Raspberries . . .158

Choosing and Storing Raspberries . . .159

Raspberry Types . . .159

RASPBERRY SALZBURGER NOCKERLN . . .160

ROSE-SCENTED RASPBERRY SAUCE . . .161

ALMOND-CRUSTED BLACK-BERRY-TANGERINE PIE . . .161

About Tapioca Starch . . .162

APPLE-BLUEBERRY CRUMB PIE WITH CARDAMOM . . .163

BLUEBERRY-WALNUT STREUSEL MUFFINS . . .164

Lingonberries . . .165

GREEK BLUEBERRY-YOGURT TART WITH OUZO (MUSTIKKAPIIRAS) . . .165

Wyman's Wild Blueberries . . .166

STRAWBERRY DEVIL'S FOOD CAKE . . .168

FRESH STRAWBERRY COULIS . . .168

STRAWBERRY-RHUBARB TART WITH WALNUT SWEET PASTRY . . .169

Pie Plant (or Rhubarb) . . .170

BERRIES:
BLACKBERRIES, BLUEBERRIES, STRAWBERRIES, & RASPBERRIES

Soft, juicy, and lusciously tart–sweet, berries of all sorts are beloved wherever in the world they grow. Their bright color makes them stand out against a green background, making them highly visible and irresistible to the animals that eat them and help disperse their seeds. All American black bears have a sweet tooth, and blueberries, raspberries, and strawberries are among their favorite foods. The bears use their lips to pluck only the ripest and sweetest berries, returning a week or so later to check on their "crop." If only we could be as picky: in our race to get the first berries to market when they start coming into season, the berries we find in supermarkets are often less than ripe. Because berries don't ripen once picked, it's best to wait for their peak season to buy them, when the price will also come down.

Blackberries may be cooked in pies, biscuits, and muffins, or left raw in all their dark shapely beauty to top European–style tarts, American pies, and to fill shortbreads. I baked my first pie filled with blackberries, thereby launching a lifelong career as a culinarian, at age eleven during a summer spent in Seattle the year of the World's Fair

(1962). The brambly blackberries grow abundantly in backyard hedges there, as in much of the Pacific Northwest, favoring its mild climate and notoriously common rain. With a girlfriend, I picked buckets of blackberries from a huge and thorny patch that formed the back wall of her backyard, and proceeded to turn them into a bubbling, indigo–colored pie. (What's a little pain in search of great ingredients?) Although not as traditional as the pie I baked in Seattle, the Almond–Crusted Blackberry-Tangerine Pie (page 161) has a delicious crust made partly from almond butter.

Blueberries are delicious eaten out of hand, but when used in baking, they are best cooked first, so their dark juices burst the skins. Raw blueberries are a rather disappointing light green under their skins. Fresh or frozen blueberries can be added to muffins and other desserts straight from the freezer. Blueberry–Walnut Streusel Muffins (page 164) are quick to make and are bound to be equally quick to disappear from your kitchen, especially if made with small, tasty wild blueberries (page 152). You wouldn't necessarily think of combining blueberries, yogurt, and ouzo together, but after tasting the Greek Blueberry–Yogurt Tart with Ouzo (page 165), with its heady yogurt-custard filling, I think you'll agree that the trio harmonizes beautifully.

For better or worse, strawberries can be found every day of the year in the supermarket, although they are all too often disappointing. It seems to me that the bigger the strawberry, the less flavor it has. There are alternatives though: frozen strawberries are usually riper and sweeter, because the ripest berries don't travel well and end up being processed. The very best strawberries are the small, fragrant, juicy but fragile local berries found in season in June at local farmers' markets. Strawberries are best used uncooked to fill shortbreads, top cakes, or layered for an English Summer Fruit Pudding (page 415).

Strawberries cooked into jam make a wonderful filling for Italian baked fruit crostatas; mixed with rhubarb and used to fill a pie, they make the perfect early spring treat in the Strawberry-Rhubarb Tart (page 169). A layer of strawberry halves on top make the tart as eye-appealing as it is delicious. For the moist Strawberry Devil's Food Cake (page 166), a dark chocolate cake with a sophisticated edge of coffee bitterness contrasts well with a filling and under-glaze of sweet fresh strawberries mixed with strawberry preserves. Top it with a coffee-flavored ganache icing and you've got a winner. In season, serve the cake with crushed sweetened fresh strawberries on the side

Although raspberries are often available in the supermarket, it's only when they are big, plump, and brightly-colored with velvety-looking skin that they are worth their usually high price. For most uses in baking, as long as they are to be cooked or baked, frozen raspberries work very well, and are much less expensive that the all-too-perishable punnets of fresh berries. Once in a while, I spot a good value on American-grown raspberries and snap them up, especially when they're in season at the local farmers' market. In this chapter, fresh or frozen raspberries go into a heavenly light-as-a-cloud baked raspberry and meringue dessert from Austria called Raspberry Salzburger Nockerln (page 160). Both frozen or fresh raspberries work equally well in the Rose-Scented Raspberry Sauce (page 161) that's great to have on hand to dress up any dessert, especially one containing chocolate, vanilla custard or cream, or almonds.

BLUEBERRIES, WILD BLUEBERRIES, AND HUCKLEBERRIES

Blueberries are America's best known native fruit–two others are cranberries and Concord grapes. Blueberries are small, round, smooth-skinned berries dusted, in most varieties, with a powdery whitish "bloom" on their velvety deep-blue skins. Their sweet, appealing flavor is best when the berries are fully ripened. If overripe, their flavor will be overly sweet without the balancing edge of tartness and they can get mushy; if underripe, they will be green and sour.

Both blueberries and their wild cousins, huckleberries, are native to North America and have been used in the kitchen extensively since Colonial times. The shrub is of the genus *Vaccinium*, from the Latin *vacca* for cow, because cows love them, a fact first noted by Captain James Cook in the late 1700s. The blossom end of each berry, the calyx, is shaped like a perfect, small five-pointed star. Native American tribal elders would tell the tale of how the Great Spirit sent these "star berries" to relieve the children's hunger during a famine. Blueberries and other berries were mixed with dried buffalo meat and animal fat into pemmican—an early version of trail mix that was crucial for Indians who spent much of their lives on the move.

On their famed 1805 expedition, Lewis and Clark found that Indians smoked wild blueberries to preserve them for winter. Lewis used some flour and made a "kind of pudding with the berries" and wrote about it in his journal: "On this new fashioned pudding four of us breakfasted, giving a pretty good allowance also to the Chief who declared it the best thing he had taisted for a long time." The Hopi called blueberries *moqui*, meaning spirits of the ancestors. Blueberries became much more widely used after the Civil War when they were canned and sent to the Union soldiers as part of their rations. Blueberries were all picked by hand until the invention of the blueberry rake by Abijah Tabbutt of Maine in 1822.

North America is the world's leading blueberry producer, accounting for nearly ninety percent of world production. The harvest runs from mid-April through early October, with its peak in July, which is National Blueberry Month.

Low-bush blueberries, *Vaccinium angustifolium*, which grow only about one foot high, thrive in Eastern Canada and Maine. These small, intensely flavored blueberries are often marketed as wild blueberries or huckleberries. They are a favorite of those who like to pick their own berries, and ready for picking from mid-late August. Wild blueberries don't tend to explode during baking and hold their shape well.

The "high-bush" blueberry, *Vaccinium corymbosum*, grows as high as fifteen feet tall, with berries that are larger and more innocuous in flavor, with Bluecrop the most important cultivar. High-bush berries are the most common commercially cultivated variety, cultivated since the 1920s. New Jersey and Michigan are the country's leading producers.

Huckleberries, *Gaylussacia baccata*, the blueberry's smaller and more intensely flavored wild counterpart, are used in similar ways. The small wild blueberry was similar to the Scottish blaeberry, the English whortleberries, the Danish bilberry, the northern German bickberren, and the southern German blauberrn. These cousins of native North American blueberries grow in Asia, Europe, and South America, from the southern tropics far to the north.

To add confusion, in some parts of the United States, blueberries and true huckleberries go by the same name. Blueberries are blue and have lots of tiny, soft seeds; huckleberries are purplish-black with fewer, harder seeds. The tiny dark bluish-purple whortleberry, *Vaccinium myrtilus*, resembles a small blueberry and is known as the bilberry in Europe.

Most wild blueberries are harvested by hand, but mechanical harvesting is now being introduced in some of the more level fields. A hand rake looks like an oval bowl with metal prongs on one side, and a handle on the other. You only have to rake the bush with the prongs and the blueberries fall into the bowl. At this point, however, the berries have most likely been damaged slightly. This is why they are almost exclusively used for processing. Hand–picking wild blueberries can be done between July first and October thirtieth, yet mechanical picking can only be done when the crop is completely ripe. Otherwise, too many green berries are harvested.

OTHER NAMES FOR LOW-BUSH BLUEBERRIES

BILBERRY • COWBERRY • CROWBERRY

FARKLEBERRY • HURTLEBERRY

LINGONBERRY • PARTRIDGEBERRY

PARKLEBERRY • WHORTLEBERRY

BEARS LOVE BLUEBERRIES

Wild bears love wild blueberries so much, they will travel ten to fifteen miles a day on an empty stomach to find the small, succulent, juicy berries in season.

CHOOSING AND STORING BLUEBERRIES

Look for blueberries that are firm, large, dry, plump, round, and free of dents and bruises. Blueberries should be deep purplish-blue to blue-black in color with a minimum of tiny green stems, and have a soft hazy white coating, which is called "bloom." Bloom is a completely natural part of the berries' defense mechanism, protecting them from the harsh rays of the sun. Blueberries that are shriveled indicate moisture loss and lack of bloom could indicate over-handling. Red-tinged or green berries are unripe, but may be used in cooking mixed with ripe blueberries. Dead-ripe blueberries will tend to split and will stain the bottom of the container. Although full-flavored, they are also prone to molding and spoilage.

Blueberries may be found almost year-round because of imports, but home-grown American berries are in season from April to October, with Canadian berries in season a bit later, from July.

Like other berries, blueberries will not continue to ripen after picking, so use them as soon as possible, or freeze them. Store blueberries refrigerated, unwashed, in their container covered with clear plastic wrap. Blueberries picked at their peak can last up to two weeks. Wash just before using them, then place on paper towels to drain.

FREEZING BLUEBERRIES

Blueberries are an excellent candidate for freezing. After thawing, they are only slightly less bright and juicy as in their original harvest state. Do not wash them before freezing as the water will cause the skins to become tough. Rinse after thawing and before eating.

To freeze for future cooking, place the berries in a rigid covered container with one inch of space for expansion. If you plan on serving them in the future in their thawed, uncooked state, pack them in a syrup made of 4 cups water plus 3 cups sugar, seal and freeze. Although it is not necessary to freeze them in syrup, it will actually help preserve the blueberries because sugar is a preservative, and will help prevent the berries from freezer-burn. For crushed or puréed blueberries, add 1 to 1 1/2 cups sugar for each quart.

FROZEN BLUEBERRIES IN BAKING

When using frozen whole blueberries in baking, do not let them thaw before adding them to your recipe. This will preserve not only their texture, but will also keep them from splitting open and bleeding. Allow about 10 minutes extra baking time if using frozen berries

Why Do Blueberries Make Batter Turn Green?

Whenever you feel like improvising by adding blueberries to a recipe, keep in mind that recipes that include an alkaline, such as baking soda, may cause a chemical reaction, creating an ugly brownish-green tinge. Baking soda is usually included in recipes using an acidic ingredient, such as buttermilk or yogurt. Try substituting regular milk for buttermilk and baking powder for the baking soda to avoid discoloration.

To keep your muffin or cake mix from turning blue when adding blueberries, coat the fruits with flour or cornstarch before mixing them into your batter.

BLACKBERRIES

Wild blackberries, *Rubus fruticosus*, are members of the *Rosaceae* (or rose) family and the largest of the wild berries. Blue to purplish black in color with shiny skin and tart flavor, these smaller, rounded berries are also known as brambleberries because they grow on thorny bushes or brambles. Like raspberries and strawberries, each blackberry consists of clumps of fruits, each containing one prominent seed. For those who enjoy sweet-tart flavors, blackberries are delicious eaten out-of-hand, especially when fully ripe and tending toward red and purplish red. They are well-suited to baking when slightly underripe.

The longer naturalized American blackberry,

Rubus laciniatus, was gathered by Native Americans all over North America, and by the colonists as well. Blackberries can be up to one and a half-inches long and equally plump. They are now widely cultivated in the United States, with Oregon and Washington known for the high quality of their berries.

CHOOSING AND STORING BLACKBERRIES

Blackberries are in peak season from June through September, though because of imports from South America, Australia, and New Zealand, they are available occasionally and at high prices throughout the year. They are sporadically available in season on the East Coast but are more prevalent on the West Coast, especially in the Pacific Northwest, where most types are grown including the closely related Loganberry, Boysenberry, and Marionberry.

Choose blackberries that are plump with full, deep purplish-blue color, and a bright, clean, fresh appearance and firm yet giving texture, with hulls, if any, that pull away easily from the berry. Berries with hulls firmly attached are underripe and will be quite tart. Overripe berries will be reddish in color, soft, and mushy, and will quickly get moldy or spoil. The berries don't ripen after picking.

Blackberries are quite fragile, especially if fully ripened. Handle blackberries gently when rinsing. Avoid pale, dented, or bruised blackberries, or berries that have broken apart or crumbled. Check the bottom of the container. If it is stained red, the berries inside may be overripe and mushy, though a little bit of stain indicates soft, dead-ripe berries.

To store blackberries for more than a day or so, transfer them to a shallow pan or tray covered with paper towels and arrange them in a single layer. Lightly cover them with a damp paper towel and use within two or three days, washing just before use. Just before using, place the berries in a colander and rinse with a gentle stream of cool water and gently pat dry with paper towel.

BLACKBERRIES AND THEIR HYBRID COUSINS

BOYSENBERRY: The Boysenberry is a blackberry probably crossed with a loganberry or a red raspberry that was first found in the late 1920s growing on an abandoned farm owned by Rudolph Boysen. This very large, reddish-purple berry is quite tart and has prominent seeds.

EVERGREEN BLACKBERRY: The evergreen blackberry, native to England and known there as cut-leaf or parsley-leafed blackberry, was brought to Oregon around 1850 by English settlers. At the time, few growers were interested in blackberries because of their sharp thorns, but when the Thornless Evergreen (also known as Black Diamond) was found and propagated in the 1920s, they became much more desirable.

LOGANBERRY: Loganberries date from the 1880s, when James Harvey Logan of California inadvertently crossed two varieties of blackberries with an old variety of red raspberries. His happy accident became the loganberry, grown mainly for juice, pies, and wine, though they also make excellent jams and preserves. Juicy and sweetly tart, loganberries turn purplish-red when very ripe. Like other berries in this list, loganberries are rarely found outside of the Pacific Northwest.

MARIONBERRY: This thorny native Oregonian berry is a cross between a Chehalem blackberry and an Olallieberry, and is named after Marion County, Oregon, where it was first popularized. The dark red to black fruit is medium to large in size, rounded in shape, though somewhat longer than wide with medium seeds. Marionberries have excellent flavor, similar to that of wild blackberries.

OLALLIEBERRY: The rare and sought after Olallieberry is a cross between a youngberry (a sweet hybrid blackberry) and the loganberry, each of which is also a cross. The berry originated in 1949 in Oregon, but is grown mostly in California, especially on the coast, on about 100 acres of land. It resembles a large, elongated blackberry and has a distinctive, sweet flavor. *Olallie* means blackberry in the Pacific Northwest Chinook language. Olallieberry pies often sell out by word of mouth during their short season: the first two to three weeks of June.

STRAWBERRIES

What's so special about strawberries? Supermarket produce aisles are loaded 52 weeks a year with green plastic strawberry crates that are filled with berries bred for their large size, which ship and keep well. Produce managers find it much easier to sell these berries because the supply is reliable year-round and often sold in the wholesale market by contract. But those often overgrown, hollow-centered, spongy-textured berries are an imitation of the real thing. You owe it to yourself to seek out the red-ripe, juicy berries that are a magnificent gift of June in many regions across the country. One day in June my mother said to me, "When I eat strawberries, they don't taste at all like the ones I remember. What happened?" I handed her a basket of locally grown small, cone-shaped berries, ruby red, tinted with orange and still fragrant from the early summer heat. She tasted them and exclaimed, "Now these are strawberries!"

It's easy to recognize locally grown berries if you know the clues. Look first at color and size: These luscious strawberries are a deep, intense red from tip to stem. You'll never see the "white shoulders" that adorn long-distance berries. Though small, these petite beauties are solid-fleshed from skin to heart and jam-packed with sweet flavor. Since berry season is short and intense, these berries are often packed in large green cardboard quart-sized punnets. Because of their juicy contents, red streaks often stain the cardboard containers of these highly perishable berries.

Supermarket strawberries are picked green and

super-cooled to extract field heat, then packed in those green plastic punnets. Trucks from California, Mexico, and Florida carry these berries cross-country. In wintertime, they are air-freighted in from New Zealand and Chile, halfway around the world. Something irreplaceable is lost in this process.

My friends, who raise strawberries organically in Bucks County at Branch Creek Farm, explained to me why it's such a labor of love. Strawberries have only a three-week growing season; not much yield for so much work. In the first year, they must constantly baby the plants and keep them covered since they are so vulnerable to frost. Strawberries don't bear any fruit at all until their second year. By the third year, the plants are no longer very productive. To get a good crop, farmers have to plant strawberries each year. Harvesting strawberries is demanding and labor intensive. After picking one season's strawberry crop, one of their workers declared, "I'll never complain about the price of strawberries again." Luckily, there are a few perks to sweeten the work: picking berries warm and fragrant from the sun and overeating all the ones that aren't perfect.

Ask for locally grown berries at your produce market. Look for them at roadside farmers' market stands, or take the family for a pick-your-own outing in June. To savor fresh-picked strawberries at their best, don't chill them, and eat them right away. Field-grown, sun-ripened strawberries are a not-to-be-missed all-American delicacy.

CHOOSING AND STORING STRAWBERRIES

Look for relatively symmetrical berries that have an appealing sheen and bright, even color, especially at the "shoulders." The berries should be clean and dry with perky green caps. Smaller is usually better for flavor and the darkest color usually indicates the sweetest berry. Berries whose punnets are stained with red will be dead-ripe to overripe. They may be too soft for slicing or dicing, but perfect for purées.

For the best flavor, don't refrigerate locally-grown strawberries berries from the farmers' market. Just eat them the day you buy them. Otherwise, store strawberries one or two days in the refrigerator, loosely wrapped in plastic. Handle the tender berries gently.

WASHING AND TRIMMING STRAWBERRIES

To wash strawberries, fill a bowl with cold water and swish the whole berries around to encourage any sand to fall to the bottom. Lift the berries from the bowl and shake off the excess water. Lay them out on paper towels to dry. Eat the berries within a day or two as they are a short-lived pleasure.

To trim strawberries, slice off the green calyx top straight across, or cut out the core in a cone-shape. Or, cut in half, leaving the curly-leafed calyx still attached to garnish a cake or other dessert. Use an inexpensive "tomato shark" to remove the core in a ball shape.

RASPBERRIES

With their velvety, giving texture, unmistakably intense fruity-tart flavor, and jewel-like color, raspberries induce rapture, though it may be fleeting. Delicate, highly perishable, and much sought-after, raspberries automatically transform any dish they're served with into a special event. Raspberries actually consist of soft, multiple fruits clumped together in a slightly conical helmet-shape around their stem. The berries are covered with tiny hairs called "styles," which are a natural part of the delicate fruit's defenses. Raspberries are usually deep blue-tinted red, though golden and black (or purple) varieties exist (at a much higher price). Their tart, intensely flavored pulp, a magnificent color fit for royalty, surrounds a small but noticeable hard seed in each small round fruit.

In the restaurant and hotel business, serving raspberries is a must for any place with high-level ambitions. These fruits are highly perishable, especially so if picked during the wet weather that is characteristic of their best growing regions, and are equally difficult to transport. This means that the market for raspberries is highly volatile, making them always high-priced, except perhaps at a farmers' market in their season of abundance (early summer with a smaller crop in the fall). A case of twelve half-pints of raspberries may sell for over one hundred dollars when they're scarce; the same case one or two days later could be worth less then ten dollars, because the fruits break down and develop mold so quickly that it would only be suitable for sauces and purées, and

that only after a lot of picking through them.

There are three main types of raspberries: black, golden, and the most common red raspberry. The red raspberry, *Rubus genus*, is indigenous to Asia Minor and North America. Two thousand years ago, the people of Troy, in Asia Minor, gathered the fruit from the wild. Records of raspberry domestication were found in the fourth-century writings of Palladius, a Roman agriculturist, and seeds have been discovered at Roman forts in Britain, so the Romans are given credit for spreading their cultivation throughout Europe. In Medieval Europe, only the rich ate raspberries. While today, their enjoyment is certainly more widespread, raspberries are still a food for the privileged.

By the seventeenth century, British gardens were lush with raspberry bushes, which flourished in the country's cool, moist climate; by the eighteenth century, raspberry cultivation practices had spread throughout Europe. When the colonists came to America, they brought the European cultivated raspberry, *Rubus idaeus*, with them, but found American Indians drying the native American wild raspberry, *Rubus strigosus*, to preserve for ease of transport for their nomadic lifestyle.

In 1761, George Washington moved to his estate in Mount Vernon, where he began to cultivate berries in his extensive gardens. By 1867, over forty varieties of raspberries were known in America. In American colonial times, raspberry shrub—a syrup of raspberries, vinegar, and sugar—was thinned with about eight parts liquid to one part shrub to make a refreshing summer beverage. In the United

States, red raspberries thrive in the relatively cool, moist, coastal climate of the Pacific Northwest, west of the Cascades. The Meeker, a late season productive summer fruiting variety with full raspberry flavor, is the most widely planted raspberry in that region. About ninety percent of fresh-market red raspberries are grown in California, Washington, and Oregon, with Michigan and New York producing more limited quantities. Washington alone accounts for nearly sixty percent of the American red raspberry crop.

CHOOSING AND STORING RASPBERRIES

Raspberries are the more fragile member of the berry family, which accounts for their high cost. Handle them gently when rinsing. (I normally don't rinse raspberries, but rather I inspect them for any bad parts or leaf pieces and wipe them off.)

Look for plump, evenly-colored berries that have a soft, hazy, gloss at their peak of ripeness. The raspberries shouldn't have any dents or bruises, a sign of poor handling and/or over ripeness. Individual fruits (called "druplets") crumbled apart from the whole berries are a sign of less than high-quality. Berries that are unevenly colored, especially if some of the individual druplets are white, are underripe. I notice this happening more commonly in the berries imported out of season from Chile and Central America.

Raspberries are quite perishable and should be refrigerated unless eaten the same day they are purchased. Keep the berries cold but not too cold, because they are very sensitive to freeze damage, and keep them dry. Wash, if at all, just before serving, spreading them out on paper towels to dry. Unless they are in exceptionally fine condition, store raspberries no more than one to two days in the refrigerator.

RASPBERRY TYPES

RED RASPBERRIES: Red raspberries are medium to light to deep red depending on the variety and where they're grown. Limited quantities are available December through March from Chile and Southern California. Red raspberries are available year-round throughout the United States, especially to the restaurant trade, but peak season is June and early September.

BLACK RASPBERRIES: Black raspberries, *Rubus occidentalis*, known as blackcaps by growers, are native to North America and common in the eastern United States and Canada. They are usually purplish black, with small seeds, a hollow core, and whitish bloom on the outside of the berry, though yellow and red forms exist. Black raspberries have a distinct jammy flavor, small seeds, and, like the red raspberry, grow around a core that is hollow once the berry has been picked off. Black raspberries are in season in July.

GOLDEN RASPBERRIES: Golden raspberries are a relatively new variety that is much rarer and always more expensive than their red cousins. They are a naturally occurring variant of red raspberries, ranging in color from clear, light yellow and golden to a gorgeous rosy-tinged apricot. Their luscious flavor and texture brings to mind soft, yielding, and delicately perfumed apricots. Golden raspberries are available in limited quantity from June to October. Look for them in farmers' markets and specialty stores.

Raspberry Salzburger Nockerln

Salzburg is a picturesque town on the Bavarian Border in Austria famous for its small hills called Nockerln. *Austrian cuisine is derived from the traditions of the Austro-Hungarian Empire and has been influenced by the foods of its bordering countries: Hungary, the Czech Republic, Italy, and Bavaria in Southern Germany. This classic Austrian dish echoes the peaked hills of Salzburg, with its pointy heaps of pink-hued meringue. Serve it with Rose-Scented Raspberry Sauce (page 161). In season, other tart red to purple berries likes boysenberries, blackberries, or red currants would also be delicious, as would bottled lingonberries. Like a soufflé, this dessert waits for no one. Serve it as soon as it comes out of the oven when it's puffy, light, and hot. This recipe is gluten-free. This recipe is dairy-free. Substitute oil for the butter.*

YIELD: 6 SERVINGS

1 tablespoon unsalted butter, softened

2 ($^1/_2$-pint) containers raspberries (1 cup), defrosted if frozen

$^3/_4$ cup sugar

Juice of 1 orange, or $^1/_4$ cup fresh orange juice

Juice and grated zest of 1 lemon (3 tablespoons juice plus 1 tablespoon zest)

4 large eggs, separated whites at room temperature

2 tablespoons Framboise (French raspberry liqueur or eau de vie), Himbeergeist (German raspberry eau de vie), or triple sec

$^1/_4$ cup potato starch

Pinch of fine sea salt

Preheat the oven to 375°F. Rub the butter into an attractive shallow oval or oblong baking dish that holds about 6 cups.

Place half the raspberries, $^1/_4$ cup of the sugar, the orange juice, and the lemon juice in a medium, heavy-bottomed, nonreactive pot. Bring to a boil and cook for about 3 minutes or until lightly thickened. Remove from the heat, cool slightly, and then gently stir in the remaining raspberries and the lemon zest. While it is still warm, pour the raspberry mixture into the baking dish.

In a medium bowl, whisk together the egg yolks, liqueur, potato starch, and starch. In the clean and greaseless bowl of a standing electric mixer and using the whisk attachment, beat the egg whites until fluffy, then add the remaining $^1/_2$ cup sugar and continue beating until the whites are firm and glossy, 4 to 5 minutes. Fold the egg whites into the yolk mixture in thirds in order not to deflate the batter. Spoon on top of the raspberry mixture, shaping into three peaked mounds to resemble the peaks of Salzburg. Bake for 25 minutes on the bottom shelf of the oven until golden and risen like a soufflé. Serve immediately right from the baking dish.

Rose-Scented Raspberry Sauce

Rose and raspberry are paired in this clear, magenta-colored sauce, giving the sauce the scent of a Persian perfumed garden. Frozen raspberries will work just as well here, if not better, than the more expensive fresh berries. You may, of course, leave out the rose water if you don't care for its heady aroma. Serve the sauce with desserts that feature chocolate, almond, custard, pears, lemons, or berries, including Zach's Almond Macaroon Cake (page 76), Velia's White Chocolate-Lemon Torta Caprese (page 78), the Australian Pavlova with Lemon Filling and Tropical Fruits (page 442), the Rose-Scented Angel Food Cake (page 467), the Torta di Savoia with Candied Citron (page 535), and the Crostata di Riso: Italian Rice Tart (page 776).

YIELD: SCANT 2 CUPS

2 ($^1/_2$-pint) containers raspberries (1 cup), defrosted if frozen

$^1/_2$ cup sugar

$^3/_4$ cup water

2 tablespoons kirsch

1 teaspoon rose water

In a small heavy-bottomed nonreactive saucepan, combine the raspberries, sugar, and water. Heat gently until the sugar dissolves and the liquid just comes to the boil.

Remove the sauce from the heat, strain through a sieve or food mill, and stir in the kirsch and rose water. Cool to room temperature. If desired, transfer to a plastic squeeze bottle and store refrigerated for up to 1 month, or freeze up to 3 months.

Almond-Crusted Blackberry-Tangerine Pie

Simple but so good, this classic American pie made with plump, juicy but tart blackberries and a double flaky butter and almond butter piecrust is well worth the effort. Blackberries do grow in other parts of the country, including the Great Lakes region and the mid-Atlantic Coast, although they are most abundant and sweetest when grown in the cool, rainy climate of the Northwest Pacific Coast. Here, a butter pie crust gets an extra dimension of flavor from brown, intensely flavored Mission almond butter. Tangerine juice and its oil-rich, fragrant zest brighten up the filling with a touch of cinnamon for kick. It is best to make this pie in a ceramic or Pyrex pie pan, which has a larger capacity and will bake more evenly than the foil or aluminum type.

YIELD: ONE 10-INCH DEEP PIE

1 $^1/_4$ pounds Butter Pie Pastry, made with 6 ounces (1 $^1/_2$ sticks) butter and 2 ounces ($^1/_4$ cup) almond butter

1 cup sugar

1 teaspoon ground cinnamon

Grated zest and juice of 1 tangerine

   (5 to 6 tablespoons juice, 4 teaspoons zest)

6 tablespoons tapioca starch, substitute

   potato or corn starch

$1/4$ teaspoon fine sea salt

8 ($1/2$-pint) containers blackberries (4 cups)

2 tablespoons (1 ounce) unsalted butter, cut into bits

Divide the pastry into two portions of $3/4$ and $1/2$ pound. Roll each portion out $3/8$ inch thick. Place the larger portion into a 10-ince pie pan without stretching the dough; press well into the corners so there are no thick spots. Trim any overhang flush with the edge. Place the smaller portion on a piece of waxed paper and reserve in the refrigerator.

Whisk together the sugar, cinnamon, tangerine zest and juice, tapioca starch, and salt. Gently fold in the blackberries. Spoon into the pie crust and dot with butter.

To make a lattice top, cut the reserved pie crust into about 12 (1-inch wide) pastry strips, using either a sharp knife or a plain or fluted dough roller. Lay half of the pastry strips on top of the filling about 1 inch apart. Fold alternate pastry strips back halfway. Lay a pastry strip crosswise on the center of the tart. Unfold the pastry strips; then alternate, folding back the remaining strips. Lay another pastry strip crosswise about 1-inch away. Fold back half the strips, lay another pastry strip crosswise about 1-inch away and repeat the weaving until lattice covers the filling. (Alternatively, make the lattice on a piece of wax paper, then refrigerate until

firm, about 20 minutes.

Use a large spatula to transfer the lattice top to the top of the tart. This is especially helpful when using a fragile sweet dough,) Trim the edges of pastry strips even with the pan, pressing the strips against the edge of the pan to seal. Form a double-thick edge and crimp or pinch in and out alternatively to form a decorative fluted border.

Preheat the oven to 450°F. Place the pie on a baking pan to catch any drips. Bake on the bottom shelf of the oven for 10 minutes, then reduce the oven temperature to 350°F and bake for 45 minutes or until the pastry is lightly browned, the berries are tender, and the filling is bubbling through the crust. Cool on a wire rack to room temperature before serving. Cover and store at room temperature for up to 2 days or refrigerate up to 4 days.

ABOUT TAPIOCA STARCH

Tapioca starch is a fine, white powder produced from specialty treated and dried bitter cassava (manioc) root, which is native to the Amazon region of Brazil. Tapioca in pearl form is commonly used to make pudding. Because tapioca starch has little flavor of its own and thickens quickly at a relatively low temperature, it is ideal for fruit pie fillings. It is also appropriate for use by people who have gluten allergies. Look for tapioca starch at Asian markets and natural food stores.

Apple–Blueberry Crumb Pie with Cardamom

A smooth and stretchy cream cheese dough forms the tender crust of this chunky, deep blue pie. A thick jammy filling of apples and blueberries is flavored with orange zest and cardamom, while a simple crumb topping adds texture and helps the whole pie hold together. Use a combination of firm and tart and soft and sweet apples here. This is a good place to use frozen blueberries, especially the small, intensely flavored wild blueberries sold by Wyman's (page 166).

YIELD: ONE 9-INCH PIE, 8 TO 10 SERVINGS

Crust

$^3/_4$ pound Cream Cheese Pastry Dough (page 565)
$^1/_2$ cup sugar

Filling

4 medium apples, preferably 2 tart and 2 sweet, peeled, cored, and thinly sliced
$^1/_2$ pound ($1^1/_4$ cups) blueberries, washed and drained, defrosted if frozen
$^3/_4$ cup sugar
$^1/_4$ cup tapioca starch
1 teaspoon ground cardamom
Grated zest of 1 orange (4 teaspoons)
$^1/_4$ cup fine dry breadcrumbs

Crumb Topping

2 ounces ($^1/_2$ cup minus $^1/_2$ tablespoon) unbleached all-purpose flour
2 ounces ($^1/_4$)cup packed dark brown sugar
2 ounces ($^1/_2$ stick) unsalted butter, cut into bits
$^1/_2$ teaspoon ground cardamom

Make the crust: Roll the dough out on a work surface lightly sprinkled with sugar to $^3/_8$-inch thick. Carefully place the dough into a 9-inch deep pie pan without stretching it; press well into the corners so there are no thick spots. Trim the edges about 1-inch beyond the edge of the pie, then fold over to make a thicker edge, and press together to seal. Crimp or pinch in and out alternatively to form a decorative fluted edge. Chill the crust for 1 hour in the refrigerator or 30 minutes in the freezer to set the shape.

Make the filling: Preheat the oven to 375°F.

In a medium bowl, combine the apples and blueberries with the sugar, tapioca starch, cardamom, and orange zest and toss until well mixed. Sprinkle the crust with the breadcrumbs, then pile the filling into the pie crust, mounding it up in the middle. Bake the pie on the bottom shelf of the oven for 30 minutes, or until the apples have softened somewhat.

Meanwhile, prepare the topping: Place the flour, brown sugar, butter, and cardamom in the bowl of a food processor. Process briefly until the mixture forms large crumbs.

Remove the pie from the oven. Pat the crumble mixture evenly over the filling and place the pie back in the oven on the bottom shelf. Bake for 35 minutes longer, or until the apples are tender, the juices are bubbling, and the crumbs are lightly browned. (If the pastry gets too dark, cover the edges with a pie shield or aluminum foil.) Cool the pie to room temperature on a wire rack before serving. Store the pie covered and at room temperature for up to 3 days.

Blueberry–Walnut Streusel Muffins

I often use frozen wild blueberries to make these classic muffins, especially the berries sold by Wyman's (page 166) because they are smaller in size with a more concentrated flavor and work especially well when fresh blueberries are out of season. If using frozen blueberries, do not defrost them before adding them to the batter. Fold them in gently, avoiding breaking up the berries so you don't end up with blue batter. I live near an area with a large Russian population and am able to find frozen lingonberries, which are wonderful in these muffins, either on their own or combined with the blueberries. When making muffins, remember these steps: mix the dry, mix the wet, combine briefly and bake.

YIELD: 24 MEDIUM MUFFINS

Streusel

2 ounces ($\frac{1}{2}$ cup minus $\frac{1}{2}$ tablespoon) unbleached all-purpose flour

2 tablespoons sugar

2 tablespoons dark brown sugar

Grated zest of 1 lemon (1 tablespoon)

2 ounces ($\frac{1}{2}$ stick) unsalted butter, cut into bits

Batter

10 ounces ($2\frac{1}{2}$ cups minus $2\frac{1}{2}$ tablespoons) unbleached all-purpose flour

$1\frac{1}{2}$ cups sugar

2 teaspoons baking powder

1 teaspoon baking soda

Pinch fine sea salt

4 large eggs

1 cup buttermilk

$\frac{1}{4}$ pound (1 stick) unsalted butter, melted and cooled

1 tablespoon lemon juice

$1\frac{1}{2}$ cups blueberries

$\frac{1}{4}$ pound (1 cup) chopped walnuts

Preheat the oven to 400°F.

Make the streusel: Combine the flour, sugar, brown sugar, and lemon zest in the bowl of a food processor and process briefly to combine. Add the butter and process again just until the mixture forms soft crumbs.

Make the batter: In a large bowl, whisk together the dry ingredients: flour, sugar, baking powder, baking soda, and salt. In a separate bowl, whisk together the liquid ingredients: eggs, buttermilk, butter, and lemon juice. Stir into the flour mixture, then gently fold in the blueberries and walnuts, mixing just long enough to combine. Divide the batter evenly among 24 muffin cups coated with cooking spray or lined with muffin papers and filling each cup about $\frac{1}{2}$-inch from the top. Crumble the streusel topping over each muffin.

Bake for 20 minutes, then reduce the heat to 350°F and bake for 15 minutes, or until lightly browned and puffy, and the muffins spring back when pressed lightly. Store covered and at room temperature for up to 2 days or bag and freeze up to 2 months.

LINGONBERRIES

Lingonberries, *Vaccinium vitis-idaea,* are small, bright red, sweet-tart berries related to both blueberries and cranberries and, like cranberries, are almost always cooked with sugar. They are native to Scandinavia, Alaska, and northeastern Canada. The first crop ripens in mid-summer, around July; the second crop ripens in the fall from late September to early November. Although most lingonberries, whether frozen or made into preserves, are imported from Scandinavia or Russia, there are a few local growers in Washington State and in the Willamette Valley region in Oregon.

The lingonberry is also known in North America as the cowberry, red whortle berry, foxberry, northern mountain cranberry, dry ground cranberry, rock cranberry, partridge berry, or whimberry. Lingonberries are picked in the wild in Newfoundland and Labrador, where they are known as partridgeberries. I find the small tasty berries imported from Russia and sold frozen and bottled in my local Russian market. The Ikea stores sell Swedish lingonberry preserves at a reasonable price. Lingonberries may be substituted for cranberries in the Cranberry-Ginger Upside-Down Cake (page 399), the Cranberry-Walnut Pound Cake (page 400), the Cranberry-Semolina Ktefa (page 401), or the Apple-Cranberry Crisp (page 403).

Greek Blueberry–Yogurt Tart with Ouzo (Mustikkapiiras)

In Greece, bilberries, Vaccinium myrtillus, *which grow in the wild, are closely related to native American wild and cultivated blueberries and huckleberries. They grow singly or in pairs instead of in clusters like blueberries. Native American wild blueberries or huckleberries—sold by Wyman's of Maine (www.wymans.com)—will be closest in flavor to small Greek bilberries. These berries go nicely with the tangy custard filling of this tart, made from some of Greece's most famous ingredients: Greek yogurt, preferably the extra-rich kind made from sheep and goat's milk; honey, Greece is famous for its wild thyme-scented honey; ouzo, the anise and licorice-infused aperitif that has a devilish way of sneaking up on you; and fresh lemon juice and zest. All the flavors work beautifully together, especially when baked in the nutty-tasting white whole wheat crust.*

YIELD: 8 TO 12 SERVINGS

$3/4$ pound Sweet White Whole Wheat Tart Pastry
   (page 863), softened

4 large eggs

$1/2$ cup sugar

$1/4$ cup honey

1 cup whole milk plain yogurt, preferably Greek yogurt

Juice and grated zest of 1 lemon
   (3 tablespoons juice, 1 tablespoon zest)

2 tablespoons ouzo, substitute Pernod or other
   anise-flavored liquor

2 tablespoons potato starch, substitute corn, wheat, or rice starch

2 cups blueberries, preferably wild blueberries

Preheat the oven to 375°F.

Dust your hands with flour and pat the dough, which will be soft and sticky, into a 10-inch tart pan. Make sure that the corners where the sides and bottom of the dough meet are not overly thick. Trim the overhang flush with the edges. Fit a piece of heavy-duty foil onto the dough and fill with beans or other pie weights. Blind bake (just the pastry crust, no filling) on the bottom shelf of the oven until the dough is cooked through but not yet browned, about 30 minutes. Remove from the oven and cool to room temperature on a wire rack.

In a medium bowl, whisk together the eggs, sugar, honey, yogurt, lemon juice and zest, ouzo, and potato starch.

Place the tart on a baking pan to catch any drips. Scatter the berries into the crust and place the pan on the bottom rack of the oven. Pull out the rack and gently pour as much filling over the berries as you can, so the berries are coated and the crust is full but not overflowing, reserving any remaining custard mix.

Bake for 30 minutes, then pour the remaining custard into the center of the tart, where the custard is still liquid. Continue baking for 20 minutes longer, or until the crust is browned and the custard is set in the middle. Remove from the oven and cool on a wire rack. Cool to room temperature before cutting into serving portions. Store covered and at room temperature up to 2 days or refrigerate and store up to 5 days.

Note: If you are using frozen blueberries, run cold water over them to rinse off the frost, which tends to absorb unwanted odors. I do this whenever I use frozen fruits or vegetables.

WYMAN'S WILD BLUEBERRIES

This family-owned company, located on the coast of northern Maine and in New Brunswick, Canada, is the largest American supplier of wild blueberries, also known as huckleberries, usually sold frozen. In 1874, Jasper Wyman founded a seafood canning company in his hometown of Milbridge, Maine. By the turn of the century, he had acquired thousands of acres of blueberry land and shifted his company to sell the Down East's superb wild blueberry. Order them frozen, in juice form, or canned (frozen works best for baking) from www.wymans.com, or look for them at the Whole Food Markets and other specialty stores.

Strawberry Devil's Food Cake

If you love chocolate-dipped fancy stem strawberries, you'll love this devilishly dark and moist cake, with its strawberry filling and topping. The contrast between the fruity strawberry glaze and the light whipped chocolate filling makes for a cake to please the most ardent chocoholic and the most dedicated fruitophilic. Strong coffee enhances the chocolatiness of dark cocoa, because they share intense, pleasingly bitter fla-

vor. A layer of strawberry glaze coats and smoothes the outside, which is then coated in shiny, smooth dark chocolate drip icing, actually the same ganache as the whipped filling. To accentuate the strawberry flavor, serve the cake with Fresh Strawberry Coulis (page 168).

YIELD: 12 SERVINGS

Cake

2 ounces ($1/2$ cup minus 1 tablespoon)
  Dutch-processed cocoa

1 cup hot, freshly brewed, extra-strong coffee

6 ounces ($1^1/2$ cups minus 1 tablespoon)
  unbleached all-purpose flour

1 teaspoon baking soda

$1/2$ teaspoon baking powder

$1/2$ teaspoon fine sea salt

$1/4$ pound (1 stick) unsalted butter, softened

1 cup packed dark brown sugar (7 ounces)

$1/2$ cup sugar

2 large eggs

Ganache

1 cup heavy cream

$1/4$ cup hot, freshly brewed, extra-strong coffee

$3/4$ pound semisweet chocolate couverture,
  coarsely chopped

Glaze

1 pint strawberries, chopped

1 cup strawberry preserves, heated and strained

1 pint strawberries, halved

Make the cake: Preheat the oven to 350°F. Spray a 9-inch springform or removable bottom pan generously with nonstick spray or rub with butter and dust with flour, shaking off the excess.

In a medium bowl, whisk together the cocoa and the coffee, making sure to break up any lumps, and set the mixture aside to cool to room temperature. In a separate bowl, whisk together the dry ingredients: flour, baking soda, baking powder, and salt, and reserve.

In the bowl of an electric mixer and using the paddle attachment, beat together the butter, brown sugar, and sugar until creamy and light, 5 to 6 minutes. Beat in the eggs, one at a time, continuing to beat until they are completely absorbed.

Alternating, add the dry ingredients and the coffee mixture to the butter mixture, beginning and ending with the dry ingredients. Pour the batter into the prepared pan, shaking back and forth to even the top.

Bake for 40 minutes, or until the cake comes away from the sides of the pan and forms a slightly rounded top, and a toothpick inserted into the center comes out clean. Cool in the pan on a wire rack. Remove the sides of the springform pan and refrigerate the cake until chilled before filling, preferably overnight. (Wrap and freeze the cake at this point for up to 3 months, if desired.)

Make the ganache: Place the cream in a Pyrex measuring bowl (or other microwaveable container) and heat to scalding or steaming hot in the microwave. Separately, combine the hot coffee and the chocolate and heat on low power in the microwave for 1 to 2 minutes at a time, until the chocolate is almost melted. Whisk till completely smooth, then gradually whisk in the cream. Continue to whisk until the mixture is completely smooth and shiny. Cool at room temperature, stirring occasionally until the icing is tepid and has reached a spreadable consistency but is still glossy, about 30 minutes. Divide the ganache in half. Chill one half until cold but still soft, about 30 minutes. Lightly beat remaining half until it is fluffy and light, but still smooth, 3 to 4 minutes.

Make the strawberry glaze: Combine the chopped strawberries and the preserves in a medium heavy-bottomed pot and bring to a boil. Boil 10 minutes, skimming off and discarding any foam that develops on top, until the glaze is thick and shiny, about 10 minutes. Strain through a fine sieve. Cool to room temperature, stirring occasionally, about 30 minutes.

Assemble the cake: Cut a very small notch, about $1/4$-inch deep, out of the side of the cake to use as a guide. Using a long, serrated knife, cut the cake horizontally into two layers.

Brush the top of the bottom layer of cake with the strawberry glaze and allow it to set about for 15 minutes in the refrigerator. Spread the whipped ganache over the glaze. Re-assemble the cake layers, using the cut notch as a guide to line up the layers in their original position. Brush the outside of the cake with the remaining strawberry glaze and allow it to set about 15 minutes in the refrigerator.

Place the cake on a wire rack over a baking pan to catch any drips. Spread the remaining (unwhipped) chocolate ganache over top, swirling to make an attractive top, and allow the excess to spill over the sides. Using an icing spatula, smooth the ganache over the sides. Chill 30 minutes to set the icing. Press a strawberry half into each portion of cake just before serving. (The strawberries will leak if placed on the cake

ahead of time.) Accompany with Fresh Strawberry Coulis, if desired. Store covered and refrigerated up to 5 days.

Fresh Strawberry Coulis

Make this fresh tasting and brightly colored sauce when you've got overripe strawberries or good-quality frozen berries. Because it is not cooked, this simple sauce has all the fresh, fruity flavor of the berries without the usual cooked "jammy" flavor. The sauce will keep for about 1 week in the refrigerator or for 2 to 3 months in the freezer.

YIELD: 1 PINT

1 pint red, ripe strawberries, cleaned, or 2 cups frozen
$1/4$ cup water
$1/4$ cup orange juice
6 tablespoons confectioners' sugar

Combine all the ingredients in the jar of a blender. Blend until completely smooth, stirring once or twice. Store tightly covered in the refrigerator up to 2 weeks, or freeze up to 3 months.

Strawberry–Rhubarb Tart with Sweet Walnut Pastry

There is a brief period every spring when local strawberries and local, intensely colored rhubarb are both at their peak. Don't wait a moment: grab them both and make this springalicious pretty-in-pink tart. The cookie-like walnut pastry can easily be made ahead and frozen. If you get a craving any other time, use frozen rhubarb (freeze your own if you can) and the juiciest, reddest strawberries you can find. Frozen strawberries will work for the filling, but you'll have to forego the fresh strawberry topping.

YIELD: 1 (10-INCH) TART, SERVES 12

3/4 pound Sweet Walnut Pastry (page 848)

3/4 cup sugar

Juice and grated zest of 1 tangerine, substitute orange
   (5 to 6 tablespoons juice, 4 teaspoons zest)

1 pound (1 bunch) fresh rhubarb, trimmed
   and cut into 1-inch lengths

2 tablespoons (1 ounce) unsalted butter, softened

2 tablespoons orange liqueur

2 tablespoons potato starch

2 pints red ripe, strawberries, hulled and sliced

1/2 cup strawberry preserves, heated till barely runny
   and strained, substitute strained red currant
   preserves

Crème fraîche or sour cream, for garnish

Make the crust: Preheat the oven to 350°F.

Roll the dough out between 2 sheets of lightly floured wax paper to about 3/8-inch thickness, then drape into a 10-inch tart pan without stretching, and press the dough well into the corners so there are no thick spots. Trim the pastry flush with the edges. Fit a piece of heavy-duty foil onto the dough and fill with beans or other pie weights. Blind bake (just pastry crust, no filling) on the bottom shelf of the oven until the dough is cooked through but not yet browned, about 25 minutes. Remove the foil and the weights, reduce the oven temperature to 325°F, and bake for 15 minutes longer, or until the dough is evenly and lightly browned. Remove from the oven and cool to room temperature on a wire rack.

Make the filling: Bring the sugar, and tangerine juice and zest to a boil in a medium heavy-bottomed nonreactive pot. Add the rhubarb and bring back to the boil, shaking occasionally so the rhubarb cooks evenly, but without stirring which will tend to break it up. Reduce the heat and simmer for 10 minutes or until the rhubarb is soft. Add the butter and shake to combine.

Whisk together the liqueur and the potato starch to make a smooth slurry and stir into the boiling liquid, continuing to cook until the mixture is clear and thickened, about 2 minutes. Fold in half the strawberries, remove the pan from the heat, and cool to room temperature.

Spoon the filling into the crust and top with the remaining strawberries. Brush the strawberries with the preserves to make a shiny glaze and chill the tart until set, about 2 hours. Serve topped with crème fraîche or sour cream. Store covered and refrigerated for up to 2 days.

PIE PLANT (OR RHUBARB)

One definition of rhubarb is "a heated dispute or controversy," maybe because the plant itself evokes such strong reactions. In my family, my mom loved rhubarb and my dad wouldn't touch it, so when she made her favorite tart and sweet stewed rhubarb, the two of us would enjoy its tart flavor and smooth, melting consistency. Is rhubarb a fruit or a vegetable? In 1947, the United States Customs Court in Buffalo, New York, ruled that rhubarb is a fruit, because that is how it was mainly used.

The scientific name for rhubarb, *Rheum rhabarbarum*, comes from the Latin, meaning root of the barbarian, so even from earliest times, this unusual plant had negative connotations. Rhubarb came originally from Asia and is related to sorrel and buckwheat. Until the nineteenth century, rhubarb was used as a medicinal tonic rather than a food. In Italy, the *amaro* (bitter) called *Rabarbaro* made from rhubarb started out as this kind of tonic.

Rhubarb's soft red color is an annual harbinger of spring. The edible portion of the plant is its thick red fleshy stalks, which end at duck-feet webbed wide green leaves, which are poisonous because of their high oxalic acid content. The leaves are normally cut off and discarded before sending the rhubarb to market. Rhubarb is always cooked with sugar or other sweeteners to balance its intense acidity and most often shows up in pies, often mixed with spring's other fruit specialty, fresh local strawberries.

There are two basic types of rhubarb: hothouse (or strawberry rhubarb) and field grown (or cherry rhubarb). Hothouse rhubarb tends to have smoother flesh, more delicate texture, and less acidity than field grown; field-grown rhubarb has deeper color, more juice, and bolder acidity. Green rhubarb is also available. Rhubarb is versatile enough to be used both for savory dishes and for desserts, especially when paired with other fruits, such as apples, raspberries, or strawberries.

Rhubarb is in season from the spring into the early parts of summer. Hothouse rhubarb is available from Washington, Michigan, and Ontario from mid-January through mid-April; field-grown rhubarb starts to come into season in April and is available, depending on the part of the country, until September. Frozen rhubarb is occasionally available at the supermarket.

BRAZIL NUTS & CASHEWS

Brazil Nuts . . .172

The Brazil Nut Effect . . .173

Cashews . . .173

Choosing and Storing Cashews

RUBY GRAPEFRUIT-ORANGE
BRAZIL NUT TORTE . . .174

BRAZIL NUT AND GUAVA SANDWICH
COOKIES (DOCINHOS DO PARA) . . .175

Quinconcé . . .176

SEPHARDIC STUFFED MONKEY . . .176

ARUBAN CASHEW CAKE . . .178

Fresh Cashews in India . . .179

Microplane Citrus Zester . . .179

BRAZIL NUTS
& CASHEWS

BRAZIL NUTS

It seems like some of my sharpest memories have to do with the candy bars I devoured shamelessly as a child. My favorite, Chunky, contained Brazil nuts, cashews, raisins, and chocolate, and came in thick squares shaped like a pyramid with the top cut off. The Chunky was first produced in the mid-1930s by New York City candy maker, Philip Silvershein, who named the candy after his granddaughter, at the time a "chunky" baby. Today, a bit "chunky" myself, I still adore chocolate mixed with lots of nuts and dried fruits.

Inside the hard-walled Brazil nut, which resembles a somewhat oddly-shaped coconut, are eight to twenty-four Brazil nuts (seeds) arranged like sections of an orange. Each three-sided nut is enclosed in a dense, hard shell. Inside, the dense ivory to white nutmeat is covered by dark brown skin and has a creamy nuttiness reminiscent of fresh coconut meat. Brazil nuts are almost fifty percent fat but are also high in protein. An old American name was the cream nut, because of their creamy texture. They are also known as butternuts and para nuts (named after Pará, a state in Brazil on the Amazon where the nuts are collected).

Brazil nuts come from a tree, *Bertholletia excelsa*, which is native to the Guianas, Venezuela, Brazil, eastern Colombia, eastern Peru, and eastern Bolivia in South America. Scattered Brazil nut trees grow in the large forests on the banks of the Amazon, Rio Negro, and the Orinoco Rivers. The trees may live for five hundred years or more, but they produce fruits only in virgin forests—forests that have not been disturbed by human activity. The reason behind this lies in how the trees are pollinated.

Large, long-tongued, female orchid bees pollinate the yellow flowers of the Brazil nut tree. The bees must be strong enough to lift the coiled hood on the flower and have tongues long enough to negotiate the complex coiled flower—whew, this flower must have true sex appeal! The orchids produce a scent that attracts orchid bees and the male bees need that scent to attract females. Without the orchid, the bees can't mate, and the fruits don't get pollinated. Forests that have been disturbed by human activity—and are therefore not virgin—usually lack this orchid. As such, Brazil nuts are collected entirely from the wild and not from farms. This trade is a good model for generating income from a tropical forest without destroying it.

The biggest importer of Brazil nuts is not Brazil but Bolivia, where the nuts are known as *almendras* (the name for almonds in Spain). In Brazil, the nuts are called *castanhas-do-Pará*, "chestnuts from Pará." Other indigenous names include *juvia* in the Orinoco, and *sapucaia* in Brazil. Unfortunately, a common slang term for the nuts in some regions of the United States was at one time "nigger-toes," though thankfully, because of its inflammatory nature, this name has virtually disappeared.

In this chapter, grapefruit and Brazil nuts are combined in the Ruby Grapefruit–Orange Brazil Nut Torte (page 174); ground brazil nuts go into the shortcrust pastry in the tender Brazil Nut and Guava Sandwich Cookies (page 175); and strong, dark espresso is mixed with the nuts in the Brazil Nut Cake with Espresso (page 373).

THE BRAZIL NUT EFFECT

In the world of science, The Brazil Nut Effect—when large items mixed with smaller items (such as Brazil nuts mixed with almonds) tend to rise to the top—is named after these extra-large nuts.

CASHEWS

The cashew fruit caipiriña cocktail I sipped at Sorriso de Dadá, a cozy old house-restaurant with an open ceiling in the heart of the old cobbledstoned Pelourinho district in Salvador de Bahia, is a tropical treat you'll have to travel to Brazil to taste.

Although the sweet, curvy, buttery-tasting cashew has long been a favorite in the kitchens of South America, India, and Asia, widespread cultivation of cashews is a twentieth-century innovation.

The cashew, *Anacardium occidentale*, is the seed of a tropical evergreen plant related to the mango, pistachio, and to poison ivy. Originating in Brazil, the cashew plant made its way to India in the sixteenth century via Portuguese sailors in yet another New World/Old World exchange. Unlike most fruits, the cashew seed hangs from the bottom of the cashew apple. Although the fresh cashew apple fruit is not only edible but delicious, it is only available in tropical regions close to where it is picked, as it is too perishable to export. Cashew apples begin to ferment as soon as they are picked and will barely last 24 hours. They are highly prized in their growing locale, where they are sometimes found canned, in jams, or used to make liqueurs, such as the feni I sampled in Goa, India.

The kidney-shaped cashew nut is surrounded by a double shell containing a caustic black substance called urushiol, the same powerful skin irritant also found in the skins of mango and in poison ivy. (Since I'm highly allergic to poison ivy, it's a good thing I don't have to shell cashews for a living, as many workers develop the rash.) In India, urushiol is said to be used by mahouts (rider/keepers) to control their tamed elephants. This black substance must be removed during the shelling process and is sold for industrial use. For this reason, cashews are never sold in the shell.

In this chapter, cashews go into the Sephardic

Stuffed Monkey (page 176), which has nothing to do with monkeys, and the Aruban Cashew Cake (page 178), which is traditional to that small island. Elsewhere, cashews are combined with coconut to make a tropical crumb crust for the Baby Banana Cream Pie (page 131). If you love turtle candies, you'll be sure to adore the Turtle Brownies with Caramel and Pecans on page 653.

CHOOSING AND STORING CASHEWS

Although cashews may be labeled as raw, they are never completely raw, because heat must be used during the shelling and cleaning process. However, they are more raw than brown roasted cashews. Raw cashews may be more difficult to find, but roasted cashews are widely available, both salted and unsalted, whole or in pieces. Dry-roasted cashews have a lower fat content than any other nut.

Cashews are highly perishable and like other nuts, can easily turn rancid quickly. Cashews in vacuum-packed jars are preferred. Store cashews in a cool, dry place in an airtight container to keep them from absorbing other food odors. If refrigerated, they can last up to four months; they may be frozen for up to six months. Cashews will become soft in baked goods and will not stay crunchy like other nuts.

Ruby Grapefruit– Orange Brazil Nut Torte

I made this unusual torte for a ladies tea party with a group of old friends. Everyone raved, including me, the most critical taster of all! Not many cake recipes call for grapefruit, especially baked right into the batter. This moist and light cake, which combines red grapefruit with ground Brazil nuts, is well worth trying. The colorful topping of red grapefruit and orange sections makes for an eye-catching presentation. This recipe is gluten-free. This recipe is dairy-free.

YIELD: 12 SERVINGS

Cake

3 large eggs, separated

$^3/_4$ cup sugar

1 teaspoon vanilla extract

Grated zest of 1 orange (4 teaspoons)

2 teaspoons grated grapefruit zest

$^1/_4$ pound (1 cup) finely ground Brazil nuts

$^1/_4$ cup ($^3/_4$ ounce) potato starch

$^1/_2$ teaspoon fine sea salt

Meringue Topping

2 ruby grapefruits, sectioned, plus extra for garnish

2 oranges, sectioned, plus extra for garnish

4 large ($^1/_2$ cup) egg whites

1 cup sugar

$^1/_4$ pound (1 cup) finely ground Brazil nuts

Make the cake: Preheat the oven to 325°F. Spray a 10-

inch round springform or removable bottom cake pan, with nonstick baker's coating or rub with softened butter and dust with potato starch, shaking out the excess.

In the bowl of a standing electric mixer and using the paddle attachment, beat together the 3 egg yolks and $^1/_2$ cup of the sugar until light and fluffy, 5 to 6 minutes. Add the vanilla, orange zest, and grapefruit zest, and beat briefly to combine. Combine 1 cup of the Brazil nuts with the starch and salt and fold into the egg mix.

In the clean and greaseless bowl of a standing electric mixer and using the whisk, beat the 3 egg whites until fluffy, then beat in $^1/_4$ cup sugar and continue beating until the whites are firm and glossy, 4 to 5 minutes. Fold the meringue into the batter in thirds so as not to deflate the whites. Spoon into the prepared pan. (You may use the same bowl to beat the egg whites without washing it for the cake topping below.)

Bake for 25 minutes, or until lightly browned and the cake has started to come away from the sides of the pan. Set on a wire rack to cool, about 15 minutes. Run a knife along the edge to loosen, release the springform sides, and invert the cake onto a wire rack. Let cool completely.

Make the meringue topping: Reduce the oven temperature to 300°F. Invert the cake onto a cake cardboard or the pan bottom for support then onto a baking sheet lined with parchment paper. Arrange the fruit sections over the cake, saving the juices for another use (or just drink them).

In the clean and greaseless bowl of a standing electric mixer and using the whisk, beat the remaining egg whites until fluffy, then add the remaining 1 cup sugar and continue beating until the whites are firm and glossy, 4 to 5 minutes. Gently fold in the remaining 1 cup of ground Brazil nuts.

Spread the meringue topping evenly over the cake and bake for 30 minutes or until the topping is lightly browned. Cool on a wire rack and transfer to an attractive cake plate. Garnish by arranging alternating sections of grapefruit and orange around the cake, and serve. This cake is best the day it is made.

Brazil Nut and Guava Sandwich Cookies (Docinhos do Pará)

Guava and Brazil nuts: two tropical ingredients that pair beautifully together, here in a New World rendition of the alfajores *cookies that originated in Spain. Light and ultra-tender ground Brazil nut shortbread cookies are paired with melted guava membrillo (fruit paste).* Membrillo *is the Spanish word for quince, from which the English word marmalade is derived, but is commonly used to denote the thick, sliceable quince paste or 'cheese' so popular in Spain. In the New World, creative cooks substituted guava and mango for the Old World quince, cooking them down until quite firm and then forming the mixture into blocks or rounds of tropical membrillo. These cookies were big winners at a Fourth of July party.*

YIELD: 36 COOKIES

$^3/_4$ pound ($2^3/_4$ cups plus 1 tablespoon)
    unbleached all-purpose flour
$^3/_4$ pound ($3^3/_4$ cups) potato starch

¹/₂ teaspoon fine sea salt

³/₄ pound (2¹/₂ cups) Brazil nuts

³/₄ pound (3 sticks) unsalted butter, softened

1 cup sugar

¹/₂ pound (about 1 cup) guava paste, diced

1 cup orange juice

Confectioners' sugar, for dusting

Line two 18 x 13-inch half sheet pans (or other large baking pans) with parchment paper or silicone baking mats. Preheat the oven to 350°F.

Whisk together the dry ingredients: flour, potato starch, and salt. Place the Brazil nuts and about 1 cup of the flour mixture into the bowl of a food processor and process until the nuts are a fine meal. Combine with the remaining flour mixture.

In the bowl of an electric mixer fitted with the paddle attachment, cream the butter and sugar until light and fluffy, 5 to 6 minutes, scraping down the sides once or twice.

Add the flour mixture, beating only long enough for the mixture to come together and form a ball. Roll out on floured work surface to ³/₈-inch thick and cut with 1¹/₂- to 2-inch cookie cutters. Arrange equidistantly in rows of 3 and 2 on the baking pans. Bake for 20 minutes, or until very light brown. Cool to room temperature on baking racks.

Meanwhile, place the guava paste and orange juice in a medium non-aluminum saucepan. Bring to a boil, whisking together until smooth or use an immersion blender. Continue to boil about 5 minutes, while stirring, until the paste is thick enough to hold its shape. Be careful not to let the paste stick and burn.

Transfer the guava filling to a metal bowl and place it inside a second larger bowl filled with a mixture of ice and water. Stirring occasionally, cool until the paste is firm and cold to the touch. Spread on half the cookies and join them in pairs, making little sandwiches. Dust the cookies generously with confectioners' sugar and serve. Store covered and refrigerated for up to 3 days.

QUINCONCÉ

I was taught by a French pastry chef to place all my cookies and pastries on the baking pan *en quinconcé*, (from the Latin *quincunx*, by fives). This is an arrangement of five units arranged as on dice, with four on the outside and one in the middle, or in rows of twos and threes so that all units are equidistant, which works especially well for small shapes on baking trays. The figure was inspired by the Greek mathematician Pythagoras, who attributed mysteries to this shape. This is the most efficient way to arrange cookies so they don't run into each other, or "kiss" as bakers say.

Sephardic Stuffed Monkey

The unusual name of this pastry has nothing to do with monkeys, but is rather the nickname for Monick's, a once-renowned London Dutch-Jewish bakery. The "stuffed monkey" is a contribution of Dutch Jews of Portuguese origin to English food, and is quite popular among English Sephardic Jews. A double-layer of pastry is filled with a mixture of raisins, candied citrus rind, and nuts, a recur-

ring theme in Jewish, especially Sephardic baking. The cashews are a legacy of early Jewish settlements in Brazil.

YIELD: 36 BARS

Dough

1 pound (3$^3/_4$ cups) unbleached all-purpose flour

1 cup sugar

1 teaspoon ground cinnamon

1 teaspoon fine sea salt

$^3/_4$ pound (3 sticks) unsalted butter,
   cut into bits and chilled until firm

2 large eggs, slightly beaten

1 teaspoon almond extract

Filling and Glaze

$^1/_2$ pound (2 cups) chopped candied orange peel,
   homemade (page 225) or purchased

$^1/_2$ pound (2 cups) chopped cashews

$^3/_4$ pound (2$^1/_4$ cups) golden raisins

1 teaspoon ground cinnamon

$^1/_2$ teaspoon ground allspice

$^1/_2$ cup light brown sugar

2 large eggs, separated

$^1/_4$ pound (1 stick) unsalted butter, melted

1 cup sliced almonds, skin-on

Make the dough: Whisk together the dry ingredients: flour, sugar, cinnamon, and salt in the bowl of a standing electric mixer. Add the butter and beat with the paddle attachment until the mixture resembles oatmeal. Add the eggs and almond extract, beating only until the mixture comes together and forms a ball.

Knead the dough briefly by hand until smooth. Transfer to a plastic bag and shape into a flattened rectangle. Chill in the refrigerator for 1 hour or in the freezer for 30 minutes until firm but still malleable.

Preheat the oven to 350°F. Prepare a 15 x 10-inch jelly roll pan by spraying with nonstick baker's coating or lining with parchment paper.

Make the filling: Combine the orange peel, cashews, raisins, cinnamon, allspice, sugar, egg yolks, and butter.

Divide the dough in half with one portion slightly larger. Roll out the larger portion between 2 sheets of lightly floured wax paper to fit the pan. Place the dough in the pan, pressing the edges up the sides of the pan and trimming as necessary. Chill the pan with the dough while rolling out the second half slightly larger than the pan.

Spoon the filling onto the dough and spread it out evenly, leaving a $^1/_2$-inch uncovered strip all around. Invert the second sheet of dough on top of the filling and press out any air pockets from the center towards the edges. Crimp the two sheets of dough together so the filling does not leak out.

Beat the egg whites lightly with 2 tablespoons water and brush all over the top. Cut small slits all over the dough to allow steam to escape, then sprinkle with the almonds, pressing them into the top lightly so they adhere. Bake for 40 minutes, or until golden-brown. Cool to room temperature on a wire rack, cut into bars, and serve. Store 3 days at room temperature

Note: If all you can find are salted, roast cashews, place them in a bowl of cold water, swish around to wash off the salt, then drain well and pat dry with paper towels.

Aruban Cashew Cake

I recently co-authored a book about the food of Aruba called Aruba Tastes & Tales, *which was published in Venezuela for sale in restaurants and other locations on the island. If you're lucky enough to make a trip to Aruba, the full-color book featuring recipes from great chefs and local cooks, makes a wonderful souvenir. For everyone else, I am including the recipe for this typical festive cake from "One Happy Island," where cashew trees, which are native to Brazil, grow. A special occasion favorite among Arubans, the cake gets its warm buttery nuttiness from ground cashews. The colorful garnish of candied cherries and lime confetti (tiny bits of shredded lime peel) is traditional, though well-drained maraschino cherries may be substituted. Be sure to use only the green part of the lime peel; the inner white pith is quite bitter.*

YIELD: 12 OR MORE SERVINGS

Cake Batter

$^1/_2$ pound (scant 1$^1/_2$ cups) unsalted cashews

6 ounces (1$^1/_2$ cups minus 1 tablespoon)
   unbleached all-purpose flour

1$^1/_2$ teaspoons baking powder

$^1/_4$ teaspoon fine sea salt

$^1/_4$ pound (1 stick) unsalted butter, softened

1 cup sugar

1 teaspoon almond extract

4 large eggs whites

1 cup milk

Icing

2 large eggs whites ($^1/_4$ cup), room temperature

$^1/_2$ teaspoon fine sea salt

$^1/_2$ pound (1$^1/_2$ cups minus 2 tablespoons)
   confectioners' sugar

$^1/_4$ pound (1 stick) unsalted butter, cut up and softened

1 teaspoon almond extract

Grated zest of 1 lime (2 teaspoons)

1 cup cashew halves

12 candied cherries

Make the cake: Preheat the oven to 350°F. Spray a 9-inch round cake pan with nonstick coating or rub with softened butter and dust with flour, shaking out the excess.

Place the cashews, flour, baking powder, and salt into the bowl of a food processor and process until finely ground, working in two batches if necessary.

In the bowl of a standing electric mixer and using the paddle attachment, cream the butter, $^1/_2$ cup of the sugar, and the almond extract until light and fluffy, 5 to 6 minutes. Transfer the mixture to a wide shallow bowl.

In the clean and greaseless bowl of a standing electric mixer and using the whisk, beat the egg whites until fluffy, then add the remaining $^1/_2$ cup sugar and continue beating until the whites are firm and glossy, 4 to 5 minutes. Fold the meringue into the creamed mixture in thirds so as not to deflate the batter. Alternately fold in the dry ingredients and the milk, beginning and ending with the dry ingredients.

Bake for 30 minutes or until the cake batter begins to come away from the sides of the pan and a toothpick or skewer stuck in the center comes out clean. Cool the cake on a wire rack and then invert to unmold. Cool completely on a wire rack before frosting.

Make the icing: In the clean and greaseless bowl of a standing electric mixer and using the whisk, beat the egg whites with the salt until light and fluffy, then add the confectioners' sugar and continue beating until the whites are firm and glossy, 4 to 5 minutes. Beat in the butter, bit by bit, and finally, add the almond extract and beat briefly to combine. Spread the icing over the cake. Sprinkle the cake with the lime zest and press the cashews and the cherries into the top of the cake in a decorative pattern. Chill for 1 hour in the refrigerator, or until the icing has set.

FRESH CASHEWS IN INDIA

I was lucky enough to taste creamy, soft fresh cashews, a rare treat at Goa's famous bustlingly busy Friday Market at Mapusa. Two young women had laboriously hand-picked the cashews for sale, selling them for the relatively high price of one rupee each (about 2 1/2 cents). Because the women were not regular market vendors, the other vendors kept chasing them away while yelling and cursing, so sales were made on the run.

MICROPLANE CITRUS ZESTER

If you don't own one already, go right out and buy a Microplane zester. It is, hand's down, the easiest, most effective way to remove the colorful oil-filled pockets of zest located on the skin of citrus fruit with none of the bitter white pith. The Microplane rasp was invented in 1990 by Richard and Jeff Grace who used a process called photo-etching to create holes in metal by dissolving it with a chemical, leaving razor-sharp edges. They initially sold it as a new woodworking tool.

In 1994, Lorraine Lee, a homemaker in Ottawa, Canada, was making an Armenian orange cake that called for several tablespoons of fresh grated zest. Out of frustration with her old grater, Lee picked up the new tool her husband had brought home from the couple's hardware store. As she rubbed the orange across the rasp, fine, lacy shreds of colorful zest peeled off its surface. The couple promptly changed the product description in their catalogue for this can't-do-without-it tool and had it made out of stainless steel. If you're left-handed like me, buy the straight version with a black plastic handle; the less expensive angled version works best for right-handers. Both are available at kitchen supply stores or order online from http://us.microplane.com.

BUCKWHEAT

Wolff's Kasha . . .183

KASHA-MUSHROOM KNISHES . . .183

UKRAINIAN BUCKWHEAT ROLLS (HRECHANYKY) . . .185

SEEDED MULTI-GRAIN SOURDOUGH BREAD . . .186

Banneton Bread Baskets . . .187

Mixed Seeds for Bread . . .187

APPLE-DATE BUCKWHEAT MUFFINS . . .188

BUCKWHEAT CINNAMON-RAISIN BREAD . . .188

Brunch with Mark Miller . . .190

BUCKWHEAT

While growing up, I enjoyed eating steaming-hot kasha as a cereal, in kasha var-nishkes (mixed with lots of browned onions and bow-tie-shaped egg noodles), and especially as the filling for hockey puck–shaped (and often hockey puck–heavy) knishes (opposite page), all dishes evocative of my Eastern European Jewish heritage. Though in America, kasha refers to only to buckwheat groats, in Russia, kasha may also refer to millet or oat porridge.

Buckwheat kasha is the roasted and sometimes crushed seeds of buckwheat, *Fogypyrum esculentum*, which is unrelated to wheat, but rather a member of the rhubarb family and also related to sorrel. Although it is thought of and used as a cereal, buckwheat is not true grass like other cereals. The three-sided, sharp-angled grain has dark brown tough skin enclosing the kernel. It gets its name from a corruption of *boek-weit*, the Dutch form of the name, meaning beech-wheat, because it resembles the triangular beech-nut.

Buckwheat is quite well known in cold places in the world, which are unsuited to growing much else. The grain is native to Siberia and reached Japan from Korea. For long centuries, buckwheat was the main food of the mountainous regions of Northern Japan, where rice wouldn't grow. Japanese soba noodles made from buckwheat flour were first produced there in the seventeenth century. Buckwheat reached Eastern Europe from Russia during the Middle Ages and was brought to Europe by crusaders who had learned of it in their travels to the east. By the fifteenth century, buckwheat was known in Germany and a bit later was to be found in Italy and France, where its name, Saracen grain (*sarrasin* in French; *saraceno* in Italian) reflects its connection with the East.

In the Alpine regions of France and Italy, places where hardy buckwheat thrives, buckwheat is a staple. In Italy's Valtellina, buckwheat flour is made into a special pasta called pizzocheri and it is also cooked into polenta. Similarly, in the French Haute Savoie, crozets, a type of buckwheat pasta cut into small squares using a special knife, is a specialty.

In the Atlantic province of Brittany, large, thin crepes are made with buckwheat flour in a dish thought to be adapted from the blini of Russia, perhaps brought to Brittany by sailors who had visited Russia. In Brittany, they are called galettes or *crêpes de sarrasin, ployes* in Acadia (French Canada), and *boûketes* in Wallonia, the French-speaking part of Belgium. Yeast-raised buckwheat pancakes were a common food in American pioneer days. In Ukraine, yeast rolls called *hrechany ky* are made from buckwheat (see the recipe on page 185).

The largest producers of buckwheat today are Russia and Poland. Dutch colonists originally brought buckwheat to North America and planted it along the Hudson River, where it was one of the first crops to be cultivated. Buckwheat is grown primarily in Northern states such as New York. Buckwheat flour is dark with a violet tint and is also known for this reason in French as *blé noir* (black wheat).

Because buckwheat is naturally free of gluten, it can be enjoyed by people who must avoid eating gluten. Buckwheat is also a good honey plant, producing a dark, strong-tasting honey. Buckwheat flour maybe added to breads, but because it has no gluten, it must be mixed with wheat flour. According to the USDA, buckwheat has an amino acid composition nutritionally superior to all cereals, including oats. Buckwheat protein is particularly rich in the beneficial amino acid, lysine.

In this chapter, buckwheat goes into the hearty filling for Eastern European Jewish Kasha–Mushroom Knishes (this page), surely better than any you've ever bought, and Ukrainian Buckwheat Rolls (page 185) from the same part of the world made with buckwheat flour. The Seeded Multi-Grain Sourdough Bread (page 186) contains buckwheat flour. Both the chewy and fruity Apple-Date Buckwheat Muffins (page 188) and the dark, fragrant Buckwheat Cinnamon-Raisin Bread (page 188) are made with buckwheat flour.

WOLFF'S KASHA

Wolff's Kasha has been produced by The Birkett Mills since 1797. Headquartered on Main Street in the village of Penn Yan (named after its original Pennsylvania and Yankee settlers) in the heart of New York's Finger Lakes region, the mill has been in continuous operation for over two centuries. Today, the company is one of the world's largest manufacturers of buckwheat products. Their products can be found in markets with a large Eastern European Jewish population and comes in fine, medium, coarse, and whole-grain versions. The buckwheat sold under the name Pocono comes from the same mill but is organic. Store kasha in the freezer.

Kasha–Mushroom Knishes

During the early part of the twentieth century, when hundreds of thousands of Eastern European Jews immigrated to America and settled in New York City, often starting out on the Lower East Side, they brought with them their family recipes for knishes. The delectable, hockey puck–shaped knish consists of a thin layer of flaky dough enclosing a hearty filling. Mashed potatoes with lots of browned onions; mushrooms and onions; liver and onions; and farmer cheese and dill are a few traditional fillings. In this filling, I combine kasha, mushrooms, dill, and shallots, all cooked in butter. Anything but light, these portable meals are well suited to eating on the go, like Spanish empanadas (pages 129, 264, 271, and 881), and Italian calzone. The stretchy cream cheese dough is an American addition.

YIELD: 24 KNISHES

1³/₄ pounds Cream Cheese Pastry Dough (page 565)

1 cup medium kasha

2 large eggs

Fine sea salt and freshly ground black pepper to taste

2 to 3 medium shallots, sliced (about 1 cup), substitute onion

2 ounces (¹/₂ stick) unsalted butter

1 pound assorted sliced mushrooms, such as baby bella, shiitake, pleurottes, and button, trimmed and sliced

2 tablespoons chopped dill

¹/₄ cup chopped flat parsley

1 large egg lightly beaten with 2 tablespoons milk, for the egg wash

Divide the dough in half. Dust each half generously with flour, then roll out on a floured work surface about ³/₈-inch thick. Cut into 5-inch diameter circles. If desired, re-roll the scraps and cut into more circles. Chill the circles while preparing the filling.

In a medium bowl, mix together the kasha and 1 egg until the grains are well coated. Heat a medium skillet (with a lid) over moderate heat and add the egg-coated kasha. Toast the kasha, separating the grains with a fork, for about 4 minutes, or until the grains are separate and toasty-smelling. Add 2 cups cold water, cover, and bring to a boil. Lower the heat and simmer for 10 minutes, or until the kasha is fluffy. Remove from the heat, season to taste with salt and pepper, and reserve.

In a separate skillet over high heat, sauté the shallots in the butter for 2 to 3 minutes, until softened. Add the mushrooms and cook until the mushroom liquid evaporates, about 6 minutes. Remove from the heat, season to taste with salt and pepper, and combine with the kasha, dill, parsley, and remaining egg. Cool to room temperature before using.

Assemble and bake the knishes: Preheat the oven to 350°F. Spoon 2 heaping tablespoons of the filling into the center of each circle, leaving a 1-inch border all around. Brush the egg wash along the border. Fold up the edges, purse style, to completely enclose the filling, then turn seam side down. Brush with egg wash and poke a fork into each knish to make air holes. Arrange on baking pans lined with parchment paper or a silicone mat and bake for 35 minutes or until nicely browned and the filling is bubbling hot. Cool slightly before serving. Store the knishes refrigerated, up to 3 days. To reheat, wrap in foil and heat in a 350°F oven for 20 minutes or until the filling is thoroughly hot.

Ukrainian Buckwheat Rolls (Hrechanyky)

These easy-to-make rolls have a dark, dramatic look and a hearty, full-bodied earthy flavor because of the combination of buckwheat and whole wheat. At the same time, they're surprisingly light in texture. The rolls would work especially well as an accompaniment to Ukrainian beet borscht, mushroom-barley soup, or chunky vegetable soup.

YIELD: 24 ROLLS

1 ($^1/_4$-ounce) package ($2^1/_4$ teaspoons) active dry yeast

$^1/_2$ cup lukewarm milk

1 tablespoon honey

$^1/_4$ pound (1 cup minus 1 tablespoon) stone-ground buckwheat flour

$^1/_4$ pound (1 cup) unbleached bread flour

6 ounces ($1^1/_2$ cups) white whole wheat flour

1 teaspoon fine sea salt, plus extra for sprinkling

2 tablespoons unsalted butter, softened, plus extra for pan

1 large egg

Vegetable oil, for brushing

In the bowl of a standing electric mixer, dissolve the yeast in the milk and stir in the honey. Allow the mixture to proof at warm room temperature for about 15 minutes, or until bubbling and puffy.

Using the paddle attachment, beat in the flours and the salt. Switch to the dough hook and continue beating for 5 to 6 minutes, until the dough is smooth and elastic and comes away cleanly from the bowl. Add the butter and egg and continue beating until the dough is smooth again.

Transfer the dough to a large oiled bowl; turn around so the dough is oiled all over. Cover with plastic wrap or a damp cloth and allow the dough to rise at warm room temperature until nearly doubled in size, about 2 hours. (It will not rise as much as wheat dough.)

Line an 18 x 13-inch half sheet pan (or other large baking pan) with parchment paper or a silicone baking mat.

Knead the dough lightly on a floured board till smooth. Divide the dough into three portions and roll into three 12-inch long ropes. Arrange the ropes, 3 inches apart, on the baking sheet. Brush the dough lightly with oil and sprinkle with fine sea salt. Using a sharp knife, make deep cuts about $1^1/_2$ inches apart without cutting all the way through the dough, to create 8 rolls from each rope. Cover with a damp towel and allow the dough to rise at warm room temperature until almost doubled in size, about 2 hours.

Preheat the oven to 350°F. Bake the rolls for 20 minutes, brush with oil, then bake for another 10 minutes, or until the rolls sound hollow when tapped on the bottom and a thermometer inserted in the center reads 190°F to 205°F. Serve warm with butter. Store in an open plastic bag for up to 2 days at room temperature or wrap and freeze up to 3 months. To reheat, wrap in aluminum foil and bake at 350°F for about 15 minutes.

Seeded Multi-Grain Sourdough Bread

It took many tries to get the proportions just right on this dark and substantial seeded bread, including more than one that went right in the trash. However, the combination of white bread flour, buckwheat, dark rye, and white whole wheat flour that gives the dough its complex flavor made it well worth my efforts. You will need to have a batch ready of the Sourdough Bread Starter (page 880) to make the bread. Like most multi-grain breads, this one tastes even better when toasted in slices. Bake it in a French banneton basket for an artisan-style bread, mixing the seeds right into the dough, or bake in loaf pans coated with a layer of seeds for sandwich bread. This recipe is dairy-free.

YIELD: 2 MEDIUM LOAVES, ABOUT 1^1/$_2$ POUNDS EACH

Sponge

1 cup Sourdough Bread Starter (page 880)

1 (^{1}/$_4$-ounce) package (2^1/$_4$ teaspoons) active dry yeast

^{1}/$_4$ cup lukewarm water

2 tablespoons honey

^{1}/$_4$ pound (1 cup) unbleached bread flour

Dough

^{1}/$_4$ pound (1 cup minus 1 tablespoon) buckwheat flour

^{1}/$_4$ pound (1 cup minus 2 tablespoons) dark rye flour

^{1}/$_4$ pound (1 cup plus 2 tablespoons) white whole wheat flour

^{3}/$_4$ pound (3 cups) unbleached bread flour

1 tablespoon fine sea salt

1 cup lukewarm water

4 tablespoons mixed bread seeds, such as natural sesame, nigella, caraway, flax, millet, poppy, anise, cumin, fennel, and/or sunflower

Cornmeal or fine semolina, for dusting

Make the sponge: In a medium bowl, combine the Sourdough Bread Starter with the yeast, water, honey, and flour and allow to rise at warm room temperature for about 1 hour or until light and bubbling.

Make the dough: In a medium bowl, whisk together the dry ingredients: buckwheat flour, rye flour, whole wheat flour, bread flour, and salt.

Stir down the sponge and transfer to the bowl of a standing electric mixer. Using the paddle attachment, beat in the water and the flour mix. Continue to beat until the dough is smooth and elastic and comes away from the sides of the bowl, 4 to 5 minutes. (If the quantity is too much for your mixer, remove the dough from the mixer, divide it in half, and beat in half of the remaining flour into each half. Knead by hand to combine both halves until the dough is smooth and elastic.)

Transfer the dough to a large oiled bowl and turn it so it is oiled all over. Cover with plastic wrap or a damp cloth and allow the dough to rise until it nearly doubles, about 3 hours, at warm room temperature. (If desired, refrigerate overnight: the dough will continue to rise slowly.)

Punch down the dough. Prepare two medium (1^1/$_2$-pound, 9 x 5-inch) loaf pans by rubbing them with oil and sprinkling with 2 tablespoons of the mixed seeds. Divide the dough in half and roll each section out into a rectangle, about the same width as the pan. Roll the dough up tightly, like a jelly roll, and place the rolls seam side down in the pans. Brush the loaves with water and sprinkle generously with the remaining 2 tablespoons of seeds.

Using a French baker's lame, a single-edged razor, or a box cutter, cut several shallow slashes into the bread. Allow the loaf to rise at warm room temperature for about 3 hours, or until almost doubled in bulk.

Preheat the oven to 400°F. Spray the loaves with water from a water mister and bake for 30 minutes or until the bread is nicely browned and has shrunk away from the sides of the pan and a thermometer inserted in the center reads 200°-205°F. Remove from the pans and cool completely on a wire rack before slicing.

Alternatively, after punching down the dough, divide it in half and form into rounds. Brush with water and sprinkle with the seeds. Place in 2 French cane *banneton* baskets that have been dusted generously with flour. Allow the breads to rise at warm room temperature for about 3 hours, or until almost doubled in bulk.

Place a pizza stone into the oven to preheat at least 20 minutes before baking. When the breads have almost doubled in size, invert them onto the pizza stone, which has been lightly sprinkled with cornmeal. Bake for 35 minutes or until a thermometer inserted in the center reads 200° to 205°F. Remove from the baskets and cool completely on a wire rack before slicing. Store the breads at room temperature in a brown paper bag or an open plastic bag for up to 2 days or wrap and freeze up to 3 months.

Note: Oil your hands to make it easier to handle sticky doughs like this one.

BANNETON BREAD BASKETS

Known in German as a *brotform* and in French as a *banneton*, these coiled natural cane bread baskets are used to shape artisanal bread dough as it rises. Dusted generously with flour, the basket coils provide a beautiful shape and decorative pattern for a traditional hearth loaf. Buy them in different shapes and sizes from Fante's (www.fantes.com).

MIXED SEEDS FOR BREAD

The Baker's Catalogue (www.bakerscatalogue.com) sells a pre-mixed Artisan Bread Topping that is perfect for this bread. It includes flax seeds, sesame seeds, nigella seeds (black caraway), mini-sunflower seeds, poppy seeds, and aniseeds. For more exotic flavor, look for Panch Phoran in Indian groceries. *Panch Phoran*, meaning five seeds, is a seed spice mixture from Bengal, India, that combines black mustard seeds, nigella seeds, cumin seeds, fenugreek, and fennel seeds.

Apple–Date Buckwheat Muffins

With its dark, earthy nuttiness, buckwheat flour provides the underlying flavor for these fruity, not-too-sweet muffins, while chunky apples and syrupy-sweet dates add chewy texture. Like all muffins, once the liquid hits the dry ingredients, thereby activating the gluten in the flour, it is important to stir the mix as briefly as possible so the muffins are tender.

YIELD: 12 MEDIUM MUFFINS

$1/4$ pound (1 cup minus 1 tablespoon) unbleached
    all-purpose flour

$1/4$ pound (1 cup minus 1 tablespoon) buckwheat flour

1 teaspoon baking powder

$1/2$ teaspoon baking soda

$1/2$ teaspoon fine sea salt

$3/4$ cup sugar

1 cup buttermilk

$1/4$ cup canola oil

1 large egg, lightly beaten

2 medium apples, peeled, cored, and finely chopped,
    preferably Fuji

$1/2$ cup chopped, pitted dates

Preheat the oven to 375°F. In a large bowl, whisk together the dry ingredients: the flour, buckwheat flour, baking powder, baking soda, and salt.

In a medium bowl, whisk together the wet ingredients: the sugar, buttermilk, oil, and egg. In a small bowl, combine the apples and dates. Set aside about $1/2$ cup of this mixture to sprinkle on top of the muffins.

Gently fold the wet mixture into the dry mixture along with all but the reserved apples and dates, working the batter as little as possible. Divide the batter evenly among 12 muffin cups coated with cooking spray or lined with muffin papers, filling each cup about $1/2$-inch from the top. Sprinkle the muffin tops with the reserved apple-date mixture.

Bake for 20 minutes or until the muffins have started to come away from the sides of the pan and the centers are puffed. Remove from the oven, cool for 5 to 10 minutes, then remove the muffins from the baking tin. Cool to room temperature on a wire rack. Store covered and at room temperature for up to 2 days or wrap and freeze up to 3 months.

Buckwheat Cinnamon–Raisin Bread

In this recipe, warm and spicy cinnamon scents a slightly sweet, dark buckwheat bread, which works very well for the sweet and savory foods often served at brunch. The original recipe came from Chef Mark Miller of Coyote Café in Santa Fe and Red Sage in Washington, D.C. (now closed), whose imaginative and elaborate chile-spiked dishes helped put Southwest cuisine on the map. I adapted the recipes and added the raisins because this bread just seemed to cry out for these intense bits of fruity sweetness. Use dark or light raisins, according to your preference, or a combination. I buy large bags of Mariani brand mixed raisins, some-

times found at warehouse club stores, to use here.

YIELD: 2 LOAVES

1 ($^1/_4$-ounce) package (2$^1/_4$ teaspoons) active dry yeast

1$^3/_4$ cups lukewarm water

$^1/_2$ cup sugar

1$^1/_4$ pounds (5 cups) unbleached bread flour

$^1/_4$ pound (1 cup minus 1 tablespoon) buckwheat flour

$^1/_2$ cup dry milk powder or dry buttermilk powder

1 tablespoon ground cinnamon

2 teaspoons fine sea salt

$^3/_4$ pound (2$^1/_4$ cups) dark or golden raisins

Prepare two medium (1-pound, 8$^1/_2$ x 4$^1/_2$-inch) loaf pans by spraying with baker's nonstick coating or rubbing with butter and dusting with flour, shaking off the excess.

In the bowl of a standing electric mixer, dissolve the yeast in $^3/_4$ cup of the lukewarm water mixed with 1 tablespoon of the sugar. Allow the mixture to proof at warm room temperature for about 15 minutes, or until bubbling and puffy.

In the bowl of a standing electric mixer, whisk together the dry ingredients: the bread flour, buckwheat flour, dry milk powder, the remaining sugar, the cinnamon, and salt. Pour in the yeast mixture and the remaining water. Beat vigorously with the dough hook attachment for 8 to 10 minutes until the dough is silky and elastic and comes cleanly away from the sides of the bowl. Add the raisins and knead them into the dough by hand.

Place the dough in an oiled bowl and turn it around in the oil until it is well covered. Cover with plastic wrap and let the dough rise at warm room temperature for 2 hours, or until it doubles in volume. Punch down the dough and let it rise again for another hour or until it almost doubles in volume again.

Divide the dough in half and roll out each half into a rectangle. Roll the dough up the short way, like a jelly roll, and place into the prepared pans with the seam sides down. Mist the dough using a spray water mister, and cover lightly with plastic wrap. Cut shallow diagonal cuts in the top of each loaf with a French baker's lame, a single-edged razor, or a box cutter. Allow the breads to rise again until the dough reaches just over the lip of the pan, 30 to 40 minutes.

Preheat the oven to 400°F.

Bake for 40 minutes or until the crust is dark golden brown, the bottom of the loaf sounds hollow when tapped, and a thermometer inserted into the center reads 190°F. Cool the breads slightly, 5 to 10 minutes, then remove from the pans and cool completely on a wire rack. Store covered and at room temperature for up to 3 days. Freeze for up to 3 months.

BRUNCH WITH MARK MILLER

In the eighties, a very exciting time in the world of American culinary expression, I worked as the chef of Apropos Bistro, where San Francisco (then Santa Fe) restaurateur Mark Miller was our guest one year for the annual Book and Cook Festival. We served a Southwest-inspired brunch menu that started with Ramos Gin Fizz cocktails and green-chile laden Bloody Mary's, and went on to chile-cured salmon gravlax, and crab cakes with green chile chutney. Pan-fried red chile quail in cider sauce were served with Texas wild boar bacon and pumpkin pecan waffles topped red chile honey. Everything was accompanied by this bread.

Trying to get ahead with the crab cake prep, I made the mistake of thinly slicing several dozen bunches of green onions, mixing the green tops and the white bottoms, as I always do, so as not to waste any part. When Mr. Miller arrived, he informed me that he only ever used the green tops, so I had to laboriously pick out all the white parts one by one, having no more green onions in the house. My mistake didn't stop him from offering me a job, though I declined.

BUTTER & OTHER ANIMAL FATS

Bog Butter ...194

Smen ...194

Butter and Baking ...194

Butter in History ...195

Advantages and Disadvantages of Baking with Butter ...196

How Butter is Sold ...196

Storing Butter ...196

Baking with Butter in Hot Weather ...197

European and American Cultured Butter ...198

Comparing American and European-Style Butter ...198

Lard and Other Animal Fats ...198

Suet ...199

Buying Leaf Lard, Suet, and Poultry Fats ...200

Rendering Poultry Fat or Suet ...200

Tips for Working with Butter or Animal Fat-Based Pastry Dough ...201

Mixing Butter and Other Animal Fats ...201

Salted or Unsalted Butter ...201

CLARIFIED BUTTER ...202

BROWN BUTTER (BEURRE NOISETTE) ...202

Freezing and Thawing Butter ...203

Butter Temperature in Baking ...203

BUTTER PIE PASTRY ...203

LARD PIE DOUGH ...204

SUET MEAT PIE DOUGH ...204

SAVORY EMPANADA DOUGH ...205

Annatto Coloring ...206

SAVORY TART PASTRY ...206

TARTE TATIN PASTRY ...206

EXOTIC MUSHROOM PUFF PASTRY PILLOWS ...207

How Does Puff Pastry Puff? ...208

About Puff Pastry ...209

Working with Puff Pastry ...209

QUÉBÉÇOISE TOURTIÈRE WITH MUSHROOMS ...210

More about Tourtière ...211

CIGARI BOREKAS WITH MOROCCAN SPICED LAMB ...212

Yufka Dough ...213

STEAK, GUINNESS, AND MUSHROOM PIE ...215

Recommended Cuts for Steak and Mushroom Pie ...215

FINANCIERS ...215

Financier Molds ...216

GERMAN BUTTER CAKE (BUTTERKUCHE) ...216

More about German Butter Cake ...217

BISCOCHITOS ...218

Biscochito History ...209

BUTTER
& OTHER ANIMAL FATS

On my way back and forth to school as a young girl, I would often puzzle over the margarine advertisements over the windows in the city bus: "Just like the higher-priced spread," they said. What in the world did they mean? It took many years until I realized they meant butter! I was so accustomed to spreading sweet whipped butter on my toasted rye bread or challah, that using margarine as a substitute was an entirely new concept.

I use pure unsalted butter for most things I bake, avoiding hydrogenated shortening or margarine. Yes, it's high in calories, but I cook and bake with butter to get the most "bang for my buck." Nothing else tastes like butter, performs like butter, or holds flavor better than butter. That's why it's so indispensable to chefs. Butter is the secret ingredient of many a restaurant dish—I was taught to always finish a pan sauce with a large pat of butter, swirled in to make it shine, and to add endless quantities of butter to mashed potatoes and mashed yams.

In America and many other countries, we have been eating more margarine than butter since the 1950s, because it is cheaper and was believed to be healthier, until recent trans-fat health problems became known. Now, we know it's actually the other way around: butter is better. Plus, shortening and margarine are just as calorific as butter, and they don't have the innate richly subtle, mouth-melting quality of butter. If I'm going to indulge in a buttercream-iced cake, I want to make sure it's made from real butter. I won't waste my precious calories on the fake "butter-substitute" sold to bakeries because it's cheap, never spoils, and doesn't melt in hot weather.

Butter is made by churning fresh or soured cream or milk until the "butter comes": when small droplets of butterfat separate from the watery whey. It takes 21 pounds of cow's milk to make just one pound of butter. While Americans are mostly familiar with cow's milk butter, elsewhere, the milk of water buffalo, camel, goats, ewes, mares, and even donkeys are used to manufacture butters with distinct flavors. Rich-tasting sheep's milk butter is used in Greece and elsewhere in the Eastern Mediterranean to make pastries like baklava.

Butter is a rich natural food with a high energy value: 750 calories per 100 grams, or about 100 calories per tablespoon, less than oil or lard (because of the water content of butter), with higher-fat European-style butters like Plugra at 130 grams per tablespoon. Like other animal fats, butter is saturated, meaning that it is solid at room temperature.

Solid butter is an emulsion (just like mayonnaise, hollandaise, peanut butter, and even soap) consisting of butterfat surrounding tiny droplets of water and milk proteins, giving the butter a creamy, smooth consistency. You can make your own butter (on purpose or by accident) by beating heavy cream until the butterfat separates from the liquid whey. If you beat ice-cold cream, you'll end up with a bowl of light, white clouds. If the cream is on the warm side, or the day is hot and humid, you might very well end up with a clump of yellow butter floating in milky liquid instead. Drain off the buttermilk, and voilà! You have just created butter. When the cream is cold, the small globules of butterfat stay suspended in the milk. If the cream gets warm, the fat molecules start to clump together, separating out of its suspension in the cream.

The color of butter ranges from creamy white to deeper golden yellow depending on the cow's diet. Commercial American butter is blended, so seasonal and regional changes are much less noticeable. Yellow butter comes from milk from a cow eating a diet rich in carotene or by having natural annatto seed added (page 206).

Butter made from pasteurized fresh cream is called sweet cream butter. This type of butter first became common in the nineteenth century, with refrigeration and the mechanical cream separator.

In Europe, cultured butter made from slightly sour, ripened cream is preferred, while sweet cream butter is the standard in the United States and Great Britain. Spreadable whipped butter is aerated with nitrogen gas; using air would encourage oxidation and rancidity. Unsalted butter is not the same as sweet butter. In the past, butter was commonly made from soured milk, in order to extract a higher percentage of butterfat. Today, almost all of American butter, salted and unsalted, is made from sweet cream. With no salt to help preserve it and disguise any off flavors, the more perishable unsalted butter must be extremely fresh and of the highest quality. The best butter for baking will always be unsalted, because it allows the baker to control the amount of salt in the recipe.

Butter browns foods best and its toasted nut flavor is especially important when cooking blander foods like eggs, pancakes, or French toast. When cooking with butter, as the butter heats, and the temperature reaches the boiling point of water, the liquid vaporizes, causing the butter to sizzle. As the temperature continues to rise, the small amount of white foam (milk solids) in the butter will turn brown and nutty flavored. However, if the butter reaches too high a temperature, the brown bits will blacken and burn, making the whole dish taste bitter.

Brown butter (called beurre noisette or hazelnut butter in French) is a wonderful ingredient in baking, adding an extra underlying flavor tone of hazelnutty goodness (see the recipe on page 202).

In this book, the small, brick-shaped French Financiers on page 215 can't be made without it. The Red Banana–Brown Butter Bars on page 133, the Almond–Sour Cherry Torte with Brown Butter on page 303, the Hazelnut–Brown Butter Cakes with Bosc Pears on page 505, the Apple–Apricot Strudel (page 121), the untraditional but delicious Chocolate–Cherry Biscotti with Cocoa Nibs (page 305), and the Chestnut Cornbread (on page 318) all depend on brown butter for their special flavors.

Butter is incredibly versatile and can be a wonderful friend to the baker. Don't be afraid to live a little dangerously. Butter tastes so good because not only does it have its own great flavor, but, as every chef and baker knows, it is an excellent carrier of flavors: spices, vanilla, citrus zest, chocolate, and other fat soluble ingredients, dispersing their flavors throughout the dish.

SMEN

In Morocco and other parts of North Africa, *smen* enhances savory dishes, especially couscous. This traditional butter-based cooking fat is made from sheep and goat milk and has a highly pungent, even stinky, smell. Considered a delicacy and prized for its penetrating aroma, smen is made by kneading butter with herbs and spices like cinnamon, then cooked, salted, and strained. The smen is poured into jugs, tightly stoppered, and buried in the ground for months, even years, and brought out for special occasions. Ethiopia's spiced version of this butter product is called *nit'r k'ibe*. Similarly, in Lebanon, *samneh* is made from butter that has been boiled until the fat in the pan is as "clear as a tear" (*dam'at el-eyn*). It is then taken off the heat and left to settle before being carefully strained through a fine sieve into sealed containers where it will keep for a year or more.

BOG BUTTER

Across northern Europe—in Ireland, Scotland, Iceland, and Scandinavia—butter was packed into barrels and buried in peat bogs, sometimes for years. This "bog butter" would develop a strong flavor as it aged, but remain edible, because of the unique cool, airless, antiseptic, and acidic environment of the peat bog. Firkins (barrels) of such buried butter have been a common archaeological find in Ireland. The practice ended before the nineteenth century. Today, Ireland is a major producer of butter for export to the European Union countries, as is Denmark.

BUTTER AND BAKING

Cookie doughs and pound cake batters are leavened by beating butter and sugar together until they are light and fluffy from the air bubbles which have been beaten in. These tiny bubbles expand in the heat of the oven and lighten the cookie or cake. Shortbread cookies have no other liquid added but the water in the butter. Pastry doughs incorporate small pieces of solid fat into the dough, which become flat layers of fat when the dough is rolled out. During baking, the fat melts away, leaving a flaky texture.

BUTTER IN HISTORY

Because even accidental agitation can turn cream into butter, it is likely that butter dates back as far as the earliest dairying, probably in the Fertile Crescent about 10,000 years ago. The earliest butter would have been made from sheep's or goat's milk; cattle are not thought to have been domesticated until about one thousand years later. In an ancient method of butter making, still used today in some parts of Africa and the Near East, a goat skin is half filled with milk, then inflated with air and sealed. It is then hung on a tripod of sticks and agitated by rocking back and forth until the butter forms.

In India, ghee, or pure, clear butterfat, has been a symbol of purity and an offering to the gods for more than 3,000 years. It has been used both as a staple food and for ceremonial purposes such as fueling holy lamps and even funeral pyres. Today, India produces and consumes more butter than any other country and almost half of its annual milk production goes into making butter or ghee.

In the warm Mediterranean climate, whole, unclarified butter would spoil very quickly and was therefore not a good method of preserving milk. The people of ancient Greece and Rome considered butter an uncouth food fit only the northern barbarians. In the cold climates of northern Europe, butter would keep longer without spoiling and so the cooking of northern Europe is based on butter as its cooking fat.

Scandinavia has been exporting butter since at least the twelfth century. Starting in the 1850s, Danish butter was exported in large quantities packed in wooden casks to Great Britain. Today, that same Danish butter produced by more than 1,000 different dairies and now sold under the name Lurpak, is found around the world.

Across most of Europe through much of the Middle Ages, butter was a common food, but one with a low reputation; it was consumed principally by peasants. Butter slowly became more accepted by the upper class, especially when, in the early sixteenth century, the Roman Catholic Church permitted its consumption during the forty days of fasting during Lent. Bread and butter became common fare among the new middle class. My favorite after-school snack when I lived in butter-rich Holland was a thick slice of white bread slathered with sweet butter and sprinkled generously with chocolate sprinkles: this treat was to be cut up and eaten with a knife and fork only, at least for the Dutch!

The Normans first popularized butter making, from methods learned from the Danes to whom dairying was long central to survival, and by the Middle Ages, butter production had become common in this Atlantic Coastal region. Normandy is still the center for the best butter in France, which is made from ripened cream, giving it a distinctive full flavor and ultra-smooth texture. This type of butter is known as cultured butter.

By the 1860s, butter was in such high demand

in France that Emperor Napoleon III offered a prize for anyone who could develop an inexpensive substitute. In 1869, a French chemist claimed the prize with the invention of margarine, originally made from beef tallow (fat) flavored with milk and worked like butter till smooth and creamy. Once hydrogenated oils (oils or fats that have been chemically altered so they are solid at room temperature) were developed around 1900, vegetable-based margarines soon followed.

ADVANTAGES & DISADVANTAGES OF BAKING WITH BUTTER

Shortening is much less expensive than butter and easier to work with because it keeps its consistency through a wide range of temperatures. Working with shortening and lard crusts enables the baker to make fancy decorations that will keep their shape in the oven without melting away. However, the all-important flavor is missing. Also, because shortening and lard are 100 percent fat, it is much easier to make a flaky, tender crust.

An alternative is to use clarified butter (see the recipe on page 202) instead of whole butter for the crust. This will result in a very flaky crust, but unfortunately, one that has less flavor, because much of the flavor in butter is contained in the milk solid bits that are removed when clarifying. That magical ingredient, brown butter (page 202), can also be used to make pastry, which has the advantage of good flavor and texture.

(see the recipe on page 202)

HOW BUTTER IS SOLD

In the United States, butter for home use has been sold in easy-to-measure quarter-pound sticks, wrapped in wax paper and packed four to a carton for the last one hundred years. One pound blocks called "prints" and larger blocks of butter are still available for commercial use. On the East Coast, long, thin sticks of butter called Elgin-pack are most common; on the West Coast, short, fat sticks of butter called Western-pack are most common, but both are packed in one pound packages.

STORING BUTTER

Butter absorbs flavors and odors easily, so keep it tightly covered and away from strong smells. Butter freezes especially well, but because it's so absorbent, the butter will taste unpleasantly "freezer-burned" if not protected from exposure to air while frozen. Store butter in the refrigerator at or below 40°F for up to one month; freeze up to four months at 20° to 30°F. I recommend the unsalted butter sold by Land-o-Lakes that is wrapped in a special layered paper that protects the butter from unwanted odors and flavors. Plugra and other European-style butters are generally wrapped in paper-lined foil, to protect it from odors.

BAKING WITH BUTTER
IN HOT WEATHER

Butter is more difficult to work with than shortening because of its low melting point and its changeable texture. Especially in hot weather, pastry cooks chill all their ingredients and utensils while working with a butter dough. Making pastry with butter is its own challenge. Because it's temperamental, costs more, and is vulnerable to spoilage, many commercial bakeries don't touch the stuff, relying on inert shortening with all that trans-fat we've been hearing about instead. No trouble, but no flavor.

Because I've always been a purist, I've learned to work with butter. It didn't come easily. When I first went to work at the old Garden Restaurant in 1977, I believed that I should be able to do everything or else I wouldn't be a "real chef." Hired in the height of summer, I proclaimed that I knew how to make puff pastry dough. Pastry chefs make this "laminated" dough by rolling out butter between layers of pastry dough, then turning, folding it into three or four layers, and rolling again. (At least they used to make it; most pastry chefs buy their puff pastry these days.) Each folding and rolling out is called a "turn." Traditionally, the number of "turns" is six, so the dough will have anywhere from 729 to 16,384 layers!

The only problem is you can't make puff pastry in a hot kitchen. Assigned to the stairwell of the sweating-hot basement kitchen, I tried anyway. The butter kept breaking out of holes in the dough, getting greasier and slipperier by the minute as I struggled. Without refrigeration for the dough or air-conditioning for both of us, I was attempting an almost impossible task. I didn't know enough to realize that my failure wasn't just due to my lack of experience.

Later I learned to make wonderful all-butter croissants by the five and six hundred while working as sous chef at the Barclay Hotel on Philadelphia's Rittenhouse Square. I would roll out endless batches of croissants, working all day in a forty-degree walk-in refrigerator so everything would stay cold, including me. Such dedication! But the croissants were the best I've ever tasted. Today, in summertime, when I make pastry dough, I combine the dry ingredients and the butter bits in a metal mixing bowl and freeze it for at least 30 minutes until the butter is firm but not rock-hard before mixing the dough.

In another major butter challenge, while working at Apropos in the 1980s, I was hired by a bride and groom to make a wedding cake. I made the most beautiful cake in the classic three tiers, filled and covered with a French vanilla buttercream tinted a lovely shade of natural green with chlorophyll derived from spinach (see the recipe on page 699) and decorated with fresh wild strawberries I snagged from a local farmer. Unfortunately, the wedding was to be held outside, the weather was hot, and the cake started to melt. I got an emergency call from the caterer and went out to rescue my cake, armed with more chilled buttercream and lots of strawberries and fresh leaves to cover any gloopy parts. I certainly learned from that experience! Today, when I ice a cake with buttercream, I make sure that the cake itself is cold (not just at room temperature) so the buttercream doesn't melt.

EUROPEAN AND AMERICAN CULTURED BUTTER

In Brittany, France, milk is allowed to ripen by the natural, lactic bacteria it contains, turning it into cultured cream, crème fraîche, which is in turn, churned into what is known as cultured butter. When cream ferments or "sours," the bacteria convert milk sugars into lactic acid and produce other aroma compounds, including diacetyl (the same ingredient used to make "butter-flavored" popcorn), which makes for a fuller-flavored, richer butter.

Today, cultured butter is usually made from pasteurized cream where fermentation is produced by the introduction of friendly bacteria. Butter may also be cultured in a kind of short-cut method by combining butter with bacterial cultures and lactic acid and then aging the butter in cold storage to develop the flavors more fully. French-style cultured butter with 86 percent butterfat content is produced by the Vermont Butter and Cheese Company (www.vtbutterandcheeseco.com) and available at Whole Foods and other specialty markets.

COMPARING AMERICAN AND EUROPEAN-STYLE BUTTER

European-style butter is higher in fat than American-style butter, which yields lighter, flakier pastry and cakes that rise higher. American butter is about 80 percent clear yellow butterfat, 18 percent water, and 2 percent milk solids; European butters and European-style butter (like Plugra) contain up to 86 percent butterfat and that much less moisture. For the same reason, it doesn't burn as easily, so you can cook at higher heat.

Although more expensive, European-style premium unsalted butter will yield cookies that are especially flavorful. I admit that I rarely use this butter for baking because of its higher price, particularly when I had to test hundreds of recipes, all of them made two, three, or even four times to perfect the recipes. If you're going to choose one place to get the most from European-style butter, reserve it for making pastry dough to produce a crust that is flakier, more tender, with better nutty flavor and less shrinkage than regular butter. Plugra, American-made European-style butter, is sold at Trader Joe's, Whole Foods, and many supermarkets including Acme and Wegman's in the Northeast.

LARD AND OTHER ANIMAL FATS

Fats from ruminant animals or those that chew their cud (cattle, sheep, and even goats) are more saturated, and harder than pork fat (lard) or poultry fat (duck, goose, or chicken fat). Beef suet, from the area surrounding the kidneys, is the hardest cooking fat; pork fat from the kidney area, known as leaf lard, is a bit softer but still quite firm. Poultry fats are softer and will be semi-liquid at room temperature.

Keep in mind that animal fats (other than butters made from milk) are almost entirely pure fat as compared to butter which contains anywhere from 15 to about 20 percent liquid and milk solids. Therefore, when substituting, you will need about 20 percent less fat to achieve the same shortening power in the dough.

The harder the fat, the crisper the pastry (the same holds true for deep-frying). Piecrusts made with lard have lighter, flakier crusts than those made with other fats. Because it has a higher melting point, the dough has time to rise higher before the fat melts out. Lard yields a puffy, flaky piecrust with a richness to the flavor that really satisfies. There is nothing like lard for tenderness and flakiness. Rolled-out shortbread-like cookies made from lard, like the Mexican Biscochitos (page 218), will be more tender and will keep their shape perfectly when baked.

Lard started to disappear from grocery store shelves after 1911, when Procter & Gamble released Crisco, hydrogenated vegetable shortening. By the mid-1930s, vegetable shortening had pretty much taken over. Even now, almost one hundred years later, lard is just starting to see a comeback, as people search for that elusive combination of flavor and flakiness in a piecrust that is unobtainable from shortening. With recent health scares about the trans fats contained in shortening, it turns out that lard is not so bad for us after all, and in fact contains less saturated fats than butter. Now a new generation of trans-fat-free all-vegetable cooking products is hitting the market, which may be less dangerous to your health, but still don't have the intrinsic good flavor of animal fats.

Lard goes into the pastry for the Québécoise Tourtière (page 210), the Quebec Maple Syrup Pie (page 555), the Pennsylvania Dutch Corn Pie (page 387), and the 'mpanatigghi Siciliano (page 331). The flaky pastry for the fruit and nut-filled Cuccidati (page 457) is made with lard while the Sardinian Sebadas (page 517) are, ideally, fried in lard for crispness and extra flavor.

Suet

Suet is the hard fat that surrounds the loins and kidneys in beef cattle and mutton, equivalent to pork leaf lard. In the United States, beef fat (or in England, also mutton fat), that is melted and strained before use is called suet. Like all animal fats, suet is saturated and solid at room temperature. Suet does add a savory depth of flavor to hearty meat-based pies like the Québécoise Tourtière with Mushrooms (page 210) and the Steak, Guinness, and Mushroom Pie (page 213).

Suet is the fat of choice in Great Britain for savory pies, steamed puddings, and for frying the crispiest fish and chips. Today, suet is often substituted there by "vegetarian suet," equivalent to American shortening. Although suet does not have a particularly meaty flavor, it does have a richness and character not found in shortening, which is essentially completely bland.

BUYING LEAF LARD, SUET, AND POULTRY FATS

Excellent-quality rendered leaf lard can be purchased at a reasonable price by mail order from Dietrich's Meats, (610) 756-6344, www.dietrichsmeats.com. Order at least 5 pounds and keep it in the freezer, defrosting overnight in the refrigerator as necessary.

Rendered duck fat is available online at www.dartagnan.com. Rendered chicken fat can sometimes be found at Jewish butcher shops. Empire Kosher Chicken Company sells rendered chicken fat in one-pound containers. Look for it in markets that have a large kosher clientele (or special order it from any market that carries Empire Products). It is also sold in bulk for food service use.

Manteca and Snowcap are both commercial brands of lard that have been hydrogenated to make them last longer. They may be found in the baking aisle of many supermarkets, especially those with an African-American, Mexican, or Caribbean clientele. While processed lard will work well in these recipes, it is not nearly as flavorful as the pure rendered lard sold by Dietrich's and other country stores. Note that the "meaty" aroma of fresh rendered lard disappears in baking. Order Manteca brand lard online from www.texmex.net. It is stable at room temperature and doesn't need refrigeration.

To find suet in America (other than the unrefined inedible type sold for bird-feeders), you'll need a friendly butcher to sell you the unrendered hard fat itself, or if you're lucky, the rendered suet. Render at home, following the directions on this page.

RENDERING POULTRY FAT OR SUET

For chicken fat, use the firm fat that can be pulled out from inside the body cavity. For duck and goose fat, also use the white fat that lies under the skin of the breast.

To render suet, chicken, duck, or goose fat, freeze the fat and connective tissue until quite firm. Grate on the large grating plate of a food processor or the large-holed side of a box grater or chop very finely. Place the fat in a heavy-bottomed pot (such as a cast-iron Dutch oven or chicken fryer, or a Creuset or other enameled cast-iron pot) along with just enough water to just cover the bottom of the pot. Set on the lowest heat and cook for several hours, stirring occasionally. Alternatively, bring the liquid to the boil on top of the stove, then cover and place the pot, covered, in a 250°F oven.

Cook as slowly as possible, stirring occasionally, until all the liquid has boiled away and the contents of the pot start to crackle, a sign that the liquid has cooked away. Once no water is left, the suet (or other fat) will quickly burn, so keep a careful watch on it. Continue cooking until the cracklings (the small pieces of tissue left after rendering out the fat) brown lightly and the temperature reaches 220°F. Carefully continue cooking until the fat is completely clear and the bits of cracklings are lightly browned (under 225°F).

Remove from the heat and, while still hot, strain through a French fine woven wire chinoise or a sieve lined with cheesecloth, without pressing the mixture.

Cool, and then pour the strained fat into jars or other containers and cool to room temperature. Or, pour into muffin tins or mini loaf pans and chill until solid, then remove from molds and wrap tightly in plastic wrap. Store frozen for up to three months or refrigerated for up to two months.

TIPS FOR WORKING WITH BUTTER OR ANIMAL FAT-BASED PASTRY DOUGH

- Keep everything as cold as possible when making the dough for a flakier, lighter crust. Chill the flour mixture and the butter or fat cut into bits in the freezer for 30 minutes before beating.
- The less you handle the dough, the flakier and more tender it will be. Use only enough water or other liquid for the dough to form a ball. Grab a clump of dough and press it together. If it holds well, you have added enough water. Note that for pure fats like lard and suet, add the whole water amount called for in the recipe, as this fat-based dough needs more water than usual.
- Pat the dough into a flattened round, then chill to relax the gluten in the flour before rolling.
- If the dough is really cold, hard, and difficult to roll out, bang it with the rolling pin to make wave-like ridges in one direction, then turn 90 degrees and bang again to make more ridges before continuing with rolling.
- Use a minimum of extra flour when rolling out dough, or roll between 2 sheets of lightly floured

wax paper, which works especially well for sticky doughs containing eggs and sugar. Roll the dough from the center out, lifting the pin after each roll and turning the round a quarter turn after each round of rolling to obtain an even circle of dough.
- Flip the dough over once or twice to ensure that it is not sticking to the work board.
- When baking a juicy fruit-filled pie, start with the oven at 425°F and bake for 15 minutes on the bottom shelf of the oven. Reduce oven temperature to 350°F and continue baking until well browned.

Mixing Butter and Other Animal Fats

A mixture of three-quarters butter and one-quarter animal fat makes for a crust with a pleasing savory taste and flaky texture: duck fat, pure rendered pork leaf lard, rendered chicken fat, goose fat, or beef suet can all be combined with butter.

SALTED OR UNSALTED BUTTER

Like most chefs, I prefer to use unsalted butter. One: because unsalted butter is necessarily fresher, because salt acts as a preservative. Two: because I want to control the amount of salt I add to a dish. If you do use salted butter, be sure to eliminate the salt from the recipe.

Clarified Butter

Clarified butter is butter with virtually all of the water and milk solids removed, leaving pure clear yellow butterfat. Clarified butter is made by heating butter slowly until it melts and separates into layers of butterfat and whey. It's easier to make in larger quantities, so start with at least 2 pounds of butter. Once clarified, the butter will keep indefinitely in the refrigerator (many people leave it at room temperature, which works fine as long as the butter doesn't have any water or impurities left at all.) I keep the tasty milky bits and solids to add to mashed potatoes and other creamy dishes.

YIELD: 3$\frac{1}{2}$ CUPS

2 pounds (8 sticks) unsalted butter, softened

Place the butter in a large Pyrex measuring cup or a bowl. Melt for about 2 minutes on medium power in the microwave, or until the layers separate. Heat 1 to 2 minutes longer if the butter hasn't completely melted. Alternatively, place the butter in a medium heavy-bottomed pot and melt over lowest heat. Keep in mind that if the butter gets too hot, it will bubble up rather than separating, so be conservative with the timing.

Once melted, skim off the flavorful white foam on top, saving it to stir into mashed potatoes or add to a cream soup. Ladle out the clear butterfat into one container. Pour the remainder into a separate container. Refrigerate both containers to solidify, several hours or overnight.

The first container, full of pure butterfat, will solidify into a grainy, yellow pure butterfat solid. In the second container, the liquid portion will remain on the bottom, while the butterfat will solidify above. Remove this solid butter, rinsing off the bottom layer under cold water to remove off any milky residues. Combine with the two portions of pure butterfat and store refrigerated for up to 3 months, reheating as needed.

Brown Butter (Beurre Noisette)

This favorite in the French kitchen is butter which is cooked after the water has evaporated so the milk solids turn brown and nutty. It is known in French as beurre noisette, *or hazelnut butter, because of its toasted nut aroma. Once cooked, the butter will keep quite well because all the water is gone and the fat that remains is quite stable.*

YIELD: 1$\frac{1}{4}$ CUPS

$\frac{3}{4}$ pound (3 sticks) unsalted butter

Melt the butter in a small, heavy-bottomed pan over low heat, then raise the heat to medium and continue cooking until all the water cooks away and the milk solids on the bottom of the pan turn medium-brown in color and nutty-smelling. The butterfat will just be starting to color. Note that when butter starts to brown, it browns quickly, so watch carefully. Remove from the heat, pour off the browned butterfat into a container, leaving behind the small browned bits. Store refrigerated for up to 2 months.

FREEZING AND THAWING BUTTER

Freezing is the best way to store butter. Just make sure the butter is well-wrapped so it doesn't pick up unwanted refrigerator or freezer odors. Thaw in the refrigerator for even consistency. You may thaw at room temperature, but the inside of the butter may still be frozen when the outside is already soft.

BUTTER TEMPERATURE IN BAKING

Butter melts between 82.4°F and 96.8°F. For creaming butter in cakes and cookies, where you want the butter to beat up light and fluffy, leave the butter to soften at room temperature about 30 minutes. For pastry, where you want the butter to stay in separate bits to make the pastry flaky, cut up the butter and freeze until firm; alternatively, grate frozen butter using a large grate. Always melt butter slowly, so it doesn't burn.

Butter Pie Pastry

This all-butter pie pastry comes out perfectly if made in a food processor, though you will need one with a relatively large capacity to make the full batch here. Alternatively, make the dough using an electric mixer or cut the butter in by hand. The key is that everything stays cold to prevent the development of toughening gluten, so I use ice water, adding only enough water so the dough is moist and just holds together. Substitute up to 25 percent (3 ounces) well-chilled transfat-free shortening, lard, beef suet, duck fat, or nut butter, such as hazelnut or almond butter, for the butter. The small amount of vinegar helps keep the pastry tender. If you are making this on a hot day, chill the flour in the freezer for 30 minutes.

YIELD: ABOUT 1½ POUNDS, ENOUGH FOR ONE 9-INCH PIE CRUST AND ONE 8-INCH PIE CRUST

¾ pound (2¾ cups plus 1 tablespoon) unbleached
    all-purpose flour
1 teaspoon fine sea salt
½ pound (2 sticks) unsalted butter,
    preferably high-fat, European-style butter
    such as Plugra, cut into bits and frozen
6 tablespoons ice water
1 teaspoon cider vinegar

Place the flour and salt in the bowl of a standing electric mixer and whisk together to combine. Add the butter and freeze in the bowl for about 30 minutes or until the mixture is quite cold but the butter is still malleable. Alternatively, freeze the butter for 30 minutes, then place the flour, salt, and butter in a food processor and proceed.

Using the paddle attachment, beat until the mixture resembles oatmeal. In a small bowl, combine the ice water and vinegar. While the mixer is running, drizzle in the water mixture and beat just until the mixture forms large clumps. (To see if the dough is moist enough, press a clump of dough between your fingers; if it sticks together, it is ready; if it crumbles, add a bit more water, kneading as little as possible so the dough doesn't toughen.)

Knead briefly to form a smooth ball. Divide the dough in half, transfer each to a plastic bag, and shape into a flattened rectangle or circle. Chill in the refrigerator for 1 hour or in the freezer for 30 minutes until firm before rolling out as desired, or freeze up to 3 months.

Lard Pie Dough

Use this rich and tender dough for savory pies like the Pennsylvania Dutch Corn Pie (page 387), the Québéçoise Tourtière (page 210), and the Maple Syrup Pie with Walnuts (page 555). Substitute duck fat, goose fat, or even rendered chicken fat for up to 25 percent of the fat or combine equal parts of lard and butter.

YIELD: 1¼ POUNDS DOUGH, ENOUGH FOR A TWO-CRUST PIE

³⁄₄ pound (2³⁄₄ cups plus 1 tablespoon) unbleached
    all-purpose flour
1 teaspoon fine sea salt
6 ounces (1¹⁄₂ cups) pure rendered leaf lard, chilled
6 tablespoons ice water

Place the flour and salt in the bowl of a food processor and process briefly to combine. Add half the lard and process until the mixture resembles oatmeal. Add the remaining lard and process again until the mixture resembles oatmeal.

With the motor running, sprinkle in the ice water a little at a time, adding just enough to moisten the dough so it comes together to form large clumps. To see if the dough is moist enough, press a clump of dough between your fingers; if it sticks together, it is ready; if it crumbles, add a bit more water, working as little as possible.

Remove from the processor and knead briefly until the dough comes together into a smooth ball. Transfer to a plastic bag and shape into a flattened rectangle. Chill in the refrigerator for 1 hour or in the freezer for 30 minutes until firm but still malleable before rolling out as desired.

Suet Meat Pie Dough

This tender, flaky dough is made with baking powder for lightness, and egg yolk for smooth texture and a bit of strength. Beef suet gives it is hearty, subtly meaty flavor and wonderful texture as does lard, which may be substituted. Use the dough for the Steak, Guinness, and Mushroom Pie (page 213) or the Pennsylvania Dutch Corn Pie (page 387), or for the topping for a chicken, beef, or turkey pot pie.

YIELD: 1¹⁄₄ POUNDS DOUGH, ENOUGH FOR A 2-CRUST PIE

10 ounces (2¹⁄₂ cups minus 2¹⁄₂ tablespoons)

unbleached all-purpose flour

1 teaspoon baking powder

1 teaspoon fine sea salt

1/4 teaspoon freshly ground black pepper

6 ounces finely shredded and chilled beef suet,
 rendered lard, or trans fat-free shortening
 (or a combination)

3 tablespoons ice water

3 large egg yolks

Whisk together the dry ingredients: flour, baking powder, salt, and pepper and place in the bowl of a food processor. Add the suet and process briefly until the mixture resembles oatmeal.

Combine the water and egg yolks, add to the processor, and process only long enough for the dough to come together to form large clumps. Leave the dough to rest for 5 minutes, then knead briefly to combine into a ball. Transfer to a plastic bag and shape into a flattened rectangle. Chill in the refrigerator for 1 hour or in the freezer for 30 minutes until firm but still malleable before rolling out as desired.

Savory Empanada Dough

This super-flaky dough is easy to work with and quite stretchable. The egg keeps it from getting soggy when filled, while a pleasing tint of orange from natural ground annatto seed gives it eye-appealing color. Note: You may substitute trans fat-free vegetable shortening (such as the kind now produced by Crisco) for lard for similar texture but less flavor.

1¹/₄ pounds (4³/₄ cups minus 1 tablespoon) unbleached
 all-purpose flour

2 teaspoons baking powder

1 teaspoon fine sea salt

1/2 teaspoon annatto powder, optional (for color)

6 ounces (³/₄ cup) pure rendered leaf lard, cut into bits
 and chilled, substitute trans fat-free shortening

6 ounces (1¹/₂ sticks) unsalted butter, cut into bits
 and chilled

1 large egg

1/2 cup ice water

Combine the flour, baking powder, salt and, annatto powder in the bowl of a food processor fitted with the steel blade. Add the lard and butter, and pulse until the mixture is the texture of oatmeal.

In a small bowl, combine the egg and water. With the processor running, slowly add the water mixture, beating just long enough for the mixture to form moist clumps that hold together when pressed. Remove from the processor and knead briefly until the dough comes together into a smooth ball. Transfer to a plastic bag and shape into a flattened rectangle. Chill in the refrigerator for 1 hour or in the freezer for 30 minutes until firm but still malleable before rolling out as desired.

Savory Tart Pastry

This seasoned dough comes out perfect when made in a food processor and is a bit sturdier because of the added egg, making it well suited to savory tarts and quiches that have liquidy filling. Omit the cayenne pepper if you use the dough for a sweet tart or pie.

YIELD: 1½ POUNDS DOUGH, ENOUGH FOR TWO 10- TO 11-INCH TART CRUSTS

¾ pound (2¾ cups plus 1 tablespoon) unbleached all-purpose flour

1 teaspoon fine sea salt

1 teaspoon freshly grated nutmeg

½ teaspoon cayenne pepper

½ pound (2 sticks) unsalted butter, cut into bits and chilled

2 large eggs

¼ cup ice water

Place the dry ingredients: flour, salt, nutmeg, and cayenne in a metal bowl and whisk together to combine. Add the butter bits and freeze in the bowl for about 30 minutes or until the mixture is quite cold but the butter is still malleable. Transfer to the bowl of a food processor and pulse until the mixture resembles oatmeal.

In a small bowl, whisk together the eggs and ice water. With the food processor running, pour in the egg mixture and pulse until the dough just comes together. Take a small handful of dough into your hands and press it together. If it is crumbly, add 1 tablespoon additional water and pulse quickly to blend together. Remove from the processor and knead briefly until the dough comes together into a smooth ball. Transfer to a plastic bag, flatten to form a fairly uniform rectangle, and refrigerate to relax the gluten, for at least 1 hour, or until firm before rolling out as desired.

Tarte Tatin Pastry

This light, flaky, fragrant, and slightly sweet dough is perfectly paired with upside-down tarts, such as the Peach and Apricot Tarte Tatin on page 616 and the Quince-Cranberry Tarte Tatin on page 753. Substitute lemon or tangerine zest for the orange zest if desired.

YIELD: 1 POUND DOUGH, ENOUGH FOR 1 TART

½ pound (2 cups minus 2 tablespoons) unbleached all-purpose flour

2 tablespoons sugar

2 teaspoons grated orange zest

½ teaspoon baking powder

½ teaspoon fine sea salt

6 ounces (1½ sticks) unsalted butter, cut into bits and chilled

3 tablespoons ice water

2 teaspoons cider vinegar

Combine the dry ingredients: flour, sugar, zest, baking powder, and salt in the bowl of a food processor. Add the butter and process until the mixture resembles oatmeal.

Combine the water and the vinegar, pour into the processor, and process again just long enough for the dough to form moist clumps. Remove the dough from the processor and knead briefly until it comes together into a smooth ball. Transfer the dough to a plastic bag and shape into a flattened rectangle. Chill in the refrigerator for 1 hour or in the freezer for 30 minutes before using, until firm but still malleable, or freeze for up to 3 months, defrosting in the refrigerator before using.

Exotic Mushroom Puff Pastry Pillows

Next time you really want to impress your guests, serve these fancy mushroom-filled puff pastry pillows. It's amazing how a simple sheet of puff pastry can turn an ordinary dish into a show-stopping centerpiece.

However, as I well know, homemade puff pastry is a labor-intensive process, which can take up to several days to complete. Today's home cook has the benefit of frozen puff pastry, although most popular brands are made with shortening, rather than the all-important butter. I use only all-butter puff pastry and find the kind made by Dufour (the same kind used in many top restaurants) in the freezer section at my local Whole Foods store. Go to www.dufourpastrykitchens.com for information about distribution. For the mushrooms in this recipe, feel free to use a nice variety, including ½ cup each of Shiitake, Black Trumpet, Hen of the Woods, Crimini, Morels, Hedgehog, Oyster mushrooms, Chanterelle, and Porcini.

YIELD: 12 APPETIZER SERVINGS; 8 MAIN COURSE SERVINGS

1 (14-ounce) package all-butter puff pastry sheets, defrosted in the refrigerator but well-chilled

1 large egg

¾ cup crème fraîche

2 ounces (½ stick) unsalted butter

1 to 2 large shallots, minced (¼ cup)

2 pounds assorted wild and exotic mushrooms, cleaned, trimmed, and sliced

¼ cup Madeira, substitute dry Marsala or dry Sherry

2 tablespoons fresh lemon juice

3 tablespoons (1 tablespoon each) chopped fresh herbs, such as chives, thyme, marjoram, chervil, sage, savory, and/or flat-leaf parsley

Salt and freshly ground black pepper

¼ teaspoon cayenne pepper

Unroll the pastry onto an 18 x 13-inch half sheet pan (or other large baking pan) lined with parchment paper or a silicone mat. Freeze for 20 minutes or until the dough is firm and cold, but not brittle.

Beat the egg with 1 tablespoon of the crème fraîche. Brush the pastry with the egg mixture, then chill again for about 20 minutes or until the glaze has set and the dough is firm and hard, but not brittle.

Transfer the pastry to a cutting board. Using a sharp knife, trim the edges of the pastry sheet so they are clean and straight. Cut the pastry into 8 rectangles or 12 squares. Arrange the pastry rectangles onto the baking pan and chill again for 20 minutes, or until firm. (The repeated chilling helps yield light, flaky, high-rising puff pastry that will hold its shape well.)

Preheat the oven to 375°F. Using a French baker's lame, a single-edged razor, or a box cutter, cut shallow scores in a decorative pattern on top of the pastry. Bake for 25 minutes or until the pastry is well browned and puffed-up.

Melt the butter in a large heavy-bottomed skillet, add the shallots, and cook slowly until translucent, about 4 minutes. Add the mushrooms, toss to combine, then cook for 10 to 12 minutes over high heat stirring occasionally, or until the liquid has evaporated. Add the Madeira and lemon juice and cook together over high heat for 3 to 4 minutes to allow the mushrooms to absorb the liquid. Add the remaining crème fraîche and cook for about 10 minutes, or until the mixture thickens and large bubbles appear to cover the surface of the sauce. Stir in the herbs and season to taste with salt, pepper, and cayenne.

Remove the pastry from the oven and allow to cool slightly. Using a serrated knife, slice off the tops and reserve both tops and bottoms. Remove any soft uncooked pastry dough from inside the bottom portion of the rectangles and discard. Arrange the pastry bottoms on heated serving plates. Spoon the filling into the bottoms, allowing some to spill out over the sides. Cover each portion with a pastry top and serve immediately.

HOW DOES PUFF PASTRY PUFF?

The key to using puff pastry is knowing what it is and how it works. There are four main ingredients: flour, butter, salt, and water. Since there is no leavener, what makes it rise up so high and fluffy? It's the way these four ingredients are combined and their reaction. A simple dough is made, which usually includes butter. The dough is then rolled around a thick slab of butter. Through a process of folding, turning, and rolling, the butter is dispersed throughout the dough creating hundreds of very thin layers of dough separated by a film of butter.

When the pastry is heated, the butter melts and boils, creating steam which lifts the successive layers of dough higher and higher. At the same time, the heat is gelatinizing the flour, hardening it around those minute air pockets, creating the puff. Properly made, stored, and cut puff pastry will expand to six or eight times its original height.

The pastry dough used in the Danish Pastry Braid with Goat Cheese and Cardamom (page 273), is made the same way, using an egg-enriched, sugar-sweetened yeast dough laminated with butter. The closely related croissant dough is made from unsweetened butter—enriched yeast dough laminated with more butter.

ABOUT PUFF PASTRY

Puff pastry, which is laminated or layered dough, was an invention of Renaissance cooks and probably perfected by the skilled pastry chefs at the courts of the dukes of Tuscany around the fifteenth century. It is thought that the pastry was brought to the royal court of France by Marie de Medici, wife of King Henry the Fourth. By the early seventeenth century, the term *puff paste* was standard in English cookbooks. Known as *pâte feuilletée* (or leaf pastry) in France, the simple but airy dough is used in many French appetizers, hors d'oeuvre, and desserts, including turnovers, en croûte dishes, beef Wellington, bouchées, vol-au-vents, Napoleons, palmiers, croissants, allumettes, turnovers, and pithiviers.

WORKING WITH PUFF PASTRY

Avoid making puff pastry on a hot, humid day, as the layers won't rise properly. Always thaw frozen puff pastry in the refrigerator to keep the layers from gluing together.

When working with puff pastry, keeping it cold is crucial so the butter stays firm and the layers stay separate. Work quickly with one piece at a time and keep the rest covered with plastic wrap in the refrigerator. Tools and room temperature should also be kept cold. Rolling the dough out on a chilled marble board will make it easier, although I get good results rolling it on my wood counter.

Puff pastry relies on heat for lift, so preheat the oven to the desired temperature 15 to 20 minutes before you plan on using it.

To cut the edges cleanly so the laminated leaves of pastry can puff up properly, the dough must be very cold, though not frozen and brittle. Pastry that is too cold will shatter when cut; pastry that is just firm and hard enough can be sliced with a sharp knife right through the layers, without mashing them together. Use a very sharp, hot knife or a pastry/pizza wheel and be sure to cut straight down and not at an angle. After you cut puff pastry, the side that was up when you cut should be down on the baking pan.

Save any scraps for other uses such as cookies, appetizer crisps, or decorations, but do not mash them together. Instead, piece the scraps together like a jig-saw puzzle, keeping horizontal and chilling again if the dough gets at all soft. Roll out, then fold into three and roll again. Chill scrap dough before using. (It will not rise as much as first roll, but will work quite well for a pastry crust.)

An egg wash glaze can be used for shine, but make sure it doesn't drip down on any of the cut sides, thereby gluing them together. If the pastry is good and cold, the egg will solidify and not run. Brush the pastry sheet with the egg wash before cutting into portions.

To reduce the rise of puff pastry (such as when using it for a super-flaky tart crust), prick it all over with a fork to allow steam to escape or use a special roller-docker.

Québécoise Tourtière with Mushrooms

I adapted this recipe from As Easy As Pie *by Susan G. Purdy, a wonderful baker and a dear friend. Purdy tells us, "In France, the traditional Christmas Eve after-Mass supper known as* Le Reveillon *features* tourtière, *a savory, spice-scented pork pie as versatile as it is delicious. In Quebec, the most common pastry is one shortened with lard or a mixture of lard and butter. The pastry crust is glazed with egg before the filling is added, to keep the lower crust crisp." I have increased the amount of mushrooms and added some intensely flavored woodsy porcini. Most traditional would be the Lard Pie Dough (page 204), but the Butter Pie Pastry (page 203) would also work well here. An untraditional but tasty alternative is the Savory Spiced Whole Wheat Pastry (page 862). The tourtière is usually served with ketchup and pickled beets or other pickled vegetables to cut its richness.*

YIELD: ONE 9-INCH DEEP-DISH PIE; 8 TO 10 SERVINGS

1 ounce dried cèpe or porcini mushrooms, soaked in warm water to cover for 20 minutes

1 pound Lard Pie Dough or Butter Pie Pastry dough (see above)

1 egg, lightly beaten with 1 tablespoon milk, for the glaze

2 ounces (½ stick) unsalted butter

1 large yellow onion, chopped

2 cloves garlic, finely chopped

½ pound crimini mushrooms, trimmed and sliced

1½ pounds coarsely ground pork, or 1 pound ground pork plus ½ pound ground veal

1 cup rich pork, veal, or beef gravy (from a roast), diluted demi-glace, or rich chicken stock

1 pound (3 medium) gold potatoes, boiled in salted water, peeled, and diced

2 tablespoons chopped flat-leaf parsley

1 tablespoon chopped celery leaves

2 teaspoons chopped fresh thyme, or ½ teaspoon dried thyme

2 teaspoons chopped fresh savory, or ½ teaspoon dried savory

Fine sea salt and freshly ground black pepper, to taste

¼ teaspoon ground allspice

Pinch ground cloves

2 large eggs, lightly beaten

Lay a dampened paper towel in a sieve set over a bowl. Scoop out the soaked porcini, chop into small bits, and reserve. Strain the mushroom liquor through the paper towel to remove any sand particles and reserve.

Divide the dough in two, with one part slightly larger. Roll the smaller portion out on a lightly floured surface to ³⁄₈-inch thick. Fold in quarters and unfold over a 9-inch diameter deep-dish pie plate or a French fluted deep-dish quiche pan. Trim the dough with scissors to ½-inch beyond the edge of the pie plate. Brush the egg wash over the bottom and up the edges of the pie, reserving the remainder. Roll out the second portion of the dough into a large circle about ³⁄₈-inch thick; trim with scissors. Refrigerate the pastry-lined pie and the dough circle while you make the filling.

Heat 2 tablespoons of the butter in a large skillet over medium heat, add the onion and sauté until transparent, 3 to 4 minutes. Add the garlic, sauté for 1 minute, then add the crimini mushrooms and reserved porcini mushrooms. Raise the heat to high and brown the mushrooms, cooking for 6 to 8 minutes, or until most of the liquid has evaporated. Remove the mixture from the pan, add the remaining 2 tablespoons butter to the pan, heat until sizzling, then add the pork and brown, cooking for 5 to 10 minutes, breaking up any clumps with a wooden spoon. Reduce the heat to medium and add the gravy and the strained mushroom soaking liquid, and cook for about 15 minutes, allowing the meat to cook thoroughly and the liquid to reduce until syrupy.

Add the potatoes, parsley, celery leaves, thyme, savory, salt and pepper, allspice, and cloves, and stir to combine. Beat in the eggs and cool the mixture to room temperature. Spoon the mixture into the prepared pastry crust.

Preheat the oven to 425°F. Position the second portion of the dough on top of the filling. Trim a $3/4$-inch overhang, then press the top edge and the bottom crust overhang together pinching together firmly to seal. Form a raised rim all around, pinching in and out alternatively to form a fluted edge. Cut several slits into the top of the dough for steam to escape and a small circle out of the center. Brush the top with the remaining egg mixture. Place the tourtière on a baking pan to catch any drips

Bake on the bottom shelf of the oven for 15 minutes. Reduce the heat to 350°F, move the pie to the center rack of the oven, and continue baking 1 hour longer, or until the pastry is golden brown and the filling bubbles up through the center. (If necessary, cover the edge of the pie with crimped heavy-duty foil or a pie shield to protect the crust from darkening too much.) Cool for at least 15 minutes on a wire rack, then serve hot or warm. Store refrigerated up to four days. Wrap in foil and reheat in a 350°F oven for 30 minutes.

MORE ABOUT TOURTIÈRE

In the predominantly French Canadian province of Quebec, tourtière is the regional specialty. Though essential for Christmas and New Year's, tourtière is served year-round, either as a main dish, filling appetizer, or lunch dish. The dish takes its name from the earthenware or metal *tourtière*, or pie dish, used in France to make filling meat-based tourtes. It is closely related to English raised meat pies like the Steak, Guinness, and Mushroom Pie on page 213.

In Quebec, a tourtière always contains pork but it is often combined with beef, veal, poultry, or game. Sometimes the filling is placed into the pastry crust uncooked, in which case it must bake for far longer. For those who avoid pork, ground dark-meat turkey makes the perfect substitute. A tourtière always contains onions for savory flavor, potatoes or breadcrumbs to absorb the pork fat and mellow the flavor, and a touch of aromatic clove, and/or cinnamon, and allspice.

Cigari Borekas with Moroccan Spiced Lamb

Borekas *are small, easily portable filled pastries that came along with the Turkish nomadic tribes in Central Asia when they moved westward to Anatolia in today's central Turkey. They are closely related to the dumplings of Central Asia along the Silk Route, such as* manti. *These pastries, found in many versions throughout the former Ottoman Empire, may have savory or sweet fillings, including this one made with lamb and aromatic spices from Morocco. You may use either Turkish yufka triangles here or phyllo dough. The yufka is rolled up around the filling, then deep-fried; the phyllo sheets are brushed with oil, then baked. You may make the pastries and freeze them and bake or fry them directly from the freezer. This recipe is dairy-free.*

YIELD: 24 BOREKAS

1 pound ground lamb

1 large onion, finely chopped

3 cloves garlic, finely chopped

4 teaspoons ras el hanout, or 1 teaspoon ground cumin, 1 teaspoon ground coriander, 1 teaspoon ground cinnamon, $1/2$ teaspoon ground ginger, $1/2$ teaspoon paprika, and $1/4$ teaspoon cayenne pepper

$1/4$ teaspoon crumbled saffron, soaked in $1/4$ cup water

Salt and freshly ground black pepper, to taste

2 large eggs, lightly beaten

2 tablespoons chopped fresh flat-leaf parsley

2 tablespoons chopped fresh cilantro

1 (14-ounce) package Turkish yufka dough (opposite page) or 1 pound phyllo pastry, defrosted in the refrigerator if frozen

$1^1/2$ cups olive oil, if using the phyllo

2 large egg whites, lightly beaten with 2 tablespoons water, for the egg wash

$1/2$ cup sesame seeds

3 cups olive oil, for frying, if using the yufka

Make the filling: Combine the lamb, onion, garlic, ras el hanout, saffron and its soaking liquid, salt and pepper in a large frying pan and cook over medium heat, uncovered and stirring occasionally, until the meat has browned and the liquid from the pan has evaporated, about 12 minutes. Remove the pan from the heat and drain off and discard any excess fat. Stir in the eggs, parsley, and cilantro and cool to room temperature.

To make the borekas using the yufka: Place a yufka triangle on your work surface with the point of the triangle facing downward, toward you. Place 2 tablespoons of filling in the center of the upper part of the triangle. Brush the edges with water and roll up tightly starting at the top wide end, folding over the sides as you go and forming a compact shape. Brush with the egg wash and sprinkle with sesame seeds. Repeat until all the pastry and filling have been used. (The pastries may be frozen at this point. Fry without defrosting.)

In a wok, a large heavy-duty frying pan, preferably cast-iron, or an electric deep-fryer, heat the oil to 365°F, or until shimmering hot, and the air about 3 inches above the oil feels hot. Add the borekas one at a time, without crowding, and fry for 2 to 3 minutes, turning once, or until browned on both sides. Drain on paper towels and serve immediately.

To make the borekas using the phyllo: Preheat the oven to 375°F. Line a baking sheet with parchment paper or a silicone baking mat. Unroll the phyllo dough and cut lengthwise through the layers into (6-inch wide) strips. Brush 1 strip lightly with olive oil and fold in half lengthwise. Lightly brush again with olive oil and place a heaping tablespoon of filling at one end. Fold at a 45-degree angle, then fold again to form a triangular pastry. Continue folding as if folding a flag. Brush with the egg wash and sprinkle with sesame seeds.

Repeat until all the pastry and filling have been used. (The pastries may be frozen at this point. Bake without defrosting at 350°F for about 35 minutes or until golden and crispy.) Arrange on the prepared baking sheet and bake for 20 minutes or until golden and crispy. Serve warm or at room temperature.

YUFKA DOUGH

Yufka, which means *thin* in Turkish, is a very thin pastry that is nearly as thin as phyllo. It seems to have originated in medieval times with Turkic tribes and may be the original phyllo dough. The dough is made from wheat flour, water, and salt, and is rolled out very thinly into a large round, which is then baked directly on a heated iron plate, called a *sac* in Turkish, then turned over and baked on the second side. It most closely resembles very thin flour tortillas or spring roll wrappers. I watched a skillful and fast-working woman prepare the giant handmade rounds of yufka in a farmers' market near Izmir, Turkey, which she stacked up like hundreds of crepes. There, the dough was sold in its full round; in America, yufka is sold in triangular shapes cut from the rounds and packaged in plastic. I find it in my local Russian market, but it can be ordered from many online Turkish food companies. The best substitute is Asian spring roll wrappers.

Steak, Guinness, and Mushroom Pie

Well-suited to the hearty fare of one of the new British "gastro-pubs," this robust pie is richly flavored with dried mushrooms, beef stock, and Worcestershire sauce. In Great Britain, the pie would always include dense, tasty kidney bits, but they are hard to come by in America and disliked by many, so I have substituted mushrooms. At one time in England, when oysters were the cheap and plentiful food of the poor, they would have enriched the pie; these days, mushrooms often take their place. Make believe you're in the movie, Tom Jones, in the old-time public house and serve this meal-in-a-pie, traditionally made with suet pastry. When working with suet, freeze it, then shred it on the large-holed side of a box grater, then freeze the shreds again until firm before mixing with the flour. If you'd prefer, make the dough with chilled lard, butter, or transfat-free shortening, or a combination of any of those, combined with twenty-five percent chilled duck fat, goose fat, or even chicken fat. Undercook the eggs because they will finish cooking in the pie. Any dark beer or porter will work well here instead of the Guinness.

YIELD: ONE 10-INCH DEEP-DISH PIE,
8 TO 10 SERVINGS

1 pound Suet Meat Pie Dough (page 204)

1 large egg yolk, lightly beaten with 2 tablespoons
   milk, for the egg wash

1/4 cup dried porcini mushrooms, soaked in warm
   water to cover 20 minutes

2 cups rich beef stock or veal demi-glaze

3 pounds beef chuck, cut into 3/4-inch cubes

Fine sea salt and freshly ground black pepper to taste

2 cups unbleached all-purpose flour,
   for dredging and thickening

1/2 cup bacon fat, rendered lard, shredded beef suet,
   or vegetable oil

1 pound crimini mushrooms, trimmed and quartered

3 to 4 large shallots, chopped (3/4 cup)

1 (12-ounce) bottle Guinness stout

2 tablespoons Worcestershire sauce

1 tablespoon chopped fresh thyme leaves

1/4 cup chopped flat-leaf parsley

6 eggs, hard-cooked only until partially set, about
   6 minutes, peeled and sliced

Make the pastry crust: Divide the dough into two parts, with one part slightly larger. Roll the smaller portion out on a lightly floured surface to 3/8-inch thick. Fold in quarters and unfold over a 10-inch diameter deep-dish pie plate or a French fluted deep-dish quiche pan. Trim the dough with scissors to 1/2-inch beyond the edge of the pie plate. Brush the egg wash over the bottom and up onto the edges of the pie, reserving the remainder. Roll out the second portion of the dough into a large

circle about 3/8-inch thick, trimming with scissors. Refrigerate the pastry-lined pie and the dough circle while you make the filling.

Make the filling: Lay a dampened paper towel in a sieve set over a bowl. Scoop out the soaked porcini, chop up into small bits and reserve. Strain the mushroom "liquor" through the paper towel to remove any sand particles and combine it with the beef stock.

Toss the beef cubes with salt and pepper to taste, then dredge in flour, shaking off the excess. Heat about half the bacon fat in a large heavy skillet, preferably cast-iron. Add the beef cubes without crowding the pan and working in batches if necessary, and brown them well on all sides. Remove the beef from the pan, then add a bit more fat, add the crimini and porcini mushrooms and brown well.

Preheat the oven to 425°F. Remove the mushrooms from the pan, add a bit more fat, and add the shallots. Sauté until wilted, about 2 minutes, then stir in 1/4 cup of the flour, cooking together for 2 to 3 minutes or until the fat is pale brown. Add the stout, stock, and Worcestershire sauce, and bring to a boil. Add the beef back into the pan and simmer for 30 minutes or until moderately tender. Remove from the heat and combine well with the mushrooms, thyme, and parsley. Cool to room temperature.

Transfer the mixture to the pastry-filled pie dish. Cover with the sliced eggs. Position the second portion of the dough on top of the filling. Trim a 3/4-inch overhang, then press the top edge and the bottom crust overhang together pinching firmly to seal. Form a raised rim all around, pinching in and out alternatively to form a fluted edge. Cut several slits into the top of the dough for steam to escape and a small circle out of the center.

Bake on the bottom shelf of the oven for 15 minutes. Reduce the heat to 350°F, move the pie to the center rack of the oven, and continue baking for 1 hour longer or until the pastry is golden brown and the filling bubbles up through the center. (If necessary, cover the edge of the pie with crimped heavy-duty foil or a pie shield to protect the crust from darkening too much.) Cool for at least 15 minutes on a wire rack, then serve hot or warm

·

RECOMMENDED CUTS FOR STEAK AND MUSHROOM PIE

I recommend beef top blade or minute steak, known as flat-iron steak when cut horizontally, which is a tender and juicy cut from the chuck, also known as petite steak when it is cut crosswise. If cut crosswise, partially freeze the meat until firm, then cut out the tough gristly layer that runs through the center of the meat. Use the trimmings to enhance a beef stock or discard. Beef chuck eye, tri-tip, or skirt steak are good choices here, but a too-lean cut like top round will result in mealy-textured beef. For more about beef cuts, see my *Field Guide to Beef*.

Financiers

These rich, buttery French almond tea cakes are made in special molds said to resemble the gold bricks hoarded by financiers. Flavored with beurre noisette (browned butter), financiers are easy to make, but the ingredients must be weighed for accuracy. When per-fectly made, the financiers are soft and springy with a characteristic bulge in the center and a slightly crunchy golden brown crust. If you don't want to bake the cookies immediately, the batter will hold in the refrigerator for a few days. The financiers must be baked in a hot oven with the molds placed on a heavy baking sheet. Once the cakes begin to rise, the temperature is reduced so the insides stay moist. Substitute mini-muffin tins for the special financier molds. Make these cookies when you have extra egg whites on hand.

YIELD: 3 TO 4 DOZEN SMALL FINANCIERS

2 tablespoons (1 ounce) unsalted butter, softened

5 ounces (1 cup) blanched almonds

3 ounces ($^3/_4$ cup minus 2 teaspoons) unbleached all-purpose flour

Pinch fine sea salt

$^1/_2$ pound confectioners' sugar, sifted

7 large egg whites (7 fluid ounces), at room temperature

7 fluid ounces Brown Butter (page 202), melted and cooled (1 cup minus 2 tablespoons)

1 teaspoon pure vanilla extract

Preheat the oven to 450°F. Place the financier molds (see page 216) on a heavy baking pan (such as a half sheet pan). Brush the molds with the softened butter.

Place the almonds, flour, and salt in the bowl of a food processor and process until very fine and powdery. Transfer to a mixing bowl and whisk in the confectioners' sugar. Whisk in the egg whites, mixing until thoroughly blended. Pour in the brown butter and vanilla and whisk until well combined. The batter will be pourable. Transfer to a Pyrex measure or other container with a spout and pour the batter into the molds, filling them almost to the rim.

Bake for 6 minutes or until the financiers just begin to rise. Reduce the heat to 400°F and bake for 6 minutes more, or until the financiers are a light, delicate brown and are beginning to firm up. Remove from the oven, cool to room temperature, then unmold. Store in an airtight container for up to 5 days.

FINANCIER MOLDS

Traditionally, financiers are baked in small, rectangular, brick-shaped molds. Another popular shape is the shallow French tart molds with pointed ends called *barquettes* (boat in French). However, both the boat-shaped and the rectangular molds can be hard to find in America, so luckily you can just as successfully use mini-muffin tins. Special silicone financier molds can be found at JB Prince (www.jbprince.com) or Bridge Kitchenware (www.bridgekitchenware .com).

German Butter Cake (Butterkuche)

German Butter Cake is the name used by bakeries for a cake of Pennsylvania Dutch origin found in German bakeries in Southeastern Pennsylvania. In earlier times, it was known as German Coffee Cake or Sour Milk Cake. Recipes for the cake, called Butterkuche *where*

Pennsylfaanisch (the German-based local language) is spoken, are common in regional cookbooks of the nineteenth and early twentieth century. Here, a light and, of course, buttery yeast dough is topped with a second layer containing even more butter that forms a yummy, gooey layer in the center of the cake.

YIELD: ONE 9-INCH CAKE, 8 TO 10 SERVINGS

Cake

2 tablespoons (1 ounce) unsalted butter, softened

$1/4$ cup fine dry breadcrumbs or cake crumbs

1 ($1/4$-ounce) package ($2 1/4$ teaspoons) active dry yeast

$1/4$ cup lukewarm water

$1/2$ cup sugar

$1/4$ pound (1 stick) unsalted butter, softened

Grated zest of 1 lemon (1 tablespoon)

$1/4$ teaspoon fine sea salt

1 cup sour cream

2 large eggs

10 ounces ($2 1/2$ cups minus $2 1/2$ tablespoons) unbleached all-purpose flour

Topping

$1/4$ pound (1 stick) unsalted butter, softened

1 cup sugar

2 ounces ($1/2$ cup minus 2 teaspoons) unbleached all-purpose flour

2 large eggs

1 egg yolk

2 tablespoons milk

1 teaspoon vanilla

$1/2$ teaspoon almond extract

½ cup sliced skin-on almonds

2 tablespoons sugar, for sprinkling

Make the cake: Prepare a 9-inch springform or removable-bottom cake pan by rubbing generously with butter and sprinkling with the breadcrumbs, shaking off the excess. Dissolve the yeast in the water, mix in 1 tablespoon of the sugar, and allow the mixture to proof in a warm place for about 15 minutes, or until bubbling and puffy.

In the bowl of a standing electric mixer and using the paddle attachment, beat the remaining sugar, the butter, lemon zest, and salt until light and fluffy, 5 to 6 minutes, then beat in the sour cream. Beat in the eggs, one at a time, and beating well after each addition. Pour in the yeast mixture and the flour and beat until smooth and shiny, about 3 minutes. (The batter will be soft and sticky.) Transfer to a large oiled bowl. Cover with plastic wrap or a damp cloth and allow the dough to rise until doubled in size, about 2 hours, at warm room temperature.

Make the topping: In the bowl of a standing electric mixer, beat the butter and sugar together until soft and creamy, 4 to 5 minutes. Add the flour, then beat in the eggs, egg yolk, milk, and vanilla and almond extracts. The mixture should be soft enough to spread easily on top of the cake.

Assemble and bake the cake: Preheat the oven to 350°F. Stir down the batter and spread evenly into the prepared pan. Spoon small dollops of the topping onto the cake from the center toward the edge smoothing them to a relatively even layer using a silicone spatula. Sprinkle with the sliced almonds and then with the 2 tablespoons of sugar. Cover with oiled plastic wrap and allow the batter to rise in a warm place until it has almost doubled again, about 1 1/2 hours. (It should reach more than half-way up the sides of the pan.)

Bake for 40 minutes or until the cake starts to come away from the sides of the pan and is golden brown on top. The gooey layer (which may fold into the heavier layer) should be crusty but almost liquid just under the crust. Cool the cake on a wire rack before cutting into serving portions. Store covered and refrigerated up to 4 days.

MORE ABOUT GERMAN BUTTER CAKE

To find out the history of German Butter Cake and to get a modern recipe, I contacted author and culinary historian, William Woys Weaver, who specializes in the cooking of Pennsylvania's German community and is the author of many books, including *Pennsylvania Dutch Country Cooking*. As with many traditional recipes, this cake is made in many versions: using yeast, baking soda, or baking powder for leavening; sweetened with honey instead of sugar; with a drippy buttery topping or a firmer topping. Weaver told me that it was customary to add flavoring to the cake including vanilla, lemon zest, or ground cassia (the stronger-flavored relative of cinnamon).

Biscochitos

Called biscochitos *(little biscuits or cookies) in Northern New Mexico, or* biscochos *in Southern New Mexico, these delicate cookies have a long tradition in that state, where they were introduced by Spanish explorers in the sixteenth century. The cookies may be flavored with anise, lemon zest, red wine, brandy, vanilla, cinnamon, or sherry. Biscochitos are most often enjoyed with red wine or hot chocolate. Lard is the traditional fat and yields cookies that are especially tender and which keep their shape beautifully if cut into the traditional fleur-de-lis, leaves, stars, hearts, or other decorative figures. This recipe is dairy-free.*

YIELD: 6 TO 8 DOZEN COOKIES

Cookies

1$^{1}/_{2}$ pounds (5$^{3}/_{4}$ cups minus 2 tablespoons)
    unbleached all-purpose flour

1 tablespoon baking powder

1 teaspoon fine sea salt

$^{1}/_{4}$ pound pure lard, substitute unsalted butter,
    trans fat free shortening, or a combination

$^{1}/_{2}$ pound (2 sticks) unsalted butter, softened

1$^{1}/_{2}$ cups sugar

2 large eggs

$^{1}/_{4}$ cup brandy

1 tablespoon aniseed, ground finely in a spice grinder

Topping

$^{1}/_{4}$ cup superfine sugar

1 tablespoon ground cinnamon

Make the dough: Line two 18 x 13-inch half sheet pans or other large baking sheets with parchment paper or silicone baking mats. In a bowl, whisk together the dry ingredients: flour, baking powder, and salt.

In the bowl of a standing mixer and using the paddle attachment, beat the lard, butter, and sugar until light and fluffy, 5 to 6 minutes.

Combine the eggs, brandy, and ground anise.

Add the flour mixture to the lard mixture and beat just long enough to combine. Add the anise mixture and beat just long enough for the dough to form large, moist clumps. Knead briefly by hand to combine into a smooth ball. Transfer to a plastic bag and shape into a flattened rectangle. Chill in the refrigerator for 1 hour or in the freezer for 30 minutes until firm but still malleable. Combine the topping ingredients and reserve.

Preheat the oven to 350°F. Remove the dough from the refrigerator and roll it out on a lightly floured work surface to about $^{3}/_{8}$-inch thick. Cut the dough into the desired shapes (fleurs-de-lis are traditional but I like leaf shapes). Sprinkle each cookie with the cinnamon-sugar and arrange on the prepared baking pans. Bake the cookies until lightly browned, 12 to 15 minutes. Cool on a wire rack and store in an airtight container for 3 to 4 days at room temperature.

BISCOCHITO HISTORY

Biscochitos originated in Spain and made their way to Mexico with the Spaniards. They are particularly popular in New Mexico where they were declared to be the official State Cookie in 1989, thanks to the efforts of biscochito baker Frances Michelle Maldonado, owner of Enchantment Delights in Albuquerque. There is no "official" recipe for biscochitos. The best bakers, however, all swear by lard, which they whip up as light as cream to give these cookies their incomparable melting texture, a cross between shortbread and a sugar cookie. The lard-based dough keeps its shape beautifully when cut into fancy shapes like the famous fleur-de-lis or iris shape, although diamonds and rounds are common, too. Treasured Spanish family recipes have been handed down for generations and biscochitos are made for every celebration.

"They're heaven's own little cakes blended delicately of sugar and spice, flour and wine and other secret ingredients, shaped by the swift fingers of the *linda señora* into small diamonds and baked until they are the delicate brown of the maiden's cheek kissed by the New Mexico sun," wrote Miguel Hambriento, an author and collector of old recipes in Mesilla, an historic town in New Mexico on the road from San Diego to San Antonio during the early 1900s. And he swore the best biscocho maker in all the state was a lovely Mesilla widow— "round and plump with eyes of a mourning dove, *la bonita* Minda makes and sells at Christmas time such biscochos that the good saints in heaven might bend down for a nibble."

CANDIED FRUITS

Comparing Ingredients
for Candied Fruit . . .223

Where to Buy High–Quality
Candied Fruit . . .223

Romanengo of Genoa . . .224

SIENNESE CAVALLUCCI . . .224

Why Cavallucci? . . .225

CANDIED CITRUS PEEL . . .225

ITALIAN WALNUT CAKE WITH
CANDIED FRUIT (TORTA DI NOCI) . . .226

ALIZA'S WEDDING CAKE . . .227

To Make a Tiered Wedding Cake . . .229

Candied Angelica . . .229

HOT CROSS BUNS WITH CURRANTS . . .230

Hot Cross Buns . . .231

SIENNESE PANFORTE . . .232

Wafer Paper . . .233

The Origins of Panforte . . .233

CANDIED FRUIT

Perhaps Americans dread candied fruit and the everlasting "regifted" fruit cake so much because we have an industrial rather than artisanal tradition of making these jewel-like fruits. Peer in the window of any number of European confectionary shops and you will see trays of sparkling, jewel-like whole candied fruits. In contrast, most American confectionary manufacturers spend the greater part of the year processing maraschino cherries, with candied fruits only a side business quickly made before Christmas. In America, fruit is candied with cheap corn syrup rather than the cane sugar syrup used in Europe.

To produce American-style candied fruits, long circular vats holding turning drums are loaded with prepared fruit. The fruit tumbles for days while dropping through a mist of sprayed corn syrup and falling back into a sugar bath. There is constant heat in the vat and the room to bake the sugar onto the candied fruit. Unfortunately, much of the American candied fruit that is available in many supermarkets is overly sweet and also contains preservatives. I wasn't able to find any American manufacturer of high-quality candied fruit in my search. I'd be happy to learn about any that are out there.

Europe follows an artisanal model in its methods. There, candied (or crystallized) fruit has been produced since at least the fourteenth century. Whole candied clementines, figs, baby eggplants, citron rinds, angelica root, pears, and apricots are a treat for the eye as well as the palate. Perfectly preserved, these fruits are the product of a painstaking process in which the natural liquid in the fruit is gradually replaced by sugar syrup while conserving the full flavor of the fruit.

To produce *fruits confits* (candied or preserved fruits in French), the chosen fruit is placed in successive 24-hour baths of sugar-syrup; each time gradually increasing the concentration of sugar. The number of baths varies depending on the fruit. Five or six days' worth of baths are required for small fruits like cherries, while several months are needed to create candied clementines, figs, and pears.

The French Provençal city of Apt, which is surrounded by the fruit orchards of the Luberon, is the capital of *fruits confits*, while Genoa, Italy, has been famed for its candied fruits since the mid-nineteenth century. Strasbourg in Alsace is known for its candied mirabelle (small yellow) plums flavored with kirsch and stuffed with fruit pâté. In Portugal, the town of Elvas also has a tradition of candying fruit by hand. Australia is known for the quality of its glazed (candied) apricots. Some of the finest apricots are grown in Australia's Barossa Valley, near Adelaide. There are more than twenty steps involved in making these luscious glazed apricots preserved in pure Australian cane sugar syrup.

In this chapter, candied fruit goes into the spiced Siennese Cavallucci (page 224), the Italian Walnut Cake (page 226), and Aliza's Wedding Cake (page 227), which I baked for my own wedding almost 25 years ago! The Hot Cross Buns with Currants (page 230) contain candied orange rind (page 225). The Siennese Panforte, a dense fruit and nut cake that dates from medieval times (page 232) lasts for months, improving as it ages.

In other chapters, candied orange goes into the Sambuca and Candied Orange Tozzetti (page 90), the fruit and nut–filled Sephardic Stuffed Monkey (page 176), the Oatmeal–Pecan Fruities (page 425), the Cuccidati: Sicilian Fig Cookies (page 457), the Maltese Kwaresimal Cookies (page 603), and the Chocolate Torte with Orange and Pistachio (page 697). Slightly bitter, sophisticated candied citron flavors the French Candied Citron and Lemon Cookies (page 534) and the Torta di Savoia with Candied Citron (page 535). Candied lemon peel enhances the lemony character of the Meyer Lemon Bundt Cake (page 533) and the Lemon Poppy Seed Biscotti (page 719). Even if you've shied away from candied citrus rinds and other candied fruits in the past, I urge you to give a try to these wonderful and uncommon recipes.

COMPARING INGREDIENTS FOR CANDIED FRUIT

Ingredients from one American brand of candied green cherries: Cherries, Corn Syrup, High Fructose Corn Syrup, Water, Citric Acid, Natural and Artificial Flavor, FD&C Blue #1, FD&C Yellow #5. Preserved with $\frac{1}{10}$ of 1% Potassium Sorbate, Benzoate of Soda, Sulphur Dioxide.

Ingredients from imported French candied fruit: lemon peel, sugar, lemon oil, citric acid, beta carotene, potassium sorbate, water

Ingredients from Romanengo of Genoa: Fresh, fully ripe fruit is coated in sugar and glucose syrup to preserve its original colors and flavors.

WHERE TO BUY HIGH-QUALITY CANDIED FRUIT

Sources for high-quality candied fruit: www. russanddaughters.com and www.thebakerscatalogue. com. Italian Harvest in San Francisco (www.italianharvest.com) carries wonderful candied fruits from Genoa's renowned confectioners, Romanengo (see page 224).

On Genoa's Via Soziglia, one of the charming old pedestrian streets that wind through the area around the Via Garibaldi, is the historic store, Pietro Romanengo fu Stefano, a hidden treasure set in the heart of the old city. The store, which has not changed one bit since the day it opened in 1814, is crammed full of artisanal food specialties. The store first sold cones of sugar in blue paper packaging and, like other confectioners of the time, produced sugared goods including preserves, candied fruit, syrups, and liqueurs; later they became chocolate makers as well. Originally from the Orient, these sugar-based products began appearing in Europe at the time of the Crusades.

Although Genoa excelled in its production as early as the Middle Ages and the Renaissance, the art of confectionery reached unheard-of levels in the eighteenth century, thanks to the influence of the French. The company's reputation soon spread beyond Genoa and it began to sell its produce to distinguished members of society, including Giuseppe Verdi and Prince Umberto of Italy, who purchased "candied fruit, demi-sucres, elegant bonbons and small metal bonbonnières decorated with pastilles" for his marriage to Margherita of Savoy in 1868. In a letter to a friend in 1881, composer Giuseppe Verdi declared, "I was unaware that Romanengo knew how to dress every kind of fruit so exquisitely."

By 1859, Genoa's candied fruit industry was producing some 200,000 kilos of candied citrus peel, as well as large amounts of other candied fruits for export to Holland, Germany, the United States, South America, and Switzerland. If you get a chance to visit Genoa, make sure to pay a visit to this beautifully maintained store.

Siennese Cavallucci

In the small, enchanting Renaissance city of Siena, bakers have been making these dense, chewy anise-scented cookies since at least the sixteenth century. Cavallucci means "little horses," and the cookies got their name from the fact that they were originally made for the servants, especially carriage drivers and those working in the stables. They are usually soaked briefly in Tuscan dessert wines such as vin santo, aleatico, or passito just before eating them. This recipe is dairy-free.

YIELD: 4 DOZEN SMALL COOKIES

10 ounces ($2^{1}/_4$ cups plus 1 tablespoon) unbleached
    all-purpose flour

2 teaspoons ground aniseed, or 1 teaspoon
    anise extract

1 teaspoon sweet mixed spices, such as Asian five spice,
    French quatres épices, or American pumpkin pie spice

1 teaspoon baker's ammonia

$^{1}/_2$ teaspoon fine sea salt

1 cup water

1 cup sugar

2 tablespoons honey

2 large egg whites ($^{1}/_4$ cup)

$^{1}/_4$ cup extra-virgin olive oil

Grated zest of 1 orange

¼ pound (scant 1 cup) chopped walnuts

2 ounces (about ½ cup) chopped candied orange peel, homemade (this page) or purchased

1 large egg white, lightly beaten with 1 tablespoon water, for the egg wash

¼ cup raw or crystallized sugar, for sprinkling

Line an 18 x 13-inch half sheet pan (or other large baking pan) with parchment paper or a silicone baking mat.

Whisk together the dry ingredients: flour, ground aniseed, mixed spices, baker's ammonia, and salt. (If using anise extract, add it to the sugar syrup after it comes off the heat—see below.)

Bring the water, sugar, and honey to the boil in a small heavy-bottomed pot over medium heat. Continue to boil until the syrup is completely clear and it reaches 225°F, or the thread stage: when a small amount of the syrup dropped from a spoon 2-inches above the pot spins a long thread. Remove from the heat and immediately combine with the flour mixture, the egg whites, olive oil, and orange zest. Fold in the walnuts and candied orange peel.

Transfer to a plastic bag and shape into a flattened rectangle. Allow the dough to rest overnight at room temperature to mellow the flavors.

Chill in the refrigerator for 1 hour or in the freezer for 30 minutes until firm but still malleable.

Preheat the oven to 300°F. Divide the dough into four to six sections and roll out with your hands on a floured board into finger-thick rolls. Cut on the diagonal into 1-inch sections and arrange on the prepared baking pans.

Brush the egg wash over the cavallucci and sprinkle with the raw sugar. Bake for 25 minutes or until firm but only lightly colored. Cool on a wire rack and leave overnight to develop the flavors before serving. Store in an air-tight tin for up to two weeks.

> ## WHY CAVALLUCCI?
>
> In Medieval times, Siena was a gateway for horse-drawn carriages traveling from the East, so many Siennese sweets have a taste of the East from ingredients like honey, spices, and dried fruits. The cookies were originally called *Berriguocoli*, the name which is featured in many documents from the sixteenth century, but got their modern name, cavallucci, because they became popular with the carriage drivers (*Cavallo* is italian for horse). These dense, hard cookies are firm, long-lasting, and easy to carry, perfect for a driver.

Candied Citrus Peel

I find chewy, slightly, bitter orange rind most stimulating to the palate, either in small amounts on its own or mixed into cookies and cakes. If you like, dip the ends of the candied rind into tempered chocolate for a classic accompaniment to a glass of after-dinner Cognac or liqueur. You can use the same recipe and method to make Candied Grapefruit Rind, a special favorite of mine. Lime rind is too bitter to candy successfully. Use this homemade candied orange peel in the many recipes in this book calling for it including Aliza's

Wedding Cake (page 227), the Chocolate Torte with Orange and Pistachio (page 697), the Cuccidati (Sicilian Fig Cookies) on page 457, the Siennese Panforte (page 232), the Hot Cross Buns with Currants (page 230), the Sephardic Stuffed Monkey (page 176), the Sambuca and Candied Orange Tozzetti (page 90), and the Oatmeal-Pecan Fruities (page 425). This recipe is gluten-free. This recipe is dairy-free.

YIELD: 2 POUNDS

8 large, brightly colored navel oranges, or other citrus fruits such as tangerines, grapefruits, or Minneolas

1 tablespoon fine sea salt, or 2 teaspoons table salt

4 cups sugar

3 cups water

1/4 cup light corn syrup

1 cup raw or crystallized sugar

Scrub the oranges with a brush to clean the skin. Cut four wedges of peel from each orange by cutting around the oranges through the skin and white pith, but not the flesh and then remove the peel. (Reserve the orange flesh for another use or slice and toss with a bit of honey, Cointreau, and lime juice and serve with cake.) Cut each peel quarter into long, thin strips.

Meanwhile bring two separate one-gallon pots of water to the boil. Add the salt to the first pot and add the strips of orange peel. Bring the liquid back to the boil and cook for 2 minutes. Drain, then run under cold water. Add the strips to the second pot of water and repeat.

Bring the sugar, water, and corn syrup to the boil in a medium heavy-bottomed pot. Add the orange strips and

simmer on very low heat for 2 hours, or until quite tender. Remove from the heat and cool the orange strips in their cooking syrup overnight or up to 2 days, covered and at room temperature. Drain the strips and arrange on one or two wire racks set over baking pans to catch the drips. Dry for 24 hours at room temperature.

Toss the partially dried strips with the raw sugar, spread out on the wire racks and dry again for 24 hours. Store the strips in an airtight container for up to 3 months.

Italian Walnut Cake with Candied Fruit (Torta di Noci)

This is a rich walnut-based fruit cake, perfect for holiday time, or wrapped in cellophane as a hostess gift. I use a combination of some of the many wonderful dried fruits found these days, including tart cherries, blueberries, black currants, pineapple, Zante currants, mango, papaya, dried and candied (glacéed) apricots, candied angelica, and candied citrus peels. (See the recipe for Candied Orange Peel on this page, if you wish to make your own.) The cake keeps quite well and the flavors mellow as the cake sits for a few days before serving. It also freezes very well. This recipe is dairy-free.

YIELD: ONE 8-INCH CAKE; 10 TO 12 SERVINGS

4 large eggs, separated

3/4 cup sugar

1/2 pound (2 cups minus 2 tablespoons) unbleached all-purpose flour

Pinch salt

10 ounces (2¼ cups) chopped walnuts

½ pound (about 2 cups) mixed dried and
    candied fruit, diced

Juice of 1 lemon (3 to 4 tablespoons juice)

Confectioners' sugar, for dusting

Preheat the oven to 350°F. Prepare an 8-inch remov-able-bottom or springform cake pan by spraying with nonstick baker's coating, or rubbing with softened but-ter and dusting with flour, shaking off the excess.

In the bowl of a standing mixer fitted with a whisk attachment, beat the egg yolks and ½ cup sugar till they are light and fluffy, 5 to 6 minutes.

In the clean and greaseless bowl of a standing elec-tric mixer and using the whisk, beat the egg whites until fluffy, then add the remaining sugar and continue beat-ing until the whites are firm and glossy, 4 to 5 minutes. Fold into the yolk mixture in thirds, so as not to deflate the meringue.

Whisk together the flour and salt and combine with the walnuts. Alternate folding in the flour mix and the candied fruits. Lastly, fold in the lemon juice.

Scrape the batter into the pan, smoothing it out with a spatula. Bake for 40 minutes or until the cake starts to come away from the sides of the pan and a toothpick or skewer stuck in the center comes out clean. Remove the cake from the oven and cool on a wire rack to room tem-perature. Remove from the pan, dust the top with the confectioners' sugar, cut into serving portions and serve. Store covered and refrigerated up to 5 days. Freeze up to 3 months, if desired.

Aliza's Wedding Cake

I married Don Reiff, who was the architect of Ristorante DiLullo where I worked as their executive chef, in 1984. Naturally, I couldn't turn over the cooking for my wed-ding reception to anyone else, so I worked day after day preparing all the food in the restaurant kitchen after hours, including this fruit-laden, sherry-soaked, white chocolate iced cake that I made in three tiers. Because the theme of the wedding was based on the abundant lilies of the valley that grew behind my tiny colonial mill worker's house, I decided to decorate the cake with these flowers that I mistakenly believed to be in the edible lily family. The day of the wedding, I found out that the tiny bell-shaped flowers were in fact poisonous! I quickly replaced them with edible violets and avoided what could have been a tragic end to our joyous occasion.

YIELD: ONE 9-INCH CAKE, 12 TO 16 SERVINGS

Cake

3 ounces (½ cup) golden raisins

½ cup diced candied apricots

½ cup diced candied angelica stem, substitute
    diced dried pineapple

½ cup diced candied orange peel, homemade
    (page 225) or purchased

1 cup vin santo, semi-dry sherry, or sweet Marsala

½ cup blanched almonds

½ pound (2 cups minus 2 tablespoons) unbleached
    all-purpose flour

1 teaspoon baking soda

½ teaspoon fine sea salt

6 ounces (1½ sticks) unsalted butter, softened

1¼ cups sugar

Grated zest of 1 lemon (1 tablespoon)

4 large egg whites (½ cup)

¼ cup brandy

Assembly

1 cup apricot preserves, melted, strained, and cooled

4 cups White Chocolate Buttercream (page 336),
  soft and spreadable

Candied violets and/or roses, for decoration or edible
fresh flowers (see page 464–466)

Make the cake: Soak the raisins, apricots, angelica stem, and orange peel in ½ cup of the vin santo overnight.

Preheat the oven to 325°F. Spray a 9-inch round cake pan with nonstick baker's coating, or rub with softened butter and dust with flour, shaking off the excess.

Place the almonds, flour, baking soda, and salt into the bowl of a food processor and process until finely ground.

In the bowl of a standing mixer and using the paddle attachment, cream the butter and ¾ cup sugar until the mixture is light and fluffy, 5 to 6 minutes. Stir in the fruit and its soaking liquid, the almond-flour mixture, and the lemon zest. Transfer the mixture to a wide shallow bowl.

In the clean and greaseless bowl of a standing electric mixer and using the whisk, beat the egg whites until fluffy, then add the remaining sugar and continue beating until the whites are firm and glossy, 3 to 4 minutes. Fold the meringue into the batter in thirds so as not to deflate the whites.

Scrape the batter into the pan and bake for 1½ hours, or until the cake starts to come away from the sides of the pan and a toothpick or skewer stuck in the center comes out clean. Cool the cake in its pan on a wire rack for 1 hour, then remove it from the pan and cool completely.

Meanwhile, soak a piece of cheesecloth in the reserved ½ cup vin santo mixed with the brandy.

Wrap the cake in the soaked cheesecloth. Place the cake in a closed container or wrap in plastic. Keep it moistened with added brushings of wine and brandy, until the cake is ready to be eaten, at least 3 days and up to 2 weeks ahead of time.

Assemble the cake: Cut a very small notch out of the side of the cake to use as a guide. Using a long serrated slicing or bread knife, cut the cake horizontally in two layers. Brush each layer with apricot preserves. Allow the glaze to set for 30 minutes at room temperature. Using an icing spatula, spread a layer of buttercream over the bottom layer of cake over the apricot glaze then press the layers together, using the cut notch as a guide to line up the layers in their original position. Spread the buttercream over the top and sides of the cake, swirling the top to make a decorative pattern. If desired, place about 1 cup of the buttercream into a plastic zipper lock freezer bag with a hole cut out of one corner or a disposable pastry bag and a star-shaped pastry tip inserted in the hole. Pipe a shell-shaped edge around the top of the cake and garnish with candied flowers. Chill for at least 1 hour before serving.

TO MAKE A
TIERED WEDDING CAKE

The above recipe makes one 9-inch cake. Bake in an 8-inch pan for the top layer. For the middle layer, double the above recipe and bake in a 10-inch cake pan as directed above until the cake starts to come away from the sides of the pan and a toothpick or skewer stuck in the center comes out clean. For the bottom tier, triple the above recipe and bake in a 12-inch cake pan as directed above, until the cake starts to come away from the sides of the pan and a toothpick or skewer stuck in the center comes out clean. (Use any extra batter to make a smaller "first anniversary cake," wrap tightly and store in the freezer for 1 year.)

Prepare a 6-times the amount of the recipe for the White Chocolate Buttercream (page 336), preparing it in two batches if necessary. Glaze and ice each cake layer separately, then chill at least 1 hour to firm the buttercream. Assemble the cake on a large decorative cake board or tray. Cut three thin wooden dowels to the height of the finished cake. To keep the tiers in place, run the dowels through the center of the assembled layers, then ice the top layer. Refrigerate the cake until serving time to keep the frosting firm. Decorate with fresh (edible) flowers at the last minute (see page 466 for suggestions).

CANDIED ANGELICA

Stalks of angelica, *Angelica archangelica*, a flamboyant looking herb in the same family as celery, parsley, and fennel, are candied in sugar syrup, especially in Europe. American pastry chefs use the closely related celery and fennel stalks to candy in the same fashion. All parts of the angelica plant are edible and taste like a combination of sweet anise–like licorice and sharp, earthy juniper berries. The long, thick, light green stems are hollow like celery and fennel. The larger the stalk; the more stringy it will be, so young, tender angelica is preferred for candying.

Vivid green candied angelica is especially popular in Sicily, where it goes into fillings for cassata and cannoli. Angelica is thought to have originated in far northern Europe in Lapland, Iceland, and Russia, and is known by such fanciful names as angel's food, herb of the angels, and root of the Holy Ghost. It is grown extensively in Europe, but not in the United States (as far as I know). Candied, it provides a lovely green decoration with clean, sweet herbal flavor and a hint of citrus. Buy organic candied angelica imported from Naples, Italy, online from http://markethallfoods.com.

Hot Cross Buns
with Currants

"Hot cross buns, hot cross buns, one a penny, two a penny, hot cross buns," was the cry of English street vendors hawking their wares for hundreds of years. These traditional English sweet buns are made from a lightly spiced yeast-risen dough enriched with butter and milk, and studded with currants and dried fruits. A cross shape is cut into the top of the buns before they are baked; after cooling, two strips of white icing are piped into the cross lines to make the characteristic design. Because of the long rising time, it is best to start this recipe a day before you want to serve the buns.

YIELD: 24 BUNS

Dough

1 pound (4 cups) unbleached bread flour

1 ($1/4$-ounce) package ($2^1/2$ teaspoons) active dry yeast

1 teaspoon fine sea salt

$1/2$ teaspoon freshly grated nutmeg

$1/4$ teaspoon ground cloves

$3/4$ cup milk

6 ounces ($1^1/2$ sticks) unsalted butter, softened

$1/2$ cup sugar

2 large eggs, separated

$3/4$ cup Zante currants

$1/4$ cup diced candied orange and/or lemon peel, homemade (page 225) or purchased

Grated zest of 1 orange (4 teaspoons)

2 tablespoons unsalted butter, melted

Glaze

6 ounces (1 cup plus 1 tablespoon) confectioners' sugar

1 tablespoon milk

1 teaspoon lemon juice

Whisk together the dry ingredients: flour, yeast, salt, nutmeg, and cloves.

Place the milk, 6 ounces butter, and sugar in a glass measure and microwave for 1 to 2 minutes, or until the butter has melted and the milk is fairly hot to the touch (about 125°F). Beat the yolks into the hot milk mixture and set aside.

In the clean and greaseless bowl of a standing electric mixer and using the whisk, beat the egg whites until they form soft peaks; reserve.

Place about half the flour mixture into the bowl of a standing electric mixer. Using the paddle attachment, gradually pour the milk mixture into the flour mix, beating until well-combined. Add the currants, candied orange peel, and orange zest and beat again until well combined. Add the egg whites and beat until absorbed. Finally, switch to the dough hook and beat in the remaining flour mixture. Continue to beat until the dough is smooth and elastic though still sticky.

Place the dough in a lightly oiled, large clean bowl. Cover tightly with plastic wrap and place in a warm place to rise until doubled in bulk, about 2 hours. Punch down the dough and refrigerate overnight, tightly covered.

Remove the dough from the refrigerator, punch down, and divide while the dough is still firm and cold. First divide into 2, then into 4, then into 8. Finally, divide each of the 8 dough balls into 3, to make a total of 24 evenly-sized buns. Roll into smooth ball shapes.

For the best rounded shape, spray 2 (12-each) medium muffin tins with nonstick baker's spray. Arrange the dough balls in the muffins cups with their smooth side up. Alternatively, arrange on baking sheets lined with parchment paper or silicone baking mats. Brush the balls with the melted butter and spray lightly using a water mister. Using a French baker's lame, a single-edged razor, or a box cutter, cut a cross onto the top of each bun. Place in a warm spot to rise until almost doubled in volume, about 1 hour.

Preheat the oven to 350°F. Bake the buns for 20 minutes, or until well-puffed and nicely browned. Remove the buns from the oven and cool to room temperature on wire racks.

Prepare the icing: Beat together the confectioners' sugar, milk, and lemon juice. Place the icing in a pastry bag with a small plain tip or in a heavy-duty plastic freezer bag and cut a small hole in the corner. Pipe the icing into the cross-shaped cuts, allow the icing to set at room temperature, about 30 minutes, then serve. Store the buns in an airtight container such as a cookie tin for up to 2 days at room temperature or wrap and freeze up to 3 months.

HOT CROSS BUNS

In the ancient Assyrian, Babylonian, and Egyptian cultures, small cakes were made to celebrate the beginning of spring. Cakes marked with a horn shape represented the horns of an ox, the animal associated with the moon. The Greeks and Romans made cakes for their moon goddesses and marked them with ox horns. (The Greek word for ox, *boun*, may have given us the word *bun*.) Little cakes were made by the Saxon conquerors of England as an offering to the goddess, Eoster, the goddess of dawn and spring, who gave her name to Easter. The buns were marked with a cross representing the four phases of the moon.

With the advent of Christianity, the cross took on a different meaning. By the fourteenth century, small spiced cakes marked with a cross were given to the poor on Good Friday. Even today, a hot cross bun baked and served on Good Friday is believed to have special powers to cure illness. If you want to take advantage of this belief, start the recipe on the Thursday before Good Friday (Maundy Thursday), because the dough must rest and rise overnight before baking. Hot cross buns became a cause of religious controversy, because they were seen by English Protestants as a holdover of Catholicism and were banned. Because they were so popular, Queen Elizabeth I allowed the buns to be sold, but only at Easter, Christmas, and to serve after funerals.

Siennese Panforte

Panforte—a chewy cross between a cake and a candy—is a classic Italian Christmas delicacy that originated in medieval times. It's a very dense, rich confection loaded with nuts, dried fruit, and spices (hence its name, which means "strong bread" in Italian). You'll need a candy thermometer here and edible wafer paper, the same kind used to line pans of Italian torrone and Spanish turron honey-nut meringue candy. The flavors of panforte mellow with time. The cake is best made at least 1 week ahead and stored at room temperature wrapped in heavy-duty aluminum foil.

YIELD: 2 LARGE CAKES, 16 TO 20 SERVINGS EACH

4 sheets edible wafer paper (see opposite page)

1 pound (3^1/$_2$ cups) hazelnuts, lightly toasted and skinned

1 pound (3 cups) skin-on almonds, lightly toasted

^{1}/$_4$ pound (1 cup minus 1 tablespoon) unbleached all-purpose flour

2 teaspoons ground coriander seed

1 teaspoon mixed spices, such as French quatres épices, Chinese five spice, pumpkin pie spice, or Speculaas Spices (page 353)

1 teaspoon baking powder

^{1}/$_2$ teaspoon fine sea salt

^{1}/$_4$ teaspoon ground cloves

.1^1/$_2$ cups sugar

1^1/$_2$ cups water

1 cup honey

^{1}/$_2$ pound candied melon, papaya, mango, and/or pineapple, diced

^{1}/$_2$ pound dried apricots, preferably California diced

6 ounces candied orange peel, homemade (page 225) or purchased, diced (1^1/$_2$ cups)

6 ounces candied citron peel, diced (1^1/$_2$ cups)

^{1}/$_4$ cup brandy

Confectioners' sugar, for dusting

Spray the sides of a 10-inch European baking ring set on a baking tray or a 10-inch removable-bottom or springform or cake pan with nonstick baker's coating, then line the bottom with edible wafer paper, cutting to fit as necessary. Cut the wafer paper to fit the top as well and reserve.

Combine the dry ingredients: ^{1}/$_4$ pound of hazelnuts, ^{11}/$_4$ pound of almonds, the flour, coriander seed, mixed spices, baking powder, salt, and cloves in the bowl of a food processor. Process until finely ground, working in two batches if necessary.

Bring the sugar, water, and honey to the boil in a medium heavy-bottomed pot. Continue cooking to the firm ball stage (250°F on a candy thermometer), or until a spoonful dropped in a glass of ice water will form a firm, but still malleable ball. Remove from the heat, cool the syrup slightly, and then while still warm, combine with the fruits, the remaining hazelnuts and almonds, the brandy, and the nut-flour mixture. (The mixture will be quite stiff.)

Oil your hands and press the mixture firmly and evenly into the pans to compact as much as possible, using your knuckles at first and then your palms. Cover with the reserved wafer paper circles, pressing well with the bottom of a glass or cup so the paper adheres to the panforte. Leave the panforte to set for 6 hours or overnight.

Preheat the oven to 325°F, then bake the panfortes for 40 minutes or until firm. Cool for about 20 minutes on a wire rack. When the cakes are cool enough to handle, use a thin-bladed spatula to loosen them from the edges of the pans. Remove completely from the pans, and cool to room temperature.

Store wrapped in heavy-duty aluminum foil for 1 week before eating, or up to 1 month. Dust generously with confectioners' sugar and then cut into thin wedges with a serrated knife to serve.

WAFER PAPER

Also called *oplatki, cialda, ostia, hostie, ouwel, obleas, hostia, pain azyme,* rice paper, and *oblaten,* the thin white sheets of edible paper are made from potato starch, water, and oil. This type of wafer originated in the host that is consecrated and used in the Catholic Church for communion. Order the sheets from www.sugarcraft.com or www.fantes.com.

THE ORIGINS OF PANFORTE

The origin of panforte in Siena may date back to the twelfth or thirteenth century, based on a perhaps fantastical interpretation of a verse in Dante's *Divine Comedy*. In a song of hell, Dante describes a certain Niccolò *"che la costuma ricca/del garofano discoperse"* (dressed in rich clothing sprinkled with cloves). Some commentators think this passage refers to Nicolo Salimbeni, who, in one of his long voyages to the East, brought to Siena breads *"mielati e pepati, profumati con chiodi di garofano"* (honeyed and peppered, perfumed with cloves), in which one can see the direct progenitors of the famed Siennese specialty.

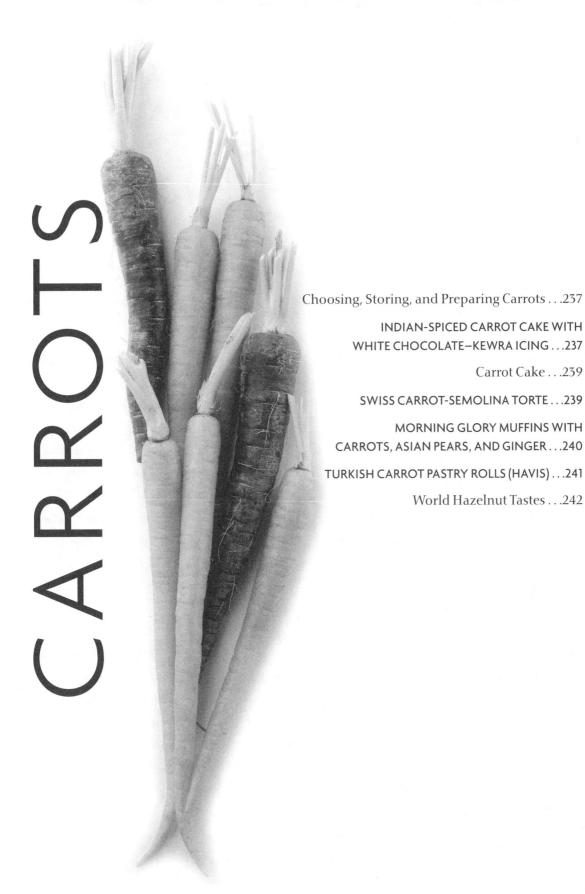

CARROTS

Choosing, Storing, and Preparing Carrots . . .237

INDIAN-SPICED CARROT CAKE WITH
WHITE CHOCOLATE–KEWRA ICING . . .237

Carrot Cake . . .239

SWISS CARROT-SEMOLINA TORTE . . .239

MORNING GLORY MUFFINS WITH
CARROTS, ASIAN PEARS, AND GINGER . . .240

TURKISH CARROT PASTRY ROLLS (HAVIS) . . .241

World Hazelnut Tastes . . .242

CARROTS

The early Celts referred to carrots as "the honey underground." Because of their inherent sweetness, carrots have long been used for sweets like Middle Eastern carrot halvah, Turkish stuffed phyllo rolls, Jewish Passover carrot candies, American carrot cake, and California carrot marmalade. The Irish make sweet carrot pudding, while the French enjoy Bavarian cream studded with candied carrot slivers. In Britain, carrot puddings often appeared in eighteenth and nineteenth century recipe books and were revived in World War II with rationing. Early New Englanders gave carrot cookies as Christmas gifts; today we make carrot quick breads for holiday gifts.

The carrot, *Daucus carota Sativus*, is a biennial plant in the Apiacea family which produces a sweet edible root. It is closely related to the wild white carrot, *Daucus carota*, known as Queen Anne's lace, which is tender enough to eat only when young as the root soon gets tough and woody. This carrot grows wild in much of Western Asia and Europe and has become a common plant of meadows and fields in eastern North America; I have a big patch growing along my front sidewalk. Other close cousins of the carrot

are celery, parsnip, and herbs like dill, fennel, chervil, and parsley. They are all members of the Apiaceae family once known as the *Umbelliferae*, because they all have umbrella-shaped seed pods along with hollow stems.

First cultivated in Afghanistan in the seventh century, carrots slowly spread into the Mediterranean region. While orange may be the familiar color of carrots today, these early carrots had purple exteriors and yellow flesh. The one-and-a-half-foot-long carrots I saw at Mumbai's oldest covered market, called Crawford Market, were the color of strawberries. In the 1600s, the Dutch bred the bright orange carrot we know today to honor their royal House of Orange. All modern-day orange-colored carrots are directly descended from these Dutch-bred carrots. Today's exotic "new" varieties of red, yellow, white, crimson, and purple-rooted carrots, all of which are fetching high prices, actually developed much earlier than the familiar orange roots.

John Parkinson (1567–1650) a great English herbalist, describes red, yellow, and white carrots and reports that the small-rooted "deepe gold yellow" variety is the best of all. He declares, that the carrot's fine-textured leaves "in Autumne will turn to be of a fine red or purple, the beautie whereof allureth many Gentlewomen oftentimes to gather the leaves, and stick them in their hats instead of feathers." This, I'd like to see. The French were especially fond of carrots and it was the famed French seed company, Vilmorin, that introduced an array of carrot varieties in the late 1800s, many of which, including the Chantenay, are still popular today.

Early European settlers brought carrots to Jamestown in 1609; Dutch Mennonites brought orange and scarlet carrots with them to Pennsylvania. Thomas Jefferson raised several types of carrots in his Monticello vegetable garden. English carrots were the first to be introduced into the colonies, where they grew larger and sweeter than in their home country. In the 1800s, carrots were more important in this country for feeding cattle and other livestock than they were for the table. Two billion pounds of carrots are grown annually in the United States alone, with California leading all other states in production. The far southern town of Holtville, California, on the bank of the Alamo River calls itself "The Carrot Capital of the World" and holds an annual Carrot Festival every year.

In this chapter, carrots add color, sweet earthy flavor, and moisture to the Indian Spiced Carrot Cake (this page), the Swiss Carrot–Semolina Torte (page 239), the Morning Glory Muffins (page 240), and the unusual and absolutely delicious Turkish Carrot Pastry Rolls (page 241).

CHOOSING, STORING, AND PREPARING CARROTS

"Bunch" carrots sold with their tops on are by necessity picked within days of sale. Not only do the tops wilt and deteriorate easily if allowed to sit around, the tops also pull moisture out of the carrot root, making for wilted carrots. Carrots are one of the most commonly found organic vegetables, sold in most supermarkets at a reasonable price.

Choose carrots with bright color, firm texture, uniform shape, and without lengthwise splitting. For bagged carrots, look for whole, evenly-sized carrots without broken-off pieces and tips and that are not at all dark or slimy. Store carrots refrigerated in a plastic bag up to 10 days. The inexpensive carrots, also known as "horse carrots" because of their large size and often given as a treat to horses, are too woody and not sweet enough for baking. For all these recipes, the carrots are peeled, topped, and tailed.

Indian–Spiced Carrot Cake with White Chocolate–Kewra Icing

A characteristic sweet of southern India is carrot halvah, a rich, sweet reduction of carrots and spices that is almost fudge-like in consistency, which is flavored with kewra or screw pine extract. This cake falls somewhere between this traditional treat and the popular American carrot cake. It has a dense texture and the unexpected flavor of cardamom. Special Indian dishes

are often decorated with varak or pure silver foil—a
microscopic thin sheet of edible, flavorless real silver,
available in Indian groceries or from www.kalusytans.
com. I have found beautiful candied whole red hibiscus
blossoms at Trader Joe's, which I pull apart into individ-
ual petals and place over the cake, although they may
be a sometime thing.

YIELD: 24 SQUARES

Cake

$3/4$ pound (6 medium) carrots, finely shredded

$1/2$ cup crushed golden pineapple, substitute canned
    crushed pineapple in light syrup, drained

2 tablespoons grated fresh ginger

$3/4$ cup chopped pistachios

$1/4$ pound (3 cups minus 3 tablespoons) unbleached
    all-purpose flour

1 teaspoon ground cinnamon, preferably milder
  true cinnamon, not cassia

$1/2$ teaspoon ground cardamom

2 teaspoons baking powder

1 teaspoon baking soda

$1/2$ teaspoon fine sea salt

4 eggs

$1^1/2$ cups sugar

$1^1/2$ cups canola oil

Icing

6 ounces white chocolate, chopped into small bits

$1/2$ pound cream cheese, softened

2 ounces (6 tablespoons minus 1 teaspoon)
    confectioners' sugar

$1^1/2$ teaspoons kewra (screw pine) extract (see page 463)

Edible silver foil or confectioners' sugar, for decorating

Candied hibiscus blossoms, for decorating

Make the cake: Preheat the oven to 350°F. Prepare a
13 x 9-inch cake pan by spraying it with nonstick baker's
coating, or rubbing with softened butter and dusting
with flour, shaking out the excess.

Combine the carrots, pineapple, ginger, and pistachios and reserve.

Whisk or sift together the dry ingredients: flour,
cinnamon, cardamom, baking powder, baking soda,
and salt and reserve.

In the bowl of a standing electric mixer fitted with the
paddle attachment, beat the eggs and sugar together
until light and fluffy, 5 to 6 minutes. Gradually beat in the
oil until the batter is lightly thickened and smooth.

Fold in the dry ingredients. Fold in the carrot mixture.
Scrape the batter into the prepared pan. Bake for 30
minutes or until the cake starts to come away from the
sides of the pan and a skewer inserted in the center
comes out clean. Cool the cake to room temperature
on a wire rack.

Prepare the icing: Place the white chocolate in a
microwaveable bowl and melt on lowest power in the
microwave, 5 to 6 minutes, or until just barely melted.
Cool to room temperature, whisking until smooth.

In the bowl of a standing electric mixer fitted with the
paddle attachment, beat the cream cheese and white
chocolate until light and fluffy, about 5 minutes, scraping
down the sides of the mixer once or twice. Beat in the
confectioners' sugar and the kewra extract and beat
again until combined. Spread the cake with the icing and

decorate the top with edible silver foil and candied hibiscus blossoms. Refrigerate the cake for 30 minutes to set the icing before cutting into 24 squares. Store covered and refrigerated up to 5 days.

CARROT CAKE

The modern American carrot cake, complete with crushed pineapple and cream cheese icing, is a direct descendent of Medieval carrot puddings that were enjoyed in Great Britain and brought to America along with carrots for planting by the early colonists. When sweeteners were scarce and expensive, carrots were much more commonly used in sweet cakes and desserts. Although George Washington was served a carrot tea cake at Fraunces Tavern in lower Manhattan in 1783, carrot cakes were noticeably absent from American cookbooks well into the twentieth century. The first carrot cake recipe in a cookbook appeared in *The Twentieth Century Bride's Cookbook*, published in 1929 by a Wichita, Kansas woman's club.

Swiss Carrot–Semolina Torte

Known in Swiss-German as Argauer Rueblitorte, *or* Argovia Carrot Cake *in English, this carrot-based cake originated in Aargau, one of the northerly cantons (provinces) of Switzerland, which is named after the river Aare. Semolina, ground from the heart of golden-colored hard durum wheat is combined with ground hazelnuts and shredded carrots in this easy-to-make cake. It is glazed first with strained apricot jam, then with a sweetened lime-sugar glaze. It is quite different from American carrot cake, which tends to be dense and quite sweet; this is lighter and more like a torte because of the ground hazelnuts it contains.*

YIELD: ONE 10-INCH CAKE; 10 TO 12 SERVINGS

Cake

$1/4$ pound ($3/4$ cup) hazelnuts, lightly toasted
   and skinned

$1/4$ pound ($1/2$ cup plus $2^1/2$ tablespoons) fine semolina

6 ounces ($1^1/4$ cups plus 1 tablespoon) unbleached
   all-purpose flour

2 teaspoons baking powder

Pinch salt

5 ounces ($1^1/4$ sticks) unsalted butter, softened

1 cup sugar

4 large eggs, separated

4 large egg yolks ($1/4$ cup)

$1/2$ cup milk

$3/4$ pound carrots, finely shredded

Coating and glaze

$3/4$ cup apricot jam, melted and strained

6 ounces ($1^1/4$ cups minus 1 tablespoon)
   confectioners' sugar

2 tablespoons lime juice

1 teaspoon grated lime zest

Make the cake: Preheat the oven to 350°F. Prepare a 10-

inch springform pan by spraying it with nonstick baker's coating, or rubbing it with softened butter and dusting with flour, shaking off the excess.

Place the hazelnuts, semolina, flour, baking powder, and salt into the bowl of a food processor and process until fine, working in two batches if necessary.

In the bowl of an electric mixer fitted with the paddle attachment, cream the butter and $1/2$ cup of the sugar until light and fluffy, 5 to 6 minutes. Beat in the 8 egg yolks, one at a time, beating well after each addition. Alternating, beat in the milk and the flour mixture. Fold in the carrots.

In the clean and greaseless bowl of a standing electric mixer and using the whisk, beat the 4 egg whites until fluffy, then add the remaining $1/2$ cup sugar and continue beating until the whites are firm and glossy, 4 to 5 minutes. Fold the egg whites into the batter in thirds so as not to deflate the meringue.

Pour the batter into the pan, shaking the pan back and forth to remove any air holes. Bake for 40 minutes or until the cake starts to come away from the sides of the pan and a skewer inserted in the center comes out clean. Cool to room temperature on a wire cooling rack, then unmold upside down.

Glaze and ice the cake: Spread the warm strained jam over the top and sides of the cake and allow it to set at room temperature, for about 30 minutes.

Mix the confectioners' sugar with the lime juice and zest, and pour over the cake, spreading a thin layer over the top and sides. Allow the icing to set at room temperature, about 30 minutes, then cut into serving portions. Store the cake at room temperature for 3 to 4 days.

Morning Glory Muffins with Carrots, Asian Pears, and Ginger

The earliest muffins in America were small, hand-held cakes made from simple ingredients like oatmeal, graham flour, cornmeal, bran, and few additions limited to apples, raisins, and nuts. In the 1970s and 1980s when people started looking for appealing and hopefully healthy grab-and-go foods to eat with their morning coffee, recipes for chunky carrot-based morning glory muffins started to show up. This one is not too sweet, yet moist, and packed with chunky fruits and nuts. The juicy Asian pears, somewhere between a hard winter pear and a crisp apple, add their own special flavor and moist texture, though winter pears like Boscs may be substituted. The touch of Asian flavor is enhanced by fresh grated ginger root.

YIELD: 18 MEDIUM MUFFINS

$1/2$ pound ($2 1/4$ cups) white whole wheat flour

2 teaspoons baking powder

1 teaspoon baking soda

1 teaspoon ground cinnamon

$1/2$ teaspoon fine sea salt

$1/2$ cup well-packed light brown sugar

$3/4$ cup sugar

$3/4$ cup grapeseed oil, canola, or vegetable oil

3 large eggs

$3/4$ pound (3 large) carrots, finely shredded

2 medium Asian pears, peeled, cored, and grated

$3/4$ cup unsweetened coconut flakes

3 ounces ($1/2$ cup) golden raisins

½ cup chopped pecans

1-inch section fresh ginger, peeled and grated (about 2 tablespoons)

Preheat the oven to 375°F. Spray muffin tins for 18 muffins with nonstick baker's coating or rub with butter and dust with flour, shaking off the excess.

In a large bowl, whisk together the dry ingredients: flour, baking powder, baking soda, cinnamon, and salt. Add both sugars and whisk to combine well.

In a bowl, whisk together the oil and eggs. Pour into the dry mixture and fold together gently until almost all combined. Avoid overbeating as this will toughen the batter. Fold in the carrots, Asian pears, coconut flakes, raisins, pecans, and ginger. Divide the batter evenly among the muffin cups, filling each cup about ½-inch from the top.

Reduce the oven temperature to 350°F. Bake the muffins for 20 minutes, or until golden brown and puffy on top. Cool on a wire rack. Store covered and at room temperature for up to 3 days.

Turkish Carrot Pastry Rolls (Havis)

I spotted the recipe for these unusual candied carrot and toasted hazelnut phyllo rolls in a large, handsome, full-color book published by the Turkish Hazelnut Promotion Group. Turkey, which grows the majority of the world's hazelnuts, had been looking for ways to promote their use and asked home cooks and professional chefs in Turkey to come up with recipes for their book, including this traditional pastry. While traveling in Turkey recently, I was told that, several years ago, Turkey had a bumper crop of hazelnuts. Faced with too many hazelnuts, the government put out a series of ads proclaiming that hazelnuts were as effective as Viagra. Hazelnuts started flying off the shelves. I'm not sure if they actually work, but this syrup-sweetened pastry is one of my favorites from this book. Serve it Turkish-style, with kaymak, if you can get it (page 251), Turkish or Greek-style thick whole-milk yogurt, or crème fraîche.

YIELD: 6 ROLLS

Syrup

1¾ cups sugar

2 cups water

2 tablespoons lemon juice plus 1 strip lemon zest

Filling and Pastry

1 pound carrots, coarsely grated

1 tablespoon unsalted butter

1½ cups sugar

1 pound hazelnuts, lightly toasted, skinned, and coarsely chopped

1 teaspoon ground cinnamon

¾ pound phyllo dough, defrosted in the refrigerator if frozen

¾ cup Clarified Butter (page 202)

¼ cup finely ground pistachios and/or grated unsweetened coconut, for garnish

Make the syrup: Combine the sugar, water, and lemon

zest strip in a medium heavy-bottomed pot. Bring to a boil, then reduce the heat and simmer for 3 to 5 minutes. Remove from the heat and stir in the lemon juice. Cool to room temperature and discard the lemon zest strip.

Make the filling and assemble: Preheat the oven to 375°F. Combine the carrots, butter, and sugar in a medium heavy-bottomed pot and cook over medium heat, stirring occasionally until the carrots are soft and most of the liquid has evaporated, about 15 minutes. Transfer to a large mixing bowl and stir in the hazelnuts and cinnamon. Cool to room temperature.

Fold a phyllo sheet in half the short way and brush lightly with butter. Spread one-sixth of the filling across the dough the short way to make an even block no more than 1 inch in diameter and leaving a 1-inch border all around. Fold over the edges of the dough, then roll up tightly to form into a log shape.

Place the roll seam side down on a baking sheet lined with parchment paper or a silicone mat. Continue with the remaining filling and dough until the filling has been used up. Push both ends of the pastry rolls toward the center to compress them and form a wrinkled surface on the rolls, which will make them crispier. Using a French baker's lame, a single-edged razor, or a box cutter, lightly score the rolls across the top, but not down the sides, of the pastry, into 6 portions each to make them easier to cut.

Bake the rolls for about 35 minutes, or until golden brown. Remove from the oven and while still hot, pour the cooled syrup over top. Sprinkle with the pistachios or coconut, and allow the pastry to cool somewhat before cutting into portions and serving. Cut through the slices into serving portions. Store covered and at room temperature for up to 3 days.

WORLD HAZELNUT TASTES

This beautiful full-color cookbook, with a big range of traditional and innovative home and restaurant recipes and photos featuring the marvelous hazelnut, is my favorite in the world of nuts. *World Hazelnut Tastes* published in Turkey, August 2003, ISBN 975-92321-1-1.

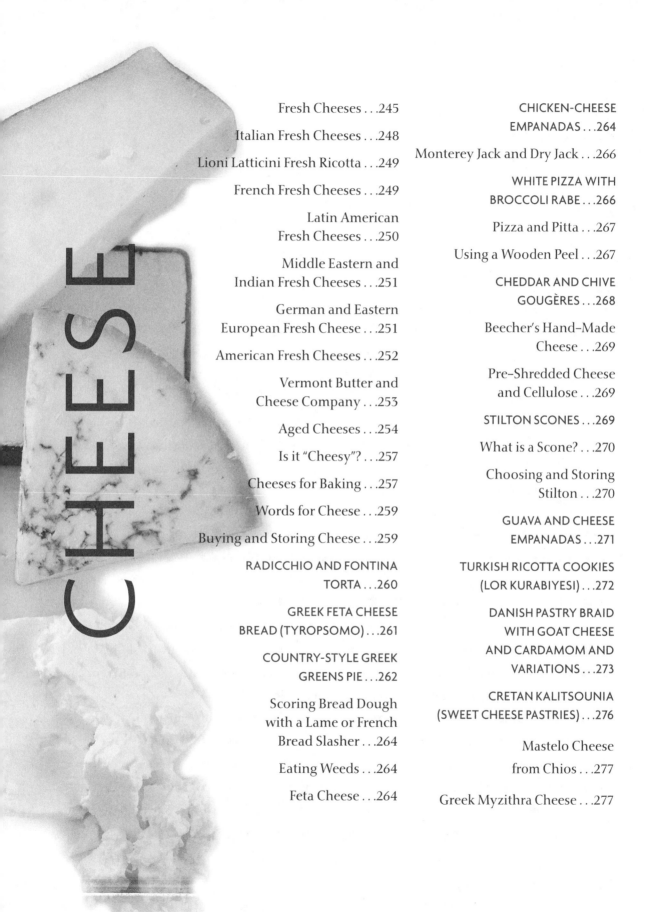

CHEESE

Fresh Cheeses . . .245

Italian Fresh Cheeses . . .248

Lioni Latticini Fresh Ricotta . . .249

French Fresh Cheeses . . .249

Latin American
Fresh Cheeses . . .250

Middle Eastern and
Indian Fresh Cheeses . . .251

German and Eastern
European Fresh Cheese . . .251

American Fresh Cheeses . . .252

Vermont Butter and
Cheese Company . . .253

Aged Cheeses . . .254

Is it "Cheesy"? . . .257

Cheeses for Baking . . .257

Words for Cheese . . .259

Buying and Storing Cheese . . .259

RADICCHIO AND FONTINA
TORTA . . .260

GREEK FETA CHEESE
BREAD (TYROPSOMO) . . .261

COUNTRY-STYLE GREEK
GREENS PIE . . .262

Scoring Bread Dough
with a Lame or French
Bread Slasher . . .264

Eating Weeds . . .264

Feta Cheese . . .264

CHICKEN-CHEESE
EMPANADAS . . .264

Monterey Jack and Dry Jack . . .266

WHITE PIZZA WITH
BROCCOLI RABE . . .266

Pizza and Pitta . . .267

Using a Wooden Peel . . .267

CHEDDAR AND CHIVE
GOUGÈRES . . .268

Beecher's Hand–Made
Cheese . . .269

Pre–Shredded Cheese
and Cellulose . . .269

STILTON SCONES . . .269

What is a Scone? . . .270

Choosing and Storing
Stilton . . .270

GUAVA AND CHEESE
EMPANADAS . . .271

TURKISH RICOTTA COOKIES
(LOR KURABIYESI) . . .272

DANISH PASTRY BRAID
WITH GOAT CHEESE
AND CARDAMOM AND
VARIATIONS . . .273

CRETAN KALITSOUNIA
(SWEET CHEESE PASTRIES) . . .276

Mastelo Cheese
from Chios . . .277

Greek Myzithra Cheese . . .277

CHEESE

My dangerous (to my waistline and my cholesterol count) love affair with cheese got serious at about age thirteen on the day I scooped my way through a gorgeously smelly high-hat Stilton cheese while visiting friends of my parents. I had never experienced anything like this funky but intriguing flavor and I only wanted more. Some years later, on a trip to Italy as a student in Marcella Hazan's cooking school in Bologna, I visited a Parmigiano-Reggiano co-op in Emilia Romagna. Great wheels of old, gold-colored cheeses were stacked like tires aging patiently for up to three years, each one hand-turned every day.

Cooking with Marcella Hazan and in the kitchens of several restaurants in Bologna, and later as the executive chef of the top-rated Northern Italian Ristorante DiLullo in Philadelphia turned me into a lifetime believer in this world-class cheese that is unparalleled for seasoning, especially for Northern Italian cooking and baking. Later, as chef at the California-influenced Mediterranean bistro, Apropos, in the late 1980s, I got hooked on the meltingly rich, Fontina from the Val d'Aosta, with its smooth, silky texture and incomparable subtle, fruity flavor that I used to make the savory tortas and upscale pizzas served from the restaurant's wood-burning oven. Authentic Italian Fontina's frankly earthy yet enticing aroma is unmistakable. (The Danish imitation in the red wax coating has an unfortunately disagreeable aroma when heated.)

I adore making and eating pizzas. Ever since my last restaurant closed, more than anything I miss bringing home pizzas from the wood-burning ovens that I would enjoy so much once the nerve-wracking hours of service were over. (I've included recipes in this book for the best of those pizzas.) I ate my all-time best pizza at DaMichele in Naples, an unassuming spot near the train station that always has a line of eager customers waiting outside. That fresh mozzarella di bufala glistening on fresh-made (twice daily!), hand-tossed, wood-oven roasted pizza was perfection on a plate.

From my first visit to that country in 1968, every Greek cheese pie I've ever tasted, as far as I can remember, has been delicious: the kind of thing I can easily overindulge in. The hand-stretched phyllo pastry pie filled with home-grown and wild greens mixed with artisanally produced Mastelo cheese from Chios, Greece (page 277) that I helped prepare and then devoured on the Greek island of Kea is a benchmark that I can only attempt to reach. I learned how good real Danish pastry can be after a romantic late night out in Copenhagen, when I (with my new friend) showed up very early in the morning at the bakery just as the first mouthwateringly buttery Danish pastry came out of the oven. Of course I had to have the cheese-filled Danish that is still my favorite kind. Because I've tasted the real thing, I'm forever ruined for the pasty, sticky, overly sweet commercial type.

This chapter is full of cheese-based (but not "cheesy") recipes for savory pastries and breads including the Radicchio and Fontina Torta (page 260) and the White Pizza with Broccoli Rabe (page 266), both from Italy and the Country-Style Greek Greens Pie (page 262) and Greek Feta Cheese Bread (page 261) from neighboring Greece. The Chicken-Cheese Empanadas (page 264) and the Guava and Cheese Empanadas (page 271) are two delicious examples of the renditions developed from the original Spanish stuffed bread found in Spain, Mexico, Central America, the Caribbean, and South America. Stilton Scones (page 269) from England and Cheddar and Chive Gougères (page 268), a French dish made with cheddar, deservedly the most popular English and American cheese, are perfect to serve as hors d'oeuvres with a glass of chilled white wine. The Danish Pastry Braid with Goat Cheese and Cardamom (page 273) is one of the more challenging types of

dough to make. But, if you follow my directions carefully, you'll be able to serve a most deliciously flaky, buttery Danish and have some in the freezer for next time. The tender, sesame-crusted Turkish Ricotta Cookies (page 272) and the Cretan Kalitsounia (page 276) use similar ingredients (butter, flour, sugar, eggs, and fresh cheese) but result in very different, though equally appetizing cookies.

FRESH CHEESES

Little Miss Muffett sat on a tuffet, eating her curds and whey. Until the spider came along, Miss Muffett couldn't stop eating her fresh white cheese. What's the connection between Miss Muffett's curds and Mexican queso blanco, German quark, Lebanese labne, Indian panir, French fromage blanc, Russian farmer cheese, Turkish lor, and English cottage cheese? They're all the simplest kind of cheese: fresh, unaged "farmhouse" or "cottage" cheeses: curds. To make fresh cheeses like these, milk is curdled by adding acids such as vinegar or lemon juice along with salt. The resulting curds are then simply drained until the cheese is thick.

Other fresh (and aged) cheeses are made by culturing milk with a "friendly" bacteria strain such as acidophilus and lactobacilus that thickens it and forms curds. The milk or cream sours as it thickens. For some types of firm quark and farmer's cheese, rennet is also added. Softer, wetter fresh cheeses like ricotta, cottage cheese, Turkish lor, fromage blanc are highly perishable, while drier, salted fresh cheeses like labne, queso blanco, and dry farmer cheese will have a longer shelf life.

Traditionally, after churning butter, a farmer or, more likely his hard-working wife, would make fresh cottage cheese from the buttermilk left after skimming the precious cream off the top to make into butter. She would set the skimmed milk in a warm place (like the back of a wood stove) until the milk had clabbered (or curdled). She would pour the resulting warm curds and whey into a cheesecloth sack and hang it up to drain. After mixing the soft curds with a little salt and fresh cream, the cheese was ready to eat within a day or so. Cottage cheese, pot cheese, farmer cheese, fromage blanc, and other fresh white curd cheeses are made essentially the same way.

Cheesemaking began as far back as 6000 BCE, when nomadic people in the warmer parts of Central Asia and in the Middle East found that when they stored milk while on the move, the milk would naturally sour and curdle. They often used the soft and supple skins of young animals as portable storage containers, which contained rennet, an enzyme mixture that promotes curdling, originally obtained from the stomach lining of young cattle, but now also produced in laboratories.

The earliest cheeses were made by draining off the watery whey through woven reed baskets (still used today) or perforated earthenware bowls and then salting and pressing the resulting curds, similar to the way ricotta salata, feta, and queso añejo are made today. Egyptian tomb murals dating to about 2000 BCE show butter and cheese being made and then stored in skin bags suspended from poles (similar to the way caciocavallo was once made in southern Italy). Certain plants, like the cardoon blossoms in the south of France, contain enzymes that will also curdle milk and have long been used for cheesemaking.

In the Old Testament, David presented ten cheeses to the captain of the army drawn up to do battle with Saul (Samuel 17:18). "And bring these ten cheeses unto the captain of their thousand." When David and the people who were with him escaped across the Jordan River, he was fed with honey, curds, sheep, and cheese of the herd, as was said, "The people are hungry and weary and thirsty in the wilderness." (Samuel 17:29). In ancient times, there was already a place near Jerusalem called "The Valley of the Cheesemakers." More than 3000 years ago, Homer referred to cheese being made in the mountain caves of Greece from the milk of sheep and goats, as is still done there today.

For centuries, quickly produced "white cheeses" were a staple food of the poor, sometimes called "white meat." Aged "yellow cheeses" were a luxury food reserved for the rich. People living close to the edge couldn't wait a year or more (as for aged Gouda or extra-sharp Cheddar) to eat their cheese. They also couldn't invest in the huge quantities of milk needed to produce this kind of cheese. Typically, the finished weight of an aged cheese represents only ten percent of the original amount of milk, and hard, long-aged seasoning cheeses like Parmigiano-Reggiano, Aged Jack, and Pecorino Romano, can yield as little as one percent of cheese from the milk.

We're each loyal to our own version of white cheese, depending on our ethnic heritage. Southern Italian immigrants brought over the techniques for making fresh ricotta and hand-kneaded mozzarella to America, while Armenians brought their string cheese, often flavored with small black nigella seeds. Lebanese labne (meaning white) is a tangy drained yogurt cheese popular in much of the Eastern Mediterranean. Broccio, a sheep's milk ricotta, comes from Corsica; ricotta salata is an aged, salted sheep's milk ricotta originating in the Sicilian heartland while the related prescinseua (page 439) is a regional specialty of Liguria, Italy.

Originally brought to market wrapped in banana leaves, Latin American fresh cheeses like panela, queso blanco, and queso fresco were made by local artisans, usually female. Like other fresh farmhouse cheeses before modern sterile cheese-making techniques, they had a shelf-life of less than a week. What makes these Hispanic cheeses different is that they keep their shape when cooked or baked, because rennet and acid are added for firm texture, similar to Indian panir and some Middle Eastern cheeses. When salted, they may be dried and aged, making them crumbly in texture, stronger-tasting, and longer-lasting.

With my Eastern European (Polish, Russian, and Lithuanian) background, I grew up eating lots of cream cheese, farmer cheese, and sour cream, all of which are made without animal rennet, off limits to Orthodox Jews, because of the forbidden mix of an animal product with its milk. In a reli-gious culture that strictly separates milk and meat, a whole cuisine of dairy dishes evolved, including blintzes, cheesecake, cheese knishes, bagels with cream cheese, and noodle-cheese kugel. I'm still crazy about these dishes and have spent many happy hours perusing the dairy aisle at my local Russian market to try the many different kinds of farmer's cheese, sour cream, and quark from Russia and all the countries of Eastern Europe.

Fresh cheeses are commonly used as fillings in baking, which also acts as a way to preserve the highly perishable curds. In this chapter, Kalitsounia (page 276), small round "oil-lamp" shaped pastries stuffed with sweetened fresh cheese, a specialty of Crete, are filled with fresh white Greek myzithra cheese. Mexican Guava and Cheese Empanadas (page 271) are stuffed with sliced guava paste and cream cheese fortified with aged, seasoning cheese. The White Pizza with Broccoli Rabe (page 266) is a pizza bianca (white pizza), a specialty of Rome that is made without tomato sauce, but rather is dotted with dollops of fresh ricotta.

Elsewhere in the book, fresh cheeses go into Spanish and Latin American empanadas (see the Guava and Cheese Empanadas, page 271), Danish pastries (page 273), Jewish cheesecake, German Buttercake (page 216), and Italian sweet ricotta pies like the Crostata della Nonna (page 676). The Torta Pasqualina Genovese (page 438), or spring pie, is made from the young fresh greens of spring and ricotta cheese or its special Genoese equivalent called prescinseua. I learned how to make the light and fluffy sesame-crusted Turkish Ricotta Cookies (page 272) in Turkey using the ricotta-like cheese called lor. The Sardinian Sebadas (page 517), fried stuffed pastry rounds with a ricotta filling, are so good, my recipe testing assistant, Betty Kaplan, told me she dreamed about eating them!

ITALIAN FRESH CHEESES

RICOTTA CHEESE: Ricotta is a fresh, soft, snowy white cheese with a pleasing, mild, slightly sweet flavor. Its texture is much like grainy, thick sour cream. Ricotta originated as a thrifty way to use the whey left over from making cheese. Technically, ricotta is not a cheese at all, but a cheese by-product. Its name, *ricotta*, means cooked again, because it was originally made by adding an acid, like vinegar, to the whey. After the whey was heated to a higher temperature, the fine whey curds would separate out. True whey cheeses (sometimes called *ricotone*) are now rare, because American, and much Italian, ricotta is now manufactured from richer whole or part-skim milk. In southern Italy, ricotta is made from the whey drained from making cheeses like mozzarella and provolone. In America, ricotta is generally made with a combination of whey and whole, low-fat, or skim cow's milk.

Ricotta is naturally low in fat, ranging from 4 to 10 percent, and is low in salt. Ricotta cheese is highly perishable. Snowy white when fresh and sweet, yellowing is an indication of age and deterioration. Ricotta that develops any bitter-tasting pink mold should be promptly discarded. Check the container for the expiration date before purchase. Store ricotta refrigerated in its container covered with its lid. Once opened, commercial ricotta will last about one week; the homemade type will last only 3 to 4 days.

MASCARPONE: Mascarpone is an incredibly rich Northern Italian slightly tangy cream cheese made from light cream (about 25 percent butterfat) that is thickened with tartaric acid, which is produced in the wine-making process. Traditionally, mascarpone was produced only in cold weather, although it is now available year round. Mascarpone is a specialty of the Northern Italian province of Lombardy (of which Milan is the capital) where it originated somewhere around the early seventeenth century. It is now also produced in America, though the domestic product is denser than its Italian counterpart.

One theory among many as to the origins of mascarpone's name is that it should actually be spelled *mascherpone* to commemorate the Cascina Mascherpa, a farmhouse that belonged to the Mascherpa family, which was once located halfway between Milan and Pavia and where mascarpone was presumably produced. (Mascherpa is still a common surname in the area.) The similar word, mascarpia, means ricotta in the local dialect and comes from the word "mascarpa," referring to dairy products made from whey, although today mascarpone isn't made from whey at all. A rather fanciful theory is that mascarpone derives from "mas que bueno," a Spanish phrase meaning "better than good" dating from this period when the Spanish controlled much of Italy. Where ever its name originated, a dollop of mascarpone is wonderful served as an accompaniment to simple Italian cakes like the Torta Boscaiola (Italian Chestnut Flour and Hazelnut Cake) (page 319) the Italian Bittersweet Chocolate-Orange Torta (page 331), and the White Bean, Chestnut, and Apricot Cake alla Povera (page 316).

LIONI LATTICINI FRESH RICOTTA

Although it is such a simple product, ricotta cheeses differ immensely among regional brands. Some are unpleasantly pasty, others mealy, others exquisitely soft and tender and delicately flavored, with a pleasing, finely grained texture. My favorite ricotta these days is the thick, snowy mounds of sweet ricotta curds made by Lioni Latticini in Brooklyn and sold packed in perforated metal containers. *Latticini* are dairy stores in Italy, where milk and fresh cheeses like ricotta are also sold. This hand-packed product is highly perishable, but better in flavor and texture than any other ricotta I've ever tasted in the U.S. It is sold at Whole Foods in the Specialty Cheese Department (go to http://lionimozzarella.com for more information).

FRENCH FRESH CHEESES

FROMAGE BLANC: *Fromage blanc* (white cheese), also known as *fromage frais* (fresh cheese), is a dairy product originating in the north of France. In Wallonia, the French-speaking part of southern Belgium, a similar cheese is known as *maquée* or *makeye*. To make it, rennet and a starter bacteria culture are added to milk, which then thickens. The curds are not allowed to solidify, but are stirred, giving fromage frais a smooth, creamy texture similar to that of yogurt.

Pure fromage blanc is virtually fat free, but cream is often added to improve the flavor, giving it a fat content as high as 8 percent. Fromage frais can be mixed with fruit similar to yogurt and is used in savory dishes such as the Alsatian Leek and Bacon Tart: Flammekueche (*Starting with Ingredients*). To make the traditional French springtime home dessert, fromage blanc is sweetened and then drained in special heart-shaped ceramic molds for Coeur à la Crème (cream hearts) and then topped with strawberries. I have adapted this idea to make the creamy white goat cheese and cream filling for the delectable Strawberry-Vanilla Coeur à la Crème Tart with Goat Cheese (page 832).

PETIT-SUISSE: Contrary to what its name suggests, Petit-Suisse (the little Swiss) comes from Normandy, France, and not Switzerland, although the cream-enriched fresh cheese was created by a Swiss woman, Madame Herould, working in a dairy in Haute-Normandie in the 1850s. This "fromage frais" (fresh cheese) is a creamy unsalted cheese made from cow's milk enriched with cream to about 40 percent fat content. Fromage blanc and Petit-Suisse work well as an accompaniment to baked fruit tarts such as the Tarte aux Pêches (page 619), the Alsatian Plum Muerbeteig (page 444) and the Peach and Apricot Tarte Tatin (page 616).

NEUFCHÂTEL: Neufchâtel is a French cheese that is similar in taste, use, and appearance to cream cheese, though moister and lighter, because it is made from milk instead of cream. It is often used in place of some of all of the cream cheese in cheese-cakes to cut down on the richness. However, because Neufchâtel contains less fat, extra flour and/or eggs must be added to the batter to keep the cake from cracking and splitting.

LATIN AMERICAN FRESH CHEESES

QUESO BLANCO: Like ricotta, queso blanco, which lies somewhere between cottage cheese and mozzarella in texture and flavor, is traditionally coagulated with lemon juice, although today it is often thickened with rennet. Queso blanco is well suited for cooking and baking because it becomes soft and creamy when heated, while maintaining its shape.

QUESO FRESCO: This spongy white cheese is grainy in texture and mildly acidic. Usually made with a combination of cow's milk and goat's milk, the cheese was brought to Mexico from Burgos, Spain. It is used to crumble over enchiladas and botanas (snacks); mild feta that has been rinsed to remove the excess salt makes the best substitute.

QUESO AÑEJO AND COTIJA: Queso añejo (aged cheese) is aged queso fresco (fresh cheese) which becomes quite firm and salty as it ages; it is to queso fresco as ricotta salata is to fresh ricotta. Queso añejo is used mainly for seasoning as in the Plantain Empanadas with Black Bean and Añejo Cheese Filling (page 129). Cotija cheese is a particular kind of hard cow's milk queso añejo named after the town of Cotija, in the province of Michoacán, Mexico. Cotija comes in two versions: The grainy type is dry, firm, and salty. In the mouth, the cheese breaks up into a sandy or grainy consistency, which adds to the texture of dishes Tajo is a moister, fattier, and less salty version of the cheese that holds its shape when cut and is used as a seasoning cheese like Italian Parmesan and Greek Feta.

REQUESÓN: The Latino equivalent of ricotta, this fresh curd cheese is traditionally sold at street markets wrapped in fresh corn husks. Requesón has a very mild and delicately sweet flavor. Like ricotta, it is white in color and has a soft, moist, grainy texture. Requesón may be substituted for ricotta in recipes like Turkish Ricotta Cookies: Lor Kurabiyesi (page 272) and Crostata della Nonna: Grandma's Ricotta Pine Nut Tart (page 000).

MIDDLE EASTERN AND INDIAN FRESH CHEESES

KAYMAK AND GAYMERA: Kaymak, or kajmak, is rich ripened thick cream, similar to clotted cream and crème fraîche and lies somewhere between thick cream and cheese. Found all over the Middle East, the Balkans, Iran, Afghanistan, India, and Turkey, kaymak may be made with water buffalo or cow's milk, and contains about 60 percent fat. Indian malai is very similar and is produced in much the same way. Kaymak is traditionally made at home (commercial versions are less desirable) by slowly simmering unhomogenized milk for hours or even days. As the milk cools, the cream rises to the top and develops a mildly tart flavor. Kaymak is sometimes made thick and solid enough to cut in sheets and roll up for topping desserts. In Iraq, the similar gaymera, a very creamy, thick white cream, is made from the milk of water buffalos. At breakfast, pieces of bread are dipped first into the gaymera and then into dibs, a sweet date syrup.

PANIR: This light-textured and mild-flavored, rather jiggly fresh cheese from India is also known as paneer, and is often used to fill samosa fritters. It is a simple unripened cheese made from whole milk heated with an acid like lemon juice until the milk proteins coagulate to form soft curds. Once drained, the panir will have a texture and delicious creamy flavor similar to ricotta, cottage cheese, and farmer cheese.

HALLOUMI: Halloumi is a cheese native to Cyprus that is traditionally made from a combination of goat's and sheep's milk though, a less interesting part cow's milk halloumi is also produced. Like mozzarella, the curds are then heated in hot water until the proteins have undergone a major transformation. Unlike mozzarella, the curds are not stretched and kneaded. Instead, the curds are salted, shaped, and left to mature. Small slabs of Halloumi are often sprinkled with salt and dried mint. The cheese is then folded to create a parcel enveloping the mint and then packed in brine as for feta.

GERMAN AND EASTERN EUROPEAN FRESH CHEESE

QUARK: Quark is an essential ingredient in German cuisine, accounting for half the country's total cheese consumption. Quite tangy and thick, quark has a tart flavor and smooth, soft, creamy texture. The more whey is drained off, the thicker the texture of the quark. Once drained, the quark may then be salted and pressed to make dry farmer cheese. Its name derives from the Slavic *tvarog*, spelled in many variations in Eastern Europe and Russia, and is also known simply as white cheese. The Polish and Lithuanian version is quite dry and compact; the German soft and tangy. Quark is now being produced in America and is usually sold in plastic tubs like yogurt. (Trader Joe's was selling it under their house brand, though I haven't seen it lately.)

FARMER CHEESE: Of Eastern European origin and closely related to quark, farmer cheese is made from just milk, cream, salt, and culture. To make farmer cheese, the curd is drained overnight in special canvas "socks." The next day, the firm, oddly shaped three-pound loaves are taken out of their socks and wrapped for sale. Because of its short shelf life, you may need to visit a Russian or Eastern European Jewish market to find farmer cheese cut from the old-fashioned three-pound loaf. There are now some smaller Russian companies making farmer cheese, sold in Russian specialty stores including the local Philadelphia company, Fresh Made.

Since childhood, I've loved the dense, tangy, firm, old-fashioned farmer cheese made by the Friendship Dairy of Friendship, New York. Founded more than 80 years ago, this family business specializes in the dairy products beloved by Eastern European Jews. After all these years, they still do most of their sales around New York, in certain Philadelphia neighborhoods, and in Miami (www.friendshipdairies.com). Farmer cheese in the traditional three-pound "sock" shape made by Breakstone's Dairy also traces its history to Eastern European Jewish immigrants. The members of the Breakstone family started out by selling milk and ice cream in New York's Lower East Side and later opened their company selling the fresh dairy products like sour cream, cream cheese, cottage cheese, and farmer cheese eaten in large quantities by people from that part of the world. With its firm texture and tangy flavor, farmer cheese is perfect for filling the Danish Pastry Braid with Goat Cheese

and Cardamom (page 273) and to make New York-style cheesecakes. Substitute up to half the cream cheese in the cheesecake recipes in this book with farmer's cheese for lighter texture and tangy flavor.

AMERICAN FRESH CHEESES

COTTAGE CHEESE: Cottage cheese is a simple, mild white curd cheese that is drained, but not pressed so some of the whey remains and is then usually washed to remove acidity. Cottage cheese was first made in cottages by the farmer's wife using buttermilk, the milk leftover after making butter. The two main types of cottage cheese are small curd, high-acid cheese made without rennet, and larger curd, low-acid cheese made with rennet, which is used to help firm the curd. Because this enzyme also hastens the curdling process, it results in cheese with lower acid content and larger curds. Salted and pressed cottage cheese becomes hoop cheese, farmer cheese, pot cheese, baker's cheese, and queso blanco. For baking, I prefer the tangier, denser curds of farmer cheese or the smaller, sweeter curds of ricotta.

CREAM CHEESE: Cream cheese is an American invention, first made by a New York dairyman named William Lawrence in 1872. In 1880, 'Philadelphia' was adopted as the brand name, after the city that was considered, at the time, to be the home of top quality food, especially dairy products. It was soon distributed in the familiar silver foil wrapper. The company was bought out by Kraft Foods in 1928, and remains the most widely-recognized brand of cream cheese world-wide. In much of the world, Philadelphia is well-known, not as the city that I call home, but as the ubiquitous brand of cream cheese.

Cream cheese is similar to French Neufchâtel in that it is made from cow's milk, but differs in that it is unripened and often contains emulsifiers to keep the water from separating out of the cream and thereby lengthen shelf-life. USDA law requires that cream cheese contain at least 33 percent fat and no more than 55 percent water, although there are low-fat and nonfat varieties now on the market, none of which I use here. I'd rather have a smaller amount of the real thing, than be frustrated by the lack of rich mouthfeel in the low-fat versions.

Cream cheese is mild, fresh-tasting, rich in body, and sweet, yet has a pleasing slight tang. At room temperature, it has a smooth and creamy texture, which gives richness to cheesecakes, frostings, bagel-schmears, and dips. Cream cheese is quite versatile in baking and shows up in the filling for the Danish Pastry Braid with Goat Cheese and Cardamom (page 273) and the Guava and Cheese Empanadas (page 271). It makes easy-to-roll, stretchable, and flaky pastry dough, as in the Cream Cheese Pastry Dough (page 565) used to make the Kasha-Mushroom Knishes (page 183) and for the Anise-Scented Date-Orange Spirals (page 423). It is essential to make American-style lusciously creamy cheesecakes like the California Apricot Cheesecake (page 118), the

Coconut Mango Cheesecake (page 482), the Key Lime Cheesecake Pie in Coconut-Pecan Crust (page 548), the Pineapple Cheesecake with Ginger-Macadamia Crust (page 683), and the July 4th Cheesecake (page 833). Cream cheese added to the batter makes a moister pound cake in the Meyer Lemon Bundt Cake (page 533) and a creamy topping baked onto the Banana-Pecan Roulade (page 132).

Cream cheese should be opened within the package dating code period and used within one week after opening. Be sure to keep it tightly wrapped. If green mold forms on the cheese, do not scrape it off and consume the rest. Unlike some hard cheeses, any mold on cream cheese makes it unsafe to eat, and it should be discarded. Because cream cheese develops mold pretty quickly, it is best to buy it in smaller packages.

VERMONT BUTTER AND CHEESE COMPANY

The Vermont Butter and Cheese Company (www.vtbutterandcheeseco.com) produces domestic mascarpone, quark, fromage blanc, and crème fraîche. The company was founded after Allison Hooper worked more than twenty years ago on a dairy farm in Brittany, France, where she learned to make crème fraîche by setting the fresh cream aside and allowing natural bacteria to create the thick, smooth, tart cultured cream.

AGED CHEESES

Cheesemaking is so old, we can't tell when it started. Like wine, beer, and sourdough bread, aged cheese is a fermented food that probably first occurred naturally. Only later did people learn how to control fermentation and consistently produce good aged cheeses. A myriad of cheeses can be made from the milk of familiar farm animals like cow, goat, and sheep, along with exotics like water buffalo, yak, camel, and even reindeer (though never pig, because its flavor is unpleasant).

To make aged cheese, the milk is curdled, or separated into soft but solid fat-laden curds and protein-rich liquid whey, using a combination of rennet, an extract taken from the stomach of a calf now also produced chemically, along with specific bacteria cultures that convert sugars present in the milk into lactic acid and help define the texture and flavor of the particular cheese, and with salt.

The type of milk and its percentage of butterfat, the flavor of the milk, which depends on the season and what the animal has been eating, the species of bacteria and molds that grow in and on the cheese, the type of salt, the methods of salting, molding, and aging, the special coatings used (such as grape seeds, vegetable ash, herbs, grape must, or chestnut leaves), and the liquids the rind is washed with (such as Marc, cider, white wine, or beer) all impact the resulting cheese. The breed of the animal also affects the milk it gives: Jersey cows produce milk with much higher butterfat content than the more numerous and higher-yielding Holstein

cows. Added flavorings such as herbs, garlic, cumin, caraway, nuts, mushrooms, truffles, or wood smoke may be mixed into the cheese itself. The location where the cheese ages is also significant: think of Roquefort, made in the same caves with the same molds present in the air and on the walls for a thousand years or the many types of cave-aged Tomme de Savoie from the French Alps.

This simple way of concentrating and preserving milk has evolved into the incredibly varied, complex, multi-dimensional, subtly nuanced, and seasonally changeable food called cheese. To make Parmigiano-Reggiano, it takes 1,100 liters (a liter contains about 34 ounces) of milk per vat to produce two wheels of cheese at about 45 kilos each (a kilo weighs 2.1 pounds). A liter of milk weighs about one kilo, so 1,100 kilos of milk yields just 90 kilos of Parmigiano-Reggiano, with an even lower yield when the cheese is premium Stravecchio, aged up to three years rather than the usual one and a half to two years. However, the long storage life of aged cheeses also allows the farmer/cheesemaker to keep a "cash-cow" on hand, turning milk that might otherwise spoil into money in the bank.

Aged cheeses generally range in color from the palest creamy white to deep orange, developing during the aging process, though sometimes natural colors are added. Schabziger (sold in the United States as Sap Sago) from Switzerland is made from cow's milk and gets its unique blue-green color from the finely chopped leaves of a mountain herb known as blue fenugreek. This cheese was first produced by monks in the Swiss Canton of Glarus in the eighth century and is still only produced there. English Sage Derby gets its green veins from rubbed sage. The orange coloring of cheeses like British Red Leicester, American orange cheddar, Dutch Gouda, and French Mimolette comes from annatto, a tropical seed with a mild flavor that is crushed to a fine deep orange powder (see page 206). Other cheeses (like Piedmontese Tetsun al Barolo) or the group of cheeses collectively known as Ubriaco (drunken), contain red wine or grape must and are sometimes rolled in crushed grape pips, giving them a purplish-red color.

Well before Roman times, cheesemaking had evolved what are still standard cheesemaking methods used today, though the industrious and well-organized Romans developed cheesemaking to a fine art. Many Roman villas had a separate cheese kitchen, called the *caseale*, and special areas where cheese could be aged. In large towns homemade cheese would be taken to a special place to be smoked for preservation. By 300 CE, Roman cheese was being exported to countries along the Mediterranean seaboard. Trade had developed so much that the Emperor Diocletian fixed maximum prices for a range of cheeses including a highly popular apple-smoked cheese. Yet another cheese was stamped and sold under the name "La Luna," (the moon) which some say is the precursor of today's Parmigiano-Reggiano.

With the collapse of the Roman Empire around 410 CE, cheesemaking spread slowly via the Mediterranean, Aegean, and Adriatic Seas to Southern and Central Europe. The river valleys provided easy access and production methods were adapted to suit the different terrain and climatic conditions mainly for cow's milk cheese production. Those cheesemakers living in remote mountainous areas would use the milk of agile goats and adaptable sheep.

Even in Roman times, cheeses from southern France and the French Alps were prized. During the Middle Ages, especially in France, monks became the innovators and developers of new types of cheese, like Port Salut and Munster, many of them still sold today. By late medieval times, French cheeses such as Brie and Roquefort were being shipped to the royal French court while Cheddar and Stilton had gained their fame in England by the eighteenth century.

Eventually, the techniques of making cheese traveled into northern Europe, where people discovered over a long period of time and through much trial and error that in colder climates cheese would keep well with much less souring and salting. Now, a new ingredient was added to the basic ingredients of cheese (milk, rennet enzymes, and salt): time. With time, lowered acidity, and salt, cheese became a hospitable medium of the growth of various microbes and enzymes, leading to the enormously varied world of cheeses we eat today. Cheeses like Camembert, Brie, Roquefort, Explorateur, Gorgonzola, and Morbier depend on naturally occurring or added molds to impart their characteristic flavor, color, and texture either on the outer rind or in veins through the inside.

As Harold McGee says, "In a sense, cheese came to life. It became capable of pronounced development and change; it entered the cyclical world of birth, maturation and decline." Real aged cheese (not chemically produced or processed cheese) has a lifetime. When young, it is mild, soft, and pliant; with maturity, its flavor and texture develops and the cheese becomes firmer; with age, it reaches its peak in flavor, but then begins to deteriorate, eventually becoming inedible, because it is too hard, too moldy, too gooey, or too smelly.

In the fertile lowlands of Europe dairying developed at a faster pace and cheesemaking from cows' milk became the norm. Salt is essential for aging cheeses, making the curd firmer and helping the cheese to age safely. In Northern Europe, especially the Netherlands, brine-salted and waxed hard-pressed salted cheeses were developed for long-term storage as sustenance in the long cold winter months. For that reason, these cheeses were also well-suited to shipping long distances. Through extensive Dutch shipping networks, their cheeses ended up in the Caribbean, where Gouda and Edam are scooped out, stuffed, and baked for queso relleno in Yucatan and in Curaçao and Aruba for keshi yena. Even today, these cheeses are still common in Latin America and the Caribbean.

The members of the Helvetica Tribe, who settled in the Swiss Alps, developed their own distinctive type of cheese–the huge wheels of cooked curd cheese called Emmenthal. In France, a large range of soft cheeses developed in the rich agricultural areas in the south and west of the country. With the luxury of comparatively the long cheesemaking season north of the Mediterranean region, soft, buttery cheeses like the square Italian Taleggio from Lombardy, the straw-patterned French Pont l'Evêque from Normandy, and the frankly breast-shaped Tetilla from Galicia, Spain developed.

Today, hundreds, if not thousands, of aged cheeses are produced in Europe from goat's, cow's, and sheep's milk or a combination in Great Britain, France, Belgium, the Netherlands, Spain, Italy, Greece, Scandinavia, the Balkans, and Turkey along with many more from the New World. The great majority of these cheeses are well-suited to baking, especially those with stronger flavors that won't get lost when mixed with other ingredients and perhaps more importantly, those that are reasonable enough in price to cook with rather than reserving them for delectation at the table.

Aged cheeses are often used as a filling and topping in baked goods including the king of cheese breads: pizza, where they lend flavor, richness, and melting texture. In baking, cheese often acts as a binder, bringing all the ingredients together. Because cheese tends to turn grainy and separate if heated too much over direct heat, it is well-suited to the moderate and even temperatures used in baking. The Greek Greens Pie (page 262), the Argentinean Chicken-Cheese Empanadas (page 264), and the Greek Eggplant and Walnut Phyllo Rolls (page 842) all depend on aged cheeses for their fillings.

Sometimes an aged cheese is incorporated

directly into the dough where it acts as a shortening similar to butter, as for the Stilton Scones (page 269), the Cheddar and Chive Gougères (page268), and A Date in a Blanket (page 421). Because of the affinity of cheese and eggs, the two are often combined, as in the French Roquefort, Apple, and Leek Tart (page 103), the Radicchio and Fontina Torta (page 260), and the Torta Pasqualina Genovese (page 438). Cheeses of the same type (i.e. soft-ripened Italian Fontina and American Monterey Jack or English Stilton and Spanish Cabrales) can normally be substituted for one another, although subtle distinctions of flavor and texture will differ.

IS IT "CHEESY"?

Something "cheesy" is cheap, inauthentic, or of poor quality. One can also be "cheesed off," upset or annoyed. Such negative connotations probably derive from the penetrating and sometimes unpleasant odor of soft-ripened cheese. Almost certainly the odor explains the term "cutting the cheese" as a euphemism for flatulence, and the term "cheesy feet" to mean feet that smell (which is actually a result of the same bacteria present in smelly cheeses). People from Wisconsin and the Netherlands, both centers of cheese production are often called "cheeseheads." Fans of the Green Bay Packers or Wisconsin Badgers can be seen in the stands wearing cheese-wedge shaped hats.

CHEESES FOR BAKING

SEMI-SOFT AND CHEDDAR CHEESES: The large category of semi-soft and cheddar-type cheeses are great melters and quite adaptable in baking. In these rennet-based cheeses, the protein matrix they contain breaks down when heated, so the cheese itself will lose its solidity and form a thick, gooey liquid. These cheeses can form part of a dough, be used as a topping, or be mixed with other ingredients, including cream and eggs, for fillings, tarts, and breads. In this book, super-creamy Italian Fontina enriches a savory Radicchio and Fontina Torta from the Veneto in Italy (page 260), while the filling for Chicken-Cheese Empanadas from Northern Mexico includes the little-known but lusciously meltable Chihuahua cheese (page 2647). Onions, sour cream, and aged cheddar fill the English-style Oatmeal-Cheddar Tart on page 573 while cheddar and curry powder go into the dough for the bite-sized sweet-savory bites called A Date in a Blanket (page 421). Blue cheeses, though in a different category, behave pretty much the same way in baking recipes like the Stilton Scones (page 269) and the French Roquefort, Apple, and Leek Tart (page 103), and the Grape, Gorgonzola, and Walnut Focaccia (page 788).

COOKED CHEESES: All these cheeses originate in the high Alpine villages where large wheels of cheese that could keep throughout the long winter months were made from the milk of cows that grazed on the high slopes. Long ago, the cheeses were made in a huge cauldron over an open fire, which was hung from a pole that swiveled so it could easily be removed from the heat. These mountain cheeses typically mature for a long time, up to six months or even a year and then are pressed, resulting in a firm texture that gets its smooth, slightly rubbery texture from the heating method used to produce them. The holes so typical of Emmenthal or Comté are caused by carbon dioxide released during maturing. With their nutty flavor, dense texture, and good melting qualities, cooked cheeses, like Swiss Emmenthal, Greek Graviera, and French Gruyère are kitchen and bakery contenders in dishes like the Chicken-Cheese Empanadas (page 264), the Greek Eggplant and Walnut Phyllo Rolls (page 842), the Country-Style Greek Greens Pie (page 262), and the Alpine Mushroom Pizza with Potato-Rye Dough (page 787).

PASTA FILATA CHEESES: *Pasta filata,* or pulled string cheeses—like Italian mozzarella and pro-volone, Mexican queso Oaxaca, and, naturally, Armenian string cheese—form long strings when melted. To make them, cheese curds are heated in a salted brine until they form a dense mass that is then kneaded by hand or by machine until it is silky smooth. Pasta filata cheeses work best as toppings or as fillings but are generally not appropriate for quiche-like egg fillings, because they can get rubbery and separate when heated. In this chapter both fresh and smoked mozzarella top the White Pizza with Broccoli Rabe (page 266). Goat cheese and moz-zarella top the Arugula and Roasted Tomato Pizza

(page 888) while the Torta Rustica (page 861) contains a cheese-lover's mixture of ricotta, Parmigiano-Reggiano, Romano cheese, and fresh mozzarella. Fresh mozzarella is packed in a light brine while dense, low-moisture mozzarella, familiar as the top-ping for commercial pizza, is sold as a firmer log.

AGED SEASONING CHEESES: Aged, seasoning cheeses are primarily used in the kitchen and for baking. They include Italian Asiago, Parmigiano-Reggiano, and its simpler cousin, Grana Padano, American aged Monterey Jack, and domestic Asiago, Swiss Sap Sago, Italian aged pecorino, Dutch aged Gouda, and Greek Kefalotyri and Kashkaval. While these cheeses won't form a creamy mass when melted on their own, because they tend to separate, when combined with other ingredients in bread and pastry doughs, fillings, and toppings, their concentrated and grainy texture shines flavor.

Pecorino Romano flavors the all-vegetable Torta Pasqualina from Genoa (page 438), the heartier meat, vegetable, and cheese Torta Rustica (page 861), and the Sicilian Pan Pizza with Zucca (page 737). Parmigiano-Reggiano tops an unusual Alpine Mushroom Pizza sprinkled with truffle oil (page 787) and a wonderful, mint-scented, dramatic-looking Sardinian Potato Torta (page 728) gets its share of Romano cheese, preferably Pecorino Sardo pro-duced in Sardinia.

GOAT CHEESES: Although they don't melt into creaminess, tangy white fresh goat cheeses work well for baking and can add creaminess and flavor to doughs, used as a topping, as an ingredient in fillings, doughs, and toppings. In this book, goat cheese fills Turkish Baked Cheese Turnovers: Puaça (page 898). Combined with cream cheese, goat cheese makes a sweet, creamy mousse-like uncooked filling for a Strawberry-Vanilla Coeur à la Crème Tart with Goat Cheese (page 832). Combined with ricotta cheese, it becomes the filling of the honey-drizzled deep-fried turnovers from Sardinia called Sebadas (page 517). The Savory Eggplant and Spiced Almond Tart (page 72) is filled with soft, creamy roasted eggplant, flavored and enriched with goat cheese and strong, salty Romano cheese. An Herbed Focaccia with Goat Cheese, Red Onion, and Black Olives (page 725) is topped with chunks of tangy, fresh goat cheese which maintains its color and shape when baked, even at high temperature.

FETA CHEESE: This rich and tangy soft cheese is of humble origin—its name comes from the word "fetid" from the Latin *foetidus*, meaning to stink, or having a strong, even offensive smell. (Some sources say its name comes from a Greek word meaning "to slice"; maybe both are true.) While some might call its characteristic aroma fetid and unpleasant, its international popularity belies this negative association. Feta cheese, which originated in Greece, is authentically made of sheep's milk, although much is now made with cow's milk or a mixture of the two, to cut down on cost. Feta is aged (but not ripened) four to six weeks in a salty whey mixture.

Actually a type of pickled, rather than aged, cheese, feta's flavor becomes sharper and saltier with age. It is creamy white in color with small holes, a crumbly texture, and is normally found in square cakes that don't have any rind packed in the brine that helps preserve the cheese—because of the high percentage of salt—but also makes it taste stronger, the longer it stays in the brine. Try the Tomato and Feta Topping for the Kea Stuffed Griddle Bread (page 144), the Greek Feta Cheese Bread (Tyropsomo) on page 261, the Country-Style Greek Greens Pie (page 262), and the Turkish Savory Cornbread (Misir Ekmegi) on page 388.

WORDS FOR CHEESE

The word for cheese in Italian, *formaggio*, refers to the forms used to shape the cheese, as does the French *fromage*; cheese in English, *queso* in Spanish, and *käse* in German all derive from the Latin *caseus* meaning cheese.

BUYING AND STORING CHEESE

Ideally, buy cheese in a hunk, avoiding any packages that show signs of white mold underneath their plastic wrap, a sign the cheese was cut too long ago. Grate the cheese as needed, because once grated, the cheese flavor quickly dissipates. Avoid industrially-produced pasteurized process cheeses, which are not naturally fermented and aged, but rather are produced quickly and cheaply in the factory and contain other ingredients including preservatives, emulsifiers, extra salt, food coloring, and whey. Pre-grated cheeses usually contain cellulose, which is added to keep the strands separate, but detracts from flavor and texture.

Store cheese in the warmer parts of your refrigerator, such as a produce drawer or the top shelf, away from the fan. While plastic wrap is acceptable for cheese purists prefer waxed paper, parchment paper, butcher paper, or aluminum foil, which allow the cheese to breathe. If cheese is wrapped in plastic, change it every few days to allow the cheese to breathe, and to keep the cheese from becoming slimy or hard. Always rewrap cheese after it has been opened using a fresh wrapping.

Wrap hard, dry cheeses such as Parmigiano-Reggiano, Asiago, or Dry Jack in plastic wrap or store in a zipper lock bag. Wrap semi-soft cheese such as Fontina or Monterey Jack in plastic wrap, parchment or waxed paper, or store in a closed plastic container. Double wrap strong, pungent cheese like Gorgonzola or Limburger or store in an airtight container to avoid having these aromas permeate the refrigerator.

If a hard cheese, like Cheddar, Swiss, Parmesan, Romano, or Gruyère develops white mold on the outside, slice off the outside layer of the cheese about half an inch below the mold to ensure that it has been entirely removed: the rest of the cheese will be fine. For semi-soft cheeses like mozzarella, Muenster, and Monterey Jack, cut away about one inch below the mold and the rest of the cheese can be eaten. Soft cheeses like Brie, Gorgonzola, and Camembert, and fresh cheeses like ricotta, cream, and cottage cheeses should be discarded or returned if they develop mold, because the mold can spread more easily through the cheese

Radicchio and Fontina Torta

In this sophisticated savory tart from Northern Italy, the bitterness of radicchio is tamed by cooking and balanced with nutty, rich, meltingly creamy Fontina cheese. The tastier but harder to grow highland radicchio di Treviso, which resembles long spears of magenta-edged Belgian endive, is ideal here, but the more common round-headed lowland radicchio di Chioggia will do fine. Serve the torta for lunch with a soup of salad, for brunch, or as part of a buffet.

YIELD: 12 APPETIZER SERVINGS; 8 MAIN COURSE SERVINGS

$3/4$ pound Savory Spiced Whole Wheat Pastry dough (page 862), Buttermilk Tart Pastry dough (page 565), or Savory Tart Pastry dough (page 206)

2 medium heads radicchio di Chioggia or 3 medium heads radicchio di Treviso

$1/4$ cup dry white vermouth or dry white wine

$1/4$ cup water

2 tablespoons unsalted butter

$1/2$ teaspoon fine sea salt, plus more to taste

$1/2$ teaspoon freshly ground black pepper, plus more to taste

2 eggs

4 large egg yolks ($1/4$ cup)

1 cup milk

$1/2$ cup heavy cream

6 ounces (about $3/4$ cup shredded) Fontina cheese, trimmed of rind, frozen until firm, then shredded

Roll out the dough on a lightly floured surface into a large round about $^3/_8$-inch thick. Fold the dough in quarters and unfold over a 10-inch diameter tart pan with a removable bottom. Lay into the pan without stretching the dough and press well into the corners so there are no thick spots. Trim any overhang with scissors. Chill the dough for 30 minutes to relax the gluten so the tart crust maintains its shape.

Preheat the oven to 375°F.

Fit a piece of heavy-duty foil onto the dough and up over the edges and fill with beans or other pie weights. Blind bake the crust on the bottom shelf of the oven (just pastry crust, no filling) until the dough is cooked through but not yet browned, about 30 minutes. Remove the foil and the weights, reduce the oven temperature to 325°F, and bake for 10 minutes longer, or until the dough is evenly and lightly browned. Remove from the oven and cool to room temperature on a wire rack before filling.

Cut out and discard the cores of the radicchio, cut in quarters then cut each quarter crosswise into $^1/_4$-inch-thick slices.

Bring the wine, water, butter, salt, and pepper to a simmer in a large heavy skillet. Add the radicchio, cover, and braise over moderately low heat, stirring occasionally, until the radicchio is wilted, about 10 minutes. Remove the cover and continue to cook over medium-high heat until the liquid has evaporated. Cool the mixture to room temperature.

Preferably in a 1- to 2-quart Pyrex measure, whisk together the eggs, egg yolks, milk, cream, and salt and pepper to taste. Distribute the cheese evenly on the bottom of the tart crust. Transfer the radicchio to the crust using a slotted spoon to drain off any juices; spread the radicchio

evenly in the pan. Pour most of the custard into the crust and bake the tart on the bottom shelf of the oven until the custard has formed a skin, about 30 minutes.

Poke a hole in the center of the custard skin and carefully pour in the remaining custard. Continue baking the tart for about 20 minutes or until the custard is completely set in the center. Cool on a rack for 15 minutes before cutting into serving portions.

To make ahead, bake 1 or 2 days before, chill, and cut into serving portions. Arrange the slices on a parchment paper–lined baking pan, cover loosely with aluminum foil, and reheat in a moderate oven about 30 minutes, or until thoroughly heated, removing the foil for the last 5 to 10 minutes of baking.

Greek Feta Cheese Bread (Tyropsomo)

Tangy, salty feta cheese crumbles enrich this light olive oil and yogurt-enriched bread dough. The bread is easy to make, keeps well for several days, and can be successfully frozen. The word tyro *or* tiro *in Greek refers to anything made with cheese; the ending* psomo *means bread. The white whole wheat flour I use here has a more delicate flavor and is lighter in color than standard whole wheat flour, which can be substituted. Bulgarian sheep's milk feta has excellent full-bodied flavor and is reasonably priced. Look for it in Greek and Middle Eastern markets.*

YIELD: 3 ($^1/_2$-POUND) BREADS

6 ounces (1¾ cups 1 tablespoon)
   white whole wheat flour
½ pound (2 cups) unbleached bread flour
1 teaspoon fine sea salt
1 (¼-ounce) package (2¼ teaspoons) active dry yeast
¾ cup lukewarm water
½ cup plain yogurt
1 tablespoon honey
¼ cup plus 2 tablespoons extra-virgin olive oil
2 tablespoons chopped fresh dill
¾ pound (about 1½ cups) crumbled feta cheese
Semolina or cornmeal, for dusting

Whisk together the dry ingredients: white whole wheat flour, bread flour, and salt. In the bowl of a standing electric mixer combine the yeast, the water, the yogurt, the honey, and ½ cup of the flour mixture. Let the mixture stand at warm room temperature for 20 minutes, or until bubbly.

Using the paddle, beat in ¼ cup of the olive oil, the dill, and about half the remaining flour mix. Switch to the dough hook and beat in remaining flour mix. Continue beating until the dough is smooth and elastic and comes away cleanly from the sides of the bowl.

Transfer the dough to a large oiled bowl; turn around so the dough is oiled all over. Cover with plastic wrap or a damp cloth and allow the dough to rise at warm room temperature until doubled in size, about 2 hours.

Punch down the dough, knead until smooth, and roll out into a large rectangle. Sprinkle with half the feta cheese and roll up into a long log shape. Cut into 3 portions and roll each portion into a round.

Turn cut side up and using a rolling pin, roll each

round out to about 6 inches in diameter. Brush the breads with the remaining 2 tablespoons olive oil. Sprinkle the breads with the remaining feta cheese, patting lightly so the cheese adheres, and tucking the rough ends of the dough underneath. Sprinkle the bread rounds with water from a plant mister, and allow the breads to rise at warm room temperature for 1 hour, or until light and puffy.

Preheat the oven to 350°F. Arrange the breads on a baking pan that has been lightly dusted with semolina or cornmeal, and bake for 30 minutes, or until well browned and the inside reads 190°F when pierced with a thermometer. Cool on a wire rack. Store at room temperature in an open plastic bag or a brown paper bag up to 3 days.

Country-Style Greek Greens Pie

While visiting the Kalamata region of Greece with the International Olive Oil Council, I happily joined one of our local guides in a hunt along the roadside for young edible wild greens to use for salad and hortopita, or greens pie. Combining the bitter, sharp, peppery, earthy, and acidic flavors and the varied textures of these greens makes for a more interesting and nutritious pie than the more common spanakopita made only with spinach. Cultivated and wild green possibilities include curly endive, young dandelion, catalogna (an Italian chicory, not dandelion though often sold as such), mustard greens, beet greens, turnip greens, sorrel, watercress, chopped fennel stalks, wild fennel greens, green onions, Swiss chard leaves, young stinging nettles, purslane, amaranth leaves, spinach, dill, flat-leaf parsley, and spearmint.

YIELD: 1 LARGE PIE, 10 TO 12 SERVINGS

3 pounds (3 bunches) assorted cooking greens
  (a combination of at least three types of greens)
$1/4$ bunch dill, chopped (about 3 tablespoons)
2 bunches green onions, thinly sliced (about 2 cups)
$1/2$ bunch flat-leaf parsley, chopped (about $1/2$ cup)
$1/2$ cup mint, preferably spearmint, chopped
  (about 3 tablespoons)
$3/4$ pound feta cheese, drained and crumbled
  (about $1^1/2$ cups)
$1/2$ pound Greek graviera or sharp Cheddar cheese,
  grated (about 2 cups)
2 eggs, lightly beaten
2 ounces ($1/4$ cup plus 1 tablespoon) semolina
  or cornmeal
Freshly ground black pepper
$3/4$ cup extra-virgin olive oil, for brushing
1 pound phyllo dough, defrosted in the refrigerator
  if frozen, preferably thicker #6 or #10 phyllo (see page
  740)

Remove the ribs and stems from the greens. Wash in a large sink full of cold water, agitating vigorously to encourage any sand to fall to the bottom. If the water looks dirty, wash again. The water should look clear when the greens are clean. Drain well.

Pour 1 cup of water into a large skillet and bring to a boil. Add the greens, turning once or twice, cooking just long enough to wilt, about 3 minutes. Drain in a colander, run under cold water to set the color, and when cool enough to handle, squeeze out as much water as possible. Chop the greens coarsely, then combine with the dill, parsley, mint, both cheeses, eggs, semolina, and pepper to taste.

Preheat the oven to 400°F. Brush a large shallow cake pan, preferably one that is 12-inches in diameter or a shallow earthenware cazuela, lightly with olive oil.

Trim the phyllo leaves to a square, discarding the remainder. Layer the pan with 8 sheets of phyllo, brushing each layer lightly with olive oil and cris-crossing the sheets each time so they cover the sides of the pan and overlap the edge by several inches. Spread the filling in an even layer over the pastry, then cover with another layer of phyllo leaves, again making an eight-deep layer of overlapping leaves, brushing each layer lightly with olive oil. Trim the top layer of overhanging edges close to the edge using scissors. Fold the overlapping dough edges over the dough and roll up at the edges tightly to form a raised edge. Bush the pie again with olive oil. Using a French baker's lame, a single-edged razor, or a box cutter, lightly score the top in large diamond shapes.

Bake the pie on the bottom shelf of the oven for 30 minutes, then reduce the oven temperature to 350°F and continue baking for 30 minutes longer or until the pastry is golden and crispy. Remove from the oven and cool for about 10 minutes before cutting into portion sizes. Store covered and refrigerated up to 3 days. Wrap in foil and reheat in a 350°F oven for 30 minutes

FETA CHEESE

Greek-made feta is so popular in its home country, where it's sold in special all-white dairy stores, that very little gets exported.

In Greece, feta often goes into *mezze*—bar snacks like tapas—because its saltiness encourages thirst. With its uncompromisingly strong flavor, feta is used in a huge number of traditional Greek savory pies and makes a good substitute for Sardinian sheep's milk cheese and Mexican queso añejo.

EATING WEEDS

City and country-born Greeks alike enjoy going out into the fields and the roadsides to gather wild greens in season, which are prized for their intense flavors and healthful, cleansing properties. Popular wild and sometimes cultivated greens include amaranth (*vlita* in Greek) one of the most common and often cultivated in kitchen gardens, sow thistle (*tsochos* or *piimaohakas*), dandelion (*rathikia*), stinging nettles (*tsouknithes* or *kōrvenōges*), mallow (*molocha* or *kassinaeris*), purslane (*glistrida, andrakles,* or *portulak*), wild fennel (*marathon*), wild carrots, as well as the more familiar sorrel, mustard greens, arugula, and many types of chicory and endive.

Chicken–Cheese Empanadas

I adapted this recipe from one shared with me by talented Argentinean chef Guillermo Pernot, with whom I co-authored the James Beard Award-winning book, Ceviche. According to Pernot, empanadas, which originated in Spain, are the national food of Argentina. Easy-to-use frozen rounds of dough called "discos" can be found at Latino markets and some supermarkets. I prefer to make my own dough to avoid the preservatives and trans-fat shortenings used in the commercial product. Inexpensive boneless, skinless chicken thighs make for a moist and tasty filling, but because commercial chicken thighs can have a rather strong, almost fishy taste due to their feed, which often contains fish meal, I use natural chicken, such as Bell & Evans, my chicken of choice. With a side of refried beans or a salad, you've got a meal that will even please kids (at least the empanada part).

$^1/_4$ cup dry white wine

$^1/_4$ cup water

Fine sea salt, to taste

$^1/_2$ pound boneless, skinless chicken thigh meat, trimmed of fat

2 tablespoons olive oil

1 medium white onion, diced

$^1/_2$ red bell pepper, diced

$^1/_2$ poblano pepper, diced, substitute bell pepper and/or jalapeño pepper

Kernels cut from 2 ears fresh corn, or $^3/_4$ cup frozen corn kernels

2 tablespoons chopped cilantro

2 teaspoons dried oregano

1 teaspoon chipotle chile flakes, or other pure chile flakes or powder

2 ounces Monterey Jack cheese, shredded ($^1/_2$ cup)

2 ounces Mexican queso añejo or feta cheese, crumbled ($^1/_2$ cup)

1$^1/_4$ pounds Savory Empanada Dough (page 205)

Cold water for brushing

1 large egg, lightly beaten with 1 tablespoon water, for the egg wash

Make the filling: In a medium pot, bring the wine, water, and salt to taste to a boil. Add the chicken and bring back to the boil. Reduce the heat to a simmer, cover, and cook for 15 minutes or until the meat is cooked through. Cool the chicken in its cooking juices.

Meanwhile, heat the olive oil, onion, red bell pepper, and poblano pepper in a large skillet. Sauté over medium heat, stirring occasionally, until the mixture is lightly browned, about 4 minutes. Add the corn and salt to taste. Cook until the peppers soften and most of the liquid has evaporated, about 3 minutes.

Drain the chicken, reserving the cooking liquid for another use (add to soup, perhaps). Pick the chicken meat, removing any fat or connective tissue, then cut into small cubes. Add to the pepper-corn mixture along with the cilantro, oregano, and chipotle flakes, and remove from the heat. Cool to room temperature, then mix in the cheeses. Refrigerate the filling until chilled, up to 2 days before assembling empanadas.

Assemble the empanadas: Fill a small bowl with cold water. Using a rolling pin, roll out the Empanada Dough about $^3/_8$-inch thick on a lightly floured surface. Using a 6-inch plate as a template, cut out circles. If desired, re-roll any scraps and cut out more circles. Spoon about $^1/_4$ cup chilled filling into the center of each circle, leaving a $^1/_2$-inch border all around. Brush the border of each circle with cold water. Fold the dough over the filling, stretching it slightly, to form a half-moon shape. Beginning at one end, press the edges together to seal, while pushing out any air pockets. Press again to ensure that the empanadas are well sealed. Using a fork or your fingers, crimp the edges to form a decorative edge. Repeat with the remaining circles and filling.

Brush the empanadas with egg wash, and refrigerate for at least 30 minutes but no longer than 2 days. (Once filled, the empanadas may be frozen and baked later, without defrosting, in a preheated 350°F oven for 40 to 50 minutes.)

Preheat the oven to 375°F. Line two 18 x 13-inch half sheet pans (or other large baking pans) with parchment paper or silicone baking mats. Arrange the empanadas on the baking sheets. Cut several small slits into the top of the empanadas to allow steam to escape. Bake for 30 minutes or until puffed and browned, and the filling is bubbling inside. Serve immediately.

MONTEREY JACK AND DRY JACK

Monterey Jack from California was originally developed in 1882 by a man of Scots origin, David Jacks. It is generally a soft, mild, buttery-tasting, and creamy-textured cheese, excellent for melting. Supermarket Jack cheese is aged about six months and contains about twenty-five percent fat. I often use Jack cheese as a nutty-tasting, warm, and rounded, though less complex, substitute for the more expensive Italian Fontina or the excellent though harder-to-find Mexican Chihuahua cheese.

Dry Monterey Jack, in my opinion, America's finest grating cheese, was first made in 1915, and is today produced exclusively by the Vella Company in California (www.vellacheese.com). It is long-aged, with a firm texture and concentrated sweet, nutty flavor. Its dark natural rind is hand-rubbed with oil, cocoa, and pepper and can be rather difficult to remove as it must be carefully cut or scraped away. The deep yellow, craggy-textured cheese is excellent for grating, well-suited to Mexican- and American-style dishes, though not commonly available, at least on the East Coast.

White Pizza with Broccoli Rabe

This white pizza, meaning that it is made without any tomato sauce, combines sweet, mild yet creamy ricotta cheese, woodsy-tasting smoked mozzarella, and milky slices of fresh mozzarella with bitter but delicious broccoli rabe that has been sautéed with plenty of garlic and hot red pepper flakes. If you don't care for the bold flavor of broccoli rabe, substitute regular broccoli, though the flavor will be less exciting. The light and slightly crunchy cornmeal pizza dough is the one I used to make hundreds, if not thousands, of wonderful wood-oven baked pizzas at the now-closed Stella Notte, in my most recent chef's position.

YIELD: 1 PIZZA, 2 TO 4 SERVINGS

$1/2$ pound ($1/2$ bunch) broccoli rabe,
   trimmed and chopped
$3/4$ pound Cornmeal Pizza Dough (page 392)
2 tablespoons extra-virgin olive oil
2 cloves garlic, finely chopped
1 teaspoon red pepper flakes
2 ounces ricotta cheese
2 ounces smoked mozzarella, diced
2 ounces fresh mozzarella, sliced

Preheat the oven to 500°F, if possible, with a pizza stone in the oven. Bring a medium pot of salted water to the boil. Add the broccoli rabe and cook for 2 to 3 minutes, or until brightly colored and crisp-tender. Drain and run under cold water to set the color.

Stretch out the pizza round to the size of wooden peel (see page 887) and sprinkle lightly with cornmeal. Alternatively, roll out the pizza and transfer it to a cornmeal dusted metal baking pan (a paella pan works well here) or a 12-inch pizza pan. Combine the olive oil, garlic, and red pepper flakes and use to brush the round, especially on the edges.

Leaving a $1/2$-inch border all around, spoon dollops of the ricotta cheese on the dough, following with small mounds of the broccoli rabe. Sprinkle the smoked and fresh mozzarella over top.

If you are using a peel, transfer the unbaked pizza to the pizza stone by placing the peel at a low angle to the stone and giving the peel a fast, vigorous thrust forward and then back, so the pizza jumps onto the stone. Bake until bubbling and well browned, about 6 minutes. If baking in a pan, allow about 8 minutes for baking. Cool slightly, then cut into 8 wedges.

PIZZA AND PITTA

There are many unrelated theories as to the origins of these Italian words. They may derive from Greek names for "bran bread" pissa, pitta, or ptea which spread through southern Italy (Magna Grecia) when it was part of the Greek Empire. According to this theory, pizza was originally poor man's bran bread. Others believe that *pizza* comes from the German word *pizzo* meaning "mouthful" (related to the English words "bit" and "bite") and was brought to Italy in the middle ages by invading Langobards.

Pizza also may derive from the Latin *pinsa*, meaning to pound or to crush, referring to the flattening out of the dough. Or, it may derive from the Italian word *pizzicare* meaning "to pluck," referring to pizza being "plucked" quickly from the oven. In yet another theory, it derives from the Latin *picea* which refers to the blackening of bread in the oven. Take your pick.

USING A WOODEN PEEL

A peel is a long-handled wooden board that is used to transfer pizza, breads, and other baked doughs to and from the oven, usually onto the brick floor of a hearth oven or a preheated pizza stone placed in a common home oven. To use the peel, sprinkle it lightly and evenly with cornmeal or fine semolina to keep the dough from sticking to the board. Stretch out the dough round to the size of the peel. Top as in the recipe without overloading the dough with topping, especially if the topping is wet, and leaving a 1-inch border all around. Note that once the dough has been topped, it must be quickly transferred to the oven otherwise the dough will begin to stick. Transfer to the pizza stone by placing the peel at a low angle to the stone and giving the peel a fast, vigorous thrust forward and then back, so the pizza jumps onto the stone. (Like I did, you may need to practice this a few times until you get the knack.) Bake as directed until the topping is bubbling and the dough is well browned, usually 6 to 8 minutes. Slide the peel underneath the baked dough to remove it from the oven and transfer it to a wooden board for cutting.

Cheddar and Chive Gougères

These airy cheese puffs are inspired by an amuse bouche (literally, "tickle the mouth" in French), a small bite before the real meal, served at the HerbFarm Restaurant outside of Seattle. The restaurant serves a prix-fixe extravaganza of nine courses, each matched with an appropriate wine and built around a different seasonal theme, including Temptations of Spice, The Hunter's Table, Truffle Treasure, The Fundamental Root, and Kobe Beef: Super Cattle. I met the owners and chef of the restaurant and just had to make a pilgrimage to this restaurant and its adjoining herb garden. In France, gougères traditionally contain Gruyère cheese; aged Cheddar is a good American alternative. The more aged and concentrated the cheese, the bolder the flavor. Use fresh chives only; dried chives lack the bright green herbal note. For best results, make on a day with low humidity.

YIELD: ABOUT 36, 12 HORS D'OEUVRE TO 16 SERVINGS

1 cup water

1/4 pound (1 stick) unsalted butter, cut into bits

Fine sea salt, to taste

1/4 pound (1 cup minus 1 tablespoon) unbleached all-purpose flour

4 large eggs, at room temperature

2 ounces extra-sharp Cheddar cheese, grated (3/4 cup)

1 bunch chives, thinly sliced

1 large egg white, lightly beaten with 1 tablespoon water, for the egg wash

Combine the water, butter, and salt in a medium heavy-bottomed pot, cover, and bring to a boil. As soon as the butter has melted, and without allowing any of the water to boil away, uncover, and add the flour all at once. Beat with a wooden spoon to combine thoroughly until the mixture forms a mass. Continue to cook for 2 to 3 minutes, stirring constantly until the dough starts to dry out and comes away from the sides of the pot.

Transfer the dough to the bowl of a standing mixer fitted with the paddle attachment. Beat on medium speed for about 1 minute, or until smooth and slightly cooled. Beat the eggs in one at a time, beating well after each addition to achieve a satiny, slightly sticky paste with the consistency between a soft dough and a thick batter. Add the cheese and chives and beat 1 minute longer, until combined well.

Preheat the oven to 375°F. Line one or two 18 x 13-inch half sheet pan (or other large baking pans) with parchment paper or silicone baking mats.

Transfer the mixture to a pastry bag fitted with a large plain tip and pipe out small high rounds onto the prepared baking pans, allowing 1 inch of space in between to allow for spreading. Alternatively, use 2 teaspoons of the dough to form balls and drop in rows on the paper, allowing 1 inch of space in between.

Brush the tips of the gougères with the egg wash. Bake for 25 to 30 minutes or until puffed and golden brown, then reduce the heat to 250°F and bake for 15 minutes longer or until the gougères are dried out, firm, and medium brown in color. Turn off the oven and allow the gougères to dry out in the oven for about 15 minutes before serving.

BEECHER'S HAND-MADE CHEESE

On a typically chilly, rainy day in Seattle, I gladly warmed up on a milk-can stool, gazing through the window of the intricate apparatus with which Beecher's cheese is made. If you want to see great cheese being made first-hand and taste the best macaroni-and-cheese and grilled cheese sandwiches anywhere (outside of my own kitchen), stop in at Beecher's, across the street from the Pike Place Market in Seattle.

This cheese-lover's haven was opened in 2003, by Kurt Beecher Dammier, a successful businessman and entrepreneur. The store quickly became known for its signature rich and creamy Flagship, a robust, nutty combination of Cheddar and Gruyère that is aged for one year. Beecher works with local dairy farmers to find milk from cows that are healthy and are not given any recombinant bovine growth hormones (rBST) for his cheese. Go to www.beechers handmadecheese.com for more information or stop in when in Seattle.

Pre-Shredded Cheese and Cellulose

While it's a bit more work to shred your own cheese, look at the ingredients of any bag of pre-shredded cheese and you'll see cellulose added. While this is an inert ingredient, added to keep the cheese from clumping back together, I'd much rather be eating pure cheese than any additives.

Stilton Scones

These meltingly tender, richly savory scones take the place of biscuits or bread and complement country-style soups like leek and potato, chunky vegetable, or cream of tomato especially well. Stilton has a nutty, not-too-strong flavor, but other blue cheeses can be substituted. Serve the scones, cut small, as an hors d'oeuvre for a cocktail party. Double the recipe if desired, roll out into a sheet, then freeze. Defrost overnight in the refrigerator, then cut out decorative shapes and bake the scones just in time for your gathering. Note that the scones reheat well in the microwave without getting rubbery.

YIELD: 12 SCONES

$\frac{1}{2}$ pound (2 cups minus 2 tablespoons) unbleached
   all-purpose flour
1 teaspoon baking powder
$\frac{1}{2}$ teaspoon dry mustard
$\frac{1}{4}$ teaspoon cayenne pepper
Fine sea salt and freshly ground black pepper, to taste
2 ounces ($\frac{1}{2}$ stick) unsalted butter,
   chilled and cut into bits
1 large egg
$\frac{1}{2}$ cup milk
$\frac{1}{4}$ pound Stilton cheese, crumbled

Preheat the oven to 400°F. Line a baking sheet with parchment paper or a silicone baking mat.

In the bowl of a standing mixer, combine the dry ingredients: flour, baking powder, mustard, cayenne pepper, salt, and pepper, whisking to combine. Add the butter and place the bowl in the freezer to chill, about 30 minutes.

Combine the egg and 2 tablespoons of the milk and reserve for the glaze.

Using the paddle attachment, beat the chilled flour mixture until it resembles oatmeal. Add the cheese and remaining milk and beat just long enough for the mixture to come together and form a ball.

Roll the dough out to $^1/_2$-inch thick between 2 sheets of wax paper, or on a lightly floured board. Cut into 2-inch rounds, place on the prepared baking sheet, and brush lightly with the egg mixture. Reroll the scraps, if desired. Bake for 15 to 18 minutes or until lightly browned. Serve warm.

WHAT IS A SCONE?

Scones are believed to have originated in Scotland and are closely related to the griddle baked flatbread known as *bannocks*. They were first made with oats, shaped into a large round, scored into four to six triangles (like shortbread), and cooked on a griddle either over an open fire or on top of the stove.

The origin of the name *scone*, correctly pronounced as *skon* or *skoan* is unclear. Some say the name comes from the place where the Kings of Scotland were crowned, the Stone (Scone) of Destiny. Others believe the name is derived from the Dutch word *schoonbrot* and the equivalent German word *sconbrot* meaning "fine (white) bread." Still others say it comes from the Gaelic *sgonn*, a shapeless mass or large mouthful, which makes the most sense to me as scones are often spooned into a rough shape before baking.

Scone dough is typically soft and sticky and contains one part liquid to three parts flour. It needs to be baked in a hot oven so the dough sets quickly, thereby producing a light scone with a light to golden brown floury top and bottom with white sides. The interior texture should be light and soft, and white in color. Drop scones are lighter and softer than rolled-out scones, because working the dough by rolling and incorporating flour in the rolling process toughens it slightly.

CHOOSING AND STORING STILTON

Stilton was first made in the early eighteenth century in the midlands of England in and around the Melton Mowbray area. The cheese takes its name from the village of Stilton (though no Stilton was ever made there) on the Great North Road. There, coaches traveling from London to Scotland and other northern destinations made their first stop for fresh horses and overnight stays. Convenient to Melton Mowbray and the surrounding area, the village became the central market place for the cheese with thousands of wheels sold every week. The blue cheese bought in Stilton became known as Stilton cheese. Today, nearly 300 years later, Stilton is still made exclusively in the surrounding counties of Leicestershire, Nottinghamshire, and Derbyshire from local milk.

Only six dairies, using the original centuries-old recipe, are licensed to produce this creamy, ivory-hued king of cheeses. It is the only British cheese with its own certification trademark. Stilton has characteristic radial veining that can look like shattered porcelain because of its extremely fine veins of mold. This gives Stilton its overall bluing–not just in pockets like other blue cheeses–and allows for even flavor. Good Stilton should have a dry, rough, brown rind and a creamy ivory interior that has plenty of bluing right to the edge. The cheese should be crumbly, but moist enough to hold its shape. Avoid Stilton that is darkened with a dry brownish crust and grayish interior. The best Stilton for cooking comes from the inner core of the cheese where it is creamiest.

Buy Stilton in larger pieces so you will end up with a good-sized section of interior. Unfortunately the rind and hard portion near the rind isn't good for cooking, though some people enjoy eating it. To keep up with the strong demand for Stilton, some lesser quality cheese can be found on the market. Poor-quality Stilton will have insufficient blue veining, because it hasn't been aged long enough, and a dry rather than creamy interior.

Guava and Cheese Empanadas

Quince or mango paste would also work well for these savory-sweet turnovers, which are good make-ahead pastries for a party. Once filled and brushed with egg wash, the flaky empanadas can be frozen, then baked directly from the freezer. The filling combines mellow cream cheese, stronger aged cheese, and intensely fruity guava. The guava paste—made from fruit pulp, sugar, pectin, and citric acid all cooked slowly until exceedingly thick and rich—is sold in bars that are firm enough to slice. Guava paste can be found in Latin markets and specialty stores and will last at least a year in the pantry, though I would refrigerate it after opening for up to three months.

YIELD: 36 EMPANADAS

1 pound cream cheese, softened

$1/2$ pound Cotija, Monterey Jack, or Manchego cheese, grated

1 (15-ounce) package guava paste

$1/2$ cup sugar

1 teaspoon ground cinnamon

1 pound Savory Empanada Dough (page 205)

1 egg, lightly beaten with 2 tablespoons water, for the egg wash

In the bowl of an electric mixer fitted with a paddle attachment, beat together the cream cheese and grated cheese until smooth. Cut the guava paste into thin slices. Combine the sugar with the cinnamon. Set the three mixtures aside.

On a lightly floured board, roll the dough out about $^3/_8$-inch thick. Place on parchment paper or wax paper–lined trays and chill again in the refrigerator for 30 minutes or 1 hour in the freezer.

Cut out 5-inch circles, using a small plate as a guide. Spread 2 tablespoons of the cheese mixture over half of each circle and then top with a slice of guava paste, leaving a $^1/_2$-inch border all around. Brush the edges of the circles with the beaten egg and fold the dough over to enclose the filling. Seal the edges by crimping with a fork. Brush the empanadas with the egg wash and sprinkle with the cinnamon sugar. Prick each empanada with a fork to allow steam to escape.

Line a baking sheet with parchment paper or a silicone mat. Arrange the empanadas on the baking sheets and chill for at least 30 minutes. (If desired, freeze the empanadas at this point. Bake directly from the freezer at 325°F for about 45 minutes or until golden brown.)

Preheat the oven to 350°F. Bake the empanadas for 25 to 30 minutes, or until golden. Cool for about 10 minutes and then serve.

Turkish Ricotta Cookies (Lor Kurabiyesi)

I learned to make these deliciously delicate sesame-crusted cookies from my Turkish friend Didem Ertan and her mother, Senay Orek. We all sat around forming the soft dough into balls, then coating them in white sesame seeds before baking them. Turkish lor is a type of fresh white cheese curd related to Italian ricotta, French fromage blanc, and Indian paneer. It is lightly tangy with a fine, smooth texture. The cookies are usually infused with aromatic piney mastic resin (see page 519), for which I've developed quite a taste, but you may leave it out.

YIELD: 36 COOKIES

$^1/_2$ pound (2 cups minus 2 tablespoons) unbleached all-purpose flour

2 ounces ($^3/_4$ cup) potato starch

1 teaspoon baking powder

1 teaspoon finely crushed mastic "tears," substitute almond or vanilla extract

1 teaspoon fine sea salt

$^1/_4$ pound (1 stick) unsalted butter, softened

$1^1/_2$ cups sugar

1 large egg

10 ounces whole milk ricotta cheese, crumbled farmers cheese, or Mastelo cheese (see page 277)

Grated zest of 1 lemon (1 tablespoon)

1 cup white sesame seeds

$^1/_2$ cup blanched almonds

Preheat the oven to 350°F. Line two 18 x 13-inch half sheet pans (or other large baking pans) with parchment paper or silicone baking mats.

Whisk together the dry ingredients: flour, potato starch, baking powder, mastic, and salt.

In the bowl of an electric mixer fitted with the paddle attachment, cream the butter and sugar until light and fluffy, 5 to 6 minutes. Beat in the egg, ricotta, and lemon zest. Add the flour mix and beat until just combined, making a soft dough. Roll the dough into

36 small balls, about the size of a walnut.

Place the sesame seeds in a bowl. Roll the balls into the seeds to coat completely. (The sesame seeds form a crust, holding the soft dough in place when baking.) Arrange the cookie balls equidistant in rows of 3 and 4 on the baking pans. Flatten each cookie lightly with the palm of your hand. Firmly press an almond into the center of each cookie.

Bake for 25 minutes, or until golden brown on the outside, but still soft in the middle. Cool on a wire rack to room temperature before serving. Store in a cookie tin or other similar container for up to 4 days.

Danish Pastry Braid with Goat Cheese and Cardamom (and Variations)

I visited Copenhagen many years ago, complete with a heavy backpack and a laughable amount of money. I ate almost exclusively from food markets and street stands. After an enchanting visit to Tivoli Gardens, I stayed up all night with a new friend, stopping at a local bakery just as they opened, about 5:00 a.m., following the irresistible aroma of fresh baked Danish pastry. Although this type of pastry originated in Vienna, with a strong influence from Turkish layered phyllo, it reaches its apotheosis in Denmark, with its abundance of good sweet butter. Danish pastry is made from a sweet yeast-raised dough that is punched down and then layered with softened butter, just like puff pastry. It is then rolled out and folded several times to make this light and flaky laminated dough. Follow this recipe and you'll have some of the best tasting Danish pastry ever, a far cry from the leaden, overly sweet commercial type served at hotel "Continental" breakfasts. The mild goat cheese filling I use is not traditional, but its dense texture and tangy aftertaste works beautifully here.

YIELD: ABOUT 2 POUNDS DOUGH, ENOUGH FOR 2 LARGE DANISH; ABOUT 1 POUND FILLING, ENOUGH FOR 1 LARGE DANISH

Dough

$1/2$ cup lukewarm milk

1 ($1/4$-ounce) package ($2 1/2$ teaspoons) active dry yeast

6 tablespoons sugar

$3/4$ pound (3 cups minus 3 tablespoons) unbleached all-purpose flour

2 ounces ($1/2$ cup minus $1/2$ tablespoon) white whole wheat flour

1 teaspoon fine sea salt

1 teaspoon ground cardamom

Grated zest of 1 orange (4 teaspoons)

1 teaspoon vanilla extract

1 large egg

2 large egg yolks

$1/4$ pound (1 stick) unsalted butter, cut into bits and softened

6 ounces ($1 1/2$ sticks) unsalted butter, chilled

Filling and Assembly

$1/2$ pound mild goat cheese, substitute farmer cheese or dry-curd cottage cheese

2 ounces cream cheese, softened

1/2 cup sugar

2 large egg yolks

1/2 teaspoon ground cardamom

Grated zest of 1 lemon (1 tablespoon)

1 teaspoon vanilla extract

2 ounces (1/2 stick) unsalted butter, melted and cooled

2 ounces (1/2 cup minus 1/2 tablespoon)
  all-purpose flour

1 large egg, lightly beaten with 1 tablespoon milk,
  for the egg wash

Crystallized or raw sugar, for sprinkling

Make the dough: In a small bowl, whisk together the milk, yeast, and sugar and allow the mixture to proof until foamy, about 10 minutes.

In the bowl of a standing mixer fitted with the paddle attachment, combine the flour, white whole wheat flour, salt, and cardamom. Add the yeast mixture, orange zest, vanilla, egg, and egg yolks, and beat until the dough is smooth and elastic, about 4 minutes. Gradually add 1/4 pound (1 stick) of the butter and continue beating until the dough is smooth again. Transfer the dough to a lightly oiled bowl, turning so all the dough is coated with the oil. Cover with plastic wrap and set aside to rise in a warm place until it doubles in bulk, about 2 hours.

Punch the dough down, cover tightly, and refrigerate until firm, about 2 hours.

Place the chilled butter on a work surface and lightly dust with flour. Using a rolling pin, beat the butter until it is malleable and about the same consistency as the dough. Keep it in a rough block shape.

Roll out the chilled dough into a large square about 16 inches on a side, forming a double-thick section in the center about the same size as the butter block. Place the butter block in the middle. Fold the edges of the dough over the butter so as to totally enclose it. Using the rolling pin, beat the dough package in parallel lines 4 or 5 times to spread out the butter evenly, then turn crosswise and beat again crosswise. This will seal the butter inside the dough package.

Turn the package upside down and roll it out into a large rectangle. Fold both edges the short way in toward the center, then fold in half, making a thick rectangular block. Cover the dough and chill for 1 hour in the refrigerator or 30 minutes in the freezer, until firm but not brittle. Roll out again and repeat the rolling and folding. Chill and repeat twice more, for a total of 4 times. This will make a many-layered dough, similar to puff pastry. (Note: If the dough ends up in a long narrow shape, cut it in half crosswise and place one section over the other to make a squarish rectangle, then roll it out lightly to flatten slightly before chilling and rolling out again.) You will need 1 pound of dough to make one large braided Danish pastry. Wrap the remaining pastry and freeze up to 3 months, defrosting overnight in the refrigerator.

Make the filling: In the bowl of a standing mixer fitted with the paddle attachment, beat together the goat cheese, cream cheese, and sugar until the mixture is smooth and creamy, 2 to 3 minutes. Add the egg yolks, cardamom, lemon zest, vanilla, and butter, and beat again until smooth, scraping down the sides several times. Add the flour, beating only long enough to blend. (The filling may be refrigerated up to 2 days before using.)

Assemble the pastry: Roll out 1 pound of the dough into a 14 x 12-inch rectangle. Transfer to a baking sheet lined with parchment paper or wax paper, and refrigerate for 1 hour or freeze for 30 minutes, until the dough is firm but not hard. Cut off the edges to make clean straight edges all around that will rise well.

Spoon about $1^1/2$ cups of filling down the center of the dough rectangle into a strip about 4 inches wide, leaving a 1-inch border at either end. (Use any extra filling for individual bear claw or pinwheel pastries or use it to fill crepes, sautéing the filled crepes in butter till brown.) Cut the edges on either side of the filling in a V-shape into strips about $3/4$-inch wide and about 4 inches long. Fold the top edge over pressing firmly to seal the ends and trimming off any excess dough. Alternate folding the strips of dough from one side over the filling followed by a strip from the other side. Repeat until all the dough strips have been folded, yielding a long pastry with a top that appears as though it is woven. Fold the bottom edge over to seal the other end, pressing firmly to seal trimming off any excess dough.

Brush the pastry with the egg wash and sprinkle with the crystallized sugar. Drape the pastry with lightly oiled plastic wrap and allow it to rise at warm room temperature for about 45 minutes or until nicely puffed.

Preheat the oven to 350°F. Bake the pastry for 25 minutes or until the dough is golden brown and well-puffed. Cool to room temperature before cutting into portions. Store covered and refrigerated for up to 3 days.

FILLING VARIATION: Use the Almond Filling in the recipe for the Rustic Fresh Fig Galette (page 454) or use the Honey-Poppy Seed Filling in the recipe for the Poppy Seed Hamantaschen (page 716) to fill the Danish.

BEAR CLAW VARIATION: Roll the pastry out into a large rectangle then cut into 4 x 3-inch rectangles. Spoon the filling down the middle the short way. Fold over the edges and press together. Cut slits about 2-inches long at $3/4$-inch intervals and fan out allowing the filling to show through. Brush with egg wash and sprinkle with crystallized sugar. Arrange on baking pans lined with parchment paper or wax paper and allow the pastries to rise at warm room temperature for about 45 minutes or until nicely puffed. Bake for 20 minutes or until golden-brown and well-puffed.

PINWHEEL VARIATION: Roll the pastry out into a large rectangle, then cut into 4-inch squares. Spoon 2 tablespoons of filling into the center of each square. Cut slits at the corners toward the center. Alternating, fold one triangular half from each corner into the center to form a pinwheel shape, pressing the points together firmly to seal. Brush with egg wash and sprinkle with crystallized sugar. Arrange on baking pans lined with parchment paper or wax paper and allow the pastries to rise at warm room temperature for about 45 minutes or until nicely puffed. Bake for 20 minutes or until golden-brown and well-puffed.

Cretan Kalitsounia (Sweet Cheese Pastries)

Kalitsounia, a specialty of Crete, are small sweet pastries, here made from an olive oil and butter-enriched dough, filled with orange and cinnamon-scented fresh cheese and usually shaped like small pointed crowns. The cookies are also known as lychnarakia *(little oil lamps) because of their resemblance to ancient, open oil burners. The best kalitsounia are said to come from the sunny villages scattered throughout the island's White Mountain Range, where they are served with a drizzle of local thyme honey. In Crete, kalitsounia are considered essential to the Easter Sunday menu, when fresh cheese is in season.*

YIELD: 40 COOKIES

Dough

3/4 pound (2³/4 cups plus 1 tablespoon) unbleached
    all-purpose flour

1 teaspoon baking powder

1/2 teaspoon fine sea salt

2 ounces (1/2 stick) unsalted butter, softened

1/4 cup sugar

3/4 cup extra-virgin olive oil

1 large egg, lightly beaten

3 tablespoons plain yogurt, not non-fat

1 tablespoon brandy

Filling

1¹/2 pounds fresh myzithra cheese (opposite page),
    substitute whole milk ricotta that has been drained
overnight in a yogurt drainer, fine wire sieve, or a colander lined with cheesecloth, farmers' cheese, or Mastelo cheese

1 teaspoon ground cinnamon

1/4 cup sugar

2 tablespoons honey

2 egg yolks

Make the dough: Line two 18 x 13-inch half sheet pans with parchment paper or silicone baking mats.

In a bowl, whisk together the dry ingredients: the flour, baking powder, and salt.

In the bowl of an electric mixer fitted with the paddle attachment, cream the butter and sugar. Beat in the olive oil, egg, yogurt, and brandy to combine well. Beat in the flour mixture only long enough to combine into a dough ball. Transfer to a plastic bag and shape into a flattened rectangle. Chill in the refrigerator for 1 hour or in the freezer for 30 minutes until firm but still malleable.

Make the filling: whisk together the cheese, cinnamon, sugar, honey, and egg yolks. Keep the filling chilled until ready to fill the pastries.

Assemble the pastries: Preheat the oven to 350°F. Divide the dough into 3 or 4 portions. Roll out a portion of the dough between two sheets of wax paper that have been lightly dusted with flour to 3/8-inch thick. Cut the dough into 3-inch circles. Continue until all the dough has been rolled out and cut, rerolling the scraps if desired.

Place about 1 tablespoons of the cheese mixture into the center of each circle. Pull the outside rim of the dough up around the cheese and, with wet fingers, pinch the edges of the dough all around to form 6 to 8 points, leaving the center open so the cheese filling shows. Repeat using all the dough and filling.

Arrange the kalitsounia on the prepared baking pans. Bake for 20 minutes until lightly browned. Allow to cool, still on the baking sheet, on a wire rack. Store covered and refrigerated up to 5 days.

flat container in which the milk is transferred, a word which came from the Romans who once occupied the island. It is excellent used as a topping for pizza, as a filling for borekas, cheese turnovers, which are made in a similar way in Chios. For more information and where to buy the cheese in America, go to www.mastelo.gr.

MASTELO CHEESE FROM CHIOS

On an all-too brief visit to the Greek island of Chios, source of the world's mastic (see page 519), I met Irene Toumazos who, with her husband, Konstantinos, produces Mastelo cheese only from the limited amount of rich high quality, full-fat cow's milk, or goat milk. She also produces an organic goat cheese. Because the local milk contains the right proteins, fats, vitamins, and salt to produce small rounds of fresh, lightly salted cheese with soft, slightly springy texture and milky aroma, no milk is imported and quantities are limited. Irene spent a whole day introducing me to her beloved island and the foods it specializes in, including her own cheese, which is served at the best restaurants on the island. Watching the full moon rise over the Aegean from an outdoor balcony at the home of her friends in the harbor of a small fishing village on the southern end of Chios was an incomparable experience.

Mastelo cheese is white, with a soft texture and no outer skin. It has a subtle flavor and is best fried, grilled, or baked. The name *mastelo* comes from the

GREEK MYZITHRA CHEESE

Fresh Greek cheeses like manouri and fresh myzithra, a type of manouri, are most often used in cheese-filled desserts. Myzithra is mild-tasting, unsalted, and soft, similar to farmer's cheese and ricotta. It is usually sold in egg-shaped balls and works well in cheese pies like the Cretan Kalitsounia on page 276. There is also an aged version that can be grated for use as a seasoning cheese.

CHEMICAL LEAVENERS

Baker's Ammonia . . .280

Using Baker's Ammonia . . .281

Buying and Storing Baker's Ammonia . . .281

Pearlash (Potassium Carbonate) . . .282

Saleratus . . .282

From Mrs. Beeton . . .282

Baking Soda . . .282

Using Baking Soda . . .283

Testing Baking Soda . . .283

Single Acting Baking Powder . . .283

Double–Acting Baking Powder . . .284

Homemade Baking Powder . . .284

Testing Baking Powder . . .284

How Much Baking Powder to Use . . .284

Rumford and Aluminum
in Baking Powder . . .285

ICED MALTED MILK COOKIES . . .285

INDIAN PUDDING CAKE . . .286

CHOCOLATE-GLAZED
PRALINE PROFITEROLES . . .287

Choux Paste . . .289

ALMOND CANTUCCI PRATESI . . .289

Comparing Baking Soda,
Baking Powder, and Baker's Ammonia . . .291

CHEMICAL LEAVENERS

We are accustomed to opening a small can of baking powder and spooning a teaspoon or two into our cookie and cake batters to help them rise. Some recipes call for baking soda, which reacts with acidic ingredients such as buttermilk, molasses, and lemon juice. Through the years, ingenious cooks have come up with all sorts of leaveners to help make their baked goods light instead of leaden. Who would have thought that the scrapings of a deer's antlers would act as both a leavener and as a natural jelly? Called hartshorn in older recipes and now known carbonate of ammonia, this strong-smelling crumbly white powder is a special favorite of mine for extra-crispy cookies. Wood ashes from a hardwood fire were made into potash by American Colonists to leaven their baked goods. In this chapter, I cover these and other more common chemical leaveners so you'll know which kind to use, how much, how its works, and how to tell if it is still effective. (Yeast is covered in its own chapter, starting on page 872)

BAKER'S AMMONIA

Baker's ammonia, also known as carbonate of ammonia, is an old-time leavener unexcelled for creating firm cookie doughs. It was used as a leavener for centuries before the predecessor of modern baking powder was developed in the middle of the nineteenth century. Just be sure not to stick your nose right into this strong-smelling chemical compound–unless you have fainted, of course, because baker's ammonia is actually the same thing as old-time smelling salts, known as sal volatile.

Baker's ammonia has unique characteristics that make it a preferred choice as a chemical leavener for some modern baking recipes. When exposed to heat and moisture, baker's ammonia will break down into ammonia, carbon dioxide, and water, all of which are sources of leavening in baked goods. As opposed to baking soda and baking powder, baker's ammonia doesn't need an acid or alkaline substance in order to react. Its unique action makes for shatteringly crisp cookies, biscotti, and crackers.

This smelly white powder is not appropriate for

muffins or cakes that typically contain a lot of liquid. It is best suited for use as a leavening agent for low-moisture products (less than 3 percent moisture in the baked product) with large surface areas that are baked at high temperatures, such as crackers, biscotti, and small, dry cookies. Baker's ammonia is often used to leaven hard Scandinavian and German cookies, such as the Crisp Swedish Coconut "Dream" Cookies (page 361), gingerbread cookies, the Almond Cantucci Pratesi (page 289), and the Crunchy Macadamia–Ginger Quaresemali (page 489), which are types of biscotti. A small amount of baker's ammonia can also be used in pâte à choux (cream puff paste) to give it an extra measure of "puff," as in the Chocolate-Glazed Praline Profiteroles on page 287.

German molded holiday cookies, such as lebkuchen and springerle, and Dutch Speculaas (page 789), where the dough is rolled out using a specially carved rolling pin, or pressed into a mold to leave decorative and fanciful imprints on the cookies, are often leavened with baker's ammonia. Once these cookies have been imprinted, they are usually left to sit out at room temperature overnight, which allows the dough's surface to dry, so the design will remain clear and sharp when the cookies are baked. Because of the long resting period, these cookies need a leavening agent that can last a long time, making baker's ammonia better suited for than more modern leaveners, which tend to lose their "oomph" more quickly.

USING BAKER'S AMMONIA

Baker's ammonia has some unique advantages over other chemical leavening agents for baking certain kinds of cookies. A small amount of baker's ammonia in cookies increases the pH, which in turn weakens the toughening gluten. The result is a cookie that spreads more, and is more tender, with a coarser, more-open crumb that quickly dries to a longer-lasting crisp.

Substitute baker's ammonia for baking powder proportionately one-to-one in cookie or cracker recipes. Unlike baking powder or soda, baker's ammonia leaves no unpleasant alkaline bitter or metallic aftertaste in baked goods. Doughs made with baker's ammonia store well, as its leavening action is only triggered by heat, not moisture. There will be a noticeable ammonia smell during baking, but I promise it will bake out of your cookies.

BUYING AND STORING BAKER'S AMMONIA

Baker's ammonia used to come in a form like rock salt, so old recipes instructed one to "crush with a rolling pin" then dissolve in liquid. However, even when powdered, it tends to form clumps and must be recrushed before mixing into dough. Look for baker's ammonia in Middle Eastern, Scandinavian, German, Mexican and Italian groceries or order it from www.thebakerscatalogue.com. Baker's ammonia is not affected by age but it does have a tendency to evaporate when exposed to air, so it should be stored in an airtight container. Keep your nose away from it when opening the container.

PEARLASH (POTASSIUM CARBONATE)

Early American colonists were surrounded by hardwood forests. The ashes from burning these trees were used to make potash and its derivative, pearlash, another old-time leavener. Like baking soda, it is an alkaline compound which reacts with an acidic ingredient–such as sour milk, buttermilk, or molasses–to produce those all-important carbon dioxide bubbles. Pearlash was popular in the seventeenth and eighteenth centuries, but because of its bitter aftertaste, it was eventually replaced by "saleratus," as baking soda was known at the time.

SALERATUS

Saleratus (aerated salt) is an old term for baking soda, which referred to either Potassium Bicarbonate or Sodium Bicarbonate. Like pearlash, potassium bicarbonate had an unpleasant aftertaste and fell from favor in the nineteenth century. Eventually, "saleratus" came to mean just sodium bicarbonate (bicarbonate of soda). Saleratus was first sold in America by John Dwight, who, with his brother-in-law, Dr. Austin Church, started manufacturing it in their kitchen, filling paper bags by hand with their product. It was called "Dwight's Saleratus" and used a cow as a trademark because of the necessity of using sour milk to activate it in

baking. Their descendants formed Church and Dwight, Co. and produced Arm and Hammer Baking Soda. The company still produces almost all the baking soda that is used in this country.

> ### FROM MRS. BEETON
>
> "CARBONATE OF SODA—Baking soda was called the mineral alkali, because it was originally dug up out of the ground in Africa and other countries: this state of carbonate of soda is called *natron*. But carbonate of soda is likewise procured from the combustion of marine plants, or such as grow on the sea-shore. . . . A small pinch of carbonate of soda will give an extraordinary lightness to puff pastes." (See page 89 for more about Mrs. Beeton.)

BAKING SODA

Baking soda, or bicarbonate of soda, comes from several sources, but most of it is derived from an ore called "trona" which is mined in the Wyoming's Green River Basin. Technology is now being developed to extract baking soda from sea water. A prime ingredient of baking powder, baking soda is alkaline in nature. When combined with an acid, such as buttermilk, lemon juice, or molasses, it creates carbon dioxide bubbles, thereby leavening doughs and batters. Because baking soda reacts with water, it should be mixed thoroughly with dry ingredients before adding liquids to ensure even leavening. Baking soda alone is normally used when sour milk, buttermilk, molasses, or other acidic liquid forms part of the recipe.

The first step for any baking recipe is to whisk together all the dry ingredients before mixing with any other ingredients. Small brown spots on the surface of muffins or quick breads are a sign that the soda was not mixed in thoroughly. Because baking powder contains both baking soda and an acid, it will create carbon dioxide bubbles even when there's extra acid present, such as buttermilk, and can be used in place of baking soda on its own. However, the acidity will be a bit more pronounced since there is no baking soda to neutralize it.

deprive the flame of oxygen. Scatter the powder directly on the fire by the handful to safely put it out.

TESTING BAKING SODA

To test baking soda, combine $1/2$ teaspoon of baking soda with 4 teaspoons white vinegar. The mixture should bubble up immediately. Baking soda will last indefinitely if stored in a closed container in a cool dry place.

USING BAKING SODA

One cup each of the following ingredients will react with $1/2$ teaspoon of baking soda and can replace 2 teaspoons of baking powder: sour milk, milk mixed with 1 tablespoon vinegar or lemon juice, sour cream, yogurt, fruit or vegetable juices, dark brown sugar, honey, molasses, and cocoa (not Dutch-processed, which has already been treated to make it alkaline).

I always keep an open box in my refrigerator to absorb unwanted odors and have it handy for baking. I also keep a large box of baking soda under my kitchen counter in case of a small grease or electrical kitchen fire. Baking soda works by depriving the fire of its fuel: oxygen. When mixed with an acidic product, the baking soda will release carbon dioxide, which will

SINGLE ACTING BAKING POWDER

Because baking soda would only work when the batter included an acidic ingredient, the next step in convenience was to include the acid in the mix so the powder only needed moisture to be activated. Baking soda was combined with cream of tartar, a fruit acid that accumulates on the inside of wine casks as a wine matures, along with cornstarch to keep the mixture dry.

When baking soda and cream of tartar are moistened in a batter or dough, they begin to react right away, producing carbon dioxide bubbles. However, the reaction also finishes quickly, so the batter has to go right into a hot oven without delay. And, no matter how dry the powders are kept, they eventually lose their potency. However, some people still prefer to use single acting baking powder, because it is made of naturally occurring ingredients.

DOUBLE-ACTING BAKING POWDER

To make double-acting baking powder, the cream of tartar is combined with two acids, one that reacts as soon as it is moistened, usually calcium acid phosphate, and a second that doesn't react until it is heated, usually sodium aluminum sulfate. Though approved by the FDA, there have been reports about potential neurological problems associated with aluminum so some people avoid this type of leavener.

Take care in substituting buttermilk for regular milk when using baking powder, as it upsets the balance of alkali to acid. Because of the acidity in buttermilk, the amount of carbon dioxide released by the baking powder will be reduced as will its leavening power. To achieve the desired result when using buttermilk instead of milk, substitute baking soda for some or all for of the baking powder. For each cup of buttermilk used in place of milk, reduce the amount of baking powder by 2 teaspoons, and replace with 1/2 teaspoon of baking soda.

High altitudes will also affect the amount of baking powder needed in a recipe. Because air pressure is lower at higher altitudes, the carbon dioxide expands more, and thus, less baking powder is needed. If you do not cut back, the texture of the product will be rough. It may take a little experimentation for your own particular high altitude. For an excellent source of detailed information about high-altitude baking, see *Pie in the Sky* by Susan Purdy.

HOMEMADE BAKING POWDER

To make your own single-action baking powder, combine 2 parts cream of tartar with 1 part baking soda. Remember, though, that recipes using this quick-acting baking powder must go *immediately* into a preheated oven to maintain their leavening power. If you plan to mix your own for storage, add about 1/4 teaspoon of cornstarch to 1 cup of baking powder mix. The cornstarch will absorb any excess moisture in the storage container and avoid a potential premature reaction.

TESTING BAKING POWDER

Commercial baking powder has about a 1-year shelf life if stored sealed in a cool, dry place. To test if your baking powder is still active, mix a teaspoon in a cup of hot water. It should start bubbling vigorously right away.

HOW MUCH BAKING POWDER TO USE

For quick breads and muffins, structural ingredients such as wheat flour (with its gluten) and eggs (with their protein) give the form, while additions like other flours that are low in gluten (corn, rye, oat, buckwheat), sugar, oils, or fats, and fold-ins (raisins, nuts, chocolate chips, and fruit) weigh down the batter and keep it from rising. The more additions, the more leavening will be needed. However, too much baking powder will cause the batter to over-rise and fall once it is removed from the oven.

Figure on at least 1 teaspoon of baking powder per quarter-pound (or 1 cup) of flour. If your recipe contains a cup or more of heavy add-ins, increase the amount of baking powder to $1^1/_2$ teaspoon per cup of flour.

RUMFORD AND ALUMINUM IN BAKING POWDER

I used Rumford's Baking Powder to test all these recipes, because it does not contain possibly harmful and bitter-tasting aluminum. Rumford's is made by Hulman and Company, a family-owned business founded in Indiana in 1848. It includes only three ingredients: calcium acid phosphate, baking soda, and corn starch. Most baking powders include sodium aluminum sulfate, which delays the reaction between the liquid and the powder until the product goes into the oven. Because Rumford's contains no aluminum, it is faster acting than common baking powder. Two-thirds of its reaction takes place in the mixing bowl; the remaining third takes place in the oven. When using Rumford's, combine the dry ingredients, then add the wet ingredients, mixing no more than necessary after adding the liquid; bake immediately in a preheated oven.

Iced Malted Milk Cookies

These delicately chewy cookies are wonderful for the kid in all of us who enjoys malted milk shakes or those malted milk ball candies. Malted milk powder flavors both the cookie dough and the shiny candy-like glaze. Children may enjoy spreading the icing on the cookies. Serve these with a glass of cold or warm milk for an indulgent, but soothing bedtime snack. Here, baking powder and baking soda are used for leavening; the baking soda is neutralized by the sour cream, while the baking powder gives the cookies extra lift.

YIELD: ABOUT 3 DOZEN

Dough

$^1/_2$ pound (2 cups minus 2 tablespoons)
   all-purpose flour

$^1/_4$ pound (1 cup) malted milk powder

2 teaspoons baking powder

$^1/_2$ teaspoon baking soda

$^1/_2$ teaspoon fine sea salt

7 ounces (1 cup packed) light brown sugar

$^1/_2$ pound (2 sticks) unsalted butter, softened

2 large eggs

$^1/_2$ cup sour cream

2 teaspoons vanilla extract

Icing

$3^1/_2$ ounces ($^1/_2$ cup packed) dark brown sugar

2 ounces ($^1/_2$ stick) unsalted butter

$^1/_4$ cup milk

2 ounces (6 tablespoons minus 1 teaspoon)
   confectioners' sugar

2 ounces (¹/₂ cup) malted milk powder

1 teaspoon vanilla extract

Make the cookies: Preheat the oven to 375°F. Line one or two 18 x 13-inch half sheet pans (or other large baking pans) with parchment paper or silicone baking mats.

Whisk together the dry ingredients: flour, malted milk powder, baking powder, baking soda, and salt.

In the bowl of a standing electric mixer and using the paddle attachment, beat together the brown sugar and butter until light and fluffy, 5 to 6 minutes. Beat in the eggs, one at a time, then beat in the sour cream and vanilla. Add the flour mixture and beat just until combined. Transfer the dough to a bowl and mix briefly with a silicone spatula so everything is evenly combined.

Drop the cookie dough by the heaping teaspoonful (or use a small ice cream scoop, #40 or #50) in rows of 2 and 3 on the baking pans, leaving at least 2-inches between each cookie. Bake until set in the middle and the edges are light golden brown, about 12 minutes. Allow the cookies to cool about 5 minutes or until firm. Remove from the baking sheets to cool on racks.

Make the icing: Combine the brown sugar, butter, and milk in a medium heavy-bottomed saucepan; cook over low heat until the butter has melted, the sugar has dissolved, and the mixture is syrupy, about 5 minutes. Remove from the heat and stir in the confectioners' sugar, malted milk powder, and the vanilla. Spread on the cooled cookies while the frosting is still warm. Allow the glaze to set for 30 minutes at room temperature. Arrange in a single layer on a wax paper-lined pan and store the cookies refrigerated for 3 to 4 days.

Indian Pudding Cake

During their early years in the New World, the colonists could only dream of the plum puddings of Old England made with wheat flour. Instead, the resourceful settlers used Native American cornmeal. By the late 1620s, dairy cattle had become a bit more plentiful and the pilgrims could enrich their "Indian" puddings with milk and cream. The West Indian molasses that sweetened the pudding was a product of the New England sea trade. Here, sour cream and molasses neutralize the alkalinity in the baking soda, while baking powder helps give the cake its light texture.

YIELD: 1 LARGE BUNDT CAKE, 10 TO 12 SERVINGS

3 ounces (³/₄ cup minus 2 teaspoons) unbleached all-purpose flour

¹/₄ pound (³/₄ cup plus 2 tablespoons) stone-ground yellow cornmeal

1 teaspoon baking powder

¹/₂ teaspoon baking soda

1 teaspoon ground cinnamon

1 teaspoon ground ginger

¹/₂ teaspoon ground mace

¹/₂ teaspoon freshly grated nutmeg

¹/₄ teaspoon ground cloves

¹/₂ teaspoon fine sea salt

4 large eggs, separated

1 cup sugar

¹/₂ cup light molasses, not blackstrap

1 cup vegetable oil

¹/₄ cup sour cream

¼ cup dark rum

Confectioners' sugar, for dusting

Preheat the oven to 350°F. Prepare a 10-inch Bundt cake pan by spraying with nonstick baker's coating, or rubbing with softened butter and dusting with flour, shaking off the excess.

In a bowl, whisk together the dry ingredients: flour, cornmeal, baking powder, baking soda, cinnamon, ginger, mace, nutmeg, cloves, and salt.

In the bowl of a standing electric mixer and using the paddle attachment, beat together the egg yolks, ½ cup of sugar, and the molasses until light, 5 to 6 minutes. Beat in the oil, sour cream, and rum and scrape into a wide, shallow bowl.

In the clean and greaseless bowl of a standing electric mixer and using the whisk attachment, beat the egg whites until fluffy, then add the remaining ½ cup sugar and continue beating until the whites are firm and glossy, 4 to 5 minutes.

Gently fold the flour mixture and the meringue alternately in thirds into the molasses mixture, beginning and ending with the flour. Spread the batter evenly into the pan and tap the pan on work surface once to release any large air bubbles.

Bake for 35 minutes or until the cake starts to come away from the sides of the pan and a skewer inserted in the center comes out clean. Cool in the pan for 10 minutes on a wire rack, then loosen the cake from the pan using a narrow metal spatula, and turn out onto a wire rack. Cool completely, then dust with confectioners' sugar and transfer to a serving plate. Store covered and at room temperature for up to 4 days. This cake freezes well.

Chocolate–Glazed Praline Profiteroles

Known in English as cream puffs and in French as profiteroles, these little airy bites are an easy-to-make classic dessert. Split and stuffed with the simplest of fillings, the lightly sweetened vanilla-flavored whipped cream, known in French as crème Chantilly, *and glazed with cofee-flavored chocolate icing, they are delightful. Hazelnut praline ground to a fine paste is available from American Almond (www.lovenbake.com), or make your own crumbly hazelnut praline using the recipe on page 509. Don't fill the profiteroles until just before serving so they stay crisp. A small amount of baker's ammonia gives the profiteroles extra lift. Note that these puffs are best made on a day with low humidity.*

YIELD: 32 PROFITEROLES

Profiteroles

½ cup water

½ cup milk

¼ pound (1 stick) unsalted butter, cut into bits

¼ pound (1 cup minus 1 tablespoon) unbleached all-purpose flour

2 tablespoons sugar

4 large eggs

Pinch salt

¼ teaspoon crushed baker's ammonia

Filling, Glaze, and Assembly

3 sheets gelatin or 1 teaspoon powdered gelatin

4 large egg yolks (¼ cup)

1/4 cup sugar

1 teaspoon vanilla

1 ounce (scant 1/4 cup) unbleached all-purpose flour

3/4 cup milk, scalded

1 cup crushed Hazelnut Praline, purchased or homemade (page 509)

1/2 cup heavy cream, chilled

1 cup Shiny Chocolate-Mocha Glaze (page 334)

Make the profiteroles: Preheat the oven to 350°F. Line two 18 x 13-inch half sheet pans (or other large baking pans) with parchment paper or silicone baking mats.

In a medium non-aluminum pot, combine the water, milk, and butter, and bring to a boil, so the liquid comes to the boil just as the butter melts. Reduce the heat to low and mix in the flour and sugar all at once, stirring with a wooden spoon or silicone spatula until the mixture comes together in a ball. Continue cooking at low heat for about 3 minutes to dry out the paste, without allowing it to color. Remove from the heat and allow the mixture to cool for 5 minutes.

Transfer the dough to the bowl of a standing mixer and beat in the eggs one by one, beating until the mixture is smooth and supple. Add the salt and baker's ammonia (without breathing in the fumes) and beat briefly to combine. Scoop the mixture into a pastry bag, if desired. Pipe or spoon into about 24 small, high rounds about 1 1/2 inches in diameter onto the pre-pared baking pans.

Bake for 30 minutes, then reduce the heat to 250°F and bake 20 minutes longer or until the puffs are dried out, firm, and medium brown in color. Remove from the oven and cool to room temperature. Cut the puffs

open horizontally, making a top and bottom. Scrape out and discard any soft, wet insides. You may place the profiteroles back in the turned-off oven to crisp up a bit more, if desired.

Make the filling: Soak the gelatin sheets in cold water to soften them, about 5 minutes. Or soak the powdered gelatin in 1/4 cup water until thickened, about 10 minutes, then heat it gently until it is clear, about 2 minutes.

In a medium mixing bowl, beat together the egg yolks, sugar, and vanilla, until well combined. Add the flour and beat briefly to combine. Gradually pour in the hot milk while constantly whisking so the mixture is smooth.

Transfer the mixture to a medium heavy-bottomed non-aluminum pot. Bring to a boil over moderate heat, stirring often. Remove from the heat, scrape the mix-ture into a stainless-steel bowl, and add the gelatin, stirring vigorously to combine well drained sheets or the melted powdered gelatin. Cool the mixture until cold to the touch by placing the bowl into a larger bowl containing a mixture of ice and water. Fold in the praline.

Meanwhile, beat the cream until firm but still bright white in color, then fold into the filling mixture in thirds so as not to deflate the cream.

Assemble the profiteroles: Warm the Shiny Chocolate-Mocha Glaze on low power in the microwave. Whisk until smooth and shiny, then transfer to a small bowl and cool until the chocolate just holds its shape but is still pourable. Dip the tops of each prof-iterole into the chocolate glaze, shaking off the excess. Allow the tops to set at room temperature, about 30 minutes.

Pipe the filling, using a second pastry bag or a heavy-duty freezer bag with the corner cut out, or spoon into the bottoms of the split profiteroles and cover with their reserved matching tops. Chill the profiteroles for 30 minutes in the refrigerator or until the chocolate has set, and serve.

CHOUX PASTE

Choux means cabbage in French and it is the name for these small miniature cabbage-like puffs, once known as *pate à chaud* (hot pastry or cooked pastry). The technique of making this twice-cooked pastry was well-known by Renaissance times. It is first cooked in the pot, then in the oven. When baked, choux pastry puffs up and becomes firm and crisp on the outside. The surface sets while the interior is still quite liquid so the air trapped inside expands and forms a large bubble (almost like blowing bubble gum).

Also known as *pâte à choux* or cream-puff dough, the same dough is used to make éclairs (page 817), gougère (page 268), and profiteroles, which may also be filled with ice cream, and served with warm chocolate or caramel sauce (page 287). When deep-fried, the same light and airy dough is rather sacrilegiously named *pets de nonne* or nun's farts. In earlier perhaps lustier times, the same dish was known as *pets de putain* (prostitutes' farts).

Almond Cantucci Pratesi

These crunchy biscotti come from the Tuscan town of Prato, about an hour by train from Florence. Although known as cantucci, this term originally referred only to the ends that were cut off the biscotti logs before slicing and baking a second time, then often given to children. In Tuscany, cantucci accompany small glasses of vin santo, the golden, honeyed fortified raisin-based dessert wine. The cantucci are then inzuppati (souped), or soaked in the wine to soften and flavor them. Stored in an airtight container, these cookies will keep well for up to one month. Baking powder on its own is used for leavening here, but an equal quantity of baker's ammonia can be substituted for extra-crisp texture.

YIELD: ABOUT 4 DOZEN

$3/4$ pound ($2^3/4$ cups plus 1 tablespoon) unbleached all-purpose flour

6 ounces ($1^3/4$ cups minus 1 tablespoon) white whole wheat flour

2 teaspoons baking powder

$1/2$ teaspoon fine sea salt

3 large eggs

3 large egg yolks

$2^1/2$ cups sugar

$1/2$ cup amaretto liqueur

$1^1/2$ teaspoons almond extract

1 pound (about 3 cups) skin-on whole almonds, lightly toasted

1 tablespoon milk

$1/2$ cup raw or crystallized sugar, for sprinkling

Preheat the oven to 400°F. Line an 18 x 13-inch baking pan with parchment paper or a silicone baking mat.

In a bowl, whisk together the dry ingredients: flour, whole wheat flour, baking powder, and salt.

In the bowl of a standing mixer and using the paddle attachment, beat together 2 of the eggs, the yolks, and the sugar until light and fluffy, 5 to 6 minutes. Beat in the amaretto and almond extract. Beat in the almonds. Add the flour mixture and beat briefly, just long enough to combine. The dough will be rather soft.

Divide the dough in half and spoon half of the dough out into small clumps lengthwise on one side of a baking pan, then repeat with the remaining dough on the other side, leaving 1 to 2 inches in between the logs and a 1-inch border along the sides.

Smooth the dough into log shapes using your lightly oiled hands.

Beat the remaining egg lightly with 1 tablespoon milk and brush over the logs. Sprinkle with the raw sugar, patting so the sugar adheres to the dough. Bake for 20 minutes or until firm on the outside but still soft on the inside, then remove from the oven and cool completely, preferably overnight. (The cookies will slice more evenly with less tendency to break if left overnight)

Preheat the oven to 350°F.

Slice each log at a 45 degree angle into $1/2$ inch-thick cookies and arrange upright on the baking tray. Bake for 20 minutes; less for a chewier cookie, longer for a crunchier cookie or until lightly browned. Cool to room temperature on a wire rack. Store in an airtight container for up to 1 week.

Freeze the dough logs either raw or baked, up to 3 months.

BAKING SODA	BAKING POWDER	BAKER'S AMMONIA
Reacts with fruits, nuts, or vegetables that contain the pigment anthocyanin, such as blueberries, blackberries, and black currants, turning the batter blue or green.	Some of the leavening power of baking powder dissipates once mixed with liquid. Double-acting baking powder will rise again when the batter or dough has been exposed to oven heat.	Batters and doughs can be made in advance and will rise well once baked. Molded cookies like springerle and Speculaas, which are usually molded then dried overnight before baking, maintain crisp, clear patterns
You must include an acidic ingredient in a recipe that uses baking soda. Without something to neutralize it, baking soda will leave a bitter, salty taste.	Most double-acting baking powders contain aluminum, which has been associated with neurological problems.	Develops a very strong odor when mixed with the dough that will dissipate once the product is cooked above 140°F.
Once mixed with liquid, the batter reacts quickly and must be baked immediately in a preheated oven to retain lift.	Batters and doughs made with non-aluminum baking powder react quickly when mixed with liquid and must be baked immediately in a preheated oven to retain lift.	Reacts rapidly in the presence of water and heat but maintains lift.
Produces baked goods with a slightly coarse or "shaggy" texture, especially if too much is used.	Produces baked goods with a finer texture than baking soda.	Increases uniformity and spread in cookies. Provides for a crisp, porous crumb and increases browning.
Allow $\frac{1}{2}$ teaspoon per 1 cup of acidic liquid.	Uses 1 to 2 teaspoons per $\frac{1}{2}$ pound of flour, depending on the weight of the added ingredients (nuts, fruits, sugar).	Uses about 1 teaspoon per $\frac{1}{2}$ pound of flour.
Lasts indefinitely if stored in a cool, dry place.	Lasts about 1 year in a cool, dry place.	Lasts indefinitely but tends to form clumps.

CHERRIES

Cherries in Disguise . . .298

The Word "Cherry" . . .298

Sweet Cherry Varieties . . .299

Sour Cherry Varieties . . .299

Sweet–Sour Cherries . . .300

Montmorencys and Hungarian
Morellos in Michigan . . .301

To Pit or Not to Pit? . . .301

Maraschino Cherries . . .301

Cherries with a Kick–
Cherries and Alcohol . . .302

Choosing and Storing Fresh Cherries . . .303

ALMOND-SOUR CHERRY TORTE WITH BROWN
BUTTER AND SOUR CHERRY SAUCE . . .303

SOUR CHERRY SAUCE . . .304

VENETIAN CORNMEAL AND
CHERRY CROSTATA . . .305

CHOCOLATE-CHERRY BISCOTTI
WITH COCOA NIBS . . .305

CHERRY-MARASCHINO CREAM PIE . . .306

TART CHERRY CLAFOUTI . . .307

CHERRIES

I celebrated my twenty-seventh birthday, May second, in Bologna, Italy, having dinner with Victor and Marcella Hazan at the classic Bolognese restaurant, Diana. The couple was acting as consultants to the exciting new Northern Italian restaurant in Philadelphia where I was to become the Executive Chef. It was my first evening in Italy and I was thrilled to be tasting the rich cuisine of Bologna la Grassa (Bologna the fat) in such august company. When our server came around offering fresh cherries for dolce (sweet or dessert), I couldn't resist and ordered a bowl of the small, rose-colored fruits. Mr. Hazan exclaimed, "Those aren't real cherries at all. It's too early in the season." At the time, I thought he was being unreasonable and "raining on my parade"; now I can see that he was right: cherries should only be eaten at their best in peak season.

This past year, I visited the Aegean Coast of Turkey and at a small local farmers' market near Izmir, I savored a wealth of superb, creamy white, crimson, and tart cherries, picked that day, spread out onto flat baskets to display them in all their intrinsic beauty, and never refrigerated. I'm sure Victor Hazan would have approved. On the same trip, the red cherries I bought at the main market in Athens were so good, I brought a big bag onto the plane for a snack and passed them out to my fellow passengers, knowing I couldn't bring them into the United States when we landed. The bad part is that I've been ruined for most American cherries, which these days, are often picked too soon in their season (the first pick obtains the highest price), shipped too far, and left to deteriorate into mushy fruit or fruit with hard, unripe parts. It seems to me that often cherries are just not as good as they were twenty or thirty years ago when I was just setting out on my culinary career and they still came in wooden crates with gorgeous labels.

Cherries are the first fruits to ripen in many places, so that "cherry" has also come to mean "new" or "the first," as in the phrase "in cherry condition", for perfect condition and in the slang "losing your cherry" for loss of virginity. Because they must be tree-ripened and therefore bruise easily, these early-fruiting stone fruits must be picked and sorted by hand. They also have to be protected from the cold. Hand-labor, relatively short season, and high-demand translates into inevitably high prices for cherries. The cherry harvest begins in early May in California, which produces a little more than a fifth of the country's sweet-cherry crop. Next, the harvest moves north to Washington State and Oregon, which together account for about 60 percent of the American sweet cherry crop between June and the end of August. Next is Michigan, which produces 70 percent of the world's tart cherry crop. Utah, Wisconsin, and Pennsylvania also have commercial cherry crops.

I simply can't resist the rare pale cream-to-rosy pink Rainier cherries during their fleeting season. As befits their fragile beauty, these cherries are quite demanding. In the spring, the branches must be thinned to give these finicky fruits enough room to grow and reach the sunlight, which gives the cherry its color and sweetness. If the weather is too hot, they spoil quickly; if the wind blows hard, they bruise from rubbing against each other; if it rains too much, their skins burst. Not to mention the quarter to a third of the small crop snatched up by birds, leaving clusters of bare pits hanging on their stems. Rainiers must be picked by their stems and placed, not dropped, into baskets. Skilled pickers pluck them from the outside of the tree in, and from top to bottom, choosing only the ripe fruits.

I adore small sour cherries, which explode with flavor in the mouth. With their thin-skins and tart, tangy flavor, sour cherries are the best choice for baking. Though excellent when eaten out of hand, sweet cherries will be insipid when baked because they lack that sharp accent. Luckily for me, several of the Amish vendors at Philadelphia's Reading Terminal Market sell sour cherries by the quart in season. Because they are esteemed in North, Central, and Eastern Europe and in Russia, I find frozen, hand-pitted sour cherries at a large local Russian market and keep a quart or two on hand for that emergency cherry tart.

The cherry is one of the world's oldest cultivated fruits, along with the apricot, and has been cultivated since at least 800 BCE, though the fruit's lineage dates back much farther. The common cherry tree, *Prunus avium*, is related to the wild fruit that was indigenous to the Black and Caspian Seas, regions of Turkey and Iran. The sour cherry seems to be a hybrid of the wild ground cherry and the sweet cherry that grew in the central and eastern Europe. Cherries grow wherever winter temperatures are not too severe and summer temperatures are moderate. They require winter cold in order to blossom in early spring.

As can be seen by its genus name, *Prunus*, cherries are members of plum, or stone fruit, family, which in turn is part of the larger rose family. Sweet cherries get their species name, *avium*, from the Latin meaning "of the birds," due to birds' obvious love of the fruit. Sour cherries, *Prunus cerasus*, get their species name from the Assyrian *karsu* and Greek *kerasos*, meaning cherry.

The cherry tree was highly regarded by the Egyptians, Greeks, and Romans for both its beautiful flowers and its versatile and delicious little fruits. They were also extremely popular with Persians and the fruit remains popular in modern-day Iran. There are more than 1,000 varieties of cherries–sweet, sour, and in–between–ranging in color from deep dark red, like my husband's favorite Oxheart cherries that grew profusely near the small upstate Pennsylvania town where he grew up, to light red and creamy white with a blush of yellow. Some of our contemporary varieties are the same ones known to the Romans, but cherries easily hybridize.

The Romans, who appreciated cherries as much as Italians do today, introduced the fruits into Britain before the first century. There, the cultivation of sour cherries was popularized in the sixteenth century by King VIII, especially in Kent. The first cherries planted by the Massachusetts colonists were the Kentish Red. When the colonists brought the cherry to New England, they had the choice of two dozen or more varieties.

In Europe, cherry orchards reach from the Iberian peninsula east to Asia Minor and are also grown to a lesser extent in the British Isles and southern Scandinavia. Iran is the world's largest cherry producer, closely followed by the United States. Just slightly below the United States in volume, Turkey is the third largest producer, with Italy and Germany fourth and fifth in production. Much of Turkey has an ideal climate to grow cherries with warm, dry summers and cool, moist winters. In fact, sweet cherries are produced throughout the country, with the harvest beginning in May near Izmir, on the Aegean Coast where I tasted those wonderful cherries, and extending into August in the mountains of east-central Anatolia.

In Japan and elsewhere in Asia, cherries are grown for the beauty of their flowers called *sakura*; most varieties don't bear fruit. Japanese people hold annual cherry blossom viewing parties called *hamani* under the blooming trees in spring. Cherry blossom season is fleeting: Full bloom (*mankai*) is usually reached about one week after the first blossoms open (*kaika*). A week later, and the blossoms drift down from the trees like soft pale pink snowflakes. In 1912, the mayor of Tokyo made a gift to the people of the United States of the blushing–pink flowering Japanese cherry trees that now surround the Tidal Basin in Washington, D.C. While growing up in that city, we eagerly awaited cherry blossom season every year. Now that I live in Philadelphia, I make sure to drive up along the Schuylkill River in Philadelphia's Fairmount Park to see the city's cherry blossom trees.

The colonists brought cherries to America in the 1600s, but commercial cherry production didn't start for more than 200 years. French colonists from Normandy brought along the cherry pits that they planted along the Saint Lawrence River, around the Great Lakes, and in gardens of cities that they established like Detroit. In 1852, a Presbyterian missionary named Peter Dougherty planted cherry trees on Old Mission Peninsula, Michigan (near Traverse City). To the surprise of the locals, cherry trees flourished and soon other residents planted more trees. The area proved to be ideal for growing cherries because the waters of Lake Michigan temper Arctic winds in winter and cool the orchards in summer.

Michigan's most important sour cherry variety originated in France and is named Montmorency, after a French dukedom in the southwest of France, famous for its cherries and, legend has it, for a duke who insisted on eating them with everything. It has been cultivated in Michigan for more than a century. Montmorencys do indeed seem to complement nearly everything and go into pies, cakes, tarts, cookies, preserves, jellies, juice, and even wine. Michigan now produces more red tart cherries than anywhere in the world and holds an annual cherry festival in the beautiful Lake Michigan resort town of Traverse City, "the cherry capital of the world." Though now rare in its native France, Michigan raises a huge quantity of French Montmorency cherries along with a significant crop of sweet cherries.

These same tart cherries are transformed by sweetening and drying to sell as a delectable (and rather pricey) alternative to raisins. During my first pregnancy, I craved those Michigan Montmorency cherries so much, I would buy them in the 10-pound food-service bags straight from the Cherry Coop in Michigan just to keep up with my appetite. Today, I buy them in more reasonable quantities in half-pound bags at the Trader Joe's stores.

In 1847, Henderson Lewelling planted the first sweet cherry orchard in western Oregon using nursery stock that he had laboriously transported by ox cart from Iowa. Lewelling Farms became known for its sweet cherries. Since the 1870s, commercial cherry production has flourished in the northern part of America, where there is enough winter cold to get the cherry buds to open properly in the spring. Today, over 85 percent of United States commercial sweet cherry production is harvested from orchards in Washington, California, and Oregon. In the Pacific Northwest, the first cherry variety harvested is the Chelan, followed by the Bing, Rainer, and others, with the peak of the season in early July.

Very seasonal in nature, fresh-market sweet cherries are sold from May through early August. California opens the market each year with its cherry season running from May through June. Shipments from Washington, on the other hand, usually begin in June. To minimize any damage to the small, easily-bruised fruit, all fresh-market sweet cherries are harvested by hand. Cherries for processing are mostly harvested by machine. Oregon and Michigan growers harvest their sweet cherries by hand as they are mostly used to manufacture maraschino cherries, which must be whole and unbruised.

In this chapter, dried sour cherries fill the Almond–Sour Cherry Torte (page 303) and make the Sour Cherry Sauce (page 304) to serve with it or over ice cream or chocolate cake. The same type of cherries fill the Venetian Cornmeal and Cherry Crostata (page 305), while dried cherries also go into the bittersweet batter for the Chocolate–Cherry Biscotti with Cocoa Nibs (page 305). Sour cherry season is the time to make the

Cherry–Maraschino Cream Pie (page 306) using the cherry-based liqueur, not the neon-red preserved cherries used to garnish cocktails, that is now gaining attention by creative bartenders. A classic baked Tart Cherry Clafouti (page 307) may be made with either pitted or whole cherries; the pits add flavor. Sweet cherries are best reserved for uses where they are uncooked, such as the filling for the Australian Pavlova with Lemon Filling and Tropical Fruits (page 442) or the French Puff Pastry Peach Galette (page 618).

CHERRIES IN DISGUISE

Cherries turn up in all sorts of guises. Green and red whole glacéed or candied cherries are seen most often decorating fruit cakes at holiday time. The pits of Mahlab or St. Lucy's cherry lend their bittersweet flavor to Middle Eastern and North African sweet pastries.

THE WORD "CHERRY"

The old Anglo-Saxon word, *ciris*, was replaced in the fourteenth century by *cherise*, borrowed from the French. English speakers quickly misinterpreted *cherise* as a plural, and so the new singular name "cherry" was coined. We use the modern French term *cerise* for an adjective meaning bright red.

SWEET CHERRY VARIETIES

Usually eaten out of hand, sweet cherries are larger than sour cherries, shaped like a heart with sweet, firm flesh. The French Bigarreau Napoleon was most likely named after Napoleon Bonaparte, his son Napoleon II, or his nephew Napoleon III. Bigarreaus have firm, crisp flesh and are best known by the variety called Napoleon, which are large pale yellow cherries tinged with light red. Their crisp, white, fragrant flesh is slightly tart. Often used to make maraschino cherries, the Bigarreau is a forebear of the Bing. It was renamed the Royal Anne or Queen Anne in America and is known as the White Napoleon in Great Britain.

The Bing, which got its name from a Chinese workman at Lewelling Farm, is the leading sweet cherry in North America. Its fruit is firm, juicy, and a deep mahogany red when ripe. Bings are exceptionally large fruits with an intensely sweet, vibrant flavor. Another sweet cherry is the Lambert, which also got its start at Lewelling Farm. This smaller, heart-shaped, red cherry closely resembles the Bing in taste and texture. Early Rivers have dark purple skins and flesh with very small stones and are very fragrant and juicy.

The exquisite, tender, and highly perishable Rainier cherry from Washington State, has golden skin with a pink-to-red blush on the side facing the sun, almost transparent flesh, exquisite sweet, delicate flavor, and fine texture.

Agronomists at the Washington State University Research Station originated the Rainier by cross-breeding the Bing and Van cherries and released it in 1960. The Rainier is easily bruised if not handled with tender loving care, so that many supermarkets are reluctant to carry them. Rainiers make a brief appearance in June and July. Only about 5 percent of Washington State cherries are Rainiers and much of the crop is exported to Taiwan and Japan, where Rainiers may sell for more than a dollar apiece. The creamy-yellow flesh is extraordinarily sweet. The State of Washington requires that Rainiers reach at least 17 brix—a measure of sweetness—before they can be picked. A peach at 13 brix is considered perfectly sweet. The best growers don't pick Rainiers until they reach at least 20 brix. Three varieties, the Bing, the Lambert, and the Rainier account for more than ninety-five percent of the Northwest sweet cherry harvest.

SOUR CHERRY VARIETIES

Normally rather tart to eat raw, sour cherries are smaller than their sweeter cousins are and more globular in shape, with thin skins and soft flesh. Sour cherries, also known as pie cherries, *griottes* in French, and *visciola* or *marasca* in Italian, grow as a shrub or small tree. The cherries are usually cooked with sugar and used for pies, preserves, and tarts, where their tart flavor balances the sweetness of the sugar. In America, the Early

Richmond variety is the first available in late spring and is bright red in color, with the Montmorency soon following, and the Hungarian Balaton following last in the season.

All cultivated European sour cherries belong to the species *Prunus cerasus*, but there are two distinct groups: morellos, with dark red skin and deep-red flesh, and amarelles with a bright "cherry red" color and yellow flesh. The morello is most commonly found in Central and Eastern Europe, as well as the Balkans, Turkey, the Caucasus, and the Middle East. It is extensively cultivated in Central Europe and the orchards of Germany's Black Forest and the hill country of northern Hungary. The farther east you go, the more these small, dark, astringent cherries are apt to be harvested from the wild.

Dark mahogany red morello cherries are both sweet and astringent, with a dark plum-like fruitiness that makes them tops for jam, preserves, and liqueurs. Long-stemmed morellos preserved in sugar syrup with alcohol are a specialty of the region around Besançon in France's Franche-Comté. The regions of Auvergne and Burgundy in France are also famed for their morellos. Early American settlers tried planting morello cherry trees in upstate New York and Massachusetts and jars of European morello cherry conserve dating from Colonial times have been unearthed in Williamsburg, Virginia.

The amarelle cherry is most common in Western Europe, especially the cultivar known as Montmorency, named after a village in the Champagne region of France. Any dish of classic French cuisine *à la Montmorency* will be made with cherries. The original base for maraschino cherries came from an eau-de-vie distilled from the small slightly bitter marasca cherry, found in Dalmatia

Gean, *guine*, and *mazzard* are very old English names for wild cherries, which have soft juicy flesh and come in many colors. The famous Swiss black cherry jam is made from intensely dark guines. The mazzard is found in England's west country, where it was probably introduced from France by Huguenots during the eighteenth century. Once the focus of a thriving market industry, the mazzard was in danger of becoming extinct, but is now being resurrected in the region.

SWEET-SOUR CHERRIES

Dual-purpose cherries have a mix of sweet and sour flavors. Known as dukes or royales, they are crosses of sweet and sour cherries and much more rare. The duke came to England from the Médoc in Bordeaux and the name was first adapted to May Duke, and then abbreviated to duke.

MONTMORENCYS AND HUNGARIAN MORELLOS IN MICHIGAN

When American fruit growers began growing sour cherries in Michigan, where the climate was suitable, they turned to high-yielding French Montmorencys, which are still most popular sour cherry in Michigan and in nearby Canada. These fruits, which bruise and discolor easily once picked, are usually dried, canned, or frozen, and are often colored with red dye for processed foods.

Michigan State horticulturist Amy Iezzoni traveled to Hungary in 1983, still during the communist era, to obtain their renowned plump, juicy morello cherries to plant in Michigan. Back home, Iezzoni named this cherry the Balaton after the famous lake in Hungary. Growers in Michigan now increasingly plant Balatons, which are a hedge against bad weather, because they ripen later than the Montmorency. It is estimated that close to five million pounds of Balaton cherries are being grown in Michigan annually, although still much less than the 300 million pounds of Montmorencys harvested.

TO PIT OR NOT TO PIT?

Pitting sour cherries seems to be largely a matter of personal choice. British author Jane Grigson had this to say on the subject, "Stoning cherries is a trying business. Avoid pampering your family in this respect. Half the fun of a cherry pie is putting the stones on the side of the plate, and counting them out later." Like beef roasted on the bone, cherries baked with their pits will be juicier and more flavorful. If you do choose not to pit the cherries, remember to warn your guests. I use a small, sharp paring knife to cut a slit into the cherry's natural cleft and then continue cutting around. I then twist off the two halves. One side will pop free, the other will contain the cherry and usually also the stem, which I scoop out. An inexpensive cherry pitter (the same as an olive pitter) will also work. Hold the cherries over a bowl when pitting them to catch their juices. In France, the Tart Cherry Clafouti (page 307) is normally made from unpitted cherries, because the slightly bitter cherry pits enhance the flavor of this batter pudding.

MARASCHINO CHERRIES

The maraschino cherry originated in Yugoslavia and northern Italy, where merchants combined liqueur with the local cherry called the Marasca. These alcohol-laced cherries were imported to the United States in the 1890s as a delicacy for the country's finest restaurants and hotels. In 1896, American cherry processors began experimenting, using a domestic sweet cherry called the Royal Anne to make their own version. Less liqueur was used in processing, with almond oil substituted. Eventually, the liqueur was eliminated altogether and by 1920, the garish, artificially colored cherries that are American bar and ice cream sundae standards became so popular, they totally replaced the original.

Millions of pounds of maraschino cherries are produced each year in America. To make them, light colored Queen Ann (Royal Ann or Napoleon) cherries are soaked in a brining liquid of sodium metabisulfate, calcium chloride, and citric acid, similar to the way pickled cucumbers are brined. Brining removes the fruit's natural color.

After pitting, the cherries are sweetened with corn syrup and fructose, then artificially flavored and colored, usually red or green, though electric blue, yellow, pink, and orange are also to be found, usually garnishing elaborate sugary cocktails. Maraschino cherries with their stems still attached are considered the top of the line and come from cherries that have been picked by hand. Gray & Company produces eighty-five percent of the maraschino cherries found in American retail markets.

CHERRIES WITH A KICK— CHERRIES AND ALCOHOL

AMARENE: Amarene are small, dark, slightly bitter cherries (*amaro* means bitter) preserved in alcohol and sugar syrup from Italy, used as a topping for ice cream and cakes. They were once bottled in Deruta pottery jars; nowadays, the glass jars are painted white.

KIRSCH: Kirsch or Kirschwasser, originally from Germany, is a clear, white fruit brandy, or eau de vie, distilled in copper pot stills from dark sweet cherries grown only in the famous Black Forest region of Germany. It takes more than 20 pounds (10 kilos) of cherries to distill each bottle. Its popularity is one of the reasons that Germany is such as large producer of both sweet and sour cherries. Use kirsch to enhance fruit cakes and tarts such as the Almond-Sour Cherry Torte with Brown Butter (page 303), the Cherry-Maraschino Cream Pie (page 306), and the July 4th Cheesecake (page 833).

CHERRY VISHNIAK: Cherry Vishniak, sometimes spelled wishniak, is brandy distilled from black cherries of Polish and Russian origin that was especially popular in the Jewish communities of that region. The name *wishniak* was picked up by one of the many small Jewish-owned soda bottlers, like Frank's, starting a century ago to slake the particular thirsts of their mostly Eastern European Jewish customers with cherry flavored soft drinks.

MARASCHINO LIQUEUR: Maraschino liqueur, originally from Dalmatia (now in Croatia) is a bittersweet cherry liqueur made from wild Marasca cherries and their crushed pits, which give it a subtle bitter-almond flavor. The cherries are processed and distilled, much like brandy, and later combined with pure cane syrup before aging and filtering.

CHERRY HEERING: Cherry Heering is a dark red, black cherry-flavored sweetened brandy that has been produced in Denmark since 1818.

KRIEK: Kriek is a traditional Belgian beer fermented with Morello cherries and produced in the area around Brussels, which gets its name from the Dutch word *kriek* for this type of cherry. Traditionally, kriek is made from the local *Schaarbeekse krieken* (a rare Belgian morello cherry), although today, other varieties of sour cherries are also used. The dark cherry-colored drink is produced using spontaneously fermented lambic beer to which sour cherries (with the pits) are added. The cherries are left to steep for a period of several months, causing a second fermentation of the additional sugar in the fruit. Typically, no sugar will be left so there will be more fruit flavor, although some krieks now have sugar added to make them a bit sweet and more approachable to Americans.

Choose firm, plump, bright, and shiny sweet cherries with smooth skin, deep color, upstanding green stalks, and sweet flavor (if you can sneak a taste.) I find that cherries imported from Chile in the winter often have pitted skins and the brownish flesh that comes from overly cold storage temperature.

Choose sour cherries that have uniformly light, bright red skins without mushiness, though they will naturally be softer than sweet cherries. Over-ripe cherries will have brown soft spots, split skins, and/or bruises. Sort cherries carefully, removing any damaged fruits, because any mold they develop will cause the others to spoil. Spread the cherries out in a shallow container so that the weight of the cherries on top won't crush those on the bottom, and allowing for air circulation—then refrigerate. Wash and pit cherries just before using.

Look for frozen pitted sour cherries, bottled sour cherries in syrup, sour cherry jam, and sour cherry juice at Eastern European, German, and Russian stores. One of the best ways to preserve cherries is to freeze them. Pit the cherries or they will pick up a bitter almond flavor from the pits. Line a shallow sheet with wax paper or a silicone baking mat and arrange the fruits in a single layer. Freeze until firm, then transfer to freezer bags, squeeze out the air, and freeze up to four months.

Almond–Sour Cherry Torte with Brown Butter and Sour Cherry Sauce

Here, an almond torte is enriched with nutty-tasting brown butter, then plumped dried tart cherries are folded into the batter. It's quite amazing how butter, cooked until the milk particles it contains turn brown, turns a simple food into a complex, multi-dimensional ingredient. With a texture like pound cake, this cake is suitable to serve on its own with afternoon tea or morning coffee. Accompany the cake with the Sour Cherry Sauce when serving it for dessert. I like to make small individual cakes baked in bar-shaped molds or in mini cups or tart pans. Bake about 30 minutes.

YIELD: ONE 9-INCH TORTE, 10 TO 12 SERVINGS

1½ cups dried tart cherries

½ cup kirsch

6 ounces (about 1 cup) blanched whole almonds

6 ounces (1½ cups minus 1 tablespoon) unbleached
   all-purpose flour

1¼ cups sugar

Pinch salt

4 large eggs, separated

1 cup Brown Butter (page 202), melted and cooled

1 teaspoon vanilla extract

1½ teaspoons almond extract

¼ cup sliced almonds, skin-on

2 cups Sour Cherry Sauce (page 304)

Confectioners' sugar, for dusting

Soak the dried cherries in the kirsch at least 30 minutes or until plump. Preheat the oven to 350°F. Spray a 9-inch round cake pan with nonstick baker's coating or rub with softened butter and dust with flour, shaking out the excess.

Place the almonds, flour, 3/4 cup of the sugar, and salt in the bowl of a food processor and process until fine, working in two batches if necessary.

In the clean and greaseless bowl of a standing mixer fitted with the whisk attachment, beat the egg whites until fluffy, then add the remaining 1/2 cup sugar and continue beating until the whites are firm and glossy, 4 to 5 minutes. Fold in the nut mixture in thirds so as not to deflate the meringue.

Whisk together the yolks, brown butter, vanilla, and almond extract and fold gently but thoroughly into the batter (the batter will deflate). Fold the cherries and any soaking liquid into the batter. Scrape the mixture into the prepared cake pan. Sprinkle the top with the sliced almonds and bake for 50 minutes, or until the cake begins to pull away from sides of the pan and a skewer inserted in the center comes out clean.

Cool the torte, upside-down, in the pan on a wire rack for 20 minutes. Flip the torte right-side up and cool completely. Dust the cake with confectioners' sugar and serve on its own or with Sour Cherry Sauce. Store covered and at room temperature for up to 3 days.

Sour Cherry Sauce

This sweet-tart mahogany-red sauce is packed with small sour cherries. Serve it with chocolate, custard, or almond desserts, or over ice cream or frozen yogurt. Use either bottled sour cherry juice, such as the one produced by Knudsen's, or the juice drained from a jar of sour cherries.

YIELD: 3 CUPS

2 cups sour cherry juice

1/4 cup sugar

1/4 cup honey

1 tablespoon cornstarch

1 pound (2 cups) pitted frozen, fresh, or bottled sour cherries

2 tablespoons kirsch or brandy

Place 1 3/4 cups of the cherry juice, sugar, and honey in a medium non-aluminum pot and bring to a boil. Boil for 10 minutes or until the mixture is thickened and syrupy.

In a bowl, whisk together the cornstarch and the remaining 1/4 cup cherry juice. Add to the pot and bring to a boil over medium heat. Cook until thickened and smooth, 1 to 2 minutes. Remove from the heat, stir in cherries and kirsch, and cool to room temperature. Store refrigerated for up to 1 month.

Venetian Cornmeal and Cherry Crostata

In the Veneto, the region of Venice and its landward surroundings, polenta, or cornmeal grits, often shows up as an accompaniment to fish and meat. Here, polenta lends its special grainy texture and distinctive corn flavor to a shallow, home-style fruit tart called a crostata in Italian. A soft almond cream acts as a bed for small sour cherries, which get baked right into the cream layer. Almonds and cherries have complementary flavors, because the two are close cousins.

YIELD: ONE 10-INCH TART, 10 TO 12 SERVINGS

1 3/4 pound Venetian Cornmeal Tart Pastry dough (page 391)

1/4 pound almond paste

2 ounces (1/2 stick) unsalted butter, softened

1/2 cup sugar

3 large eggs

2 tablespoons amaretto liqueur, substitute brandy

1 teaspoon almond extract

1 ounce (1/4 cup minus 1 teaspoon) unbleached all-purpose flour

1/4 pound (1 1/4 cups) almond meal or finely ground skin-on whole almonds

1 1/2 pounds (3 cups) pitted sour cherries, partially defrosted if frozen

Roll out the pastry about 3/8-inch thick between two sheets of lightly floured wax paper. Without stretching the dough, place it in a 10-inch tart pan with a removable bottom. Alternatively, press the dough out by hand into the bottom and 2 inches up the sides of a 10-inch springform or removable-bottom cake pan, making sure the pastry is even and not too thick, especially at the corners, where the sides meet the top. Chill the crust for 1 hour in the refrigerator or 30 minutes in the freezer to set the shape.

Preheat the oven to 350°F. Place the almond paste, butter, and sugar in the bowl of a food processor and process until light and creamy. Add the eggs, amaretto, and almond extract and process again until well combined. Whisk together the flour and almonds, add to the creamed mix, and process briefly to combine. Spoon the filling into the pastry-lined tart pan. Spoon the cherries and any juices over top.

Bake on the bottom shelf of the oven for 30 minutes, then reduce the oven temperature to 325°F and bake for 30 minutes or until the center is set. If necessary, cover the crostata with aluminum foil during last 30 minutes to prevent excessive browning. Cool to room temperature on a wire rack. Store covered and at room temperature for up to 3 days.

Chocolate–Cherry Biscotti with Cocoa Nibs

These crumbly, yet crisp biscotti are loaded with crushed bitter chocolate nibs (the inside of the cocoa bean), dark red Dutch process cocoa, and dried sweetened sour cherries. Almond extract and kirsch intensify

the cherry flavor. These biscotti are not at all traditional, but they sure are delicious, easy to make, and
long-keeping. Baker's ammonia will make them extra-
crisp, but baking powder may be substituted. For more
information about cocoa nibs, see page 340.

YIELD: ABOUT 48 COOKIES

14 ounces (3^1/$_4$ cups plus 2 tablespoons) unbleached
    all-purpose flour

2 ounces (^{1}/$_2$ cup minus ^{1}/$_2$ tablespoon) Dutch
    process cocoa

2 teaspoons baker's ammonia, substitute baking powder

^{1}/$_2$ teaspoon fine sea salt

3 large eggs

1^1/$_2$ cups sugar

^{1}/$_2$ cup Brown Butter (page 202), melted and cooled

^{1}/$_4$ cup kirsch

1^1/$_2$ teaspoons almond extract

1 teaspoon vanilla extract

5 ounces (1 cup) crushed cocoa nibs

1^1/$_2$ cups dried tart cherries

^{1}/$_2$ pound (1^1/$_2$ cups) hazelnuts, lightly toasted, skinned,
    and roughly chopped

^{1}/$_2$ cup raw sugar, for sprinkling

Preheat the oven to 350°F. Line two baking sheets with
parchment paper or silicone baking mats.

In a medium bowl, whisk together the dry ingredients: flour, cocoa, baker's ammonia, and salt.

In the bowl of a standing mixer fitted with the paddle attachment, beat the eggs and the sugar until light
and fluffy, 5 to 6 minutes. Slowly beat in the brown but-

ter, then add the kirsch, almond extract, and vanilla,
and beat lightly to combine. Fold in the flour mix, then
fold in the cocoa nibs, cherries, and hazelnuts.

Lightly oil your hands and form the dough into two
logs, each about 1^1/$_2$ inches wide and ^{3}/$_4$-inch thick.
Arrange the logs on the prepared baking sheets equidistant from each other with at least 2 inches of space
in between. Sprinkle the dough with raw sugar, patting
so the sugar adheres. Bake for 25 minutes or until lightly
browned but still soft in the center. Cool to room temperature on a wire rack.

Reduce the oven temperature to 325°F. Using a sharp
knife, slice the logs diagonally into ^{1}/$_2$-inch thick slices.
Arrange the slices upright onto the baking sheets. (The
cookie slices will be somewhat fragile.) Bake again for
about 20 minutes, or until crispy. Store in an airtight
container. The cookies will keep for at least a month in
dry weather. You may freeze the dough before or after
baking up to 2 months.

Cherry–Maraschino Cream Pie

*When I made this pie during my seemingly endless recipe
testing phase, it disappeared in minutes and got rave
reviews from some tasters who were getting pretty tired
of an overly bountiful array of sweets. A flaky all-butter
piecrust is topped with a layer of sweetened, lightly
thickened sour cherries (which may be fresh, frozen, or
from a jar), then topped with an easy almond-scented
cream based on sweetened condensed milk.*

3/4 pound Butter Pie Pastry dough (page 203)

Filling

1/4 cup sugar

2 tablespoons cornstarch

2 cups frozen pitted sour cherries, defrosted and
drained, with juices saved, plus 1/2 cup tart cherry
juice, or 2 cups pitted sour cherries in glass jar plus
1/2 cup liquid

1/4 cup maraschino liqueur, substitute kirsch

Topping

1 (14-ounce) can sweetened condensed milk

1/2 cup fresh-squeezed lemon juice

1 teaspoon vanilla extract

1 teaspoon almond extract

1/2 cup heavy cream, whipped

Make the pie crust: Roll the dough out between two sheets of lightly floured wax paper or on a lightly floured work surface to 3/8-inch thick. Drape into a 9-inch pie pan without stretching the dough. Form a double-thick edge and crimp or pinch in and out alternatively to form a fluted border. Chill for 1 hour in the refrigerator or 30 minutes in the freezer.

Preheat the oven to 375°F. Fit a piece of heavy-duty foil onto the dough and fill with beans or other pie weights. Blind bake (just pastry crust, no filling) on the bottom shelf of the oven until the crust is cooked through but not yet browned, about 30 minutes. Remove the foil and the weights, reduce oven temper-

ature to 325°F, and bake for 10 minutes longer, or until the dough is evenly and lightly browned. Remove from the oven and cool to room temperature on a wire rack.

Make the topping: In a bowl, whisk together the sugar and cornstarch and beat in any cherry juices and the liqueur. Transfer to a small pot and cook over low heat until thickened and clear, about 5 minutes. Cool to room temperature, then add the cherries. Spoon into the pie crust.

Make the filling: In a bowl, whisk together the condensed milk and the lemon juice. (The mixture will thicken.) Add the vanilla and almond extract and whisk lightly to thin, then fold in the whipped cream. Spoon on top of the cherry filling. Refrigerate the tart until set, at least 1 hour before serving. Store refrigerated up to 2 days.

Tart Cherry Clafouti

This classic French peasant dish is from the Limousin, a rural region close to the center of l'Hexagon (France is shaped like a hexagon). The clafouti is classically made by baking fresh fruit, especially cherries, with a pancake-like batter in a ceramic baking dish. The dish got its name from the old Occitan language spoken in Occitania, the region that included Southern France, parts of Italy, and northern Spain, from a word meaning "to fill up," as in filling the batter with cherries. Once a purely regional dish, the easy-to-make clafouti spread throughout France during the nineteenth century, where it is made in many versions. Purists insist that the cherries not be pitted, as the pits release a subtle bitter cherry flavor when cooked.

YIELD: 6 SERVINGS

2 tablespoons (1 ounce) unsalted butter, softened

1/2 cup plus 2 tablespoons sugar

1 pound (2 cups) fresh tart cherries, pitted if desired,
    drained bottled sour cherries, or partially defrosted
    frozen sour cherries

2 ounces (1/2 cup minus 1/2 tablespoon) unbleached
    all-purpose flour

Pinch salt

4 large eggs

1 cup milk

6 tablespoons brandy

Confectioners' sugar, for sprinkling

Preheat the oven to 350°F. Butter a wide shallow baking
dish that holds about 6 cups and sprinkle with 2 tablespoons of sugar. Sprinkle the cherries into the dish.

In a bowl, whisk together the flour, remaining 1/2 cup
sugar, and the salt. Make a well in the center. Separately
whisk together the eggs, milk, and brandy. Beat into the
flour mixture and whisk together until the mixture is
smooth and the consistency of pancake batter, without overbeating.

Pour the batter over the cherries and bake for
45 minutes or until the clafouti is set in the middle and
puffy. (It will sink slightly as it cools.) Sprinkle with
confectioners' sugar just before serving the clafouti
hot or warm.

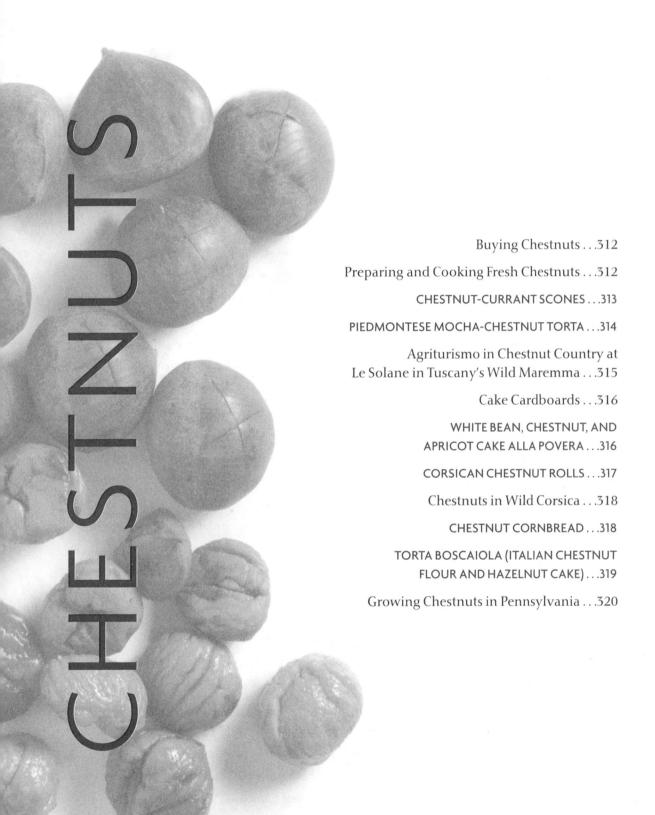

CHESTNUTS

Buying Chestnuts . . .312

Preparing and Cooking Fresh Chestnuts . . .312

CHESTNUT-CURRANT SCONES . . .313

PIEDMONTESE MOCHA-CHESTNUT TORTA . . .314

Agriturismo in Chestnut Country at
Le Solane in Tuscany's Wild Maremma . . .315

Cake Cardboards . . .316

WHITE BEAN, CHESTNUT, AND
APRICOT CAKE ALLA POVERA . . .316

CORSICAN CHESTNUT ROLLS . . .317

Chestnuts in Wild Corsica . . .318

CHESTNUT CORNBREAD . . .318

TORTA BOSCAIOLA (ITALIAN CHESTNUT
FLOUR AND HAZELNUT CAKE) . . .319

Growing Chestnuts in Pennsylvania . . .320

CHESTNUTS

On a culinary tour of "sunny Naples" and the surrounding region in November a few years ago, I found myself shivering in the penetrating damp and cold even in my fully-lined raincoat. My souvenir from an expedition by bouncing ferry boat to the nearby island of Capri, was a stylish down jacket. I shipped my raincoat back home and proceeded to warm myself up from the inside out with an infusion of hazelnut cream-topped espresso from Caffé Il Professsore and a burningly-hot handful of big creamy-sweet Campanian chestnuts roasted over oak charcoal by a hatted, gloved, and scarfed street vendor. On the streets of Manhattan, that same sweet, smoky aroma wafts over fast-moving New Yorkers enticing them to pause briefly for a paper sack of roasted chestnuts, likely imported from Campania.

Chestnuts, *Castanea sativa*, but also various Asian varieties, mostly *Castanea mollissima*, are a wonderful ingredient for baking. Chestnuts are less known in America today than in Europe and Asia, mostly because the once magnificent groves of native American chestnuts died out early in the twentieth century. In Italy, market vendors and restaurants create artful displays of glossy mahogany-colored chestnuts in their spiky outer shells set over big fans of their shiny green leaves. Chestnuts have long been an important food in forested portions of Europe, especially on the island of Corsica, where they are a staple, because this nutritious food could be gathered freely from wild trees. Chestnuts contain twice as much starch as potatoes and contain less oil than other nuts. In the chestnut-growing regions of Italy and France, chestnuts are ground into sand-colored, slightly sweet flour, excellent as a gluten-free starch for cakes, cookies, and breads.

Chestnuts are one of the earliest foods eaten by humans. The chestnut tree dates back to prehistoric times and was first introduced to Europe via Greece. Native Americans feasted on America's native chestnut, *Castanea dentata*, long before European immigrants introduced their stock to this country. In 1904, diseased Asian chestnut trees planted on Long Island, New York carried a fungus that devastated America's chestnuts. Today, most chestnuts eaten by Americans are imported from Japan, China, Spain, and Italy.

Chestnuts are abundant in the southern Italian region of Campania, where some of the world's highest quality chestnuts are grown. In Italy, these starchy nuts are given to the poor as a symbol of sustenance on the Feast of Saint Martin; in Tuscany, they are traditionally eaten on Saint Simon's Day. Legend has it that the Greek army survived on their stores of chestnuts during their retreat from Asia Minor in 401–399 BCE. Such was the economic value of the chestnut tree that people in many parts of Italy called it "the bread tree."

Chestnuts grow encased in a spiky husk, with one to three nuts per each prickly burr. When mature, the fruit falls to the ground and is then gathered. Although we refer to chestnuts as nuts, the meat inside their woody brown shell is soft and starchy, more akin to a grain rather than an oil-rich nut. A single large nut grows inside the spiky outer casing of the cultivated European chestnut, *marrone* in Italian and *marron* in French. These are graded by size and condition from A to AAA. The top grade contains the most creamy flesh and the least wrinkled folds that teach a valuable lesson in patience in the course of attempting to remove all the stubborn bits of woody skin. In my chef years, I would buy Italian chestnuts in 50 pound burlap sacks, but only those graded AAA. Years of shelling hot roasted chestnuts deadened the nerves on my fingers so that now I can pick up hot plates without pain.

Two to three smaller nuts grow inside the casing of the European wild chestnut, *castagna* in Italian and *châtaigne* in French. Smaller, sweeter, and rather sticky Asian chestnuts have thinner skins and can be found in season at Korean markets. Asian chestnuts are also being grown in America, along with some hybrids of Asian and American chestnuts. Look for starchier, nutty-tasting dried European chestnuts at Italian groceries; look for softer, fruitier dried Asian chestnuts at Asian markets.

In baking, chestnuts are incredibly versatile, whether as whole fresh chestnuts, dried chestnuts, chestnut flour, vacuum-packed whole chestnuts, chestnuts in sugar syrup, or candied chestnuts. In this chapter, the British Chestnut–Currant Scones (page 313) are made with chestnut flour, while the White Bean, Chestnut, and Apricot Cake from Italy (page 316) includes both chestnut flour and candied chestnuts. The Corsican Chestnut Rolls (page 317) comes from that wild and isolated Mediterranean island. The Chestnut Cornbread (page 318) is a variation on the American favorite, while the Italian Torta Boscaiola (page 319) is a "woodlands" cake made with chestnut flour and hazelnuts. The dense, moist, flourless Mocha-Chestnut Torta (page 314) from the foothills of the Alps in Piedmont, Italy, is made from sweetened chestnut purée, dark chocolate, and espresso coffee.

BUYING CHESTNUTS

Harvested from October through March, December is the prime month for fresh chestnuts. Choose the largest, smoothest, shiniest chestnuts that feel heavy for their size. Chestnuts that have cracked shells will likely be moldy on the inside. Chestnuts that rattle inside their shells are dried out. Because fresh chestnuts easily turn moldy, store in the refrigerator up to a month or freeze whole chestnuts in their shells for up to four months. Freeze cooked chestnuts, either whole, chopped or puréed, in an airtight container up to six months.

Dried chestnuts are a bit sweeter and less floury in texture than fresh roasted, albeit not as flavorful. The dried form is reconstituted by soaking in water before using in equal quantities as fresh ones. Soak them as you would dried beans for about two hours before cooking. Store dried chestnuts like dried legumes, in a dry place and in an airtight container, preferably in the freezer, for up to six months.

While nothing beats the flavor of fresh-roasted chestnuts, even for a food fanatic like me, preparing chestnuts (see right) is quite a challenge. I often buy the vacuum-packed chestnuts from France and Italy that come in glass jars or the vacuum-packed plastic packages of frozen chestnuts sold at Trader Joe's in season, and European (and now American) chestnut flour. I have also found small bags of softer, sweeter, peeled whole Chinese chestnuts in my local Asian market. Sweetened chestnut purée in cans is usually imported from France. Clement Faugier (www.clementfaugier.com), which has been producing chestnut products since 1882 is a excellent brand found in American specialty stores.

While visiting the shop of a top Tuscan confectioners in January, I lusted for the huge copper pan tucked into a corner of the small shop. Its perforated top portion was crammed full of freshly-made candied chestnuts, still dripping sugar syrup into the bottom section. Exquisitely tender and sweet *marrons glacés* (candied large chestnuts) may be found in specialty stores especially in winter though because of the extensive labor involved, they are always a luxury. According to the Genoese, the marron glacé was invented there in 1790 at a time that it was controlled by the French. However in 1667, the famed French chef, La Varenne, had written in his book, Le Parfaict Confiturier (The Perfect Preserve Maker) of a method to preserve chestnuts.

PREPARING AND COOKING FRESH CHESTNUTS

Chestnuts must be thoroughly cooked before being eaten in order to avoid digestive discomfort, because of the high levels of tannic acid they contain. The thin but tough outer shell as well as the bitter inner brown skin must be removed before eating. To prepare fresh chestnuts, make a crisscross cut on the domed side of each chestnut, taking care not to slip off the smooth, slippery tough shell. This is an important step, because the chestnuts can potentially explode from internal pressure if not pierced.

To oven-roast, place the chestnuts on a baking sheet and roast at 425°F for about 20 minutes, or until the chestnuts start to darken and the shells split open. Cool slightly and pull off the outer shells, taking care to remove all of the brown inner skin as well. It's easiest to do when the chestnuts are quite warm, so work with only a few at a time, keeping the rest in the pot or oven, and don heat resistant gloves to make peeling easier. To roast in a fire or over a grill, use a special chestnut roaster (available from Fante's: www.fantes.com, which also sells the special small Italian chestnut knife I like to use), or a disposable aluminum pie plate punched with rows of holes. Fill the roaster with chestnuts, and place in on a grill over white hot coals or in the embers of a fire and grill, shaking occasionally, until the shells have started to blacken. Peel while still hot.

To boil, cover with cold water, bring to a boil, and simmer for 3 minutes. Remove from heat. Scoop out a few chestnuts at a time and peel off the shell and skin with a sharp knife. As they cool, the chestnuts become more difficult to peel, so keep them in hot water until you are ready to peel. To boil and cook chestnuts completely in their skins, simmer for 15 to 25 minutes, then peel and use, but don't be disappointed if they fall apart as you peel them. This boiling method is best used when you will be mashing the chestnuts or pushing them through a sieve for purée. Restaurants will often cook the whole chestnuts in the deep-fryer, where the direct high heat encourages the shells to separate from the meats. A home deep-fryer would serve the purpose as well.

Chestnut–Currant Scones

These easy-to-make drop scones are moist, rich, crumbly, and full of woodsy chestnut flavor. You don't even have to roll them out: simply scoop the batter with an ice cream scoop or a rounded soup spoon onto a baking sheet and bake. Not too sweet, the surprise of small bits of currant combined with chestnut flour make these scones out of the ordinary.

YIELD: 18 SCONES

$1/4$ pound ($3/4$ cup plus 1 tablespoon) chestnut flour

$1/2$ pound (2 cups minus 2 tablespoons) unbleached
    all-purpose flour

$1/2$ cup sugar

2 teaspoons baking powder

1 teaspoon ground coriander

$1/2$ teaspoon fine sea salt

$1/2$ pound (2 sticks) unsalted butter, cut into small bits

$1/2$ cup Zante currants

1 large egg

1 cup heavy cream

Line an 18 x 13-inch half sheet pan (or other large baking pan) with parchment paper or a silicone baking mat.

In the bowl of a standing mixer, whisk together the dry ingredients: chestnut flour, flour, sugar, baking powder, coriander, and salt. Add the butter to the bowl and place in the freezer to chill for 30 minutes, or until butter is quite cold and firm.

Preheat the oven to 375°F.

Using the paddle attachment, beat until the mixture

resembles oatmeal, then add the currants.

Separately, whisk together the egg and cream. Add to the mixture and beat just long enough to form large moist clumps. Do not over-mix or the batter will toughen. Scoop the batter into mounds by the quarter cup onto the baking pan. Bake for 16 minutes or until lightly browned. Cool to room temperature on a wire rack before serving. Scones are best fresh made.

Piedmontese Mocha–Chestnut Torta

Rich and dark, this moist cake—which is more like a chocolate-chestnut pudding than a cake—combines the sophisticated Piedmontese mountain flavors of chestnuts, espresso, and dark chocolate. Dense, sweet, and starchy chestnut cream substitutes here for flour. The trio of ingredients is found in many forms in Piedmont and its capital city of Torino (Turin). I have traveled in this far northern part of Italy several times, enjoying its richly indulgent, old-fashioned, French-influenced food, most recently as a delegate to the Slow Food Terra Madre, a gathering of producers and chefs from around the world. This recipe is gluten-free.

YIELD: ONE 9-INCH TORTE; 10 TO 12 SERVINGS

Torta

10 ounces bittersweet chocolate, chopped

1 (17^1/$_2$-ounce, 500 g) can sweetened chestnut purée

^{1}/$_2$ pound (2 sticks) unsalted butter, softened

4 large eggs, separated

1 tablespoon finely ground espresso or 1 tablespoon coffee extract

Pinch salt

1 teaspoon vanilla extract

^{1}/$_4$ pound (^{3}/$_4$ cup) chestnut flour

^{1}/$_2$ cup sugar

Glaze and Decoration

6 ounces bittersweet chocolate, chopped

^{1}/$_4$ cup hot brewed espresso

2 tablespoons dark rum, substitute brandy, bourbon, or more coffee

2 ounces (^{1}/$_2$ stick) unsalted butter, softened

^{1}/$_4$ cup chocolate-covered espresso beans, optional for garnish

Make the cake: Preheat the oven to 350°F. Spray a 9-inch round removable-bottom or springform cake pan with nonstick baker's coating, or rub with softened butter and dust with flour, shaking off the excess.

Place the chocolate in a microwaveable bowl and melt in the microwave on lowest power for 2 minutes at a time, or until just barely melted. Whisk until smooth and cool to room temperature.

In the bowl of a standing mixer fitted with the paddle attachment, beat the chestnut purée with the butter until light and fluffy, 5 to 6 minutes. Beat in the egg yolks, one at a time, then add the ground espresso, salt, and vanilla. Fold in the chocolate and the chestnut flour and transfer to a wide shallow bowl.

In the clean and greaseless bowl of a standing mixer fitted with the whisk attachment, beat the egg whites until fluffy, then add the sugar and continue beating until the whites are firm and glossy, 4 to 5 minutes. Fold into the chestnut mixture in thirds so as not to deflate the meringue.

Spread the batter evenly into the pan and shake back and forth several times to smooth the top. Bake for 50 minutes or until the cake rises somewhat and looks dry and slightly cracked on top. (The center should be soft but not liquidy). Cool in the pan for 1 hour on a wire rack, or until it has reached room temperature (it will fall). Invert the cake onto a 9-inch cake cardboard or onto the bottom of a 9-inch cake pan. Place the cake onto a wire cake rack over a baking pan.

Make the glaze: Place the chocolate in a microwaveable bowl and melt on low power in the microwave, 2 minutes at a time, or until just barely melted. Add the espresso and whisk together until the chocolate melts completely and the mixture is smooth and shiny. Whisk in the rum and butter and allow the glaze to cool until it is thick enough to hold its shape.

Spoon the glaze over the cake, using an icing spatula to spread it evenly over the top and sides. Use the spatula to swirl the icing in a decorative pattern on top of the cake. Arrange the chocolate-covered espresso beans around the top outside edge of the cake.

Chill the cake for 30 minutes in the refrigerator or until the glaze is set. Cut into portions using a knife dipped into hot water and wiped dry in between each cut and taking care not to drip any water onto the icing (which will cause unsightly spots). Store covered and refrigerated for up to 5 days. (You may freeze the cake before icing it for up to 3 months.)

AGRITURISMO IN CHESTNUT COUNTRY AT LE SOLANE IN TUSCANY'S WILD MAREMMA

One taste of Maya Eisner and Claudio Roncoroni's smooth, luscious chestnut-chocolate Crema di Marroni, and I wanted more. This spread, which comes from my friends' agriturismo farm and inn, Le Solane, in Tuscany's wild Maremma near the Tyrrhenian Sea, is best described by Maya. "It is an antique local recipe coming from the Monte Amiata that is the highest mountain in the area, which is covered by chestnut trees. The local women used to prepare this cream in winter time when the chestnut harvest was abundant, but in recent years, the production of this kind of cream was abandoned by most people. We tasted it in the house of an old farmer who told us the story and gave us his grandma's recipe. So we decided to revive this old tradition and produce our own, made from only chestnuts, chocolate, and vanilla."

Built in the eighteenth century, Le Solane was a thriving farm covered with olive and Mediterranean pine trees until it was abandoned fifty years ago. The intrepid couple restored Le Solane as a working farm and inn where they also make strawberry-vin santo, fig-walnut, and quince preserves from home-grown fruits and nuts. The surrounding region is filled with lovely ancient walled towns renowned for their culture, art, history, and rustic confections, and baked goods, many featuring the combination of woodland chestnuts and intensely flavored dark chocolate. For more information, go to: www.lesolane.it and tell them Aliza sent you.

White Bean, Chestnut, and Apricot Cake alla Povera

As the author of an entire book about beans, (Beans: More than 200 Wholesome, Delicious Recipes from Around the World), *I am always fascinated with unusual uses for legumes. This cake is called* alla povera, *meaning "poor people's style" in Italian, because it is made with what were, years ago, the foods of the poor. Chestnuts could be gathered for free; honey could be collected at little expense; and beans were a stalwart peasant staple. These days, chestnuts, especially when candied as* marrons glacées, *are a luxury food, as is chestnut flour, because in America, most of it is imported from Europe. This cake is well worth making for your more adventurous friends. It is moist and light, combining the intriguing flavors of apricot, chestnut, and mild white beans. Accompany slices of the cake with the Apricot-Brandy Sauce (page 123) if desired. This recipe is gluten- and dairy-free.*

YIELD: ONE 9-INCH CAKE, 10 TO 12 SERVINGS

$1/4$ pound (1 cup) dried apricots,
   preferably California, diced

$1/4$ cup brandy

2 ounces ($1/2$ cup plus 2 tablespoons) potato starch

2 ounces ($1/4$ cup plus $2^1/2$ tablespoons) chestnut flour

1 teaspoon baking powder

$1/2$ teaspoon fine sea salt

1 (15-ounce) can cooked white beans,
   drained and rinsed

5 large eggs, separated

$1/2$ cup honey

6 ounces (about 8) marrons glacés (candied chestnuts)
   or drained chestnuts in syrup, roughly chopped

$3/4$ cup sugar

Confectioners' sugar, for dusting

Soak the apricots in the brandy for at least 1 hour and up to 2 days ahead of time, or until plump and soft. Spray a 9-inch springform or removable-bottom cake pan with baker's nonstick coating, or rub with softened butter and dust with flour, shaking out the excess.

Sift together the dry ingredients: potato starch, chestnut flour, baking powder, and salt.

In a food processor, process the beans until smooth and then, if desired for smoother texture, strain using a food mill or a sieve to remove skins.

Preheat the oven to 350°F. Scrape the bean purée into a mixing bowl, add the egg yolks and honey and whisk together to combine. Fold in the starch mixture, then fold in the apricots with their soaking liquid and the chestnuts.

In the clean and greaseless bowl of a standing mixer

using the whisk attachment, beat the egg whites until fluffy, then add the sugar and continue beating until the whites are firm and glossy, 4 to 5 minutes. Fold into the bean mixture in thirds so as not to deflate the meringue.

Scrape the batter into the pan and bake for 25 minutes, reduce oven temperature to 325°F and continue baking 25 minutes longer, or until the cake has started to come away from the sides of the pan and the center has puffed up slightly. Cool to room temperature on a wire rack, then dust with confectioners' sugar before cutting into serving portions. Store covered and at room temperature up to 3 days.

Corsican Chestnut Rolls

Bon'appetittu *is what they say in Corsica when serving this traditional bread, made from the flour of the chestnut trees that grow all over the island. A traditional Corsican product, chestnut flour is the base for numerous dishes. To make the flour, the chestnuts are picked and shelled, the placed in a dryer where a carefully regulated fire dehydrates them over a period of several days. Darker and sweeter than wheat flour, chestnut flour goes into Corsican breads like this one and other baked goods. Here, simple ingredients yield delicious, nutty-tasting small rolls with a delicate but definite chestnut flavor, attractive warm buff-color, and firm, crunchy crust. This recipe is dairy-free.*

YIELD: 16 ROLLS

1 ($^1\!/_4$-ounce) package ($2^1\!/_2$ teaspoons) active dry yeast

$1^1\!/_2$ cups lukewarm water

1 pound (4 cups) unbleached bread flour

$^1\!/_4$ pound ($^3\!/_4$ cup plus 1 tablespoon) chestnut flour, plus more for sprinkling

2 teaspoons fine sea salt

In the bowl of a standing mixer fitted with the paddle attachment, combine the yeast, water, and $^1\!/_4$ cup of the flour. Allow the mixture to proof for about 10 minutes or until bubbling. Beat in the remaining flour, the chestnut flour, and the salt. Change to the dough hook and continue beating until the dough is smooth and elastic and comes away from the sides of the bowl.

Transfer the dough to a large oiled bowl; turn around so the dough is oiled all over. Cover with plastic wrap or a damp cloth and allow the dough to rise until doubled in size, about 2 hours, at warm room temperature.

Punch down the dough and divide it evenly into 16 portions. Roll each portion into a smooth ball. Dip the smooth tops of each roll into a small bowl of chestnut flour. Arrange the rolls on a baking pan lined with parchment paper or a silicone baking mat. Score the tops of the rolls with a French baker's lame, a single-edged razor, or a box cutter in a criss-cross shape. Allow the rolls to rise until almost doubled in bulk, about 1 hour at room temperature, covering the rolls with a damp kitchen towel to keep them from forming a crust.

Preheat the oven to 425°F. Place the rolls in the hot oven, throw a handful of ice cubes onto the bottom of the oven to create steam, and then reduce the temperature to 375°F. Bake for 20 minutes or until the bread is browned and the inside reads 190°F to 205°F when

pierced with a thermometer. Cool to room temperature on a wire rack before serving.

This bread freezes well for up to 2 months. To reheat,
wrap in aluminum foil and bake at 350°F for 20 to 30
minutes or until hot and crusty inside.

CHESTNUTS IN WILD CORSICA

The *castagnu* is the emblematic tree of this wild
and isolated island, filled with ancient chestnut tree
forests. The often strangely-shaped tree is considered as a magical sentinel in Corsican lore. On this
Mediterranean island, the chestnut was a staple
food and the chestnut tree was known as *u arburu a
pane*, the bread tree, in Corsican. (Similarly, the
Cherokee tribes in the American Northeast called it
the bread tree—*tili tlugvi*, in the Cherokee language.) Chest-nuts were already an important part
of the Corsican economy during the Roman occu-
pation almost two thousand years ago. Today,
chestnuts and chestnut flour are used to make
polenta, cakes, pies, muffins, ice-cream, superb
honey, jam, crêpes, marrons glacés, chestnut beer,
and chestnut liqueur (*liqueur de châtaigne*), and are
celebrated during the island's Chestnut Week in
early December.

Chestnut Cornbread

*This unusual cornbread, which combines woodsy
chestnut flour, honey, buttermilk, and the special nutty
flavor of brown butter, would be perfect to serve on
Thanksgiving, as it features two early American staples:
chestnuts and cornmeal. It is moist and dense in texture
with a complex flavor that belies how easy it is to make.*

YIELD: 8 TO 10 SERVINGS

6 ounces (1¼ cups plus 1 tablespoon) stone-ground
   yellow cornmeal
¼ pound (¾ cup plus 1 tablespoon) chestnut flour
2 ounces (½ cup minus ½ tablespoon) unbleached
   all-purpose flour
1 teaspoon baking powder
½ teaspoon baking soda
1 teaspoon fine sea salt
3 large eggs
½ cup honey
1 cup buttermilk
½ cup Brown Butter, melted (page 202)

Preheat the oven to 350°F. Spray an 8-inch square baking pan with nonstick coating.

In a large mixing bowl, whisk together the dry ingredients: cornmeal, chestnut flour, flour, baking powder,
baking soda, and salt. In a second bowl, whisk together
the eggs, honey, buttermilk, and brown butter. Pour
the egg mixture into the cornmeal mixture and stir
until just combined, without overbeating. Pour the
batter into the prepared pan and bake for 30 minutes,

or until set in the middle and the cornbread has begun to come away from the sides of the pan. Cool on a wire rack for 10 minutes, then cut into portions and serve warm or at room temperature. Store covered and refrigerated for up to 3 days, reheating before serving.

Torta Boscaiola (Italian Chestnut Flour and Hazelnut Cake)

Boscaiola means "from the woodlands" or "woodlands style" in Italian, which poetically describes this dark, rich-tasting wheat-free cake. Because it is so flavorful and moist, the cake can be served to your most discerning, sophisticated friends. Chestnut flour is a delicious slightly sweet, nutty-tasting alternative flour that can be purchased from Italian markets and many online sources including the American-grown chestnut flour from Delmarvelous Chestnuts (www.buychestnuts. com). Serve the cake with sweetened whipped mascarpone and accompany with strong espresso or Cognac. This recipe is gluten- and dairy-free.

YIELD: ONE 10-INCH BUNDT CAKE; 10 TO 12 SERVINGS

$^{1}/_{2}$ pound (1$^{1}/_{2}$ cups) hazelnuts, lightly toasted and skinned

6 ounces (1$^{1}/_{4}$ cups plus $^{1}/_{2}$ tablespoon) chestnut flour, plus additional for dusting

1 teaspoon baking powder

$^{1}/_{2}$ teaspoon fine sea salt

6 large egg yolks (6 tablespoons)

1 cup honey, preferably dark

1 cup sugar

$^{3}/_{4}$ cup extra-virgin olive oil

1 cup Zante currants

4 large egg whites ($^{1}/_{2}$ cup)

Confectioners' sugar, for dusting

Preheat the oven to 350°F. Prepare a 10-inch Bundt pan by spraying with nonstick baker's coating, or rubbing with oil and dusting with chestnut flour, shaking out the excess.

Combine the hazelnuts, chestnut flour, baking powder, and salt in the bowl of a food processor. Process until the nuts are finely ground.

In the bowl of a standing mixer fitted with the paddle attachment, beat the egg yolks, honey, and $^{1}/_{2}$ cup of the sugar until thick and pale, 5 to 6 minutes. Slowly beat in the oil and continue beating until the mixture is creamy again. Add the flour mixture and mix at low speed just until just combined. Fold in the currants by hand. Transfer the batter to a wide shallow bowl.

In the clean and greaseless bowl of a standing mixer fitted with the whisk attachment, beat the egg whites until fluffy, then add the remaining $^{1}/_{2}$ cup sugar and continue beating until the whites are firm and glossy, 4 to 5 minutes. Fold the meringue into the batter in thirds so as not to deflate the meringue. Spread the batter in the pan and rap the pan on a work surface once to release any large air bubbles.

Bake for 30 minutes then cover the cake with aluminum foil (to prevent the top from over-darkening)

and bake 30 minutes longer or until the cake starts to come away from the sides of the pan and a wooden pick or skewer inserted in center of cake comes out, for a total of 1 hour baking time. (The cake is naturally dark on top.) Cool the cake in the pan on a wire rack for 30 minutes, then remove from the pan. Cool the cake to room temperature, then dust with confectioners' sugar just before serving. Store covered and at room temperature for up to 5 days.

Note: To measure honey, rub the inside of a measure, preferably Pyrex, with oil before adding the honey. It will slide right out.

GROWING CHESTNUTS IN PENNSYLVANIA

A couple who left the corporate world and put their entire savings into starting a chestnut farm are finally, after fifteen long years, starting to see the results of their work and the saplings that they planted on the Delmarva (Delaware-Maryland-Virginia) Peninsula in Townsend, Delaware. The chestnuts themselves are a hybrid of the original American chestnuts and a Chinese variety that is resistant to the deadly blight that, beginning in 1904, wiped out the immense chestnut trees that towered up to eighty feet high in our forests. The nuts are on the small side, more like Asian chestnuts than the much larger Italian-grown marrone chestnuts. They have buttery-yellow flesh, and sweet, dense, coconut-like flesh with an inner skin that is relatively easy to peel off.

Co-owner Gary Petit's father had long struggled to reintroduce the long-lost American chestnuts to the Allegheny Forest near his Pennsylvania home. Petit's wife and co-owner, Nancy, is a Master Gardener in the state of Delaware, who enjoys traveling to farmers' markets and stores to show people how to use these once common, but now rather exotic, nuts. The fresh chestnuts are sold entirely by mail-order at www.buychestnuts.com as long as the crop lasts, along with dried chestnuts, chestnut flour, and even chestnut saplings if you want to grow your own.

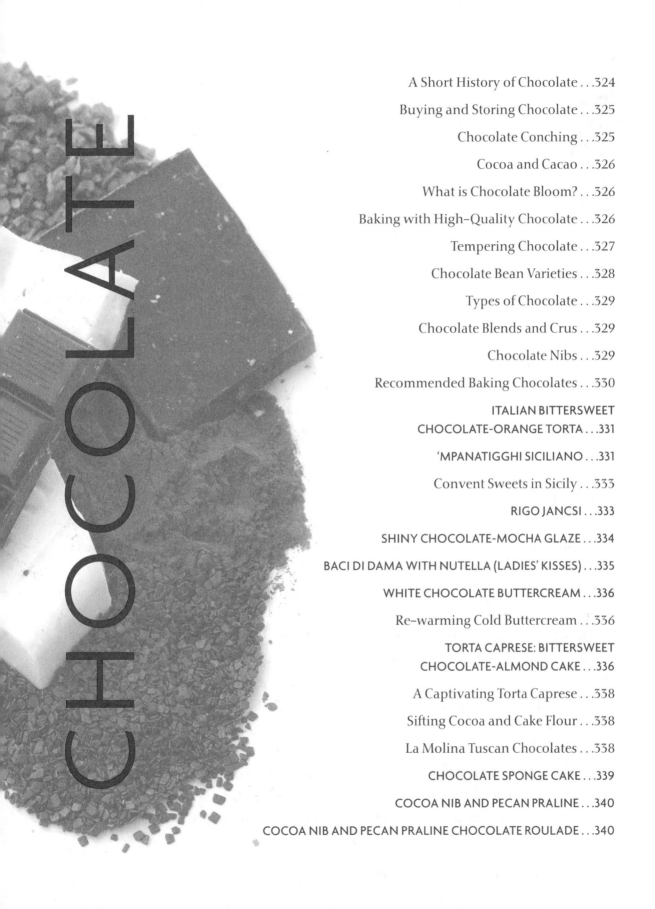

CHOCOLATE

A Short History of Chocolate . . .324

Buying and Storing Chocolate . . .325

Chocolate Conching . . .325

Cocoa and Cacao . . .326

What is Chocolate Bloom? . . .326

Baking with High–Quality Chocolate . . .326

Tempering Chocolate . . .327

Chocolate Bean Varieties . . .328

Types of Chocolate . . .329

Chocolate Blends and Crus . . .329

Chocolate Nibs . . .329

Recommended Baking Chocolates . . .330

ITALIAN BITTERSWEET
CHOCOLATE-ORANGE TORTA . . .331

'MPANATIGGHI SICILIANO . . .331

Convent Sweets in Sicily . . .333

RIGO JANCSI . . .333

SHINY CHOCOLATE-MOCHA GLAZE . . .334

BACI DI DAMA WITH NUTELLA (LADIES' KISSES) . . .335

WHITE CHOCOLATE BUTTERCREAM . . .336

Re–warming Cold Buttercream . . .336

TORTA CAPRESE: BITTERSWEET
CHOCOLATE-ALMOND CAKE . . .336

A Captivating Torta Caprese . . .338

Sifting Cocoa and Cake Flour . . .338

La Molina Tuscan Chocolates . . .338

CHOCOLATE SPONGE CAKE . . .339

COCOA NIB AND PECAN PRALINE . . .340

COCOA NIB AND PECAN PRALINE CHOCOLATE ROULADE . . .340

CHOCOLATE

In America, chocolate is all about indulgence, extravagance, sin, and transcendent experience. One pastry chef I know got dipped in the nude into a warm vat of liquid chocolate and I've seen the photos to prove it! How about a Chocolate Almost Better Than Sex Cake or even a Chocolate Better Than Sex Cake? Better than a psychologist's visit is a Chocolate Therapy Cake. If you're passionate, a Burning Love Chocolate Cream Cake is called for. Better than meditation is a Chocolate Divine Cake. If religion is on your mind, try a Chocolate Damnation, or Chocolate Sin. If you feel like going all out, there is Chocolate Intemperance, Chocolate Decadence, and Chocolate Indulgence. Be careful not to lose your senses when eating a Chocolate Obsession Cake, Chocolate Oblivion, or even risking Chocodeath. You may feel like a Divinely Decadent Chocolate Cake, or a Died-and-Went-To-Heaven Chocolate Cake at first but try a Chocolate Sigh Cake after Chocolate Torture after indulging in a Chocolate Lover's Torte.

Unlike America, where chocolate is about indulgence, Europeans and Latin Americans consider chocolate, concentrated, high-energy food to be fed to children to make them stronger. An Italian friend remembers being fed chocolate, always bittersweet, as a restorative. For this reason, European chocolate recipes are generally less sweet and made with lots of dark chocolate.

Hershey chocolate bars were standard issue in rations for American soldiers during World War II, because they were a quick energy booster that didn't spoil. Of course, it didn't hurt Hershey's business when the soldiers came home with a taste for chocolate. The Andalusian Bittersweet Chocolate–Sherry Cake (page 55), Bitter Chocolate–Hazelnut Torta with Pears (page 645), and 'mpanatigghi Siciliano (page 331) feature European-style bittersweet chocolate.

In my early years as a would-be chef, whenever I worked with chocolate, I'd end up with far too much smeared on my apron, arms, and sometimes even my hair. I judged my developing pastry skills on how clean I could keep myself, a measure of how much the chocolate controlled me and how much I could control this maddeningly messy material. Cocoa butter, or cocoa fat, has the unique ability to melt at well below body temperature, so that it quickly melts in the warm palms of your hands. One of the secrets of working with chocolate is to handle it quickly with cooler fingertips. Tempering chocolate so that it hardens to a glossy solid that breaks with a snap, can be a real challenge. Luckily, you won't need to temper the chocolate for these recipes.

The botanical term cacao, refers to the tree, the pods and their contents; cocoa, refers to the fermented cocoa beans and to the powder made from them. Cocoa beans are the seeds of the cacao tree, native to the dense tropical forests of the Amazon and a hugely important crop in tropical regions. The top world producers are Ivory Coast, Ghana, Indonesia, Cameroon, Nigeria, Brazil, and Ecuador. About 5 million metric tons (one metric ton equals 1,000 kilos, or 2,200 pounds) of cocoa beans are produced annually.

The tree's thick husks start out green, turns yellow, orange, and then red, often all at the same time. Traditionally, cacao trees are grown under shade trees but with plenty of moisture and nutrients, but trees are now raised in the sun, greatly increasing yields. Not that different from their human keepers, cocoa trees live up to 100 years and are at their prime 30 to 40 years after maturity, though unlike humans, they begin bearing fruits at about 5 years of age.

The large (6 to 10 inches long) pods can grow directly off the truck of the tree. Inside are 20 to 40 from white to purple "beans," actually seeds, each plump oval about 1¼-inches long and all enclosed in a gooey white pulp called the placenta. A mature cocoa tree will develop about 100 pods a year, although many drop off. The pods are cut from the branches by hand then opened to remove the beans and their pulp, which are fermented and dried for about 5 days and turned so that they ferment or "cure" properly to brown or partly purple. The beans are placed in shallow trays to dry in the sun, or in rainy areas, dried mechanically, to prevent mold.

The chocolate maker roasts the beans to bring out its complex flavors and aromas. The beans are then winnowed to remove their shells, leaving only the edible nibs. The nibs are ground into a thick, viscous liquid called chocolate liquor made up of about half cocoa solids and about half cocoa fat. Coarsely chopped natural unsweetened cocoa nibs are a new ingredient in the baker's repertoire. See the Chocolate–Cherry Biscotti with Cocoa Nibs (page 305) and the Cocoa Nib and Pecan Praline Chocolate Roulade (page 340).

To make the ultra–smooth, glossy confection called chocolate, chocolate liquor is conched, finely ground in a machine that got its name because the earliest ones were shaped like conch shells. The process was invented, perhaps by happy accident, in 1879 by Swiss chocolatier, Rodolphe Lindt. It's the combination of cocoa butter and solids in various proportions that determines the type of chocolate. The cocoa mass is mixed with sugar, flavored with vanilla or its artificial substitute, vanillin, and lecithin. (Lecithin is an emulsifier extracted from egg yolks or soy that help keep the chocolate from separating.

A SHORT HISTORY OF CHOCOLATE

As many people know and believe, especially women who sometimes get irresistible monthly cravings, chocolate's genus name, *Theobroma*, means "food of the gods." Chocolate, *Theobroma cacao*, gets its name from the Aztec word, xocalatl, meaning bitter liquid. The Aztecs allowed only men to drink this love potion which the Aztec king Montezuma drank in golden goblets before visiting his wives. (Like other aphrodisiacs, it works as long as you believe it will.) William Hickling, in his 1838 History of the Conquest of Mexico wrote that Montezuma "took no other beverage than the chocolatl, a potation of chocolate, flavored with vanilla and spices, and so prepared as to be reduced to a froth of the consistency of honey, which gradually dissolved in the mouth and was taken cold."

The Mayas established the earliest cocoa plantations around 600 CE in the Yucatan. From early times, Central American peoples used cacao beans as a form of payment. By 1200, the Aztecs were taking chocolate as tribute from conquered Mayans. In 1528, the Spanish explorer, Hernando Cortez brought cocoa beans to Spain, impressed by the fact that the Aztecs used them as currency. Cortes described chocolate as, "The divine drink which builds up resistance and fights fatigue." He built plantations on Trinidad, Haiti, and the West African island of Bioko to grow cacao to trade with Aztecs for gold. Spain maintained a virtual monopoly of the cocoa market for almost a century after that.

By the early 1700s, chocolate houses started opening up in England. At that time, chocolate was drunk as a hot beverage, like tea and coffee. In 1828, a clever Dutch chemist named Coenraad Van Houten figured out how to extract cocoa butter from chocolate liquor and began making the cocoa powder still sold by that company. By 1848, Van Houten had combined cocoa butter, sugar, and chocolate liquor to create the first "eating chocolate." Van Houten treated the cocoa with an alkalizing agent to improve the color and flavor in a process that became known as "Dutching," and cocoa processed this way is still called Dutch or Dutched chocolate with characteristic red-brown color.

The first American chocolate factory was established in Dorchester, Massachusetts, in 1765 by John Hannon and Dr. James Baker using West Indian cocoa beans. An American named Sam German created a sweet baking chocolate bar for the Baker's Chocolate Company in 1852 that is still sold today. In the same year, during the heady California Gold Rush, an Italian native, Domingo Ghirardelli established his first chocolate factory at Ghirardelli Square, San Francisco, its location for more than 60 years. An early modern chocolate bar was produced in England by Joseph Fry & Son by mixing cocoa butter back into the "Dutched" chocolate, and added sugar, creating a paste that could be molded. The chocolate bars were displayed at an English exhibition in 1849 by Joseph Fry & Son and Cadbury Brothers companies, which evolved into today's British chocolate giant, Cadbury's.

Switzerland has an abundance of milk from dairy cows, so in 1875, Daniel Peter and Henri Nestlé combined chocolate and milk powder and created the first milk chocolate bar. In 1879, Rodolphe Lindt of Berne, Switzerland invented the "conching" machine, which heated and rolled chocolate in order to refine it and make its texture finer, thereby allowing chocolate artisans to create all sorts of molded chocolates.

BUYING AND STORING CHOCOLATE

The easiest way to buy, store, and use chocolate is to purchase it in small, easily-melted chocolate discs or wafers, packed for restaurants and bakeries in 5 kilo boxes and for home use in smaller 1, 2, and 5 pound boxes. Many fine chocolate companies now produce their version of these disks, which are available at specialty stores or from online sources. Dark chocolate keeps well for up to one year as long as it is covered and stored in a cool place. I buy the easy-to-melt chocolate discs in a 5 kilo (11 pound) box, which under halfway normal circumstances (not when I am testing recipes) lasts me about six months. Perhaps you can buy a box and split it with a friend.

Wrap chocolate tightly in its own paper or in heavy-duty aluminum foil and keep it away from heat and light. Ideally, store in a cool, dry place between 60 and 65°F. In hot climates or during the summer, store chocolate in the refrigerator, well-wrapped to prevent it from absorbing odors. Like fine wines, dark chocolate actually improves with age when stored in an airtight container at cellar temperature.

CHOCOLATE CONCHING

The conch grinds the cocoa solids, aerating the cocoa paste while evenly coating the tiny cocoa bits and added sugar crystals with cocoa butter while developing the flavor of the chocolate through friction, thereby releasing aromatic volatile oils. During conching, the chocolate mass is placed in a container filled with metal beads, which act as grinders and produce cocoa and sugar particles smaller than the tongue can detect. The length of the conching process determines the final smoothness and quality of the chocolate. Top-quality chocolate is conched for as long as 78 hours, lesser grades four to six hours. Once conched the chocolate particles will typically be between 19 and 40 microns in diameter (human hair is 100 microns in diameter).

COCOA AND CACAO

The word *cacao*, first learned by the Spanish from the Maya, has its origins in the Olmec civilization of 3,000 years ago. In America, the word is used to describe all products made from the cacao seeds before they are processed. After processing they are called 'chocolate.' In Great Britain, 'cocoa' is basically used to describe what is known in the U.S. as 'cacao,' while in the States, 'cocoa' only refers to cocoa powder or the hot drink made from it. However, in the world commodity market for cacao products, based in New York, *cocoa* is the term used.

WHAT IS CHOCOLATE BLOOM?

There are two forms of "bloom" that can appear on the surface of chocolate: fat bloom and sugar bloom. If the storage temperature exceeds 75°F, large white cocoa butter crystals may appear on the surface, causing the chocolate to develop a whitish cast, known as "bloom." It is often accompanied by numerous minute cracks that dull the appearance of the chocolate.

Sugar bloom is grainy crystallization of the sugar crystals on the surface of the chocolate. It is caused by high humidity and the formation of condensation on the surface of the chocolate when it is brought from a cold environment into a warm room. Fat bloom will feel oily and melt when touched; sugar bloom will feel grainy to the touch. To prevent either type of bloom, it is important not to expose chocolate to wide fluctuations in temperature; instead, make all temperature changes gradually. Though not as attractive, the chocolate will still be fine for eating and baking.

BAKING WITH HIGH-QUALITY CHOCOLATE

If you have a favorite chocolate cake or brownie recipe, try making it with great chocolate. All of a sudden, your cake will taste like your restaurant favorites. Low-grade chocolates just can't compare in flavor to specialty American brands and imports. Inexpensive chocolates rely on waxy-textured inexpensive vegetable fats rather than on lusciously melting cocoa butter, use less complex bean varieties, and aren't ground fine enough. It's like the difference between brand-name canned Robusta coffee and freshly ground Arabica beans. Once you've tasted the best, it's hard to go back to ordinary. Luckily, there are lots of good quality chocolates available now even in the supermarket. Check the ingredients: you should see only chocolate liquor, cocoa butter, sugar, lecithin, and vanilla on the label.

TEMPERING CHOCOLATE

Tempering is the tricky process of crystallizing the molecules of cocoa butter in a particular way that makes the chocolate stable, hard, and shiny. There are five different forms that the cocoa fat crystals can take as they cool down and harden, but only one produces desirable glossy, firm chocolate. These good beta crystals are encouraged to grow and then harden into well-tempered chocolate that will shrink and pull away from a mold, and display beautiful shine and crystalline snap. If the chocolate is not properly tempered when melted, it will form large crystals as it hardens, causing the chocolate to appear mottled and matte and have a crumbly texture.

To temper chocolate, it must be melted slowly and evenly until all the chocolate is completely liquefied. Next, it is cooled to below its setting temperature, so it begins to crystallize. This may be done in several ways, either mechanically using a chocolate tempering machine, or by hand. The old-fashioned way is to spread the fully melted chocolate out on a marble slab using the natural cooling properties of marble to cool the chocolate until enough of the proper crystal "seeds" develop along the edges of the spread-out chocolate.

In the second method, finely chopped chocolate (one-third solid chocolate to two-thirds melted chocolate) is added to the melted chocolate. The mixture is then stirred until its temperature is brought down far enough to begin to crystallize on the edges. This method uses the already formed crystals present in the solid chocolate to "seed" the melted chocolate. Once the proper crystallization has begun, the chocolate is then rewarmed until it is melted and can be worked with.

Since I've discovered the special pure Beta 6 cocoa butter crystals sold by Albert Ulster (www.ausi.com) the frustrating process of tempering chocolate is now a cinch. All you need is a microwave, an instant-read thermometer, and the crystals. These cocoa butter crystals in their most stable form work so well that even a novice can temper chocolate. The crystals are sold in 1.25 kg containers ($2^3/4$ pounds), a large quantity and not cheap, but they do work. To use them, melt chocolate couverture (chocolate that is high in cocoa fat) to 95°F. Add 1 percent by weight (about 1 tablespoon for a pound of chocolate) of the crystals, stir well, wait ten minutes, and the chocolate is ready to use.

CHOCOLATE BEAN VARIETIES

The three most important cacao varieties—Forastero, Criollo, and Trinitario—have cross-bred and been hybridized, so that the distinctions are not clear. Cacao trees are difficult to grow and cultivate and will only grow twenty degrees north and twenty degrees south of the equator. If the temperature drops below 60°F, the tree will be damaged. Most cocoa farmers grow several varieties and due to cross-pollination, single trees with all the characteristics of a specific variety are rare unless the grower has planted cuttings of a single "mother" tree.

The Criollo, the rarest and most expensive cocoa bean on the market, was the most important variety at the time of the Spanish explorers. Today, it represents only about two to eight percent of the crop and grows in Mexico, Nicaragua and Guatemala. It can also be found in Venezuela, Colombia, Trinidad, Jamaica, and Grenada. Criollo also grows on the Indian Ocean islands of Madagascar and the Comoros and in Java. Criollo beans are particularly challenging to grow, as they are vulnerable to a variety of environmental threats and produce low yields and so many plantations have switched to less demanding Forasteros.

Criollo pods are usually deeply ridged and warty, with pointed ends. Inside, the beans range from white to shades of pink. The pale soft, thin-skinned, light-colored pods yield reddish tinged chocolate. Known for its mild fruitiness, the flavor of Criollo beans is slightly bitter, delicate, yet complex, with rich and long-lasting secondary notes that combine strength and delicacy. It is mildly astringent and low in tannin, is noted for its finesse, and is comparable to Arabica coffee beans.

The rare Porcelana from Venezuela is a pure subtype of Criollo that is light in color and delicately fruity in flavor with mild tannins and acids, and nutty, caramel notes. This varietal is made by Amedei and Domori in Italy into luxury-priced chocolate bars meant for savoring.

The Forastero a large group of wild and cultivated cacaos, is by far the most common of the three main varieties and represents 80 to 90 percent of world cocoa production. With its thick walls, the Forastero is disease-resistant and highly productive. Believed to be indigenous to Brazil's northern Amazon River, it grows in Peru, Colombia, Brazil, Guyana, and Venezuela. The great majority of African cocoa beans in Ivory Coast, Ghana, Cameroon and São Tomé Island are Forasteros. Comparable to Robusta coffee beans, earthy Trinitarios can be forcefully aromatic with moderate acidity and pungent aroma though lacking in finesse.

Ecuador's highly aromatic Arriba (the national bean of Ecuador and also known as Nacional) is a Forastero with large, green, wrinkled pods and big large purple beans that produce dark, tannic cacao with strong jasmine notes and nutty aftertaste. This varietal is grown in small quantities only in Ecuador.

The Trinitario, which represents 10 to 15 percent of world production is a natural hybrid of the Criollo and Forastero that originated in Trinidad (hence its name) in the mid-1700s after Forastero mixed with local Criollos. Trinitario grows in Trinidad and nearby islands as well as Java, Papua-New-Guinea, Sri Lanka, and Cameroon. Well suited to commercial cultivation, the highly aromatic Trinitarios ranges from spicy and earthy to fruity and acidic, combining the traits of both its forebears.

TYPES OF CHOCOLATE

Baking, bitter, or unsweetened chocolate is ground and conched cocoa beans formed into bars that contain only cocoa solids and cocoa fat. Bittersweet, semisweet, and sweet chocolates each have different amounts of sugar added, with bittersweet having the least. Lecithin, an emulsifier or stabilizer made from egg yolks, is added to the chocolate so that it is smooth and resists separating or turning grainy. Pure vanilla flavors the best chocolates; artificial vanillin is more common.

To make couverture (coating chocolate) meant for fancy chocolate-dipped candies, extra (expensive) cocoa butter is added so the chocolate will be shiny, shrink away from any mold, and break with a clean snap. Couverture must contain at least 32 percent cocoa butter, so that it melts to a thinner consistency that hardens into the thin shell desirable for chocolate confections. For the recipes in this book, couverture is not necessary.

Milk chocolate is enriched with milk solids and is generally quite sweet and extra smooth. Long America's favorite chocolate, milk chocolate is making a comeback among pastry chefs.

Technically not a true chocolate at all, white

chocolate is made from cocoa butter, milk solids, and sugar. The solid cocoa part of the cocoa bean is removed, leaving only the cocoa fat. Because of its high fat and sugar content, white chocolate is notoriously temperamental. Melt white chocolate at extra low temperatures (10 percent power in the microwave or in a double-boiler over steaming, not boiling water) to keep it smooth and creamy.

Much of the "chocolate" we eat really isn't. For "confectionery" or "summer coating," (not the same as couverture) manufacturers replace expensive, finicky cocoa butter with easier-to-handle vegetable fats that melt at higher temperatures. While this enables a factory to run all year round, the waxy mouthfeel of this quasi-chocolate is a big disappointment for aficionados. The chocolate morsels used for chocolate chip cookies are generally made from this type of "chocolate" for shelf stability and because they resist melting, desirable in a chocolate chip cookie, but not in cake or cookie batter.

In this book, I call mostly for bittersweet chocolate, though you may easily substitute semisweet chocolate for slightly sweeter flavor. I occasionally use milk chocolate and white chocolate. Substitute chopped bits of high-quality chocolate with the powdery bits sifted out for chocolate chips. The small round coin-shaped discs of high-quality chocolate sometimes found in smaller quantities at specialty stores make excellent "chocolate chips."

CHOCOLATE BLENDS AND CRUS

Blending chocolate varieties allows companies to achieve a consistent product year after year, similar to blended whiskeys like Johnny Walker. The newest thing in chocolate is single-origin chocolates, which have distinctive flavors and may vary from year to year, comparable to single-malt scotch. Just about every top chocolate company now produce single-origin chocolate bars. Eager tasters can then compare chocolate from different regions and get to use winespeak descriptions like "spicy yet fruity, with raisin notes," "fresh coffee flavor with undertones of strawberries and honey" and "fruity blueberries and red berries accented by spices and wood."

CHOCOLATE NIBS

Chocolate nibs are the heart of the cocoa bean from which all chocolate is made. After the outer husks of the individual beans have been removed, the nibs are roasted and broken into small bits. When finely ground, the nibs become chocolate liquor, the basis for all eating chocolate. The nibs are the essence of chocolate, for those who prefer their chocolate intense and bitter. Chocolate nibs add crunchy texture and intense bitter chocolate flavor to baked goods and make a great substitute for roasted nuts or chocolate chips, although you may have to increase sugar to compensate for their bitterness. Store cocoa nibs tightly wrapped and at room temperature away from the light up to one year. Order cocoa nibs from www.artisanconfection.com or from specialty chocolate companies.

RECOMMENDED BAKING CHOCOLATES

CALLEBAUT, a well-known Belgian chocolate, melts easily and is excellent for icings. It is often found broken into smaller blocks at candy stores and specialty food stores and is relatively reasonable in price. Look for their Intense Dark Chocolate or the 811 in 5-kilo (11 pound) blocks that I used for years for all my restaurant baking.

GHIRARDELLI is high-quality domestic chocolate sold in smaller bars at specialty stores and some supermarkets (look in the candy aisle, not the baking aisle). Their Bittersweet Chocolate Baking Bar is a good choice.

GUITTARD is another domestic chocolate and my choice these days for baking. I buy their 61 percent bittersweet chocolate discs in 5-kilo (11 pound) from a wholesale supplier (see CaviarAssouline in Sources). They also make semi-sweet chocolate chips, excellent for cookies.

SCHARFFEN BERGER'S, from San Francisco, makes 9-ounce chocolate bars of semisweet, bittersweet, and unsweetened chocolate that are perfectly sized for the home baker. For more ambitious bakers (or those with lots of friends), they sell easy-to-melt petite chocolate squares in 5-pound bags.

LINDT SWISS CHOCOLATE, sold in high-priced bars in the candy aisle, is considered one of the finest in the world. The Swiss are known for their super-smooth light and sweet milk chocolates, so Lindt is a good choice for milk chocolate.

PETER'S CHOCOLATE is the oldest and some say the best block chocolate. The large chunks of broken-up chocolate bars sold in specialty candy and gourmet food stores are often made by Peter's. In my early years in kitchens, Peter's was just about only chocolate I could buy in big blocks. It's still an excellent choice for baking, especially when price is important.

VALRHONA is a favorite of top pastry chefs. This chocolate is expensive, but its line of custom-blended chocolates is for the true connoisseur. Try Caraque, a mellow, deep red semisweet chocolate, the intense Caraïbe, made from dark roasted Caribbean beans, or Manjari, noted for its acidic fruitiness.

EL REY from Venezuela is a personal favorite, for its rich, deep flavor and smooth mouthfeel and because it's the only chocolate grown and processed in its country of origin. Try their single-origin Apamate, Gran Saman, Mijao and Bucare dark chocolates, their Caoba milk chocolate, and Icoa white chocolate.

TRADER JOE'S sells good-quality bittersweet, semisweet, and white Belgian chocolate in 500-gram bars (a bit more than a pound) at a very reasonable price and also chocolate bits, both under their store brand. Use the blocks for melting and mixing in batters; use the bits for cookies.

Italian Bittersweet Chocolate–Orange Torta

My friend Velia de Angelis made this sophisticated and intense bittersweet chocolate torte scented with orange zest and orange liqueur for me at the bakery owned by her hard-working friend, Iliana, in Orvieto, Italy. It is one of Velia's favorite cakes. I like to make the cake in a ring shape, but you can use a round pan, if you prefer. This recipe is gluten-free.

YIELD: ONE 9-INCH CAKE, 10 TO 12 SERVINGS

5 ounces bittersweet chocolate, roughly chopped

$1/4$ pound (1 stick) unsalted butter, cut into bits

2 ounces ($1/2$ cup minus 1 tablespoon) Dutch process cocoa

2 ounces ($1/2$ cup plus 2 tablespoons) potato starch

1 teaspoon baking powder

Pinch salt

4 large eggs, separated

1 cup sugar

$1/2$ cup heavy cream

$1/4$ cup Cointreau, Triple Sec, or other orange liqueur

Grated zest of 1 orange (4 teaspoons)

1 egg white

Confectioners' sugar, for dusting

Preheat the oven to 350°F. Spray a 9-inch tube pan with nonstick baker's coating, or rub with softened butter and dust with flour, shaking off the excess.

Place the chocolate and butter in a microwaveable bowl and melt on low power in the microwave for 2 minutes at a time, or until just barely melted. Whisk until smooth and cool to room temperature.

In a bowl, whisk together the dry ingredients: cocoa, potato starch, baking powder, and salt.

In a standing mixer fitted with a whisk attachment, beat the egg yolks and $1/2$ cup of the sugar until light and fluffy, 5 to 6 minutes. Beat in the chocolate mixture, then add the cream, orange liqueur, and orange zest, and beat until combined. Gently fold in the flour mixture.

In the clean and greaseless bowl of a standing mixer fitted with the whisk attachment, beat the 5 egg whites until fluffy, then add the remaining $1/2$ cup sugar and continue beating until the whites are firm and glossy, 4 to 5 minutes. Fold into the chocolate mix in thirds, so as not to deflate the meringue.

Spread the batter in the pan and rap the pan on work surface once to release any large air bubbles. Bake for 35 minutes or until the cake starts to come away from the sides of the pan and the middle of the cake has cracked all around. Cool completely on a wire rack, then dust with confectioners' sugar before serving.

'mpanatigghi Siciliano

I first tasted and loved these unusual chocolate-filled pastries in Florence, at a trade fair featuring Italy's best artisanal chocolate makers. It is a very old recipe found only in the Moderate region of Sicily, famed for its sweets. Its Sicilian dialect name, 'mpanatigghi, comes from the Spanish word empanadilla *(or small, bread-*

based turnover) and dates from the years of Spanish rule, starting in 1282 and lasting for 400 years, when Sicily was quite isolated. The traditional Sicilian kitchen is full of meat-based pastries, dating from its earlier days under Arab rule (832–1091). Here the Arab tradition of meat-filled pastries is combined with chocolate, brought from Spanish colonies in the New World to Sicily, a Spanish colony in the Old World. Together, they make a moist and delicious filling that's just got to be tried. The veal is so mild, you wouldn't know it's the secret to making the juicy filling unless someone told you. This recipe is dairy-free.

YIELD: 60 COOKIES

Pastry

6 ounces ($^3/_4$ cup) lard or trans fat-free shortening

6 ounces ($^3/_4$ cup) sugar

6 egg yolks (6 tablespoons)

1 pound ($3^3/_4$ cups) unbleached all-purpose flour

Filling

$^1/_2$ pound finely ground veal

1 cup sugar

1 pound (3 cups) whole almonds,
  lightly toasted and ground

$^1/_4$ pound bittersweet chocolate, grated

$^1/_2$ teaspoon ground cinnamon

4 large egg whites ($^1/_2$ cup)

Confectioners' sugar

Make the pastry: In the bowl of a standing mixer fitted with the paddle attachment, beat the lard and sugar together until light and fluffy, 5 to 6 minutes. Beat in the egg yolks one at a time. Add the flour and beat only long enough to combine. Transfer the dough to a plastic bag and shape into a flattened rectangle. Chill in the refrigerator for 1 hour or in the freezer for 30 minutes until firm but still malleable.

Make the filling: Cook the veal in a large nonstick skillet, breaking it up as it cooks for 3 to 4 minutes, or until it is no longer pink. Remove from the heat and combine with the sugar, almonds, chocolate, cinnamon, and egg whites. Cool the filling to room temperature, or refrigerate up to 2 days ahead of time.

Assemble the pastries: Preheat the oven to 375°F.

Roll out the pastry dough to a thin, even sheet about $^3/_8$-inch thick, dusting it with flour to prevent sticking. Cut into 3-inch rounds with a biscuit or cookie cutter. Chill the rounds before filling if they get soft.

Place one spoonful of filling on each circle of dough, fold the circle in half, and crimp or roll the edges, making sure the pastries are well-sealed. As they are completed, place the pastries on a baking sheet lined with parchment paper or a silicone baking mat. (If you're not baking these immediately, freeze the stuffed pastries on the pan, then transfer to an airtight plastic container with wax paper separating the layers of pastry, and freeze for up to 3 months.)

Cut a cross-shaped slit in the top of each pastry and bake for 20 minutes, or until the filling bubbles out of the top. (If the pastries are frozen, do not defrost them before baking, simply bake at 350°F for about 35 minutes or until browned and the filling bubbles out of the top.) Cool to room temperature, then dust with confectioners' sugar and serve. Store refrigerated for up to 3 days.

For centuries, nuns were the main producers of pastries, which they sold to the public to support their religious orders. Each convent had its own specialty, like the *pasta reale* produced by the Martorana convent in Palermo. *Pasta reale* (royal pastry) or marzipan, is made from finely ground Sicilian almonds, sugar, and egg whites, is painted and sculpted into fanciful life-like fruits, vegetables, and small figures. The meat-based sweets made by the nuns of the Origlione Monastery in Palermo and the Mazzarino convent of the Ennese are also quite famous.

Rigo Jancsi

I've been making small squares of this delectably rich and creamy cake since my earliest catering days more than thirty years ago. The pastry is named after the handsome Gypsy violinist who played with his orchestra all around Europe in the early twentieth century. Once, he played at a restaurant where the Belgian duke of Chimay was dining with his young beautiful wife, the daughter of an American millionaire. She was entranced by his music, but even more so by his passionate black eyes. Scandalously, the duchess left her husband for Jancsi and accompanied him on his tours. So, watch out, because this delectable pastry may be as dangerous as the Gypsy for whom it was named!

YIELD: 48 SQUARES

Cake

6 ounces unsweetened chocolate, finely chopped

$^3/_4$ pound (3 sticks) unsalted butter, softened

1 cup sugar

8 large eggs, separated

$^1/_4$ pound (1 cup minus 1 tablespoon) unbleached
    all-purpose flour

Pinch salt

Filling and Glaze

2 cups heavy cream

14 ounces semisweet chocolate, finely chopped

$^1/_4$ cup dark rum

2 teaspoons vanilla extract

2 cups Shiny Chocolate-Mocha Glaze (page 334)

Make the cake: Preheat the oven to 350°F. Line an 18 x 13-inch half sheet pan (or other large baking pan) with parchment paper or a silicone baking mat. Place the chocolate in a microwaveable bowl and melt on low power in the microwave for 2 minutes at a time, or until just barely melted. Whisk until smooth and cool to room temperature.

In the bowl of a standing mixer fitted with the paddle attachment, beat the butter with $^1/_2$ cup of the sugar until the mixture is light and fluffy. Beat in the egg yolks one at a time, then add the melted chocolate and mix to combine.

In the clean and greaseless bowl of a standing mixer fitted with the whisk attachment, beat the egg whites until fluffy, then add the remaining $^1/_2$ cup sugar and continue beating until the whites are firm and glossy, 4 to 5 minutes. Fold about one-third of the meringue into the chocolate mixture, then pour the chocolate mixture over the rest of the whites. Sprinkle the flour and salt lightly on top. Gently fold the mixture together until almost no white streaks remain. Pour the batter into the prepared pan, spreading it evenly.

Bake in the middle of the oven for 20 minutes, or until the cake shrinks slightly away from the sides of the pan and a skewer inserted in the middle comes out clean. It will still be very flat. Loosen the cake from the pan by running a sharp knife around the sides, and turn it out onto a rack to cool. (Put the rack on top of the pan and flip the whole thing over to keep the cake from breaking.)

Make the filling: Place the cream in a microwaveable bowl and heat to scalding or steaming hot in the microwave. Add the chocolate and allow it to melt from the heat of the cream. Stir until completely melted. (If necessary, microwave for 30 seconds longer and then stir until melted.) Whisk in the rum and the vanilla and cool for 1 hour in the refrigerator, stirring occasionally or until the mixture is cool but not cold, with the texture of chocolate pudding.

Transfer the chocolate cream to a standing mixer fitted with the whisk attachment and beat until it is smooth and creamy and forms soft peaks. Be careful not to overbeat, or the filling will separate. If this happens, melt it, cool it completely, and beat again.

Cut the cake into two halves. Spread the filling over one layer and place the other layer on top. Smooth out the edges with a spatula. If one of the cake layers should break, use it on the bottom. Refrigerate on a rack for about 1 hour.

Glaze the cake: Warm the Shiny Chocolate-Mocha Glaze on low power in the microwave. Whisk until smooth and shiny, then cool until the chocolate just holds its shape but is still pourable. Place the rack with the cake on it onto an 18 x 13-inch half sheet pan (or other large baking pan) to catch the drips. Pour the glaze over the cake, smoothing with an icing spatula. If necessary, scrape up some of the drips with a rubber spatula and pour back over the cake. Note that once the glaze starts to set, it will lose its shine if you continue to spread. Refrigerate the cake until the glaze is firm, about 30 minutes. Serve by cutting into 48 small, equal pieces, 6 across and 8 down, using a sharp knife dipped into hot water and wiped dry in between each cut. Store the cake refrigerated up to 4 days, but for maximum flavor, allow it to come to room temperature before serving.

Shiny Chocolate–Mocha Glaze

This easy-to-make shiny glaze is dark and chocolaty. It will keep quite well in the refrigerator for up to three months. Reheat at low power in the microwave until it is mostly melted, then whisk to combine. Use it to glaze the Rigo Jansci (page 333) and the Torta Gianduia (page 506) or the Chocolate-Glazed Praline Profiteroles (page 287).

YIELD: ABOUT 2 CUPS, ENOUGH TO GLAZE 1 LARGE CAKE, OR THE RIGO JANSCI

3/4 cup sugar

6 tablespoons strong brewed espresso

½ pound bittersweet or unsweetened chocolate, finely chopped

In a small, heavy saucepan, bring the sugar and coffee to the boil, stirring, until the sugar is completely dissolved. Add the chocolate and heat until it has melted completely, whisking to combine the mixture into a smooth, shiny glaze. Allow the glaze to cool for about 10 minutes, or until it is thick enough to hold its shape, but remain pourable.

Baci di Dama with Nutella (Lady's Kisses)

The fancifully named baci di dama *("lady's kisses" in Italian) are small, delicate cookies paired with a rich, creamy filling that are found in many* pasticcerie *(pastry shops) in Northern Italy. Here I use Nutella, the creamy Italian cocoa and hazelnut spread now sold in American supermarkets, to join together the pair of cookies. If you love hazelnuts as much as I do, substitute them for the almonds. Who wouldn't like a kiss like this?*

YIELD: 36 COOKIES

7 ounces (2 cups) unbleached all-purpose flour
7 ounces (2¼ cups minus 1 tablespoon) potato starch, substitute corn, wheat, or rice starch
Pinch salt
¼ pound (¾ cup) whole blanched almonds
½ cup sugar

7 ounces (1¾ sticks) unsalted butter, softened
5 ounces (1 cup minus 2 tablespoons) confectioners' sugar
1 large egg
1 teaspoon almond extract
1 cup Nutella

Line an 18 x 13-inch half sheet pan (or other large baking pan) with parchment paper or a silicone baking mat.

In a bowl, whisk together the dry ingredients: flour, potato starch, and salt. Place the almonds and sugar in the bowl of a food processor and process until finely ground.

In the bowl of a standing mixer fitted with the paddle attachment, beat the butter and confectioners' sugar until light and fluffy, 5 to 6 minutes, then add the almond-sugar mixture and beat until combined. Next, add the flour mixture and beat briefly, just long enough to combine. Finally, beat in the egg and the almond extract, beating just long enough to combine. Transfer to a plastic bag and shape into a flattened rectangle. Chill in the refrigerator for 1 hour or in the freezer for 30 minutes until firm but still malleable.

Preheat the oven to 325°F.

Divide the dough into small balls, either by hand or using a small ice cream scoop, making about 6 dozen balls. Arrange the balls equidistant on the prepared baking sheets. Bake for 18 minutes or until the cookies are slightly flattened and lightly browned on the edges. Remove from the oven and cool to room temperature. Spread half the cookies with a thin layer of Nutella and sandwich in pairs. Store covered and refrigerated up to 3 days.

White Chocolate Buttercream

This silky-smooth French buttercream is made from hot sugar syrup beaten with egg yolks to make a luscious, buttery, shiny cake frosting with an elegant ivory color. Use it to ice Aliza's Wedding Cake (page 227), the Chocolate Sponge Cake (page 339), or the Macaroon Cake (page 76). I used it to ice the Torta Caprese (page 336) as a birthday cake for a chocolate-loving friend who can't have wheat.

YIELD: ABOUT 1 QUART, ENOUGH TO ICE A 9-INCH LAYER CAKE

6 ounces white chocolate, finely chopped

1 cup sugar

1 cup water

4 large egg yolks ($^1/_4$ cup)

$^1/_2$ pound (2 sticks) unsalted butter, cut into bits and softened

1 teaspoon vanilla extract

1 tablespoon brandy

Grated zest of 1 lemon (1 tablespoon)

Place the white chocolate in a microwaveable bowl and melt on low power for 2 minutes at a time, or until just barely melted. Whisk until smooth and cool to room temperature.

Combine the sugar and water in a small heavy-bottomed pot and bring to a boil. Continue boiling until the syrup reaches the soft-ball stage, 238°F on a candy thermometer, or when a spoonful dropped in a glass of ice water forms a soft ball.

Meanwhile, beat the yolks in the bowl of a standing mixer fitted with the whisk attachment for 1 minute or until sticky. Reduce the mixer speed to low and pour in sugar syrup into the center of the bowl, while still beating. Continue beating until the mixture reaches room temperature, about 10 minutes.

Beat in the chocolate, then add the butter, beating well until combined and completely smooth. Add the vanilla, brandy, and lemon zest and beat until smooth and fluffy.

Store the buttercream tightly covered in the refrigerator for up to 2 weeks, but always use soft, fluffy buttercream when icing a cake.

RE-WARMING COLD BUTTERCREAM

To rewarm buttercream, place the bowl containing the cold buttercream over a bowl of hot water and allow it to partially melt, breaking the mass up with a spoon, transfer to the bowl of a standing mixer. Then beat it until it is soft and fluffy but firm enough to barely hold its shape.

Torta Caprese: Bittersweet Chocolate–Almond Cake

This dark, slightly crumbly flourless chocolate cake was served in the early 1930s at the historical "Strandpension Weber" in the Italian village of Marina

Piccola. It was created by two Austrian spinsters, heirs of the painter August Weber, who landed in Capri ship-wrecked in a dilapidated row boat. The cake unites almonds, abundant in Southern Italy, with chocolate, brought to Europe by the Spanish, in a sophisticated bittersweet cake that quickly became famous throughout the Gulf of Naples and beyond. Today, Torta Caprese is prepared in many versions, including white chocolate flavored with fragrant, locally-grown lemon peels (page 530). If desired, drizzle slices of cake with a simple warm chocolate sauce made by scalding 1 cup of heavy cream then whisking in $^1/_2$ a pound of finely chopped bittersweet chocolate until smooth. This recipe is gluten-free.

YIELD: ONE 10-INCH CAKE, 12 TO 16 SERVINGS

5 ounces bittersweet chocolate, chopped

7 ounces (scant $1^1/_2$ cups) blanched almonds

1 ounce ($^1/_4$ cup) Dutch process cocoa

1 ounce ($^1/_4$ cup plus 1 tablespoon) potato starch

Pinch fine sea salt

5 ounces (1 stick plus 2 tablespoons) unsalted butter, softened

5 large eggs, separated

$^3/_4$ cup sugar

$^1/_4$ cup brandy

Confectioners' sugar, for sprinkling

Preheat the oven to 325°F. Place the chocolate in a microwaveable bowl and melt in the microwave on lowest power for 2 minutes at a time, or until just barely melted. Whisk until smooth and cool to room temperature.

Place the almonds, cocoa, potato starch, and salt into the bowl of a food processor and process till the mixture is finely ground.

Rub a 9-inch removable-bottom or springform pan with 1 tablespoon of the butter and dust with some of the almond mixture, shaking off the excess. (You may also line the bottom with a circle of parchment paper, especially if using a standard cake pan).

In the clean and greaseless bowl of a standing mixer fitted with the whisk attachment, beat the egg whites until white and fluffy, then add half of the sugar and continue beating until the whites are firm and glossy, 4 to 5 minutes. Scrape the meringue into another bowl.

Using the same mixer bowl (it is not necessary to wash it) and the paddle attachment, cream the remaining butter and sugar until light and fluffy, 5 to 6 minutes. Beat in the egg yolks one at a time and continue to beat until they have been fully absorbed and the mixture is smooth and creamy. Transfer to a wide, shallow bowl.

Fold in the almond mixture, then fold in the chocolate and brandy. Fold in the meringue in thirds, so the batter doesn't deflate. Spread the batter evenly into the pan and shake the pan back and forth to even the top. Bake for 40 minutes or until the cake starts to come away from the sides of the pan and a toothpick stuck in the middle comes out mostly dry (a little moisture in the middle is fine). Cool to room temperature on a wire rack, then remove from the pan and sprinkle with confectioners' sugar. Handle gently because the cake is fragile. Serve drizzled with warm chocolate sauce if desired.

Store the cake wrapped in aluminum foil at room temperature for up to 3 days, or wrap well, first in wax paper and then in foil, and freeze up to 2 months.

A CAPTIVATING TORTA CAPRESE

For Maria Teresa Berdondini, owner of the exclusive custom Italian travel company, Tuscany by Tuscans (www.tuscanybytuscans.com), Torta Caprese will be forever the sweetest love memory she has. She told me, "About fifteen years ago, a charming man from the dreamy southern Italian island of Capri, tired of my excuses for postponing dates with him, and told me over the phone, 'If you don't want to go out with me, I will come to your home and cook dinner, dessert included.' I laughed to myself, but this guy had serious intentions. He came and prepared a delicious meal with a lot of tomatoes and oregano. The *piece de resistance* was a fabulous cake from his native Capri, dark and soft without flour or baking powder and not too sweet. I was a bit skeptical at the beginning, but the first bite conquered me totally. Now Giuseppe is the companion of my life, even if—like every Italian man—he prefers to have the cake made for him, preferably by his mother, back in Capri."

SIFTING COCOA AND CAKE FLOUR

I normally whisk the dry ingredients together to combine them as it is not necessary to use a sifter for all-purpose flour. However, when using cocoa and/or cake flour, which are quite fine and tend to clump, it is important to sift either with a sifter or by putting through a fine wire sieve.

LA MOLINA TUSCAN CHOCOLATES

I visited the small, unassuming workshop of La Molina chocolate in the small town of Quarrata, in the heart of Tuscany's emerging artisanal "Chocolate Valley." The chocolates are produced by two young brothers, Riccardo and Massimiliano Lunardi, who based their business on a love for their land, its traditions, and a passion for local Tuscan ingredients and seasonings. Riccardo and Massimiliano are *figli d'arte*, an Italian phrase for those born to the art, because they grew up watching their father Luigi prepare the exquisite creations for the family's bakery, Dolce Forno (sweet oven), which I also visited in the same town.

After spending time learning about fine chocolates in France, the two brothers created La Molina, named after La Molina, Anne of Austria's personal maid. When the Hapsburg-Spanish princess married Louis XIII of France in 1615, she brought her intended an elaborate casket of chocolate. She also brought La Molina, who was responsible for preparing her mistress' chocolate. This happy pairing thereby brought royal cachet to the new European craze for chocolate.

La Molina produces simple, high-quality chocolates in innovative flavors based on Tuscan traditions, like rosemary, sage, wild fennel, and mixed sweet spices. Their stunning packaging was designed by artist Riccardo Fattore, a close friend of the Lunardi Brothers, and is the result of a harmonious collaboration among the staff of this young and vibrant Italian company. Find them online at www.lamolina.it. They are sold in America by Gustiamo, www.gustiamo.com.

Chocolate Sponge Cake

This is an adaptable, easy-to-make, light cake that is perfect for the Florentine Chocolate Nut Zuccotto (page 58) and Cocoa Nib and Pecan Praline Chocolate Roulade (page 340). You'll need one and a half jelly roll cakes to make the zuccotto and one half sheet or jelly roll cake to make the chocolate roulade. Wrap any extra cake with plastic wrap or wax paper, then with aluminum foil and it will freeze perfectly up to two months.

YIELD: TWO 15 X 10-INCH JELLY ROLLS, ONE 10-INCH ROUND CAKE, TWO SHALLOWER 9-INCH ROUND CAKES, OR ONE 18 X 3-INCH HALF SHEET PAN PLUS ONE 9-INCH ROUND CAKE

3 ounces ($^3/_4$ cup minus $1^1/_2$ tablespoons) Dutch process cocoa

3 ounces ($^3/_4$ cup minus 1 tablespoon) unbleached all-purpose flour

$^1/_2$ teaspoon fine sea salt

12 large eggs, separated and at room temperature

2 cups confectioners' sugar

2 teaspoons vanilla extract

Confectioners' sugar, for rolling the cake

Preheat the oven to 350°F. Spray the cake pans with nonstick baker's coating, or rub with butter and dust with flour.

Sift together the dry ingredients: cocoa, flour, and salt, making sure that there are no lumps.

In the bowl of a standing mixer fitted with the pad-dle attachment, beat the yolks and 1 cup of the confectioners' sugar until light and fluffy, 5 to 6 minutes. Transfer to a wide shallow bowl.

In the clean and greaseless bowl of a standing mixer fitted with the whisk attachment, beat the egg whites until fluffy, then add the remaining 1 cup confectioners' sugar and continue beating until the whites are firm and glossy, 4 to 5 minutes.

Alternating with the cocoa mix and beginning and ending with the meringue, fold the meringue and cocoa mix into the yolk mix in three parts so as not to deflate the meringue. Spoon the batter into the prepared pans, smoothing the tops. Bake for 20 to 30 minutes or until the cake springs back when touched in center and starts to come away from the sides of the pan. Remove from the oven and cool to lukewarm temperature, then invert the cake onto a wire rack and cool to room temperature.

Note: Bake the 10-inch round cake for 20 minutes; the 2 (9-inch) cakes for 25 minutes; and the half sheet pan for 25 minutes.

Note: To use this cake as a roulade, while it is still warm, unmold it onto a sheet of wax generously dusted with confectioners' sugar. Roll up the cake and allow it to cool. Carefully unroll, remove the wax paper, spread with whipped cream or other filling, and roll back up.

Cocoa Nib and Pecan Praline

Small bits of bitter cocoa nibs and toasted pecans flavor this untraditional praline mixture. Crush it up and sprinkle it in or on ice cream and mix into pancake, muffin, pound cake, or cookie batter. I like to serve apple wedges sprinkled with praline for a grown-up caramel apple. Like all caramel products, praline is best made on a day with low humidity. Stored in an airtight container, the praline will keep for several months, ready to use.

YIELD: 3 CUPS

1 cup sugar

$1/2$ cup light corn syrup

2 tablespoons dark brown sugar

2 tablespoons (1 ounce) unsalted butter, softened

$1/2$ teaspoon fine sea salt

$1/2$ cup crushed cocoa nibs

$1/4$ pound (1 cup) pecans, lightly toasted, chopped, and kept warm

Line an 18 x 13-inch baking pan with parchment paper or a silicone baking mat.

Place the sugar, corn syrup, brown sugar, butter, and salt into a medium heavy-bottomed pot, preferably copper. Bring to a boil, then continue cooking until the sugar browns and reaches 340°F on a candy thermometer. Immediately stir in the cocoa nibs and pecans using a wooden spoon or a silicone spatula.

Spread the mixture onto the prepared pan while still hot; it will start to stiffen as it cools. Allow it to cool to room temperature. When cool and hard, break into irregular pieces or shards using a hammer or a meat pounder. Place the shards in a food processor and process just long enough for the mixture to form fine chunks. Store airtight in single layer at room temperature.

Cocoa Nib and Pecan Praline Chocolate Roulade

A roulade is the French term for what Americans call a jelly roll, though it is often not filled with jelly at all. Here, an airy chocolate sponge cake is rolled up with a sophisticated cocoa-nib, pecan praline, and whipped cream filling. Once the three parts are ready, it's an easy cake to make with an impressive presentation, especially served on a decorative long, narrow platter. First you must make or assemble the components: a chocolate sponge roll cake (which can be frozen and defrosted), the crushed cocoa-nib and pecan praline (which can also be made ahead and stored for months), and the whipped cream filling. For a quicker shortcut, substitute 1 cup crushed toffee candy plus $1/2$ cup crushed cocoa nibs for the Cocoa-Nib and Pecan Praline.

YIELD: 1 ROULADE, 8 TO 10 SERVINGS

1 cup heavy cream, chilled

$1/2$ cup sour cream

6 tablespoons confectioners' sugar

$1^1/2$ cups Cocoa Nib and Pecan Praline (this page)

1 Chocolate Sponge Cake (page 339),
  baked in a half sheet pan
2 tablespoons Dutch process cocoa

In the bowl of a standing mixer fitted with the whisk attachment, beat the cream and sour cream until firm but not stiff, about 3 minutes Add 4 tablespoons of the confectioners' sugar and beat again until firm. (Note: on a hot day, freeze the bowl, the beater, and the cream for 20 minutes before beating.) Fold in the praline. Spread the mixture evenly over the bottom side of the cake, leaving a 1-inch border along one short side. Starting with the cream-filled end, roll the cake up as tightly as possible. Place strips of wax paper lengthwise down both sides of a long, narrow serving platter to cover the edges. Place the cake seam side-down on the platter.

Whisk together the cocoa and remaining confectioners' sugar and sift evenly over top of the cake. Carefully remove the wax paper strips and discard. Chill the cake for at least 1 hour before slicing on the diagonal into serving portions. Cover and store up to 2 days in the refrigerator.

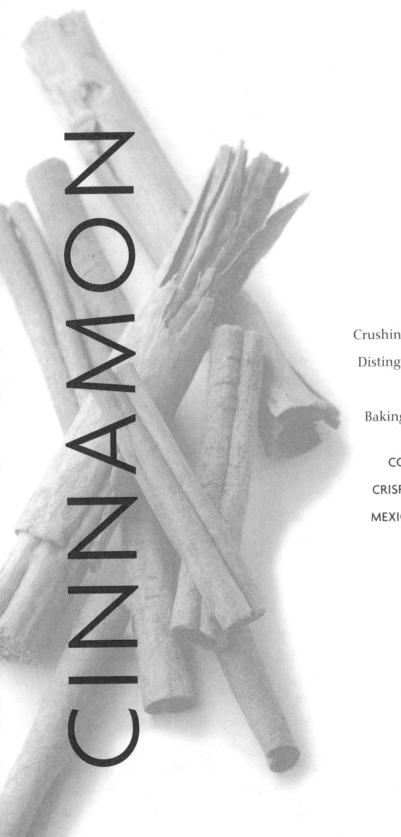

CINNAMON

Cinnamon and Cassia ...346

Crushing Cinnamon and Cassia Sticks ...348

Distinguishing Cinnamon and Cassia ...349

SPICED POLVORONES ...349

Baking Two Pans or Cakes At A Time ...350

HAZELNUT-CINNAMON THUMBPRINT
COOKIES WITH RED CURRANT JAM ...350

CRISPY LEMON-CINNAMON COOKIES ...351

MEXICAN SPICED COCOA MERINGUES ...352

SPECULAAS SPICES ...353

CINNAMON

All those bakers of cinnamon buns and sticky buns at highway rest stops and mall food courts are well aware how difficult it is for anyone to resist the sweet, warm, slightly sharp, and lively aroma of cinnamon. In fact, it's almost impossible to imagine baking without it, especially when mixed with apples or butter and sugar: not in apple pie, betty, crisp, or crumble; not in coffee cake, oatmeal cookies, raisin bread, or snickerdoodles (a Pennsylvania–German specialty)?

Cinnamon is one of the oldest spices in the world, mentioned several times in the Torah (the Jewish Bible); the spice was used as a fragrant oil in sacred oil to anoint the priests. Cinnamon comes from the tropical cinnamon tree, which is in the same family as the Mediterranean bay laurel and Jamaican allspice. The word *cinnamon* comes from the Greeks, who borrowed it from the Phoenicians, who took it from the Hebrew *kinamom* and Aramaic *qunimun*. All these names may ultimately derive from an early Malaysian language and would therefore be related to the modern Indonesian *kayu manis* or "sweet wood." Italians call it *canella*; the French call it *cannelle*, and the Spanish, *canela*, all meaning "little cane" or

"little tube," an apt description.

Native to Sri Lanka (known as Ceylon until 1972), true cinnamon, *Cinnamomum zeylanicum*, dates back in Chinese writings to 2800 BCE, and is known as *kwai* in Chinese today. Cinnamon was commonly used on funeral pyres in Rome. The Emperor Nero is said to have burned a year's supply of cinnamon at the funeral for his wife, Poppaea Sabina. The origin of this desirable spice was a highly–guarded secret of Arab, traders who first brought it from the east via caravan to the port of Alexandria, Egypt. Canny Arab traders concocted a number of magical myths to hide the location of the trees and enhance cinnamon's mystique. Venetian traders, who themselves held a monopoly on Europe's spice trade, in turn brought cinnamon to Europe. When the Venetian trade was disrupted by Ottoman Turks and others, Europeans started to search for other routes to Asia to obtain this rare and wonderful spice.

Portuguese traders arrived in Ceylon at the end of the fifteenth century, and used the salagama caste, the caste of traditional cinnamon growers, to produce cinnamon exclusively for them. The Portuguese established a fort on the island in

1518, and were able to protect their cinnamon monopoly for over a hundred years. However, the Dutch allied themselves with the inland Ceylonese kingdom of Kandy and seized control of the "cinnamon island" in the seventeenth century from the Portuguese.

When the Dutch learned that cinnamon was also grown along the Southwestern coast of India, they forced the local king to destroy the crop, thus preserving their monopoly. The Dutch East India Company eventually began to cultivate trees rather than harvesting cinnamon from the wild. In 1795, the British gained control of this island so fragrant that its aroma wafted many miles out to sea.

By 1833, the cinnamon monopoly had started to come apart when it was found that cinnamon could be grown in other tropical regions including Indonesia, Mauritius, Réunion, and Guyana. Today, cinnamon is grown in Sri Lanka; Tellicherry in southern India, also known for its high quality peppercorns; Java and Sumatra in Indonesia, where forty percent of the world's cinnamon crop is grown; China; the Caribbean; Brazil; Madagascar; Zanzibar; Egypt; and Vietnam.

It takes twenty to thirty years of growth before cinnamon can be harvested from a tree, but the trees will produce cinnamon for many years. At harvest time, native farmhands gather and travel to the sometimes remote areas where the trees grow. For cinnamon sticks, the upper, more tender branches are carefully cut and the inner bark removed.

Cinnamon is harvested just after the rainy season when the bark is moist and soft. Skilled workers cut around the stem using small pointed knives to peel the bark from the trees. To loosen the valuable tender inner, pale reddish-brown bark, they rub the stripped stems with brass rods that will not discolor the cinnamon. The bark, which curls naturally into friable quills, is left to dry and ferment for about twenty-four hours. These smaller quills are painstakingly rolled by hand into large compound quills that may be as much as 3 feet long. Cinnamon sticks are attractive and uniform, but relatively mild in flavor. For ground cinnamon, large chunks are removed from the stronger and more flavorful lower, older branches. Most cinnamon in America actually comes from the more pungent cassia, *Cinnamomum cassia*, from Indonesia.

The closely related, but stronger Chinese cassia was more common in the West until the sixteenth century when true cinnamon started to become available. Cassia, or Chinese cinnamon, is similar but bolder and more peppery-tasting than true cinnamon. The quills are thicker and tougher with a dark brown, rough outer surface. In the United States, cinnamon may refer to either cinnamon or cassia; in Europe and Australia it is illegal to sell cinnamon that is actually cassia. In Europe, cassia is generally found in Chinese markets.

The powdered cinnamon sold in supermarkets in the United States is actually cassia. It is much more mucilaginous in consistency than true cinnamon, noticeable when it is steeped in milk used to make custard or ice cream. European health agencies have recently warned against consuming large amounts of cassia, due to a toxic component called coumarin, contained in much lower dosages in Ceylon or true cinnamon.

In this chapter, cinnamon's warm, pleasingly spicy fragrance enhances Spiced Polvorones cook–ies (page 349), Hazelnut–Cinnamon Thumbprint Cookies (page 350), Crispy Lemon–Cinnamon Cookies (page 351), and Mexican Spiced Cocoa Meringues (page 352). Throughout this book are many recipes calling for cinnamon, especially those that contains apples, pumpkin, and rice.

CINNAMON AND CASSIA

TRUE CINNAMON: The name *cinnamon* is correctly used to refer only to Ceylon Cinnamon, also known as "true cinnamon" (from the botanical name *Cinnamomum verum*, an alternative name to *C. zeylanicum*). Ceylon cinnamon is native to Sri Lanka, though also grown in India, the East and West Indies, and Central America. The cultivated variety grows 8 to 10 feet tall and resembles a shrub rather than a tree. Most of the true cinnamon in the United States is sold in the stick form.

True cinnamon has very smooth bark, is pale reddish-brown in color, and has a highly fragrant, citrusy aroma. The quills are thinly layered (1 millimeter or less), soft, and relatively easy to crumble. Ceylon cinnamon has a much lower volatile oil content than other types (between 1 and 2 percent), but its flavor has a subtle complexity. When ground, Ceylon cinnamon has a fine, light, and rather crumbly texture and a delicate, complex aroma with citrusy overtones that blends well with other seasonings. True cinnamon is unfamiliar to many Americans, though it is prized in Europe and Mexico and heavily used in its place of origin, Sri Lanka and in India and is called for

wherever Persian or Arab influence is felt: West and Central Asia, North and East Africa, and Mexico.

CEYLON SOFTSTICK CINNAMON: Softstick cinnamon comes from the young shoots of the true cinnamon tree. It is rolled into fat quills of papery-thin bark that can be easily crumbled by hand. This sweet, subtly aromatic, pale-colored cinnamon is the most delicate of all members of its family and is preferred in Europe and Mexico, where it is used to flavor chocolate, especially drinking chocolate. Look for softstick cinnamon, also known as *canela*, in the United States at Mexican groceries.

CHINESE CASSIA: Chinese cassia, *Cinnamomum cassia*, also known as Cassia cinnamon or Chinese cinnamon, is native to Southeast Asia, especially southern China and northern Vietnam, and has the strong, spicy-sweet flavor most Americans are familiar with.

In China, the bark is typically peeled from the trees starting at ten years of age and continuing as long as thirty years. Cassia quills are hard and woody in texture, and thicker than true cinnamon, as all of the layers of bark are used. It has a strong fragrance with an edge of bitterness and astringency. Because it is often not carefully peeled, the outer surface will be uneven and rough, and dark brown in color; the inside medium reddish brown. The bark chunks will be very thick (3 millimeters to 1 centimeter) and strong but brittle. Because the bark cannot be rolled up regularly, cassia is often sold in small pieces of irregular shape. In flavor, it is similar to Vietnamese cinnamon, but less intense. I buy long sticks of unpeeled thick cassia bark at my local Asian market.

TUNG HING CASSIA: Tung Hing, a rarer form of cassia produced in China, tastes spicy and more peppery than Indonesian cassia. This cinnamon has a high content of natural oil (3 to 4 percent) and is appreciated for its rich, sweet, spicy flavor.

VIETNAMESE CINNAMON: In China and Japan, Vietnamese cinnamon, *Cinnamomum loureirii*, is considered to be the finest in the world. Vietnamese cinnamon was known in earlier times as Saigon cinnamon, a species closely related to cassia and often marketed as cassia (or, in North America, as "cinnamon"). Vietnamese cinnamon has an intense flavor and aroma because of its exceptionally high percentage of essential oils, similar to Tung Hing cassia cinnamon, but more powerful. The quills resemble cassia in color, but are smaller and thinner. When ground, the dark powder has a rich, distinctly sweet, spicy flavor, and an intense color.

Up to the 1960s, Vietnam was the world's most important producer of Saigon Cinnamon. With the disruption of the trade caused by the Vietnam War,

production of cassia in the highlands of Sumatra in Indonesia was increased and Indonesia remains one of the main exporters of this type of cassia today. Vietnamese cinnamon has only become available again in the United States since the beginning of this century.

Vietnamese cinnamon comes from the remote north and west regions of Vietnam where people here have been harvesting and cracking cinnamon for over 400 years (maybe even longer). Large thick sticks (2 to 3 millimeters) about 18 inches long and 2 inches in diameter are brought in from the countryside to be cleaned and sorted into varying grades. The strength of the spice depends upon the essential oil content: the higher the level, the stronger the flavor. The sticks are stored in large, colonial-style warehouse rooms. When orders for cinnamon come in, the large sticks are cracked into slightly smaller pieces and packed into burlap bags for shipment. Most of the work is done by local farmers to supplement the meager income they receive from their rice crops.

INDONESIAN CASSIA CINNAMON: Indonesian cinnamon, *Cinnamomum burmannii,* which is cultivated in Java and Sumatra, is thicker than and less breakable than Vietnamese cinnamon (up to 3 millimeters). The quills are thicker than Ceylon cinnamon, reddish-brown on the outside, but dark, grayish-brown on the inside. This type is popular in the Netherlands and in the United States. Sweet, fragrant, and mellow, Indonesian cassia cinnamon is the "cinnamon" Americans are most familiar with and the type sold in most supermarkets. It is highly aromatic like Ceylon cinnamon, but is slightly bitter and astringent and less complex and subtle than true cinnamon.

INDONESIAN KORINTJE CINNAMON: Korintje cinnamon, a subtype of *Cinnamomum cassia*, grows only on the slopes of Mount Kerinci in Sumatra, an island in Indonesia. The government protects the slopes where the cinnamon trees grow wild. From the mountain slopes, where the light reddish brown bark is harvested a bit earlier in the season than Chinese and Vietnamese cinnamons, the bark is trucked down to the port town of Padang where it is graded A, B, and C, and washed, then either cracked for Korintje A, or cut for sticks.

Korintje translates as "thick quill" and is judged for quality based on the part of the tree that is harvested (trunk or branch) and on the length of the bark peeled from the tree. It is milder than Chinese cassia with smooth flavor, more fragrance, and less bite than cassia and considered to be superior to the common Indonesian cinnamon found in supermarket brands.

CASSIA AND CINNAMON BUDS: Less common, cassia buds, which resemble cloves, are the unripe fruits of the cassia cinnamon tree and have flavor similar to cassia, but sweeter, sharper, and more flowery. The buds must be finely ground to release their fragrance. In China, through centuries of careful observations, it was determined at which precise point to pick the buds from the cassia tree in order to maintain its powerful oils, which act as a natural preservative. The "Mother Cassia Tree," was planted by careful mathematical calculations, as to where and when it would be placed, because the buds were also highly valued for their spiritual nature. In ancient Taoist temples, cassia buds were used to perfume the air at spiritual gatherings and it was the custom to give a pair of cassia bud "twins" to newly married couples. Not easy to find in America, cassia buds may be purchased from www.thespicehouse.com.

Cinnamon buds, although less aromatic than the bark, have a mild, pure, and sweet fragrance. The buds are used regionally as a spice in the western coastal state of Gujarat, India. I have not found them for sale in the United States but hope to try them on my travels.

CRUSHING CINNAMON AND CASSIA STICKS

Ground cinnamon quickly loses the subtle, fruity nuances of its aroma, leaving the less delicate notes, so it is best to crush, then grind your own every few months. The raggedy-edged quills of softstick cinnamon found in Mexican and Latin American markets is pale in color and soft enough to crumble with your hands and then grind. To grind cassia or harder cinnamon, first crush up 4 to 6 quills with a meat cleaver, pounder, or hammer. Then grind the crushed pieces in a coffee grinder, spice grinder, or using a mortar and pestle to a fine powder.

DISTINGUISHING CINNAMON AND CASSIA

In America, cinnamon sticks are almost invariably cassia and not true cinnamon. True cinnamon quills usually curl in a spiral shape, while cassia quills curl in from both sides in a double scroll shape. True cinnamon sticks (or quills), especially softstick cinnamon, have many thin, friable layers and can easily be crushed into powder using a mortar and pestle, coffee or spice grinder. (Small pieces of the quills are known as quillings.) Cassia sticks are much harder, made up of one thick layer, and are too woody to grind without crushing them up finely first using a mortar and pestle or industrial machinery.

It is a bit more difficult to tell ground cinnamon from ground cassia, although true cinnamon will be light reddish tan in color with a warm, sweet flavor while powdered cassia is medium reddish brown in color with a pungent, slightly bitter aroma, coarser in texture than cinnamon. Cassia and Indonesian cassia cinnamon may be labeled as cinnamon, Indonesian cinnamon, or "bastard" cinnamon in America.

Spiced Polvorones

Also known as Mexican Wedding Cookies, these sandy-textured shortbread-type cookies are made with a combination of delicately nutty white whole wheat flour, all-purpose flour, and typical Mexican sweet spices: citrus scented, mild softstick cinnamon, called canela in Mexico, allspice (native to the New World), and potent ground cloves. The cookies are baked and then rolled in a mixture of sugar, grated chocolate, and spices.

YIELD: 48 COOKIES

Coating

1 cup superfine sugar

2 ounces bittersweet chocolate, finely grated

1 teaspoon ground softstick cinnamon (canela)

$1/2$ teaspoon ground allspice

Pinch ground cloves

Cookies

$3/4$ pound ($2^3/4$ cups plus 1 tablespoon)
    unbleached all-purpose flour

$1/4$ pound (1 cup plus 2 tablespoons) white
    whole wheat flour

2 teaspoons baking powder

2 teaspoons ground softstick cinnamon (canela)

1 teaspoon ground allspice

$1/4$ teaspoon ground cloves

$1/4$ teaspoon fine sea salt

1 pound (4 sticks) unsalted butter, softened

1 cup confectioners' sugar

$1/4$ cup milk

1 teaspoon vanilla extract

Make the coating: Combine the sugar, chocolate, cinnamon, allspice, and cloves in shallow bowl. Set aside in the refrigerator.

Make the cookies: Line one or two 18 x 13-inch half sheet pans (or other large baking pans) with parchment paper or silicone baking mats.

In a bowl, whisk together the dry ingredients: flour, whole wheat flour, baking powder, cinnamon, allspice, cloves, and salt.

In the bowl of a standing mixer fitted with the paddle attachment, cream the butter and confectioners' sugar together until light and fluffy, 5 to 6 minutes. Pour in the milk and vanilla and beat briefly to combine. Add the flour mix and beat again just long enough to combine. Transfer to a plastic bag and shape into a flattened rectangle. Chill in the refrigerator for 1 hour or in the freezer for 30 minutes until firm but still malleable.

Preheat the oven to 325°F. Scoop 48 small balls of the batter, about 1-inch in diameter (using a #40 ice cream scoop). Arrange in rows of 4 and 3 on the baking pans, placing the balls at least 1 inch apart. Bake for 20 minutes or until lightly colored. Cool on the baking pan for 2 minutes, or until slightly cooled and firmed up.

Roll each cookie in the coating mixture, coating well all over. Cool to room temperature on wire racks, then store in an airtight container 2 to 3 days, or refrigerated up to 1 week.

BAKING TWO PANS OR CAKES AT A TIME

When baking two cakes or baking pans, switch their positions and their directions halfway through baking and allow 5 to 10 minutes longer baking time.

Hazelnut–Cinnamon Thumbprint Cookies with Red Currant Jam

Hazelnuts and red currants are a time-honored duo in the former Austro-Hungarian Empire (Austria, Northern Italy, Hungary, Czechia, Slovakia, Serbia, and parts of Poland, among others). Both ingredients are less common in the United States, though they deserve to be stars. Here, small balls of buttery cinnamon-scented cookie dough are rolled in ground hazelnuts, then pushed down in the center to make an indentation for the jam. After baking, a dollop of ruby-colored tart red currant jam fills the center, creating a palate-pleasing contrast of flavor and texture. Either the dough itself or the portioned out dough balls can be frozen to bake later.

YIELD: 30 COOKIES

$1/2$ pound (2 cups minus 2 tablespoons) unbleached all-purpose flour

$1^1/2$ teaspoons ground cinnamon

$1/2$ teaspoon fine sea salt

$1/2$ pound ($1^1/2$ cups) hazelnuts, lightly toasted and skinned

$1/2$ pound (2 sticks) unsalted butter, softened

$3/4$ cup sugar

4 large eggs, separated

1 teaspoon vanilla extract

$1/2$ cup red currant jam

Line two 18 x 13-inch half sheet pans or other large baking

sheets with parchment paper or silicone baking mats.

Whisk together the dry ingredients: flour, cinnamon, and salt. Place the hazelnuts into the bowl of a food processor and grind finely.

In the bowl of a standing mixer fitted with the paddle attachment, cream the butter and sugar until light and fluffy, 5 to 6 minutes. Beat in the egg yolks, one a time, then beat in the vanilla. Add the flour mixture and beat just long enough to combine. Transfer to a plastic bag and shape into a flattened rectangle. Chill in the refrigerator for 1 hour or in the freezer for 30 minutes until firm but still malleable.

Preheat the oven to 325°F.

In a small bowl, beat the egg whites lightly. Place the hazelnuts in another bowl.

Scoop the dough into 30 evenly sized balls using a small ice cream scoop or your hands. Dip each ball first in the egg whites, turning to coat completely and shaking off any excess, then in the hazelnuts to coat. Place the cookie balls 1-inch apart on the baking sheets. Press your thumb into the center of each cookie to make an indentation.

Bake the cookies for 18 minutes or until lightly browned. (If baking two sheets at once in one oven, switch their positions and their directions halfway through baking.) Remove from the oven and, while still hot, press your thumb, the back of a melon baller, or the back of a round teaspoon into the center of each cookie to accentuate the depression. Place the cookie sheets back in the oven and bake 2 to 3 minutes, or until lightly browned. Cool the cookies on the baking sheets for 10 minutes or until firmed up, then use a wide spatula to transfer them to a wire rack to cool completely.

Warm the jam until it is barely pourable, then spoon 1 teaspoon jam into the center of each cookie. Allow the jam to set at room temperature in cold weather, in the refrigerator in hot weather. Store the cookies at room temperature for 2 to 3 days, or refrigerated up to 1 week.

Crispy Lemon–Cinnamon Cookies

These simple cookies are flavored with cinnamon and an abundance of grated lemon zest. The baker's ammonia used for leavening gives them their special shatteringly crisp texture. Baking powder may be substituted in equal amounts and will result in good crisp, though not brittle, cookies. For a special Scandinavian-style garnish, the cookies are sprinkled with white pearl sugar, which does indeed resemble small white pearls. It is available from the Baker's Catalogue (www.bakerscatalogue.com) and online from many Scandinavian companies.

YIELD: 36 COOKIES

1 pound (3¾ cups) unbleached all-purpose flour

2 cups sugar

2 teaspoons ground cinnamon

2 teaspoons powdered baker's ammonia

½ teaspoon fine sea salt

½ pound (2 sticks) unsalted butter, chilled
    and cut into bits

3 large eggs, lightly beaten

Grated zest of 3 lemons (3 tablespoons)

1 large egg white, lightly beaten with 1 tablespoon
　water, for the egg wash
Pearl sugar or raw sugar, for sprinkling

Line an 18 x 13-inch half sheet pan (or other large baking
pan) with parchment paper or a silicone baking mat.

In the bowl of a standing mixer fitted with the whisk
attachment, whisk the flour, sugar, cinnamon, baker's
ammonia, and salt. Switch to the paddle attachment,
add the butter, and beat until the mixture resembles
oatmeal. Beat in the eggs and lemon zest, mixing only
long enough for a ball to form. Transfer the dough to a
plastic bag and shape into a flattened rectangle. Chill in
the refrigerator for 1 hour or in the freezer for 30 minutes until firm but still malleable.

Preheat the oven to 375°F.

Divide the dough into 4 sections and roll each section out between 2 sheets of lightly floured wax paper,
leaving the other sections in the refrigerator to keep
cold. If the dough gets warm and sticky, refrigerate
again still between the sheets of wax paper.

Cut out the cookies using a 3-inch cookie cutter.
Arrange them on the prepared baking pans. Brush the
cookies with the egg wash and sprinkle generously
with pearl sugar. Bake for 12 minutes or until golden.
Remove to a wire rack to cool to room temperature.

Mexican Spiced
Cocoa Meringues

*If you're looking for some sophisticated yet easy-to-
make cookies, try these cocoa, almond, and sweet spiced
meringues dipped in chocolate. Softstick cinnamon,
known in Mexico as canela, is essential to the balance of
flavor in the sweet spices used here. If you have a stock
of egg whites in the freezer, this is a perfect time to use
them. Melt frozen egg whites by placing their container
in a bowl of hot water. Like all meringues, these cookies
will come out best if prepared on a day with low humidity, common in winter. This recipe is gluten- and
dairy-free.*

YIELD: 48 COOKIES

$1/4$ pound ($3/4$ cup) blanched almonds

2 cups sugar

3 ounces ($3/4$ cup minus $1 1/2$ tablespoons)
　Dutch process cocoa

2 ounces ($1/2$ cup plus 2 tablespoons) potato starch

2 teaspoons ground softstick cinnamon (canela)

$1/2$ teaspoon ground allspice

Scant $1/4$ teaspoon ground cloves

8 large egg whites (1 cup), at room temperature

$1/4$ pound semisweet chocolate, finely chopped

2 tablespoons (1 ounce) unsalted butter

Preheat the oven to 200°F. Line two 18 x 13-inch half
sheet pans or other large baking sheets with parchment
paper or silicone baking mats.

Place the almonds and 1 cup sugar into the bowl of a

food processor and process until finely ground. Add the cocoa, potato starch, cinnamon, allspice, and cloves, and pulse just until well mixed.

In the clean and greaseless bowl of a standing mixer fitted with the whisk attachment, beat the egg whites until fluffy, then add the remaining 1 cup sugar and continue beating until the whites are firm and glossy, 4 to 5 minutes. Gently fold the cocoa mixture in thirds into the meringue just until blended so as not to deflate. (A few streaks of white may remain.)

Drop heaping spoonfuls of the batter 1 inch apart onto the prepared baking sheets, or pipe it through a pastry bag fitted with a $1/2$-inch star or plain tip. Bake, using both oven racks, for $1^1/2$ hours, alternating the position and direction of the pans halfway through the baking time. Turn off the oven and allow the meringues to cool in the oven for 1 hour.

Peel the cooled meringues off the parchment paper or silicon mat. Place chocolate and butter into a microwaveable bowl and melt on low for 2 minutes at a time, or until just barely melted. Whisk until smooth. Dip the tops of the meringues into the chocolate to cover partially. Let the meringues stand, chocolate-side up, until the chocolate has set, about 30 minutes at room temperature. Store in an airtight container for up to 2 weeks.

Speculaas Spices

Known as speculaaskruiden, *just about everyone who makes speculaas cookies in Holland has their own version of this cinnamon-based spice mix, which can also be found ready-mixed in the Netherlands. The Dutch prefer to use Indonesian korintje here, a legacy of their years of colonial rule. Use this mix for the Dutch Almond-Filled Spice Tart (Gevulde Speculaas) (page 74) and the Dutch Speculaas with Rye (page 789). Fresh ground spices will yield the best, most aromatic flavor.*

YIELD: $1/2$ CUP SPICES

3 tablespoons ground cinnamon

1 tablespoon ground ginger

1 tablespoon ground aniseed

2 teaspoon ground coriander

$1^1/2$ teaspoons freshly grated nutmeg

$1^1/2$ teaspoons ground cardamom

1 teaspoon ground allspice

1 teaspoon ground mace

$1/2$ teaspoon ground cloves

Combine all the spices. Store, preferably in a spice tin, in a cool dark place, for up to 4 months.

COCONUT

Stages of Coconut . . .357

Choosing and Storing Coconut . . .358

Dried and Frozen Grated Coconut . . .359

Opening and Grating Fresh Coconut . . .359

HONDURAN COCONUT BREAD
(PAN DE COCO) . . .360

CRISP SWEDISH COCONUT
"DREAM" COOKIES (DROMMAR) . . .361

What is a Baker's Dozen? . . .361

COCONUT CREAM–FILLED
COOKIE TURNOVERS . . .362

CHOCOLATE-DIPPED
COCONUT MACAROONS . . .363

COCONUT

After 28 hours and three cramped flights, I finally arrived in Cochin, India, to join a culinary tour of Southwest India with a group of fellow women chefs. Two hours more by car and I reached Kumarakom, a resort on the banks of Vembanad Lake in Kerala's backwaters, a long chain of brackish lagoons and lakes inland from the Arabian Sea. My first taste of India was a cool drink of juice straight out of one of the coconuts picked from the many tall, gently swaying palms. A few days later when I was regretting yielding to temptation and sipping a mug of toddy, fermented coconut sap, in a small backwater village toddy house, I was again served fresh coconut juice as the best of restoratives. Indeed coconut water is highly nutritious and full of electrolytes. As in other tropical regions, coconut is a staple, providing food, beverage, shelter, even cosmetics, and desserts in Kerala.

Coconuts are the fruit of the coconut palm, botanically known as *Cocos nucifera*, with *nucifera* meaning "nut-bearing." The coconut's name is a bit of a misnomer, since it is botanically classified as a drupe (a type of fruit with outer flesh surrounding a hard pit) containing an extra-large seed rather than a nut. The fruit-bearing palm trees are native to Malaysia, Polynesia, and southern Asia, but their light, fibrous husks allowed them to float easily to islands throughout the Indian Ocean, Africa, the Pacific islands, the coasts of the Americas, and the Caribbean. Today, coconuts are prolific in South America, India, the Pacific Islands, Hawaii, and Florida. Most American coconuts come from Honduras, the Dominican Republic, and Puerto Rico.

Intrepid fifteenth-century Spanish and Portuguese seamen found a resemblance to a monkey's face in the three round indented markings or "eyes" found at the base of the coconut and they began using the Spanish and Portuguese word coco, meaning monkey's face, for the coconut. In the sixteenth century, the Spanish introduced coconuts to Puerto Rico, and the Portuguese brought them to Brazil, although they may have arrived on their own by floating across the oceans.

In northern India, the coconut is the fruit of the "Tree of Life," and coconuts are kept by priests to dispense as a fertility symbol to women who wish to conceive. In Bali, women are forbidden to touch coconut palms for fear of draining the fertility of the tree into the woman. In New Guinea, it is believed that the palm sprouted from the head of the first man to die. On the Nicobar Islands in the Indian Ocean, whole coconuts were used as currency for the purchase of goods until the early part of the twentieth century.

In Sanskrit, the coconut palm is known as *kalpa vriksha*, meaning "tree which gives all that is necessary for living," because nearly all parts of the tree can be used. Coconut milk, coconut flesh, coconut sugar, and coconut oil all derive from the fruit. The husk is burned for fuel, but it also functions as its own dish and cup. A fiber called coir is taken from the husk and used to make brushes, mats, fishnets, and rope, while a potent fermented toddy or drink is also made from the sap of the coconut palm. Although it takes up to a year for coconuts to mature, the trees bloom up to thirteen times a year, so fruit is constantly forming, yielding a continuous harvest year-round. An average harvest from one tree runs about sixty coconuts, with some trees yielding three times that amount.

From Thailand and Sri Lanka to Bahia, Brazil, and Trinidad in the Caribbean, coconut milk shows up in every part of the meal, including baked goods and desserts. Coconut milk, or the richer, fattier coconut cream, is extracted from the meat of the ripe coconut. It is sold in cans either plain (unsweetened) or sweetened, so check the can carefully. The unsweetened kind is what you want for cooking; the sweetened kind works best for cocktails. In the tropical regions where coconuts abound, unsweetened coconut cream is used to flavor, enrich, and thicken sauces and for puddings. For baking, coconut cream, especially the extra-rich kind thick enough to spoon, makes a good substitute for heavy cream and behaves in much the same way in recipes. Coconuts are high in saturated fats, so coconut fat or oil, like butter, is solid at room temperature.

In this chapter, coconut goes into the moist, slightly sweet Honduran Coconut Bread (page 360), the Crisp Swedish Coconut "Dream" Cookies (page 361), the custard filling for the Coconut Cream–Filled Cookie Turnovers (page 362), and the easy Chocolate-Dipped Coconut Macaroons (page 364). Elsewhere in the book, dried coconut goes into the crusts for the Key Lime Cheesecake Pie (page 548) and the Baby Banana Cream Pie (page 131), and the pastry for the Coconut Mango Cheesecake (page 482).

STAGES OF COCONUT

Like people, the lifetime of a coconut has several different "ages." The coconut, a large hollow nut with creamy white flesh enclosed in a woody brown shell grows inside a fruit. When young, the fruit's outer shell will be green, turning to reddish brown as it matures, and finally grayish brown. Between this outer fruit shell and the woody coconut is a thick layer of coarse brownish fibers called coir, which is pulled off, leaving behind a few strands of rough hair, enough so that if it were a man, he could do a "comb-over."

In a very young coconut, the inner meat of the kernel is soft and the liquid is abundant, but doesn't taste good. As the fruit ripens to the "green coconut" stage, the inner white kernel gradually firms up to a creamy, jellied texture and its liquid becomes the sweet and refreshing drink, called coconut juice or coconut water that I sipped through a straw poked into the fruit in Kerala. One kind of green coconut, called Sweet Young Coconut, is now imported from Thailand and sold by Melissa's at supermarkets (www.melissas.com) and also can be found in Asian markets. Their green outer shell has been cut away leaving a layer of light tan coir then shrink-wrapped in plastic. Under the coir is a relatively soft pinkish-tan shell, which contains the flesh and juice.

The hard hairy brown coconuts at the market are fully mature. At this stage of the coconut's life, the juices no longer will taste good as all of its sweet richness has been absorbed into the coconut meat, which is now the edible portion.

CHOOSING AND STORING COCONUT

Young green and mature coconuts are available year-round, with peak season in fall and winter. Mature coconuts have a shelf life of about two months, but it can take longer for them to reach the market, because they are shipped by boat. It's likely that some of these coconuts will be moldy or dry inside, so it's important to check carefully before buying.

A fresh coconut in good condition should feel heavy for its size and contain enough liquid to slosh audibly when shaken. If you don't hear it, the liquid has leaked out through a crack and the coconut's meat is likely spoiled.

A coconut has three "eyes" at one end. Two are "blind" and one, the "soft eye" is where the embryo develops. At the top of the coconut three ridges meet at a point between the eyes forming angles. The soft eye contained in the wider angle is also the place where the coconut will first show signs of spoilage. The "eyes" should be dry and there should be no moldy spots or sour, alcoholic smell. Moist patches are a sign that the liquid has escaped through a crack in the shell and the coconut will have likely fermented. Older coconuts will be gray-ish rather than rich brown in color; newly matured coconuts will be light tan.

Store a fresh unopened coconut at room tem-perature for up to two months, depending on how long ago it was picked. Store grated fresh coconut in a covered container or plastic bag, refrigerated, for up to four days, or frozen for up to six months. Store dried coconut in a covered container or plastic bag up to six months refrigerated. Store unopened canned coconut at room temperature for up to eighteen months. Once opened, canned coconut or coconut cream should be refrigerated and used within five to seven days. Because of its high oil content, coconut meat or coconut cream can quickly turn rancid.

DRIED AND FROZEN GRATED COCONUT

You can buy minimally processed dried or desiccated unsweetened coconut flakes that are finely grated or chips that are thinly sliced in natural foods markets. The sweetened coconut in plastic bags or small cans in the supermarket baking aisle is moist and quite sweet, but also full of preservatives.

While fresh-grated coconut is absolutely delicious, it is a real challenge to prepare. I use frozen fresh-grated coconut sold in 14-ounce packages in the freezer case in Latin American and Asian groceries. It is inexpensive, easy to use, and far closer to the fresh, both in flavor and texture than either the rather fibrous desiccated coconut or the preservative-laden, overly sweet shredded coconut. Look for the La Fe or Goya brand in Latin markets. Imported from Thailand, it is sold under various names in Asian markets.

OPENING AND GRATING FRESH COCONUT

The coconut has three "eyes," one of which is soft. This is the one you want to poke open, using an awl or a sharpening steel. Drain and discard the coconut liquid. Don't skip this step, because you will be baking the coconut next. If not opened and drained, the coconut could explode.

Preheat the oven to 350°F. Bake the coconut for 25 minutes, and then cool. The flesh will shrink away from the shell. Some shippers carve a shallow cut around the coconut's circumference about one-third of the way down from the top. Ideally, tap the shell with a hammer at the horizontal line until it cracks apart. Otherwise, tap the coconut near the center until it cracks.

Insert a thin, flexible icing spatula between the shell and the meat to pop the meat away from the shell. (Don't substitute a knife, because you could end up stabbing yourself.) Leave the dark brown skin on for a natural look and less work. Use a sharp paring knife or a swivel-bladed peeler to remove the skin, leaving creamy-white coconut meat. Peeling will be easier if the coconut is warm.

Cut thin shavings for garnish using a French mandoline, Japanese Benriner cutter, deli-style meat slicer, or Microplane. Place the shavings in a bowl of ice water so they'll curl up and stay moist. Various mechanical and electric graters are common in places where coconuts grow. These graters are used to scrape out the meat of a split coconut, working from the inside out. Look for this special tool in an Indian or Thai grocery.

Honduran Coconut Bread (Pan de Coco)

Some of the best food in Honduras is made by the Garifuna people, descendants of African slaves who arrived on the shores of St. Vincent Island in 1635 after surviving the sinking of a Dutch slave ship on which they were being transported. The escaped Africans merged with the local natives and became known as the Garifuna, which means "cassava eating people." Two hundred years ago, the Garifuna were exiled from the hills of St. Vincent to the Caribbean coast of Central America. Here they maintained their African traditions transformed by their time spent among the Arawak and Carib Indians and by their new countries of Honduras, nearby Belize, and Guatemala. Coconut is used for many traditional Garifuna dishes including this coconut bread. A special handmade tool devised for "gratering" coconut (the term used by the Garifuna of Belize) is made of a slab of wood shaped into a figure eight and embedded with small, sharp pebbles. This moist, delicately flavored, slightly sweet bread is wonderful toasted.

YIELD: ONE 2³/₄-POUND LOAF

1 (¹/₄-ounce) package (2¹/₂ teaspoons) active dry yeast

¹/₄ cup lukewarm water

2 tablespoons sugar

1¹/₂ pounds (6 cups) unbleached bread flour

1 (14-ounce) can unsweetened coconut milk

2 tablespoons (1 ounce) unsalted butter, softened

1¹/₂ teaspoons fine sea salt

¹/₂ pound (2 cups) frozen grated coconut, defrosted, substitute 2 cups desiccated coconut soaked for 15 minutes in warm milk to cover, then drained

In the bowl of a standing mixer fitted with the paddle attachment, combine the yeast, water, sugar, and ¹/₄ cup of the flour. Allow the mixture to proof for about 10 minutes or until bubbling. Beat in the coconut milk, butter, salt, and about half the remaining flour.

Switch to the dough hook and beat in the remaining flour and the coconut. (If the dough is too much for your mixer, beat it in two batches.) Continue beating until the dough is smooth and elastic and mostly comes away from the sides of the bowl (it will still be a bit sticky). Transfer the dough to a large oiled bowl and turn it around so it is oiled all over. Cover with plastic wrap or a damp cloth and allow the dough to rise until doubled in size, about 2 hours, at warm room temperature.

Punch down the dough and form it into a large smooth ball. Place it on a baking pan lined with parchment paper or drop it into a flour-lined bread-rising basket called a banneton (page 187) with the smooth side down. Cover the bread with a damp kitchen towel to keep it from forming a crust and allow it to rise at room temperature until almost doubled in bulk again, about 3 hours. (If desired, once the bread has mostly risen, cover it and place it in the refrigerator. The bread will continue to rise slowly overnight. The next day, allow the bread to come to room temperature, then bake.)

Preheat the oven to 375°F. If you are using the banneton, place a baking stone in the oven to preheat, as well, for at least 30 minutes. To bake the bread, turn it out of the basket directly onto the stone. Alternatively, simply place the baking pan with the bread on it into the hot oven. In either case, throw a handful of ice cubes onto the bottom of the oven to create steam, and bake the bread for 45 minutes, or until it is well browned and the inside reads 190°F to 205°F when pierced with a thermometer. Cool to room temperature on a wire rack before slicing. Store at room temperature in a bown paper bag for up to 3 days. Freeze if desired up to 3 months.

Crisp Swedish Coconut "Dream" Cookies (Drommar)

Baking Drommar, or 'dreams', are a Christmas tradition in Sweden and among Swedish-Americans. These simple butter and coconut cookies are extra-crispy because of the baker's ammonia used for leavening. Best of all, the cookies are easy enough for children to make: the dough is rolled into balls, dipped into coconut, then baked.

YIELD: 3 DOZEN COOKIES

$1/2$ pound (2 cups minus 2 tablespoons) unbleached all-purpose flour

$1/2$ teaspoon fine sea salt

1 teaspoon baker's ammonia, crushed to a fine powder

$1/2$ pound (2 sticks) unsalted butter, softened

$1^1/4$ cups sugar

1 teaspoon almond extract

2 cups unsweetened flaked coconut

Line two 18 x 13-inch half sheet pans (or other large baking pans) with parchment paper or silicone baking mats,

or rub with butter and dust with flour, shaking off the excess.

Whisk together the dry ingredients: flour, salt, and baker's ammonia, keeping away from your nose.

In the bowl of a standing mixer fitted with the paddle attachment, beat together the butter and sugar until light and fluffy, 5 to 6 minutes. Beat in the almond extract and $1^1/2$ cups of the coconut. Add the flour mixture, beating just long enough for the mixture to form a ball. Transfer to a plastic bag and shape into a flattened rectangle. Chill in the refrigerator for 1 hour or in the freezer for 30 minutes until firm but still malleable.

Preheat the oven to 300°F. Roll the dough into 36 (1-inch) balls, then roll them in the remaining $1/2$ cup of coconut. Arrange the balls 1 inch apart on the baking pans. Bake in batches in the upper third of oven for 18 minutes or until pale golden around edges. Transfer the cookies to a wire rack to cool to room temperature. Store in an airtight container at room temperature for up to 1 week.

WHAT IS A BAKER'S DOZEN?

The oldest known source and most likely origin for the expression "a baker's dozen" dates to the thirteenth century and comes from one of the earliest English statutes, instituted during the reign of Henry III in the thirteenth century, called the Assize of Bread and Ale. Bakers who were found to have shortchanged customers could lose a hand to an axe. To avoid punishment, a baker would give 13 for the price of 12, to be certain of not being known as a cheat and allowing for one of the dozen to be lost, eaten, burnt, or ruined in some way. The practice can be seen in the guild codes of the Worshipful Company of Bakers in London.

However, the tidy way 13 disks (cookies, biscuits, and small cakes) can pack a rectangular baking sheet is another reason for the baker's dozen. Modern standard–sized baking sheets have a 3:2 aspect ratio, and the most efficient array is hexagonal close packing with six–fold symmetry, meaning that each mound of dough will be equidistant from its six nearest neighbors. The corners of a cookie sheet or baking pan heat up and cool off faster than the edges and interior, so any item placed near a corner will not bake at the same rate as the other items. Rows or 3 and 2 or 4 and 3 provides the dense hexagonal packing while avoiding corners. This arrangement would have been discovered empirically by bakers with the goal of baking the maximum number per batch with optimal uniformity. Continued use of the baker's dozen also stems from tradition, which customers see as a sign of appreciation from the baker for their continued patronage.

Coconut Cream–Filled Cookie Turnovers

Years ago, I worked at the QVC network preparing the food for camera. At the time, I did hundreds of shows featuring cookbooks, food products, cookware, and gadgets. These cookies date from the time that I prepared everything I could think of to show off a set of turnover makers, similar to the plastic Chinese dumpling makers with ruffled edges found in Asian markets and kitchen supply stores. These cookies are meant for coconut lovers: a sweet sugar cookie dough is rolled out thinly, cut in circles, then filled with luscious coconut cream, and topped with shredded coconut and baked.

YIELD: ABOUT 4 DOZEN COOKIES

Cookie Dough

18 ounces (4^1/4 cups) unbleached all-purpose flour

1 teaspoon baking powder

^{1}/2 teaspoon fine sea salt

^{1}/2 pound (2 sticks) unsalted butter, softened

^{3}/4 cup sugar

4 large eggs

Filling

1 cup milk

2 ounces (^{1}/2 stick) unsalted butter

^{1}/2 cup sugar

2 large eggs

2 teaspoons vanilla extract

1 teaspoon almond extract

2 ounces (^{1}/4 cup minus 1 teaspoon) unbleached

all-purpose flour

1 cup shredded unsweetened coconut

Topping

1 large egg, lightly beaten with 1 tablespoon milk,
  for the egg wash

1/2 cup shredded unsweetened coconut

Make the dough: Whisk together the dry ingredients: flour, baking powder, and salt.

In the bowl of a standing mixer fitted with the paddle attachment, cream the butter and sugar, until light and fluffy, 5 to 6 minutes. Beat in the eggs, one at a time. The mixture will resemble scrambled eggs, but don't worry. Add the flour mix, beating only until the mixture forms a ball. Transfer to a plastic bag and shape into a flattened rectangle. Chill in the refrigerator for 1 hour or in the freezer for 30 minutes until firm but still malleable.

Make the filling: Place the milk and butter in a glass quart measure or bowl. Heat for 2 to 3 minutes in a microwave until steaming.

Combine the sugar, eggs, vanilla, and almond extract, and beat to combine. Whisk in the flour. Slowly pour in the hot milk mixture, beating until smooth. Pour into a (non-aluminum) medium saucepan and bring to a boil over medium heat, whisking constantly so the mixture cooks evenly. Remove from the heat, then stir in the coconut. Transfer the mixture to a bowl, preferably stainless-steel, and cool by placing it over a second bowl filled with a mixture of ice and water, stirring often. Cover tightly and cool for at least 30 minutes in the refrigerator, or until firm.

Roll out the cookie dough between 2 sheets of lightly floured wax paper, then chill again until firm. Cut into 4-inch circles, using a plain or fluted cutter, chilling until all the circles have been cut out. If desired, collect all the dough scraps and roll out again, then chill until firm and cut out more circles. Spoon a heaping teaspoon of filling into each round, then brush the edges with the egg wash. Fold the dough circles over to form turnovers, pressing the edges to seal. Note that some of the filling will inevitably break through the cookie tops or edges. Arrange on baking pans lined with parchment paper or silicone mats.

Preheat the oven to 350°F. Brush the cookie tops with the egg wash, then sprinkle them generously with the coconut. Bake for 20 to 25 minutes, or until lightly browned.

Note: the unbaked cookies will freeze perfectly. Arrange the frozen cookies on baking sheets lined with parchment paper or silicone mats and bake for 30 to 35 minutes, or until lightly browned.

Chocolate–Dipped Coconut Macaroons

The story goes that macaroons made from ground almonds, sugar, and egg whites were invented in an Italian monastery in 1792. During the French Revolution, two Carmelite nuns from Italy were hiding in the town of Nancy. They baked and sold macaroons to earn their living, and became known as the Macaroon Sisters. The recipe was then passed on to Jews living in France, who made them a staple of Ashkenazi Passover baking, because the cookies are unleavened and made without wheat flour. The small cookies get their name from the Italian maccherone *(like macaroni in English)* because almond paste is similar in color and even consistency to pasta or macaroni dough. In North America, coconut is commonly substituted for the more expensive almonds to make dense, moist, and sweet macaroons like these, which use a traditional American ingredient: sweetened condensed milk for creamy sweetness and a touch of the more exotic rosewater for its heavenly aroma. This recipe is gluten-free.

YIELD: 24 MACAROONS

1 (14-ounce) can sweetened condensed milk

3 large egg whites (6 tablespoons),
   at room temperature

1 teaspoon vanilla extract

1$\frac{1}{2}$ teaspoons rosewater, substitute almond extract

1 pound (3 cups) shredded unsweetened coconut

$\frac{1}{4}$ pound semisweet chocolate, finely chopped

2 tablespoons (1 ounce) unsalted butter

Preheat the oven to 325°F. Line two 18 x 13-inch baking pans with parchment paper or silicone baking mats.

In the bowl of a standing mixer fitted with the paddle attachment, beat the condensed milk, egg whites, vanilla, and rosewater. Add the coconut, mixing until well combined.

Wet your hands and make 24 balls of the mixture. Arrange evenly spaced on the baking pans (macaroons won't spread) and bake for 15 minutes, or until light golden. Cool to room temperature on a wire rack.

Place the chocolate and butter into a microwaveable bowl and melt on low power for 2 minutes at a time, or until just barely melted. Whisk until smooth. Dip the tips of the macaroons into the melted chocolate and arrange on baking sheets. Allow the chocolate to set at room temperature for 30 minutes before serving. Store the macaroons in an airtight container for up to 1 week.

COFFEE

Growing the Best Coffee . . .369

Arabica and Robusta Coffee . . .370

Blending and Roasting Coffee . . .370

Storing Coffee . . .370

Espresso . . .371

Instant and Freeze–Dried Coffee . . .372

Decaffeinated Coffee . . .372

Coffee Tips . . .372

Coffee Roasts . . .372

BRAZIL NUT CAKE WITH ESPRESSO
(TORTA DE CASTANHÀ-DO-PARÀ) . . .373

Grinding Nuts . . .374

CHOCOLATE-KAHLÚA SILK PIE . . .374

Samel the Limo Driver and Ethiopian Coffee . . .376

MOCHACCINO SWIRL COOKIES . . .376

WHITE CHOCOLATE, HAZELNUT,
AND ESPRESSO DACQUOISE . . .377

COFFEE

Coffee is both the perfect companion to cake, cookies, or other sweet treats, and a source of potent flavor for desserts that balances their sweetness. White, dark, and milk chocolate all blend with coffee as do hazelnuts, while sweet spices like cardamom, clove, and cinnamon mellow its bitterness. Although that twist of lemon zest served with espresso in "authentic Italian" restaurants doesn't exist in Italy, I successfully combine the two in my White Chocolate, Hazelnut, and Espresso Dacquoise (page 377). In Ethiopia, home of coffee (buna in Ethiopian), green coffee beans are toasted over an open fire, often with cardamom just before brewing and while burning frankincense, the aromatic tree sap resin whose use dates from Biblical times. My antique dark carved wood coffee mortar and pestle from Ethiopia is a most treasured possession.

I never was a coffee drinker until I got a restaurant job that involved coming in early in the morning to a cold kitchen with a damp concrete floor and washing bushel after bushel of spinach in large sinkfuls of icy water. That cup of steaming hot coffee became my lifesaver. Later, I would begin every evening's dinner service with a dou-

ble espresso on ice, giving me that extra kick needed for the fast-moving, demanding "rush" hours. While I have sadly had to cut way down on my coffee habit, I do make an exception when the coffee is irresistibly good, as in Italy, Greece, and Turkey. Luckily, I've found that the penetrating aroma of perfectly roasted, fresh ground, just brewed coffee is almost as intoxicating as the real thing.

The history of coffee is as dark and murky as unfiltered coffee stirred up by plenty of controversy. The coffee tree probably originated in the province of Kaffa (ultimately the source of the word coffee) in Ethiopia. Sometime before 1000 CE, members of the Galla tribe in Ethiopia noticed that they would get extra energy when they ate certain berries ground and mixed with animal fat, probably after observing goats munch on the same berries. The habit of consuming the succulent outer flesh of the coffee bean in nearby Sudan was carried to Yemen and the Arab world by captured slaves who were transported through the great port of the day, Mocha.

Sometime after, Arab traders began cultivating the coffee plant in Yemen, boiling the green beans into a beverage called qahwa (pronounced kahveh), meaning "that which prevents sleep," in Turkish. Luxurious coffee houses serving as gathering places for men to play chess, listen to music, and tell tales opened first in another port city, Mecca. Known as "Schools of the Wise," they became centers for political agitation. In 1511, Khair Beg, the notably corrupt governor of Mecca, tried to ban coffee to prevent political opposition. Instead, the sultan decried that coffee is sacred and had the governor executed.

By about 1350, Turkish traders began dry-roasting the beans, making them easier to transport and also strengthening the brew. Ottoman Turks brought coffee, most likely from Yemen, to Constantinople in 1453. In 1471 or 1475, the first coffeehouse, Kiva Han, was established; the first coffeehouse in Damascus, Syria, opened in 1530. I spotted Starbucks all over Istanbul and was told that the chain is popular there because, unlike traditional Turkish coffee houses, they are places where both men and women can gather. During the fifteenth and sixteenth centuries, the Arabs planted thousands of acres of coffee trees throughout the Arabian Peninsula and Yemen and trade in coffee beans flourished.

In 1529, a Viennese who had lived in Turkey, Franz Georg Kolschitzky, helped lead relief forces through enemy lines, defeating the Turks in their attempt to capture Vienna. Although the Turks were routed, they left behind an enduring legacy: sacks of coffee beans that Kolschitzky claimed as his reward. Kolschitzky then opened a coffeehouse, the first in central Europe, refining his brew by filtering out the grounds and mixing in sugar and milk.

Coffee arrived in Italy in 1615 through the vibrant trade between Venetian and Arab traders. Canny Venetian merchants introduced it as a rare beverage priced for the rich sold in chemist's shops. The first coffeehouse opened in Venice in 1683. Still thriving, Caffé Florian, on Piazza San Marco opened in 1720. (If you get to Venice, don't miss enjoying a small and expensive caffé for a bit of time travel to the early eighteenth century.)

Advised that coffee was the "devil's beverage" and should be banned, Pope Clement VIII wisely decided that "this beverage is so delicious that it would be a sin to let only misbelievers drink it! Let's defeat Satan by blessing this beverage, which contains nothing objectionable to a Christian." By 1763, Venice had over 200 caffés and by the late eighteenth century, other Italian cities had their own caffés where men would partake of this stimulating "intellectual beverage."

In Rome, Caffé Greco was frequented by literary lions like Stendhal, Goethe, and Keats. When I stopped there for an espresso a few years back, the marble-topped tables, gold and red damask walls, and old mirrors didn't look like they had changed at all since Caffé Greco opened in 1760 on Via Condotti. In 1732, the German, Johann Sebastian Bach composed his Kaffee-Kantate which includes the aria, "Ah! How sweet coffee tastes! Lovelier than a thousand kisses, sweeter far than muscatel wine! I must have my coffee."

The first person known to brew coffee in England was a Cretan Jew named Nathaniel Conopios, who was studying at Balliol College, Oxford. In 1650 Jacob, a Lebanese Jew, opened England's first coffee house in Oxford, later moving it to London. British coffeehouses became places for discussion and learning called "penny universities"—the price of a cup of coffee. Opened in 1688 Edward Lloyd's London Coffee House was frequented by merchants and maritime insurance agents and evolved into today's world-famous company.

The origin of coffee was kept secret by the same Arab traders who controlled the lucrative market in spices. Coffee beans are sterile, so it was necessary to get the actual plants. In 1690, the Dutch were able to smuggle a coffee plant from Mocha, Yemen and began cultivating it in Ceylon (now Sri Lanka) and in Java (now Indonesia.)

Coffee was first cultivated in the Caribbean in the 1720s, when Gabriel Mathieu de Clieu, a French naval officer serving in Martinique, acquired a single coffee tree in Paris, which he brought back with him. Although his ship was attacked by pirates, survived a terrible storm, and a saboteur on board tried destroy it, that single plant survived and was planted in Martinique. By 1777, official surveys counted nineteen million coffee trees there. In 1727 the Brazilian government sent Lieutenant-Colonel Francisco de Melo Palheta to Guiana to arbitrate a border dispute between French and Dutch colonies. While there, he began a secret liaison with the governor's wife.

Upon Palheta's departure, she presented him with a bouquet in which she had hidden fertile coffee seeds—the basis for Brazil's coffee plantations.

Coffee reached New Amsterdam with the early Dutch colonists, but tea was preferred until the Boston Tea Party made drinking coffee a patriotic act. Out West, cowboy coffee was prepared as in Ethiopia by roasting green coffee "cherries" over an open fire, grinding them with mortar and pestle, and then boiling the grinds with water. One company, Arbuckle's, put a peppermint stick in each bag of coffee. Camp cooks had no trouble finding a volunteer for grinding, because that person would get the peppermint stick.

During World War I, American soldiers got in the habit of drinking coffee brewed in giant mess-hall percolators and from the packets of instant Maxwell House issued in their rations. Coffee sales boomed during Prohibition and by 1940, the United States was importing seventy percent of the world coffee crop. Coffee breaks began during World War II when war industry factories would allow workers a short rest and a hit of caffeine.

In 1886, Joel Cheek, a former wholesale grocer, named his popular coffee blend "Maxwell House," after the hotel in Nashville, Tennessee where it was served. Its slogan, "good to the last drop," came from a declaration made by President Theodore Roosevelt in 1907. The many small local coffee-roasting shops began to die out after 1900 when the Hills Brothers began packing roast coffee in vacuum tins.

In 1971, Starbucks opened its first unassuming

store in Seattle's Pike Place public market and started a national (and now international) craze for strong, fresh-roasted whole-bean coffee. Today, because fresh-roasted coffee is again in demand, artisanal coffee roasters can be found in many cities, including my local Chestnut Hill Coffee Company, started by an Afghani and a Seattleite (www.chestnuthillcoffee.com).

Pleasingly bitter, earthy coffee marries perfectly with chocolate in creamy ganache fillings in the Strawberry Devil's Food Cake (page 166), the English Millionaire's Shortbread (page 769), and the Frangelico Mousse Cake (page 771). I make the Peanut-Chocolate Bars with Espresso (page 627) using a trio of New World ingredients–peanut, chocolate, and coffee. In very different form, the same three flavor the Peanut Meringues with Spiced Bittersweet Chocolate Puddings (page 630). Dark chocolate, earthy chestnuts, and equally dark coffee combine in the moist, flourless Piedmontese Mocha-Chestnut Torta (page 314). In this chapter, coffee flavors the whipped cream filling for the Brazil Nut Cake with Espresso (page 373) and half the dough for the Mochaccino Swirl Cookies (page 376).

GROWING THE BEST COFFEE

The most desirable coffee is grown in altitudes of about 3,000 feet, where its complex flavors develop best. The fruit (also known as beans, cherries, or berries) must be hand-picked from trees that bear flowers, and green and ripe fruit all at the same time. The outer pulp and parchment of the coffee fruit are removed to reveal a pair of pale green to dark yellow beans, which are then cleaned, dried, graded, and hand-inspected. The beans are packed in burlap sacks and exported "green" for roasting, blending, and grinding.

Today, coffee is grown worldwide, and is the number one food product traded internationally. Coffee is one of the few crops that small farmers in third-world countries can profitably export, and conscientious consumers now demand Fair Trade certified coffee to ensure that the world's coffee farmers (who are small holders) get a fair price for their harvests.

Jamaican Blue Mountain Coffee from the island's highlands is noted for its mild flavor and minimal bitterness. One of the most expensive and sought-after coffees in the world, Kona coffee, is cultivated on about 400 farms on mountain slopes in the Kona Districts of Hawaii. The rare coffee known as Bourbon Pointu was a favorite of France's King Louis XV and Honoré de Balzac. By the mid-twentieth century, this coffee from Réunion Island in the Indian Ocean had almost disappeared. Yoshiaki Kawashima, a second-generation coffee expert was able to track down 30 coffee plants growing in the wild, kicking off a successful five-year project to revitalize the island's coffee industry.

ARABICA AND ROBUSTA COFFEE

The two most important species of coffee beans are *Coffea arabica*, and *Coffea robusta*. Coffea arabica originated in Ethiopia and migrated to the rich coffee belts of Brazil, Columbia, and other countries located between 25 degrees North and 30 degrees South latitude. Arabica beans grow best at high altitudes and produce superior coffees with mellow, rich flavor and complex aromas with about half the caffeine of robusta beans. Arabica production represents eighty percent of the world's coffee trade, however, only ten percent is suitable for specialty coffee companies.

Robusta beans grow at lower elevations and have higher yields and better disease resistance than Arabica. The beans have a woody, astringent flavor and are used to increase coffee's caffeine content and for its lower price. A small percentage is typically added to Italian espresso blends to increase the desirable crema—the fine creamy bubbles that cover the surface when espresso is brewed properly by an expert barista.

BLENDING AND ROASTING COFFEE

As coffee beans age, they turn from green to yellow and at the same time lose their moisture. The skilled roaster must gauge the moisture content, ripeness, and consistency of the beans, as well as when they were picked and where they were grown, to judge how best to roast them.

Coffee beans are quite fragile and easily broken. Broken beans make for unevenly roasted coffee and therefore unevenly brewed coffee. The best-tasting coffees are carefully handled so they contain the maximum percentage of whole beans.

Anywhere from three to six types of beans may be combined to make signature blends. According to some roasters, the best coffees are pre-blended and then roasted together so the results are mellower, rounder, with more depth of flavor due to the exchange of flavorful volatile aromas during the roasting process. The best coffee is roasted in smaller batches at about 800°F, so all the various factors can be better controlled, using green (or unroasted) coffee beans that have been stored for less than one month before roasting.

STORING COFFEE

Store whole roasted beans in an airtight container in a cool, dry place for up to two weeks. For longer storage, place beans in a zipper lock bag with the air removed or any other airtight container filled to the top with no airspace, and freeze up to three months.

Refrigerate freshly ground coffee in an airtight container. Use freshly ground coffee quickly since it begins to lose its flavor after only two days.

ESPRESSO

The term espresso, not expresso, comes from the Italian, meaning both "quick," because the coffee is quickly brewed with the help of steam, and "pressed out" referring to the process of pushing the freshly fine-ground bean essence through a special machine, again with the help of steam. This process extracts much more flavor from the grounds and results in a highly concentrated brew with a thin layer of thick, creamy, dark beige froth called crema on the coffee's surface.

The espresso machine was invented in 1903 by Luigi Bezzera, a manufacturer who was looking for a quick way to brew coffee, although he made little money from his invention. Desidero Pavoni bought the rights to Bezzera's espresso machine patent in 1905 and successfully introduced the beverage to the Italian market. The iconic aluminum Moka Express was invented by Alfonso Bialetti in 1933. This simple two-part stovetop coffee maker uses pressurized boiling water forced through the grounds into the top portion of the pot. Today, it (or its many imitators) is found in just about every Italian home. In 1927, the first espresso machine in America was installed at Cafe Reggio in Greenwich Village, New York. The splendid original bronze and chrome machine, made in 1902, is still displayed there (www.cafereggio.com).

With the availability of steam in the machines, cappuccino, named for the color of the robes of Capuchin monks, developed. Cappuccino is a cup of espresso topped with a thick layer of foamy hot steamed milk. It first became popular in Italy at the beginning of the nineteenth century, and soon after was introduced in America by the original owner of Cafe Reggio, Domenico Parisi.

It is said that Naples has the best coffee in Italy because at the turn of the twentieth century, when cholera abounded, Neapolitans searched out the source of pure water used by the Romans. They believe that the best coffee is made with this water that has run through limestone and is full of minerals. Outside of Naples, the best coffee is made with the highest quality, freshest, most evenly roasted whole beans handled properly by a skillful barista and always using filtered water.

According to standards now being established by the Italian parliamentary Agricultural Commission, true Italian espresso should be hazelnut-colored with flourishes of red and a smokiness that creates a uniform tiger-stripe pattern. The desirable crema, which sits on top, must fit the coffee like a tight sweater with very fine bubbles that remain for a long time on the surface of the liquid without breaking, and without holes opening in its center. At the end of the coffee, the crema should form a crown around the rim of the cup. Marco Lion, the head of the commission, says, "The taste should be aristocratic, elegant, noble, sensual, tasty, rigorous, clean, and sincere as well as large, rich, vivid, valuable, fragrant, and progressive in the way that various flavors evolve in succession, which delight those in search of new thrills and emotions."

The Italian National Espresso Institute (www.espressoitaliano.org) describes the perfect espresso as having an intense scent with notes of flowers, fruits, toasted bread, and chocolate, all of which are also sensed in its long-lasting aftertaste. The taste of espresso should be round, substantial, and velvety, while sour and bitter tastes will be well balanced with barely perceptible astringency. The perfect cappuccino should have 1 part espresso (25 ml, or about 5 teaspoons) to 5 parts (125 ml or about ½ cup) steamed milk. The froth should be white, speckled with chocolate and hazelnut, with hints of dried fruit, toasted cereal, and caramel, while the body of the drink should have an almost imperceptible acidity.

INSTANT AND FREEZE-DRIED COFFEE

Powdered coffee gained popularity at the Buffalo Pan-American Exposition in 1901. In 1930, the Brazilian government approached the Swiss company Nestlé to develop coffee that could be made simply by adding water, yet would retain its flavor. After seven years of research and testing, the results were marketed as Nescafé, a combination of Nestlé and coffee. Instant coffee is a powder made of heat-dried freshly brewed coffee. It is useful in baking to add directly to batters. Freeze-dried coffee is first brewed then frozen into a slush before the water is evaporated in a more expensive process than instant that produces coffee with superior flavor.

DECAFFEINATED COFFEE

Decaffeinated coffee was first developed by Dr. Ludwig Roselius of Bremen, Germany. General Foods popularized decaffeinated coffee in the 1930s with Sanka, named from the French *sans* (meaning without) caffeine. The caffeine is removed from coffee beans before roasting using a chemical solvent (which disappears completely when the beans are roasted) or with the Swiss water process, in which the beans are steamed and the caffeine-laden outer layers are removed. Most higher-priced coffees are decaffeinated using the water process.

COFFEE TIPS

The finer the grind, the stronger the flavor. The fresher the brew, the more complex and rich the flavor.

- Add a pinch of fine sea salt to coffee grounds to help neutralize the acid.
- Spice up coffee by adding a pinch of ground cardamom, cinnamon, clove, or allspice to the ground coffee when brewing.
- For baking, use instant coffee or instant espresso granules, or make double-strength brewed coffee and let it cool to room temperature. Coffee extract is about the easiest way to add coffee flavor to baked goods. Look for the pure coffee extract made by the Neilsen Massey company of

COFFEE ROASTS

- American roast beans are medium-roasted to produce a moderate brew.
- French roast and dark French roast beans are heavily-roasted to a deep chocolate brown which produces a more intensely-flavored coffee.
- Italian roast produces noticeably glossy, brown-black colored beans that are strong in flavor and used for espresso and is usually made with a blend of beans.
- European roast combines two-thirds darker-roast beans with one-third regular-roast.
- Viennese roast is the opposite: one-third darker-roast beans blended with two-thirds regular-roast.

Brazil Nut Cake with Espresso (Torta de Castanhà–do–Parà)

Castanhà-do-Parà *is the native Brazilian name for this (not surprisingly) native Brazilian nut. Here, the dense, creamy, coconut-like flesh of the nuts is finely ground and mixed with meringue and fine dry breadcrumbs for a light Viennese-style torte. A luxurious topping of whipped cream flavored with espresso and coffee liqueur is easy to make. The whole cake makes an excellent presentation and would be perfect to serve after a Brazilian or Latin American-themed dinner. Once the cake is filled and topped with the whipped cream, it will only keep for about two days in the refrigerator. However, the cake itself may be made two to three days ahead of time. Wrap with heavy-duty aluminum foil and store in the refrigerator until filling and serving.*

YIELD: ONE 10-INCH CAKE; 10 TO 12 SERVINGS

Cake

2 tablespoons (1 ounce) unsalted butter, softened

$3/4$ cup fine dry breadcrumbs, or panko

$3/4$ pound (2 $1/4$ cups) Brazil nuts

Pinch salt

8 large eggs, separated

$1 1/2$ cups confectioners' sugar

Filling

1 cup heavy cream, chilled

$1/4$ cup confectioners' sugar

2 tablespoons cold strong espresso or coffee extract

2 tablespoons coffee liqueur or brandy

1 tablespoon finely ground coffee, for garnish

Make the cake: Rub a 10-inch springform pan with butter and dust with 2 tablespoons of the breadcrumbs. Place the remaining breadcrumbs, the Brazil nuts, and salt into the bowl of a food processor and process until finely ground.

In the bowl of a standing mixer fitted with the paddle attachment, beat the egg yolks with $3/4$ cup of the confectioners' sugar until the mixture is light and fluffy, 5 to 6 minutes. Fold in the ground nut mixture.

Preheat the oven to 325°F.

In the clean and greaseless bowl of a standing mixer fitted with the whisk attachment, beat the egg whites until fluffy, then add the remaining $3/4$ cup confectioners' sugar and continue beating until the whites are firm and glossy, 4 to 5 minutes. Fold the meringue into the nut mixture in thirds so as not to deflate it. Scrape the batter into the prepared pan and bake for 1 hour, or until the cake is set in the middle and has started to come away from the sides of the pan. Turn off the oven and allow the cake to cool with the door open for 5 minutes, then remove it from the oven and cool to room temperature.

Make the filling and assemble the cake: Beat the cream until firm enough to hold its shape, but not stiff or yellow. (Note: on a hot day, super-chill the bowl, the beater, and the cream in the freezer for 20 minutes before beating.) Add the confectioners' sugar, the espresso, and liqueur and beat again briefly to combine.

Cut a very small notch, about $1/4$-inch deep, out of the side of the cake to use as a guide. Using a long, serrated knife, cut the cake horizontally into two layers. Spread half the cream on the top of the bottom layer, then cover with the second layer. Re-assemble the cake, using the cut wedge as a guide to line up the layers in their original position. Spread the remaining cream in the center of the cake, leaving a (1-inch) border all around. Sprinkle the top with ground coffee, then chill the cake for at least 1 hour before cutting into serving portions.

GRINDING NUTS

Nuts grind much more finely and without getting oily if they are frozen first. It's best to grind the nuts together with some sort of starch or flour, again to keep them from getting oily while allowing you to grind them as fine as possible. Although ground nut flours are available in many natural foods markets, I find that they lack flavor; once ground, the natural aroma and taste of the nuts seem to quickly dissipate.

Chocolate–Kahlúa Silk Pie

Kahlúa is a well-known Mexican coffee-flavored liqueur that has a strong, but sweet flavor. It has been produced since before World War II, and is the second largest liqueur brand in the world, made in different versions and strengths, depending on the market. The more expensive, more potent, and less sweet Kahlúa Especial is made with premium Arabica coffee beans. Here, I use the liqueur to flavor the silky-smooth filling for an easy-to-make tart made in a pecan crumb crust. Of course, other coffee liqueurs, such as Tia Maria, may be substituted. Chocolate-covered espresso beans make the most appropriate garnish and the tart can be prepared one or two days ahead of time.

YIELD: ONE 10-INCH TART, 10 TO 12 SERVINGS

Crust

$^1/_2$ pound (2 cups) pecans

1 cup fine dry breadcrumbs or panko

$^1/_2$ cup packed dark brown sugar

$^1/_2$ teaspoon ground cinnamon

$^1/_4$ pound (1 stick) unsalted butter, melted and cooled

Filling

$^3/_4$ pound bittersweet chocolate, coarsely chopped

$^1/_4$ pound (1 stick) unsalted butter, melted and cooled

2 tablespoons instant coffee powder

6 large egg yolks (6 tablespoons)

$^3/_4$ cup dark brown sugar

$^1/_4$ cup Kahlúa liqueur or other coffee liqueur

1 cup heavy cream, chilled

Chocolate-covered coffee beans

Make the crust: Place the pecans, breadcrumbs, brown sugar, and cinnamon in the bowl of a food processor and grind until fine. Pour in the butter and process briefly to combine. Press the mixture into the bottom and 2 inches up the sides of a 10 inch tart pan with a removable bottom. Chill for 1 hour in the refrigerator or 30 minutes in the freezer to set its shape.

Preheat the oven to 375°F. Fit a piece of heavy-duty foil onto the crust and up over the edges and fill with beans or other pie weights. Blind bake (just pastry crust, no filling) on the bottom shelf of the oven until the crust is cooked through but not yet browned, about 30 minutes. Remove the foil and the weights, reduce the oven temperature to 325°F and bake for 10 minutes longer, or until the dough is evenly and lightly browned. Remove from the oven and cool to room temperature on a wire rack before filling.

Make the filling: Place the chocolate, butter, and coffee powder in a medium heavy-bottomed, non-aluminum pot and melt over low heat until the chocolate and butter are almost completely melted. Remove from the heat and whisk until smooth.

In the bowl of a standing mixer fitted with the paddle attachment, beat the egg yolks and sugar until thick and light about 3 minutes. Temper by gradually whisking about one-quarter of the hot chocolate mixture into the yolks. Add the yolk mixture to the hot chocolate in the pot and whisk to combine. Stirring constantly, cook for 1 to 2 minutes over moderate heat, or until the mixture thickens visibly and reads 165°F on a thermometer. Remove the pot from the heat and transfer the mixture to a bowl, preferably stainless steel, and cool by placing over a second bowl filled with a mixture of ice and water, stirring often. Stir in the Kahlúa. Spread two-thirds of the chocolate mixture into the baked crust.

In the bowl of a standing electric mixer and using the whisk attachment, beat the cream until firm. Fold the whipped cream into remaining chocolate mixture by thirds so as not to deflate the cream. Spread or pipe the cream over the dark chocolate layer. Garnish with chocolate-covered coffee beans. Chill the tart for 2 hours, or until firm before cutting into portions.

Mochaccino Swirl Cookies

Ellen Gray, former pastry chef at Stella Notte Restaurant where I was chef and partner, would prepare these not-too-sweet spiraled cookies to serve with gelato. Their name comes from the fact that half the cookie dough is flavored and colored with dark cocoa and ground espresso powder. These are great make-ahead cookies to keep in the freezer for whenever you need some good-looking, grown-up cookies. Make the roll, wrap it tightly in parchment paper, and freeze up to six months. Defrost in the refrigerator only until quite firm but just sliceable, then slice and bake.

YIELD: 30 COOKIES

2 tablespoons Dutch process cocoa

1 tablespoon finely ground espresso powder

2 tablespoons hot brewed coffee

1/2 pound (2 cups minus 2 tablespoons) unbleached all-purpose flour

1/2 teaspoon baking powder

1/2 teaspoon fine sea salt

1/2 pound (2 sticks) unsalted butter, softened

1 cup sugar

1 large egg yolk

2 tablespoons heavy cream

1 teaspoon vanilla extract

Combine the cocoa, espresso powder, and coffee in a small bowl and whisk to a smooth paste. Cool to room temperature.

Whisk together the dry ingredients: flour, baking powder, and salt.

In the bowl of a standing mixer fitted with the paddle attachment, cream the butter and sugar together until light and fluffy, 5 to 6 minutes. Combine the egg yolk, cream, and vanilla and beat in until well combined. Add the dry ingredients and beat briefly, just long enough to combine into a ball. Divide the dough in half. Wrap one half in plastic wrap and refrigerate. Add the cocoa mixture to the other half, kneading briefly to combine evenly. Wrap the mocha dough in plastic and refrigerate. Chill both doughs at least 4 hours or overnight.

Roll the mocha dough out between two sheets of lightly floured wax paper into an 8 by 12-inch rectangle. Repeat the process with the vanilla dough. (If the dough gets soft, chill it for 30 minutes in the refrigerator.) Pull off the top sheet of wax paper and invert the vanilla dough onto the mocha dough. Press lightly all over so both doughs adhere to each other. Using a sharp knife, trim the edges. Roll the doughs up the long way into a cylinder, wrap in parchment paper, and chill for at least 4 hours or overnight.

Preheat the oven to 375°F. Unwrap the dough log and cut it into $1/4$-inch thick slices. Arrange the cookie slices onto baking sheets lined with parchment paper and bake for 10 minutes or until set and lightly colored. Cool completely on a wire rack. Store the cookies in an airtight tin up to 1 week.

White Chocolate, Hazelnut, and Espresso Dacquoise

I made this scrumptious meringue torte for a recent pot-luck dinner with a group of friends who are always willing to be guinea pigs for my culinary experiments. Their reaction: Wow! I agree. Here, toasted hazelnut and ground espresso flavor crunchy meringue layers, cutting down on the natural sweetness of the meringue. The crunchy grains of espresso and aromatic lemon zest provide welcome contrast with the delicate sweetness of white chocolate. Like any meringue-based dessert, it's best not to attempt this show-stopping dessert on a hot, humid day. It does keep and freeze well, so you can make it one to two days ahead of time. This recipe is gluten-free.

YIELD: ONE 10-INCH TORTE, 12 TO 16 SERVINGS

Meringue

$1/2$ pound ($2^1/4$ cups) confectioners' sugar

$1/2$ pound ($1^1/2$ cups) hazelnuts, lightly toasted and skinned

2 tablespoons ground espresso

10 egg whites ($1^1/4$ cups), at room temperature

$1/2$ cup sugar

Filling

1 cup heavy cream

$1/2$ pound (2 sticks) unsalted butter, cut into bits

1 pound white chocolate, finely chopped or grated

Grated zest of 1 lemon (1 tablespoon)

$1/4$ cup confectioners' sugar

2 tablespoons espresso powder

Make the meringues: Preheat the oven to 300°F. Line two 18 x 13-inch half sheet pans (or other large baking pan) with parchment paper or silicone mats. Using the bottom of an 8-inch cake pan for a guide, draw 3 circles onto the parchment paper with a colorful marker. Turn the paper over so the circle shows through.

Place the confectioners' sugar, hazelnuts, and espresso powder in the bowl of a food processor and process to a fine powder.

In the clean and greaseless bowl of a standing mixer fitted with the whisk attachment, beat the egg whites until fluffy, then add the sugar and continue beating until the whites are firm and glossy, 4 to 5 minutes. Transfer the meringue to a large wide bowl. Fold the hazelnut mixture into the whites in thirds so as not to deflate the meringue.

Divide the mixture into 3 evenly-sized portions. Spread one portion evenly onto each parchment paper circle using a silicone spatula or pipe through a pastry bag with a large open tip or no tip. Bake for 45 minutes, then switch the position and direction of the pans, so the meringues bake evenly.

Reduce the oven temperature to 250°F and continue baking for 45 minutes or until the meringues are firm. Cool completely on a wire rack.

Remove the parchment paper from the meringues. Note: the meringues should be crunchy and pull away easily from the paper. If they are sticky, they need more time in the oven to dry.

Make the filling: In a medium heavy-bottomed non-aluminum pot, heat the cream and butter together until the cream is steaming hot and the butter has melted. Remove from the heat and immediately stir in the chocolate and the lemon zest. Whisk occasionally until the chocolate has melted completely. Transfer the mixture to a bowl, preferably stainless-steel, and cool by placing over a second bowl filled with a mixture of ice and water, whisking occasionally so it cools evenly. Note: you may cool the mixture in the refrigerator, but be careful to whisk it often and cool only until the mixture is firm enough to hold its shape and still maintain its shine.

When the filling is cool to the touch and firm enough to hold its shape when whisked, transfer to the bowl of a standing mixer fitted with the whisk attachment, and whip the cream until fluffy and firm enough to hold its shape, 1 to 2 minutes. Be careful not to overbeat, because the cream could separate.

Assembly: Fill a plastic gallon-size freezer bag with the cream, then cut a pencil-sized hole cut out of one corner (or cut a larger hole and attach a small pastry tip). Pipe a small circle of the filling onto a large, flat cake plate to secure the cake. Press one meringue layer, rough side up, onto the cream to secure. Pipe out half the filling from the bag onto the meringue, spreading it all the way to the edges with a silicone spatula.

Top with a second round of meringue, turning and gently pushing down so it attaches well to the filling. Top with the remaining filling and spread to the edges as before. Top with the third meringue circle, this time with the smooth side of the meringue facing up. Make sure to turn and gently push down on the meringue to attach it to the underlying cream. Chill the dacquoise for at least 2 hours to set up the cream filling.

Using a serrated knife, trim the outer edge of the cake to make an even edge. Sprinkle the top with confectioners' sugar. Place a paper doily on top and sprinkle the espresso powder over top. Gently remove the doily so as not to disturb the design. Refrigerate until ready to serve (up to 1 day ahead) or wrap well and freeze to serve at a later time. Use a serrated bread knife to cut the dacquoise into wedges.

CORN & CORNMEAL

Types of Corn . . .383

Cornmeal and Cornstarch . . .384

Nixtamalized Corn . . .385

Corn Syrup . . .386

"Eating the Cornbread" . . .387

PENNSYLVANIA DUTCH CORN PIE . . .387

Hard–Cooked (Not Boiled) Eggs . . .388

TURKISH SAVORY CORNBREAD (MISIR EKMEGI) . . .388

BRUSTENGOLO (UMBRIAN CORNMEAL,
PEAR, RAISIN, AND NUT CAKE) . . .389

Mistrà . . .390

TORTA SBRISOLONA ALLA LOMBARDA
(LOMBARDIAN CRUMBLY CAKE) . . .390

VENETIAN CORNMEAL TART DOUGH . . .391

CORNMEAL PIZZA DOUGH . . .392

SHINY CORNSTARCH GLAZE . . .393

CORN

Corn, the New World's most important contribution to world diet, reaches its apogee in the Americas. Cornbread, corn pone, corn spoon bread, Indian pudding (steamed cornmeal pudding) (see the "Indian Pudding" Cake, page 286), grits, pound cake (see the Cornmeal and Rosewater Pound Cake, page 469), corn spoon bread, flap–jacks, grits, and cornmeal mush are just a few of the ways Americans bake with corn and cornmeal.

The English word *corn* originally meant any grain or grain–like object, as in the corns of salt used to make corned beef. Its scientific *Zea mays*, derived from the Aztec word *maize*, which is used in many languages, aside from American English including French *maïs* and Spanish *maíz*. Genetic evidence suggests that corn was first domesti–cated about 9,000 years ago, perhaps in the high–lands of central Mexico. Cultivated since at least 3500 BCE, corn began to spread widely and quickly about 1500 BCE becoming the staple food of the Incas, Mayas, and Aztecs. During the first millennium CE, corn cultivation spread into the American Southwest where in 1540, the explorer Coronado found Pueblo Indians growing corn under irrigation. One of the oldest forms of corn,

popcorn, was found in Bat Cave, New Mexico and has been dated to 3600 BC.

About a thousand years later, corn reached the North American East Coast where the inhabitants cleared large forest and grasslands to grow the new crop. Because corn is relatively easy to grow allowing people enough free time to think beyond basic survival, corn–centric civilizations began to flourish. In 1608, the Jamestown Colony learned how to grow corn from local Indians, and corn helped keep the Pilgrims alive during the bitter winter of 1620.

Columbus brought corn back with him to Spain, where, as early as 1498, it was grown in Andalusia as a curiosity. Within one generation, Southern European farmers were raising corn and by the end of the eighteenth century corn was planted from Gibraltar to the Black Sea. Because the new grain was often planted on land that for–merly lay fallow and it ripened at a season when food was scarce, corn became the food of the poor, who ate it mostly in the form of polenta (cornmeal grits mush) and fed it to their animals.

Corn reached Italy, not from the West and Spain, but from the East. It's not known just who brought corn to Italy. Perhaps the Venetians exchanged Mexican corn for sugar cane, or it may have arrived in Italy through Venetian trade with Turkey. The word for corn in Turkish is *misir*, meaning Egyptian and in Italian, it is *granoturco* meaning Turkish grain, both names indicating confusion about the origin of this new crop. Starting about 1650, Italians in the Veneto switched from cooking *grano saraceno* (buckwheat, literally Saracen grain) to corn for their polenta, laboriously stirred in the unlined copper bucket known as a *paiolo* swinging over an open fire. Corn is the main grain grown along Turkey's Black Sea coast and the region's cuisine features many cornmeal specialties including the Turkish Savory Cornbread (page 388) with feta, olives, and dill in this chapter. Corn bread is also a common food in Georgia, which borders Turkey on the eastern coast of the Black Sea; mamaliga, similar to polenta, is the staple food of nearby Romania.

Fresh sweet corn, almost unknown outside of North America, goes into corn spoon bread, corn pudding, and Pennsylvania Dutch Corn Pie (page 387). Sweet corn (*Zea mays, var. saccharata*) probably originated from a mutation of a Peruvian corn called *Chuspillo* that keeps the sugar contained in the kernel from converting to starch. The Papoon corn grown by the Iroquois in 1779 was an early sweet corn although there was little interest in sweet corn until about a hundred years ago, when seed sellers in the eastern United States first began marketing it. From the Civil War onward, the popularity of sweet corn in America has continued to

increase. Silver Queen is the standard to which other varieties are compared though now mostly substituted with the longer-lasting Silver King. Kandy corn is extra-sweet. Dantings Early was one of the first named sweet corn varieties, while Golden Bantam, released in 1902, became one of the most important open-pollinated varieties.

In this chapter, fresh (or frozen) corn kernels go into the filling for the Pennsylvania Dutch Corn Pie (page 387). Ground yellow cornmeal goes into the Turkish Savory Cornbread (page 388) studded with black olives and white feta cheese. The dense and fruity Umbrian country-style cake called Brustengolo is made with cornmeal (page 389), while a crumbly Torta Sbrisolona (page 390) from Mantova in Lombardy, Italy, depends on cornmeal for its texture. The Venetian Cornmeal Tart Dough (page 391) made with cornmeal is sweetened with honey. Cornstarch mixed with water and boiled into until thick and smooth are the simple ingredients for the Jewish-style baker's Shiny Cornstarch Glaze (page 393) brushed on breads like the Sauerkraut Rye (page 784).

TYPES OF CORN

Corn is one of the most diverse grains and through selection by nature and by humans, we now have flint, flour, dent, pop, sweet, and waxy corn. Flint and dent corn are grown for animal feed, popcorn is grown for its "popability," flour corn is grown for cornmeal, and sweet corn is eaten as a fresh vegetable. Flint corn kernels have hard, glassy flesh and smooth, hard skins. Flour corn kernels contain soft starch within thin skins. Dent corns have hard sides and soft starchy cores that cause the end of the kernels to dent during drying. Waxy corn produces amylopectin, a complex starch.

Field corn contains about 4 percent sucrose in its milky stage compared to 10 percent in sweet corn. In standard sweet corn varieties, the kernels can lose as much as half their starch if kept at room temperature for 24 hours, the reason that seed companies and growers have been switching to the Super-Sweets.

Popcorns are either pearl-type with smooth, pearl-shaped crowns or white rice-types which are pointy. Popcorns are basically small-kernelled flint corns with hard flesh surrounding a small amount of soft, moist starch, which expands into steam when heated, causing the flesh to explode. After popping, popcorn can be either mushroom or butterfly-shaped. Mushroom types are easier to coat with syrup for caramel corn; butterfly has better mouth-feel, so it is best for movie-watching. Pueblo tribes grow red, yellow, white, blue, black, and multicolored corns, with each color having a cultural significance, blue corn is the most important. Ground into flour, blue corn is coarser, sweeter, and nuttier.

Modern corn varieties are hybrids, meaning they must be grown from special seed corn, a boon to seed companies, though many specialty growers raise open-pollinated yellow, white, bi-color, red, blue, and mixed-color "Indian" corns grown from saved kernels. Miniature corn is just infant regular corn, picked young enough so the cobs are tender enough to eat. Golden-

yellow kernels of super-sweet hybrids contain twice as much sugar as other sweet corns and that sugar is slow to convert to starch. The kernels actually get sweeter after harvest and stay sweet up to two weeks, so that this type is ideal for freezing. However, to my taste, the milky-sweet corn flavor is eclipsed by over-bearing sugar in these varieties.

CORNMEAL AND CORNSTARCH

Dried corn is found in many forms: whole, crushed, and finely ground into flour. Steel-ground yellow cornmeal, the type found in the supermarket aisle in the United States, has the husk and germ of the maize kernel almost completely removed. This type keeps almost indefinitely if stored in an airtight container in a cool dry place, but it is relatively bland and uninteresting in flavor.

Stone-ground cornmeal retains some of the hull and germ, lending more flavor and better nutritional value to recipes. It is more perishable and tends to gets buggy, but will keep well if refrigerated or frozen. White cornmeal is more traditional in Africa, where it is known as mealie meal, and is also popular in the Southern United States for making cornbread. Blue cornmeal is made from the rarer blue corn, one of the oldest types of corn.

Cornstarch is the fine white powdery starch of the corn or maize grain. It is also ground from the endosperm, or white heart, of the corn kernel. Corn flour may be the same as cornmeal, but usually more finely ground. In Great Britain, corn flour refers to cornstarch. In America, corn flour may also refer to *masa harina*, the flour of hominy: dried corn treated with slaked lime.

Cornstarch has a distinctive bright white appearance and feel when mixed raw with water or milk. This mixture is called a "slurry" and has the property of giving easily when gently pressed but resisting if pressed forcefully. Confectioners' sugar is mixed with three percent cornstarch to prevent caking. Corn-starch is a quick and easy way to thicken mixtures containing liquid, like pie filling and pastry cream. Its disadvantage is that it can produce a rubbery texture if overused and its thickness is less stable than that produced by the use of flour. If stirred too much, the sauce or filling can thin out.

Masa (Spanish, from the Latin *massa*, or "mass") is an ancient method of making dough by adding water to flour. *Masa nixtamalera* is made from corn boiled with slaked lime and ground into a wet dough. Sold in Mexican groceries, *masa harina* is flour made from lime-processed dough. *Masa de maíz*, sometimes also confusingly called *masa harina*, is made from finely ground untreated corn. Both masa nixtamalera and masa de maíz are used for making tortillas, tamales, and pupusas in Mexico, Central, and South America.

NIXTAMALIZED CORN

Nixtamalization, a word of Aztec origin, is the process whereby dried corn kernels are soaked and cooked in an alkaline solution, usually limewater, to cause the transparent outer hull of the corn kernel, called the pericarp, to separate and slip off the grain. Nixtamalized hominy is nutritionally superior to cornmeal because the lime (calcium oxide, not the citrus fruit) adds calcium to the dough. It also makes the niacin in the cornmeal nutritionally available, helping to prevent pellagra and making the corn easier to digest.

The ancient Maya and Aztecs used ashes to create alkaline solutions for treating corn, while North American Indians used sodium carbonate, also known as washing soda or soda ash, made from wood ash, or oyster shells. The Hopi Indians would get alkali from ashes of juniper trees, while the Maya today use the ashes of burnt mussel shells.

Although Europeans quickly accepted corn, they did not adopt the nixtamalization process, perhaps because they had more efficient milling processes. Because of the lack of understanding of the importance of this process, in places where corn became a staple grain, such as Alpine Italy, people suffered from a disease caused by vitamin and protein deficiency called pellagra. In parts of Africa, a related disease called kwashiorkor shows up in places where untreated corn is the staple food. Because of this, in Europe, corn had the reputation as a grain that could prevent starvation but also lead to malnourishment. Polenta was long considered to be fit only for the poor in Italy until recently, when it gained status as gourmet rustic food.

CORN SYRUP

Corn syrup is composed mainly of glucose and is produced through a series of enzymatic reactions that convert corn starch to corn syrup. It is widely used in products labeled "all natural" in the United States. Because of its mild sweetness, corn syrup is often combined with high intensity sweeteners like sugar and honey in jams and jellies.

Corn syrup is used for sweetening, to soften texture, add volume, and prevent sugar crystallization. Light corn syrup is clear and light yellow in color; dark corn syrup is made with refiners' syrup, a type of molasses. Light corn syrup is used when delicate sweet flavor is desired, such as in fruit sauces and jams. With its robust flavor, dark corn syrup goes into the filling for pecan pie and sticky bun smear.

Glucose syrup is often made from corn starch, but it can also be produced from wheat, rice, or potato starch. Glucose syrup is less sweet than normal sugar, but has technical advantages that make it useful in the food industry. Until recently, the corn syrup sold in supermarkets was high in glucose. Today, high fructose corn syrup (HFCS), as in Karo Syrup, is now most common. To make HFCS, other enzymes are used to convert glucose into fructose, yielding sweeter and more soluble syrup.

The complex process for making HFCS was developed in the 1970s. By the late 1990s, the use of sugar declined, not because Americans were eating less sweet foods, but because producers were including more HFCS. This syrup has the same sweetening power as an equal amount of cane or beet sugar sucrose, but it is much more complicated to make, requiring fermentation and enzyme action in large chemical plants in the Corn Belt. In spite of this, HFCS is cheaper than sugar and is easy to transport: the liquid is piped into tanker trucks. Its major use is in commercially prepared foods to thicken and help retain moisture.

Just about every processed food in America contains corn syrup, especially baked goods, confections, and frozen desserts. Look on the ingredient labels for beverages, soda, breads, breakfast cereals, breakfast pastries, candy bars, condiments, cookies and cakes, dairy products, syrups, pastries, and snacks; all contain high fructose corn syrup. Corn syrup prevents the formation of ice crystals in frozen desserts and sweetens less expensive jams and preserves.

Although I generally avoid highly processed foods like HFCS, I do use it to prevent sugar syrup from crystallizing, because it is difficult for home cooks to obtain glucose syrup. I use it to make the syrup in which I simmer orange rind (page 225), for the Candied Walnuts (page 847), and in the glaze for the Sesame Honey Cones (page 800). The Amish Black Walnut Oatmeal Pie (page 575) contains dark corn syrup. Its filling is similar in consistency to pecan pie. In many versions, the filling for the Maple Syrup Pie (page 555) is adulterated with corn syrup, in the same way that inexpensive pancake syrups are made from corn syrup rather than maple syrup.

Pennsylvania Dutch Corn Pie

I adapted this recipe from one shared with me by my longtime neighbor and friend, Barry Brommer, who grew up in Columbia, Pennsylvania, and got it from his mother. Relatively unknown, the lovage I use to flavor the pie is an intensely celery-scented herb that is common in Pennsylvania Dutch cooking with leaves that resemble giant flat-leaf parsley. I have a stalwart lovage plant in my herb garden with giant roots and stalks that grow taller than me every summer. If you bake the pie in a foil pan, double the pan to make it more rigid. You can use the second pan for your next pie.

YIELD: ONE 10-INCH PIE; 8 TO 10 SERVINGS

1 pound Lard Pie Dough (page 204)

1 cup half-and-half

Pinch saffron, crumbled

3 cups fresh white corn kernels, substitute frozen white corn kernels, rinsed, drained, and patted dry

1 (15-ounce) can creamed corn, substitute 2 cups fresh corn ground in the food processor with 1/2 cup heavy cream and 2 tablespoons flour

2 tablespoons chopped lovage, substitute flat-leaf parsley or dill

2 tablespoons chopped flat-leaf parsley

1 heaping tablespoon instant (Wondra) or all-purpose flour

Fine sea salt and freshly ground black pepper

4 hard-cooked eggs, sliced (see sidebar on next page)

2 tablespoons (1 ounce) unsalted butter, chilled and cut into bits

Divide the dough in two on a floured work surface, with one section slightly smaller. Roll out the smaller section into a round about 12 inches in diameter and about 3/8-inch thick. Roll the larger piece out into a round about 14 inches in diameter, trimming off the rough edges with scissors. Place both dough rounds on baking pans lined with parchment paper or wax paper and chill for 30 minutes.

Fold the smaller round of dough in quarters, lift it up, and drape it into a 10-inch pie pan. Trim the crust to 1/2-inch beyond the edge of the pan using scissors.

Preheat the oven to 350°F.

In a small bowl, combine the half-and-half and the saffron and allow the mixture to steep for about 15 minutes or until the liquid is bright yellow. Combine the half-and-half mixture with the corn, creamed corn, chopped herbs, flour, and salt and pepper to taste.

Spoon the mixture into the pie crust. Top with the eggs and sprinkle with additional salt and pepper. Scatter the butter bits over top.

Cover with the top crust, pressing the edges firmly together to seal. Crimp the rim with a fork or a pie crimper. Cut slits in the crust to vent. Place the filled pie on a baking sheet and bake on the bottom shelf of the oven until lightly browned and the filling is bubbling, about 1 hour. Cool on a wire rack for 15 minutes before slicing into serving portions.

HARD-COOKED (NOT BOILED) EGGS

For the creamiest whites, tender, sunshine-yellow yolks, and no nasty green ring, never boil your eggs! Instead, place 6 to 10 large eggs in a medium heavy-bottomed pot and cover with cold water. Add salt, cover, and bring to a boil. Boil for 1 minute only, turn off the heat, and allow the eggs to set in the water for 6 to 8 minutes.

To test, remove 1 egg from the pot and crack the shell using the back of a spoon or the side of a knife. Feel the egg: a still-soft egg will feel mushy and liquidy, a perfectly cooked egg will be medium-firm with a bit of give to the white. (For the recipe above, the eggs should feel soft inside but not completely liquidy, as they will cook further when baked in the pie.) When the eggs are ready, immediately drain them and run under cold water to keep them from cooking further.

Turkish Savory Cornbread (Misir Ekmegi)

Trabzon, formerly known as Trebizond, is a city on the Black Sea coast of north-eastern Turkey, which for thousands of years has been a critical meeting point for international trade, due to its strategic location at the crossroads of east-west (Asia-Europe) and north-south (Russia-Middle East) trading routes. The city's inhabitants were early adopters of corn, perhaps from the east or through trade with Venetians. I'd like to know the story of how New World corn made its way to Eastern Turkey. Kuymak (Turkish polenta made with cornmeal and lots of butter and cheese), is a local specialty. This moist, savory cornbread studded with black olives and black nigella seeds (see page 899 for more information), feta, dill, and red pepper flakes, is another. Vary the recipe by substituting the grated zest of one lemon for the feta, and increasing the salt as necessary.

YIELD: 16 SQUARES

$1/2$ pound ($1 3/4$ cups) stone-ground yellow cornmeal

$1/4$ pound (1 cup minus 1 tablespoon) unbleached all-purpose flour

2 teaspoons baking powder

$1/2$ teaspoon fine sea salt

3 large eggs

1 cup whole milk yogurt

$3/4$ cup extra-virgin olive oil

$1 1/2$ cups crumbled feta cheese

$1/2$ cup pitted, sliced oil-cured black olives and/or Kalamata olives

1 teaspoon red pepper flakes

$^{1}/_{4}$ cup chopped dill

1 tablespoon nigella seeds

Preheat the oven to 375°F. Spray a 9-inch square baking pan with nonstick baker's coating or rub lightly with oil and dust with the dry ingredients mix.

Whisk together the dry ingredients: cornmeal, flour, baking powder, and salt.

In a large bowl, beat the eggs, yogurt, and oil together just to combine, then fold in the flour mix in three parts. Fold in three-quarters of the feta, three-quarters of the olives, three-quarters of the pepper flakes, three quarters of the dill, and three quarters of the nigella seeds. Spoon the batter into the prepared pan and top with the remaining feta, olives, pepper flakes, dill, and nigella seeds. Bake for 45 minutes or until the cornbread is firm in the center and starts to come away from the sides of the pan. Cool on a wire rack before cutting into serving portions. Store covered and refrigerate for up to 3 days.

Brustengolo
(Umbrian Cornmeal, Pear, Raisin, and Nut Cake)

This hearty, rustic cornmeal torte from Umbria is a typical autumn dessert that was originally a food of the poor, especially the region near Perugia. In the past, especially in the countryside, cornmeal was used for baking because it was abundant and inexpensive. In the traditional recipe, cornmeal was mixed with boiling water

and the mixture rested overnight. In the morning, raisins, pine nuts, walnuts, hazelnuts, and thin slices of apple were added, then the cake was baked. In another version, the dough is fried in lard or olive oil. I've also seen a Brustengolo made in a pastry crust with the fruits baked inside as a filling. Here, I combine wheat flour and cornmeal with baking powder for leavening to make a lighter cake. Although usually made with apples, here I substitute firm, juicy winter pears in honor of Umbria's long tradition of using pears for both sweet and savory dishes.

YIELD: ONE 10-INCH CAKE; 10 TO 12 SERVINGS

$5^{1}/_{2}$ ounces (1 cup) golden raisins

$^{1}/_{2}$ cup mistrà (see 390), substitute anisette or Pernod

2 pounds (about 4) Bosc pears, cored, and sliced

Juce and grated zest of 1 lemon (3 tablespoons juice and 1 tablespoon zest)

$^{1}/_{2}$ pound ($1^{3}/_{4}$ cups) stone-ground yellow cornmeal

$^{1}/_{2}$ pound (2 cups minus 2 tablespoons) unbleached all-purpose flour

2 teaspoons baking powder

$^{1}/_{2}$ teaspoon fine sea salt

4 large eggs

$2^{1}/_{4}$ cups sugar

$^{1}/_{2}$ pound (2 sticks) unsalted butter, melted and cooled

1 cup extra virgin olive oil

$^{1}/_{4}$ pound (scant 1 cup) walnuts, lightly toasted and coarsely chopped

$^{1}/_{2}$ cup pine nuts, lightly toasted

Soak the raisins in the mistrà for at least 1 hour, and up to overnight.

Preheat the oven to 350°F. Spray a 10-inch springform pan with nonstick baker's coating, or rub with softened butter and dust with flour, shaking off the excess.

Combine the raisins and any soaking juices with the pears, lemon juice, and lemon zest.

In a medium bowl, whisk together the dry ingredients: cornmeal, flour, baking powder, and salt.

In the bowl of a standing mixer fitted with the paddle attachment, beat the eggs and 2 cups of sugar until light and fluffy, 5 to 6 minutes. Slowly, beat in the butter and oil. Continue to beat until the mixture is entirely incorporated and the batter is thick and creamy. Fold in the flour mixture. Fold in half the pear mixture, half the walnuts, and half the pine nuts. Scrape the batter into the pan and cover the top with the remaining fruits and nuts. Sprinkle with the remaining $^1/_4$ cup of sugar.

Bake on the bottom shelf of the oven for 45 minutes, then reduce the heat to 325°F. Continue baking for 45 minutes or until the cake starts to come away from the sides of the pan and a skewer inserted in the center comes out clean. Cool completely on a wire rack before slicing.

MISTRÀ

Mistrà, an anise-infused liqueur typical of Umbria and the Marches, flavors this cake; anisette, Pernod, or ouzo may be substituted. In fact, it may be that Mistrà actually came to this part of Italy from Greece because Mistrà is both the name of a town in the Peloponnesus and an alternate name in Greek for ouzo.

Torta Sbrisolona alla Lombarda (Lombardian Crumbly Cake)

*This crumbly cake—*sbrisolona *means crumbly—comes from the region of Lombardy, Italy. It's a very traditional cake, dating from the time when few could afford the ingredients of richer cakes or pastries. It is found in many versions in bakeries, especially in the town of Mantova, where it is a specialty. Serve the cake at room temperature in summer as an accompaniment to sliced peaches mixed with sweet dessert wine or accompanied by the Sour Cherry Sauce on page 304. This cake keeps quite well for 3 to 4 days, stored in a cake tin or other sealed container. This recipe is dairy-free.*

YIELD: ONE 10- TO 11-INCH TART; 8 TO 10 SERVINGS

$^1/_4$ pound ($^3/_4$ cup) blanched almonds

5 ounces (1$^1/_4$ cups minus 4 teaspoons) unbleached all-purpose flour

5 ounces (1 cup plus 1 tablespoon) finely ground stone-ground yellow cornmeal

$^1/_2$ teaspoon fine sea salt

$^3/_4$ cup sugar

Grated zest of 1 lemon (1 tablespoon)

1 teaspoon vanilla extract

2 large eggs

$^1/_4$ cup extra-virgin olive oil

2 tablespoons ice water

2 tablespoons amaretto liqueur

$^1/_4$ pound ($^3/_4$ cup) whole skin-on almonds

Confectioners' sugar, for dusting

Preheat the oven to 350°F. Spray a 10- to 11-inch tart pan with nonstick baker's coating, or rub with softened butter and dust with flour, shaking off the excess.

Place the almonds, flour, cornmeal, and salt in the bowl of a food processor and process until the almonds are very finely ground. Add the sugar, lemon zest, vanilla, eggs, and oil, and process briefly, just until the dough is crumbly.

Combine the water and amaretto and pour into the processor. Process briefly, just long enough to moisten the mixture so it forms large crumbs like streusel. Lightly toss the mixture together with the whole almonds. Pat the mixture lightly into the pan, without mashing the crumbles together. Bake for 30 minutes, or until lightly colored. Cool completely before removing from pan. Dust generously with confectioners' sugar and serve. Portions should be broken off, not sliced.

Venetian Cornmeal Tart Dough

This is one of my all-time favorite pastry doughs. A crunchy cornmeal-based dough from Venice, it is flavored with honey, vanilla, and the ubiquitous Italian pastry ingredient: lemon zest. Because it is soft and sticky, the dough is best patted into place by hand or chilled till firm, then rolled out between two sheets of wax paper. Because it is somewhat fragile, it works best as a shallow crust to line a shallow tart pan like a French removable-bottom fluted tart pan. Use it for the Italian Hachiya Persimmon Meringue Torte (page 662) and the Venetian Cornmeal and Cherry Crostata (page 305).

YIELD: 1¹/₂ POUNDS DOUGH, ENOUGH FOR 2 TART CRUSTS

¹/₂ pound (2 cups minus 2 tablespoons) unbleached all-purpose flour

¹/₄ pound (³/₄ cup plus 2 tablespoons) stone-ground yellow cornmeal

¹/₂ cup sugar

¹/₂ teaspoon fine sea salt

6 ounces (1¹/₂ sticks) unsalted butter, chilled and cut into bits

4 egg yolks (¹/₄ cup)

¹/₄ cup honey

2 teaspoons vanilla extract

Grated zest of 1 lemon (1 tablespoon)

In the bowl of a standing mixer fitted with the paddle attachment, combine the dry ingredients: flour, cornmeal, sugar, and salt. Add the butter and beat until the pieces resemble oatmeal.

Separately, beat the yolks, honey, vanilla, and lemon zest. Add to the flour mixture and mix just until the dough comes together. Form the dough into a large, flat oblong, wrap well, and chill for 1 hour in the refrigerator or 30 minutes in the freezer. (If desired, store the dough, tightly wrapped, in the freezer for up to six months.) Use as directed in the individual recipes.

Note: when blind-baking a tart crust (see page 30) made from this extra-rich dough, bake it at 350°F for

20 minutes, then remove the foil lining and the beans, reduce the oven temperature to 325°F and bake for 10 minutes longer, or until lightly browned and firm.

Cornmeal Pizza Dough

I have used this light but slightly crunchy pizza dough to make hundreds, if not thousands, of fabulous pizzas in the wood-burning oven in my last restaurant. Although traditional Neapolitan pizza dough is made only with flour, yeast, salt, and oil, this one combines bread flour for strength, all-purpose flour for tenderness, and cornmeal for flavor and texture. It makes a delicious slightly crunchy dough for any pizza recipe. It is especially good in the White Pizza with Broccoli Rabe (page 266) and the Sicilian Pan Pizza with Zucca (page 737).

YIELD: 2 POUNDS DOUGH, ENOUGH FOR 2 LARGE OR 3 SMALLER PIZZAS

$^1/_2$ pound (2 cups minus 2 tablespoons) unbleached all-purpose flour

$^1/_2$ pound (2 cups) unbleached bread flour

$^1/_4$ pound ($^3/_4$ cup plus 2 tablespoons) stone-ground yellow cornmeal

2 teaspoons fine sea salt

$^1/_2$ cup lukewarm water

1 tablespoon honey

1 ($^1/_4$-ounce) package (2$^1/_2$ teaspoons) active dry yeast

$^3/_4$ cup lukewarm milk

$^1/_4$ cup extra-virgin olive oil

In a medium bowl, whisk together the dry ingredients: all-purpose flour, bread flour, cornmeal, and salt.

In the bowl of a standing mixer fitted with the paddle attachment, whisk together the water, honey, and yeast and allow the mixture to proof for 10 minutes or until bubbling. Beat in the milk and oil. Beat in the flour mixture, then switch to the dough hook and beat on low speed for about 10 minutes, or until the dough is smooth and elastic. The finished pizza dough should be soft and slightly sticky: you should be able to press a finger into the dough and pull it away cleanly after it sticks briefly.

Transfer the dough to a lightly oiled bowl, turning it so all the dough is coated with oil. Cover with plastic film and set aside in a warm place. Allow the dough to rise at warm room temperature until doubled in volume, about 1 hour.

Divide the dough into 2 or 3 portions and form into smooth rounds. Roll out or stretch out by hand into the desired size: 12 to 14 inches is common.

Note that pizza dough doesn't freeze very well, although it may be made one day, allowed to partially rise, then refrigerated overnight for use the following day or even punched down again and kept chilled for use the second day. Allow the dough to come to room temperature before rolling or stretching into a circle or tongue shape.

Shiny Cornstarch Glaze

*Brush this shiny glaze on hearty breads like the
Sauerkraut Rye (page 784), the Black Olive Herb Bread
(page 889), and the Currant-Walnut Baguette (page 761)
to give them a professional-looking finish. It is the same
glaze you see on bakery Jewish rye and pumpernickel
breads.*

YIELD: 1¼ CUPS GLAZE, ENOUGH FOR 8 LOAVES

1 cup water
2 tablespoons cornstarch
¼ cup cold water

Bring the water to a boil in a small pot.

Meanwhile, in a small bowl, whisk together the cornstarch and cold water to make a thin, soupy slurry. While
constantly whisking the water in the pot, pour the slurry
into the boiling water until the mixture is well combined.
Cook for 1 to 2 minutes, or until the mixture is thickened,
smooth, and shiny. Remove from the heat and continue
to whisk occasionally (to prevent a skin from forming)
until it reaches room temperature.

Use the glaze to brush on breads after shaping and
before rising and once again as soon as the bread comes
out of the oven. Store covered and refrigerated up to
2 weeks.

CRANBERRIES

Choosing and Storing Cranberries . . .398

Cranberry Cooking Tips . . .398

Heirloom Cranberries at
Paradise Hill Farm . . .399

CRANBERRY-GINGER UPSIDE-DOWN CAKE . . .399

CRANBERRY-WALNUT POUND CAKE . . .400

CRANBERRY-SEMOLINA KTEFA . . .401

Making Brik Pastry Leaves . . .402

HOT APPLE-CRANBERRY CRISP WITH
OATMEAL-ALMOND TOPPING . . .403

CRANBERRIES

The big, red cranberry that Americans and Canadians enjoy in muffins, sauces, tarts, pies, cakes, and quick breads is a native wetland fruit that grows on trailing vines which spread their roots like strawberries. These cranberries, *Vaccinium macrocarpon*, belong to a large family of low, scrubby, woody plants that thrive in the poor and acidic soil of moors, mountainsides, and especially bogs. In America and Canada, cranberries thrive in bogs formed by glaciers more than 10,000 years ago.

Smaller European cranberries have been eaten by Arctic peoples for millennia and are harvested from the wild in Scandinavia and Russia. In the boggy lands of northern England and Scotland, people would gather cranberries to mix with sugar and bake into tarts. One English name is fenberry, because they grew in the fens (marsh lands). The European cranberry's botanical name, *Vaccinium oxycoccos*, comes from the Latin *vacca*, meaning cow because cows seem to be fond of them. The fruits are related to the tiny red lingonberries, *Vaccinium vitis-idaea*, (page 165) popular in Scandinavia and Russia and to native American blueberries. Although similar in appearance,

highbush cranberries, *Viburnum trilobum*, are a completely different fruit of the honeysuckle family, which grow on a shrub and have pointed leaves and a single seed that must be strained out. They can be substituted in any recipe using puréed cranberries.

Thinking that the vine blossom resembled the neck, head, and bill of a crane, German and Dutch settlers called them *kranebeere*. Cranes are also fond of the berries, which grow in the bogs where cranes live. Others names are bounceberries because they literally bounce if dropped when fresh, and bearberries because bears also love them. In Canada, cranberries are called *atoca*, their Iroquois Indian name, or mossberry. In French Canada, the fruits are called *canneberge*, a word of unknown origin, or *pommes de pré* (meadow apples).

In New England, the natives called cranberries *sassamanash* and likely introduced them to starving settlers in Massachusetts. Pequot Indians called them *ibimi*, or "bitter berry." Native Americans recognized that their wax skin contains a natural preservative (benzoic acid) and would mix them into pemmican (dried meat mixture) for long journeys. New Englanders also valued cranberries for long-keeping through the long, cold winter. Lenni-Lenape Indians in New Jersey harvested the fruits they called *pakim*, meaning "noisy berry." John Webb established a cranberry bog in Ocean County, New Jersey in 1840 although today only 3,000 acres remain in that state.

By 1680, settlers were bartering with Native Americans for cranberries to be cooked into sauces served with the region's wild turkey, likely adapted from English Cumberland Sauce made with red currants. In the early 1800s Henry Hall, a Revolutionary War veteran from Dennis, Massachusetts noticed that sand blown over cranberry bogs from nearby dunes helped the plants grow faster and slowed the growth of weeds and insects. Today, New England growers spread sand on their bogs every three years.

Ship merchants bought cranberries and sold them to whalers who kept them in barrels of cold water for sailors to eat to prevent scurvy. In response to a slowing ship building industry, former ship builders and sea captains began to cultivate cranberries. They financed their bogs the same way they had financed their ships, by selling sixty-fourth interests in them. Some Cape Cod bogs are still owned by people who inherited them through these shares. A cranberry vine can survive indefinitely; some vines on Cape Cod are more than 150 years old and still bear fruit.

Growers take advantage of the fact that cranberries contain small air pockets and float in water by flooding the fields for harvest. Mechanical beaters agitate the fruits, freeing them from their stalks, floating them in acres of crimson that are rafted or pumped into collecting points at the water's edge. The great majority of cranberries are harvested using this method and are used for processed foods like juice and sauce. For the much smaller fresh market, cranberries are dry harvested–the fruit "combed" from the vines using picking machines. Once picked, the berries are bounced down a stair-stepped processor to cull out the old berries (which do not bounce) from the fresh.

As early as 1686, the colonists began exporting cranberries to England. An 1769 English cookbook gives these directions for preserving them: "Get your cranberries when they are quite dry, put them into dry clear bottles, cork them up close and set them in a dry cool place" and use them to "garnish your dishes all the Winter." In America, cooks made cranberries into sauces, preserves, and pies. In American Cookery, published in 1796, Amelia Simmons gave directions for a cranberry tart, "Stewed, strained and sweetened, put into paste No. 9, and baked gently."

By the 1840s, cranberries were cultivated on Cape Cod and New Jersey, at a time when sugar became more affordable, so that it could be used to sweeten cranberry tarts and pies. About the same time, Christmas trees were decorated with homemade ornaments which soon featured American cranberries strung with American popcorn to make red and white holiday garlands.

Cranberry sauce was first canned commercially

in 1912 as "Ocean Spray Cape Cod Cranberry Sauce." The same company is famous for their cranberry products, including the baker's favorite: dried, sweetened cranberries, also called "craisins," which can be substituted for raisins in any muffin, cake, or cookie recipe. The most important cranberry-growing areas are New Jersey, Massachusetts, Oregon, Washington, Wisconsin and British Columbia and Quebec in Canada.

Once generously sweetened, their tart flavor complements cakes, pies, muffins, and tarts. In this chapter, fresh (or frozen) cranberries go into the Cranberry-Ginger Upside-Down Cake (page 399), the Cranberry-Semolina Ktefa (page 401), and the Hot Apple-Cranberry Crisp with Oatmeal-Almond Topping (page 403), while fresh and dried cranberries flavor the Cranberry-Walnut Pound Cake (page 400).

CHOOSING AND STORING CRANBERRIES

Before they ripen, cranberries are actually white. Autumn's combination of warm, sunny days and cool nights give the cranberries their brilliant red color. Cranberries picked early in the season will be pale and super-sour. Those picked later in the season will have fully developed color and will be less acidic and bitter. Cranberries are at their peak in November, one reason they've come to be so closely associated with Thanksgiving.

Choose brightly colored, bright to dark red cranberries that are shiny, plump, and whole. Pale, greenish, or pink berries are underripe and will be bitter; shriveled berries or those with brown spots are old. Truly fresh cranberries will actually bounce if you drop them and will be quite firm to the touch. Cranberries will keep in the refrigerator for at least one month and can be frozen for up to six months. Use them straight from the freezer but allow 10 to 15 minutes extra baking or cooking time.

CRANBERRY COOKING TIPS

Use a food processor it to chop cranberries quickly, pulsing them until chunky.

- Add a pinch of baking soda to the pot when cooking cranberries to neutralize some of their acid, so that you'll need less sugar.
- Sugar toughens the skin of cranberries in cooking, so don't overdo it.
- Cook cranberries just until they pop, otherwise they will get mushy and bitter-tasting.
- Substitute dried, sweetened cranberries for raisins in baking recipes for a tangy, colorful change. If desired, plump them like raisins by soaking them in hot water and letting them stand for 15 to 20 minutes or soak them in apple jack or brandy to cover until plump, about 2 hours and don't drain them before adding them to recipes.
- It is not necessary to defrost frozen cranberries before using them in recipes, although you may need to allow about 10 minutes extra baking time.

HEIRLOOM CRANBERRIES AT PARADISE HILL FARM

Paradise Hill Farm has been in Mary Ann Thompson's family since 1890. Her grandmother won a silver medal at the Buffalo Exposition in the early 1900s, and Mary Ann is continuing that tradition today. The farm spans over 800 acres in the Pine Barrens, with 200 acres planted with red and white cranberries. Located east of Philadelphia in Burlington County, Paradise Hill Farm is committed to conserving New Jersey's unique and precious Pine Barrens. The farm specializes in cranberries and blueberries, and is dedicated to preserving heirloom varieties like Mariposa, Early Richard, and Centennial. They are a transitional farm on their way to organic growing and use no sprays. Their heirloom cranberries tend to have thinner skins and less pulpy flesh than commercial high-production varieties, with a mild, less tart flavor and more tender texture when cooked.

Cranberry–Ginger Upside–Down Cake

A tradition in American home baking, an upside-down cake is made by placing fruits at the bottom of the pan before the batter is poured in, so they form a decorative topping once the cake is inverted. The most common upside-down cake is made with canned pineapple slices with maraschino cherries in the center. In this delightfully different, brightly-colored tart, whole cranberries are mixed with spicy candied ginger and brown sugar to make an eye-catching topping for an uncommon, uncommonly delicious cake that's also easy to make.

YIELD: ONE 10-INCH CAKE, 10 TO 12 SERVINGS

Topping

1/4 pound (1 stick) unsalted butter

1 cup packed light brown sugar

3/4 pound (3 cups) cranberries, fresh or frozen

1/2 cup finely chopped candied ginger

Cake

6 ounces (1 1/2 cups minus 1 tablespoon) unbleached all-purpose flour

2 teaspoons ground ginger

1 teaspoon baking powder

1/2 teaspoon ground cinnamon

1/4 teaspoon freshly grated nutmeg

1 teaspoon fine sea salt

1/4 pound (1 stick) unsalted butter, softened

1 cup light brown sugar

2 large eggs

1/2 cup milk

1 teaspoon vanilla extract

Make the topping: Melt the butter and brown sugar together in a 10-inch heavy oven-proof skillet, preferably cast-iron over medium heat. Cook for 2 to 3 minutes or until thick and bubbling, then turn off the heat. Arrange half the cranberries on top of the butter and sugar mixture, sprinkle with the ginger, then top with the remaining half of the cranberries.

Make the cake: Preheat the oven to 350°F. Whisk

together the dry ingredients: flour, ginger, baking powder, cinnamon, nutmeg, and salt.

In the bowl of a standing mixer fitted with the paddle attachment, cream the butter and brown sugar until light and fluffy, 5 to 6 minutes. Beat in the eggs one at a time, beating well after each addition.

Combine the milk and vanilla in a small bowl. Beginning and ending with dry ingredients, add the dry ingredients and milk mixture alternately into the creamed mixture, beating after each addition. Carefully spoon the batter evenly over the cranberries. Knock the pan on the counter several times to settle the batter.

Bake for 30 minutes, or until the cake starts to come away from the sides of the pan and a skewer stuck in the center comes out clean. Remove from the oven, and let the cake stand for 15 minutes to cool and firm. Run a thin sharp knife around the edges of the cake to loosen. Invert gently onto a serving plate and serve warm or at room temperature. Store covered and refrigerated up to 3 days.

Cranberry–Walnut Pound Cake

This simple, colorful, and moist pound cake studded with fresh and dried cranberries along with toasted walnuts is a keeper. Plus, it freezes well. It's a great cake to have on hand for unexpected guests at holiday time and would make a perfect hostess gift. Bake the cake in mini-loaf pans, wrap them in cellophane, and tie them with a cranberry-colored ribbon and you have a holiday gift that will be welcomed by all. The cake comes

out best if it is baked in a light-colored aluminum pan rather than a dark-colored coated pan, which will yield a cake with a darker crust. If you are making this in mini-loaf pans, adjust the baking time to about 25 minutes.

YIELD: ONE 9 X 5-INCH LOAF, 8 TO 10 SERVINGS

6 ounces (1 1/2 cups minus 1 tablespoon) unbleached all-purpose flour

1 teaspoon ground cinnamon

1/2 teaspoon fine sea salt

1/4 teaspoon baking soda

1/4 pound (1 stick) unsalted butter, softened

1 1/2 cups sugar

4 large eggs, at room temperature

1 teaspoon vanilla extract

1/2 cup sour cream

1 cup walnuts, lightly toasted and coarsely chopped

1 cup fresh cranberries

1/2 cup dried cranberries

Preheat the oven to 350°F. Prepare a large (1 1/2 pound, 9 x 5-inch) loaf pan by spraying with nonstick baker's coating, or rubbing with softened butter and dusting with flour, shaking off the excess.

Whisk together the dry ingredients: flour, cinnamon, salt, and baking soda.

In the bowl of a standing mixer fitted with the paddle attachment, cream the butter and sugar together until light and fluffy, 5 to 6 minutes. Beat in the eggs, one at a time, then beat in the vanilla. Fold in the flour mixture alternating with the sour cream, beginning and ending with the flour, and scraping down the sides of the bowl once or twice to get rid of any lumps.

Combine the walnuts and cranberries and fold about three-fourths of the mixture into the batter, reserving the remainder. Scrape the batter into the prepared pan and sprinkle with the remaining nut-fruit mixture. Bang the pan on the counter once or twice to get rid of any air bubbles. Bake for 1 hour, or until the cake is well risen and deep golden and a toothpick inserted in the center emerges clean.

Cool the cake in the pan on a wire rack for about 10 minutes or until somewhat cooled, then unmold and cool completely. Store covered and at room temperature for up to 5 days.

Cranberry–Semolina Ktefa

Ktefa is an elegant dessert served in some of Morocco's most exclusive restaurants. Traditionally, large, circular sheets of ouarka or brik leaves are deep-fried, layered with ground almonds, sugar, and cinnamon, and covered with warm semolina custard. Here I use a colorful American cranberry coulis flavored with orange zest to complement the orange blossom-scented creamy semolina filling. Unless you live in an area with a North African community, it is difficult to find the brik leaves, but Asian spring roll wrappers make a great substitute. Everything can be made ahead of time, even frying the leaves, but the individual layered desserts must be assembled just before serving so the layers stay crisp.

YIELD: 6 TO 8 SERVINGS

Coulis

6 ounces (1^1/$_2$ cups) cranberries

1 cup sugar

1 cup orange juice

Zest of 1 orange (4 teaspoons)

Cream

1 cup milk

1 cup heavy cream

^{1}/$_2$ teaspoon ground cinnamon

^{1}/$_2$ teaspoon ground cardamom

2 ounces (^{1}/$_4$ cup plus 1 tablespoon) semolina

2 tablespoons sugar

1^1/$_2$ teaspoons orange blossom water

Assembly

^{1}/$_2$ pound (1^1/$_2$ cups) blanched almonds, coarsely ground

^{1}/$_2$ cup superfine sugar

2 teaspoons ground cinnamon

1 quart grapeseed or canola oil, for frying

1 (6-ounce, 170 g) package brik leaves, each cut into quarters, substitute spring roll skins. Defrost in the refrigerator if frozen

Make the coulis: Place the cranberries, sugar, and orange juice in a medium, heavy-bottomed, non-aluminum pot and bring to a boil. Add the orange zest, reduce the heat to low, and simmer for about 10 minutes, or until the syrup is brilliant red and the cranberries have nearly disintegrated. Strain the mixture through a sieve, pressing lightly to extract the liquid. Discard the solids and reserve the liquid.

Make the cream: In a medium heavy-bottomed, non-aluminum pot, scald the milk and cream with the cinnamon and cardamom. Whisk in the semolina and sugar. Bring to a boil, stirring constantly, and cook over medium heat until thickened and smooth, about 5 minutes. Remove from the heat and whisk in the orange blossom water. Transfer the cream to a stainless-steel bowl and chill until thick enough to be pourable but still hold its shape.

Assemble the dessert: Combine the almonds, sugar, and cinnamon in the bowl of a food processor. Process briefly to chop the almonds roughly.

In a wok, a large heavy-duty frying pan, preferably cast-iron, or an electric deep-fryer, heat the oil to 365°F, or until shimmering hot, and the air above the pot feels hot when you hold your hand about 3 inches above the oil. Add the brik leaf quarters without crowding the pan and working in batches if necessary. Fry for 2 to 3 minutes or until browned on both sides. Drain on a wire rack, a brown paper bag, or paper towels.

For each portion, layer three fried leaves, sprinkling with the almond mixture in between each layer. Pour over the cream, then top with three more leaves, each sprinkled with the almond mixture. Drizzle the coulis over the top and around the plate and serve immediately.

MAKING BRIK PASTRY LEAVES

Also known as *ouarka, warka, malsouqa, dioul*, and *feuilles de brick*, these very thin rounds of cooked dough are a specialty of the Maghreb (North Africa). I watched the dough being made using a fascinating and imaginative technique. A round griddle is heated while a soft dough is made. The cook takes the dough, which is rolled into a ball, and taps it against the griddle, making thin, small circles. He or she continues to tap the dough in this manner until it is a large round made up of lots of overlapping, individual circles.

The thin, round leaves are then filled, rolled, or folded into the desired shape—which is different in every country and region—then deep-fried. In France, even the corner grocery sells the leaves, but they are difficult to find in America. I order mine from www.caviarassouline.com, one of the few vendors that has them for sale in the United States. The best substitute is thicker phyllo dough, Asian spring roll wrappers, or French crepes.

Hot Apple–Cranberry Crisp with Oatmeal–Almond Topping

Apple crisp was probably the very first dessert I made for my family, at about the age of ten. This one is not so different, but the combination of apples and cranberries makes a sweet and tart filling in a lovely shade of rosy-pink. The toasted almonds give an interesting texture to the crumble topping. A combination of at least two kinds of apples makes for a more complex flavor. This dessert is easy enough for almost anyone to make successfully.

YIELD: 8 SERVINGS

Filling

1 cup sugar

$1/2$ cup sour cream

$1/2$ teaspoon ground cinnamon

1 teaspoon vanilla extract

2 tablespoons unbleached all-purpose flour

6 large apples, peeled and sliced, preferably
   3 Granny Smith and 3 Fuji

$1/2$ pound (2 cups) cranberries

Topping

2 ounces ($1/2$ cup minus $1/2$ tablespoon) unbleached
   all-purpose flour

$1/2$ cup packed light brown sugar

Pinch salt

6 ounces ($11/2$ sticks) unsalted butter, chilled and cut
   into bits

3 ounces ($1/2$ cup) oatmeal (not instant)

6 ounces (1 cup) skin-on almonds, roughly chopped

Preheat the oven to 350°F.

Make the filling: In a bowl, whisk together the sugar, sour cream, cinnamon, and vanilla. Stir in the flour. Combine with the apples and the cranberries. Spread the mixture in the bottom of a shallow 6-cup baking dish.

Make the topping: Place the flour, brown sugar, salt, and butter in the bowl of a food processor. Process briefly, just until the mixture resembles oatmeal. Add the oatmeal and almonds and process again briefly to combine. Lightly crumble the topping over the fruit. Bake for 35 minutes, or until the fruit is bubbling and the topping is lightly browned. Serve while still hot.

Store covered and refrigerated up to 3 days. Cover and reheat at 350°F. for 20 minutes, uncovering for the last 5 minutes to crisp the top.

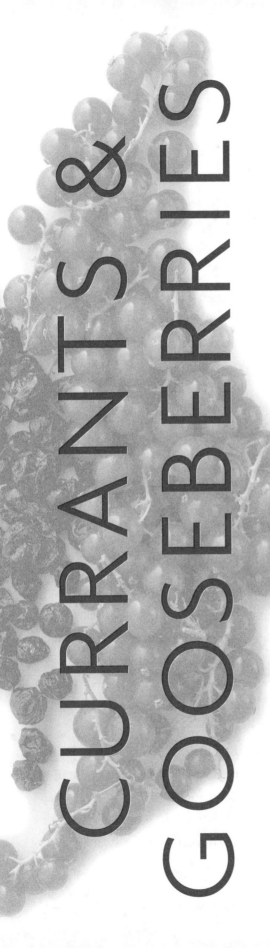

CURRANTS & GOOSEBERRIES

Gooseberries . . .406

John Parkinson on Gooseberries . . .408

Red, White, and Black Currants . . .408

Bar–le–Duc Seedless Currant Jelly . . .409

Ribes Fruit Season . . .410

Buying Gooseberries and Currants . . .410

GOOSEBERRY COBBLER WITH
WALNUT CRUNCH . . .410

BLACK CURRANT-APPLE LINZER TORTE . . .411

HUNGARIAN RED CURRANT-
HAZELNUT TORTE . . .413

ENGLISH SUMMER FRUIT PUDDING
WITH LEMON AND MINT . . .415

CURRANTS
& GOOSEBERRIES

Travel to France, Switzerland, Holland, Northern Italy, or elsewhere in Northern Europe in the summer and early fall and you'll see delicate branchlets of clear, jewel-colored red currants garnishing desserts, topping fruit macedoines (macerated fruits with liqueurs), tarts, pies, and cakes. If you visit the British Isles in the same season, you'll likely be served a gooseberry tart, pudding, or preserves to spread on crumpets. With their intense tart flavor, currants and gooseberries are both closely related members of the genus Ribes.

Highly appreciated in Northern Europe and Italy, but little known in America today, gooseberries and currants were brought to this country by the early colonists. Both currants, especially black currants, and gooseberries act as host to a fungus that attacks the white pine, one of the most valuable trees in America. A mildew disease wiped out American-grown gooseberries in 1905 and growing all Ribes fruits was restricted for many years. At one time, an unsuccessful effort was made to eradicate all wild and domestic gooseberries and currants in America. Growing restrictions were imposed on cultivated red currants from 1906 to 1966. With the development of new disease-resistant varieties, restrictions on Ribes cultivation in American are being relaxed.

Today, red and black currants and gooseberries are grown in Washington's Puyallup Valley–once the center of the state's berry industry–by George Richter, who is famed for the quality of his raspberries. Richter is a third-generation farmer whose family has been living off the land in the region for more than a century. With more farmers now growing these small fruits, it's time to pay a bit more attention to these petite beauties. I have found fresh gooseberries in season at my local Whole Foods market in early summer, a clear sign that appreciation for the fruit is growing. Red currants imported from Chile are found in the wintertime, although most of the crop goes to Europe, and locally-grown currants are occasionally found in summer at farmers' markets, especially in the Pacific Northwest.

GOOSEBERRIES

Gooseberries were first cultivated by the skillful gardeners of the low countries of Europe from the beginning of the sixteenth century. The Dutch name for the fruit, *kruisbezie*, was likely corrupted into their English name, gooseberry. They are known as *groseille maquereau* in French, meaning "mackerel currants," because a sauce made from these tart green berries traditionally accompanies dishes of oily mackerel fish in France and in England. Their old English name, fea-berry, came about because their juices were used to reduce fevers. A "gooseberry" is British slang for a person who is seen as a fifth wheel.

The fruits were probably first introduced into England in the mid-sixteenth century during the reign of Queen Elizabeth I. Toward the end of the eighteenth century, the gooseberry became a favorite of English cottage-horticulture, especially in Lancashire, where cotton-spinners raised numerous gooseberries in an effort to cultivate ever larger and sweeter varieties. Gooseberries, a fruit that does well in colder climates, are used in Northern Europe and Scandinavia for sauces, pies, sauces, puddings, chutneys, jams, and desserts. Because of their high pectin content, gooseberries also make excellent jelly.

It is believed that gooseberries were brought from England to the new colonies in 1629 by the Massachusetts Bay Colonists. The European gooseberry, however, was subject to mildew in the warm, humid summers of the East. Even today, few European varieties are grown in the East and the fruits thrive best in the cool coastal regions of the Pacific Northwest. Gooseberries are common in the British Isles, where they grown in copses (thickets of small trees and shrubs), hedgerows (thick bushes grown as borders), and around old ruins.

The European gooseberry, *Ribes grossularia*, is native to the Caucasus Mountains in North Africa; the American gooseberry, *Ribes hirtellum*, is native to northeastern and north-central United States and nearby Canada. European gooseberries can be as large as a small plum, but are usually about 1 inch long. American gooseberries are smaller (up to ½ inch long), perfectly round, and pink to wine-red when ripe. They are more productive then their European cousins, but are also more bland and innocuous in flavor. European cultivars are pure species, but virtually all American cultivars also have European genes.

The gooseberry, which grows singly or in pairs, is the size of a marble with tiny hard seeds in the middle and darker longitudinal lines that make them resemble mini world globes. The fruits range in color from green, white (gray-green), and yellow to shades of red from pink to purple and almost black. The gooseberry has a tart, but pleasing flavor all its own, and a smooth, almost creamy texture, somewhere between a strawberry and a grape, but must be cooked before eating.

RED, WHITE, AND BLACK CURRANTS

Currants are small berries with juicy flesh that may be red, white, gold, pink, or black. They are closely related to gooseberries. Red currants were collected from the wild for medicinal use as early as the fifteenth century. The three European varieties—red, white, and black—of this semi-transparent sweet-tart berry have been cultivated since well before the sixteenth century; the golden currant is a native American variety. Red and white currants were probably first cultivated as garden plants in Holland, Denmark, and the coastal plains surrounding the Baltic.

The berries have been known as corans or currans since 1550 in England, because they resemble the unrelated tiny Corinth grapes from the Greek Ionian island of Zante, sold as Zante currants when dried and Champagne grapes when fresh. Red currants were also known in England as "red gooseberries," and their alternate English name was "beyond-the-sea gooseberries." The French and Dutch names—groseilles d'outre mer (gooseberries from over the water) and overzee (over the sea)—indicate that the fruits may have first been imported, possibly by the Danes and Normans. The much older English name, ribes, is of ancient Indo-European origin and is common to many other languages.

Red currants are most popular in northern Europe and Scandinavia. Only a small amount of red currants are grown commercially in the United States. Red currants from Chile are now being marketed here, though most of that crop still goes to northern Europe, where demand is high.

Both red and black currant juice are popular in Germany and Eastern Europe. I find currant juices and preserves in my local Russian market. Frozen red currant purée is also available (see page 410). Red currants make an exceptionally tasty and quivering clear jelly, perfect to glaze a colorful fruit tart.

White currants are albino red currants, which arise spontaneously in several species. More versatile but less colorful than the red, white currants are good for cooking, but because of their lower acidity, they are also good to eat fresh. The best white currants are nearly transparent. Pink currants, which have colorless skin and pink flesh, fall between red and white types.

Black currants have a characteristic sweet but earthy aroma and are highly esteemed in Northern Europe. Their leaves also release the scent when rubbed and are used for tea. The dark blue-black fruits are astringent and must be cooked before eating. Black currants are best known for their use in making the famed cordial, crème de cassis, from the town of Cassis, near Dijon, France. Originally, black currants were used primarily for herbal medicines as they are outstandingly rich in vitamin C, and are high in antioxidants. Today currants are used primarily for juice, and the syrup that is essential for the kir cocktail–white wine and cassis syrup. The cocktail is named after Félix Kir, longtime mayor of Dijon, who popularized the drink by offering it at receptions to visiting delegations.

BAR-LE-DUC SEEDLESS CURRANT JELLY

In the 1300s, the monks of the town of Bar-le-Duc in Lorraine, France had the idea of removing the seeds from the red and white currants that grow in the region to make a particularly delicate preserve. Originally made only from rare white currants, today red and white currants go into the legendary crystal-clear jelly. Packaged in crystal jars, the exquisite confiture was a favorite of European nobility. In the late 1500s, Mary Stuart, Queen of France, called Bar-le-Duc "a ray of sunshine in a jar." After World War II, however, production of this highly labor-intensive specialty declined, and by the early 1970s, only one producer—91-year-old René Amiable—was left; and he'd decided it was time to close shop. When Jacques Dutriez, who was already in the preserves business in Bar-le-Duc, begged Amiable not to let this ancient art die, Amiable trained Dutriez and then sold him the business.

To create this unique product, which has been likened to sweet caviar on the tongue that bursts with flavor with the "pop" of each currant, fragile bunches of the small red and rare white currants unique to the Bar-le-Duc area are cut from their bushes as they ripen each July. Only two varieties of currants—the Versaillaise and the Roudom—are used. Women called *epepineuses* (seed extractors) use goose quills to flick out the tiny seeds without disturbing the delicate flesh of these fragile berries. The berries are then simmered in sugar syrup and poured into small, faceted glass jars. All the work must be done in a single day so the fruit stays at its peak of perfection. Depending on the harvest, annual production ranges from five- to twenty-thousand jars, which, despite their necessarily high price, disappear quickly off the shelves in fine stores.

Gooseberry Cobbler with Walnut Crunch

Gooseberries, which grow profusely in the hedgerows of England, are easily found at the market. In America, we are just starting to see fresh gooseberries for sale in our supermarkets. While they are in season—a short two weeks or so in summer—serve them in this tangy pale green cobbler with its flaky biscuit topping. The acidity of the fruit, offset by the sweetness of sugar, is mellowed by the buttery biscuit topping. Tapioca flour thickens the filling. See page 162 for more about tapioca. Serve it, as in England, with spoonfuls of impossibly rich and equally delicious Devonshire clotted cream, or with vanilla ice cream or Crème Anglaise, known in England as pouring custard (page 835).

YIELD: 6 TO 8 SERVINGS

Biscuits

6 ounces (1^1/$_2$ cups minus 1 tablespoon) unbleached
    all-purpose flour

^{1}/$_4$ cup sugar

1^1/$_2$ teaspoons baking powder

^{1}/$_4$ teaspoon fine sea salt

2 ounces (^{1}/$_2$ stick) unsalted butter, chilled
    and cut into bits

^{1}/$_2$ cup buttermilk

Filling

1 cup sugar

2 tablespoons tapioca flour, or substitute potato,
    wheat, rice or cornstarch.

1/2 teaspoon freshly grated nutmeg

Pinch salt

1 quart gooseberries

Assembly and Topping

1 tablespoon unsalted butter, softened

1/4 cup heavy cream

1/2 cup coarsely-chopped walnuts

1/4 cup well-packed light brown sugar

1/2 teaspoon ground cinnamon

Make the biscuits: Combine the dry ingredients: flour, sugar, baking powder, and salt in the bowl of a food processor. Pulse to combine, then add the butter and process until the mixture resembles oatmeal. Add the buttermilk and process just long enough for the mixture to form a ball. Transfer the dough to a plastic bag and shape into a flattened rectangle. Chill in the refrigerator for 1 hour or in the freezer for 30 minutes until firm but still malleable.

Make the filling: In a small bowl, combine the sugar, tapioca flour, nutmeg, and salt. Toss with the gooseberries and pour into the baking dish.

Assemble and bake: Preheat the oven to 375°F. Prepare an 8-inch baking dish, preferably ceramic or Pyrex glass by rubbing with 1 tablespoon of butter.

Roll out the dough about 1/2-inch thick, working the dough as little as possible so it doesn't toughen. Using a 3-inch fluted or plain round biscuit or cookie cutter, cut out the biscuits. Gently press together the scraps and reroll, cut out more biscuits, discarding any excess. Arrange the biscuits over the fruit, slightly overlapping. Brush the biscuits with the cream.

In a small bowl, combine the walnuts, brown sugar, and cinnamon. Sprinkle over the biscuits. Bake for about 40 minutes or until the fruit is bubbling and the biscuits are golden. Serve hot or warm.

Store this for 2 to 3 days refrigerated, but warm again before serving (cover with aluminum foil and bake at 350°F for about 20 minutes).

Black Currant– Apple Linzer Torte

Linzer torte originated in Linz, Austria, and is very distinctive looking, with its beautiful golden brown crust, filled with ruby red preserves peeking through the pretty lattice design. Printed recipes for this torte started to appear in the early 1700s. As far as recipes go, this one has stood the test of time as the dough is still made with ground almonds, sugar, butter, flour, and egg yolks, although sometimes ground hazelnuts are substituted.

The other change is the type of preserves that are used to fill a Linzer torte. Tradition tells us to use black currant preserves. But because they are hard to find in North America, we usually substitute raspberry preserves, although apricot and cranberry make the occasional appearance. The crust of a Linzer torte may be either white or brown in color, depending on whether you use blan-ched or toasted nuts in the dough (I prefer the more intense flavor of toasted nuts). Sometimes recipes even include cocoa powder (about 1 tablespoon) along with the toasted nuts, so if you are a chocolate fan, you may want to include this in your recipe. The secret to the melting texture of this dough is the cooked egg yolks, which add a silkiness that also absorbs the juices of the fruits as it bakes.

Dough

6 ounces (1 cup) skin-on hazelnuts, lightly toasted

$1/2$ pound (2 cups minus 2 tablespoons) unbleached
    bread flour

2 teaspoons ground cinnamon

$1/2$ teaspoon ground cloves

Pinch salt

$1/2$ pound (2 sticks) unsalted butter, softened

$1^{1}/_{2}$ cups sugar

Yolks of 4 hard-cooked eggs

Grated zest of 1 lemon (1 tablespoon)

Filling

3 pounds (6 to 8 medium) sweet-tart apples, such as
    Granny Smith or Fujis, peeled, cored, and diced

1 cup sugar

1 cup fresh black currants, washed and destemmed, or
$3/4$ cup black currant purée, or $1/2$ cup black currant
    preserves (cut the sugar to $3/4$ cup)

Make the dough: Place the hazelnuts, flour, cinnamon, cloves, and salt into the bowl of a food processor. Process until finely ground.

In the bowl of a standing mixer fitted with the paddle attachment, cream the butter and sugar until light and fluffy, 5 to 6 minutes. Beat in the egg yolks and lemon zest. Add the hazelnut mixture and beat just until the mixture comes together in moist clumps. Knead briefly until the dough comes together into a ball.

Divide the dough into two portions, about one-third and two-thirds each. Place the smaller portion in a plastic zipper-lock bag, press into a flattened block and chill for 1 hour in the refrigerator or 30 minutes in the freezer. Press the larger portion of the dough into a 10- to 11-inch tart pan. Make sure that the corners, where the sides and bottom of the dough meet, are not overly thick. Trim the edges, then chill for 1 hour in the refrigerator or 30 minutes in the freezer to set the shape.

Make the filling: Place the apples and sugar in a large non-aluminum heavy-bottomed saucepan and bring to a boil. Reduce the heat to low and simmer for 45 minutes, stirring often, until the mixture is quite thick. Add the black currants and cook another 15 minutes, or until the mixture is thick enough to show a clear streak on the bottom of the pot when stirred. Spread the dense mixture onto a baking sheet lined with parchment paper and set aside to cool completely. The filling should be quite firm.

Roll the reserved dough out between two sheets of wax paper. (Chill again until firm if the dough seems too soft.) Using a fluted-edged pastry wheel or a sharp knife, cut the dough into $1/2$ inch-wide strips. Arrange the strips on a baking pan lined with wax paper and chill until firm but still malleable, about 20 minutes.

Preheat the oven to 350°F. Spread the fruit filling evenly over the bottom of the chilled crust.

To make the lattice topping, lay six dough strips, evenly spaced, across the torte. Fold back every other strip on top of itself to about 2 inches from the edge of the torte. Place a dough strip perpendicular to the folded edges and unfold the strips. Next, fold the previously unfolded set of strips back on themselves in the same fashion and repeat, placing another crosswise strip against the folded edges and unfolding the strips. Repeat until the whole torte is covered by the woven lattice. Trim the edges of the strips that stick out from the edges. Use the remaining strips of dough to form an edge. Lay the strips (it's okay if they are in pieces) around the edge of the torte. Using a fork, press the strips into the edges of the bottom crust to seal the edges.

Place the torte on a baking pan to catch any drips and bake for 45 minutes. When done, the crust will be golden brown and start to shrink away slightly from the sides of the pan. The filling will be set but the tart will not be firm until it cools. Remove from the oven and cool completely on a wire rack before unmolding. If desired, refrigerate for up to 3 days before serving, but serve at room temperature.

Hungarian Red Currant–Hazelnut Torte

This Viennese-style nut torte combines hazelnuts and red currants—two ingredients favored by those living in the former Austro-Hungarian Empire. The light, nut-thickened cake is split and filled with red currant preserves, and a classic buttercream mixed with more toasted hazelnuts is spread over the cake. If you're lucky enough to find fresh red currants, garnish the cake with the small branchlets, but make sure your guests remove the fruits from their stems before eating them.

YIELD: ONE 9-INCH TORTE; 10 TO 12 SERVINGS

Cake

$1/4$ pound ($1/4$ cup) hazelnuts, toasted

$1/4$ pound (1 cup minus 2 tablespoons) cake flour or 3 ounces unbleached all-purpose flour plus 1 ounce potato starch

1 teaspoon baking powder

$1/2$ teaspoon fine sea salt

6 large eggs, separated

$3/4$ cup sugar

1 teaspoon vanilla extract

2 ounces ($1/2$ stick) unsalted butter, melted and cooled

Buttercream and Assembly

3 large egg yolks

$1^1/2$ cups confectioners' sugar

1 teaspoon vanilla extract

2 tablespoons potato starch, substitute corn, wheat, or rice starch

$3/4$ cup whole milk, scalded

$1/2$ pound (2 sticks) unsalted butter, cut into bits and softened

6 ounces (1 cup) hazelnuts, toasted

1 cup red currant preserves, heated

$1/2$ pint fresh red currants, for garnish

Make the cake: Preheat the oven to 350°F. Prepare a 9-inch springform or removable bottom cake pan by spraying with nonstick baker's coating, or rubbing with softened butter and dusting with flour, shaking off the excess.

Combine the hazelnuts, flour, baking powder, and salt in the bowl of a food processor and process until finely ground.

In the bowl of a standing mixer fitted with the paddle attachment, beat the egg yolks, $1/2$ cup of the sugar and the vanilla until the mixture is light and fluffy, about 5 minutes. Pour in the butter and beat again until the mixture is smooth. Fold in the hazelnut mixture. Transfer to a wide shallow bowl.

In the clean and greaseless bowl of a standing mixer fitted with the whisk attachment, beat the egg whites until fluffy, then add the remaining $1/4$ cup sugar and continue beating until the whites are firm and glossy, 4 to 5 minutes. Fold the meringue into the yolk mixture in thirds so as not to deflate it. Spread the batter evenly into the pan and rap the pan on a work surface to release any large air bubbles.

Bake for 35 minutes or until the cake starts to come away from the sides of the pan and a skewer inserted in the center comes out clean. Transfer the pan to a wire cooling rack. Cool until the cake is warm to the touch, then remove the pan bottom and cool to room temperature.

Make the buttercream: In a medium bowl, whisk together the egg yolks, 1 cup of the confectioners' sugar, and the vanilla. Add the potato starch and beat briefly to combine, then pour in the hot milk, whisking to combine into a smooth cream. Transfer the mixture to a medium, heavy-bottomed, nonreactive pot. Bring to a boil over moderate heat, whisking constantly, especially at the edges, until the custard thickens and just starts to bubble, about 3 minutes. Remove from the heat, transfer to a mixing bowl, and cool to lukewarm, whisking often to prevent it from forming a skin. Beat in the butter. (If the custard is lumpy, transfer it to the bowl of a food processor and process until smooth.)

Combine the hazelnuts and the remaining $1/2$ cup of confectioners' sugar in the bowl of a food processor and process until finely ground. Beat the hazelnut mixture into the custard and refrigerate until firm, about 1 hour. Or scrape the mixture into a stainless-steel bowl and cool over a mixture of ice and water.

Assemble the cake: Using a long, serrated knife, cut a very small notch, about $1/4$-inch deep, out of the side of the cake to use as a guide. Cut the cake horizontally into two layers. Place one layer, cut-side up, on a 9-inch-diameter cake pan bottom or cardboard round. Spread the red currant preserves evenly on the cake layer. Re-assemble the cake, using the cut wedge as a guide to line up the layers in their original position, and pressing down lightly so the layers adhere. Chill until the jam is set, about 30 minutes.

Transfer the buttercream to the bowl of a standing mixer and beat with the whisk for about 5 minutes or until light and fluffy. Spread the buttercream over the top and sides of the cake. Arrange the fresh red currants (if available) over the top of the cake. Refrigerate until the buttercream sets, at least 1 hour. (The torte can be made 1 to 2 days ahead. Allow the torte to come to room temperature before serving.) The cake freezes well up to 2 months (without the currants).

English Summer Fruit Pudding with Lemon and Mint

English cookbooks abound with substantial steamed sweet puddings suitable for the cold, damp winter. Once summer finally arrives, people look forward to summer pudding, made from summer's abundant berries, sweetened and layered with firm white bread to soak up their juices and left overnight to set. (Sometimes angel food cake is used instead of bread, but to me this makes an overly sweet pudding.) Any of the following red fruits are used in England: raspberries, strawberries, pitted red cherries, red currants, black currants, gooseberries, and even cooked rhubarb. In this recipe, I've combined berries with peaches and mangoes for contrast of color and texture, with a hint of refreshing mint and lemon. Crème Anglaise (English pouring custard) is the traditional and essential accompaniment for summer pudding.

YIELD: 8 TO 12 SERVINGS

1 pint red currants or raspberries

1 pint blueberries

1 pint red or green gooseberries, small stems picked off, or more blueberries

2 sprigs fresh mint, preferably spearmint

1 lemon, 2 ribbons of zest peeled with a potato peeler, then juiced

$1/2$ cup sugar

1 pint blackberries, or Marionberries, olalliberries, or loganberries

3 firm but ripe peaches, preferably free-stone, diced

2 firm but ripe mangoes, preferably Ataulfo (Champagne mangoes), peeled and diced or more peaches

$1^1/2$ pound loaf day-old firm white sandwich bread, sliced and crusts removed (such as Buttermilk Sourdough White Sandwich Bread, page 00)

3 cups Crème Anglaise (page 835)

Sprigs of fresh mint, preferably spearmint, for garnish

Place the red currants, blueberries, gooseberries, mint, lemon zest, lemon juice, and sugar in a medium nonreactive pot and heat until the blueberries turn dark and shiny. Remove from the heat, discard the lemon zest and mint, and stir in the blackberries, peaches, and mangoes.

Rub a high-sided container, such as a large French charlotte mold or a soufflé dish, lightly with oil. Line it with plastic wrap, fitting it tightly to the mold and allowing the edges to overhang. Cut the bread to fit the bottom and sides of the dish, using triangles for the bottom, middle, and top layers, and 1- to $1^1/2$-inch wide strips of bread for the walls. Arrange the triangles tightly fitted together to form the bottom layer (which will become the top), and then place the wide strips against the wall of the mold, fitting the strips tightly together.

Spoon in half the fruit mixture, cover with a layer of the bread cut into triangles, and repeat, ending with more bread. Cover with the plastic wrap, and then top with a plate, cake pan, or tart bottom to fit just inside the bowl and place a weight on top, such as a can of tomatoes. Refrigerate overnight to set the pudding.

To serve, unwrap the plastic wrap and carefully run a knife round the edges to loosen, then invert the pudding on to a shallow serving dish with a lipped edge. Remove the plastic wrap.

Serve cold with Crème Anglaise and a sprig of mint for each portion. Store the pudding refrigerated for 2 to 3 days.

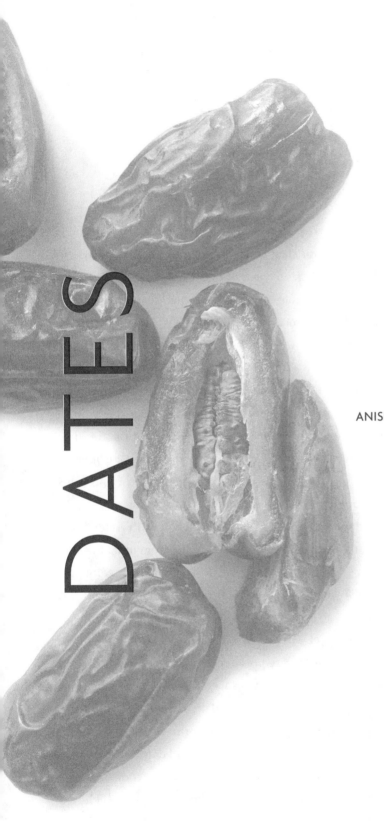

DATES

Date Varieties . . .420

A DATE IN A BLANKET . . .421

MAKROUD (TUNISIAN SEMOLINA
COOKIES STUFFED WITH DATES) . . .422

ANISE-SCENTED DATE-ORANGE SPIRALS . . .423

OATMEAL-PECAN FRUITIES . . .425

DATES

Like the nomads of antiquity and modern times, traveling with my heavy backpack across Canada, I found that dates satisfied my sweet tooth with a ready to eat snack that tasted just as good then as when nomads traveling in camel caravans would gather the fruits in desert oases. The hugely swollen bottom lip I got from a wasp that stung that tender inner flesh as I munched my dates on the side of the road while waiting for a ride is a less felicitous, though equally enduring memory.

Date palms may exceed 100 feet and never stop growing until they eventually topple over. A date palm will live about 5 years, with each year's growth emerging from above the previous year's. One date palm can produce 150 kilos (330 pounds) of dates, or about 1000 date fruits. Even in California, date growers use Arabic terms to describe the stages of a date. When the fruit has reached its full size and color and is ready to pick, it is at the *khala* stage. Next comes the *rutag* stage, when the date softens, darkens, and begins to shrink. The final stage, *tamar* (date in Arabic) is reached when the fruit is fully cured and ready for packing.

According to legend, the date, *Phoenix dactylifera*, flourished in the Garden of Eden, located also bylegend, near the junction of the Tigris and Euphrates rivers in the Fertile Crescent. In ancient Phoenicia, a deep-purple dye long reserved for royalty was derived from the Murex shellfish. Both Phoenician and "phoenix," the legendary bird reborn in the flames, derive from the Greek *phoinix*, meaning "purple-red." Phoenix was probably adopted as the genus name for the date because the fruits are tinted purple. *Dactylifera* is a Greek word meaning finger, because the fruits grow in clusters of dark-brown "fingers."

Dates originated somewhere with water in the hot dry region that stretches from India through the Middle East to North Africa. Date palm gardens were well-established in Mesopotamia 4,000 to 5,000 years ago, its sweet fruit essential to their diet. They were a staple food in Egypt where the fruits were preserved by two methods still used today. Firm dates were dried in the sunlight for two or three days and then left in the shade to dry completely to tamar form. Moist dates were pressed into baskets made of date palms and left for several days similar to sweet, chewy pressed dates from Iran. According to Egyptian folklore, a handful of dates soaked in fresh goat's milk overnight and ground in the same milk the next morning improves sexual performance.

The date palm flourished in Israel near Jericho since the Neolithic period. The ancient Greeks and Romans were fond of dates and imported the best from Jericho. Persian poets extolled the date palm's "three hundred and sixty" uses. The Chinese began importing dates from Persia during the T'ang dynasty (618–907 CE).

According to the Psalms, "The righteous bloom like a date palm, they thrive like a cedar in Lebanon... They shall still bring forth fruit in old age." In the Song of Songs the beloved is described: "Thy stature is like a palm tree and thy breasts to clusters of grapes. I said, I will go up to the palm tree, I will take hold of the boughs thereof." For the harvest holiday of Sukkot, the Jews were commanded to take "date branches, the branch of a thick tree (myrtle), and willows of the creek," which they gathered into a bundle and waved about during prayers

One Christian story about dates relates to the flight of Joseph and Mary to Egypt. Having left their country in great haste, they had taken no food with them. As they entered the date palm groves of Egypt, one of the trees gently bent its head towards them so deeply that they could feast on its sweet fruits while the cherubs who were seated on the fronds welcomed them by singing and wishing them peace.

In Arab tradition, dates were created not from the clay used for other plants, but rather from material left over after creating Adam. A story is told of a man who asked the Prophet Mohammed "'How can I know that you are the Prophet of God?' Prophet Mohammed answered, 'I can call the date fruits from that tree to come down', and so he did. After that he ordered the date fruits to return up again and be reconnected to the tree and the fruits obeyed. Then the Arabian man believed that the Prophet Mohammed was the Prophet of God."

The Spanish introduced dates into California in 1765 near Mission San Ignacio. Today, dates grow in dry, hot parts of the United States, especially California and Arizona, although the country is not one of the world's top date producers. One hundred million date palms grow in the world today, more than half in the Arab world. Egypt and Saudi Arabia are the largest producers, though Algeria, Iran, Iraq, and Pakistan also have significant crops.

Moroccan royalty considered Medjool dates the ultimate delicacy and kept the fruit only for their personal use. However, in the 1920s, disease threatened the Medjools and only the trees growing in the Bou Denib oasis survived. In a radical move to save the precious trees, the Chariff of Morocco presented the United States with eleven date palms, which were successfully planted in the Coachella Valley in California's southern desert. Today, the Bard Valley Growers Cooperative produces seventy percent of all Medjools in California, the largest Medjool date region in the world.

There are three types of dates: soft dates have

soft, giving flesh, are high in moisture and low in sugar; semi–dry dates have firm flesh, are low in moisture, and high in sugar; dry or bread dates have dry, hard flesh, are low in moisture, and high in sugar. Nearly all the dates sold in America are of the semi–dry type. Dry or soft dates are eaten out–of–hand and may be seeded and stuffed with fillings such as almonds, candied orange and lemon peel, and marzipan. Dates can also be chopped and used in a range of sweet and savory baked goods and puddings.

Dates are processed into cubes, paste, spread, date syrup or "honey" called "dibs," powder (date sugar), vinegar, and alcohol. In India, North Africa, Ghana, and Côte d'Ivoire, date palms are tapped for their sweet sap which is converted into palm sugar (known as jaggery or gur), molasses, or alcoholic beverages. In times of scarcity, the finely ground seeds are mixed with flour to make bread.

Dates keep very well and do not need to be refrigerated, although they will continue to shrink and can develop sugar crystals as they dry. Ripe dates are about eighty percent sugar with the remainder consisting of protein, fat, and minerals. In this chapter, I fill the savory cheddar cheese and curry pastries called A Date in a Blanket (page 421) and the Makroud (Tunisian Semolina Cookies) (page 422) with dates. The Anise–Scented Date-Orange Spirals (page 423) are filled with a soft, sweet date filling, and the Oatmeal–Pecan Fruities are studded with chopped dates. Elsewhere, I combine chewy dates and crunchy apples for my Apple–Date Buckwheat Muffins (page 188).

DATE VARIETIES

DEGLET NOOR: This semi-dry date originated in Tunisia and was imported to the United States from Algeria. It makes up ninety percent of California's crop. The Deglet Noor is popular in the United States and is important in Europe. It has a delicate flavor and firm, textured, translucent flesh with amber to light red color and is quite sweet, though mild in flavor.

HALAWI: This medium-sized soft, golden brown date originated in Iraq. Its name means "sweet" and it is in fact quite sweet with caramel-like texture.

MEDJOOL: This large, luscious fruit averages over two inches in length and is prized in America and the Middle East. To obtain the maximum size for these huge, plump dates, growers thin out about eighty percent of the fruits. The dates are harvested by hand by men who must climb the forty-foot tall palms to pick them. The fruits are also hand-packed. In winter, colorful red boxes of Medjools appear in the produce aisle at local supermarkets. Medjools are not cheap and must be pitted, although this is easy: just cut a slit down the middle and pull out the large, hard pit.

THOORY: Often known as the "bread date," the dry, though sweet and nutty Thoory is the staple date of desert nomads and has hard flesh and chewy texture. It is also grown in California.

ZAHIDI: The oldest-known cultivar, the semi-dry Zahidi is consumed in great quantity in the Middle East. Introduced into California about 1900, this medium-sized fruit is sugary-sweet, cylindrical in shape, and light golden-brown in color. Because of their high sugar content, Zahidis are used in the Middle East to make date syrup, or dibs (a very early use of dates).

KHADRAWI: This small, dark, mahogany-colored date, which originated in Iraq, has a dry flaky skin. This heavy-cropping fruit is high in moisture.

A Date in a Blanket

In this recipe, a light curry-infused cheddar cheesy pastry dough blankets a whole date, which has been stuffed with a blanched almond. So, in one mouthful, you get savory, sharp cheese, aromatic curry spice, honeyed chewy fruitiness, and crunchy, mellow almond. What a combination! When two ex-sisters-in-law, Ruth and Dena Lefkowitz, came for lunch, we couldn't stop eating these dainty sweetmeats. As I served the little tidbits, the two asked me if they were "pigs in a blanket." "No," I replied, "They're dates in a blanket." Dena said, "Why not call them 'A Date in a Blanket'? Who doesn't want one of those?" The smaller Deglet Noor dates that are the most common type found in the supermarket work best here.

YIELD: 60 HORS D'OEUVRE PASTRIES

½ pound (2 cups minus 2 tablespoons) unbleached all-purpose flour

2 teaspoons curry powder

½ teaspoon cayenne pepper

½ teaspoon fine sea salt

¼ pound (1 stick) unsalted butter, softened

½ pound extra-sharp Cheddar cheese, grated (about 2 cups)

¼ cup milk

1 pound whole pitted dates

1 cup blanched almonds

1 large egg, lightly beaten with 1 tablespoon milk, for the egg wash

Line an 18 x 13-inch half sheet pan (or other large baking pan) with parchment paper or a silicone baking mat. Whisk together the dry ingredients: flour, curry powder, cayenne pepper, and salt.

In the bowl of a standing mixer fitted with the paddle attachment, beat the butter and cheese until well blended and creamy, 4 to 5 minutes. Add the flour mixture and the milk and beat just until the mixture forms a ball. Transfer to a plastic bag and shape into a flattened rectangle. Chill in the refrigerator for 1 hour or in the freezer for 30 minutes until firm but still malleable.

Meanwhile, split the dates open using a paring knife. Stuff each date with an almond, then press the edges back together. (Don't worry if you happen to split some of the dates in half. Simply press the almond on one half and cover with the second half.)

Roll out the dough to ³⁄₈-inch thick and cut out 3-inch circles, rerolling the scraps if desired. Wrap each stuffed date in a circle of dough, completely encasing the date and forming a small cylinder.

Preheat the oven to 375°F.

Roll each date in the egg wash. Arrange the date cylinders on the baking pan and bake until golden brown, about 25 minutes.

(If desired, make the dough ahead and refrigerate up to 3 days or freeze up to 3 months. Or freeze the filled pastries, baking them as needed at 350°F for about 40 minutes.) Store covered and at room temperature up to 3 days.

Makroud (Tunisian Semolina Cookies Stuffed with Dates)

These date-filled cookies are a specialty of the city of Kairouan in southern Tunisia and are also a favorite in Algeria. In Libya, a slightly different version flavored with ginger, called macrute, *were traditionally prepared to celebrate the Jewish springtime holiday of Purum. To make the makroud, you prepare a soft, slightly mealy semolina dough enriched with olive oil and butter (the butter is perhaps a legacy of the many years of French influence in the region). After shaping the dough into a trough, you fill it with a mixture of sweet, spiced dates scented with orange blossom water, a favorite combination in the Maghreb (North Africa) and cover it with more dough. After cutting into individual lozenges, the cookies are deep-fried, drained, and soaked in honey syrup. Makroud get their name from an Arabic word meaning rhomboid, referring to their special shape. (See the Syrian Mahmoul on page 466 for a related cookie.)*

YIELD: 5 DOZEN COOKIES

Dough

1½ pounds (4 cups minus 1 tablespoon) fine semolina

½ teaspoon fine sea salt

Pinch of ground turmeric, optional for golden color

Pinch of baking soda

5 ounces (1 stick plus 2 tablespoons) unsalted butter, melted and cooled

6 tablespoons extra-virgin olive oil

Filling

10 ounces pitted dates

½ cup water

2 tablespoons unsalted butter

2 teaspoons orange blossom water

1 teaspoon ground cinnamon

½ teaspoon ground allspice

Pinch ground cloves

Grated zest of 1 orange (4 teaspoons)

Syrup

1 cup water

1 cup sugar

½ cup honey

Assembly

2 teaspoons orange blossom water

1 cup water

1 quart grapeseed, rice bran, or canola oil, for frying

Make the dough: Combine the semolina, salt, turmeric, baking soda, butter, and oil, and let the mixture rest for at least 2 hours, or up to overnight, at room temperature until thickened.

Make the filling: Check the dates for pits. Combine the dates with the water in a microwaveable bowl and microwave for 3 to 4 minutes, or until the dates are tender and the liquid has been absorbed. (Alternatively, place the dates on a steamer rack over a pot of boiling water, cover and steam for about 10 minutes, or until quite tender.)

Place the dates, butter, orange blossom water, cinnamon, allspice, cloves, and orange zest in the bowl of a food processor and process to a paste. Transfer the mixture to a bowl and cool to room temperature, or refrigerate for up to 3 days before use.

Make the syrup: Bring the water, sugar, and honey to the boil in a medium heavy-bottomed pot, skimming off the white foam. Keep the syrup hot, or reheat when needed.

Assemble the cookies: Finish the dough: Rub the dough mixture between your fingers to make it crumble finely like couscous. Using a wooden spoon or a silicone spatula, combine the dough with the orange blossom water and the water to make a soft dough. Divide the dough into 4 pieces.

Roll each portion of dough into a tube about 3 inches long and 1 inch wide. Press a channel into the tube with your forefinger, without breaking through the dough. Fill the channel with the date mixture, then close the channel to cover the filling completely. Flatten the log a bit with your hands, then cut it on the diagonal into lozenge shapes, about 1 inch in length.

In a wok, a large heavy-duty frying pan, preferably cast-iron, or an electric deep-fryer, heat the oil to 365°F, or until shimmering hot, and the air above the pot feels hot when you hold your hand about 3 inches above the oil. Lay the cookies into the oil and fry for 3 to 4 minutes or until golden brown, working in batches. Scoop the cookies from the oil using a slotted spoon or a wire skimmer and drain on a wire rack.

As soon as all the cookies have been fried and drained, dip each one thoroughly into the hot syrup. Drain and allow the cookies to dry. Store in an airtight container up to 5 days at room temperature.

Anise-Scented Date-Orange Spirals

These thin cookie spirals are filled with chewy date purée flavored with orange juice, orange zest, and aniseed. Though anise complements the intensely sweet flavor of the dates, if you don't care for its licorice-like flavor, substitute 1$\frac{1}{2}$ teaspoons ground cinnamon. The filling is spread in a layer over a rich and easy-to-roll cream cheese dough, then rolled up and refrigerated till firm. The cookies are then ready to slice and bake whenever you need an interesting accompaniment to coffee or tea. Make sure all the dates are pitted; even if you buy pitted dates, there will inevitably be one last hard pit that will get caught in the blade of the food processor if you don't check them carefully. (Of course, if you do conscientiously check for pits, you probably won't find any.)

YIELD: 3 DOZEN COOKIES

Dough

7 ounces (2 cups) unbleached all-purpose flour

1/2 teaspoon baking powder

1/4 teaspoon baking soda

1/2 teaspoon fine sea salt

1/4 pound (1 stick) unsalted butter, softened

1/4 pound cream cheese, softened

1/2 cup sugar

1 large egg yolk

1 teaspoon vanilla extract

Filling

3/4 pound (1 3/4 cups) dates, preferably Medjool, pitted

1/4 cup sugar

Grated zest of 1 orange (4 teaspoons)

1 tablespoon finely ground aniseed

1 cup orange juice

Make the dough: Whisk together the dry ingredients: flour, baking powder, baking soda, and salt.

In the bowl of a standing mixer, beat together the butter, cream cheese, and the sugar until light and fluffy, 5 to 6 minutes. Add the egg yolk and vanilla, and beat together to combine. Add the flour mixture and beat just long enough for the mixture to come together and form moist clumps. Knead the dough briefly by hand just until it forms a ball. Transfer to a plastic bag and shape into a flattened rectangle. Chill in the refrigerator for 1 hour or in the freezer for 30 minutes.

Make the filling: Combine the dates, sugar, orange zest, and the aniseed. Purée about one-quarter of the mixture at a time in the food processor, adding the orange juice as needed to make a soft, gooey paste.

Continue until all the dates have been puréed and combine with any remaining orange juice.

Roll the dough out between two sheets of lightly floured wax paper into an even rectangle about 3/8-inch thick, then chill for 30 minutes again or until cold.

Spoon the date mixture in small dollops evenly over the dough. Oil your hands and spread the date mixture evenly over the dough, leaving a 1/2-inch border at the edges. Starting with the long side of the dough, roll the dough, jelly roll fashion, into a tight log. Chill the log, wrapped in wax paper for at least 4 hours or until firm, or up to 3 days.

Preheat the oven to 350°F. Line two 18 x 13-inch half sheet pans (or other large baking pan) with parchment paper or silicone baking mats.

Using a sharp knife, slice the dough log into 1/3-inch thick rounds and arrange about 2 inches apart on the baking pans. Bake the cookies in batches in the middle of oven, for 12 minutes or until pale golden. Cool to room temperature on a wire rack.

Store at room temperature in an airtight container for 4 to 5 days. Alternatively, freeze the roll or part of the roll. Defrost just long enough for the dough to be firm but malleable, slice, and bake.

Oatmeal–Pecan Fruities

They may be old-fashioned, but they sure are packed full of chunky fruits and nuts. Here, instead of the more familiar additions of raisins and walnuts, the cookies get a share of bittersweet candied orange peel, sweet, chewy dates, tart red dried cranberries, and chopped pecans. For more colorful cookies, reserve a portion of the fruits and the nuts and press a few of each into the top of eazch cookie before baking. Once the dough balls have been formed, they will freeze perfectly, ready for baking. Spread in a single layer on a pan lined with parchment or wax paper and freeze until hard. Transfer to zipper-locked freezer bags with the air squeezed out and freeze.

YIELD: 36 TO 48 COOKIES

¼ pound (1 cup plus 2 tablespoons) white whole wheat flour

¼ pound (1½ cups) oatmeal, not instant

½ teaspoon fine sea salt

½ teaspoon baking soda

¼ pound (1 stick) unsalted butter, softened

½ cup sugar

½ cup well-packed dark brown sugar

2 teaspoons vanilla extract

2 large eggs

2 ounces (6 tablespoons chopped) candied orange peel, homemade (page 225) or purchased

¼ pound (¾ cup) pitted dates, sliced

2 ounces (½ cup plus 2 tablespoons) dried cranberries

6 ounces (1½ cups) pecans, roughly chopped

Preheat the oven to 350°F. Line two 18 x 13-inch half sheet pans with parchment paper or silicone baking mats.

In a large bowl, whisk together the dry ingredients: flour, oatmeal, salt, and baking soda.

In the bowl of a standing mixer fitted with the paddle attachment, cream the butter, sugar, dark brown sugar, and vanilla until light and creamy, 5 to 6 minutes. Beat in the eggs, one at a time. Add the flour mixture and beat just enough for the mixture to come together and form moist clumps. Add the candied orange peel, dates, cranberries, and pecans, and beat briefly to combine.

Scoop or spoon the dough into walnut-sized balls. Arrange the balls equidistant from each other in rows of 3 and 2 on the baking pans and press down with your palm to flatten slightly. Bake for 18 to 20 minutes or until lightly browned. Cool to room temperature on a wire rack.

Store at room temperature in a cookie tin or similar container for up to 1 week.

EGGS

Egg Grades . . .430

Parts of the Egg . . .430

Separating Eggs . . .431

Egg Yolks . . .431

Copper Egg White Bowls . . .432

Egg Whites . . .432

Blood Spots in Eggs . . .433

Freshness of Eggs . . .433

Buying and Storing Eggs . . .434

From Molecular Gastronomy
Expert Hervé This . . .434

SMOKED SALMON AND
SPINACH QUICHE . . .434

Lox, Nova, Smoked, and
Kippered Salmon . . .435

From Molecular Gastronomy
Expert Hervé This . . .436

B'STILLA OF CHICKEN . . .436

TORTA PASQUALINA GENOVESE . . .438

About Ligurian Prescinseua . . .439

BONÈT PIEMONTESE: CHOCOLATE-
AMARETTI BAKED CUSTARD . . .439

Amaretti . . .440

PAN DI SPAGNA . . .441

SEPHARDIC PAN LEVI COOKIES . . .442

AUSTRALIAN PAVLOVA WITH LEMON
FILLING AND TROPICAL FRUITS . . .442

GERMAN MUERBETEIG DOUGH
(MELLOW DOUGH) . . .444

EGGS

I happen to love anything made with eggs: give me a baked custard, savory or sweet flan, crème brulée, quiche, nut meringue, sponge cake, gelato, semifreddo, or macaroon and I'm happy. Eggs are almost indispensable in baking: just think how hard it would be to bake without them, as vegans and people who are allergic to eggs well know. Eggs, along with flour, provide the structure to baked goods, acting as the "glue" to bind all the other ingredients together. They provide leavening along with golden color, velvety mouthfeel, and rich flavor to doughs and batters.

In this book, I use only chicken eggs, though duck eggs work quite well for baking. Other eggs, such as goose and quail are not generally used for baking. It's becoming much more common to find all-natural eggs, even in standard supermarkets, which will be generally firmer, with deeper-colored and richer yolks, and thicker shells.

When beaten either whole or separately, at room temperature or heated over steaming water, egg proteins trap the air incorporated into them in small bubbles, which expand in the heat of the oven, causing the product to rise. Eggs, especially lecithin-rich yolks (a natural emulsifier) act as a thickener in custards, flans, and pastry cream. Thinned out with water, milk, or cream, whole eggs, whites, or yolks are painted onto baked goods like breads, tarts, and cookies for shine. Egg whites go into meringues and similar products like macaroons and meringue and nut meringue cake layers.

The magical egg, which symbolizes the annual rebirth of the earth, played a central role in the springtime rituals of ancient cultures. Once the long, dark winter was over, the earth burst with green and was reborn just as the egg miraculously burst with life. The Romans, Gauls, Chinese, Egyptians, and Persians all cherished the egg as a symbol of the universe. With the advent of Christianity, the symbolism of the egg came to represent, not nature's rebirth, but the rebirth of man. Early Christians maintained that every good Christian should eat at least one egg on Easter: easy to do with all the egg-filled Easter breads made in places like Italy and Greece, including the Torta Pasqualina Genovese (page 438).

The ancient Persians painted eggs for their New Year festival, *Nowrooz*, which falls on the spring equinox, a tradition alive today. During the ritual Jewish Seder dinner held at the beginning of the springtime holiday of Passover, a roasted hard-boiled egg dipped in salt water symbolizes both new life and the sacrifice once offered at the Holy Temple in Jerusalem. After a funeral, Jewish mourners eat a simple meal of hard-cooked eggs and bread: the egg representing new life in the midst of death, the bread the basic food of life. The egg became intertwined with Passover and the often concurrent Christian celebration of Easter. (Because of their connectedness, in Italian, both Easter and Passover are called *Pasqua*.)

Leghorns and other chicken breeds with white feathers and earlobes, lay white eggs; Rhode Island Reds, Plymouth Rocks and other breeds with red feathers and earlobes lay brown eggs. Americans prefer white eggs, except in New England where brown shells are preferred. Because brown eggs come from larger birds that eat more, brown eggs are usually more expensive and develop thicker shells. I prefer brown eggs for the sensory pleasure of handling these warm brown eggs and for their thick, easy to peel shells. Specialty farmers now raise chickens that lay blue eggs, called Araucan, a hybrid of two South American breeds: the Collonca and the Quetros.

In this chapter, a combination of whole eggs, for light, yet firm texture, and egg yolks, for richness and unctuous mouthfeel, go into the baked custard filling for the Smoked Salmon and Spinach Quiche (page 434). In the Moroccan B'stilla of Chicken (page 436), an elaborate saffron-infused chicken pie, partially scrambled eggs combined with chicken act as a binder; the eggs set completely when baked. In the Torta Pasqualina (Easter Pie) (page 438) from Genoa, Italy, whole eggs are broken into hollows made in a vegetable filling with spring greens and artichokes.

In the Pan di Spagna (Spanish bread or cake in Italian) (page 441), an Italian egg-foam cake with Sephardic Jewish origins, egg yolks are beaten with sugar until very light, then combined with the separately beaten whites and just enough flour to provide structure. It is similar in result the classic French Genoise cake (cake from Genoa), in which whole eggs are beaten over steaming hot water until warm, light, and thick. Flour, and sometimes a bit of butter, is folded in and the cake is baked. See the Chocolate Sponge Cake (page 339) and the Torta Gianduia (page 506) for cake using the Genoise method. The Sephardic Pan Levi Cookies (page 442) are basically Pan di Spagna batter formed into cookies and baked until crispy and dry.

Because sponge cakes are rather dry, made with little if any fat, they are often soaked in liqueur-laden syrup and layered with creamy fillings. The elaborate Torta di Zabaglione (page 480) combines Pan di Spagna, the light egg-yolk and Marsala wine cooked foam called *zabaglione* in Italian and *sabayon* in France, and crunchy oven-dried egg white meringue chunks. The Australian Pavlova with Lemon Filling and Tropical Fruits (page 442) is made from egg white meringue thickened with a small amount of starch and a touch of vinegar to keep it tender. Eggs, cream, and chocolate form the Bonèt Piemontese: Chocolate–Amaretti Baked Custard (page 439); crushed amaretti macaroons add crunch. The German Muerbeteig Dough: Mellow Dough (page 444) gets its richness from egg yolks.

EGG GRADES

We buy eggs by grade, according to the thickness of the shell and the firmness of the white. AA is the best, followed by A (most supermarket eggs), B–grade eggs have thin shells and watery whites. You can buy perfectly adequate inexpensive tray eggs (30 to the tray) in warehouse clubs, but note that they will have thin, easily broken shells. Eggs are sized from medium to jumbo (as in condoms, there is no such thing as small), with pee–wees at less than 1 pound per dozen the exception to the rule. At the other end of the size spectrum, jumbos weigh 2 pounds per dozen.

PARTS OF THE EGG

The egg consists of the thick, clear white (albumen)—about two-thirds of the egg's total weight—and the yellow, gold, or even red yolk—about one-third of its weight. The protein in egg whites coagulates at 150°F; the protein in the egg starts to coagulate at 158°F, but it fully thickens without curdling at 165°F, the temperature to which custards are heated.

The ropy strand of material that anchors the yolk in the center of the white is called the chalazae. The more prominent the chalazae, the fresher the egg. Although, it is perfectly fine to eat, the more squeamish may prefer to pull it off, or strain it out of beaten eggs before cooking for perfectly smooth texture.

An egg defends itself against bacterial contamination with its calcium-rich eggshell. Thousands of tiny pores in the shell allow moisture and carbon dioxide out and air in. When the egg is laid, the hen puts a protective coating on the outside. USDA regulations require that eggs be washed, sanitized, and then coated with tasteless, natural mineral oil for protection.

As an egg ages, air forms a pocket in the empty space between the white and shell, usually (though not always) at the large end of the egg. A large air pocket is a sign of an old egg; a fresh egg will have little to no air pocket. The air pocket will be especially noticeable when the eggs have been hard-cooked and shelled..

SEPARATING EGGS

It is easier to separate eggs when they are cold, although for baking, eggs work best if they are at room temperature. Separate the eggs, cover the bowls and leave them at room temperature for about 20 minutes before proceeding with the recipe. It is important not to allow any fatty yolk to mix in with the whites, which will prevent the whites from achieving their full volume when whipped. The safest way to do this is to have three bowls ready. Crack the egg in half and transfer the yolk back and forth between the two shell halves shell allowing the white to drain into one bowl. Put the yolk, which ideally will still be whole, into the second bowl. Continue, using the third bowl for one egg white at a time, so if some yolk gets mixed in with the white, you'll only lose one egg (save it for an omelet or egg wash).

If you do happen to get some egg yolk in with the white, remove the unwanted yolk by using an empty eggshell, because the yolk will stick to the shell. Egg yolks will immediately start to form a skin after being separated. Cover the yolks directly with plastic wrap or with a thin layer of water to keep them moist and refrigerate up to two days before use. Egg yolks may be frozen, but they must first be mixed with sugar or salt to keep them from coagulating.

Always use the size egg that is called for in the recipe. If the size is not given, assume it is large. If your eggs are not the right size, measure them by volume following the guidelines in the Equivalents Chart (page 44). For the most part, eggs used in baking will

work best at room temperature. To warm eggs, place them in a bowl of hot water for 5 to 10 minutes, turning them once or twice so they warm evenly.

EGG YOLKS

Egg yolks add structure, tenderness, and golden color to baked goods. The yolk, or yellow contains all the fat, a bit less than half the protein, and most of the egg's vitamins, and measures about 1 tablespoon in a large egg. Hens fed yellow corn and alfalfa meal will lay eggs with deeper-yellow yolks. Hens fed wheat or barley will lay eggs with lighter-colored yolks. I can still remember how years ago, I found it hard to bring myself to eat the unappetizingly pale yolks served to me in London.

In Italy, egg yolks are deep orange and are called the "red" instead of the "yellow." They are the secret of tender hand-rolled fresh pasta in Emilia-Romagna and the custard-based crema gelato flavored with orange zest and vanilla beans that first delighted the court of Catherina de Medici. Look for the double-yolk eggs sometimes found at farmers markets or buy eggs from free-range hens. I have noticed especially deep yolk color in the eggs from Land o' Lakes, so much so that they make other yolks look pale and insipid.

A fresh egg yolk will be rich in color and will stand upright. Blood spots are not harmful and will disappear with age.

Some recipes call for beating egg yolks and sugar until thick and light, and the mixture forms a ribbon.

This means beating the yolks and sugar together until the batter drops from the beaters in a slow ribbon-like shape (this takes about five minutes at high speed). The ribbon forms when the sugar has completely dissolved in the yolks. I use the phrase "beat the eggs and sugar until light and fluffy," instead.

COPPER EGG WHITE BOWLS

Perhaps you've seen those special copper bowls used for beating egg whites. I do have a large copper egg white bowl hanging from my tool rack that I use occasionally, but mostly enjoy for its decorative value. Copper bowls have been used in France since the eighteenth century to stabilize beaten egg whites. The copper in the bowl helps create a tighter bond in the sulfur contained in the egg whites; using a silver-plated bowl will have the same result. Copper is poisonous in large quantities, but the miniscule amount imparted by reaction with the bowl is perfectly safe to eat and is far less than normal daily intake through other means. The results of hand-beating are definitely superior: the air bubbles are smaller and more stable, but it's just too much for most people, especially when beating more than two or three whites, so I use a mixer in these recipes.

EGG WHITES

Egg whites add lightness to baked goods through their ability to capture air bubbles and help build structure. The albumen, or egg white contains more than half the egg's protein and minerals, about 2 tablespoons in a large egg. Egg whites thin out as the egg ages. Fresh egg whites will be cloudy because they contain carbon dioxide. The white of older eggs will be more transparent, due to its loss of carbon dioxide.

To get maximum volume when beating egg whites, the eggs should be at room temperature. Make sure both bowl and beaters are clean and free of grease. (If they are too cold, place the egg whites in a microwavable bowl and microwave on low power (10 to 20 percent) for 1 minute.)

Copper is the best type of bowl to use, especially if you're planning to beat the eggs by hand. When whites are over-beaten, losing their gloss and breaking up into clumps, the protein molecules lose their elasticity and the whites become dry and flaky and won't hold as much air. (If this happens, add another white and beat again only until the whites are creamy and glossy or discard and start again, especially if you have extra egg whites on hand.) I save extra egg whites in zipper lock bags in the freezer, so I always seem to have some to spare.

When adding beaten egg whites to your batter, always fold the whites into the heavier mixture; not vice versa. Fold gently and quickly so as not to deflate the mixture, adding the meringue in three stages preferably folding with a silicone spatula. Cut down and through the batter making sure not to over-mix. A few unmixed streaks are fine. The most important thing is not to deflate the egg whites, which will expand in the heat of the oven to provide leavening.

One way to help stabilize egg whites is to add a small amount (usually a $1/4$ or $1/2$ teaspoon) of cream of tartar (potassium bitartrate), a by-product of wine-making, to the bowl. This acid lowers the pH level of the egg white to the acidic range resulting in more stable foam, and is an alternative to using a copper bowl (see previous page). To avoid the potential over-beating, I always beat the whites with some of the sugar called for in the recipe and therefore, I don't generally use cream of tartar.

BLOOD SPOTS IN EGGS

The little red blood spot you sometimes see are caused by the rupture of a blood vessel while the egg is being formed. Today, blood spots do not indicate a fertilized egg, because roosters are kept out of contact with hens. These eggs are perfectly safe to eat. Remove the spot if desired with the tip of a knife. An egg with a blood spot is not harmful but is also not kosher. Growing up in a kosher household, we would carefully separate eggs, one at a time into a dish, discarding any with a spot. At the kosher restaurant where I consulted, Max and David's (www.maxanddavids.com), the *mashgiach* (or *mashgicha*), the kosher supervisor, has to check every batch of cracked eggs for forbidden blood spots.

FRESHNESS OF EGGS

Egg cartons display the date the eggs were packed in the form of a Julian date representing the consecutive days—January 1 is one, December 31 is three-hundred and sixty-five. Eggs can be stored in the refrigerator for four to five weeks beyond packing date with minimal quality loss.

The freshness of an egg is only partly due to when it was laid. The temperature and humidity at which the eggs are stored, and how they are handled are also factors in freshness. A one-week old egg, stored under ideal conditions (temperature under 40°F and humidity of about seventy-five percent) can be fresher than an egg left at room temperature for just one day. Most eggs reach supermarkets within a few days of leaving the laying house. An egg with a pale yellow yolk and watery white has likely been sitting in storage for several weeks, or months..

A fresh egg will sink to the bottom of a bowl of cold water; an old egg will float or turn sideways. Because eggshells are porous, an air pocket forms at one end of the egg as the egg ages, so the egg becomes light enough to float.

FROM MOLECULAR GASTRONOMY EXPERT HERVÉ THIS

Eggs have a property of expansion because of the water they contain (90 percent for the white; 50 percent for the yolk). To maximize the expansion, we need to heat it from below because steam becomes trapped under the coagulated layer of egg and pushes it up. "Soufflés, macaroons, puff pastries, and choux should therefore be baked on the floor or the bottom shelf of the oven."

Smoked Salmon and Spinach Quiche

Real men and *real women both eat quiche, especially this smoky-salty quiche, laden with sweet onions and spinach. This luscious quiche can be prepared one to two days ahead of time, cut into individual slices, and reheated in a 325°F oven. Frozen whole spinach leaves, rinsed under running water to remove any frost and gently squeezed out, can be substituted for fresh spinach. Although washed baby spinach is the most convenient way to buy spinach, fresh bunch spinach with flat or curly leaves is also a good choice; just be sure to wash very well in a large bowl of cold water to avoid a sandy quiche. Spicy arugula may be substituted for the spinach.*

YIELD: 8 TO 10 SERVINGS

$3/4$ pound Buttermilk Tart Pastry dough (page 565), Savory Tart Pastry dough (page 206), or Savory Spiced Whole Wheat Pastry dough (page 862)

1 tablespoon unsalted butter

1 large sweet onion, diced

6 ounces baby spinach leaves, or other spinach, trimmed if necessary, washed and drained

$1/4$ pound cold-smoked salmon, cut into small squares

4 large eggs

2 egg yolks

2 cups heavy cream

$1/2$ cup sour cream

Fine sea salt

$1/2$ teaspoon freshly ground black pepper

$^1/_2$ teaspoon freshly grated nutmeg

Roll out the pastry $^3/_8$-inch thick to fit into a deep-fluted French quiche pan (about 9 inches in diameter). Drape the pastry loosely into the pan without stretching and press firmly into the bottom and sides. Trim the edges and chill for 1 hour in the refrigerator or 30 minutes in the freezer.

Preheat the oven to 375°F. Fit a piece of heavy-duty foil onto the dough and fill with beans or other pie weights. Blind bake (just pastry crust, no filling) on the bottom shelf of the oven until the crust is cooked through but not yet browned, about 30 minutes.

Remove the foil and the weights, reduce oven temperature to 325°F and bake for 15 minutes longer, or until the crust is evenly and lightly browned. Remove from the oven and cool to room temperature on a wire rack.

Melt the butter in a medium skillet and sauté the onion until crisp-tender, 3 to 4 minutes. Remove from the heat, add the spinach, and stir once or twice so the spinach wilts in the heat of the pan. Mix in the salmon and spoon the mixture into the pastry crust.

Whisk together the eggs, egg yolks, cream, sour cream, salt, pepper, and nutmeg. Pour two-thirds of the egg mix over top the spinach mixture and stir to combine.

Place the filled crust on a baking pan to catch any drips and cover with foil. Cut a few slashes into the foil to allow steam to escape, and place the baking pan on the bottom shelf of the oven. Bake for 45 minutes or until the custard forms a skin. Uncover and poke a hole in the middle and pour in the remaining custard so the filling puffs up in the center. Continue baking until the custard has set in the middle, about 45 minutes longer.

Cool on a wire rack for 20 minutes, or cool to room temperature and refrigerate overnight. To reheat, cut into portions, arrange the slices on a baking sheet, and bake at 350°F for 20 minutes or until thoroughly heated.

LOX, NOVA, SMOKED, AND KIPPERED SALMON

Lox, which means "salmon" in Yiddish, is salmon fillet that has been cured with water, salt, sugar, and spices. It is important to Ashkenazi Jewish cuisine and was introduced to America by Eastern European Jewish immigrants. Nova lox or Nova Scotia salmon comes from a time when much of the salmon served in the bagel capital of America, New York City, came from Nova Scotia. This type of salmon is cured with a milder, less salty brine, then cold smoked. Other types of cold-smoked salmon, such as Scottish-style or Scandinavian-style are cured using slightly different methods. Any of these would work well for the quiche above, as long as you adjust for the differences in salt content. Some delis sell belly lox, which is fattier but tasty and costs less; smoked salmon trimmings would also work if you're willing to do a little knife work. Kippered salmon is hot-smoked, meaning the temperature of the smoke is hot enough to cook the flesh. It is less desirable here, because its texture is a bit dry.

B'stilla of Chicken

Ancient in origin the b'stilla is the great centerpiece of every Moroccan banquet. The traditional version is a pie made of incredibly thin, delicate, and highly decorated ouarka pastry enclosing a medieval mix of pigeon meat, lemon, honey-flavored scrambled eggs, and chopped almonds with sugar and cinnamon. Crispy ouarka (also known as brik, brick, dioul, malsouqa) leaves are sometimes available in the United States. Ouarka leaves are unique to North Africa and give pastries made with them a distinctive North African identity. They are incredibly crispy and light when cooked. They are made by tapping a soft sticky dough of semolina flour on a hot pan, repeatedly until a complete circle has been made without gaps. Many recipes, including this one, substitute phyllo dough and shredded chicken for the pigeon, here moist, flavorful chicken thighs. Although it may sound a bit strange, the confectioners' sugar, cinnamon, and almond topping provides the perfect flavor and texture contrast.

YIELD: ONE 10-INCH PIE, 8 TO 10 SERVINGS

$^{1}/_{2}$ pound (about 1$^{1}/_{2}$ cups) whole skin-on almonds, lightly toasted

$^{1}/_{2}$ cup confectioners' sugar

4 teaspoons ground cinnamon

1 quart chicken stock

1 medium onion, diced

2 tablespoons finely chopped fresh ginger, or 2 teaspoons ground ginger

1 teaspoon saffron

Salt and freshly ground black pepper

3 pounds bone-in skinless chicken thighs

1/4 cup chopped flat-leaf parsley

1/4 cup chopped cilantro

8 large eggs

Juice of 1 lemon

1 1/2 cups Clarified Butter (page 202)

3/4 pound brik pastry or phyllo dough, defrosted in the
refrigerator if frozen

Place the almonds, confectioners' sugar, and 1 teaspoon
of the cinnamon in the bowl of a food processor. Process
until the mixture is coarsely ground and reserve.

In a large soup pot, combine the stock, onion, ginger,
the remaining 3 teaspoons (1 tablespoon) cinnamon,
saffron, and salt and pepper to taste, and bring to a
boil. Add the chicken and bring back to a boil, skimming
off any foam as necessary. Reduce the heat to medium-
low and cook for 25 minutes or until the chicken comes
away easily from the bones.

Remove the chicken from the broth, reserving the
liquid, and set aside to cool. Pick the chicken meat from
the bones and shred it roughly. Mix the chicken with
the parsley and cilantro and reserve.

Pour the chicken cooking liquid into a medium pot
and cook over medium heat for about 15 minutes, until
the liquid has reduced by about three-quarters to 2
cups, and is syrupy. Cool the liquid somewhat.

In a bowl, whisk together the eggs, lemon juice, 2
tablespoons of the clarified butter, and salt and pepper
to taste. Add the reduced liquid and whisk together to
combine. Cook the mixture over medium-low heat in a
large skillet, stirring constantly until the mixture cooks

into soft, loose curds. Remove from the heat and add
the chicken. Cool to room temperature.

Preheat the oven to 350°F. Brush the bottom and sides
of a 10-inch removable bottom or springform cake pan
with butter. Trim the pastry leaves to a square – discarding the excess.. Brush one of the leaves with clarified
butter, and place it, buttered side up, in the bottom of
the pan so the excess dough dangles over the side.
Repeat with a second sheet, crosswise to the first, using
8 sheets altogether.

Spread half the nut mixture on top of the pastry.
Spread the chicken mixture over top. Cover with 8
sheets more of phyllo, buttering each one and laying it
into the pan in alternating directions. Fold the dangling
edges over the top and brush this final layer with butter. Place the pan on a second baking pan to catch the
drips and bake 40 minutes on the bottom shelf of the
oven or until the top is golden. Remove from the oven
and cool about 10 minutes.

Flip the b'stilla onto an ovenproof platter or a baking
pan lined with parchment paper and return to the
oven. Bake for 30 minutes longer, or until the top is
golden. Remove from the oven and cool about 10 minutes. Transfer to a serving platter and sprinkle with the
remaining almond mixture. Cut into serving portions.

Store the b'stilla refrigerated up to 2 days. Wrap in
aluminum foil and reheat in a 350°F oven for about 30
minutes, uncovering for the last 10 minutes of baking so
the pastry crisps up.

Torta Pasqualina Genovese

This substantial Torta is flavored with borage, boraggio in Italian, the most important herb of the narrow coastal province of Liguria. The large, hairy leaves of this wild and cultivated plant have a faint cucumber fragrance and a light flavor. Because of its hairiness, it is best cooked. Wild nettles are also gathered for this torta, which combines the young wild greens of spring with the season's artichokes and eggs, once also a seasonal food. Before industrialization, egg laying was almost entirely concentrated in the spring. According to tradition, the torta should be made of exactly thirty-three very fine, almost transparent layers, one to mark each year of Jesus' life. Modern cookbooks generally call for twelve to sixteen layers. The traditional recipe, which dates back to the 1500s, also calls for prescinseua, a soft curd cheese (see below) that is a specialty of Liguria.

YIELD: 8 TO 12 SERVINGS

Filling

$1/4$ cup extra virgin olive oil

$1/2$ cup finely chopped fennel branches and fronds

1 pound Swiss chard or beet greens, or a combination, trimmed of ribs, washed, cooked briefly, then drained and excess water squeezed out

$1/4$ cup chopped borage leaves, substitute chervil or tarragon or a combination

Fine sea salt, freshly ground black pepper, and grated nutmeg, to taste

1 (12-ounce) package frozen artichoke wedges, defrosted and rinsed under cold water

$1/2$ cup grated pecorino Romano

$1/2$ cup grated Parmigiano-Reggiano or Grana Padano cheese

1 (15-ounce) container whole milk ricotta

2 tablespoons chopped marjoram leaves

2 large eggs

Pastry

1 pound ($3 3/4$ cups) unbleached all-purpose flour

2 tablespoons extra virgin olive oil

3 large egg yolks

$3/4$ cup cold water, as needed

Assembly

$1/2$ cup extra virgin olive oil

8 large eggs

1 egg yolk, lightly beaten with 1 tablespoon milk, for the egg wash

Make the filling: In a medium skillet, heat 2 tablespoons of the olive oil and sauté the fennel until brightly colored, about 3 minutes. Add the cooked chard and the borage and cook over high heat for about 5 minutes or until any liquid has evaporated. Season with salt, pepper, and nutmeg. Cool the greens to room temperature and then chop.

In a medium skillet, sauté the artichokes in the remaining 2 tablespoons olive oil until they just start to brown about 5 minutes. Set aside to cool.

Combine the grated cheeses, ricotta, marjoram, eggs, and more salt, pepper, and nutmeg. Mix with the greens and artichokes and divide in two portions.

Make the pastry: Place the flour, oil, and egg yolks in

the bowl of a food processor and process to combine. Pour in only enough of the water so the mixture forms a ball. Remove from the processor and knead on a floured board until smooth. Form a long roll of the dough and cut it into 16 portions. Roll each portion out into a very thin round, large enough to cover the bottom of a 10-inch removable bottom or springform cake pan.

Assembly: Preheat the oven to 350°F. Stack half of the dough sheets into the pan, brushing each with oil and offsetting them so they partially cover the sides of the pan. Top with half the vegetable and ricotta mixture, spreading it out evenly. Make seven hollows in the filling—six around the outside and one in the middle. Carefully break open an egg and pour it into one of the hollows. Repeat with the remaining eggs and hollows. Spoon the second half of the vegetable mixture carefully over top so as not to break the eggs. Top with the remaining pastry sheets, brushing each with oil.

Brush the top of the pie with the egg wash. Place on a baking pan to catch any drips and bake on thje bottom shelf of the oven for 1 hour, or until the pastry is golden brown and the filling is bubbling hot. Allow the pie to cool for at least 15 minutes before cutting into portions. Serve hot or at room temperature. Store refrigerated for 2 to 3 days, and bring to room temperature before serving.

ABOUT LIGURIAN PRESCINSEUA

This soft, fresh cheese has an unusual name the origins of which are unknown and hails from the province of Liguria. It is traditionally made from the milk of sheep that graze in the Apennine Mountains, although these days the cheese is most commonly made from cow's milk. It is a highly perishable cream cheese with a sour taste similar to yogurt, made by allowing cow's milk to sour. Because it spoils so quickly, this cheese is purely a regional specialty. In earlier times, the milky curds were sold in small earthenware containers, though today plastic or glass is used instead. In Genoa, Liguria's most important city, this cheese is a must for Torta Pasqualina. In America, we must substitute fresh ricotta, sheep's milk ricotta, if possible.

Bonèt Piemontese: Chocolate–Amaretti Baked Custard

This dessert is a triumph of Piedmontese home-style baking. Every woman from the region will have her own version and will proudly serve it to guests or at family get-togethers. In the local French-influenced dialect, bonèt *means "bonnet." These baked chocolate custards are so named because the earliest molds were in the shape of a small round hat. Today, they are made in molds lined with caramel, similar to Spanish flan. What makes the dish particularly Italian is the dark chocolate and bits of crunchy bittersweet macaroons called* amaretti. *Substitute dried almond or even hazelnut macaroons (see page 504 for a recipe) with a few drops of almond extract. Some people flavor the custard with lemon zest instead of rum. In Torino, where many people own large copper pans just for this purpose, the sugar is caramelized directly in the mold over the heat. This recipe is gluten-free.*

YIELD: 8 SERVINGS

1³/₄ cups sugar

3 tablespoons potato starch, substitute corn,
    wheat, or rice starch

2 ounces (¹/₄ cup minus ¹/₂ tablespoon)
    Dutch process cocoa, sifted

4 large eggs

1¹/₂ cups milk, scalded

1¹/₂ cups heavy cream, scalded

¹/₄ cup dark rum

2 ounces bittersweet chocolate, melted

16 amaretti biscuits, crumbled (about 6 ounces)

Preheat the oven to 325°F. Arrange 8 ramekins or custard cups that hold about ¹/₂ cup each in a baking pan.

In a small heavy-bottomed, nonreactive pot with a lid, mix ¹/₄ cup of water with 1 cup of the sugar. Bring to a boil, then cover with the lid ajar and cook over moderate heat, shaking occasionally, until the water cooks away and the sugar starts to turn brown and just begins to redden in color (350°F on a candy thermometer), about 10 minutes. Quickly but carefully pour the caramel into the ramekins, but don't worry if the bottoms aren't evenly coated; the caramel will melt in the oven.

In a large bowl, whisk together the potato starch, cocoa, and the remaining ³/₄ cup sugar. Add the eggs, milk, and cream, and whisk together until smooth. Add the rum and melted chocolate and whisk together until smooth.

Pour the custard mixture into the molds, filling them as much as possible because the custard will shrink as it bakes. Sprinkle the molds with about three-quarters of

the amaretti crumbles, reserving the remainder for garnish. Place the baking pan with the molds onto the pulled out shelf of the oven. Pour enough hot water into the baking pan to come at least 1-inch up the sides of the pan.

Cover the entire pan with foil and cut slits in several places in the foil to allow steam to escape. Gently push the shelf back into the oven so as not to spill out any hot water. Bake for 45 minutes or until the custards have completely set in the middle but have not begun to puff up. Remove the molds from the pan, cool, and refrigerate for 2 to 3 hours.

Sprinkle each custard with a few bits of the remaining crumbled amaretti just before serving in the ramekins.

AMARETTI

Amaretti, meaning "small bitter bits" in Italian, are a kind of small, brown macaroon that is crisp and crunchy on the outside and soft inside. They originated in Venice during the Renaissance. Amaretti are made from either ground sweet almonds mixed with bitter almonds or apricot pits, or from almond paste, along with sugar and egg whites. The biscuits are often crushed and added to desserts like trifle and semifreddo (frozen mousses) for a bit of crunch and flavor.

One version of the story of the origin of the famed Amaretti di Saronno tells that a young baker and his lovely fiancée who both came from the town of Saronno invented the cookies in the 1700s during a surprise visit from the Bishop of Milan. To honor him, the two young lovers, Giuseppe and Osolina, quickly baked up a mixture of sugar, apricot kernels, and egg whites, creating crisp, airy cookies with an unusual bittersweet flavor which they wrapped in pairs to symbolize their love.

Pan di Spagna

The name of this classic sponge cake means "bread of Spain." It first entered Italian cuisine—especially in Naples, Sicily, and Sardinia, where the kings of Spain known as the Bourbons once ruled—in the eighteenth century. The light, delicate, and versatile cake became enormously popular at the courts of the city-states of Italy, especially Parma and Bologna. Pan di Spagna eventually became the most important basic cake in Italian cuisine, used to make any number of layered desserts, including Venetian tiramisù (in the form of ladyfingers made from the same batter), Zuppa Inglese, created to please British tourists, and Florentine Chocolate Nut Zuccotto (page 58). For use in the Zabaglione Cake (page 480) and the Lemon-Blackberry Bavarese (page 481), it is preferable to make the cake one day ahead and let it rest at room temperature overnight, so it will slice more evenly with less crumbling. This recipe is dairy-free.

YIELD: TWO 9-INCH CAKES, OR ONE HALF SHEET CAKE

5 large eggs, separated, at room temperature

$1^1/_2$ cups sugar

1 teaspoon vanilla extract

Grated zest of 1 lemon (1 tablespoon)

A few gratings of nutmeg

$^1/_4$ pound (1 cup minus 1 tablespoon) unbleached all-purpose flour

Preheat the oven to 350°F. Spray two 9-inch cake pans with nonstick baker's coating or rub with butter and dust with flour, shaking off the excess. (If baking in the half sheet pan, prepare the pan the same way or line with parchment paper or a silicone baking mat.)

In the bowl of a standing mixer fitted with the paddle attachment, beat the egg yolks with $^3/_4$ cup of the sugar until the mixture is light and fluffy, 5 to 6 minutes. Beat in the vanilla, lemon zest, and nutmeg, and then transfer the batter to a wide shallow bowl.

In the clean and greaseless bowl of a standing mixer fitted with the whisk attachment, beat the egg whites until they are fluffy, then beat in the remaining $^3/_4$ cup sugar and continue beating until firm and glossy. Using a silicone spatula, fold one-third of the meringue gently but thoroughly into the egg yolk mixture, sprinkle with some of the flour, then fold in another portion of whites, and sprinkle with more flour, and repeat. Scrape the batter into the prepared pans and bake for 45 minutes (30 minutes if using the half sheet pan), or until the cake starts to come away from the sides of the pan and a skewer stuck in the center comes out clean. Cool to room temperature on a wire rack. Store at room temperature, wrapped in plastic wrap, for 2 to 3 days, or wrap and freeze up to 3 months.

Sephardic
Pan Levi Cookies

These delicate, airy cookies are one of the oldest and still most popular recipes of Curaçao's Sephardic Jews. Related to Pan di Spagna (page 441), they are traditionally baked for all holidays and other festive occasions and are often sent to the sick. The cookies are a must dunked in Spanish-style rich, dark, hot drinking chocolate at every brit milah *(circumcision ceremony), on the eighth day after a boy's birth. This recipe is dairy-free.*

YIELD: 2 DOZEN COOKIES

$1/4$ pound (1 cup minus 1 tablespoon) unbleached
    all-purpose flour
$1/2$ teaspoon baking powder
Pinch fine sea salt
$1/2$ teaspoon ground cinnamon
$1/2$ teaspoon ground mace
4 large eggs
$1/2$ cup sugar

Preheat the oven to 325°F. Line two 18 x 13-inch half sheet pans or other large baking sheets with parchment paper or silicone baking mats.

Whisk together the dry ingredients: flour, baking powder, salt, cinnamon, and mace.

In the bowl of a standing mixer fitted with the paddle attachment, beat the eggs and sugar until light, and fluffy, 5 to 6 minutes. Fold in the flour mixture by hand. Spoon or pipe tablespoons of the batter about 2 inches apart on the baking sheets, leaving room for the cookies to spread.

Bake for 10 minutes, then reduce the oven heat to 275°F, and bake for 5 minutes, or until the cookies are lightly browned at the edges. Turn off the oven and allow the cookies to dry out and crisp, about 10 minutes. Store in a tightly covered container such as a cookie tin for up to 1 week.

Australian Pavlova
with Lemon Filling
and Tropical Fruits

This iconic dessert was created in the 1930s by an imaginative Australian chef, Herbert Sachse, as a cake suitable to serve at afternoon tea. It is named in honor of the Russian ballerina, Anna Pavlova, who visited Australia in the 1920s. New Zealand has a similar dessert dating from the same era and also lays claim to creating it. A meringue-based cake, the Pavlova has a soft, sweet center and a crisp outer crust that is obtained by folding a little vinegar and cornstarch or potato starch into the meringue. Here, I spread the Pavlova with Lemon Filling and top it with an assortment of colorful, freshly-cut fruits. (A filling of sweetened, vanilla-scented whipped cream is more traditional and can be substituted.) Use an assortment of passion fruit, red papaya and starfruit, to equal about 2 cups of cut-up fruit, keeping in mind contrast of color and texture. Kiwi is especially appropriate here, for its striking green color and firm, though yielding, texture and also because it is native to New Zealand, which rivals Australia in claiming to be the creator of the

Pavlova. You can also serve the lemon filling spooned over the Majorcan Lemon-Almond Cake (page 77), or use it as a filling for a pie.

YIELD: 8 SERVINGS

Meringue

1 cup sugar

1 tablespoon potato starch

$1/2$ teaspoon fine sea salt

4 large egg whites ($1/2$ cup), at room temperature

2 teaspoons cider vinegar

Filling

$1^1/2$ cups freshly squeezed lemon juice (about 8 lemons)

2 tablespoons potato starch

4 large eggs

4 large egg yolks ($1/4$ cup)

1 cup sugar

Grated zest of 2 lemons (2 tablespoons)

6 tablespoons unsalted butter, softened

Topping

2 kiwi fruit, peeled and diced

$1/4$ golden pineapple, firm but ripe, peeled and diced

1 mango, firm but ripe, diced

$1/2$ pint container strawberries, trimmed, and diced

 Substitute blueberries or blackberries

Juice of 1 lime

2 tablespoons honey

Make the meringue: Place a rack in the center of the oven, and preheat the oven to 250°F. Line a baking sheet with parchment paper and draw a 10-inch circle on the paper. Turn the paper over so the ink is on the back.

In a small bowl, whisk together $1/2$ cup of the sugar, the potato starch, and the salt.

In the clean and greaseless bowl of a standing mixer fitted with the whisk attachment, beat the egg whites until light and fluffy, then add the remaining $1/2$ cup of the sugar and continue beating until the whites are firm and glossy, 4 to 5 minutes. Transfer the meringue to a wide shallow bowl.

Sprinkle about one-quarter of the sugar-starch mixture over the top of the meringue and fold in using a silicone spatula, continuing until all the sugar-starch mixture has been used. Sprinkle the vinegar over top and fold in. Spoon the meringue onto the parchment paper circle, making the meringue shallower in the center, make a nest shape.

Bake for 1 hour and 15 minutes or until the outside of the meringue is dry and takes on a very pale cream color. Turn the oven off, leave the door slightly ajar, and let the meringue cool completely in the oven. (The outside of the meringue will feel firm to the touch if gently pressed and the inside soft and marshmallow-like.) You should be able to easily pull the meringue off the parchment paper; if it sticks, turn the oven back on and bake the meringue for 15 to 30 minutes longer, or until dry on the bottom. (Pull the paper from the bottom. At this point, you can store the Pavlova, wrapped in aluminum foil, in a cool, dry place, for 2 to 3 days, as long as the weather is nice and dry. It is best not to make the Pavlova on a humid day, as it will tend to be sticky.)

Make the lemon filling: In a small mixing bowl, mix together $1/4$ cup of the lemon juice with the potato starch until smooth.

In a medium bowl, combine the remaining lemon juice, the eggs, egg yolks, and sugar, whisking or stirring until smooth. Fold in the lemon-starch mixture. Transfer to a heavy-bottomed, two-quart nonreactive (not aluminum, unless it is coated on the inside) pot, Place the pot over low to medium heat and whisk until the lemon filling thickens and just begins to bubble. Remove from the heat, then whisk in the lemon zest and butter. Transfer the filling back to a bowl, preferably stainless steel, over a second bowl filled with ice and water and stir occasionally until cool and thick. Note that you will have extra filling. (At this point, you may store the filling, covered and refrigerated, up to 2 weeks.)

Assemble the Pavlovas: Toss the fruit lightly with the lime juice and honey.

Place the Pavlova onto an attractive serving plate. Spread about 1 cup of the Lemon Filling over top, leaving a 1-inch border all around. Spoon the fruit over top. Serve immediately, cutting into 12 portions.

German Muerbeteig Dough (Mellow Dough)

Translated, muerbeteig means "mellow dough," and it is appropriately mellow in flavor and crumbly in texture because of the ground almonds it contains. Basically, it is based on the principle of using one part sugar by weight, double the weight of butter and triple the weight of the flour. It must be weighed for the most accurate measurement, as I have done for all the recipes in this book. Use the muerbeteig for the Alsatian Plum Muerbeteig (page 710) and as an alternate pastry for the French Apricot Tart (page 120), the Strawberry-Rhubarb Tart (page 168), the Blackberry-White Chocolate Tart (page 483), the Minneola Orange Tart (page 600), or the Butterscotch-Ginger Pear Tart (page 641). The dough may be either rolled out between two sheets of wax paper or pressed by hand into the pan. Well-wrapped, the dough may be frozen for up to 2 months. Defrost overnight in the refrigerator.

YIELD: ABOUT 2 POUNDS, ENOUGH FOR 2 MEDIUM TO LARGE TARTS

$3/4$ pound ($2^3/4$ cups plus 1 tablespoon) unbleached all-purpose flour

$1/2$ cup sugar

1 teaspoon baking powder

$1/2$ teaspoon fine sea salt

$1/4$ pound ($3/4$ cup) blanched almonds

$1/2$ pound (2 sticks) unsalted butter, hilled and cut into bits

1 large egg

2 large egg yolks

1 teaspoon vanilla extract

1 tablespoon dark rum, substitute brandy

Grated zest of 1 lemon (1 tablespoon)

In the bowl of a standing mixer fitted with the whisk attachment, combine the dry ingredients: flour, sugar, baking powder, and salt.

Place the almonds and about 1 cup of the dry ingredient mixture into the bowl of a food processor and process until the almonds are finely ground. Combine the almond mixture with the remaining flour mixture, switch to the paddle attachment, and beat in the butter until the mixture resembles oatmeal.

Separately, combine the egg, egg yolks, vanilla, rum, and lemon zest. Add to the mixer bowl and beat just long enough for the mixture to come together and form a soft dough.

Transfer to a plastic bag and shape into a flattened rectangle. Chill in the refrigerator for 1 hour or in the freezer for 30 minutes until firm but still malleable.

FIGS

Fig Season . . .450

Choosing and Storing Fresh Figs . . .450

Fig Newtons . . .451

Choosing and Storing Dried Figs . . .451

Fig Varieties . . .451

LADY BALTIMORE CAKE . . .452

From Lady Baltimore by Owen Wister . . .454

RUSTIC FRESH FIG GALETTE . . .455

SWEET FIG FOCACCIA
(FICATOLLA DEL CHIANTI) . . .455

Focaccia . . .456

CUCCIDATI (SICILIAN FIG COOKIES) . . .457

FIGS

Slowly munching on a couple of dried figs while cracking the seeds has long been one of the ways I get my sugar fix while striving to maintain a reasonable weight. That fruity, figgy, honeyed flavor is so satisfying, it's hard to decide which is better: plump, chewy, dried figs or luscious velvety-skinned fresh figs dripping with juices from their split bottoms. Figs are a wonderful ingredient in baking, adding their mild but distinctive flavor, moisture, and dense texture to cookies, muffins, and cakes. The rarer fresh fig, with its short season and higher price, is quite a delicacy cut in half and baked cut-side up in fruit tarts. Cooked figs and fig syrup have been used for sweetening for millennia in North Africa and the Middle East.

Figs, *Ficus carica*, are plump, soft, yielding fruits, oval to round with a pointy protruding stem. When properly honey-ripe, figs are quite delicate in texture and flavor with milky juices, sweet soft pulp, and tiny, edible, crunchy seeds. Figs are native to Turkey and are one of the oldest fruits known. Today, Turkey is still the top fig producer in the world, mostly growing in the Aegean region of Izmir, called Caria in earlier time, fol-

lowed by Egypt and other countries of the Mediterranean region. Sumerian stone tablets dating back to 2500 BCE record the usage of figs. Nine fossilized figs dating more than 11,000 years back were found in the early Neolithic village Gilgal I, a village in the Lower Jordan Valley, near the ancient and still thriving city of Jericho.

Figs are believed to have been among the earliest cultivated crops, one thousand years before wheat and rye. In the Book of Genesis, Adam and Eve covered their bodies with fig leaves after eating from the Tree of Knowledge. Ever since, fig leaves or paintings of fig leaves have been used to cover the genitals of nude figures in painting and sculpture, often added long after the original work was completed.

The fig is lovingly referred to in the Biblical Song of Songs, "The fig-tree putteth forth her green figs, and the vines in blossom give forth their fragrance. Arise, my love, my fair one, and come away." The biblical phrase "each man under his own vine and fig tree" was used to describe the fair life that would be led by settlers in the American West. The Zionist leader Theodor Herzl, in his vision of the land of Israel, used the same phrase. Fig trees are also mentioned in the Koran in many places.

In Egypt, Cleopatra hid the poisonous asp she used to end her life in a basket of fresh figs. The Greeks believed the fig was a gift of Demeter, and it was made sacred to Dionysus. Figs were also a much loved food for the Romans, and the fruit is still prized today in Italy. From Central Africa to the Far East, the fig tree is believed to be the Tree of Life and Knowledge. The Bo tree, under which Buddha meditated, was a type of fig tree. The term *sycophant*, meaning a servile, self-seeking flatterer, translates literally to "one who shows the fig." The term dates back to the ancient Greek fig trade and referred to a despicable person who informed on fig smugglers. The English phrase "I don't care a fig" originates from the profligate abundance of this fruit.

Fig trees can live as long as 100 years and grow to 100 feet tall, although they are normally kept pruned to a height of about 16 feet. There is an enormous fig tree growing at Bartram's Garden's in Philadelphia, planted by pioneer American botanist, John Bartram, or one of his descendants (www.bartramsgarden.com). Philadelphia is on the border of a climate zone and is actually too cold to grow figs. However, if the fig tree is babied by wrapping it in burlap to protect it in the winter months, or bent over to be put to bed and covered for the winter in a trench in the ground, and if it is planted in a place with lots of sunlight, ideally facing south, figs will actually grow here, as attested to by the many large unwieldy-looking bundles of wrapped fig trees found in backyard gardens in Italian neighborhoods all over the city.

Although we consider the fig to be a fruit, botanically, it is actually a flower with blossoms that form inside of the fruit, creating thousands of tiny internal flowers. In the small opening visible on the bottom of the fruit is an even smaller, narrow passage, which allows a special fig wasp to enter the fruit and pollinate the flower. The skins of figs can be light green, black, brown, purple, light pink, or a variegated combination. When ripe, the flesh can be pale green, creamy white, deep red, brownish purple, or opal. If you can get them, large-fingered, fresh green fig leaves make a lovely natural bed on which to serve small pastries, cookies, a cake, or cheese. For grilling, wrap pieces of cheese or other foods in the leaves, which are completely edible.

The Spanish conquistadores brought dark-purple Smyrna figs, originally from Smyrna, now Izmir on Turkey's Aegean coast, to Mexico in 1520. In the late eighteenth century Franciscan monks brought Smyrna figs with them to their San Diego mission. As these figs spread to missions along California's coast, they became known as Mission figs. Except for backyard figs, all fresh figs eaten in the United States come from California, where the climate is perfect for producing this seductive fruit. California grows five varieties of figs: Calimyrna, Kadota, Adriatic, Mission or Black Mission, and Brown Turkey.

Figs don't ripen once they are picked, so they must be harvested at their peak when they are quite fragile with skin that bruises and tears easily. Cut open a fresh fig and its juicy, soft, crimson to yellow flesh will be packed with minuscule edible seeds. In Italy, where food and love are inextricably intertwine, the male form, *fico*, for fig, refers to the fruit but the female form, *fica*, is a pleasing euphemism for a woman's genitals. A short season plus the difficulty in transporting fresh figs make this highly perishable fruit a high-priced delicacy. But, luckily, figs are also delicious dried and are well-suited to most baking recipes in that form.

The Lady Baltimore Cake (page 452) is a three-layered Madeira-sprinkled specialty of Charleston, South Carolina, not Baltimore, slathered with meringue icing, and filled with sliced dried figs and toasted pecans. In the Rustic Fresh Fig Galette (page 454) fresh figs halves nestle in a layer of almond cream baked in a free-form pastry crust. In the Tuscan Sweet Fig Focaccia (page 455), I combine fresh fig halves with walnuts and anise seed baked on yeast-raised sweet dough. I grind figs, dried figs, golden raisins, candied orange peel, Zante currants, walnuts, and pine nuts and then stuff the mixture into rich cookie dough to make Cuccidati (Sicilian Fig Cookies) (page 457), a Sicilian Christmas tradition.

FIG SEASON

Beginning in June, the fig tree grows its first crop of fruit on branches from the previous year. A second crop grown on new green branches ripens in August through September. The first figs are picked in July in America, but those picked a bit later in the season, when they have had the chance to ripen more fully in the heat of the summer sun, will be sweeter and have more deeply concentrated flavor.

CHOOSING AND STORING FRESH FIGS

Ripe figs are fragile and sweet-smelling. When you find ripe figs, hurry them home and use them fast, or else stash them in the refrigerator. Most will hold for a few days, but ripe figs can spoil, even in the fridge (they can get expensive, and you'll want to savor every one).

Sometimes you'll see the bottom skin splitting open to reveal the flesh. When choosing figs, reach for the ones that you might think should be left behind. A fig with a slightly shriveled neck and a split at the bottom end, oozing with sweetness, is perfectly ripe and ready to eat. Both the skin and interior should be soft and yielding; the thin skin will have lost its shine and will be moist, fragrant, and sweet. An underripe fig will be firm to the touch with a rather dry, undeveloped center.

Unfortunately, ripe figs are fragile and don't travel well. Figs that have flattened sides or are slumped in their containers have probably been exposed to too much heat in transport. They will probably also have an unpleasant alcoholic smell and should be avoided. If possible, leave the figs at room temperature for up to two days before, because, like tomatoes, figs taste best if they've never been refrigerated. Handle all figs with tender, loving care, because their fragile skins bruise and tear easily. Store fully ripened figs in the refrigerator up to 2 days; bring to room temperature before serving, peeled or not as desired.

FIG NEWTONS

About the only way many Americans have eaten figs is in the chewy filling of Fig Newton cookies, originally baked by the Kennedy Biscuit Works of Cambridgeport, Massachusetts, and now by Nabisco. There are many stories about where the cookie got its name, but the most reliable source attributes it to the nearby town of Newton, Massachusetts, a town near the manufacturing plant. The company already had several lines of cookies named after regional areas to help drum up local business.

CHOOSING AND STORING DRIED FIGS

The figs strung into rings called crowns grow in the Kalamata region of Greece, also famous for its olives, and are in season from October through December. Their chewy flesh is tender and honey-sweet. Choose plump dried figs that are soft enough to give slightly when squeezed. Avoid hard or shriveled dried figs, any displaying white mold or with a sour smell. As figs dry, sugar from inside the fig migrates to the surface and form white crystals. Although figs with sugar crystals are quite edible, they will often be dense and mealy in texture.

FIG VARIETIES

CELESTE: This tender, small to medium-sized fig has purple-tinged medium-brown skin and sweet, juicy, and creamy white pulp. Its main crop ripens in mid-June. Because the Celeste is more cold-hardy than other types and grows on a large, vigorous, and very productive tree, it is a favorite for backyard gardens, like those found all over Philadelphia, especially in Italian neighborhoods. It is excellent for eating fresh with a rich sweet flavor and can also be used for fig preserves.

CALIMYRNA: This fig gets its name from a contraction of California and Smyrna and is the most common fig grown in California. Calimyrnas are California's version of the Smyrna variety originally from that region of Turkey, now called Izmir, which grows in Turkey, Greece, and North Africa. When fresh, they will have golden to light yellowish-green skin, pale amber-pink flesh, and a characteristically nutty flavor. Because of their thick skin, these figs are usually peeled when eaten fresh, but they are most often sold dried. Fresh Calimyrna figs are in season in July and August.

KADOTA (DOTTATO IN ITALY): The Kadota has firm, yellowish-green skin and amber to violet flesh with few seeds. They are eaten fresh but are often found canned. They are good fresh and dried and in Kadota fig honey. Fresh Kadotas are in season from May through October.

MISSION OR BLACK MISSION: Named by the Franciscan monks who first planted them in San Diego, they have dark purple skins with light strawberry-colored flesh, a strong, concentrated flavor, and high sugar content. They are in season from May through November and may be found in quart or pint-size baskets. They are also found dried and have good flavor, especially for fig purées, where their reddish-purple color can be appreciated. For cutting and mixing in batters, I prefer lighter colored dried figs.

BROWN TURKEY: The dangling testicle-sized and shaped Brown Turkey figs are medium to large in size with copper-colored skin, whitish to pink pulp and few seeds. These figs are in season from May through December and are often sold from cases each nestled into an individual mold.

Lady Baltimore Cake

Despite its name, this fig lover's cake comes from Charleston, South Carolina, and not Baltimore. Owen Wister (1860–1938), a popular novelist of the time, picked Charleston, South Carolina, as the setting of his new romance novel, Lady Baltimore, *modeling the main character, named Lady Baltimore, after one of the city's famous belles, Alicia Rhett Mayberry. A cake that Wister ate in Charleston's Women's Exchange tea room was said to serve as his inspiration. Toward the end of the nineteenth century, Florence and Nina Ottelengui, who managed Charleston's Lady Baltimore Tea Room*

for a quarter of a century, made their own version of the cake based on the Queen Cake of that period. They are said to have baked and shipped a cake to Owen Wister annually. Another good place to use up extra egg whites: this cake and its icing take 13 whites in all!

YIELD: ONE 9-INCH LAYER CAKE, 12 TO 14 SERVINGS

Cake

$^1/_2$ cup finely chopped dried figs

3 ounces ($^1/_2$ cup) raisins, chopped

$^1/_2$ cup Madeira or Amontillado sherry

$^3/_4$ pound ($2^3/_4$ cups plus 1 tablespoon) unbleached all-purpose flour

1 tablespoon baking powder

Pinch salt

$^1/_2$ pound (2 sticks) unsalted butter, softened

2 cups sugar

1 teaspoon vanilla extract

1 teaspoon almond extract

1 cup milk

7 large egg whites (7 fluid ounces), at room temperature

Icing and Filling

2 cups sugar

$^3/_4$ cup water

6 large egg whites ($^3/_4$ cup), at room temperature

$^1/_2$ teaspoon fine sea salt

2 teaspoons vanilla extract

1 teaspoon almond extract

1 cup pecans, lightly toasted and chopped fine

1 cup dried figs, trimmed and sliced, for garnish
Pecan halves, for garnish

Soak the figs and raisins in the Madeira for at least 1 hour or until soft and plump, preferably overnight.

Make the cakes: Preheat the oven to 325°F. Spray three 9-inch cake pans with nonstick baker's coating.

In a bowl, whisk together the dry ingredients: flour, baking powder, and salt.

In the bowl of a standing mixer fitted with the paddle attachment, beat the butter and 1½ cups of the sugar until light and fluffy. Beat in the vanilla and the almond extracts. Add the flour mixture in batches alternately with the milk, until it is just combined.

In the clean and greaseless bowl of a standing mixer fitted with the whisk attachment, beat the egg whites until fluffy, then add the remaining ½ cup sugar and continue beating until the whites are firm and glossy, 4 to 5 minutes. Fold into the batter in thirds so as not to deflate the meringue.

Divide the batter among the prepared pans, smoothing the tops. Bake for 30 minutes or until the cakes start to come away from the sides of the pans and a skewer inserted in the center comes out clean.

Remove the cakes from the oven and let them cool in the pans on racks for 10 minutes. Turn them out onto the racks, and let them cool completely. (The cake layers may be made 1 week in advance and kept wrapped well in plastic wrap and frozen. Let the layers thaw before proceeding with the recipe.)

Make the icing: In a medium, heavy-bottomed pot, combine the sugar and water, and bring to a boil, shaking to combine without forming crystals, until the mixture forms a clear syrup, about 3 minutes. Continue to cook to the firm ball stage (250°F on a candy thermometer), or until a spoonful dropped in a glass of ice water will form a firm, but still malleable ball, about 6 minutes.

When the sugar is almost ready, in the clean and greaseless bowl of a standing mixer fitted with the whisk attachment, beat the egg whites and salt together till they form medium peaks. With the mixer on low speed, pour the hot syrup into the center of the bowl. Continue to beat until the meringue is firm, glossy, and at room temperature, about 10 minutes. Add the vanilla and almond extracts and beat briefly to combine.

Drain the liquid from the figs and raisins and reserve. For the filling, fold the chopped figs, raisins, and chopped pecans with 2 cups of the meringue, reserving the remainder for the icing.

Arrange one of the cake layers on a serving plate. Sprinkle it with half of the reserved soaking liquid from the fruits, spread it with half the fig and raisin filling, and top with another cake layer. Sprinkle the cake with the remaining half of the soaking liquid and spread with the remaining dried-fruit filling. Cover with the third cake layer.

Spread the top and side of the cake with the reserved icing, swirling it to make an attractive pattern, and decorate with the sliced figs and the pecan halves. Store the cake at room temperature for up to 4 days, ideally covered with a glass cake dome (though a large overturned pot will do) to keep the cake from sticking to the cover.

Rustic Fresh Fig Galette

This country-style tart is easier and less intimidating to make than a fancier tart made in a fluted pan. A light, kirsch-flavored almond cream is layered inside a pizza-like pastry crust, figs cover the top, and sliced almonds are sprinkled over top for a crunchy texture and an interesting look. Vary the tart by filling it with plums, apricot halves or peach wedges.

YIELD: 10 TO 12 SERVINGS

Filling

2 ounces (1/4 cup minus 1 teaspoon) unbleached all-purpose flour

1/2 cup blanched almonds, whole or sliced

1/4 pound almond paste

2 ounces (1/2 stick) unsalted butter, softened

1/4 cup sugar

2 large eggs

1/4 cup kirsch, substitute brandy

Topping and Assembly

1 pound Sugar Pastry dough (page 823)

1 1/2 pounds (8 to 10) large, firm but ripe figs, stems trimmed and sliced

1 egg, lightly beaten with 2 tablespoons milk, for the egg wash

1/2 cup sliced skin-on almonds

1 cup strained red currant jam, optional

Make the filling: In the bowl of a food processor, combine the flour and almonds, and process until finely ground. (The flour keeps the almonds from turning oily.) Remove from the processor and reserve.

Combine the almond paste, butter, and sugar in the bowl of the processor and process until smooth. Add the eggs and process again until smooth. Add the flour-almond mixture and the kirsch and process again briefly, just long enough to combine. Transfer to a bowl, cover with plastic wrap, and chill for 30 minutes in the refrigerator, or until the mixture is firm enough to hold its shape. (Refrigerate up to 4 days before using, if desired.)

Preheat the oven to 350°F. Roll the dough into a large circle (about 14 inches in diameter) and place onto a 12-inch diameter round pizza pan with the edges hanging out. (Or shape a pan out of several layers of heavy-duty aluminum foil.) Trim the edges of the pastry with scissors so it is even. Spread the almond filling over the pastry to the rim of the pizza pan. Arrange the figs in tight concentric rings over the filling cut side up. Fold the edges of the dough up, pleating as you go, to form a rough border.

Brush the egg wash over the dough border, then sprinkle with the sliced almonds. Bake for 45 minutes, or until the pastry edges are brown and the filling is bubbling. Remove from the oven and cool to room temperature.

In a small pot or in the microwave, melt the jam until just hot to the touch. Brush the fig slices with the jam. Allow the jam to set before cutting the tart into serving portions. Store covered at room temperature up to 2 days.

Sweet Fig Focaccia (Ficatolla del Chianti)

This sweet focaccia from the Chianti region of Tuscany is made with a soft, egg-enriched yeast-raised dough that is patted out into a large rectangle, then filled with fresh fig halves, walnuts, and flavored with ground aniseeds. Anise and figs make a marriage that was meant to be, while walnuts make the mixture an amiable ménage a trois. *Serve the focaccia with salty cheese like Pecorino Romano or a blue cheese like Gorgonzola and a glass of red wine from Chianti.*

YIELD: 10 TO 12 SERVINGS

Sponge and Dough

1 ($\frac{1}{4}$-ounce) package (2$\frac{1}{4}$ teaspoons) active dry yeast

3 tablespoons honey

1 cup lukewarm water

2 large eggs, at room temperature

18 ounces (4$\frac{1}{4}$ cups) unbleached all-purpose flour

1 teaspoon fine sea salt

3 ounces ($\frac{3}{4}$ stick) unsalted butter, softened

Topping

1 pound (6 to 8) fresh figs, sliced

1 cup chopped walnuts

$\frac{1}{4}$ cup raw sugar

1 tablespoon ground aniseed, optional

Prepare a 15 x 10-inch jelly roll pan by lining with parchment paper or wax paper.

Make the sponge: In the bowl of a standing mixer fitted with the paddle attachment, combine the yeast, honey, and water, and allow the yeast to dissolve. Allow the mixture to proof in a warm place for about 10 minutes, or until bubbling and puffy. Beat in the eggs, then beat in about half the flour to make a soft sponge. Cover with plastic wrap or a damp cloth and allow the sponge to rise at warm room temperature until doubled in size, about 1$\frac{1}{2}$ hours.

Make the dough: Using the dough hook, beat in the remaining flour and the salt and until the dough is smooth and elastic, about 6 minutes. Then beat in the butter, continuing to beat until the butter has been completely incorporated into the dough. The dough should be firm enough to hold its shape but still soft and sticky. (The dough will stick to the bowl.) Transfer the dough to a large oiled bowl; turn around so the dough is oiled all over. Cover with plastic wrap, and allow it to rise at warm room temperature until doubled in size, about 1½ hours.

Punch down the dough, then pat and stretch it out to fit into the baking pan. Spray lightly, using a plant mister, with water and allow the dough to relax for 10 minutes at room temperature. Stretch the dough out again so it fully covers the baking pan. Dimple the dough all over using your knuckles.

Arrange the figs over the dough cut side up. Combine the walnuts, sugar, and aniseed, then sprinkle over the figs. Spray again lightly with water using a plant mister and leave to rise at warm room temperature until well-puffed, about 1 hour.

Preheat the oven to 400°F.

Bake the focaccia for 20 minutes, reduce the oven temperature to 375°F, and continue baking for 20 minutes longer, or until the top is golden. Cool for about 15 minutes in the pan, then remove and cool completely on a wire rack. Store covered at room temperature up to 3 days.

FOCACCIA

Focaccia is a flat, oven-baked Italian bread, which may be topped with onions, herbs, cheese, nuts, cured meats, or even fruit, as in the recipe above from Tuscany. Its name comes from the Latin word *focus*, meaning both "center" and "fireplace," as the quick-cooking bread was originally baked in the hearth in the center of the house. Related to pizza, focaccia is thought to have originated with the Etruscans or ancient Greeks, but today, it is a regional specialty of Liguria, made in countless variations, both savory and sweet. On a recent visit, I spotted bakeries all over Genoa baking fresh focaccia twice a day for sale to eager customers.

To make the bread, the dough is rolled out or pressed by hand into a thick layer and then baked in a hearth oven. Bakers often pierce the bubbles appearing on the surface of the bread. It is also common to dot the bread by making indentations all across the bread using the knucklesr or the wooden handle of a kitchen utensil. The dough is usually brushed with olive oil before baking.

Cuccidati
(Sicilian Fig Cookies)

These festive cookies from Sicily have a filling made of figs, dried fruit, and nuts that tastes like the best Fig Newton you can imagine. At one time, the famed ripe, sweet figs of Sicily would be stuck on cinnamon stick skewers and left to dry in the sun and then used to make these cookies at Christmastime. Cuccidati, cuddureddi, and buccellati are all names for the cookies that channel the exotic flavors of Sicily's long-ago Arabic heritage and are often made for holidays and weddings. You can use either light or dark figs, as long as they are moist and tender. Lard does make the lightest, most tender dough here, but try to use the unprocessed, non-hydrogenated type (see page 198 for more about lard.) If possible, grind the filling using a meat grinder, so it is evenly-textured and chunky. Otherwise, pulse in a food processor so it doesn't turn to mush. Cut decorative slits into the cookies, using your imagination to create the lacy patterns and then sprinkle the cookies with colorful nonpareils. This recipe is dairy-free.

YIELD: 2 DOZEN COOKIES

Pastry

1 pound (3³/4 cups) unbleached all-purpose flour

¹/2 cup sugar

1 teaspoon baking powder

¹/2 teaspoon fine sea salt

6 ounces lard, substitute transfat-free shortening
   or unsalted butter

³/4 cup milk

Filling

1 pound dried figs, trimmed and cut into bits,
   soaked in lukewarm water to cover for 30 minutes
   or until soft and plump

¹/4 cup golden raisins

¹/4 cup chopped candied orange peel
   (homemade, see page 225 or store bought)

¹/2 cup Zante currants

¹/2 cup chopped walnuts

¹/4 cup pine nuts

Grated zest of 1 lemon (1 tablespoon)

¹/4 cup honey

1 teaspoon ground cinnamon

¹/2 teaspoon ground cloves

1 large egg, lightly beaten with 1 tablespoon milk,
   for the egg wash

¹/2 cup colorful nonpareils, optional, for garnish

Line two 18 x 13-inch half sheet pans (or other large baking pans) with parchment paper or silicone baking mats.

Make the pastry: In the bowl of a standing mixer fitted with the whisk attachment, whisk together the dry ingredients: flour, sugar, baking powder, and salt. Switch to the paddle attachment, add the lard and beat until the mixture resembles oatmeal. Add the milk and beat just long enough for the mixture to come together and form large moist clumps. Knead briefly on a floured board to mix completely, then pat into a flattened block and wrap in plastic film. Chill for 1 hour in the refrigerator or 30 minutes in the freezer.

Make the filling: Preheat the oven to 350°F. Drain the figs and combine with the raisins and candied orange peel. Preferably using a meat grinder, grind the mixture to a chunky paste. Alternatively, place in the bowl of a food processor and pulse until the mixture is sticky but still chunky. Combine with the Zante currants, walnuts, pine nuts, lemon zest, honey, cinnamon, and cloves.

Roll the dough in batches out on a floured work surface to about $^3/_8$-inch thick. Cut into 3 x 4-inch rectangles. Spoon a tablespoon of filling the long way evenly along the center of the rectangle, leaving a $^1/_2$-inch border all around. Fold the edges over to make a neat long rectangular package, pressing the edges together after moistening lightly with a bit of water.

Turn the packets seam side down. Using a single-edged razor or a sharp paring knife, cut small slits in a decorative pattern all over the top. Alternatively, fold the pastry in half and press the two edges together. Cut slits along the joined edge one long edge about halfway to the other edge and at $^1/_2$-inch intervals. Bend the pastry to fan out the cut edge, allowing filling to show (like a bear claw pastry). Brush each pastry with the egg wash, then sprinkle with nonpareils.

Arrange the filled pastries on the baking pans and bake for 25 minutes or until the pastries are golden brown. Cool on a wire rack. Store in a cookie tin or other similar container for up to one week.

Note: When working with lard, it is important to add all the liquid to the dough, even though the dough will come together without it. Because lard is one hundred percent fat, the dough will be too crumbly and tender to roll out unless enough liquid has been added to form the gluten.

FLOWERS

Rosewater . . .461

Rose–Scented Loukum in Istanbul . . .462

Rose Syrup from Italy's Valle Scrivia . . .463

Orange Blossom Water . . .463

Kewra Water . . .463

How to Use Flower Waters . . .464

Lavender . . .464

Lavender Syrup . . .464

Using Candied and Fresh Flowers . . .464

Make Your Own Candied Flowers . . .464

Common Edible Flowers . . .465

Buying Flower Waters, Syrup,
Fresh, and Candied Blossoms . . .466

MAHMOUL (SYRIAN PISTACHIO-STUFFED
SEMOLINA COOKIES WITH ROSEWATER) . . .466

ROSE-SCENTED ANGEL FOOD CAKE . . .467

Angel Food Cake Tips . . .468

CORNMEAL AND ROSEWATER POUND CAKE . . .469

Elizabeth Goodfellow and Eliza Leslie . . .469

Pound Cake or Quatres Quarts . . .470

ORANGE BLOSSOM BRIOCHES . . .470

ORANGE BLOSSOM GLAZE . . .471

HONEY GLAZED LAVENDER-LEMON CAKE . . .472

The Famous Bundt Cake Pan . . .473

FLOWERS

I opened a bottle of rosewater made from hand-picked red roses from Dubai and let out a genie: a blast of the most incredible intoxicating perfume, far more potent than any other rosewater I've ever used, that could easily fuel a magic carpet ride. A smaller bottle contains deliriously honeyed jasmine water from Thailand; the same haunting fragrance flavors Sicilian gelsomino (jasmine blossom) gelato and the syrup for fruit fritters. Another bottle contains Pakistani floral, fruity kewra water that transports me instantly to faraway lands. The water is also produced in Northern India. I also have a small blue plastic bottle (along with some of the now empty older blue glass bottles) of sweetly fragrant orange blossom water produced by A. Monteux in France near Grasse, perfume capital of the word.

Today, innovative pastry chefs are experimenting with some of the oldest and most potent flavorings in the world: floral essences. Often known as flower waters, these flavorings have traditionally been used in Middle Eastern, Greek, Turkish, Iranian, and Indian cooking and baking. Rose and orange water were also quite commonly used as flavorings starting in medieval times in Europe,

especially in Spain, southern France, Italy, particularly Sicily, though also in the British Isles.

Flower waters result from the steam distillation process used to extract essential oils from flowers and contain the water-soluble essence of that particular flower. Flower waters are also known as *hydrosols*, referring to the water condensate produced during the steam-distillation of plants for its essential oil. Both rosewater and orange blossom water were first distilled in the tenth century, followed by lavender water in the twelfth century.

In the Arab and Indian world, jasmine, iris, geranium, and kewra water (in India) are also used in the kitchen and bakery for their aromatic qualities. Jasmine and geranium water scent North African and Sicilian sweets, while kewra water, from the Pandanus tree blossom, goes into Indian sweets. Elderberry blossom fritters are an old-time season specialty once made by German-Americans, while batter fritters dipped in jasmine-scented honey and sugar syrup in the Arab style are a Sicilian floral specialty.

In this chapter, semolina-stuffed Mahmoul cookies are scented with rosewater in a Syrian specialty (page 466) as is a classic American angel food cake (page 467) and a colonial-era cornmeal pound cake (page 469). Small French buttery brioches are stuffed with orange marmalade and flavored with orange blossom water (page 470), both products of the bitter orange tree. For even more orange intensity, an orange blossom glaze (page 471) is drizzled over top and that can also be used to glaze shortbread cookies and the like. Lavender and lemon flavor a honey-glazed cake in a combination inspired by the flavors of the south of France (page 472). An Indian spiced carrot cake with cardamom gets a smooth, rich white chocolate and cream cheese icing with a touch of tropical kewra water (page 237).

ROSEWATER

Rose perfumes are made from attar of roses, or rose oil, which is a mixture of volatile essential oils obtained by steam-distilling the crushed petals, a process first developed in Persia and later Bulgaria. Because of the perfume industry's immense demand for rose oil, rosewater, which is a byproduct of this production, is inexpensive. Rosewater was first produced by chemists in medieval times in Persia (now Iran). Historians believe that Moorish conquerors carried the rose from Persia to Spain, spreading from there into France and other parts of Europe.

The large rose family originated in the region that stretches from Western Europe to East Asia with most European rose varieties stemming from the *Rosa gallica*, which grows wild in the Caucasus Mountains. The production of rosewater by steam distillation was probably first done by the renowned tenth-century Persian physician, Avicenna. About 2,000 rose blossoms yield only one gram of rose oil along with its rosewater, the part used in the kitchen.

Classically, rosewater is made using the many-petaled, fragrant damask rose, *Rosa damascena*, first grown in Persia (now Iran) and Bulgaria, but now also found in Spain, Italy, and France. In the south of France and North Africa, rose oil is obtained from *Rosa centifolia*. In the famed Bulgarian Rose Valley in central Bulgaria, also known as the Kazanlak Valley, rosewater is distilled from the damask rose. Cultivated in the region for over 300 years this rose produces blossoms with an extraordinarily high percentage of essential oil. Indian rose essence is extracted from small deep-red roses with a double row of petals grown specifically for their inimitable fragrance, which is then diluted to make rosewater. Today, the countries of the Middle East are the largest producers of rosewater, because of demand and the availability of damask roses.

Rosewater has a distinctive flavor and is used heavily in South Asian, West Asian and Middle Eastern cuisine–especially in sweets. For the uninitiated, especially in America, the first reaction is usually "it tastes like soap," because that is our association in the West. Elsewhere, rose is as common a culinary flavoring as is vanilla and cinnamon in the States. Red rose, white mastic (see page 519), and green bergamot (a rare and highly fragrant Mediterranean citrus fruit) are the three traditional flavors for *loukoumia*, the Greek name for the sweet chewy confection known as

Turkish delight in English and *loukum* in Turkish. In India, rosewater flavors the small globes of fried dough called *gulab jamun*. In Iran, rosewater is used in small but potent quantities to flavor tea, ice cream, cookies, and other sweet pastries.

Rosewater is a key flavoring for Indian sweet lassi, a drink made from yogurt, sugar, and fruit juices, and in jallab, a sweet syrup made from dates, grape molasses, and rosewater that is popular in the Middle East and India. Turks dissolve rose-scented loukum (Turkish delight) into their coffee, and in Iran, honey and jams are scented with rose petals. Farther east, in Malaysia and Singapore, rosewater is mixed with milk, sugar, and pink food coloring to make a sweet drink called *bandung*. Rose ice cream is enjoyed in many Middle Eastern countries and even tobacco is scented with rose in Turkey.

Rose preserves made with petals simmered in heavy sugar syrup are sold in Indian groceries. While visiting the Greek island of Chios, home of mastic (see page 519), I bought a jar of locally made, pastel-colored, transparent rose petal preserves. Vitamin-C packed rose hips jam is popular in Central Europe. In France, red rose petals from Provence are candied and used to decorate cakes. Rose syrup and rose jam are also produced in Italy, especially in Liguria. In Western Europe today, rosewater shows up in macaroons–including the Ispahan, filled with rose-scented cream and topped with a fresh rose petal, created by Pierre Herme (www.pierreherme.com)–marzipan, meringues, pound cakes, and other sweets. It was popular in American colonial times as a flavoring for pound cakes such as the Cornmeal Pound Cake on page 469, although these days, it is rare to find it in American kitchens.

Fresh rose petals, rosewater, sweet rose syrup, candied rose buds, and dried rose buds are all used in baking. When using fresh roses, make sure they are organic, as insect repellent sprays can be poisonous. When using dried rosebuds, separate the petals from the calyx before using the petals only.

ROSE-SCENTED LOUKUM IN ISTANBUL

While wandering the endlessly fascinating streets of Istanbul, I came across a beautifully preserved and restored shop opened in 1777 in the Eminön district, near the Galata Bridge and Topkapi Palace. A favorite of the sultans and known as Turkish Delight, loukum has been produced in Turkey since the fifteenth century, but it was in this shop that Ali Muhiddin Haci Bekir became famous when he began producing rose-scented chewy loukum candy from a new recipe using starch and refined sugar. Originally, the confection was called *rahat loukum*, meaning "comfortable morsel," because it was soft enough even for those with bad teeth to enjoy. Today, the fifth generation of the Haci Bekir family runs the small shop. While pistachios, walnuts, almonds, and even chocolate flavor their loukum today, the original rosewater flavor is still a favorite. For more information, go to www.hacibekir.com.

ROSE SYRUP FROM ITALY'S VALLE SCRIVIA

I happily carried a small bottle of superb, deep-red rose syrup produced in the Valle Scrivia in the mountains north of Genoa back to my kitchen. At one time, this rose syrup was found in every Genovese kitchen. The syrup had become a rarity, although in the year 2000, a new producers association was organized with help from Slow Food (www.slowfood.com). The best rose to make this syrup is the wild rose, or *Rosa rugosa*, which originated in Japan and Manchuria, China, and the Gallica, already grown in the gardens of the Greeks and Romans. The two-hundred year old confectionary store, Romanengo (see page 224) uses roses from this region to infuse their exquisite candies and liqueurs and sells the Ligurian rose syrup. Buy it from Italian Harvest (www.italianharvest.com

ORANGE BLOSSOM WATER

Fragrant orange blossom water is distilled from the flowers of the bitter orange tree, *Citrus aurantium*, also known as Seville orange, sour orange, or Bigarade orange. Many varieties of bitter oranges are distilled for their essential oil, which is used in perfume, as a flavoring, and in herbal medicines. The same thick-skinned, dimpled orange is prized for making marmalade, because of its high pectin content, and for liqueurs such as Curaçao and Grand Marnier (see page 595 for more). Orange blossom water is lighter and less intensely perfumed than rosewater, although that varies greatly by brands and country of origin. Some are sweeter, others more floral. In the Middle East, orange flower water is diluted in hot water to make "white coffee." The A. Monteux orange flower water from France has a very floral fragrance, almost like a perfume. The Middle Eastern orange flower water is from Lebanon and is labeled as orange blossom water. The nose is definitely more orange and citrusy with an earthy character and no sweetness to the palate. Cortas is the most commonly found brand of orange blossom water (and rosewater) in the United States.

KEWRA WATER

Kewra water is distilled from the male flowers of the palm-like blossoming pandanus tree, *Pandanus odoratissimus*, also known as screw pine. Widely cultivated in India, it is used to flavor sweets, syrups, beverages, and halvas in India, especially the Northern Indian province of the Punjab. The water has a delicate, floral scent similar to rose but sweeter, fruitier, and more tropical with vanilla-like notes.

Though pandanus trees grow all over tropical Asia, kewra water is mainly a Northern Indian, especially Punjabi flavoring. Indian emigrants have transported the trees to other tropical regions and it is now used as a flavoring from Australia to Polynesia. Look for kewra water in small bottles at Indian groceries and note that a little bit goes a long way.

HOW TO USE FLOWER WATERS

Try a few drops of rosewater, mixed with slivered almonds, in ice cream, rice pudding, or custard. Or, make simple syrup using one part of rosewater to three parts water, plus sugar and add to ice tea or drizzle on plain cakes or sliced fruit. Rosewater also pairs nicely with ricotta cheese, mango, raspberry, and peach.

Orange blossom water is an ingredient in Persian and Arabic food. It has a stronger flavor than rosewater and should be used sparingly so the other flavors are not overwhelmed. Add a few drops to fruit mace-doines, or to flavor desserts made with almonds, pistachios, apples, apricots, figs, pears, or dates.

LAVENDER

Fresh or dried lavender flowers can be used to make simple syrup for fruit, ice cream, cake, or pastries. Lavender works well with berries, black currants, cherries, figs, plums, or paired with gin-ger, lemon, orange, or vanilla flavors. With laven-der, it's important to err on the conservative side, as its flavor gets stronger with cooking or baking and can easily become overpowering, even for a lavender-lover like me.

LAVENDER SYRUP

To make lavender-infused simple syrup, combine 1 cup of water and 3/4 cup sugar in a saucepan and bring to a boil. Add 1 tablespoon fresh lavender flowers and stir, making sure the flowers are immersed in the liquid. Remove from the heat, cover, and let the mixture steep for 30 minutes. Strain into a pitcher and use immediately or refrigerate up to three months in a glass jar with a tightly closed lid. Use the syrup to flavor meringues, to soak cakes and pastries, or to dress mixed fruit Macedonia.

USING CANDIED AND FRESH FLOWERS

Candied violets or violas are produced commer-cially in the scented flower–growing region of the south of France at Toulouse. Fresh and candied flowers make exquisite garnishes for special occa-sion desserts and cakes. Try violets or roses on anything chocolate or chestnut. Yellow candied mimosa work with vanilla or white chocolate and other delicate flavors.

MAKE YOUR OWN CANDIED FLOWERS

To make your own candied flowers, gather perfect violets, deep-colored rose petals, mimosa blos-soms, or lilac blossoms on a dry day. Wash the flowers gently and quickly in cold water, then allow them to dry completely on paper towels.

Lightly beat one egg white until it is frothy. Dip each flower or flower petal first into the egg white, then roll in super-fine sugar to coat evenly, but lightly. Arrange on wax paper to dry for one day. Store in an airtight tin, layered between waxed paper.

COMMON EDIBLE FLOWERS

Be very careful that any blossoms are, in fact, edible. The blossoms of edible herbs will also be edible and have a sweet, honeyed herbal perfume. Edible flowers must be organically grown as many insect repellents are poisonous.

BORAGE BLOSSOMS, *Borago officinalis,* also known as star flower, are small five-pointed star-shaped flowers in an exquisite and unmistakable beautiful shade of periwinkle blue with a black center. Like borage leaves, the blossoms taste like cucumber.

CALENDULA, *Calendula officinalis,* also known as Pot Marigold, is a wonderful edible flower with flavors ranging from spicy to bitter, tangy to peppery. Sprinkle the petals on cakes or other desserts for garnish.

ELDERBERRY BLOSSOMS, *Sambucus species,* are pale creamy white in color with a sweet scent and taste. Do not wash the blossoms as that removes much of the fragrance. Instead check them carefully for insects. The blossoms are dipped in fritter batter and deep-fried.

HIBISCUS BLOSSOMS, *Hibiscus rosa-sinensis,* are quite large. They have a mild cranberry-like flavor with citrus overtones and may be candied.

JOHNNY-JUMP-UPS, *Viola tricolor,* have lovely small yellow, white, and purple blooms with a mild wintergreen flavor.

LAVENDER FLOWERS, *Lavendula species,* have a highly aromatic sweet, floral flavor, with lemon and citrus notes.

LILAC, *Syringa vulgaris,* is generally very fragrant, with a slightly bitter flavor and a distinct lemony taste.

NASTURTIUM BLOSSOMS, *Tropaeolum majusm,* are large, intensely colored, and have a spicy flavor similar to watercress, with the hook-shaped bottom portion the sweetest, honeyed part of the flower.

PANSIES, *Viola x wittrockiana,* have a mild grassy flavor but come in exquisite colors.

ROSES, *Rosa rugosa, Rosa damascene,* and *Rosa gallica officinalis,* taste like a combination of strawberries and green apples. All roses are edible, but darker varieties will have a stronger flavor. Be sure to remove the bitter white portion of the petals and the calyx before using.

SAGE, *Salvia officinalis,* has small, fragrant flowers that are violet-blue, pink, or white, and are small, tube-like, and clustered together in whorls along the stem tops. The flowers have a honey-sage scent.

SCARLET RUNNER BEANS, *Phaseolus coccineus,* have strikingly beautiful blossoms that are edible. In England, they are often grown as ornamentals.

SCENTED GERANIUMS, *Pelargonium species*, have a flower flavor that generally corresponds to the variety. Rose and lemon geranium work well for desserts. Their colors are generally pinks and pastels.

VIOLETS, *Viola* species, have a sweet, perfumed flavor, and are used in old-fashioned desserts, creams, and candies. Pick them from the wild in season.

BUYING FLOWER WATERS, SYRUP, FRESH, AND CANDIED BLOSSOMS

Rosewater, syrup, and dried roses are available all year from Middle Eastern and Indian groceries and online from Sadaf (www.sadaf.com), which specializes in Iranian foods, and other sources. Candied violets, roses, mimosa blossoms, and lilacs are available from many online suppliers, including www.markethallfoods.com. Rose and orange blossom waters in clear glass bottles produced by Cortas of Lebanon are the easiest brand to find in the United States. Orange blossom water is also produced in northwestern Morocco and sold in this country under the name Mustapha's, among others. Both Pakistani and Indian kewra water are available from Kalustyan's (www.kalustyans.com, as is the superb rose water from Dubai. Kewra essence is a more concentrated oil made from the same blossoms. It is sold in tiny bottles in Indian and Southeast Asian markets.

The candied chestnuts sent to me from Romanengo of Genoa were nestled among candied violets and picked up a heavenly aroma just from being in their general vicinity. Order both online at www.romnengo.com or from their American distributer. www.italianharvest.com.. Meadowsweets is a family business in New York's Schoharie Valley, which is reviving the delicate art of crystallizing edible flowers. The process, done by hand, one at a time, preserves the exquisite detail and brilliant natural color of the flowers. Order pansies, violas, Johnny-jump-ups, lavender, and miniature roses, with daisies and cornflowers available in season from www.candiedflowers.com. Occasionally, small plastic clamshells of edible flowers may be found in the specialty produce section of the supermarket. These can be used as is or candied.

Mahmoul (Syrian Pistachio–Stuffed Semolina Cookies with Rosewater)

Mahmoul are small pastries made from faintly grainy semolina dough and related to the Tunisian Makroud (page 422). They are made by the hundreds by the patient women of a bridegroom's family (for the wedding is given by the man's side). Because they are a pastry made for feasts and other celebrations, they are filled with costly pistachios and scented with rosewater, a heavenly flavor combo.

YIELD: 24 COOKIES

Dough

1 pound (2$\frac{1}{2}$ cups plus 2 tablespoons) fine semolina

$\frac{1}{4}$ pound (1 cups minus 1 tablespoon) unbleached
all-purpose flour

10 ounces (2$\frac{1}{2}$ sticks) unsalted butter,
melted and cooled

Filling

1 pound pistachios, finely chopped

1 cup sugar

2 teaspoon rosewater

Confectioners' sugar, for dusting

Make the dough: In a medium bowl, combine the semolina, flour, and butter. Let mixture stand, covered, for 1 hour. Knead in about 1 cup water, enough to make a soft, but not sticky, dough.

Preheat the oven to 375°F.

Make the filling: In a food processor, combine the pistachios, sugar, and rosewater, and process until the mixture turns into a stiff, smooth dough, about 2 minutes.

Roll a walnut-sized piece of dough into a ball and, holding it in your cupped palm, press with your finger to form a deep depression in its center. Press in 1 tablespoon of filling and pinch the edges of the dough firmly together to enclose filling. Continue forming cookies in the same manner, arranging them seam side down and 1 inch apart on two greased baking sheets. Bake until pale gold, about 25 minutes. Cool and then dust with confectioners' sugar.

Rose-Scented Angel Food Cake

Angel food cakes were probably baked first by African-American slaves in the South because whipping the egg whites by hand requires a strong arm and tireless beating. Slave cooks escaping north up the Mississippi River brought along their knowledge and skill in making this fluffy white cake first to St. Louis. Angel food cakes are traditionally served after a funeral in the African-American community, perhaps as a wish that the angels would shine on the departed. Note that if you don't have superfine (or bar) sugar, spin the sugar in a blender or coffee grinder until it is powdery. I like to tint the glaze with a touch of rose coloring paste to accentuate its pinkness. Use the gel colors sold by Wilton or Ateco, as liquid colors are too thin and watery. Look for rose syrup and edible dried roses at Middle Eastern and Indian markets. This recipe is dairy-free.

YIELD: ONE 10-INCH CAKE, 10 TO 12 SERVINGS

Cake

3 ounces unbleached all-purpose flour plus 1 ounce
potato starch or $\frac{1}{4}$ pound cake flour

1$\frac{1}{2}$ cups superfine sugar

12 large egg whites (1$\frac{1}{2}$ cups), at room temperature

$\frac{1}{2}$ cup lukewarm water

$\frac{1}{2}$ teaspoon fine sea salt

1 teaspoon cream of tartar

2 teaspoons rosewater

1 teaspoon vanilla extract

Glaze

$^1\!/_4$ pound (1$^1\!/_4$ cups) confectioners' sugar

4 teaspoons lime juice (1 lime)

1 tablespoon rose syrup, substitute grenadine syrup or
  framboise liqueur plus 1 teaspoon rose water

Touch of rose coloring paste, optional

Fresh or dried rose petals and leaves for garnish, optional

Make the cake: Preheat the oven to 325°F. In a small bowl, whisk the flour and potato starch and $^3\!/_4$ cup of the sugar together.

In a standing mixer fitted with a whisk attachment, beat the egg whites and water at medium speed until frothy, add the salt, cream of tartar, rosewater, and vanilla, and beat briefly to combine. Slowly add the remaining $^3\!/_4$ cup sugar and continue beating until the whites are moist and glossy and just firm enough to form soft, drooping peaks. Take care not to overbeat the whites, which will cause a dry and ill-formed cake.

Transfer the mixture to a large, wide bowl. Sift enough of the flour mixture to dust the top of the foam. Using a spatula, fold in gently. Continue dusting and folding until all of the flour mixture is incorporated.

Carefully spoon the batter into an ungreased 10-inch tube pan, preferably a special angel food pan. Using an icing spatula, cut through the batter with a circular motion to remove any large air bubbles and to draw the batter into any unfilled spaces. Shake the batter back and forth to even the top.

Bake for 45 minutes, or until the cake is springy to the touch and a metal skewer or toothpick comes out clean. If the pan has feet, invert it over a work surface; otherwise invert it over the neck of a bottle so that the cake hangs downward. Cool for at least 1 hour before removing the cake from the pan. Run a thin knife around the edge of the pan and the inside tube to loosen the cake. Then tap the pan against the counter until the cake detached from the pan onto a cake plate.

Make the glaze: In a small bowl, whisk together the confectioners' sugar, lime juice, rose syrup, and rose coloring paste, until smooth and thick. Drizzle the glaze over the cake, let the cake stand for 10 minutes, or until the glaze is set, and garnish it with the rose petals. (I like to decorate the cake as my artistic daughter Ginevra suggested: a narrow band of individual rose petals surrounding the inner edge of the cake and a matching band around the outer edge.)

ANGEL FOOD CAKE TIPS

Sift the flour several times to incorporate as much air as possible and handle the flour lightly. Beat the egg whites until they are just firm enough to hold up in soft, drooping peaks and are moist and glossy for the lightest cake with finest grain. Underbeaten egg whites will result in a heavy, compact, and undersized cake because not enough air has been incorporated while overbeaten whites will result in a dry cake of poor volume because of loss of air and moisture. Add any flavoring to the mixture before you add the flour. It will then be thoroughly blended without the extra folding that would be necessary if it were added last. In combining ingredients, fold the mixture just enough to blend ingredients. Undermixing makes an uneven grain in cake. Overmixing makes the cake heavy, undersized, close-grained, and tough. Use a serated knife to sice the cake.

Cornmeal and Rosewater Pound Cake

This recipe originated at the cooking school of Elizabeth Goodfellow in Philadelphia around 1810. Mrs. Goodfellow was one of the most influential cooks and pastry chefs in the country until her death in 1851. According to culinary historian William Woys Weaver, her cake is deceivingly sophisticated; its success depends upon an ingenious chemical reaction that will not take place unless rosewater is present. The result is the most luscious, goldenrod-colored pound cake. Weaver uses white cornmeal; I love the color and flavor of the yellow. For a more subtle rose flavor, you may cut the rosewater quantity to four tablespoons.

YIELD: ONE 10-INCH RING CAKE, 10 TO 12 SERVINGS

3/4 pound (2 1/2 cups plus 2 tablespoons) stone ground white cornmeal

1/4 pound cake flour, or 3 ounces all-purpose flour plus 1 ounce cornstarch or potato starch

2 teaspoons baking powder

1 tablespoon freshly grated nutmeg

1 teaspoon fine sea salt

1 pound (4 sticks) unsalted butter, softened

1 1/2 cups superfine sugar

8 large eggs, at room temperature

6 tablespoons rosewater (yes, 6 tablespoons)

Dried rose petals, for sprinkling

Confectioners' sugar, for dusting

Preheat the oven to 350°F. Prepare a 10-inch cake pan, preferably ring-shaped, by spraying with nonstick baker's coating, or rub with softened butter and dust with flour, shaking off the excess.

Whisk together the dry ingredients: cornmeal, flour, baking powder, nutmeg, and salt, then set aside on the stove to keep warm.

In the bowl of a standing mixer fitted with the paddle attachment, cream the butter and sugar until very light and fluffy, 6 to 8 minutes, then beat in the eggs one at a time. Fold in the cornmeal mixture in thirds, then add the rosewater and beat only enough to combine it with the batter thoroughly. Scrape the batter into the prepared pan. Bake for 45 minutes or until the cake starts to come away from the sides of the pan and a skewer inserted in the center comes out clean.

Separate the rose petals from their calyxes and crumble into bits with your hands. Dust the cake with sugar and then sprinkle with the rose petal bits.

Note: Edible dried rose buds are available from Indian, Middle Eastern, and Pakistani groceries or from www.kalustyans.com.

ELIZABETH GOODFELLOW AND ELIZA LESLIE

Elizabeth Goodfellow (1768–1851) was an American pastry cook, confectioner, and cooking school instructor, probably born in Maryland. It is not known where and how she got her extraordinary culinary training, but by 1808, she had established herself as one of the leading pastry cooks and confectioners in the country. Goodfellow was a firm believer in American ingredients and an American style of cooking, and was one of the most creative forces in American cookery during the early nineteenth century. Goodfellow is credited for introducing lemon pudding, the prototype for lemon meringue pie, in her Philadelphia shops. She was also famous for her rose jumbles: delicate, crisp, ring-shaped sugar cookies scented with rosewater.

Eliza Leslie was a top student at Goodfellow's school who went on to publish more than a dozen influential American cookbooks. Her first book, probably derived from recipes she learned at Goodfellow's school, was titled *Seventy-Five Receipts for Pastry, Cakes and Sweetmeats,* and was published in 1828. She also wrote a book called *The Indian Meal Book,* published during the Irish potato famine to teach the Irish how to use American cornmeal.

POUND CAKE OR QUATRES QUARTS

English pound cake and French *quatres quarts* (four quarters) from Brittany were the most popular kinds of cakes into the twentieth century. Both are made by weighing equal amounts of eggs, flour, sugar, and butter, pushing to the maximum the amount of butter and sugar that the foundation structure provided by the flour and eggs are able to hold. Any more butter or sugar and the cake would collapse under the weight. Before electric mixers, it was hard work to beat the sugar and butter together until it was full of the air bubbles that would expand to lighten the cake as it baked.

Orange Blossom Brioches

These dainty little brioches are full of orange flavor: sultry, sweet perfume from their blossoms, oily fragrance from their colorful skins, and a filling of Seville (or bitter orange) marmalade, making them quite sophisticated. Gild the lily (or the brioche) with an orange blossom and orange juice glaze and watch them fly off the table. I make them in 1-cup fluted ceramic brioche molds (purchased from www.bakerscatalogue .com) and fill the indented center with orange marmalade before baking. When they cool, I pipe the Orange Blossom glaze in circular patterns over the top so they resemble lush, overblown flower blossoms. Use 1-cup custard cups or muffin tin if you don't have brioche molds.

YIELD: 3 DOZEN SMALL BRIOCHES

1 cup lukewarm milk

1 cup sugar

1 ($\frac{1}{4}$-ounce) package (2$\frac{1}{4}$ teaspoons) active dry yeast

Grated zest of 2 oranges or tangerines (8 teaspoons)

1 tablespoon orange blossom water

8 large egg yolks ($\frac{1}{2}$ cup)

1 teaspoon fine sea salt

1$\frac{1}{2}$ pounds (5$\frac{3}{4}$ cups minus 2 tablespoons) unbleached all-purpose flour

10 ounces (2$\frac{1}{2}$ sticks) unsalted butter, cut into piece-sand softened

1 cup Seville orange marmalade

1 cup Orange Blossom Glaze (opposite page)

In a small bowl, combine the milk, $\frac{1}{4}$ cup of the sugar, and the yeast, and let stand until foamy, about 10 minutes.

In the bowl of a standing mixer fitted with the paddle attachment, combine the yeast mixture, the remaining $^3/_4$ cup of the sugar, the orange zest, orange blossom water, egg yolks, and the salt. Beat until well-combined, about 30 seconds. Using the paddle attachment, beat in about two-thirds of the flour, continuing to beat until the dough is smooth and elastic, though still soft. Add the butter, a little at a time, beating until the butter has been completely incorporated and no lumps remain. Beat in the remaining flour, continuing to beat until the dough is smooth and elastic, though still rather sticky.

Transfer the dough to a large oiled bowl; turn around so the dough is oiled all over. Cover with plastic film or a damp cloth and allow the dough to rise at room temperature until doubled in size, about 2 hours. (Note that if the ambient temperature is too warm, the butter will start to melt and leak out of the brioches. You may refrigerate the dough at this point up to overnight. The dough will continue to rise but more slowly.)

Punch the dough down to remove air bubbles. Grab a small clump of dough, enough to fill the chosen mold about half full. Smooth the clump into a ball, pulling the rough portion under, and press into the mold with the smooth side up. Continue doing this until all the dough has been shaped. Gently press down the centers to form a nest. Spoon about 2 teaspoons marmalade into the center of each nest. Arrange the molds on a baking pan, spray with water from a plant mister and set aside to rise at warm room temperature until almost doubled, about $1^1/_2$ hours.

Preheat the oven to 375°F. Bake the brioches for 20 minutes, or until puffed and golden brown. Remove from the oven and cool to room temperature.

Arrange the brioches on a wire rack placed over a baking pan or a sheet of wax papers. Drizzle 1 to 2 teaspoons of Orange Blossom Glaze over each brioche, allowing the excess to drip off. In cool weather, the glaze will set at room temperature. In warm weather, place them in the refrigerator for about 30 minutes to set the glaze. Store the brioches covered and in a single layer for up to 2 days at room temperature.

Orange Blossom Glaze

Use this simple, orange-tinted glaze to drizzle on cakes such as the rose scented Angel Food Cake (page 00) substituting the orange blossom water for the rose water or the Pan di Spagna (page 00).

YIELD 2$^1/_2$ CUPS

$^1/_4$ cup orange juice concentrate, defrosted
1 tablespoon orange blossom water
Grated zest of 1 orange (4 teaspoons)
2 cups confectioners' sugar

In a medium bowl, combine the orange juice concentrate, orange blossom water, and orange zest. Whisk in the confectioners' sugar to form a thick, barely pourable glaze. Spoon drizzle or pipe over cakes or cookies and allow the glaze to set for 30 minutes at room temperature. Store covered and refrigerated up to 3 weeks, though the glaze may thin out. Beat in more confectioners' sugar if necessary.

Honey Glazed Lavender–Lemon Cake

Three flavors redolent of Provence come together in this easy-to-make but impressive cake: honey, lemon, and lavender. I still get a strong déja-vu feeling when I sniff lavender, bringing back the memory of seemingly endless fields of waving lavender fronds on a visit to Provence when I was about twelve. I process the lavender buds with the flour mix for the cake batter and with the confectioners' sugar for the glaze, sieving out the pieces and leaving behind a subtle but unmistakable lavender flavor to both.

YIELD: ONE 10-INCH BUNDT CAKE, 10 TO 12 SERVINGS

Cake

10 ounces (2¼ cups plus 1 tablespoon) unbleached all-purpose flour

2 ounces (½ cup plus 2 tablespoons) potato starch

1 tablespoon dried lavender blossoms

2 teaspoons baking powder

1 teaspoon baking soda

½ teaspoon fine sea salt

½ pound (2 sticks) unsalted butter, softened

1½ cups sugar

4 large eggs

Grated zest of 2 lemons (2 tablespoons)

¾ cup buttermilk

6 tablespoons freshly squeezed lemon juice (2 to 3 lemons)

Glaze

1 cup confectioners' sugar

1 tablespoon dried lavender blossoms

½ cup honey, preferably wildflower

1 tablespoon fresh squeezed lemon juice

Lavender sprigs (dried or fresh) for garnish, optional

Make the cake: Place an oven rack in the lower third of the oven. Preheat the oven to 325°F. Spray a 10-inch Bundt or ring pan with nonstick baker's coating, or rub with softened butter and dust with flour, shaking out the excess.

In the bowl of a food processor, combine the dry ingredients: flour, potato starch, lavender blossoms, baking powder, baking soda, and salt. Process until the lavender is ground finely. Sift the flour mix through a fine sieve to remove any lavender bits.

In the bowl of a standing mixer fitted with the paddle attachment, cream the butter and sugar until light and fluffy, 5 to 6 minutes, scraping down the sides once or twice. Beat in eggs one at a time, beating well after each addition, then beat in the lemon zest.

Whisk together the buttermilk and lemon juice. With the mixer on lowest speed, beat in the flour mix alternating with the buttermilk mixture, beginning and ending with the flour mix.

Spoon the batter into the prepared pan, knocking once or twice against the counter to remove any air bubbles. Bake for 1 hour or until the cake starts to come away from the sides of the pan and a toothpick or skewer stuck in the center comes out clean. Cool completely on a wire rack. Turn the cake out onto a wire rack set over a sheet of wax paper.

Make the glaze: Place the confectioners' sugar and the lavender blossoms in the bowl of a food processor. Process until the lavender is ground finely into powder. Sift the mixture through a fine sieve to remove any lavender bits.

Place the honey in a medium microwaveable bowl and heat on low power for 1 minute, or until warm to the touch and runny in consistency. Add the sugar mixture and lemon juice and whisk together until smooth. Drizzle the glaze over the cooled cake and allow it to set before cutting into serving portions. Garnish the cake with sprigs of lavender. Store the cake, covered and at room temperature, for up to 4 days. Note that this cake, unglazed, freezes well up to three months. Defrost and then glaze.

THE FAMOUS BUNDT CAKE PAN

In 1950, a group of Minneapolis women of Eastern European Jewish background and members of the influential Jewish women's organization, Hadassah, approached the owner of Nordic Products, H. David Dalquist, to ask him to make an aluminum version of the iron Turk's head pan used in European, especially Austro-Hungarian, baking. Happy to oblige, Dalquist made up a few pans for the members with some extra to sell to the public.

Ten years later, the new *Good Housekeeping Cookbook* showed a decorative pound cake that had been baked in one of pans. After that, cakes baked in this easy-to-use pan started to show up in and win national baking contests. Today, more than fifty million pans exist in America. A few of the originals were honored by being included in the Smithsonian Institute's collection. I prefer my two old, plain aluminum original Bundt pans, rather than the more modern dark-colored non-stick treated pans I bought a few years ago. Cakes come out lighter and more evenly colored in the aluminum pans and I never have a problem with sticking as long as I spray the pans with nonstick baker's coating.

GELATIN

European Sheet Gelatin...478

Fruit Enzymes that Prevent
Gelatin from Setting...479

Working with Gelatin...479

TORTA DI ZABAGLIONE...480

LEMON-BLACKBERRY BAVARESE
WITH LIMONCELLO...481

COCONUT MANGO CHEESECAKE...482

BLACKBERRY-WHITE CHOCOLATE TART...483

Fixing Lumpy Pastry Cream...484

GELATIN

The sparkling fruit jelly layered with jewel–like fruits in the window at Milan's world–famous food emporium, Peck, caught my eye. I snapped a few shots to bring home and inspire me to make my own version, until the gentleman inside shook his head no. Clear, colorful, home-made fruit jellies were once the hallmark of a skillful cook. Most of us no longer know how to make our own because it's much easier to open a box of Jell-O or other prepared gelatin dessert. Gelatin is another secret ingredient for bakers, used to help give more body to creamy fillings.

Valued for their brilliant shimmering appear-ance, jellies were originally based on a home-made gelatin, rich with body from gelatinous calves' feet. For cooks in earlier times, making jelly demanded a great deal of time and technical skill. Fancy molded jellies became the symbol of a well-to-do household. Two hundred years ago, jellies were served in fancy glasses, sometimes in ribbons–layers of jellies in different colors. In Vic-torian times, jellies were often set in elaborate copper molds in all sorts of fanciful shapes. The clear fruit preserves also known as jellies get their thickness from pectin, the soluble fiber present in many fruits, especially those that are quite tart, not from animal-based gelatin.

Multi-talented inventor Peter Cooper (also the founder of the nation's first free university: Cooper Union in New York City) obtained the first patent for a gelatin dessert in 1845. By the begin-ning of the twentieth century, Americans began to switch from homemade jellies to Jell-O, the fruit-flavored powdered gelatin dessert mix that has been a pantry staple for over 100 years. More than one million packages of Jell-O gelatin are pur-chased or eaten every day and the Jell-O name is recognized by 99 percent of Americans. It didn't take long for Jell-O to become the symbol of American plenty and family values. For a time, immigrants entering Ellis Island were served Jell-O as a "Welcome to America." The company hired artist Norman Rockwell to create memorable ads showing the ease of making Jell-O: a little girl unmolding a Jell-O treat for her doll, a grand-mother making Jell-O with her grandchildren.

It's easy to see why Jell-O took off so fast and so far; we already loved jellied desserts. My 1923 Fanny Farmer Boston Cooking School Cookbook has 20 pages of fresh fruit, liqueur, and wine-flavored desserts, all using unflavored gelatin as a base. Farmer flavors the jellies with kumquat, pineapple, coffee, cider, sauternes, loganberry, and apricot-wine. She makes a fruit chartreuse in a deep, rounded bowl with a clear layer filled with a creamy fruit mousse. She called her vari-colored ribbon jelly layered with fruits, Macédoine pudding, after the multi-ethnic region of Macedonia.

Jell-O and other jellied desserts (like Bavarian cream and panna cotta) get their body from gelatin, derived from collagen–present in skin, connective tissue, and bones–particularly from young animals. Yes, it is the same collagen (or elasticity) that we lose as our skin ages. French Chef Marie Antoine Carême (1784–1833) the extraordinarily gifted chef and founder of La Grande Cuisine Française, taught chefs that the best aspics are made with calves' feet and veal knuckle–this is still true.

Years ago, I saw an irresistible picture in my *Time-Life Good Cook Classic Desserts Cookbook* of a sunshine-tinted orange jelly mold made with a homemade clear gelatin. I just had to make it, so as recommended by Carême, I ordered calves' feet from my meat purveyor. Nobody really understood what I was looking for because homemade jelly was a dish so out of style at the time, but they agreed to take my order. The next day, I came to work looking forward to the challenge of recreating the jelly. My order arrived and I opened the box to find calves feet. Just what I wanted. The only trouble was, they came complete with hooves and fur. I tried again; this time, ordering another gelatin-rich

cut, veal knuckle, and had better luck. The jelly was absolutely delicious; shimmering, brightly colored, and it held its shape without being rubbery. I still like to experiment with gellied fresh fruit juices and layered berries and other soft fruits, although these days I use the clear, thin sheets of European gelatin instead of making my own. One day, I'll succeed in re-creating Peck's magnificent jellied fruit terrine.

Gelatin is important in cookery and the food industry because of its ability to transform large amounts of liquid into an apparently solid substance, a gel. If the mixture is beaten while syrupy and thick but not yet fully set, the gelatin is elastic enough to stretch around and hold air bubbles, resulting in a mousse (the word for "sea foam" in French). Gelatin is used in making ice cream because it interferes with the formation of large ice crystals, so the ice cream maintains a smoother texture.

Transparent and almost colorless, unflavored gelatin is sold as a dehydrated powder. Gelatin granules swell up to approximately ten times their original size when moistened, trapping water molecules in the process. One envelope of gelatin, containing about $2\frac{1}{2}$ teaspoons of the powder, will gel 2 cups of liquid. European pastry chefs prefer using the glassy, thin, fragile sheets of gelatin. Both types are mixed with liquids and flavorings and used to "set" savory aspics if they don't contain enough naturally occurring gelatin and for desserts.

Modern jellied desserts are descended from

medieval dishes prepared from calves' feet or other gelatin-rich meat stocks, which were carefully clarified and then flavored. Medieval cooks knew a wide range of gelling agents besides meat broth, including isinglass and hartshorn. Isinglass is collagen extracted from the sounds or swimming bladders of certain fish such as sturgeon, hake, and cod. Because of its special chemical structure, isinglass is used for clarifying wines and beers. At one time, isinglass used to be equally important for culinary purposes. Although it is not used today in the kitchen, there is renewed interest in fish-derived gelatins. In Italian, gelatin is called *colla de pesce*, or fish gelatin, although it seems that it is actually made from gelatin-rich pig's skin along with cartilaginous calves' bones rather than fish. In England in the seventeenth and eighteenth centuries, hartshorn shavings were used to produce a special jelly, the same hartshorn that was also processed to be used as a leavener (see baker's ammonia on page 280).

There are also non-animal sources of gelatin extracted from seaweed. Carrageenan, also known as Irish Moss, is a seaweed mostly found off the coast of Ireland. Agar-agar is a reddish-purple seaweed from Asia used to make kosher (vegetarian) fruit jelly desserts. Agar-agar (kanten, grass jelly, or seaweed jelly) is a powerful gel. It is unique in being able to withstand temperatures near boiling, making it ideal for making jellied sweet dishes in tropical climates without melting. However, it tends to liquefy when combined with acidic fruits.

EUROPEAN SHEET GELATIN

European and American pastry chefs prefer using glassy-thin, fragile sheets of gelatin, an extremely refined form of gelatin that results in a clearer, more delicately gelled product without any rubberiness. Sheet gelatin is becoming more widely available in America and is sold by the Baker's Catalogue (www.bakerscatalogue.com) in packets of 20 sheets and from CaviarAssouline (www.caviarassouline.com) in 1 kilo packages. It is, naturally, more expensive than powdered gelatin.

To use the sheets, soak them in cold water to cover until they're soft and limp, 5 to 10 minutes. Remove them from the water and drop them directly into hot liquid, stirring until they are completely dissolved. For making panna cotta, in which barely set, jiggly consistency is essential, sheet gelatin is ideal. This type of gelatin comes in different grades, from bronze to silver, gold, and platinum. No matter what the grade, each sheet gels the same amount of liquid; the difference is in how refined it is. The highest grades have the least odor. Three sheets of gelatin equal about 1 teaspoon powdered gelatin.

FRUIT ENZYMES THAT PREVENT GELATIN FROM SETTING

Uncooked pineapple contains the enzyme *bromelain*, which will stop gelatin from setting properly by breaking down the gelatin. Papaya contains the enzyme *papain*, kiwi fruit contains *actinidin*, and figs contain *ficin*, all of which have similar effects when used raw. Cooking denatures the enzyme, a necessary step if jelling these fruits. Canned pineapple is already cooked, so it's fine to use as is.

WORKING WITH GELATIN

Unprepared gelatin has an indefinite shelf-life as long as it is wrapped airtight and stored in a cool, dry place.

- Keep gelatin dishes chilled until ready to serve; they can melt easily in hot weather or a hot kitchen.
- To avoid clumping, "bloom" powdered gelatin by mixing it with a little cold water or other liquid for about 5 minutes to moisten and plump the gelatin granules until the liquid has been absorbed before heating the mixture.
- Store gelatin desserts in a tightly closed container to avoid the formation of a thick rubbery skin on the surface.
- Too much sugar can prevent gelatin from setting. The more sugar in the recipe, the softer the jelly will be.
- You can melt down and re-chill gelatin several times before the mixture loses its thickening ability. Melt it in a double-boiler over low heat.
- Gelatin takes twice as long to dissolve when combined with cream or milk.
- When combining sugar with unflavored gelatin, mix the sugar and gelatin first before dissolving.
- To suspend fruits in gelatin, chill the mixture until it is syrupy and about the consistency of cold egg whites. Then mix in the additions and chill until completely set.
- Drain solids of their liquid before adding to gelatin to avoid watering down the gelatin.
- To easily unmold gelatin, spray the mold with cooking oil before filling. To avoid an oily film which might cloud the surface when using spray oil, briefly rinse the mold with cold water before filling. To unmold, dip the mold into warm (not hot) water as far up on the outside as the filling on the inside for 5 to 10 seconds, loosen the edges with a silicone spatula, and unmold. Return to the refrigerator for 20 minutes to refirm before serving.
- Two hours of chilling should be enough for most clear molds; four hours for gelatin molds containing cream and other additions. Layered gelatins must be individually chilled and firmed before adding the next layer.
- When doubling a gelatin-based recipe that calls for 2 cups of liquid, use only $3^3/_4$ cups of liquid in the doubled recipe.
- Do not bring gelatin mixtures to a full boil or you risk losing the gelatin's thickening properties.
- To easily center a mold on a plate, rinse the plate with cold water before unmolding the gelatin, so the gelatin it won't slide around.

Torta di Zabaglione

There is only one real *Harry's Bar. Located on Venice's Calle Vallaresso, near the Piazza San Marco, this legendary restaurant has been, for six decades, the meeting place for artists, writers, royalty, maestros, divas, celebrities, the very rich, and lots of ordinary, though discerning, Americans and Europeans. I ate like a queen on my own there many years ago with a full window view of the Grand Canal. My meal, which was perfect in every detail, consisted of a white peach Bellini, chicken and vegetable risotto, and a slice of this justly famed fluffy cake.*

YIELD: 12 SERVINGS

Filling

3 sheets gelatin, or 1 teaspoon powdered gelatin

4 large egg yolks ($1/4$ cup)

$1/2$ cup sugar

3 tablespoons unbleached all purpose flour

1 cup dry Marsala

Grated zest of 1 lemon (1 tablespoon)

$1^1/2$ cups heavy cream, chilled

Assembly

1 Pan di Spagna cake (page 441)

About 12 Italian Meringues (page 836)

Soak the gelatin sheets in cold water to soften them, about 5 minutes. Or soak the powdered gelatin in $1/4$ cup water until thickened, about 10 minutes, then heat it gently until it is clear, about 2 minutes.

In the bowl of a standing mixer fitted with the paddle attachment, beat the egg yolks and sugar until the mixture is thick and pale yellow. Add the flour 1 tablespoon at a time and beat in thoroughly. Beat in the Marsala and lemon zest.

Transfer the mixture to a heavy-bottomed saucepan and cook over medium heat, whisking constantly, until it just begins to boil. Remove from the heat and whisk in the drained gelatin sheets or the melted gelatin powder, stirring until completely dissolved.

Transfer the mixture to a bowl, preferably stainless-steel, and cool over a second bowl filled with a mixture of ice and water. Whisk the mixture from time to time to keep a crust from forming,

In the bowl of a standing mixer fitted with the whisk attachment, whip the cream until stiff but still bright white and not at all yellow. Fold into the egg mixture.

Cut a very small notch, about $1/4$-inch deep, out of the side of the Pan di Spagna cake to use as a guide. Using a long, serrated knife, cut the cake horizontally into three layers. Place the bottom layer of cake on a platter and spread it with about one-third of the filling. Place the second layer on top using the cut notch as a guide to line up the layers in their original position. Using a board or the bottom of a cake pan, press gently on the cake to secure. Smooth the filling that oozes out on the sides. Use the remaining filling to ice the sides and top of the cake.

Break the meringues into small pieces, about 1-inch long, and stick them all around the cake. Keep the cake refrigerated, up to 2 days, before serving. Note that the meringues will be crunchy at first, gradually softening. Use a knife dipped into hot water and then wiped dry to cut into serving portions.

Lemon–Blackberry Bavarese with Limoncello

This light and lusciously lemony molded dessert is adapted from one made famous by the French pastry chef Gaston Lenôtre, called a rosace *and made with oranges. Here, I've adapted it, using poached lemon slices and Limoncello liqueur. I also added a dark, tart layer of blackberries for contrast of color, texture, and flavor. Soft and creamy, the bavarese belongs to that category of desserts called* dolci al cucchiao, *or spoon-desserts, in Italy. You'll need to start one day ahead to simmer and then soak the lemon slices to sweeten them and mellow out the bitterness of their white pith. The less seedy the lemons, the easier they will be to work with. To make it easier, use a purchased sponge cake and purchased Limoncello instead of making your own.*

YIELD: 12 TO 14 SERVINGS

Lemon Syrup

6 large lemons (allowing for extra in case any break)

2 cups sugar

2 cups water

$^3/_4$ cup Limoncello, homemade (page 537)
    or purchased

Filling and Assembly

8 sheets gelatin, or $2^1/_4$ teaspoons powdered gelatin

7 large eggs

2 cups whole milk

$^3/_4$ cup sugar

2 ounces ($^1/_2$ cup minus 2 teaspoons) unbleached
    all-purpose flour

Pinch salt

$^1/_2$ cup fresh lemon juice (from about 3 lemons)

Grated zest of 2 lemons (2 tablespoons)

$^1/_4$ cup Limoncello, homemade (page 537)
    or purchased

1 cup heavy cream, chilled

1 Pan di Spagna cake (page 441)

1 pint blackberries, washed and drained well

Make the syrup: Scrub the lemons, trim off the ends, and slice them thinly and evenly, preferably using a mandoline or a deli-style meat slicer. Pick out any pits and discard.

Bring the sugar and water to a boil in a medium, nonreactive pot, and boil until the mixture is completely clear, about 3 minutes. Remove the syrup from heat and stir in Limoncello. Spoon out one half of the syrup and reserve. Add the lemon slices to the remaining syrup in the pot. Bring to a boil and then simmer on lowest heat for 1 hour, or until the lemons are tender but still whole. Remove from the heat, transfer gently to a container or bowl, and marinate overnight at room temperature, turning occasionally so all the lemons are covered with the syrup.

Make the filling: Soak the gelatin sheets in cold water to soften, about 5 minutes or soak the powdered gelatin in $^1/_4$ cup water until thickened, about 10 minutes, then heat it gently until it is clear, about 2 minutes.

In a medium bowl, whisk the eggs and $^1/_4$ cup of the milk until smooth. In a small bowl, whisk together the sugar, flour, and salt. Sprinkle the flour-sugar mixture into the eggs and whisk to combine well. Place the remaining $1^3/_4$

cups milk into a microwavable container, preferably a Pyrex measure, and scald until steaming hot in the microwave. Gradually pour in the hot milk, whisking until the mixture is smooth. Transfer the mixture to a medium, heavy-bottomed, nonreactive pot and heat over low heat, while constantly whisking, especially at the edges, until the mixture thickens evenly and comes to a boil.

Remove from the heat and immediately stir in the drained gelatin sheets (or powdered gelatin mixture), the lemon juice, lemon zest, and Limoncello. Transfer to a stainless-steel bowl and set the bowl over a second bowl filled with ice and water. Cool the mixture to room temperature, whisking often—the gelatin will have just begun to set.

In the bowl of a standing mixer fitted with the whisk attachment, beat the cream until it is firm, but not at all yellow in color. Fold into the pastry cream in thirds, so as not to deflate the mixture.

Assemble the dessert: Prepare a 9-inch cake pan by brushing lightly with the syrup, then line evenly with plastic film, allowing the edges to overhang.

Cut the Pan di Spagna horizontally into 2 (½-inch) thick slices (you will have extra cake; reserve for cake crumbs).

Drain the lemon slices well, discarding the soaking liquid, which will be rather bitter. Use the slices to line the pan, covering the entire surface and the sides, making sure to overlap them in an even pattern, especially on the bottom, which will become the top.

Spoon one-third of the pastry cream into the pan without dislodging the lemons. Cover with a layer of Pan di Spagna and brush generously with the reserved syrup. Spoon one-third more of the pastry cream mix-

ture over the cake. Arrange the blackberries over the cake. Spoon the remaining pastry cream over the blackberries, filling completely. Top with a second layer of Pan di Spagna and brush with more syrup.

Cover the surface with plastic wrap and chill the bavarese for at least 4 hours, preferably overnight, to set. (The bavarese may be assembled up to 2 days ahead.)

When ready to serve, uncover the top and invert onto an attractive serving platter. Pull off the plastic film and serve, cutting into 12 or more slices.

Coconut Mango Cheesecake

This unbaked "refrigerator" cheesecake is creamy, luscious, and tastes of a tropical island. It was inspired by one served at the Buccaneer Restaurant on the Dutch island of Aruba. Look for pure mango purée in specialty food markets or in the freezer section at Latin American and Mexican markets. The coconut pastry is so good, why not double recipe and freeze the rest? It would make a perfect crust for a key lime pie. The bottled mango slices sold in the refrigerator section at the supermarket or frozen mango pieces make a perfect easy garnish.

YIELD: 16 SERVINGS

Coconut Crust
½ pound (2 cups minus 2 tablespoons) unbleached all-purpose flour

6 tablespoons sugar

6 ounces (1½ sticks) unsalted butter, chilled
   and cut into bits

½ teaspoon fine sea salt

¼ pound (2 cups) shredded unsweetened coconut

1 large egg

1 teaspoon almond extract

Filling

Juice of 3 limes (6 tablespoons)

1 (¼-ounce) package (2½ teaspoons) powdered gelatin

1 pound cream cheese, softened

1 cup sugar

1½ cups mango purée (the flesh of 2 large mangoes
   puréed in the food processor)

2 teaspoons grated lime zest

2 tablespoons dark rum

1 firm but ripe fresh mango, cut into slices and mixed
   with a bit of lime juice

Make the crust: In the bowl of a food processor, combine the flour, sugar, butter, and salt. Process to combine well. Add the coconut, egg, and almond extract, and process only long enough for the mixture to come together. Transfer the mixture to a bowl and work by hand briefly to combine well.
Press the dough into the bottom and 2-inches up the sides of a 10-inch springform pan, smoothing the edges so they're even. Chill for 1 hour in the refrigerator or 30 minutes in the freezer to set the shape.

Preheat the oven to 375°F. Fit a piece of heavy-duty foil onto the dough and fill with beans or other pie weights. Blind bake (just pastry crust, no filling) on the bottom shelf of the oven until the crust is cooked

through but not yet browned, about 30 minutes. Remove the foil and the weights, reduce the oven temperature to 325°F, and bake 20 minutes longer, or until the crust is evenly and lightly browned. Remove from the oven and cool to room temperature on a wire rack.

Make the filling: In a small microwaveable bowl, combine the lime juice with the gelatin and allow the gelatin to "bloom," or thicken and absorb all the juice, about 10 minutes. Place the bowl in the microwave and heat on low power for 1 to 2 minutes, or until the gelatin has melted and there are no more granules visible. Cool to room temperature.

Place the cream cheese and sugar in the bowl of an electric mixer fitted with the paddle attachment and beat until smooth, scraping down the sides once or twice to eliminate any lumps. Add the mango purée, lime zest, rum, and the gelatin mixture, and beat briefly to combine. Scrape the mixture into the baked pastry crust. Top with the fresh mango slices. Chill in the refrigerator for at least 4 hours, or until set. Cut into portions using a hot, wet knife, washed clean in between every cut.

Blackberry–White Chocolate Tart

Though rich, and roluptuous white chocolate on its own is quite sweet and a bit bland, pair it with tart and tangy dark blue-black blackberries and it really shines. Make this tart during late summer's blackberry season. Be extra careful when melting white chocolate. It burns quite easily. Either melt it over steaming water or use melt it in a microwave set on 10 or 20 percent power for to 2 minutes at a time until the chocolate is barely melted.

YIELD: ONE 10-INCH TART; 10 TO 12 SERVINGS

³/₄ pound Sugar Pastry dough (page 823)

White Chocolate Pastry Cream

3 sheets gelatin, or 1 teaspoon powdered gelatin

4 egg yolks (¹/₄ cup)

¹/₄ cup sugar

Scrapings of 1 vanilla bean

Grated zest of 1 lemon (1 tablespoon)

1 ounce (¹/₄ cup) unbleached all-purpose flour

1¹/₂ cups milk, scalded

3 ounces white chocolate, melted and cooled

Topping

1¹/₂ pints blackberries

1 cup red currant jelly, melted and cooled until thickened but still pourable

Roll out the dough into a large round, ³/₈-inch thick, on a lightly floured surface. Transfer to a 10-inch tart pan with a removable bottom and press into the pan without stretching the dough, pressing well into the corners so there are no thick spots. Trim any overhang and smooth the edges. Chill the pastry crust for 30 minutes to relax the gluten and so the tart crust maintains its shape well.

Preheat the oven to 375°F. Fit a piece of heavy-duty foil onto the dough and fill with beans or other pie weights. Blind bake (just pastry crust, no filling) on the bottom shelf of the oven until the crust is cooked through but not yet browned, about 30 minutes. Remove the foil and the weights, reduce oven temperature to 325°F and bake for 10 minutes longer, or until the crust is evenly and lightly browned. Remove from the oven and cool to room temperature on a wire rack before filling.

Soak the gelatin sheets in cold water to soften, about 5 minutes or soak the powdered gelatin in ¹/₄ cup water until thickened, about 10 minutes, then heat it gently until it is clear, about 2 minutes.

In a medium mixing bowl, beat together the egg yolks, sugar, vanilla bean scrapings, and lemon zest until well combined. Add the flour and beat briefly to combine. Gradually pour in the hot milk while constantly whisking until the mixture is smooth.

Transfer the mixture to a heavy-bottomed non-aluminum pot and bring to a boil over moderate heat, stirring often. Remove from the heat and, beat in the gelatin and the white chocolate. Continue to stir until smooth. Scrape the mixture into a stainless-steel bowl and cool to room temperature over a larger bowl filled with ice and water.

Pour the filling into the pastry crust and smooth with a spatula. Arrange the blackberries over the filling, tightly packed together with stem ends down. Brush with the melted jelly and chill until set, about 1 hour.

FIXING LUMPY PASTRY CREAM

If it is not constantly whisked while heating, pastry cream can easily turn lumpy, especially in the corners where the whisk doesn't reach. If this happens, transfer the mixture to a food processor and process until smooth.

GINGER

Young Ginger...488

Mature Ginger...488

Hawaiian Ginger...488

Buying, Storing, and
Preparing Fresh Ginger...488

Preserved Ginger...489

Crystallized Ginger...489

Ground Ginger...489

CRUNCHY MACADAMIA-
GINGER QUARESEMALI...489

About Macadamias...490

STORING MACADAMIA NUTS...490

GINGER FIG SCONES...491

CANADIAN MAPLE–BLACK
WALNUT GINGERBREAD...491

SWEDISH GINGER-SPICE
COOKIES: PEPPARKAKOR...493

PECAN-GINGER CAKE
WITH CARAMEL ICING...494

GINGER

Now that the gnarled, bumpy roots of fresh ginger are sold at almost every supermarket, we've become accustomed to grating this refreshingly peppery and sweetly pungent rhizome (a kind of root) into all sorts of savory and sweet dishes. Ginger, *Zingiber officinale*, resembles a thick-fingered knobby hand and is actually sold in "hands." The root has khaki-colored papery skin with succulent and aromatic flesh that is creamy white and pinkish when young, pale-yellow when mature, turning greenish yellow when aged. Piquant fresh ginger has a wonderful fragrance that often shows up in perfumes, and a pungent, zesty flavor. Ginger's name developed from the Middle English *gingivere*, but its 3,000 year-old Sanskrit name shringaverna means "horn root," an apt description.

Ginger has been a key ingredient in Chinese cooking for more than 2,500 years. In Japan, which got its taste for ginger from China about 2,000 years ago, mioga ginger (*Zingiber mioga*) is used, rather than the underground rhizomes, for its young buds and stems—especially in its pink pickled form. Arab traders carried ginger from its place of origin in Asia to the countries of the Mediterranean in the first century, and the root is mentioned in the Koran. In spite of the ready availability of fresh ginger in many places, dried ginger is used for seasoning in the Middle East, North Africa, and Eastern Europe. In times past, perishable fresh ginger would spoil on the long voyage from the East and so the taste developed for the dried spice.

At the old and revered University of Salerno, Italy which reached the height of its influence between the tenth and the thirteenth century, the professors taught that eating ginger brought about a happy life in old age, enabling you to love and be loved as in your youth! Because of ginger's potent reputation as an aphrodisiac, the Portuguese expanded the cultivation of the rhizome in their slave colonies in West Africa and Brazil, feeding it to their male slaves to increase desire and help increase their population. The root was seen to resemble a small man—and it does, in fact, have physical dilating effects on the pertinent organs. Even today, ginger is used by the Arabs to increase sexual desire, and in Senegal, women make themselves ginger belts to arouse their husbands. Today, ginger is a basic seasoning in West Africa and the Afro-Brazilian cuisine of Bahia and other parts of Brazil.

Although well-known to the ancient Romans, ginger nearly disappeared in Europe after the fall of the Roman Empire. The Venetian explorer, Marco Polo, reported seeing vast ginger plantations when he traveled to China in the thirteenth century. When he brought the spice back to Europe, it began a new craze for this much sought-after, though expensive spice. Because of its rarity and cost, the many Northern European ginger-seasoned baked goods (German lebkuchen, Dutch speculaas, French pain d'épices, English gingerbread) were prepared only for holidays. Important visitors to the court of Queen Elizabeth I of England received likenesses of themselves in the form of gingerbread men.

In the eighteenth century, after the Brothers Grimm tale of Hansel and Gretel described a house made of bread with a roof of cake and windows of barley sugar, German bakeries began offering gingerbread houses with icing snow on the roofs and candy trimmings, along with gingerbread Christmas cards, and elaborately decorated molded cookies. In America, in the Pennsylvania Dutch (actually German) community of Lancaster County, at holiday time, children would cut out and decorate foot-high gingerbread men and women with rows of buttons and big smiles and place them in the front windows of their houses.

The Spaniards planted ginger in Jamaica to have a ready source of this much-loved spice. Ginger grows wild in the Caribbean Islands and is quite a common seasoning there. Jamaican ginger is especially sought-after, because of its strong, bright flavor. The island is the most important producer of ginger today, followed by India, Africa, and China. In America, top-quality ginger is raised in Hawaii.

Versatile ginger is indispensable in baking in its fresh juicy form, its concentrated, dried, powdered form, and in crunchy bits of candied ginger, so ginger-flavored recipes show up throughout this book in cakes, cookies, muffins, scones, and, of course, gingerbread. The Morning Glory Muffins with Carrots, Asia Pears, and Ginger (page 240) are a great way to wake-up. The Cranberry-Ginger Upside-Down Cake (page 399) gets an unexpected spiciness from chopped candied ginger. The Butterscotch-Ginger Pear Tart (page 641), flavored with fresh grated ginger, makes an excellent wintertime dessert.

In this chapter, the Crunchy Macadamia–Ginger Quaresemali (page 489) are an untraditional, but captivating treat. Serve the Ginger Fig Scones (page 491) studded with bits of candied ginger at teatime. The Canadian Maple–Black Walnut Gingerbread (page 491) combines two native American ingredients: black walnuts and maple syrup, along with the more tropical fresh ginger in a moist gingerbread with a light, silky maple-meringue icing. For pecan lovers, try the impressive Pecan-Ginger Cake with Caramel Icing (page 494), an old-fashioned layer cake with a shiny caramel icing and a caramel-flavored cream filing.

YOUNG GINGER

Young ginger, or spring ginger, is harvested just five months after planting and has pale, thin skin that doesn't need to be peeled. Its flesh is tender, juicy, and not at all stringy. Its flavor is mild and sweetly spicy. Look for young ginger in Asian markets in the springtime. This is the type of ginger used to prepare candied ginger and ginger in syrup. It is quite perishable.

MATURE GINGER

Mature ginger has dun-colored, flaky, thick skin that must be peeled, and is the most common type of ginger in the market. Because this ginger stays in the ground longer, it develops more gingerol, the substance that gives ginger its hot and pungent flavor.

HAWAIIAN GINGER

Hawaiian ginger, not surprisingly, grows only in Hawaii and is considered by many, including me, to be the best quality available. Twenty years ago, the ginger industry in Hawaii was a collection of small backyard operations catering entirely to the local market. By 1997, it had become an important local industry, producing more than twelve million pounds a year of this outstanding product. Look for the Hawaiian ginger sticker on the hand of ginger.

BUYING, STORING, AND PREPARING FRESH GINGER

Fresh ginger can be found all year, though it is at the height of its season from spring through the beginning of fall. Choose plump, ideally whole "hands" of ginger with smooth, taut, slightly shiny skin and a minimum of broken off pieces. Ginger that is wrinkled, soft, very light in weight, with greenish flesh, or any white mold on the broken ends is old and is apt to be stringy. However, if this is the only kind to be found, the bad parts can be cut away and the root finely chopped and the juice squeezed out. Ginger roots with a minimum of protruding knobs and branches will be the easiest to peel. Look for top-quality fresh ginger in Asian and Caribbean markets, where the turnover is fast.

To prepare fresh ginger, cut off any small knobs that stick out, then peel the remaining piece with a sharp knife or a swivel peeler. (Chop up the knobs and simmer them in sugar syrup and use to poach fruit, like pears or quince to sweeten iced tea or make caramel sauce.) Asian chefs patiently use the back of a spoon to scrape off the thin outer layer of skin at the root. For baking, fresh ginger should be finely chopped or grated. Unless I'm planning to use a lot of ginger within 2 weeks or so, I freeze the root, grating it in small amounts while still frozen. (The finely grated peel will be unnoticeable when cooked or baked.) Or I cut off a larger chunk to peel and then chop or grate.

PRESERVED GINGER

Young ginger is preserved in a sugar and salt brine to make this confection, which may be used on its own, or added to desserts. Look for it in Asian and specialty markets. Trader Joe's sells tender non-stringy cubes of candied, but not crystallized ginger that are excellent for baking

CRYSTALLIZED GINGER

Also known as candied ginger, this type of ginger is simmered in sugar syrup until tender and then coated with sugar. It is commonly chopped up and added to desserts. Look for inexpensive candied ginger slices in Asian markets, making sure that it is tender and pliable, not brittle and/or stringy.

GROUND GINGER

Also referred to as powdered ginger, this dried, ground spice is more peppery than the fresh root, which is fruitier. Look for inexpensive ground ginger in Asian or Caribbean markets or in the supermarket spice aisle.

Crunchy Macadamia–Ginger Quaresemali

In earlier times, people in Rome would make a baked sweet of leavened dough, sugar, pine seeds, and raisins as a treat during Lent, when many pleasures were restricted. These twice-baked cookies are named after the forty days of Lent, called the quaresemali *in Italian. On the first Friday of March, young men would present them to their sweethearts, sometimes even hiding a ring inside. You don't have to wait for March or Lent to make these sensational biscotti. The dough is leavened with baker's ammonia giving these sweets an extra-crispy bite. While neither macadamias nor candied ginger is traditionally used in Italy, the two make an irresistible combination.*

YIELD: ABOUT 4 DOZEN COOKIES

1 pound (3³⁄₄ cups) unbleached all-purpose flour

1 teaspoon baker's ammonia, crushed to a fine powder

¹⁄₂ teaspoon fine sea salt

2 cups sugar

4 large eggs

¹⁄₄ pound (1 stick) unsalted butter, melted and cooled

1 pound whole macadamia nuts, rinsed and dried
   if salted

¹⁄₄ pound candied or crystallized ginger, chopped

1 large egg white, lightly beaten with 1 tablespoon
   water, for the egg wash

Line two 18 x 13-inch half sheet pans (or other large baking pans) with parchment paper or silicone baking mats.

In a bowl, whisk together the dry ingredients: flour, ammonia, and salt.

In a medium bowl, lightly beat together the sugar and eggs, then stir in the butter. Add the dry ingredients, then stir in the macadamia nuts and ginger. (The dough will be sticky.) Oil your hands and divide the dough into four. Form each piece into a log about 1½ inches wide and ¾ inch thick. Arrange the logs on the baking sheets with at least 2 inches of space in between. Brush the logs with the egg wash and chill for 30 minutes in the refrigerator to set their shape.

Preheat the oven to 350°F. Bake the logs for 25 minutes, or until lightly browned but still soft in the center. Cool to room temperature and transfer the logs to a cutting board.

Reduce the oven temperature to 325°F.

Using a sharp knife, cut the logs diagonally into ½-inch thick slices. Arrange the slices upright on the baking sheets. (The cookie slices will be somewhat fragile.) Bake again for 15 minutes, or until crispy and lightly but evenly browned. Cool on a wire rack to room temperature. Store in an airtight container, such as a cookie tin. These cookies will keep for at least 1 month in dry weather.

ABOUT MACADAMIAS

Macadamia nuts are closely associated with Hawaii, and for good reason: Hawaii is the largest exporter of macadamia nuts, providing ninety-five percent of the world's crop. Yet, this buttery-tasting nut is native to Australia and comes from a tree that was originally grown only for ornamental purposes. The tree was introduced to Hawaii in 1880, where it thrived in the tropical environment. Today, California also produces a sizable macadamia nut crop.

The macadamia nut is encased in an extremely hard shell that is difficult to crack, which is the main reason it took so long for the inner nutmeat to be discovered as a tasty food source. The tree was named for chemist John MacAdam by his friend and colleague, Baron Ferdinand von Mueller, Director of the Royal Botanical Gardens in Australia. MacAdams died shipboard while en route to taste the nut named for him.

Shelled macadamia nuts are about the size of a marble and have a rich, sweet, delicate, buttery flavor that is especially good in baked goods. Because the shell is so difficult to crack (much like black walnuts), you'll find them in the market always shelled, either raw or roasted, salted or unsalted. Due to the labor involved in shelling the nuts, the tropical environment required to grow them, and the long distances to market, macadamias are typically more expensive than other nuts. Prices have dropped dramatically in the past twenty years due to new strains with softer shells and with expanded production. Look for reasonably priced macadamias at Trader Joe's markets.

Macadamia nuts have a very high fat content and must be stored carefully to avoid rancidity. The nuts should be light in color. They will darken with age as the oil they contain turns rancid. Vacuum-packed nuts are the best choice for the freshest product, though cellophane packages can also be good. Refrigerate unopened nuts in an airtight container up to six months or freeze up to a year. Once opened, refrigerate and use macadamia nuts within 3 months.

Ginger Fig Scones

Many of the scones sold at coffee shops are overly large and overly mealy. These ginger and dried fig–studded scones are light as can be because they are made from a dough that is too soft to roll out. Instead, it is simply scooped and dropped like cookies, making these scones easy to make and more delicious than you'd have ever believed a scone could be. Like all scones, they are best the day they're made.

YIELD: ABOUT 18 SCONES

$1/2$ pound (2 cups minus 2 tablespoons) unbleached all-purpose flour

$1/2$ cup sugar

1 tablespoon ground ginger

1 teaspoon baking powder

Pinch salt

$1/4$ pound (1 stick) butter, chilled and cut into bits

2 tablespoons chopped candied orcrystallized ginger or well-drained ginger in syrup

6 ounces dried figs, trimmed and cut into small pieces

$1/2$ cup buttermilk

$1/2$ cup heavy cream

Preheat the oven to 375°F.

In the bowl of a standing mixer fitted with the whisk attachment, combine the dry ingredients: flour, sugar, ground ginger, baking powder, and salt. Switch to the paddle attachment and add the butter, beating until the mixture resembles oatmeal. Add the crystallized ginger and figs and beat again briefly to combine. Pour in the buttermilk and beat just long enough for the dough to come together in large, moist clumps.

Turn out the dough and knead briefly by hand to combine into a smooth, sticky dough. Using a scoop, form the dough into small mounds and arrange on an 18 x 13-inch half sheet pan (or other large baking pan). Brush the scones with cream and bake for 12 minutes or until golden. Scones are best the day they are made.

Canadian Maple–Black Walnut Gingerbread

Molasses, ginger, and maple syrup are inextricably linked with early Canadian foods. The first two came as part of the English navy rations, the other from the native inhabitants. Black walnuts (page 840), which are indigenous to North America, have a distinctive bittersweet flavor and

a smooth, buttery texture that takes this easy cake out of the ordinary. Of course, you may substitute English walnuts if they are not available. Although I almost always use a 12-cup standing mixer, here, the icing quantity is too small and a hand mixer is the best choice.

YIELD: 16 SQUARES

Gingerbread

1/2 pound (2 cups minus 2 tablespoons) unbleached all-purpose flour

2 ounces (1/2 cup plus 1 tablespoon) white whole wheat flour

1 teaspoon baking soda

1 teaspoon fine sea salt

2 large eggs

1 cup maple syrup, preferably grade B

1 cup sour cream

3 ounces (3/4 stick) butter, melted and cooled

2-inch section fresh ginger, peeled and finely grated (about 3 tablespoons)

3 ounces (3/4 cup) black walnuts, lightly toasted and chopped

Icing

1 cup maple syrup, preferably grade B

2 large egg whites (1/4 cup)

1/4 pound (1 stick) unsalted butter, cut up and softened

3 ounces (3/4 cup) black walnuts, lightly toasted and chopped

Make the gingerbread: Preheat the oven to 350°F. Prepare a 9 x 9-inch cake pan by spraying with nonstick baker's coating or rub with butter and dust with flour, shaking off the excess.

Whisk together the dry ingredients: all-purpose flour, whole wheat flour, baking soda, and salt.

In the bowl of a standing mixer fitted with the paddle attachment, combine the eggs, maple syrup, sour cream, butter, and ginger, and beat briefly to combine. Add the flour mix and beat just long enough to combine. Fold in the walnuts by hand.

Pour the batter into the pan and bake for 35 minutes, or until the cake pulls away from the sides of the pan and a toothpick stuck in the center comes out clean. Remove from the oven and cool to room temperature on a wire rack. Unmold and turn upside-down.

Make the icing and assemble cake: Bring the maple syrup to a boil in a small, heavy-bottomed pot. Boil to the firm ball stage (250°F on a candy thermometer), or until a spoonful dropped in a glass of ice water forms a firm, but still malleable ball.

Meanwhile, in a clean and greaseless bowl and using an electric hand mixer, beat the egg whites until fluffy.

Pour the hot syrup slowly into the center of the bowl over the egg whites, beating constantly with the electric mixer. Beat until the mixture reaches room temperature, about 10 minutes. Beat in the butter and continue beating until smooth. (Chill the icing for 30 minutes in the refrigerator if it is too soft to hold its shape.) Spread the icing in big swirls on the cake and sprinkle with the walnuts. Chill the cake for 1 hour in the refrigerator before cutting into serving portions. Store refrigerated up to 4 days. The uniced cake freezes well.

Swedish Ginger–Spice Cookies: Pepparkakor

Pepparkakor, or pepper cookies, are Swedish spice cookies that are a must at Christmastime. They are another of the large family of Northern European ginger and spice breads that date back to medieval times, when spices were so rare and expensive, they could only be used on the most important of occasions. Children can help form the dough balls, flatten them, and sprinkle with raw sugar. If you happen to have any extra cookies, freeze them to use for gingerbread crumb crusts.

YIELD: ABOUT 5 DOZEN COOKIES

18 ounces ($4^{1}/_{4}$ cups minus 4 teaspoons) unbleached all-purpose flour

1 tablespoon ground ginger

2 teaspoons ground cinnamon

$1^{1}/_{2}$ teaspoons baking soda

1 teaspoon fine sea salt

1 teaspoon freshly ground black pepper

1 teaspoon ground cardamom

$^{1}/_{2}$ teaspoon ground allspice

$^{1}/_{4}$ teaspoon ground cloves

5 ounces ($1^{1}/_{4}$ sticks) unsalted butter, softened

$^{3}/_{4}$ cup sugar

$^{3}/_{4}$ cup dark brown sugar

1 large egg

Grated zest of 1 lemon (1 tablespoon)

5 ounces ($^{1}/_{2}$ cup plus 2 tablespoons) golden syrup, substitute light corn syrup

5 ounces ($^{1}/_{2}$ cup plus 2 tablespoons) heavy cream

1 egg white, lightly beaten with 1 tablespoon water, for the egg wash

$^{1}/_{2}$ cup raw or crystallized sugar, for sprinkling

Line two 18 x 13-inch half sheet pans (or other large baking pans) with parchment paper or silicone baking mats.

In a bowl, whisk together the dry ingredients: flour, ginger, cinnamon, baking soda, salt, pepper, cardamom, allspice, and cloves.

In the bowl of a standing mixer fitted with the paddle attachment, cream the butter and both sugars until light and fluffy, 5 to 6 minutes. Beat in the egg, lemon zest, golden syrup, and cream. Beat in the dry ingredients, beating only long enough for the dough to form a ball. Cover the dough and chill for 30 minutes or until soft, but cold to the touch.

Preheat the oven to 350°F.

Scoop the dough into about 60 balls about the size of a walnut. Lightly oil your hands and roll the balls of dough until smooth. Arrange the dough balls in rows of 3 and 2 on the baking pans. Cut a piece of wax paper into about a 4-inch square. Lay the wax paper on a cookie ball and use the flat bottom of a ceramic ramekin or a juice glass to flatten the ball to about $^{1}/_{3}$-inch thick. Brush the cookies with the egg wash, then sprinkle with the raw sugar.

Bake the cookies for 12 minutes or until crisp at the edges, repeating the process for the remaining cookies. (If baking two sheets at once, switch their directions and positions after 6 minutes and bake a total of 15 minutes.) Cool the cookies to room temperature on a wire rack, then store overnight in an airtight container to allow the flavors to mellow. Store up to 2 weeks. The unbaked dough freezes well.

Pecan–Ginger Cake with Caramel Icing

A shiny layer of caramel cream icing coats this torte, which is inspired by the nut cakes of Vienna, but made here with native American pecans, spicy, aromatic fresh ginger, and dark rum. The same caramel lightened with whipped cream and chunky with chopped toasted pecans fills the split cake. This is a good make-ahead cake for parties, as it can be completed 2 to 3 days ahead of time and will stay nice and moist. The only challenge here is cooking the caramel: once you begin to see the color just start to turn red, immediately add the hot cream.

YIELD: ONE 9-INCH LAYER CAKE, 12 TO 14 SERVINGS

Cake

$1/4$ pound (1 cup) pecans, lightly toasted

$1/4$ pound (1 cup minus 2 tablespoons) cake flour, or 3 ounces unbleached all-purpose flour mixed with 1 ounce potato starch or other starch

1 tablespoon baking powder

2 teaspoons ground ginger

$1/2$ teaspoon fine sea salt

6 large eggs, separated

3 ounces ($3/4$ cup well-packed) light brown sugar

2 ounces ($1/2$ stick) unsalted butter, melted and cooled

2-inch section fresh ginger, peeled and finely grated or finely chopped

2 tablespoons dark rum

Filling and Icing

$1^1/2$ cups sugar

$1/2$ cup water

1 cup heavy cream, scalded

1 cup heavy cream, chilled

2 ounces ($1/2$ cup) pecans, lightly toasted and chopped

12 pecan halves, lightly toasted, for garnish

Make the cake: Preheat the oven to 350°F. Spray two 9-inch cake pans with nonstick baker's coating, or rub with softened butter and dust with flour, shaking off the excess.

In the bowl of a food processor, combine the pecans, flour, baking powder, ground ginger, and salt, and process until finely powdered, working in two batches if necessary.

In the bowl of a standing mixer fitted with the paddle attachment, beat the egg yolks and $1/2$ cup of the brown sugar until light and fluffy, 5 to 6 minutes. Pour in the butter and beat again until the mixture is smooth. Fold in the grated ginger, rum, and the pecan mixture. Transfer to a wide shallow bowl.

In the clean and greaseless bowl of a standing mixer fitted with the whisk, beat the egg whites until fluffy, then beat in the remaining $1/4$ cup of the brown sugar and continue beating until firm and glossy, 4 to 5 minutes. Fold into the yolk mixture in thirds so as not to deflate the batter. Divide the batter evenly between the pans.

Bake for 35 minutes or until the cakes start to come away from the sides of the pan and a skewer inserted in the center comes out clean. Transfer the pans to a wire rack to cool for about 30 minutes, or until no longer hot to the touch. Remove the cakes from the pans, and let them come to room temperature on the wire racks. (In hot weather, chill the cakes in the refrigerator for 30 minutes before continuing with the recipe.)

Make the icing: Combine the sugar and water in a medium heavy-bottomed, nonreactive pot, preferably copper, and bring to a boil, stirring, until the syrup is clear. Continue cooking over medium heat—shaking the pot or stirring with a wooden spoon or silicone spatula so the sugar cooks evenly—until the syrup reaches 350°F on a candy thermometer and the sugar is medium brown in color with a touch of redness, about 8 minutes. (WORK CAREFULLY AS CARAMEL IS EXTREMELY HOT!) Slowly pour in the scalded cream, being careful as you pour because it can bubble up and create hot steam. Stir with a wooden spoon to combine into a smooth cream. If there are any hardened pieces of sugar, heat the mixture for 2 to 3 minutes, or until they have completely liquefied. Remove from the heat, and cool to room temperature, stirring occasionally, and over ice, if desired.

Make the filling: Beat the chilled cream, either by hand or using a hand mixer, until firm but not at all yellowed. Pour in $1/4$ cup of the cool caramel mixture reserving the remainder and beat again until firm. Fold in the chopped pecans. Cover tightly and chill for 30 minutes in the refrigerator to firm.

Place one cake on a serving platter (or cake board), and spread with the caramel cream filling. Top with the second cake, pressing down lightly so the cake adheres. Transfer the filled cake to a wire rack with a baking pan underneath to catch the drips. Pour the remaining caramel mixture directly onto the center of the cake, allowing it spread over the top and drip down the sides. If the caramel has hardened too much to pour, warm at low power in the microwave or over a double boiler. Allow the icing to set for about 5 minutes, and then press the pecan halves into the top. Chill again for about 30 minutes before cutting into 12 serving portions. Store the cake covered and refrigerated up to 5 days. The uniced cake freezes well.

HAZELNUTS

TURKISH SEEDED HAZELNUT BREAD . . .502

ONE-BOWL HAZELNUT
CORNMEAL BISCOTTI . . .503

TURKISH HAZELNUT MACAROONS . . .504

Turkish Hazelnuts in Germany . . .505

HAZELNUT-BROWN BUTTER
CAKES WITH BOSC PEARS . . .505

TORTA GIANDUIA . . .506

HOMEMADE GIANDUIA . . .508

The Story of Gianduia . . .508

HAZELNUT PRALINE . . .509

HAZELNUTS

The ancient Celts equated hazelnuts with wisdom, expressed succinctly in the timeless phrase, "all in a nutshell." The Gaelic words for hazelnuts and wisdom–*cno* and *cnocach*–are closely related. Revered by the Celts as a magical plant, hazelnut trees were used in fertility rites and the fire festivals of midsummer. Sacred groves of hazel could be found throughout Scotland, which was known as Caledonia, meaning "Hill of the Hazel". (In Gaelic, *coll* means "hazel tree" and *dun* means "hill"–as in sand dunes.) In Ireland, the unauthorized felling of this tree, holy to the Celts, was a capital offense.

According to archeologists, the range of hazel trees expanded rapidly during the Mesolithic period (11,000 to 6,000 years ago). Because animals don't disperse the nuts very far from the trees, the people of that time are believed to have carried the nuts with them for food. Hazelnuts, which were plentiful and an easily stored source of protein, were often ground and mixed with flour to be made into nourishing breads, not that different from the Turkish Seeded Hazelnut Bread (page 502), from the birthplace of hazelnuts.

Scottish mythology tells of a sacred pool around which nine hazel trees grew. These trees would drop their nuts into the water, thereby feeding a group of salmon revered by the Druids, the learned priests of the ancient Celtic society. The number of bright spots on the salmon equaled the number of nuts they had eaten and presumably how wise they were. (In an Irish variation of the legend, a single salmon ate all these magical nuts.) A Druid master, wishing to gain wisdom, caught one of the salmon, and instructed his pupil to cook the fish. When hot juices from the cooking fish spattered onto the apprentice's thumb, he thrust it into his mouth, thereby gaining the fish's knowledge. Named Fionn MacCumhail (or Finn McCool), he became a heroic leader in the country's mythology.

In Ireland, whole villages would gather hazelnuts at just the right time. If they were picked too early, the nuts would lack taste and not store long. Too late, and the jays and squirrels would have eaten them all. "Nutting" used to be a euphemism for courting, because gathering the nuts in the woods gave plenty of opportunity for young couples to meet for love. In England, Holy Cross Day, September 14, was traditionally a school holiday for children to go nutting, a custom which persisted until World War I. Halloween was once known in part of Britain as Nutcrack Night, when the stored nuts were opened. On this night, you could find your true love by observing the behavior of hazelnuts placed on a fire. Some parishioners were in the habit of taking hazelnuts to church on the following Sunday to be cracked noisily during the sermon.

Hazelnuts have grown wild since the Ice Age and are believed to be native to Anatolia in Central Turkey. Archeological records have also shown fossilized remains of hazelnuts that were 5,000 years old in prehistoric excavations from China, although the nuts aren't much used in Chinese cuisine. Hazelnuts spread from Turkey through Greece into Italy especially Campania in the south and Piedmont in the north, and from there into Spain, France, Germany, and England. All filberts are hazelnuts, but not all hazelnuts are filberts, which are the English variety of hazelnut. European hazel trees produce larger, thin-shelled nuts; native North American hazel trees produce small, thick-shelled nuts.

The English name, hazelnut, comes from the Anglo-Saxon *haesel knut*, haesel meaning "cap" or "hat," referring to the cap of ruffly green leaves that grow over hazelnuts on the branch. The cultivated hazelnuts called filberts may take their name from St Philibert's Day, August 20, when hazelnuts were supposed to start ripening. Or, it may come derive from the German vollbart, meaning "full beard." With a little imagination, the filbert, which resem-

bles an acorn without its cap, can be seen as a fellow with a neatly barbered, pointy beard. The term "Cob nuts" comes from a nineteenth century children's game known as Cob played with hazelnuts, a precursor to marbles.

The old Italian name for the hazelnut tree, *avellano*, derives from the ancient city of Abella (today Avella) in the region of Avellino in Campania, Italy. The city is also commemorated in hazelnut's scientific name, *Corylus avellana*, and in its old French name, avelline. In modern Italian, hazelnuts are known as *nocciole*, a diminutive of noci, used for all nuts in general and walnuts in particular, indicating just how basic these small nuts are to Italian cuisine and particularly its pastry artists.

Pliny (23–79 CE) in his *Historia Naturalis*, wrote that hazelnuts were taken to Italy from the Pontus Euxinus (Black Sea) coasts and named Ponticae Nuces or Nux Pontice. From the third century BCE, Latin writers from Cato to Virgil attested to the presence of hazelnuts in Campania. In the excavations at Herculaneum, the Roman town lost along with Pompeii in the eruption of Mount Vesuvius beginning on August 24, 79 CE, there is a colorful fresco portraying hazelnuts and even some charred remains. Until the mid-nineteenth century, hazelnuts exported from the port of Naples to France and Holland were so important that at the end of the seventeenth century, the Kingdom of Naples had a special office to measure the nuts.

I've heard people in the southern Italian province of Campania argue vociferously that their hazelnuts are the best; equally strong in their opinions as to the superiority of their own hazelnuts are the residents of Piedmont in the north, which is famed for its hazelnut–chocolate confection, Gianduia (page 508). Toward the end of the eighteenth century, Vincenzo De Caro, a historian from Salerno, wrote, "it is known to all that the hazelnut tree flourishes wonderfully in most areas of our property."

The Tonda di Giffoni (Giffoni Round), a top Italian variety that originates and grows in Campania, was awarded IGP recognition in 1997. Inside its reddish–brown skin, this nut, which takes well to roasting, is white and firm with aromatic flesh and skin that is easy to remove. In Piedmont, the famous Tonda Gentile delle Langhe (round and mild Langhe nut), which received IGP status in 1994, is prized for its subtle flavor and crunchy texture, while its round shape lends itself to mechanical shelling. According to one proud grower, "Piedmont hazelnuts are, without a doubt, the best hazelnuts known; the unmistakable smell of this marvelous nut is now well-known throughout the world."

Turkey, where hazelnuts originated, still raises 75 to 80 percent of the world's crop largely from orchards near the Black Sea, which has a temperate climate with mild winters and moderate summers similar to that of Oregon. In Turkey, hazelnuts are picked by hand from trees that often grow in the wild. Grown in Campania, Sicily, and Piedmont, Italy is the second-largest producer of hazelnuts with about 15 percent of the world's crop. Italians have a voracious appetite for these small nuts, consuming virtually all of their own production and importing even more hazelnuts, mostly from Turkey.

Only three percent of the world's hazelnut crop comes from the United States, almost all of that from orchards scattered through the Willamette Valley, in the western portion of Oregon, with a much smaller crop from Washington. Although Spain ranks fourth in hazelnut production, its baking tradition focus more on the almonds brought there by the Moors than on hazelnuts.

The American hazelnut, *Corylus cornuta var. californica*, native to Oregon and California, provided food for indigenous peoples throughout the Northern Hemisphere. During their journeys in the Oregon Territory, local inhabitants bartered hazelnuts to the explorers Lewis and Clark in 1805, and to botanist David Douglas, in 1825. Shortly after 1847, Henderson Lewelling, an early Oregon nurseryman, first imported the European hazelnut, with 'Cob' filberts from England and 'Red Aveline' nuts from Hapsburg, Austria. By 1885, Felix Gillet, a French nurseryman, had started selling specific hazelnut cultivars throughout the Northwest, including the Barcelona, which is widely planted in Oregon today along with the Ennis.

Lewis and Clark returned with hazelnut plants to be used as nursery stock at the Prince Nursery in Flushing, New York, the first commercial nursery in the United States established by Robert Prince in 1737. During the Revolutionary War,

General Washington sent armed guards to surround and protect the nursery's valuable stock of American filbert trees and Barcelona filbert trees imported from Spain. The name filbert was used by early French settlers to America, who likely first introduced the European filbert into Oregon. At first, filbert was employed for the smaller American nuts, while hazelnut was reserved for the larger, plumper European nuts but today, filbert is mostly used in Oregon; elsewhere the nuts are known are hazelnuts.

Hazelnuts are green as they develop but darken to reddish or chocolate-brown as they mature. Once picked, the hazelnuts stay in their hard shells until six weeks later, after they have been dried. The nuts, which are about the size of acorns, grow in clusters of up to 12 nuts, and usually mature during the last week of August. They are harvested during the last of September, mechanically in the United States and by hand in Europe.

It's no wonder I kept running out of hazelnuts no matter how many I bought when testing the recipes for this book. Looking back over my recipes, I used hazelnuts in several dozen cakes, pastries, fillings, cookies, and breads from the Hungarian Red Currant Hazelnut Torte (page 413), to the Egyptian Flatbread with Dukkah Sprinkle (page 890). Until recently, most Americans hadn't taken to hazelnuts the way Europeans do partly because we don't grow nearly as many hazelnuts as we do almonds, walnuts, and pecans–the last two of which are native to America. With mountains of Nutella, oceans of hazelnut lattes, and travels to Italy, France, Switzerland, and other places where hazelnuts rule the patisseries and chocolatiers, Americans' taste for hazelnuts has grown, so much so that it can be difficult to track down supplies. Note that when buying hazelnuts, it's important to taste them first, because too often, those sold in American stores have turned rancid.

For bakers in Italy, France, Germany, Austria, Switzerland, and Turkey, the small, reddish-brown skinned, hazelnut is the nut of choice, because it is rich in sweet, flavorful oil, the nuts are dense enough to substitute for flour when ground, and its bittersweet flavor imparts distinctive character to cakes, cookies, pastry doughs, and even breads. The flavor of hazelnuts is accentuated by toasting and complement raspberries, chocolate, cherries, pears, red currants, carrots, coffee, dried fruits, honey, and sweet spices.

Although the two originate in very different parts of the world, hazelnuts and chocolate have made a long-lasting marriage in European pastry and confectionary, especially in Northern Italy with the classic Torta Gianduia (page 506) from Torino, the Torta Boscaiola, a gluten-free chestnut flour and hazelnut cake (page 319), the Bitter Chocolate–Hazelnut Torte with Pears (page 645), the Florentine Chocolate Nut Zuccotto (page 58), the Nutella–filled Baci di Dama cookies (page 335), and the Sambuca and Candied Orange Tozzetti (page 90).

The One-Bowl Hazelnut Cornmeal Biscotti (page 503) get their intense hazelnutty flavor from both chopped nuts and hazelnut oil. The Turkish Hazelnut Macaroons (page 504) contain just three ingredients: hazelnuts, egg whites, and sugar, and feature a thin, crunchy outside and a chewy, toasty inside. Hazelnuts and brown butter flavor the Hazelnut-Brown Butter Cakes with Bosc Pears (page 505), perfect for wintertime. The Torta Gianduia (page 506) is my version of the iconic Torinese specialty made now elsewhere in Northern Italy.

The famed tortes of the former Austro-Hungarian Empire wouldn't be the same without the bittersweet hazelnuts that help balance their richness. The Black-Currant-Apple Linzer Torte (page 411) comes from Austria; the Red Currant-Hazelnut Torte (page 413) from the similar baking traditions of Hungary. The Carrot-Semolina Torte with hazelnuts (page 239) comes from Aargau, Switzerland. The Carrot Pastry Rolls (Havis), the Hazelnut Macaroons (page 241), and Semolina Sponge Cookies (Sekerpare) all come from Turkey, where hazelnuts first grew wild. The White Chocolate, Hazelnut and Espresso Dacquoise (page 377) is my own creative interpretation of the classic French pastry made famous by Chef Ferdinand Point of La Pyramide. Hazelnuts and caramel form a complementary duo in the Hazelnut Praline (page 509), used in the Chocolate-Glazed Praline Profiteroles (page 287).

Turkish Seeded Hazelnut Bread

Not surprisingly, this hazelnut-studded bread comes from Turkey, thought to be the original home of the hazelnut and the world's largest producer of the nuts today. Finely ground kasha (buckwheat grouts) adds its own dark and slightly sweet nuttiness to this tasty bread. The pungent and slightly acrid black nigella seeds, sprinkled on the outside, are a typical seed spice in that part of the world, along with the sesame seeds. This recipe is dairy-free.

YIELD: 2 SMALL LOAVES

1 ($\frac{1}{4}$-ounce) package (2$\frac{1}{2}$ teaspoons) active dry yeast

1 tablespoon honey

1 cup lukewarm water

1 pound (4 cups) unbleached bread flour

1 cup fine kasha (buckwheat groats)

6 ounces (1 cup) hazelnuts, coarsely chopped

1 teaspoon fine sea salt

Cornmeal or semolina for dusting

1 large egg white, lightly beaten with 1 tablespoon water, for the egg wash

2 tablespoons sesame seeds

2 teaspoons nigella seeds

In the bowl of a standing mixer fitted with the paddle attachment, combine the yeast, honey, and water, and let sit until bubbling, about 10 minutes.

In a bowl, whisk together the dry ingredients: flour, kasha, hazelnuts, and salt. Pour into the yeast mixture and mix, adding 1 cup more water to form a soft moist dough that doesn't stick to your hands. Continue to beat until smooth and elastic. Transfer to a lightly oiled bowl, cover with a damp cloth, and leave to rise at warm room temperature until doubled in size, about 2 hours.

Preheat the oven to 400°F. Lightly sprinkle two 18 x 13-inch half sheet pans (or other large baking pan) with cornmeal or semolina.

Divide the dough in half and form each half into a round. Arrange the breads with their smooth sides up on the prepared baking pans and allow the breads to rise again until doubled in size. Brush the breads with the egg wash, then sprinkle with sesame and nigella seeds. Bake the breads for 35 minutes or until they sound hollow when tapped and a thermometer inserted in the center reads 190°F. to 205°F. Remove the breads from the pan and cool to room temperature on a wire rack. This bread freezes well.

One-Bowl Hazelnut Cornmeal Biscotti

Could these cookies be any easier to make? The combination of hazelnuts and cornmeal can be found in Northern Italy, especially in the Veneto, where cornmeal polenta is historically the accompaniment to every meal and shows up in all sorts of baked goods. This recipe calls for the addition of hazelnut oil to the cookie batter, which intensifies the flavor of the biscotti. If you have enough time, let the baked cookie log sit out overnight, so it gets firmer and a bit stale, creating slices with cleaner edges. This recipe is dairy-free.

YIELD: 40 COOKIES

1$^1/_2$ cups sugar

6 ounces (1$^1/_2$ cups minus 1 tablespoon) unbleached all-purpose flour

$^1/_4$ pound ($^3/_4$ cup plus 2 tablespoons) stone ground yellow cornmeal

1 teaspoon ground cinnamon

1 teaspoon baking powder

$^1/_4$ teaspoon fine sea salt

$^1/_2$ pound (1$^1/_2$ cups) skin-on hazelnuts, lightly toasted, skinned, and coarsely chopped

$^1/_4$ cup hazelnut oil, substitute grapeseed or canola oil

$^1/_4$ cup grapeseed or canola oil

4 large egg whites ($^1/_2$ cup)

Preheat the oven to 375°F. Line two 18 x 13-inch half sheet pans (or other large baking pans) with parchment paper or silicone baking mats.

In a medium mixing bowl, whisk together the sugar, flour, cornmeal, cinnamon, baking powder, and salt. Add the hazelnuts, hazelnut oil, and grapeseed oil, and stir with a wooden spoon until well blended. Add the egg whites and stir until dough comes together. It should be slightly sticky. Allow the dough to rest at room temperature for 10 minutes.

Using lightly oiled hands, divide the dough in half. Form each half into a fat log about 1$^1/_2$ inch-thick and place onto the prepared baking pans allowing 2-inches in between the logs. Bake for 25 minutes or until golden brown. Allow the biscotti to cool to room temperature on a wire rack overnight.

Preheat the oven to 325°F. Slice each log on the diagonal into $^1/_2$-inch thick slices. Arrange the slices standing up on the baking pans. (Cut into ½-inch slices, the biscotti will be thick enough to stand up so they brown evenly and you won't need to turn them over.) Bake for 20 minutes or until lightly browned. Cool completely and store in airtight container up to 2 weeks.

Turkish Hazelnut Macaroons

On a visit to my friend Didem Ertan's family, I spent a day with her slim, tanned, fashionista sister, Sinem Sagel, at her lovely beach house near Çesme, on Turkey's Aegean Coast. The long, shallow beach, low rolling waves, and breezy sunshiny day was very relaxing. Before leaving for the beach, we sat outside in Sinem's lush garden and savored a typical Turkish breakfast, complete with watermelon slices, olives, and feta cheese. A plateful of some rather large and irresistible chewy, toasted hazelnut macaroons accompanied tea served in traditional small hourglass-shaped Turkish tea cups. I brought home a taste for macaroons and two dozen tea cups emblazoned with a blue eye to bring good fortune. Waiting for the crust to form on these cookies is the critical step here. This recipe is dairy-free. This recipe is gluten-free.

YIELD: ABOUT 48 MACAROONS

½ pound (1½ cups) whole hazelnuts,
    toasted and skinned

1 pound confectioners' sugar
½ cup sugar
½ teaspoon fine sea salt
6 large egg whites (¾ cup), at room temperature

Line two 18 x 13-inch half sheet pans (or other large baking pans) with parchment paper or a silicone mat.

In the bowl of a food processor, combine the hazelnuts, half of the confectioners' sugar, the sugar, and salt. Process until the nuts are finely ground.

In the bowl of a standing mixer fitted with the whisk attachment, beat the egg whites until light and foamy, then add the remaining confectioners' sugar and beat until firm and glossy, 4 to 5 minutes. Transfer the mixture to a wide, shallow bowl so it's easier to fold in the nuts without deflating the meringue. Fold in the ground hazelnut mixture in thirds so as not to deflate the meringue.

Pipe or spoon the batter into small rounds onto the pans, allowing about ½ inch of space in between. Allow the macaroons to rest at room temperature for 30 minutes or until a thin skin forms over the top of the macaroons.

Preheat the oven to 350°F. Bake for 15 minutes or until the macaroons are pale brown on the outside but still soft on the inside. Cool to room temperature on a wire cooling rack before removing the macaroons from the pan. Store in a cookie tin or other airtight container up to 2 weeks.

TURKISH HAZELNUTS IN GERMANY

The story of hazelnut production in Turkey dates back to the period of the Ottoman Empire. During this period, people in Germany wanted to have close economic ties to the Ottoman Empire. In fact, later, Turkey became an ally of Germany. Germany had many things to sell, but few to buy. So they thought, 'What can we buy from the Ottoman Empire?' They saw that Turkey had an abundance of high-quality hazelnuts, which could work very well with German-produced chocolates and tortes. So they offered to purchase Turkish hazelnuts and, in return, sell them industrial products. This abundance of hazelnuts led to the nut being used in all sorts of baked goods in Germany and in the Austro-Hungarian Empire, parts of which had been conquered and influenced by Turkish culture already.

Hazelnut–Brown Butter Cakes with Bosc Pears

Hazelnuts, especially when toasted, have a flavor that resembles the brown butter used in this cake to enrich the batter. The firm, spicy Bosc pears, in season in the cold weather months, add juiciness and full-bodied fruit flavor to these small cakes, while chewy diced dried pears accentuate their pear flavor. Because these cakes use only the egg white, the recipe is a good place to use up some of those egg whites you may have in the freezer. Serve the small cakes while still warm, perhaps

with hazelnut syrup-flavored espresso or small glasses of Italian Frangelico hazelnut liqueur mixed with brandy or rum to cut down on its sweetness.

YIELD: 8 SERVINGS

$^1/_4$ pound ($^3/_4$ cup) hazelnuts, toasted and skinned

$^3/_4$ cup sugar

2 ounces ($^1/_2$ cup minus $^1/_2$ tablespoon) unbleached all-purpose flour

1 teaspoon ground cinnamon

$^1/_2$ teaspoon fine sea salt

Grated zest of 1 lemon (1 tablespoon)

6 large egg whites ($^3/_4$ cup), at room temperature

1 cup Brown Butter (page 202)

$^1/_4$ cup diced dried pears, soaked in warm water to cover for 30 minutes

2 Bosc pears, stemmed, cored, and sliced crosswise

2 tablespoons (1 ounce) unsalted butter, melted and cooled

2 tablespoons sugar

Spray 8 ($^3/_4$-cup to 1-cup) ramekins, custard cups, or muffin cups with nonstick baker's coating, or rub with butter and sprinkle with flour, shaking out the excess.

In the bowl of a food processor, combine the hazelnuts, $^1/_2$ cup of the sugar, the flour, cinnamon, salt, and lemon zest, and grind until finely powdered.

In the clean and greaseless bowl of a standing mixer fitted with the whisk attachment, beat the egg whites until fluffy, then add the remaining $^1/_4$ cup sugar and continue beating until the whites are firm and glossy, 4 to 5 minutes. Transfer to a wide shallow bowl so it's easier to fold in the nuts without deflating the meringue.

Preheat the oven to 350°F. Fold the meringue into the nut mixture in thirds so as not to deflate the batter. Gradually fold in the brown butter, stirring until well blended, then fold in the drained dried pears. Arrange a layer of pear slices on the bottom of each ramekin, then spoon the batter equally among the ramekins over top. Overlap more pear slices on the tops in a circular pattern. Brush the pears with the butter and sprinkle with sugar.

Bake for 45 minutes or until the cakes start to come away from the sides of the ramekins and a toothpick inserted in the center comes out clean. Cool on a wire rack 10 to 15 minutes. To remove the cakes from the ramekins, run a thin-bladed knife between each cake and ramekin to loosen; invert to unmold, then set upright. Serve warm or at room temperature. Store covered and refrigerated up to 3 days but allow the cakes to come to room temperature before serving.

Torta Gianduia

One of my signature cakes in my years at Ristorante DiLullo was this Torta Gianduia, flavored with the signature hazelnut praline and chocolate confection of Torino, Italy, called Gianduia (see page 508 for more information). I translated the original recipe from a metric version in an Italian cookbook and came up with a homemade version of the Gianduia itself, as it is difficult to find in America. While it is one of the more elaborate recipes in this book, it is well worth the effort, serving a lot of happy eaters. If your chocolate writing skills are good, do as they do in pasticcerie (pastry shops) in Italy and write "Gianduja" or "Gianduia" across the top of the cake with melted chocolate.

YIELD: ONE 10-INCH CAKE, 14 TO 16 SERVINGS

Cake

3 ounces ($3/4$ cup minus 2 teaspoons) unbleached all-purpose flour

3 ounces (1 cup minus 1 tablespoon) potato starch, substitute corn, wheat, or rice starch

1 ounce ($1/4$ cup) Dutch process cocoa

$1/2$ teaspoon fine sea salt

6 large eggs

3 large yolks

1 cup sugar

$1/4$ cup honey

1 teaspoon vanilla

$1/4$ pound Gianduia, purchased, or homemade (page 508), melted and cooled

Filling

1 cup heavy cream

$1/2$ pound Gianduia (purchased or homemade, see page 508), melted and cooled

Syrup

$1/2$ cup water

$1/2$ cup sugar

2 tablespoons Maraschino liqueur, substitute kirsch or more brandy

2 tablespoons brandy

Assembly

1 cup strained apricot jam

2 cups Shiny Chocolate Mocha Glaze
   (page 334), lukewarm

Make the cake: Preheat the oven to 350°F. Prepare a 10-inch cake pan by spraying it with nonstick baker's coating, or rub with softened butter and dust with flour, shaking off the excess.

Sift together the dry ingredients: flour, starch, cocoa, and salt.

Heat a medium pot of water to boiling. Combine the eggs, egg yolks, sugar, and honey in a large stainless-steel bowl and place over the pot of boiling water to make a water bath, without allowing the bottom of the bowl to touch the water. Heat while whisking often until the mixture is hot to the touch, and reaches 140°F on a thermometer.

Remove the bowl from the heat and immediately scrape out the contents into the bowl of a standing mixer fitted with the whisk attachment. Add the vanilla and beat the mixture until it is cool, thick, and fluffy, about 10 minutes.

Fold about one-third of the egg mixture into the Gianduia to lighten it, then fold the Gianduia mixture into the remaining egg mixture. Fold in the flour mixture, then scrape the batter into the prepared pan. Bake for 50 minutes, or until the cake starts to come away from the sides of the pan and a skewer inserted in the center comes out clean. Allow the cake to cool on a wire rack. (You may allow the cake to rest overnight before filling and icing, if desired.)

Make the filling: Place the cream in a microwavable bowl and scald. Add the cream to the Gianduia and whisk to combine into a thick cream. Transfer the mixture to a bowl, preferably stainless steel and cool by placing over a second bowl filled with a mixture of ice and water, stirring often until the mixture is cold to the touch, but still soft.

Transfer the cream to the bowl of a standing mixer fitted with the whisk and beat for 1 to 2 minutes, or until the cream is light in color and firm enough to hold its shape, taking care not to overwhip and separate the cream.

Make the syrup: In a small pot, bring the water and sugar to a boil and whisk until clear. Remove from the heat and stir in the Maraschino and brandy.

Assemble the cake: Cut a very small notch, about $1/4$-inch deep, out of the side of the cake to use as a guide. Using a long, serrated knife, cut the cake horizontally into two layers. Brush each layer on the cut side with the syrup.

Spread the whipped Gianduia filling over the bottom layer of the cake. Reassemble the cake using the notch as a guide to reassemble in their original position, twisting the layers back and forth to encourage the filling to spread out evenly inside. Smooth the cream at the edges using an icing spatula, then refrigerate the cake for 30 minutes to set the filling.

Warm the jam and brush it all over the cake. Chill for 30 minutes in the refrigerator to set the apricot glaze.

Place the cake on a wire rack over a baking pan to catch the drips. Pour the Mocha-Chocolate Glaze over the cake, smoothing with an icing spatula. If necessary, scrape up some of the drips with a rubber spatula and pour back over the cake. Note that once the chocolate glaze starts to set, it will lose its shine if you keep spreading. Chill the cake for at least 30 minutes before cutting into 16 portions using a hot knife, dipped in hot water and dried in between each cut. The uniced cake freezes well. Store the cake refrigerated for up to 5 days.

Homemade Gianduia

Gianduia, a chocolate confection made from chocolate and the ground, toasted hazelnuts grown throughout Piedmont, is sold by many local confectioners in Italy, but is difficult to find in America. One source is Surfas in Los Angeles (www.surfasonline.com). I have developed this recipe for homemade Gianduia, made from purchased or homemade hazelnut praline, milk chocolate, and cocoa. It has a soft, creamy consistency, melts well, and works for the ganache-type filling used in the Torta Gianduia (page 506) and mixed into the cake batter itself.

YIELD: ABOUT 2 POUNDS

1 pound milk chocolate, chopped into small bits
1 (15-ounce) can hazelnut praline, or 15 ounces
  Hazelnut Praline (page 509)
1 ounce ($1/4$ cup) Dutch process cocoa

Place the chocolate in a microwaveable bowl and melt in the microwave on lowest power for 2 minutes at a time, or until just barely melted. Whisk until smooth and cool to room temperature.

Rub an 8-inch square metal pan with butter.

Place the praline into the bowl of a food processor and process until smooth and creamy-looking, like peanut butter. Add the melted chocolate and the cocoa and process again to combine into a smooth creamy paste. Scrape the mixture into the pan and chill until set, about 2 hours. Use as needed. Cover and store refrigerated for up to 3 months.

THE STORY OF GIANDUIA

In the middle of the nineteenth century, the winds of revolution in Italy became the inspiration for what was to become a Piedmontese confectionery classic. Because cocoa and cocoa butter were rationed during those turbulent years, Piedmontese artisans circumvented the problem with a new kind of chocolate, made by blending precious cocoa with the local *Tonde Gentili delle Langhe* hazelnut. The chocolates were piped by hand into a small, oblong shape and named *givu*, a Piedmontese word meaning "cigarette butt."

The godfather of the confection's new name was Giovanni del Boccale, also known as *Gianduja* or *Gian d'la duja*. This local farmer is credited for inventing the delightful mascot of Piedmont, featuring a short-braided tail of hair pointing upwards and a tricorn hat. Gianduia became the symbol of the battle for independence which was fought in Piedmont in 1799. During the Carnival celebrations of 1865, the playful and beloved Gianduja rewarded crowds with the wonderful new chocolates that were dubbed Gianduiotti (little Gianduia). The new chocolate-

Hazelnut Praline

Pralines started out in France as whole almonds individually coated in caramelized sugar, prepared by the chef of the seventeenth century sugar magnate, Marshal du Plessis-Praslin. When ground into a chunky mixture, powder, or thick paste, it is known as pralin *in French. The American version, made with pecans and brown sugar, is popular in Louisiana (see page 651).*

YIELD: 3 CUPS

1 cup sugar

$^1/_2$ cup water

$^1/_2$ pound ($1^1/_2$ cups) hazelnuts, toasted and kept warm in a 200°F oven

Prepare a metal baking pan with shallow sides by spraying generously with nonstick spray or line with a silicone baking mat.

In a medium, heavy-bottomed (preferably copper for best heat conduction) pot with a lid, mix the sugar and water together, taking care not to splash up the sides which would encourage sugar crystals to form. Cover the pot and heat on low to moderate heat until the sugar melts entirely and the liquid is clear, about 3 minutes

Raise the heat to medium-high and continue cooking with the lid on, checking often. The sugar will first start to show thick bubbles all over and then will start to brown lightly at the edges. This is when the extremely hot caramel can burn easily. The caramel is ready when it reaches 350°F on a candy thermometer and the sugar is medium brown in color with a faint touch of redness. PAY CAREFUL ATTENTION HERE AS CARAMEL IS EXTREMELY HOT.

Mix the nuts with the caramel, using a wooden spoon, and pour the still hot mixture out onto the prepared baking sheet. Allow the praline to cool at room temperature until it is hard.

Use your hands to break the praline into shards, then break it up further with a meat pounder or a clean hammer. Place the broken-up pieces in the bowl of a food processor and process until the praline is in fine pieces. Remove from the processor and store in an airtight container for up to 6 months.

HONEY

Measuring Honey . . . 517

The Word Honey . . . 517

Top American Honey Varieties . . . 517

SARDINIAN SEBADAS: FRIED STUFFED
ROUNDS WITH RICOTTA CHEESE . . . 517

GREEK HONEY-NUT COOKIES WITH MASTIC
(MELOMAKARONA WITH MASTIHA) . . . 518

About Mastic . . . 519

Mastihashop . . . 520

SFRATTI DI PITIGLIANO . . . 520

About Albergo Guastini . . . 522

TORTA DI MIELE (ITALIAN JEWISH HONEY CAKE) . . . 522

GERMAN BEE-STING CAKE: BIENENSTICH . . . 523

HONEY

Baking with honey is intriguing and challenging, because each type of honey imparts its own distinctive flavors to the recipe, so using different types of honey produces different results. Honeys vary in color, texture, clarity, flavor, and amount of crystallization (if any). Because the sweetening power and flavor of sugar has been standardized, it is easier but less interesting to work with. Until sugar came to dominate the baking of Western Europe, honey, the "thick, barely pourable liquid produced in a mysterious way by honey bees from flower nectar," was one of the few sweeteners. (Date and fig honey, or dibs, were well-known in the Middle East and still popular today.)

Bees have been producing honey just as they do today for at least one hundred and fifty million years as food for the hive during the long months of winter when flowers aren't blooming and little or no nectar is available. The bee that produces practically all the honey in the world today, *Apis mellifera*, seems to have originated in Asia and arrived in Europe by way of the Middle East. These honeybees produce an abundance of honey, far more than the hive can eat, and

humans harvest the excess. Today, European honeybees can be found in beekeepers' hives around the world.

Collecting honey was gratifying because it was a matter of luck with just enough risk to heighten the appetite and the pleasure in finding it. Animals love honey as much as humans do. Bears and primates will stick a paw into a bee hive when they smell the honey and some monkeys have learned to stick a branch into the nest and suck the honey from the stick. Rock paintings in Spain about 12,000 years ago show a man clinging to vines or ropes and putting one hand into the hold while holding a basket to take the honey with the other with bees flying all around him. Two honey pots from Egyptian New Kingdom tombs (about 1400 BCE) still contain honey.

In Old Testament times, honey was gathered from wild bees, rather than cultivated in domestic hives. Because the land was highly cultivated during the later Biblical period, the pronouncements of the prophets of a return to "the land of milk and honey" indicated that the cultivated land would return to its natural state. Jonathan, King Saul's son, and also David's beloved friend, brought victory to the embattled Jewish armies in their war against the fearsome Philistines. After the battle, Jonathan was faint and tired until he chanced upon a beehive. He drew some honey from it using the edge of his cane, ate it, "and his eyes lit up."

Honey cakes date back to the Egyptians, who baked them as offerings to placate their vengeful gods. The Greeks and Romans made their own honey cakes and offered them to their equally jealous gods. They viewed honey as an important food, but also as a healing medicine. In the fifth century BCE, Euripides, the great Greek playwright of sophisticated tragedies, described a cheesecake as "steeped most thoroughly in the rich honey of the golden bee." The ancient Greeks made a kind of honey pudding in which slightly fermented honey was mixed with boiled milk to make it curdle. The mixture was drained and served with fruit.

The fine art of beekeeping flourished throughout the Roman Empire and Virgil, the Roman poet, wrote about "the heavenly gift of honey." The Romans would bake special honey cakes called *quinquagesima liba* for people reaching their 50th birthdays (a great age back then and still an accomplishment today) made of wheat flour, grated cheese (even today, it seems like everything in Italy is seasoned with grated cheese), honey, and olive oil. First made by the Chinese, honey bread (or cake) was carried in the saddlebags of Genghis Kahn's Mongol horseman because it was a long-keeping, energy-rich food. Turks and Arabs learned how to makes the cakes

from the Mongols. European Crusaders later encountered the cakes in the Holy Land.

In 1596, France's King Henry VI of Navarre, granted the Corporation of Spice-bread Makers its own statutes, separate from that of the Pastry cooks. In 1694, the first *Dictionnnaire de l'Académie Française* defined *pain d'épices* as "a kind of cake made with rye flour, honey and spices." Until the end of WWII, the only ingredients in traditional French spice-bread were honey, buckwheat honey from Brittany if possible, an equal amount of flour (wheat in Dijon, rye in Reims, which is further north), and spices. The "mother dough" was kept cool in wooden tubs and aged for several months or even several years, so the honey brought about a delicious fermentation.

In the fourteenth century *Canterbury Tales*, Geoffrey Chaucer mentions the "roial spicerye and Gyngebreed" brought as a gift to Sir Thopas. Up until the seventeenth century, English gingerbread consisted of equal quantities of breadcrumbs and honey, along with spices like ginger, pepper, and cinnamon. This stiff dough was molded until hardened and sold at traveling fairs. In England, molasses began to replace honey during the seventeenth century Restoration. The entire related family of gingerbreads from Great Britain, the lebkuchen and pfeffernusse of Germany and Scandinavia, and the pain d'épices in France are still baked at holiday time, especially for Christmas. In this book, the dense, honey-sweet Siennese Panforte (page 232), chunky with fruit and nuts, dates back to Renaissance times.

Once Christianity was established in Europe, both honey and beeswax production increased greatly, with the beeswax needed to meet the demand for church candles. Honey, was the luxury sweetener of the Middle Ages until Renaissance times when the sugar native to India began to arrive from the East by way of Arab traders. By the seventeenth century, sugar had taken over the pastry-cooks kitchen.

In the sixteenth century, conquering Spaniards found that the natives of Mexico and Central America had already developed beekeeping with the distinct family of stingless honeybees native to the Americas, *Melipona beecheii*. The Mohawks and Algonquin tribes of Canada would stuff small pumpkins with honey, cider, and beaver fat and bake them in the embers of their fires. They would crush strawberries in honey and use the preserves for winter provisions. (Doesn't that sound incredibly good?) A Cheyenne Indian myth says that the first men lived on honey and wild fruits and were never hungry. The native peoples called the European honeybees brought by Europeans "white man's flies."

Ships crossing the Atlantic carried European honey bee colonies to Virginia and Massachusetts in the early seventeenth century. The forest clearings of early colonial America were ideal for the honeybees, which used the plentiful nectar and pollen available from the abundant trees and shrubs of the eastern United States to produce their honey. European settlers took bee hives with them as they traveled westward across the coun-try. Honeybees reached Florida by 1763 and west of the Mississippi by 1800. Russian settlers carried bees to Alaska in 1809 and to California by 1830, although the Spanish may have brought them from Mexico before that date.

Bees are social insects that have evolved along with nectar-producing flowering plants, the two helping each other. To make honey, bees extract nectar as they fly from one flower to the next, gathering pollen on their feet at the same time. The more fragrant the flower, the more bees it attracts. Honeybees will gather nectar from about two million flowers to make just one pound of honey. Honey is primarily composed of fructose, glucose, and water along with enzymes, minerals, vitamins, and amino acids. In most honeys, fructose predominates, so the honey is on the average 1.25 to 1.5 times sweeter than sugar.

The bees fill their honey sacs with nectar from the flowers, which they begin to convert into extra-sweet invert sugars on the way back to the hive. The bees deposit this thin liquid honey into the hexagonal wax cells of their combs. To concentrate it further, worker bees ingest and regurgitate the honey, beating their wings to ventilate the hives. It takes about five quarts of nectar to make one of honey. Once the honey is ready, they seal the cells with a substance secreted by special wax-making bees.

Beekeepers harvest honey in the summer, with the first harvest and the best quality honey, from May to June. The second, less-valued harvest is at the end of the summer. The beekeepers open the hives when the sun is at its height. It is well-known that fine weather will encourage the worker bees to leave the hives and go into the fields. The quality of the honey depends on the flowers visited by the bees, because it retains their fragrance, minerals, and other properties. Not surprisingly, hives in a natural environment rich in wild flowers will give honey of better quality than from plants grown with fertilizers or in polluted places.

Bees have a traveling range of a few kilometers (a mile or so) so in order to collect the more highly-valued single-species honey the beekeeper must observe which flowers the bees have visited and harvest each type separately. Even in ancient times, beekeeping was migratory, with the hives being moved sometimes great distances with the seasons. Bees know their own hives, so the hives themselves have to be moved, not just the bees.

The bees are basically migrant farm workers and their beekeepers their bosses. In Scotland, beekeepers moved the hives to the heathers on the moors in summer to produce heather honey. In the American Southeast, orange blossom and gallberry (a plant related to holly) honeys are collected early in the season. The hives and their keepers would then travel up to New York to set out hives out for clover, goldenrod and basswood. During blueberry season in Maine and Michigan bees that produce orange blossom honey earlier in the season in Florida switch over to blueberry honey.

There are as many flavors of honey as there are flowers, because the type of flower nectar gathered by the bees directly affects the flavor of the honey. Honey's flavors range from mild and floral to aromatic and spicy, to bittersweet and resinous. Because honey has so many subtle nuances of flavor and sugar has only its one-dimensional sweetness to offer (except when caramelized), with the decline of honey, we all became less discerning in our collective sweet tooth. About 300 different single-flower honeys are collected in the world today. Some of the most valued are orange blossom, acacia, chestnut, buckwheat, and lavender. (See page 517 to learn about the unusual Sardinian bitter honey.)

To process honey, the honeycomb is removed from the hive and spun in a centrifuge to separate the liquid from the wax. The honey is then heated to 155° to kill the yeast. The honey is then strained, blended if necessary, and then filtered under pressure to remove pollen grains and tiny air bubbles that would keep it from being clear. (Some honeys are sold in their unfiltered state.)

Although it is quite stable, honey can spoil, because it contains moisture and will absorb more from the air when the humidity level is higher than 60 percent, allowing sugar-tolerant yeasts to grow on the honey. For this reason, it is best to store honey in a tightly closed container. Honey, which is a more or less viscous liquid.

In France and Germany, light, sweet, thin, pale gold acacia honey is common. In Provence, pale, thick, and aromatic lavender honey can be found. In Sardinia, bitter honey, from the flowers of the strawberry gum tree is a specialty (see page 000). In Tuscany and Piedmont, thick, slightly crystallized and faintly bitter chestnut honey is prized. The famed Greek thyme honey from Mount Hymettus was by legend beloved by the gods; people still enjoy it today. Even in Roman times, cunning beekeepers would place their hives in the thyme fields of Spain to make a pseudo-Mount Hymettus honey sold on the ancient Via Sacra in Rome in luxury shops. Buckwheat honey was once common in Brittany, where buckwheat was the main grain and traditionally used to make pain d'épices. Although buckwheat and its honey are no longer found in Brittany, dark, strong-tasting buckwheat honey is relatively common in the United States.

For baking, this miraculous substance presents its own challenges and rewards. When cooking with honey, remember that honey is 25 to 50 percent as sweet as sugar because of its higher fructose content. It imparts a pronounced and distinctive flavor rather just adding sweetness, especially in darker varieties. Because of its natural acidity, honey will react with alkali baking powders and baking soda to lighten baked goods. It also acts as a preservative to baked goods, helping to maintain moistness because of the water it contains. When baking, I usually combine honey and sugar, because honey alone tends to dominate. Honey burns more easily than sugar, so reduce the heat about 25 degrees (F) when cooking or baking.

Honey has a special affinity with nuts, which are often glazed with honey, or mixed together in cakes and other sweets such as the Torta di Miele: Italian Jewish Honey Cake (page 522), the honey-drenched wreath of puffy fried dough bits known as *Tieglach* or *Cicerchiata* (page 587), and the Greek Honey cake with Yogurt (page 903). Sardinia is famed for its distinctive bitter honey, which is drizzled over the Sebadas: Fried Stuffed Rounds with Ricotta Cheese (page 517).

In Greece, which is famed for its aromatic and resinous thyme blossom honey and the piney mastic sap used as a seasoning (see page 519), honey is simmered into a syrup to coast Greek Honey-Nut Cookies with Mastic (Melomakarona with Mastiha) (page 518). Both Ashkenazi and Sephardic Jewish traditional sweets often feature honey mixed with nuts.

The honey-walnut filled Sfratti di Pitigliano (page 520) taste just like the honey-walnut candies called simply *nuss* (nuts) or *nuant* that my Polish-born grandmother would make and drop onto wax paper to set. The addition of orange zest marks the recipe as Italkeni (or Italian-Jewish) rather than Ashkenazi. The German Bee-Sting Cake: Bienenstich (page 523) is topped with a layer of chewy, honey-almond cream candy.

Sardinian Sebadas: Fried Stuffed Rounds with Ricotta Cheese

Sebadas resemble large round ravioli stuffed with ricotta cheese—sheep's milk ricotta in its original version—that are fried until puffy and light, and then drizzled with the special bitter honey of Sardinia. The pastries are a specialty of the mountainous Barbagia region south of the central part of Sardinia. Called Miele Amaro di Corbezzolo *in Sardinia, the honey is collected after three months of pollination of the flowers of the rare* Arbutus unedo *plant. This plant is known as the strawberry tree in English because its fruits resembles round, spicy strawberries. I gorged myself on more than one of these sebadas at Dallas' Arcodoro and Pomodoro ("rainbow and tomato" in Italian), a restaurant that specializes in the foods of this fascinating island. The owner of both the restaurant and the specialty food importing company is Sardinian native, Efisio Farris, who I've had the pleasure of meeting. Find the bitter honey at his website, www.gourmetsardinia.com.*

YIELD: 4 TO 6 SERVINGS

Filling

1/2 pound whole milk ricotta

2 ounces mild goat cheese

Grated zest of 1 lemon (1 tablespoon)

2 large eggs

2 tablespoons sugar

Dough and Assembly

$1/4$ pound (1 cup minus 1 tablespoon) unbleached all-
    purpose flour

2 ounces ($1/2$ cup minus $1/2$ tablespoon) bread flour

$1/4$ pound ($1/2$ cup plus $2^{1}/2$ tablespoons) fine semolina

$1/2$ teaspoon fine sea salt

$1/2$ cup warm milk

$1/4$ pound (1 stick) unsalted butter, melted and cooled

3 cups lard, olive oil, or canola oil, for frying

Confectioners' sugar

$1/2$ cup bitter or chestnut honey, warm, substitute wild-
    flower or buckwheat honey

Make the filling: Combine the ricotta, goat cheese, lemon zest, eggs, and sugar in a mixing bowl and blend well. Set aside.

Make the dough: In the bowl of a standing mixer fitted with the whisk attachment, combine the all-purpose flour, bread flour, semolina, and salt.

In a separate bowl, whisk together the milk and butter. Pour the mixture into the flour mixture, change to the paddle attachment, and beat until a ball of dough forms. Beat 1 minute longer, or until the dough is smooth, wrap well, and chill for 1 hour in the refrigerator or 30 minutes in the freezer.

Using a pasta machine dusted with flour or a rolling pin on a flour-dusted work surface, roll the dough out to less than $1/4$-inch thick. Using a sharp knife and the bottom of a bowl or container, cut 5-inch diameter circles from the pastry. Spoon about 2 tablespoons of the filling onto half of the dough rounds, leaving a $1/2$-inch border around the filling. Brush the border with water and then cover with a second dough round. Press the edges of the dough rounds together firmly to seal.

In a wok, a large heavy-duty cast-iron frying pan, or an electric deep-fryer, heat the lard to 365°F, or until shimmering hot and the air about 3 inches above the lard feels hot. Place the pastries, one at a time, in the lard without crowding, and working in batches if necessary. Fry until light brown and crispy, about 4 minutes. Scoop from the lard, drain on a wire rack, and keep warm in a 200°F oven while you fry the remaining sebadas.

While the sebadas are still warm, sprinkle them with confectioners' sugar, drizzle with the honey, and serve immediately. If any are left, wrap in aluminum foil and refrigerate up to three days. Reheat in the foil in a preheated 350ºF oven for about 15 minutes or until hot, then uncover the foil and heat 5 minutes longer to crisp them.

Greek Honey–Nut Cookies with Mastic (Melomakarona with Mastiha)

These festive honey-soaked cookies, also called phoenikia, *are dipped into a honeyed syrup flavored with mastic-infused ouzo. They are a specialty of the fascinating Aegean island of Chios, which I had the chance to visit recently. Either dip the cooled cookies in hot syrup, or the hot cookies in cold syrup, so they'll absorb it better. Greek thyme honey would work well here, as would wildflower honey.*

YIELD: 48 COOKIES

Cookies

1 pound (3³⁄₄ cups) unbleached all-purpose flour

¹⁄₄ pound (¹⁄₂ cup plus 2¹⁄₂ tablespoons) fine semolina

¹⁄₄ cup confectioners' sugar

1 teaspoon baking powder

1 teaspoon ground cinnamon

Pinch powdered cloves

1¹⁄₂ cups orange juice

Grated zest of 1 orange (4 teaspoons)

2 cups extra-virgin olive oil

2 ounces (¹⁄₂ stick) unsalted butter, melted

¹⁄₂ pound (2 cups) walnuts, finely chopped

Syrup

1 cup water

1 cup sugar

1 cup honey

¹⁄₂ cup Mastiha liqueur, or ¹⁄₂ cup ouzo plus
    2 teaspoons crushed mastic, or 6 tablespoons
    vodka plus 2 tablespoons anisette

Juice of ¹⁄₂ lemon

Preheat the oven to 350°F. Line two 18 x 13-inch half sheet pans (or other large baking pans) with parchment paper or silicone baking mats.

Make the cookies: In a large bowl, whisk together the dry ingredients: flour, semolina, confectioners' sugar, baking powder, cinnamon, and cloves.

Separately, whisk together the orange juice, orange zest, olive oil, and butter. Using a wooden spoon or silicone spatula, fold the orange juice mix into the flour mixture. Do not overwork the dough, which will be soft and rather oily in consistency.

Divide the dough into 4 portions and form each part into logs about 1¹⁄₂ inches in diameter. Using a sharp knife, cut each log on the diagonal into ³⁄₈-inch thick slices. Arrange on a baking pan about 2 inches apart. Using the palm of your hand, press each slice to flatten into an oblong shape. Bake for 20 to 25 minutes until golden, firm and crisp, then cool completely on a wire rack.

Make the syrup: In a medium nonreactive pot, bring 1 cup of water and the sugar to a boil over medium heat and simmer for 1 minute. Add the honey, liqueur, and lemon juice and keep hot.

Dip the cookies (as many as will fit in a single layer in the pot) into the hot syrup, using a spatula to hold them down for about 1 minute to absorb the syrup. Remove the cookies with a wire skimmer or slotted spoon, allowing some of the excess syrup to drip off.

Arrange on a large serving sheet in layers, sprinkling each layer of cookies generously with the walnuts before topping with another layer of cookies. Store the cookies covered with wax paper and at room temperature for 4 to 5 days.

ABOUT MASTIC

The Greek island of Chios lies just five miles off the Turkish coast in the northern Aegean Sea. The purported birthplace of Homer and Hippocrates, Chios is best known as the world's source of mastiha, or mastic, a crystalline resin produced from the bark of the mastic tree (*Pistacia lentiscus var. Chia*) that has been cultivated there for millennia. During the annual fall harvest, the trees are cut—known on the island as "hurting" the tree—to produce its "tears," the clear drops of resin that harden into mastic.

In ancient times, mastic was well-known from Carthage to Egypt and Arabia. The healthful properties of mastic resin were first documented by the Greek physician and botanist Dioscorides (first century BCE), generally considered the "father of pharmacology." Dioscorides praised Chios mastic for its health benefits and for its tranquilizing and aphrodisiac effects. Aristocratic women in the Roman and Byzantine empires cleaned and whitened their teeth with mastic toothpicks, while Ottoman sultans reserved the island's finest and largest "tears" for the women in their harems. One sultan satisfied (or at least attempted to) his more than three hundred concubines after regularly consuming a potent potion made of pepper, cloves, nutmeg, bay leaves, aniseed, sugar, and mastic. The Genoese, who ruled Chios from 1346 to 1566, brought organized trading to the island, shipping its famed mastic to London, Venice, Pisa, Marseilles, Damascus, Florence, Cyprus, and Odessa.

In Greece, mastic is traditionally brought out of the cupboard on Christmas and Easter to be pounded and used as a seasoning in holiday breads and biscuits. The intriguing musky, slightly piney, incense-like spice is also exported for use by chefs and food producers worldwide. Mastiha flavors Greek cakes, breads, pastries, ice cream, chocolate, jams, liqueurs, aperitifs, and natural chewing gum, and is much used in Turkey and the Middle East, where most of the island's product is exported. Mastic "tears" or powdered mastic may be purchased at Greek and Middle Eastern groceries, including Kalustyan's (www.kalustyans.com). The larger the tear, the higher the price.

MASTIHASHOP

The Chios Gum Mastic Growers Association has opened a chain of stylish mastic boutiques on the island of Chios, in Athens airport, and other places including their newest store in New York's Lower East Side. I happened to be walking on Orchard Street, well-known for its clothing bargains, and came upon the tiny, but fully-stocked store, which had just opened that day (www.mastihashopny.com)! Lucky for me, I was able to stock up on some of the hauntingly flavored mastic specialties that I had loaded up on in Chios, including my favorite: mastic halvah. Unfortunately, because of state liquor laws, the store is not allowed to sell the mastiha-infused ouzo that I use in the cookies above, but they have everything else you can think of, including a line of all-natural mastic-infused cleansers, cosmetics, and toothpaste.

Sfratti di Pitigliano

I made a special pilgrimage to the small southern Tuscan town of Pitigliano, which had a longstanding and influential Jewish community. While there, I sampled several different versions of this iconic pastry, shaped like a thick stick. I also interviewed (in Italian) Signore Guastini, the owner of the one local hotel, to get her recipe for this wonderful cookie, which was the basis of this recipe. In the often ironic humor of the Jews, something especially good—the sweet and delicious walnut-honey filled cookies—commemorate something bad—the hated and feared wooden bats that were used to force Jews back into the ghetto at night. The outside pastry is like a sugar cookie dough while the orange-scented honey filling is chewy and chunky with nuts.

YIELD: ABOUT 2 DOZEN PASTRIES

Dough

$^3/_4$ pound ($2^3/_4$ cups plus 1 tablespoon) unbleached
  all-purpose flour

$^1/_2$ cup sugar

2 teaspoons baking powder

$^1/_2$ teaspoon fine sea salt

6 ounces ($1^1/_2$ sticks) unsalted butter, chilled
  and cut into bits

4 large eggs

$^1/_4$ cup dry white wine

Grated zest of 1 lemon (1 tablespoon)

Filling

2 cups honey

$^1/_2$ pound walnut halves, roughly chopped

$^1/_2$ cup fine dry breadcrumbs or panko

Grated zest of 1 orange (4 teaspoons)

1 egg yolk, lightly beaten with 1 tablespoon water,
  for the egg wash

Make the dough: In a bowl, whisk together the flour, sugar, baking powder, and salt. Beat in the butter until the pieces are the size of oatmeal.

In a bowl, whisk together the eggs, wine, and lemon zest. Beat this mixture into the flour mixture and continue to beat until the dough forms large, moist clumps. Finish by briefly kneading by hand until a smooth ball is formed. Flatten into a rectangular shape, cover with plastic wrap, and refrigerate for 1 hour or until firm.

Make the filling: Simmer the honey for 15 minutes, until it reaches the soft-ball stage, 238°F on a candy thermometer, or when a spoonful dropped in a glass of ice water forms a soft ball. Immediately add the walnuts and continue cooking 10 minutes longer or until the honey has darkened slightly and the mixture is thick. Test in ice water to make sure the mixture is firm enough to hold its shape, but is still malleable.

Immediately, remove from the heat and stir in the breadcrumbs and the orange zest. Mix well, then set aside to cool to room temperature.

Divide the filling into 4 portions, roll each portion into a log shape, and refrigerate until firm, about 2 hours.

Divide the dough into 4 portions and roll out each portion between 2 floured sheets of wax paper into a rectangle about 8 by 3 inches and about $^1/_4$ inch thick. Refrigerate again until firm, about 30 minutes.

Place one log of the filling in the center of each dough rectangle. Fold over the dough edges, trimming off any excess dough especially at the ends. Roll up to completely enclose the filling. Repeat with the remaining dough and filling.

Brush the logs with egg wash and cut 4 small slits in the top of each. Arrange on an 18" x 13" baking pan that has been lined with parchment paper or a silicone mat seam side down and freeze for 20 minutes.

Preheat the oven to 375°F. Bake for 20 minutes or until the logs are well browned and the filling is just starting to bubble. Note that the filling often oozes out. Trim off any drips once the logs cool, and discard. Cool to room temperature, then cut on the diagonal into lozenge shapes. Store covered and at room temperature for up to five days. Baked but uncut, the sfratti logs freeze beautifully up to three months, wrapped in aluminum foil or freezer paper.

About Albergo Guastini

Pitigliano is a small medieval town, barricaded on its long edge by soft tufa stone, a type of volcanic rock. The houses of the old Jewish ghetto rise from the upper edges of the cliff, seemingly right from the tufa. The small, family-owned Guastini Hotel and Restaurant has been housing visitors since 1905. It is the only hotel in the old town centre. It has about 60 beds, placed in single, old-fashioned rooms. Most of the hotel's rooms enjoy striking views. The restaurant offers food typical of the region, traditional recipes, and some Jewish dishes.

Torta di Miele (Italian Jewish Honey Cake)

Honey cakes have been part of Jewish tradition since medieval times, especially in Germany. Young children just starting school would be fed with honey cake to make their learning sweet. In this moist Italian Jewish honey cake, sweet spices, lemon juice and its fragrant zest, golden raisins, and rum flavor the cake, while olive oil provides richness, moisture, and fruity flavor. This is a simple cake that keeps well, mellowing in flavor after a few days at room temperature. Serve it with hot brewed tea. This recipe is dairy-free.

YIELD: 2 SMALL LOAVES

$3/4$ pound ($2^3/4$ cups plus 1 tablespoon) unbleached all-purpose flour

1 tablespoon baking powder

1 teaspoon ground cinnamon

Pinch ground cloves

$1/2$ teaspoon fine sea salt

1 cup honey

$1/4$ cup sugar

$1/2$ cup hot water

$1/4$ cup dark rum, or brandy

4 large eggs

Juice of 1 lemon (3 tablespoons)

Grated zest of 1 lemon (1 tablespoon)

$1/2$ cup extra-virgin olive oil

$5^1/2$ ounces (1 cup) golden raisins

$1/4$ pound (1 cup chopped) walnuts, lightly toasted

Preheat the oven to 375°F. Prepare two small ($3/4$-pound) 8 x 4-inch loaf pans by spraying them with nonstick baker's coating or rubbing with oil and dusting with flour, shaking out the excess.

In a medium bowl, whisk together the dry ingredients: flour, baking powder, cinnamon, cloves, and salt.

In a large bowl, combine the honey, sugar, water, and rum, stirring until the sugar is dissolved. Beat in the eggs, lemon juice, and zest until well combined. Slowly beat in the olive oil. Fold in the flour mixture, then fold in the raisins and walnuts.

Pour the mixture into the pans and bake for 35 minutes. The center of the cakes should be puffed up and cracked, and a skewer inserted in the center should come out clean. Cool on a wire rack before slicing.

Store at room temperature, covered, for 4 or 5 days or wrap and freeze up to 3 months.

German Bee-Sting Cake: Bienenstich

I've been lucky enough to gather recipes from all sorts of generous people, who are happy to share their treasures. One evening at a party, I met Jens Langlotz from Germany, who offered to get his mother's recipe for this cake. In the message that accompanied the recipe, he said, "I hope this is going to turn out as delicious as I remember it from Germany." I certainly hope so, because it sure is good! His mother uses bitter almond oil to flavor the cake, which is illegal in America because large quantities of bitter almonds are poisonous. I've substituted almond extract in this recipe. The cake gets its name because, as the story goes, a bee was attracted to the gooey honey topping and the baker was stung. Not too much of a sacrifice in the pursuit of a wonderful cake recipe in my mind. In Jens, mother's version, the pastry cream filling is mixed with the tart, thick, white yogurt-like cream called quark, which I happen to love. However it got its name, this is one delicious cake.

YIELD: ONE 9-INCH CAKE, 10 TO 12 SERVINGS

Cake

1 cup lukewarm milk

$^1/_2$ cup sugar

1 ($^1/_4$-ounce) package (2$^1/_4$ teaspoons) active dry yeast

1 teaspoon almond extract

18 ounces (4$^3/_4$ cups minus 1 tablespoon) unbleached all-purpose flour

Filling

4 large egg yolks

$^3/_4$ cup sugar

2 ounces ($^1/_2$ cup minus $^1/_2$ tablespoon) unbleached all-purpose flour

1 ounce ($^1/_4$ cup plus 1 tablespoon) potato starch, substitute corn, wheat, or rice starch

1$^1/_2$ cups milk, scalded

1 teaspoon almond extract

$^1/_2$ vanilla bean, split open and seeds scraped out, substitute 1 teaspoon vanilla

$^1/_2$ cup quark, substitute crème fraîche, chilled

Topping

$^1/_2$ cup sugar

2$^1/_2$ ounces (5 tablespoons) unsalted butter

$^1/_4$ cup heavy cream

$^1/_4$ cup honey

3 ounces ($^3/_4$ cup) sliced skin-on almonds

Make the cake: Spray a 9-inch cake pan with nonstick baker's coating, or rub with softened butter and dust with flour, shaking out the excess. Line the edge of the pan with a strip of folded and buttered wax paper, to hold in the filling.

In the bowl of a standing mixer fitted with the paddle attachment, combine $^1/_4$ cup of the milk, 1 tablespoon of the sugar, the yeast, and the almond extract. Allow the mixture to proof in a warm place for about 15 minutes, or until the mixture is bubbling and puffy. Beat in the remaining milk and remaining sugar. Beat in the flour, switch to the dough hook, and continue beating until the dough is smooth and elastic, though still soft and sticky.

Transfer the dough to a large oiled bowl; turn around so the dough is oiled all over. Cover with plastic wrap or a damp cloth and allow the dough to rise until doubled in size, about 2 hours, at warm room temperature.

Punch down the dough, then roll it out on a lightly floured work surface to a 9-inch round. Transfer the dough to the pan and allow it to rise at warm room temperature for about 1 hour, or until puffy.

Preheat the oven to 350°F. Bake the cake for 30 minutes or until golden brown and the cake has begun to come away from the sides of the pan. Cool to room temperature on a wire rack.

Make the filling: In a medium bowl, beat the egg yolks and sugar together to combine. Whisk in the flour and potato starch. Slowly pour in the scalded milk. Transfer the mixture to a medium nonreactive pot and bring to a boil over low heat, whisking often. As soon as the mixture boils, remove it from the heat and whisk in the almond and vanilla extracts.

Transfer the mixture to a bowl, preferably stainless-steel and cool by placing over a second bowl filled with a mixture of ice and water, stirring often.

In the bowl of a standing mixer fitted with the whisk attachment, whip the quark to stiff peaks, then fold into the pastry cream. Refrigerate until ready to use.

Make the topping: Combine the sugar, butter, cream, honey, and almonds in a medium, heavy-bottomed, nonreactive pot and bring to a boil. Cook until the mixture reaches the soft-ball stage, or 238°F on a candy thermometer, and is thickened enough to start to come away from the sides of the pan, about 10 minutes. Remove from the heat, transfer to a metal bowl, and cool to room temperature, or until the mixture is firm enough to hold its shape.

Spread the topping on the cooled cake and set aside until the topping has set. Remove the wax paper lining.

Assemble the cake: Cut a very small wedge, about $1/4$-inch deep, out of the side of the cake to use as a guide. Using a long, serrated knife, cut the cake horizontally into two layers. Cut the top half only into twelve wedges. Spread the custard filling onto the cut side of the bottom layer of cake. Arrange the 12 wedges around the top of the custard in a circular shape.

Chill the cake for 30 minutes or until the custard has set. Using a knife dipped in hot water and dried thoroughly in between each cut, cut the cake top into 12 portions and serve. Store the cake covered and refrigerated for up to 2 days.

LEMONS & CITRONS

Lemon Varieties . . . 530

Citron . . . 531

LEMON GALATABOUREKO . . . 532

MEYER LEMON BUNDT CAKE . . . 533

FRENCH CANDIED CITRON AND LEMON COOKIES . . . 534

TORTA DI SAVOIA WITH CANDIED CITRON . . . 535

BISCOTTI ROCOCÒ . . . 536

HOMEMADE LIMONCELLO . . . 537

LIGHT LEMON PASTRY CREAM . . . 538

FRESH LEMON SAUCE . . . 539

LEMONS
& CITRONS

One of my earliest culinary experiments involved lemons, actually a lemon meringue pie that my mother was baking for her dinner party. I was no more than about four years old and for some mischievous reason, I decided to pour salt into the sugar bowl. Yes, my mother did make that pie with salt and serve it to her guests. Hopefully, she has forgiven me by now!

Quite a few years later, I immersed myself in learning to cook and bake the simple, fresh ingredient–based food of Italy, where light and lively lemon juice and the essential oils contained in the fruit's bright yellow skin wafts through the air of home kitchens, restaurants, and bakeries.

Throughout the Mediterranean, the precious oils on the outside of the lemon's skin, often foolishly discarded by American cooks, scent pastries, cakes, and cookies as often as vanilla in American counterparts. Because vanilla was and is expensive and had to be imported from far away, cooks in the region, especially in Italy and Greece, used close-at-hand lemons instead, often from trees planted in their own courtyards.

It's apparent that lemon is an essential flavor in the many Italian recipes in this book. Small shreds of yellow zest scent cakes like the White Chocolate–Lemon Torta Caprese (page 78), the crumbly cornmeal Torta Sbrisolona (page 390), and the Torta di Miele (page 522) and pastry doughs like the Pasta Frolla (page 62) and the Venetian Cornmeal Tart Dough (page 391). The Lemon Poppy Seed Biscotti (page 719) are chunky with bits of candied lemon rind. Lemon features in the lemon–custard filled Lemon-Pine Nut Tart (page 675), the sweet rice–filled Crostata di Riso (page 776), and even Rosemary and Rye Breadsticks (page 783) get their lively acidity from fresh-squeezed lemons and a beguiling aroma from lemon zest. Babàs al Limoncello (page 56) get their lemon four ways infused lemon zest in the batter: lemon juice and zest in the Light Lemon Pastry Cream filling (page 538), and a soaking in lemon juice and Limoncello liqueur (page 537) sugar syrup. Because all these recipes call for aromatic lemon zest and less call for acidic lemon juice, it's no wonder I keep ending up with too many naked lemons–lemons that have had their protective cloak of oily zest grated off!

Several years ago, I visited an organic cooperative lemon orchard high above the rock-strewn

Mediterranean coastline on the Amalfi coast. The farmers planted groves of the special Sorrento lemon tree grafted onto the sturdy root stock of bitter oranges (the same kind used to make marmalade and orange blossom water). Using completely biodegradable building materials, they protect the precious trees from the wind by building *pergolati* (roofless shelters) constructed of thin flexible chestnut wood branches cut from trees grown in the orchard especially for this purpose. Because the trees bear fruit throughout the year, in winter, workers climb up and cover the pergolas straw mats to protect the fussy trees from the cold. Huge olive trees tower over the lemon trees, providing shade in the summer and keeping the pampered lemon trees relatively cool. Ladders made from wood poles lashed together with reeds and biodegradable iron bands allow the workers access to the top "floors" to hand-pick the gigantic, lumpy, and extraordinarily fragrant tree-ripened Sorrento lemons.

As a restaurant chef, I refused to use metallic-tasting bottled lemon juice although, in spite of my reputation as a food fanatic, I would compromise and used freshly-squeezed, then frozen lemon juice sold by the quart. It is not ideal, however, because these lemons are mechanically juiced, the juice tends to pick up a bitter aftertaste from squeezing the lemon's white pith too hard. I search out plump lemons with thinner skin and therefore juicier flesh and try not to forget to first grate off the zest before squeezing the fruits for juice. (Store the grated zest covered and refriger-

ated up to two weeks, mix it with sugar to make syrup for lemonade, or let it dry and sprinkle on vegetables, fruit, poultry, and fish).

Botanists believe that the lemon and its cousin, the citron, originated in the eastern Himalayan region of India and adjoining areas, because natural hybrids of citron and lemon are abundant there. However, the common Mediterranean lemon has not been found growing wild in any part of that region or elsewhere else, so its beginnings are still a mystery. Others scientists cite evidence that the lemon is native to southeastern China and was well known and cultivated before the Sung dynasty (960 to 1279). One book of the time mentions lemons: "In the fourth year of K'ai Pao, two bottles of lemon juice were allowed to be presented to the Emperor." Lemons were grown in Egypt before 900 CE and Arab agronomists were familiar with the lemon, as were the Persians, who called the fruit *limu*, and the Iraqis, who called it *hasia*.

A mosaic tile floor found in a Roman villa at Carthage, (Tunisia) probably of the second century CE shows recognizable fruit-bearing lemon trees. Lemons reached the Amalfi Coast of Italy by about the second century and by the fourth century, skillful Italian gardeners were already raising lemons. Citrons, lemons and oranges attached to freshly cut branches covered with green leaves adorn a vaulted ceiling built for the Emperor Constantine (274 to 337). However, after the Lombard invasion of 568, the luxurious gardens and their delicate citrus trees of Italy were destroyed.

The Arabs had introduced the citron, sour

orange, lemon, and shaddock (precursor of the grapefruit) to Spain and North Africa by about 1150. By the end of the eleventh century, returning Crusaders brought back lemons, apricots, and sour oranges from Asia Minor.

At the palace of Louis the XIV, known as "the Sun King," witty diversions, balls, and theatre entertained the resident courtesans, who were presented with lemons and oranges on special occasions. Casanova believed that the lemon was a miraculous aphrodisiac but Catalan priests excommunicated the lemon, claiming that the devil had not succeeded in making it as round and perfect as the orange and that this deformed fruit was unworthy of Christians.

According to Bartolome de las Casas in his *Historia de las Indias* (1520 to 1559), Columbus, and his fleet of 17 vessels, stopped in the Canary Islands for supplies including lemon seeds. On his second voyage to the New World in 1493, Columbus planted lemons and oranges in Haiti where he established the settlement of Isabella. At about the same times, the Portuguese introduced lemons into Brazil. By 1653 Peru grew small lemons and the large lemons known as Royals. Ships full of colonists brought lemons from Brazil across the southern oceans to Australia in 1788.

Lemons arrived in Florida with the early Spanish explorers and colonists some time between 1513 when Ponce de Leon first landed in Florida, and 1565 when St. Augustine, the first colony in Florida, was established. Wild groves of citrus fruits including lemons became common in

Florida and the state led the United States in lemon production until a heavy freeze in 1835 interrupted development of the industry. At first Florida and then California began raising lemons commercially to offset America's heavy imports of lemons from Sicily, which still raises nine out of ten lemons produced in Italy. The great freeze of 1894–95 killed the Florida lemon groves and production switched to California.

Lemons and oranges grew in the mission gardens of Baja California. In 1769 when the Jesuits were expelled from the region, they moved north into California, bringing along lemon and orange trees. But, it took the California gold rush of 1849 to establish a commercial lemon industry. With the huge influx of would-be prospectors, food, especially fresh fruits and vegetables, were scarce and high-priced. Due to the shortage of vitamin C, scurvy was widespread. Flush with gold, the miners were willing to pay $1 apiece for lemons, a sure cure for scurvy. By 1856, the lemon industry in California was well-established.

Lemons grow on attractive small, widely branched thorny evergreen tree that can grow ten to twenty feet high. They are quite demanding, intolerant of frost and extreme heat. In the best conditions lemon trees can produce flowers and fruit almost year-round. (In Italy some trees produce four crops a year.) One tree may bear as many as 3,000 lemons a year, which are green when immature, turning yellow in the cool nights of autumn and winter .

Since 1950, California has produced about one-quarter of the world's supply of lemons, though Arizona is now also a major grower. Italian lemons for export are harvested as early as possible and are naturally "cured" in transit. In the early days, California and Florida lemons were allowed to remain on the trees until they became quite large. Now, growers pick the fruits as soon as they contain 25 percent juice by hand, because the fruits have to be handled gently and can't be picked when they're at all wet.

In Southern Mexico, and Guatemala lemons are grown mostly for their aromatic oil and for dehydrating into lemon powder. Lemons have long been an important commercial crop in the Mediterranean countries of Portugal, Greece, and Italy and two islands: Sicily and Corsica, along with Turkey. The biggest lemon producers aside from California are Italy, Spain, Greece, Turkey, Cyprus, Lebanon, South Africa, and Australia. About one million cases of lemons of often extra-seedy Spanish lemons ship to America every year. In South America, Argentina is the leading producer, with Chile a distant but growing second.

Lemons contain up to forty percent juice, (averaging 3 tablespoons of juice per lemon) which is five percent citric and ascorbic acid and about 1 tablespoon of heavily scented zest. Aside from flavoring desserts on its own, lemon juice is also valuable to sprinkle on white fruits like bananas, pears, and apples preventing them from turning an unappetizingly brown as the fruit reacts with the oxygen in the air.

Although I know they're preferable, I usually can't bring myself to pay the high price of organic lemons (sometimes $3.50 each!). Conventional lemons are treated with diphenyl, an ethylene gas that keeps the skins yellow and fresh-looking and sometimes coated with wax, so I wash the lemons in hot water with detergent, and then rinse them well under running cold water.

Because of their versatility in baking, lemons appear in many guises in this book. The delicate Majorcan Lemon–Almond Cake (page 77) takes advantage of two locally grown Majorcan crops: lemons and almonds. Aromatic lemon zest and ground true cinnamon scent the Crispy Lemon–Cinnamon Cookies (page 351). Lemon and garden mint scent the English Summer Fruit Pudding (page 415), which would be perfect served with iced minted lemonade on a hot summer's day. The clean, floral scent of lavender in the Honey Glazed Lavender–Lemon Cake (page 472) relies on lemon's bright acidity as a sharp counterbalance.

The Lemon–Blackberry Bavarese (page 481) is a creamy lemon creation layered with tart blackberries for flavor and color contrast. The Lemon Galataboureko (page 532), a layered phyllo pastry from Greece gets a light creamy semolina custard filling, the whole thing drenched in lemon and lemon liqueur syrup. Cream cheese enriches the batter for the dense, smooth, and silky Meyer Lemon Bundt Cake (page 533), which is lavishly scented with fragrant, short-lived Meyer lemons.

LEMON VARIETIES

Lemons come in a variety of shapes and sizes and colors, usually with a "neck" on the stem end and a "nipple" on the blossom end. The fruits can be very large or very small, have thick or thin, smooth or knobby skin; and more or less acidic juice, but they all have one thing in common: their skin contains valuable aromatic essential oils in their yellow skin.

AMERICAN LEMONS: The Eureka, long America's most common lemon, was born from young Italian lemon plants (probably Lunario) introduced to California in 1850. The vigorous trees have few thorns and pink-tinged flowers. The big oblong fruits are very juicy with a high acid content that accents their "lemony" flavor and not many seeds. The main harvest matures in late winter and early spring. The Armstrong usually bears seedless or almost-seedless fruits but otherwise resembles the Eureka.

The Lisbon lemon originated in Portugal and traveled the world, reaching Australia in 1824. It was first catalogued in Massachusetts in 1843, and reached California about 1849 and was again introduced from Australia in 1874. (It may be the same as the Portugal lemon grown in Morocco and Algeria). Its fruits are almost identical to the Eureka and now surpasses it in numbers harvested.

MEYER LEMONS: Agricultural explorer, Frank N. Meyer introduced his namesake fruit into the United States in 1908 after finding it growing as an ornamental pot-plant near Peking, China. It is con-sidered either an orange-lemon or a mandarin-lemon hybrid. Because it is thin-skinned and quite perishable, the Meyer lemon became a garden tree planted in California backyards, rather than a com-mercial crop. About 1980, someone who had a Meyer lemon tree growing in their yard brought the fruits to Chez Panisse, where the fruits became a signature ingredient of the restaurant.

The tree produces flowers and fruit almost all year round, with the main harvest from December to April. Now raised for the commercial market by spe-cialty growers, Meyer lemons will be on the expensive side, but well worth the extra cost for their complex flavor and aroma, hinting of sweet lime, lemon, and mandarin. The fruits contain about four times the sugar of a common lemon and are succu-lent, inordinately juicy, and highly aromatic, with a pronounced floral fragrance in their soft rind. Bright, shiny Meyer lemons with richly colored orangey-yel-low rind are a sign that the fruits were picked when fully ripe. With their soft, thin rind and juicy flesh, Meyer lemons deteriorate quickly—after a few days they begin to shrivel, and the rinds become hard and dry. Even so, they'll usually be fine on the inside, how-ever. Cut away and discard any soft or mushy parts.

EUROPEAN LEMONS: Small Fino lemons from Spain grow on thorny trees with lots of thorny shoots. The lemons are have smooth, thin rind, and a medium number of seeds. The Verna, also from Spain, is oval-shaped with a pronounced nipple, short neck, rough-textured, medium-thick peel that clings tightly, and few to no seeds. This winter lemon is the leading variety of Spain and also important in Algeria and Morocco. The Femminello Ovale, one of the oldest Italian lemons accounts for three-quarters of Italy's lemon crop. This prized lemon is short and rounded with a blunt nipple and rounded base. Its flesh is tender and juicy and high in the acid that accentuates lemon flavor.

CITRON

The shiny sunny-yellow locally-grown *cedri di Amalfi* I saw piled up for sale in Amalfi, Italy were giant-sized. Across the plaza, those same citrons were transformed into chocolate-dipped new moon-shaped candied sections at Pasticceria Pansa (see page 57) and in small dice, mixed into their super-hard Rococò cookies (see page 536). If Americans are familiar at all with the lemon's almost juiceless, thick-skinned cousin, the citron, it is usually in the form of the candied rind dreaded by many (and included in a recent list of America's most hated foods).

The citron, *Citrus medica Linn.*, is called *cedrat* or *citronnier des Juifs* (Jewish citron) in French, *cidra* in Spanish, and *cedra* in Italian. Shaped like a rather large and bumpy lemon, the citron is faintly ribbed with the ribs more prominent in the Etrog variety grown in Israel for ritual use. It thick flesh is greenish-yellow to bright yellow, with little juice, but an abundance of seeds.

The legendary citron's place of origin is unknown; citron trees grow wild in the hills of northern India and seeds of the fruit were found in Mesopotamian excavations dating back to 4000 BCE. The fruit was imported into Greece from Persia (now Iran) and Greek colonists began growing citrons in Palestine about 200 BCE. A Jewish coin dating from 136 BCE depicts the citron. Citrons were introduced to Italy in the third century, but were mostly destroyed by the Lombard invaders only one hundred years later. However, citron trees growing in the Kingdom of Naples, Sardinia, and Sicily survived, and the region is still a strong citron growing area today. By the turn of the millennium, citrons growing in Salerno on the Amalfi Peninsula were presented as tribute to the Norman lords. For centuries, this area supplied citron to the Jews in Italy, France, and Germany for the fall Feast of the Tabernacles (Sukkot) ceremony. The special Etrog cultivar is raised in Israel for the same holiday and perfect specimens sell for prices comparable to gold.

Citrons were introduced into Puerto Rico in 1640, where they are grown in the same central, mountainous regions as coffee and are also grown commercially in Brazil. Although citrons have been raised in California since 1880, the most important growing areas today are Sicily, Corsica and Crete and other islands off the coasts of Italy, Greece and France, and nearby mainland regions, and in Israel, where they are raised with great care for ritual use.

The striking Buddha's Hand or Fingered Citron, sometimes seen at specialty markets in wintertime, is a mutant citron variety that splits off into about five long, pointed, finger-like segments and has little to no flesh or seeds. This highly perfumed fruit, commonly grown in China and Japan, is placed as an offering on Buddhist temple altars. In central and northern China, it is the custom to carry a ripe, fragrant citron in the hand or to place it on the table to perfume the air.

To make the candied citron used in baking, especially for those dreaded fruit cakes, the fruits are halved and the pulp is scraped out. Next the fruits are soaked in seawater or salt water to ferment for about forty days to soften their thick peel. Next they are boiled to further soften their peel and remove some of its bitterness (just as I do with the Candied Citrus Peel on page 225). Finally, the peel is candied in a sugar syrup and then sun-dried. Candying is done mainly in Italy, England, France, and the United States, although top-quality candied citron without preservatives is imported from Italy.

Of course, as I am attracted to all bold and unusual flavors, especially those with such a fascinating history as citron, I love using candied citron, but never the nasty kind cured with chemicals, but rather the all-natural type described above. In this chapter, the diced rind goes into delicate and elegantly thin French Candied Citron and Lemon Cookies (page 534), the French and Jewish-influenced Torta di Savoia (page 535) that I adapted from an old Piemontese cookbook, and the extra-crunchy spice and citron-laden ring-shaped Biscotti Rococò (page 536) from the Amalfi Coast of Italy.

Lemon Galataboureko

I learned this version of galataboureko from Greek culinary expert, Aglaia Kremezi while taking a course at her island cooking school. (galata means milk in Greek) This traditional Greek dessert features a creamy, sweetened milk and egg custard thickened lightly with grainy semolina, baked between layers of phyllo, then soaked with lemon-scented sugar syrup. In the Greek town of Ioannina, the capital of the Romaniot Jews, a slice of galataboureko was traditionally eaten to break the Yom Kippur fast, along with a glass of well-watered ouzo, the Greek anise-flavored liqueur. While no one knows exactly when the first Jews arrived in Greece, legend has it the Romanist Jews escaped from a slave ship traveling from Jerusalem to Rome. Maybe I should switch from bagels and lox to this make-ahead, light pastry to break my annual fast.

YIELD: 24 SQUARES

Pastry

4 cups milk

2 ounces ($1/2$ stick) unsalted butter

$1/2$ cup sugar

$1/4$ pound ($1/2$ cup plus $2 1/2$ tablespoons) fine semolina

4 large eggs

1 tablespoon grated lemon zest

1 teaspoon vanilla extract

1 cup Clarified Butter (page 202), melted and cooled

$3/4$ pound phyllo dough, defrosted if frozen (you will have $1/4$ pound leftover)

Syrup

1½ cups sugar

1 cup water

1 cinnamon stick, crushed

2 whole cloves

Grated zest of 1 lemon (1 tablespoon)

2 tablespoons Limoncello, homemade (page 537) or
  purchased, or lemon-infused vodka

Assemble the pastry: Scald the milk in a large heavy-bottomed, non-aluminum saucepan, then stir in the butter and sugar. Gradually add the semolina, whisking constantly, and slowly bring the mixture just to a boil.

In a large bowl, beat the eggs lightly. Slowly beat in the hot semolina mixture, whisking constantly. Stir in the lemon zest and vanilla. Transfer the mixture to a bowl, preferably stainless steel, and cool by placing over a second bowl filled with a mixture of ice and water, stirring often.

Brush a 13 x 9-inch baking pan with clarified butter. Unroll the phyllo and drape it with a dampened towel. Place a layer of phyllo in the pan, allowing it to overhang the sides. Brush the sheet lightly with the clarified butter. Repeat, making 5 more layers, changing the direction of the sheets each time and brushing each sheet with the clarified butter. The bottom and sides of the pan should be completely covered with 2 to 3 inches of phyllo hanging over the edges on all sides. Pour in the cooled custard and spread it out evenly over the pastry leaves.

Preheat the oven to 350°F. Cover the custard with 6 more layers of phyllo, this time cut to fit the top of the pan, brushing each layer with clarified butter. Trim the overhanging edges to about 1 inch beyond the edge. Roll up the overhang to form a raised edge to the pastry. Using the tip of a very sharp knife, shallowly score the top phyllo layer into 24 square or diamond shapes. Bake for 1 hour, or until the pastry is golden brown and crisp. Cool for 5 minutes on a wire rack.

Make the syrup: Place the sugar, water, cinnamon stick, cloves, and lemon zest in a small pot. Bring to a boil, then reduce the heat and simmer for 10 minutes, or until the syrup thickens slightly. Remove from the heat, strain and stir in the Limoncello. Cool the syrup until it is lukewarm, then pour it evenly over the hot pastry. Cool thoroughly to room temperature before cutting and serving. Store covered and at room temperature for 2 days or cover and refrigerate up to 1 week.

Meyer Lemon Bundt Cake

Meyer lemons look and taste like a cross between an ultra-fragrant lemon and a sweet-tart orange. Because they're a specialty crop and grown on a smaller, though growing scale in California, Meyers are only available for a short season, usually January through March, and at a relatively high price. I do treat myself to these seasonal citrus fruits once or twice a year though, because they are unique. This rich, smooth pound cake takes advantage of all their perfume. Substitute two parts lemon to one part orange if Meyer lemons are not available.

YIELD: 1 LARGE BUNDT CAKE OR
2 (6 CUP) LOAF PANS, 12 TO 16 SERVINGS

Cake

$^3/_4$ pound ($2^3/_4$ cups plus 1 tablespoon) unbleached
 all-purpose flour

2 teaspoons baking powder

$^1/_2$ teaspoon fine sea salt

$^3/_4$ pound (3 sticks) unsalted butter, softened

$^1/_2$ pound cream cheese, softened

3 cups sugar

$^1/_4$ cup Meyer lemon juice

Grated zest of 3 Meyer lemons (3 tablespoons)

1 tablespoon vanilla extract

4 large eggs, separated

$^1/_4$ cup chopped candied lemon peel, optional

Glaze

$^1/_4$ cup Meyer lemon juice

Grated zest of 1 Meyer lemon (1 tablespoon)

2 cups confectioners' sugar

2 Meyer lemons, thinly sliced and pitted, or 2 table
 spoons chopped candied lemon peel, for garnish

Make the cake: Preheat the oven to 325°F. Spray 1 (10-inch) Bundt pan or 2 (6 cup) loaf pans with nonstick coating.

In a medium bowl, whisk together the dry ingredients, flour, baking powder, and salt. In the bowl of a standing mixer fitted with the paddle attachment, cream the butter, then add the cream cheese and beat until the mixture is soft and creamy, scraping down the sides once or twice. Beat in the sugar, lemon juice, zest, and vanilla. Beat in the

eggs, one at a time, then stir in the flour mixture and candied lemon peel. Scrape the batter into the pan.

Bake for 1 hour, or until the cake starts to come away from the sides of the pan and a skewer stuck in the center comes out clean. Cool to room temperature.

Make the glaze: In a bowl, whisk together the lemon juice, zest, and confectioners' sugar until smooth. Spoon over the cooled cake and leave to set, about 15 minutes. Press the lemon slices around the cake in a decorative pattern, then allow to set about 20 minutes longer before serving. Alternatively, decorate the cake with chopped candied lemon rind. Store covered and at room temperature for up to two days, or cover and refrigerate up to 1 week. This cake freezes well, wrapped in foil or freezer paper, up to three months.

French Candied Citron and Lemon Cookies

These fragrant, lemony cookies are very quick and easy to make. They are shaped, like many American cookies, by pushing the batter from a spoon. They are then flattened by tapping the baking sheet vigorously several times on the work surface so they spread out enough to get crisp. Small bits of candied citron add an intriguing flavor and fragrance along with chewy texture.

YIELD: 60 COOKIES

7 ounces ($1^1/_2$ cups plus $1^1/_2$ tablespoons) unbleached
 all-purpose flour

½ teaspoon baking powder

¼ teaspoon fine sea salt

7 ounces (1¾ sticks) unsalted butter, softened

1¼ cups sugar

4 large eggs

Grated zest of 3 lemons (3 tablespoons)

¼ pound (½ cup) diced candied citron

Line two 18 x 13-inch half sheet pans (or other large baking pans) with parchment paper or silicone baking mats.

Whisk together the dry ingredients: flour, baking powder, and salt.

In the bowl of a standing mixer fitted with the paddle attachment, cream the butter and sugar until light and fluffy, 5 to 6 minutes, scraping down the sides once or twice. Beat in the eggs, one at a time, beating well after each addition. Add the lemon zest and candied citron and beat briefly to combine. Add the flour mixture and beat just long enough to combine. Let the batter stand for 15 minutes at room temperature.

Preheat the oven to 400°F.

To shape the cookies, take 1 teaspoon of batter and use another teaspoon to push the batter onto the baking sheet, spacing the cookies about 2-inches apart because they spread. Tap the baking pans vigorously several times on the counter to spread the cookies.

Bake for 7 minutes, or until the cookies are medium-brown at the edges and the centers are lightly colored. Transfer to a wire rack to cool. Store the cookies up to 1 week in an airtight container.

Torta di Savoia with Candied Citron

Related to Pan di Spagna (page 441) and made from equal weights of eggs, sugar, and flour, this cake is called Gâteau di Savoja in the French-influenced Italian town of Piedmont. I adapted this recipe from Il Cuoco Piemontese, *an influential cookbook published in Torino in 1766. Count Amadeo di Savoia is said to have served this cake to Charles of Luxembourg in 1438, after which he was appointed Duke and Imperial officer, thus beginning the rise to power of the future royal Italian House of Savoy. That's some cake! The use of citron indicates a Jewish connection, because the fruits are used during the annual harvest holiday of Sukkot. The cake, which was originally flavored with toasted citron blossoms, must have been made in one huge pan, probably copper, like the large tin-lined copper mold I brought back from Torino in the 1970s. I have substituted a mixture of lemon and lime for the citron, along with the candied citron that I adore. If you happen to have access to fresh citron, by all means use it here. This recipe is dairy-free.*

YIELD: ONE 10-INCH BUNDT CAKE, 12 TO 16 SERVINGS

½ pound (2 cups minus 2 tablespoons) unbleached all-purpose flour

2 ounces (½ cup plus 2 tablespoons) potato starch, substitute corn, wheat, or rice starch

½ teaspoon fine sea salt

5 large eggs, separated

10 ounces (1⅓ cups) sugar

Grated zest of 1 lemon (1 tablespoon)

Grated zest of 1 lime (2 teaspoons)

¼ cup Limoncello, homemade (page 537)
    or purchased

¼ pound (¾ cup) diced candied citron, substitute
    candied lemon, optional

Preheat the oven to 350°F. Spray a 10-inch ring or Bundt pan with nonstick baker's coating or rub with flour and dust with flour, shaking off the excess.

Whisk together the dry ingredients, flour, starch, and salt. In the bowl of a standing mixer fitted with the paddle attachment, beat the egg yolks with ½ cup of the sugar until the mixture is light and fluffy, 5 to 6 minutes. Beat in the lemon zest and lime zest, and then transfer the batter to a wide shallow bowl.

In a separate clean and greaseless bowl of a standing mixer, beat the egg whites until they are fluffy, then beat in the remaining sugar and continue beating until firm and glossy, 4 to 5 minutes.

Using a silicone spatula, fold one-third of the meringue gently but thoroughly into the yolk mixture, sprinkle with some of the flour mixture, sprinkle with Limoncello and candied citron, then fold in another portion of whites, and sprinkle with more flour, and repeat.

Scrape the batter into the prepared pan and bake for 1 hour, or until the cake starts to come away from the sides of the pan and a skewer stuck in the center comes out clean. Cool to room temperature on a wire rack. Store at room temperature, wrapped in plastic wrap, for 2 to 3 days, or wrap and freeze up to 3 months.

Biscotti Rococò

These crunchy ring-shaped cookies are a specialty of Pasticceria Pansa in Amalfi (page 57). I carried a bag of them with me on my solo drive from Naples to Spoleto, sustaining me, along with several stops for espresso, on a long, rainy drive. These rustic cookies are baked in the small family farms of Campania mainly at Christmastime. Traditionally, they are leavened with baker's ammonia, which gives them a glassy texture, though baking powder is often substituted. Superb tangerines with their abundant perfumed oil also grow in the region, but orange zest may be substituted.

YIELD: 48 COOKIES

¾ pound (2¾ cups plus 1 tablespoon) unbleached
    all-purpose flour

6 ounces (1 cup) blanched almonds

2 teaspoons finely crushed baker's ammonia, substitute
    baking powder

1 teaspoon ground cinnamon

½ teaspoon freshly grated nutmeg

½ teaspoon fine sea salt

1¼ cups sugar

2 ounces (½ stick) unsalted butter, cut up and softened

Grated zest of 1 lemon (1 tablespoon)

Grated zest of 1 tangerine, substitute orange
    (4 teaspoons)

½ cup sweet Marsala, Sherry or Madeira

2 eggs, lightly beaten

¼ pound (1 cup) diced candied citron peel, substitute
    candied orange or lemon

1 egg, lightly beaten with 1 tablespoon water,
  for the egg wash

Line two 18 x 13-inch half sheet pans (or other large baking pans) with parchment paper or silicone baking mats.

In the bowl of a food processor, combine the flour, half the almonds, the baker's ammonia, cinnamon, nutmeg, and salt, and process until finely ground. Remove from the processor and reserve. In the processor, chop the remaining almonds to a medium coarse texture.

In the bowl of a standing mixer fitted with the paddle attachment, beat the sugar, butter, and lemon and tangerine zests until creamy, 4 to 5 minutes. Beat in the Marsala, then the eggs (don't worry if the mixture resembles scrambled eggs). Beat in the citron peel and chopped almonds, and then add the flour mixture. Beat only until combined enough for the mixture to form large, moist clumps.

Knead lightly by hand just until the mixture forms a ball, then allow the dough to rest at room temperature for about 15 minutes.

Preheat the oven to 325°F. Divide the dough into about 48 small balls about the size of a walnut. Roll each ball on a lightly floured work surface into a stick about 1/2-inch-wide and 3 inches long. Shape each stick into a ring, overlapping the ends and pressing them together to seal. Transfer the rings to the pans, allowing about 1 inch in between. Brush the rings with the egg wash and bake for 20 minutes or until lightly colored and firm. Remove from the oven and cool to room temperature on a wire rack. Store in a cookie tin or an airtight container for up to 1 week.

Homemade Limoncello

Limoncello is a lemon-yellow sweet liqueur made in the spectacularly beautiful region of the Amalfi Coast in Campania, where the celebrated fragrant Sorrento Oval lemon grows in orchards overlooking the Mediterranean. Many people in the region make their own Limoncello, and just about every restaurant meal ends with a tiny glass of this homemade spirit. Pure grain alcohol (190-proof, sold as Everclear) will extract the volatile oils from the lemons more quickly and completely, though vodka will also work. Increase the amount of sugar syrup if you prefer a sweeter, less potent liqueur. Organic lemons are best here, because you are only using the zest, which can also contain insecticides and preservatives. If they are not available, scrub your lemons especially well in hot, soapy water and rinse well before using. One part of the yellow, highly potent infused liquid is combined with two parts sugar syrup to yield a liqueur that is about 60 proof or 30 percent alcohol.

YIELD: 3 QUARTS

2 pounds (8 to 12) lemons, well scrubbed,
  preferably organic
1 quart grain alcohol (190 proof)
2 cups sugar

Carefully zest the lemons using a potato peeler, making sure to avoid the white pith. Mix the lemon zest with the alcohol, and set it aside at room temperature it to infuse for 48 hours. Strain, discarding the zest.

Heat the sugar with 6 cups water until boiling and clear. Cool the syrup to room temperature. Add to the strained alcohol, and transfer to an attractive bottle. Store in the freezer indefinitely until ready to serve chilled in small liqueur glasses or to flavor desserts.

Light Lemon Pastry Cream

Use this delectable, airy, lemon-scented pastry cream to fill the fabulous Babàs al Limoncello Pansa from Amalfi (page 56), or as an alternative filling for the Praline Cream Puffs (page 000). The gelatin helps the cream hold its shape but may be omitted. If you choose to do so, increase the flour by 1 1/2 tablespoons to thicken the cream. Fragrant Meyer lemons make a wonderful filling that reminds me of the fabulous Sorrento lemons found in Amalfi, where the recipe for this filling originates.

YIELD: ABOUT 3 CUPS

3 sheets gelatin or 1 teaspoon powdered gelatin

1 1/4 cups milk

3 large egg yolks

3/4 cup sugar

2 ounces (1/2 cup minus 1/2 tablespoon) unbleached all-purpose flour

Pinch salt

Grated zest of 2 lemons (2 tablespoons)

Juice of 2 lemons (6 tablespoons)

1/2 vanilla bean, split open and seeds scraped out, substitute 1 teaspoon vanilla extract

1/2 cup heavy cream, chilled

Soak the gelatin sheets in cold water to soften, about 5 minutes. Or soak the powdered gelatin in 1/4 cup water until thickened, about 10 minutes, then heat it gently until it is clear, about 2 minutes.

Place 1 cup of the milk in a microwavable container, preferably a Pyrex measure, and scald in the microwave until steaming, about 2 minutes.

In a medium bowl, whisk together the egg yolks and sugar until combined. Add the remaining 1/4 cup of milk and whisk to combine. Fold in the flour and salt. Slowly pour in the scalded milk while whisking to combine. Transfer the mixture to a medium nonreactive pot and bring to a boil over low heat, whisking often, especially at the edges. As soon as the mixture thickens and starts to bubble, remove it from the heat and whisk in the gelatin, lemon zest and juice, and vanilla seeds, making sure the gelatin has dissolved completely. (If the cream is at all lumpy, either strain through a fine wire sieve or transfer to a food processor and process until smooth.)

Transfer the mixture to a bowl, preferably stainless-steel, and cool by placing over a second bowl filled with a mixture of ice and water, stirring often.

In a chilled medium bowl and using a hand mixer or a large whisk, whip the cream to stiff peaks, then fold into the lemon cream. Cover tightly and store refrigerated up to 3 days.

Note: To quickly chill a bowl, swirl a handful of ice cubes around the empty bowl then discard the ice cubes.

Fresh Lemon Sauce

When I was testing recipes for this book, I used the zest of so many lemons, I decided to include this light and versatile sauce as a way of using up the juice of all the extra lemons. If all your lemons are naked, their bright skins zested for other recipes, substitute about $^{1}/_{4}$ teaspoon of pure lemon oil for the fresh lemon zest. Serve this sauce over fresh berries, alongside a fruit tart, or with angel food cake. Or serve it warm in a bowl and dip strawberries, peaches, and pound cake in it as a kind of fondue.

YIELD: ABOUT 1$^{1}/_{2}$ CUPS

3 large eggs

$^{1}/_{2}$ cup sugar

$^{1}/_{2}$ cup freshly squeezed lemon juice (2 to 3 lemons)

Grated zest of 1 lemon (1 tablespoon)

2 tablespoons (1 ounce) unsalted butter

In a medium bowl, beat together the eggs and sugar until light. Beat in the lemon juice, zest, and butter. Make a double boiler by bringing about 2 inches of water to a boil in the bottom of a medium pot. Transfer the lemon mixture to a stainless steel bowl or a nonreactive pot that can fit on top of the second pot without touching the water. Cook over medium heat, stirring constantly, until the sauce thickens visibly. Remove from the heat, whisk in the butter and either serve warm or transfer to a stainless steel bowl, and place plastic wrap directly on the custard to keep a skin from forming. Store refrigerated up to 1 week.

LIMES

Choosing and Storing Limes . . . 544

ALMOND-LIME BARS . . . 545

MEXICAN LIME AND TEQUILA TART
WITH MANGO TOPPING . . . 546

LIME CORNMEAL COOKIES . . . 547

KEY LIME CHEESECAKE PIE IN
COCONUT-PECAN CRUST . . . 548

LIMES

Craig Claiborne had it right when he wrote, "All citrus fruits possess refreshing powers, but the lime more than most, seems to lift the spirit." Just about any tropical fruit benefits from a splash of lime, especially coconuts, mangoes, pineapples, papayas, and bananas. Key Lime Pie in its many iterations–here a luscious Key Lime Cheesecake Pie (page 548)–is a dessert that always sells in American restaurants, from the grittiest roadside diner to the finest "white tablecloth" establishment.

Americans on the East Coast call them Key limes and on the West Coast and the Southwest, they are Mexican limes. These small, seedy and highly acidic yellowy green limes, *Citrus aurantifolia*, grow on thorny trees that are quite sensitive to cold. Key limes are a bit larger than a walnut, almost round in shape, with thin yellowish skin that easily develops splotchy brown spots. Though full of seeds, Key limes are highly aromatic with distinctive bouquet and are very juicy, with a stronger and more complex flavor than Persian limes. Both Persian and Key limes have a higher sugar and citric acid content than lemons, though Key limes are more acidic than Persians, a quality which is essential to thickening the filling for Key Lime Pie.

Although its name refers to the Florida Keys, this lime originated in the Indo–Malayan region. Returning Crusaders brought limes back home to Europe and the Mediterranean; Arabs probably carried the fruits from the Middle East and across North Africa into Spain and Portugal. By the mid-thirteenth century, Italians and probably also French gardeners were growing limes. In the early sixteenth century, Spanish and Portuguese explorers brought the fruit to southern Florida, South America, the Caribbean, and Mexico where it became naturalized. People in Florida planted lime trees in their yards and after the 1906 hurricane, when farmers abandoned their pineapple groves, they began to plant limes instead. Key limes grew commercially in southern Florida and the Keys until the 1926 hurricane wiped them out in all but backyard gardens. Currently, Mexico is the leading producer, with the Caribbean and Egypt next. Most of the Key limes sold in 1-pound green net bags in supermarkets come from Mexico and Central America; ninety percent of American-grown Key limes come from Florida.

The larger Persian or Tahitian lime is shaped

like a small fat lemon with tough thick tightly clinging skin and juicy, pale green flesh divided into 10 segments, and are almost always seedless. Their skin is vivid green when immature, ripening to pale-yellow, though growers pick the fruits when they're still green, partly to distinguish them from lemons. Although its origin is unknown, botanists believe that the Tahitian lime is a hybrid of the Mexican lime and the citron. This lime, which grows on medium to large trees with nearly thornless trees and wide-spreading, drooping branches, has only in recent years been given its botanical name, *Citrus latifolia Tan.*

The Persian lime was introduced into the Mediterranean region by way of Persia (now Iran) although the fruit doesn't grow there today. For centuries, a virtually identical lime called *Sakhesli* has been cultivated on the island of Djerba off the coast of Tunisia and in parts of Algeria. Its name means "from Sakhos," an old Arabic name for Chios, the Greek island close to the Turkish coast famed for its citrus and mastic trees. Portuguese traders probably carried the fruit to Brazil, and it was apparently taken to Australia from Brazil about 1824. It reached California from the Pacific island of Tahiti between 1850 and 1880, picking up its name along the way.

This far-voyager next traveled eastward to Florida, where it had arrived by 1883 and quickly took the place of the more cold-sensitive Key lime and the lemon. Today, Florida produces 90 percent of America's limes for use fresh and for processing, especially in limeade concentrate. Following World War I, the Tahitian lime became a well-established commercial crop. At first, there was market resistance, buyers viewing the Tahiti lime as a "green lemon," and, for a long time, Canadians would not accept it because they were accustomed to the more flavorful Mexican lime.

In the eighteenth century, scientists learned that citrus juice would prevent scurvy, a disease which had devastated the British navy more than any enemy. In 1795, the British Admiralty officially issued lemon juice to sailors who, in the next twenty years, drank well over one million gallons of lemon juice along with their daily ration of rum. The switch from lemon to lime came about for two reasons. Great Britain was often at war with the Mediterranean countries that exported lemons, so limes imported cheaply from the its colony of Jamaica became the better choice. Also, doctors realized that limes contain a higher percentage of the ascorbic acid that prevented scurvy, so the Royal Navy switched to lime juice for its sailors, who became known as "limeys."

The wild lime fruit, *Citrus hystrix*, and its highly perfumed leaves are a favorite flavoring in Thai, Malaysian and Indonesian cuisines. Its shiny deep green leaves look as though one leaf grows from the end of another at a slightly different angle. Once known as kaffir lime, this name, deriving from an Arabic word for a non-believer, became a derogatory name for black Africans in South Africa and wild lime is its preferred name today. The fruits are small and rounded with a slightly elongated neck, yellowish-green to deep green wrinkly skin with prominent bumps. Although they do contain small quantities of very sour juice, wild limes are valued for their aromatic skin and even more for their leaves, which release an intense sweet fragrance when crushed. Substitute several crushed lime leaves for the vanilla beans in the Crème Anglaise (English Vanilla Custard Sauce) (page 835), straining them out after cooking the custard. Finely mince 1 or 2 leaves and add them to the batter for the Italian Meringue Twists and Topping (page 836) or the filling for the Coconut Cream–Filled Cookie Turnovers (page 362).

Because bananas have creamy, delicately sweet flesh but lack acidity, two banana recipes in this book, the Baby Banana Cream Pie in Coconut–Cashew Shell (page 131), and the Red Banana–Brown Butter Bars (page 133) call for lime as an accent. The plentiful cashew trees brought to the Caribbean island of Aruba from their native Brazil provide the cashews ground into flour for the Aruban Cashew Cake (page 178). The traditional confetti of lime zest shreds livens its look and tingles the nose.

Lime is a surprising but complementary flavor for the Swiss Carrot–Semolina Torte's (page 239), although limes grow nowhere near Switzerland. Lime cuts the sweetness of the meringue crust in the diced fruit macedoine that tops the Australian Pavlova with Tropical Fruits (page 442). Just like Key Lime Pie, an unbaked tropical Coconut Mango Cheesecake (page 482) depends on the thickening power of acidic lime mixed with sweetened condensed milk, plus cream cheese. Lime suits hot weather foods best, as in the creamy Southern Million Dollar Pie (page 685), where it accents coconut, pineapple, and strawberries.

Rose and lime are another unexpected but compatible couple, spotted together in the Rose-Scented Angel Food Cake (page 467) and in the mango topping for the Mexican Lime and Tequila Tart (page 546). In this chapter, I make Almond-Lime Bars (page 545), a variation on the ever-popular lemon bars, with a ground almond shortcrust base and lime juice custard topping accented by its bitter but aromatic zest. Crunchy yellow cornmeal and plenty of lime juice and flavor the Lime Cornmeal Cookies (page 547). The Key Lime Cheesecake Pie in Coconut-Pecan Crust (page 548), combines two American winners, cheesecake and Key lime pie for a super creamy pie in a crunchy coconut and pecan crumb crust.

CHOOSING AND STORING LIMES

Look for brightly colored, firm Tahitian limes that are heavy for their size, so they'll be juicy. Small brown patches on the skin of either Persian or Key limes won't affect their flavor, but they are a sign that the fruits are deteriorating and should be used soon. Unfortunately, at certain times of year, these limes will have very hard or shriveled skin and are likely to be full of dry pulp with little juice. Tahitian limes are available year-round. Store them refrigerated up to 10 days.

Almond–Lime Bars

Everyone in America probably knows and loves lemon bars. These are a delicious and extra-tart variation made with limes and an almondy crust. I like to tint the yellowy-green filling a light and lovely green with natural chlorophyll coloring, but it is optional (see the recipe on page 699). Garnish each square with thin slices of lemon or mint sprigs.

YIELD: 24 BARS

Crust

1/2 pound (2 cups minus 2 tablespoons) unbleached all-purpose flour

1/4 pound (3/4 cup) blanched almonds

1/2 cup confectioners' sugar, plus extra for dusting

1/4 teaspoon fine sea salt

1/2 pound (2 sticks) unsalted butter, chilled and cut into bits

1 teaspoon almond extract

Topping

1 1/2 cups sugar

4 large eggs

1 ounce (2 tablespoons) unbleached all-purpose flour

1 teaspoon baking powder

3/4 cup fresh lime juice

Grated zest of 1 lime (2 teaspoons)

1 teaspoon Chlorophyll, (page 699), optional for green color

Confectioners' sugar, for dusting

Make the crust: Preheat the oven to 350°F. Line a 13 x 9-inch baking pan with parchment or wax paper.

In the bowl of a food processor, combine the flour, almonds, confectioners' sugar, and salt, and process to a medium-fine texture. Add the butter and almond extract and process again just until moist clumps form. Remove from the processor and lightly knead to form a smooth dough. Press onto the bottom of the prepared pan.

Bake for 20 minutes or until the center is lightly colored and set and the edges are golden. Leave the oven hot.

Make the topping: In a large bowl, whisk together the sugar and eggs, add the flour and baking powder, and whisk to combine well. Finally, beat in the lime juice, zest, and chlorophyll. Pour the topping over the hot crust and bake until the topping is set and lightly golden, about 25 minutes. Cool to room temperature in the pan on a wire rack. Sift confectioners' sugar over top. Cut into 24 squares. Store at room temperature for up to 2 days, or refrigerated for 4 to 5 days.

Mexican Lime and Tequila Tart with Mango Topping

For those who love the lime and tequila in a margarita, this Mexican tart is a perfect choice. A pecan crumb crust is filled with a mixture similar to that of Key lime pie that has been spiked with tequila and lightened with meringue. Brazilian cachaça, a kind of white lightning made from cane syrup, makes a good substitute for the tequila and an equally good cocktail. If fresh Key limes aren't available, substitute the slightly less acidic standard Persian limes, a better choice to my mind than using the bottled juice, which seems to have a metallic aftertaste. The fresh mango topping is mixed with fragrant rosewater, a lovely combination.

YIELD: ONE 9-INCH TART, 6 TO 8 SERVINGS

Crust

$1/4$ pound dry lightly sweetened biscuits,
    such as Maria cookies, or biscotti

$1/4$ pound (1 cup) pecans

2 tablespoons sugar

3 ounces ($3/4$ stick) unsalted butter, melted and cooled

Filling

1 (13-ounce) can sweetened condensed milk

4 large egg yolks

$1/2$ cup fresh squeezed Mexican lime (Key lime) juice

Grated zest of 1 of the limes (2 teaspoons)

$1/4$ cup white tequila

2 large egg whites ($1/4$ cup)

$1/4$ cup sugar

Topping

2 large, firm but ripe mangoes

1 tablespoon freshly squeezed Mexican lime
    (Key lime) juice

2 tablespoons sugar

1 teaspoon rosewater, optional

Make the crust: In the bowl of a food processor, combine the biscuits, pecans, and sugar, then process until medium-fine. Pour in the butter and process again briefly until the mixture starts to form clumps and a handful sticks together when pressed. Press the mixture firmly, about $1 1/2$-inches high, into a 9-inch removable bottom or springform cake pan.

Make the filling: Preheat the oven to 325°F. Whisk together the condensed milk, egg yolks, lime juice, zest, and tequila.

In the clean and greaseless bowl of a standing mixer fitted with the whisk attachment, beat the egg whites until fluffy, then add the sugar and continue beating until the whites are firm and glossy, 4 to 5 minutes. Fold the meringue into the lime mixture in thirds so as not to deflate the meringue. Spoon the filling into the crust and bake for 30 minutes, or until the filling puffs up slightly and sets in the center. Cool the tart completely on a wire rack. Chill until cold, at least 2 hours and up to 8 hours.

Make the topping: Peel the mangoes, then thinly slice or dice them, and combine them with the lime juice, sugar, and rosewater. Cut the tart into serving portions and spoon the mangoes and their juices over top of each portion. Store the tart (without the mangoes) refrigerated up to 2 days.

Lime Cornmeal Cookies

These golden-colored, rich cookies are crumbly with cornmeal and tangy with fresh lime in both the batter and the glaze. The cookies are easy to make and don't need to be rolled out. Form the batter into small balls, then flatten them with a glass to shape them quickly and evenly. Either green Persian or the more acidic, yellowy-green Key limes will work fine here. Once made, the batter will freeze beautifully, ready to bake and glaze whenever you want.

YIELD: 6 DOZEN COOKIES

Cookies

$3/4$ pound ($2^3/4$ cups plus 1 tablespoon) unbleached all-purpose flour

$1/2$ pound ($1^3/4$ cups) stone-ground yellow cornmeal, plus extra for dusting

$1/2$ teaspoon fine sea salt

1 pound (4 sticks) unsalted butter, softened

2 cups sugar

2 large eggs

$1/2$ cup freshly squeezed lime juice

Grated zest of 2 limes (4 teaspoons)

2 teaspoons pure almond extract

Glaze

1 pound ($4^1/2$ cups) confectioners' sugar

$1/2$ cup lime juice

Grated zest of 2 limes (4 teaspoons)

Make the cookies: Whisk together the dry ingredients: flour, cornmeal, and salt.

In the bowl of a standing mixer fitted with the paddle attachment, cream the butter and sugar until light and fluffy, 5 to 6 minutes, scraping down the sides once or twice. Beat in the eggs one at a time, beating well after each addition. Beat in the lime juice, zest, and almond extract.

With the mixer on low speed, add the flour mixture and beat just until the mixture comes together and forms moist clumps. Knead the dough briefly by hand until it is smooth, then transfer to a plastic bag and shape into a flattened rectangle. Chill in the refrigerator for 1 hour or in the freezer for 30 minutes until firm but still malleable.

Preheat the oven to 350°F. Line two 18 x 13-inch half sheet pans (or other large baking pans) with parchment paper or silicone baking mats.

Using a small ($1^1/4$ inch) ice-cream scoop or a tablespoon, form marble-sized balls of dough. Place the balls on the prepared baking pans about 3 inches apart. Dip the flat bottom of a glass or a ramekin into a bowl filled with cornmeal. Flatten the balls with the bottom of glass until the dough is about $1/4$-inch thick.

Bake the cookies for 15 minutes or until crisp and light golden brown around the edges. Transfer to a wire rack, and let the cookies cool completely.

Make the glaze: In a medium bowl, whisk together the confectioners' sugar, lime juice, and zest until smooth and just liquid enough to pour. Place a wire rack on top of a sheet of wax or parchment paper or a baking pan to catch the drips. Spread the glaze evenly over each cookie, allowing the excess to drip off the edges. Let the glaze set. Store the cookies in an airtight container up to 1 week.

Key Lime Cheesecake Pie in Coconut–Pecan Crust

Tart and tangy, yet voluptuously creamy, this no-bake cheesecake is easy as can be. A crunchy, coconutty, pecan crumb crust ideally made in a deep, French fluted quiche pan encloses the smooth filling. Make the cheesecake a day or two ahead of time. I like to decorate it with paper-thin slices of Persian limes (Key limes have too many seeds). Last time I made this pie, I broke the rule of not using anything for garnish that's not in the dish by arranging colorful Clementine orange segments in pairs around the outside of the pie with thin slivers of green candied angelica sticking out of their ends like stems.

YIELD: ONE 9-INCH PIE, 10 TO 12 SERVINGS

Crust

1/4 pound (1 cup) shredded unsweetened coconut

1/4 pound (1 cup) pecan pieces

1/4 pound biscotti or graham cracker cookies, crumbled

Pinch salt

1/4 cup sugar

6 ounces (1 1/2 sticks) unsalted butter, melted and cooled

Filling

1/2 pound cream cheese, at room temperature

7 fluid ounces sweetened condensed milk

7 fluid ounces fresh Key lime juice

Grated zest of 1 Key lime (2 teaspoons)

1 lime, thinly sliced

Make the crust: In the bowl of a food processor, combine the coconut, pecans, cookie crumbs, salt, and sugar, and process until medium-fine. With the processor running, pour in the butter, continuing to process until well combined. Press the mixture firmly into a 9-inch fluted French quiche pan (or a 9-inch springform cake pan). Chill for 30 minutes to set the crust.

Preheat the oven to 375°F. Fit a piece of heavy-duty foil onto the dough and fill with beans or other pie weights. Blind bake (just pastry crust, no filling) on the bottom shelf of the oven until the crust is cooked through but not yet browned, about 30 minutes. Remove the foil and the weights, reduce the oven temperature to 325°F, and bake for 10 minutes longer, or until the crust is evenly and lightly browned. Remove from the oven and cool to room temperature on a wire rack.

Make the filling: In the bowl of a standing mixer fitted with the paddle attachment, beat the cream cheese until smooth and shiny, scraping down the sides of the bowl once or twice. Add the condensed milk, lime juice, and zest, and beat until smooth. Whisk by hand to ensure that no lumps remain in the batter. Spoon the filling into the crust. Decorate with the paper-thin slices of lime, and chill to set, at least 2 hours. Store lightly covered and refrigerated up to two days. Wrap in foil or freezer paper and freeze (without the lime slices) up to one month.

MAPLE

Buying and Storing Maple Syrup . . . 551

Other Maple Products . . . 552

NEW ENGLAND CRANBERRY-MAPLE-RAISIN PIE . . . 552

MAPLE CORNMEAL MUFFINS
WITH PINE NUTS AND CURRANTS . . . 553

QUÉBÉÇOISE MAPLE BREAD PUDDING . . . 554

MAPLE SYRUP PIE WITH WALNUTS:
TARTE AU SIROP D'ERABLE . . . 555

MAPLE

On a very chilly fall night, when I had foolishly chosen fashion over warmth, I traveled with a group of fellow culinarians to a Quebec sugar shack to learn how this North American delicacy was produced and to sample it in local dishes. Thankfully, the first thing I learned was how the locals keep warm: we arrived in open wagons at the large wood cabin and found a great bonfire glowing in the forecourt. An iron cauldron suitable for a witch's brew hung over the fire and was filled to the brim with Caribou. This treacherously intoxicating, though thankfully hot, firewater brew contains various wines and spirits, typically brandy, vodka, sherry, and port. After downing a glass, I was ready for maple sugaring, music, food, loud conversation, and more.

The sugar maple, *Acer saccarum*, also known as the hard maple or rock maple, and *Acer nigrum*, or black maple, are the two trees with the sweetest sap. Although maple trees grow in Europe, Europeans didn't know how to tap their sweet sap until American colonists learned how to do it from Native Americans, who had long been using maple sap for its sweetness. Native Americans traded what they called *sweet water* with the

colonists, and after the 1764 Sugar Act, which imposed high tariffs on imported sugar, maple sweeteners gained popularity as a proud local product of the new colony.

The colonists soon realized that the traditional method of slashing the trees to retrieve the sap led to waste and also damaged the trees. They switched to tapping the trees, collecting the sap in troughs and buckets. Nowadays, no more than three taps are inserted per tree to avoid damage, and the sap is still collected via spouts from hanging galvanized metal buckets. The annual production of maple sap is unpredictable, depending on the trees themselves and weather patterns. The North American sugaring season begins as early as January and continues into April. In the old days, the sap was boiled in huge troughs to evaporate the water, or it was frozen, the lighter water rising to the top; the sweeter, heavier syrup sinking to the bottom.

Maple syrup is only produced in North America, where weather conditions encourage the trees to produce large amounts of sap. The clear sap usually contains 2 to 3 percent sugar, although some trees can produce up to 6 percent sugar. The sap is boiled in a "sugar house" (also known as a "sugar shack" or in Quebec, a *cabane à sucre*), a special building that is louvered at the top to vent the steam from the enormous vats of boiling sap. Most pure maple syrup is still made by boiling the water out and then filtering the syrup to remove impurities. The sap becomes syrup when it reaches 7 degrees over the boiling point of water, a temperature that varies with elevation. An experienced sugar maker can tell when the syrup is ready by the sheets or aprons that the syrup form as it drips off the paddle.

The specific density of the syrup must reach about 66.6 percent, measured in degrees Brix using a hydrometer. Syrup that is too thin will be runny and susceptible to fermentation and souring. Syrup that is too thick can crystallize during storage. It takes approximately 36 gallons of maple tree sap to make only 1 gallon of maple syrup.

Vermonters celebrate the early spring sugaring season by snacking on an unusual sweet and sour combination of maple syrup, plain raised doughnuts, and dill pickles. They dip each bite of doughnut in syrup and eat it interspersed with bites of dill pickles. Making maple syrup taffy, also called Sugar On Snow, is also a favorite activity in the region at sap time. In Quebec, one company, Maison des Futailles, even produces two maple whiskies. Fine Sève is distilled from maple wine and then aged in oak barrels. Sortilège, a combination of Canadian whisky and maple syrup, was first made on the Île d'Orléans in Quebec City hundreds of years ago. These I have to try! For more information, go to www.futailles.com.

In this book, the Canadian Maple–Black Walnut Gingerbread (page 491) combines spicy hot ginger with sweet, slightly resinous maple syrup both in the batter and the icing. In this chapter, maple lovers will find a colorful New England Cranberry–Maple–Raisin Pie (page 522) chunky with fruits; the uncommon, hearty Maple Cornmeal Muffins with Pine Nuts and Currants (page 553); an incredibly rich and delectable Québécoise Maple Bread Pudding (page 554); and the equally rich Maple Syrup Pie with Walnuts (Tarte au Sirop d'Erable) (page 555).

BUYING AND STORING MAPLE SYRUP

In general, the lighter the color, the more delicate the flavor. In America, Grade AA Light Amber (Fancy) is a light, amber-colored syrup with mild flavor, usually made from the first sap of the season. Grade A Medium Amber, is amber in color with a more pronounced maple flavor and is typically poured over pancakes. Grade A Dark Amber has a deeper caramel-like color and stronger flavor. Grade B is my maple syrup of choice for baking as its robust molasses-like flavor shines in baked goods. Canadian Grades differ.

Maple syrup should be kept in a cool, dark place for up to two years until opened. Refrigerate after opening up to one year. Because maple syrup will not freeze, it can be kept in the freezer almost indefinitely. Improperly stored maple syrup can grow harmful moldy toxins, in which case it must be discarded. (I have had this happen.)

OTHER MAPLE PRODUCTS

Although maple syrup is most familiar, the sap is also transformed into grainy maple sugar, maple honey (thicker than syrup), maple cream (almost as thick as peanut butter), and maple butter (thick enough to be spreadable). I have been sampling a new product called Equinox maple flakes, which resemble the bran flakes in Raisin Bran cereal in texture and appearance. Made using an advanced technological process, the all-natural flakes make a wonderful light, crisp topping for muffins, cookies, and to top the Québécoise Maple Bread Pudding (page 000). Look for the flakes at Whole Foods stores.

New England Cranberry–Maple–Raisin Pie

This colorful and chunky pie would make a welcome addition to the Thanksgiving table or a holiday buffet, especially because it can be made several days ahead of time. The flaky all-butter pie crust is filled with a mixture of cranberries, golden raisins, and orange zest that is sweetened with maple syrup and sugar and thickened with tapioca flour. The pie is topped with a flaky and decorative lattice top. Because cranberries freeze so beautifully, you can make this pie even in the darkest days of winter. I always buy a few extra bags of cranberries to freeze, because once their short season is over, it can be difficult to find frozen cranberries, although I have seen them occasionally. Lingonberries make a wonderful substitute. I find them frozen at my local Russian market. You may also find the small, tart berries in a Scandinavian or German market.

YIELD: ONE 9-INCH PIE, 8 TO 10 SERVINGS

1 pound Butter Pie Pastry dough (page 203)

18 ounces cranberries, fresh or frozen and defrosted

5 1/2 ounces (1 cup) golden raisins

1/2 cup sugar

3/4 cup pure maple syrup, preferably grade B

1/4 cup tapioca starch

1 teaspoon vanilla extract

1 tablespoon brandy

Grated zest of 1 orange (4 teaspoons)

2 tablespoons unsalted butter, cut into bits

1 large egg, lightly beaten with 1 tablespoon milk, for the glaze

2 tablespoons sugar, for sprinkling

Line a baking sheet with parchment paper or wax paper and set aside. Divide the dough in half. Lightly dust a clean work surface with flour, and roll each piece of dough into an 11-inch circle. Press one circle into a 9-inch pie plate, preferably Pyrex (so you can see when the pastry crust has browned), or aluminum (for good head conduction), and chill for 1 hour in the refrigerator or 30 minutes in the freezer.

Make the filling: In a large mixing bowl, combine the

cranberries, raisins, sugar, maple syrup, tapioca starch, vanilla, brandy, and orange zest. Pour into the chilled bottom crust. Dot the top with the butter.

Make the lattice top: Cut the second circle into about 12 ($^3/_4$-inch wide) pastry strips, using a sharp knife or a plain or fluted dough roller. Lay half of the pastry strips on top of the filling about 1 inch apart. Fold alternate pastry strips back halfway. Lay a pastry strip on the center of the tart crosswise. Unfold the pastry strips; now fold back the remaining strips. Lay another pastry strip crosswise about 1 inch away. Fold back half the strips, lay another pastry strip crosswise about 1 inch away and repeat the weaving until lattice covers the filling. (Alternatively, especially if working in hot weather, make the lattice on a piece of wax paper, then refrigerate until firm, about 20 minutes. Use a large spatula to transfer the lattice top to the top of the tart.) Trim the edges of the pastry strips even with the pan, pressing the strips against the edge of the pan firmly to seal. Brush the edge of the pie with the glaze, then sprinkle with the sugar.

Preheat the oven to 425°F. Place the tart on a baking pan to catch any drips. Bake on the bottom shelf of the oven for 20 minutes. Reduce the oven temperature to 350°F and continue to bake for 50 minutes or until the crust is golden brown and juices in the center of the pie start to bubble. (If the top starts to darken too much, drape with aluminum foil.)

Cool the pie to room temperature on a wire rack before cutting into serving portions. Store at room temperature for up to 2 days or refrigerate and store up to 5 days.

Maple Cornmeal Muffins with Pine Nuts and Currants

The original recipe for these not-too-sweet, maple-flavored muffins, chunky with toasted pine nuts and bittersweet currants came from star chef, Mark Miller, who was a guest chef at Apropos Bistro one year for Philadelphia's Book and Cook Festival. Of course, his recipe made more than 200 muffins, so I've adapted it considerably. Piñon pine trees grow in the American Southwest, the region which inspired much of Miller's cooking at his Santa Fe restaurant, Coyote Café. I first met Chef Miller when he worked with equally famous star chef Jeremiah Tower, both recent alumni of Chez Panisse, at their Fourth Street Grill.

YIELD: 1 DOZEN MUFFINS

6 ounces (1$^1/_2$ cups minus 1 tablespoon) unbleached all-purpose flour

$^1/_4$ pound ($^3/_4$ cup plus 2 tablespoons) stone-ground yellow cornmeal

2 teaspoons baking powder

1 teaspoon ground cinnamon

$^1/_2$ teaspoon freshly grated nutmeg

$^1/_2$ teaspoon fine sea salt

1 large egg

$^1/_4$ pound (1 stick) unsalted butter, melted and cooled

1 cup buttermilk

$^3/_4$ cup pure maple syrup, preferably grade B

$^1/_4$ cup sugar

1 teaspoon vanilla extract

$^1/_4$ pound (about 1 cup) pine nuts, lightly toasted

$^1/_2$ cup Zante currants

Preheat the oven to 325 °F. Line a 12-cup medium muffin tin with muffin papers, or spray with nonstick baker's coating.

In a large bowl, whisk together the dry ingredients: flour, cornmeal, baking powder, cinnamon, nutmeg, and salt.

Beat together the egg, butter, buttermilk, maple syrup, sugar, and vanilla. Pour over the dry ingredients and fold together lightly and gently to blend. Reserve 2 tablespoons each of the pine nuts and the currants, then add the remainder of both into the batter.

Scoop the batter into the muffin papers or tins and sprinkle with a portion of the reserved pine nuts and currants. Bake for 30 minutes or until the muffins puff on top and the batter has started to come away from the side of the pans. Cool to room temperature on a wire rack before serving. Muffins are best the day they are baked.

Québécoise Maple Bread Pudding

Two homey ingredients come together in this rich custardy bread pudding: baguettes and maple syrup. Stale bread works best to cube without tearing. I've coated the outside of the mold with Maple Flakes, a new-fangled but deliciously regional product from Quebec (see page 552). Substitute dark brown sugar if you can't find the flakes. And if you don't want to indulge quite so freely, you could always use 3 cups of milk and 1 cup of heavy cream instead of the recommended amounts below. Serve with coffee and/or brandy.

YIELD: 8 TO 10 SERVINGS

1 French baguette (about $3/4$ pound), preferably stale, cut into $3/4$-inch cubes

1 tablespoon unsalted butter, softened

2 cups milk

2 cups heavy cream

6 large eggs yolks

2 large eggs

$3/4$ cup pure maple syrup, preferably grade B

$1/4$ cup packed dark brown sugar

$1/2$ teaspoon fine sea salt

$1/4$ cup Maple Flakes (page 552), or more dark brown sugar

Preheat the oven to 350°F. Spread the bread cubes in a single layer on a baking pan and toast for 15 minutes, or until lightly colored. Transfer to a large mixing bowl. Butter an 8-inch round or square pan, preferably ceramic.

Combine the milk and cream in a large microwavable container, preferably a Pyrex measure, and scald in the microwave until steaming hot.

In a large bowl, beat together the egg yolks, eggs, maple syrup, brown sugar, and salt. Slowly whisk in the scalded cream and milk. Add the bread cubes and toss well so the bread soaks up the liquid. Cover tightly with plastic wrap. Place a plate slightly smaller than the bowl on the plastic wrap in order to submerge the bread pieces in the liquid mixture. Allow the bread to soak for 30 minutes or until it is thoroughly soft and most of the liquid has been absorbed.

Remove and discard the plastic wrap. Spoon the

bread and custard mix into the baking dish, and sprinkle with the maple flakes (or more dark brown sugar). Cover the pan with foil, pricked to allow steam to escape, and place the pan in a second pan filled with hot water.

Bake for 1 hour, removing the foil for the last 10 minutes, or until the custard is just set in the center. Remove the pan from the hot water and uncover. Allow the pudding to cool somewhat before cutting into portions and serving.

If making ahead, arrange the cut pieces onto a baking pan lined with parchment paper (so they won't stick) and reheat in a 350°F degree oven for about 15 minutes.

Maple Syrup Pie with Walnuts: Tarte au Sirop d'Erable

This classic sweet of old Quebec has a smooth, rich filling. Sugar or molasses pies like this one were popular in every region of Canada and in the United States in pioneer days. When ingredients were scarce, molasses was a standby for baking. In Quebec, this Maple Syrup Pie and Sugar Pie (Tarte au Sucre) were made from maple syrup and maple sugar when available, or brown sugar for economy. Backwoods Pie, using brown sugar plus maple or corn syrup, appears in early Nova Scotia cookbooks. Molasses Pie (Tarte a la Ferlouche or Tarte a la Melasses in Quebec) and Lassy Tart (in Newfoundland) were lightly spiced and thickened with breadcrumbs. Shoofly Pie, most common in American

Mennonite areas, had a molasses and brown sugar filling with crumbs on top.

YIELD: ONE 9-INCH PIE, 8 TO 10 SERVINGS

$^3/_4$ pound Sweet White Whole Wheat Tart Pastry (page 863)

2 cups maple syrup, preferably grade B

1 cup heavy cream

2 ounces ($^1/_4$ cup minus 2 teaspoons) all-purpose flour

$^1/_2$ teaspoon fine sea salt

5 large eggs

$^1/_4$ pound (1 cup) walnuts and/or black walnuts, chopped, optional

Roll out the dough out between two sheets of lightly floured wax paper to about $^3/_8$-inch thick. Drape the dough, without stretching it, into a 9-inch pie pan, preferably aluminum or Pyrex for better browning. Trim the edges evenly, then crimp or pinch in and out alternatively to form a decorative fluted edge. Chill the crust for 1 hour in the refrigerator or 30 minutes in the freezer to set the shape.

Preheat the oven to 400°F. In bowl, whisk together the maple syrup, cream, flour, salt, and eggs; stir in the nuts. Pour into the crust and bake on the bottom shelf of the oven for 15 minutes. Reduce the heat to 350°F and bake for 35 minutes longer or until pastry is golden and the filling is slightly puffed and looks dry but still trembles. Cool to room temperature on a wire rack before cutting in serving portions. Store covered and refrigerated up to 5 days.

MILK, CREAM, & BUTTERMILK

Cream . . . 559

Sour Cream . . . 560

Clabber . . . 560

Evaporated Milk . . . 560

Sweetened Condensed Milk . . . 561

Buttermilk . . . 561

PAPIAMENTO BREAD PUDDING
WITH PONCHE CREMA . . . 562

ARGENTINEAN ALFAJORES COOKIES . . . 563

PILAR'S TRES LECHES CAKE . . . 564

BUTTERMILK TART PASTRY . . . 565

CREAM CHEESE PASTRY DOUGH . . . 565

DULCE DE LECHE . . . 566

The History of Dulce de Leche . . . 567

Many Versions of Dulce de Leche . . . 567

MILK, CREAM & BUTTERMILK

Humans have been drinking animal milk since the earliest days of animal husbandry. By about 7000 BCE, cattle were being herded in parts of Turkey. Domestic cows, which existed throughout much of Europe and Asia, were introduced to the New World and other colonies during the Age of Exploration. The fatty, opaque white liquid is produced by the mammary glands of female mammals. In addition to female cows, ewe sheep, nanny goats, mare horses, donkeys, camels, yaks, water buffalo, and reindeer all produce milk that is enjoyed by people in different parts of the world. In Russia and Sweden, even small moose dairies exist.

By law, American milk is pasteurized, a process named after its inventor, French scientist Louis Pasteur. To pasteurize liquid like milk, it is briefly heated and immediately cooled in order to destroy viruses, bacteria, molds, yeasts, and all such harmful microorganisms. Pasteurized milk is still perishable and must be kept stored cold.

Conventional milk is pasteurized using the high temperature short time pasteurization. It is heated to a minimum of 170°F for 19 seconds, producing milk with a shelf life of about two weeks.

Most organic dairies ultra-pasteurize their milk, heating the milk to 280°F for two seconds, then immediately chilling it, giving it a slightly "cooked" taste. Dairy products pasteurized by the second, higher-heat method will typically have a shelf life of about two months. Milk or cream that is pasteurized at a lower temperature tastes fresher, lighter, and cleaner. The same method with the same "cooked" taste is used to make ultra-pasteurized heavy cream, practically the only kind to be found on supermarket shelves.

Milk has a tendency to separate into a small top layer that is lighter in weight, though higher in fat, over a larger bottom layer that is heavier in weight, though lower in fat. This high fat cream layer that rises to the top is skimmed off to sell separately. Since 1932, American milk has been homogenized to prevent this separation. It is pumped at high pressure through very narrow tubes, breaking up the fat globules. Homogenized milk tastes blander but feels creamier in the mouth than unhomogenized milk; it is whiter in color and more resistant to developing off flavors. Unhomogenized milk just needs vigorous shaking to make it smooth again.

In 1961, the world's first aseptic carton was released by the Swedish company, Tetra-Pak, which included a thin aluminum layer embedded into the packaging material. With the new packaging and the new short-term/high temperature method of sterilization, milk (and other perishable liquids) could remain shelf-stable for months without refrigeration, a significant improvement in Europe and much of the developing world where refrigeration is limited or nonexistent. In 1989, the Institute of Food Technologists placed aseptic packaging first on its list of the ten most important scientific innovations of the century. We mostly see this type of milk in small sizes for children's lunch boxes, but in Europe and many other places, it's the most common packaging for all milk.

Back in the 1920s, Americans could buy fresh raw milk, clabber and buttermilk, naturally yellow butter, fresh farm cheeses, and cream in various colors and thicknesses. Many people feel that what's needed today is a return to humane, pasture-based dairying and small-scale traditional processing rather than the factory dairies common today. I can still remember the delicious fresh milk topped with a rich layer of cream that I drank every morning while camping outside of London as a young backpacker. Unhomogenized milk has made a small comeback in a few areas, including the Sonoma, California-based Straus Family Creamery, which sells organic milk with the cream still on top in old-fashioned glass bottles similar to the kind I drank in London. "Raw" or untreated milk straight from the cow has its vocal proponents, who claim that it is more healthful as long as the milk is produced from grass-fed and organically-fed animals in a super-clean environment.

CREAM

Cream is the higher butterfat layer skimmed from the top of milk, produced industrially using centrifuges called "separators." Cream produced by cows (particularly Jersey cattle) grazing on natural pasture often contains some pigments from the plants they eat, giving the cream a light yellow tint. Cream from grain-fed cows is pure white. In my years as a chef, I insisted on buying only extra rich heavy cream from a local dairy that didn't ultra-pasteurize its milk to make my Italian gelato. When whipped, the cream would hold its air bubbles for hours and it yielded sauces with lots of body, ultra-smooth mouthfeel, and rich flavor.

Half-and-half, often used to whiten coffee, ranges from 10 to 18 percent milkfat. Light cream, ranges from 18 to 30 percent fat. Whipping cream has 30 to 36 percent fat, heavy whipping cream contains over 36 percent fat, while extra-heavy cream may be up to 40 percent fat. Crème fraîche is heavy cream from 30 to 40 percent milk fat that is ripened and lightly soured with a bacterial culture. It is not as thick or as sour as American sour cream, but unlike sour cream, it can be boiled without separating.

Mexican *crema* (or *crema espesa*, "heavy cream" in Spanish) is similar, though lighter in body to crème fraîche. In Great Britain, clotted cream, which contains more than 50 percent fat, is processed with heat, so it is pale yellow in color and just about thick enough to cut with a knife. It is *de rigueur* for "cream tea" served with scones. Light cream is called single cream in Britain; heavy cream is called double cream.

Sour Cream

I still can't seem to get enough of sour cream, which has 16 to 21 percent butterfat. Sour cream gets its characteristic tangy flavor from the lactic acid created by the bacteria that thickens it. American sour cream often contains additional ingredients such as gelatin, rennet, and vegetable enzymes. Sour cream derives from *smetana*, a thick, extra-rich sour cream popular in Russia and Central and Eastern Europe. Like sour cream in America, smetana is widely used in Eastern European Jewish cooking, mixed into cheesecake and coffeecake batters, and used as a topping for fried potato latkes and potato and fruit-filled dumplings like the Austrian Apricot Dumplings (page 000). Its consistency can range from thin (about 10 percent butterfat) to extra-thick (as much as 70 percent butterfat). In Russia, the additions of thickeners, like the gelatin often used in America, is regarded as cheating, creating a substandard product. I wish all American producers of sour cream felt the same way.

CLABBER

I remember my grandmother's clabber, which she called sour milk, sitting on the countertop of her Brooklyn second-floor apartment kitchen. Somehow I could never bring myself to drink it. Clabber, which is related to French crème fraîche, is produced by allowing unpasteurized milk to sour at the proper humidity and temperature. Over time, the milk thickens or curdles into a yoghurt-like liquid with a strong, sour flavor. In the rural South, clabber was sweetened and eaten for breakfast. Clabber was originally a Scottish and Anglo-Irish word meaning wet, gooey mud. It appears to have arrived in the United States with the many Scottish nannies who cared for the privileged children of Virginia gentry.

You can, however, make your own clabber by adding a couple tablespoons of commercial buttermilk to a glass of milk. Add the buttermilk to cream and, in a few days, you will get crème fraîche.

EVAPORATED MILK

Swiss-born John Baptist Meyenberg immigrated to the United States from Switzerland and began Helvetia Milk Condensing Company, which produced sweetened condensed milk. In 1892, the company started producing evaporated milk without added sugar. Evaporated milk has had about sixty percent of its water removed via evaporation and is then subjected to a complex process before it is canned. The high heat gives evaporated milk a cooked taste and a slightly darker color than fresh milk.

SWEETENED CONDENSED MILK

Before the nineteenth century, drinking fresh milk could be a health hazard because dairies were not kept especially clean and the milk was not kept especially cold. The idea for an easily portable canned milk that wouldn't spoil came to Gail Borden during a transatlantic trip on board a ship in 1852. The cows in the hold became too seasick to be milked during the long trip, and an immigrant infant died from lack of milk. By 1854, Borden had produced his first condensed milk. At first, Borden thought that condensing the milk made it more stable (and in fact thinner liquids spoil more easily than those that are more concentrated). But, he realized that the key was in heating the milk to kill the bacteria and microorganisms that caused spoilage.

Borden was granted a patent for sweetened condensed milk in 1856 with the sugar added to help preserve the product. It took time for customers, who in those days were accustomed to drinking watered-down milk, with chalk added to make it white, and molasses added for sweetness, color, and creamy texture, to accept this new product. When the dangerous practice of feeding New York cows on distillery mash was exposed in *Leslie's Illustrated Newspaper*, Borden's condensed milk business greatly benefited. In 1861, the Union Army purchased Borden's condensed milk for field rations, which led to further success.

Sweetened condensed milk goes through less processing than evaporated milk. Though the same sixty percent of the water has been removed from condensed milk, sugar has been added, making it 40 to 45 percent sugar and very useful for baking. When mixed with an acidic ingredient like Key limes, the sweetened condensed milk thickens naturally without heat.

BUTTERMILK

Old-fashioned homemade buttermilk is the slightly sour, residual liquid which remains after butter has been churned, similar to the whey left after curdling for cheese. This true buttermilk is flecked with tiny spots of golden butter that hadn't been skimmed. It takes one gallon of milk to yield one-half pint of true buttermilk. Modern, commercial buttermilk is made by adding a lactic acid bacteria culture to pasteurized sweet whole milk or more commonly skim milk or non-fat milk and then it is left to ferment for about twelve hours. Salt is usually added for flavor. Buttermilk is excellent in baked goods, where its acidity neutralizes the alkalinity of baking soda, improves browning, and helps develop finer texture. Its tangy, fresh flavor goes especially well with peaches, cherries, and berries.

Papiamento Bread Pudding with Ponche Crema

Aruba's Papiamento is a family-owned restaurant housed in a historic cunucu, or Aruban farmhouse built in the early nineteenth century and complete with thick walls, a sloped roof, and a cistern to gather the rain that falls so infrequently on the island. One of the house specialties is this sweetly aromatic and tender bread pudding flavored with fresh ginger, cinnamon, and nutmeg. Thick, custardy Ponche Crema liqueur, a local specialty similar to egg nog (see page 63 [Aruban Ponche Crema Liqueur recipe in Alcohols] for the recipe), adds the final fillip. If you have to have leftover Pan Dushi (page 891), by all means, use it here, but cut back on the sugar and raisins to one-half cup each to compensate for the bread's sweetness. If you're lucky enough to get to Papiamento (www.papiamento restaurant.com), tell them Aliza sent you.

YIELD: 10 TO 12 SERVINGS

2 loaves (about 2$\frac{1}{2}$ pounds) stale, firm white bread, crusts removed, cut into 1-inch cubes

1 quart whole milk

8 large eggs

$\frac{3}{4}$ cup sugar

14 ounces sweetened condensed milk

1$\frac{1}{2}$-inch section fresh ginger, peeled and grated or finely chopped (about 2 tablespoons)

1 teaspoon ground cinnamon

$\frac{1}{2}$ teaspoon freshly grated nutmeg

Pinch salt

2 ounces ($\frac{1}{2}$ stick) unsalted butter, cut into bits

$\frac{3}{4}$ cup golden raisins

1 cup Ponche Crema liqueur from Aruba, substitute Rum-Vanilla Custard Sauce (page 61)

In a large bowl, combine the bread and milk, and set aside at room temperature to soak for 2 hours.

In a medium bowl, combine the eggs, $\frac{1}{2}$ cup of the sugar, the condensed milk, ginger, cinnamon, nutmeg, and salt, and beat lightly. Add this mixture to the bread, toss lightly to coat, and let soak in the refrigerator for 2 hours.

Add the butter bits to the bread mix and stir to combine.

Preheat the oven to 350°F. Use the remaining butter to grease a large baking dish.

Add the raisins to the bread mixture, then spoon the mixture into the baking dish, pushing the raisins down into the mixture so they don't burn. Sprinkle the top with the remaining sugar, cover with lightly oiled foil, and bake for 1 hour. Remove the foil, and bake 30 minutes longer, or until browned on top. Remove from the oven, let cool slightly, and cut into portions. Top with the liqueur, and serve warm. Store covered and refrigerated up to five days. Wrap in foil and reheat in a preheated 350°F oven for about 20 minutes or until heated through, then uncover and heat 10 minutes longer to crisp the top.

Argentinean Alfajores Cookies

These shortbread-like cookies are made with a combination of all-purpose flour, potato or another type of starch, and confectioners' sugar, making them light and almost powdery in texture. Lemon zest, lots of butter, egg yolks, and brandy complete the dough. The cookies are then spread with a thin layer of dulce de leche, the Latin American caramel made from sweetened condensed milk. It's actually pretty easy to make your own dulce de leche following the recipe on page 566, but you can buy it in Latin American markets and well-stocked supermarkets.

YIELD: 24 COOKIE SANDWICHES

$3/4$ pound ($2^3/4$ cups plus 1 tablespoon) unbleached all-purpose flour

$1/4$ pound ($1^1/4$ cups) potato starch, substitute corn, wheat, or rice starch

2 teaspoons baking powder

$1/2$ teaspoon fine sea salt

$1/2$ pound (2 sticks) unsalted butter, softened

1 cup (5 ounces) confectioners' sugar, plus extra for sprinkling on top

4 large egg yolks

Grated zest of 1 lemon (1 tablespoon)

$1/4$ cup brandy

1 cup Dulce de Leche, homemade (page 566) or purchased

Whisk together the dry ingredients: flour, potato starch, baking powder, and salt. Line two 18 x 13-inch half sheet pans (or other large baking pans) with parchment paper or silicone baking mats.

In the bowl of a standing mixer fitted with the paddle attachment, cream the butter and confectioners' sugar until light and fluffy, 5 to 6 minutes. Beat in the egg yolks, one at a time, beating well until the mixture is creamy again. Add the lemon zest and brandy and beat again briefly to mix. Add the flour mixture and beat only long enough to combine. The dough should be soft and a bit sticky, but not crumbly.

Transfer to a plastic bag and shape into a flattened rectangle. Chill in the refrigerator for 1 hour or in the freezer for 30 minutes until firm but still malleable.

Roll out half the dough between two sheets of lightly floured wax paper to about $3/8$-inch thick, then repeat with the remaining dough. Refrigerate the rolled out dough for 30 minutes or until firm but still malleable. Cut into 2-inch rounds or other decorative shapes, using a fluted cookie cutter if desired. Re-roll the trimmings once if desired. (Freeze any leftover dough up to 2 months.)

Preheat the oven to 350°F. Arrange the rounds equidistant from each other in rows of 4 and 3 on the pans. Dust the cookies with confectioners' sugar and bake for 13 minutes, or until lightly browned on the edges, taking care not to over-bake the cookies. Cool the cookies to room temperature on a wire rack, then dust again with more confectioners' sugar.

If the dulce de leche is firm, warm it at low heat in the microwave so it is spreadable. Working gently because the cookies are fragile, spread half the cookies with a thin layer of dulce de leche. Cover with a second cookie, twisting back and forth to encourage the filling to spread out evenly inside. Refrigerate the cookies for about 30 minutes before serving. Store the cookies refrigerated up to 1 week, but bring to room temperature to serve.

Pilar's Tres Leches Cake

This is a cake for those days when you have a demanding sweet tooth to satisfy. There are innumerable variations on this Latin American favorite, popular now practically everywhere, though it was probably first made in Mexico in the early nineteen hundreds with condensed milk imported from America. This recipe comes from Pilar Sydow, a native of Venezuela. This delicious and easy treat consists of a sponge cake that is soaked in a sweet syrup made of three milks: evaporated milk, condensed milk, and heavy cream. For a light and fruity version, serve this topped with diced tropical fruits such as papaya, mango, passion fruit, star fruit, and pineapple. To make a Quatro Leches Cake, spread the top with a thin layer of dulce de leche (page 566) just before serving.

YIELD: ONE 13 X 9-INCH CAKE, 10 TO 12 SERVINGS

6 ounces ($1\frac{1}{2}$ cups minus 1 tablespoon) unbleached all-purpose flour

1 teaspoon baking powder

$\frac{1}{2}$ teaspoon fine sea salt

$\frac{1}{4}$ pound (1 stick) unsalted butter, softened

1 cup sugar

4 large eggs

$1\frac{1}{2}$ teaspoons vanilla extract

1 cup whole milk

6 ounces evaporated milk

7 ounces sweetened condensed milk

6 tablespoons dark rum

1 cup heavy cream

$\frac{1}{2}$ cup confectioners' sugar

Preheat the oven to 350°F. Spray a 13 x 9-inch baking pan with nonstick baker's coating or rub with butter and dust with flour, shaking off the excess. Sift the flour, baking powder, and salt together and set aside.

In the bowl of a standing mixer fitted with the paddle attachment, cream the butter and sugar together until light and fluffy 4 to 5 minutes. Beat in the eggs, one at a time, then add $\frac{1}{2}$ teaspoon of the vanilla. Beat well until creamy. Add the flour mixture, in 3 to 4 batches, mixing only until blended. Pour the batter into the prepared pan and bake for 30 minutes or until the cake is set in the middle and starts to come away from the sides of the pan. Remove the cake from the oven and while it is still hot, pierce it in 8 or 10 places with a fork or skewer, then let it cool to room temperature.

Combine the whole milk, evaporated milk, condensed milk, and rum, and pour the mixture over the top of the cooled cake. Refrigerate for at least 2 hours before serving.

Just before serving, beat the cream until firm but still bright white in color, then add the confectioners' sugar and remaining vanilla and beat again briefly to combine. Spread over top of the cake. Cut the cake into serving portions and serve chilled, spooning any excess milk mixture onto the serving plates. Store tightly covered and refrigerated up to five days.

Buttermilk Tart Pastry

This unsweetened pastry dough is made with butter-milk, either fresh or in dried form, which makes a particularly flaky short crust dough because the acidity in it tenderizes the dough. Use it for savory tarts like the Smoked Salmon and Spinach Quiche (page 434) and for the Radicchio and Fontina Torta (page 260). I like to keep a package of the dry buttermilk powder made by the Saco company in my pantry. Look for it in the baking aisle of well-stocked supermarkets. If you can't find the buttermilk powder, substitute $1/2$ cup liquid butter-milk whisked together with 1 egg, instead of the dry buttermilk and 3 beaten eggs in the recipe.

YIELD: ABOUT 1¼ POUNDS DOUGH, ENOUGH FOR 1 LARGE OR 2 SMALL TARTS

$3/4$ pound (3 cups minus 3 tablespoons) unbleached all-purpose flour

1 teaspoon fine sea salt

$1/4$ cup dry buttermilk powder

$1/2$ pound (2 sticks) unsalted butter, cut into bits

3 large eggs, lightly beaten

In the bowl of a standing mixer fitted with the paddle attachment, combine the flour, salt, and buttermilk powder, and mix together lightly. Add the butter bits, but don't mix them in. Place the bowl in the freezer for 30 minutes to chill.

Beat the chilled flour mixture until it resembles cold and crumbly oatmeal. Add the eggs and beat until the mixture just comes together into a ball. Place the dough in a large zipper lock bag and flatten the dough to fill the bag. Chill for at least 30 minutes before rolling out. The dough can be refrigerated for up to 2 days before using or frozen up to 3 months.

Cream Cheese Pastry Dough

This flaky, easy-to-roll dough was probably first developed in America by the Philadelphia Cream Cheese Company as a way to get customers to buy more of their product. Whoever invented it, the dough is a winner. Use it to make rugelach filled with jam, chocolate, or nuts and raisins (see Starting with Ingredients). In this book, I use the dough for the Apple-Blueberry Crumb Pie (page 163) and for the classic Kasha-Mushroom Knishes (page 183).

YIELD: 1¾ POUNDS DOUGH, ENOUGH FOR TWO TARTS OR PIES

6 ounces (1½ sticks) unsalted butter, softened

6 ounces cream cheese, softened

1 pound ($3¾$ cups) unbleached all-purpose flour

1 teaspoon fine sea salt

1 large egg

In the bowl of a standing mixer fitted with the paddle attachment, cream the butter and cream cheese until smooth, scraping down the sides of bowl once or twice. Add the flour and salt and beat until just combined. Add the egg and beat just long enough for the dough to form a ball. Transfer the dough to a plastic bag and shape into a flattened rectangle. Refrigerate for 1 hour or freeze for 30 minutes until firm but still malleable. Store tightly wrapped in the freezer for up to two months.

Dulce de Leche

Dulce de leche, *which means "milk candy" in Spanish, is a rich caramel-like sauce prepared by very slowly heating sweetened milk until the sugars darken. Although the transformation that occurs is often called caramelization, it is actually a Maillard reaction: the chemical reaction responsible for the browning of cooked food. The development of sweetened condensed milk (page 561) made it easy to make dulce de leche at home. Traditional home recipes for dulce de leche call for boiling the cans until the contents darken and thicken. There is the small possibility that the cans could explode while simmering, so it's best to use the method in the recipe below for similar, but safer, results.*

YIELD: ABOUT 3 CUPS

2 (14-ounce) cans sweetened condensed milk

Pierce the tops of the can twice using a triangular can opener and remove the paper from the cans. Cover the tops of the cans tightly with heavy-duty aluminum foil and place them in a heavy-bottomed saucepan. Add enough hot water to reach 1/2-inch from the tops of the cans. Cover the pan and bring the water to a boil, then reduce the heat to low and cook the cans for 3 hours, adding more water to the pot if necessary.

Turn off the heat, cool the cans to room temperature, about 30 minutes. Speed the cooling up, if desired, by placing the cans in a pan filled with ice and water. Use a can opener to remove the tops and scrape out the contents into a bowl. For smoother texture, process the dulce de leche in a food processor until smooth. Store refrigerated in an airtight container up to 3 months.

THE HISTORY OF DULCE DE LECHE

There are several legends about the origins of dulce de leche. In one, an Uruguayan servant was heating milk for some soldiers. Because she was angry with her master for ordering her to heat so much milk, she added lots of sugar into it to make it impossible for the soldiers to drink. She then left the milk heating, and when she came back, she found that the milk had turned into a brown jam. Her master was about to punish her, but a soldier tasted the jam and discovered how good it was.

In another story, the maid of a nineteenth-century Argentinean leader, Juan Manuel de Rosas, was making *lechada*—a drink made with boiled sugar and milk—when she heard someone knock at the door. She left the lechada on the stove. When she returned, the lechada had overcooked and turned into a thick, sweet brown jam: dulce de leche.

It may be that dulce de leche had its origins in French *confiture de lait* (milk preserves). A similar story dating from the fourteenth century in Normandy involves a military cook who had the same culinary accident while making sweet milk for breakfast.

MANY VERSIONS OF DULCE DE LECHE

Dulce de leche is well-known in Latin America, where it is enjoyed in Argentina, Brazil, Chile, Uruguay, the Dominican Republic, Cuba, Paraguay, Bolivia, Peru, Puerto Rico, Nicaragua, Costa Rica, and Panama. The texture of dulce de leche ranges from spreadable to cuttable. In Mexico, it is known as *cajeta*, named after the small wooden boxes in which the dark caramel cream was traditionally packed. A specialty of Celaya in the state of Guanajuato, the Mexican version is made with half goat's milk and half cow's milk, and has a stronger aftertaste from the goat's milk.

In Peru, the milk-sweet is known as *natillas;* in Colombia and Venezuela it is known as *arequipe*. In Coro, Venezuela, *dulce de leche* is sold as *dulce de leche con chocolate* when chocolate is swirled in. French *confiture de lait* is very similar to the spreadable forms of dulce de leche. Formerly a Latino specialty food, dulce de leche has entered the American mainstream. Häagen Dazs introduced their hugely successful dulce de leche ice cream in 1998, while in 2007, Starbucks began offering dulce de leche flavored lattes and Frappuccinos.

OATS

SAVORY OATMEAL-CHEDDAR TART . . . 573

GUINNESS OATMEAL BREAD . . . 574

AMISH BLACK WALNUT OATMEAL PIE . . . 575

CANADIAN DATE-OATMEAL SQUARES . . . 576

OATMEAL-APPLE UPSIDE-DOWN TART . . . 577

OATS

Alexander the Great fed his fabled horse, Esepheus, only with oats because he claimed that this most nutritious of grains made his horse run faster. For much the same reasons, oats, which contain about sixteen percent protein and have high levels of complex carbohydrates and fiber that slow digestion, are a staple food for many athletes. In classical times Greeks and Romans regarded oats as coarse, barbarian fare, using them mainly as animal fodder, but the Romans did foster the growing of oats in Britain. In the northern regions of England, Wales, and Ireland and even more so in colder Scotland, oats are the most important grain, valued as a cereal grain that thrives in moist, cool climates where even tolerant barley won't grow.

Oats, *Avena sativa*, originated as a weed in wheat and barley fields, accidentally harvested with the rest of the crop that eventually came to be cultivated in their own right. The word *oat*, which derives from the Old English "ate" is pure English, with no known relatives in other languages. Wild oats drop off their heads and scatter as soon as they ripen (just like those proverbially sown by the young), so that they spread easily but are dif-

ficult to harvest. Cultivated oats keep their heads much longer, as do those of us who, sadly, are done with sowing our own wild oats.

Today's oatmeal cookies descend from the ancient bannocks and oatcakes that were a basic food for the Celtic peoples of the British Isles. Oatcakes were also known as "haverbread," from *haver*, a word of Anglo-Saxon/Germanic origin meaning oats, and the source of haversack, a bag for oats. In Scotland, oats show up in porridge, bannocks, beverages, and desserts like cranachan, made from toasted oats mixed with fresh whipped cream, berries, and whisky. Bannocks are usually griddle or girdle cakes made from oatmeal or barley. From the pagan times in Scotland, special kinds of bannocks were made to mark each season. On February first, the Bonnach Bride (St. Bride's bannock) celebrated the first day of Spring; the Bonnach Bealtain (Beltane bannock) celebrated the first day of summer; Bonnach Lunastain (Lammas bannock) the first day of autumn; and the Bonnach Samhtain (Hallomas bannock) the first day of winter.

Oats are so important in Scotland that at one time, its universities had an holiday called Meal

Monday, so that students could return to their farms and collect oats for food. Many people, especially those of Scottish heritage, believe that the marked success of canny and frugal Scots in their homeland and in adopted countries can be credited to their diet of oats. In Lancashire, in cold northwest England, where leavened and unleavened oat-bread are typical, it is said that, "Handsomer and more muscular men are not reared in any part of the British dominions, than in those countries where the oatmeal diet is predominant."

In England in the seventeenth century, once lowly flummery, made with oatmeal to achieve the desirable smooth and gelatinous texture, was served in elaborate molds to delight diners. In 1747, Hannah Glasse's *The Art of Cookery, Made Plain and Easy; Which far exceeds any Thing of the Kind Ever Yet Published* appeared in England, a cookbook so important that many could not believe a woman had written it. Glasse's much-reprinted book including a recipe for oat flummery sweetened with sugar and flavored with orange blossom water. Glasse also used oatmeal to make hasty pudding, which in America, evolved into cornmeal mush or pudding and an unappetizing sounding "Water Gruel" made of oatmeal and water suitable for invalids.

People that had made the long voyage advised new immigrants to Australia to bring along oatmeal and oatcakes. Rib-sticking, lightweight, and easy to store, oatmeal traveled to the North Pole with Admiral Richard Byrd, to the South Pole with Ronald Amundsen, to Mt. Everest with Sir Edmond Hillary, and orbited the earth with American astronauts.

An adventurous sea captain, Bartholomew Gosnold, brought oats to the New World, where in 1602, he planted them on one of the Elizabeth Islands off the southern coast of Massachusetts. The Dutch grew oats in New Netherlands by 1626, and by 1648, oats were cultivated in Virginia. Scottish, Dutch, and other northern European immigrants used sturdy oats in porridges, puddings, and baked goods. In 1764, George Washington experimented with oats on his farm at Mount Vernon. By 1787, he had 400 acres of oats planted. Today, oats, which are grown mostly in the cold regions of the upper Midwest, are America's third most important cereal crop (after wheat and corn) and are the fourth most important cereal crop worldwide.

In 1854, Ferdinand Schumacher, a miller from Akron, Ohio, introduced oatmeal porridge to Americans. Known as "The Oatmeal King," Schumacher traveled about promoting oatmeal and founded The German Mills American Oatmeal Company. Henry D. Seymour and William Heston developed rolled oat, made by steaming and rolling pinhead oatmeal, and established the Quaker Mill Company in 1877. In 1901, the Quaker Mill Company merged with Schumacher's German Mills and several others and became the Quaker Oats Company.

People bought oatmeal in the familiar cylindrical container with the directions for making porridge printed on the back. Soon, oatmeal became a popular cooking and baking ingredient. Recipes published in eighteenth and nineteenth-century American cookbooks including oatmeal blanc-mange, Scottish and English griddle-baked oat cakes, muffins made from leftover cold cooked oatmeal, bread and biscuits.

Oats are graded according to the grind, including coarse, pin(head), and fine. Irish steel-cut, or pinhead, oats first have their hulls removed, leaving only the oat groat, or inner grain. A cutting machine with rotating steel discs cuts each groat into about two to four small angular pieces. While they take much longer to cook than the familiar American quick-cooking oats, steel-cut oats have a distinct nutty flavor and pleasing firm texture.

In the twentieth century all sorts of new oatmeal recipes were published, including cakes, cookies, wafers, drops, macaroons, quick breads and yeast breads, muffins, scones, pancakes, and the famous Neiman-Marcus chocolate chip cookies made with oat flour. Today, oats are turned into streusel toppings for pies and crisps like the Hot Apple-Cranberry Crisp with Oatmeal-Almond Topping (page 403) and are added to breads, muffins, and cookie batters like the Oatmeal Pecan fruities (page 000) because they retain moisture well, helping to keep baked goods fresh.

A short-lived "oat bran craze" swept the U.S. in the late 1980s After reports found that oats can help lower cholesterol. In 1997, when the FDA (Food and Drug Administration) ruled that foods high in oats can carry a label that they may reduce the risk of heart disease when combined with a low-fat diet, the sales of oats soared again. Oats contain little gluten (the stretchiness that forms into bubbles that fill with fermented gasses and leaven bread), so that breads made from these grains alone will be coarse, dense, and crumbly. However, that same quality makes oats easier to digest for people with gluten intolerances.

Mixed with other flours, rolled oats and oat flour add a welcome nutty flavor to breads. It's pretty easy to substitute up to twenty percent protein-rich oat flour for wheat in cookie and pastry recipes. Cake recipes are more finicky, so it's probably not a good idea to substitute there. It's best to use common American rolled oats or oat flour, as required in the recipe for baking.

One of the tastiest pastry doughs in this book is used in the Savory Oatmeal-Cheddar Tart (opposite page), filled with sharp cheddar and browned onions. Guinness Stout provides the liquid for a purely Irish Guinness Oatmeal Bread (page 574). The frugal Amish, renowned for their intense sweet-teeth, combine oatmeal with the black walnuts harvested from trees growing all over Lancaster County, Pennsylvania, with eggs and dark syrup to make a "transparent" Amish Black Walnut Oatmeal Pie (page 575). Whisky-spiked Canadian Date-Oatmeal Squares (page 576) are easy-to-make bar cookies with an oatmeal crumble topping and a dense, chewy date filing. Oatmeal-Apple Upside-Down Tart (page 577) is a hearty variation on the theme of fruit-topped tarts and cakes and distantly related to French tarte tatin.

Savory Oatmeal–Cheddar Tart

Rolled oats make a slightly crumbly short crust pastry crust here, which is filled with caramelized onions and sharp Cheddar cheese in a sour cream custard. Make a big pot of rib-sticking split pea soup and serve it with wedges of this tart for a pleasing wintertime meal. The tart keeps well for four or five days. Wrap the wedges in aluminum foil and reheat in a moderate oven for 20 to 30 minutes before serving. Substitute yogurt or crème fraiche for the sour cream if desired. Use the oatmeal pastry for any of the other savory quiche-like tarts either in this book or from your own collection.

YIELD: ONE 10-INCH TART,
8 TO 10 SERVINGS

Crust

6 ounces (1 cup) rolled oats

2 ounces (½ cup plus 1 tablespoon) white whole wheat flour

2 ounces (½ cup minus ½ tablespoon) unbleached all-purpose flour

1 teaspoon paprika

¼ teaspoon cayenne pepper

1 teaspoon fine sea salt

¼ teaspoon ground black pepper

¼ pound (1 stick) unsalted butter, chilled and cut into bits

3 tablespoons ice water

Filling

2 ounces (½ stick) unsalted butter

1 large onion, thinly sliced

1 cup sour cream

6 ounces (about ¾ cup shredded) extra-sharp Cheddar cheese, shredded

2 large eggs

2 large egg yolks

Fine sea salt

Freshly ground black pepper

Freshly grated nutmeg

Cayenne pepper

Make the crust: In the bowl of a food processor, combine the oats, whole wheat flour, all-purpose flour, paprika, cayenne pepper, salt, and pepper. Process briefly to combine, then add the butter and process until the mixture resembles oatmeal. With the machine running, add the ice water and process just long enough for the dough to come together and form a ball. Transfer to a plastic zipper lock bag and shape into a flattened rectangle. Chill in the refrigerator for 1 hour or in the freezer for 30 minutes, until firm but still malleable.

Preheat the oven to 375°F. Roll out into a 10-inch tart pan with a removable bottom, pressing well into the corners so there are no thick spots. Trim overhang even with the edge. Fit a piece of heavy-duty foil onto the dough and fill with beans or other pie weights. Blind bake (just pastry crust, no filling) until the crust is cooked through but not yet browned, about 30 minutes. Remove the foil and the weights and bake for 10 minutes longer, or until the crust is evenly and lightly browned. Remove from the oven and cool to room temperature.

Make the filling: In a large skillet over low heat, melt the butter. Add the onion, cover the skillet, and cook for 10 minutes, stirring once or twice, until the onion is tender. Uncover the skillet, raise the heat to medium, and cook, stirring occasionally, for 10 minutes or until the onion is golden brown. Remove from the heat and cool to room temperature.

Preheat the oven to 375°F. Whisk together the sour cream, cheese, eggs, and egg yolks. Season to taste with salt, pepper, nutmeg, and cayenne. Add the onions and stir to combine. Spoon the filling into the crust and place the tart pan on a baking pan to catch any drips. Reduce the oven temperature to 350°F and bake for 30 minutes, until the filling has just begun to puff up in the center. Remove from the oven and cool slightly before serving. Store covered and refrigerated up to three days. Wrap in foil and reheat in a preheated 350ºF oven for 20 minutes or until heated through. Unwrap and heat 10 minutes longer to crisp the dough.

Guinness Oatmeal Bread

Made with a combination of bread flour, whole wheat flour, cornmeal, and oatmeal, this hearty yet light-bodied bread is quick to make, and makes excellent toast and sandwiches. Serve it with Cheddar or Stilton, pickles, pickled onions, a slice of pâté, beet salad, apple wedges, and, of course, a bottle of Guinness or other beer, for a traditional English ploughman's lunch. The bread freezes beautifully. This recipe is dairy-free.

YIELD: 2 MEDIUM LOAVES

1 (1/4-ounce) package (2 1/4 teaspoons) active dry yeast

1/4 cup lukewarm water

1/4 cup maple syrup

10 ounces (2 1/2 cups) unbleached bread flour

1/4 pound (1 cup plus 2 tablespoons) white whole wheat flour

1/4 pound (1 1/3 cups) oatmeal

6 ounces (1 1/4 cups plus 1 tablespoon) stone-ground white cornmeal

2 teaspoons fine sea salt

1 (12 fluid ounce) bottle Guinness stout, at room temperature (flat is OK)

1 egg white, lightly beaten with 1 tablespoon water, for the egg wash

2 tablespoons sesame seeds

Spray two medium (1-pound, 8 1/2 by 4 1/2-inch) loaf pans with nonstick baker's coating.

In a small bowl, combine the yeast, water, and maple syrup, and set aside to proof, about 10 minutes, or until the mixture is bubbly.

In the bowl of a standing mixer fitted with the paddle attachment, combine the dry ingredients: bread flour, whole wheat flour, oatmeal, cornmeal, and salt, and beat briefly with to combine. Beat in the stout, then switch to the dough hook attachment and continue beating until the dough is smooth and elastic and comes away from the sides of the bowl, about 5 minutes.

Transfer the dough to a large oiled bowl; turn over to coat with oil, cover with plastic wrap or a damp cloth, and allow the dough to rise at warm room temperature until doubled in size, about 2 hours.

Punch the dough down and cut it in half. Using a rolling pin, roll each section into a rectangle about 9-inches wide and about 1-inch thick, and then roll the dough up tightly into a log shape. Fit the dough, seam side down, into the pans. Brush with the egg wash, then sprinkle with the sesame seeds. Using a single-edged razor or a French baker's lame, cut 3 diagonal slits into each doug log. Set the dough aside to rise at warm room temperature, for about 1 hour, or until the logs have risen just above the edges of the pans.

Preheat the oven to 400°F. Bake the breads for 40 minutes or until the bread sounds hollow when tapped on the bottom, and a thermometer inserted in the center reads 200°F. Cool on a wire rack for 10 minutes, then remove the breads from the pans (to keep them from getting soggy), and cool completely before slicing. Store in a brown paper bag or a plastic bag open at the end for up to three days, or tightly wrap in foil or freezer wrap and freeze up to 1 month.

Amish Black Walnut Oatmeal Pie

When the Amish arrived in the new American colonies in about 1737, they moved beyond Philadelphia to a region "rich with limestone soil, where black walnut trees grew." In autumn, the ground in Pennsylvania's Amish country is littered with their spongy green fruits covering gnarly, rock-hard, black shells that quite effectively protect the bittersweet nut meats inside. Though delicious and often free for the taking, shelling black walnuts requires a good amount of patience and determination, two character traits admired by the Amish. Here, black walnuts, oatmeal and other pantry ingredients fill a dark, sweet pie that would be served at community gatherings including funerals.

YIELD: ONE 9-INCH PIE, 8 TO 10 SERVINGS

$^3/_4$ pound Butter Pie Pastry dough (page 203)

3 large eggs, lightly beaten

1 cup well-packed dark brown sugar

$^1/_2$ cup dark corn syrup

$^1/_2$ cup heavy cream or evaporated milk

3 ounces($^1/_2$ cup) oatmeal

1 cup coarsely chopped black walnuts

2 ounces ($^1/_2$ stick) unsalted butter, melted and cooled

1 teaspoon vanilla extract

Pinch salt

Roll out the dough to a large circle and transfer it to a 9-inch pie plate. Trim and flute the edges and refrigerate for 30 minutes.

Preheat the oven to 350°F.

In a large mixing bowl, whisk together the eggs, brown sugar, corn syrup, cream, oatmeal, walnuts, butter, vanilla, and salt.

Place the pie plate on a baking pan to catch any drips and place the pan in the oven. Pour in the filling. Crimp aluminum foil over the edge of the pastry to prevent over-browning, or cover the edge with a metal pie shield. Bake for 40 minutes, remove the foil and bake for 15 minutes, or until the top is deep golden brown and just beginning to puff in the center. Remove from the oven and cool completely on a wire rack before cutting into serving portions. Store covered and at room temperature for up to two days.

Canadian Date–Oatmeal Squares

These chewy cookie squares come from Canada and use pantry ingredients like rib-sticking oatmeal, honey-sweet dried dates, with a shot of Canadian whisky. Most Canadian whiskies are blended from grain spirits, often mainly rye, which does well in its cold climate. A great deal of Canadian whisky crossed the border illegally into America with the so-called bootleggers during Prohibition in the 1920s. These easy to make bar cookies freeze beautifully. I'd serve them with hot coffee spiked with whisky, Canadian, of course.

YIELD: 32 BARS

Filling

1 cup chopped dates

$^{1}/_{2}$ cup dark brown sugar

1 tablespoon cornstarch

1 cup chopped walnuts

2 tablespoons Canadian whisky

Dough

6 ounces ($1^{1}/_{2}$ cups minus 1 tablespoon) unbleached all-purpose flour

$^{3}/_{4}$ pound (2 cups) oatmeal

$^{1}/_{2}$ teaspoon baking soda

Pinch fine sea salt

6 ounces ($1^{1}/_{2}$ sticks) unsalted butter, softened

1 cup dark brown sugar

Make the filling: Combine the dates, brown sugar, cornstarch, and $^{3}/_{4}$ cup of water in a medium pot and cook over moderate heat, stirring constantly, until thickened, about 10 minutes. Remove from the heat, stir in the walnuts and whiskey, and cool to room temperature.

Make the dough: Spray a 13 x 9-inch baking pan with nonstick baker's coating, or rub with softened butter and dust with flour, shaking off the excess.

In a bowl, whisk together the dry ingredients: flour, oatmeal, baking soda, and salt.

In the bowl of a standing mixer fitted with the paddle attachment, cream the butter and brown sugar until light and fluffy. Gradually add the flour mixture to make a stiff but crumbly dough. Turn out onto a work surface and knead the dough lightly with your hands until relatively smooth, about 2 minutes. Divide the dough in half and press one half into the bottom of the pan.

Preheat the oven to 350°F. Spread the filling over the bottom crust in the pan, then crumble the remaining dough over top. Bake for 40 minutes, or until the top is medium brown. Remove from the oven, cool to room temperature, and cut into squares. Store covered and at room temperature for up to two days or cover and refrigerate up to five days. Wrap in foil or freezer paper and freeze up to two months.

Oatmeal–Apple Upside–Down Tart

This is a variation on the classic French upside-down apple tart known as tarte tatin. Here, the flaky pastry is made with oatmeal, giving it a substantial texture and full-bodied flavor. The apples are mixed with orange zest and orange marmalade, and are then simmered in caramel. Make the tart in a French tin-lined copper tarte tatin pan or in a well-seasoned cast-iron skillet and serve it right from the pan. The tart is at its best the same day it is made. After a day or so, the tart's texture will be compromised.

YIELD: ONE 9-INCH TART, 8 TO 12 SERVINGS

Crust

6 ounces (1¼ cups plus 1 tablespoon) unbleached
    all-purpose flour

3 ounces (½ cup) oatmeal

½ cup sugar

1 teaspoon baking powder

½ teaspoon fine sea salt

6 ounces (1½ sticks) unsalted butter,
    cut into bits and chilled

3 tablespoons ice water

1 teaspoon cider vinegar

Filling

Juice and grated zest of 1 orange

¼ cup orange marmalade

2 tablespoons brandy

Pinch ground cloves

3 pounds mixed tart baking apples, such as Fuji,
    Golden Delicious, or Granny Smith

¾ cup unsweetened crème fraiche, optional,
    for serving

Caramel

1 cup sugar

2 ounces (½ stick) unsalted butter, cut up

Make the crust: In the bowl of a food processor, combine the dry ingredients: flour, oatmeal, sugar, baking powder, and salt, and process. Add the butter and process until the mixture resembles oatmeal.

Combine the ice water and the vinegar, pour into the food processor, and process again just long enough for the dough to form moist clumps. Remove the dough from the processor and knead briefly until the dough comes together into a smooth ball. Transfer the dough to a plastic zipper lock bag and shape into a flattened rectangle. Chill in the refrigerator 1 hour or in the freezer for 30 minutes until firm but still malleable. (The dough may be frozen up to 3 months, defrosting in the refrigerator before using.)

Roll out the dough on a lightly floured surface into a large round about 10-inches in diameter and about ⅜-inch thick. Transfer to a sheet of parchment or wax paper and refrigerate for at least 30 minutes or until firm.

Preheat the oven to 425°F.

Make the filling: In a large bowl, combine the orange juice and zest, marmalade, brandy, and the cloves. Peel and core the apples, then cut them into eighths. Add the apple wedges to the orange juice mixture and stir to combine.

Make the caramel: In a heavy, ovenproof (preferably cast-iron) 9-inch skillet over medium heat, cook the sugar and butter, stirring occasionally with a wooden spoon, until the sugar turns medium amber in color, about 6 minutes. Swirl the pan occasionally so the sugar colors evenly to a deep, rich brown with a hint of red. Immediately remove the pan from the heat.

Carefully (as the pan will be hot), arrange a ring of apple wedges laying on their sides and with their narrower core edges facing towards the center around the outside of the pan to make a border. Arrange more apples wedges neatly and tightly overlapping in a single layer of more or less concentric rings inside the border. (This layer will become the top when the tart is served.) Spoon the remaining apples and any juices over top, mounding the apples up in the middle. Place the pan back on the stove and cook over medium heat until the caramel is bubbling thickly, about 15 minutes, shaking gently once or twice to prevent burning. Remove from the heat and cool for about 10 minutes, or until the apples are no longer steaming, although still hot.

Drape the dough round over the fruit. Trim the pastry to about 1-inch over the edge with scissors or a paring knife. Allow the dough to soften slightly from the heat of the fruit, about 2 minutes, then tuck the edges down around the fruit. Cut several slits in the pastry to allow steam to escape. Place the pan on a baking pan to catch any drips and bake on the bottom shelf of the oven until the crust is golden and the filling is bubbling and thick, about 45 minutes.

Remove the tart from the oven and cover with a piece of aluminum foil. Place a plate smaller than the diameter of the skillet on top of the foil and weigh the plate down with one or two cans. Set the tart aside to cool for about 45 minutes, or until the tart is still warm but the fruit has set.

Remove the weight, plate, and foil, and cover the skillet with a large cake platter. Hold the skillet and the pan together and flip them over so the fruit is on top. Cut into portions and serve with a dollop of crème fraîche. This tart is best the day it is made.

OIL
FOR BAKING & FRYING

Baking with Oil . . . 580

Frying with Oil . . . 581

Italian Flour . . . 583

TARALLI: BOILED AND BAKED
"PRETZELS" FROM PUGLIA . . . 584

SPANISH HONEY-DIPPED SPIRAL
PASTRIES (HOJUELAS) . . . 585

KOURAMBIEDES WITH
OLIVE OIL . . . 586

TEIGLACH OR CICERCHIATA . . . 587

MARIA'S CUSCUROLS . . . 588

OILS
FOR BAKING & FRYING

BAKING WITH OIL

Because oil is liquid at room temperature, it cannot perform one of its main functions in cake batters: trapping small air bubbles when solid fat (butter) is creamed (or beaten until light and airy) with sugar, which then expand with heat, helping the product to rise. Oil will, however, tenderize batter and help keep it moist, so it is often used in fruity, dense, quick-breads and muffins that are leavened with baking powder, as in the Apple–Date Buckwheat Muffins (page 188) and the Morning Glory Muffins with Carrots, Asian Pears, and Ginger (page 240). Just remember that once the dry (flours) and wet (egg, buttermilk, oil, etc.) ingredients are combined, mixing must be kept to a minimum to prevent developing tough strands of gluten.

Fat tenderizes pastries when it is dispersed through the dough, allowing the small particles to coat the starch granules, keeping them separate and preventing gluten from forming. Pastry, especially puff pastry doughs, relies on fat to help separate the layers of gluten and starch formed in the dough. The fat melts as the pastry bakes, leaving minute air pockets. The liquid in the dough produces steam, which causes the layers to rise while evaporating, while the fat keeps the layers separate. In pie pastry, the same melting action produces a flaky crust. Because it is pure fat, oil doesn't produce any steam, so dough made with oil doesn't get flaky when baked, though it will be tender. (Knishes and borekas are often made with an oil–based dough.)

The ratio of fat to flour, whether the fat is solid or liquid, and if the fat and has not melted before you put it in the oven, influences whether or not you get a flaky pie crust, tender cake, or cookies that don't spread much when baked. Texture or mouthfeel is especially important in baking, where fats are required to produce a fluffy or flaky and tender product. In baking, fat acts both as a leavening agent (causing the dough to rise) and as a tenderizer by actually shortening the gluten strands in the dough.

In cakes, well-creamed fat creates small empty cell pockets, which hold the steam and the carbon dioxide produced by the reaction of the baking powder, allowing the cake to rise. Solid fats disperse easily throughout the batter, making for a smoother texture, while oil can result in baked goods with a grainy texture.

In the countries of the Mediterranean, where olive oil is produced, many pastries are made using this age-old fat, sometimes combined with butter. A mild tasting olive oil works well in many cake and pastry recipes. For frying, the International Olive Oil Institute recommends using what is now labeled simply as "olive oil." Once known as "pure olive oil," it is a combination of refined olive oil and virgin or extra-virgin oil. I often mix highly flavored extra-virgin olive oil with a more neutral oil for baking and frying. I also like to use sweet but mild grapeseed oil, which I'm able to buy at a reasonable price at my local Asian market. Otherwise, a neutral oil like canola or vegetable (usually soy) oil works best.

Cakes like the Florida Tangerine Kiss-Me Cake (page 602), dense with chopped raisins and oranges, is shortened with oil, as is the equally fruity (or vegetable-y) Indian-Spiced Carrot Cake (page 237). The "Indian Pudding" Cake (page 286) is leavened by the reaction of acidic buttermilk and molasses with basic (or alkaline) baking soda, but it gets it moistness from oil. In Italy, olive oil is added to cake batters, such as in the Torta Boscaiola: Italian Chestnut Flour and Hazelnut Cake (page 319), the Brustengolo: Umbrian Cornmeal, Pear, Raisin, and Nut Cake (page 389), and the Torta di Miele: Italian Jewish Honey Cake (page 522).

The simple, moist Spanish Orange and Olive Oil Cake (page 599) benefits from the addition of fruity green olive oil, which enhances its fruity character. The Greek Tahini Cake: Tahinopita (page 802) is shortened, not by olive oil, but with tahini paste, smooth and rich peanut butter–like mashed sesame seeds. Because oil is 100 percent fat, and butter is only about 80 percent fat (unless it is first clarified, see page 202), 20 percent less oil will achieve the same shortening effect.

Small amounts of oil often flavor, enrich, and tenderize breads, such as the olive oil added to the Greek Feta Cheese Bread: Tyropsomo (page 261), the Moroccan Sesame-Anise Bread (page 87), and the Fig and Pine Nut Bread (page 674). The Central European Sauerkraut Rye Bread (page 784) is enriched with vegetable or canola oil, while the Taralli: Boiled and Baked "Pretzels" (page 584) from Puglia get a good share of olive oil in the dough, so they are both crunchy and rich. The One-Bowl Hazelnut Cornmeal Biscotti (page 503) get their richness from a combination of intensely flavored hazelnut oil and mild grapeseed oil.

FRYING WITH OIL

I'm a big fan of baking with olive oil, probably because I love all the olive oil–based cuisines of North Africa, Southern France, Eastern Spain, Italy, Greece, Turkey, Israel and the surrounding region. In many of these places, people don't have ovens in their kitchens, or if they do, the ovens are really small. Only the local baker has a big oven. Instead, many traditional deep-fried pastries and other sweets have developed. While traveling through the olive oil-producing region of Kalamata, Greece, several years ago, I had the chance to taste some wonderful pastries made with local olive oil, including the rich and crumbly Kourambiedes with Olive Oil (page 586).

Also, through my ongoing research into my own Jewish culinary heritage, I have realized how important the art of frying has been in Jewish cuisine. There is a religious origin for the skill, but it is also based on historical limits to Jewish trades and on using the limited ingredients on hand. For the Feast of Lights, or Chanukah, celebrating the miracle of the oil that burned for eight days and nights, Jews all over the world prepare oil-fried foods. In India, the Bene Israel, said to be descendents of oil pressers from Galilee who survived a shipwreck somewhere in the Arabian Sea, prepared a special nut-and-fruit version of Kerala's neyyappam for the holiday.

One of the few trades permitted to Roman Jews in times past was as *friggitori*, cooks who specialized in frying small bits of foods. In the several thousand-year old Jewish community of Italy, *fritelle di riso*—rice, raisin, and pine nut fritters that remind me of New Orleans's Calas (page 773)—and anise and raisin dough dipped in honey syrup are prepared for Chanukah. Tunisian Jews make *yoyo*, fried ring-shaped doughnuts dipped into honey syrup that I happily munched on years ago from a street stand while hostelling in Paris.

The holiday is celebrated in Israel by frying *sufganiot* (jelly doughnuts). In this chapter, Spanish Honey-Dipped Spiral Pastries (Hojuelas) (page 585) and the fried bits of dough simmered in honey syrup and then formed into a decorative wreath known as *Teiglach* in Yiddish and *Cicerchiata* in Italian (page 587) are both deep-fried. In other chapters, Caribbean Plantain Empanadas filled with Black Beans (page 129) are fried, as are the Cigari Borekas with Moroccan Spiced Lamb (page 212).

If done properly, these crispy brown pastry treats can be as light as anything you can imagine. For deep-fat frying especially, it is important to use a fat with a high smoke point, as foods are best fried at temperatures between 365°F and 375°F. For best results, use a frying thermometer. Alternatively, wait until the oil is shimmering and feels hot when you (carefully) place your hand about 3 inches above it. At lower temperatures, the outside won't form a protective crust right away, so the food will absorb the fat and becomes greasy. At higher temperatures, the outside will darken too much before the inside is cooked through, and the oil will break down quickly, start smoking, and have to be replaced.

Less expensive, though more bland, refined oils, rather than cold-pressed virgin oils, are highly filtered and work best for deep-frying. Cold-pressed oils, which are more flavorful, are best for pastries. Unrefined oils also have low smoke points, so they can't be used for deep-frying. Cold-pressed oils should always be stored in a cool, dark place, though not the refrigerator, because they are less stable than refined oil and will get rancid more easily.

Refined (not extra-virgin) olive oil, peanut, and soy oil (often bottled as vegetable oil) all start to smoke at about 450°F and are good choices for deep-frying. Refined canola oil can get even hotter: 460°F. Grapeseed oil starts to break down at 420°F (a good choice, but perhaps too expensive) so it can be used for frying, while the rice bran oil found in Asian markets can get as hot as 490°F before it starts to smoke.

When frying in oil, always use a pot that is large enough to contain the layers of bubbles that form as the food fries without pouring out of the pot. The standard steel wok I bought in Chinatown works best for me, because you don't need much oil to get a good depth. The metal is an excellent heat conductor so the oil heats quickly. An electric deep-fryer is another good choice, though more difficult to clean. I also use a heavy, splayed pot (called a Windsor) that has more volume at the top, to allow for bubbling up and less at the bottom, so you don't need as much oil.

At the "flash" point, about 600°F for oil, tiny wisps of flame will appear on the surface of the oil. At the burning point, about 700°F, the oil will ignite. If your oil does ignite, do not attempt to put it out with water. The oxygen in the water will just spread the fire. Instead, smother the fire with a tight-fitting lid or suffocate it with baking soda. I remember heating a French omelet pan for too long on my old, unfortunately electric, stove. All of a sudden, I heard a sound like an explosion. I looked over at the stove and the whole pan of oil was burning! What to do? I didn't have a handy box of baking soda, so I gingerly moved the pot to my enamel sink and let it burn out. Now I keep a big box of baking soda right near my stove, just in case.

Note that the smoke point of any oil decreases with use. I do save and filter oil that I have used for deep-frying. But I always combine used oil with at least an equal quantity of new oil. To filter frying oil, allow it to cool somewhat, until it is still rather hot and thin, but not dangerous to handle. Carefully pour the oil through a paper towel or a large paper coffee filter placed inside a sieve or china cap (a perforated metal cone commonly used in restaurants) to hold it in place over a completely dry container. (You don't want to have any water in the frying oil, because it pops and spatters.)

ITALIAN FLOUR

In Italy, flour is classified as 1, 0, or 00, depending on how finely it is ground and how much of the bran and germ have been removed. *Doppio zero* (double zero) is the most highly refined, and is talcum-powder soft, basically equivalent to American unbleached all-purpose flour. Higher protein flours may also be milled to 00 fineness, but if suitable for making bread, it will be labeled as *panifiable* (can be made into bread).

In the original Italian recipe for the taralli, 00 flour from Italy was specified. I made two batches that were exactly the same except for the difference of the flour, one with unbleached American all-purpose flour and the second with imported Italian 00.

While both worked well, the 00 batch was definitely lighter in texture and easier to roll out. You can find 00 flour, sometimes called pizza or pasta flour, at many Italian gourmet or specialty shops. There are also numerous online sources, such as Todaro Brothers (www.todarobros.com), which sells the flour in large quantities, and will ship to any location in the United States.

Taralli: Boiled and Baked "Pretzels" from Puglia

Taralli are crunchy, ring-shaped biscuits that are boiled, then baked, like an Italian pretzel. They are common to several regions of southern Italy, but are taken to another level in Puglia, where bread is revered. Taralli al Finocchio are a popular version, flavored with toasted fennel seed, but they may also be flavored with hot pepper flakes, garlic, oregano, cheese, and black pepper. What makes taralli so irresistible is the fruity, slightly burning taste of their most important ingredient, extra-virgin olive oil. With groves of more than 50 million olive trees, some dating as far back as 5000 BCE, Puglia annually produces more than 200 million liters of some of the finest extra-virgin olive oils in the world. Do not be afraid of the wetness of the dough. Just flour your board and your hands well and it will roll out easily with a light touch. This recipe is dairy-free.

YIELD: 6 TO 8 DOZEN SMALL "PRETZELS"

1 ($\frac{1}{4}$-ounce) package (2$\frac{1}{4}$ teaspoons) active dry yeast

$\frac{1}{2}$ cup dry white wine, lukewarm

$\frac{1}{2}$ cup water, lukewarm

$\frac{3}{4}$ pound (3 cups minus 3 tablespoons) all-purpose flour

$\frac{1}{2}$ pound (1$\frac{1}{4}$ cups plus 1 tablespoon) fine semolina

$\frac{1}{2}$ cup extra-virgin olive oil

1 teaspoon fine sea salt

2 tablespoons fennel seeds, lightly crushed

OR 1 tablespoon cracked black pepper plus 1 tablespoon granulated garlic

OR 1 tablespoon crushed red pepper flakes plus 1 tablespoon dried oregano

In the bowl af a standing mixer fitted with the paddle attachment, scatter the yeast over the wine and water and set aside to proof for about 10 minutes, until the mixture is bubbly. Stir to mix well. Beat in the flour, semolina, oil, and salt. Switch to the dough hook attachment, and continue beating until the dough is smooth and elastic about 5 minutes. Add the fennel seeds (or alternate flavorings) and beat briefly to combine. Transfer the dough to a large oiled bowl; turn it around so the dough is oiled all over. Cover with plastic wrap or a damp cloth and allow the dough to rise at warm room temperature until doubled in size, about 2 hours.

Punch the dough down and divide it into 60 to 72 small pieces. Roll each piece into a long, slim pencil about the thickness of your pinky. Cut it into 3-inch lengths and bring the two ends together to form a doughnut-like shape, pressing the ends firmly together.

Preheat the oven to 375°F. Bring a pot of salted water to a rolling boil and drop the taralli in, a few at a time. When they float to the top, scoop them from the water and arrange them on a clean kitchen towel to dry.

Place the drained taralli on a baking pan lined with parchment paper or a silicone baking mat and bake for 35 minutes or until golden brown and crisp. Store in a cookie tin or other airtight container at room temperature for up to two weeks.

Spanish Honey–Dipped Spiral Pastries (Hojuelas)

Arranged in a big bowl, these crunchy pastries look like big flower blossoms. To make them, long strips of thin, leaf-like dough are deep fried, rolled up and dipped in honey syrup, then sprinkled with sesame seeds. Some also sprinkle them with cinnamon and chopped walnuts. Their name in Spanish means "leaves," because of the thinness of the dough. These pastries are made for celebrations. I served them at a New Year's party and they were gone in an instant. Hojuelas are a specialty of Jews of Spanish/Sephardic origin in the countries of their diaspora, including Colombia, Venezuela, and Turkey. They are also made in Greece where they are known as diples. While one person can both roll and fry the pastries (as I did for testing), it's easiest if one person rolls and cuts the strips and another person fries them. This recipe is dairy-free.

YIELD: ABOUT 24 PASTRIES

Dough

1³/₄ pounds (6¹/₂ cups minus 1 tablespoon) unbleached all-purpose flour

¹/₂ teaspoon fine sea salt

¹/₂ cup orange juice

¹/₄ cup lemon juice

Zest of 1 lemon (1 tablespoon)

³/₄ cup olive oil

Syrup

1 cup sugar

1 cup honey

1 cinnamon stick, crushed

Assembly

6 cups mild olive oil, or olive oil plus canola, soy, or peanut oil, for frying

¹/₂ cup white sesame seeds

Make the dough: In the bowl of a standing mixer fitted with the paddle attachment, combine the flour, salt, orange juice, lemon juice, lemon zest, olive oil, and 1 cup of water, and beat until the dough is smooth. Cover with plastic wrap and allow the dough to rest at room temperature for 30 minutes (it will soften).

Make the syrup: In a medium saucepan over medium heat, combine the sugar, honey, 1 cup of water, and cinnamon, bring to a boil, skimming off and discarding the white foam. Remove from the heat and set aside to cool. Strain the syrup into a medium bowl.

To shape the pastries, you'll need to work with pieces of dough about the size of a small fist. Using a pasta machine or a rolling pin, roll out the dough into long strips, about 2 feet long. Sprinkle the dough with flour, if necessary, to keep it dry. Using a fluted pastry wheel, trim the edges then cut the strips lengthwise into 2-inch wide strips. Arrange the strips on a work surface sprinkled with flour, to keep them from sticking to each other.

Preheat 4 cups of the oil to 365°F or until the oil is shimmering and feels hot when you place your hand about 3 inches above it. (Add more oil as needed.) Loop the dough loosely around your four fingers to make spirals, pressing the end of the strip firmly against the spiral so it adheres well. Drop the spirals one at a time into the oil without crowding. The dough will inevitably start to uncurl as it fries. Use a pair of tongs to press the uncurled end back into shape. When the pastries are lightly golden on all sides, after about 5 minutes, remove them from the oil and drain on a wire rack. (This method makes slightly heavier pastries but is faster.)

Alternatively, loop one end of a strip of dough in between the tines of a large metal serving fork to secure it in place. Holding the opposite end of the strip in your other hand and supporting it over your arm, place the fork-wrapped end into the oil and fry until light brown. Roll the fried end of the dough one or two turns on the fork, allowing another portion of the dough strip to dip into the oil, frying until the dough is light brown . Continue frying and rolling until the strip has been completely fried and rolled up into a spiral, pressing the end of the dough against the spiral to prevent it from unraveling. Turn the spiral of fried dough over once so that it browns evenly. Repeat, rolling and frying another strip of dough. (This method yields a lighter pastry, because the fried dough rolls up loosely, but it takes more time and a bit more skill to do.) Drain the fried spirals on a wire rack placed over a baking pan to catch the drips, or on paper towels.

One by one, dip the fried hojuelas into the syrup, then sprinkle with sesame seeds. Serve warm or at room temperature. Store up to 1 week at room temperature, covered.

Kourambiedes with Olive Oil

I first tasted these tender, crumbly cookies made with fruity olive oil while visiting an olive oil press in the Kalamata region of Greece, where the pointy-ended purple Kalamata olives come from as well as lots of high-quality olive oil. Because no air is whipped into the dough, baking soda and baking powder help leaven the cookies. Similar to Mexican wedding cookies and Russian tea kisses, these cookies are also made with almonds and olive oil, giving them Mediterranean flavors. Kourambiedes are served in the Greek community at Christmas and other festive occasions. Each cookie is studded with a whole clove as a symbol of the Magi's gift of spices to the newborn baby Jesus. Kourambiedes freeze very well, so you can double the recipe and make the cookies as needed. They also make a good holiday gift. This recipe is dairy-free.

YIELD: 3 DOZEN COOKIES

$3/4$ pound ($2^3/4$ cups plus 1 tablespoon) unbleached
   all-purpose flour

½ pound (1¾ cups) blanched almonds

1 teaspoon baking powder

½ teaspoon baking soda

½ teaspoon fine sea salt

¼ teaspoon ground cloves

1 cup extra virgin olive oil

¾ cup sugar

¼ cup brandy

Juice and grated zest of 1 lemon
   (3 tablespoons juice, 1 tablespoon zest)

Whole cloves, for garnish

Confectioners' sugar, for dusting

Preheat the oven to 350°F. Line two 18 x 13-inch half sheet pans (or other large baking pans) with parchment paper or silicone baking mats.

In the bowl of a food processor, combine the flour, almonds, baking powder, baking soda, salt, and ground cloves, and process until finely ground, working in two batches if necessary.

In the bowl of a standing mixer fitted with the paddle attachment, combine the oil, sugar, brandy, lemon juice and zest, and beat to combine. Add the flour mixture, beating only until a dough ball forms. (The dough should be firm.)

Scoop or spoon the dough into small balls. Squeeze each ball in your hand to form points at either end, then shape into a fat crescent. Arrange the crescents equidistant and about 1½ inches apart on the prepared baking pans. Stick a whole clove in the center of each cookie.

Bake for 15 to 18 minutes or until very lightly colored. Cool to room temperature in the pan on a wire rack,

then sift confectioners' sugar generously over the cookies. Store at room temperature in a cookie jar or other covered container up to 1 week.

Teiglach or Cicerchiata

Teiglach *comes from the Yiddish meaning "little bits of dough." This dessert originated in Italy where it is called,* cicerchiata, *from the word for "little bits of chickpeas." They are small, fried bits of puffy pasta-like egg dough, that are simmered in honey syrup with toasted nuts and/or raisins. Brought by Jewish traders from Italy to Central europe where they were renamed Teiglach, they are traditionally eaten for celebratory occasions, including Rosh Hashanah, Sukkot, Simchat Torah, Purim, weddings, and births. This festive teiglach is similar in nature to the French* croquembouche, *though it is made in the shape of a crown, not a mountain. It is a spectacular centerpiece with its clusters of dough and nuts, and is totally addictive. This recipe is dairy-free.*

YIELD: 1 LARGE RING, 12 TO 16 SERVINGS

Dough

½ pound (2 cups minus 2 tablespoons) unbleached
   all-purpose flour

½ teaspoon fine sea salt

3 large eggs, slightly beaten

Flour, for dusting

3 cups olive oil, grapeseed oil, or canola oil

Syrup

1 1/2 cups honey

5 unces (1 cup) hazelnuts, lightly toasted, skinned, and
   coarsely chopped

Grated zest of 1 lemon (1 tablespoon)

1 tablespoon fresh lemon juice

Colorful candy sprinkles, for decoration

Make the dough: Spray a large pizza pan with nonstick baker's coating, or rub with oil.

In the bowl of a standing mixer fitted with the paddle attachment, combine the flour, salt, and eggs, and beat until combined into a soft dough. Turn the dough out onto a floured surface and knead until smooth, about 5 minutes. Shape it into a ball, flatten it with your hands and sprinkle it lightly with flour. Roll the dough out to a rectangle about 1/4-inch thick. Using a sharp knife or a pizza cutter, cut into thin strips (about 1/4-inch wide) and dredge the strips in flour. Cut the strips cross-wise into chickpea-size bits and dredge again with flour to prevent them from sticking to each other.

In a wok, a large heavy-duty frying pan, preferably cast-iron, or an electric deep-fryer, heat the oil to 365°F, or until shimmering hot and the air above the pot feels hot when you hold your hand about 3 inches above the oil. Scoop up the dough bits into a large sieve and shake to remove excess flour.

Drop a handful of the dough bits into the oil and fry until golden, stirring so they cook evenly. They will puff up. Fry until light golden brown, about 4 minutes. Scoop from the oil using a slotted spoon or a wire skimmer. Drain on paper towels and cool to room temperature. Repeat with the remaining dough bits.

Make the syrup: In a large, heavy-bottomed pot, bring the honey to a boil and cook over moderately high heat for 3 minutes or until slightly thickened. Add all the dough balls, the hazelnuts, lemon zest, and lemon juice. Reduce the heat and cook 6 minutes longer, stirring constantly, or until the syrup has darkened slightly and has mostly been absorbed.

Pour the hot dough and nut mixture into the pizza pan and allow the mixture to cool until it can be handled. Shape the mixture into an open circle, using heat-proof gloves, or lightly oiled hands and a wooden spoon or silicone spatula. While still warm sprinkle with colorful candy sprinkles and allow the teiglach to cool thoroughly at room temperature (it will harden a little).

Eat by breaking off pieces with your fingers or by cutting it into 2-inch segments. Store, covered and at room temperature for up to three days.

Maria's Cuscurols

A Portuguese home-cook's specialty, the delectably light and crispy dough triangles known as cuscarols are fried, drained, and then sprinkled with cinnamon sugar. It is a testament to my long-term friendship with Maria Mata, an excellent cook, that she was willing to share this recipe with me. Although her friends have been begging her for it for years, she always puts them off, saying, "I don't have it right now. I'll have to get it to you." As Maria does, you may double the batch of dough, freezing half for up to three months. "These always come out so good," says Maria, and she is so right! We couldn't stop ourselves from grabbing just one more. . . . The secret is her use of beer for lightness and a few spoons of port wine for flavor and a bit of tang. This recipe is dairy-free.

YIELD: 3 DOZEN CUSCUROLS

1 pound (3³/₄ cups) unbleached all-purpose flour

1 teaspoon baking powder

1 teaspoon fine sea salt

³/₄ cup beer, lukewarm

2 ounces (¹/₂ stick) unsalted butter,
    melted and cooled

1 large egg

2 tablespoons port wine

Grated zest of 1 lemon (1 tablespoon)

1 quart olive oil, peanut oil, or vegetable oil,
    for frying

1 cup sugar

1 teaspoon ground cinnamon

In the bowl of a standing mixer fitted with the whisk attachment, combine the dry ingredients: flour, baking powder, and salt.

In a medium bowl, whisk together the beer, butter, egg, wine, and lemon zest.

Switch the attachment on the mixer to the paddle attachment. Add the beer mixture to the bowl and beat until the dough is smooth, about 5 minutes. Allow the dough to rest at room temperature for about 10 minutes to relax the gluten.

Turn the dough out onto a lightly floured work surface and roll it out into thin sheets. Cut the dough sheets into rough triangles, about 3 to 4 inches on a side. Cut two parallel slits in the center of each triangle, leaving a border about 1-inch all around.

In a wok, a large heavy-duty frying pan, preferably cast-iron, or an electric deep-fryer, heat the oil to 365°F, or until shimmering hot, and the air above the pot feels hot when you hold your hand about 3 inches above the oil. Place about six of the dough triangles into the oil, one at a time. Fry them for 3 to 4 minutes, or until golden brown. Drain on a wire rack over a baking pan to catch any drips. Keep warm in a 200°F oven until all the dough has been fried.

Combine the sugar and cinnamon. Place the cuscurols in a large bowl and dust generously with the cinnamon sugar. Serve immediately while still hot. Store the cuscarols (if they last that long) covered and at room temperature for up to three days.

ORANGES & TANGERINES

Orange Varieties . . . 594

Buying and Storing Oranges . . . 597

Cutting an Orange . . . 597

Tangerines . . . 597

Preparing Tangerines . . . 598

Buying and Storing Tangerines . . . 599

SPANISH ORANGE AND OLIVE OIL CAKE . . . 599

MINNEOLA ORANGE TART . . . 600

ORANGE OR TANGERINE CARAMEL SAUCE . . . 601

FLORIDA TANGERINE KISS-ME CAKE . . . 602

MALTESE KWARESIMAL COOKIES . . . 603

Blood Oranges in Malta . . . 604

TANGERINE SEMOLINA TORTA . . . 605

ORANGES & TANGERINES

Anyone who has read M.F.K. Fisher's *The Art of Eating* can almost taste the sections of tangerines that Fisher dried in her small apartment on Strasbourg's Boulevard de l'Orangerie. "In the morning, in the soft sultry chamber, sit in the window peeling tangerines, three or four. Peel them gently; do no bruise them. . . . Separate each plump little pregnant crescent. . . ." Handling a vibrantly-colored orange or a brilliant tangerine while lightly scratching its oily surface to release its sunny fragrance brightens my mood in the short days of winter, when citrus fruits are at their best. When flying, I always carry an orange or two in my bag, because the fruits keep so well and don't bruise, providing a welcome fresh taste and therapeutic aroma in the miserably stale, dead air.

Wild oranges probably originated in China and India, but the earliest citrus fruits in China were actually mandarins or tangerines. The sour orange was the first orange to arrive in the West and by the eleventh century was already thriving (as it still does) in Sicily. Also known as the Seville oranges, they were cultivated near Seville, Spain by the end of the twelfth century. For 500 years, the sour orange was the only orange in Europe

and the first orange to reach the New World. Sir Walter Raleigh took sour orange seeds to England to plant in Surrey. The trees began bearing fruit in 1595, but were killed by cold in 1739. Soon, due to increased trade with Southern Europe, strange and exotic fruits like oranges, lemons, and even pomegranates began to reach the England. In Victorian times, poor children in England would dream of getting a golden orange as a Christmas present, although they had probably never tasted one before. Because a vast network of national and international transportation means that they are available, though not necessarily at their best, throughout the year, these days we tend to take oranges and other citrus fruits for granted.

After Portuguese explorers discovered the sea route around the Cape of Good Hope past South Africa in 1498, they established several colonies in India, where they learned to eat oranges. In the early sixteenth century, Portuguese explorer Vasco da Gama brought a single orange tree root from China to Portugal, which is thought to be the forbear of all the oranges of Portugal, Spain, France, and even Israel.

On his second voyage to the New World in

1493, Christopher Columbus brought orange, lemon and citron seeds to Haiti. Spanish explorer Ponce de Leon brought oranges and lemons to Florida in 1513. By 1656, oranges were being raised in Florida, but the trees were destroyed by soldiers during the first Seminole War. By 1739, orange grew in Baja California and they reached Hawaii in 1792. The orange was naturalized in Mexico by 1568 and in Brazil by 1587. Oranges were first cultivated in South Africa in 1654 and in Australia after 1788.

Long the only orange known in Europe, the bitter orange, *Citrus aurantium*, has very sour juice and highly aromatic zest. Neroli oil, used in many perfumes and as a flavoring in baking, is distilled from its fragile blossoms. Neroli gets its name from Anne Marie Orsini, princess of Nerola, a small town near Rome, Italy who, towards the end of the seventeenth century, made this essence a fashionable fragrance. Marmalade, used in the Orange Blossom Brioches (page 470) takes advantage of the abundant pectin contained in the bitter orange's pulpy white, bitter pith and its many seeds.

The plump, rounded sweet orange, *Citrus sinensis*, is full of sweet-tart, juicy, bright-orange flesh that can be squeezed for its juice or cut into slices or sections for use in baking. Brought to Europe from India by Portuguese traders in the fifteenth century, the sweet orange quickly displaced the bitter, and is now the most common type of orange. The ancient name orange derives from the Sanskrit word *naranga*, very close to the Spanish *naranja* of today. Today, two-thirds of the world's oranges are grown in Brazil, Florida and California, with Spain also a significant producer.

Because of climate and soil differences, the same orange variety grown in Florida or in California will differ in color, skin thickness, juiciness, and acidity. Sweeter Florida oranges have thin orange to yellow skins, often marked with blemishes, and sometimes exhibiting a greenish cast. Though not beauty queens, their juicy, easy-to-squeeze flesh makes them excellent for juicing. Firmer, more acidic California oranges are usually solid orange in color, because they are grown in a drier climate with cooler nights. With their thick skin and pulpier flesh, they are best suited to eating out of hand or cutting into sections for fruit salad or garnish.

Throughout the Mediterranean, the fragrant oils in the orange's skin are an essential flavoring for cakes, cookies, and pastry doughs like the Biscotti Rococò (page 536), the Tarte aux Pêches (French Baked Peach Tart) (page 619), the Greek Tahini Cake (Tahinopita) (page 802), and the Torta di Zucca (Squash Cake with Pine Nuts and Apricots) (page 741).

When it comes time for dessert, beautifully cut suprêmes of orange–the French way of sectioning citrus fruits, leaving only the sections of shiny, juicy brightly colored fruit–make a beautiful garnish. Easiest to cut from with seedless navel oranges, I use these colorful sections in the Chocolate Torte with Orange and Pistachio (page 697), the almondy Tangerine Semolina Torta (page 605), the Spanish Orange and Olive Oil Cake (page

599), and the Ruby Grapefruit–Orange Brazil Nut Torte (page 174). The Orange Caramel Sauce made from cooked-down orange (or tangerine) juice with its zest and sugar can be drizzled over the Ruby Grapefruit–Orange Brazil Nut Torte, or the Italian Bittersweet Chocolate–Orange Torta (page 331). The chunky, fruity Florida Tangerine Kiss–Me Cake (page 602), made with a whole ground tangerine, is a good make-ahead cake that will last at least a week. The Maltese Kwaresimal Cookies (page 603), made ideally with the tart blood-red oranges for which the island of Malta is famed, shows the influence of nearby Sicily, where quaresemali biscotti (page 489) are also made. When you have lots of oranges, don't make orangeade, or rather do make it with the juice, but save the skins including white pith to make your own Candied Citrus Peel (page 225).

ORANGE VARIETIES

CARA CARA ORANGE: These oranges originated at the Hacienda de Cara Cara in Venezuela. They have orangey-pink skins and pink to raspberry-colored flesh and are usually seedless. Their sweet flavor has a definite undertone of grapefruit bitterness. Cara Caras are in season from late December through March from specialty growers.

CLEMENTINE: The early-maturing sweet Clementine, the fruit of a variety of mandarin named in 1902, is especially popular in North Africa. This small orange is thought to be a natural mutation discovered by a monk in Algeria named Father Clement, who tended a garden of mandarin trees in the orphanage of Misserghim and named it the "clementino." Others believe that the fruits, which are virtually identical to the Canton mandarin, originated in China and eventually found their way to the Mediterranean.

These small easily-peeled and usually seedless oranges were first brought to the United States in 1902, but didn't gain popularity until 1997 when a devastating freeze in Florida made domestic oranges scarce and expensive. Clementines are in season from the end of October through February, but are quite perishable. Separated into their natural sections and with any extraneous strands of white pith removed, Clementines make a lovely fresh garnish for cakes.

JAFFA ORANGE: These oval-shaped oranges are sweet and tangy in flavor with a strong aroma. Their thin, smooth, yellow-orange peel is easy to remove and their flesh has concentrated nectar-like juices. The first fruits to carry the name Jaffa orange, known as the Shamouti among Arab residents of the region, came from the agricultural colony of Sarona established 1871 in Israel. The Jaffa orange was developed by Jewish and Palestinian growers from the Baladi, a small, round and bittersweet orange thought to be the first variety to arrive in the region following the Arab conquest in the seventh century.

By the time of Napoleon's invasion of the land of Israel in 1799, Jaffa's citrus orchards were already famed for the quality of their oranges. (See *City of Oranges: An Intimate History of Arabs and Jews in Jaffa* by Adam LeBor to learn about the history of these oranges and the growers in the region.) The Jaffa was introduced into Texas in 1883 from Palestine and is considered by some, but not all, to be a blood orange. Those grown in the cooler winter in Texas tend to have flecks of red pigment and light colored flesh.

NAVEL ORANGE: In 1820, a single mutation in an orchard of sweet oranges planted at a monastery in Brazil yielded the navel orange, also known as the Washington, Riverside, or Bahia navel. The mutation causes navel oranges to develop a tiny secondary conjoined twin orange at the blossom end of the original fruit. From the outside, the smaller undeveloped twin at the bottom of the fruit recalls the human navel. Now the most important eating orange in the world, the tart full-bodied navel orange thrives in the Mediterranean, Australia, California, and Argentina. Navel oranges mature early, are usually large and seedless, easy to peel, and easy to segment. California navels are somewhat more acidic and flavorful than those grown in Florida but have thicker and sometimes hard to peel skin. Navel oranges are best suited for eating out of hand or sectioning. Once squeezed, their juice quickly turns bitter, even when refrigerated. American navels are in season November through April. The sweet, low acid Chinese navel orange is grown in California mostly for export to Hong Kong.

SEVILLE, BIGARADE, OR BITTER ORANGE: Seville oranges have thick, rough skin and extremely tart, bitter flesh that is full of seeds. Because of their high acid content and the generous amounts of pectin contained in their white pith and seeds, Sevilles are favored for marmalades as well as liqueurs like Curaçao and Cointreau. Most of Spain's Seville orange crop is shipped to Britain to be cooked into thick, chunky marmalade. Seville oranges are also raised in Florida. In season from December through April, they can be found in Latin American markets.

VALENCIA ORANGE: The Valencia, which came from the Azores and probably originated in Portugal, has a thin rind that is easiest to peel when the fruits are mature. Medium to large in size, it is noted for its plentiful, deeply-colored juice, and few seeds. Valencias leads production in California and Florida, accounting for about half the orange crop each year. Florida Valencias are considered the best juice oranges. Valencias are in season March through June.

BLOOD ORANGES: Though I expected the tall dark red glass of juice to be tomato, instead it was squeezed from blood oranges. My first sip of blood orange juice at a hotel on the Italian Adriatic Coast turned me into a lover of these dark-streaked, extra-tangy fruits. As a chef, I began buying Sicilian blood oranges in the late 1970s, when they were rare and quite expensive but essential to my authentic Italian menu. With their outstanding flavor and distinctive red color, blood oranges are especially popular in Italy as juice and in desserts. Try using them in the Spanish Orange and Olive Oil Cake (page 599), the Maltese Kwaresimal Cookies (page 603), or the Tangerine Semolina Torta (page 605).

The first blood oranges started appearing in Sicily in the seventeenth century, perhaps due to a mutation that produced their sunset-colored flesh and skin. In Great Britain, the fruits are known as Maltese oranges, because they also grew on this island long ruled by Britain and may have originated there concurrently, as it is close to Sicily. Blood oranges are grown in large quantities in Sicily for local use and for export. The most popular varieties are the Tarocco, the Moro, and the Sanguinaccio.

All blood oranges tend to contain few seeds, with more or less red-pigmented peel and flesh. The red pigmentation varies with climate and is most apparent when the fruits grow in regions where the days are hot and the nights are cold. Their red color comes from anthocyanin, which is not typically found in citrus, but is abundant in blueberries and blackberries and other red fruits.

Spanish and Italian immigrants first brought blood oranges to North America but Americans were squeamish about their bloody color and wouldn't buy them. Only within the last decade or so have these colorful fruits caught on in America. They are now imported, especially from Sicily, but also from Spain, and are grown domestically, The best-known varieties include the rounded Moro, the slightly elongated Tarocco (named for its resemblance to a child's toy top), and the egg-shaped darkest red

Sanguinaccio (bloody one). The Moro and Sanguinaccio are usually seedless and most intensely colored, while the Ruby is lightly flecked and has seeds.

Although the varieties may be the same, blood oranges from Sicily tend to have deeper reddish orange coloring and are both more tart and more sweet than oranges from Florida, California or Texas due to geography, storage and/or handling. California blood oranges resemble small navels with smooth, thick peel and deep, blood-red color. The Ruby, Moro and Tarocco grow in Florida, although red coloration is reduced because of its steady warm, humid climate. Coastal southern California blood oranges ripen from February to May, November to February in the low desert and February to May in the northern coast. Gulf Coast and Texas fruits ripen from December to March. In Florida, Moros begin their season in October. Ruby and Moro ripen from late November to early January, while the Sanguinaccio matures in February or March.

VOLCANO ORANGE®: The red-orange Tarocco, sold in America as the Volcano orange, has been recognized by the European Union with the "Indicazione Geografica Protetta" (geographically protected variety) and are raised only on the slopes of the Sicily's volcano, Mount Etna. These deep red oranges are sweet and juicy with a distinct flavor They are prized for the color and flavor of their juice, especially for spremuta or fresh-squeezed red orange juice, sold in glass bottles in the United States. Volcano oranges come into season in mid-March. Look for the juice and the fruits at specialty stores.

BUYING AND STORING ORANGES

Oranges are always picked when they are ripe and do not ripen once picked. Each type of orange will be at its best at the midpoint of its growing season. Choose firm oranges with thinner skin that are heavy for their size as these will be the juiciest. Brown streaks or spots don't affect quality flavor or texture. Juice oranges generally have smoother skin than thicker "chicken-skinned" Navels. Some oranges, especially those grown in Florida, are colored with vegetable dye, though this is not permitted in California or Arizona. Florida oranges are often slightly greenish; California oranges are usually solid orange in color. Although ripe, the skin color may revert back to green if there are blossoms on the tree at the same time as the fruit, in a natural process called re-greening. These oranges may actually be sweeter because they are extra-ripe.

Oranges keep well for up to two weeks in the refrigerator but they keep almost as well at room temperature without wrapping. For this reason, I almost always carry along an orange or two in my travel food emergency kit. Oranges will also yield more juice at room temperature. Do not store in a closed or unperforated plastic bag, because the moisture trapped inside encourages the growth of mold. Remove and discard any oranges with mold so it doesn't spread to the rest of the fruit.

Although oranges from somewhere in the world are to be found in the supermarket produce aisle all year round, the American crop starts appearing in October and runs through the end of March or beginning of April. Florida oranges are in season from November through May, California and Arizona oranges are in season from December through May.

CUTTING AN ORANGE

Halve unpeeled oranges crosswise for juicing. For garnishing, halve an orange "through the poles," then cut each half crosswise into thin wedges. To cut an orange into skinless slices or sections, or *à vif* (to the quick) in the French phrase, cut a round of peel from the top and bottom so the flesh is exposed. Cut slices of peel longitudinally from top to bottom through to the flesh. For orange rings, slice the peeled fruit crosswise. For sections, run a thin, sharp knife along the sides of dividing membranes to the core; twist the knife at the core to release the sections, working over a bowl to catch the juices.

TANGERINES

Tangerines, *Citrus reticulata*, are more squat in shape than oranges, with tangy, faintly bitter, juicy flesh and highly perfumed skin. All tangerines have easily peelable zipper skin attached to the flesh with a net-like membrane, *reticulata* in Latin, and can easily be pulled apart into segments. Often more deeply colored than oranges, tangerines are full of abundant juices with a concentrated flavor. Lately, I've been happily buying tangerine juice, which seems to be a new product on the market, and wonderful to use in baking recipes. And, I never miss the chance to grate off the oily, intensely colored zest to add to cookies, cakes, and other batters.

The first tangerines were being grown in the United States by the 1840s, and were all known then as mandarins, referring to their origin in China. The newer name tangerine originated toward the end of the nineteenth century, when mandarins, which were thought to come from Tangiers in Morocco, started to become more common.

Confusingly, all tangerines are mandarins, but not all mandarins are tangerines. Some of these fruits are still known as mandarins (especially those all-too-familiar peeled segments found in small cans and on top of salads in just about every chain restaurant.) Unlike tangerines, mandarins have light orange-colored, smooth skin with few seeds and mild, sweet, though rather unexciting, flavor. The wild citrus fruit, from which mandarins are descended, probably grew in northeast India, where wild mandarins are still found. Mandarins were already being cultivated in China thousands of years ago, but it was not until 1804 that they fruit was first carried from China as far as England and became known as the mandarin orange.

Satsumas, which were developed in Japan in the sixteenth century, are sometimes placed in a separate species, *Citrus unshiu*. Tangors, *Citrus x nobilis*, like the Temple Orange and the Honey Murcott, are a cross between tangerines and oranges that tend to be large, rounder in shape, and similar, though sweeter, than oranges.

Tangelos, *Citrus x paradisi x Citrus reticulata*, are a tangy, sweet-tart hybrid of grapefruit and tangerine developed by the U. S. Department of Agriculture and released in 1931 that include the Minneola and the Honeybell. Prized for their extra juicy, nearly pulpless flesh, these fruits have a distinctive hump resembling a fat little nose at their stem end. Minneolas are a personal favorite of mine with full-bodied, concentrated flavor that really shines when used in baking. I buy as many as I can of these extremely juicy oranges with their sweetly fragrant zest for eating out of hand and for desserts like the Minneola Orange Tart with Orange Caramel Sauce (page 600). Minneolas are in season from mid-December through April, though the choice Minneolas known as Honeybells are only in season in January and February, and often sold by mail-order from specialty growers.

PREPARING TANGERINES

If peeling the tangerine, make sure to remove the oily zest first for later use. Most tangerines are full of seeds. To remove them, cut a small slit in the inside center of each segment and squeeze out the seeds that surround the opening. Alternatively, cut the tangerine in half through its equator, exposing the seeds. Use the tip of a sharp knife to pick out the seeds.

Spanish Orange and Olive Oil Cake

Spain is a major world grower of the two main ingredients in this cake: oranges and olives. In Spain, oranges flavor all sorts of desserts, including flan (baked caramel-topped custard), cakes with almonds, and tarts. In Moorish-influenced Andalusia, mermelada de naranja ácida—*marmalade made from the region's bitter or Seville oranges—is used for its body and intense bittersweet flavor in desserts and savory dishes. This moist, syrupy cake of Sephardic Jewish origin became a big hit when made with almond milk and baked in the shape of a Star of David at Max and David's (www.maxanddavids.com), the kosher restaurant for which I designed the menu.*

YIELD: ONE 8-INCH CAKE, 10 TO 12 SERVINGS

Cake
7 ounces (2 cups) unbleached all-purpose flour

$1/2$ teaspoon baking powder

$1/2$ teaspoon baking soda

teaspoon fine sea salt

3 large eggs, separated

$1^1/4$ cups sugar

1 cup milk, substitute almond milk

$1/2$ cup extra-virgin olive oil

Grated zest of 1 orange (4 teaspoons)

Syrup
2 oranges

$1^1/2$ cups orange juice

$1^1/2$ cups sugar

Make the cake: Preheat the oven to 350°F. Spray an 8-inch cake pan with nonstick baker's coating, or rub with softened butter or oil and dust with flour, shaking off the excess.

Whisk together the dry ingredients: flour, baking powder, baking soda, and salt.

In the bowl of a standing mixer fitted with the paddle attachment, beat the egg yolks with $1/2$ cup of the sugar until light and fluffy, 5 to 6 minutes.

In a bowl or quart-size measuring cup, whisk

together the milk, olive oil, and orange zest. Add to the egg yolk mixture and beat to combine. Add the flour mixture, beating just long enough to combine.

In the clean and greaseless bowl of a standing mixer fitted with the whisk attachment, beat the egg whites until fluffy. Add the remaining $3/4$ cup sugar and continue beating until the whites are firm and glossy, 4 to 5 minutes. Fold the meringue into the batter one-third at a time, so as not to deflate the meringue. Pour the batter into prepared cake pan and bake for 45 minutes, or until the cake begins to come away from the sides of the pan and a toothpick or skewer stuck in the center comes out clean. Remove the cake from the oven, let it cool on a wire rack until it is warm to the touch, then invert and cool completely.

Make the syrup: Using a swivel-blade peeler, remove the rind from both oranges into long, thin strips with a minimum of white pith. Cut the strips crosswise into thin slices. Section both oranges and reserve. Bring a small saucepan of water to a boil, add the orange zest strips and bring the liquid back to a boil over high heat. Boil 1 minute, then drain.

In a large saucepan, combine the orange juice, sugar, and the blanched orange zest strips. Bring to a boil, reduce the heat, and simmer for 15 minutes, or until the syrup is slightly thickened, skimming as necessary. Strain the syrup and reserve the orange strips along with $1/2$ cup of the syrup. Use a toothpick to poke holes in the top of the cake, and then pour the remaining syrup all over the cake.

Place the $1/2$ cup syrup and the strips of zest in a small saucepan, bring to a boil and cook down until the syrup thickens and just begins to darken, about 5 min-

utes. While the mixture is still hot, use a spatula to spread the thick glaze over the top of the cake. Place the cake on a serving platter. Pare the oranges of all their pith and membrane so that only flesh is left and section. Arrange the reserved orange sections on top of the cake, cut into serving portions, and serve. Store covered and at room temperature up to 3 days.

Minneola Orange Tart

The juice and zest of sweet-tart Minneola oranges flavor the filling for this sugar crust tart, a variation on a lemon curd tart. Additional oranges are sliced and arranged on top of the tart for a colorful and zippy topping. Note that the filling will keep quite well in the refrigerator. Depending on the size of the tart pan used here, you may have extra filling. Cover and refrigerate up to three weeks and use as a sauce over fruit salad, pound cake, or angel food cake.

**YIELD: ONE 10-INCH TART,
8 TO 12 SERVINGS**

$3/4$ pound Sugar Pastry dough (page 823)

$1^{1}/2$ cups sugar

Juice and grated zest of 2 Minneola oranges
(about $3/4$ cup juices and 8 teaspoons zest)

$1/4$ cup fresh lemon juice

6 large eggs

2 large egg yolks

Pinch flour

¼ pound (1 stick) unsalted butter,
    cut into bits and softened
4 Minneola oranges

Roll out the dough on a lightly floured surface into a large round, ³/₈-inch thick. Transfer the round to a 10-inch tart pan with a removable bottom and press into the pan without stretching the dough. Press well into the corners so there are no thick spots. Trim any overhang flush with the edge. Chill the dough for 30 minutes to relax the gluten and set the tart shape.

Preheat the oven to 375°F. Fit a piece of heavy-duty foil onto the dough and fill with beans or other pie weights. Blind bake on the bottom shelf of the oven (just pastry crust, no filling) until the crust is cooked through but not yet browned, about 30 minutes. Remove the foil and the weights, reduce oven temperature to 325°F and bake for 10 minutes longer, or until the crust is evenly and lightly browned. Remove from the oven and cool to room temperature on a wire rack.

In a medium-sized metal bowl, combine the sugar, orange juice and zest, lemon juice, eggs, egg yolks, and flour, and whisk to blend. Set the bowl over a saucepan of simmering water and whisk constantly for about 12 minutes, until the mixture thickens substantially and a thermometer inserted into the mixture registers 175°F (do not allow the mixture to boil). Remove the bowl from the heat and stir in the butter while the mixture is still hot, whisking until smooth. Press plastic wrap directly onto the surface of the mixture and cool to room temperature.

Preheat the oven to 325°F.

Spread the filling evenly into the cooled crust. Place the tart back in the oven and bake for 20 minutes, or until the filling has set in the middle. Remove from the oven and cool for about 10 minutes, or until the filling is somewhat firm.

Pare the oranges of all their pith and membrane so that only flesh is left. Cut the oranges into thin slices. Arrange the slices on top of the filling. Chill the tart in the refrigerator for about 1 hour. Cut the tart into serving portions and serve. Store covered and refridgerated up to 2 days.

Orange or Tangerine Caramel Sauce

This simple three-ingredient sauce depends on sugar browning into caramel, losing some of its sweetness in the process, but gaining a complex flavor profile. The slight bitterness of the oily orange zest imparts its own aroma. The key here is to use a heavy-bottomed pot. I have two copper pots that I always use for making caramel, browning it evenly without any burnt spots. If tangerines are in season, use them to make a sauce that is highly aromatic and deeper in color. The tangerine juice now sold in cartons at Whole Foods, Trader Joe's, and other stores will work well, but be sure to buy a couple of fresh tangerines for their incomparable zest. Warm this sauce slightly to thin it out and serve it over the Italian Bittersweet Chocolate-Orange Torta (page 331), or the Crostata della Nonna: Grandma's Ricotta-Pine Nut Tart (page 676), or mix it half and half with sweetened whipped cream and spoon over scones or pound cake.

YIELD: ABOUT 2 CUPS

1 cup sugar

2 cups orange juice, substitute tangerine juice

Grated zest of 2 oranges or tangerines (8 teaspoons)

In a medium, heavy-bottomed pot, preferably copper, over low heat, combine the sugar and 1 cup of the juice. Heat until the liquid comes to the boil and the syrup is clear, about 4 minutes. Raise the heat to medium and continue boiling until the syrup thickens and starts to brown, about 8 minutes. As the sugar melts, shake the pot carefully (CARAMEL IS EXTREMELY HOT!), so the syrup cooks evenly, or stir with a wooden spoon, until it reaches 350°F on candy thermometer and the sugar is medium brown in color with a faint touch of redness. Immediately remove the pot from the heat and pour in the remaining 1 cup orange juice (the juice will bubble up and release hot steam and the caramel will harden). Whisk into the sauce, reheating briefly over medium heat to melt the caramel. Store the sauce for about 3 months in the refrigerator, warming it before use.

Florida Tangerine Kiss–Me Cake

The original recipe for this chunky, fruity cake won the Pillsbury Bake-off grand prize in 1950, submitted by Lily Wuebel of Menlo Park, California. Florida is the Orange Blossom State, so it's appropriate that in my version of the cake, I flavor the fluffy tangerine icing with orange

blossom water. The combination of orange blossom water and cinnamon imparts a hint of spice, redolent of North Africa, though the buttery pecans that are also added are purely American. Either use a deeply colored tangerine or a tangelo, such as the Minneola, Honey Bell, or Honey Murcott, with its seeds removed. In Israel today, a similar cake is made using local Jaffa oranges, though I'm not sure if it was adapted from the American cake or created separately.

YIELD: ONE 10-INCH CAKE, 12 TO 16 SERVINGS

Cake

$1/2$ pound (2 cups minus 2 tablespoons)
    unbleached all-purpose flour

1 teaspoon baking soda

$1/2$ teaspoon baking powder

$1/2$ teaspoon fine sea salt

$1/2$ teaspoon ground mace

$1/2$ cup toasted wheat germ

1 tangerine, cut into wedges, seeded,
  and white membrane removed

$5^1/2$ ounces (1 cup) golden raisins

$1/4$ pound (1 cup) pecans, lightly toasted and chopped

2 large eggs

1 cup sugar

$3/4$ cup grapeseed or canola oil

1 cup tangerine juice

Icing

2 large egg whites ($1/4$ cup)

1 cup sugar

2 tablespoons corn syrup

Juice and grated zest of 1 tangerine
  (6 tablespoons juice and 4 teaspoons zest)
6 ounces (1½ sticks) unsalted butter, softened
1 teaspoon orange blossom water
¼ pound (1 cup) pecans, lightly toasted

Preheat the oven to 350°F. Spray a 10-inch cake pan with baker's nonstick coating or rub with butter and dust with flour, shaking off the excess.

Whisk together the dry ingredients: flour, baking soda, baking powder, salt, and mace. Stir in the wheat germ.

Using a meat grinder or a food processor, grind or process the tangerine wedges, raisins, and about two-thirds of the pecans together, making sure not to turn them into purée; the mixture should be chunky.

In the bowl of a standing mixer fitted with the paddle attachment, beat the eggs and sugar until light and fluffy, 5 to 6 minutes. Slowly beat in the oil, continuing to beat until the oil has been completely absorbed. Beating on low speed, alternate adding the flour mixture and the tangerine juice, beginning and ending with the flour. Fold in the ground raisin-nut mixture.

Spoon the batter into the prepared pan and level the top. Bake for 40 minutes, or until the cake starts to come away from the sides of the pan and a skewer stuck in the center comes out clean. Cool to room temperature on a wire rack.

Make the icing: In the bowl of a standing mixer fitted with the whisk attachment, combine the egg whites, sugar, corn syrup, and tangerine juice. Set the bowl onto a medium saucepan filled with about 1-inch of simmering water. Cook, over medium heat, stirring constantly until the syrup is clear and is hot enough to start to steam, 160°F on a thermometer, about 8 minutes.

Remove the bowl from the heat and beat with the whisk attachment on medium-high speed until the mixture is glossy and firm and has cooled to room temperature. Beat in the butter, scraping down the sides once or twice, continuing to beat until the mixture is smooth. Fold in the tangerine zest and the orange blossom water.

Refrigerate the icing for 30 minutes, until firm enough to hold its shape. Spread the icing over the cake and sprinkle with the remaining pecans. Chill the cake for 30 minutes to set the icing, before cutting into serving portions. Store the cake in the refrigerator up to 1 week.

Maltese Kwaresimal Cookies

These super-crunchy, intensely orange-flavored cookies originated in Sicily, where they are called quaresemali *(see page 489 for a recipe). The cookies are made without any animal products especially for Lent. Malta is known for its blood oranges, used here for their juice and fragrant zest. In French cuisine, any dish with* Maltaise *in its name will be made with blood oranges. Sweetly perfumed orange blossom water, an ingredient of Arabic origin, known as* ilma zahar *in Malta, and common in both Sicily and Malta, lends its scent to the cookies along with candied orange rind and orange liqueur. In an unusual method, once the dough is baked the first time (in a sheet, not in the more common logs); it is brushed with honey and sprinkled with sliced almonds before a second baking. This recipe is dairy-free.*

YIELD: 6 DOZEN COOKIES

$1/4$ pound ($3/4$ cups) blanched whole or slivered
   almonds

14 ounces ($3^1/4$ cups plus 2 tablespoons) unbleached
   all-purpose flour

2 teaspoons baking powder

1 teaspoon ground cinnamon

$1/2$ teaspoon fine sea salt

$1^1/2$ cups sugar

1 cup mild olive oil, grapeseed, or canola oil

$3/4$ cup blood orange juice, substitute orange juice

$1/2$ cup orange liqueur, such as Triple Sec or Curaçao

2 teaspoons orange blossom water

Grated zest of 2 blood oranges, substitute tangerines
   or oranges (8 teaspoons)

$1/2$ pound ($1^1/2$ cups) slivered almonds or chopped
   whole almonds, lightly toasted

$1/4$ pound candied orange rind, diced (1 cup)

Topping

1 cup honey

1 cup sliced almonds, preferably skin-on

Preheat the oven to 350°F. Line an 18 x 13-inch half sheet pan (or other large baking pan) with parchment paper or a silicone baking mat.

In the bowl of a food processor, combine the blanched almonds, flour, baking powder, cinnamon, and salt. Process until finely ground, working in two batches if necessary.

In a large bowl, whisk together the sugar, oil, orange juice, orange liqueur, orange blossom water, orange zest, toasted almonds, and the candied orange rind. Fold in the flour mixture to make a soft, sticky dough. Spread the dough out evenly onto the baking pan and bake for 35 minutes, or until lightly browned on the outside but still soft on the inside.

Remove the pan from the oven, and immediately brush the top with the honey and sprinkle with the sliced almonds. Allow to cool completely at room temperature, at least 1 hour, or up to overnight.

Cut the cookie into evenly-sized sticks, about 3-inches by 1-inch.

Preheat the oven to 350°F. Arrange the cookies on the baking pans and bake for 20 minutes, or until the cookies are lightly browned and crisp at the edges. Store in a cookie tin or other similar container up to 2 weeks.

BLOOD ORANGES IN MALTA

With three oranges on its emblem, the town of Lija stakes its claim as Malta's fruit basket. Famed for its deep-red blood oranges, the motto of the village is *Suavi Fructo Rubeo* ("with sweet fruits I redden"). The branches of the orange tree are covered with thorns, which could also have contributed to their name, along with their bloody color. The flavor of these oranges, which is claimed by the Maltese as being of local origin, is an intriguing mix of oranges, raspberries, and concord grapes.

Tangerine Semolina Torta

In this simple Italian torta, nutty and grainy fine semolina is combined with ground blanched almonds for a slightly crumbly, light, and tasty cake. In a method that reached Europe with the Arabs, and used in many Greek and Turkish desserts, a sweet tangerine syrup scented with its oily perfumed zest is poured over the warm cake and allowed to soak in. While oranges may be substituted here, there is something special about the faintly bitter intense flavor of tangerines that makes this cake out of the ordinary.

YIELD: ONE 9-INCH CAKE, 10 TO 12 SERVINGS

Cake

$^1\!/_2$ pound (1$^1\!/_2$ cups) blanched almonds

9 ounces (1$^1\!/_2$ cups plus 1 tablespoon) fine semolina

Pinch salt

6 ounces (1$^1\!/_2$ sticks) unsalted butter, softened

$^3\!/_4$ cup sugar

3 eggs

Grated zest of 1 tangerine (4 teaspoons)

$^3\!/_4$ cup tangerine juice

Syrup

1 cup sugar

1 cup tangerine juice

2 tablespoons Napoléon tangerine liqueur, substitute orange liqueur

Make the cake: Preheat the oven to 350°F. Spray a 9-inch cake pan with nonstick baker's coating, or rub with softened butter and dust with flour, shaking off the excess.

In the bowl of a food processor, combine the almonds, semolina, and salt, and grind until finely powdered, working in two batches if necessary.

In the bowl of a standing mixer fitted with the paddle attachment, cream the butter and sugar until light and fluffy, 5 to 6 minutes. Beat in the eggs, one at a time, beating well after each addition, then beat in the tangerine zest. Beat in the flour mix, alternating with $^3\!/_4$ cup of the tangerine juice, beginning and ending with the flour mix. Scrape the batter into the pan, banging it once or twice on the counter to remove any large bubbles.

Bake for 40 minutes or until the cake starts to come away from the sides of the pan and a toothpick or skewer stuck in the center comes out clean. Remove from the oven and cool on a wire rack for 15 minutes.

Make the syrup: In a medium, heavy-bottomed, nonreactive pot over high heat, combine the 1 cup tangerine juice and sugar. Bring to a boil, then reduce the heat and simmer for 10 minutes, or until the syrup thickens slightly. Remove from the heat, stir in the liqueur and cool slightly.

Drizzle half the syrup over the cake while. Let it sit for 10 minutes, or until the syrup has been absorbed. Turn the cake out onto a plate and brush the remaining syrup over top. Cool to room temperature before slicing. Store covered and at room temperature for up to 4 days.

PEACHES & NECTARINES

Clingstone and Freestone Peaches . . . 613

White Peaches and Nectarines . . . 613

Choosing and Ripening
Peaches and Nectarines . . . 614

Donut Peaches . . . 614

Pitting Peaches and Nectarines . . . 615

WHITE PEACH AND SOUR CREAM PIE . . . 615

PEACH AND APRICOT TARTE TATIN . . . 616

CARAMELIZED NECTARINE AND GINGER
SHORTCAKES WITH SOUR CREAM . . . 617

FRENCH PUFF PASTRY PEACH GALETTE . . . 618

TARTE AUX PÊCHES (FRENCH
BAKED PEACH TART) . . . 619

PEACHES & NECTARINES

In Roald Dahl's 1961 children's classic, *James and the Giant Peach*, the young orphan, James, escapes from his cruel spinster aunts and travels about inside a giant peach that had magically grown in their backyard. After many adventures, James and his crew of child-size insects land on the Empire State Building and are honored with a suitably magnificent parade. James retires to his peach pit home in Central Park where he spends his time relating stories of his adventures. Although I've never traveled about in a peach, eating a peach that has been tree-ripened, preferably nearby, to coax out the utmost in natural fruit sugars and drippy, sticky nectar can indeed be a magical experience.

Peaches have long inspired artists and writers. I had the distinct pleasure of hearing eloquent California peach farmer, Mas Masumoto, speak about his search for the perfect peach. In *Epitaph for a Peach*, Masumoto tells of his (successful) attempt to rescue a truly sweet and juicy peach from dying out in this world of cold-storage and cross-country transport. He turns the bulldozers away from his family's orchards and vows to find a home for the Sun Crest peach, which he describes as "one of

the last remaining truly juicy peaches. When you wash that treasure under a stream of cooling water, your fingertips instinctively search for the gushy side of the fruit. Your mouth waters in anticipation. You lean over the sink to make sure you don't drip on yourself. Then you sink your teeth into the flesh and the juices trickle down your cheeks and dangle on your chin. This is a real bite, a primal act, a magical sensory celebration announcing that summer has arrived."

Throughout the ages, artists have extolled the beauty of peaches in all manners of expression. Jeffrey Steingarten wrote in *Vogue* about his obsessive search for that elusive perfect peach: "Why has humankind labored to cultivate and propagate this high-maintenance fruit for the past 10,000 years? There can be only one reason–a perfect, fresh peach is one of the most delicious things on earth. The purpose of a ripe peach is pure delight. Simply ask a human who has just eaten one, or simply ask a peach." The French artist, Renoir, who was known for perfectly depicting the soft, rosy flesh of women's breasts, started by painting peaches–in a bowl, on a plate, with almonds, with chestnuts, and with grapes. The

American blues-rock band leader Steve Miller sang, "You're the cutest thing, That I ever did see, I really love your peaches, Want to shake your tree." But not all peach metaphors refer to women. A Pathan poem says, "There is a boy, across the river, With a bottom like a peach. But alas, I can't swim."

The curved cleft that divides a downy peach in two plump halves invites inevitable anatomic comparisons, while its warm skin, blushing with deeper rose on the side that soaked up the sun, seems to be painted just for the pleasure of the eye. Grape growers in the Lyonnais region of France would plant a peach pit at the end of each row of grapes. As these *Pêches de Vigne* (vineyard peaches) grew, they acted as a signal to growers. As long as all was well and the capricious peaches showed no signs of disease or insect damage, farmers knew that their hardier and more valuable grapes were thriving. Covered with soft grayish down, these small fruits are succulent as their deep red flesh suggests.

The French peach, *Téton de Venus* (breast of Venus), is a variety known since 1667 that is sought after for its meltingly tender flesh. In a reversal of the more common journey, these prized peaches were brought from France to Italy where they grew under the name *Poppa di Venere*. Giorgio Gallesio writes, in his *La Pomona Italiana (Italian Pome Fruits 1817-1839)*, that this variety is the most beautiful of white-fleshed peaches. "The fruit is large and rounded, and ends with a point best described as a nipple: the skin, whitish underneath, is colored on one side with a beautiful purplish red, the flesh is white, freestone, and full of juice." (my translation).

Wild peaches originated in prehistoric China and Tibet, but these fruits were so small, sour, and hairy, it's difficult to believe they are the ancestors of today's sweet, tender fruits. The temperamental peach tree does not flourish in hot climates and will die if frozen, yet it requires cold nights in order to set its buds. Peaches and nectarines must lure animals (including humans) to carry off their large, heavily armored seeds using only their seductive scent and attractive color. It must work, because humans have become the most important propagators of this prized fruit, cultivating them for at least 2,000 years.

From ancient China, humans brought peach trees along Silk Road trade routes to regions with suitable climates, such as Kashmir, India, Turkey, and Persia. Peaches flourished for so long in Persia (now Iran), that people assumed it was a native fruit, as reflected in its botanic name: *Prunus persica* (Persian Plum). Alexander the Great is said to have brought peaches from Persia's orchards back to Greece. Eventually the peach spread to the rest of Europe, arriving in France and England only in the seventeenth century. In Queen Victoria's day, no formal meal was complete without a fresh peach presented in a folded napkin to be eaten with fruit knife and narrow-tined fork, of course, because peaches were too blatantly suggestive in that repressed time to consume whole.

Early French settlers brought peaches to their small settlement on the Gulf of Mexico coast in 1562. Spanish conquistadors brought peach trees to Mexico and to St. Augustine, Florida, where they arrived in 1565. Native American peoples carried peaches north from Mexico, planting seeds first in the southern United States as they roved the country. Peaches were noted by John Smith in Jamestown as early as 1629; William Penn observed wild peaches as far north as Philadelphia in 1683. European settlers in Virginia regarded peaches as a luxurious delicacy and planted them in enormous quantities, often as hedges, ultimately defining a distinctive American form of the fruit quite different from those of European tradition.

William Bartram, the Philadelphia botanist, explorer, and son of the renowned John Bartram, wrote in 1773 about visiting the ruins of a French plantation near Mobile, Alabama: "I ascended the bank of the river, and penetrating the groves, came presently to old fields, where I observed ruins of ancient habitations, there being abundance of Peach and Fig trees, loaded with fruit, which affording a very acceptable dessert after the heats and toil of the day." Thomas Jefferson wrote in an 1807 letter, "I am endeavoring to make a collection of the choicest kinds of peaches for Monticello." Early American settlers used the abundant fruits to ferment into the peach cider called mobby, sometimes distilling it into peach brandy. Jefferson experimented with the "black plumb peach" of Georgia, sold today as the "Indian Blood Peach," a natural hybrid cross of the French Sanguinole (bloody) and naturalized peach trees grown by the Indians.

From Virginia, intensive peach culture spread as far north as Pennsylvania, where Swedish botanist Peter Kalm observed on his tour of America, "Every countryman had an orchard full of peach trees which were covered with such quantities of fruit that we could scarcely walk in the orchard without treading upon the peaches that had fallen off, many of which were left on the ground." Peach trees merged into the surrounding vegetation so completely that even botanist John Bartram assumed that the peach was a native tree. Mary Randolph's influential 1824 cookbook, *The Virginia Housewife*, contains six recipes using peaches, including ice cream, peach preserves, and boiled, sugared, and sun-dried peach chips.

In the nineteenth century, American farmers began commercial peach production in Maryland, Delaware, Georgia, and Virginia. The peach industry took off in Georgia after the Civil War, when the emancipation of the slaves led to the end of cotton as king. Georgians viewed peach country as a kind of Eden, and printed peach crates with Bible verses. In the 1880s, the Elberta, the first modern clingstone, and the Georgia Belle were two new varieties developed in Georgia. Today, Georgia grows more than 40 varieties of peaches in orchards run by third-, fourth-, and even fifth-generation growers.

To me, the two most important categories of peaches are "woolly and inedible" or "juicy and ripe." Peaches are often picked before sugars are able to develop fully, so that they might withstand the stress of mechanical picking, sorting, and packing, followed by long-distance shipping. The peaches that appear in stores in the winter, which have been imported from the Southern Hemisphere, can be in cold storage for four to six weeks. If stored at cold temperatures for longer than a week without a chance to warm up, peaches turn dry and mealy, or hard and leathery, and brown on the inside through a phenomenon called internal breakdown. Unfortunately, these symptoms only emerge after the peach has been ripened and can't be detected until that first miserably disappointing bite.

Sadly, many peaches grown commercially in the United States have had their disease resistance, flavor, aroma, and immunity to insects and diseases bred out by hybridizers in favor of uniformity and durability. Peaches piled high in supermarkets make an eye-catching display, but the fruits must be hard and unripe in order not to be crushed. Because consumers in America shy away from fuzzy peaches, supermarket peaches have had their skins brushed mechanically after harvest. Visit farmers' markets for the best in peaches and nectarines, where growers present fuzzy peaches in quart-size containers so their tender flesh won't bruise. They may be a bit spotty, oddly-shaped, or even have a bruise or two, but they'll be satisfying, fragrant, and juicy. Don't be put off by the fuzz; you might miss the most exquisite peach, ripe enough for its juices to drip down your chin.

Perhaps if peaches were treated more as precious jewels and less like baseballs to be knocked around, our peaches would taste better. Buying good peaches is definitely a crap shoot: sometimes the peaches from my local farmers' market and even the supermarket ripen so perfectly that I can easily demolish two or even three on my own, that is, if I can get to them before my fruit-loving progeny. Other times, they never make it into the land of the sublime. A "pinch ripe" peach, plucked gently from its branch, handled with TLC, and eaten as soon as possible is a treasure, an experience to recall with pleasure. But the best fully ripened peach is perched on the edge of disaster, because decay begins almost immediately, and in just a few days, it can dissolve into a mushy mess.

With more than 2,000 peach varieties and even more being created all the time, there is always a new peach to anticipate. Each peach variety has its own personality, and each taster has a different preference. Many Asians prefer the low-acid, honeyed sweetness of white peaches, also a favorite in Pennsylvania. I live for the bold tanginess and firm, though giving texture of late-harvest yellow peaches. White peaches and nectarines have little balancing acid, but their penetrating floral aromas and soft voluptuous flesh are exceptional. These fragile white fruits are usually reserved for eating out of hand, but now that they've become more common, I also bake with them, as in the White Peach and Sour Cream Pie (page 615).

As a peach ripens on the tree, its green chlorophyll fades, and its underlying warm, reddish-gold hues develop both as the background and foreground color of its skin and its flesh, with deeper hues close to the pit. The peach's legendary fragrance develops and its flesh softens, beginning at the shoulders, eventually ripening into juicy succulence. The scent from a bowl of ripe peaches should fill a room. Bite into one, and its honeyed sweetness should be balanced by just enough acidity to give the fruit character. Although a peach picked too soon will soften and get juicier as the pectin that glues the cells together begins to break down, the fruit will never develop the full-bodied flavor and heady scent of tree-ripened fruit. A peach contains only the amount of sugar it started with when it was picked, but tastes sweeter because its acid content decreases as the fruit ripens.

NECTARINES

The smooth-skinned nectarine, *Prunus persica, Nucipersica group*, is the product of an incestuous relationship in which the nectarine originated as a mutant of the peach, or the peach evolved from a nectarine-like ancestor. According to American horticulturalist, Luther Burbank, the peach's fuzz acted as protection from excess sunshine, moisture, wind, and insects and that lacking this shield, the smooth nectarine did not thrive as well. Nectarines, whose origin is still a mystery, get their name from the Greek *nekter*, the honeyed liquid imbibed by the gods. Because fuzziness is genetically dominant, sometimes fuzzy peach trees bear a few smooth nectarines or visa versa. Nectarines, which may have either white or gold flesh, are noted for the spicy "zing" of their aroma and a pronounced flavor .

Because it is impossible to tell which nectarine seeds will produce nectarine-bearing trees, commercial growers graft nectarine branches onto peach trees. Smooth-skinned nectarines are often smaller and rounder in shape than peaches and have more sugar and acid. Their flesh is denser than that of peaches and their deep reddish-orange skin doesn't change color significantly as the fruit ripens. Yellow-fleshed varieties have a distinct pink tinge, although white nectarines with pale, creamy-pink flesh also exist. There are more than one hundred freestone and clingstone varieties of nectarines, which are more delicate than peaches, bruising even more readily.

Nectarines were first described in print in England in 1587, although they've been around much longer, perhaps even longer than peaches. White nectarines were so prized by England's royalty, that people would harvest the precious fruits and place them on a pillow as a gift for their King or Queen.

Two cousins, peaches and apricots, cut into plump halves fill the French Peach and Apricot Tarte Tatin (page 616). Spicy-fleshed nectarines sautéed in butter and sugar fill the Caramelized Nectarine and Ginger Shortcakes with Sour Cream (page 617). The French Puff Pastry Peach Galette (page 618) combines sliced peaches layered on an almond cream base in a crackly butter puff pastry shell. In the surprisingly easy Tarte aux Pêches (French Baked Peach Tart) (page 619), peach wedges nestle in a soft, sweet, buttery crust.

CLINGSTONE AND FREESTONE PEACHES

With flesh that ranges from creamy, pale pink to deep mango-orange, the thousands of varieties of peaches are classified according to how firmly the flesh attaches to the pit. Clingstones are the first to be harvested. Even when ripe, their flesh clings to the stone, maddening when you're trying to section them for a tart but beneficial for canners because they're quite firm. Peaches survive canning better than most fruits, so much of the world's production ends up on the grocery aisle, not the produce department. Semi-freestones are a newer hybrid of the clingstone and freestone, good both fresh and canned.

Freestones have flesh that easily pulls away from the pit, making them a good choice for eating fresh and for baking in tarts and pies because they're easy to cut into regular wedges. Most East Coast peaches are freestones, which tend to be larger than clingstones, with less juicy, but sweet and acid-balanced flesh. My favorite is the Red Haven peach. These freestones have prominent red streaks radiating out from the pit, are tart, firm, and juicy, and peel readily. Another good choice is the Cresthaven, a medium-to-large peach with golden skin blushed with red. Its firm, juicy, yellow flesh resists browning, an advantage when baking.

Peach season starts in California in May, moving across the country to Georgia, and then South Carolina in June and continues with some late varieties until September or even the beginning of October. Many peach varieties yield their fullest flavor in August. Clingstones are the first to market, followed by semi-clings, and finally freestones. The nectarine season in American begins in early May. As with peaches, as the season progresses, the fruit size becomes larger, reaching maximum size in August. The season peaks in July and August, ending in October.

WHITE PEACHES AND NECTARINES

White-fleshed stone fruits have occurred in nature for thousands of years and have long been cultivated. White-fleshed peaches and nectarines are savored for their honeyed fragrance, lusciously creamy texture, and subtle color. Records of white-fleshed peach varieties can be traced to the mid-1600s; white-fleshed nectarines to the late 1700s. Until World War II in America, all nectarines had white flesh, but because they are easily bruised, white fruits declined in popularity as Americans moved to cities far from orchards. In the 1980s, when the Asian markets opened up, they preferred low-acid, white-fleshed fruits and were willing to pay top dollar. Ten years ago, white-fleshed stone fruit (including cherries) represented only one percent of the American fruit crop. Today, that number is almost fifteen percent and white-flesh peaches and nectarines represent almost twenty percent of the peach and nectarine crop.

CHOOSING AND RIPENING PEACHES AND NECTARINES

The key to choosing both peaches and nectarines is their background color, which should contain no hint of green. A fully mature, plump peach (and we know that maturity and plumpness are both beautiful, at least in this case) will have rounded shoulders and a full, bulging line that runs from top to bottom alongside the cleft. Avoid peaches with tan circles, an early sign of decay. Look for nectarines with smooth, unwrinkled skin and without bruises. Farmers' market peaches and nectarines will often exhibit small blemishes, which do not affect quality. The fruits should give slightly at the cleft when pressed with your thumb.

Ripe, yellow-fleshed peaches and nectarines will taste sweeter because their acid content decreases almost fifty percent during the ripening process. White-fleshed peaches and nectarines start out with low acid levels, which don't change as they ripen. So, a firm white nectarine or peach will taste just as sweet as a fully ripened fruit, making them well-suited to baking, as firm flesh is easier to work with.

To ripen peaches and nectarines, store them in a single layer enclosed in a brown paper bag. If you leave these delicate fruits in the open, they will tend to dehydrate and shrivel before they ripen, because their skin contains no natural protective oils. Note that white-flesh peaches and nectarines will ripen almost twice as fast as yellow-flesh fruits. Store fully-ripened fruits in the refrigerator for three to five days. Once fully ripened and refrigerated, a peach can have shriveled skin, but inside, be incredibly rich, juicy, and succulent because excess water has evaporated.

DONUT PEACHES

These small, odd-looking, but intriguing flat peaches are descendants of a flat peach called the Peen-to or Chinese Saucer Peach, introduced to the United States from China in 1869. These freestone fruits are shaped like small, fat doughnuts with a sunken center and a small, nearly round pit. Their pale yellow skin has a rosy blush, with exquisitely sweet, meltingly tender, and juicy flesh, intense peach flavor, and hauntingly perfumed fragrance. New varieties like Saturn, Jupiter, UFO, and even the Sweet Bagel peach from Florida have made quite a splash on the American market since the 1990s. Los Angeles specialty producer distributor, Frieda Kaplan, came up with their catchy name. In season in July and August, Donut peaches should be reserved for eating out of hand, or to cut into funny, squat wedges to add to the fruit mixture for the Australian Pavlova (page 442).

Start with firm but ripe freestone peaches and nectarines. Use a sharp paring knife and, starting at the stem end, cut through the natural cleft and then all the way around, ending back at the stem end and making sure to cut all the way through to the stone. Firmly grasp the two halves and twist them in opposite directions. One half will pop off, leaving the second half with the stone. If the peach resists giving up its stone, repeat, scraping at the stone to make sure you have cut all the way through. Use a spoon to scoop out the stone, or cut the second half-peach in half again, cutting through to the stone again. Twist off the first wedge. The remaining wedge will have the stone attached and is easy to twist off. If all you have are clingstones, use a paring knife to cut away the flesh of clingstone fruits as closely as possible from their stones. I rarely peel peaches and never peel nectarines, because when baked, their flavorful and deeply colored skins bleed attractively and add flavor.

White Peach and Sour Cream Pie

Make this lovely pale-pink pie at the height of summer when locally-grown white peaches are sold at farmers' markets. Pennsylvania specializes in white peaches, so I can often find them in season, but they are now being grown on a much bigger scale commercially, so they are not hard to find. Their delicate flavor, succulent texture, and heady floral perfume all come through in this old-fashioned pie. I don't peel the peaches, because their thin skin adds flavor and color.

YIELD: ONE 9-INCH PIE, 8 TO 10 SERVINGS

Pie

3/4 pound Butter Pie Pastry dough (page 203)

1 cup sour cream

1/2 cup packed light brown sugar

1 teaspoon almond extract

1/4 teaspoon fine sea salt

1 large egg

1 ounce (2 tablespoons) unbleached all-purpose flour

2 1/2 pounds (5 to 6) firm but ripe white peaches, sliced

Topping

2 ounces (1/4 cup minus 2 teaspoons) unbleached all-purpose flour

2 ounces (1/2 stick) unsalted butter, chilled and cut into bits

1/4 cup light brown sugar

1/2 cup sliced skin-on almonds

Make the pie: Roll out the dough out between two sheets of lightly floured wax paper to a large round about 3/8-inch thick. Drape the dough round, without stretching the dough, into a 9-inch pie pan, preferably aluminum for better browning. Trim the edges evenly, then crimp or pinch in and out alternatively to form a decorative fluted edge. Chill the crust for 1 hour in the refrigerator or 30 minutes in the freezer to set the shape.

Preheat the oven to 400°F.

In a large bowl, combine the sour cream, brown sugar, almond extract, salt, and egg, and whisk together to combine. Fold in the flour and peaches, then spoon the filling into the pie crust.

Place the pie on a baking pan to catch any drips. Bake on the bottom shelf of the oven for 15 minutes, then reduce the oven temperature to 350°F and continue baking for 30 minutes, or until the filling is mostly set in the center. Remove from the oven and cool slightly. Leave the oven set at 350°F.

Make the topping: In the bowl of a standing mixer fitted with the paddle attachment or in food processor, combine the flour, butter, brown sugar, and almonds, and beat just long enough to form crumbs. Sprinkle the topping evenly over the pie. Bake an additional 15 minutes or until the topping is lightly browned. Cool to room temperature on a wire rack before cutting. Store covered and refridgerated for up to 3 days

Peach and Apricot Tarte Tatin

I've combined sweet, plump peaches with tangy apricots in this delicious variation on the classic French tarte tatin, an upside-down fruit tart best made in a special French heavy copper and tin tarte tatin pan or a cast-iron skillet. I checked recent prices: though beautiful and perfectly suited to caramelizing the fruit bottom, the genuine French pan costs about $200, so buy one only if you plan to make a lot of tarts! Make sure to bring this colorful, decorative tart to the table whole before slicing it into individual portions. Once cut, the tart will look kind of messy, though so good to eat! Rich, slightly tart unsweetened crème fraîche makes the best accompaniment, though Vanilla Custard Sauce (page 835), full of tiny vanilla bean specks, would also be wonderful and very French!

YIELD: ONE 9- TO 10-INCH PIE, 8 TO 10 SERVINGS

$^3/_4$ pound Tarte Tatin Pastry dough (page 206)

$^3/_4$ cup sugar

2 ounces ($^1/_2$ stick) unsalted butter

1 firm but ripe peach, halved and pitted

2 pounds (about 6) firm but ripe peaches, pitted and cut into thick wedges

1 pound (about 8) firm but ripe apricots, pitted and cut into thick wedges

$^3/_4$ cup unsweetened crème fraîche, for serving

Roll out the dough on a lightly floured surface into a large round about 2 inches larger than the diameter of the pan and about $^3/_8$-inch thick. Transfer to a sheet of parchment or wax paper and refrigerate for at least 30 minutes.

In a heavy, ovenproof (preferably cast-iron) 9- or 10-inch diameter skillet set over medium heat, cook the sugar and butter, stirring, until the sugar dissolves. Increase the heat to high and bring the mixture to a boil, without stirring, until the sugar caramelizes and turns medium amber in color, occasionally swirling the pan so the sugar browns evenly, about 5 minutes.

Immediately remove from the heat and cool for 2 minutes or until the caramel is moderately hot.

Place 1 peach half, rounded-side down, in the center of the pan. Arrange alternating peach and apricot wedges very close together, rounded-side down, in concentric circles around the peach half. Nestle any remaining peach and apricot wedges, rounded-side down, over the first layer. Place the pan back on the stove and cook over medium heat until the caramel is bubbling thickly, about 15 minutes, shaking occasionally to prevent burning. Remove from the heat and cool about 10 minutes, or until hot, but no longer steaming.

Preheat the oven to 425°F.

Trim the dough round to a 10-inch circle, and drape it over the hot fruit. Let the tart stand for 2 minutes to soften the dough. Tuck the dough edges around the fruit. Cut several slits in the pastry to allow steam to escape. Bake the tart on the bottom shelf of the oven until the crust is golden and the filling is bubbling and thick, about 30 minutes.

Remove the tart from the oven and cover it with a piece of aluminum foil. Place a plate smaller than the diameter of the skillet on top of the foil and weigh the plate down with one or two cans. Set the tart aside to cool for about 30 minutes, or until the tart is still warm but the fruit has set.

Remove the weight, plate, and foil, and cover the skillet with a large cake platter. Hold the skillet and the platter together and flip them over so the fruit is on top. Cut into portions and serve with a dollop of unsweetened crème fraîche. This tart is best the day it is made

Caramelized Nectarine and Ginger Shortcakes with Sour Cream

These shortcakes are made up of extremely light and gingery biscuits paired with sweet and slightly spicy nectarines that have been sautéed with brown sugar and butter. A topping of cold, tangy sour cream excites the palate. The biscuits are good enough to eat on their own, perhaps dunked in a cup of tea. Make these shortcakes in late summer when good, red-skinned nectarines are in season.

YIELD: 10 SERVINGS

Biscuits

½ pound (2 cups minus 2 tablespoons) unbleached
    all-purpose flour

¼ cup sugar

1 teaspoon baking powder

2 teaspoons ground ginger

½ teaspoon fine sea salt

¼ pound (1 stick) unsalted butter, chilled
    and cut into bits

½ cup whole milk

1 large egg

¼ cup chopped crystallized ginger

Filling

2 pounds (about 6) firm but ripe nectarines,
    peeled, pitted, and sliced

¾ cup well-packed light brown sugar

1 tablespoon fresh lemon juice

Assembly

1/2 cup sour cream

1/2 cup confectioners' sugar

2 teaspoons vanilla extract

Make the biscuits: Preheat the oven to 400°F. Line an 18 x 13-inch half sheet pan (or other large baking pan) with parchment paper or a silicone baking mat.

In the bowl of a food processor, Combine the dry ingredients: flour, sugar, baking powder, ginger, and salt, and process briefly to combine. Add the butter and process until the mixture resembles oatmeal.

Separately, whisk together the milk and egg. Add the milk mixture to the processor and process just long enough for the dough to form moist clumps. Add the crystallized ginger and process briefly, just long enough to combine. Turn the dough out onto a lightly floured work surface. Knead the dough briefly by hand until it forms a smooth ball. With floured hands, shape the dough into a fat log about 2 inches thick, and cut it crosswise into 10 rounds. Pat each round to 1-inch thickness and place them on the baking pan.

Bake the biscuits for 15 minutes, or until they are puffed in the center and light brown. Keep warm.

Make the filling: In a heavy large skillet over high heat, combine half the nectarines, half the brown sugar, and half the lemon juice, and cook, shaking the pan every now and then, until the fruit is just tender and the juices bubble thickly, about 5 minutes. Transfer to a bowl and repeat with the remaining nectarines, brown sugar, and lemon juice. Combine both batches of nectarines.

To assemble the shortcakes: In a bowl, fold together the sour cream, confectioners' sugar, and vanilla.

Cut the biscuits in half horizontally. Place 1 biscuit bottom in each of 10 serving bowls. Spoon about 1/4 cup of the nectarine mixture onto each biscuit along with a portion of the cooking juices. Top with a spoonful of the sour cream mixture, cover each serving with a biscuit top and serve immediately.

French Puff Pastry Peach Galette

Only the best all-butter puff pastry will do in this recipe. I recommend Dufour brand (page 207), sold at Whole Foods and other specialty food stores. Most of the popular brands are unfortunately made from shortening. They have the look, but none of the tender, impossibly flaky texture of the real thing. Make this country-style galette in late summer when the best freestone peaches are in season. In a pinch, or when you're getting sick of winter, make the tart with frozen peach wedges that have been defrosted and drained. A thin layer of almond cream provides a flavorful bed for the peaches and absorbs any excess liquid, so the pastry stays crisp.

YIELD: 8 TO 10 SERVINGS

1 (14-ounce) package all-butter puff pastry,
  thawed in the refrigerator

1/4 pound (3/4 cup) blanched almonds

2 ounces (1/2 stick) unsalted butter, softened

1/2 cup confectioners' sugar

1 teaspoon ground cinnamon

1 teaspoon rosewater, substitute almond extract

1 teaspoon vanilla

2 large eggs

1 large egg white, lightly beaten with 1 tablespoon water, for the egg wash

1½ pounds (about 4) firm but ripe peaches, pitted and thinly sliced

2 tablespoons sugar

¼ cup apricot jam, melted and strained

2 tablespoons brandy

Line an 18 x 13-inch half sheet pan (or other large baking pan) with parchment paper or a silicone mat. On a lightly floured surface, unfold the puff pastry and roll it out to a larger rectangle about ³⁄₈-inch thick. Place on the prepared pan and freeze for 30 minutes or until quite firm.

Turn the pastry out onto a lightly floured work surface and trim the edges on all sides to expose the layers and help them separate. Freeze again for 30 minutes or until firm.

In the bowl of a food processor, combine the almonds, butter, confectioners' sugar, cinnamon, rosewater, and vanilla, and process to a fine paste. Add the eggs and process again until smooth. Spread the almond filling in a thin layer over the pastry leaving a 1-inch border at the edges. Fold the edges over to form a border about 1-inch wide on each side, trimming off the excess pastry at the corners. Prick the pastry (not the borders) all over to prevent it from puffing up. Brush the border with the egg wash. Chill the pastry again until firm, then cut away a thin slices from the doubled-over outside edges exposing the layers of puff pastry.

Preheat the oven to 400°F. Arrange the peach slices in closely overlapping rows on top of the almond cream and sprinkle with the sugar. Bake the galette on the bottom shelf for 25 minutes, or until the edges are just golden brown. (If it puffs up in the center while baking, prick it several times.) Transfer to a wire rack to cool to room temperature.

Whisk together the apricot jam and the brandy. (You may rewarm the mixture, but keep in mind that if that brandy gets too warm, it can ignite.) Brush the peaches with the jam mixture and let the galette sit for 5 minutes before cutting into serving portions.

Tarte aux Pêches (French Baked Peach Tart)

Sometimes the best discoveries are those made by accident, as for this tart. My assistant, Betty Kaplan, and I had an extra batch of sautéed peaches and a dough that was too soft to roll out for cookies. Rather than throwing them out, I suggested that we might as well combine the two and see what happened. As it turned out, this baked fruit tart came out not only beautiful to look at, with rosy-edged peach wedges scattered over the top of puffy golden brown pastry, but it was just as good when we tasted it. The proof was the fact that by morning, every piece had been eaten. Glazing the fruits with a shiny mixture of their cooked down juices was the perfect finishing touch to an easy but delicious tart, best made in peach season. I have to admit that we made our tart during January's mid-winter doldrums when a dis-

play of surprisingly fragrant, soft, ready-to-eat peaches (yes, from Chile) were impossible to pass up.

YIELD: 10 TO 12 SERVINGS

Dough

½ pound (2 cups minus 2 tablespoons) unbleached all-purpose flour

2 teaspoons baking powder

½ teaspoon fine sea salt

¼ pound (1 stick) unsalted butter, softened

1 cup sugar

4 large eggs

2 tablespoons orange juice

2 teaspoons orange zest

1 teaspoon vanilla extract

Filling

2 pounds (about 8) firm but ripe peaches, cut into six wedges each

¾ cup well-packed light brown sugar

1 tablespoon fresh lemon juice

Make the dough: Preheat the oven to 350°F. Spray a 10- to 11-inch tart pan with baker's nonstick coating or rub with butter and dust with flour, shaking off the excess.

Whisk together the dry ingredients: flour, baking powder, and salt.

In the bowl of a standing mixer fitted with the paddle attachment, cream the butter and sugar together until light and fluffy, 5 to 6 minutes. Beat in the eggs, one at a time, beating well after each addition. Beat in half the flour mixture, then add the orange juice, orange zest, and vanilla. Add the remaining flour mixture, beating only long enough for the dough to come together.

Make the filling: In a large bowl, combine the peaches, brown sugar, and lemon juice. Spoon about half the mixture into a heavy large skillet. Cook over highest heat until the fruit is just tender and the juices bubble thickly, shaking the pan so the fruit cooks evenly, about 5 minutes. Transfer the mixture to a bowl and repeat with the remaining fruit mixture, then combine both batches. Drain the fruit in a colander or sieve, saving the juices for the glaze.

Spread the dough into the pan, smoothing it as much as possible. Spoon the fruit evenly over the batter. Place the tart pan on a baking pan to catch any drips. Bake for 30 minutes or until lightly browned and puffy. Cool to room temperature on a wire rack.

Pour the reserved fruit juices into a small pot and boil for 3 to 4 minutes or until thick and syrupy. Brush the glaze only on the fruit wedges, then allow the tart to cool until set before cutting into serving portions. Store covered and refrigerated up to 3 days.

PEANUTS

Peanut Varieties . . . 625

Introducing Mr. Peanut . . . 625

Buying and Storing Peanuts
and Peanut Products . . . 625

AMISH PEANUT BUTTER CREAM PIE . . . 626

PEANUT-CHOCOLATE BARS WITH ESPRESSO . . . 627

PEANUT BUTTER AND JELLY CAKE . . . 629

PEANUT MERINGUES WITH SPICED
BITTERSWEET CHOCOLATE PUDDINGS . . . 630

PEANUTS

It's only in America that pastry chefs create fanciful, peanut-centric desserts like peanut butter chocolate chip cake, chunky peanut butter cheesecake, Southern cola cake with broiled peanut butter icing, and white chocolate and peanut ice cream lasagna. Peanuts are a favorite ingredient for creative American pastry chefs looking to adapt European techniques to American ingredients, often while humorously recreating childhood favorites. Thus, the reconstructed peanut butter sandwich: chocolate fudge tart with caramelized bananas, red wine caramel sauce and peanut butter ice cream and the peanut Dacquoise: nut meringue with peanut nougatine (caramel and chopped toasted peanuts), peanut butter, and milk chocolate cream, topped with coffee crunch.

In this chapter, I've included peanut creations that are just as delicious, but less elaborate than today's restaurant specialties that can call for six to eight separately made components. (I do include several more complex recipes in the book for times when you really want to show off or just master a challenging recipe.) The sophisticated but easy Peanut–Chocolate Bars with Espresso (page 627)

combine two complementary flavors: peanuts and coffee. (I start most days with peanut butter spread on an oatmeal granola bar to drink with coffee–or nowadays, tea.) The Peanut Butter and Jelly Cake (page 629), Peanut Meringues with Spiced Bittersweet Chocolate Puddings (page 630), and Amish Peanut Butter Cream Pie (page 626), get their earthy flavor and full-bodied texture from peanuts and peanut butter.

Peanuts are also known as earthnuts, ground nuts, goobers, jack nuts, pinders, manila nuts, and monkey balls (referring to the whole pod, which contains the nuts in a rather testicle-like sac). These underground legumes are so ingrained in American culture, especially in sweets like Philadelphia's favorite Peanut Chews, peanut brittle, and fork-pressed peanut butter cookies, that it's hard to believe they were once scorned as a food fit only for slaves or animals.

The peanut is a legume, along with beans, chickpeas, lentils, and favas, defined as a having a pod that contains two or more beans and opens along a seam on two sides, although the peanut pod does not open on its own. Unlike other legumes, after its flower has been fertilized, the peanut buries itself underground, where its pod develops two to three or as many as five to seven nuts, depending on the variety. Peanuts are nutritious and high in energy, containing forty to fifty percent oil and between twenty and thirty percent protein.

Peanuts, *Arachis hypogaea*, probably originated in Brazil or Peru, and for about 3,500 years–as long as people have been making pottery in South America–they have been making jars shaped like blobby peanuts or decorated with peanut shapes. The Incas of Peru first cultivated wild peanuts, which they called *ynchic*, and offered them to the sun god. Peanuts were also widely cultivated in Ecuador, Bolivia, and Brazil, where female farmers wouldn't allow men to tend the plants because they believed they would only bear fruit for a woman. Old Incan graves found along the dry, western coast of South America often contained jars filled with peanuts to provide sustenance in the afterlife.

Spanish conquistadors found peanuts offered for sale by vendors at the market in Tenochtitlan (today's Mexico City) under the name *tlalcacahuatl* (*nahuatl* meaning earth and *cacahuatl* meaning cacao). So, that all-American dessert duo–chocolate and peanut–goes back as far back as their Aztec name, which describes them as a kind of underground cocoa bean. When the Spanish explorers first encountered peanuts, they were hesitant to eat them. Eventually the Indians shared their knowledge of peanut cultivation and even traded peanuts for Spanish goods.

Spanish and Portuguese explorers took peanuts back to Europe from Brazil, though they did not thrive back home, because the climate was unsuitable and the new food was considered bizarre. But they quickly became a staple food of the tropical regions of West Africa, where many Africans regarded the peanut as one of several plants possessing a soul. (With a little imagination, peanuts in the shell do resemble a tiny person.) About one-tenth of the world's crop is grown in the United States, nearly half of that in Georgia. The United States, China, and Argentina are the world's three top exporters of peanuts.

Spain's galleons, connecting the port of Acapulco with Manila, carried silver, peanuts, and other valuables to the East where they were traded for spices, silk, and porcelain. The peanut was introduced to China by Portuguese traders in the 1600s, where they became quite popular. Today, China is the world's largest peanut producer. It is via this long-running trade route that peanuts became a common food in Indonesia and Southeast Asia.

In the 1700s and 1800s, hundreds of thousands of slaves were taken from West Africa to Southern plantations, nourished along the way with peanuts and corn, two inexpensive and easily transportable foods. Once they reached America, the slaves planted peanuts throughout the southern states. Because of their connection to the slave community, peanuts were long denigrated. During the Civil War, there was a critical shortage of food, and many days, in both the North and the South, peanuts were the only food to be found.

Hungry soldiers would roast peanuts over a campfire, grinding them into an ersatz coffee. It may have been these soldiers who transformed the Bantu name for peanut, *nguba*, into goobers or goober peas. Once back home, Union soldiers introduced peanuts to their friends and families, some of them even began working as peanut vendors on the streets of Northern cities.

With new mechanical equipment built around 1900, the once difficult and time-consuming to harvest peanut came into demand for its oil, for roasted and salted nut snacks, and to grind for peanut butter. In 1870, Phineas T. Barnum, of Barnum and Bailey's Circus, started selling bags of roasted peanuts for sale at circus performances. People loved them. Roasted peanuts soon appeared at other gathering places like baseball games and the theater. The cheap, high balcony seats started to be known as "the peanut gallery," because the patrons would snack on this inexpensive (and noisy) food in the faraway upstairs seating. About half the peanuts grown in the United States end up in peanut butter and one-quarter more are sold roasted and, usually, salted.

Peanuts are essential for iconic America sweets like Philadelphia's Tastykake Peanut Butter Kandy Kakes; the 1914 peanut and molasses taffy Mary Janes, named after their creator's aunt; and the peanut butter cream–filled chocolates, Reese's Peanut Butter Cups, created in 1928 by Harry Burnett Reese, a former farmer who worked for chocolate magnate Milton S. Hershey. Today, six of the top ten candy bars sold in America contain peanuts and/or peanut butter.

Hot "honey roasted" peanuts are a South American and Cuban culinary tradition, so on the streets of New York and other major cities, vendors roast peanuts (and other more expensive nuts) with water and sugar (not honey), sometimes sprinkling them with vanilla to entice customers with its scent. A single vendor can sell 6,000 pounds a week of peanuts alone; there are more than one hundred nut carts in New York City.

Although the Incas were known to have used peanuts to make a type of paste, today's peanut butter was invented by Dr. John Kellogg (who also invented corn flakes) in 1890, as a convenient and healthy protein food that was easy to digest for patients with no teeth. The first peanut-butter making machine was patented in 1903, and by 1904, the throngs of people who visited the St. Louis Universal Exposition had the chance to sample peanut butter. J.L. Rosefield perfected a process to keep the oil from separating in peanut butter in 1912. He marketed his product as churned peanut butter under the name Skippy, still one of the top peanut butter brands in America today. The United States ranks third in world peanut production but is the world's largest peanut butter supplier and consumer. China is by far the largest grower of peanuts, with more than double the production of India, which is ranked second. Peanuts grown outside of the United States are usually harvested for their oil and for animal feed. Peanut growers harvest their crop in the fall, when fresh shell peanuts are found for sale.

PEANUT VARIETIES

RUNNER: This peanut is America's most important variety, because of its attractive appearance, uniform kernel size, and large yield. Mainly grown in Georgia, Alabama, Florida, Texas, and Oklahoma, more than half the runners end up in peanut butter.

SPANISH: These small, rounded peanuts are covered with loose-fitting reddish-brown skin. In America, they are used for snacks and peanut butter, but most go into peanut candies. Primarily grown in Oklahoma and Texas, Spanish peanuts are also crushed to extract their large content of oil.

VALENCIA: Mainly grown in New Mexico, these peanuts are quite sweet and preferred for the fresh, boiled peanuts eaten as a snack in the South, or for roasting in the shell. Valencias contain two or three small, oval-shaped kernels, tightly crowded into their pods, and are covered in bright-red skin.

VIRGINIA: The Virginia peanut, also called the Virginia bunch peanut, provides most of the peanuts eaten whole in the United States as "ballpark peanuts." Virginias are grown mainly in Virginia and parts of North and South Carolina. Prized for their large size, crunchy texture, and excellent flavor, larger Virginias are roasted for gourmet snack peanuts. Years ago, people would soak these peanuts in water to remove their skins before roasting (actually frying), causing the peanuts to "blister" in small bubbles, making them extra-crunchy. These blister peanuts are still sought after today.

INTRODUCING MR. PEANUT

Amedeo Obici, founder of the Planter's Peanut Company, was born in Oderzo, Italy, and immigrated to America in 1889. Misdirected on his way to Scranton, he got off the train in Wilkes-Barre, Pennsylvania, where he worked in an Italian family's fruit store. They had a peanut roaster with a fan that blew the fragrance of the roasting peanuts out to the street to lure customers. Obici built his own peanut cart from scrap yard parts. A genius at promotion, Obici would put one letter of his last name in each bag of peanuts, putting the letter O in one of every fifty bags. Customers who got the O won a gold-colored watch. Mr. Peanut, the company's beloved and enduring mascot, with top hat, monocle, and cane, was the winning entry in a 1916 contest that he sponsored for school children.

BUYING AND STORING PEANUTS AND PEANUT PRODUCTS

Buy raw, shelled peanuts in bags at a natural foods store or an Asian market. Use these peanuts when you're going to further toast or fry the nuts. Peanuts can keep for up to 12 months if stored properly. Raw peanuts should be stored in the refrigerator in a tightly covered container or in the freezer. Store roasted peanuts in a porous bag, such as a brown paper bag. Keep them in a cool dry place and maintain good air circulation, for up to one week. Don't store peanuts in plastic or mold might form.

Though dry-roasted peanuts are oven-roasted rather than fried, they are not especially low in calories because peanuts themselves are high in fat.

Commercial peanut butter is a blend of ground, shelled, and roasted peanuts mixed with vegetable oil (which is usually hydrogenated) and salt. Some types also contain sugar and other additives as stabilizers to prevent oil separation and to enhance flavor. Natural peanut butter normally contains only peanuts, oil, and perhaps salt, and will eventually separate, the lighter oil rising to the top of the dense, heavy peanut pulp. To help postpone this action, turn the container upside-down occasionally to redistribute the oils and then stir vigorously to recombine the peanut paste with its oil. Or, scoop out chunks of the solid pulp and combine them with the oil by running in the food processor until the mixture is smooth and creamy.

For baking, natural peanut butter works best because it has a fresher, peanuttier flavor, although I admit that I usually buy commercial peanut butter. Natural peanut butters should be refrigerated after opening and will keep for up to six months. Commercial peanut butter requires no refrigeration and can be kept at room temperature up to six months after opening. Store unopened jars of peanut butter up to one year in a cool, dark place.

Amish Peanut Butter Cream Pie

This old-time recipe comes from the large Amish community in Indiana and was made from simple pantry ingredients. In order to be frugal and not waste anything, the egg yolk–based custard filling is covered with an egg white–based meringue topping. Sandwiched between the two is a layer of candy-like peanut crumble. The surprisingly flaky whole wheat tart shell adds a rich, nutty flavor of its own, hearty enough to stand up to the strong earthiness of peanuts.

YIELD: ONE 9-INCH PIE, 8 TO 10 SERVINGS

3/4 pound Sweet White Whole Wheat Tart Pastry
    dough (page 863)

Peanut crumble

1/2 cup confectioners' sugar

1/4 pound (1/2 cup) smooth or chunky peanut butter

3 ounces (1/2 cup chopped) peanuts, rinsed
    and dried if salted, optional

Filling

3 cups whole milk, or half-and-half

1/2 cup sugar

6 large egg yolks

2 ounces (1/2 cup minus 1/2 tablespoon) unbleached
    all-purpose flour

1 teaspoon fine sea salt

2 tablespoons (1 ounce) unsalted butter

1 teaspoon vanilla extract

Topping

3 large egg whites (6 tablespoons)

$^3/_4$ cup sugar

1 teaspoon vanilla extract

1 ounce ($^1/_4$ cup plus 1 tablespoon) potato starch,
  substitute corn, wheat, or rice starch

Preheat the oven to 375°F. Roll out the dough into a large round, $^3/_8$-inch thick, on a lightly floured surface. Transfer to a 9-inch pie pan, preferably aluminum, and press into the pan without stretching the dough and pressing well into the corners so there are no thick spots. Trim the overhang to about 1-inch from the edge and double over, pressing together well so the layers adhere. Crimp or pinch in and out alternatively to form a decorative fluted border. Chill the dough for 30 minutes to relax the gluten and so the crust maintains its shape.

Fit a piece of heavy-duty foil onto the dough and fill with beans or other pie weights. Blind bake (just crust, no filling) on the bottom shelf of the oven until the crust is cooked through but not yet browned, about 30 minute,. Remove the foil and the weights, reduce oven temperature to 325°F and bake for 15 minutes longer, or until the crust is evenly and lightly browned. Remove from the oven and cool to room temperature on a wire rack before filling.

Make the crumble: In the bowl of a standing mixer fitted with the paddle attachment, beat together the confectioners' sugar, peanut butter, and chopped peanuts, until the mixture is crumbly; reserve.

Make the filling: Place the milk in a medium, heavy-bottomed non-aluminum pot and heat to scalding.

In a medium bowl, whisk together 1/4 cup of the sugar and egg yolks until smooth, then whisk in the flour and salt. While whisking, pour in the hot milk to temper the mixture, then transfer the mixture to the pot. Cook over medium-low heat, stirring constantly, especially at the edges, until the mixture bubbles up in the center and thickens. Remove from the heat and immediately stir in the butter and vanilla. Remove from heat and let the custard cool over a second bowl filled with ice and water to make it cool faster, whisking often to prevent a skin from forming.

Make the topping: In the clean and greaseless bowl of a standing mixer fitted with the whisk attachment, beat the egg whites until fluffy, then add the remaining $^1/_2$ cup sugar and vanilla and continue beating until the whites are firm and glossy, 4 to 5 minutes. Sprinkle the potato starch over top and fold into the meringue.

Preheat the oven to 350°F. Pour the custard into the crust, then sprinkle with the peanut crumble. Spoon or pipe the meringue on top of the pie. Bake for 1 hour, or until the meringue is golden brown and crusty. Cool to room temperature on a wire rack before serving. Store refrigerated up to 3 days.

Peanut–Chocolate Bars with Espresso

One of my favorite combinations is peanuts with coffee, and when you add chocolate, it gets even better. The Aztec word for peanuts translates to something like earth-cocoa beans, so the combination of peanuts and chocolate goes far back into the mists of history. If you chop good quality chocolate to add to these quick and easy crunchy bars, the chocolate will partially melt into the bars, making them even richer. Top the bars with a smooth icing made from coffee, chocolate, and a little butter, and you've got a winner.

YIELD: 32 BARS

Bars

$1/4$ pound (1 cup minus 1 tablespoon) unbleached
    all-purpose flour

6 ounces (1 cup) oatmeal

1 teaspoon baking soda

$1/4$ teaspoon fine sea salt

6 ounces ($1 1/2$ sticks) unsalted butter, softened

$1/2$ cup sugar

$1/2$ cup well-packed dark brown sugar

$1/2$ cup creamy, or chunky peanut butter

$1/4$ cup espresso or strong coffee,
    cooled to room temperature

2 tablespoons coffee extract, substitute Kahlúa,
    other coffee liqueur, or more coffee

1 large egg

1 teaspoon vanilla extract

$1/4$ pound semisweet chocolate, chopped finely,
    substitute semisweet chocolate bits

1 cup roasted peanuts, chopped

Glaze

6 ounces semisweet chocolate, chopped finely

$1/4$ cup espresso or strong coffee

2 ounces ($1/2$ stick) unsalted butter, softened

$1/2$ cup roasted peanuts, chopped

Make the bars: Preheat the oven to 350°F. Spray a 13 x 9-inch baking pan with baker's nonstick coating or rub with butter and dust with flour, shaking off the excess.

Whisk together the dry ingredients: flour, oatmeal, baking soda, and salt.

In the bowl of a standing mixer fitted with the paddle attachment, cream the butter, sugar, brown sugar, and peanut butter until light and fluffy, 5 to 6 minutes, scraping down the sides once or twice. Beat in the espresso, coffee extract, egg, and vanilla. Add the flour mixture and beat just long enough to combine. Fold in the chocolate and peanuts.

Spread the batter into the pan and bake for 25 minutes or until lightly browned. Cool on a wire rack to room temperature.

Make the glaze: Place the chocolate in a microwaveable bowl and melt in the microwave on lowest power for 2 minutes at a time, or until just barely melted. Whisk until smooth, then whisk in the coffee and the butter and whisk until smooth. Cool the icing until it's firm enough to hold its shape, then spread over the top of the bars. Sprinkle evenly with the peanuts, then chill for 30 minutes to set the glaze before cutting into bars. Store covered and refrigerated up to 5 days.

Peanut Butter and Jelly Cake

This cake is for PB and J lovers everywhere, and is well suited for both grown-ups and children. A light, peanutty torte made partially with white whole wheat flour is split and filled with strawberry or raspberry jam or jelly, then a light and fluffy buttercream, with peanut butter standing in for some of the butter, is spread over top. It would make a wonderful birthday cake and can be made two or three days ahead of time. Use smooth or chunky peanut butter, according to taste.

YIELD: ONE 10-INCH CAKE, 12 TO 16 SERVINGS

Cake

6 ounces (1 1/4 cups minus 1 tablespoon) unbleached all-purpose flour

1/4 pound (1 cup plus 2 tablespoon) white whole wheat flour

1 teaspoon baking soda

1 teaspoon fine sea salt

6 ounces (1 1/2 sticks) unsalted butter, softened

2 cups sugar

4 large eggs, separated

1/2 pound (1 cup) peanut butter, smooth or chunky

1 teaspoon vanilla extract

1 cup buttermilk

Buttercream and Filling

1 cup sugar

4 large egg yolks

1/2 pound (1 cup) peanut butter, smooth or chunky

6 ounces (1 1/2 sticks) unsalted butter, cut into bits and softened

1 teaspoon vanilla extract

1 cup strawberry or raspberry preserves

1/2 cup roasted peanuts (may be salted, but rub in a towel to remove some of the salt), chopped

Make the cake: Preheat the oven to 350°F. Spray a 10-inch cake pan with baker's nonstick coating or rub with butter and dust with flour, shaking off the excess.

Whisk together the dry ingredients: all-purpose flour, whole wheat flour, baking soda, and salt.

In the bowl of a standing mixer fitted with the paddle attachment, cream the butter and 1 cup of sugar until light and fluffy, 5 to 6 minutes. Beat in the egg yolks, one at a time, beating well after each addition. Beat in the peanut butter and the vanilla. Transfer the batter to a wide shallow bowl. Alternating, fold in the flour mix and the buttermilk, beginning and ending with the flour mixture.

In the clean and greaseless bowl of a standing mixer fitted with the whisk attachment, beat the egg whites until fluffy, then add the remaining 1 cup sugar and continue beating until the whites are firm and glossy, 4 to 5 minutes. Fold into batter in thirds, so as not to deflate the meringue.

Spread the batter evenly into the pan and rap once or twice on a work surface to release any large air bubbles. Bake for 50 minutes or until the cakes starts to come away from the sides of the pan and a toothpick or skewer stuck in the center comes out clean. Cool the cake in the pan on wire racks for about 30 minutes. Remove the cake from the pan, and cool completely on a wire rack.

Make the buttercream: Combine the sugar and 1 cup of water in a small heavy-bottomed pot and bring to a boil. Continue boiling until the syrup reaches the firm-ball stage, 250°F on a candy thermometer, or when a spoonful dropped in a glass of ice water forms a firm ball.

Meanwhile, place the egg yolks in the bowl of a standing mixer fitted with the whisk attachment. Beat for 1 minute or until the mixture is sticky. Reduce the mixer speed to low and pour in the sugar syrup into the center of the bowl while still beating. Continue beating until the mixture reaches room temperature, about 10 minutes. Beat in the peanut butter, then add the butter and vanilla, beating well until combined and completely smooth. (Store the buttercream tightly covered in the refrigerator for up to 2 weeks, but always use soft, fluffy buttercream when icing a cake.)

Cut a very small notch, about ¼-inch deep from the side of the cake to use as a guide. Using a long serrated knife, split the cake into two even layers, then spread the cut side of the bottom layer with the preserves. Cover with the top layer, then spread the buttercream over the top and sides of the cake. Then re-assemble the cake using the cut notch as a guide to line up the cut layers in the original position. Then spread the buttercream over the top and sides of the cake. Sprinkle the cake with the peanuts and chill for at least 1 hour, or until the icing has set, before cutting into portions.

Peanut Meringues with Spiced Bittersweet Chocolate Puddings

The duo of peanuts and chocolate dates back to Aztec times. In this Mexican dessert, ground peanuts are folded into sweet meringue and piped into sticks. The light golden brown meringues come out looking a bit like peanuts in their shell or those peanut marshmallow candies. Accompanying the meringues are small, spiced chocolate puddings, scented with cinnamon, allspice, and cloves in the Mexican way with chocolate. You'll need to buy roasted but unsalted peanuts or rinse and dry salted ones. The meringues are best made on a dry day as humidity will make them sticky.

YIELD: 12 SERVINGS

Meringues

6 ounces (1 ¼ cups) roasted peanuts,

2 ounces (½ cup minus 2 teaspoons) unbleached
   all-purpose flour

½ teaspoon fine sea salt

½ pound (2 cups plus 2 tablespoons) confectioners'
   sugar

8 large egg whites (1 cup), at room temperature

¾ cup sugar

Puddings

2 tablespoons (1 ounce) unsalted butter, softened

½ pound bittersweet chocolate, finely chopped

4 large eggs

¼ cup sugar

1 cup milk, scalded

$^1\!/_2$ cup heavy cream, scalded

$^1\!/_2$ cup strong hot coffee

$^1\!/_4$ cup Kahlúa, or other coffee liqueur

$^1\!/_2$ teaspoon ground cinnamon

$^1\!/_4$ teaspoon ground allspice

Pinch ground cloves

1 teaspoon vanilla extract

$^1\!/_4$ pound (1 cup) roasted peanuts, finely chopped

Make the meringues: Preheat the oven to 275°F. Line an 18 x 13-inch half sheet pan (or other large baking pan) with parchment paper or a silicone baking mat.

In the bowl of a food processor, combine the peanuts, flour, salt, and confectioners' sugar, and process until finely ground.

In the clean and greaseless bowl of a standing mixer fitted with the whisk attachment, beat the egg whites until fluffy, then add the sugar and continue beating until the whites are firm and glossy, 4 to 5 minutes. Transfer the meringue to a wide shallow bowl, then fold in the peanut mixture. Spoon or pipe the batter onto the baking pan into 2-inch long tubes. Bake for 45 minutes, then reduce the oven temperature to 225°F and continue baking for 30 minutes or until lightly colored and firm. Cool completely on a wire rack.

Make the puddings: Preheat the oven to 325°F. Rub 12 small ramekins or custard cups that hold about $^1\!/_2$ cup each with the softened butter. Place the chocolate in a microwaveable bowl and melt in the microwave on lowest power for 2 minutes at a time, or until just barely melted. Whisk until smooth and cool to room temperature.

In a large bowl, whisk together the eggs and sugar. Whisk in the warm melted chocolate, the milk, cream, coffee, Kahlúa, cinnamon, allspice, cloves, and vanilla. Transfer the batter to a large spouted measuring cup or pitcher and fill the ramekins to about $^1\!/_2$-inch from the top. Sprinkle each pudding generously with chopped peanuts. Arrange the ramekins in a large baking pan filled with enough hot water to come about halfway up the side of the pan, Cover the pan with foil, and prick the foil to allow steam to escape and bake for 25 minutes or until the center is just set in the center. Serve the puddings while still hot accompanied by the meringues. (If made ahead, reheat the puddings on medium power 2 minutes at a time or until just heated through.)

PEARS

Choosing, Storing, and
Ripening Pears . . . 637

Winter Pear Varieties . . . 638

Summer (or Butter) Pear Varieties . . . 639

Harry and David's "Royal Riviera" Pears . . . 640

Antique Italian Pear Varieties at
Archeologia Arborea in Umbria . . . 641

Modern Italian Pear Varieties . . . 641

BUTTERSCOTCH-GINGER PEAR TART . . . 641

To Poach Pears . . . 643

OATMEAL PEAR CRISP WITH DRIED CHERRIES . . . 643

PEAR AND TOASTED PECAN BUNDT CAKE
WITH BROWN SUGAR GLAZE . . . 644

BITTER CHOCOLATE-HAZELNUT
TORTA WITH PEARS . . . 645

PEARS

Not many years ago, I would happily buy wood crates of pears from Oregon's Hood and Rogue River Valleys, each delicately wrapped with a sheet of tissue paper to keep the fruit warm and protected from bruising, each crate identified with an artful label. Today, too many pears are picked too green and hard, and while they're no longer packed in wood, they are often handled as if they're made from wood–and in fact, sometimes, they taste like they're made of it, as well. But simply by paying attention to the fruit we buy, choosing for quality and variety, not just price, and buying local whenever possible, we can help encourage caring growers to continue their necessary work. People like Isabelle dalla Ragione, whom I met in Italy. This caring grower is rescuing antique pear trees in Umbria–some as old as two hundred and fifty years–and propagating them at the arboretum started by her and her late father, Livio dalla Ragione (for more information, see page 641).

Pears can be added to cakes, tarts, and pies raw or pre-cooked. Winter pears are firmer and good for poaching, baking, and roasting; soft pears, like Bartletts and Anjou (or d'Anjou) can be eaten out of hand or gently poached. Even canned pears, usually Bartletts, taste good in baked goods and other desserts. Like French couture fashion and fine restaurants, pears automatically have cachet, which I took advantage of in my chef years. Make a tart or cake with apples, and it'll be homey; use pears instead, and the dessert will automatically garner that French panache that makes it worth more money in a restaurant. Classic French desserts like pear frangipane tart (pears baked over almond cream) and poires Belle Helene (poached pears over vanilla ice cream, topped with chocolate sauce) depend on buttery, ripe, juicy pears like the ultra-creamy French Comice pear.

People have been eating fresh and dried pears for thousands of years. The various names for this fruit–*poire* in French, *pera* in Italian and Spanish, *peer* in Dutch, and even *birnbaum* (pear tree) in German–all originate from a language older than our Indo-European ancestral language. Because of this, it seems the fruit was cultivated from the Caspian Sea as far west to the Atlantic. It is unlikely that the common pear, *P. communis*, was gathered and eaten from the wild because it would have been too small, hard, and gritty to be palatable.

Three pear species account for the vast majority

of this fruit: the European pear, *Pyrus communis*, cultivated mainly in Europe and North America; the Chinese white pear (*bai li* in Chinese) *Pyrus × bretschneideri*; and the Nashi Pear, *Pyrus pyrifolia*, also known as the Asian Pear or Apple Pear. Chinese pears are thought to have originated in the western part of the country in the foothills of the Tian Shan Mountains, spreading east and west from there along the mountain chains and evolving into more than twenty varieties. Pears have been cultivated in China for approximately 3,000 years, about the same amount of time as European pears. Both Asian species grow mainly in eastern Asia and each has thousands of cultivars. Native to central and southern China, the Nashi Pear was probably the first to be domesticated, because even the fruits of wild trees are edible. Asian pears traveled from China to Japan, Korea, and Taiwan, where they are extensively cultivated today.

European pears probably originated in Central Asia, spread into the Fertile Crescent and then to Greece, Italy, and Western Europe. Pears are widely distributed throughout temperate Europe and traces of cultivated pears have been found in the oldest Swiss lake-dwellings. The Greek poet, Homer, in the eighth century BCE, referred to pears as a "gift of the gods." Evidently, the Romans agreed, and proceeded to use grafting techniques to develop more than fifty varieties, also introducing the pear to other parts of Europe including England. Wall paintings in Pompeii (destroyed by the eruption of Mount Vesuvius in 79 CE) show birds on a tree laden with small pears and a bird pecking at pears not much different from those of today. At the time of the Norman Conquest, the *Domesday Book*, the great survey of England executed for William "the Conqueror" and completed in 1086, mentions the use of pear trees as boundary markers.

Early in the ninth century, several varieties of pears were already being cultivated in France, which by the eleventh century, had already established itself as the pear center of Europe. King Louis the XIV of France knew that a perfect pear has no peer. He would meticulously peel the fruit in a single long strip so he could cleverly wrap its skin back into place, bestowing his conceit upon one of his flavored courtiers or courtesans. His French subjects knew of three hundred varieties of pears, but connoisseurs considered only twenty-five worth eating.

These best of fruits were quite challenging to raise in the open orchards of the time, because they would ripen at different times, rather than all at once. French Monks used the espalier technique developed by the Romans, but first seen on an Egyptian wall painting, to train fruit trees, particularly apples, figs, and pears, into flattened shoulder-height forms to grow against a sunny wall. The French *espalier* comes from the Italian *spalla* (shoulder) and *spalliera*, something to rest the shoulder against. The technique transformed pears growing near Paris, because the crop could be easily controlled and harvested. Pears grew in elaborate espaliered configurations in the king's garden at Versailles. Most pears of the time were best suited to baking; soft dessert pears only appeared after the mid-sixteenth century.

Horticulturists in the French province of Anjou began cultivating the Doyenne du Comice in the 1850s, still the reigning queen of pears. Anjous, known originally as d'Anjou Beurré (buttered pear of Anjou, today's Angers) are America's most common dessert pear. Small pears with white down on the under surface of their leaves are used in France to make *perry*, the pear-equivalent of cider. Other small-fruited pears are found growing in the wild in western France, and in Devonshire and Cornwall in Western England, although these trees are likely the seeds of cultivated trees deposited by birds, which then reverted into wild spine-bearing trees.

Among the pears known in the sixteenth century Europe was the Popering, mentioned by Mercutio in Shakespeare's *Romeo and Juliet*, probably a Flemish variety, named for Popering in Flanders. Until the fourteenth century, all the pears grown in Britain originated in France. Even in 1860, most of the hundreds of pear varieties described in Robert Hogg's *The Fruit Manual*, had French names like Albertine, Beurre d'Amanlis, Ambrette d'Hiver, Arbre Superbe, Belle d'Esquerme, Duc de Brabant, Vert Longue, and Jalousie de Fontenay. La Juive (the Jewess) was described as, "Fruit medium sized, pyramidal. Skin of a uniform pale yellow color, mottled with pale brown russet, and thickly covered with russet dots. Eye small and open, with short, erect segments even with the surface. Stalk about an inch long, stout, and tapering into the fruit, or obliquely inserted. Flesh yellowish, buttery, and melting, very juicy, sugary, and rich."

Thought to date back to Roman times, the earliest British cultivar was the Warden pear, cultivated by the skillful Cistercian monks of Warden Abbey in England, founded in the twelfth century. These large, coarse-fleshed baking pears were baked in the Warden pies colored with saffron mentioned in Shakespeare's *A Winter's Tale*. Because they were quite long-lasting, wardens were used to feed English troops. When Queen Elizabeth I visited the city of Worcester in August 1575, a Warden pear tree, heavily laden with fruit, was planted by the gate by which Her Majesty was to enter the city. The Queen admired the tree and its fruit and directed that three of these pears be added to the coat of arms of the city.

The Bartlett pear was first propagated by in seventeenth-century England in Berkshire by a schoolmaster named John Stair from a wildling. Stair sold some of his cuttings to a horticulturist named Williams, who further developed the variety and renamed it after himself. Seedlings from these pears crossed the Atlantic with the early colonists. In 1812, nurseryman Enoch Bartlett, of Dorchester, Massachusetts, started distributing the same pear under his own name, apparently unaware that it already had a name. Ever since, this fruit has been known as the Bartlett in the United States and as the Williams elsewhere. Bartlett pear trees traveled West in the covered wagons of the 49ers heading for the Great California Gold Rush.

In the 1800s, pears growing in the Pacific Northwest escaped fire blight, a disease that limited pear cultivation in the east. Today, more than ninety percent of the American pear crop is grown in that region. The Rogue Valley in southern Oregon has long been known for the high quality of its Bosc and Comice pears. It the 1970s, it was the first area to raise the newer red skinned pears. Excellent growing conditions and bountiful harvests have made Oregon's Hood River County America's largest producer of pears. Over 12,000 acres are dedicated to the production of green and red Anjou, Bartlett, Comice, Bosc, Forelle, and Seckel pears.

In the United States, almost sixty percent of pears are sold in the fresh market, the rest are mostly canned. Americans eat over five pounds of pears per person. Pears can be categorized as grainy hard or winter pears, best cooked or baked, and soft, melt-in-your-mouth dessert or butter pears. Sweet, crisp Asian pears, known for good reason as sand pears, are juicy eaten right out of hand, though their slightly gritty texture can take a little getting used to.

In this book, diced, juicy Asian pears add flavor and appealing light texture to the Morning Glory Muffins with Carrots, Asian Pears, and Ginger (page 240). In Umbria, pears have long been a favorite fruit for cooking and baking. The traditional Brustengolo: Umbrian Cornmeal, Pear, Raisin, and Nut Cake (page 389) is chunky and moist with pears. A trio of dried and fresh pears, toasted hazelnuts, and brown butter complement each other perfectly in the Hazelnut–Brown Butter Cakes with Bosc Pears (page 505). Fresh ginger lends a spicy note to the smooth butterscotch pudding filling topped with poached pear fans in the Butterscotch–Ginger Pear Tart (page 641).

Easy enough for children to make (apple crisp is one of the first desserts I ever made), the homey Oatmeal Pear Crisp with Dried Cherries (page 643) combines pears with tangy mahogany-red dried cherries. Grated pears make for a moist Pear and Toasted Pecan Bundt Cake with Brown Sugar Glaze (page 644), a favorite of my daughter, Ginevra. The sophisticated Bitter Chocolate–Hazelnut Torta with Pears (page 645) comes from Northern Italy, where barely sweetened chocolate is preferred, and combines three European favorites: dark chocolate, toasted hazelnuts, and pears.

CHOOSING, STORING, AND RIPENING PEARS

It is said that one must sit up all night to catch a pear at its precise moment of ripe perfection, although pears are one of the few fruits that do not ripen well on the tree. The fruits must be harvested by hand when they are fully mature, but not yet ripe.

Choose pears that are bright and fresh looking though not overly green, and without bruises. Note that because Comice have very fragile skins, they may appear bruised on the surface, but this does not usually indicate damage on their juicy interiors. Take special care in handling these fruit even before they ripen.

Pears ripen after they are harvested but only Bartletts change color noticeably as they ripen from light green to pale yellow. The best test for ripeness is aroma: if the pears give off a peary fragrance, it's ready. Alternatively, test for ripeness by pressing gently near the stem: the pear should give to gentle pressure. Because pears ripen from the inside out, pears that are soft around the middle will generally be over-ripe.

Store unripe pears in a single layer in a warm place in a fruit bowl or in a brown paper bag to encourage ripening, checking the fruit every day. Pears produce ethylene as they ripen, so avoid storing them next to ethylene-sensitive produce such as bananas, tomatoes, avocadoes, honeydew melons, and apples. Pears may also absorb odors produced by onions and potatoes, while the ethylene given off by ripe pears will impart a bitter flavor to carrots. Store ripe pears 3 to 4 days in the refrigerator.

WINTER PEAR VARIETIES

BOSC: Also known as Beurre Bosc, Gold Bosc, Golden Russet Bosc, and Kaiser Alexander, these large, firm, winter pears are the aristocrat of the pear family. Boscs originated in Belgium, cultivated first in 1807 by Van Mons who named them Calebasse Bosc in honor of Monsieur Bosc, a distinguished Belgian cultivator. The Bosc has a silhouette that is unique among pears, sitting on a plump bottom that tapers elegantly to a curved point. Its russeted (rough) warm earthy-brown skin does not change colors as the fruit ripens. The firm, crisp, creamy-white flesh is slightly fibrous, though saturated with syrupy juices, and with hints of vanilla and spice. Boscs have the highest sugar content of all commercial pears and hold their shape particularly well, so they are ideal for baking and poaching.

KIEFFER: This hybrid cross of a Chinese Sand Pear and a Bartlett originated in Pennsylvania and was named in 1876 by its grower, Peter Kieffer. Kieffers grew extensively in the United States in the early 1900s and can still be found in small orchards and at farmers' markets. This small pear is squat and rounded in shape, with greenish yellow-skin often blushed with dull red, and large russet dots. Its white, coarse-textured flesh is crisp and juicy with a definite musky flavor. Best suited to baking or poaching, the Kieffer is a late pear, in season from mid-September to mid-October. If allowed to remain on the tree, it becomes softer and sweeter, though it will not ripen further after harvest.

SECKEL: Seckel pears, also known as Sugar or Honey pears, were named by Mr. Seckel, who, discovered and propagated the wild seedling pear he found growing near Philadelphia in the early 1800s. The smallest of all commercially grown pears, Seckels have rotund bodies, small necks, and short stems. Their smooth, thin olive-green to brownish skin has a prominent red blush. Firm, sweet, and spicy, with cream to ivory flesh and crisp though somewhat grainy texture makes them best for cooking, preserves, or canning. Their small size and attractive appearance makes Seckels ideal for autumn holiday garnishes or to serve with a cheese course. Seckels don't change color when they ripen.

SUMMER (OR BUTTER) PEAR VARIETIES

ANJOU AND RED ANJOU: In America, these squat pears are known as Anjou; in France, as d'Anjou or Beurré d'Anjou. They were introduced to England early in the nineteenth century and brought to America about 1842. Anjous have a larger rounded bottom that gradually tapers to a smaller rounded top, and they keep their light green color even when ripe. They have thin skin, and smooth, cream to ivory flesh full of tart juices when ripe. They are the most common pear in America because of their notable ability to resist the hazards of cold storage and long-distance transport. Anjous are a useful but not prized pear, because they are not quite as sweet or flavorful as other varieties. However, Anjous are readily available and their firmer texture makes them good candidates for cooking or baking.

The much newer Red Anjous, also known as Gebhard Red or LeRoi, originated in the United States in 1956. They have deep, rich, maroon color, mild, sweet flavor, and smooth flesh that is full of juices when ripe.

BARTLETT AND RED BARTLETT: To me, the Bartlett pear, called the William's or William's Bon Chrétien (good Christian) in England and France, is the finest eating pear—excluding the expensive, though exquisite, Comice. Given the choice between a Bartlett and an Anjou, often found for sale at the same time, I'll always choose the Bartlett. Seventy-five percent of all pears grown in the United States are Bartletts, which have the quintes-

sential pear shape: a rounded bell on their bottom half, a well-defined sloping shoulder, with a smaller neck. Bartletts' thin, pale green skin mellows to a warm yellow when ripe. The pear has juicy flesh with a smooth, buttery texture. When ripe, Bartletts give off a distinctive musky aroma that can fill a room. The Bartlett is America's favorite pear, although much of the crop ends up in cans and some are dried in halves. The saying goes that this summer pear should never see the October page of the calendar.

The Bartlett is the same pear you'd find in a bottle of Swiss Poire Eau de Vie. (But don't buy the bottle with the pear, even though it's as surprising as seeing a ship in a bottle, because, as I found from personal experience, the pear actually tastes terrible.) These pears are excellent for eating out of hand, and baking in tarts, pies, and cakes, and cobblers.

The Red Bartlett or Williams Rouge originated in the United States in 1934. Their bright red skin is extremely thin and smooth; their fine-grained, buttery flesh is fine-grained and full of sweet, highly perfumed, winey juices

COMICE: The Comice, short for Doyenne de Comice, originated in France in 1849 and is still considered by pear connoisseurs, including myself, to be the finest eating pear. In America, the best of these fat, lumpy-looking, rotund, yellowish-green pears are grown in Southern Oregon. This large, often russeted or red blushed pear has smooth, meltingly buttery flesh, copious juices, and a full-bodied, fruity fragrance. Comices will display almost no color change as they ripen. Their relative rarity and high price means that they're usually eaten out of hand, though they are wonderful when poached. I still remember the melting poached Comice pears I enjoyed at Chez Panisse more than twenty years ago. Take special care in handling these pears even before they ripen.

FORELLE: The small green and red speckled Forelle pear is also called the "trout pear" (*forelle* is the German word for "trout") because its spotted markings are similar to those on the fish. The Forelle has been known under that name in Saxony since the early eighteenth century, but the variety itself is thought to be much older. Its symmetrical, bell-shaped body rests on a small round base that tapers evenly to a short neck with a long, narrow stem. Forelles have attractive, thin, yellow skin freckled with crimson lenticles (which allow the pear to breath), and firm cream to ivory flesh. Forelles are sometimes tricky to ripen, but can be very sweet and juicy, with firm, slightly grainy flesh.

PACKHAM PEAR: Also known as Packham's Triumph, this fruit was first bred in Australia in 1897 as a cross between a Bartlett and the Yvedale St. Germain. It is the Australian pear of choice and is grown extensively throughout the Southern Hemisphere. This later season pear resembles the Anjou in overall shape and size, though it is less symmetrical and has smooth, thin, green skin. Its flesh is a bit coarse with strings close to the core. When fully ripe, Packhams are juicy and sweet and are excellent eaten out of hand, but are also well-suited to baking and cooking.

HARRY AND DAVID'S "ROYAL RIVIERA" PEARS

Samuel Rosenberg, father of Harry and David, was a successful hotel owner in Seattle, Washington, but his true love was agriculture. In 1910, he traded his luxurious Hotel Sorrento for 240 prime acres of pears in Southern Oregon's Rogue River Valley. Following Sam's death just a few years later, his two sons, who had been trained in agriculture at Cornell University, took over the family business. The brothers decided to specialize in the luscious, though easily bruised, Comice pear, for which there was high demand from Europe's grand hotels and restaurants.

It turned out that the Rogue Valley was even better suited to raising the Comice pear than its native France. Naming their super-deluxe pears "Royal Riviera" set them apart. Throughout the Roaring 20s, their fame spread, and business boomed. With the Crash of 1929 and the Great Depression that soon followed, the market disappeared overnight. To find new buyers, the two brothers came up with the innovative idea of selling their pears by mail. In 1934, they made sales trips to San Francisco and New York, where they successfully pitched their pears as an ideal business gift. Today the company is the largest employer in the Rogue River Valley. To order pears from Harry & David, go to www.harryanddavids.com.

ANTIQUE ITALIAN PEAR VARIETIES AT ARCHEOLOGIA ARBOREA IN UMBRIA

Some of the antique pear varieties that have been rescued and propagated at this pear rescue farm in the hills of Umbria include the unusual pink-fleshed Pera Briaca (also known as Cocomerina) that is quite sweet and juicy. The Brutta e Buona (ugly and good) is an almost round-shaped pear that dates from late medieval times and grows in small bunches. Its light green skin is completely russeted (rough brown papery covering), its flesh is white, juicy, crunchy, flavorful, and slightly grainy, suited to candying in sugar syrup or roasting with honey and red wine. Of the many pears growing on the farm (along with other fruits like peaches, plums, apples, and cherries) are the small cinnamon-red bottomed Pera Cannella (cinnamon pears), the long green Pera de Curato (Curate's pear), and the turban-shaped Pera Marzola. For more information and to order the book *Archeologia Arborea, Diario di Due Cercatori di Piante* (*Archeological Arboretum, Diary of Two Plant Explorers*), now available in English, go to www.archeologiaarborea.org.

MODERN ITALIAN PEAR VARIETIES

ABATE: An elongated fall pear with rust-green skin that is good cooked and raw.

COSCIA: A small summer pear with light yellow skin that is best raw.

DECANA: A large fall pear with light yellow to rust skin that is best raw.

KAISER: A tapered fall pear, with russeted skin that is good raw and cooked.

MARTIN SEC: A small fall pear that should be cooked.

Butterscotch-Ginger Pear Tart

In this tart, a nutty, sweet pastry crust is topped with fanned pear halves nestled in whisky-spiked butterscotch custard. When you come across good quality Bartlett pears, this is an excellent tart to make. I prefer American-grown Bartletts, as I've found that imports don't ripen well because they have to be picked too green to survive long-distance shipping. Though softer than and not as flavorful as homemade poached pears, drained canned pear halves will also work here. Use a melon baller or Parisienne cutter to easily remove the pod of seeds from the center of the pears.

YIELD: ONE 10-INCH TART,
10 TO 12 SERVINGS

Pie Crust

3/4 pound Sweet White Whole Wheat Tart Pastry
dough (page 863)

Pears

2 cups dry white wine

1 cup sugar

1 cinnamon stick, crushed

1 bay leaf

4 ripe yet firm Bartlett pears, unpeeled, halved and
cored

Filling

4 large egg yolks

1-inch section fresh ginger, peeled and grated
(about 1 tablespoon)

1/4 pound (3/4 cup firmly packed) dark brown sugar

2 ounces (1/4 cup minus 1 teaspoon) unbleached all-
purpose flour

1/2 teaspoon fine sea salt

1 1/4 cups milk, scalded

2 ounces (1/2 stick) unsalted butter, cut into bits

Make the crust: Roll out the dough on a lightly floured surface into a large (11- to 12-inch) round about 3/8-inch thick. Transfer to a 10-inch tart pan with a removable bottom. Lay into the pan without stretching the dough and press well into the corners so there are no thick spots. Trim any overhang with scissors. Chill the dough for 30 minutes to relax the gluten so the crust maintains its shape well.

Preheat the oven to 375°F. Fit a piece of heavy-duty foil onto the dough and up over the edges and fill with beans or other pie weights. Blind bake (just crust, no filling) on the bottom shelf of the oven until the crust is cooked through but not yet browned, about 30 minutes. Remove the foil and the weights, reduce the oven temperature to 325°F, and bake for 10 minutes longer, or until the crust is evenly and lightly browned. Remove from the oven and cool to room temperature on a wire rack before filling.

Make the pears: In a heavy-bottomed, non-aluminum saucepan just large enough to hold the pears in one layer, combine the wine, sugar, cinnamon stick, and bay leaf, and bring to a boil over moderately high heat, stirring until the liquid is clear. Place the pears, into the pot, and bring the liquid to a boil again, then reduce the heat to a slow simmer and cook for 15 minutes, or until they are just tender when pierced. Allow the pears to cool in the syrup.

Make the filling: In a standing mixer fitted with a whisk attachment, beat the egg yolks, ginger, and brown sugar until well combined. Beat in the flour and salt, then slowly pour in the scalded milk, beating to combine. Transfer the mixture to a medium, heavy-bottomed, non-aluminum pot and bring to a boil over moderate heat, whisking often. As soon as the mixture boils, remove it from the heat and whisk in the butter. Transfer the mixture to a bowl, preferably stainless-steel and cool by placing the bowl over a second bowl filled with a mixture of ice and water, stirring often, until the mixture is cool.

Preheat the oven to 350°F.

Drain the pears well, reserving the syrup. Cut the pears into fan shapes by cutting narrow slices from the bottom three-quarters of the way to the stem end. Spread the pears out from the bottom to form a fan.

Spread the filling into the baked crust. Arrange the

pear fans equidistant from each other on top of the filling, pressing them in gently so they adhere to the filling. Bake for 35 minutes or until the filling is light brown and puffy. Cool to room temperature.

Cook the pear poaching liquid down over moderately high heat until it is thick and syrupy, about 5 minutes, remove the cinnamon stick and bay leaf.and drizzle over each portion before serving.

TO POACH PEARS

Select hard winter pears, like Bosc or Seckel, or use firm but not hard butter pears, especially Bartletts. Make a light sugar syrup, enough to cover the pears, using equal quantities of sugar and water (two cups of each is a good amount to start with). Add flavorings as you wish: a whole vanilla bean split length- wise, soft-stick cinnamon, whole allspice berries, bay leaves, strips of lemon or orange zest, cardamom seeds in their pod, and/or several whole cloves, along with the juice of one lemon. Bring the liquid to a boil.

You may also substitute honey or maple syrup for part of the sugar. Use half as much honey as the sugar it is replacing (honey is half again as sweet as sugar) when making the syrup. Peel the pears and split them in half from the stem to the bottom, leaving the stems attached. Using the smaller end of a melon baller, scoop out around the round ball of flesh containing the seeds. Everything else is edible. Place the pears into the boiling liquid . Slowly bring back to a boil. Simmer until the pears are almost tender through when pricked, about 20 minutes. Remove from the heat and allow the pears to cool in their liquid.

Oatmeal Pear Crisp with Dried Cherries

This fruit crisp is comfort food with a twist: juicy, ripe pears contrast with tangy, mahogany-colored dried cherries. Desserts that combine cold and hot are always exciting to the palate, so serve this hot or warm with a scoop of vanilla ice cream or a dollop of crème fraîche. Be sure the pears are ripe enough to be aromatic and juicy; hard pears will result in a disappointing dessert.

YIELD: 8 TO 10 SERVINGS

5 ounces ($3/4$ cup) rolled oats

1 ounce ($1/4$ cup) white whole wheat flour

$3/4$ cup light brown sugar, packed

1 teaspoon ground cinnamon

$1/2$ teaspoon ground mace

$1/2$ teaspoon fine sea salt

$1/4$ pound (1 stick) unsalted butter,
    chilled and cut into bits

6 firm but ripe Bartlett pears

Juice of 1 lemon

$1/2$ cup dried tart cherries

$3/4$ cup unsweetened crème fraîche, for serving

Preheat the oven to 375°F.

In the bowl of a standing mixer fitted with the paddle attachment, combine the dry ingredients: oats, flour, $1/4$ cup of the brown sugar, the cinnamon, mace, and salt. Add the butter and beat until the mixture resembles oatmeal.

Peel, core, and dice the pears into 1-inch chunks.

Combine with the lemon juice, cherries, and the remaining ½ cup brown sugar. Spoon the mixture into a 9-inch baking dish, preferably ceramic. Sprinkle the top with the oat mixture.

Bake for 40 minutes, or until the pears are soft and bubbling and the topping is brown. Serve hot or warm with a dollop of crème fraîche.

Pear and Toasted Pecan Bundt Cake with Brown Sugar Glaze

This moist, fruity cake is topped with a thin layer of crackly brown sugar glaze and keeps well for four or five days, so it can easily be made ahead. Pears comple-ment the earthy bittersweet flavor of native American pecans, especially when they're toasted—their flavor recalls that of brown butter. Instead of slicing the pears, I grate them without peeling the fruit as the skins disap-pear when cooked. If you have a food processor with a grating plate, the task can be accomplished in minutes.

YIELD: ONE 10-INCH BUNDT CAKE,
12 TO 16 SERVINGS

Cake
³/₄ pound (3 cups minus 3 tablespoons) unbleached
    all-purpose flour
1 teaspoon baking soda
1 teaspoon fine sea salt
1 teaspoon ground cinnamon

2 cups sugar
4 large eggs
2 teaspoons vanilla extract
1½ cups grapeseed or canola oil
4 large Bosc pears, peeled, cored, and grated
4½ ounces (1 cup) pecans, lightly toasted
    and finely chopped

Glaze
¼ pound (1 stick) unsalted butter, cut into bits
½ cup firmly packed dark brown sugar
1 tablespoon milk

Make the cake: Preheat the oven to 350°F. Spray a 10-inch Bundt pan with baker's nonstick coating or rub with butter and dust with flour, shaking off the excess.

Whisk together dry ingredients: flour, baking soda, salt, and cinnamon.

In a standing mixer fitted with the whisk attachment, beat the sugar, eggs, and vanilla until light and fluffy, 5 to 6 minutes. Slowly beat in the oil, allowing it to be fully absorbed before adding more. Transfer to a wide shallow bowl. Fold in the pears with their juices and the pecans. Fold in the flour mixture. Pour the batter into the prepared pan, banging down once or twice on the counter to remove any air bubbles.

Bake the cake for 1 hour, or until a toothpick stuck into the batter comes out clean and the cake has started to pull away from the sides of the pan. Cool the cake for 15 to 20 minutes or until no longer hot, then turn it right side up onto a cake rack placed over a bak-ing pan. Cool to room temperature.

Make the glaze: Combine the butter, brown sugar,

and milk in a small pot and bring to a boil, whisking occasionally. Boil for 2 minutes, or until the mixture is thickened and creamy looking. Cool the glaze until it's just barely warm to the touch and firm enough to hold its shape. (If the glaze separates, add a teaspoon or so more of milk and/or blend until creamy.)

Spoon the icing over cake, allowing it to drip down the sides. If desired, scrape up the excess, using a silicone spatula, and spoon it over the cake again. Let the cake cool completely before cutting into serving portions. Store refrigerated 4 to 5 days.

Bitter Chocolate–Hazelnut Torta with Pears

I picked up a copy of an Italian culinary magazine while in Italy several years ago, and a picture of this easy but sophisticated torta caught my eye. What makes it special, other than the very Italian combination of dark bitter chocolate and roasted hazelnuts, is the way the pears are set into the torta: thin slices of pears are arranged vertically in soldier-like rows across the cake. After baking, the pears get soft and more concentrated in flavor, while the rum mellows the bitterness of the chocolate. If you can make brownies, you can make this cake.

YIELD: 16 SQUARES

$1/2$ pound bittersweet chocolate, finely chopped

5 ounces ($1^1/4$ sticks) unsalted butter, cut into bits

$1/4$ cup dark rum

$1/2$ pound ($1^1/2$ cups) hazelnuts, lightly toasted

3 large firm, but ripe Bartlett pears and skinned

1 cup sugar

4 large eggs

Preheat the oven to 350°F. Spray a 9-inch square baking pan, preferably light-colored aluminum, with nonstick baker's coating, or rub with softened butter and dust with flour, shaking off the excess.

Place the chocolate and butter in a large microwaveable bowl and melt in the microwave on lowest power for 2 minutes at a time, or until just barely melted. Whisk until smooth. Whisk in the rum and then cool the mixture to room temperature.

Cut the pears in half, vertically, and core them, cut off and discard the tips and ends, and slice them thinly crosswise.

Place the hazelnuts and sugar in the bowl of a food processor and process until fine. Fold into the chocolate mixture, then beat in the eggs. Spoon the mixture into the prepared pan. Stand the pear slices vertically, in a regular pattern, with their skin skin-side out, into the batter, leaving about $1/2$-inch of pear showing.

Bake for 25 minutes or until the cake starts to come away from the sides of the pan and the center is set. The batter will still be sticky and soft. Remove from the oven and cool to room temperature on a wire rack before cutting into 16 squares. Store covered and refridgerated up to 4 days.

PECANS

Buying and Storing Pecans . . . 649

Hickory Nuts . . . 649

CREOLE PECAN PRALINES . . . 650

Pralines in Louisiana . . . 651

HEIRLOOM SWEET POTATO-PRALINE PIE . . . 651

RUM PECAN-PRALINE SANDIES . . . 652

TURTLE BROWNIES WITH CARAMEL AND PECANS . . . 653

CRANBERRY-CARAMEL PECAN TART . . . 654

PECANS

Americans love soft, golden-brown pecans, and they show up in all sorts of American baked goods in this book, and everywhere else. Butter pecan ice cream is very popular (it's still my favorite), and almost every restaurant in America serves pecan pie. In this book, these delectable nuts are showcased in the Cocoa Nib and Pecan Praline Chocolate Roulade (page 340) and the Oatmeal–Pecan Fruities (page 425), taking oatmeal raisins cookies a step beyond the norm, adding dates, pecans, dried cranberries, and candied orange rind. The Pecan–Ginger Cake with Caramel Icing (page 494) is an old-fashioned layer cake right out of an idealized mirror-backed revolving glass dessert case at the highway diner– if they used lots of pecans, real vanilla, and butter, that is. And the Key Lime Cheesecake Pie in a Coconut–Pecan Crust (page 548) is an easy, no-bake pie that is sure to be a big hit. And there's so much more. . . .

Native to the Mississippi River Valley, the versatile and buttery pecan is a member of the hickory family and is closely related to the walnut. Pecan trees are better known for their wood, which is used for smoking, than their nuts, which are notoriously difficult to shell. The pecan nut's original botanical name, *Hicoria pecan*, was changed to *Carya illinoinensis* in the late seventeenth century after fur traders brought the nuts to the Atlantic coast from Illinois, calling them Illinois nuts or Mississippi nuts. The English term, *pecan*, which first appeared in print in 1773, comes from the Algonquin word *paccan* or *pakan*, which also refers to walnuts and hickory nuts. The term means "a nut so hard, it has to be cracked with a stone." Native American tribes north and south of the border depended on pecans as readily available for food in autumn.

By the late 1770s, the economic potential of pecans was realized by French and Spanish colonists settling along the Gulf of Mexico. By 1802, the French had begun exporting pecans to the West Indies–although this trade may have started even earlier with Spanish colonists.

In 1822, Abner Landrum of South Carolina discovered a pecan budding technique, which provided a way to graft plants derived from superior wild trees. However, this invention was lost or overlooked until 1876 when an African–American slave from successfully propagated pecans by grafting a superior wild pecan to seedling pecan stocks at Louisiana's Oak Alley plantation. This clone was named "Centennial" because it won the Best Pecan Exhibited award at the Philadelphia Centennial Exposition in 1876. A landmark planting that year of 126 Centennial trees was the first official orchard of these improved pecans. Starting in the 1880s, Louisiana and Texas nurserymen learned of pecan grafting and began propagation on a commercial level. Today, Georgia, Oklahoma, and Texas all produce large amounts of pecans.

BUYING AND STORING PECANS

Purchase unshelled pecans that feel heavy for their size, and are uncracked and free of blemishes. Shake the nuts—if they rattle in the shell, avoid them. Rattling is an indication of age. Pecans have a high oil content and can go rancid quickly. Avoid bulk bins of shelled pecans and stick with those that are in sealed packages or tins with expiration dates.

Available year-round, fresh pecans are generally at their peak the first three weeks after harvesting season in the fall. After that, they will slowly begin their decline into rancidity. Properly stored at room temperature, unshelled pecans will keep up to three months. Once they are shelled, they should be stored in a sealed container (to prevent them from absorbing unwanted odors) in the refrigerator up to six months or up to a year in the freezer. Pecans can be frozen shelled or unshelled; shelled pecans should always be kept in a closed container.

HICKORY NUTS

The large American shagbark hickory tree, *Carya ovata*, can easily by recognized by its shaggy bark, and can live for two hundred years. The word *hickory* is derived from the word *pawcohiccora*, an Algonquin term for a ground meal made from the nuts and used as a sort of spread or sauce. The nuts are gathered in the fall in the eastern part of the United States from Maine to eastern Texas. Though seldom grown commercially, hickory nuts are prized for their sweet and very rich flavor that has no trace of tannic bitterness. These nuts can replace pecans in any recipe. The hard wood of the tree is typically used for smoking meats like ham and bacon, and an extract from the bark is used to make a sweet syrup with a slightly bitter, smoky flavor.

Along with the pecan, the hickory nut was a staple food for Native Americans and early colonists. Native Americans would gather the nuts and cure them in a dry spot for about a week. Then, with great patience, they would extract the precious flesh from the hard, white shells, using a special tool. Because these nuts are so hard to crack, they can be fairly expensive. Order them in season from Ray's Hickory Nuts in Wisconsin (www.rayshickorynuts.com).

Creole Pecan Pralines

A specialty of Louisiana and the surrounding region, locals that have been making these soft, slightly grainy brown sugar and pecan candies for years are able to judge the perfect moment of readiness by eye and by texture. readiness by eye and by texture. The superior heat-conducting properties of a heavy copper pot will work best for melting and cooking the sugar evenly. For the rest of us, a candy thermometer also makes it easy to judge when the sugar syrup is ready. These tender caramel-flavored pralines are ground up to make the topping for the Heirloom Sweet Potato-Praline Pie (page 651).

YIELD: ABOUT 36 PRALINES

4 cups sugar

$^3/_4$ pound (3 cups) pecans, lightly toasted
   and kept warm

$^1/_4$ pound (1 stick) unsalted butter,
   cut into bits and softened

2 teaspoons vanilla extract

1 teaspoon fine sea salt

Line three 18 x 13-inch half sheet pans (or other large baking pans) with silicone baking mats or wax paper.

Combine 3 cups of the sugar and 1 cup of water in a medium-to-large, heavy-bottomed pot. Bring the mixture to a boil. Continue to cook until the mixture is thickened and bubbling and it reaches the soft-ball stage, 238°F on a candy thermometer, or when a spoonful dropped in a small bowl of ice water forms a soft ball.

Immediately remove from the heat and keep warm.

Meanwhile, place the remaining 1 cup of sugar in a small, heavy-bottomed pot, preferably copper, and cook over low heat until the sugar begins to melt and turns golden, about 8 minutes. As the sugar melts, shake the pot carefully (CARAMEL IS EXTREMELY HOT!) so the sugar cooks evenly or stir it with a wooden spoon, until the sugar is medium brown in color with a faint touch of redness. Carefully add this dark caramel to the warm sugar syrup, and stir with a long wooden spoon to combine. Heat the mixture over medium high heat until it again reaches the soft ball stage, 238°F on a candy thermometer, or when a spoonful dropped into a small bowl of ice water forms a soft ball.

Immediately remove from the heat and stir in the pecans, butter, vanilla, and salt. Mix with the wooden spoon until the mixture thickens enough to hold its shape. Use two spoons to scoop by the tablespoonful onto the wax paper, scooping with one spoon and using the second spoon to scrape the mixture off into a rounded mound onto the pan. Cool the pralines completely at room temperature, then remove them from the mats or wax paper. Store in a tightly covered container for 2 to 3 days. The pralines will be at their softest and creamiest on the first day.

PRALINES IN LOUISIANA

Like the city of New Orleans, the praline grew from aristocratic French roots but evolved into something quite different in America. According to French food historians, the seventeenth-century French chef of the diplomat Marshal Duplessis-Praslin first developed a technique for coating almonds in caramelized sugar, which he then presented as gifts to the ladies he courted. The confections traveled with French colonists to the new lands in Mississippi, where both sugar cane and nuts grew in abundance. In Louisiana kitchens, locals substituted native pecans for the almonds and add cream or butter to mellow and soften the praline's slightly grainy and crumbly texture. Its proper pronunciation in New Orleans is "prah-lean," not "pray-lean."

Even before the Civil War, free women of color already specialized in making and selling the pralines for "pin money." The 1901 *Picayune's Creole Cook Book* published by the Daily Picayune newspaper explained that "the word 'Praline' is entirely associated in New Orleans with the delicious...brown [candies], made of pecans and sugar, which are sold by the old Creole negro women of New Orleans. The *Pralinieres,* as they are called, may always be found . . . going about the streets of the Old French Quarter, selling their wares of an evening." In his 1945 book, *Gumbo Ya-Ya,* Louisiana folklorist Lyle Saxon described African-American women dressed in gingham with starched white aprons and *tignons,* (head wraps), fanning their soft praline candies with palmetto leaves to keep them cool while enticing passersby with their cries of *"belles pralines!"*

Heirloom Sweet Potato–Praline Pie

This pie originated in Oklahoma, where pecans can be picked right off the tree after the first frost, perfect for Thanksgiving. It's wonderful served warm or at room temperature. I prefer to use yellow (sometimes called white) sweet potatoes like the Hayman, Nancy Hall, and Jersey Yellow, because they are denser with a chestnut-like texture and flavor, but the choice is yours.

YIELD: ONE 9-INCH PIE, 8 TO 10 SERVINGS

$^3/_4$ pound Butter Pie Crust (page 203)

1 pound (1 large or 2 medium) sweet potatoes

2 large eggs

1 cup well-packed light brown sugar

2 ounces ($^1/_2$ stick) unsalted butter, melted and cooled

$^1/_2$ cup heavy cream

1 teaspoon ground cinnamon

1 teaspoon ground ginger

$^1/_2$ teaspoon freshly grated nutmeg

$^1/_2$ teaspoon fine sea salt

$^3/_4$ cup crumbled Creole Pecan Pralines (page 650)

Roll out the pastry into a large round about $^3/_8$-inch thick and use it to line a 9-inch pie pan. Chill for 1 hour in the refrigerator or 30 minutes in the freezer to set the shape.

Place a steamer basket inside a medium pot with a lid and add enough water to come up 1-inch in the pot. Add the sweet potatoes, cover, and steam over moderate heat for 40 minutes or until tender, checking to make sure the water hasn't boiled away. Drain well and cool slightly. When cool enough to handle, peel the sweet potatoes and transfer to a medium bowl. Coarsely mash the potatoes (you should have about 2 cups). Add the eggs, brown sugar, butter, cream, cinnamon, ginger, nutmeg, and salt, and mash thoroughly.

Preheat the oven to 400°F. Spread the sweet potato mixture over the bottom of the crust. Sprinkle the crumbled pralines over top.

Bake the pie on the bottom shelf of the oven for 10 minutes, then reduce the oven temperature to 350°F and bake until the filling is set in the center and just beginning to puff, about 45 minutes. Set the pie on a wire rack to cool to room temperature. Store covered and at room temperature for up to two days or refrigerated up to five days.

Rum Pecan–
Praline Sandies

These melt-in-your-mouth shortbread cookies are made with nothing but pecans, sugar, butter, more sugar, more pecans, and enough flour to give them body. White whole wheat flour makes them even nuttier. You start by making a sugar caramel without any water, so it ends up quite hard and not at all sticky, best for making praline. If you don't have a copper pot, use the heaviest small pot in your kitchen for even melting of the sugar.

YIELD: ABOUT 4 DOZEN COOKIES

1 cup sugar

$^1/_4$ pound (1 cup) pecans, lightly toasted and kept warm

$^3/_4$ pound (2$^3/_4$ cups plus 1 tablespoon) unbleached all-purpose flour

$^1/_4$ pound (1 cup plus 2 tablespoons) white whole wheat flour

2 teaspoons baking powder

1 teaspoon fine sea salt

1 pound (4 sticks) unsalted butter, softened

1 cup confectioners' sugar

1 teaspoon vanilla extract

$^1/_4$ cup dark rum

1 cup ($^1/_4$ pound) pecan halves

Preheat the oven to 325°F. Line an 18 x 13-inch half sheet pan or other large baking pan with parchment paper or a silicone baking mat.

Make the pecan praline: Place the sugar in a medium, heavy-bottomed pot, preferably copper, and cook over low heat until the sugar begins to melt and turns golden, about 8 minutes. As sugar melts, shake the pot carefully (CARAMEL IS EXTREMELY HOT!), so the sugar cooks evenly, or stir with a wooden spoon, until it reaches 350°F on a candy thermometer and the sugar is medium brown in color with a faint touch of redness.

Immediately, remove from the heat and stir in the first quantity of pecans, using a wooden spoon. Immediately spread the mixture into the prepared pan and cool to room temperature.

Dump the contents of the pan onto a chopping board and crush into small chunks with a meat mallet, the side of a heavy knife, or a hammer. Transfer the chunks to the bowl of a food processor and process until medium-fine. The praline may be made several weeks ahead. (Store in a tightly covered glass jar or tin, not in plastic.)

Whisk together the dry ingredients: flour, wheat flour, baking powder, and salt.

In the bowl of a standing mixer fitted with the paddle attachment, cream the butter and confectioners' sugar until light and fluffy, 5 to 6 minutes. Beat in the vanilla and rum, then add the flour mixture, and beat briefly to combine. Fold in the praline. Scoop the dough into walnut-sized balls and arrange in rows of 2 and 3 on baking pans lined with parchment paper. Press a pecan half into the center of each cookie and bake for 18 minutes or until lightly colored. Cool on a wire rack.

Store covered and at room temperature for up to five days. Note that the well-wrapped unbaked dough may be frozen for up to three months. Defrost in the refrigerator then scoop and bake. Alternatively, freeze the dough balls on a wax paper-lined baking tray until firm, then transfer to a zipper bag and freeze. Arrange on a baking tray, allow the balls to defrost about 30 minutes and then bake.

Turtle Brownies with Caramel and Pecans

The turtle candies on which these scrumptious brownies are based got their name from their shape, which does indeed resemble a turtle. To make them, toasted cashews or pecans are coated with soft, chewy caramel, and covered with chocolate in an impossible to resist

combination. Here, I make dark chocolate brownies studded with toasted pecans, then top them with a layer of homemade, vanilla-scented, chewy caramel. A layer of shiny bittersweet chocolate glaze finishes these definitely over-the-top brownies.
I like to pipe large the chocolate glaze in interlocking circles for an easy, but dramatic pattern.

YIELD: 16 TO 24 BROWNIES

Brownies

1/2 pound (2 sticks) unsalted butter, cut into bits

1/2 pound bittersweet chocolate, chopped

4 large eggs

1 1/2 cups packed dark brown sugar

1/2 cup sugar

2 teaspoons vanilla extract

1/4 pound (1 cup minus 1 tablespoon) unbleached
    all-purpose flour

Pinch fine sea salt

1/2 pound (1 1/2 cups) pecans, lightly toasted

Topping and Glaze

1 cup sugar

1/2 cup heavy cream

1/4 pound (1 stick) unsalted butter, cut into bits

2 teaspoons vanilla extract

1 cup Chocolate Glaze (see recipe for Rigo Jansci
  on page 333)

Make the brownies: Preheat the oven to 350°F. Spray a 13 x 9-inch baking pan with nonstick baker's coating, or rub with softened butter and dust with flour, shaking off the excess.

Place the butter and chocolate in a microwaveable bowl and melt in the microwave on lowest power for 2 minutes at a time, or until just barely melted. Whisk until smooth and cool to room temperature.

In the bowl of a standing mixer fitted with the paddle attachment, beat the eggs, both sugars, and vanilla until light and fluffy. Fold in the chocolate mixture, then fold in the flour and salt until just combined. Pour the batter into the prepared pan. Sprinkle the pecans on top of the batter.

Bake for 40 minutes or until the top is shiny and crackling and the batter is just starting to come away from the sides of the pan. Cool to room temperature on a wire rack.

Make topping and glaze: Combine the sugar and $1/2$ cup of water in a medium, heavy-bottomed pot (preferably copper), and then bring to the boil over moderate heat, about 3 minutes or until clear. Continue boiling until the water evaporates and the syrup thickens, about 5 minutes, then turns light tan, and, finally, turns light reddish brown and reaches 350°F on a candy thermometer.

Immediately, remove from the heat and carefully add the cream—the liquid will bubble up and form hot steam. Stir in the butter and vanilla and whisk until the sauce is smooth. Transfer the sauce to a bowl, preferably stainless-steel, and let cool until it is barely warm and spreadable. Spread the caramel over the brownies and chill until the caramel is set, about 1 hour.

Place the Chocolate Glaze in a plastic bag with the corner cut out (insert a small plain tip inside for more even piping, if desired). Pipe the chocolate in a decorative pattern all over the caramel layer, then chill again for about 30 minutes or until the chocolate is set.

Cranberry–Caramel Pecan Tart

While testing the many recipes in this book, I was assisted by Betty Kaplan, an experienced and caring cooking teacher, and an exuberant and hard-working assistant. She was generous enough to share the recipe for this colorful tart. Perfect for the fall and winter holiday season, the tart is filled with a combination of caramel, cream, cranberries, and toasted pecans, baked in a sugar pastry crust. The tart keeps well for three to four days at room temperature and is great to have on hand for unexpected visitors. Keep a bag of cranberries in the freezer and you can make this whenever the urge strikes, defrosting the cranberries first.

YIELD: ONE 10-INCH TART, 10 TO 12 SERVINGS

$3/4$ pound Sugar Pastry dough (page 823)

1 cup sugar

$1^1/4$ cups heavy cream, scalded

6 ounces ($1^3/4$ cups) cranberries ($1/2$ bag)

$1/2$ pound pecan pieces, lightly toasted and chopped

Pinch fine sea salt

Make the crust: Preheat the oven to 375°F. Roll out the dough on a lightly floured surface into a large round about $3/8$-inch thick. Transfer to a 10-inch tart pan.

Carefully transfer the dough to the pan, without stretching it, and press well into the corners so there are no thick spots. Trim any overhang. Chill for 30 minutes to relax the gluten so the crust maintains its shape well.

Fit a piece of heavy-duty foil onto the dough and up over the edges and fill with beans or other pie weights. Blind bake (just pastry crust, no filling) on the bottom shelf of the oven until the dough is cooked through but not yet browned, about 30 minutes. Remove the foil and the weights, reduce the oven temperature to 325°F and bake for 10 minutes, or until the dough is evenly and lightly browned. Remove from the oven and cool to room temperature on a wire rack before filling.

Make the filling: Melt the sugar in a medium, heavy-bottomed sauce pan over low heat until it is deep golden brown and just beginning to turn red, about 8 minutes. Note that at first, it will seem like the sugar will never melt, but after about 5 minutes or so, it will begin melting from the bottom. Swirl the pot, rather than stirring (which would encourage sugar crystals to develop), so the sugar melts evenly. When most of the sugar has melted and browned, stir with a wooden spoon so it melts evenly. When almost all the sugar has melted, add the cream, keeping in mind that it will bubble up and create hot steam. Once the cream hits the sugar, the sugar will harden at first. Keep stirring until the mixture is smooth and combined. Heat briefly to melt any hardened caramel, especially at the edges of the pot. Remove from the heat and strain through a sieve into a metal bowl (to remove any still-hardened caramel bits). Allow the mixture to cool for 10 minutes or until moderately hot.

Add the cranberries, pecans, and salt to the caramel, and mix to combine. Spoon this mixture into the crust. Bake for 25 to 30 minutes or until the cranberries have mostly split open and the juices are bubbling. Remove from the oven and cool on a wire rack for 30 minutes, or until the tart is warm. Remove the pan and cool completely to room temperature before cutting into serving portions.

PERSIMMONS

Persimmon Varieties . . . 660

Choosing, Ripening,
and Storing Persimmons . . . 662

ITALIAN HACHIYA PERSIMMON
MERINGUE TORTE . . . 662

Using a Butane Torch . . . 663

SPICED FUYU PERSIMMON BARS . . . 664

SPICED HONEY–ALMOND RINGS
WITH BRANDIED PERSIMMON BITS . . . 665

PERSIMMON-BLACK WALNUT BREAD . . . 666

PERSIMMONS

Traveling through Tuscany and Umbria in late fall, I saw many picturesque persimmon trees lining many winding roads. Though the trees were bare of leaves, their branches were laden with brilliant Hachiya persimmons, left on the trees to soften and sweeten. If I didn't know better, I'd have sworn the trees were covered with lacquered Christmas ornaments. In Japan, as in Italy, persimmon trees bear heart-shaped, deep green, waxy leaves that turn butter-yellow to bittersweet-orange in the fall. Persimmon wood is among the hardest known to man, and is prized by Japanese artists for carving and furniture-making.

Although there is a native American persimmon, many Americans tend to stay away from the fruit, not knowing how to enjoy it. There is a wry saying in persimmon country–the American Southeast–that persimmons are only "good for dogs, hogs, and 'possums.'" This chapter aims to change that notion and clarify the confusion among the essential differences between the most common persimmons: the native American persimmon, the Sharon fruit grown in Israel and South Africa, the Japanese Hachiya persimmon, and the Japanese Fuyu, or Fuyugaki, persimmon.

Some persimmons will begin to appear in the markets in late September, but November and December are when they're most plentiful.

The plum, tomato, or heart-shaped fruit ranges in color from burnt orange to red-orange, with more than 1,000 cultivars. Once you know how to choose persimmons, how to fully ripen them, and how best to use them, you'll find that they make a fine moist, sweet, subtly-flavored addition to baked goods.

The most widely cultivated persimmon is the Japanese or Kaki persimmon, *Diospyros kaki*, or *shizi* in China. When ripe, this orange-colored fruit comprises thick, pulpy jelly encased in a waxy, thin skin. Now the dominant variety sold in the United States, this fruit is native to China, though it was introduced to Japan at an early date. It has become Japan's national fruit and is one of the traditional foods for the Japanese New Year.

The smaller, rounder, lighter orange Sharon fruit and Fuyu persimmons are good to eat when firm; native American and Hachiya persimmons must be soft enough for the pulp to resemble orange Jell-O. Because they contain high levels of tannin, persimmons will pucker your mouth if eaten when under-ripe, leaving a distinctly unpleasant feeling similar to those that accompany eating an unripe mango. Sharon fruits are actually Fuyu persimmons that were given a new name by market-savvy Israeli horticulturalists who wished to give the fruit new appeal.

Most of the world calls persimmons *kaki*, or *caqui* in Spanish. In the United States, we call them persimmons after the Algonquin Indian name, *putchamin* (or other similar words) for the native American fruit, *Diospyros virginiana*. The small, rounded fruits are also known as possum persimmons, because they are favored by the plump marsupials. Early American settlers found the grape-sized, seedy local persimmons inedible until Native Americans told them the fruits would not be ready to eat until the first frost. The settlers assumed this meant that frost was necessary to improve the fruit's taste, but it actually meant that the fruit should be left on the tree until well-ripened, often into October.

Hernando de Soto and his Spanish conquistadors found Native Americans eating a kind of bread made from what they called "prunes," or dried persimmons. The settlers of Jamestown, Virginia, described persimmons as "very sweet and pleasant to the taste, and yields on distillation, after fermentation, a quality of spirits." Captain John Smith was quoted as saying, "If it be not ripe it will drawe a mans mouth awrie with much torment; but when it is ripe, it is as delicious as an Apricock."

When Commodore Matthew Perry opened Japan to the West in 1855, he changed the persimmon scene forever when he returned to the United States with persimmon trees that he had found growing on the coast of Southern Japan. Sometime in the mid 1800s, the first persimmon cultivar arrived in California. In 1828, the earliest Japanese persimmons in the United States sprouted from seeds in Washington, DC, but were unsuccessful because of the unusually cold winters during that period. The USDA introduced grafted cultivars of Japanese persimmons into California and Georgia beginning in 1870. Many experimental persimmon tree trials were planted by Professor Hume in Central Florida in the early 1900s at the University of Florida in Gainesville. The trees were a sensation because of their prolific early-bearing fruit that ripened into colorful, juicy, sweet fruit in late fall when very few fresh delicacies were in season.

A sub-tropical plant, the persimmon grows well in California and the Southeastern United States. Most American persimmons are grown in the San Joaquin Valley and the foothills of the Sierra Nevada. Japanese persimmons are grown in great numbers by California orchardists and the fruit begins showing up in supermarkets, but especially in Asian markets, around Thanksgiving. They may be stored unripe for two months in the refrigerator, and then ripened at room temperature.

Because the Hachiya variety is so delicate in its ripe state, it is always picked and shipped to market while still hard and unripe. I bought an entire case of large, heart-shaped Japanese Hachiya persimmons to use for testing, although minus the sturdy wood crate and artfully designed label in which I would buy them during my chef years. (Persimmons, grapes, and pears were some of the last holdouts of the lost American craft of designing fruit labels to paste on wood crates for shipping.) As the persimmons ripened, I would freeze them, until I had enough for a recipe. It took a full month before the final fruits fully ripened to their ambrosia–like state. But frozen persimmons will keep perfectly well for months.

Persimmons figure prominently in old–time American country baking traditions, especially puddings, pie fillings, and quick breads. I'd like to revive that tradition with recipes like the Italian Hachiya Persimmon Meringue Torte (page 662), with its dense, creamy, pudding–like filling in a nutty whole wheat crust. The Spiced Fuyu Persimmon Bars (page 664) are made from firm, ripe Fuyu persimmons or Sharon fruits. The Spiced Honey–Almond Rings with Brandied Persimmon Bits (page 665) are studded with bits of dried persimmon bits that have been plumped in brandy. The quickly made, moist Persimmon–Black Walnut Bread (page 666) combines two native American foods: persimmons and black walnuts, and would make a perfect tea or coffee cake to feed the family on Thanksgiving weekend.

PERSIMMON VARIETIES

AMERICAN PERSIMMON: The highly astringent American persimmon, *Diospyros virginiana*, is native to eastern North America. Juicy, pinkish-orange American persimmons contain a few seeds and have a natural juicy, sweet, fruity taste when fully ripened. They should be left on the tree until plump, quite soft to the touch, and completely ripe, from September into October.

JAPANESE FUYU: The Japanese Fuyu persimmon is a non-astringent variety, meaning that it tastes good and sweet even when firm and may be eaten like an apple, shiny skin and all. The brownish-orange Fuyu has a squat shape and a flat bottom, close to the appearance of a medium-sized tomato. The fruit has been grown in Asia for many centuries where it is revered and offered to Buddha. Fuyus were brought to California in the early part of the twentieth century. With increased immigration from Japan, China, the Philippines, and most recently Southeast Asia, demand for this fruit has grown. Fuyus are available at farmers and Asian markets from October to December. After harvest, Fuyus can be kept for two to three weeks at room temperature, gradually softening.

JAPANESE HACHIYA: The beautiful heart-shaped Hachiya persimmon, with its pointed end and red-orange coloring, is a soft type that must be full ripened and jelly-like before eating or using for baking, otherwise it is unbearably astringent. A perfect

Hachiya persimmon will feel like a water balloon, and have a jelly-like texture, a honey-sweet apricot-like taste, and a smooth, slippery texture. These persimmons are especially good for baking, where their sweet flavor and soft texture shine.

OTHER PERSIMMONS: The black persimmon also known as the black sapote, *Diospyros digyna*, is native to Mexico. It has green skin and white flesh, which turns black when ripe. The mabolo or velvet-apple, *Diospyros discolor*, is native to the Philippines and turns bright red when ripe. The date-plum, *Diospyros lotus*, is native to southwest Asia and southeast Europe, and was known to the ancient Greeks as "the fruit of the Gods," hence its scientific name. This species is mentioned in the Odyssey as being so delicious, those who ate it forgot about returning home and wished only to stay among the lotus-eaters.

ASIAN DRIED PERSIMMONS: Called *hoshigaki* in Japanese, these persimmons are peeled and dried whole over a period of several weeks in a painstaking method that requires patience, careful monitoring, and a fair amount of dexterity. Through a combination of hanging to dry and delicate hand-massaging, the sugars contained in the fruit form a delicate surface dusting of sugar crystals that resemble frost. Hoshigaki are succulently tender and moist, with concentrated persimmon flavor. Traditional to Japan, the craft of hoshigaki-making came to America with Japanese American farmers and is also practiced in Korea, China, and Vietnam.

The flattened brownish-orange fruits, with their characteristic four-petaled rounded calyx, are eaten as a snack or dessert and added to the spicy Korean punch called *sujeonggwa*. I can almost always find hoshigaki for sale at my local Korean market, where they are known as *gotgam*. The mature, fermented fruit is used to make the fruity persimmon vinegar that is believed to have a wide variety of holistic properties and sells for prices as high as any aged Balsamic vinegar.

SHARON FRUIT: Sharon fruit is grown in Israel's Sharon Valley, and has become quite popular in Europe and the United States. The smallish seedless fruit has shiny light orange skin and an exceptionally sweet, versatile flavor. As a non-astringent persimmon, it can be enjoyed firm like an apple or soft like a peach. Small brown spots that may appear on the surface and inside of the fruit are an indication that its sugar has crystallized and created super-sweet pockets. Sharon fruit may be refrigerated up to ten days and will soften at room temperature in two days. Sharon fruit is now also raised in Spain and South Africa and is imported to the United States from December until the end of February.

CHOOSING, RIPENING, AND STORING PERSIMMONS

Persimmons are available October to January. Look for plump, smooth, highly colored fruit with green caps intact. To fully enjoy persimmons, wait until they are fully ripe before eating them or adding them to recipes. Ripening them at room temperature until they are very soft will bring out their maximum sweetness. Fuyu persimmons and Sharon fruit should be purchased when firm. Enjoy them as they are, crunchy and sweet, or allow them to soften a bit at room temperature. There are several varieties of Fuyu, some with sizeable black seeds, others entirely without seeds. The less common but especially tasty reddish-orange Gosho persimmon and the bright yellow-orange Eureka persimmon sometimes turn up at farmers' markets on the West Coast.

Once ripe, persimmons don't keep well. They should be eaten right away or refrigerated for a day or two. If you're waiting for several to ripen at once, you'll discover they can have minds of their own, each one choosing a different time to ripen. Simply freeze each persimmon as it ripens until you have the required amount. Lengthen the short persimmon season by storing firm Hachiyas up to one month in the refrigerator before setting them out at room temperature to ripen. To enjoy them out of season, freeze them for six months before ripening.

Italian Hachiya Persimmon Meringue Torte

Traveling in Italy in late November, I noticed that most of the trees were bare except for persimmon trees, which had the vivid orange fruits hanging from their leafless branches. Called cachi *(or kaki) in Italy (after their Brazilian name,* caqui*), the heart-shaped fruit are sweet, with flesh that is almost transparent and jelly-like when ripe. Here, a smooth and luscious persimmon curd fills a crunchy, Venetian-style cornmeal and honey pastry shell with a smooth and velvety meringue topping.*

YIELD: ONE 10-INCH TART, 10 TO 12 SERVINGS

3/4 pound Venetian Cornmeal Tart Pastry dough (page 391)
6 very ripe Hachiya persimmons
1 1/2 cups sugar
2 tablespoons potato starch, substitute corn, wheat, or rice starch
1/2 teaspoon ground mace
Juice and grated zest of 1 lemon (3 tablespoons juice and 1 tablespoon zest)
1/2 teaspoon fine sea salt
2 ounces (1/2 stick) unsalted butter, melted and cooled
4 eggs, separated

Preheat the oven to 350°F. Roll out the dough between two sheets of lightly floured wax paper to 3/8-inch thickness. Transfer it to a 10-inch tart pan with a removable bottom and press into the pan without stretching the dough, pressing well into the corners so there are no thick spots. Alternatively, press the dough out by hand into the bottom and up the sides of the tart pan, making sure that the pastry is even and not too thick. Chill the crust for 30 minutes to relax the gluten so the tart crust maintains its shape.

Fit a piece of heavy-duty foil onto the crust and fill with beans or other pie weights. Blind bake (just pastry crust, no filling) on the bottom shelf of the oven until the crust is cooked through but not yet browned, about 25 minutes. Remove the foil and the weights, reduce the oven temperature to 325°F, and bake for 10 minutes longer, or until the dough is evenly and lightly browned. Remove from the oven and cool to room temperature on a wire rack before filling.

Make the filling: Pull off the four-petaled tops of the persimmons. Cut them into quarters, place them in a blender or food processor, and process to a fine purée—you'll need 2 cups of pulp. Combine the pulp, 1/2 cup of the sugar, the potato starch, mace, lemon juice and zest, and salt in a medium non-aluminum pot and bring to a boil. Reduce the heat to moderate and cook for 5 minutes, or until the mixture is lightly thickened.

Separately beat together the melted butter and egg yolks. Temper the mixture by mixing in a small amount of the persimmon mixture, then add the entire butter mixture to the pot and mix to combine. Return to the heat and cook, constantly stirring, for about 5 minutes, or until the mixture starts to bubble. Cool to room temperature, stirring often to prevent a skin from forming. Pour into the crust and chill for 30 minutes in the refrigerator to allow the filling to set.

Make the meringue topping: In a small, heavy-bottomed pot, combine the remaining 1 cup sugar with 1 cup water and bring to a boil, shaking to combine until the mixture forms a clear syrup. Continue to cook until the syrup is thickened and bubbling and reaches the soft-ball stage, 238°F on a candy thermometer, or when a spoonful dropped in a small bowl of ice water forms a soft ball.

When the sugar is almost ready, beat the egg whites to form medium peaks. With the mixer going on low speed, beat in the hot sugar syrup. Raise to high speed and continue to beat until the meringue is firm, glossy, and at room temperature, about 10 minutes. Spoon the meringue over the cooled pie or transfer the meringue to a large pastry bag fitted with a large star-shaped tip and pipe over the pie in an attractive pattern. Either place under a hot broiler for 2 to 3 minutes, watching carefully so it doesn't burn, or use a culinary blowtorch to brown the top. Chill at least 4 hours before cutting into serving portions and serving.

USING A COMMON BLOW TORCH

It's much easier to control the browning of meringue or burnt sugar toppings (as for crème brulée) if you use a small chef's butane torch. I used to use a full-sized propane torch, but found that the smaller type that fits onto a standard can of butane fuel works just as well. When using the torch, make sure you work in an area where there's nothing nearby that can catch on fire. Be sure to light the torch while it's pointed away from yourself. For extra safety, store the can and the torch attachment separately. Asian markets are a good place to find inexpensive cans of butane fuel.

Spiced Fuyu Persimmon Bars

These dark, moist, and fruity bars look like brownies, but have an intriguing flavor from ripe persimmons. Use well-ripened Fuyu or Sharon fruit here. Although these persimmon varieties are sweet even when firm, they should be soft enough to make a rather soupy purée. The persimmons are spiced with cinnamon, nutmeg, and cloves, and combined with brown sugar and toasted walnuts for crunch, and Zante currants for tiny bits of bittersweet flavor and chewy texture.

YIELD: 24 BARS

$1/2$ pound (2 cups minus 2 tablespoons) unbleached
   all-purpose flour

1 teaspoon baking soda

1 teaspoon ground cinnamon

$1/2$ teaspoon freshly grated nutmeg

$1/4$ teaspoon ground cloves

$1/2$ teaspoon fine sea salt

3 ripe Fuyu persimmons or Sharon fruit

Juice of 1 lemon, 3 tablespoons

1 cup light brown sugar, packed

$1/2$ cup grapeseed or canola oil

1 large egg

6 ounces ($1^{1}/2$ cups) walnuts, lightly toasted
   and chopped

$1/4$ pound (1 cup) Zante currants

24 walnut halves, for garnish

Preheat the oven to 350°F. Spray a 13 x 9-inch baking pan with baker's nonstick coating or rub with butter and dust with flour, shaking off the excess.

In a medium bowl, whisk together the dry ingredients: flour, baking soda, cinnamon, nutmeg, cloves, and salt.

Make the filling: Pull off the four-petaled tops of the persimmons. Cut them into quarters, place them in a blender or food processor, and process to a fine purée—you'll need $1^{1}/2$ cups of purée. Transfer the persimmons to a large mixing bowl and whisk in the lemon juice, brown sugar, oil, egg, walnuts, and currants. Fold in the flour mix. Scrape the batter into the pan and arrange the walnut halves evenly over the top in 4 rows of 6 so they will be in the center of each bar when cut.

Bake for 40 minutes or until the bars start to come away from the sides of the pan and a toothpick stuck in the center comes out clean. Cool on a wire rack to room temperature, then cut into bars. Store in a covered container at room temperature up to four days.

Spiced Honey–Almond Rings with Brandied Persimmon Bits

I was curious about the flattened, deep-orange dried fruits speckled with fine sugar crystals in my local Asian market, so I had to buy some. It turns out that they are hoshigaki, *a carefully prepared Japanese specialty of dried persimmons. Their concentrated flavor is delicately sweet; their flesh succulently tender and moist. Here, I soak them in brandy and mix them in a spiced almond dough that has been flavored with coriander, ginger, and lemon. I form the soft dough into figure-eight shapes, roll them in sugar, then bake them. With their slightly mysterious flavor, I'd serve these aromatic cookies after an Asian or Indian meal.*

YIELD: ABOUT 40 COOKIES

6 dried persimmons, trimmed and diced,
   substitute diced apricots
1/4 cup brandy
10 ounces (2 1/2 cups minus 2 1/2 tablespoons)
   unbleached all-purpose flour
1 teaspoon baking powder
1/2 teaspoon baking soda
1/2 teaspoon fine sea salt
1 teaspoon ground coriander
1 teaspoon ground cinnamon
1/2 pound (1 1/2 cups) blanched almonds
1/2 cup honey
1/2 cup brown sugar, packed
1/2 cup sugar

Juice and grated zest of 1 lemon (3 tablespoons juice
   and 1 tablespoon zest)
2 large eggs
1-inch piece fresh ginger, peeled and grated
1 teaspoon almond extract
Sugar, for rolling

Soak the persimmons in the brandy to soften, about 1 hour or up to overnight.

Whisk together the dry ingredients: flour, baking powder, baking soda, salt, coriander, and cinnamon. Place 1 cup of the dry ingredients and the almonds in a food processor, and process until finely ground. Add to the flour mixture and whisk to combine.

In a large non-aluminum saucepan over moderate heat, combine the honey, brown sugar, sugar, and lemon juice and zest, and cook, stirring, just until the sugars are dissolved and the mixture is clear, about 3 minutes. Remove from the heat and let the mixture cool about 5 minutes, or until no longer steaming hot.

In a large bowl, whisk together the eggs, ginger, and almond extract. Add the honey mixture and whisk to combine. Stir in the persimmons with their soaking liquid, and fold in the flour mixture. Wrap the dough in plastic and let it rest at room temperature for 4 hours, or refrigerate overnight, to develop the flavors.

Preheat the oven to 350°F. Line two 18 x 13-inch half sheet pans (or other large baking pans) with parchment paper or silicone baking mats.

Divide the dough into 40 balls. Roll each piece out on a work surface that has been sprinkled with sugar and, using the palms of your hands, form into 3- to 4-inch sticks. Form each stick into a ring or figure-eight shape, pressing the ends together to seal. Arrange the cookies on the baking pans and bake for 15 to 20 minutes, or until they are firm and lightly colored. Cool completely on a wire rack. Store in a cookie tin or similar container up to one week.

Persimmon–
Black Walnut Bread

I put this moist, dark, brandy-spiked tea bread on the brunch menu at Azalea, the restaurant at the Omni Hotel at Independence Park for which I designed the original regional menu. It combines two native American ingredients common to the Pennsylvania Dutch region south and west of the city: persimmons and black walnuts, along with a generous pour of brandy. Use a light-colored pan here as the bread tends to darken on the outside. Persimmons freeze beautifully; purée them for this recipe, skin and all. Substitute milder-tasting English walnuts for the black walnuts if desired.

YIELD: 2 SHALLOW, MEDIUM-SIZED LOAVES

1 pound (2 to 3) ripe Hachiya or American persimmons

$^1/_2$ pound (2 cups minus 2 tablespoons) unbleached all-purpose flour

1 teaspoon baking powder

1 teaspoon baking soda

1 teaspoon fine sea salt

6 ounces (1$^1/_2$ sticks) unsalted butter, softened

1 cup light brown sugar, packed

3 large eggs, separated

$^1/_4$ pound (1 cup) chopped black walnuts

$^1/_4$ cup brandy

Preheat the oven to 350°F. Spray two (1-pound, 8$^1/_2$ x 4$^1/_2$-inch) loaf pans with baker's nonstick coating.

Pull off the four-petaled tops of the persimmons and remove the seeds. Purée them in a food processor. You'll need 1 cup purée. (Freeze any extra or mix with sugar and lemon juice and use for dessert sauce.)

Whisk together the dry ingredients: flour, baking powder, baking soda, and salt.

In the bowl of a standing mixer fitted with the paddle attachment, cream the butter and $^1/_2$ cup of the brown sugar together until light and fluffy, 5 to 6 minutes. Beat in the egg yolks, one at a time. Alternating, and beginning and ending with the dry ingredients, fold the persimmon purée and the flour mixture into the batter. Fold in the walnuts and the brandy.

In the clean bowl of a standing mixer fitted with the whisk attachment, beat the egg whites until fluffy, then add the remaining brown sugar and continue beating until the whites are firm and glossy, 4 to 5 minutes. Fold into the batter in thirds so as not to deflate the whites. Scrape the batter into the prepared pans.

Bake for 50 minutes, or until the bread starts to come away from the sides of the pan and a toothpick or skewer stuck in the center comes out clean. Note that the breads will fill the pans only about two-thirds after baking. You may also bake the breads in smaller loaf pans, reducing the baking time accordingly.

PINE NUTS

Buying and Storing
Mediterranean Pine Nuts . . . 670

Toasting Pine Nuts . . . 671

Traditional Harvesting of Pine Nuts
in the American Southwest . . . 671

Gathering Pine Nuts in Lebanon . . . 671

Pine Nut Oil . . . 672

CATALAN FLATBREAD WITH SPINACH,
ONION, AND PINE NUT TOPPING . . . 672

Catalan Coca . . . 673

Escalivada . . . 673

FIG AND PINE NUT BREAD . . . 674

LEMON–PINE NUT TART . . . 675

CROSTATA DELLA NONNA:
GRANDMA'S RICOTTA-PINE NUT TART . . . 676

PINE NUTS

There was a magnificent old Mediterranean pine tree growing in the lush garden of my Turkish friend's family home near Izmir. I was so excited to taste the lovable little nuts right off the tree. We gathered the cones with no problem, but when we went to look for the shell-covered seeds nestled at the base of their rough brackets, we found that industrious squirrels had beaten us to them. What a disappointment! Buying small packets of the precious nuts the following day in a small, local farmers' market was the next best thing. I only wish I had sprung for a few more packages, because I quickly used up my stash, sprinkling them on the Catalan flat bread in this chapter and the Brustengolo cake from Umbria.

The long, thin, torpedo-shaped seeds of the Stone Pine, *Pinus pinea*, which grows at quite low altitudes, are prized throughout the Mediterranean. Evidence of their use in the Middle East going back to Biblical times. True Mediterranean pine nuts most resemble almonds in their flavor and dense, almost chewy, texture, but they are more resinous and spicy.

About eighty percent of the pine nuts sold in American supermarkets and warehouse clubs now come from China, which ships about two million pounds of the tiny nuts (about 1,500 pine nuts in a pound) here every year. The fact that Chinese pine nuts are reasonably priced means that they are accessible to more bakers in America, but we are basically limited to only these rather bland nuts unless you search out other varieties in Mediterranean or Indian groceries. More flavorful Mediterranean pine nuts sell for three to four times as much as those from China, but many knowledgeable cooks and bakers insist on them, or at least prefer them. One of the best and certainly tastiest souvenirs I have from a recent women chef's tour of India is a large bag of Chilgoza pine nuts harvested in the Himalayas that I snagged in Mumbai's historic Crawford Market shown in the photo on this page. I also carried precious packets of long, narrow Mediterranean pine nuts that I bought in an Izmir farmer's market home from Turkey.

Native Americans, people from the Mediterranean region, and Asians all have a venerable tradition of gathering and eating the small, soft nuts. Pine nuts, pine seeds, pine kernels, piñon, pinyon, pignoli, and pignoles are all names for the small, edible seeds extracted from between the scales of pinecones. While all pines produce seeds, only certain types are large and tasty enough to be worth the trouble of shelling them.

The nuts have also long been a staple of the diet of indigenous peoples of Siberia and far Eastern Russia. In the course of 180 million years, the original tall pines of northern Asia ended up as the small desert trees found in Mexico and the American Southwest. It takes anywhere from fifteen to twenty-five years for the trees to begin producing seeds, and even more time for them to reach top production. Harvesters gather the cones in late autumn or early winter, from wild trees in China and from groves plantedin Europe, picking up fallen cones, climbing up ladders to cut them off, or using long-handled hooks to break them off. The cones are then sun-dried or heated to encourage the brackets to open, making their hoard easier to reach. The nuts are then either extracted by hand or further processed to remove their hard outer shells.

Not only are they delicious, but pine nuts also have a reputation as a powerful aphrodisiac throughout the Mediterranean and Asia. Maybe this is why pine nuts were found in the ruins of Pompeii? In *Ars Amatoria, The Art of Love*, the Roman poet Ovid recommends "the nuts that the sharp-leafed pine brings forth" as an aphrodisiac. Apicius, in his Roman cookbook, *De Re Coquinaria*, suggests pine nuts with onions, white mustard, and pepper to enhance physical love. Galen, the renowned Greek physician of the second century,

advises that eating a mixture of pine seeds, honey, and almonds before bedtime for three consecutive evenings should produce the desirable effects. The early sixteenth-century Sheik Nefzaoui wrote in *The Perfumed Garden*—the Arabic love guide, "He who feels that he is weak for coition should drink before going to bed a glassful of very thick honey and eat twenty almonds and one hundred grains of the pine tree." Perhaps this is the reason why Greeks and Romans preserved their pine nuts in honey.

Many believe that the most effective pine nuts for love come from the Chilgoza Pine or Noosa Pine, *Pinus gerardiana*, which grows only at extremely high elevations in the northwestern Himalayas from Afghanistan to Tibet. Chilgoza pine nuts are a staple food for the inhabitants of Kunawar, a Himalayan region known for its high birthrate. Attempts have been made to cultivate the Chilgoza pine outside the Himalayas, but without success. I don't know if pine nuts work as a love stimulant, but they're legal, fun to eat, and couldn't do any harm.

The two most important pine nut trees in North America are the Piñon Pine, *Pinus edulis*, the state tree of New Mexico, and the Mexican Pinyon, *Pinus cembroides*. Enthusiasts in nearby Nevada, Arizona, Utah, and parts of California claim that the soft seeds of the Singleleaf Piñon, *Pinus monophylla*, Nevada's state tree, are the best to be had.

From prehistoric times, the indigenous peoples of the entire Southwest from Texas to California relied on the small piñon pine for the food, fuel, building materials, and medicines that allowed them to establish the cultures of the Hopi, Zuñi, Pueblo, and Navajo peoples. Spanish explorers who arrived in the American Southwest in the sixteenth century found Native Americans grinding pinõns for flour on stone *metates*. The nuts were also eaten raw, roasted, boiled, or mashed and spread on corn cakes like peanut butter.

The cuisines of Greece, Italy, Spain, Portugal, Southern Italy, Turkey, Lebanon, Morocco, Tunisia, and Italy all make good use of the nuts, often in baked goods reserved for special occasions. I adore the petite nuts and use them in recipes of both Mediterranean and American origin. In this chapter, I combine pine nuts, maple syrup, and cornmeal in the Maple Cornmeal Muffins with Pine Nuts and Currants (page 553). For the Spanish Baked Quince with Pine Nuts and Dried Fruit (page 754), the aromatic but rock-hard fruits are stuffed with pine nuts, Zante currants, dried apricots, and cherries, then baked in an aromatic red wine and honey syrup with sweet spices until soft, tender, and oozing with syrupy juices.

On the Cycladic island of Kea in Greece, I learned to make a chunky, tasty eggplant and beef filling studded with toasted pine nuts for the Kea Stuffed Grilled Bread (page 144). In Sicily, pine nuts go into many traditional dishes, including the Cuccidati (Sicilian fig and pine nut stuffed cookies) (page 457). My friend, Chef Michael Tuohy from Woodfire Grill in Atlanta, sprinkles the nuts on his Duck Confit Pizza (page 859).

And whether it's Turkish or Armenian in origin, the Lahmacun (also spelled lamajoun) that I learned to make in Çesme, Turkey, was topped with a little ground beef, fresh tomato purée, and pine nut mixture before being baked in a wood-burning oven. In this chapter, the savory Catalan flatbread (page 672) is topped with the familiar Mediterranean combo of spinach, currants, and pine nuts, along with caramelized onions accented with a little red wine vinegar.

Figs and pine nuts are a time-honored pair, especially in southern Italy from which the Fig and Pine Nut Bread (page 674) comes. In the Lemon–Pine Nut Tart (page 675), the nuts are ground into a delicate pastry that is filled with an equally delicate lemon custard and baked. The old-fashioned Crostata della Nonna: Grandma's Ricotta Pine-Nut Tart (page 676) is a classic Italian sweet, made by grandmothers up and down the boot-shaped peninsula.

BUYING AND STORING MEDITERRANEAN PINE NUTS

I have found Mediterranean pine nuts, called *snober* or *snoober* in Arabic, for sale online from Kalustyan's at about $33 per pound (www.kalustyans.com). The Spanish Table in Seattle (www.spanishtable.com) also sells them. Store pine nuts in the freezer to prevent the oil-rich nuts from becoming rancid.

TOASTING PINE NUTS

Toasting pine nuts brings out their flavor. There are many ways of toasting nuts, all of which require close attention because they burn very easily. For the most evenly browned pine nuts, roast them in oil. Place one cup of pine nuts in a very small saucepan and barely cover with a neutral oil (such as canola). Heat the pot over low heat and cook until the nuts are golden brown, shaking occasionally, about eight minutes. Be careful once the nuts start to take on some color, because they quickly pass from golden and nutty to black and bitter.

After straining the nuts from the oil, pour the oil into a glass jar and allow the solids to settle to the bottom so that the oil is clear. Use this pine nut-flavored oil for salad dressings. Oven-toast pine nuts by placing them in a baking dish large enough to hold them in a single layer. Bake at 300°F for 8 minutes, then shake and place back in the oven for 4 minutes longer, until light golden brown. Use a timer, because if the pine nut aroma is powerful enough for you to notice, it's probably already too late.

Traditional Harvesting of Pine Nuts in the American Southwest

The Hopi, Zuñi, Pueblo, Navajo, Washo, Shoshone, and Paiutes all harvested this wild crop. At harvest time, there was a great gathering in the sacred lowland piñon forests. The men would pull the cones from the trees using a large willow branch with a sturdy V-shaped hook at the end, while the women and children would pile the cones in large conical wicker baskets carried on their backs with a cordage band across their foreheads.

In camps surrounding the forest, the pine cones would be roasted on a basket tray over hot coals that was kept in constant motion, throwing them up and swirling the tray to encourage the shells to open, similar to the way we roast chestnuts. When they turned brown, the piñons were then placed on a winnowing tray and thrown repeatedly into the air so the cracked shells could be carried off by the wind. The nutmeats were then roasted, stored, and eventually ground into flour. Until the 1920s, piñon nuts were commonly collected and sent to large cities on the East Coast to be sold as "Indian nuts." Buy them in season (and in the shell) from www.pinenut.com.

GATHERING PINE NUTS IN LEBANON

During the summer holidays in the Lebanese mountains, Anissa Helou, author of the outstanding cookbook, *Lebanese Cuisine,* used to gather pinecones. "After we gathered enough cones, we sat by a flat stone and with another small stone, we started cracking the hard kernels open. The secret was how to scale the strength of the hit so that we broke the shell without crushing the nut, a feat we occasionally achieved." They would also eat soft immature or "green" pine nuts dipped in salt.

Catalan Flatbread with Spinach, Onion, and Pine Nut Topping

This flatbread, made with a crunchy cornmeal dough, is an example of a coca, a pizza-like specialty of Catalonia in northeastern Spain. The coca is traditionally formed into a long, tongue-shaped oval and baked in a wood-burning oven, though I have prepared it in a rectangle here. (If you have a wood-burning oven, shape the coca by hand into the tongue shape before baking it directly on the floor of the oven.) Cut the coca into small rectangles to serve as tapas with wine or drinks. Another popular Catalan version is topped with roasted sweet red peppers, chorizo sausage bits, and Spanish goat cheese. Coco is also delicious topped with the Catalan roasted vegetables called *escalivada (see opposite page).*

YIELD: 8 TO 12 APPETIZER SERVINGS

Dough

$1/2$ pound (2 cups minus 2 tablespoon) unbleached all-purpose flour

$1/4$ pound ($3/4$ cup plus 2 tablespoons) yellow stone-ground cornmeal

1 ($1/4$-ounce) package ($2 1/4$ teaspoons) active dry yeast

1 teaspoon fine sea salt

$1/2$ cup lukewarm water

1 tablespoon honey

2 tablespoons extra-virgin olive oil

Topping

3 tablespoons extra-virgin olive oil

2 large yellow onions, peeled and thinly sliced

2 tablespoons red wine vinegar

$1/4$ cup Zante currants, soaked in warm water to cover 30 minutes, or until plump

Fine sea salt and freshly ground black pepper

1 pound fresh spinach, stems removed or 1 pound frozen spinach, defrosted

$1/4$ cup pine nuts, lightly toasted

Make the dough: In the bowl of a standing mixer fitted with the whisk attachment, combine the dry ingredients: flour, cornmeal, yeast, and salt, and whisk to combine.

Combine the water, honey, and oil, and pour the mixture into the dry ingredients. Switch to the paddle attachment, and beat until the mixture forms a soft, smooth dough, about 3 minutes. It will still be a bit sticky. Transfer the dough to a lightly floured surface and knead briefly to form a smooth, round ball. Cover lightly with a damp cloth and set aside at room temperature to rest for 30 minutes to relax the gluten.

Make the topping: In a large skillet, combine 2 tablespoons of the oil and the onions and cook over moderate heat, stirring often, until the onions are quite tender and lightly browned, about 20 minutes. Add the vinegar and stir to combine, then remove from the heat and transfer to a mixing bowl. Drain the currants and add to the onions. Season the mixture with salt and pepper to taste.

In large, wide pot over medium-high heat, cook the spinach with just the water that clings to the washed leaves, stirring often, until wilted, 3 to 5 minutes. Drain, then rinse under cold water to set the color, and squeeze out the excess moisture. Alternatively, squeeze out the excess liquid from the defrosted spinach, without cooking. Place the spinach in a medium bowl and season with salt and pepper to taste.

Assemble the flatbread: Coat an 18 x 13-inch half sheet pan (or other large baking pan) with baker's nonstick cooking spray. Roll the dough out on a lightly floured surface into a rectangle a bit larger than the pan. Transfer the dough to the prepared pan. Roll the dough edges under to make a thicker rim of crust. Brush the remaining 1 tablespoon oil over the edge of the crust. Scatter the spinach over the crust, leaving a 1-inch border all around. Top with the caramelized onion mixture and sprinkle with the pine nuts. Allow the coca to rise 30 minutes at warm room temperature or until puffy.

Preheat the oven to 425°F. Bake for 25 minutes or the crust is golden brown and crispy. Transfer to a cutting board and use a pizza cutter to cut the coca into small rectangles. Serve hot or at room temperature.

CATALAN COCA

The flat and oval-shaped Catalan *coca* (*coques* is the plural) can range in texture from dry and flaky to moist and spongy. The toppings can be savory (*bacala*—salt cod, *chicharrones*—pork cracklings, and *escalivada*—roasted vegetables) or sweet (sugar and anisette, or pine nuts and candied fruit). Traditionally, different coques are made for feast days, including the version made for the midsummer's eve, called *coca de Sant Joan*, topped with green and red candied cherries and glazed for shine.

ESCALIVADA

The Catalan word *escalivar* means "to char or roast in hot wood ashes," as the vegetables are traditionally cooked by mountain shepherds over the embers of a hardwood fire, thereby permeating the vegetables with a smoky flavor. To make escalivada, combine sweet red peppers, eggplant, onion, and tomatoes with olive oil, salt, and pepper, and roast in a 400°F oven until nicely browned, about 30 minutes, then peel the vegetables, and cut them into strips.

Fig and Pine Nut Bread

If you love figs and pine nuts as much as I do, this slightly sweet Mediterranean-style bread is for you. Chunky bits of chewy dried figs, toasted pine nuts, freshly ground aniseed, and fruity extra-virgin olive oil enrich and flavor the bread. Toast slices, top with mild goat cheese, and toast again for a quick and delicious snack or lunch. Mediterranean pine nuts are the most appropriate for this bread, though inexpensive Chinese pine nuts will work fine.

YIELD: 1 LARGE OR 2 MEDIUM ROUND LOAVES
(3 POUNDS)

2 ($\frac{1}{4}$-ounce) packages ($4\frac{1}{2}$ teaspoons) active dry yeast

1 tablespoon honey

$2\frac{1}{2}$ cups lukewarm water

1 pound (4 cups) unbleached bread flour

6 ounces ($1\frac{1}{2}$ cups) white whole wheat flour

2 ounces wheat germ

2 teaspoons fine sea salt

$\frac{1}{4}$ cup extra-virgin olive oil

1 tablespoon ground aniseed

$\frac{1}{2}$ pound dried figs, such as Calimyrna,
     stemmed and cut into thin strips

$\frac{1}{4}$ pound pine nuts, lightly toasted

Cornmeal, for sprinkling

In the bowl of a standing mixer fitted with the paddle attachment, combine the yeast, honey, and $\frac{1}{2}$ cup lukewarm water. Allow the mixture to proof in a warm place for about 15 minutes, or until bubbling and puffy.

Whisk together the dry ingredients: bread flour, whole wheat flour, wheat germ, and salt. Beat the remaining 2 cups water, the olive oil, and aniseed into the yeast mixture then beat in the flour mixture. Continue beating until the dough is smooth and elastic and comes away cleanly from the bowl 5 to 6 minutes. Transfer the dough to a large oiled bowl; turn around so the dough is oiled all over. Cover with plastic wrap or a damp cloth and allow the dough to rise at warm room temperature until doubled in size, about 2 hours.

Turn the dough out onto a lightly floured work surface. Pat the dough into a large, flat oval and sprinkle evenly with half the figs and pine nuts. Roll up the dough into a log shape. Pat it into a flat oval again and sprinkle evenly with the remaining figs and nuts. Roll up again. Shape into one large round loaf or two medium loaves, gently pulling the surface taut from the bottom. Using a French baker's lame or a single-edged razor, cut several shallow slashes into the top of the bread. Place the bread on a parchment-lined baking sheet sprinkled with cornmeal. Spray with a water mister, cover loosely with plastic wrap, and let rise at warm room temperature until doubled in size, about 2 hours.

Preheat the oven to 425°F. Bake the bread for 15 minutes, then lower the oven temperature to 375°F and bake for 35 minutes more or until the bread sounds hollow when tapped on the bottom and a thermometer inserted in the center reads 200°F. Cool completely on a wire rack before slicing. Store the bread, wrapped loosely in plastic wrap or aluminum foil, at room temperature for up to five days, or freeze up to 3 months.

Lemon–Pine Nut Tart

This delicate tart from Provence is best served the day it is made and at room temperature, for its subtle flavor and creamy texture to be at its best. Crushed pine nuts add flavor and texture to the egg-enriched, lemony crust, while a topping of lemon sections is sprinkled with confectioners' sugar and caramelized. For best flavor, use Mediterranean pine nuts if possible, especially for sprinkling over the top. (See page 670 for more about them.)

YIELD: ONE 11-INCH TART, 8 TO 12 SERVINGS

Crust

$^3/_4$ pound ($2^3/_4$ cups plus 1 tablespoon) unbleached
    all-purpose flour

$^1/_4$ pound (1 cup) pine nuts

$^1/_4$ cup sugar

$^1/_2$ teaspoon fine sea salt

$^1/_2$ pound (2 sticks) unsalted butter, frozen and
    cut into bits

2 large eggs

2 tablespoons light rum, substitute vodka

Grated zest of 1 lemon (1 tablespoon)

Filling

4 large eggs, at room temperature

1$^1/_2$ cups sugar

Grated zest of 2 lemons (2 tablespoons)

1 cup fresh lemon juice

$^1/_2$ cup heavy cream

Pinch flour

Confectioners' sugar, for sprinkling

2 lemons, sectioned, pits removed, and set on paper
    towels to blot excess liquid

1 ounce ($^1/_2$ cup) pine nuts

Make the crust: Combine the dry ingredients: flour, pine nuts, sugar, and salt in the bowl of a standing mixer fitted with the paddle attachment. Add the butter and mix until the mixture resembles oatmeal.

In a small bowl, whisk together the eggs, rum, and lemon zest. Pour the egg mixture into the mixer and beat until just combined and the dough comes together in moist clumps. Briefly knead by hand to combine well. Press the dough into an 11-inch tart pan and refrigerate until firm, at least 45 minutes and up to overnight. (You will have extra dough: freeze for another time or roll out, cut into decorative shapes, sprinkle generously with confectioners' sugar, and bake along with the tart.)

Preheat the oven to 375°F. Fit a piece of heavy-duty foil onto the dough and fill with beans or other pie weights. Blind bake (just pastry crust, no filling) on the bottom shelf of the oven until the crust is cooked through but not yet browned, about 30 minutes. Remove the foil and the weights, reduce oven temperature to 325°F and bake for 10 minutes longer, or until the dough is evenly and lightly browned. Remove from the oven and cool to room temperature on a wire rack.

Raise the oven temperature to 375°F. Make the filling: Lightly beat the eggs, sugar, lemon zest, lemon juice, cream, and flour until well mixed. Place the crust on a baking sheet, and place in the oven. Pull the shelf out, carefully ladle the filling into the crust, and push the shelf back into the oven. Bake for 10 minutes then reduce the oven temperature to 350°F. Bake for 20 minutes or until the filling jiggles slightly when pan is shaken. Remove from the oven.

Preheat the broiler to high. Sift the confectioners' sugar through a shaker or a fine sieve evenly over the surface of the tart. Arrange the lemon segments in an attractive pattern around the edge of the tart. Sprinkle the center with the pine nuts. Cover the crust edges with foil to keep it from burning. Broil the tart about 5 inches from the heat source, watching carefully, until the sugar begins to caramelize, about 2 minutes, rotating the tart to brown evenly. Alternatively, brown the top of the tart using a chef's blow torch (see page 663). Cool to room temperature, then cut into wedges and serve. Store covered and refrigerated up to four days.

Crostata della Nonna: Grandma's Ricotta– Pine Nut Tart

Sweet wine-soaked golden raisins, toasted pine nuts, lemon zest, and nutmeg add aromatic flavor and chunky texture to this Tuscan tart. You would likely need an invitation to someone's home to taste the tart in Italy. Because its fresh ricotta filling doesn't last more than two or three days, Crostata della Nonna is not usually found in bakeries there. Like other traditional desserts including Torta Caprese (page 336), Zuccotto (page 58), and Panforte (page 232), this torta is made in many versions. Accompany the crostata with small glasses of syrupy Vin Santo or sweet or dry Marsala, the same wine that makes the raisins plump, juicy, and a bit boozy. In Italy, the filling is often made with extra-rich and creamy sheep's milk ricotta. Though much less common than cow's milk ricotta here, some American artisanal producers are now selling sheep's milk ricotta. By all means, substitute it here.

YIELD: ONE 10- TO 11-INCH TART, 10 TO 12 SERVINGS

$1/2$ cup golden raisins

$1/4$ cup Vin Santo, or sweet or dry Marsala

$3/4$ pound Pasta Frolla dough (page 62)

1 (15 ounce) whole milk ricotta

$1/2$ cup sugar

3 large eggs

Juice and grated zest of 1 lemon (3 tablespoons juice and 1 tablespoon zest)

$1/2$ teaspoon freshly grated nutmeg

$1/2$ cup pine nuts, lightly toasted

Soak the raisins in the Vin Santo for 30 minutes or until plump.

Roll the dough out between two sheets of lightly floured wax paper to about $3/8$-inch thick. Transfer to a 10-inch tart pan with a removable bottom. Lay into the pan without stretching the dough and press well into the corners so there are no thick spots. Trim any overhang flush with the edge. Alternatively, press the dough by hand into the pan. Chill the crust for 30 minutes to relax the gluten so the crust maintains its shape.

Preheat the oven to 350°F.

In a medium bowl, beat together the ricotta, sugar,

eggs, lemon juice and zest, and nutmeg, until creamy and smooth. Stir in the pine nuts and the raisins with their soaking juices. Spread the filling evenly into the crust. Sprinkle on crystallizd sugar, if using. Bake on the bottom shelf of the oven for 45 minutes, or until the crust is brown and the filling has set in the middle and is light brown at the edges. Remove from the oven, cool on a wire rack, and serve warm or at room temperature. Store covered and refrigerated up to four days.

PINEAPPLE

Pineapple Varieties . . . 681

Choosing, Ripening, and Storing Pineapple . . . 682

PINEAPPLE CHEESECAKE WITH
GINGER-MACADAMIA CRUST . . . 683

PINEAPPLE-COCONUT FLAN WITH DARK RUM . . . 684

PINEAPPLE RUM–PECAN BARS . . . 685

SOUTHERN MILLION-DOLLAR PIE . . . 685

PINEAPPLE COCONUT SHORTBREAD
BARS WITH MACADAMIA NUTS . . . 687

PINEAPPLE

The pineapple, Ananas *comosus*, is indigenous to Brazil and Paraguay and was spread by the region's native peoples through South and Central America to the West Indies. Pineapples were a favorite fruit of the fierce Carib tribes who inhabited the islands of the Caribbean Sea. Portuguese sailors on ships trading to and from Brazil spread the name for the fruit used by the Brazilian Tuli Indians: *anana*. Today, this name, meaning "excellent fruit," is still used in most languages to refer to the pineapple. In Spanish, pineapples are called *ananá* or *piña*. The fruit's English and Spanish names come from the similarity of the fruit to a pine cone.

On his second voyage to the Caribbean, in 1493, Christopher Columbus and his crew explored the lush, volcanic island of Guadeloupe, where they found a deserted Carib village. They saw pots filled with human remains and, more pleasingly, fresh vegetables and fruits, including pineapples. The fruits were eaten and enjoyed by his sailors, who described the unusual new fruit as having a rough, segmented exterior like a pinecone and a firm interior like an apple. In Europe, the fruit, so full of natural syrupy-sweetness, was prized by royalty and envied by the hoi polloi. In the 1600s, King Charles II of England posed for an official portrait receiving a gift of a pineapple, "the fruit of kings," as a symbol of royal privilege.

In the American colonies, where the home was the center of community social life, the pineapple was held in high esteem and became symbolic of hospitality and graciousness. A pineapple would crown the most important feasts, placed on a special pedestal. So important was this fruit's symbolic value that pineapples were rented out by the day to decorate hostesses' tables. Later, the same fruit would be sold to other, wealthier customers who would actually eat the fruit (ripened along the way, no doubt). Pineapples also became a favorite motif of American craftspeople, decorating gateposts, weather vanes, china, and tablecloths, carved onto the backs of chairs, and painted onto chests.

While ships brought preserved, candied, and glazed pineapples from Caribbean islands as expensive sweetmeats, the fresh fruit was even more rare. Only the fastest ships in the best weather conditions could deliver fresh, unspoiled pineapples to the finest shops of colonial America. The search for a way to grow pineapples in England stimulated the development of the greenhouse, although it would be two hundred years before pineapples were successfully reproduced. Instead, pineapples spread around the world via sailing ships that carried the fruit as protection against scurvy.

Spanish sailors brought pineapples to their colony in the Pacific, the Philippines, from where they spread into Southeast Asia, now the region of the world that dominates production. The Spanish also are thought to have brought the fruit to Hawaii early in the sixteenth century. Toward the end of the nineteenth century, James Dole, a horticulture graduate of Harvard University, arrived in Hawaii. Within fifteen years, Dole had developed the pineapple into Hawaii's second-largest industry (after sugarcane). By the 1950s, the word "pineapple" was practically synonymous with Hawaii, which then accounted for about eighty percent of world production.

Hawaii still leads production in fresh pineapples in the United States; the best are jetted to the mainland and carry a tag that proclaims that fact. However, today, pineapples come into mainland United States from Puerto Rico, Thailand, the Philippines, Costa Rica, Mexico, and Honduras. I'm a particular fan of the sweeter, less acidic gold-fleshed pineapples.

In the kitchen, pineapples add color, sweetness, acidity, and texture. They are versatile enough to grill in slices, perhaps as an accompaniment to the Pineapple–Coconut Flan (page 684); they can be caramelized and flamed with rum and served with cake, such as the Swiss Carrot–Semolina Cake (page 239). Pineapple can be added to cake batters, as in the Indian–Spiced Carrot Cake (page 237); while dried, candied pineapple bits add flavor and texture to the Siennese Pan forte (page 232). Fresh pineapple, along with other tropical fruits like papaya, kiwi, mango, and star fruit, fill a soft meringue cloud in the Australian Pavlova with Lemon Filling and Tropical Fruits (page 442).

PINEAPPLE VARIETIES

BABY SUGAR LOAF: This variety originated in Mexico, where it is still grown, and was brought to Hawaii, where it grows sweeter, meatier, and more yellow in color. This pineapple can be picked ripe and shipped without reducing its shelf life.

DEL MONTE GOLD™: This large and heavy gold-fleshed pineapple, introduced by Del Monte in 1996, is twice as sweet as most white-fleshed pineapples and is low in acid. It is plump and heavy with a squarish, barrel-like appearance, chunky shoulders, and firm, but juicy flesh.

KONA SUGARLOAF: This round to conical-shaped pineapple grown in Hawaii weighs 5 to 6 pounds and is too tender for shipping, so you'll have to travel there to taste its sweet, juicy flesh. Inside, it is cream to gold in color and its leaves pull out easily.

NATAL QUEEN: This small, conically shaped pineapple from South Africa weighs only 2 to 3 pounds with spiny leaves, dark yellow skin, deep-set eyes, and a small, tender core. The juicy fruit has crisp, golden-yellow flesh, and keeps well after ripening.

RED SPANISH: This spiny-leafed squarish pineapple, which weighs 2 to 4 pounds, is the most popular cultivar in the Caribbean, Venezuela, and Mexico, and is well suited for long distance shipping. It has a pleasing aroma, orange-red skin, deep-set eyes, pale yellow flesh, coarse, though flavorful flesh, and a large core.

SMOOTH CAYENNE OR SWEET SPINELESS: This cylindrically shaped fruit introduced to Hawaii from Cayenne, French Guiana in 1820, is the most widely planted pineapple in Hawaii, and the most common type found in the mainland United States. Weighing 5 to 6 pounds, its leaves are smooth; its skin is orange with shallow eyes. The Smooth Cayenne has soft flesh and not much fiber. Its pale yellow flesh is juicy, mildly acidic, quite sweet and rich in flavor.

SOUTH AFRICAN BABY PINEAPPLE: This golden-skinned South African pineapple has been grown year-round since the mid-1980s. The entire pineapple is just about 5 inches long and 3 inches wide. Its bright yellow flesh is sweet, very juicy, and tender, and its core is crunchy and edible. I like to cut these pineapples in half, scoop out the flesh and mix it with ice cream and rum or a frozen mousse mixture, then cover with meringue and glaze with a torch for a pineapple baked Alaska.

CHOOSING, RIPENING, AND STORING PINEAPPLE

Pineapples are picked ripe because, once off the tree, any starch remaining in the fruits will not convert to sugar. However, the fruit will continue to soften and get juicier when ripened after purchase. Pineapples with yellow to orange skin will be sweeter and juicier than those with green to yellow skin, because these are picked when riper. These are usually "Jet-fresh" pineapples, which will be more expensive but of higher quality than those shipped by boat. A pineapple that has been properly handled will have lively looking, deep green leaves. The larger the fruit, the greater the proportion of edible flesh, so pick a big one.

Dark spots develop in pineapples which are subjected to temperature changes, so ripen at cool room temperature for up to one week, or until the fruit has a distinct sweet pineapple aroma, and a leaf can be pulled out with little resistance. Pineapples ferment easily, which is signaled by dry, brownish leaves, dull yellow skin, or an alcoholic aroma. Cut away and discard any brown spots. Once cut, wrap the pineapple well or place in a covered container to prevent its aroma from spreading to other foods and store in the refrigerator for about three days.

Pineapple Cheesecake with Ginger–Macadamia Crust

A far cry from the more familiar canned pineapple-topped diner cheesecake, in this recipe, freshly chopped pineapple is folded into the creamy filling, which is then sprinkled with chopped candied ginger, and baked in a sweet and spicy gingersnap and macadamia nut crust. The cake comes out golden studded with shiny bits of light brown ginger. I like to serve this cake on a platter surrounded by pineapple leaves arranged in a spoke pattern.

YIELD: ONE 9-INCH CAKE, 12 TO 14 SERVINGS

Crust

6 ounces (2 cups) gingersnap cookies, crushed

1/4 pound (1 cup) macadamia nuts

2 tablespoons chopped candied ginger

1/4 cup light brown sugar, packed

2 ounces (1/2 stick) unsalted butter, melted and cooled

Filling

1 1/2 pounds cream cheese, softened

1/2 pound (1 cup plus 2 tablespoons) light brown sugar, packed

2 large egg yolks

2 large eggs

1/4 cup dark rum

2 tablespoons unbleached all-purpose flour

1/2 golden pineapple, peeled, quartered, and cut into small chunks (reserve the rest for another use) or 1 1/2 cups canned pineapple chunks in natural juices, drained

1/4 cup finely chopped candied ginger, optional

Pineapple leaves, for garnish

Make the crust: Preheat the oven to 350°F. Prepare a 9-inch removable bottom or springform cake pan by spraying with nonstick baker's coating, or rub with softened butter and dust with flour, shaking off the excess.

In the bowl of a food processor, combine the cookies, macadamia nuts, ginger, and brown sugar, and process until finely ground. Add the butter and process again briefly to combine. Press the mixture into the bottom and 1 1/2-inches up the sides of the pan. Bake until the crust is set, about 12 minutes. Transfer to a wire rack and cool to room temperature.

Make the filling: Reduce the oven temperature to 300°F.

In the bowl of a standing mixer fitted with the paddle attachment, combine the cream cheese and brown sugar, and beat until light and fluffy, scraping down the sides of the mixer once or twice to get rid of any lumps. Beat in the egg yolks, then the eggs, one at a time, beating just until the batter is smooth. Add the rum and the flour and beat to combine. Fold in the pineapple.

Wrap the bottom and sides of the pan in a sheet of aluminum foil, preferably heavy-duty. Scrape the batter into the cake pan and sprinkle the top with the ginger.

Place the pan in a roasting pan with high sides and pour in enough hot water to come halfway up the sides of the cake. Bake for 1 hour and 30 minutes, or until the center is set and the cake doesn't jiggle in the center when shaken. Check often near the end of baking time to be sure the filling doesn't begin to rise and crack. Remove from the oven and cool to room temperature. Garnish the platter with pineapple leaves and serve. Store refrigerated up to 5 days.

Pineapple–Coconut Flan with Dark Rum

Start this rum-spiked tropical flan a day ahead of time to allow the caramel base to liquefy, making a built-in sauce. Because fresh milk and cream were so hard to come by in the isolated Caribbean islands, flan was and still is often made with canned unsweetened coconut milk, evaporated milk, or sweetened condensed milk. In this Caribbean-style flan, I have combined cream and coconut milk for lightness. You may wish to grate fresh coconut, or you can use the frozen grated coconut available at Asian and Caribbean markets. It is inexpensive, easy to use, and a great product to keep in the freezer. Unsweetened dried coconut can be substituted, but it won't be as juicy.

YIELD: 8 SERVINGS

1 cup sugar

1 cup crushed pineapple in natural juices, drained

1 cup heavy cream

1 (13-ounce) can unsweetened coconut milk

4 large eggs

2 large egg yolks

Pinch all-purpose flour

$1/4$ cup light brown sugar, packed

$1/4$ cup dark rum

$1/4$ cup fresh grated or frozen grated coconut (defrosted if using frozen)

Make the topping: Have a 9-inch round cake pan or a 2-quart ceramic baking dish ready. Measure out $1/2$ cup of water and place it, along with the sugar, in a small, heavy-bottomed pot over medium heat. Bring to a boil, and let boil until the sugar begins to melt and turns golden, about 8 minutes. Shake the pot carefully (CARAMEL IS EXTREMELY HOT!), so the sugar cooks evenly or stir with a wooden spoon or silicone spatula until it reaches 350°F on a candy thermometer and the sugar is medium brown with a faint touch of redness. Remove the pot from the heat and pour into the bottom and part way up the sides of the pan, swirling so the caramel coats the bottom more or less evenly.

Make the flan: Preheat the oven to 325°F.

Combine the cream and coconut milk in a microwavable container, preferably a Pyrex measure, and heat in the microwave for 1 to 2 minutes until it is scalding (steaming hot).

In a medium mixing bowl, beat the eggs, egg yolks, flour, brown sugar, and rum until well combined. Gradually add the cream mixture, constantly whisking until smooth. Stir in the coconut. Pour the custard into the prepared pan, cover with aluminum foil that has been pricked to allow steam to escape, and place the pan in a large roasting pan with high sides. Fill the roasting pan with hot water so it reaches 2 inches up the sides of the custard pan. Bake for $1^{1}/2$ hours or until the custard has set in the center and a skewer inserted into the center comes out clean. Cool to room temperature, then chill for at least 2 hours or until firm and cold.

To serve, place a dished serving platter on top of the pan and invert the custard. Lift the pan off. If any of the caramel topping remains in the pan, place the pan back in a 325°F oven for 10 minutes or until it has melted, then pour over the flan. Store the flan covered and refrigerated for 3 to 4 days.

Pineapple Rum–Pecan Bars

It's hard to believe how easy it is to make these chewy bar cookies. My family and my tasters quickly snapped them up. The cookies are made with pantry ingredients, including pecans and canned pineapple. If you don't have dark rum, which underscores the sugary sweetness of the pineapple, substitute brandy or bourbon.

YIELD: 36 BARS

6 ounces (1½ cups minus 1 tablespoon) unbleached
   all-purpose flour
1 teaspoon baking powder
½ teaspoon fine sea salt
1 (20-ounce) can pineapple chunks in natural juices,
   well-drained
2 cups sugar
¼ pound (1 stick) unsalted butter, melted and cooled
4 large eggs
2 tablespoons dark rum
½ pound (2 cups) pecans, lightly toasted
   and chopped

Preheat the oven to 350°F. Line a 15 x 10-inch jelly roll pan with wax paper.

Whisk together the dry ingredients: flour, baking powder, and salt.

Reserve ½ cup of the pineapple, and place the remaining pineapple in the bowl of a food processor. Process briefly to chop finely, without turning it to mush, or chop by hand.

In a medium bowl, whisk together the sugar, butter, eggs, and rum. Add the flour mixture and beat just to combine. Fold in the chopped pineapple and pecans. Pour the mixture into the prepared pan. Scatter the reserved pineapple chunks over top. Bake for 35 minutes or until lightly browned and the batter has started to come away from the sides of the pan.

Remove from the oven and cool to room temperature. Cut into 36 bars. Cover well and store at room temperature up to 2 days, or refrigerate up to 5 days.

Southern Million–Dollar Pie

Ambrosia in a coconut crumb crust, this luxurious pie was a bit hit back in the fifties, when a million dollars was a lot more money than it is now (when we measure our rich by the billion. Hey, I'd still take a million…). This no-bake filling pie has many versions and has been featured in any number of community cookbooks. In my version, I use fresh gold pineapple (though canned will also work); ripe, local strawberries; lime juice and its slightly bitter, but bitingly refreshing, zest; and a shot of dark rum. Be sure to grate only the green part of the lime zest, which is best accomplished with a Microplane zester (page 179).

YIELD: ONE 9-INCH PIE, 8 TO 10 SERVINGS

Crust

2 ounces ($^1/_2$ cup) pecans

2 ounces ($^1/_2$ cup) unsweetened flaked coconut

$^1/_4$ pound graham crackers or biscotti

$^1/_4$ cup dark brown sugar, packed

$^1/_2$ teaspoon ground cinnamon

2 ounces ($^1/_2$ stick) unsalted butter, melted and cooled

Filling

6 sheets gelatin, soaked in cold water to soften,
    or 2 teaspoons powdered gelatin

1 cup diced fresh pineapple or canned pineapple
    chunks in natural juices (not crushed pineapple),
    chopped and drained, juice reserved

Juice and grated zest of 1 lime, (2 tablespoons juice
    and 2 teaspoons zest)

2 tablespoons dark rum

$^1/_2$ pound cream cheese, softened

$^1/_2$ cup sugar

$^1/_4$ pound (1 cup) pecans, lightly toasted and chopped

$^1/_4$ pound (1 cup) unsweetened flaked coconut

1 quart strawberries, 6 of the best-looking kept whole
    for garnish, the remainder cored and diced

1 cup heavy cream, chilled

2 tablespoons confectioners' sugar

2 teaspoons vanilla extract

Thinly sliced pineapple and mint sprigs,
    for garnish, optional

Make the crust: Combine the pecans, coconut, graham crackers, brown sugar, and cinnamon in the bowl of a food processor and grind until fine. Add the butter and process briefly to combine. Press the mixture into a deep 9-inch pie pan. Chill for 1 hour in the refrigerator or 30 minutes in the freezer.

Preheat the oven to 350°F. Bake the crust until the dough is cooked through, about 15 minutes or until evenly and lightly browned. Cool to room temperature on a wire rack before filling.

Make the filling: If you are using gelatin sheets, combine the lime juice and pineapple juice in a small microwavable measuring cup for a total of $^3/_4$ cup liquid. Microwave on low power until hot to the touch, then add the drained gelatin sheets and the rum, and whisk until combined and the liquid is clear.

If you are using the powdered gelatin, combine the lime juice and pineapple juice in a small microwavable measuring cup for a total of $^3/_4$ cup liquid. Add the powdered gelatin and set it aside to bloom (soak up all the liquid) for about 10 minutes. Heat on low power in the microwave until the liquid is clear, and then whisk in the rum.

In the bowl of a standing mixer fitted with the paddle attachment, beat the cream cheese, sugar, and lime zest until light and fluffy, 4 to 5 minutes, scraping down the sides of the mixer once or twice to get rid of any lumps. Whisk in the gelatin mixture (which should still be hot so it mixes in completely). Fold in the pecans, coconut, strawberries, and pineapple.

In a separate chilled bowl, beat the cream until firm, add the confectioners' sugar and vanilla, and beat again briefly to combine. Fold into the cream cheese mixture. Spoon the filling into the crust. Garnish with the reserved strawberries, and the sliced pineapple.

Refrigerate the pie for at least 4 hours or overnight, then garnish with the mint sprigs before cutting into serving portions, using a knife dipped in hot water and wiped dry in between each slice. Store the pie 2 to 3 days (if it lasts that long) covered and refrigerated.

Pineapple Coconut Shortbread Bars with Macadamia Nuts

Although macadamia nuts originated in Australia, they were introduced to Hawaii in 1880 where they have thrived ever since (see page 490 for more about macadamias). I've combined three Hawaiian specialties: coconut, pineapple, and macadamias in an easy to make yet oh-so-good recipe for bar cookies. A gingery shortbread pastry bottom, nutty with white whole wheat flour is covered with a creamy topping chunky with pineapple, coconut, and macadamias, scented with aromatic cardamom, a cousin of ginger. I use the frozen grated coconut available at Asian and Caribbean markets here, giving the bars all the delicate flavor and juicy, crunchy texture of fresh coconut with much less work!

YIELD: 32 BARS

Shortbread pastry

$1/4$ pound (1 cup minus 1 tablespoon) unbleached all-purpose flour

$1/4$ pound (1 cup plus 2 tablespoons) white whole wheat flour

$1/2$ teaspoon fine sea salt

2 teaspoons ground ginger

$1/2$ cup firmly packed dark brown sugar

$1/2$ pound (2 sticks) unsalted butter, cut into $1/2$-inch slices and softened

Filling

2 ounces ($1/2$ cup minus $1/2$ tablespoon) unbleached all-purpose flour

1 teaspoon baking powder

1 teaspoon ground cardamom

$1/2$ fine sea salt

4 large eggs

1 cup firmly packed light brown sugar

$1/8$-ounce (1) package frozen grated coconut, defrosted, or 2 cups fresh grated coconut

1 (20-ounce) can crushed pineapple, drained

$1/2$ pound (2 cups) chopped toasted macadamia nuts (rinsed and patted dry if salted)

Make the shortbread: Preheat the oven to 350º F. Line a 13 x 9-inch baking pan with parchment paper with the sides extending several inches outside the pan to make it easier to remove the finished bars.

Combine the all-purpose and white whole wheat flours, the salt, ginger, dark brown sugar, and butter in the work bowl of a food processor. Process until well blended and the mixture forms large, moist clumps. Pat the dough evenly into the bottom of the pan. Bake 20 minutes on the bottom shelf of the oven, or until lightly browned. Cool 30 minutes or to room temperature.

Make the filling: In a small bowl, whisk together the flour, baking powder, cardamom, and salt. In a medium bowl, whisk together the eggs with the light brown sugar to combine. Fold in the coconut, pineapple, and the macadamia nuts. Gently fold in the flour mixture just to combine.

Spread the topping mixture over the baked crust and bake 45 minutes, or until the topping is set and lightly browned on the edges. Cool to room temperature and then chill one hour. Cut into 32 bars. Store covered and at room temperature for up to 1 day, or cover and refrigerate up to 5 days.

PISTACHIOS

Zenobia Pistachios . . . 693

PISTACHIO BIRD'S NEST PASTRIES . . . 693

Kadayif Pastry . . . 695

M'HANCHA: THE SERPENT . . . 695

MILK CHOCOLATE AND PISTACHIO COOKIES . . . 696

CHOCOLATE TORTE WITH
ORANGE AND PISTACHIO . . . 697

PISTACHIO CUSTARD SAUCE
OR PISTACHIO GELATO . . . 698

CHLOROPHYLL (NATURAL
GREEN COLORING) . . . 699

PISTACHIOS

Strolling past a small corner bakery on the quieter and less touristy Asian side of Istanbul, my eyes were instantly drawn to the bright green pistachios garnishing the *kadayif*–rolls of pistachio–filled shredded wheat pastry (see the recipe for Pistachio Bird's Nests on page 693). Pistachios are a big deal in Turkey, Syria, and Iran, the region that has long been the center of world production. Those pistachios destined to decorate pastries are shelled and finely ground while still raw, so they maintain their bright green color. Most pistachios are roasted to split open their shells, which changes the color of the nut meats to yellow or brownish–green.

The most unusual way of preparing pistachios I've come across was on the Greek island of Chios, home of the wild pistachio tree, which is tapped for mastic resin (see page 519). There and on several other Greek islands, immature pistachios with soft, edible shells are cooked whole in sweet syrup until tender to make the Greek specialty called spoon fruits. A small spoonful of these syrupy fruits are offered to guests upon arrival as a sign of hospitality, as they were served to me at an organic farm on Chios that raises pistachios.

The pistachio, *Pistacia vera*, is the edible nut of a small, evergreen tree, related to the cashew and the mango, that is native to the mountainous and high desert regions of Turkmenistan, Iran, and western Afghanistan. Insides its thin, hard, ivory-colored shell, the pistachio kernel ranges in color from yellowish green to light green and even to deep forest green. In general, the deeper the shade of green, the higher the value of the pistachio because of better flavor and more appealing color.

There are nine other species in the genus *Pistacia*, including *Pistacia lentiscus*, the tree also known as the lentisk, that is tapped for mastic only on the Greek island of Chios; and another wild pistachio, *Pistacia terebinthus*, whose tender shoots are pickled and eaten in the Greek Cycladic Islands. These species are native to the Mediterranean and southwest Asia, and have much smaller nuts, without the hard shell of *Pistacia vera*, or the "true pistachio." The turpentine-flavored nuts of the lentisk and the wild pistachio were quite popular in antiquity. Persia (now Iran) is still the world's top grower of pistachios, mostly in the southeastern region of Kerman. The English word "pistachio," ultimately derives from an Old Persian word *pistak*.

Pistachio trees mature rather slowly, reaching significant production seven to ten years after planting, with peak production reached only after about twenty years. The trees can live and produce nuts for centuries, alternating one heavy crop year with one light crop year. The nuts grow in grape-like clusters inside an outer skin, or hull, covered with a shell. When the pistachio nuts ripen, their hulls turn rosy, indicating they are ready for harvest, usually in September. Grown under ideal conditions of cool winters and hot, long summers with moderate humidity, pistachio shells will split open with an audible pop just before harvest and resemble a laughing face. To harvest pistachios, the trees are shaken and the ripe nuts simply fall to the ground. Following harvest, the nuts must be hulled and dried within twenty-four hours to maintain their freshness and unblemished appearance.

Pistachios were already being eaten in Turkey and the Middle East by about 7000 BCE. According to the Roman historian, Pliny, the pistachio was introduced to Italy from Syria during the reign of Tiberius, early in the first century BCE. Although well known to the Romans, the true pistachio, *Pistachio vera*, was little known elsewhere in Europe before medieval times. Pistachios were probably introduced to Sicily at an earlier date, either by the Phoenicians or by Greek colonizers. By the ninth-century, the Saracen Arab rulers of Sicily encouraged the cultivation of these tasty nuts. Arab growers in Sicily began the practice of deeply pruning pistachio trees every two years to increase nut production.

Turkey's pistachios are considered to be some of the world's best. I agree with that assessment, having greedily sampled pistachios at a farmers' market near the city of Izmir. The Turkish Antep pistachio, with its distinctive green color, comes closest to the top Iranian variety, which is very hard to find in the United States. These small nuts are rather difficult to open, but are well known for their vivid, tantalizingly flavor. Both larger, red-skinned pistachios and smaller, deep-green pistachios are common in Turkey. Turkey is the largest exporter of pistachios to the United States, with most of its production in the southeastern regions of Gaziantep and Urfa close to Syria and Iran. Turkey also sells its pistachios to Syria, Russia, and Lebanon, and imports even more pistachios from Iran. Pistachios also grow in Syria for sale to Lebanon and other Arab countries, and in Greece, where they are mostly reserved for domestic use.

With their long history on the island of Sicily, pistachios found their way into many of its traditional sweet confections, which were made with another ingredient introduced by the Arabs: cane sugar. Today, small, vibrant green pistachios are grown in the area around Mount Etna and in the Bronte area of Sicily, sold with their reddish outer skins removed. Sicilian pistachios are slightly longer and thinner than those grown in the Middle East. They also have a stronger, more distinctive flavor, perhaps due to the volcanic soil in which they're grown. While they are not exported in large quantities, these deep green nuts can be found (for a high price) at specialty importers like Kalustyan's (www.kalustyans.com) and Albert Ulster Imports (www.auiswiss.com). Top pastry chefs prize them for decorating their creations.

Pistachios were first imported to America in the 1880s by traders who sold them mostly to people of Middle Eastern origin. At first, pistachio shells were dyed red to hide the blemishes that develop easily in their bone-colored shells. A Brooklyn street vendor specialized in selling red-shelled pistachios as a way to draw customers and to distinguish the nuts he sold from those of his competitors. The idea caught on, especially on the East Coast, where red pistachios became the standard. Today, only about fifteen percent of American pistachios are dyed. It took the advent of vending machines in the 1930s for pistachios to gain popularity in America. The pistachios, which were dyed red to stand out in the machines, became a popular snack. As I remember, there were never enough pistachios for my nickel or dime.

Before the overthrow of the Shah of Iran in 1979, virtually nobody grew pistachios commercially in the United States. A series of political events led to the American trade embargo against Iran. Iran leads the world in pistachio output, but an import tax upwards of three hundred percent to import Iranian pistachios certainly discourages anyone from importing them into the United States. Because most of the pistachios eaten by Americans had been imported from Iran, California farmers saw an opportunity to corner the

market and planted the trees in great numbers. Today, about three hundred million pounds of pistachio nuts are harvested annually in California. Almost all are the Kerman variety that originated in Iran's region of that name. These are preferred in California for their large size and widely split shells.

Importers of Turkish and Iranian pistachios describe California grown nuts as beautiful but lacking in flavor. California producers in turn, claim their pistachios taste just as good, but are larger, fresher, and easier to open. Most of the production in California comes from the San Joaquin and Sacramento Valleys. Today, about ninety percent of American pistachios are roasted and salted in their shells for snacking. The rest are shelled, mostly for use in baking, ice creams, and confectionary, though they also show up in sausages, pâtés, and other savory preparations.

In this book, most of the pistachio recipes have Middle Eastern or Arabic origins, including the Pistachio Bird's Nest Pastries (opposite page) made with kadayif, sometimes known as shredded wheat dough; and the M'hancha: The Serpent (page 695), a Moroccan pastry made for celebrations. In other chapters, Mahmoul: Syrian Pistachio-Stuffed Semolina Cookies with Rosewater (page 466) comes from Syria's rich tradition of pistachio dishes. The Sesame Honey Cones with Ricotta and Sun-Dried Fruits (page 800) mix pistachios and colorful bits of dried and candied fruits in the ricotta filling, while the Turkish Semolina Sponge Cookies: Sekerpare (page 869) are sprinkled with ground pistachios for garnish. An herb, nut, and spice mixture used for dipping bread, Egyptian Dukkah (page 890) includes pistachios, hazelnuts, and sesame seeds.

Not all pistachio recipes in this book have Middle Eastern or Arabic origins, however. One exception is the all-American Milk Chocolate and Pistachio Cookies, an easy variation on chocolate chip cookies (page 696). The Chocolate Torte with Orange and Pistachio (page 697) combines bittersweet chocolate, orange juice and zest, and pistachios in an Italian-style rich, dense cake. The Pistachio Custard Sauce (page 698), which can be served as is or frozen for Pistachio Gelato, comes from France and Italy. And the Indian-Spiced Carrot Cake (page 237) includes pistachios instead of the usual walnuts.

This chapter also includes a recipe for natural green Chlorophyll (page 699), extracted from spinach, so you can tint the Pistachio Custard Sauce to a lovely color that echoes that of the nut meats. It is completely unlike the unsavory "pistachio green" often found in artificially dyed ice creams and custard sauces.

ZENOBIA PISTACHIOS

Zenobia Nuts, based in the Bronx, was founded in 1926 by Joseph Zaloom, a Syrian immigrant who named the company after the third century Syrian Queen, Zenobia. For more than eighty years, Zenobia has been known for its top quality Turkish and California pistachios packed in foil bags for freshness. During World War II, the company's owner arranged to ship Iranian pistachios across the Atlantic on Liberty ships. Avoiding German submarines to deliver their cargo, the pistachios brought to America on these ships were the country's only wartime supply. For more information and to order pistachios from Zenobia, go to www.nutsonthenet.com.

Pistachio Bird's Nest Pastries

In this recipe, pistachios fill the rounds of shredded wheat dough known as kadayif *in Turkish,* kunefa *in Arabic, and shredded phyllo dough in English. The dough, which is wrapped up to resemble a skein of wool, is first pulled apart then tossed with butter and rolled up in a nest shape around the filling or drizzled with butter after rolling. In Turkey, special unroasted pistachios—still bright green—are sold ground into an emerald powder that is used as an appealing garnish. To make this powder myself, I chopped the greenest pistachios I could find in a food processor, then strained the nuts through a fine sieve. I used the chunky pieces for the filling and the fine powder for the garnish. The best alternative to kadayif, also spelled kadaif, is phyllo dough.*

YIELD: 12 ROLLS

Filling and Pastry

1/2 pound (2 cups) shelled pistachios,
    as green as possible, roughly chopped
1/2 cup apricot preserves
1/2 teaspoon ground cinnamon
Grated zest of 1 orange or tangerine
    (4 teaspoons)
About 6 ounces kadayif pastry, defrosted
    if frozen (opposite page)
3/4 cup Brown Butter (page 202) or
    Clarified Butter (page 202)

Syrup

1/2 cup honey
1 cup sugar
1/2 lemon
1 cinnamon stick, crushed

Preheat the oven to 350°F. Spray a 12-cup muffin tin with nonstick baker's coating or rub with butter.

Combine the pistachios, apricot preserves, cinnamon, and orange zest. Place the pistachios in the bowl of a food processor and chop roughly. Strain the pistachios through a fine wire sieve, reserving the chopped pistachios for the filling and the powdery pistachios for garnish. Pull a small handful of kadayif strands apart, spreading it out about 1-inch wide. Fold the dough over itself the long way to make a piece about 6 inches long.

Spoon about 2 tablespoons of the pistachio mix onto one end of the dough. While pulling on the bunch of strands with one hand, roll up the pastry to form a compact bird's nest shape. Repeat with the remaining kadayif until you have 12 nests. (To substitute phyllo, brush one sheet with butter, then fold it over to make a long strip about 1-inch wide. Spoon about 2 tablespoons of the pistachio mix onto one end of the strip, then roll up into a compact bird's nest shape. Continue until you have twelve "nests.") Place each round into a muffin cup to maintain its shape while it takes. Using a plastic squeeze bottle if possible, drizzle each roll lightly and evenly with brown butter.

Bake for 25 minutes or until the pastry is golden brown and crispy. Cool for about 10 minutes or until relatively firm, then remove from the tins, placing the nests on a wire cooling rack over a baking pan to drain off any excess butter.

Make the syrup: In a medium, heavy-bottomed saucepan, combine the honey, 1 cup of water, the sugar, lemon, and cinnamon stick. Bring to a boil, skimming off any white foam. Simmer until the sugar is completely dissolved and the syrup is clear, about 5 minutes. Allow the syrup to cool until warm to the touch; then strain through a fine sieve, discarding the lemon and the cinnamon stick.

Transfer the rolls to a baking dish just large enough to hold them tightly in a single layer. Drizzle the syrup over the pastries, making sure to cover each roll. Let them sit at room temperature for 2 to 3 hours, turning them over once so they absorb the syrup evenly, then turn back upright. Sprinkle the center of each bird's nest with the powdered pistachios. Store the rolls at room temperature in an airtight container for up to 1 week.

KADAYIF PASTRY

The very fine vermicelli-like threads of kadayif pastry, also spelled kadaif, are also known as shredded phyllo. Masses of these dough threads are layered or rolled about a filling to make sweet pastries and desserts similar to those made with phyllo in the same region. Kadayif is produced by drizzling streams of thin flour- and-water batter through a container pierced with fine holes onto a special turning hot plate, so it dries into long threads resembling shredded wheat.

Just like wool, the pastry threads are then collected into skeins for sale. The dough is usually sold frozen in America and can be found at Middle Eastern and Greek groceries. Go to www.athens.com and look under the name "shredded fillo dough" for store locations to buy it. Or, buy kadayif online from www.minosimports.com, which has a large selection of kadayif along with phyllo dough in different thicknesses and strudel dough.

M'hancha: The Serpent

The "serpent" is made of a tube of phyllo dough, filled with an almond and pistachio mixture, then rolled up into a fat coil. It is often served at weddings and other celebrations in Morocco. I like to tint the yellowy-green filling with a bit of natural green chlorophyll for a more appealing color that emphasizes the pistachio, but that is not necessary. Rosewater is typically combined with pistachio in the Arab world, but if you don't care for its

aroma, substitute 2 teaspoons of vanilla or orange blossom water.

YIELD: 1 RING, 12 TO 16 SERVINGS

6 ounces (about 1 cup) blanched almonds

6 ounces (1 cup) pistachios, preferably Sicilian skinned pistachios, see page 691

1 cup sugar

6 ounces almond paste

2 ounces ($^1/_2$ stick) unsalted butter

2 tablespoons rosewater

1 teaspoon Chlorophyll (page 699), optional

2 large egg whites ($^1/_4$ cup)

$^1/_2$ cup Clarified Butter, (page 202) melted and cooled

$^1/_2$ cup mild olive oil

About $^1/_2$ pound phyllo sheets, defrosted if frozen

Confectioners' sugar, for garnish

$^1/_4$ cup finely chopped pistachios, for garnish

In the bowl of a food processor, combine the almonds, pistachios, and sugar, and process until finely ground but not at all oily. (It helps if the nuts are frozen or at least cold.) Transfer to a medium mixing bowl. (It is not necessary to wash out the processor bowl.)

In the bowl of a food processor, combine the almond paste, butter, rosewater, Chlorophyll, and egg whites, and process until smooth and creamy. Add to the almond-pistachio mixture, beating with a wooden spoon until smooth. Turn the filling out onto a floured board, and shape it into a long, snake-like log, about 1-inch in diameter. You can also make 2 or 3 shorter logs. Chill in the refrigerator 30 minutes or until moderately firm.

Combine the clarified butter and the olive oil. Working on a long table, arrange about 4 feet of parchment or waxed paper on the table. Brush with the butter. Lay 3 overlapping sheets of phyllo dough next to each other, going the long way making a strip about 4-feet long. Repeat until you have 3 layers of pastry. Place the filling about 1-inch from the edge of the table, pressing together to form a single roll, if necessary. Fold the edges of the phyllo pastry under and roll up tightly forming a long log-shape.

Prepare an 8- to 9-inch cake pan by brushing with butter. Working from the outside in and using the waxed paper to help roll, gently roll up the pastry log in a spiral shape to form the snake, trying not to crack the pastry. (It is helpful to have someone else support the roll.) Place the "snake" into the cake pan to help it keep its shape while baking. Brush again with the butter-oil mixture. Chill the pastry if desired for up to 2 days before baking.

Preheat the oven to 350°F

Bake the pastry for 30 minutes or until lightly browned. Remove from the pan, flip over onto a parchment paper or silicone mat-lined baking pan, and bake again until well browned, about 15 minutes.

Cool to room temperature on a wire rack. Dust with confectioners' sugar and then with chopped pistachios. Store covered and at room temperature for up to 5 days.

Milk Chocolate and Pistachio Cookies

A variation on basic chocolate chip cookies and just as easy to make, these cookies have melted milk chocolate added to the batter along with chopped chocolate folded into the batter for texture. Using a tip I learned as a television food stylist, reserve some of the chopped milk chocolate bits and pistachios to press into the top of each cookie before baking.

YIELD: 4 DOZEN COOKIES

Dough

6 ounces milk chocolate, coarsely chopped, for melting

$^4/_6$ pound (1 cup) unbleached bread flour

$^1/_4$ pound cake flour or 3 ounces unbleached all-purpose flour plus 1 ounce potato starch

1 teaspoon baking powder

$^1/_2$ teaspoon baking soda

$^1/_2$ teaspoon fine sea salt

6 ounces (1$^1/_2$ sticks) unsalted butter, softened

6 ounces (1 cup) dark brown sugar, firmly packed

2 large eggs

1 teaspoon vanilla extract

6 ounces shelled pistachios, coarsely chopped ($^1/_4$ cup)

$^1/_4$ pound milk chocolate, coarsely chopped

Topping

2 ounces pistachios, coarsely chopped

2 ounces coarsely chopped milk chocolate, optional, for garnish

Place the chocolate in a microwaveable bowl and melt in the microwave on lowest power for 2 minutes at a time, or until just barely melted. Whisk until smooth and cool to room temperature.

Sift together the dry ingredients: flours, baking powder, baking soda, and salt.

In the bowl of a standing mixer fitted with the paddle attachment, cream the butter and sugar until light and fluffy, 5 to 6 minutes, then beat in the eggs one at a time, scraping down the sides once or twice. Beat in the melted chocolate and the vanilla. Add the flour mixture and beat only long enough to combine. Fold in the pistachios and the 1/4 pound of chopped milk chocolate.

Form the dough, which will be soft, into two logs roughly 2 inches in diameter, and wrap in waxed paper, parchment paper, or plastic wrap. Chill the logs in the refrigerator for 1 hour, or until firm but still malleable. Re-roll the dough logs to make them evenly rounded. Chill the logs again for at least 1 hour or until quite firm, or up to 4 days. Alternatively, scoop the batter into small walnut-sized balls and chill them for 1 hour to set their shape.

Preheat the oven to 350°F. Line two 18 x 13-inch half sheet pans (or other large baking pans) with parchment paper or silicone baking mats.

Cut each log into 3/8-inch thick slices and arrange on baking sheets, or arrange the dough balls on baking pans. Sprinkle each cookie with pistachio and milk chocolate bits, pressing lightly so they adhere, and bake for 18 minutes or until lightly browned around the edges. Cool on a wire rack before removing from baking sheets. Store in a cookie tin or other airtight container at room temperature up to 5 days. If desired, wrap the unbaked dough well and freeze up to 3 months, defrosting in the refrigerator before slicing or scooping.

Chocolate Torte with Orange and Pistachio

In this sophisticated, almost flourless torte, I have combined a trio of my favorite flavors: bittersweet chocolate, orange, and pistachio. The batter is made with melted bittersweet chocolate fortified with Dutch process cocoa powder and flavored with orange zest, orange juice, and orange liqueur. The shiny glaze combines the trio of flavors again, while a garnish of chopped green pistachios and diced candied orange peel gives it an elegant finish. Serve the individual servings of the cake over a small pool of Pistachio Custard Sauce (page 698) for a fancy finale to a dinner party.

YIELD: ONE 10-INCH CAKE, 10 TO 12 SERVINGS

Cake

1/2 pound bittersweet chocolate, chopped

1/4 cup orange juice concentrate, defrosted

Grated zest of 1 orange (4 teaspoons)

1/4 cup Cointreau or other orange liqueur

1/4 pound (1 cup) shelled pistachios

2 ounces (1/2 cup minus 2 teaspoons) unbleached
  all-purpose flour

1 ounce (scant 1/4 cup) Dutch process cocoa

1/2 teaspoon fine sea salt

1/2 pound (2 sticks) unsalted butter, softened

1 cup sugar

5 large eggs, separated

Glaze

6 ounces bittersweet chocolate, chopped

1/2 cup orange juice

2 ounces (¹⁄₂ stick) unsalted butter,
  cut into bitsand softened

2 tablespoons pistachios, split in half
  (as green as possible)

2 tablespoons diced candied orange peel,
  homemade (page 225) or purchased

Preheat the oven to 325°F. Spray a 10-inch springform cake pan with nonstick spray.

Place the chocolate in a microwaveable bowl and melt in the microwave on lowest power for 2 minutes at a time, or until just barely melted. Whisk until smooth, then whisk in the orange concentrate, zest, and liqueur. Cool to room temperature.

Combine the pistachios, flour, cocoa, and salt in the bowl of a food processor and process to a fine powder.

In the bowl of a standing mixer fitted with the paddle attachment, cream the butter and ¹⁄₂ cup of the sugar until light and fluffy, 5 to 6 minutes. Beat in the egg yolks one at a time. Fold in the chocolate mixture, then fold in the flour mix.

In the clean and greaseless bowl of a standing mixer fitted with the whisk attachment, beat the egg whites until fluffy, then add the remaining ¹⁄₂ cup sugar and continue beating until the whites are firm and glossy, 4 to 5 minutes. Fold the meringue into the batter in thirds so as not to deflate batter. Scrape the batter into the prepared pan and rap the pan on work surface once to release any large air bubbles.

Bake for 50 minutes, or until firm but still moist in the center and the cake has begun to come away from the sides of the pan. Cool to room temperature on a wire rack, then remove from the pan, inverting back onto a

wire rack set on top of a baking pan.

Make the glaze: Place the chocolate in a microwaveable bowl and melt in the microwave on lowest power for 2 minutes at a time, or until just barely melted. Whisk until smooth and cool to room temperature. Heat the orange juice to boiling in a microwaveable bowl, and then beat in the melted chocolate and the butter. Cool until the mixture is firm enough to hold its shape.

Spoon the chocolate glaze over the cake, smoothing the top and sides with an icing spatula. Decorate with the pistachios and candied orange peel, pressing into the glaze so they adhere.

Chill for 30 minutes in the refrigerator to set the glaze. Bring the cake to room temperature before serving. Cut with a sharp knife that has been dipped in hot water and wiped dry in between each slice. Store the cake covered and refrigerated up to 5 days, allowing it to come to room temperature before serving.

Pistachio Custard Sauce or Pistachio Gelato

This pale green pistachio-infused variation of the basic custard sauce called Crème Anglaise is tinted a lovely shade of green with natural chlorophyll. Although the chlorophyll is optional, on its own, the sauce is a less appealing shade of yellowish green. Most pastry chefs simply combine pistachio paste with vanilla custard sauce. You may do the same by purchasing pistachio paste from American Almond (www.lovenbake.com) and substituting about a half cup of the paste for the pistachios, decreasing the amount of sugar to 1/2 cup. However, to me, the pistachio flavor here, derived by steeping ground pistachios in milk, is more subtle and fresh Tasting. Serve the sauce with the Chocolate Torte with Orange and Pistachio (page 697), the Swiss Carrot-Semolina Torte (page 239), the Torta Caprese: Bittersweet Chocolate-Almond Cake (page 336), the French Puff Pastry Peach Galette (page 618), or the Tarte aux Pêches (French Baked Peach Tart) (page 619). Alternatively, freeze the mixture in an ice cream machine and serve it in small scoops as gelato to accompany the same desserts.

YIELD: 3 CUPS, 10 TO 12 SERVINGS

2 cups milk

1 cup heavy cream

$^1/_4$ pound pistachios, finely ground

$^1/_2$ vanilla bean, split

8 large egg yolks

$^3/_4$ cup sugar

Pinch flour

$^1/_2$ teaspoon fine sea salt

1 teaspoon Chlorophyll, optional

Place the milk, cream, pistachios, and vanilla bean in a large Pyrex measure or other microwavable container and heat in the microwave until steaming hot. Allow the mixture to cool to room temperature, then refrigerate overnight or up to 4 days to infuse.

In a medium bowl, whisk together the egg yolks and sugar until they are light and fluffy, 5 to 6 minutes. Meanwhile, scald the pistachio-infused milk in the microwave until steaming hot.

Sprinkle the yolk mixture with the flour and salt, then whisk in a little of the hot milk mixture to temper the mixture. Add the remaining milk mixture and then transfer to a heavy-bottomed pot. Heat over medium heat until the sauce visibly thickens and reads 165°F on a thermometer.

Strain through a fine sieve, pressing well to extract all the liquid and discarding the solids. Whisk in the chlorophyll. Serve warm or cold. To store, cool and then refrigerate up to 5 days in a covered container.

To make gelato, run the custard in an ice cream freezer, following the manufacturer's directions.

Chlorophyll (Natural Green Coloring)

I learned how to make this natural green coloring from my treasured book, The Art of Confectionery, *published in Boston in 1866 (page 808). The book says, "These receipts are from the best New York, Philadelphia, and Boston confectioners' and include a large number from the French and other foreign nations." While working with Georges Perrier and his pastry chef on* Georges Perrier: Le Bec-Fin Recipes, *I found that the chef prepares his chlorophyll using the exact same method. Whisk a small spoonful of chlorophyll into the Pistachio Custard Sauce or into the topping for the Almond-Lime Bars (page 545) to give them an appealing natural green color. A teaspoonful of the chlorophyll is enough to tint most recipes.*

YIELD: 2 TO 3 TABLESPOONS

1 pound spinach, washed and drained,
  stems discarded
1 cup water

Process the spinach leaves and water to a purée. Strain
through a fine sieve or use a juicer to extract the
spinach pulp. Only the raw spinach juice should remain.

Place the spinach juice in a small nonreactive pot
and gently heat until the green chlorophyll coagulates
with clear liquid underneath. Remove from the heat
and cool about 10 minutes, or until warm.

Dampen a paper towel and set it inside a wire sieve.
Gently pour the liquid through the sieve, discarding the
clear juice (or save for vegetable stock). Using a silicone
spatula, scrape the green off the paper towel. This is
the chlorophyll. Transfer to a covered container and
refrigerate to use as needed, up to 2 weeks.

PLUMS & PRUNES

Choosing, Ripening, and Storing Plums . . . 705

Plum Varieties . . . 706

PLUM GINGERSNAP BROWN BETTY . . . 708

RED PLUM STREUSEL CAKE . . . 708

ALSATIAN PLUM MUERBETEIG . . . 710

BRANDIED PRUNE POUND CAKE . . . 710

Slivovitz, Brandy Distilled from Plums . . . 711

PLUMS & PRUNES

In seventeenth century England, a plum was a slang term for £1,000, a large sum of money for the day, which evolved to a "plum job" for a political job involving little work and lots of money. With similar soft, yielding textures, risen bread dough and soft-fleshed women were also called plums. The fruits were so desirable in England, even sweets containing no plums (or prunes), like Christmas plum pudding and plum cake, kept the word in their name. Sugarplums were a confection that, although not actually made from plums, resembled them in shape and size and often came equipped with little wire stalks for suspending them from a Christmas tree. The Sugarplum Fairy is a character in Tchaikovsky's 1892 *Nutcracker* ballet.

When it comes to prunes, in America, we're leery of this dried form of the plum, because they have become associated with elderly people suffering from constipation. Marketers have now renamed them dried plums, although I prefer the original *prune*, now a fashion color in Italy and France. When I bought a pair of velvety, thin-wale corduroy pants in Naples, the saleswoman was adamant that their color was *prugne not violette.*

Plums, which range from light yellow to rose-red to clear red to purple and even blue-black, are now the second-most cultivated fruit in the world, second only to apples. The plum, *Prunus domestica*, forms another branch of the *Prunus* family that also includes cherries, apricots, peaches, and nectarines. Plums and cherries are close cousins; the main difference is in size, so that plums may be substituted for cherries in many recipes. Wild plums are common throughout the temperate parts of the Northern Hemisphere. It seems likely that *Prunus domestica* is indigenous to Central Europe, although the time and manner of its origin are uncertain. Plum trees must be grafted onto rootstock because plum trees grown from seeds revert back to the wild blackthorn that has grown wild in the forests of western Asia for thousands of years.

Alexander the Great brought plums from his travels in the East to the Mediterranean region. Plums were known in Egypt; prunes have been found among the provisions for the afterlife stored in the tomb of Kha, the architect of Thebes. Plums were prominent in the writings and songs of Confucius and the earliest cultivation of the trees took place in China. The plum tree plays a significant role in Chinese mythology and is associated with great age and wisdom. Blossoms of the plum tree carved on jade are a symbol of resurrection.

In 65 BCE, Pompey the Great introduced the plum to the orchards of Rome. The Etruscans knew of the wild plum and the Roman natural historian Pliny speaks of the "great crowd of plums" that was the glory of Roman orchards. According to Roman physician and philosopher Galen, prunes from Spain were the best. The Iberians of Catalonia probably improved on wild plums brought to them by the Phoenicians and Greeks.

Plums were cultivated in the gardens of medieval monasteries in England, and Chaucer refers to a garden with "ploumes" and "bulaces" (*bullace* is another kind of plum, as is the *gage*). By the early seventeenth century, the British were importing the best plums in Europe, reputed to grow in the Balkans and Southern Europe, particularly Moravia in Southern Germany. Plum cultivation became increasingly important in the seventeenth and eighteenth centuries in England and Western Europe.

The famed French Reine-Claude plum commemorates Queen Claude, wife of Francois I. She was described as "far from pretty, but so good, kind, and sweet" that the naturalist Francois Belon thought of her at once when he needed a name for the plum he had brought to the French province of Touraine from the East. Plums grow so well in the region that it is said that the plum is made for Touraine, and Touraine for the plum. During the eighteenth century, Sir William Gage took the Reine-Claude to England, where it acquired a new British name, the Green Gage.

The Damson, a small dense-fleshed oval plum, and the somewhat rounder bullace are classified as *Prunus institutia*. This species, native to Eastern Europe and Western Asia, is considered to be older then *Prunus domestica*, the plum proper. Growing wild in hedgerows, the damson is small and sour, best suited to making jam and fruit butter. The damson had been known in Western Europe since prehistoric times–remains have been found in excavations of prehistoric Swiss lake dwellings–but it was also grown in the Near East. The damson got its name, a variation of Damascus, because it was from this Syrian city famed for its plums that the fruit reached Italy well over 2,000 years ago.

About the year 1200, the Duke of Anjou brought the Damascene plum back to France from a Crusade. Older fruits of the same species already known in Europe were called Damson. The British took a prominent role in improving damsons, developing varieties from it that include the Farleigh and Bradley's King, along with the Black and White bullaces. Damsons are also made into damson "cheese," a stiff fruit paste reminiscent of the Spanish quince membrillo paste and the Latin American guava membrillo paste.

Ever since medieval times, the English word *prune* has referred to an extra-sweet variety of plum that has been dried. In France, the fresh fruit is called *prune* and the dried fruit is *pruneau*; in Italian it is *prugna* and *prugne*. Prunes all come from a group of oval, black-skinned plums with a very high level of sugar that allows them to be sun dried without fermenting, and a "free" or easily detached pit, uncommon among plums. Prunes turn black in drying as the result of enzyme action. It takes about three pounds of fresh plums to produce one pound of prunes.

The superb Prune d'Agen comes from a town in Aquitaine in the southwest of France. The Agen plum came from Damascus during the Crusades and ended up in the town of that name, where it was known in the early eighteenth century as Robe de Sergent (sergeant's coat), because the fruit was the same color as police officer uniforms of the time. If you ever try prunes macerated in Armagnac, the special brandy also from this region, you'll know why they are considered to be a delicacy.

The Agen plum, now grown all over western France, is not picked; the trees must be shaken and the fallen fruits then sorted on cloths spread under the trees. Before they ripen, these plums have already been thinned on the tree in order to encourage larger fruits. Once the plums are gathered, they are set out to dry for several days and turned frequently. Most prunes in America derive from La Petite d'Agen, a plum brought from Agen to the United States by two French brothers, Pierre and Louis Pellier who followed the prospectors West with the California Gold Rush and started a nursery business in 1856 using plum cuttings they had brought from France.

The Quetsche, the pride of Alsace, is a delicious plum, elongated like the Agen plum, juicy and fragrant. The true Alsatian Quetsche, when bought in France, should have its place of origin specified on its packaging. If it is anonymous, it may well have come from Italy, where, according to the French at least, the variety has less flavor, scent, and sugar. Not far from Alsace is Lorraine, home to the Mirabelle plum of Nancy. Deep golden, with a fine perfume, small, tender Mirabelles should be admired and sniffed before they are actually eaten.

Plums end up distilled in potent liquor in Alsace, Lorraine, and bordering Germany. Both Quetsche and Mirabelle are distilled into eau de vie, or clear white liqueur. Mirabelle eau de vie has been known since the sixteenth century and makes a softer and more full-bodied liqueur than Quetsche. The Bokhara plum, *Prunus bokhariensis*, is dried extensively for use in the savory cuisines of Central Asia, Georgia, and the northern fringe of India. Some plums, such as the Portuguese Elvas, are candied, probably the progenitor of the plumless sugarplum known in England.

In America, several varieties of indigenous wild plums, well known to Native Americans before the arrival of Europeans to the continent, are still common and often made into jam or jelly. The best-known is the wild beach plum, *Prunus maritima*, found growing in beach dunes from New England to Virginia. The cherry-sized crimson or purple fruits were among the first foods that the early colonists adapted to their own recipes. Because of their tartness and high pectin (soluble fiber) content, beach plums make an excellent jelly.

Inland, the American wild plum, *Prunus ameri-*

cana, sometimes called the sloe, is widespread. In the north, the hardy Canadian plum, *Prunus nigra*, is common. In the southeast, the Chickasaw plum, *Prunus angustifolia*, often produces large, red plums. Several of these native plums, edible even in the wild, have been the source of cultivated varieties, especially in the southern states where *Prunus domestica* will not thrive.

The early colonists brought European plums along with them to the East Coast. The first kinds they raised were a mixture of European and native plums. Some of these can still be found today. In 1790, William Prince planted the pits of twenty-five quarts of Green Gage plums, which produced trees yielding fruit of every color. By 1828, Prince's nursery offered one hundred and forty different kinds of plums for sale. The opening up of California coincided with the introduction of the Asian plum, *Prunus salicina*, from Japan. Asian plums, such as the Burbank, Santa Rosa, El Dorado, and President, dominate the California crop, by far the largest in North America.

With their dense, pulpy flesh, large range of rich colors, and sweet, slightly tangy flavor, all sorts of fresh plums work well when baked into tarts, such as the Alsatian Plum Muerbeteig (page 710), a lovely array of plum halves baked into the rich, crumbly cookie crust called *muerbeteig* in German and adapted as a specialty of the German-influenced province of Alsace. Plums and ginger are matched in the Plum Gingersnap Brown Betty (page 708), a dark and delicious take on an old-fashioned dessert. A layer of tart red plum wedges nestled in moist cake batter is topped with a layer of soft, creamy custard and finished with crumbly streusel in the Red Plum Streusel Cake (page 708). In dried form, prunes add concentrated jammy flavor in the Brandied Prune Pound Cake (page 710).

CHOOSING, RIPENING, AND STORING PLUMS

Choose plump plums that have intense color, smooth, matte skins, and that are firm with few, if any, cracks or blemishes. The natural powdery bloom on some plums does not affect quality. Most important is that the plums be picked in season and not stored for long before sale. In wintertime, American supermarket shelves abound with plums grown in the Southern Hemisphere, especially Chile, but I believe that this is the time to wait for plum season, because the fruit so often turn out to be cottony and tasteless. Once in a while, I spot good quality, slightly waxy, juicy-looking plums from Chile, the major exporter of stone fruit, with none of the pitting on the skin often found in these imported plums.

To ripen plums, spread the fruits out into a single layer on the counter, turning them daily to prevent soft, mushy spots on the bottom. Once the skins lose their shine and begin to look waxy and a bit dull, the plums are ripe, although they will not actually develop more sugar. Refrigerate ripe plums for four to five days. Never stack ripe fruit more than three high because the weight of the top fruits will bruise the bottom fruit. Note that plum skins are thin and edible, with a bit of tart flavor; the small pit is discarded. Fresh plums are in season from May to late October.

PLUM VARIETIES

ANGELENO: The Angeleno is a huge purple plum with yellow, very sweet, and meaty flesh. When fully tree-ripened, it develops a full, robust flavor and is quite versatile. It is in season from mid-August through the beginning of September.

BLACK AMBER: This super-large, super-beautiful plum with shiny black skin has a slightly floral bouquet. Best used for pies and sauces, Black Ambers should be cooked with the skin left on because it will color the flesh a deep, stained-glass red and add tartness. This plum is in season mid-June through mid-July.

BURBANK: The famed Burbank plum was imported by Luther Burbank from Japan. It has red and golden yellow skin and apricot-colored flesh, which is firm, sweet, aromatic, juicy, and uniquely flavored. A semi-freestone, the Burbank is in season in mid-August.

CASSELMAN: This bright red plum is considered to be the best late-season variety. Its deep amber flesh is very sweet and meaty with an old-fashioned tangy taste, similar to some French plums. It is in season late August to late September.

DINOSAUR EGG PLUOT: The fancifully named Dinosaur Egg is a hybrid of a plum and an apricot, commonly known as a pluot, that mainly retains the characteristics and flavor of a plum. Its skin is a light reddish-yellow in color with small but noticeable speckles. It is very sweet and tends to bruise easily when ripened, so handle with care. It is in season from August through September.

EL DORADO: This plum is dark with nearly black skin and firm, amber-colored flesh. Medium to large in size, with a flattened shape, it has pleasing flavor and sweetness and will still be firm when fully ripe. The El Dorado has bright red to reddish skin with purple highlights and amber flesh with mellow, sweet flavor. It stays firm during cooking, making it a great plum for canning. It is in season in mid-July.

ELEPHANT HEART: Often found at farmers' markets, the delicate skin of this variety requires very gentle handling. A large, heart-shaped plum, it has dark reddish-purple mottled skin and sweet, juicy, richly flavored, firm red flesh. Look for it beginning the third week in July.

FRIAR: This large, deep blue to purplish black–skinned plum has amber-colored, sweet, juicy flesh. An excellent eating plum, it is also recommended for preserves, sauces, and tarts. Friars are sweetest and most delicious late in their season, which begins in August and ends in the fall.

ITALIAN PRUNE PLUM: As it ripens, this small, slender plum's color changes from a reddish blue to a purple-blue, showing a powder-white bloom when fully ripe. Its flesh is rich in flavor and very sweet when fully ripe and is excellent for cooking and preserving. A freestone plum, it is in season in late summer and is very popular in areas with large Italian communities.

KELSEY: A distinctively heart-shaped plum with thin, greenish-yellow skin blushed with red, it is large, firm, and aromatic with rich flavor. It tends to have a hard supplementary core near the pit that must be cut away before eating. It is low in acid, has a small pit, and is a freestone. The Kelsey is in season the third week in June and keeps well.

LARODA: This is a dark reddish-purple plum similar to Santa Rosa, but larger, and is harvested approximately five to six weeks later. Not quite round in shape, the highly flavored Laroda is quite tart but develops wonderful sweetness when fully tree-ripened. It is in season the second week in July.

NUBIANA: This farmers' market favorite is an old-fashioned plum with delightful flavor. Flattened in shape, its skin is shiny black, and its flesh is deep amber. Its flavor is slightly wild with a hint of musk. It is fragrant and holds very well after being picked in late July.

RED BEAUTY: A fully tree-ripened Red Beauty plum will be dark red-purple in color and slightly soft to the touch. Its amber flesh is sweet, aromatic, and juicy; its skin is slightly tart. This plum is almost exclusively used for fresh eating and it keeps quite well. It is in season from mid-May through the beginning of June.

SANTA ROSA: Often considered to be the queen of all plums, the Santa Rosa, developed by Luther Burbank, is the most popular plum in California and Arizona. Juicy, tangy, and flavorful, its skin is reddish-purple and its amber flesh is tinged red. Santa Rosas account for more than one-third of the California plum harvest. Among the most flavorful plums in the world, the Santa Rosa has only a twenty four–hour window between being too green and too ripe. Its season begins in early July.

SATSUMA PLUM: A longtime favorite plum in California, this Japanese plum is mottled maroon over green skin with dark red meaty flesh. Its flavor is sweet, mild, and not tart, and it is excellent for jam. It is in season in late July.

WICKSON PLUM: This large, heart-shaped, greenish-yellow plum has very sweet, amber-yellow, and translucent flesh, and little or no tartness at the skin or the pit. Its flesh is a bit coarse, somewhat fibrous, and firm, and it keeps and ships well. Its season begins the third week in June.

Plum Gingersnap Brown Betty

Brown Betty is an English sweet pudding closely related to French apple charlotte (see page 108) and has been popular in America since colonial times. The bubbling dark baked pudding, made here with plums instead of apples, gets a spicy kick from gingersnaps. Make a double batch of the Swedish Pepparkakor (page 493) and use some of them to make this homey and homely, but so delicious dessert. Although the origin of its name is unknown, perhaps the dessert is named after the small, unassuming-looking brown teapot known as a Brown Betty produced in Stoke-on-Trent, England, since the end of the seventeenth century. Bake the Betty in an attractive ceramic dish so it can be served from it at the table.

YIELD: 8 TO 10 SERVINGS

6 ounces gingersnaps (about 16 small cookies), purchased or homemade (page 493 [Pepparkakor])

$1/2$ cup dark brown sugar, packed

1 teaspoon ground ginger

$1/2$ teaspoon ground nutmeg

$1/2$ teaspoon ground cinnamon

2 ounces ($1/2$ stick) unsalted butter, melted

$1/4$ cup apple juice

2 tablespoons sugar

Juice and grated zest of 1 lemon (3 tablespoons juice and 1 tablespoon zest)

$2^1/2$ pounds firm but ripe plums (about 9), preferably red or black, pitted and sliced (skin left on)

$3/4$ cup unsweetened crème fraîche, for serving

Preheat the oven to 350°F.

In the bowl of a food processor, combine the gingersnaps, brown sugar, ginger, nutmeg, and cinnamon, and process to fine crumbs. Add the butter and process again briefly to combine.

In a large bowl, combine the apple juice, sugar, lemon juice and zest. Add the plums and toss well to combine. Spoon half the fruit into a 9-inch baking dish, preferably ceramic. Sprinkle with $1/2$ cup of the gingersnap crumb mixture, spoon the remaining fruit mixture on top, then cover with the remaining crumbs.

Bake for 45 minutes or until the fruit is tender and the crumbs are nicely browned. Serve hot or warm, accompanied by crème fraîche. Store refrigerated for up to 5 days, reheating before serving. (Cover with foil and bake at 350°F for about 30 minutes or until piping hot.)

Red Plum Streusel Cake

This fruity, four-layered cake starts with a layer of moist orange and nutmeg-flavored batter. Next is a layer of deep red plum wedges tightly packed together with a sour cream custard poured over top. A sprinkling of buttery oatmeal streusel tops it off. For the most intense color, make the cake in late fall when the darker plums come into season. If tangerines are in season, use both their juice and fabulously fragrant zest instead of orange.

YIELD: ONE 9-INCH CAKE, 8 TO 10 SERVINGS

Streusel

2 ounces ($\frac{1}{2}$ cup minus 2 teaspoons)
   unbleached all-purpose flour

3 ounces ($\frac{1}{2}$ cup) oatmeal

2 tablespoons sugar

2 tablespoons dark brown sugar

Grated zest of 1 lemon (1 tablespoon)

$\frac{1}{2}$ teaspoon grated mace, substitute ground nutmeg

3 ounces ($\frac{3}{4}$ stick) unsalted butter, chilled and
   cut into bits

$\frac{1}{2}$ cup sliced almonds

Cake

$\frac{1}{4}$ pound (1 cup minus 1 tablespoon) unbleached
   all-purpose flour

1 teaspoon baking powder

1 teaspoon fine sea salt

$\frac{1}{2}$ teaspoon freshly grated nutmeg

2 ounces ($\frac{1}{2}$ stick) butter, softened

$\frac{1}{2}$ cup sugar

2 large eggs

2 tablespoons orange or tangerine juice

Grated zest of 1 orange or tangerine (4 teaspoons)

1 teaspoon vanilla extract

$2\frac{1}{2}$ pounds (about 9) firm but ripe plums, preferably
   red, pitted and cut into six wedges each

Filling

1 cup sour cream

2 large eggs

2 tablespoons orange juice concentrate,
   substitute orange or tangerine juice

2 tablespoons potato starch,
   substitute corn, wheat, or rice starch

Spray a 9-inch springform pan with nonstick baker's coating, or rub with softened butter and dust with flour, shaking off the excess.

Make the streusel: In the bowl of a food processor, combine the flour, oatmeal, sugar, brown sugar, lemon zest, and mace. Process briefly to combine, then add the butter and almonds and process again just long enough to combine into large crumbs.

Make the cake: Preheat the oven to 350°F.

Whisk together the dry ingredients: flour, baking powder, salt, and nutmeg.

In the bowl of a standing mixer fitted with the paddle attachment, cream the butter and sugar until light and fluffy, 5 to 6 minutes, scraping down the sides once or twice. Beat in the eggs one at a time, then beat in the orange juice, orange zest, and vanilla. Add the flour mixture and beat briefly, just long enough to combine. Scrape the batter into the pan. Nestle the plum wedges in the batter, skin side up.

Make the topping: In a bowl, whisk together the sour cream, eggs, orange juice concentrate, and potato starch and pour evenly over the plums. Sprinkle with the streusel.

Bake for 1 hour or until the topping is golden brown and the cake has begun to come away from the sides of the pan and a toothpick or skewer stuck in the center comes out clean. Cool to room temperature on a wire rack before cutting into serving portions. Store covered and at room temperature for up to 4 days.

Alsatian Plum Muerbeteig

This large, shallow tart filled with spiced plum halves is made with muerbeteig, *a rich shortcrust pastry of German origin (see page 444). I bake it in a pizza pan to mimic the large shallow tart pans used in Alsace. The small oval-shaped Italian prune plums, known as* quetsche *in Alsace, in season in late summer and early fall, are ideal for this tart. The dusty-looking dark blue plums were common in the former Austro-Hungarian Empire where they were used to make* slivovitz *(plum brandy), tarts like this one, and cakes like the Brandied Prune Pound Cake (page 710). The same plums grow abundantly throughout Northern Italy, especially in Trentino-Alto Adige and Friuli-Venezia Giulia, which were once part of the same empire. The fruits are known in Italian as* prugne *when fresh and* prugne secchi *when dried.*

YIELD: 10 TO 12 SERVINGS

1 pound Muerbeteig dough (page 444)

1¹/₂ cups plum jam

¹/₄ cup plum brandy (slivovitz), substitute brandy
    or quetsche

¹/₂ cup sugar

1 teaspoon ground cinnamon

¹/₂ teaspoon ground mace

Grated zest of 1 lemon (1 tablespoon)

3 pounds (about 24) Italian prune plums, pitted and
    halved

³/₄ cup unsweetened crème frâiche, for serving

Roll out the dough between two sheets of lightly floured wax paper to a circle about 13-inches in diameter. Lay into the bottom of a 12-inch pizza pan without stretching the dough and crimp to form a decorative edge. (Alternatively, press the dough out by hand into the pan.) Chill the crust for 30 minutes to relax the gluten and so the crust maintains its shape well.

Preheat the oven to 350°F.

Combine the plum jam, brandy, sugar, cinnamon, mace, and lemon zest and spread over the crust. Arrange the plum halves, cut side up in closely overlapping circles over the plum jam mixture.

Place the filled tart on a sheet of aluminum foil and crumple it up around the edges to prevent drips. Bake the tart on the bottom shelf of the oven 45 minutes, or until the crust is golden brown and the plums are bubbling and juicy and the crust is golden brown. Cool to room temperature, then cut into portions and serve with a dollop of unsweetened crème frâiche. Store covered and at room temperature for up to 2 days or cover and refrigerate up to 4 days.

Brandied Prune Pound Cake

In this recipe, I soak prunes (I refuse to call them dried plums) in plum brandy (or brandy, if it is not available) until plump. I mix the dried fruit with a pound cake batter that gets its subtle tanginess from yogurt and sweet spiciness from ground allspice and mace., I substitute potato or other starch for part of the unbleached all-purpose flour for lightness instead of using bleached cake flour. Like other pound cakes, this one keeps quite well and freezes beautifully.

YIELD: ONE 10-INCH CAKE, 12 TO 16 SERVINGS

1 cup diced dried plums

$1/2$ cup slivovitz (plum brandy)

10 ounces ($2^1/2$ cups plus 1 tablespoon) unbleached all-purpose flour

2 ounces ($1/2$ cup plus 2 tablespoons) potato starch, substitute corn, wheat, or rice starch

$1/2$ teaspoon baking soda

$1/2$ teaspoon fine sea salt

$1/2$ teaspoon ground allspice

$1/2$ teaspoon ground mace

$1/2$ pound (2 sticks) unsalted butter, softened

3 cups sugar

4 large eggs

1 cup rich yogurt, not non-fat

Grated zest of 1 orange (4 teaspoons)

1 teaspoon vanilla extract

1 teaspoon almond extract

In a medium bowl, soak the plums in the slivovitz for at least 30 minutes or until plump.

Preheat the oven to 325°F. Spray a 10-inch tube pan with baker's nonstick coating or rub with butter, then dust with flour, shaking off the excess.

Whisk together the dry ingredients: flour, potato starch, baking soda, salt, allspice, and mace.

In the bowl of a standing mixer fitted with the paddle attachment, cream the butter and sugar until light and fluffy, 5 to 6 minutes, scraping down the sides once or twice. Beat in the eggs, one at a time, beating well after each addition.

In a small bowl, whisk together the yogurt, orange zest, vanilla, and almond extracts. Beat in the flour mix alternating with the sour cream mix, beginning and ending with the flour mix. Fold in the plums and any soaking liquid.

Pour the batter into the pan, banging down on the counter once or twice to deflate any large air bubbles. Bake for 1 hour and 10 minutes or until the cake starts to come away from the sides of the pan and a toothpick or skewer stuck in the center comes out clean. Let the cake cool in the pan about 30 minutes, or until warm but not piping hot. Run an icing spatula around the edge of the pan to loosen, then invert onto a wire rack and allow the cake to cool to room temperature. Store, covered, at room temperature for 4 to 5 days.

SLIVOVITZ: BRANDY DISTILLED FROM PLUMS

Slivovitz is the local fruit brandy of Serbia and Bosnia-Herzegovina. It is traditionally made from the black plum called the Madjarka, which imparts a rich, heady scent to the spirit. These black plums are crushed along with their stones and fermented very slowly for about three months. The liquor is double-distilled and then aged in casks of Slovenian oak. Sometimes, whole plums are thrown in to macerate in the spirit while it ages about five years. Slivovitz is the national drink of Serbia where about eighty percent of local plum production is used to create it. The brandy is a traditional after-dinner digestive drink for Ashkenazi Jews. Because it is made from plums without any fermented grain, slivovitz is also considered kosher for Passover. Quetsche, made in Alsace, France, and Mirabelle, made in Lorraine are other types of clear, distilled plum beverages. All three are also produced in nearby parts of Europe including Germany, Luxembourg, and Italy.

POPPY SEEDS

Choosing and Storing Poppy Seeds . . . 715

ONION POPPY SEED KICHELS . . . 715

HONEY-POPPY SEED HAMANTASCHEN . . . 716

Hamantaschen and Jewish History . . . 717

BLACK KUGELHOPF . . . 717

Kugelhopf History . . . 719

LEMON POPPY SEED BISCOTTI . . . 719

POPPY SEEDS

Poppy seeds, Papaver *somniferum,* are small, blue–black or creamy white, *Papaver somniferum var. album*, seeds gathered from the same plant from which opium is produced. It is currently illegal to grow poppies in the United States, although it is perfectly legal to cook with the seeds or oil, as witnessed by all the poppy seeded bagels, challah breads, and poppy-filled Hamantaschen sold in this country every year. However, some gardening suppliers will not ship or sell the seeds.

The poppy originated in the Eastern Mediterranean, where 3,500 years ago, the ancient Sumerians called it "plant of joy." Known to the early Egyptians, the poppy was mentioned in Homer's *Iliad* and had reached India and China by 800 CE. The ancients valued poppy seeds for their oil, though their narcotic and pain–killing powers were also well known.

After the exquisite, papery, red poppy blooms and dies off, large parchment–colored, capsules form, topped with a small pronged crown. Milky opium latex is extracted from immature pods by cutting small slits into the sides. When fully developed, the pods divide into chambers housing myr-

iad tiny seeds–one pound of poppy pods contains one to two million seeds. The seeds have virtually no narcotic content, although people who eat poppy seeds may test positive for opium in drug tests. Cold-pressed poppy oil is produced in small quantities for the kitchen or bakery; heat–extracted oil is produced for use in artist's paints.

Both the slightly larger, oilier, blue–black poppy seeds (Hungarian or Dutch) and the smaller, creamy–white poppy seeds (White Persian or Indian) have a sweet, pleasant aroma and a mild, nutty taste. Blue poppy seeds are stronger in flavor, especially after roasting, and are popular in Eastern Europe, Holland, Germany, and Austria, where they appear in stollen, tortes, dumplings, Bohemian kolache, and noodle casseroles. In Ashkenazi Jewish cookery, poppy seeds top breads like challah, bagels, and bialys. They are crushed to make "mohn" or poppy seed filling for Jewish Hamantaschen cookies and Hungarian strudel. Mild white poppy seeds are prized for their thickening properties, especially for creamy Mogul Indian korma sauces and flavored breads, cakes, and cookies in Scandinavia.

CHOOSING AND STORING POPPY SEEDS

Most baking recipes call for the stronger tasting blue-black poppy seeds rather than milder, creamy white poppy seeds, though they can be substituted in the Lemon Poppy Seed Biscotti recipe and used in other cookie and cake recipes. Look for white poppy seeds in Indian, Middle Eastern, and Scandinavian food stores. Look for blue poppy seeds and mohn (ground poppy filling) in German, Russian, and Central European markets. It is best to buy small quantities of poppy seeds from stores with high turnover, or from specialty spice purveyors. Because poppy seeds are extremely hard, a special poppy seed grinder is often used to grind the seeds. Purchase canned poppy seed paste from American Almond (www.lovenbake.com). Purchase a special poppy seed grinder (resembling a hand-cranked meat grinder) from www.cooking.com or from Otto's Hungarian Import Store & Deli and other online sources.

Because they are high in oil, poppy seeds are prone to rancidity. The seeds also tend to get buggy, so they are best stored in the freezer.

Onion Poppy Seed Kichels

My maternal great-grandmother lived a long life, well into her nineties, along with my great-grandfather, who owned a coal business run out of the large brownstone house they owned in the Williamsburg section of Brooklyn. I have a wonderful photo of her with her children taken just before they boarded the ship bound for New York from her native Galicia in Poland. The story is told that she cut off the boys' payess (earlocks) just before the photo, because as she said, "They don't wear them in America." She died when I was about thirteen years old and though I don't have that many memories of her, the memory of the taste and the smell of her golden raisin challah and tzibla (onion) and poppy seed kichels (small biscuits) have stayed with me.

YIELD: ABOUT 3 DOZEN BISCUITS

3/4 pound (3 3/4 cups) unbleached all-purpose flour

1/4 pound (1 cup plus 2 tablespoons) white
    whole wheat flour

1 tablespoon baking powder

1 tablespoon fine sea salt

1/2 teaspoons black pepper

1 pound (2 medium) onions, finely grated with juices

2 large eggs

3/4 cup vegetable oil

1/4 cup blue poppy seeds

Preheat the oven to 350°F. Line an 18 x 13-inch half sheet pan (or other large baking pan) with parchment paper or a silicone baking mat.

In a bowl, whisk together the dry ingredients: flour, wheat flour, baking powder, salt, and pepper.

In the bowl of a standing mixer fitted with the paddle attachment, combine the onions, eggs, oil, and poppy seeds, and mix. Add the flour mixture and beat until just combined. Cover and allow the dough to rest at room temperature for about 15 minutes to relax the gluten.

Roll out the dough (which will be sticky) in portions on a floured work surface to $3/8$-inch thick, then cut it into 3-inch circles, rerolling the scraps. Use a spatula to move the circles onto the baking pans, placing them in rows of four and three, about 1-inch apart.

Bake for 25 minutes or until light tan in color and crispy. While these kichels are best the day they are made, you can store them in a cookie tin or other container at room temperature up to 2 days.

Honey–Poppy Seed Hamantaschen

A popular Eastern European pastry called mohntashen *(poppy seed pockets) was transformed into Hamantaschen (Haman's pockets) by Ashkenazi Jews. To make them, circles of sweet buttery dough are filled with poppy seed, apricot, cherry, or prunes mixtures. The circles are folded into a tricorn to represent the hated Haman's hat before baking. Observant Jews replace the butter with non-dairy margarine or oil, because the cookies would usually be served after a meat meal. To maintain the kosher separation of dairy and meat, no dairy is eaten for several hours after the meal. Start a day ahead to soak the poppy seeds, or use canned poppy seed filling also called* mohn, *available at German and Eastern European specialty shops and online from www.lovenbake.com or from www.parthenonfoods.com. If you're making your own filling, grind the poppy seeds using a special poppy seed grinder (page 715), a spice grinder, coffee grinder, or a mortar and pestle.*

YIELD: 3 DOZEN COOKIES

$1/4$ pound blue poppy seeds

Dough

$3/4$ pound (2 cups minus 2 tablespoons) unbleached all-purpose flour

2 teaspoons baking powder

1 teaspoon fine sea salt

$1/2$ pound (2 sticks) unsalted butter, softened

$1/2$ cup sugar

2 large eggs

2 tablespoons orange juice

2 teaspoons orange zest

1 teaspoon vanilla extract

Filling

2 ounces ($1/2$ stick) unsalted butter, softened

$1/4$ cup honey

$1/2$ cup coarsely ground walnuts

2 ounces ($1/2$ cup) golden raisins

2 teaspoons grated orange zest

Place the poppy seeds in a bowl and add about 1 cup boiling water, enough to cover the seeds by about 1 inch. Soak overnight at room temperature.

Make the dough: Preheat the oven to 350°F. Line two 18 x 13-inch half sheet pans (or other large baking pans) with parchment paper or silicone baking mats.

Whisk together the dry ingredients: flour, baking

powder, and salt.

In the bowl of a standing mixer fitted with the paddle attachment, cream the butter and sugar until light and fluffy, 5 to 6 minutes. Beat in the eggs one at a time, beating well after each addition. Beat in half the flour mixture, then add the orange juice, zest, and vanilla. Add the remaining flour mixture, beating only long enough for the dough to come together in moist clumps.

Knead the dough briefly by hand until it forms a ball. Transfer to a plastic bag and shape into a flattened rectangle. Chill in the refrigerator for 1 hour or in the freezer for 30 minutes.

Make the filling: Drain the poppy seeds well and grind them finely with a special poppy seed grinder or a coffee or spice grinder or using a mortar and pestle. (Substitute 1 cup poppy seed filling.)

In the bowl of a standing mixer fitted with the paddle attachment, cream the butter and honey until light and fluffy, 5 to 6 minutes. Beat in the walnuts, raisins, orange zest, and ground poppy seeds. Chill the filling for 1 hour in the refrigerator or 30 minutes in the freezer, until firm.

Preheat the oven to 375°F.

Divide the dough into 2 or 3 sections and roll each one out between 2 sheets of lightly floured wax paper lightly dusted with flour to about 3/8 inch thick. If the dough gets warm and sticky, refrigerate it again, still between the sheets of wax paper. Cut the dough into 3-inch rounds, rerolling the scraps if desired. Spoon about 1 tablespoon of the filling into the center of each circle. Fold up the edges on three sides to form open triangles. Pinch the corners together firmly. Bake for 20 minutes or until delicately browned. Store refrigerated up to 1 week.

HAMANTASCHEN AND JEWISH HISTORY

These triangular poppy seed–filled cookies hail from the Ashkenazi tradition and commemorate the Jewish holiday of Purim. In the fifth century BCE, in the reign of King Achashverosh of Persia, Morde-chai, a Jew, refused to prostrate himself before Haman, the King's vizier. Offended, Haman set out "to destroy all the Jews that were throughout the whole kingdom of Achashverosh" (from the Book of Esther). The Jews were saved from Haman's deadly plan by the intervention of Mordecai's beautiful cousin, Esther, who had been chosen as queen a few years earlier. The pastries are made in the shape of Haman's tricorn hat. Symbolically, this long-ago enemy of the Jewish people is destroyed by gobbling up the cookies. In Italy, another version of the pastries are called *orecchie di Aman* (Haman's ears), and are consumed just as quickly.

Black Kugelhopf

This sweet, yeast-raised cake gets its rich dark color from poppy seeds and bittersweet chocolate and its spicy flavor from cinnamon, cloves, and lemon zest. Spelled in any number of variations, a kugelhopf is baked in a special tall, narrow tube pan with a swirled pattern embossed on the side that resembles a turban. This pan, also known as a Turk's head or turban pan, is the inspiration for the American Bundt cake pan (page 26). Kugelhopf is popular in Germany, Austria, and especially Alsace. Start a day ahead to soak the poppy seeds and make sure all the ingredients are at room temperature. I make my kugelhopf using a silicone Turk's head mold, available at Fante's (www.fantes.com), along with other choices in just about every other shape and material you can imagine.

YIELD: 12 SERVINGS

2 ounces ($^1/_2$ cup) poppy seeds

1 ($^1/_4$-ounce) package (2$^1/_2$ teaspoons) active dry yeast

$^1/_4$ cup lukewarm water

2 tablespoons honey

7 ounces (2 cups) unbleached all-purpose flour

1 teaspoon fine sea salt

$^1/_2$ teaspoon ground cinnamon

$^1/_4$ teaspoon ground cloves

$^1/_4$ pound (1 stick) unsalted butter, softened

$^1/_2$ cup sugar

2 large egg yolks

2 large eggs

$^1/_4$ pound bittersweet chocolate, grated

Grated zest of 1 lemon (1 tablespoon)

1 teaspoon vanilla extract

Confectioners' sugar, for dusting

Place the poppy seeds in a bowl and add about 1 cup boiling water, enough to cover the seeds by about 1 inch. Soak overnight at room temperature.

Spray an 8-inch diameter Kugelhopf or Turk's head mold with nonstick baker's coating, or rub with softened butter and dust with flour, shaking off the excess.

In a small bowl, combine the yeast, lukewarm water,

and honey. Allow the mixture to proof in a warm place for about 15 minutes, or until bubbling and puffy.

In another bowl, whisk together the dry ingredients: flour, salt, cinnamon, and cloves.

Drain the poppy seeds well and grind them finely with a special poppy seed grinder or a coffee or spice grinder.

In the bowl of a standing mixer fitted with the paddle attachment, cream the butter and sugar until light and fluffy, 5 to 6 minutes. Beat in the egg yolks and eggs one at a time and blend well. Beat in the poppy seeds, chocolate, lemon zest, and vanilla. Add the flour mixture and beat until the dough is smooth and elastic though still sticky. Transfer the to the pan, filling the mold evenly. Tent the pan with oiled plastic wrap and allow the dough to rise until doubled in size, about 2 hours, at warm room temperature.

Preheat the oven to 425°F. Bake for 20 minutes. Reduce the heat to 350°F and bake for 20 minutes or until the bread sounds hollow when tapped on the bottom and a thermometer inserted in the center reads 190°F.

Remove from the oven, invert the cake over a wire rack, loosen from the pan and cool completely. Dust the top with confectioners' sugar. Store in an airtight tin or other container up to 3 days at room temperature.

KUGELHOPF HISTORY

The kugelhopf is thought to have originated in Vienna, commemorating the Hapsburg defeat of the Turks at the city's gates in 1683. The cake is made in the shape of the sultan's turban, which, like the hamantaschen (page 716), is eaten as a way of symbolically destroying the enemy. The Turkish-crescent-shaped croissant is also said to date back to this watershed battle that established the strength of the Habsburg Empire. Today, kugelhopf, also spelled kougel or gugel, hupf or hopf, is a bakery specialty of Alsace, France. Alsatians have an unlikely, if charming, tale of the Magi, the Three Kings, who walked all the way from Bethlehem to Cologne and received hospitality from a pastry chef named Monsieur Kugel. In his honor, the Magi made a cake in a turban shape. A Fête de Kugelhopf held every June in Alsace celebrates that event.

The traditional Alsatian baking mold is made from terra cotta glazed only on the inside which yields kugelhopf with a smooth, dark outer crust and fine, moist inner crumb. According to Chef André Soltner, a native of Alsace, in times past, a wedge of kugelhopf would be served as sustenance before the lengthy marriage ceremonies held in Alsace's churches and synagogues. The bride's mother would also bake kugelhopfs as gifts for the priest, the pastor, or rabbi, the mayor, the schoolteacher, the midwife, and her neighbors as a token of goodwill.

Lemon Poppy Seed Biscotti

Poppy seeds and citrus complement each other especially well, as in these crunchy, lemony biscotti enriched with fruity olive oil and flavored with fragrant lemon zest and plenty of freshly squeezed lemon juice. If you have mild and creamy-tasting Indian white poppy seeds, mix them here with the black poppy seeds. Like all biscotti (at least all those that I've ever made), once formed into logs, the dough keeps perfectly in the freezer up to three months. Alternatively, bake the logs then freeze them, so all you need to do is allow them to defrost, then slice and re-bake. This recipe is dairy-free.

YIELD: ABOUT 40 BISCOTTI

1¼ pounds (4¾ cups minus 1 tablespoon) unbleached all-purpose flour

2 cups sugar

1 tablespoon baking powder

1 teaspoon fine sea salt

¾ cup extra-virgin olive oil

3 large eggs

½ cup fresh lemon juice

Grated zest of 2 lemons (2 tablespoons)

¼ pound (1 cup) diced candied lemon rind

¼ cup poppy seeds

1 egg white lightly beaten with 1 tablespoon water, for the egg wash

½ cup raw or crystallized sugar, for sprinkling

Preheat the oven to 375°F. Line an 18 x 13-inch half sheet pan (or other large baking pan) with parchment paper or a silicone baking mat.

In the bowl of a standing mixer fitted with the whisk attachment, combine the dry ingredients: flour, sugar, baking powder, and salt. Whisk to combine.

In a small bowl, whisk together the olive oil, eggs, lemon juice, zest, candied lemon rind, and poppy seeds. Add this mixture to the flour mixture, switch to the paddle attachment, and beat just long enough for the mixture to form large moist clumps. Knead the dough by hand to combine well.

Turn the dough out onto the baking pan and form two evenly-shaped logs about 2-inches wide and 2 inches apart. Brush the logs with egg wash and sprinkle with the crystallized sugar, pressing into the top lightly so it adheres.

Bake for 25 minutes or until light golden brown but still soft in the center. Cool on a wire rack to room temperature.

Preheat the oven to 350°F.

Using a serrated knife, slice each roll diagonally into $1/2$-inch thick slices. Arrange the cookie slices standing up on a baking pan. Bake for 15 minutes or until lightly colored at the edges. Cool to room temperature on a wire rack. Store in a cookie tin or other covered container for up to 2 weeks.

POTATOES

Gluten–Free Baked Goods in this Book . . . 723

Types of Potatoes . . . 724

HERBED FOCACCIA WITH GOAT CHEESE,
RED ONION, AND BLACK OLIVES . . . 725

BUTTERMILK-SOURDOUGH
WHITE SANDWICH BREAD . . . 726

DILLED POTATO-ONION ROLLS . . . 727

SARDINIAN POTATO TORTA (COCCOI PRENA) . . . 728

MEXICAN CHOCOLATE TEQUILA SOUFFLÉ CAKE . . . 729

POTATOES

Potatoes might not be the first ingredient you think of when it comes to baking, but their starchiness and moisture content makes them a natural for breads and fillings and to thicken batters. Potatoes have many positive effects on bread: yeast loves it, while the bread itself will be softer in texture and will stay fresh longer. Potato bread was first made in the nineteenth century by the Irish as a way of using up leftover mashed potatoes. In America, many commercial bakeries specialize in light and fluffy potato-based breads, although because these breads also usually contain additives and preservatives, I prefer to make my own.

In this chapter, I use fresh potatoes, instant potato flakes, and potato starch. The tender Herbed Focaccia with Goat Cheese, Red Onion, and Black Olives (page 725) is made with instant potato flakes, which, as professional bakers know, are an easy way to add moisture. (It's not often that you'll see me in the instant potato aisle!) I make my sourdough starter by boiling potatoes and using the nutrient-rich cooking liquid to jump-start the fermentation process. The Buttermilk-Sourdough White Sandwich Bread (page 726) makes great sandwich bread with more body than the commercial type and with a subtle, sour aftertaste from its potato-based starter. My Dilled Potato-Onion Rolls (page 727) get their moistness and light texture from potatoes, and the delicious Sardinian Potato Torta (page 728) is filled with potatoes and enriched with pecorino cheese and lots of refreshing mint. The Tequila Soufflé Chocolate Cake (page 729) is just one example of using potato starch as a substitute for bleached cake flour taking advantage of its light thickening power and tender texture. It also yields cakes appropriate for people with gluten allergies.

Potatoes are so much a part of our cuisine, we forget that until Columbus made his famous travels to the Americas, no one outside of South America had ever seen one. Native tribes in the Andes began cultivating the wild potatoes they found high in the mountains as early as 7,000 years ago. Even today, Peru is the world's potato capital, with a huge diversity of native potatoes in odd shapes and colors. These early potatoes were small, knobby, and bitter, so the indigenous peoples developed special techniques to remove their bitterness. Wild potatoes continue to be eaten in the Andes and are known as *papas criollas* (native potatoes). Potatoes in today's market may be lumpy or smooth, leather-skinned or paper-skinned, small as one ounce or large as one and a half pounds, in colors ranging from cream to rose to yellow, red, brown, purple, and blue, and gold to brown. And they are used in every part of the meal–including dessert.

The Spanish brought the potato back to the Old World about 1570, where they were first used to feed hospital inmates. From there, potatoes spread throughout much of the world, eventually becoming a staple food, especially for the poor. Like tomatoes, potatoes were first thought to be poisonous because they are members of the family that includes deadly nightshade. Indeed, the leaves of the potato plant are poisonous, as are potatoes left in the light long enough to turn green, which indicates the presence of solanine, a substance that causes illness and, in large quantities, can be toxic. (Cut away any green skin or flesh on potatoes before cooking to avoid solanine.)

It took two centuries before the potato was commonly accepted. The British King Charles II recommended that large quantities of potatoes be grown in case of war or famine. About 1780, the people of Ireland adopted the rugged crop and by the mid-nineteenth century, the vast majority of the Irish population had become totally dependent on the potato for food. When the potato blight destroyed crops in the years 1845, 1846, and 1848, thousands starved to death while others emigrated, mainly to North America and Britain.

In France, Antoine Parmentier, a pharmacist, chemist, and employee of King Louis XV, recognized that the potato's nutritional benefits and high yields could be a blessing for the French farmer. While being held prisoner by the Prussians during the Seven Years War, Parmentier became so convinced of the benefits of the potato, he was determined to make it a staple of the French diet. After failing to convince conservative French farmers of its advantages, he found a more effective way of making his point: Parmentier acquired a miserable and unproductive field near Paris where he planted fifty acres of potatoes. During the day, a guard would stand over the field, drawing much attention. In the evening, when the guard was relaxed, locals came to investigate. Believing whatever was being guarded must be valuable, many peasants "acquired" potatoes and were soon growing them in their own gardens. Potatoes became fashionable in France after they were taken up by the French court of Louis XVI. In French cuisine, any dish that bears the name à la Parmentier is sure to include potatoes.

GLUTEN-FREE BAKED GOODS IN THIS BOOK

Many people have gluten allergies or intolerances so that they must avoid foods made with grains that contain gluten, the material that adds stretchability to baked goods. Wheat, especially bread flour, has a high level of gluten; rye, barley, and, to a lesser extent, oats, contain less. But, even someone that can't tolerate gluten can enjoy a delicious cake, cookie, or other dessert using the recipes listed here. Here I replace wheat and other flours containing gluten with ground nuts, potato starch, rice flour, chestnut flour, chestnut purée, and even ground white beans. Because potato starch is very useful in gluten-free baking, lending its thickening ability to cake batters, I have listed the gluten-free baked goods in this chapter.

Andalusian Bittersweet Chocolate-Sherry Cake (page 55)

Bonèt Piemontese (page 439)

Chocolate-Dipped Coconut Macaroons (page 364)

Frangelico Mousse Cake with Gianduia-Rice Crunch (page 771)

Italian Bittersweet Chocolate-Orange Torte (page 331)

Italian Meringue Twists and Topping (page 836)

Majorcan Lemon-Almond Cake (page 77)

Mexican Chocolate Tequila Soufflé Cake (page 729)

Mexican Spiced Cocoa Meringues (page 352)

Piedmontese Mocha-Chestnut Torta (page 314)

Raspberry Salzburger Nockerln (page 160)

Ruby Grapefruit-Orange Brazil Nut Torte (page 174)

Torta Boscaiola: Italian Chestnut Flour and Hazelnut Cake (page 319)

Torta Caprese: Bittersweet Chocolate-Almond Cake (page 336)

Turkish Goat's Milk Rice Pudding (page 774)

Velia's White Chocolate-Lemon Torta Caprese (page 78)

White Bean, Chestnut, and Apricot Cake alla Povera (page 316)

White Chocolate, Hazelnut, and Espresso Dacquoise (page 377)

TYPES OF POTATOES

There are innumerable varieties of potatoes in supermarkets and at farmers' markets, but they all fall into three main categories:

ALL-PURPOSE POTATOES: As their name implies, these are potatoes that have a medium starch level, smooth, light tan skin, and white flesh. Several varieties of all-purpose potatoes, which may be called round whites, Irish, Chef's, Maine, or Katahdin potatoes, are grown and used most often in the Eastern United States as an "all-purpose potato". They are creamy in texture, hold their shape well after cooking, and are available year-round at a reasonable price. If you simply buy "potatoes," this is the kind you'll get.

NEW POTATOES: New potatoes are freshly dug potatoes that have not reached their maturity and have never been kept in storage. They have a thin skin and fine-textured, quick-cooking, creamy flesh. They are in season from late winter or early spring through midsummer and are often found fresh-dug at farmers' markets. They would be used in baking for topping a tart or pizza, but not for dough because of their low starch content.

STARCHY POTATOES: Starchy or mealy potatoes, such as Russets, are more commonly known as Idaho potatoes (although only Russet potatoes grown in Idaho may be properly called Idaho potatoes). The potato cells in starchy potatoes separate more easily upon cooking because of their high starch levels. When cooked, they have a glistening appearance and a dry, fluffy texture. Because they're starchy, they're well suited for making gnocchi, potato dumplings, and other potato-based doughs.

Herbed Focaccia with Goat Cheese, Red Onion, and Black Olives

Focaccia has become quite the rage in America as an alternative to overladen pizzas. The soft, sticky dough is quite light when baked, puffing up around the sparse but flavorful bits of goat cheese, thin red onion wedges, and earthy oil-cured black olives in this recipe. In Genoa, I saw more fresh herbs used than in any other part of herb-loving Italy, so it's perfectly appropriate that I've added a generous quantity of resinous herbs to this dough. Although I avoid dried herbs, which just don't have the lively freshness of their fresh counterparts, they are acceptable, though not ideal, when added to a dough like this one.

YIELD: 1 FOCACCIA, 8 TO 12 SERVINGS

$1/4$ cup olive oil

$1^1/2$ pounds ($5^1/2$ cups plus 2 tablespoons) unbleached all-purpose flour

$1/4$ pound ($1^1/2$ cups) instant potato flakes

2 teaspoons fine sea salt

3 tablespoons chopped fresh resinous herbs, such as rosemary, thyme, savory, marjoram and/or sage, or 1 tablespoon crumbled Herbes de Provence

1 ($1/4$-ounce) package ($2^1/2$ teaspoons) active dry yeast

$2^1/2$ cups lukewarm water

Freshly ground black pepper

1 red onion, thinly sliced

$1/2$ cup pitted and halved Kalamata olives

$1/4$ pound mild goat cheese, crumbled

Generously coat an 18 x 13-inch half sheet pan (or other large baking pan) with 2 tablespoons of the olive oil.

In a large mixing bowl, whisk together the flour, potato flakes, salt, and herbs.

In the bowl of a standing mixer fitted with the paddle attachment, combine the yeast and lukewarm water, allowing the yeast to dissolve. Stir in about 1 cup of the flour mix and allow the mixture to proof in a warm place for about 15 minutes, or until bubbling and puffy. Beat in the remaining flour mixture.

Switch to the dough hook and beat until the mixture comes together in a ball and is smooth and elastic but is still soft and sticky, 5 to 6 minutes. The dough should stick briefly to your hand then pull away. Lightly oil your hands, then punch down the dough.

Press the dough into the pan without folding it over

(don't worry if it doesn't reach all the way into the corners). Leave the dough to rest and rise at warm room temperature for about 1 hour, or until light and puffy.

Press the dough out to the edges of the pan. Using your index finger, poke indentations over surface of dough about every inch or so. Brush the dough with the remaining olive oil and grind fresh black pepper over top.

Scatter the red onions all over the dough, leaving a 1-inch border around the edges, and press them to adhere to the dough. Repeat with the olives and goat cheese. Allow the focaccia to rise at warm room temperature until soft and puffy, about 45 minutes.

Preheat the oven to 400°F.

Bake the focaccia for 20 minutes, or until nicely browned on both top and bottom. Remove from the oven, cool about 5 minutes, then remove the focaccia from the pan and allow it to cool on a wire rack. Cut into squares to serve. Store loosely covered at room temperature up to 2 days, or wrap tightly in aluminum foil and freeze. Reheat frozen focaccia still wrapped in foil in a preheated 375°F oven about 15 minutes, then cool slightly before serving.

Buttermilk–Sourdough White Sandwich Bread

This firm yet light white bread is perfect for sandwiches and makes excellent toast. The sourdough starter is made from the water in which I've boiled potatoes, which is full of nutrients to help the fermentation process. I like to sprinkle the top of this bread with poppy seeds for color contrast, but white sesame seeds (or no seeds) are also fine. The bread freezes very well as long as it is well-wrapped. You'll need to begin making the starter about a week ahead of time.

YIELD: ONE 1³/₄-POUND LOAF

1¼ pounds (4³/₄ cups minus 1 tablespoon) unbleached all-purpose flour

2 teaspoons fine sea salt

1 (¹/₄-ounce) package (2¹/₂ teaspoons) active dry yeast

cup Sourdough Starter with Potato (page 880)

2 cups buttermilk

2 tablespoons honey

1 large egg, lightly beaten with 1 tablespoon milk, for the egg wash

Poppy seeds, for sprinkling

Spray a large (1¹/₂ pound, 9 x 5-inch) loaf pan with non-stick baker's coating or rub with butter and dust with flour, shaking off the excess.

In the bowl of a standing mixer fitted with the paddle attachment, combine the dry ingredients: flour, salt, and the yeast, and beat briefly to combine.

In a small bowl, whisk together the starter, buttermilk, and honey. Beat into the flour mixture. Switch to the dough hook and beat until the mixture forms a smooth and elastic dough ball that cleans the sides of the bowl, about 5 minutes.

Transfer the dough to a large oiled bowl; turn the dough so it is oiled all over. Cover with oiled plastic wrap or a damp cloth and allow the dough to rise at warm room temperature until doubled in size, about 2 hours.

Turn the dough out to a lightly floured work surface. Punch it down and roll into a rectangle about 9 inches long, then fold up in thirds like a letter, pressing the edges together so they adhere. Place the dough in the loaf pan, seam side down.

Gently brush the loaf with the egg wash then sprinkle with the poppy seeds. Cover with plastic wrap that has been lightly oiled. Allow the bread to rise at warm room temperature for about 2 hours, or until it rises over the lip of the pan.

Preheat the oven to 400°F.

Place the bread in the oven and reduce the oven temperature to 375°F and bake for 35 minutes, or until the bread sounds hollow when tapped on the bottom and a thermometer inserted in the center reads 190°F. Cool to room temperature on a wire rack before slicing. Store in an opened plastic bag at room temperature for up to 2 days or wrap and freeze up to 3 months.

Dilled Potato–Onion Rolls

Spicy ground dill seed and fresh dill flavor these rolls along with dried shallot. These moist and tender yet chewy rolls make a wonderful burger roll, especially for salmon, portabello mushroom, turkey, or tuna burgers. Or fill them with tuna or salmon salad for sandwiches. Although the quantity of salt may seem like a lot, bread dough, like all starchy foods, sucks up flavor, especially salt, so if you cut the quantity, the bread will taste flat.

YIELD: ABOUT 20 (2-OUNCE) ROLLS OR 12 (3-OUNCE) BURGER ROLLS

1 ($^{1}/_{2}$-pound) russet or Idaho potato

2 teaspoons fine sea salt

$^{1}/_{2}$ pound (2 cups minus 2 tablespoons) unbleached all-purpose flour

$^{1}/_{4}$ pound (1 cup) unbleached bread flour

2 teaspoons dill seed, finely ground

1 ($^{1}/_{4}$-ounce) package (2$^{1}/_{2}$ teaspoons) active dry yeast

1 tablespoon honey

$^{1}/_{2}$ cup lukewarm milk

$^{1}/_{4}$ cup chopped fresh dill

3 large shallots, finely chopped

2 ounces ($^{1}/_{2}$ stick) unsalted butter, melted and cooled

Place the potatoes in a pot with enough cold water to cover by about 2 inches along with 1 teaspoon of the salt. Bring to a boil, then reduce the heat and boil for 15 minutes or until the potatoes are quite soft. Strain, reserving $^{1}/_{2}$ cup of the cooking liquid. Cool the liquid to room temperature. Mash the potatoes with a potato masher or a heavy whisk.

Line an 18 x 13-inch half sheet pan (or other large baking pan) with parchment paper or a silicone baking mat.

Whisk together the dry ingredients: flour, bread flour, dill seed, and the remaining salt.

In the bowl of a standing mixer fitted with the paddle attachment, combine the reserved potato water, the yeast, and honey. Stir in about 1 cup of the flour mixture and allow the mixture to proof in a warm place for about 20 minutes, or until bubbling and puffy. Beat in the milk, fresh dill, and shallots, then beat in the remaining flour mixture.

Switch to the dough hook and continue beating until the dough is smooth and elastic and mostly comes away from the sides of the bowl, about 10 minutes. Set the dough aside to rest, covered, for 10 minutes.

Divide the dough into the desired roll sizes. Shape each piece into a smooth ball, pulling the surface dough underneath. Place the balls on the prepared pan, smooth side up and evenly spaced, allowing at least 1½-inches between them. Brush each roll with butter and allow them to rise at warm room temperature until they've almost doubled in bulk, about 1 hour.

Preheat the oven to 350°F. Bake the rolls for 25 minutes, or until they're golden brown. Cool about 10 minutes, then remove the rolls from the pan to cool on a wire rack so they don't get soggy underneath. Store in an opened plastic bag at room temperature for up to 2 days or wrap and freeze up to 3 months.

Sardinian Potato Torta (Coccoi Prena)

This stuffed bread is a specialty of the region of Ogliastra, in the center of Sardinia's Eastern Coast between the Gennargentu Mountains and the Tyrrhenian Sea. Made from a light and fluffy semolina and potato bread dough, it is filled with a mixture of potato, sautéed onion, pecorino cheese, extra-virgin olive oil, and mint. Coccoi preno (stuffed bread) is also made in individual portions, shaped, according to Sardinians, like the rays of the sun. The bread is deli-

cious hot, warm, or at room temperature. Don't be tempted to add too much liquid to the dough as the potatoes will continue to exude water.

YIELD: 12 SERVINGS

2½ pounds gold potatoes

1 (¼-ounce) package (2¼ teaspoons) active dry yeast

¼ cup lukewarm water

1 tablespoon honey

6 ounces (1½ cups minus 1 tablespoon) unbleached all-purpose flour

6 ounces (1 cup) fine semolina

Fine sea salt and freshly ground black pepper

6 tablespoons extra-virgin olive oil

1 large yellow onion, finely chopped (2 cups)

2 tablespoons finely shredded fresh mint, preferably spearmint

¼ pound feta cheese

¼ pound aged pecorino cheese, preferably pecorino Sardo

1 large egg

Bring a pot of salted water to a boil, add the potatoes, and boil until tender, about 20 minutes.

Meanwhile, combine the yeast, lukewarm water, and honey in the bowl of a standing mixer fitted with the dough hook. Allow the mixture to proof in a warm place for about 15 minutes, or until bubbling and puffy.

Drain the potatoes and peel them while they are still hot (wrap your hands in a clean towel or use silicone dishwashing gloves to protect your hands). Mash or rice the potatoes, then scoop ½ pound of the potatoes into the bowl of the mixer, reserving the remainder for the filling. Add the flour, semolina, salt to taste, 2 tablespoons of the olive oil, and the yeast mixture. Beat to combine, and continue beating until the dough is smooth and elastic and comes away cleanly from the bowl, about 5 minutes. Transfer the dough to a large oiled bowl; turn the dough so it is oiled all over. Cover with oiled plastic wrap or a damp cloth and allow it to rise at warm room temperature until doubled in size, about 2 hours.

Meanwhile, make the filling: Heat 2 tablespoons of the olive oil in a medium skillet, add the onions, and fry until lightly golden. Combine with the reserved mashed potatoes, and add the mint, cheeses, egg, and black pepper to taste (salt is unnecessary because the cheese is salty).

Preheat the oven to 400°F.

Punch down the dough, roll it into a ball, then roll it out on a lightly floured work surface into a large circle about 16 inches in diameter and about $^3/_8$-inch thick. Place the dough into a 10-inch cake pan; you should have about 4 inches of overlapping dough that will become the top of the torta. Spoon the filling into the pan, then fold over the edges of the dough to cover the top, leaving a hole in the center about 4 inches around. Roll any leftover dough into ropes and use to decorate the rim of the hole and around the top of the torta. Brush the torta with the remaining 2 tablespoons of olive oil and bake for 30 minutes or until well browned. Cool on a wire rack and serve warm or at room temperature.

Mexican Chocolate Tequila Soufflé Cake

This light, flavorful chocolate cake gets a warm afterglow from a generous amount of white tequila. The cinnamon and cloves used to flavor the chocolate here came with the Spanish through the Moors, who brought the spices from the East to Spain. Today in Mexico and Latin America, dense, grainy bars of chocolate are made from dark, bitter chocolate mixed with sugar crystals, cinnamon, and sometimes almonds. Because only potato starch is used to thicken this flourless cake batter, it is gluten-free. Serve this rich cake in small wedges accompanied by a dollop of Mexican crèma or crème frâiche. This cake is gluten-free.

YIELD: ONE 9-INCH CAKE, 12 TO 16 SERVINGS

$^1/_2$ pound bittersweet chocolate, chopped

$^1/_2$ pound (2 sticks) unsalted butter, cut into bits

$^1/_4$ pound (1$^1/_4$ cups) potato starch, substitute corn,
   wheat, or rice starch

$^1/_2$ teaspoon fine sea salt

1 teaspoon ground cinnamon

$^1/_4$ teaspoon ground allspice

Pinch ground cloves

5 large eggs

1$^1/_4$ cups light brown sugar, packed

6 tablespoons white tequila

Confectioners' sugar, for garnish

Mexican crèma, for serving

Preheat the oven to 350°F. Spray a 9-inch removable

bottom cake pan or springform pan with nonstick baker's coating, or rub with softened butter and dust with flour, shaking off the excess. Place a parchment paper or waxed paper circle into the bottom of the pan. Wrap the bottom and sides of the pan in a single sheet of aluminum foil, preferably heavy-duty, to prevent drips.

Place the chocolate and butter in a microwaveable bowl and heat in the microwave on lowest power for 2 minutes at a time, or until just barely melted. Whisk until smooth and cool to room temperature.

In a medium bowl, sift together the potato starch, salt, cinnamon, allspice, and cloves.

In the metal mixing bowl of a standing mixer, combine the eggs and brown sugar. In a pot that is about the same diameter or a bit smaller then the metal mixing bowl, bring about 1 inch of water to a boil. Place the metal bowl over the boiling water and whisk until the mixture is evenly hot to the touch and reads 150°F on a thermometer.

Place the mixing bowl on the standing mixer and beat with the whisk attachment until the mixture is very light and thick and cools to room temperature, about 10 minutes. Sprinkle the potato starch mixture over top and fold in using a silicone spatula. Fold in the chocolate and the tequila. Scrape the batter into the pan.

Bake for 1 hour or until the cake starts to come away from the sides of the pan and it puffs up. (A skewer inserted in the center will not come out clean.) Cool completely before removing the sides of the pan. Sprinkle with confectioners' sugar and cut into serving portions using a knife that has been dipped in hot water then wiped dry in between each slice. Serve with dollops of Mexican crèma.

Store covered and refrigerated up to 4 days. Cut the cake while cold, but bring to room temperature before serving.

PUMPKIN & SQUASH

Homemade Pumpkin Spice Mix . . . 733

Roasting Squash . . . 733

Cooking Squash in the Microwave . . . 733

Steaming Squash . . . 733

Choosing and Storing Butternut Squash . . . 733

Preparing Butternut Squash . . . 734

Winter Squash for Baking . . . 734

DURUM WHEAT BREAD WITH SQUASH,
TOMATOES, ONIONS, AND PEPPERS . . . 736

Cucuzza Squash in Louisiana . . . 737

SICILIAN PAN PIZZA WITH ZUCCA . . . 737

GREEK PHYLLO PUMPKIN PIE
(KOLOKYTHOPITA) . . . 739

Working with Phyllo Dough . . . 740

Soaking with Sugar Syrup . . . 740

TORTA DI ZUCCA (SQUASH CAKE
WITH PINE NUTS AND APRICOTS) . . . 741

BOURBON-SPICE PUMPKIN CAKE . . . 742

Pumpkin Pies . . . 743

PUMPKIN & SQUASH

What, you might ask, are pumpkin and squash doing in a baking book? Think pumpkin pie, pumpkin muffins, and zucchini bread and it starts to make sense. In other parts of the world, pumpkins and other squashes are used in both savory and sweet baking. Cuccuzzara, a durum wheat and squash bread from Southern Italy is made with the Old World gourd squash, though firm New World butternut squash would work just as well. From Sicily comes a layered pan pizza, ideally baked in a heavy blue steel Sicilian pizza pan (page 000) that is ideal for a party as it makes a large pie.

The word "squash" is derived from the Algonquin word askutasquash–something that is eaten green, or in an unripe state, like summer squash, where smaller is better. When we say "squash," we usually mean winter squash–like butternut, acorn, and calabaza–which have a hard inedible peel. The peels of summer squashes–like zucchini and yellow crookneck–are entirely edible. The difference is also apparent in the seeds. Winter squashes have large, tough skinned seeds that are edible only if roasted and shelled: a popular snack throughout Greece,

Turkey, the Middle East, and North Africa. Summer squashes have smaller, tender-skinned seeds that are almost nonexistent in young squash, though more apparent in larger, more mature specimens. Although zucchini bread, a sweet quick bread, is one of the best ways to use overly large summer squash, I prefer baking with firm winter squash.

Although pumpkins were unknown in Greece until after Columbus's voyages, they have been used well since, as in the Greek Phyllo Pumpkin Pie (page 000), a squash-filled sweet pastry drenched in sweet syrup like baklava. In Italy after World War II, no one wanted to eat zucca squash or chestnuts anymore, because those were some of the few foods they had to eat during the war years. These days, the once-disdained squash has regained its reputation in delicious offerings like the Torta di Zucca (page 000). This moist, squash-based cake from Northern Italy includes raisins soaked in grappa, almonds, and candied citron. The Bourbon-Spice Pumpkin Cake (page 000) is easy to make from canned pumpkin purée (although fresh will work well also).

HOMEMADE PUMPKIN SPICE MIX

Combine 2 tablespoons ground cinnamon, 4 teaspoons ground ginger, 2 teaspoons ground allspice, 2 teaspoons freshly grated nutmeg, 1 teaspoon ground mace, and $\frac{1}{2}$ teaspoon ground cloves. Store in a tightly covered tin or jar away from the light up to 1 year. Use 1 to 2 teaspoons in any baking recipe calling for squash.

ROASTING SQUASH

Prick the squash all over with a fork, then roast it whole after at 375°F for about 1 hour. Alternatively, cut the squash in half, scoop out the seeds, then roast at 375°F for about 40 minutes. When the squash is cooked enough to be soft when pierced, it's easy to scoop away the flesh from the hard shell–like skin.

COOKING SQUASH IN THE MICROWAVE

Cut the squash in half, scrape out the seeds and strings, and microwave on high power for 8 to 12 minutes, or until tender when stuck with a fork. Let cool for 5 to 10 minutes, then scoop out the flesh.

STEAMING SQUASH

Set up a metal steamer basket placed in a pot filled with about 2 inches of salted water. Cover and bring to a boil. Meanwhile, peel the squash, cut it in half and scoop out the seeds. Cut the squash into 1-inch cubes and then steam until tender—but not mushy—when pricked with a fork, about 8 minutes.

CHOOSING AND STORING BUTTERNUT SQUASH

Choose large butternuts with a relatively small bottom and a long "neck." This neck portion contains solid meat without any seeds, making it easy to cut up. The bottom end contains the seed cavity and is surrounded by flesh that is softer in texture with noticeable strings. The skin should be dry, uniformly hard, and free of soft spots and bruises. Despite the tough exterior (which preserves the squash during lengthy storage), butternuts need careful handling because they will bruise if roughly handled. To store for several weeks, keep in a cool, dry place with good air circulation. The soft, moist flesh surrounding the seedpod will deteriorate quickest. If that area is mushy, you've stored your squash too long. However, the "neck" area will probably be firm and quite usable.

PREPARING BUTTERNUT SQUASH

One of the few disadvantages of this squash is that it can be difficult to peel. To eliminate this rather tedious step, some supermarkets now sell pre-peeled butternut squash chunks. If your butternut is whole, cut off a thin slice from the top and bottom end of the squash so it will stand upright. Cut in half at the point where the narrow neck meets the bulgy bottom, so you have one easy-to-peel cylindrical section and one more difficult-to-peel rounded section. Peel with a standard swivel-bladed potato peeler or a paring knife. Or avoid peeling and roast the squash "in its coat." Once cooked, it's easy to pull the flesh away from the hard shell–like skin.

WINTER SQUASH FOR BAKING

Some of the major winter squash species are: *Cucurbita maxima*, which includes varieties like Hubbard, blue and red Kuri, Rouge Vif d'Etampes, and buttercup squash; *Cucurbita moschata*, which includes varieties that grow only in warmer climates including butternut, winter crookneck, some pumpkins, and calabaza; *Cucurbita pepo*, which includes acorn squash, summer squash, Carnival, spaghetti, and pumpkin; and *Cucurbita mixta*, which includes the golden striped and green striped cushaw.

ACORN SQUASH: Acorn squash, which may be buff, orange, or dark green in color, is the most widely available small winter squash. It has smooth, sweetish flesh that is rather stringy; buff varieties have the most concentrated flavor. The skin is usually edible after baking, though it may have been waxed.

BUTTERCUP SQUASH: Buttercup squash weigh two to four pounds, are stocky in shape with a beanie top like a turban. This top enlarges as the squash matures. Many people consider buttercup to be the best hard squash. When baked, the fine, dry flesh is smooth and tastes of roasted chestnuts and sweet potato.

CALABAZA: Calabaza is a general name for warm-climate pumpkins. In the United States, calabaza has become the name for a large round or pear-shaped squash with mottled skin that may be deep green-orange, amber, or buff and speckled or striated, but always relatively smooth and hard-shelled when mature. Calabaza is often sold in large wedges. Unlike other pumpkins, it is grown primarily in warmer climates and is thus available year-round, especially at Latino markets.

CARNIVAL SQUASH: Carnival Squash is a trademarked name for a cross between an acorn and a Sweet Dumpling squash and weighs two to four pounds. It is flattened in shape with ivy-green marbling mixed with orange. Its flesh is deep yellow and is sweeter and more concentrated in flavor than the acorn, though a bit coarse in texture.

HUBBARD: Hubbard is a term for a group of large to huge squash that may be bluish, gray, orange, or dark to light green in color, are mostly teardrop or top-shaped with dense flesh, and which weigh up to 50 pounds! This squash was named after Mrs. Elizabeth Hubbard of Marblehead, Massachusetts, around 1850, who provided the seeds for this previously unnamed variety.

ITALIAN GOURD SQUASH: The Italian gourd squash, *Lagenaria siceraria*, variously known as Italian Edible Gourd, Serpent of Sicily, Cucuzza, Longissima, Bottle Gourd, Calabash, Zucca, or Suzza Melon, is in another botanical family entirely. This long, thin, serpent-like squash is a vine-like annual plant with white flowers (New World squash all have yellow flowers) that may grow up to twenty-five feet long. The female flowers produce long cylindrical gourds that may be straight, twisted, or coiled up like snakes, light green in color with smooth (though sometimes hairy) skin. Although they can reach up to three feet in length, cucuzzi are best harvested when they are immature and less than one foot long. The thick, tender, creamy white flesh can be bitter if harvested when fully mature. Cucuzzi are sold with stem intact, which will continue nourishing the squash up to one month after picking. The tender young shoots, called tennerumi, are much appreciated in Italy, where I've seen them sold in local street markets in season.

JARRAHDALE PUMPKIN: Jarrahdale Pumpkin is an Australian cultivar that looks like a smaller classic pumpkin with heavily lobed sides and a distinctive celadon-green, smooth, and relatively thin skin. Its deep orange flesh is extremely smooth and creamy.

KABOCHA: Kabocha is a marketing name in the United States applied to many strains of Japanese pumpkin and winter squash with rough mottled skin, including Delicata and green or orange Hokkaido. All have tough skin, deep flavor with honeyed sweetness, and fine grained, extremely dense sweet-potato-like flesh.

KURI: Kuri, or Orange Hokkaido, is a teardrop-shaped Japanese Kabocha squash with smooth, red-orange skin and dense yellow-orange flesh that is similar to the Golden Hubbard. It is an ideal squash for baking, as its chestnut-like flesh doesn't contain much water. Also, because it is such a long-lasting squash, you can enjoy gazing at this beautiful persimmon-colored squash for several months until you get around to cooking it.

PUMPKIN: A pumpkin is almost anything as long as it's a hard-skinned squash. What is considered "pumpkin" changes from country to country and region to region. In the United States, the term generally means a large, rounded, orange squash of the type used for Jack o'Lanterns. Miniature pumpkins are cream or orange in color with sweet, firm, flavorful flesh. Some may have edible skin. Pie pumpkins or sugar pumpkins are shaped like a large curved crookneck squash with hard, bright orange skin and dense flesh that is suitable for pie.

ROUGE VIF D'ETAMPES: This striking persimmon-orange pumpkin has been cultivated in France since the mid 1800s and was later introduced to American gardeners. It weighs 15 to 20 pounds and has a dense, sweet flesh and mild flavor. It's easy to see why it's also called Cinderella pumpkin; it would make a perfect coach.

SWEET DUMPLING SQUASH: This Japanese variety is solid and plump, cream in color with ivy-green stripes inside the ridges. Sweet Dumplings weigh about one pound each and ripen to butter and orange color. The pale yellow flesh is fine and dry textured like a potato with a fresh sweetness.

TURK'S HEAD: Turk's Head is a medium to large variety that is best known as a decorative squash, with its brilliant orange and dark green markings. It resembles a Turkish-style hat. Though edible, it has a hard, woody rind that is difficult to remove.

ZUCCA: Zucca (zucchini is a diminutive) is a hard Italian squash that may be squat or rounded, ridged and bumpy. Either orange or gray-blue with a green tinge, it is shaped like a giant zucchini with dense deep orange flesh. Available in late fall and winter, and like the Caribbean calabaza, it is often sold in sections. The delicious tender shoots, called teneri di zucca, may be found in local markets. In the central Italian region of Emilia-Romagna, the flesh of the dense sweet squash, called zucca barucca, fills slightly sweet tortelli di zucca mixed with crushed amaretti biscuits and Parmigiano cheese.

Durum Wheat Bread with Squash, Tomatoes, Onions, and Peppers

This vegetable-laden bread comes from Southern Italy, where cucuzza, the Old World gourd squash would be used. The firm, baseball bat-sized zucca squash, a New World squash adapted to that region, would be another possibility. The durum wheat used here is a high protein, hard wheat that is excellent for chewy breads and essential for milling the good dried pasta for which the region is famed. Look for pale yellow durum wheat at Italian markets and natural foods stores or order online at www.bakerscatalogue.com. You may substitute fine semolina for similar flavor, but slightly grainy texture.

YIELD: 1 LARGE RING-SHAPED LOAF

$3/4$ cup extra-virgin olive oil

1 medium red onion, thinly sliced

3 cloves garlic, thinly sliced

1 red bell pepper, roasted, skinned, and cut into strips, or 1 roasted pepper from a jar, drained and cut into strips

$1/2$ cup oven-roasted plum tomatoes, homemade (page 888) or purchased, cut into strips

2 teaspoons dried oregano

1 teaspoon red pepper flakes

1 tablespoon fine sea salt

1 cup lukewarm water

1 ($1/4$-ounce) package ($2 1/2$ teaspoons) active dry yeast

2 pounds (7 cups) durum flour

1¼ pounds butternut squash, peeled and finely grated (about 3 cups)

Spray a 10-inch ring pan with nonstick baker's coating or rub with oil.

In a medium skillet over medium-low heat, combine ¼ cup of olive oil, the red onion, and the garlic, and cook until softened but not browned, about 6 minutes. Stir in the bell pepper, tomatoes, oregano, red pepper flakes, and 1 teaspoon of the salt. Cool to room temperature.

In the bowl of a standing mixer using the paddle attachment, combine ½ cup of the lukewarm water with the yeast and about ¼ cup of the flour and allow the mixture to proof for 10 minutes.

Beat in the remaining ½ cup of the oil and the remaining ½ cup of water. Beat in the remaining flour and the squash and beat until the dough is smooth and elastic and comes away cleanly from the sides of the bowl. (The squash will give off its moisture as its sits, so the dough should be quite firm at this point. Add a little water only if needed for the bread to come together in a ball.)

Transfer the dough to an oiled bowl, cover, and allow it to rise at warm room temperature until doubled, about 2 hours. Punch down the dough and roll it out into a large rectangle, about 16 x 8-inches. Spread evenly with the vegetable mixture, leaving a 1-inch border all around. Roll up tightly. Place the bread, seam side down, into the prepared pan, bringing the ends around and joining them to make a ring. Cover loosely with oiled plastic wrap and allow the bread to rise at warm room temperature until doubled again, about 1 hour.

Preheat the oven to 375°F. Bake the bread for 40 minutes or until golden brown and a thermometer inserted into the center reads 190°F. Remove from the oven, wait 5 minutes, then turn out the bread onto a wire cooling rack to prevent the bread from getting soggy. If desired, place the bread on a baking pan back in the oven for about five minutes to crisp the outside. Store the bread in an open plastic bag at room temperature for up to 3 days, or refrigerate for up to five days.

CUCUZZA SQUASH IN LOUISIANA

The *cucuzza*, which could be translated as "big, long squash," originated in Italy from the Old World gourd family. Today, this special squash is grown in Ruston, Louisiana, by Christopher Marco Cordaro at the largest cucuzza farm in the country. Cordaro grows the squash, which are in season from June until the first frost, from heirloom seeds that have been in his family for generations. Go to www.cucuzzasquash.com for more information.

Sicilian Pan Pizza with Zucca

In New York and Philadelphia, where there are large Sicilian communities, many pizza shops sell Sicilian pizza by the square. These thick pizzas have their roots in the sfincione of Palermo, Sicily, on which Chicago's deep-dish pizza is based. In a bakery, this pizza would be baked in a

*heavy, blue-steel Sicilian pizza pan; here, I use a half
sheet pan or other large baking pan. Use the Cornmeal
Pizza Dough for an extra-crunchy crust, or the Woodfire
Grill Pizza Dough for a lighter, chewier crust.*

YIELD: 10 TO 12 SERVINGS

¹⁄₄ pound (about 1 cup) Oven-Roasted Plum
    Tomatoes, homemade (page 888) or purchased

1 pound Cornmeal Pizza Dough (page 392)
    or Woodfire Grill Pizza Dough (page 858)

1¹⁄₂ cups whole-milk ricotta

2 ounces (¹⁄₂ cup) grated Parmigiano-Reggiano
    or Grana Padano cheese

1 large egg

2 tablespoons each chopped flat-leaf parsley
    and fresh basil

¹⁄₂ teaspoon freshly grated nutmeg

Fine sea salt and freshly ground black pepper

2 pounds fresh spinach or Swiss chard, trimmed
    and cooked until wilted

Olive oil, as needed

3 large cloves garlic, crushed or finely chopped

1¹⁄₂ pounds zucca (hard Italian pumpkin), butternut,
    sugar pumpkin, calabaza, or other firm, deep-col-
    ored squash, peeled, seeded, and cut into thin
    half-moon slices (no more than ¹⁄₄ -inch thick)

¹⁄₂ teaspoon red pepper flakes

1 red onion, thinly sliced

¹⁄₂ pound thin-sliced pancetta, capicola ham,
    or Italian salami, such as Genoa

Place the tomatoes in a microwavable bowl and warm

briefly in the microwave until any congealed oil around
them melts. Drain the tomatoes, reserving both the oil
and the tomatoes. Brush some of the tomato oil onto
an 18 x 13-inch half sheet pan (or other large baking pan).

Roll out the pizza dough on a lightly floured surface
thinly so it is somewhat larger than the pan, rolling the
ends under to make a thicker border. Brush the dough
with more of the reserved tomato oil.

In a medium bowl, combine the ricotta, grated
cheese, egg, parsley, basil, nutmeg, and salt and pepper
to taste; reserve.

Squeeze out any excess water from the spinach and
chop it roughly. Toss the spinach with about 2 tablespoons of the tomato oil (or olive oil if you've used all
the tomato oil), the garlic, and salt and pepper to taste.

Toss the zucca with 2 tablespoons more of the
tomato oil (or olive oil), the red pepper flakes, and salt
and pepper to taste. Toss the onion with a little oil.

In the following order, arrange the pizza toppings in
1-inch-wide strips diagonally across the pizza dough:
the ricotta mixture, the spinach, the onion, the zucca,
the pancetta, and the tomatoes and repeat until the
pizza is covered and all the fillings have been used.
Allow the pizza to rise at warm room temperature until
light and puffy, about 30 minutes.

Preheat the oven to 425°F. Bake the pizza for 20 minutes or until the dough and toppings are lightly
browned. Cut into 12 portions. Store covered and
refrigerated up to 2 days. Wrap cut portions in aluminum foil and reheat in a 350°F oven for about 20
minutes or until hot, uncovered for the last 5 minutes
baking to crisp up the dough.

Greek Phyllo Pumpkin Pie (Kolokythopita)

The Old and the New World come together in this pumpkin-filled phyllo pastry: the pumpkins from the New World, the phyllo, honey, and walnuts from the Old. This dish is a specialty of the region of Ileia, on the West coast of the Peloponnese peninsula of Greece. Start this recipe one day ahead, to give yourself time drain the pumpkin.

Although not traditional, I recommend the dense Japanese pumpkins, like the persimmon-colored Kuri and the dark green Kabocha. Mixing in semolina, which helps absorb excess moisture so the filling is pleasingly firm though light in texture is one of the secrets of phyllo pies like this one and the Lemon Galataboureko (page 532.

**YIELD: ONE 9-INCH SQUARE PIE,
10 TO 12 SERVINGS**

Pie

3 pounds sugar pumpkin, calabaza, or other firm, deep-colored squash, seeded and cut into large chunks

1/2 pound phyllo dough, defrosted in the refrigerator if frozen

1/4 cup sugar

1/4 cup honey

1/4 pound walnuts, finely chopped

1/4 pound (1/2 cup plus 2 1/2 tablespoons) fine semolina

1 teaspoon ground cinnamon

3/4 cup Brown Butter (page 202) or Clarified Butter (page 202)

Syrup

1/2 cup honey

1/2 cup sugar

2 cups water

Juice of 1 lemon

1 teaspoon rosewater, optional

Make the pie: Set a steamer basket in a pot filled with about 2 inches of water. Add the pumpkin, cover the pot, and steam over moderate heat until the pumpkin is soft and tender, about 20 minutes. Drain, cool to room temperature, and remove any skin. Place the pumpkin in a food processor and purée. Transfer to a colander set over a bowl and let the pumpkin drain overnight in the refrigerator. Alternatively, place the pumpkin in cheesecloth and squeeze out any excess liquid by hand.

Preheat the oven to 350°F.

In a large bowl, combine the pumpkin, sugar, honey, walnuts, semolina, and cinnamon.

Lightly oil a 13 x 9-inch baking pan and line with 8 sheets of phyllo, allowing the sheets to overlap the edges, alternating directions each time, and brushing each sheet lightly with oil. Spoon in the pumpkin mixture. Trim the remaining sheets to fit the inside of the pan more or less exactly. Lay the trimmed phyllo sheets on top, brushing each with butter. Roll the overlapping edges over to form a border around the pie. Lightly score 2-inch diamond shapes into the top of the phyllo. Mist the top of the pastry with a spray water mister, then bake for 40 minutes or until browned and crispy on top. Remove from the oven and cool on a wire rack.

Make the syrup: When the pie is cool, combine the honey, sugar, and water in a small pot, and bring to a boil. Boil for 5 minutes or until the mixture is clear and slightly thickened, then remove from the heat, stir in the lemon juice, and pour over the cooled pie.

Store covered and at room temperature for up to 1 day. Store covered and refrigerated up to 3 days, allowing the pie to come to room temperature before serving.

WORKING WITH PHYLLO DOUGH

If you live in an area with a large Middle Eastern, Greek, Turkish, or Lebanese population, you may be able to find phyllo dough that has never been frozen. I buy mine from Bitar's, a Lebanese grocery near Philadelphia's Italian Market. If you've struggled with stuck-together or crumbling sheets of phyllo, the fresh type will be a revelation, because it's so much easier to work with.

If your phyllo has been frozen, thaw it overnight in the refrigerator. About 1 hour before using it, allow the dough to come to room temperature. Carefully unroll the roll of phyllo sheets onto a smooth, dry surface. Drape the dough sheets with plastic wrap and a damp towel. (Keep the phyllo covered, uncovering only as needed to avoid drying out the dough.)

If you are brushing butter onto your phyllo, melt it in the microwave and cool to lukewarm first.

Brush each sheet of phyllo lightly and evenly. To prevent the fragile edges of the sheets from cracking, brush them first, then work into the center.

Make sure that any filling you use with phyllo is cool or cold and not too moist. Sprinkle the dough with breadcrumbs or cookie or cake crumbs, or add semolina to the filling to absorb excess moisture.

Phyllo dough is numbered according to thickness, the lower the number, the thinner the dough. Number 4—standard phyllo—is thin and pliable, good for light desserts such as Galataboureko (page 532) and hors d'oeuvres, such as Cigari Borekas (page 212). Number 7 is medium thick. This flexible, easy-to-handle dough is good for more substantial dishes like B'stilla (page 436) and Greek Phyllo Pumpkin Pie (page 739). Number 10 is most like hand-rolled phyllo and strudel dough. It is good for pies like Greek Greens Pie (page 262) and strudels such as the Apple-Apricot Strudel (page 121) and Quince and Sour Cherry Strudel (page 751). You can buy all different types of phyllo including hand-made plus strudel dough on-line from www.minos imports.com.

SOAKING WITH SUGAR SYRUP

For cakes or pastries to absorb the maximum amount of syrup, there must be a temperature difference between the cake or pastry and the syrup. If the cake is hot, the syrup should be cold, or visa versa.

Torta di Zucca (Squash Cake with Pine Nuts and Apricots)

One of my special discoveries for this book was this moist, satisfying cake. It is baked in a ring pan and topped with a sprinkling of small, tasty pine nuts. Roasted winter squash is folded into the batter, along with colorful and tangy apricot bits that have been soaked in grappa and grated orange zest. In Italy, zucca would be used in this cake. In the United States, butternut squash, sugar pumpkin, or calabaza are the closest equivalents. It's an easy cake that's out of the ordinary and absolutely delicious. The colorful, tender dried apricots from California work best in this cake. To make this a dairy-free cake, substitute ³/₄ cup less 2 tablespoons mild olive oil for the butter.

YIELD: ONE 9-INCH CAKE, 10 TO 12 SERVINGS

¹/₄ pound (³/₄ cup) dried apricots, preferably California, diced

¹/₄ cup grappa, substitute white rum

1¹/₂ pounds (1 large) butternut squash

¹/₂ pound (2 cups minus 2 tablespoons) unbleached all-purpose flour

2 teaspoons baking powder

¹/₂ teaspoon freshly grated nutmeg

1 teaspoon fine sea salt

4 large eggs, separated

1¹/₂ cups light brown sugar, packed

¹/₄ pound (1 stick) unsalted butter, melted and cooled

¹/₂ cup (2 ounces) pine nuts

Grated zest of 1 orange (4 teaspoons)

Soak the apricots in the grappa at room temperature for at least 1 hour and up to overnight.

Preheat the oven to 350°F. Spray a 9-inch ring cake pan with baker's nonstick coating or rub with butter and dust with flour, shaking off the excess.

Pare the squash, scrape out any seeds, and cut into large chunks. Measure out one pound of the squash and place in a roasting pan. Roast for 45 minutes or until the squash is tender when pierced. Purée the squash in a food processor or mash by hand. (You should have about 1¹/₂ cups.)

Whisk together the dry ingredients: flour, baking powder, nutmeg, and salt.

In the bowl of a standing mixer fitted with the paddle attachment, beat the egg yolks and ³/₄ cup of the brown sugar until light and fluffy, 5 to 6 minutes. Fold in the melted butter and beat again until smooth and creamy. Add the flour mixture and beat just long enough to combine. Transfer the batter to a wide shallow bowl. Fold in the mashed squash, then add the apricots and their soaking liquid, half the pine nuts, and the orange zest.

In the clean and greaseless bowl of a standing mixer fitted with the whisk attachment, beat the egg whites until fluffy, then add the remaining ³/₄ cup brown sugar and continue beating until the whites are firm and glossy, 4 to 5 minutes. Fold the meringue into the batter in thirds so as not to deflate it. Pour the batter into the prepared pan and rap the pan on a work surface once to release any large air bubbles. Sprinkle the top with the remaining pine nuts.

Bake for 50 minutes, or until the cake starts to come away from the sides of the pan and a toothpick or skewer stuck in the center comes out clean. Remove from the oven, cool for 20 minutes, then turn out onto a wire rack and cool to room temperature. Store the cake at room temperature for 3 to 4 days.

Bourbon–Spice Pumpkin Cake

This moist, lightly spiced cake has a subtle, warm after-glow that comes from the bourbon. It is made with a combination of white and white whole wheat flour, giving it a nutty-tasting rustic quality. The cake is easy to make using canned pumpkin purée and will keep quite well for up to one week because of the bourbon. It would be perfect for an adult Halloween party or for Thanksgiving instead of the ubiquitous pumpkin pie. When I left this cake on the counter, it sure disappeared in a hurry around my young adult son and his hungry friends.

YIELD: ONE 10-INCH BUNDT CAKE, 10 TO 12 SERVINGS

$1/4$ pound (1 cup minus 1 tablespoon) unbleached all-purpose flour

$1/4$ pound (1 cup plus 2 tablespoons) white whole wheat flour

2 teaspoons baking soda

1 teaspoon ground cinnamon

$1/2$ teaspoon freshly ground nutmeg

$1/4$ teaspoon ground cloves

1 teaspoon fine sea salt

$1^1/_2$ cups canned or fresh pumpkin purée

$3/4$ cup buttermilk

$1/4$ cup bourbon

2 teaspoons vanilla extract

$1/2$ pound (2 sticks) unsalted butter, softened

1 cup dark brown sugar, packed

1 cup sugar

4 large eggs

Confectioners' sugar, for dusting

Preheat the oven to 375°F. Spray a 10-inch Bundt cake pan with nonstick baker's coating, or rub with softened butter and dust with flour, shaking off the excess.

In a large mixing bowl, whisk together the dry ingredients: flour, whole wheat flour, baking soda, cinnamon, nutmeg, cloves, and salt.

In a separate bowl, combine the pumpkin, butter-milk, bourbon, and vanilla.

In the bowl of a standing mixer fitted with the paddle attachment, cream the butter and both sugars until light and fluffy, 5 to 6 minutes, scraping down the sides once or twice. Beat in the eggs one at a time, beating well after each addition. Alternate beating in the flour and pumpkin mixtures, beginning and ending with the dry ingredients.

Scrape the batter into the prepared pan. Bake for 15 minutes, then reduce the oven temperature to 350°F and continue baking for 30 minutes, or until the cake starts to come away from the sides of the pan and a toothpick or skewer stuck in the center comes out clean. Cool for 20 minutes on a wire rack, then turn the cake out and continue cooling on the rack to room temperature. Dust with confectioners' sugar, then cut into portions. Store, covered, at room temperature for up to 4 days. This cake also freezes well.

PUMPKIN PIES

Although this book doesn't include a recipe because it is not one of my personal favorites and there are so many recipes available, pumpkin pie is a seasonal treat in America. The pie gets its characteristic seasoning from pumpkin pie spice, a blend of "warm" sweet spices like cinnamon, ginger, nutmeg, clove, allspice, and mace that works well for most squash-based baked goods. Many companies produce seasonal pumpkin pie–flavored foods, including ice cream, pancakes, muffins, and even coffee. Most pumpkin pies are made using canned pumpkin purée, because the familiar Jack o'Lantern pumpkins are too stringy. If you want to make your own pumpkin pie, a sugar pumpkin, butternut squash, calabaza, or Japanese Kuri or Kabocha squash are firm enough to use, and are also good choices for any of the baking recipes in this chapter.

QUINCE

Slow Food Ark of Taste . . . 748

Quince Varieties . . . 748

Choosing, Ripening, and Storing Quince . . . 749

Preparing Quince . . . 749

SPICED QUINCE JAM . . . 749

SPICED QUINCE AND WALNUT
THUMBPRINT COOKIES . . . 750

QUINCE AND SOUR CHERRY STRUDEL . . . 750

Phyllo Dough from Hand–Made
to Machine–Made . . . 752

QUINCE-CRANBERRY TARTE TATIN . . . 753

BAKED QUINCE WITH
PINE NUTS AND DRIED FRUIT . . . 754

QUINCE

Have you ever wondered about the mysterious fruit, sometimes seen at farmers' markets or in Asian groceries, that looks like a large, lumpy apple or a squat pear? Those lumpy yellow fruits, sometimes coated with fuzz, are quince, a rock-hard fruit that tastes like a cross between an apple and a pear, and which is best cooked before eating. Naturally, because I have an affinity with all odd and neglected ingredients, I adore quince, even though they are not the easiest fruit to prepare.

Although once relatively common in America, at least in the big cities of the East Coast, this old-time cousin of the pear and apple has been neglected in modern times, partly because it quite hard and tart when raw and partly because the fruit is often covered with thick, tan-colored fuzz that can be a little daunting. But for those adventurous enough to try them poached or baked, the quince turns a lovely carnelian color, somewhere between pink and orange, and has a wonderful perfume and concentrated jammy flavor.

Native to the Caucasus mountain region, the quince, *Cydonia oblonga*, is one of the earliest-known fruits, already familiar to the ancient Akkadians, who flourished in Mesopotamia, from 2350 to 2000 BCE. Many believe that both the forbidden fruit in the Garden of Eden and the "apple" mentioned in the Song of Solomon were actually quince. The quince's genus name, *Cydonia*, refers to the ancient city of Cydon (modern-day Khania) on the island of Crete. The English name, *quince*, originated in the fourteenth century as a plural of *quoyn*, via the Old French *cooin*, and ultimately from the Greek *kydonion malon*, meaning Kydonian apple or golden apple. According to Greek mythology, the Trojan War was fought because Helen of Troy bribed Paris to award a quince to Aphrodite as the prize in a beauty contest, naming her more beautiful than the goddess Athena.

According to the classical Roman naturalist, Pliny, the quince was carried from Crete to Italy and the western Mediterranean. The quince eventually spread throughout Asia to the east, as far as Great Britain to the west, and eventually to the United States. Medieval cooks regarded the quince as the most useful of fruits, and spiced it with black pepper, cinnamon, ginger, cloves, and nutmeg–flavors that still work well with the fruit today. In Europe and the Eastern Mediterranean region, the quince was an important fruit, widely grown in Britain from the sixteenth to the eighteenth century. The quince was among the first fruits to have been introduced to the new colonies by the colonists. Quince seeds were mentioned in the Massachusetts Company in 1629. By 1648, quince were growing in Virginia, and by 1720, they were commonly cultivated.

Eventually, however, the popularity of the quince was eclipsed by sweeter, softer fruits that took its place. Today, only a small portion are consumed as fresh fruit; the majority go into preserves, especially the thick paste known as *membrillo* in Spanish-speaking countries and as lovely preserves of diced quince packed in clear jelly enjoyed in Greece and Turkey. In Britain, the most common use for them is as a pastry filling. Quince is often combined with apples to bring an attractive pale pink color, extra body, and an interesting flavor and scent to the dish. The quince is still, however, especially popular in much of Latin America and Mexico, where apples don't thrive. There are large quince plantations in Uruguay.

Quince are often covered by a felty coating that wipes off easily, revealing a waxy skin that emanates a sweet, fresh fragrance. This unique fragrance, hinting of pineapple, guava, and pear, can easily perfume a room. It was said by traders on the Silk Route that one quince could perfume an entire caravan! When cooked, the quince's hard, dry flesh becomes softer and sweeter. It is a favorite for baking and preserving because of its pleasing sweet-sour flavor and high levels of pectin. The fruit's sharp, distinctive flavor comple-

ments a wide variety of baked goods and sweets. The term "marmalade," which originally referred only to thick quince jam, derives from the Portuguese word for the quince, *marmelo*.

In Spain, quince is cooked into a thick, sweet, orangey-red paste that is eaten with cream cheese and used to fill tarts and empanadas (page 271). This paste is called *membrillo*, which is also the Spanish name for quince. In Italy, quince, called *melacotogna*, are popular for stuffing Sardinian ravioli and in the fruit tarts called crostatas. In France, the fruits are known are *coing*, and show up in Provençal dishes. But it is in Turkey where the quince is most common. There, people distinguish the various kinds of quince from *ekmek ayvasi*, or apple-quince, which are rounded, yellow, and sweet, and *limon ayvasi*, or lemon quince, which are larger, oblong, and green, with a lemony tartness.

Once common in American orchards, quince are now considered to be a rare fruit, raised on limited acreage in California. Many of the quince in North American markets come from Argentina. They may be found in Asian markets, as they are popular in Asian, particularly Korean, cuisine. The quince season runs from August into January or February, when a few quince are imported from Chile.

I'm here to get you to try this fruit that is as rewarding as it is demanding. In this chapter, I make a Spiced Quince Jam (page 749) to use as a filling for the Spiced Quince and Walnut Thumbprint Cookies (page 750). I combine quince and sour cherries to fill a strudel (page 751). Quince and cranberry make a harmonious duo in the Quince–Cranberry Tarte Tatin (page 753). The extraordinarily good Spanish Baked Quince with Pine Nuts and Dried Fruit (page 754) are also well worth trying, even if you've never eaten a quince in your life. Also, the Brown Bread Apple Charlotte with Rum–Vanilla Custard Sauce (page 108) is wonderful if made with all or some quince. The Brazil Nut and Guava Sandwich Cookies (page 175) may be filled with quince membrillo instead of guava membrillo, and the Guava and Cheese Empa–nadas (page 271) are also excellent made with quince membrillo.

SLOW FOOD ARK OF TASTE

The Ark of Taste was created in Italy in 1996 at the first Salone del Gusto in Turin, which was sponsored by Slow Food, a giant artisanal foods show that I was lucky enough to attend in 2006. The Ark seeks to preserve endangered tastes like quince and to celebrate them by introducing them to the general public through media, public relations, and events. The goal is to promote artisan foods and heirloom varieties by stabilizing production techniques and establishing production standards to guarantee them a viable and profitable future. Find out more online at www.slowfoodusa.org/ark.

QUINCE VARIETIES

MEECH'S PROLIFIC: This historic American quince variety was discovered in Connecticut in the middle of the nineteenth century. It is a particularly fragrant quince, combining the aromas of apples, flowers, and vanilla. It is named after Reverend William Meech, who introduced the fruit as the "Pear-Shaped Orange Quince" in an 1883 botanical article. He popularized the fruit as Meech's Prolific in his definitive book, *Quince Culture*, published in 1888. In the book, he described the fruit as the "most uniformly prolific of all known varieties." Others described it as "the perfect quince." This variety has been included in the Slow Food Ark of Taste (see below), which is dedicated to "saving cherished Slow Foods, one product at a time."

PINEAPPLE QUINCE: The light-skinned, white-fleshed Pineapple Quince smells like its tropical namesake. It is the main variety of quince available in American supermarkets, grown in California on about 300 acres in the San Joaquin Valley. It looks like a knobby pear, though large, smooth, and golden yellow in color, with white flesh and a distinct pineapple aroma as its ripens.

OTHER QUINCE VARIETIES: The Perfumed Quince has an oval shape with tapered ends, smooth yellow skin, and white flesh. The Champion is a late-season variety that is quite fuzzy and pear-shaped with delicate flavor. The Portugal, a rare quince from Portugal, is giant, bulbous, and football-shaped, with deep, rich flavor.

CHOOSING, RIPENING, AND STORING QUINCE

Quince are usually lumpy in shape, so if you buy a small one, there won't be much edible fruit left after trimming. Instead, choose quince that are firm, yellow rather than green, and as large as possible. Quince ripen slowly at room temperature, turning from green to yellow, with the flesh remaining firm but turning from shiny to waxy as the fruit ripens. Note that although quince bruise easily, any small marks on the skin won't affect their quality. Avoid softened, shriveled, or overly bruised quince.

The best quince can often be found at Asian, especially Korean markets, where they are in high demand. Fresh quince are most commonly available from October to December, but I've found them at my local Korean market at odd times throughout the year (except maybe in summer and during the time that I was searching for them to complete my testing). Store unripe quince at room temperature, keeping them from touching each other, until they are yellow and fragrant. Store ripe quince in a plastic bag in the refrigerator for up to two months.

PREPARING QUINCE

Quince are usually peeled, either before or after cooking. This can be done with a potato peeler or a small, sharp paring knife. Then cut the fruit away from its large, fibrous seed pocket. Another method is to half-cook the (whole) quince in simmering water, then remove it from the liquid and let it cool before peeling and cutting it up. Peeling will be much easier with softer, partially cooked fruit.

Spiced Quince Jam

Because of their very high pectin content and dense, aromatic flesh, quince make a wonderful thick jam. This recipe makes a jam that is gently spiced with coriander seeds, cinnamon, and black peppercorns. The quince are simmered in a mixture of white wine, honey, sugar, and a bit of lemon to keep them from darkening. As they cook, the fruits turn a lovely shade of orange-pink. Although I use the jam as a filling for the Thumbprint Cookies on page 750, it is also delicious spread on toasted bread or toasted pound cake.

YIELD: ABOUT 3 CUPS

1 cup dry white wine

3 bay leaves

1 cinnamon stick, lightly crushed

2 teaspoons coriander seeds

2 teaspoons peppercorns

1 cup honey

1 cup sugar

4 large quince, cut in half

Juice of 1 lemon

In a Dutch oven set over high heat, combine the wine, bay leaves, cinnamon stick, coriander seeds, peppercorns, honey, and sugar, and bring to a boil. Lower the heat and simmer for 20 minutes.

Strain the liquid, discarding the solids. Return the liquid to the Dutch oven, add the quince, and bring back to a boil.

Preheat the oven to 325°F.

Cover the Dutch oven, place it in the oven, and bake until the quince are tender, about 2 hours.

Uncover the Dutch oven and while still in the pot, mash the quince with the back of a spoon or a potato masher. Set aside to cool to room temperature. Strain the entire contents of the pot through a food mill or a sieve to remove skins and seeds.

Heat the oven to 275°F. Spread the quince into a shallow, oven-proof casserole (not metal), such as Pyrex, and bake for 2 hours, stirring once or twice, until the jam is deep reddish-orange in color and quite thick. Transfer the jam to a bowl and allow it to cool to room temperature, stirring occasionally so it doesn't form a skin. Pack the jam into a glass jar or other covered container and refrigerate. The jam can keep for several months in the refrigerator.

Spiced Quince and Walnut Thumbprint Cookies

Thumbprint cookies, with a spoonful of jam in the center, have a pleasing look and an even more pleasing flavor when they are homemade. These quince-filled, walnut-dusted cookies are a far cry from the red and orange ones sold in commercial bakeries and supermarkets. You may freeze part or all of the dough up to three months. If you don't want to make your own jam, use store-bought Turkish quince jam or melted membrillo instead.

YIELD: 6 TO 8 DOZEN COOKIES

$^3/_4$ pound ($2^3/_4$ cups) walnuts

2 ounces ($^1/_2$ cup plus 2 tablespoons) potato starch, substitute corn, wheat, or rice starch

1 pound ($3^3/_4$ cups) unbleached all-purpose flour

1 cup sugar

1 pound (4 sticks) unsalted butter, chilled and cut into bits

2 teaspoons vanilla extract

2 tablespoons heavy cream

3 cups Spiced Quince Jam (page 749)

In the bowl of a food processor, combine the walnuts and starch and grind until medium-fine. Transfer to the bowl of a standing mixer fitted with the paddle attachment, and add the flour and sugar. Mix to combine, then add the butter, and beat until the mixture resembles oatmeal. Sprinkle in the vanilla and cream, and beat again briefly, until the mixture comes together in moist clumps. Knead briefly until the mixture forms a ball, then transfer the dough to a plastic bag and shape into a flattened rectangle. Chill in the refrigerator for 1 hour or in the freezer for 30 minutes until firm but still malleable.

Preheat the oven to 325°F.

Form the dough into small, walnut-sized balls, using a small ice cream scoop, if desired. Place the balls on ungreased baking sheets about 2 inches apart. Press a deep indentation into the center of each cookie with the small end of a melon baller or your thumb. Bake for 12 to 15 minutes, or until light golden in color. Remove the cookies from the oven and, while they are still warm, press the melon baller or your thumb into the depression again to deepen it. Cool to room temperature.

Spoon or pipe about 1 teaspoon of the quince jam into the center of each cookie. Allow the jam to set 30 minutes at room temperature or 15 minutes refrigerated. Store covered and in a single layer (so the jam doesn't stick) up to 2 days at room temperature and up to 5 days refrigerated.

Quince and Sour Cherry Strudel

Fragrant quince, with its firm texture and apple-pear-like flavor, is combined here with tender, tangy sour cherries, and membrillo (quince paste) to make an off-beat but superb strudel filling. A sprinkling of cake crumbs helps absorb any excess liquid and is a great way to use stale cake (keep a bag in the freezer). Plain toasted breadcrumbs or cookie crumbs will also work.

The strudel, made with phyllo dough, is formed into a great horseshoe shape. If quince paste is not available, apple butter can be substituted or it may be omitted altogether, with a small loss of flavor and body.

YIELD: 10 TO 12 SERVINGS

3 ounces (6 tablespoons) unsalted butter

4 large ripe quince (about 2 pounds), peeled, cored, and diced

1 cup sugar

1/4 teaspoon ground cloves

1 pound fresh sour cherries, stemmed and pitted, or 1 (24-ounce) jar, 2 cups, drained bottled sour cherries, or 2 cups frozen sour cherries, partially defrosted

1/4 cup membrillo, substitute cherry preserves or apple jelly

1/4 cup kirsch, substitute brandy

2 ounces (1/2 cup) chopped walnuts

1 cup Clarified Butter, (page 202) melted and cooled

3/4 pound phyllo dough, defrosted if frozen

1 cup cake crumbs, substitute cookie crumbs, or plain breadcrumbs

1/4 cup raw sugar

Line an 18 x 13-inch half sheet pan (or other large baking pan) with parchment paper or a silicone baking mat.

In a large, heavy skillet over moderate heat, melt the butter, add the quince, and sauté. When the fruit has softened slightly, about 8 minutes, add the sugar and cloves, increase the heat to high, and continue to cook until the sugar starts to brown, about 8 minutes longer, shaking the pan often. Stir in the cherries and the membrillo and cook 5 minutes longer or until the pan juices are thick and syrupy.

Remove from the heat, stir in the kirsch and walnuts, and cool to room temperature. To speed the cooling, transfer the mixture to a bowl, preferably stainless steel, and cool by placing over a second bowl filled with a mixture of ice and water, stirring often.

Preheat the oven to 400°F.

Arrange a 2-foot length of wax paper on a work surface. Brush the paper lightly with butter, then place 2 sheets of the phyllo overlapping by about 2-inches the long way on the wax paper. Brush lightly and evenly with butter. Repeat 5 more times, for a total of 6 layers of phyllo, brushing each layer with butter.

Sprinkle the phyllo with the cake crumbs. Spoon the cooled filling in a long, even strip about 1 inch from the front edge. Tuck the ends under and roll up the strudel from the long side of the phyllo. Gently form the strudel into a horseshoe shape and transfer to the baking pan. (It helps to have someone there to support the strudel.) Brush the top with butter, then sprinkle with raw sugar. Cut shallow slits 1½-inches apart across the top of the strudel keeping the sides intact.

Bake for 40 minutes, or until well browned. Note that the filling will inevitably ooze out of the pastry. Drain off any excess melted butter. Cool slightly and cut into serving portions with a serrated knife through the slits. Serve warm. Store the strudel covered and at room temperature for up to 3 days. Store covered and refrigerated for up to 5 days. Cover with foil and reheat in a 350°F oven for 20 minutes.

PHYLLO DOUGH FROM HAND-MADE TO MACHINE-MADE

An a young boy in his native Cyprus, Evripides Kontos worked after school at a bakery. During the holiday season, this bakery would often be unable to produce enough of its hand-stretched phyllo dough. So, Kontos left school at age 16 to start a business, producing the dough for bakeries in Cyrus. At the urging of his American uncle, Kontos eventually set off for the United States, and by 1968 he was making and selling hand-stretched phyllo dough to restaurants and bakeries in the New York area. In 1971, he and a partner designed the first machine to make phyllo dough. With increased availability of this machine-made product, Americans, especially chefs, started using the dough more and more. Although hand-stretched dough is still the best, those packages of frozen phyllo at the supermarket are certainly convenient. Today, pastry chefs can even buy pre-buttered (or oiled) phyllos, a product that's sure to start showing up in retail markets soon. The company also makes phyllo in various thicknesses from thin to thick. Go to www.kontos.com for more information.

Quince–Cranberry Tarte Tatin

One of the easiest and most attractive pastries you can make is a tarte tatin, the famed upside-down tart created in 1889 by the two sisters, Stéphanie and Caroline Tatin, at the Hotel Tatin in Lamotte-Beuvron, France. In early summer, make the Apricot Peach and Tarte Tatin on page 616; in fall make this colorful and full-bodied tart, perhaps for Thanksgiving; in winter, make the Oatmeal Apple Upside Down Tart (a tarte tatin by another name). I love the combination of meaty quince and brightly colored, tangy cranberries sweetened with the inimitable maple syrup.

YIELD: 8 SERVINGS

$^3/_4$ pound Tarte Tatin Pastry dough (page 206)

6 large quince

Juice of 1 lemon

$^3/_4$ cup sugar

2 ounces ($^1/_2$ stick) unsalted butter

12 ounces fresh cranberries

$^1/_2$ cup pure maple syrup, preferably grade B

1 cup crème fraîche

Roll out dough on a lightly floured surface into a large round about 12 inches in diameter and about $^3/_8$-inch thick. Transfer to a sheet of parchment or wax paper and refrigerate for at least 30 minutes.

Preheat the oven to 400°F.

Quarter each quince, core, peel, and slice into $^1/_2$-inch thick wedges. Place in a bowl and add the lemon juice and enough cold water to cover.

In a heavy, ovenproof (preferably cast-iron) 9- or 10-inch skillet over medium heat, stir the sugar and butter until the butter melts, about 3 minutes. Increase the heat to high and let the mixture boil, without stirring, until the sugar caramelizes and turns medium amber in color, occasionally swirling the pan so the sugar browns evenly, about 5 minutes. Remove from the heat and cool for 2 minutes or until the caramel is moderately hot.

Drain the quince and arrange the slices in a closely packed, spiral pattern over the caramel. Sprinkle the cranberries over top. Cover the cranberries with any remaining quince. Drizzle the maple syrup evenly over the fruit.

Trim the dough to a 10-inch circle, then drape it over the fruit. Tuck the edges around the fruit. Cut several slits in the dough to allow steam to escape. Cover the pan with foil. Bake for 45 minutes, or until the pastry is browned and the filling is bubbling up through the slits..

Remove the tart from the oven and cover with a piece of aluminum foil, then a plate smaller than the diameter of the skillet, and then a can, to weigh down the fruit. Cool about 30 minutes, or until it reaches room temperature. Remove the weight, plate, and foil, and cover the skillet with a large cake platter. Hold the skillet and the plate together and flip over so the fruit is on top. Cut into portions and serve with a dollop of unsweetened crème fraîche. This tart is best the day it is made.

Baked Quince with Pine Nuts and Dried Fruit

When I made these stuffed quince halves, baked in red wine and honey syrup, I couldn't get over just how good they were. In fact, I kept warming them and eating them day after day, and believe me, with all the sweet baked goods I needed to make for this cookbook, I had plenty of other choices. The quince cook up to a sweet, fragrant, soft yet dense texture; the chunky fruits and pine nuts provide textural and visual contrast, while the syrup just gets better and better, the longer it cooks. I would serve these with dry cookies, the kind that would be called biscuits *in England and* petits fours secs *in France, such as the Spanish Sesame-Anise Cookies (page 799) or the Pan Levi (page 442). This is a wonderful make-ahead dessert that improves when reheated.*

YIELD: 12 SERVINGS

6 large ripe quinces (3 to 4 pounds)

$1/2$ cup honey

2 cups dry red wine

2 bay leaves

6 tablespoons pine nuts

$1/4$ cup dried apricots, diced

$1/4$ cup dried cherries

$1/4$ cup golden raisins

$1/2$ cup dark brown sugar

Pinch ground cloves

$1/2$ teaspoon ground cinnamon

Preheat the oven to 375°F.

Place the quinces in a baking dish large enough to hold them.

In a small bowl, whisk together the honey and wine, and pour over the quince. Add the bay leaves, then cover the dish with aluminum foil and bake for 1 hour, 15 minutes, or until the quince are moderately tender when pierced. Remove from the oven and cool to room temperature.

In a medium bowl, mix the pine nuts, apricots, cherries, raisins, brown sugar, cloves, and cinnamon.

Drain the quince, reserving the pan juices. Using an apple corer, scoop out the center core and pits, keeping the fruit as intact as possible for stuffing. Alternatively, cut around the center core from one end of the quince using a small, sharp paring knife. Turn over the quince and cut around the center core from the other end. Push out the core with the back of a wooden spoon or the end of a sharpening steel. Cut each quince in half through its "equator." Use a melon baller or a spoon to scoop out any remaining seeds. Arrange the quince, cut sides up, in a ceramic or glass baking dish just large enough to hold them. Spoon some of the pine nut mixture into the center of each quince and over the top. Bake again, uncovered at 375°F, until the quince are tender and the juices are syrupy, about 45 minutes. Cool and serve topped with syrup from the baking dish.

Store covered and at room temperature up to 1 day, or cover and refrigerate up to 5 days. Cover with foil and reheat at 350°F for 30 minutes or until hot and bubbling.

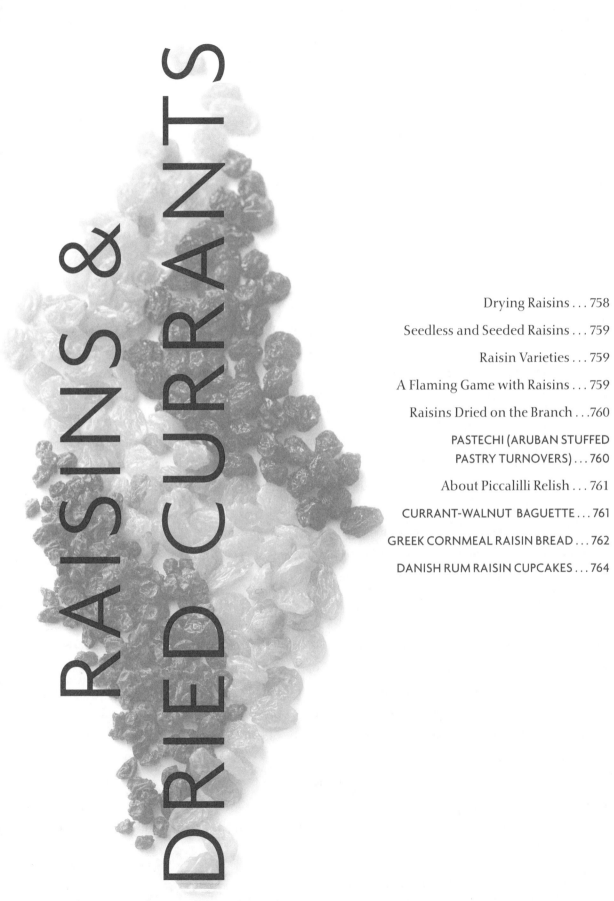

RAISINS & DRIED CURRANTS

Drying Raisins . . . 758

Seedless and Seeded Raisins . . . 759

Raisin Varieties . . . 759

A Flaming Game with Raisins . . . 759

Raisins Dried on the Branch . . . 760

PASTECHI (ARUBAN STUFFED
PASTRY TURNOVERS) . . . 760

About Piccalilli Relish . . . 761

CURRANT-WALNUT BAGUETTE . . . 761

GREEK CORNMEAL RAISIN BREAD . . . 762

DANISH RUM RAISIN CUPCAKES . . . 764

RAISINS & DRIED CURRANTS

My memories of my great-grand-mother are few and rather fuzzy (she died when I was about thirteen), but those that remain are inevitably connected to food. Every Friday, in preparation for Shabbat (the Sabbath), she would prepare a pair of large, braided challah breads studded with plenty of golden raisins. To this day, the only challah that tastes right to me contains those raisins, and the only raisins that taste right to me are those tangy golden beauties. Although with new types of raisins on the market, like the large Monukka and Red Flame raisins, I'm learning to expand my repertoire.

In the winter months of times past, when supermarket aisles full of fresh (and often flavorless) produce didn't exist, people relied on dried and preserved food from their pantries and cold cellars to carry them through until summer's bounty ripened. The small, chewy, dense, and sweet dried grapes called raisins were used in both sweet and savory dishes to take advantage of their ability to plump up by absorbing liquids. Raisins are quite concentrated: it takes four and a half pounds of fresh grapes to produce one pound of raisins.

The word *raisin* comes from the Latin *racemus*, and means "a cluster of grapes or berries." While in the United States, the term "raisin" refers to any form of dried grape, in Great Britain and its former colonies, raisins are commonly known as *sultanas* (which in America refers to a particular type of raisin). In France, fresh grapes are known as *raisins* while raisins are known as *raisins secs*. In Australia and other countries, specific dried grape varieties are given separate names, so in Australia, *raisins* are largest, *sultanas* are medium-sized, and *currants* are the smallest.

Humans probably discovered raisins when they happened upon grapes drying on a vine. The peripatetic-trading Phoenicians established the earliest vineyards in Greece and southern Spain, while Armenians created vineyards in Persia (parts of today's Turkey, Iran, and Iraq). These areas not only had perfect climates for growing raisins, but they were also close to the important markets in Greece and Rome. Phoenicians and Armenians traded raisins with the Greeks and Romans, and the fruit soon became a favorite in these regions. The Roman Emperor Augustus feasted on small roasted birds stuffed with raisins, and Hannibal brought raisins as rations to feed his troops while as they crossed the Alps (perhaps creating the first "trail mix"). Greeks and Romans decorated places of worship with raisins and handed them out to winners in sporting contests. Roman physicians prescribed raisins to cure anything from mushroom-poisoning to old age.

Crusader knights first introduced raisins to Europe in the eleventh century, when they returned home from the Eastern Mediterranean. Because raisins were easy to pack and ship, they were soon found throughout northern Europe. By the fourteenth century, raisins had become an important part of European cuisine, and raisin prices skyrocketed. The English, French, and Germans all attempted to grow grapes for raisins, but their climates were too cold for drying the fruit.

In Greece today, raisins—mainly sultanas—are produced in the areas of Peloponnesus, Crete, and the smaller islands. The larger and darker Corinthian, or black raisin, is cultivated near the city of Corinth. The Zante currant, from the Ionian island of Zakynthos (Zante in English), is one of the oldest raisins, known as early as 75 CE when Pliny wrote of a tiny Greek grape, thin-skinned, juicy, and sweet, that grows in exceedingly small bunches. The tiny, seedless, tangy dried black grapes are called "currants" when dried—the name evolved from "Corinth," the port where the fruits were first shipped to western Europe. These small treats are the dried versions of the tiny, so-called Champagne grapes often used to garnish cheese trays.

Zante currants were first introduced into the United States dates in 1854, although they were not successful until cuttings from the Greek village of Panariti, noted for the high quality of its raisins, were planted in California. They are still a specialty crop grown in small quantities.

Muscat grapes from the vineyards of Spain eventually ended up in California, brought by missionaries sent to Mexico by Spain's Queen Isabelle. The missionaries who raised grapes for sacramental wine passed on their knowledge of viticulture and planted these same grapes for raisins. But it wasn't until 1851 that farmers near San Diego, California, began growing a commercially marketed raisin grape, the Egyptian Muscat.

Eventually, because San Diego did not have enough water, the farmers moved to the San Joaquin Valley, perfect for growing, with its long, hot growing season and plenty of sunshine. In 1873, a massive heat wave hit the San Joaquin Valley just before harvest. Most of the grapes that had been planted to make wine dried on the vine, spelling financial disaster throughout the region. In desperation, enterprising growers took their dried grapes to San Francisco, where they were marketed as "Peruvian Delicacies." They were the hit of the season and sold out immediately.

By the late 1800s, many Armenians—descendents of the same people who cultivated the earliest vineyards in Persia—began settling the San Joaquin Valley. The development of this area of California as the world's largest producer of raisins can be credited, in great part, to these

Armenian growers who still dominate the industry. Today, the majority of the world's supply of raisins comes from California, dried from Thompson seedless grapes (95 percent), muscadine grapes, or Black Corinth grapes (Zante currants).

Raisins are one of the most important additions to baking recipes, used in both savory and sweet baking and just about every cuisine. They can be used straight from the box or plumped first in wine, spirits, or simply warm water. While I concentrate on raisin recipes in this chapter, there are lots of varied recipes throughout the book that call for raisins and smaller Zante currants. Although I don't use them in this book, raisin juice and raisin paste are often added to "low-fat" desserts to add moisture.

The Pastechi (Aruban Stuffed Pastry Turnovers)(page 760) have a delicious, savory-sweet meat filling similar to Spanish picadillo. The dense, fruit and nut–laden Currant-Walnut Baguette (page 761) is excellent served with cheese, especially tangy goat cheese. The Greek Cornmeal Raisin Bread (page 762) is an unusual and tasty bread flavored with mastic and coriander seed, with orange juice used as the liquid. The Danish Rum Raisin Cupcakes (page 764) are definitely for grown-ups only, as the raisins are soaked in a full half-cup of dark rum. In other chapters, look for the German Apple and Rum-Raisin Custard Torte (page 54), the Zaleti: Venetian Cornmeal Cookies with Grappa Raisins (page 60), the Buckwheat Cinnamon-Raisin Bread (page 188), the Brustengolo (Umbrian Cornmeal, Pear, Raisin, and Nut

Cake (page 389), and the New England Cranberry-Maple–Raisin Pie (page 552) among many others that call for raisins.

DRYING RAISINS

Most raisins are dried in the vineyards naturally, by sun, although some are mechanically dehydrated. Once they are sun dried, a process that takes two to four weeks, they are then graded, cleaned, and packed. Light-colored raisins are kept golden in color with the addition of sulfur dioxide (sulfites).

SEEDLESS AND SEEDED RAISINS

Seedless raisins are made from grapes with no seeds. Seeded raisins are made from grapes with seeds, which are removed before or after drying. The two are not generally interchangeable because the flavor is quite different. Seeded raisins, such as Muscats, are more difficult to find than the common seedless variety carried on most market shelves. Muscats are often only available during autumn and winter seasons for the holidays.

RAISIN VARIETIES

MONUKKA: These large, dark, seedless raisins come from the grapes of the same name. They're produced in limited quantities and can be found at natural foods and specialty stores.

MUSCAT: Also known as Spanish Málaga, or Muscatels, these oversized, thin-skinned, raisins have lots of seeds and superb flavor. Large and brown, with an intensely fruity flavor, these premium raisins are made from the greenish-gold Muscat grapes planted by the Phoenicians in many parts of Spain over two thousand years ago and brought to California by the Spanish missionaries. The seeds are removed by pushing them out through the skins, bringing sugar onto the surface of the grapes, and making them sticky. Once seedless Thompsons took over the raisin market, Muscats became a specialty item. Because they are so sweet and moist, Muscats are excellent in baking. They can be found at natural foods and specialty stores and are available in a five-pound box from Sunmaid. Go to www.sunmaid.com to find them.

SMYRNA SULTANA: Smyrna Sultanas, from the Western Coast of Turkey, are seedless and pale yellow, with a fine flavor. Quite popular in Europe, these raisins come from a seedless yellow grape and are usually softer and sweeter than other varieties.

THOMPSON SEEDLESS: Also known as the Oval Kishmish or Sultanina, these are entirely seedless yellow grapes with low acidity. They were introduced in California in 1876 by a Scottish farmer named William Thompson. When sun-dried, these grapes become the dark raisin so familiar to Americans today. Later, it was discovered that they would keep their original light gold color if processed with the use of sulfur. Today, ninety-five percent of both light and dark California raisins are made from Thompson seedless grapes grown in the San Joaquin Valley.

ZANTE CURRANT: Not to be confused with the red, black, or white currant in the *Ribes* genus (page 408), Zante currants are tiny, seedless, and sweet dark grapes. They are native to the island of Zante, Greece, and are now also sold fresh as Champagne grapes.

A FLAMING GAME WITH RAISINS

Snapdragon was a wintertime parlor game played in England and the United States from about the sixteenth to the nineteenth centuries, often on Christmas Eve. In a dim or dark room, a large shallow bowl filled with brandy and raisins was set alight so blue flames could be seen playing across the brandy. The aim of the game was to pluck the raisins from the bowl and eat them without getting burned. In the dark, with the flames jumping about, the participants would themselves resemble demons as they snatched out the raisins.

Pastechi (Aruban Stuffed Pastry Turnovers)

The versatile pastechi is a fried pastry turnover stuffed with spicy meat, shrimp, or fish. Pastechi are served in Aruba at all times of the day, with coffee for breakfast, tea in the afternoon, or cocktails in the evening. The large, half moon–shaped turnovers may be found at take-out restaurants, beach parties, and on the buffet table of elegant parties. Unlike the related Spanish empanadas, Aruban pastechi are made with a slightly sweet dough and a smaller amount of filling. Make the pastechi up to two days ahead of time, frying just before serving. Or fry earlier in the day and reheat in the oven. Any cut of beef, preferably from a roast or stew will work. Ground beef is not appropriate.

YIELD: 4 DOZEN TURNOVERS

Filling

1 pound cooked beef, cut into chunks

1 tablespoon vegetable oil

1 medium onion, finely chopped

1 small green bell pepper, finely chopped

1 celery rib, finely chopped

2 tablespoons raisins

1 tablespoon piccalilli relish, substitute sweet pickle relish, finely chopped

Hot red pepper, preferably habañero, finely chopped, to taste

2 tablespoons soy sauce

$1/2$ teaspoon freshly ground black pepper

$1/2$ teaspoon freshly ground cumin

$1/2$ teaspoon freshly ground nutmeg

Dough

1 pound ($3^3/4$ cups) unbleached all-purpose flour

1 tablespoon baking powder

1 teaspoon salt

2 tablespoons sugar

2 tablespoons (1 ounce) unsalted butter, softened

2 tablespoons vegetable shortening

1 egg, lightly beaten

1 cup ice water

1 quart peanut, canola, or vegetable oil for frying

Make the filling: Place the meat into the bowl of a food processor and process briefly until well-chopped.

Alternatively, chop by hand into small bits. Reserve.

In a large frying pan heat the oil and sauté the onion, green pepper, and celery until softened but not browned, about 5 minutes. Stir in the raisins, relish, red pepper, soy sauce, pepper, cumin, and nutmeg, and cook until well-combined and any juices have evaporated, about 5 minutes. Remove the mixture from the pan, combine with thte beef, and chill.

Make the dough: In a bowl, whisk together the flour, baking powder, salt, and sugar, and reserve.

In the bowl of a standing mixer fitted with the paddle attachment, cream the butter and shortening until light and fluffy. Beat in the flour mixture, then add the egg and enough of the ice water to make a smooth and pliable, but not sticky dough. Roll the dough into a thin sheet, then cut out circles about 6 inches in diameter.

Place one spoonful of filling in the center of each pastry circle, leaving a 1-inch border all around. Fold over and press firmly to seal the pastry. Arrange the stuffed pastechi in a single layer on a baking sheet lined with wax paper. At this point, you may refrigerate the pastechi up to 4 hours before frying.

In a wok, a large, heavy-duty frying pan, preferably cast-iron, or an electric deep-fryer, heat the oil to 365°F, or until shimmering hot, and the air above the oil feels hot when you hold your hand about 3 inches above it. Add one pastechi at a time to the oil and fry without crowding the pan until golden brown, 3 to 4 minutes. The pastechi may be kept warm in a 200°F oven until serving.

ABOUT PICCALILLI RELISH:

This pickled vegetable relish, once known as Indian pickle, is quite popular Great Britain as well as Aruba and is of Anglo-Indian origin. It is a mixture of finely chopped firm vegetables such as cabbage, cauliflower, carrots, celery, green tomatoes, sweet peppers, and onions, seasoned with vinegar, sugar, salt, along with mustard and other spices, especially turmeric for its yellow color. Although popular in Great Britain since the mid-eighteenth century, piccalilli has never really caught on in the United States. Its name is a play on "pickle." Piccalilli is closely related to chow-chow, although that relish is of Chinese origin.

Currant–Walnut Baguette

This earthy brown bread, shaped into a long, rather plump baguette loaf and densely packed with tiny flavor-packed Zante currants and toasted walnuts, is virtually impossible to stop eating. A portion of full-bodied oat flour gives it extra flavor. Serve the bread in thin slices to accompany a cheese board or toast and spread with butter, cream cheese, or mild goat cheese and serve with a bowl of hearty soup. The bread also freezes quite well.

YIELD: 1 LONG BAGUETTE

$^3/_4$ pound (3 cups) unbleached bread flour
$^1/_4$ pound ($^3/_4$ cup plus 2 tablespoons) oat flour

2 teaspoon fine sea salt

1 (¼-ounce) package (2½ teaspoons) active dry yeast

2 tablespoons honey

1¼ cups lukewarm water

¼ pound (1 cup) walnuts, lightly toasted and chopped

¼ pound (1 cup) Zante currants

1 large egg, lightly beaten with 1 tablespoon water,
   for the egg wash, or 2 tablespoons Shiny Cornstarch
   Glaze (page 393)

Line an 18 x 13-inch half sheet pan (or other large baking pan) with parchment paper or a silicone baking mat.

In a medium bowl, whisk together the dry ingredients: flour, oat flour, and salt.

In the bowl of a standing mixer fitted with the paddle attachment, dissolve the yeast and the honey in ¼ cup of the lukewarm water and let stand until foamy, about 10 minutes. Add the remaining 1 cup water, then beat in half the flour mixture. Add the walnuts and currants and beat until well combined, then beat in the remaining flour mixture. Switch to the dough hook and continue beating until the dough is smooth and elastic and comes away cleanly from the sides of the bowl.

Coat a large bowl with oil. Transfer the dough to the bowl and turn it around so it is oiled all over. Cover with plastic wrap or a damp cloth and allow the dough to rise at warm room temperature until doubled in size, about 2 hours.

Turn the dough out onto a lightly floured board. Punch it down to remove the air bubbles. Roll the dough into a rectangle about 16 x 8 inches. Roll the dough up tightly into a long cylinder, pinching the edges to seal. Transfer the dough roll, seam side down, to the pan.

Brush the loaf with the egg wash. Using a French baker's lame, a single-edged razor, or a box cutter, make 5 to 6 shallow slashes on the diagonal across the bread. Cover with oiled plastic wrap and allow the bread to rise at warm room temperature until it is almost doubled in bulk, about 45 minutes.

Preheat the oven to 375°F. Bake for 35 minutes, or until the bread sounds hollow when tapped on the bottom and a thermometer inserted in the center reads 190°F, and the loaf is well-browned. Cool to room temperature on a wire rack before slicing.

Greek Cornmeal Raisin Bread

This raisin bread comes from the beautiful island of Mykonos in Greece. Many older Greek people loathe raisins because in the 1930s, the government made it compulsory for anyone buying any kind of bread to buy a loaf of raisin bread, too, in order to increase the consumption of the large crop of Zante currants from the island of Corinth. This wonderful orange and spiced raisin bread is good enough to change even the most confirmed raisin hater to a raisin lover. The mastic resin imparts a mysterious and pleasing piney aroma and flavor to the bread, but may be omitted. This recipe is inspired by a recipe in Aglaia Kremezi's gorgeously photographed book, The Foods of Greece. *You must start the sponge a day ahead of time.*

YIELD: TWO 1½-POUND LOAVES

Sponge

$^1/_2$ cup Sourdough Starter (page 880)

$^1/_4$ pound (1 cup minus 1 tablespoon) unbleached
all-purpose flour

$^1/_2$ cup lukewarm water

Dough

1 pound (3$^3/_4$ cups) unbleached all-purpose flour

$^1/_4$ pound ($^3/_4$ cup plus 2 tablespoons) stone-ground
yellow cornmeal

2 teaspoons fine sea salt

1 teaspoon ground mastic (page 519), optional

1 teaspoon ground coriander seed

1 teaspoon ground cinnamon

Pinch ground cloves

1 ($^1/_4$-ounce) package (2 $^1/_2$ teaspoons) active dry yeast

1 cup orange juice

Grated zest of 1 orange (4 teaspoons)

$^1/_4$ cup honey

$^1/_2$ pound (1$^1/_2$ cups) raisins, gold, dark or mixed

Olive oil, for brushing

2 tablespoons sesame seeds, for sprinkling

In the bowl of a standing mixer fitted with the whisk attachment, combine the starter, flour, and water. Cover with plastic wrap and allow the sponge to rest overnight at warm room temperature.

Spray two medium (1-pound, 8$^1/_2$ x 4$^1/_2$-inch) loaf pans with baker's nonstick coating or rub with butter and dust with flour, shaking off the excess.

in a large bowl, whisk together the dry ingredients: flour, cornmeal, salt, mastic, coriander, cinnamon, and cloves.

Sprinkle the starter with the yeast and whisk to combine.

In a medium microwavable container, preferably a Pyrex measure, combine the orange juice, zest, and honey, and microwave for 1 minute on medium power to lukewarm, or until the liquid is just warm enough to dissolve the honey.

Switch to the paddle attachment, add the orange juice mixture to the sponge, and beat to combine. Beat in half of the flour mixture, then the raisins. Beat in the remaining flour mixture and continue to beat until the dough is smooth and elastic and comes away cleanly from the sides of the bowl, 5 to 6 minutes.

Transfer the dough to a large oiled bowl, turning it around so the dough is oiled all over. Cover with plastic wrap or a damp cloth and allow the dough to rise at warm room temperature until doubled in size, about 3 hours. (If you press the dough with your finger and it sprigs back, it needs to rise further; if the dough stays depressed, it is ready.)

Punch down the dough, then turn it out onto a lightly floured work surface and roll it up into a fat log. Cut the log into 2 even portions, using a scale to weigh them if desired. Roll each portion out into a 12 x 8-inch rectangle about $^3/_4$-inch thick. Roll up tightly and fit each portion into a pan, seam side down. Brush each loaf with olive oil, then sprinkle with sesame seeds, pressing lightly so they adhere. Cover the pans with oiled plastic wrap and leave to rise at warm room temperature for about 2 hours, or until the dough is light and puffy and has risen above the edges of the pans.

Preheat the oven to 375°F. Bake the loaves for 45 minutes or until golden brown on top and a thermometer inserted into the center reads 190 to 205°F. Remove the loaves from the pans about 5 minutes after they come out of the oven, so they don't get soggy. Cool to room temperature on a wire rack before slicing. Store the breads in an open plastic bag at room temperature for up to 4 days, or wrap and freeze for up to 3 months.

Danish Rum Raisin Cupcakes

Loaded with raisins that have been soaked until plump in dark rum, these cupcakes are definitely only for grown ups. The simple buttery batter is tangy with sour cream, and have an undertone of freshly grated nutmeg. You'll have to start one day ahead of time (or more) to soak the raisins. Myer's Dark Rum from Jamaica (page 53) has the intense dark brown sugar flavor that complements the raisins, though other dark rum may be substituted.

YIELD: 12 CUPCAKES

1 cup dark raisins

$^1/_2$ cup dark rum

$^1/_2$ pound (2 cups minus 2 tablespoons) unbleached all-purpose flour

1 teaspoon baking powder

1 teaspoon baking soda

$^1/_2$ teaspoon fine sea salt

1 teaspoon freshly grated nutmeg

$^1/_4$ pound (1 stick) unsalted butter, chilled and cut into bits

$^3/_4$ cup sugar

1 cup sour cream

1 large egg

1 teaspoon vanilla extract

Soak the raisins in the rum overnight at room temperature. Drain the raisins and reserve the rum.

Line 12 muffin cups with paper cups, spray each cup with nonstick baker's coating, or rub with butter and dust with flour, shaking off the excess.

In the bowl of a standing mixer whisk together the dry ingredients on low speed: flour, baking powder, baking soda, salt, and nutmeg. Switch to the paddle attachment, then beat in the butter until the mixture resembles oatmeal.

In a small bowl, whisk together the sugar, sour cream, egg, and vanilla until smooth. Add this mixture to the flour mixture, and beat only long enough to combine. Fold in $^3/_4$ cup of the raisins and their soaking liquid by hand, so as not to toughen the dough by overbeating. Fill each muffin cup with about $^1/_2$ cup of batter, filling them no more than three-quarters full. Sprinkle the remaining raisins on top.

Preheat the oven to 375°F. Bake the cupcakes for 20 minutes, or until puffed up and browned and a toothpick or skewer stuck in the center comes out clean. Cool to room temperature on a wire rack. Serve immediately or store covered up to 2 days at room temperature. Wrap and freeze up to 3 months, if desired.

RICE

Forms of Rice ... 769

English Millionaire's Shortbread ... 769

FRANGELICO MOUSSE CAKE WITH
GIANDUIA-RICE CRUNCH ... 771

CALAS (NEW ORLEANS RICE FRITTERS) ... 773

From Africa to Bahia and New Orleans ... 774

TURKISH GOAT'S MILK RICE PUDDING (SUTLAÇ) ... 774

Turkish Baldo Rice ... 775

Creamy Rice Pudding ... 775

CROSTATA DI RISO: ITALIAN RICE TART ... 776

RICE

Warm, soft, sweet, and comforting, rice pudding is one of those "nursery foods" that grown-ups in Great Britain, India, Turkey, Greece, Italy, Latin America, and the United States still love to eat. Riz à l'Imperatrice (Rice Pudding Empress Style) from France is studded with a royal treasure house of candied and glazed fruits, while the same idea is expressed in the Chinese Eight Treasures Rice, enriched with candied lotus seeds, red dates, candied kumquats, and more. The simpler, but no less delicious, Turkish Goat's Milk Rice Pudding: Sutlaç (page 774) is lusciously soft and creamy with a tangy aftertaste from goat's milk.

However, this chapter is not all about puddings. Here, rice starch lightens shortbread dough when it is mixed with wheat flour to make the delicately crumbly, three-layered English Millionaire's Shortbread (page 769) and the similarly "barely there" dough for the Argentinean Alfajores Cookies (page 563). An extravagant Frangelico Mousse Cake with Gianduia–Rice Crunch (page 771) is a light genoise (heated egg foam) cake thickened with rice starch, with a crunchy layer of gianduia (hazelnut and caramel milk chocolate), puffed rice cereal, and toasted hazelnuts on the bottom. It's hard to believe this cake is gluten-free. The puffy, slightly sour rice fritters called Calas (New Orleans Rice Fritters) (page 773) originated in West Africa, the home of America's most skilled rice farmers.

In Italy, especially in the areas near the Po River Valley, center of rice culture in Italy for about 2,000 years, rice pies are made in many versions. Basically, partially cooked rice pudding is finished by baking it in a rich shortcrust pastry shell. In this chapter, I make Crostata di Riso (page 776), a creamy rice-filled tart flavored with almonds and amaretti biscuits. The rice may be cooked, mixed with eggs and cheese, and formed into a "crust" which is then filled with cooked vegetables, olives, capers, and anchovies. Or, like the sweet crostata, a savory pastry shell is filled with savory cooked rice and other tasty ingredients and baked.

Rice is a grass plant with long, slender leaves and small seeds. It is native to tropical and subtropical southeastern Asia, where it grows in wetlands. The cultivation of rice is best-suited to regions with high rainfall and plenty of people, as requires abundant water and is very labor-intensive to cultivate. However, rice can be grown practically anywhere, even on steep hillsides, though usually requiring the help of insecticides. The word *rice* has an Indo-Iranian origin, and came into English from the Greek *óryza*, via the Latin *oriza*, the Italian *riso*, and the Old French *ris* (today *riz*).

Rice is the world's third-largest crop, behind maize (corn), and wheat. Although native to South Asia and parts of Africa, long centuries of trade and exportation have made it common practically everywhere in the world. All the rice grown in the world comes from two main species: *Oryza sativa*, native to subtropical southern Asia, and *Oryza glaberrima* (African rice), native to tropical southeastern Africa. Rice provides more than one-fifth of the calories consumed worldwide by humans and is a staple throughout Eastern, Southern, and Southeast Asia.

Rice is often grown in paddies–shallow flooded fields–taking advantage of the rice plant's tolerance to water as well as the benefits the water adds in preventing weeds, pests, and vermin. Once the rice is established in the field, the water can be drained in preparation for harvest. Whether it is grown in a paddy or a field, rice requires a great amount of water, making it a controversial crop in some areas, particularly in the United States and Australia, where rice farmers use large amounts of water to generate relatively small crop yields. However, in places that have a periodical rainy season and typhoons, rice paddies help keep the water supply steady and prevent floods from reaching dangerous levels.

Rice cultivation probably began simultaneously in many countries over 6,500 years ago. Common wild rice (not related to the dark brown grains of American native wild rice) was likely the ancestor of Asian rice, which appears to have originated in the foothills of the Himalayas. In Japan, dry-land rice was introduced about 1000 BCE and wet-paddy rice agriculture about seven hundred years later. African rice, which originated in the Niger River delta as far west as Senegal, has been cultivated in the region for 3,500 years. However, this variety never developed far from its original region. Instead, its cultivation declined in favor of Asian rice, possibly brought to Africa by Arabs between the seventh and eleventh centuries.

Rice was introduced to the Middle East at the time of the ancient Greeks and was familiar to both Greek and Roman writers. By the first century, rice was being grown in Iran and in Italy's Po River Valley, still great centers of rice production and consumption. The Moors brought rice to the Iberian Peninsula when they conquered it in 711. The Spanish in turn carried rice to South America at the beginning of the eighteenth century. By the second half of the fifteenth century, rice had spread throughout Italy and then France.

Rice first reached the United States in 1694 in South Carolina, probably from Madagascar. South Carolina and Georgia amassed great wealth from the huge rice plantations cultivated by slaves. At the port of Charleston, through which passed forty percent of all American slaves, West African slaves from the Senegambian region brought the highest prices because they were experienced in the complex techniques of rice culture. With the loss of slave labor after the Civil War, rice production became less profitable and it died out in its original region about one hundred years ago. Today, the delicate, adaptable grains of Carolina Gold rice are once more being grown with help from the Carolina Gold Rice Foundation (www.carolinagoldricefoundation.org). It can be purchased from Anson Mills (www.ansonmills.com).

Rice has been grown in southern Arkansas, Louisiana, and east Texas since the mid 1800s, with Cajun farmers raising it in wet marshes and low lying prairies. Rice cultivation began in California during the California Gold Rush, when about 40,000 Chinese laborers immigrated to the state, although commercial production didn't begin until 1912. By 2006, California was second only to Arkansas in rice production. In California, the rice grown is mainly short and medium-grain japonica varieties, such as Calrose, which makes up as much as eighty five percent of the state's crop.

To process rice, the seeds are milled to remove the chaff (the outer husks), therby making brown rice. The germ and the remaining husk, called the bran, are then removed to make white rice. White rice may be also polished with glucose or talc powder, parboiled, or processed into flour, and is enriched by adding back some of the nutrients lost in processing. Rice is washed to remove the starchy coating. The moist inner layer of the husk, called the bran, *nuka* in Japan, is heated to extract oil with a high smoking point that makes it well suited to deep-frying.

Most varieties of rice are processed into white rice at the mill, where the grains are polished to remove the husk, bran, and part of the germ. This processing strips some of the nutrients, but makes the rice tender and fast-cooking.

The more than 24,000 registered varieties of rice which exist in the world can be classified as short, medium, or long-grain. Each behaves differently when cooked because of size and shape, but mainly because of variations in the ratio of two starches: amylose and amylopectin. In short and medium-grain rice (like Spanish bomba, Italian arborio, and Japanese sushi rice) amylopectin dominates, so the grains tend to cling together when cooked. In long-grain rice (like most American supermarket rice, Indian Basmati, and Chinese rice), amylose dominates, so the cooked grains are dry, fluffy, and stay separate. (For more information about rice varieties, see my previous book, *Starting with Ingredients*.)

Glutinous rice has little amylose and a high level of amylopectin, giving it its sticky quality. The difference in this type of rice has been traced to a single mutation that was selected for by farmers. Glutinous rice is used in Southeast Asia, China, and Japan, and has been grown in the region for over 1,000 years—according to Chinese legend, it has grown there for at least 2,000 years. Tests have confirmed that rice was used as a key ingredient in the mortar joining the bricks in the Great Wall of China. In Japan, it is used to make *mochi*, glutinous rice balls, and as a glutinous coating for mochi ice cream, a fusion of Japanese mochi covering balls of American ice cream.

FORMS OF RICE

PUFFED RICE: Rice can be puffed (or popped), taking advantage of its inner moisture content. The method involves heating grain pellets in a special chamber.

RICE FLAKES OR BEATEN RICE: To make rice flakes, rice is dehusked and beaten to make small flat flakes, called *atukulu*, *bajil*, or *aval* in India. These flakes are used to make roti (flat bread), breakfast porridge, and dessert puddings. *Pinipig* is pounded, dried glutinous rice flakes, used by Filipino cooks to make desserts and beverages.

RICE STARCH: Rice starch is another source of pure starch that is also valuable in baking for its gentle thickening properties. It is used in baking for people on a gluten-free diet and to make beverages like horchata, rice milk, and sake. Because of all the different characteristics, natural "native" rice starches appropriate to the needs of food processors can be found without having to chemically modify them, as with cornstarch.

RICE FLOUR: This flour is made from rice that is husked, washed, soaked, dried, and ground into a flour that has the texture of very fine sand. Rice starches are known for their very clean taste profile, which will not interfere with the final flavor of a food, so that other flavors come through cleaner and quicker on the palate. It is also easy to digest. The flour is raw and must be cooked before eating. Its aroma is subtle and the taste is smooth and gentle.

Rice flour can be used to thicken sauces or fillings, or to give structure to doughs and batters. It is soft and slightly grainy when used to thicken sauces, elastic in doughs, and adds crispness to batters. Japanese mochi flour is ground from sticky rice. Mochiko Blue Star Brand Sweet Rice Flour can be found in Asian markets and works well to thicken pastry cream and other fillings. Store in an airtight jar and use within 4 months or freeze.

RICE MILK: This is a milky liquid processed mostly from brown rice. Its natural sweetness comes from the natural enzymatic process that breaks down the carbohydrates into sugar, especially glucose. It is an alternative to dairy and soy products for people with allergies and may be substituted (with varying results) for milk in many baking recipes.

English Millionaire's Shortbread

If you can't actually be a millionaire, you can at least eat like one. This luxurious British shortbread consists of three delicious layers: a buttery shortbread, smooth milky caramel, and chocolate. Biting into one of these delectable bars is like enjoying both a cookie and a candy bar at the same time. The confection starts with a baked shortbread base made with rice flour to make it crumbly and tender. Next comes a layer of dulce de leche (Spanish milk caramel) thickened and smoothed with sweet butter. The top layer is a combination of bittersweet chocolate and a little butter to help it shine, even when refrigerated. If you can resist eating them, make these bars a day ahead to give the flavors time to mellow.

YIELD: 16 SQUARES

Shortbread

¼ pound (1 cup minus 1 tablespoon) unbleached all-purpose flour

2 ounces (½ cup) rice flour

1 teaspoon fine sea salt

6 ounces (1½ sticks) unsalted butter, softened

¼ cup sugar

1 teaspoon vanilla extract

Filling

¼ cup milk, chilled

2 tablespoons potato starch, substitute corn, wheat, or rice starch

1 cup homemade Dulce de Leche (page 566), or 7-ounce block Dulce de Leche, such as Goya

¼ pound (1 stick) unsalted butter, softened

Topping

6 ounces bittersweet chocolate chopped

¼ cup hot coffee

2 tablespoons (1 ounce) unsalted butter, at room temperature

Chocolate decors, for garnish

Make the shortbread: Preheat the oven to 350°F. Line a 9-inch square baking pan with parchment or wax paper (so you can remove the shortbread.)

Whisk together the dry ingredients: flour, rice flour, and salt.

In the bowl of a standing mixer fitted with the paddle attachment, cream the butter and sugar until light and fluffy, 5 to 6 minutes, scraping down the sides once or twice. Beat in the vanilla, then add the flour mix and beat just until the dough comes together to form a dough ball. Lightly flour your hands so the dough doesn't stick, then press the dough onto the bottom of the pan, smoothing it out with the palm of your hand.

Bake for 20 minutes, or until the shortbread is pale golden in color. Remove from the oven and place on a wire rack to cool to room temperature while you make the filling.

Make the filling: If you are using a homemade Dulce de Leche, combine the milk and starch in a small bowl and whisk to make a slurry.

Place the dulce de leche in a small pot and heat over low heat until it melts. Whisk in the slurry and heat until bubbling and thick, 2 to 3 minutes. Remove from the heat and beat in the butter. Transfer the mixture to a bowl, preferably stainless steel, and cool by placing over a second bowl filled with a mixture of ice and water, stirring often.

If you are using packaged firm dulce de leche, cut the block into cubes and microwave it at low power for 5 to 6 minutes, then stir until smooth. If there are any lumps, place it back in the microwave and heat at low power for 2 to 3 minutes. Remove from the microwave and cool to lukewarm. Place the dulce de leche in the bowl of a standing mixer fitted with the paddle attachment, add the butter, and beat until smooth and creamy, 2 to 3 minutes. Cool to room temperature.

Spread the dulce de leche over the shortbread.

Make the topping: Place the chocolate, coffee, and butter in a microwaveable bowl and heat in the microwave on lowest power for 2 minutes at a time, or until just barely melted. Whisk until smooth and cool until the chocolate is thick enough to hold its shape, then pour over the dulce de leche. It will be cool to the touch but not cold. Sprinkle with chocolate decors, and chill until set, about 1 hour in the refrigerator.

Cut the shortbread into 16 squares using a sharp knife dipped into hot water and wiped dry in between each slice. Store the shortbread, covered and refrigerated, up to one week.

Frangelico Mousse Cake with Gianduia–Rice Crunch

Make this killer cake when you want to serve a really extravagant dessert. Starting from the bottom up, the milk chocolate hazelnut confection called gianduia *is mixed with chopped and toasted hazelnuts and puffed rice cereal to make a candy-bar layer. Next comes a layer of the light sponge cake called* genoise, *here thickened with rice flour and dark cocoa and enriched with hazelnut oil. Once baked, the cake is moistened with Frangelico liqueur. A super-creamy layer of gianduia mousse comes next, topped by another layer of cake. The cake is then covered with a coffee-flavored chocolate ganache icing. Wow! Although there are several components to be made here, this cake can be made one to two days ahead of time. Just cover and store refrigerated. This recipe is gluten-free (be sure to check the ingredients on the cereal).*

YIELD: ONE 9-INCH CAKE, 10 TO 12 SERVINGS

Cake

1½ ounces (¼ cup plus 2 tablespoons) rice flour

1½ ounces (½ cup) Dutch process cocoa

½ teaspoon fine sea salt

4 large eggs

¾ cup light brown sugar

¼ cup hazelnut oil, substitute Clarified Butter (page 202), melted and kept warm

1 tablespoon coffee extract or finely ground espresso coffee

1 teaspoon vanilla extract

¼ cup Frangelico liqueur, substitute dark rum or brandy

Gianduia–Rice Crunch

½ pound Gianduia, purchased or homemade (page 508), chopped

¼ pound (1 cup) hazelnuts, toasted, skinned, and finely chopped

1 cup puffed rice cereal (such as Rice Krispies)

Mousse and Glaze

½ pound Gianduia, purchased or homemade (page 508), chopped

1 cup heavy cream

2 ounces (½ cup) hazelnuts, toasted, skinned, and finely chopped, for garnish

Make the cake: Preheat the oven to 350°F. Spray a 9-inch cake pan with nonstick baker's coating or rub with butter and dust with flour, shaking off the excess.

Sift the flour, cocoa, and salt together.

In a the bowl of a standing mixer, combine the eggs and light brown sugar. In a pot that is about the same diameter or a bit smaller than the bowl of the mixer, boil about 1-inch of water. Place the mixing bowl over the boiling water and whisk the eggs and sugar until the mixture is evenly hot to the touch and reads 150°F on a thermometer, about 5 minutes. Immediately transfer the bowl to the standing mixer and beat with the whisk attachment until the mixture is very light and thick, and has cooled to room temperature, about 8 minutes. Fold in the flour mixture in thirds, so as not to deflate the batter.

In a medium bowl, combine the hazelnut oil, coffee extract, and vanilla. Add 1 cup of the cake batter and fold it in with a silicone spatula. Gently fold this mixture into the remaining cake batter. Scrap the batter into the pan, shaking back and forth to smooth the top.

Bake for 25 minutes, or until the cake starts to come away from the sides of the pan and the top springs back slightly when gently pressed. Cool completely in the pan on a wire rack. Using a serrated knife, cut the cake horizontally into two layers.

Make the crunch: Line the bottom of a 9-inch removable bottom or springform cake pan with a circle of parchment or wax paper. Place the gianduia into a microwaveable bowl and melt over low power for 2 minutes at a time, until just barely melted. Fold in the hazelnuts and the rice cereal. Spread the crunch evenly over the bottom of the pan. Immediately place one cake layer, cut side down, on top of the crunch layer, pressing

gently so it adheres. Brush the cake with 2 tablespoons of the Frangelico. Chill while making the mousse layer.

Make the mousse layer: Place the gianduia in a medium microwaveable bowl and heat over low power for 2 minutes at a time until just barely melted.

Place the cream in a small microwaveable bowl or a Pyrex measure and microwave for 1 to 2 minutes on high power until steaming hot. Whisk the cream into the gianduia until the mixture is smooth.

Transfer one half of the mixture to the clean bowl of a standing mixer. Set the other half of the mixture aside to cool at room temperature until it is thick enough to hold its shape, but is still pourable. This will be the glaze.

Place the standing mixer bowl over a second bowl filled with a mixture of ice and water, and whisk occasionally until the mixture is cold to the touch, but still liquid. Transfer the bowl to the mixer and, using the whisk attachment, beat just until soft peaks form and the mousse is firm enough to hold its shape about 2 minutes taking care not to overbeat. Spread the mousse evenly over the cake in the pan. Cover with the top layer of the cake and brush with the remaining 2 tablespoons Frangelico. Cover and chill for at least 2 hours, or until the mousse is firm. (The cake can be prepared 2 days ahead at this point, keeping it refrigerated.)

Run an icing spatula between the cake and the pan sides to loosen. Carefully remove the pan sides from the cake; smoothing the sides with the icing spatula. Place the cake on a wire rack set over a baking pan. Pour the glaze over top and use an icing spatula to smooth the top and sides. If the glaze has gotten too cold, warm it in the microwave for 1 minute on lowest power until it is barely pourable, then whisk until smooth.

Place the hazelnuts in a small bowl. Hold the cake in one hand and use the other hand to scoop up a small handful of hazelnuts and pat them onto the sides of the cake, about 1 to 2 inches up from the bottom. Try to keep your hand from touching the chocolate ganache. Place the cake on a decorative platter and chill for 30 minutes or until the icing has set. Cut into serving portions using a knife rinsed under hot water and wiped dry in between each cut. Store covered and refrigerated up to 3 days.

Calas
(New Orleans Rice Fritters)

I was surprised when I couldn't find a recipe for the famous rice fritters called calas *in my facsimile edition of the great classic of Creole cooking, the 1901 edition of* The Picayune Creole Cook Book. *Perhaps it is because calas were street food, eaten for breakfast with hot coffee or café au lait, and not made in the home at all. Fresh, hot fritters were peddled by African American street vendors in the city's French Quarter, with the cry, "Calas, bels calas Madame, tout chauds!" ("Calas, beautiful calas, Madam, all hot"). For the best airy, slightly tangy fritters, start the batter at least 4 hours ahead, preferably overnight, and allow another hour the next day to rise the batter again just before frying. Peanut oil and rice bran oil have very high smoking points, so they work well for light and greaseless deep-frying. Serve the calas with strong, hot coffee, flavored with chicory, New Orleans style.*

YIELD: ABOUT 24 FRITTERS

1 teaspoon fine sea salt

$1/2$ cup long-grain rice

$1/2$ cup sugar

1 ($1/4$-ounce) package ($2^{1}/_{2}$ teaspoons) active dry yeast

$1/4$ pound (1 cup minus 1 tablespoon) unbleached all-purpose flour

$1/2$ teaspoon freshly grated nutmeg

2 large eggs

$1/2$ cup milk

1 teaspoon vanilla extract

1 quart rice bran oil, for frying, substitute peanut or canola oil

Confectioners' sugar, for dusting

In a small pot, bring $1^{1}/_{2}$ cups of water to a boil. Add the salt and rice, and bring to another boil. Reduce the heat to a simmer, cover, and cook until the rice is soft and slightly mushy, about 30 minutes. Cool to lukewarm.

In a small bowl, combine $1/2$ cup water, the sugar, and yeast, and allow the mixture to bubble about 10 minutes at warm room temperature. Stir in the rice, cover the bowl with plastic wrap, and leave at room temperature for at least 4 hours, or until light and bubbling.

Mash the rice against the sides of the bowl with a wooden spoon to break it up into smaller bits, but don't make it mushy. (At this point, you may continue cover and refrigerate the rice mixture to use the next day.)

In a small bowl, whisk together the flour and nutmeg.

In a medium bowl, lightly beat the eggs, milk, and vanilla. Fold in the flour mixture and the rice mixture. The batter should be a bit thicker than pancake batter.

Cover with plastic wrap and allow the batter to rise at warm room temperature until puffy, about 1 hour.

In a wok, a large heavy-duty frying pan, preferably cast-iron, or an electric deep-fryer, heat the oil to 365°F, or until shimmering hot, and the air above the pot feels hot when you hold your hand about 3 inches above the oil. Drop the batter by tablespoonfuls into the oil and cook, turning, until golden brown on both sides, about 3 minutes, working in several batches. Drain on a wire rack placed over another pan to catch the drips and keep warm in a 200°F oven while preparing the remaining calas. Sprinkle the fritters generously with confectioners' sugar before serving.

FROM AFRICA TO BAHIA AND NEW ORLEANS

I was lucky enough to visit Bahia, Brazil, some years back, where I sampled the savory black-eyed pea fritters called *acarajé*, sold by women in traditional all white lace blouses and skirts with African-style head wraps. I just knew these fritters had a connection to the calas of New Orleans, especially when I read that originally calas were also made from black-eyed peas. Eventually, the black-eyed pea calas evolved into New Orleans-style calas made from rice grown in the region. As it turns out, the names for calas and acarajé both derive from several African languages: the Nupe *kárá*, for fried cake, the Yoruba for *akara*, (which became *acarajé* in Bahia) for ground bean cake, and from the Bantu *kada* to fry.

Turkish Goat's Milk Rice Pudding (Sutlaç)

My Turkish friend's mother Senay Ornek gets her goat's milk fresh from the farm whenever she makes this soft, light pudding. I visited the goat farm near her home to pick up our supply of milk for the pudding. Along with several playful goats wandering in a nearby field, the farmer also kept pigeons and chickens, grew lots of fresh herbs, and various kinds of squash. A lush grape arbor and a tree full of tiny plums provided shade and tree-ripened fruit, Sutlaç was the classic moist and creamy rice pudding made for the sultans in the Ottoman Palace kitchens, and is usually flavored with mastic or rosewater. Cinnamon and vanilla make excellent substitutes. The dark brown or even burnt crust on top is considered by many to be the best part. This recipe is gluten-free.

YIELD: 8 TO 12 SERVINGS

Fine sea salt

$^3/_4$ cup short to medium-grain rice, such as Turkish Baldo, Italian Arborio, or Spanish bomba

1 quart goat's milk

1$^1/_2$ cups sugar

1 teaspoon crushed mastic, substitute 1-inch section cinnamon stick

1 teaspoon rosewater, substitute 1 teaspoon vanilla extract

2 ounces ($^1/_2$ cup) rice flour

$^1/_2$ cup superfine sugar, for glazing

In a medium bowl, soak the rice in cold water to cover for 30 minutes; drain and rinse.

In a medium, heavy-bottomed, nonreactive pot that holds about 3 quarts, bring 1½ cups of lightly salted water to a boil. Add the rice, cover the pot, and lower the heat to low. (If you are using the cinnamon stick, add it to the pot.) Simmer for about 25 minutes, or until the rice is soft and has absorbed the water. (If using the cinnamon stick, discard after the 25 minutes.)

Stir in the milk, sugar, and mastic, rosewater, and a little more salt .

Whisk together the rice flour and ¼ cup cold water to make a thin paste, then slowly pour it into the pudding while beating constantly. Raise the heat to moderate and bring to a boil, stirring often with a wooden spoon or silicone spatula until the pudding thickens and you see bubbles on the surface, about 5 minutes. Reduce the heat to low and simmer for 20 minutes, stirring often, or until the pudding is thick and creamy. Turn the heat off and allow the pudding to cool for about 10 minutes or until thickened enough to hold its shape.

Ladle the pudding into 8 to 12 shallow ovenproof ramekins. Cool to room temperature. Meanwhile, preheat the broiler to high.

Sprinkle 1 to 2 tablespoons of superfine sugar evenly on top of each portion. Arrange the bowls on a baking sheet and place on the upper rack of the oven. Broil for 3 to 4 minutes or until the tops form a deep brown skin. Allow the puddings to cool to room temperature and serve, or chill in the refrigerator and serve cold. Store, covered and refrigerated, up to 3 days.

Note: Superfine sugar caramelizes quicker and more evenly, though granulated sugar may be substituted.

TURKISH BALDO RICE

This excellent medium-grain rice is grown in Piedmont, Italy, and in Turkey. Its grains are stickier than other varieties of rice that are often used for risotto, such as Arborio, Carnaroli, and Vialone Nano. Limited quantities of Baldo rice are now being cultivated in the United States. Baldo, imported from Turkey can be ordered from a number of online Turkish food stores. (Pirinç is an excellent brand.) It is an outstanding choice for this rice pudding.

CREAMY RICE PUDDING

What makes rice pudding creamy? Of the three main types of rice–short, medium, and long grain–the one you choose for your pudding will affect the outcome. The key is the type of starch, which acts as a thickener in the pudding. Plants store glucose sugars as starch–sugar molecules hooked together to make bigger molecules–in either long, straight chains (amylose), or small, branched shapes (amylopectin). When amylose has been heated, it thickens. When it cools and dries, it forms hard crystals. Long-grain rice has more amylase than medium- or short-grain rice, so, if you use long-grain rice for pudding, it can become hard when chilled. Medium- or short-grain rice are your best bets for pudding.

Crostata di Riso:
Italian Rice Tart

Whether it's called a crostata *(same derivation as the word "crust") or a* torta *(meaning "cake" or "pie"), this creamy rice tart is a winner. The crostata is flavored with lemon zest, almonds, and the small, crunchy, apricot-pit macaroons called* Amaretti di Saronno, *along with amaretto liqueur, and a bit of almond extract to give to the filling that slight edge of bitter almond. If you happen to have some leftover Turkish Hazelnut Macaroons (page 504), use them instead of the amaretti.*

YIELD: 8 TO 10 SERVINGS

$^3/_4$ pound Pasta Frolla dough (page 62)

4 cups whole milk

$^3/_4$ cup sugar

1 teaspoon fine sea salt

Grated zest of 1 lemon (1 tablespoon)

1 cup Arborio rice, or other short grain

6 large Amaretti di Saronno cookies or
  other macaroons, crumbled

6 ounces (about 1 cup) whole blanched almonds,
  lightly toasted and chopped

2 large egg whites, at room temperature

3 large eggs

$^1/_4$ cup amaretto liqueur

1 teaspoon almond extract

On a lightly floured surface, roll out the dough to a 13-inch round, about $^3/_8$-inch thick. Transfer to a 10-inch tart pan with a removable bottom. Press into the pan without stretching the dough, pressing well into the corners so there are no thick spots. Trim any overhang. Chill the crust for 30 minutes to relax the gluten and so it maintains its shape well.

Preheat the oven to 350°F. Fit a piece of heavy-duty foil onto the crust and fill with beans or other pie weights. Place the crust on a baking pan to catch any drips. Blind bake (just crust, no filling) on the bottom shelf of the oven until the crust is cooked but not yet browned, about 20 minutes. Remove the foil and the weights, reduce the oven temperature to 325°F, and bake for 10 minutes longer, or until the dough is evenly and lightly browned. Remove from the oven and cool to room temperature on a wire rack before filling.

In a medium heavy-bottomed saucepan, combine the milk, $^1/_4$ cup of the sugar, the salt, and the lemon zest, and bring to a boil over medium heat. Add the rice, reduce the heat to low, and simmer, uncovered and stirring occasionally, until the rice is tender and the milk has been absorbed, about 40 minutes.

Transfer the rice to a large bowl, and cool to room temperature, stirring often to prevent a skin from forming.

Mix the amaretti and almonds into the cooled rice.

In the clean and greaseless bowl of a standing mixer fitted with the whisk attachment, beat the egg whites until fluffy, then add $^1/_4$ cup sugar and continue beating until the whites are firm and glossy, 4 to 5 minutes. Fold the meringue into the rice mixture in thirds so as not to deflate.

Preheat the oven to 375°F. Without cleaning out the mixer (it's not necessary), beat the eggs with the remaining $^1/_4$ cup of sugar until they are light and fluffy, 5 to 6 minutes. Fold into the rice mixture along with the amaretto liqueur and almond extract. Pour the batter into the prepared pan, shaking pan lightly to distribute batter evenly. Place the pan on the bottom shelf of the oven, and bake for 35 minutes, or the until top of cake is golden brown and a skewer inserted in the center comes out clean. Cool on a wire rack to room temperature before unmolding. (The cake can be prepared up to a day ahead. Let cool, cover, and refrigerate. Bring to room temperature before serving.)

RYE

Maslin Bread . . . 782

Pain Bouilli . . . 782

Rye and St. Anthony's Fire . . . 783

Working with Rye Flour . . . 783

RYE AND ROSEMARY
BREADSTICKS WITH LEMON . . . 783

SAUERKRAUT RYE BREAD . . . 784

POTATO-RYE PIZZA DOUGH . . . 786

ALPINE MUSHROOM PIZZA WITH
POTATO-RYE DOUGH . . . 787

GRAPE, GORGONZOLA, AND
WALNUT FOCACCIA . . . 788

DUTCH SPECULAAS WITH RYE . . . 789

Tips for Molded Speculaas . . . 790

History of Speculaas . . . 791

RYE

The Roman naturalist, Pliny the Elder, wrote that rye "is a very poor food and only serves to avert starvation." Even after rye is mixed with wheat, he says, "to mitigate its bitter taste . . . even then [it] is most unpleasant to the stomach." I have to disagree. One of the most satisfying aspects of working on this book was discovering the robust flavors of often disdained grains, like oats, barley, and rye, and using these grains in interesting ways.

When I think of rye, I taste the chewy, tangy, caraway-topped Jewish rye bread, Russian black bread covered with pyramid-shaped charnushka seeds (or nigella), swirled marble rye bread, and dense sour corn rye from the bakeries of my youth in Washington, DC, and New York City. Rye bread was such a constant in my house, when I visited a friend's house where they had soft, sliced, and crustless white bread, I would eat it like candy. But rye bread spread with sweet whipped butter is still my benchmark of what good bread should be.

While working on this book, I came to realize how much flavor and texture rye flour, especially dark rye, can add to bread, pizza, and even cookie doughs. I still haven't attempted to make my own real Jewish rye because the process is so complex—with a three-stage sourdough starter—and requires the use of *altus*, soaked and squeezed out bits of stale sour rye bread. I'm getting ready to try my hand at it, though.

Starting somewhere around the fifth century, rye has been cultivated in Central and Eastern Europe and Western Russia. It is the main bread grain east of France and north of Hungary. The early history of rye is unclear, as its wild ancestor has not been identified with certainty. Cultivated rye, *Secale cereale*, could have originated either from wild rye found in southern Europe and nearby parts of Asia, or from wild rye found in Syria, Armenia, Iran, and Turkestan.

At first, rye was a weed that originally grew in wheat and barley fields in southern Asia. It had apparently evolved along with wheat and barley for over 2,000 years until its value as a crop was recognized. Domesticated rye has been found at a number of Neolithic sites in Turkey, but is not found in central Europe until the Bronze Age (1800 to 1500 BCE). It is possible that rye traveled west from Turkey with wheat, and was only later cultivated on its own, much the same as with oats.

Rye breads, including dark pumpernickel, are widely eaten in Northern and Eastern Europe, and rye is also used to make Scandinavian crisp bread. In Europe, dark bread made from cheaper rye was long a food of the poor as white bread made from wheat was a food of the rich. In medieval times, more expensive wheat was grown in soil fertilized by generous amounts of manure, and the poor, who did not have animals to produce the manure, grew barley, oats, and rye instead.

The venerable French *pain d'épices* (spice bread), another type of gingerbread, is made with a combination of rye and other flours, along with sweet, fragrant spices, and honey for sweetening. By 1571, the bakers of pain d'épices won the right to their own guild, or professional organization, separate from the other pastry cooks and bakers. Dijon, Reims, and Paris are all noted for their pains d'épices, then and now a favorite at holiday time. Dutch speculaas cookies (page 789), originally made entirely with rye flour, date from the same time.

As France and England got wealthier, wheat displaced rye. The same thing is happening today in the Baltics and elsewhere in the former Soviet Union. Rye breads were once the basic fare of Poland and Lithuania also centers of Jewish baking traditions. The large waves of Jewish immigrants in the late nineteenth and early twentieth centuries from Eastern Europe and the former Soviet Union brought along their penchant for rye breads, eespecially to the cities of the Northeast.

Rye grain was first brought to the New World by English and Dutch settlers to the northeastern United States. Probably the best known uses of rye in America are in rye whiskey, Jewish-style rye bread, and German-style pumpernickel bread. Today, the leading states in rye production are South Dakota, Georgia, Nebraska, North Dakota, and Minnesota. Less than half the rye grown in America is harvested for grain, and about half of that is used for livestock feed or exported. The rest goes into alcoholic beverages and food. The remaining rye is grown as pasture, to make hay, or as a cover crop.

The famous dark rye loaf called pumpernickel is made with a combination of rye flour and coarser rye meal and a sourdough starter. This bread has long been associated with Westphalia, Germany. The bread gets its name from the German words *pumpen*, meaning "fart", and *nickel*–or devil. A basic translation would be "devil's fart." The bread is baked at a low temperature in a steam-filled oven in covered, long narrow pans, so the bread has time to develop its sweet, dark chocolate and coffee flavors and earthy aroma without forming a crust. Lighter, chewier American-style pumpernickel breads are colored with almost burnt caramel, molasses, coffee, or cocoa, and mixed with wheat for lighter texture.

The structure of pure rye–flour breads, like traditional German pumpernickel, is formed by a network of starches, not of gluten as in wheat bread. Rye flour is low in gluten, so today it is usually combined with twenty to fifty percent wheat flour for lightness of texture. Rye also contains a higher proportion of beneficial soluble fiber than wheat, which accounts for its sticky texture in dough form.

In this chapter, the Sauerkraut Rye Bread (page 784) is dark and delicious with the tang of sauerkraut, the hot spiciness of mustard, and bittersweet flavor from molasses. Rye and Rosemary Breadsticks with Lemon (page 783) have a delicious earthy flavor from the rye, and are fragrant with lemon zest and rosemary. The same dough may be used to form handmade pretzels (great with beer, of course). Two Teutonic favorites, rye and potato, go into the surprisingly light Potato-Rye Pizza Dough (page 786) from the Southern Tyrol, the region of far Northern mountainous Italy that was once part of Austria. The dough works perfectly with the hearty flavors of the Alpine Mushroom Pizza (page 787), but it would also work beautifully with the Woodfire Grill Duck Confit Pizza (page 859). A portion of rye flour imparts robust character to the Grape, Gorgonzola, and Walnut Focaccia (page 788). The Dutch Rye Speculaas (page 789) are quite crunchy and full of mellow spices, while the deep earthy flavor of rye gives the cookies their full-bodied character mixed with wheat flour for lightness.

MASLIN BREAD

Originally, rye was just a weed that grew alongside wheat. Eventually, farmers gave up trying to separate the two, and harvested the fields as maslin. The duo of grains served as insurance against crop failure. In colder, wetter weather, the rye would thrive; in warmer, drier weather, the wheat would thrive. The two grains were ground together into flour and then made into tasty maslin bread, the rye adding sweetness and moistness, the wheat adding lightness and chewy structure.

PAIN BOUILLI

Pain Bouilli (known as *po buli* in the local dialect) is a boiled bread that comes from the tiny village of Villar d'Arène in the French Haut Alpes. The inhabitants, called *les Faranchins*, make a dough out of rye flour and boiled water only–no salt or leavening–and bake it for seven hours. From the eighteenth century until as recently as 1960, the villagers would bake their bread only once a year, in late fall. Because wood was so scarce at that high altitude, the oven was fired only once a year. The cool dry mountain air then dried out the bread so it could be kept for a whole year. These days the villagers have access to other breads, so while still they bake their traditional bread in the village oven, they keep it for months rather than a year.

RYE AND ST. ANTHONY'S FIRE

Because of its tendency toward ergot poisoning, which results from a fungus that grows on rye, it still has somewhat of a stigma. The first major outbreak of ergot poisoning was documented in 857 CE in the Rhine Valley. The disease is known as Holy Fire or St. Anthony's Fire, after men from the order of St. Anthony built hundreds of hospitals to treat victims of the disease. France became the center of many severe epidemics because the country's cool, wet climate was conducive to the development of the fungus, and rye was the staple crop of the poor.

In 1670, a French physician, Dr. Thuillier, realized that the consumption of rye infected with ergot was responsible for the disease. Although the ergot fungus, called "cockspurs" by French farmers, was well known, it had never been considered harmful. The disease occurred in Russia in 1926, with 10,000 reported cases, in England in 1927 with 200 cases among central European Jewish immigrants (who ate a lot of rye bread), and in Provence in 1951.

Despite the poisonous effects of the fungus, various beneficial medicines have been extracted from ergot, including ergonovine, used to cause contractions of the uterus during childbirth and to treat psychiatric disorders. In 1935, Albert Hofmann synthesized ergonovine at Sandoz Laboratories in Switzerland. This synthesized fungus later became widely known as the hallucinogen, LSD. Through careful screening and safer planting practices, ergotism is now rare, but unfortunately there has never been a variety of rye that has developed a resistance to the fungus.

WORKING WITH RYE FLOUR

To find bold, dark rye flour, the type I call for in these recipes, it's best to shop at a well-stocked natural foods market. You can also order it online, as I do, from Bob's Red Mill (www.bobsredmill.com). Pumpernickel flour is dark rye flour that is ground somewhat coarse than rye flour and is used for pumpernickel bread and Boston brown bread (see the recipe for Steamed Brown Bread in my *Beans: More than 200 Wholesome Delicious Recipes from Around the World.*). Light or medium rye flour may be substituted, but they are more innocuous in character.

Store rye flour in the freezer, but let it come to room temperature before using it. (You may place the flour in a microwavable bowl and heat it one minute to take the chill off quickly.) Keep in mind that doughs made with rye will inevitably be stickier than wheat doughs, so don't be alarmed.

Rye and Rosemary Breadsticks with Lemon

Rye, rosemary, and lemon may be an unexpected combination, but they complement each other quite well in these light, crunchy breadsticks from Italy's Alpine region. The dough is easy to roll by hand into long, thin sticks. A fresh lemony undertone marries well with piney rosemary to produce an intriguing addition to any picnic basket, buffet table, or formal dinner. Form the sticks into pretzels shapes, or wrap them in Fontina cheese, pro-

sciutto, or bresaola and serve as bocconcini (small bites) with a glass of Piedmontese Barbera or Barbaresco.

YIELD: 30 BREADSTICKS

10 ounces (2$\frac{1}{2}$ cups minus 2$\frac{1}{2}$ tablespoons)
    unbleached all-purpose flour

$\frac{1}{2}$ pound (1$\frac{3}{4}$ cups) dark rye flour

2 teaspoons fine sea salt

$\frac{1}{2}$ teaspoon baking soda

1 ($\frac{1}{4}$-ounce) package (2$\frac{1}{2}$ teaspoons) active dry yeast

2 tablespoons light molasses, not blackstrap

$\frac{1}{2}$ cup lukewarm water

$\frac{1}{2}$ cup fresh lemon juice (from about 3 lemons)

Grated zest of 2 lemons (2 tablespoons)

2 tablespoons finely chopped fresh rosemary

2 tablespoons grapeseed or canola oil

1 large egg

Cornmeal, for sprinkling

2 egg whites, lightly beaten with 2 tablespoon
    water, for egg wash

Pretzel or kosher salt, for sprinkling

In a medium bowl, whisk together the flour, rye flour, salt, and baking soda.

In the bowl of a standing mixer fitted with the paddle attachment, combine the yeast, molasses, and water. Stir in about 1 cup of the flour mixture and allow the mixture to proof in a warm place for about 30 minutes, or until bubbling and puffy. Add the lemon juice, zest, rosemary, oil, and egg, and beat well. Beat in the remaining flour mixture and continue beating until the dough comes together and is elastic, and mostly comes away from the sides of the bowl, 4 to 5 minutes. (The dough will still be sticky because of the rye flour.) Transfer the dough to a large oiled bowl; turn around so the dough is oiled all over. Cover with plastic wrap and allow the dough to rise at warm room temperature until doubled in size, about 2 hours.

Punch the dough down and turn it out onto a lightly floured work surface. Divide the dough into 30 pieces. Using the palms of your hands, roll each piece into a stick about 12 inches long. (You will have a more even-looking stick if you place the dough on a firm surface and roll your hands across the top, moving from the center outward.) Arrange the sticks 1 inch apart on baking pans that have been lightly sprinkled with cornmeal. Brush them lightly with egg wash and sprinkle lightly with salt. Allow the sticks to rise in a warm place for 15 minutes or until soft and puffy.

Preheat the oven to 350°F.

Bake the sticks for 30 minutes, or until well browned. Cool to room temperature on a wire rack. Store the breadsticks in a covered container at room temperature for up to 1 week. Rewarm them in a 300°F oven for about 20 minutes.

Sauerkraut Rye Bread

While this is the only recipe in this book using sauerkraut, the unexpected ingredient makes for a wonderfully chewy bread. It is dark and slightly sharp, with a nice sour aftertaste, and a slight sweetness from the rye and molasses. I prefer to use fresh bag-packed sauerkraut like

Kissing's, made in Philadelphia since 1949, rather than the cooked sauerkraut packed in cans. This loaf makes the best bread for pastrami or corned beef sandwiches and is even better for Reuben sandwiches.

YIELD: ONE 2¼-POUND LOAF

³⁄₄ pound (3 cups) unbleached bread flour

6 ounces (1¼ cups plus 1 tablespoon) dark rye flour

¼ pound (1 cup plus 2 tablespoons) white whole wheat flour

1 tablespoon ground caraway seed

2 teaspoons fine sea salt

2 (¼-ounce) packages (5 teaspoons) active dry yeast

³⁄₄ cup lukewarm water

¼ cup light molasses, not blackstrap

Cornmeal or semolina

¼ pound (³⁄₄ cup) sauerkraut, drained and finely chopped (juices reserves)

¼ cup grapeseed, canola, or olive oil

2 tablespoons Dijon mustard

1 egg white, lightly beaten with 2 tablespoons water, for the egg wash, or 2 tablespoons Shiny Cornstarch Glaze (page 393)

1 tablespoon nigella seeds or whole caraway seed, for sprinkling

Whisk together the dry ingredients: bread flour, rye flour, white whole wheat flour, ground caraway, and salt.

In the bowl of a standing mixer fitted with the paddle attachment, combine the yeast, water, and molasses. Stir in about 1 cup of the flour mixture and allow the mixture to proof in a warm place for about 20 minutes, or until bubbling and puffy. Sprinkle a large baking pan with cornmeal or semolina.

In a medium bowl, combine the sauerkraut, ½ cup of the sauerkraut juice, the oil, and mustard. Add to the yeast mixture and beat briefly to combine. Add the remaining flour mixture and beat to combine. Switch to the dough hook and continue beating until the dough is smooth and elastic and forms a sticky, shaggy mass that mostly comes away from the sides of the bowl. Transfer the dough to a large oiled bowl; turn around so the dough is oiled all over. Cover with plastic wrap or a damp cloth and allow the dough to rise at warm room temperature until doubled in size, about 2 hours. Punch the dough down. (At this point, you may cover and refrigerate the dough overnight. Allow it to come to room temperature before proceeding with the recipe.)

Using a rolling pin and sprinkling the dough with a little flour if it is too sticky, flatten the dough into a large rectangle about ³⁄₄-inch thick. Square the edges by pushing the ends toward the middle. Roll into a tight log, sealing at each turn with the heel of your hand and squaring the ends off. Place the loaf, seam side down, on the baking pan that has been lined with a silicone baking mat or a sheet of parchment paper. Brush with egg wash and sprinkle with nigella or caraway seeds. Using a French baker's lame, a single-edged razor, or a box cutter, cut 5 or 6 shallow diagonal slashes across the loaf. Mist the loaf with water from a plant sprayer and allow the loaf to rise again at warm room temperature until almost doubled in bulk, about 2 hours.

Preheat oven to 425°F. Place the bread in the oven, reduce the oven temperature to 375°F and bake for 40 minutes or until the bread sounds hollow when tapped on the bottom and a thermometer inserted in the center reads 205°F. Cool completely on a wire rack before slicing. Store in an open plastic bag at room temperature for up to 3 days, or wrap well and freeze up to 3 months.

Potato-Rye Pizza Dough

This unusual pizza dough comes from the far north of Italy in the part called the Southern Tyrol, where German ingredients like potatoes, rye, and beer are common. The potatoes provide moistness and lightness while the rye gives an earthy, hearty flavor and darker color to the dough, and the beer helps it rise. Like professional bakers, you may substitute three-quarters of a cup of reconstituted packaged mashed potatoes for the fresh potatoes here.

YIELD: ABOUT 1$\frac{1}{2}$ POUNDS DOUGH, ENOUGH FOR TWO 12-INCH PIZZAS

2 teaspoons fine sea salt

6 ounces Russet potatoes, peeled and cut into large chunks

10 ounces (2$\frac{1}{2}$ cups minus 2$\frac{1}{2}$ tablespoons) unbleached all-purpose flour

$\frac{1}{4}$ pound (1 cup minus 2 tablespoons) dark rye flour

1 ($\frac{1}{4}$-ounce) package (2$\frac{1}{2}$ teaspoons) active dry yeast

6 tablespoons (3 ounces) lukewarm milk

$\frac{1}{4}$ cup beer

2 tablespoons extra-virgin olive oil

Bring a medium pot of water to a boil.. Add 1 teaspoon of the salt and the potatoes and boil until tender, about 15 minutes. Drain and mash the potatoes.

Whisk together the dry ingredients: flour, rye flour, and the remaining 1 teaspoon of salt.

In the bowl of a standing mixer fitted with the paddle attachment, combine the yeast, milk, and beer. Beat briefly, then allow the mixture to proof in a warm place for about 15 minutes, or until bubbling and puffy. Beat in the olive oil, potato, and flour mixture. Switch to the dough hook and continue beating until the dough is smooth and elastic. Transfer the dough to a large oiled bowl; cover with plastic wrap or a damp cloth and allow the dough to rise until doubled in size, about 2 hours, at warm room temperature.

The dough may be made one day, allowed to partially rise, then refrigerated overnight for use the following day or even punched down again and kept chilled for use the second day. Allow the dough to come to room temperature before rolling or stretching into a circle or tongue shape.

Divide the dough into 2 portions and form into smooth rounds. Roll out or stretch out by hand into the desired size: 12 to 14 inches is common. Note that this dough freezes well. Allow it to come to room temperature before rolling or stretching out.

Alpine Mushroom Pizza with Potato-Rye Dough

Wild mushrooms are avidly sought after in the forests of Alpine Italy, where this pizza comes from. Here Italian Fontina from the high Val d'Aosta in Italy and an assortment of wild or exotic cultivated mushrooms top a pizza made from the dark and delicious Potato-Rye Pizza Dough. Top the pizza with white or black truffle oil. Although fresh white truffles are very expensive, if you have the chance to use the intoxicatingly aromatic truffles, do so. Of course, you may half the recipe and make one pizza at a time. Defrost the dough, overnight in the refrigerator if you'd like, and allow it to come to room temperature before proceeding with the recipe.

YIELD: TWO 12-INCH PIZZAS, 4 TO 8 SERVINGS

Topping

6 ounces imported Italian Fontina, trimmed

$\frac{1}{4}$ cup extra virgin olive oil

2 medium red onions, thinly sliced

2 teaspoons finely chopped rosemary

2 teaspoons finely chopped sage

2 teaspoons finely chopped thyme

1 pound crimini mushrooms, trimmed and sliced

4 cloves garlic, thinly sliced

Fine sea salt and freshly ground black pepper

Assembly

Cornmeal, for sprinkling

1$\frac{1}{2}$ pounds Potato-Rye Pizza Dough (page 786)

$\frac{1}{2}$ cup (2 ounces) grated Parmigiano-Reggiano

or Grana Padano cheese

2 tablespoons (or more, if desired) white or

black truffle oil, for sprinkling

2 tablespoons chopped flat-leaf parsley, for garnish

Freeze the cheese until firm, about 20 minutes, then shred it.

In a large skillet over medium-high heat, heat 2 tablespoons of the olive oil, then add the onions and sauté, stirring often, until the onions are soft and just beginning to brown, about 4 minutes. Transfer the onions to a bowl and stir in the herbs, reserving the skillet. Add the remaining 2 tablespoons of olive oil to the skillet, the mushrooms, and the garlic, and sauté until the mushrooms are soft and just beginning to brown, about 4 minutes. Season with salt and pepper and set aside.

Preheat the oven to 500°F. Sprinkle two 12-inch pizza pans (or other large baking pans) lightly with cornmeal.

Punch down the dough and divide it into two portions. Roll each portion into a smooth ball. Roll out the dough on a lightly floured work surface or stretch it out by hand to fit into the pans. Sprinkle the Fontina cheese onto the dough then top with dollops of the onions and mushrooms. Sprinkle with Parmigiano cheese.

Bake both pizzas about for 10 minutes, or until bubbling and well browned, switching the positions and directions of the pans halfway through baking. Remove from the oven and sprinkle with truffle oil and chopped parsley. Cut the pizzas into 8-wedges each and serve immediately. To reheat, wrap the pizza in aluminum foil and bake at 375°F for 15 minutes.

Grape, Gorgonzola, and Walnut Focaccia

In this recipe, red grapes, potent but lusciously creamy Italian Gorgonzola, and soft-textured walnuts top soft, light, and earthy part-rye focaccia. Red globe grapes would be fabulous here, though they do have pits. In their short fall season, inky blue Concord grapes bake up dark and sweet. While any blue cheese will work, genuine Italian Gorgonzola has a full-bodied flavor and super-creamy texture that really works here to balance the sweetness of the grapes. Its funky character balances the robust, slightly bitter flavor of the rye.

YIELD: 1 LARGE RECTANGULAR FOCACCIA, 12 TO 16 SERVINGS

$3/4$ pound ($3^3/4$ cups) unbleached all-purpose flour

$1/4$ pound (1 cup minus 2 tablespoons) dark rye flour

2 teaspoons fine sea salt

1 ($1/4$-ounce) package ($2^1/2$ teaspoons) active dry yeast

$1^1/2$ cups lukewarm water

$1/4$ cup extra virgin olive oil

Freshly ground black pepper

$1/4$ pound large red grapes, halved and pitted
    if necessary

3 ounces Gorgonzola cheese, cut into small bits

3 ounces ($3/4$ cup) walnuts, roughly chopped

Line an 18 x 13-inch half sheet pan (or other large baking pan) with parchment paper or a silicone baking mat.

In a medium bowl, whisk together the dry ingredients: flour, rye flour, and salt.

In the bowl of a standing mixer fitted with the paddle attachment, combine the yeast, $1/4$ cup of the water, and $1/2$ cup of the flour mixture. Allow the mixture to rest until it is bubbling, about 15 minutes. Beat in the remaining flour mixture. Switch to the dough hook and continue beating until the mixture comes together in a rough and shaggy ball and is elastic, 5 to 6 minutes.

Transfer the dough to a large oiled bowl; cover with plastic wrap or a damp cloth and allow the dough to rise until doubled in size, about 2 hours, at warm room temperature. The dough may be made one day, allowed to partially rise, then refrigerated overnight for use the following day or even punched down again and kept chilled for use the second day. Allow the dough to come to room temperature before proceeding.

Punch down the dough and use oiled hands to press the dough into the pan without folding it over (don't worry if it doesn't reach all the way into the corners). Leave the dough to rest and rise at warm room temperature for about 1 hour, or until light and puffy. Using your index finger, poke indentations over the surface of the dough about every inch or so. Brush the dough with the remaining olive oil and grind fresh black pepper over top.

Press the grapes into the dough, leaving a 1-inch border around the edges. Sprinkle the cheese and walnuts onto the dough, then mist with water from a plant mister. Allow the focaccia to rise at warm room temperature until soft and puffy, about 30 minutes.

Preheat the oven to 425°F. Bake the focaccia for 25 minutes, or until nicely browned. Remove from the oven, cool for about 10 minutes, then remove the focaccia from the pan and cut into squares to serve.

Store loosely covered at room temperature up to 2 days or wrap tightly in aluminum foil and freeze. Reheat frozen focaccia still wrapped in foil in a pre-heated 375°F oven for about 20 minutes.

Dutch Speculaas with Rye

Called speculaas *in Holland and* speculoos *in Flanders (Flemish Belgium), these cookies are one of the oldest Dutch/Flemish culinary specialties, dating from medieval times. They were once made entirely from rye flour, but in modern times, wheat flour is added for lightness. These warmly spiced cookies, related to gingerbread cookies, are formed on specially carved wooden forms. Typically made in winter, they are associated with the feast of "Sint Nicolaas" or Saint Nicholas, the original Santa Claus. Baker's ammonia gives these cookies an extra-crisp texture, but baking powder may be substituted.*

YIELD: 18 TO 24 LARGE COOKIES

1 pound (3¾ cups) unbleached all-purpose flour

6 ounces (1¼ cups plus 1 tablespoon) dark rye flour

2 tablespoons Speculaas Spices (page 353), or pumpkin pie or apple pie spices

1 teaspoon baker's ammonia, crushed to fine powder, substitute baking powder

1 teaspoon fine sea salt

½ pound (2 sticks) unsalted butter, softened

1 pound (2¼ cups packed) light brown sugar

Grated zest of 1 lemon (1 tablespoon)

Grated zest of 1 orange (4 teaspoons)

½ pound (1¾ cups) skin-on almonds or hazelnuts, ground

2 large eggs, lightly beaten

¼ cup heavy cream

1 large egg, lightly beaten with 1 tablespoon milk, for the glaze

1 cup whole blanched almonds, for decoration, optional

Potato starch, or corn, wheat, or rice starch, for rolling

Line two 18 x 13-inch half sheet pans or other large baking sheets with parchment paper or silicone baking mats.

In a medium bowl, whisk together the dry ingredients: flour, rye flour, speculaas spices, baker's ammonia, and salt.

In the bowl of a standing mixer fitted with the paddle attachment, cream the butter, sugar, and lemon and orange zests until light and fluffy, 5 to 6 minutes. Add the almonds and flour mixture and beat briefly to combine.

Separately, combine the eggs and cream and add it gradually to the mixture, beating until the dough comes together in a ball. Transfer the dough to a plastic bag, shape into a flattened rectangle, and let it rest overnight in the refrigerator to develop the flavors.

Remove the dough from the refrigerator 30 minutes before rolling, so that the dough can soften enough to be firm but still malleable. Divide the dough into 3 or 4 sections and roll out one section at a time on a work surface lightly dusted with starch about ⅜ inch thick. (On a hot day, refrigerate the remaining sections to keep them from getting too soft.) Use either a cookie cutter or real Dutch wooden Speculaas molds to cut out and form the cookies.

If you use the mold, sprinkle the molds liberally with starch. Cut the dough into a strip a bit wider than the mold. Press the strip into the mold, making sure that the dough fills all the spaces. Form the cookies, tapping the molds upside down on the worktop to free the cookies from the mold. Trim the sides to make a neat form, and arrange the cookies on the baking pans. If using the molds, it is best to allow the cookies to rest lightly covered and at room temperature overnight to dry the surface of the dough so that the designs maintain their definition when baked. Continue, sprinkling the molds with starch each time you press fresh dough into it If using cookie cutters, cut out into the shapes and arrange on the baking pans, continuing until all the dough has been rolled out. (When using cookie cutters, it is not necessary to dry out the cookies overnight before baking.)

Preheat the oven to 375°F. Brush the cookies lightly with the egg wash. Press almonds into the cookies as desired in a decorative pattern.

Bake the cookies for 20 minutes, then reduce the oven temperature to 325°F and continue baking for 15 minutes, or until the cookies are medium brown. Cool them completely on a wire rack. Store in an airtight tin for two to three weeks.

TIPS FOR MOLDED SPECULAAS

TO PREVENT STICKING: Spray the molds with nonstick cooking spray or lightly wipe them with cooking oil.

TO MAKE MOLDED COOKIES: Roll the dough out $3/8$-inch thick. Brush confectioners' sugar or starch into the mold image, then press the dough into the mold with your fingers and working from center outward. Trim the edges with a knife or pastry wheel. Using a rolling pin, lightly roll over the back of the cookie to smooth it before turning it out of the mold.

DRYING MOLDED COOKIES: Molded cookies should be dried at least 2 and up to 24 hours before baking (depending on humidity) or until a skin develops on the surface. Drying helps preserve the image during baking. Test-bake one cookie first.

REMOVING BUBBLES: Flat areas of larger cookies can bubble up when baking. Remove the tray from the oven and, using a potholder or baker's mitt, press down by hand. Place back in the oven and continue baking.

HISTORY OF SPECULAAS

One of my most treasured possessions is an antique wooden speculaas cookie mold from Holland, dating from about 1750. The board is about two feet long, with five hand-carved images on each side. The images represent the daily life of the times, including a man holding a sign that reads, "Niews van der dag" (news of the day), a large sailing ship, children riding a horse-drawn sleigh, a girl milking a cow, a lamplighter with his ladder, a girl picking apples, and a man with a work horse.

Speculaas get their name from the Latin *speculum*, meaning mirror, because the biscuits had the carved figure of the mold shown in mirror image. Old wooden cookie molds show biblical scenes, historic events, ships, windmills, mermaids, and, of course, images of Saint Nicholas with the small children he had saved according to legend. Young singles might receive a *vrijer* or *vrijster* (male or female loved one), which could be considered a marriage proposal from the giver. These cookies are shaped into large dolls, similar to gingerbread men, and are decorated with colored icing, silver dragées, almonds, and even gold leaf.

The oldest recipes for Speculaas were made from rye flour and honey. These cookies were so hard, they could only be eaten when crumbled and soaked in liquid to make a sweet porridge. Nothing went to waste: crumbled Speculaas would be sprinkled on buttered bread for sandwiches or mixed into puddings.

SESAME SEEDS

Choosing and Storing
Sesame Products . . . 796

SESAME SPINACH BOREKAS . . . 796

Borek, Bourekas, Brik, and Boureki . . . 798

About Za'atar . . . 798

TURKISH SESAME-COATED BREAD RINGS
(SUSAMLI SIMIT) . . . 798

SPANISH SESAME-ANISE COOKIES . . . 799

SESAME HONEY CONES
WITH RICOTTA FILLING . . . 800

GREEK TAHINI CAKE (TAHINOPITA) . . . 802

SESAME SEEDS

"Open sesame" is the magic phrase in the tale of Ali Baba and the Forty Thieves from *The Thousand and One Nights*, and though there are no jewels and precious stones in this chapter, there is a treasure of recipes using sesame seeds in their many forms. The phrase "open sesame" probably comes from the tendency of the small, sausage-shaped pods of the sesame plant, *Sesamum indicum* (*indicum* means "from India"), to burst open with a pop, much like a lock springing open, and scatter their seeds when ripe. Because of this, the pods are often harvested by hand before they are fully ripe. The English word "sesame" comes from the Arabic *simsim*, and the early Egyptian *semsent*.

Sesame seeds are believed to be one of the first condiments, as well as one of the first plants, to be used for its edible oil. Sesame is an annual herb that can grow as high as seven feet. Inside the pods are tiny seeds with hulls that vary from white to yellow, tan, brown, and black according to variety, although all are white inside. The hulls are often removed because they contain a small amount of oxalic acid, which imparts a bitter flavor.

Sesame was cultivated for its oil in ancient Babylonia and is mentioned on a clay tablet dat-ing from the sixth century BCE listing the accounts at Nebuchadnezzar's palace. Sesame was also listed in the Ebers Papyrus, a 65-feet-long scroll that dates from 1550 BCE listing ancient herbs and spices named after the famous German Egyptologist, Georg Ebers. The source of the papyrus is unknown, but it was said to have been found between the legs of a mummy. The earliest recorded use of any spice comes from an Assyrian myth that the gods drank sesame wine the night before they created the earth.

The chewy, golden-yellow semolina bread sprinkled with sesame seeds and baked at neighborhood Italian bakeries in Philadelphia date back to Sicily, where the bread has been baked since ancient times. Sesame seeds and sesame oil have long been closely associated with Mizrahi (or Eastern) Jewish cooking. As a neutral (neither meat nor dairy) plant food, sesame was used for cooking, baking, and confectionery by Jews living in Palestine, Syria, Egypt, and Spanish Jews living in Turkey. Sesame tahini is a basic food in Israel today as it is in the surrounding region.

Sesame has long been grown in Persia (now Iran) and India, and was probably introduced into China from Persia early in the first millennium. The tiny tear-shaped seeds have a mild, nutty flavor that seems to be almost universally appealing. The seeds contain about fifty percent oil by weight and though growing sesame for its oil is even less productive than olives, it is a popular cooking and seasoning oil in many places, especially in the Middle East. Asian sesame oil extracted from toasted seeds is called "fragrant oil" in China and is a common savory ingredient in Korea, Japan, and the Sichuan province of China.

Sesame was cultivated from early times in Egypt and Ethiopia, but also in East and West Africa. It was from West Africa that sesame seeds traveled to the American colonies along with slaves from the same region, who called the seeds *benne*. The crisp, buttery little cookies sprinkled with the seeds called benne wafers date from the seventeenth century when the seeds were first brought to the Low Country, through the port of Charleston, a major slave market.

In the Eastern Mediterranean, close to the plant's first area of cultivation, sesame seeds are essential to cooking, as oil, tahini (crushed sesame paste), and halvah (a dense, sweetened crushed sesame seed confection). In India, where the seeds are known as *gingili* or *gingelly*, sesame is sprinkled on breads, pastries, and biscuits. In Asia, especially China and Japan, and the Middle East, sesame seeds flavor and add texture to confections and fried sweet titbits. Sesame is now grown mostly in India, China, Mexico, and the Sudan.

In this book, the chewy ring-shaped breads sold by Turkish street vendors called Susamli Simit (Turkish Sesame-Coated Bread Rings) (page 798) are rolled in sesame seeds. They top the Moroccan Sesame-Anise Bread (page 87), while the same combination of sesame and anise shows up in the Spanish Sesame-Anise Cookies (page 799). The soft, tender Turkish Ricotta Cookies with Sesame Seeds (page 272) are coated in sesame seeds. Sesame Honey Cones with Ricotta and Sun-Dried Fruits (page 800) combine the fried cannoli of Sicily with the sesame seeds and sugar syrup of North Africa. The Spanish Honey-Dipped Spiral Pastries (Hojuelas) (page 585) are sprinkled with sesame seeds, a touch that likely dates from Arabic rule of Spain. Sesame seeds also feature in the dairy-free Greek Tahini Cake (page 802), served during Lent; and the Garlic-Sesame Grissini (page 885), crispy breadsticks from Northern Italy.

Tiny sesame seeds add nutty flavor and rich, slightly crunchy to texture to the Turkish flatbread called Pide (page 900), made in many versions, including one spread with tahini and grape molasses and topped with sesame seeds. The za'atar topping for the Sesame Spinach Borekas (page 796) is a mixture of sesame seeds, za'atar herb, and ground sumac. The Egyptian Flatbread with Dukkah Sprinkle is dipped in a similar mixture of sesame seeds, herbs, and nuts. The Cigari Borekas with Moroccan Spiced Lamb (page 212) are rolled in sesame seeds before frying until crisp.

CHOOSING AND STORING SESAME PRODUCTS

SESAME OIL: Cold-pressed sesame oil is gently heated to preserve its delicate natural aromas; hot-pressed sesame oil yields greater quantities of less subtly flavorful oil. Milder cold-pressed sesame oil can be used in cakes or muffin batters that call for oil, such as the Sambuca and Candied Orange Tozzetti (page 90), the Fuji Apple Cake (page 105), the Apple-Date Buckwheat Muffins (page 188), or the Indian-Spiced Carrot Cake (page 237). With its much stronger flavor, toasted sesame oil is used for seasoning, and not generally for baking.

SESAME PASTE: In the Middle East, sesame seeds are ground and pressed into a dense paste and mixed with sweet syrup and honey to make halvah, or ground into tahini. In Asia, the seeds are roasted before being ground into much stronger tasting and darker colored sesame paste. The Turkish flat bread called *pide* is spread with tahini and the Greek Tahini Cake (Tahinopita) (page 802) relies on tahini to add structure, flavor, and richness to this vegan cake.

SESAME SEEDS: The small seeds have a nutty, slightly sweet flavor and aroma which is enhanced by toasting. Look for white (hulled) sesame seeds, the most delicate form, at specialty spice stores and Indian, Asian, and Middle Eastern markets. Look for black sesame seeds at Asian markets; look for unhulled (natural) tan sesame seeds at natural foods stores. Sesame seeds purchased in bulk can be much less expensive that those packed in spice jars. The seeds are harvested between September and April. After that time, the seeds found in the market will likely be from the new crop and will be fresher.

Sesame seeds tend to get rancid quickly, so it is best to store them refrigerated up to six months or frozen up to one year. Sesame oil, whether cold-pressed or roasted, is quite stable and will keep for years without turning rancid, even in hot climates.

To toast sesame seeds, spread them out in a light-colored baking pan and toast in a 350°F oven for about 8 minutes, shaking once or twice so they toast evenly.

Sesame Spinach Borekas

These small, savory turnovers are filled with a mixture of spinach and pine nuts and then sprinkled with the Levantine sesame seed, sumac, and herb mix called za'atar. The base dough is made with lemon juice, which lends its tart flavor and helps tenderize the dough (just like adding a teaspoon of vinegar to pie dough). Then the dough is dabbed with butter and folded many times to make a laminated (or layered dough), creating flaky perfection. This type of dough originated in Turkey, but its descendents are found in French puff pastry and croissants, Danish pastry, Middle Eastern phyllo, Moroccan ouarka, Tunisian brik, and in the layered dough in the Torta Pasqualina Genovese (page 438).

YIELD: ABOUT 36 TURNOVERS

Dough

1 pound (2 cups minus 2 tablespoons) unbleached
  all-purpose flour

2 teaspoons fine sea salt

1/2 pound (2 sticks) unsalted butter, softened

1/4 cup extra-virgin olive oil

Juice of 1 lemon

3/4 cup ice water

Filling

1 pound fresh spinach or Swiss chard, stemmed,
  or 1 pound frozen spinach, thawed

1/4 cup extra virgin olive oil

1 medium yellow onion, finely chopped

2 ounces (1/4 cup plus 1 tablespoon) fine semolina

1 large egg

1/4 cup pine nuts, lightly toasted, optional

Fine sea salt and freshly ground black pepper

1 large egg, lightly beaten with 1 tablespoon water,
  for egg wash

1/4 cup Za'atar Mix (page 798), substitute sesame seeds

Make the dough: In the bowl of a standing mixer fitted with the paddle attachment, combine the flour, salt, and 2 ounces of the butter.

Separately, in a small bowl, whisk together the olive oil, lemon juice, and water and pour it into the flour mixture. Beat until the dough comes together in moist clumps, 2 to 3 minutes. Knead the dough lightly by hand until smooth. Cover and allow the dough to rest at room temperature for 15 minutes to relax the gluten. Sprinkle a handful of flour on a work surface and roll out the dough into a large, evenly-shaped rectangles, about 3/8-inch thick. Place small dabs of the butter all over the dough.

Fold dough into thirds like a letter. Cover with plastic wrap and refrigerate for 30 minutes or until firm.

Roll out the dough again, working in the opposite direction as the first time. Fold the dough in thirds again and return to the refrigerator for 30 minutes longer. Repeat the rolling, working in the opposite direction, folding the dough in thirds, and refrigerating once more. Finally roll the dough again into a large thin rectangle about 3/8-inch thick. Chill for 30 minutes to relax the dough.

Meanwhile make the filling: Line two 18 x 13-inch half sheet pans (or other large baking pans) with parchment paper or silicone baking mats.

Place the spinach in a large microwavable bowl and moisten with 2 tablespoons of water. Microwave on high for 2 minutes to wilt the spinach, turning and heating for 1 minute longer if necessary. Run the spinach under cold water to set the color, then squeeze out all the excess water. Chop the spinach.

In a medium skillet over moderate heat, warm the oil, then add the onion and sauté until it is softened, about 3 minutes. Remove from the heat and add to the spinach, along with the semolina, egg, pine nuts, and salt and pepper to taste.

Preheat the oven to 350°F. Cut the dough into 3-inch squares. Place 1 heaping teaspoon of the filling on each square, taking care to keep it away from the edges and leaving a border all around. Fold the dough in half to form a triangle, pinching the edges to seal well. Brush each pastry with egg wash and sprinkle with the za'atar. Arrange the borekas on the pans and bake for 30 minutes or until golden brown.

Store covered and refrigerated up to 3 days. Wrap in foil and reheat in a 350°F oven for 20 minutes.

BOREK, BOUREKAS, BRIK, AND BOUREKI

Borek originated with the Turks of Central Asia and are made with yufka dough or other types of dough including phyllo and flaky yogurt pastry. The word *börek* comes from the Turkish root *bur*, meaning "to twist". Whatever their shape, borek in Turkey may be filled with feta cheese, potato, and parsley, chopped meat or sausage along with vegetables like spinach, nettles, leeks, eggplant, and zucchini. In Armenia, the pastries are called *boeregs* and are filled with cheese, spinach, or ground beef. The borek was brought to the Serbian town of Niš in 1498 by a famous Turkish baker, Mehmed Oglu, who came there from Istanbul. The town now holds an annual borek festival.

The Russian version, called *cheburek*, is made from unleavened dough and filled with ground lamb, onions, and spices, and fried in oil. This is a common street food in Russia, the Ukraine, and Georgia. In Greece, *boureki* or *bourekaki* (the diminutive form), are small pastries made with phyllo or pastry dough. All sorts of bourekas are served in Israel, often made from puff pastry, and filled with cheese, mashed potato, spinach, eggplant, and mushrooms, each in a different shape to indicate its filling. The famous Tunisian brik is another form of borek, this time a large triangle made of special brik pastry and filled with whole egg, chopped onions, and parsley, and often canned tuna and then fried until crisp.

ABOUT ZA'ATAR

In Jordan, Lebanon, Israel, and the Palestinian Territories, *za'atar* is an Arabic word that refers both to the specific herb—a highly resinous type of thyme, *Thymbra spicata*, with long spiky leaves that have an intense thyme-like flavor. Syrian marjoram, *Maiorana syriaca* and other local herbs are also known as za'atar. The mixture usually consists of the za'atar herb, ground sumac, and toasted sesame seeds. It is often sprinkled on pita bread and baked, or plain pita bread may be dipped first in olive oil and then into the za'atar or za'atar mixed with yogurt.

To make your own, combine 2 tablespoons crushed dried thyme, summer savory, oregano, or marjoram (or a mixture), 2 tablespoons toasted sesame seeds, 1 tablespoon ground sumac, and fine sea salt to taste. Store in a spice tin out of the light at room temperature for a month or two.

Turkish Sesame–Coated Bread Rings (Susamli Simit)

Simit is fast-food bread sold in the streets of Turkey, and often eaten as a breakfast food with jam or yogurt, though they are also delicious on their own. Susamli is the Turkish word for "sesame". The best simit are light and flaky, baked to a gold color, and encrusted with sesame seeds. They have a subtly tangy flavor from the yogurt in the dough. The simit are formed into large, open rings rather like a bagel, and are often braided or twisted. They are the Turkish equivalent of Philadelphia's soft pretzels and New York bagels.

Dough

1 ($\frac{1}{4}$-ounce) package ($2\frac{1}{2}$ teaspoons) active dry yeast

$\frac{1}{2}$ cup lukewarm water

1 tablespoon honey

$\frac{3}{4}$ pound (3 cups minus 3 tablespoons) unbleached
   all-purpose flour

2 teaspoons fine sea salt

2 tablespoons extra-virgin olive oil

2 tablespoons (1 ounce) unsalted butter,
  melted and cooled

$\frac{3}{4}$ cup plain yogurt, not non-fat

Topping

$\frac{1}{2}$ cup milk

$\frac{1}{2}$ cup light molasses, not blackstrap

2 to 3 cups white sesame seeds

Make the dough: Line two 18 x 13-inch half sheet pans
(or other large baking pans) with parchment paper or
silicone baking mats.

Dissolve the yeast in $\frac{1}{4}$ cup of the water along with
the honey and allow the mixture to proof in a warm
place for about 15 minutes, or until bubbling and puffy.

In the bowl of a standing mixer fitted with the paddle attachment, combine the flour and salt.

Separately, whisk together the remaining $\frac{1}{4}$ cup
water, the olive oil, butter, and yogurt. Beat in the yeast
mixture, then add it to the flour mixture and beat until
the dough forms a soft ball, is smooth and elastic, and
comes away cleanly from the sides of the bowl.
Transfer the dough to a large oiled bowl; turn it around

so the dough is oiled all over. Cover with plastic wrap
or a damp cloth and allow the dough to rise at warm
room temperature until doubled in size, about 2 hours.

Punch down the dough, then turn it out onto a lightly
floured work surface and divide the dough into 16 portions. (The dough freezes well for up to three months at
this point. Defrost and allow it come to room temperature
before rolling out.)Using the palms of your hands, roll each
piece into cigar shapes, about 10 inches long with pointy
ends. (You will have a more even-looking stick if you place
the dough on a firm surface and roll your hands across the
top, moving from the center outward.) Twist the ends
of the "cigars" together to make a circle and arrange on
the baking pan. Repeat until all the dough is used.

Make the topping: Whisk together the milk and
molasses. Dip each simit into the mixture allowing the
excess to drip off, then dip them in a bowl of the
sesame seeds, rolling to coat completely. Allow the
simit to rise at warm room temperature for 45 minutes
or until light and puffy.

Preheat the oven to 375°F. Bake for 30 minutes, or until
golden brown and crispy on top. Cool on a wire rack
before serving. Simit are best eaten the day they are made.

Spanish
Sesame–Anise Cookies

*The combination of sesame and aniseed in these crunchy,
nutty cookies from Spain is a legacy of the many years of
control by the Moorish Arabs, who brought the two
ingredients to the country. The same combination shows*

up in the Moroccan Sesame-Anise Bread (page 87). The cookies contain no butter or other animal products, so they are appropriate for vegans (and for those who keep kosher, they are pareve, or neutral, including neither meat nor dairy). Rather they are enriched with olive oil and almonds, moistened with white wine, and seasoned with cinnamon and citrus zests, along with the sesame and aniseed. These delicious cookies get mellower and softer if they're allowed to age a few days before serving.

YIELD: 24 COOKIES

14 ounces (3³/₄ cups plus 2 tablespoons) unbleached
   all-purpose flour

2 teaspoons baking powder

1 teaspoon ground cinnamon

¹/₂ teaspoon fine sea salt

1 cup extra-virgin olive oil

³/₄ cup dry white wine

¹/₄ cup white sesame seeds

1 tablespoon aniseed, ground

Grated zest of 1 lemon (1 tablespoon)

Grated zest of 1 orange (4 teaspoons)

1¹/₂ cups sugar

¹/₄ cup sliced almonds

Line two 18 x 13-inch half sheet pans with parchment paper or silicone baking mats.

In the bowl of a standing mixer fitted with the whisk attachment, mix the dry ingredients: flour, baking powder, cinnamon, and salt.

In a separate bowl, combine the oil, wine, sesame seeds, aniseed, lemon zest, orange zest, and 1 cup of the

sugar. Pour into the flour mixture and beat with the paddle attachment just long enough for the mixture to come together in moist clumps. Briefly knead by hand to combine well. Wrap in plastic and allow the dough to rest at room temperature for 30 minutes.

Preheat the oven to 350°F.

Roll the dough into 24 walnut-sized balls. Roll each ball in the remaining sugar. Arrange them on the baking pan in rows of three and two. Using the flat bottom of a ceramic ramekin or a glass covered with a square of wax paper, flatten each cookie to about 3 inches in diameter. Press 6 to 8 almond slices gently but firmly into the top of each cookie.

Bake for 30 minutes, or until the tops of the cookies are golden brown at the edges. Cool to room temperature on a wire rack. Store up to 2 weeks in an airtight container, such as a cookie tin.

Sesame Honey Cones with Ricotta Filling

These small "horns of plenty" are rather fancifully inspired by the ricotta-filled cannoli of Sicily and the syrup-moistened pastries of North Africa. The cones are made from sesame seed dough moistened with fragrant orange blossom water. The creamy ricotta cheese filling is chock-full of dried apricots macerated in amaretto liqueur, dark chocolate bits, and (ideally) Sicilian green pistachios (page 691). Start at least an hour and up to three days ahead to soak the fruits and make the dough. You'll need metal cream horns or cannoli tubes, both available from www.fantes.com.

$^1/_2$ cup diced California apricots

$^1/_4$ cup amaretto

Cones

2 ounces ($^1/_4$ cup plus 1 tablespoon) sesame seeds

$^1/_4$ pound (1 cup minus 1 tablespoon) unbleached
   all-purpose flour

$^1/_2$ teaspoon baking powder

$^1/_4$ teaspoon fine sea salt

1 large egg yolk

2 tablespoons orange blossom water

3 tablespoons unsalted butter, melted and cooled

1 large egg white, lightly beaten

1 quart grapeseed or canola oil, for brushing and frying

Syrup

$^1/_4$ cup honey

$^1/_2$ cup light corn syrup

Juice of 1 orange

Filling and Assembly

1 (15-ounce) container whole milk ricotta

$^1/_2$ cup confectioners' sugar, plus extra for dusting

2 teaspoons vanilla extract

2 ounces semisweet chocolate, finely chopped,
   or mini chocolate chips

$^1/_4$ cup pistachios, preferably Sicilian, finely chopped

Soak the apricots in the amaretto for at least 1 hour at room temperature.

Make the dough: In the bowl of a standing mixer fit-ted with the paddle attachment, combine the sesame seeds, flour, baking powder, and salt.

In a small bowl, lightly beat together the egg yolk, orange blossom water, and butter. Add to the flour mixture and beat until well combined, firm, and smooth. Transfer the dough to a plastic bag and shape into a flattened rectangle. Chill in the refrigerator vat least 30 minutes, or until firm. Roll out on a lightly floured work surface (or use a pasta machine) to about $^1/_8$-inch thick.

Using a knife and the bottom of an individual tart pan, the bottom of a jar, or a large cookie cutter, cut into 4-inch rounds. Roll out each round into a thin oval about the thickness of pasta dough or 1/16th-inch thick. Brush each metal cone with a little cold oil. Wrap the dough around the metal cone or tube, sealing the edges with a little egg white to form a cone shape or a tube shape. Using the tip of a knife, separate the top edge of the dough from the cone at the open end or at both ends of the metal tube to make a larger opening.

In a wok, a large heavy-duty frying pan (preferably cast-iron), or an electric deep fryer, heat the oil to 365°F, or until shimmering hot, and the air above the oil feels hot when you hold your hand about 3 inches above it. Place the tubes one by one in the oil, and fry until golden brown on all sides, turning as needed, 3 to 4 minutes. Drain on a wire rack or paper towels.

Make the syrup: In a small pot over high heat, combine the honey and corn syrup, and bring to a boil. Remove from the heat and stir in the orange juice. Cool slightly, then dip each cone into the syrup. Place on a wire rack set over a baking pan to catch the drips. Turn the cones once or twice until all the excess syrup drips off.

Make the filling: Combine the ricotta with the confectioners' sugar and the vanilla. Fold in the apricots with their soaking liquid, the chocolate, and pistachios. Place the filling in a heavy-duty zipper lock bag and cut away the corner of the bag. Store refrigerated. Just before serving, fill the cones with the ricotta cream until they are overflowing. Store the cones in an airtight container such as a cookie tin at room temperature for 2 to 3 days before filling, if desired, but note that in humid weather they may lose their crispness.

Greek Tahini Cake (Tahinopita)

This tender cake reminds me of eating dense, sweet sesame halvah, something I've loved since childhood. Tahinopita is frequently made in Greece during Lent as it is contains no animal products such as eggs or milk. This tahini-based cake would also be good for vegans and to serve after a meat-based meal for those who keep kosher. Tahini (ground sesame seed paste) is available at most supermarkets, natural foods stores, or Middle Eastern groceries. If the tahini has separated (like natural peanut butter) into oil and solid pulp, scrape it all into a food processor and process until smooth.

YIELD: 12 TO 16 SERVINGS

10 ounces (2 1/2 cups minus 2 1/2 tablespoons) unbleached all-purpose flour

1 tablespoon baking powder

1/2 teaspoon baking soda

1/2 teaspoon ground allspice

1/2 teaspoon fine sea salt

1 cup tahini paste

1 cup sugar

Grated zest of 1 orange (4 teaspoons)

1 cup fresh orange juice, strained

1/4 pound (1 cup) walnuts, lightly toasted and finely chopped

1/4 pound (3/4 cup) golden raisins

2 tablespoons white sesame seeds

Preheat the oven to 350°F. Prepare a 9-inch tube pan by spraying with nonstick baker's coating, or rub with softened butter and dust with flour, shaking off the excess.

Whisk together the dry ingredients: flour, baking powder, baking soda, allspice, and salt.

In the bowl of a standing mixer fitted with the paddle attachment, beat the tahini, sugar, and orange zest until light and creamy, about 10 minutes, then gradually beat in the orange juice. Beat until smooth and creamy, about 2 minutes. Add the flour mixture and beat just long enough to blend. Add the walnuts and raisins and beat briefly to combine.

Scrape the batter into the pan, knocking the base of the pan on the table top to settle the batter. Sprinkle the top with the sesame seeds. Bake for 45 minutes or until the cake starts to come away from the sides of the pan and a toothpick or skewer stuck in the center comes out clean.

Cool on a wire rack, then invert and leave for 2 to 3 minutes before lifting the pan from the cake. Cool to room temperature and then turn right side up. Store the cake, covered, at room temperature for up to 5 days.

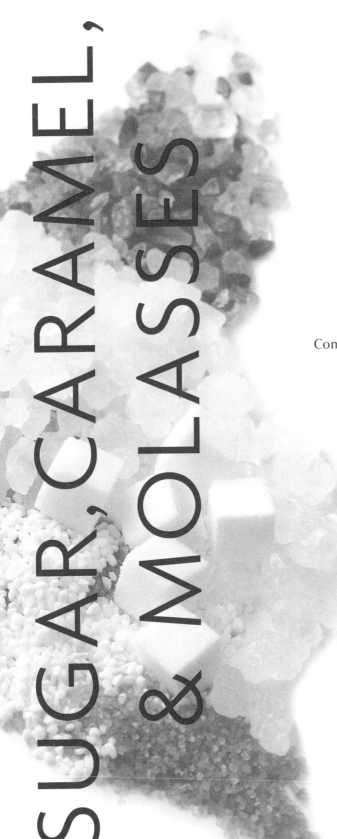

SUGAR, CARAMEL, & MOLASSES

Guarapo . . .808

Chewing on Sugar Cane . . . 808

The Art of Confectionery . . .808

"The Different Degrees of Sugar–
Boiling for a Variety of Purposes" . . . 809

An Old Way to Refine Sugar . . .809

Types of White Sugar . . . 809

Comparing Cane Sugar and Beet Sugar . . . 813

Steen's Cane Syrup . . . 813

Caramel . . . 814

Caramel Cooking Tips . . . 815

C & H Sugar . . . 815

Molasses . . . 816

Types of Molasses . . . 817

CHOCOLATE CARAMEL ÉCLAIRS . . . 817

History of Éclairs . . . 819

MOLASSES-GINGER BRANDY SNAPS . . . 819

MELTING CARAMEL CAKE:
CARAMEL COULANT . . . 820

BROWN SUGAR-PECAN
SWEET DREAM COOKIES . . . 821

VANILLA CARAMEL SAUCE . . . 822

SUGAR PASTRY . . . 823

SUGAR, CARAMEL
& MOLASSES

It's difficult to conceive of writing a baking book without using sugar (unless it is a book for special diets). Even though I love using alternate sweeteners like honey, maple, dates, and figs, sugar in its many forms is by far the most adaptable and useful sweet ingredient. The hard edges of granulated sugar beaten to a cream with butter help lighten pound cake and cookie batters, while tiny crystals of superfine sugar dissolve easily to make the smoothest meringues, and melt evenly to a lovely, reddish-amber caramel. Light brown sugar moistens and subtly flavors pie and strudel fillings, upside-down cakes, and cobblers, while dark brown sugar imparts more moisture along with its bolder molasses-edged flavor to devil's food cake, gingerbread, and oatmeal cookies.

Today, we take it for granted that we can buy inexpensive five-pound bags of pure, refined white sugar that can be used straight from the bag. Not that long ago, sugar was sold in rock-solid loaves that had to be cut off in chunks with special iron sugar nippers, then boiled with water into syrup and skimmed repeatedly until clear, then cooled until it crystallized again. Even the finest quality refined sugar had to be crushed and sifted before use. In Western Europe and the Americas, we are accustomed to making sweet cakes and pastries with crystallized sugar. In the Arab world, North Africa, Greece, Turkey, and India, many cakes and pastries are baked or fried then soaked in sugar syrup, a method that dates back to when large stalks of sugar cane would be crushed to obtain their syrupy juices.

Sugar is the refined and crystallized juice extracted from either the sugar cane plant, *Saccharum officinarum* (and other species), which resembles bamboo and has sappy, sweet, pulp-filled stems; or from the sugar beet, *Beta vulgaris*, a large root vegetable. Fully refined white sugars have little flavor apart from their sweetness; the differences lie in whether they have been refined from cane or beets (see below), and in the size of their crystals. Partially refined sugars, like turbinado sugar, raw sugar, or muscovado sugar have their own special flavors from residual plant substances or those created in the manufacturing process. Dark brown cakes of unrefined sugar, known as *kuro-zato*, are sold in Japan; in Mexico, cone-shaped loaves of medium-brown sugar are called *piloncillo*, and in Colombia, loaf sugar is called *panela*. In India and Southeast Asia, cones of unrefined dark palm or cane sugar are called *jaggery* or *gur*.

Sugar was once made by pressing short lengths of sugarcane stalks through a roller mechanism to extract the juices, which were then boiled until granules of sugar began to crystallize in the thick molasses. It was then packed in barrels. The molasses was allowed to drain out of the barrels, which were then sent to the refiners for further processing, or were sold as raw, or muscovado, sugar. While cooling, the raw sugar would leak molasses (treacle in Great Britain) which wouldn't crystallize, but was certainly edible.

Cones of sugar were wrapped in indigo blue paper to protect them from the light and to highlight their whiteness. The exquisite candied whole fruits I ordered from the historic confectionery store, Romanengo, in Genoa, came wrapped in this same blue paper, dating back to the eighteenth century, when this company first started selling sugar in loaf form. The blue paper was often re-used to dye linens light blue.

Sugar cane is a grass that is thought to have developed in New Guinea, about 8,000 years ago, moving from there into Southeast Asia and India. The Chinese claim to have been the first to produce cane sugar, but it seems likely that they learned the method from the Indians, because the canes have long grown in India, especially in the Ganges River delta. According to legend, Buddha's ancestors came from Gur, or the land of sugar, now Bengal. The Ramanyana, the Sanskrit epic dating to about 1200 BCE, describes a place where "the drinking water tastes like sugar cane juice."

It wasn't until the Gupta dynasty (around 350 AD) that the Indians developed a method to transform sugar cane juice into grainy crystals that were easy to store and transport. It was then that sugar use really started to take off. Early refining methods involved grinding or pounding the cane in order to extract the juice, then boiling it down or drying it in the sun to gravelly solids. From this process comes the Sanskrit word for sugar (*sharkara*), which also refers to gravel, and the Chinese term "gravel sugar" for table sugar. The Greek word for sugar, *zahari*, also refers to either sugar or pebble. The English word ultimately derives from the Sanskrit *sharkara*.

When the Persian Emperor Darius attacked India in 510 BCE, the men in his army discovered "a reed that gives honey without the aid of bees," which they brought home. Indian sailors helped spread sugar through various trade routes, and in Southern Asia, the Middle East, and China, sugar became an ingredient in cooking and desserts. It is also thought that Alexander the Great and his army brought sugar from India back to Europe from where it spread to Africa. Trading caravans eventually spread sugar throughout the Middle East and to the Black Sea. Sugar was also used in Egyptian and Phoenician medicine, and later that of the Greeks and Romans, as well.

Arabs adopted the techniques of sugar production from India and set up the first sugar plantations, mills, and refineries on the island of Crete around the year 1000. The Arabic name for the island, *Quandi*, means crystallized sugar (or candy).

Crusaders brought sugar to Europe after their campaigns in the Holy Land, where they encountered caravans carrying this "sweet salt." The Moors brought sugar to the Iberian Peninsula (Spain and Portugal) when they conquered it in the eighth century, with early plantings in the Canary Islands and Madeira. One lovely, though unsubstantiated, story claims that Christopher Columbus stopped in the Canary Islands in 1492, for wine and water, intending only a brief visit. He became romantically involved with the Governor of the island, Beatrice de Bobadilla and stayed there a month. When he departed, she presented him with cuttings of sugarcane, which became the first to reach the New World.

The Portuguese brought sugar to Brazil, and by 1540 there were 2,000 plantations in Demerara (the name for raw sugar in Great Britain) and Surinam on the north coast. After 1625, the Dutch carried sugarcane from South America to the Caribbean Islands, the region which became the world's largest source of sugar. The economies of entire islands, such as Guadeloupe and Barbados, became based on sugar production. By 1750, the French colony known as Saint-Domingue (now Haiti) had become the largest sugar producer in the world.

It is impossible to separate the history of sugar from the history of slavery in the New World. As sugar production increased, slaves from Africa became the plantation workers for this arduous and too often fatal work. Four million slaves were sent to work in the British West Indies, but only 400,000 were alive after slavery ended in the British Empire in 1838. Jamaica was also a major producer of sugarcane in the eighteenth century. Between 1701 and 1810, almost one million slaves were brought to work in Jamaica and Barbados. Rum was distilled from the by-products of the sugar industry in the notorious three-way trade with Africa, the Caribbean, and New England. Slaves from Africa, destined for backbreaking work in the sugarcane fields of the Caribbean islands, were paid for by rum distilled in New England, using molasses made from sugarcane grown in the Caribbean.

Due to increased production during the eighteenth century and a seemingly endless appetite for the sweet crystals, sugar became enormously popular as Europeans began eating jams, candy, tea, coffee, cocoa, cakes, puddings, and pies in ever increasing amounts. As they established sugar plantations on the larger Caribbean islands like Cuba and Jamaica, prices fell, especially in Britain. Candy-makers had already developed a repertoire of complex, varied, and much-loved candies in seventeenth-century Europe. As sugar became cheaper and more available, sugar confectionery became even more important and elaborate. Dutch settlers in New England brought their small sweet cakes called *koekjes* (cookies) to America, and they became one of the most popular sugar products that Americans bake.

Sugarcane quickly exhausts the soil in which it grows, so new areas of production are often sought out. Cuba became the richest land in the Caribbean because its terrain was not mountainous and it was well-suited to grow sugarcane. This made it the world's largest producer after the Haitian Revolution (1791–1804) ended slavery on the island of Santo Domingo. Sugar production then spread to the newer European colonies in Africa and in the Pacific, where it became especially important in Fiji. Today's largest producer of sugarcane is Brazil, where sugarcane is also used to distill the spirit called *cachaça*, and *bagasse* (the waste left after refining) is used as fuel.

While no longer grown by slaves, sugar from developing countries has an on-going association with workers earning minimal wages and living in extreme poverty. Sugarcane is harvested mechanically or by hand, with hand harvesting still accounting for more than half of the world's production, especially in the developing world. When harvested by hand, the field is first set on fire to burn away dead leaves and kill poisonous snakes living among the canes, leaving the moist stalks and roots unharmed. Using large (and lethal) cane knives or machetes, harvesters cut the standing cane just above the ground. A skilled harvester can cut about 1,000 pounds of sugarcane in just one hour.

Until the nineteenth century, and even into the early part of the twentieth century (in England), refined sugar was sold in solid form, in cones, blocks, or loaves. Large, wealthy households would buy expensive highly refined white sugar in tall, conical loaves that weighed anywhere from five

pounds to over 30 pounds. From these loaves, pieces would be broken off using special iron sugar-nippers, like heavy pliers with sharp blades on the cutting sides. The finest sugar, packed in smaller loaves of only three to four pounds, came from the island of Madeira, one of the earliest places that sugarcane was planted in Europe.

Seventeenth-century immigrants to the new American colonies were advised to wait to buy sugar until they reached their destination, because it would be much cheaper than at home. By the eighteenth century, sugar was regularly advertised in Boston newspapers. According to culinary historian William Woys Weaver, muscovado sugar was advertised in the *Philadelphia America Weekly Mercury* of 1719. Although considered to be a lower grade of dark, minimally refined sugar, today muscovado sugar fetches a high price as an imported specialty food.

By 1807 in Philadelphia, Havana white, Havana brown, Muscovado (first, second, and ordinary quality), and West India clayed white and clayed brown sugars were for sale. Colonial cooks used many grades and kinds of sweetening, in both solid and liquid form. Because molasses was much cheaper than crystallized sugar, it was consumed in vast quantities in the American colonies, which still has a strong tradition of molasses-sweetened dishes like Indian pudding (page 286).

I use sugar in all its many forms throughout this book. In this chapter, the Brown Sugar–Pecan Sweet Dreams (page 821) takes advantage of the deeper flavor and moist quality of brown sugar.

Vanilla Caramel Sauce (page 822) is a versatile good-keeping sauce made from caramelized sugar, heavy cream, and vanilla. Serve it over ice cream, slices of pound cake, and in the batter for the Melting Caramel Cake (page 820). The Sugar Pastry (page 823) is flaky and slightly sweet and is a favorite pastry for French tarts. Of course, any pastry dough than contains sugar will inevitably be a bit more difficult to work with as the sugar makes the dough sticky. Elsewhere, homemade Dulce de Leche (page 566), a Latin American favorite, is made from sweetened condensed milk, which itself contains a high proportion of sugar. I use raw sugar or the more expensive clear crystallized sugar to add sparkle to cookies like the Siennese Cavallucci (page 224), the Swedish Ginger-Spice Cookies: Pepparkakor (page 493), the Almond Cantucci Pratesi (page 289), and the Lemon Poppy Seed Biscotti (page 719). Small, lightweight balls of white pearl sugar from Sweden top the Crispy Lemon-Cinnamon Cookies (page 351).

GUARAPO

On the streets of Sao Paolo, Brazil, and Miami, Florida, vendors use small mechanical presses to extract cut sections of peeled sugarcane stalks to make the fresh sugarcane juice called *guarapo*. Much appreciated by the locals as a refreshing though calorie-laden drink, *guarapo* may be mixed with lime or lemon juice or pineapple to give it an acidic edge.

CHEWING ON SUGAR CANE

At the age of eleven, I spent three months living and traveling in Mexico with my family. I remember visiting a small village for its annual fiesta and seeing people chewing on what looked to me like wood. I was horrified that the people didn't have anything else to eat. Although they were no doubt quite poor, I didn't realize at the time that they were chewing on sections of sugarcane to get at the sweet juices contained inside. Today, trendy restaurants serve their cocktail concoctions with sugarcane swizzle sticks and skewer shrimp on them for grilling. For dessert, skewers of fruits stuck on sugarcane sticks can be grilled and served with pound cakes and shortbread cookies.

THE ART OF CONFECTIONERY

My precious copy of *The Art of Confectionery*, published in Boston in 1866, has this to say about sugar: "Of sugar there are three varieties: double-refined, refined, and brown. Double-refined sugar must be perfect white, inodorous, dry, and of a fine grain: this is used for conserves, candies, and all things which are designed to remain without color. Refined sugar is the next in quality and price: this should be white and dry. It serves for pastry, chocolate, pickles, and similar preparation, in which whiteness is not important. Brown sugar is used for ginger, barley-sugar, and like preparations."

"THE DIFFERENT DEGREES OF SUGAR-BOILING FOR A VARIETY OF PURPOSES

There are seven distinct degrees in sugar-boiling: 1. *lisse*, or the thread, large or small. 2. *perle*, or the pear, large and small. 3. *soufflé*, or the blow. 4. *plume*, or the feather. 5. *boulet*, or the ball, large or small. 6. *cassé*, or the crack or snap. 7. *caramel*, or hard-baked. [These terms came from the French and correspond to today's thread, soft ball, firm ball, hard ball, hard crack, and caramel stages].

To prepare Granite sugar: Take a pound of the finest loaf-sugar, break it up in very small lumps and put these on a clean marble slab; use the end of a rolling pin to break up these lumps much smaller without necessarily bruising the sugar, as this would dull its crystallized appearance; riddle this through a rather coarse wire sieve, and then sift it through a hair sieve in order to free it from the finer powered sugar. What remains in the sieve, if the process has been properly conducted, will present the appearance of a rather coarse yet even-grain kind of gravelly sand. This is what is called by confectioners granite sugar.

Instructions for the Use of Royal Icing [egg whites mixed to a stiff white paste with confectioners sugar]. It requires a knowledge of drawing, good taste, and practice, to produce a variety of neat or elegant designs or ornamentation; but you must not be deterred from trying your hand on accounts of these difficulties: for, you must remember that industry and perseverance overcome all obstacles."

AN OLD WAY TO REFINE SUGAR

One method of refining sugar involved crushing the coarse sugar, boiling it in water mixed with slaked lime (the same kind used to treat corn for masa harina, page 385), and mixing it with ox blood or egg white. This was done so that the impurities in the sugar would attach to the coagulated blood or egg white, similar to the way a meat stock is clarified. After repeated boiling and skimming, the sugar was poured into inverted cone-shaped molds, perforated at the tip. From the opening, clear sugar syrup trickled down into a bottle, finally ready for use.

TYPES OF WHITE SUGAR

BAKERS' SPECIAL SUGAR: The extra-small crystals of this sugar were developed especially for the baking industry. It is used to sprinkle on doughnuts and cookies, as well as in some commercial cake recipes, especially high-ratio cakes (made with an extra-high proportion of sugar), to create a fine crumb texture.

CANE SYRUP: Cane syrup a is thick, sweet aromatic syrup used to drizzle over biscuits or pancakes, and for sweetening baked goods. This is a specialty of

Southern Louisiana that is similar to British treacle. Although many small mills in the region once produced cane syrup, Steen's Cane Syrup is the only one still made today (www.steensyrup.com).

COARSE SUGAR: As its name implies, the crystal size of coarse sugar is larger than that of "regular" sugar. To make coarse sugar, molasses-rich sugar syrup that is high in sucrose is allowed to crystallize. The large crystal size of coarse sugar makes it highly resistant to color change or inversion (natural breakdown to fructose and glucose) in cooking and baking, characteristics that are important when making fondant icings, candies, and liqueurs.

CONFECTIONERS' SUGAR: Confectioners' sugar, or powdered sugar, is granulated sugar ground to a powder, sifted, and then mixed with three percent cornstarch to prevent caking. Confectioners' sugar is ground into three different degrees of fineness. The type commonly available in supermarkets, 10X, is the finest; 6X and 4X are progressively coarser. 10X sugar is used in icings, candies, to sweeten whipping cream, and to sprinkle on cookies and cakes. The other two types are used by commercial bakers.

CRYSTALLIZED SUGAR: Also known as sanding sugar, this consists of large shiny crystals coated with carnuba wax to keep the crystals separate. The large crystals reflect light and give the product a sparkling appearance. It is often sold colored for decorating holiday and special occasion cookies.

CUBE SUGAR: To make these perfect little cubes, granulated white sugar is moistened with sugar syrup and pressed into shape. It is not generally used in baking, though the cubes may be rubbed against the skin of citrus fruits to absorb their oils and then added to batters.

FRUIT SUGAR: Fruit sugar or fructose is slightly finer than "regular" sugar and is used in dry mixes such as gelatin and pudding desserts, and powdered drinks. Fruit sugar has a more uniform small crystal size than "regular" sugar. The uniformity of crystal size prevents separation or settling of larger crystals to the bottom of the box, an important quality in dry mixes.

GRANULATED SUGAR: This is the type of sugar most commonly used in baking in recipes that call for "sugar." Granulated sugar has medium-sized crystals. It may be refined from sugarcane or sugar beets.

INVERT SUGAR: Sucrose can be split into its two component sugars (glucose and fructose). This process is called inversion, and the product is called invert sugar. Commercial invert sugar is a liquid made from equal amounts of glucose and fructose. Because fructose is sweeter than either glucose or sucrose, invert sugar is sweeter than white sugar. Invert sugar is used by food manufacturers to prevent the crystallization of sugar and to retain moisture in packaged foods. Pastry chefs use invert sugar to make thick sugar syrups and sorbets that resist crystallization. In the home kitchen, sugar, water, and a bit of lemon juice, or sugar, water, and a small amount of corn syrup boiled together can be used as the equivalent.

LUMP SUGAR: Rough cubes of white or light brown sugar, often imported from France and served at fancy restaurants to sweeten coffee. I've found similar cubes at a lower price in my local Korean market.

PEARL SUGAR: White, small, lightweight clumps of sugar used to sprinkle on cakes, pastries, and cookies. The sugar keeps its white color after baking. It is especially popular in Sweden.

PRESERVING OR COARSE SUGAR: These large crystals are processed from the purest sugar liquor so it resists color change or inversion (the natural breakdown into fructose and glucose) at high temperatures. Preserving sugar is used for canning fruits and making preserves and jellies.

ROCK SUGAR OR ROCK CANDY: Rock sugar is made by growing large crystals, usually on white cotton strings, in a strong sugar solution. It may be found in brown and white lumps or crystallized on stirring sticks to be served with coffee. Yellow or clear Chinese rock sugar is used in Chinese cuisine and may be found in Asian groceries. Rock candy, usually flavored with aniseed, is served as a mouth freshener after meals in India. Children in Mexico make rock candy in the shapes of skulls and then decorate them with icing and jewels for the Day of the Dead.

SUCROSE: Sucrose is white granulated sugar that has been dissolved in water to make clear syrup. Amber liquid sugar is the equivalent made from brown sugar.

SUPERFINE SUGAR: Also known as ultrafine or bar sugar, it is the finest of all the types of granulated white sugar. The superfine crystals make this type of sugar ideal for delicately textured cakes such as angel food cake and meringues, to melt for hard caramel, as well as for sweetening fruits and iced drinks because it dissolves easily. In England, similar sugar is known as caster or castor, named after the type of shaker in which it is often packaged.

SUGAR SYRUP: Sugar syrup is used to drench pastries of Arabic and Turkish origin. It is made by boiling equal quantities of sugar and water until the liquid is clear. Other ingredients like honey, orange blossom water, rose water, vanilla beans, and cinnamon may be added to the syrup for extra flavor. Once boiled, the syrup will then need to be skimmed to remove any impurities; the more additions to the syrup, the more it will need to be skimmed so the syrup is clear.

GOLDEN SYRUP: This is a term found in British cooking for syrups made in the process of refining sugarcane. The lightest treacle produced from the first boiling of the sugarcane juice is called light treacle or golden syrup. Lyle's Golden Syrup is the most commonly found brand in the United States.

TYPES OF BROWN SUGARS

BROWN CANE SUGAR: Brown sugar retains some of the surface molasses syrup that develops on the sugar during the refining process, giving it a deeper, more complex flavor than white sugar. Dark brown sugar is dark because it contains more molasses and has a stronger flavor and moister consistency. Brown cane sugar, a combination of sugar and molasses, produced naturally while refining white cane sugar is made by the traditional method, crystallization.

BROWN BEET SUGAR: Beet sugar is made by refining sugar all the way to the final white granular stage, stripping off all the molasses because beet molasses is unfit for human consumption (it's used to feed cattle). To make brown sugar from beets, cane sugar molasses is added back into the beet sugar through a process called painting, in which the crystals are coated with the molasses. Because the molasses doesn't penetrate the crystals, it can sometimes be rubbed right off.

FREE-FLOWING BROWN SUGAR. This is a powdery brown sugar that is drier than common brown sugar and does not clump or turn into hard bricks, though less flavorful because it contains less molasses.

DEMERARA OR RAW SUGAR: These are larger crystals of sugar which have been partially processed so only the surface molasses has been washed off. It has a blond color and mild brown sugar flavor, and is often used in home baking. I use it to sprinkle on cookies for sparkle instead of the more expensive and harder to find crystallized sugar. Demerara gets its name from the Demerara in Guyana, the original source of this sugar. Today, it is produced mainly in Mauritius.

MUSCOVADO OR BARBADOS SUGAR: Muscovado sugar, a British specialty brown sugar, is very dark brown and has a strong molasses flavor. The crystals are coarser and stickier in texture than American brown sugar. Unrefined muscovado sugar gets its full-bodied flavor and color from sugarcane juice. It was one of the most prominent exports of the Philippines from the 1800s until the late 1970s. It is commonly used in cookie recipes.

SUCANAT: Sucanat (the word combines sugar and natural) is grainy, pure dried cane juice that retains the full bodied flavor of the molasses contained in the juice. It is generally found in natural foods stores as an unrefined alternative to white and light brown sugar that works well in baking.

TURBINADO SUGAR: Also known as turbinated sugar, this sugar cane extract is made by steaming unrefined raw sugar. Turbinado sugar is similar in color to Demerara or raw sugar with large free-flowing crystals. A popular brand name is Sugar in the Raw. In general, light brown sugar, demerara or raw sugar, and turbinado sugar can be substituted for each other in recipes, although only clear crystalline turbinado sugar and demerara or raw sugar work wells for sprinkling.

COMPARING CANE SUGAR AND BEET SUGAR

Both beet and cane sugars are 99.95 percent sucrose, but many bakers believe that the remaining .05 percent of trace minerals and proteins makes a difference, and that cane sugar performs better. Many manufacturers don't specify whether their product is beet sugar or cane sugar. Generally, if the source is not specified, it's probably beet sugar. I've found that beet sugar is a bit wet, with a texture like damp sand, and doesn't perform as well in delicate meringues, in making caramel, and in angel food and other cakes.

Much of the small but significant differences come from the fact that cane and beets are two different plants altogether. Cane sugar contains trace minerals that are different from those in beet sugar and it's these minerals that expert pastry chefs say make cane sugar preferable to use. As professional bakers have long noticed, cane sugar has a low melting-point, absorbs fewer undesirable odors, blends easily, and is less likely to foam up. The differences are most apparent between brown cane sugar and brown beet sugar (beet sugar coated with cane sugar molasses, because beet sugar molasses has an unpleasant flavor).

Beets are a root, growing below ground; cane is a grass, waving in the breeze. Cane was once the dominant sugar in United States markets, but within the last few years beet has taken the lead and beet sugar is quite common in Northern Europe. Beet now accounts for over half of the ten million tons of refined sugar consumed in the United States each year. Beet sugar is cheaper to produce because it requires just one refining process at a single plant while traditional sugarcane refining calls for two stages of processing at two different facilities. Beets can also thrive in a wider range of climates. This large, rather homely root is cultivated in 12 states, whereas cane can grow in just four. Hawaii alone has lost more than 60 percent of its cane fields over the last five to ten years because of urban growth and conversion to higher value crops like macadamia nuts and coffee.

STEEN'S CANE SYRUP

In 1910, in an effort to save his crop of sugarcane that had frozen, Mr. C.S. Steen started collecting sugarcane juice to create syrup. At first, Mr. Steen peeled the sides of the cane, revealing the juicy, sugary pulp. The cane was then brought to a syrup mill, where the cane juice was mashed with large mule–powered rollers, and heated with a hard wood fire. Seven to ten gallons of raw juice boil down to one gallon of syrup. Using a mule, the mill could produce several barrels of syrup a day. Today, mechanical equipment cuts the sugarcane, strips off the leaves, and loads it onto carts that carry it to the mill to be boiled into syrup. Eighty–five years later, the family still produces cane syrup in Louisiana. Go to www.steensyrup.com to order their syrup or to get more information.

CARAMEL

After chocolate, caramel is about the most important flavoring ingredient used in baking. Especially in recent years, pastry chefs have been exploring the potential for this complex ingredient by presenting caramel tasting plates. In making caramel, heat transforms sugar, a single molecule into hundreds of different molecules rich with complex buttery, milky, fruity, flowery, roasted, and rum-like flavors.

Caramel is sugar cooked until it first melts and then darkens. To make caramel, sugar is cooked to a temperature range between 320 to 356°F. At over 375°F, the caramel will turn dark brown and then black. Sometimes the caramel is made separately, melting the sugar on its own, or it is mixed with a little lemon juice or corn syrup to prevent the syrup from crystallizing as it thickens.

Caramel can provide the flavor in puddings and desserts, a filling in candies, or a topping for custards and ice creams. The easiest way to make caramel is to mix sugar with water and boil it into syrup. This makes it possible to cook the sugar over high heat without burning it. The longer cooking process also gives the caramel time to develop more flavors. As the sugar darkens, it becomes less sweet and more acidic, eventually turning bitter as it reaches the burning point. However, a slight edge of bitterness is desirable to balance caramel's sweetness.

The barely-colored just-melted sugar syrup is called light caramel. As the sugar syrup continues to cook, it reaches the golden stage, followed by the slightly darker amber stage and then the dark stage. If the color becomes excessively dark, the caramel will be bitter and can quickly burn. If you undercook it, its flavor won't be fully developed.

Caramel and butterscotch are made in similar ways to toffee, as is fudge. The difference is in the degree of boiling temperature and the ways in which they are cooled.

Light caramel will harden into a very hard, glasslike sheet. Dark caramel will harden into a softer texture; the darker the caramel, the softer it will be when it hardens and the more flavorful it will be. Except for caramel sauce, do not attempt to make caramel in humid or rainy weather, because it will be sticky and won't harden well unless your kitchen is cool and air-conditioned.

In this book, a variety of candies, confections, and desserts are made with caramel in its many forms. See the Pecan-Ginger Cake with Caramel Icing (page 494), the Orange or Tangerine Caramel Sauce (page 601), the Cranberry-Caramel Pecan Tart (page 654), the Chocolate Caramel Éclairs (page 817), the Melting Caramel Cake: Caramel Coulant (page 820), the Vanilla Caramel Sauce (page 822), and the French Caramel Puff Pastry Fruit Tart (page 830). Three different upside-down tarts, called tarte tatin in France, start with caramel poured into the pan, which is topped with fruit and then pastry: Peach and Apricot Tarte Tatin (page 616), Quince-Cranberry Tarte Tatin (page 753), and the Oatmeal-Apple Upside-Down Tart (page 577).

CARAMEL COOKING TIPS

Caramel is extremely hot and sticky. If you're just learning how to make it, keep a large deep bowl filled with ice and water nearby. If by chance a drop of caramel lands on your hand, plunge it into the ice water. Also, wear an oven mitt to protect your hands.

Use a heavy-bottomed pot or skillet to make caramel, so the sugar melts and darkens evenly. I use a heavy, nickel steel-lined copper pot. The traditional French caramel and preserving pot is made from uncoated copper. Although copper is poisonous in larger quantities, here the copper doesn't react with the sugar so it is quite safe to use.

It's also important to be able to see the color of the caramel as it cooks, so the inside of the pot should be light in color, such as stainless or nickel steel, heavy cast-aluminum, or enameled cast-iron. Note that anything cooked in stainless steel, including sugar, tends to stick, so shake the pot often for even cooking. Avoid using any nonstick coated pot, as the high heat can damage the coating and cause undesirable compounds to be released.

If the recipe calls for adding liquid to the caramel, like heavy cream, use a large pot such as a Dutch oven, as the mixture will bubble up as soon as the liquid is added. Also, keep your face averted from the opening of the pot when adding the liquid to avoid steam burns. Place a wire sieve over the pot before pouring the liquid through the strainer to prevent anything from splattering on you.

When making liquid caramel with sugar and water syrup, be sure to start with a perfectly clean pot and clean, cold water, because jagged-edged sugar crystals tend to form on any impurities. This crystallizing is desirable if you're making rock candy, fondant, or Creole Pecan Pralines (page 650).

Avoid stirring the sugar syrup as this will encourage the dissolved but still present sugar crystals to reform. Instead, tilt the pot from side to side so the caramel cooks evenly without burning. I often cover the pot when I'm making caramel so the moisture that collects on the inside of the lid drips down into the pot, keeping it from crystallizing. Once the syrup starts to brown, I remove the lid and shake the pot so the caramel cooks evenly.

To clean a pot with burnt-on caramel, fill the pot most of the way with water and bring it to a boil on the stove so the burnt caramel melts into the water. You may have to do this several times, but eventually the pot will come clean.

C & H SUGAR

In 1906, the California and Hawaiian Sugar Refining Company began refining pure cane sugar from raw cane sugar grown in Hawaii in the small town of Crockett, California, near San Francisco. More than one hundred years later, this pure cane sugar is preferred by top West Coast pastry chefs, though it is unfortunately not available in the East. (Go to: www.chsugar.com for more information.)

MOLASSES

Cane molasses is a delicious by-product which is extracted during the sugarcane refining process used to make sugar crystals. The sugar cane is crushed to remove the juice, which is then boiled vigorously. Machines utilize centrifugal force to extract the sugar crystals from the syrup. The remaining medium to deep brown syrup becomes molasses. The term is also used in the Greece, the Middle East, North Africa, and Turkey for syrups made from cooked down pomegranate juice (pomegranate molasses), date syrup, (date molasses or dibs), fig juices, and grape syrup. Molasses made from sugar beets is too bitter for eating. It is fed to animals instead.

The word "molasses" comes from the Portuguese *melaco*, itself derived from the Latin *mel* for honey. The earliest use of the word "molasses" in English was in a book published in 1582 translated from *First Booke of the Histoire of the Discoverie and Conquest of the East Indies* by Lopez de Castanheda, in which he describes 'Melasus' as a 'certine kind of Sugar made of Palmes of Date trees.'

Molasses became the most common American sweetener in the eighteenth century because it was much cheaper than sugar and was part of the triangular trade route that brought molasses to New England to be made into rum, which was then shipped to West Africa to be traded for slaves, who were in turn traded for molasses in the West Indies.

By the end of the nineteenth century, molasses and maple syrup were the sweeteners of choice in Eastern North America, but when sugar prices dropped after World War I, both molasses and maple syrup dropped in popularity.

The highest grade of molasses is made from clarified, reduced, and blended sugarcane juice without any sugar extracted. This is the kind called for here and found in supermarkets (but usually not natural foods stores) under the brand name Grandma's Original (or Gold Label) Molasses and Brer Rabbit Mild Molasses. Bitter-tasting blackstrap molasses is obtained from the last boiling and contains the least sugar and the most vitamins, minerals, and trace elements, but is too strong for baking use. The flavor and color of molasses varies depending on how early or late in the process the molasses is extracted. The lighter the color of the molasses, the sweeter and milder it will be.

In this book, I use molasses in the Molasses-Ginger Brandy Snaps (page 819), the Rye and Rosemary Breadsticks with Lemon (page 783), the Sauerkraut Rye Bread (page 784), and in the glaze for the Turkish Sesame-Coated Bread Rings (page 798). The Tahini and Grape Molasses Pide (page 901) is made with cooked down grape juice molasses. Of course, all the many recipes in this book that call for brown sugar also contain molasses, which helps to moisten the product and adds its own darker, faintly bittersweet flavor.

TYPES OF MOLASSES

LIGHT MOLASSES: This is syrup remaining after the first processing of the sugar. It is generally unsulphured and is the lightest and the sweetest, variety. It is often used as syrup for pancakes and waffles or stirred into hot cereals such as oatmeal. It contains 65 percent sucrose.

MEDIUM OR DARK MOLASSES: This type of molasses remains after the second processing of the sugar. It is not as strong as blackstrap. It contains about 60 percent sucrose.

BLACKSTRAP MOLASSES: The syrup remaining after the third extraction of sugar from sugar cane. Blackstrap (derived in part from the Dutch *stroop*, meaning syrup) refers to the color of the molasses, which is extremely dark. It has a very strong, bittersweet flavor with a heady aroma. This variety is best used in recipes rather than as a straight sweetener such as pancake syrup. It contains many of the nutrients left behind by refined sugar crystals. By measure, it is 55 percent sucrose, the least sweet of the varieties.

DARK TREACLE: True treacle dates from Victorian times in England. This dark, viscous syrup is notably sweeter and has a much mellower flavor than American molasses. Nowadays, treacle is a blend of molasses and refinery syrup. It is particularly suited for baking dark fruitcakes and to make toffee candy. British dark treacle can be substituted for molasses in most recipes, but much less frequently will molasses work as a replacement for treacle. If you do substitute molasses for treacle, use the lightest, unsulphured molasses you can find. Lyle's Dark Treacle is one brand available in the United States.

SORGHUM MOLASSES: This sweet syrup comes from the sorghum plant, a cereal grain that is grown specifically for molasses rather than for refined sugar. Also called West Indies or Barbados molasses, the syrup is made from the juice of the stalk, which is cooked and clarified. The result is smooth with a clear amber color, without sediment or graininess. It contains no sulphur but does generally contain preservatives added to lengthen its otherwise short shelf life.

Chocolate Caramel Éclairs

An éclair is a delicate pastry made with choux paste, the same eggy, puffy dough used to make the small rounds called profiteroles (page 287). The dough is first cooked on top of the stove, eggs are beaten in, and it is then piped into small mounds or strips and baked. The water contained in the dough turns to steam in the heat of the oven while the starch and gluten contained in the flour and the proteins in the eggs act like a bubble to contain the air that is released. To make the éclairs, the dough is piped into fat strips and baked until crisp and hollow inside. Éclair is the French word for lightning, a fanciful name used for the pastry, perhaps because the pastries shine with the icing. Like all choux paste prod-

ucts, it is best to wait for a day that is low in humidity for crisp éclairs.

YIELD: 15 ÉCLAIRS

Éclairs

3 ounces (³/₄ stick) unsalted butter, cut into bits

¹/₂ teaspoon fine sea salt

5 ounces (1¹/₄ cups) unbleached bread flour

4 large eggs

Cream

1 cup superfine sugar

2 cups milk

4 large egg yolks

1 ounce (¹/₄ cup plus 1 tablespoon) potato starch

1 ounce (¹/₄ cup) unbleached all-purpose flour

Scrapings of 1 vanilla bean, or 2 teaspoons
    vanilla extract

3 ounces (³/₄ stick) unsalted butter, softened

Glaze

¹/₄ pound bittersweet chocolate, finely chopped

2 tablespoons unsalted butter

Make the éclairs: Line an 18 x 13-inch half-sheet pan (or other large baking pan) with parchment paper or a silicone baking mat.

In a medium, heavy-bottomed, non-aluminum pot, bring 1 cup of water, the butter, and salt slowly to a boil so that the butter has a chance to melt before the water boils. Reduce the heat to low and mix in the flour all at once, stirring with a wooden spoon or silicone spatula until the mixture comes together in a ball. Continue cooking at low heat for about 3 minutes to dry out the paste, without allowing it to color. Remove from the heat and allow the mixture to cool for 5 minutes.

Preheat the oven to 375°F.

Transfer the mixture to the bowl of a standing mixer fitted with the paddle attachment, and beat in the eggs one by one, beating until the mixture is smooth and supple. Scoop the mixture into a piping bag fitted with a ¹/₂-inch plain or fluted tip. Pipe or spoon into 15 éclairs (5 rows of 3) in 4 x 1-inch lengths, maintaining the same thickness.

Bake for 25 minutes, then reduce the oven temperature to 325F° and bake 25 minutes longer or until the éclairs are dried out, firm, and medium brown in color. Turn off the oven. Remove the éclairs from the oven and, using a serrated knife, split in half lengthwise, scraping out and discarding any soft paste on the insides and replacing the top on their matching bottoms. Place the éclairs back in the turned off oven to dry out for 20 minutes or until crisp.

Make the cream: In a medium heavy-bottomed saucepan, preferably copper, over moderate heat, cook the sugar, stirring often with a wooden spoon or silicone spatula. When the sugar turns reddish brown in color, immediately pour in 1¹/₂ cups of the milk. (The milk will bubble up and make steam, so stand clear.) The caramel will harden once the milk has been added, so heat the liquid, stirring often, until the caramel has melted completely. Set aside.

In a medium bowl, lightly beat together the egg yolks, the remaining ¹/₂ cup of milk, the potato starch, flour, and vanilla bean scrapings. Pour a little of the caramel mixture onto the egg mixture to temper it, whisking to combine, and then return the whole mixture to the pan, whisking to combine. Cook over low heat for 3 to 4 minutes, or until the mixture thickens and starts to form bubbles, stirring constantly. (If the pastry cream does forms lumps, place an immersion blender into the cream and blend until smooth.) Turn off the heat and beat in the butter, stirring until the butter has been completely incorporated.

Transfer the cream to a stainless steel bowl and cool by placing over a second bowl filled with a mixture of ice and water, stirring often until it is cool and thick. (This may be made up to three days ahead of time.)

Make the chocolate glaze: Place the chocolate and butter in a microwaveable bowl and microwave on low power, 2 minutes at a time, or until just barely melted. Cool the mixture until it is thick enough to barely hold its shape.

Assemble the éclairs: Scoop the caramel pastry cream into a piping bag fitted with a ½-inch plain or fluted tip. Alternatively, scoop the pastry cream into a zipper lock freezer bag and cut out a corner forming a ½-inch opening. Pipe the filling onto the éclair bottoms.

One by one, dip the éclair tops into the chocolate glaze, allowing any excess to drip off. Cover each filled bottom with its matching top. Arrange the éclairs on a baking pan lined with wax paper and chill for 30 minutes to set the filling. Serve immediately, or refrigerate up to two days (although they won't be as crisp, the éclairs will be pleasingly mellow after a day or two.)

HISTORY OF ÉCLAIRS

Éclairs originated in France around the turn of the nineteenth century, perhaps made first by Marie-Antoine Carême, the highly influential famous pastry chef to royalty. The first American recipe for the pastry appeared in the *Boston Cooking School Cook Book* published in 1884.

Molasses–Ginger Brandy Snaps

These crisp cookies were a popular type of fairing, a special food, usually sweet, served at each town or country fair in England. Brandy snaps in many shapes were made from sugar, honey, treacle, or after the 1880s, from golden syrup. These crisp cookies contain very little flour so they spread out into a thin layer of bubbly dough that gives them an open lacy texture. Use Grandma's Original or Brer Rabbit light molasses here, the only two brands that I know of that are light in flavor without the bitterness of blackstrap molasses. I've found these brands in the supermarket, not in natural foods stores, which generally sell only stronger blackstrap molasses. Make these cookies on a dry day (wintertime is best) so they stay nice and crisp. They are a perfect accompaniment to coffee, ice cream, or creamy mousse desserts. When still warm and pliable, the cookies can easily be molded into curved "roof tiles" or cups.

YIELD: 2 DOZEN COOKIES

1/4 pound (1 stick) unsalted butter

1/2 cup sugar

1/2 cup light molasses, not blackstrap

1-inch section fresh ginger, peeled and finely grated

1 teaspoon ground ginger

1/2 teaspoon ground cinnamon

Grated zest of 1 orange (4 teaspoons)

1/4 pound (1 cup minus 1 tablespoon) unbleached
    all-purpose flour

2 tablespoons brandy

Preheat the oven to 375°F. Line two 18 x 13-inch half-sheet pans (or other large baking pans) with parchment paper or silicone baking mats.

In a medium heavy-bottomed pot over high heat, combine the butter, sugar, molasses, fresh ginger, ground ginger, cinnamon, and orange zest. Bring the mixture to a boil, stirring until well-combined, and then remove from heat. Stir in the flour and brandy. Allow the mixture to cool for about 10 minutes or until it is thick but still pourable. Place the pot in a bowl of hot water to keep the mixture at about the same temperature. (If it gets too cold, the batter will be too stiff to spread out for the lacy look and delicate texture.)

Drop the batter, about 2 inches apart, by the table-spoonful onto the pans. Bake for 12 minutes or until browned and lacy cooking.

If desired, while the cookies are still warm, drape them over rolling pins or a broomstick to form curved shapes. Reheat the cookies briefly if they start to harden before they've all been shaped. Store in an air-tight cookie tin or other container for up to 4 days.

Melting Caramel Cake: Caramel Coulant

The molten chocolate cake was originally developed by France's renowned Valrhona chocolate company as a way to show off their single variety chocolates. It now appears in one form or another in restaurants across the United States, France, and now, Italy and elsewhere. While it is deservedly a crowd-pleaser, this caramel cake with its melting buttery caramel is good enough to give the chocolate version some strong competition. Best of all, you bake the little cakes ahead of time and then reheat them in the microwave to melt the center. Serve with unsweetened whipped cream or crème fraîche.

YIELD: 12 INDIVIDUAL CAKES

6 large eggs

1/2 cup sugar

1 1/2 cups Vanilla Caramel Sauce (page 822),
    at room temperature

1 teaspoon fine sea salt

1/4 cup Clarified Butter (page 202), melted and cooled

2 teaspoons vanilla

6 ounces (1 1/2 cups minus 1 1/2 tablespoons) unbleached
    all-purpose flour

1 cup unsweetened whipped cream or crème fraîche,
  for garnish

Preheat the oven to 425°F. Prepare 12 (4-ounce) ramekins or a muffin tin that holds twelve muffins by spraying with baker's nonstick coating. If desired, line the muffin cups with papers and spray the papers with the nonstick coating.

In the bowl of a standing mixer fitted with the paddle attachment, beat the eggs and sugar until light and fluffy, 5 to 6 minutes. Add $3/4$ cup of the caramel sauce, salt, clarified butter, and vanilla, and beat to combine. Fold in the flour by hand. Transfer the batter to a large measuring cup with a spout and pour the batter into the prepared ramekins. (They will be completely filled.)

Bake for 10 minutes until golden brown and well-puffed on top, but the centers are still liquid. Invert the ramekins or the muffin cups onto a baking pan lined with wax paper. Serve immediately or cool to room temperature. To serve later, heat the cakes in the microwave for 20 seconds so the centers are warm and melted. In a small pot, heat the remaining caramel sauce until hot to the touch. Serve the cakes immediately drizzled with the remaining warm caramel sauce and a dollop of unsweetened whipped cream or crème fraîche.

Brown Sugar–Pecan Sweet Dream Cookies

These delicate buttery cookies are chock-full of buttery-tasting toasted pecans with the warm spice tones of cinnamon and ginger. A skilled bread baker and an imaginative but down-to-earth pastry chef, Mary Ellen Hatch, shared this easy recipe with me. I worked with her at Apropos American Bistro in the late 1980s. Later at the Dock Street Brewing Company, she made all the homemade breads and desserts for the menu I designed. Hatch went on to become head baker for one of Philadelphia's

top artisan bakeries: Baker Street Bread Company, and then pastry chef at the long-time Philadelphia neighborhood favorite, The Rose Tattoo Café.

YIELD: 6 DOZEN COOKIES

$3/4$ pound ($2^3/4$ cups plus 1 tablespoon) unbleached all-purpose flour

$1^1/2$ teaspoons baking soda

2 teaspoons ground cinnamon

2 teaspoons ground ginger

1 teaspoon fine sea salt

$1/2$ teaspoon freshly grated nutmeg

$3/4$ pound (3 sticks) unsalted butter, softened

$1^1/2$ cups dark brown sugar, packed

$3/4$ cup sugar

2 large eggs

1 tablespoon vanilla extract

$3/4$ pound (3 cups) pecans, lightly toasted and coarsely chopped

Whisk together the dry ingredients: flour, baking soda, cinnamon, ginger, salt, and nutmeg.

In the bowl of a standing mixer fitted with the paddle attachment, cream the butter, brown sugar, and sugar until light and fluffy, 5 to 6 minutes, scraping down the sides once or twice. Beat in the eggs, one at a time, then beat in the vanilla. Add the flour mixture, beating only long enough for the mixture to form moist clumps. Add $1/2$ pound (2 cups) of the pecans and beat briefly, just long enough to combine. Scoop the dough into small (1 tablespoon) balls and arrange on a wax paper-lined tray. Refrigerate for 1 hour or until firm. If desired, freeze the balls until firm then transfer to a zipper-lock freezer bag with the excess air squeezed out. Allow the balls to defrost until they are chilled but not frozen before baking as below.

Preheat the oven to 350°F. Line two 18 x 13-inch half-sheet pans (or other large baking pans) with parchment paper or silicone baking mats. Arrange the chilled dough balls equidistant on the baking pans, in rows of threes and twos. Flatten the cookies lightly with your palm. Press a few of the remaining pecans into the top of each cookie.

Bake for 12 minutes or until medium brown. Remove from the oven and cool on a wire rack. Store the cookies in a cookie tin or other container for up to 1 week at room temperature. You may freeze the cookie balls or the dough up to three months.

Vanilla Caramel Sauce

While this recipe makes more caramel sauce then you'll need, it's difficult to make this smooth, deep-colored caramel sauce in smaller quantities. Never fear: the sauce will keep for up to three months, refrigerated. Simply warm briefly in the microwave and drizzle over ice cream, pound cake, or chocolate cake.

YIELD: 2$\frac{1}{2}$ CUPS

2 $\frac{1}{4}$ cups sugar

$\frac{1}{2}$ cup heavy cream

$\frac{3}{4}$ cup milk

2 tablespoons (1 ounce) unsalted butter

2 teaspoons vanilla extract

In a medium heavy-bottomed pot (preferably copper), heat the sugar and $\frac{1}{2}$ cup water until boiling and the syrup is clear, then continue to boil until the water evaporates and the sugar syrup turns a deep reddish-brown.

Immediately pull the pot off the heat and pour in the cream and milk, taking care as they will bubble up and form hot steam. Lastly, stir in the butter and whisk until the sauce is smooth. Place the pot back on the heat for 1 to 2 minutes, heating until the mixture is bubbling and completely smooth. Stir in the vanilla, then transfer the sauce to a bowl, preferably stainless-steel, to cool to room temperature. Store covered and refrigerated for up to three months.

Sugar Pastry

Not quite as fragile as the Pasta Frolla (page 62), this sweet pastry is equivalent to the French pâte brisée. Use it for any fruit tart, either rolling it out between two sheets of wax paper or pressing it into the shell. Note that the more sugar that is included in pastry dough, the more difficult it will be to roll out, due to the stickiness of the dough. Chill the dough if it starts to get too soft. The almond and vanilla extracts here give the dough a subtle fragrance. I use this adaptable pastry in the Blackberry-White Chocolate Tart (page 483), the Minneola Orange Tart (page 600), the Cranberry-Caramel Pecan Tart (page 654), and the Strawberry-Vanilla Coeur à la Crème Tart with Goat Cheese (page 832).

YIELD: 1 1/2 POUNDS, ENOUGH FOR TWO
9- TO 10-INCH TARTS

1/2 pound (2 sticks) unsalted butter, cut into bits

1/2 cup sugar

3/4 pound (3 cups minus 3 tablespoons) unbleached
   all-purpose flour

1 teaspoon fine sea salt

1 egg, lightly beaten

1 1/2 teaspoons almond extract

1 1/2 teaspoons vanilla extract

2 tablespoons ice water

In the bowl of a standing mixer, combine the butter, sugar, flour, and salt. Chill in the freezer until the butter is firm but not hard, about 30 minutes.

In a separate bowl, whisk together the egg, almond extract, vanilla extract, and ice water, and reserve, refrigerated.

Using the paddle attachment, beat the butter and flour mixture until the pieces are the consistency of oatmeal. Pour in the egg mixture and beat until just combined and the dough forms large, moist clumps. Form the dough into a flattened round, wrap in plastic, and chill for 1 hour in the refrigerator or 30 minutes in the freezer, until firm but still malleable before rolling out. Store refrigerated for up to 5 days or freeze up to 3 months, defrosting before use.

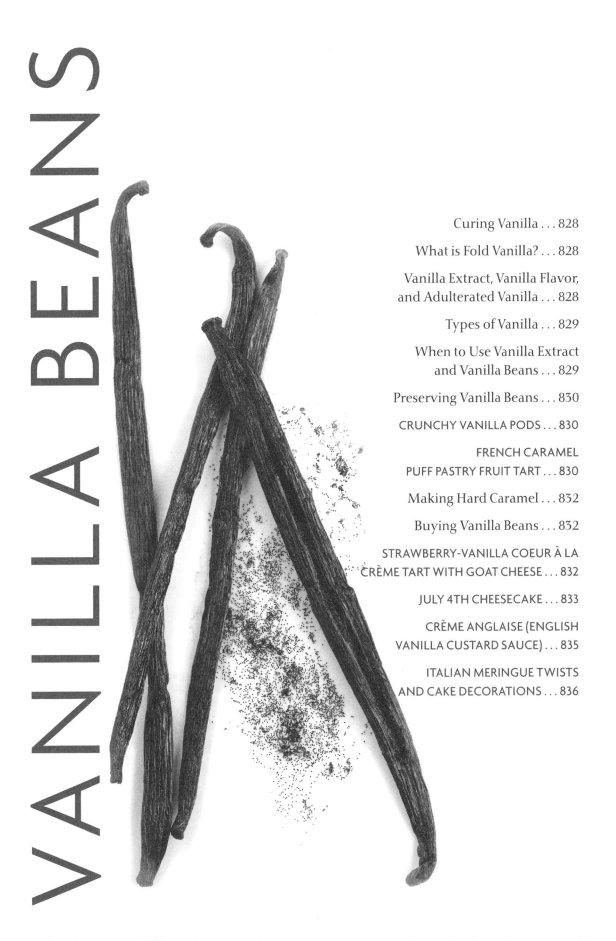

VANILLA BEANS

Curing Vanilla . . . 828

What is Fold Vanilla? . . . 828

Vanilla Extract, Vanilla Flavor,
and Adulterated Vanilla . . . 828

Types of Vanilla . . . 829

When to Use Vanilla Extract
and Vanilla Beans . . . 829

Preserving Vanilla Beans . . . 830

CRUNCHY VANILLA PODS . . . 830

FRENCH CARAMEL
PUFF PASTRY FRUIT TART . . . 830

Making Hard Caramel . . . 832

Buying Vanilla Beans . . . 832

STRAWBERRY-VANILLA COEUR À LA
CRÈME TART WITH GOAT CHEESE . . . 832

JULY 4TH CHEESECAKE . . . 833

CRÈME ANGLAISE (ENGLISH
VANILLA CUSTARD SAUCE) . . . 835

ITALIAN MERINGUE TWISTS
AND CAKE DECORATIONS . . . 836

VANILLA BEANS

Vanilla is the one flavoring used in baking that appeals to everyone. I have never yet met anyone who says they don't care for its delicately fruity, floral, faintly woody flavor. As long as the vanilla is pure, it is virtually almost impossible to overdo this marvelously subtle yet complex spice. Whether you like floral Tahitian vanilla or sweet, creamy Mexican vanilla, there is a vanilla flavor for everyone. As the culinary purist that I am, I never have used artificial vanilla, even in a restaurant or other commercial operation. I'd rather leave it out altogether than try to fool people into thinking that they're eating the real thing.

The peaceful Totonaca Indians of the Gulf coast of Mexico around Veracruz were probably the first people to cultivate vanilla. According to their mythology, the tropical orchid was born when Princess Xanat, forbidden by her father from marrying a mortal, fled to the forest with her lover. The lovers were captured and beheaded. Where their blood touched the ground, the vine of the tropical orchid grew. While other tribes paid tribute to the Aztecs in the form of maize or gold, the Totonaca paid in vanilla beans. In the fifteenth century, Aztecs from the central highlands of Mexico conquered the Totanaca and learned the secrets of the vanilla vine. The conquerors soon developed a taste for the vanilla bean which they named *tlilxochitl*, or "black flower," because the ripe fruit shrivels and turns black shortly after it is picked.

Vanilla gets its name in every language, except the original Totonaca, from the Spanish *vainilla*, a diminutive of *vaina*, (closely related to "vagina") meaning the sheath covering a sword, perfectly appropriate for this aphrodisiac seasoning. Its species name, *planifolia*, comes from the plant's flat leaves. The word "vanilla" entered the English language in 1754, when botanist Philip Miller wrote about the plant in his *Gardener's Dictionary*.

Vanilla was unknown in the Old World before the Spanish conquistadores brought it back to Spain. When Cortez returned to Spain in 1521, he brought sacks of cocoa and vanilla along with the gold, silver, and precious jewels of Montezuma's lost empire. Within half a century, Spanish factories were preparing vanilla-flavored chocolate for drinking, a beverage long enjoyed only by the nobility and the wealthy. In 1602, Hugh Morgan, apothecary to Queen Elizabeth I, suggested that vanilla could be used as a flavoring on its own and the versatility of the exotic bean was finally uncovered. Spanish and Portuguese sailors and explorers brought vanilla to Africa and Asia in the sixteenth century.

Mexico was the original and chief producer of vanilla until the mid-nineteenth century. In 1819, French entrepreneurs shipped vanilla beans to French colonies on the East Indian Ocean islands of Réunion and Mauritius, with the hope of producing vanilla there. Although the plants grew, they disappointingly did not bear fruit. In 1836, a Belgian botanist named Charles Morren found that common insects could not pollinate the orchid. In Mexico, a tiny bee, the Melipone, found only in the vanilla districts of Mexico is uniquely equipped to pollinate the flowers. Because the bees didn't survive outside Mexico, Morren began laboriously hand-pollinating the blossoms of vanilla growing in the East Indian Ocean islands. Edmund Albius, a twelve-year-old former slave from Réunion Island, developed a more efficient method of pollinating the vanilla blossom with a bamboo splinter that is still used today.

Of the thousands of varieties of orchids, the vanilla plant is the only one that produces an edible fruit. The small, trumpet-like flower grows on a vine, and is only open for part of one day. It takes 5 to 6 pounds of freshly picked pods to make one pound of vanilla beans, which are cured either in the air or over a fire. The result is supple, black, oily, smooth pods with a delectable fragrance. Because the flowers open at different times, vanilla growers must check each plant daily for its flowering. Once the flower is open, it must be hand-pollinated to produce the fruit, except in its native Mexico.

Soon the tropical orchids were sent from Réunion to the Comoros Islands and Madagascar along with instructions for pollinating them. By 1898, Madagascar, Réunion, and the Comoros Islands were producing about eighty percent of the world's crop. Today, Madagascar and Indonesia together produce ninety percent of the world's vanilla bean crop. Mexico, where the vanilla orchid originated and which once produced about 500 tons of vanilla beans annually, now produces only a small percentage of the harvest, about ten tons in 2006.

Although pure vanilla extract and vanilla bean scrapings flavor many of the baked goods in this book, but in this chapter I focus on recipes where the accent is on the vanilla. I use vanilla in the custard filling for French Caramel Puff Pastry Fruit Tart (page 830), the filling for the Strawberry-Vanilla Coeur à la Crème Tart with Goat Cheese (page 832), the filling for the July 4th Cheesecake (page 833), the classic Crème Anglaise: English Vanilla Custard Sauce (page 835), and the Italian Meringue Topping and Meringue Twists (page 836).

CURING VANILLA

The unfermented vanilla fruit pods have none of the sought-after vanilla flavor. In order to produce the flavor, vanilla beans (technically fruits, not beans at all) are cured in a process that can take from three to six months. In Mexico, the beans are wrapped in blankets, then bundled in straw mats and heated in ovens for 24 to 48 hours. In Bourbon, the beans are blanched to start. The beans are then laid out in the hot sun to cure, then wrapped back up and allowed to sweat overnight. This process is repeated until the beans are properly cured. Other curing processes are used elsewhere.

Once the vanilla beans have been hand-selected, the flavor is extracted using heat. Nielsen-Massey (www.nielsenmassey.com), a producer of prime-quality vanilla extract, uses an exclusive cold extraction process to preserve vanilla's delicate flavor bouquet. Without heat, the liquid must gently recirculate over and through the beans in a process that takes weeks, rather than days, as when heat is used. Making a batch of vanilla extract using this method takes from three to five weeks, depending on the final strength of the product.

WHAT IS FOLD VANILLA?

The strength of vanilla is measured in folds, its strengths established by the Federal Food and Drug Administration. Single-fold vanilla contains the extract of 13.35 ounces of vanilla beans to one gallon of liquid. Two-fold vanilla contains 26.7 ounces per gallon, three-fold vanilla contains 40.5 ounces per gallon, and powerful four-fold contains 53.4 ounces per gallon (a gallon contains 128 ounces). Typically, vanilla sold in retail stores is single-fold. Stronger fold vanillas are more commonly used commercially where large batches of product are being flavored.

VANILLA EXTRACT, VANILLA FLAVOR, AND ADULTERATED VANILLA

In order to be labeled pure vanilla "extract," the product must contain at least 35 percent alcohol by volume. If it has less, it is pure vanilla flavor. About 95 percent of what is sold as "vanilla" contains artificial vanillin, produced from lignin, derived from wood. The necessity of manual pollination outside Mexico makes vanilla one of the most expensive spices, so that all too often vanilla extract is adulterated, usually with vanillin or, especially in Mexico, with tonka bean, which contains hypnotically fragrant coumarin, now suspected of being a carcinogen and therefore illegal in many places.

TYPES OF VANILLA

Today, vanilla beans are grown in four main areas of the world, each region producing beans with their own distinctive characteristics and attributes. Madagascar, an island off the east coast of Africa, is the world's largest producer of vanilla beans that produce what is called Madagascar or Bourbon vanilla. The term "Bourbon" applies to beans grown on the Bourbon Islands, which include Madagascar, Comoro, the Seychelles, and Réunion, and has nothing to do with Kentucky bourbon. Madagascar Bourbon vanilla is considered to be the highest quality pure vanilla available, with a creamy, sweet, smooth, mellow flavor. Madagascar (mostly the fertile region of Sava) accounts for half of the global production of vanilla.

Indonesia is the second largest producer of vanilla. Its vanilla is woody, astringent, and phenolic (similar to alcohol).

Produced in small quantities, Mexican vanilla is creamy, sweet, smooth, and spicy.

The last of the four major vanilla-producing regions is Tahiti. Tahitian vanilla grown from a different genus of vanilla orchid, *Vanilla tahitensis*, is smooth, quite flowery, and fruity, with a note of anise.

WHEN TO USE VANILLA EXTRACT AND VANILLA BEANS

I generally use pure vanilla extract (try the high-quality extracts from Nielsen-Massey: www.nielsenmassey.com) for adding to cookie batters, dark cake batters, and other places where color isn't important. For custard sauces, flans, and infused syrups, I generally use vanilla beans, because I love their subtler, more complex flavor and the look of the miniscule black seeds speckling the dessert. Once you add vanilla bean scrapings to a dessert (or savory dish), it is automatically elevated to a higher level.

In this book, I use vanilla beans in the Rum-Vanilla Custard Sauce (page 61), Pistachio Custard Sauce (page 698), and Crème Anglaise (page 835). They also go into the batter for the California Apricot Cheesecake (page 118), the filling for the German Bee-Sting Cake (page 523), the filling for the Chocolate Caramel Éclairs (page 817), and the Strawberry–Vanilla Coeur à la Crème Tart (page 832). Vanilla extract flavors most of the European and American-style sweet baked goods in this book in recipes too numerous to mention here.

PRESERVING VANILLA BEANS

Store vanilla beans in a tightly sealed container or plastic bag in the refrigerator to keep them moist. I store my vanilla beans in a jar of brandy so the flavor is gradually extracted into the brandy. I then use the liquid portion instead of vanilla extract. When I want to use the seeds, it's easy to split open the softened beans and scrape out the seeds and the gel that surrounds them. If the beans sit in the brandy for several months so that they're quite plump and soft, you can actually squeeze out the vanilla beans from the top of the bean, which seems to open up on its own. (If not, simply cut off a small slice from the tip. When the bean is mostly emptied, I place it back into the brandy to keep giving off its flavor. This method works very well for me; I have been using it for years.

Crunchy Vanilla Pods

I learned this imaginative way of using empty vanilla pods from Argentinean chef Guillermo Pernot, with whom I co-authored the James Beard Award-Winning cookbook, Ceviche: Seafood, Salads, and Cocktails with a Latino Twist *(Running Press 2001). While Pernot would use the pods as garnish for his creative ceviches, they also work well as garnish for desserts, especially puddings and ice creams. The crunchy pods are quite delicious to munch on.*

YIELD: 4 TO 6 GARNISH SERVINGS

2 vanilla beans, halved or quartered lengthwise
$^1/_4$ cup sugar

Scrape the tiny vanilla seeds and their dark, gooey pulp from the pods, reserving them for another use or combine with $^1/_4$ cup brandy or whiskey and use later as vanilla extract.

Preheat the oven to 300°F.

Bring a small pot containing 2 cups of water to a boil. Add the vanilla pods and boil for about 15 minutes, or until soft and tender. Drain the pods, discarding the water, and clean out the pot. Add 1 cup of water, the sugar, and the pods to the pot. Bring to a boil, reduce the heat to moderate, and boil for about 10 minutes, or until the pods are shiny and glazed. Drain off any remaining syrup (saving it for another use if desired, such as poaching fruit or to sweeten cocktails or iced tea) and spread the pods out on a small baking pan. Bake for 15 minutes, or until crisp, dark, and shiny. Store at room temperature in an airtight container for up to 2 weeks. Serve as a garnish.

French Caramel
Puff Pastry Fruit Tart

Puff pastry is not the easiest dough to work with, especially on a hot humid day, but once you know its secrets, it is so rewarding to be able to magically transform a flat strip of dough into an impossibly flaky, multi-layered pastry. For this colorful pastry strip, with puffed sides, I spread a thin layer of caramel along the bottom for bit-

tersweet flavor, crunchy texture, and to keep the pastry from getting soggy. Next I spread a layer of vanilla bean pastry cream over top. I then arrange a series of strips of colorful seasonal fruit on the diagonal and then glaze the fruit with ruby red and tangy currant glaze. This fabulous presentation will make anyone believe that you must have studied to become a professional pastry chef!

YIELD: 12 SERVINGS

1 (14-ounce) package all-butter puff pastry sheet, defrosted in the refrigerator, but well-chilled

1 large egg, lightly beaten with 1 tablespoon milk, for the egg wash

$^3/_4$ cup superfine sugar

1 tablespoon fresh lemon juice

2 cups White Chocolate Pastry Cream (page 484)

1 pint blackberries

2 firm but ripe peaches, plums, or mangoes, sliced into thin wedges

2 firm but ripe kiwi fruit, peeled and sliced

1 cup firm cherries, halved and pitted

1 cup red currant jelly, melted and cooled until thickened but still pourable

Line an 18 x 13-inch half-sheet pan (or other large baking pan) with parchment paper or waxed paper (not a silicone mat because you're going to be cutting on the pan).

Without unfolding the pastry, roll it out on a lightly floured work surface into a rectangle about 18 x 10 inches. Place it on the prepared pan and chill for 30 minutes in the freezer or until it is firm and cold, but not brittle.

Using a sharp knife, trim the edges of both sides of the pastry to make clean, straight lines. Brush a strip about 3 inches wide lengthwise on both sides of the pastry with the egg wash. Fold the edges over onto the egg-glazed pastry to make two parallel borders, each about 2 inches wide. Chill again in the freezer about 20 minutes or until the egg wash has set and the dough is firm and hard, but not brittle.

Preheat the oven to 375°F. Using a sharp knife, trim off a thin strip of pastry about $^1/_4$ inch wide to cut away the folded outside edges of the pastry, thereby forming a long border of double-thick pastry along each side. Using a French baker's lame, a single-edged razor, or a box cutter, cut shallow scores through the border strips in a decorative crisscross pattern on top of the pastry. Poke the center portion of the pastry all over with a fork. (This prevents the pastry in the center from puffing up too much.)

Bake the crust for 15 minutes, then using the fork, poke the center portion again to let out the air bubbles from the center of the pastry until it flattens out again. Continue baking 10 minutes longer or until the pastry crust is well-browned and puffed-up. Cool to room temperature on a wire rack.

In a medium heavy pot with a lid, preferably copper, combine the sugar and lemon juice. Slowly heat until the sugar melts and begins to turn color at the edges, shaking occasionally so the sugar melts evenly. Uncover and continue to cook until the sugar just starts to turns reddish-brown. Immediately pour the caramel evenly down the center of the baked pastry crust. Using a wooden spoon or a silicone spatula, spread the caramel as evenly as possible along the pastry crust, but don't worry if it hardens and leaves a few spots bare. Cool the caramel completely before spreading the pastry cream evenly over top.

Arrange the fruits in contrasting rows on the diagonal and tightly pack together over the filling. Brush with the melted jelly and chill until set, about 30 minutes in the refrigerator. Cut into portion sizes and serve. This pastry is best served the same day it is made.

MAKING HARD CARAMEL

When making a hard caramel (starting with sugar and a bit of lemon juice, rather than with sugar syrup that is cooked down) it is best to use superfine or bar sugar. The tiny crystals will melt more evenly and quickly. If substituting granulated sugar, keep the heat low and shake the pot often so that it melts evenly without burning. Be patient—the sugar will eventually melt. A copper pot is ideal here, because the heat conduction is so good that it's easy to melt the sugar.

BUYING VANILLA BEANS

The market price of vanilla rose dramatically in the late 1970s due to a typhoon, with prices becoming more stable through the early 1980s, despite the pressure of newly introduced Indonesian vanilla. By the mid-1980s, the cartel that had controlled vanilla prices and distribution since its creation in 1930 disbanded. Prices dropped seventy percent over the next few years, to about $10 per pound. Typhoon Huddah, which struck in early 2000, along with political instability and poor weather, drove vanilla prices back up to more than $250 per pound in 2004. Since then, prices have dropped dramatically, although that is not always seen when buying vanilla in small amounts.

Strawberry–Vanilla Coeur à la Crème Tart with Goat Cheese

Coeur à la crème, which translates to "cream heart" from the French, is an easy-to-make sweetened cream cheese mousse that's drained overnight to remove excess liquid. This is a tangier version made from cream cheese, crème fraîche (French thickened cream), and mild goat cheese. The bright white color of the mousse is accented by the deep jewel tone of the strawberries, while the soft texture and acidic edge of the berries cuts the richness of the cheese. While it's not absolutely necessary to use whole vanilla beans here, the miniscule black specks and warm, tropical fragrance take this luscious tart to a higher level. Start two days ahead to prepare and drain the filling. In a pinch, wait one day only. The filling won't be quite as thick, but will still work well.

YIELD: ONE TART, 10 TO 12 SERVINGS

3/4 pound cream cheese, softened

3/4 cup confectioners' sugar

1 vanilla bean, seeds scraped out

6 ounces mild goat cheese

1 cup crème fraîche, purchased or homemade
  (see *Starting with Ingredients*)

3/4 pound Sugar Pastry Dough (page 823) or Sweet
  White Whole Wheat Dough (page 863)

1 quart small ripe strawberries, cored and halved

3/4 cup red currant preserves, melted and strained

In the bowl of a standing mixer fitted with the paddle attachment, combine the cream cheese, confectioners' sugar, and vanilla seeds until smooth and creamy, scraping down the sides of the bowl several times to break up any small lumps. Add the goat cheese, and beat again until smooth.

Separately, whip the crème fraîche until light and firm, then fold into the cream cheese mixture.

Line a wire sieve with dampened cheesecloth so the edges hang out, and place it over a bowl. Fill the sieve with the cream cheese mixture and cover with the over-hanging cheesecloth so the mixture is enclosed. Allow the mixture to drain in the refrigerator for 48 hours or until nicely thickened.

Roll out the pastry between two sheets of lightly floured wax paper to about 3/8-inch thick. Without stretching the dough, drape it into a 10-inch French tart pan, preferably at least 1 1/2-inches deep. Trim off any overhanging edges, then chill the crust for 1 hour in the refrigerator or 30 minutes in the freezer to set the shape.

Preheat the oven to 350°F.

Fit a piece of heavy-duty foil onto the crust and fill with beans or other pie weights. Blind bake (just pastry crust, no filling) on the bottom shelf of the oven until the crust is cooked through but not yet browned, about 25 minutes,. Remove the foil and the weights, reduce the oven temperature to 325°F, and bake for 10 minutes longer, or until the dough is evenly and lightly browned. Remove from the oven and cool to room temperature on a wire rack before filling.

Spoon the cheese mixture into the tart crust and spread it out evenly. Arrange the strawberries over top, placing them as close together as possible. Brush with the red currant preserves and chill for 30 minutes to set the glaze before cutting into serving portions. Store refrigerated up to 2 days.

July 4th Cheesecake

It doesn't have to be the fourth of July to make this strikingly beautiful cake. But, in commemoration of the Fourth, red and blue berries glazed with shiny red cur-rant jelly top a white cheesecake base dotted with tiny black vanilla bean seeds. The crumb crust is a perfect place to use up any broken biscotti bits or the crusty ends, though graham crackers will work too. Made in a 10-inch cake pan to give plenty of room for the colorful topping, the cake can easily serve sixteen happy people. Substitute brandy or light rum for the kirsch, although kirsch will emphasize the berry flavors here. Even better would be the rare but wonderful framboise, an eau de vie distilled from raspberries.

YIELD: ONE 10-INCH CHEESECAKE,
12 TO 16 SERVINGS

Crust

3 ounces (about 1 cup) almond biscotti or
   graham crackers, crushed

1/4 pound (3/4 cup) hazelnuts, lightly toasted and
   skinned, substitute skin-on almonds

1/4 cup dark brown sugar, packed

1 teaspoon ground cinnamon

2 ounces (1/2 stick) unsalted butter, melted and cooled

Filling

2 pounds cream cheese, softened

1 cup sugar

1 cup full-fat Greek yogurt or sour cream

3 large eggs

2 large egg yolks

Grated zest of 1 lemon (1 tablespoon)

Scrapings of 1 vanilla bean, or 2 teaspoons
   vanilla extract

Topping

1/2 cup full-fat Greek yogurt or sour cream

2 tablespoons sugar

2 tablespoons kirsch, substitute brandy,
   light rum, or framboise

Fruit

1 pint raspberries

1 pint blueberries

1 pint small ripe strawberries, halved
  (leaving the green calyxes attached)

1 pint blackberries

1 cup red currant jelly, or strained red currant jam,
melted and cooled until slightly thickened

Preheat the oven to 350°F. Spray a 10-inch springform pan with nonstick coating.

In the bowl of a food processor, combine the biscotti, hazelnuts, sugar, and cinnamon. Process until fine crumbs form, then add the butter, and process 1 minute to combine. Press the mixture firmly into the bottom of the pan.

Place the pan on a baking pan to catch any drips and bake for 20 minutes or until lightly browned. Cool and reserve.

Lower the oven temperature to 300°F.

In the bowl of a standing mixer fitted with the paddle attachment or a food processor, combine the cream cheese and sugar, and beat until smooth, scraping down the sides of bowl with a silicone spatula to prevent lumps. Add the yogurt, eggs and egg yolks, lemon zest, and vanilla bean scrapings, and beat until smooth, scraping down to get rid of any stubborn lumps. Whisk briefly by hand to insure that the batter is smooth.

Wrap the bottom and sides of the pan in a single sheet of aluminum foil, preferably heavy-duty. Scrape the batter into the crust, place the pan into a larger baking pan, and pour in about 1-inch of hot water. Carefully place the baking pan in the oven and bake for about 1 hour, or until the center of the cheesecake is just barely set and no longer jiggly when shaken. Check often near the end of the baking time to be sure the filling doesn't begin to rise and crack (or it will fall and crack even more). Remove from the oven and cool to room temperature or cool and refrigerate overnight.

Make the topping: Preheat the oven to 400°F.

In a small bowl, whisk together the yogurt, sugar, and kirsch, and spread it evenly over the cooled cheesecake. Bake the cheesecake in the upper third of the oven for 5 minutes, or until the topping is just set. Cool to room temperature.

Arrange the berries in lengthwise strips over the cheesecake, alternating blueberries and raspberries, then blackberries and strawberries. Press the fruit in slightly so it adheres to the topping. Brush the fruit with the jelly and chill for 1 hour in the refrigerator. Insert a thin-bladed icing spatula between the edge of the cake and the pan sides to separate them and remove the sides. (Pastry chefs use a hand-held torch to heat the sides of the metal pan just enough to release the cake.) Cut the cake into portions using a hot wet knife, rinsed under hot water in between each slice. Store covered and refrigerated for up to 3 days.

Crème Anglaise (English Vanilla Custard Sauce)

This versatile sauce is commonly referred to by its French name, crème anglaise (English cream), but is also called "English pouring custard," differentiating it from a fully set baked custard. With its mild flavor and soft texture, it is typical of the nursery foods served to well-to-do English children, who traditionally ate their meals in the nursery (or children's quarters), fed by their nannies. Use a split-open fresh vanilla bean if at all possible, for its full-bodied fragrance and also for the aesthetic pleasure of the miniscule black seeds speckled into the creamy pale yellow sauce. Note this same sauce can be chilled and run in an ice cream machine to make delectably rich, French-style vanilla ice cream.

YIELD: 2½ CUPS

1 cup milk

1 cup light or heavy cream

1 vanilla bean, split lengthwise, or 2 teaspoons vanilla extract

4 large egg yolks

½ cup sugar

Combine the milk, cream, and vanilla bean in a microwaveable 1-quart glass measure or heavy-bottomed, nonreactive pot and heat until scalding. Cover, and set aside for 15 minutes.

Meanwhile, beat the egg yolks and the sugar together until combined.

Reheat the milk mixture until steaming hot, then whisk it into the egg mixture. Transfer the mixture to the saucepan and heat, stirring often, over medium-low heat until the custard has visible thickened (you will be able to see streaks in the pan when you stir the sauce with a wooden spoon or silicone spatula) or reaches 165°F on a thermometer. Immediately remove from the heat. Scrape out the insides of the vanilla bean using a small sharp knife and add to the mixture, discarding the pod (or rinse it well, dry it, and store it in a bowl of sugar). Transfer the custard to a metal bowl to cool, whisking often to prevent a skin from forming. Serve warm or refrigerate up to 4 days before serving.

Italian Meringue Twists and Cake Decorations

These crispy meringues are quite sweet with an airy, melt-in-the-mouth texture and delicate lemon, vanilla, and almond flavors. Crumbled meringues make a simple decoration for a cake like the Torta di Zabaglione (page 480). Meringues must be baked at a very low temperature, in fact, they are really dried rather than baked. The longer they're baked or allowed to dry, the drier and crisper their centers will be. If the meringues are baked for a shorter time, they will be crisp on the surface but be soft and chewy inside and will tend to soften easily. Meringues are best made on a day with low humidity. Substitute 2 teaspoons coffee extract for the vanilla and almond extract and the lemon juice to make coffee meringues. This recipe is gluten-free. This recipe is dairy-free.

YIELD: ABOUT 24 (8-INCH) MERINGUES

1 cup sugar

4 egg whites ($^1/_2$ cup), at room temperature

$^1/_2$ teaspoon fine sea salt

2 teaspoons vanilla extract

1 teaspoon almond extract

1 teaspoon fresh lemon juice

In a medium, heavy-bottomed pot, combine the sugar with $^1/_2$ cup water and bring to a boil, shaking to combine without forming crystals, until the mixture forms a clear syrup. Continue to cook until the mixture is thickened and bubbling and it reaches the soft-ball stage, 238°F on a candy thermometer, or when a spoonful dropped in a small bowl of ice water forms a soft ball.

When the sugar is close to the soft ball stage and has thick bubbles all over the surface (about 230°F), beat the egg whites and salt together to form medium peaks. With the mixer going on low speed, beat the hot sugar syrup into the center of the bowl (to minimize splashing). Continue to beat until the meringue is firm, glossy, and at room temperature, about 10 minutes. Beat in the vanilla, almond extract, and lemon juice.

To make meringues for decorative cookies: Preheat the oven to 200°F. Line two 18 by 13-inch baking pans with parchment paper or silicone baking mats. Transfer the meringue to a piping bag fitted with a medium star tip and pipe into figure-8 shapes, 3 to 4 inches in length. Bake for 1 hour or until dry and firm.

To make meringue sticks for decorating cakes: Preheat the oven to 200°F. Line two 18 by 18-inch baking pans with parchment paper or silicone baking mats. Transfer the meringue to a piping bag fitted with a medium plain tip or heavy-duty plastic freezer bag with the corner cut out, and pipe the mixture into long strips about 3 to 4 inches in length Bake for 1 hour or until dry and firm.

Turn off the oven and let the meringues dry out several hours or overnight. Note that when the meringues come away easily from the pan, they are done. If they stick to the pan in the center, put them back in a 200°F oven and bake for 30 minutes longer, or until they are crisp. Remove the meringues from the pan carefully, and store them in a dry place up to two weeks.

WALNUTS & BLACK WALNUTS

Black Walnuts . . . 840

Hammons Black Walnuts . . . 841

Choosing and Storing Walnuts . . . 841

GREEK EGGPLANT AND WALNUT PHYLLO ROLLS . . . 842

LE BEC-FIN'S FRUITED WALNUT BREAD . . . 843

CALIFORNIA WALNUT-ROSEMARY BREAD . . . 844

POTICA (SLOVENIAN HONEY-WALNUT RING) . . . 845

CANDIED WALNUTS . . . 847

SWEET WALNUT PASTRY . . . 848

WALNUTS & BLACK WALNUTS

I'm a nut-a-holic, I admit. It all goes back to one of my early tasks in a very influential kitchen: toasting walnuts with a great deal of trepidation to make sure I didn't burn a whole expensive batch. It had long been my goal to work at Kathleen Mulhern's The Garden restaurant in Philadelphia, and I finally landed a job in the pantry, just in time for their madly busy summer. At the time, The Garden was just about the only restaurant around that boasted an outdoor garden, and it was always mobbed for lunch, especially by business people. One of my jobs was toasting a huge tray of walnuts every day for the chicken salad. Perhaps because I didn't get much time to eat anything else except the toasty ends of French baguettes discarded by customers, I managed to gorge myself daily on those soft, buttery-tasting toasted nuts. They are still among the foods that I can't resist, especially when toasted.

Walnuts are the fruit of the English walnut tree, *Juglans regia*, a Latin contraction of *Jovis glans*, meaning "regal nut of Jupiter" or "nut of the Gods," also known as the Persian walnut. According to Roman lore, the gods feasted on walnuts while their lowly subjects subsisted on lesser nuts

such as acorns, beechnuts, and chestnuts. Some scholars say the term "walnut" derives from the Teutonic German *wallnuss* or *welsche nuss*. Others believe it comes from the Anglo-Saxon word *wealh* meaning "foreign" or "alien" and *hnutu* meaning "nut." Walnuts were brought to Europe through Persia in early history and got the name English walnut, because they were brought from Asia Minor to England aboard English boats.

The walnut tree, which grows widely in temperate zones throughout the world, goes so far back in human history, no one knows where it originated, although the ancient Romans believe it originated in Persia. Early cultivation of the walnut tree spanned from southeastern Europe to Asia Minor to the Himalayas. Greek usage of walnut oil dates back to the fourth century BCE, nearly a century before the Romans. Walnut oil has been used for centuries in the preparation of fine paints for artists.

It's easy to imagine why ancient Romans considered the walnut to be a tree version of the human brain. The shell represented the skull, while the two nut halves resembled a miniature brain. Walnuts were thrown to Roman wedding guests by the groom to bring good health, to ward off disease, and to increase fertility. Young boys eagerly scrambled for the tossed walnuts, as the groom's gesture indicated his passage into manhood. In Rome, the walnut was thought to enhance fertility, yet in Romania, a bride would place one roasted walnut in her bodice for every year she wished to remain childless. During the Middle Ages, Europeans believed walnuts would ward off fevers, witchcraft, epileptic fits, the evil eye, and even lightning.

Franciscan priests brought the walnut to California in the United States around 1770. The Carpathian walnut is a cold, hardy strain found in the northern states of the American Midwest while the black walnut is native to North America. In much of Europe, walnuts are so basic, they are simply known as nuts (*noci*) in Italian, French (*noix*), and Spanish (*nuez*).

Walnut trees can grow up to 100 feet tall, with trunks up to twelve feet in diameter. Of the fifteen edible species of *Juglans*, the Persian or English variety is the most delectable and the most widely-used. English walnuts have a thin shell which is easily cracked. The soft curly nutmeat halves have a sweet flavor with a touch of the bitterness and astringency from the golden to dark-brown paper edible skin. Other varieties include black walnut, Chinese walnut, Japanese walnut, and white walnut, also often called butternut. The roots of the black walnut and butternut produce a substance called *juglone* which can be toxic to many plants and trees near the tree's root system;

but there are plants that can co-exist with the tree.

When the outer husk of the nut begins to crack and the thin divider separating the still-moist nut kernels inside becomes brittle, it's time to harvest walnuts. Commercial walnuts are hulled, washed, and dried by machines. Walnuts grown in France are said to be the finest, at least in France. French walnut oil is esteemed, although good quality walnut oil is now being produced in California. Walnut oil is an excellent, albeit expensive, choice for baked goods and cold dressings, but not for cooking. I use walnut oil in the California Walnut-Rosemary Bread (page 844) to enrich the dough and enhance its walnut flavor.

With their rich, buttery texture, and mild pleasing flavor, walnuts are a natural in baking, used wherever the nuts are grown. In this book, the adaptable walnut goes into savory baked goods like the Currant-Walnut Baguette (page 761) and the Grape, Gorgonzola, and Walnut Focaccia (page 788). I rely on walnuts in sweet baked goods like the Blueberry-Walnut Streusel Muffins (page 164), the Italian Walnut Cake with Candied Fruit (page 226), the Cranberry-Walnut Pound Cake (page 400), the English Gooseberry Cobbler with Walnut Crunch (page 410), the Maple Syrup Pie with Walnuts (page 555), the Spiced Quince and Walnut Thumbprint Cookies (page 750), and the Greek Honey Walnut Cake with Yogurt (page 903).

In this chapter, walnuts fill the savory Greek Eggplant and Walnut Phyllo Rolls (page 842), the Fruited Walnut Bread from Philadelphia's famed LeBec-Fin Restaurant (page 843), the California

Walnut–Rosemary Bread (page 844), and the Potica (Slovenian Honey–Walnut Ring) (page 845). The soft, dark caramel–colored Candied Walnuts (page 847) are delicious on their own but are also added to the dense and delicious Candied Walnut Apple Pie (page 109) from Philadelphia. Rich and tender Sweet Walnut Pastry (page 848) is used in the Strawberry–Rhubarb Tart (page 168).

BLACK WALNUTS

The saying "a tough nut to crack" surely must refer to the black walnut, as it requires extreme force and determination to get to the meat. Black walnuts are notoriously difficult to crack, with thick, ridged shells and hulls that adhere to the shell, so they remain a regional specialty product. I, of course, adore them, as I go for all sorts of strong, distinctive flavors. This native American delicacy is especially favored for baking and is used to flavor ice cream and confections like fudge.

Eastern black walnuts, *Juglans nigra*, are native to the central and eastern United States and grow wild throughout the Midwest and East-Central United States. In season, I can find hand-shelled black walnuts at the Amish stands at Philadelphia's venerable Reading Terminal Market, because large stands of the trees grow in nearby Lancaster and Chester Counties, and the nuts are cracked and picked by family members who run the stands.

Although the meat to nut ratio is small, the robust flavor of black walnuts is incomparable in baked goods; English walnuts are best for eating out of hand while black walnuts contribute their rich taste and texture to all sorts of American baked goods and sweets.

Dark, hard, sticky shells protect the dark-skinned white nutmeats which must be cured after harvesting. Many find the easiest way to hull black walnuts is to spread them in a layer over the driveway and just drive over them with a car. Once cracked, the meat must be painstakingly coaxed from the shell. Because the oil in the shells leaves an indelible brown stain on the hands, it is advisable to wear rubber gloves when handling black walnuts.

In this book, I use black walnuts in the Canadian Maple-Black Walnut Gingerbread (page 491), the Amish Black Walnut Oatmeal Pie (page 575), and the rich and moist Persimmon-Black Walnut Bread (page 666). I had to stop myself from using these faintly funky nuts more often. Although they are quite delicious with a marvelous bittersweet aftertaste, they are not easy to find and are rather expensive.

HAMMONS BLACK WALNUTS

In 1946, Ralph Hammons found that he couldn't keep enough black walnuts on the shelves of his grocery store in the small town of Stockton, Missouri. Seeing the potential of this local crop, Ralph bought a cracking machine and began buying wild nuts from the hard-working Ozark people who gathered them each fall. Since then, the company has survived short crops, fad diets, and even a destructive tornado to become the world's leading supplier of American black walnuts. Three generations of Hammonses have kept the world supplied with these nuts for over sixty years.

Black walnuts are one of the few harvested crops still picked by hand, and they are a hands-on product, from planting to harvest to final processing. Hammons still buys its nuts from the wild, gathered across sixteen states by thousands of people. Each year, the company buys millions of pounds of nuts gathered in the fall from approximately 250 buying locations. To crack the nuts, they use special nutcrackers unique to the industry, consisting of large steel wheels that crack the shells. Then they pass through another series of rollers with saw-like teeth that separate the nutmeats from the shells. Once separated from their shells, the nut kernels are graded into various sizes. I buy my black walnuts every year from them, online at www.hammonsproducts.com.

CHOOSING AND STORING WALNUTS

Walnut halves are the most expensive type of walnut sold, but because they are whole, their flavor and texture are tops. Walnut pieces are appropriate for most baking applications, though sometimes the bags contain lots of powdery bits and skin pieces at the bottom. I shake the walnuts through a sieve to get rid of these before baking.

Walnut meal is ground walnuts, sometimes found at natural foods stores. I prefer to grind my own in the food processor. Once ground, the nuts lose their flavor and start to deteriorate very quickly.

There is a long tradition of pressing nuts for their oil in France. A French company based in the Loire River Valley has now opened a sister operation in the United States selling specialty oils including high-quality walnut oil. Go to www.latourangelle.com for more information. Walnut oil should be refrigerated to maintain its flavor and prevent spoilage, as it tends to get rancid easily. Allow it to come to room temperature before using.

Avoid rubbery, shriveled, or blackened shelled walnuts. The best walnuts are whole, firm, and snap easily. Nuts that grow on the sunnier side of the tree will have a darker skin and a richer flavor, but many bakers prefer light walnuts because of their milder, more adaptable flavor.

Walnuts can quickly turn rancid due to their high oil content. The best walnuts will always be those that you shell yourself, but even for me, that is pretty ambitious, at least to obtain them in quantities big enough for baking.

For long-term storage, it's best to buy unshelled nuts and store them in the refrigerator for 2 to 3 months or freeze them up to 1 year. Shelled, bagged nuts are commercially available, but you might think twice about using them after hearing how they are processed. Commercially-packaged walnuts are often treated with ethylene gas, fumigated with methyl bromide, dipped in hot lye or a solution of glycerin and sodium carbonate to loosen their skins, and then rinsed in citric acid. Perhaps it's worthwhile to seek out organic walnuts, in spite of their necessarily higher price.

Store shelled walnuts in an airtight container refrigerated and away from any strong-smelling foods for up to 1 year and 2 years in the freezer. If you freeze the nuts, use them soon after removing them from the freezer to ensure freshness.

Greek Eggplant and Walnut Phyllo Rolls

These fat, crunchy rolls are filled with a savory mixture of roasted eggplant, walnuts, Greek Graviera cheese, and ground cumin. Serve them cut into smaller lengths with cocktails, ideally Greek ouzo diluted with water and lots of ice. I spent a wonderful (though extremely hot) week on the Greek Cycladic Island of Kea, attending a cooking course given by Aglaia Kremezi. She taught me to gently push the ends of the logs toward the center to form a wrinkled surface on the rolls and

make them bake up crisper. We picked all the vegetables straight out of her vegetable and herb garden so the eggplants we used for these hearty vegetarian rolls were plump and sweet as possible. Start one hour ahead to soak the eggplants.

YIELD: 8 TO 10 SERVINGS

3 pounds (2 large) eggplant, cut into 1-inch cubes

Fine sea salt and freshly ground black pepper

1 pound leeks, white and pale green inner portion thinly sliced

1½ cups extra-virgin olive oil, for frying and brushing pastry

½ pound (2 cups) grated Graviera or sharp Cheddar cheese

¼ pound (1 cup) grated kefalotyri or pecorino Romano cheese

6 ounces (1¼ cups) chopped walnuts

2 teaspoons ground cumin

1 pound phyllo dough, defrosted if frozen, or 1 pound Turkish yufka dough

Sprinkle the eggplant cubes lightly with salt and pepper and drain in a colander for at least 1 hour.

In a medium skillet over medium heat, fry the leeks in 2 tablespoons of the olive oil until they are soft, about 5 minutes.

Preheat the oven to 400°F.

Rinse the eggplant under cold running water, drain and pat dry with paper towels. Spread the eggplant out on a baking pan lined with parchment paper or a silicone mat. Roast for 30 minutes, stirring once, or until the eggplant is soft and brown on the edges. Cool to room temperature.

Chop the eggplant and combine it with the leeks, both cheeses, the walnuts, cumin, and pepper to taste.

Set the oven to 375°F.

Fold a sheet of phyllo dough in half the short way and brush with olive oil. Spread about ¼ cup of the eggplant mixture across the dough to make an even form, no more than 1 inch in diameter and leaving a 1-inch border all around. Fold over the edges of the dough, then roll up tightly to form into a log. Place the log, seam side down, on a baking pan lined with parchment paper or a silicone mat. Continue with the remaining filling and dough until the filling has been used up.

Gently push the ends of the logs toward the center to form a wrinkled surface on the rolls, which will make them crispier. Using a French baker's lame, a single-edged razor, or a box cutter, lightly score the rolls into six portions each to make them easier to cut into portions. Bake about 1 hour, or until golden brown. Remove from the oven and allow the rolls to cool somewhat before cutting into portions and serving.

Le Bec–Fin's Fruited Walnut Bread

One of the hallmarks of a fine French restaurant is the care taken with the cheese course, served at the end of the meal. Anyone who has traveled and eaten in France remembers the superb farm cheeses served there. We have more limits here on the types of cheeses we can serve, but at Le Bec-Fin they serve slices of this home-made fruit bread, with a selection of perfectly ripened French cheeses to make a special memory. Use the exquisite peeled green pistachios from Sicily here, as they do at "Le Bec" for the best color and flavor (see page 691).

YIELD: 2 LOAVES

1¼ pounds (4¾ cups minus 1 tablespoon) unbleached
    all-purpose flour

¼ pound (1 cup plus 2 tablespoons) white
    whole wheat flour

2 teaspoons fine sea salt

1 (¼-ounce) package (2½ teaspoons) active dry yeast

2 cups lukewarm water

¼ cup honey

2 ounces (½ stick) unsalted butter, melted and cooled

3 ounces (¾ cup) walnuts, lightly toasted and chopped

3 ounces (¾ cup) pistachios

3 ounces (¾ cup) dried tart cherries

3 ounces (¾ cup) dried apricots, cut into small pieces

¼ pound (1 cup) dried figs, stemmed and
    cut into small pieces

1 large egg white lightly beaten with 1 tablespoon
    water, for the egg wash

Spray two medium (1-pound, 8$\frac{1}{2}$ x 4$\frac{1}{2}$-inch) loaf pans with baker's nonstick coating or rub with butter and dust with flour, shaking off the excess.

In a bowl, whisk together the dry ingredients: all-purpose flour, whole wheat flour, and salt.

In the bowl of a standing mixer fitted with the paddle attachment, dissolve the yeast in $\frac{1}{2}$ cup of the water. Beat in the honey and about 1 cup of the flour mixture and allow the mixture to proof at warm room temperature for about 15 minutes, or until bubbling and puffy.

Beat in the remaining 1$\frac{1}{2}$ cups water, then beat in half the butter. Beat in the remaining flour, then switch to the dough hook and continue beating until the dough is shiny and elastic and comes away cleanly from the sides of the bowl, about 5 minutes. Beat in the remaining butter, the walnuts, pistachios, cherries, apricots, and figs. Transfer the dough to a large oiled bowl; turn it around so the dough is oiled all over. Cover with plastic wrap or a damp cloth and allow the dough to rise at warm room temperature until doubled in size, about 2 hours.

Punch down the dough, then turn it out onto a lightly floured work surface and roll it into a fat log. Cut the log in half. Roll each half out into a rectangle about 8 inches wide, 12 inches long, and $\frac{3}{4}$ inch thick. Roll the rectangles up tightly and fit each into a pan, seam side down. Brush the tops of the breads with egg wash. Cover the breads with plastic wrap that has been lightly oiled. Allow the breads to rise at warm room temperature until they are puffy and light, about 2 hours.

Preheat the oven to 350°F. Bake both breads for 35 minutes or until golden brown on top and a thermometer inserted into the center reads 205°F. Remove the loaves from the pans about 5 minutes after they come out of the oven, so they don't get soggy. Cool to room temperature on a wire rack before cutting into thin slices.

Store the breads in an open plastic bag for up to 4 days at room temperature, or wrap and freeze for up to 3 months.

California Walnut–Rosemary Bread

The original recipe for this soft, light, and extra walnutty bread dates back to the late 1980s, when I served as chef of the California-Mediterranean bistro called Apropos. At that time, the only way we could serve good bread was to make our own, because, at least in Philadelphia, the artisanal bread movement hadn't yet caught on. Twenty years later, the picture has certainly changed, but I still enjoy making my own bread, especially this one, redolent of piney rosemary. I am such a walnut-fiend, that when they're freshly toasted, I can't help munching on a handful, so I always toast extra.

YIELD: 2 LARGE LOAVES

Sponge

1 ($\frac{1}{4}$-ounce) package (2$\frac{1}{2}$ teaspoons) active dry yeast

1$\frac{3}{4}$ cups lukewarm milk

$\frac{1}{2}$ pound (2 cups minus 2 tablespoons) unbleached all-purpose flour

2 tablespoons honey

Dough

3/4 pound (3 cups) unbleached bread flour

1/2 cup walnut oil

1 tablespoon fine sea salt

6 ounces (1 1/4 cups) walnuts, lightly toasted and chopped

2 tablespoons finely chopped rosemary

Make the sponge: In the bowl of a standing mixer fitted with the paddle attachment, beat together the yeast, milk, flour, and honey until the mixture is smooth and creamy, about 3 minutes. Cover loosely with plastic wrap and let rest at warm room temperature for about 1 hour, or until bubbly.

Make the dough: Beat about half the bread flour into the sponge, then beat in the oil and salt. Add the walnuts, rosemary, and the remaining bread flour, a little at a time, until a soft, shaggy dough is formed that clears the sides of the bowl, 5 to 6 minutes.

Turn the dough out onto a lightly floured work surface and gently knead until smooth and springy, about 3 minutes, adding a bit more flour as necessary to prevent sticking. Push any walnuts that fall out back into the dough. The dough should be moist and soft, yet firm enough to hold its shape. Place the dough in a oiled bowl, turn over to coat completely with oil, cover with plastic wrap, and let rise at warm room temperature until doubled in bulk, about 2 hours.

Turn the dough out onto the work surface and divide into 2 portions. Shape each portion into a round or oblong loaf. Place the loaves smooth side up on a greased or parchment-lined baking sheet or into two lightly oiled (1-pound, 8 1/2 x 4 1/2-inch) medium loaf

pans. Cover the loaves loosely with plastic wrap and let stand at room temperature to rise until doubled in bulk, about 45 minutes.

Preheat the oven to 375°F. Bake both loaves for 40 minutes, or until the bread sounds hollow when tapped on the bottom and a thermometer inserted in the center reads 190°F. Cool 5 minutes, then invert onto a wire cooling rack. Cool completely before slicing. Store at room temperature for 1 day, or wrap in aluminum foil and refrigerate up to 5 days (or freeze up to 3 months.)

Potica (Slovenian Honey–Walnut Ring)

A sweet yeast-raised bread with a delicious honey and walnut filling, potica must be rolled by hand, pulled and stretched so the dough covers the counter, ready for the filling of nuts, honey, eggs, and vanilla. Rolled into a spiral and shaped into a ring, the potica is then baked. I adapted this recipe from Lee Butala's mother, a native of Slovenia. Mr. Butala is the Executive Producer of "Cultivating Life" (www.cultivatinglife.com), a public television show featuring outdoor living and cooking, on which I made the Country-Style Greek Greens Pie on page 262. Says his mom, "Rolling the dough out on a clean, floured glass towel will allow you to roll the loaves more easily." Like all traditional baked goods, potica is made in many variations especially at holiday time and has many names including povitica and orehnjaca,.

YIELD: 2 LARGE RINGS

Dough

1½ pounds (5¾ cups minus 2 tablespoons)
   unbleached all-purpose flour

1 teaspoon freshly grated nutmeg

1 teaspoon fine sea salt

1 (¼-ounce) package (2½ teaspoons) active dry yeast

¼ cup lukewarm water

½ lukewarm milk

½ cup sour cream

¼ pound (1 stick) unsalted butter, softened

¼ cup sugar

3 large eggs

Filling

1 pound (3¾ cups) walnuts, chopped fine

1 cup honey

¼ pound (1 stick) unsalted butter, melted

1 cup milk

Grated zest of 1 lemon (1 tablespoon)

2 teaspoons vanilla extract

3 eggs, separated

½ cup sugar

2 tablespoons (1 ounce) unsalted butter, softened

Make the dough: Whisk together the dry ingredients: flour, nutmeg, and salt.

Dissolve the yeast in the water, add ¼ cup of the flour mixture and allow the mixture to proof in a warm place for about 10 minutes, or until bubbling.

In the bowl of a standing mixer fitted with the paddle attachment, beat together the milk, sour cream, and butter until smooth, then beat in the sugar. Beat in the eggs, one at a time, and then beat in the yeast mix-

ture. Beat in the remaining flour mixture and continue beating until the dough is smooth and elastic, about 5 minutes. Transfer the dough to a large oiled bowl; turn it around so the dough is oiled all over. Cover with plastic wrap or a damp cloth and allow the dough to rise until doubled in size, about 2 hours, at warm room temperature.

Make the filling: In a medium, heavy-bottomed pot over low heat, combine the walnuts, honey, butter, milk, lemon zest, vanilla, and egg yolks. Heat, stirring constantly, until the mixture has begun to thicken and just starts to bubble at the edges. Remove from the heat and cool to room temperature, stirring occasionally so the mixture doesn't form a skin.

In a standing mixer fitted with a whisk attachment, beat the egg whites until fluffy, then add the sugar and continue beating until the whites are firm and glossy. Fold into the nut mixture.

Assemble the poticas: Butter two 10-inch ring pans or angel food pans.

Punch the dough down and turn it out onto a lightly floured work surface. Divide the dough in half; roll each half out very thinly until each piece is about 18 x 24 inches. Spread half of the nut mixture evenly over each piece of dough, leaving a border of about ½-inch all around. Roll up the dough the long way, like a jelly roll, and place it seam side up in the pans, tucking the ends into one another to form a complete ring. Cover with oiled plastic wrap and allow the poticas to rise at warm room temperature for 30 minutes or until lightly puffed.

Preheat the oven to 375°F. Bake both poticas for 10 minutes, then reduce the oven temperature to 325°F and bake for 35 to 40 minutes or until the poticas are lightly browned and the dough has begun to shrink away from the sides of the pan. After 20 minutes switch the positions of the poticas so that they bake evenly. Cool for about 10 minutes, then invert onto a wire rack and cool to room temperature. Store covered and at room temperature for up to 3 days or wrap and freeze up to 3 months.

Note: Use a pastry brush to remove any excess dry flour from the dough before rolling it up, as this flour will get pasty. Anytime you roll out a dough with flour, it's a good idea to brush away the excess for lighter results.

Candied Walnuts

To make these toasty, nutty, caramel-coated nuts, I use a three-step process that I learned many years ago from Chinese chef and prolific cookbook author, Eileen Yin-Fei Lo. First, the nuts are soaked in cold water, then they are simmered in boiling water. These first steps soften the nuts and extract their bitter tannins. The nuts are then simmered in sugar syrup so they absorb the sweetness all the way through. Finally, they are toasted in the oven. Is it worth it? Try them and let me know. They're the best version I've ever tasted. This recipe is gluten-free and dairy-free..

YIELD: 3 CUPS

1 pound (3³⁄₄ cups) walnut halves

1 cup sugar

1 cup water

¹⁄₂ cup light corn syrup

2 tablespoons vegetable oil

Wash the walnuts well under running water, then soak them in cold water for 10 to 15 minutes or until pale and soft. Drain well.

Bring a large pot of water to a boil. Add the nuts and simmer for 10 minutes or until the water turns dark and the nuts are beige-white in color. Drain well.

In a medium heavy-bottomed pot over medium-high heat, bring the sugar, water, and corn syrup to a boil, stirring to dissolve the sugar. When the syrup is clear and bubbling, add the walnuts, reduce the heat to low, and stir with a wooden spoon. Simmer the nuts in the syrup for 25 minutes, stirring occasionally until they are coated with the syrup and shiny. Turn off the heat and allow the nuts to cool in the syrup for 10 minutes.

Preheat the oven to 350°F. Drain the nuts and toss them with the oil. Spread the nuts evenly onto a baking pan lined with parchment paper or a silicone mat. Bake for 15 minutes, or until the nuts are crisp, browned, dry, and caramelized. Remove them from the oven and cool on a wire rack. Store in a tightly covered container up to three weeks.

Sweet Walnut Pastry

This is a somewhat fragile but delicious pastry dough that works well with berry and peach fillings that contrast with its rich, buttery taste and nutty texture. Use it for the Strawberry-Rhubarb Tart (page 168) and the French Apricot Tart (page 120). The dough freezes quite well, so it's worth making in a large batch to have on hand for fresh fruit tarts. You may either roll out the dough between two sheets of wax paper or press it into a tart pan by hand.

YIELD: ABOUT 2½ POUNDS PASTRY,
ENOUGH FOR 3 TARTS

1 pound (3¾ cups) unbleached all-purpose flour

½ cup sugar

½ teaspoon fine sea salt

¼ pound (scant 1 cup) walnuts

1 large egg

2 large egg yolks

Grated zest of 1 lemon

2 tablespoons dark rum

¾ pound (3 sticks) unsalted butter, frozen
   and cut into bits

In a medium bowl, whisk together the dry ingredients: flour, sugar, and salt. Place the walnuts and about 1 cup of the flour mixture into the bowl of a food processor and process until the walnuts are finely ground.

In a separate bowl, whisk together the egg, egg yolks, lemon zest, and rum, and reserve.

Transfer the walnut mixture to the bowl of a stand-ing mixer fitted with the paddle attachment, and combine with the remaining flour mix. Add the butter and beat until the mixture resembles oatmeal. Pour in the egg mixture and beat just long enough for the dough to form a ball. Transfer the dough to a plastic bag and shape into a flattened rectangle. Chill in the refrigerator at least 30 minutes, or until firm before rolling out. This dough freezes well up to 3 months.

WHEAT & SEMOLINA

Types of Wheat . . . 853

Types of Flour . . . 854

Antico Molino Caputo . . . 857

Giusto's Artisanal Bread Flours . . . 857

WOODFIRE GRILL PIZZA DOUGH . . . 858

Vera Pizza Napoletana . . . 859

WOODFIRE GRILL DUCK CONFIT PIZZA . . . 859

CARAMELIZED SWEET ONIONS . . . 860

TORTA RUSTICA . . . 861

SAVORY SPICED WHOLE WHEAT PASTRY . . . 862

SWEET WHITE WHOLE WHEAT TART PASTRY . . . 863

TUNISIAN SEMOLINA GRIDDLE BREAD . . . 864

CHAKCHOUKA (TUNISIAN VEGETABLE STEW) . . . 865

SPICY HARISSA SAUCE . . . 866

LAHMACUN: ARMENIAN LAMB FLATBREAD . . . 866

Is Lahmacun Turkish or Armenian? . . . 867

Aleppo Pepper . . . 868

About Tamarind . . . 868

To Prepare Tamarind . . . 868

TURKISH SEMOLINA SPONGE COOKIES (SEKERPARE) . . . 869

WHEAT & SEMOLINA

Out of the more than 350 recipes in this book, over 300 call for wheat flour. Wheat is the most fundamental ingredient for baking in a tradition that stretches back into the earliest civilizations of the Fertile Crescent. By planting wheat, grains could be stored without spoiling, carried from place to place, and prepared in any number of ways. Wheat grain could be used for trade, leading to the development of commerce and a way of feeding people in cities far from distant fields.

Today, it is estimated that one-third of the world's population depends on wheat for their nourishment. The great wheat-producing countries of the world are the United States, China, and Russia, but India, France, Italy, Canada, Argentina, and Australia are also important producers. Unfortunately, large-scale mechanized farming and continual planting of wheat without crop rotation have exhausted the soil of large wheat-growing areas.

Wheat provides structure that contains the gas bubbles in yeast-risen doughs, holds shorteners like butter and oil that make for flaky doughs, sugar that sweetens the dough and makes it more tender, and eggs that lighten the dough and assist in the formation of dough structure. There are all sorts of wheat flours milled for specific purposes, including cake flour, pastry flour, pizza flour, bread flour, hi-gluten flour, clear flour, whole wheat flour, white whole wheat flour, semolina, and durum wheat flour. In this book, I've limited the wheat flour I use to unbleached white flour, unbleached white whole wheat, semolina flour, bread flour, cake flour, and durum flour.

Freshly milled wheat flour is yellowish in color. Although flour can be aged naturally with similar results, to speed up the process, manufacturers in America bleach flour to lighten its color and to help develop the gluten that provides structure to baked goods. Cakes made with bleached flour require less flour and can absorb more sugar, while fat particles will disperse more evenly in the cake making for finer and tenderer crumbs. However, I prefer not to use bleached flour, which is forbidden in the European Union and Australia due to health concerns about the chlorine bleach and peroxides used in the process. In Europe, flour is whitened and its gluten strengthened by adding small amounts of fava bean or soy flour. I generally combine unbleached all-purpose flour with potato starch for lighter cakes and pastries.

To adapt your own recipe, substitute up to twenty percent of all-purpose flour with potato starch. With all unbleached flours, it is best to store them in the refrigerator or the freezer, especially in hot weather.

Wheat, *Triticum spp.*, is an annual grass that is probably derived from a perennial, though distinctions between the various species are not always clear. A handful of different wheats have been grown from prehistoric times until today. The simplest wheat is einkorn, which has two sets of chromosomes,. Somewhere close to one million years ago, wild wheat mated with wild goatgrass, producing wheat with four sets of chromosomes, giving the world the two most important wheats of the ancient Mediterranean: emmer and durum.

About 8,000 years ago, mating between tetraploid wheat and goatgrass gave us our modern bread wheats, with six sets of chromosomes. The extra chromosomes are thought to contribute to the agricultural and culinary diversity found in modern wheats. This wheat's most important characteristic is the elasticity of the gluten proteins that allow bread to rise, leading to a whole world of bread-making. When the gluten contained in wheat is mixed with water, the gluten proteins bond together, forming an elastic mass that can expand to hold the gas bubbles produced by the yeast. Ninety percent of the wheat grown in the world today is hexaploid bread wheat. Most of the remaining ten percent is durum wheat, used mainly for making dried pasta. Others types of wheat are cultivated on a much smaller scale.

Wheat, which was first cultivated in the Neolithic period, was one of the earliest of grains domesticated by humans. Bread wheat was already being grown in the Nile valley by 5000 BCE. From there it spread to the Fertile Triangle (the Indus and Euphrates Valleys) by 4000 BCE, to China by 2500 BCE, and England by 2000 BCE. From the dawn of agriculture, wheat has been the chief source of bread for Europe and the Middle East. The civilizations of Western Asia and Europe are largely based on wheat, known as the staff of life, rice is more important in East Asia and maize (corn) in Mexico, Central, and South America. Wheat is considered sacred in some parts of China, while Greek, Roman, Sumerian, and Finnish mythology all had gods and goddesses of wheat.

The Spanish conquistadores first brought wheat to the New World, in Mexico, in 1520. English colonists brought wheat to Virginia early in the seventeenth century, but it didn't do well in the humid climate of the East Coast colonies. Wheat reached the Great Plains by 1855, and perhaps as early as 1839 in Kansas. The five thousand Russian Mennonites who settled in Kansas between 1874 and 1884 brought Turkey Red winter wheat along with them, one of the winter wheats suitable for bread-making that was grown throughout Europe and Northern Asia. In 1900, scientists at the United States Department of Agriculture introduced wheats from eastern Europe, which, together with Mennonite wheat, provided the basis for the highly important hard red winter wheat crop of the Great Plains.

Cyrus McCormick's invention of the mechanical reaper in 1831 made it possible to harvest wheat much more efficiently than harvesting by hand. A farmer working by hand could cut only two acres of wheat a day; using the amazing reaper, farmers could cut quadruple their production.

About three-quarters of the wheat grown in the United States is winter wheat, planted in the fall. Hard winter wheats have a higher content of protein and gluten, and are often used for yeast-raised breads. Durum is the hardest winter wheat and is primarily used for making pasta, though almost all durum wheat grown in North America is spring planted. Soft spring wheats are used in the United States to make all-purpose flour. In Canada, spring wheat is labeled as cake flour.

Sixty to sixty-three million acres of wheat produced in forty-two states are harvested each year in the United States using giant combines that cut an acre of wheat in less than six minutes. Soft red winter wheat and soft white wheats are grown east of the Mississippi River. West of the Mississippi, the wheats grown include hard red winter, hard red spring, durum, hard white, and soft white. Soft white wheat is grown in the Pacific Northwest, while spring and durum wheats are grown in the Northern Plains. Today, the Ameri-can wheat belt covers the Ohio Valley, the prairie states, and Eastern Oregon and Washington; Kansas leads the states in production.

In this chapter, I have included a recipe for classic pizza dough, borrowed from my friend, Michael Tuohy, chef/owner of Atlanta's Woodfire Grill (page 859), along with his outstanding Woodfire Grill Duck Confit Pizza (page 859). The Italian Torta Rustica (page 861) is made with simple yeast-raised wheat dough. I make two pastry doughs using part white whole wheat, one savory (page 862) and one sweet (page 863). The Tunisian Semolina Griddle Bread (page 864) is an unusual and deliciously flaky bread cooked on a hot griddle that I learned from master baker and Tunisian native Taieb Dridi (www.couscoussier.com). I learned to make Lahmacun (page 866), an Armenian/Turkish flatbread that is covered with lamb and tomato, baked until soft and chewy, and eaten rolled up as some of the best street food you've ever had, from my Turkish friend's mother and the owner of a restaurant with a wood-burning oven. The recipe for the tender Turkish Semolina Sponge Cookies: Sekerpare (page 869), made with that golden-yellow nutty-tasting flour, came from a cooking class I took in Istanbul.

TYPES OF WHEAT

DURUM WHEAT: Durum wheat, *Triticum turgidum durum*, is the most important of the tetraploid wheats with four sets of chromosomes. Durum wheat arose in the Near East and spread to the Mediterranean before Roman times. Emmer (see below) was better suited to humid climates and had a starchy grain; durum was better suited to semi-arid conditions and had a glassy grain. Both are used to make breads, bulgur, couscous, and the large, flat steamed Ethiopian bread called injera.

Durum wheat, or macaroni wheat, is the only tetraploid wheat widely cultivated today. Durum is the hardest of all wheats. Its high protein content and gluten strength make durum good for pasta and bread. It is not, however, very good for cakes, which are made from soft wheat for tenderness. Most of the durum grown today is amber durum, the grains of which are amber-colored and larger than other types of wheat. Durum wheat sells at a premium to other varieties. Worldwide, durum wheat is grown in the former Soviet Union, Argentina, India, Turkey, Morocco, and Algeria, with United States and Canada also being major producers. In Europe, durum is mainly raised in southern and central Italy. The largest producer of durum is Canada, where it is grown mostly in Saskatchewan. In the United States, durum wheat is primarily grown in North Dakota.

Although I've easily made thousands of pounds of pasta dough using durum flour and eggs, in this book I only use durum flour in one recipe, the Durum Wheat Bread with Squash, Tomatoes, Onions, and Peppers

(page 736). I'd like to explore more recipes in the future for this flavorful flour.

EINKORN WHEAT: According to archeological evidence from the Fertile Crescent, einkorn wheat, *T. monococcum*, was probably the first wheat to be cultivated, about 10,000 years ago. Although einkorn is rarely grown today, because its gluten is sticky and fluid and unsuited to making bread, nutritionists have renewed interest in it, because einkorn is high in protein and minerals.

EMMER WHEAT: Emmer wheat, *T. turgidum dicoccum*, was probably the next wheat to be cultivated according to archeologists. Suited to warmer climates, emmer became the most important cultivated wheat from the Near East through North Africa and Europe. By early Roman times durum and bread wheats took over. Emmer, known as farro in Italian, is still common in Tuscany, used in its whole form to thicken and add body to soups form and ground into flour. Emmer is an important crop in Ethiopia and a minor crop in Italy.

KAMUT: Kamut (Egyptian for "wheat") is a registered trademark for a high-protein subspecies of durum wheat. It has large grains and is high in protein, though the gluten is of a type that is best suited to making pasta rather than breads.

SEMOLINA: The inner endosperm of durum is called semolina, a hard, grainy, golden-yellow substance with the consistency of cornmeal and a pleasing, mildly nutty flavor. Semolina is used in baking for its special texture and thickening properties. In Middle Eastern, Turkish, and North African baking, semolina is added to fillings to help absorb excess liquid.

As you can see from the number of recipes that include semolina in this book, I think it's a wonderful ingredient. Try the Swiss Carrot-Semolina Torte (page 239), the Cranberry-Semolina Ktefa (page 239), the Makroud (Tunisian Semolina Cookies Stuffed with Dates) (page 422), the Mahmoul (Syrian Pistachio Stuffed Semolina Cookies with Rosewater) (page 466), and the Tangerine Semolina Torta (page 605). I also thicken the filling for the Sesame Spinach Borekas (page 796) and the Greek Phyllo Pumpkin Pie (page 739) with semolina.

SPELT: Spelt, *T. spelta,* is an important wheat species (or sub-species) in southern Germany, where it has been grown since 4000 BCE and known as *dinkel,* It is naturally high in fiber, and is higher in protein than modern wheat varieties. The grain is covered by a tough husk, making it more difficult to process. That same husk, which is removed just before milling, protects the kernel and helps to retain nutrients, so that health-conscious consumers now search it out, especially for making breads..

WHEAT BERRIES: These are whole wheat seeds or kernels, containing the entire grain, including the endosperm, bran, and germ. Hulled wheat berries are similar to hulled barley and are the best type to use for fillings and puddings in recipes like the Neapolitan Torta Pastiera (Italian Easter Pie) in *Starting with Ingredients,* and the Turkish specialty, Noah's Pudding (Ashure in Turkish). The berries are usually soaked overnight to soften before cooking; they may also be cooked in a pressure-cooker. Soft white wheat berries will cook up quicker and tenderer. Look for wheat berries in natural food stores and Middle Eastern markets.

TYPES OF FLOUR

ALL-PURPOSE FLOUR: A blended wheat flour with a moderate gluten level, usually 9 to 12 percent protein. It is the most adaptable type of flour and works well for most home baking. Bleached all-purpose flour is treated with chlorine, peroxide, or nitrogen dioxide. Natural aging occurs by allowing the flour to oxidize slowly with the oxygen in the air, however, this creates a flour that is more expensive because of the time involved. I only use unbleached all-purpose flour, usually Ceresota (Hecker's on the West Coast), King Arthur, or Whole Food's store brand. Gold Medal also produces unbleached all-purpose flour that can be found in many supermarkets.

BREAD FLOUR: Bread flour contains about 12 to 13 percent protein, allowing for large bubbles of gas that produce well-risen, chewy loaves of bread. I only use unbleached bread flour, usually King Arthur or Whole Food's store brand. I often combine other lower or non-gluten flours such as buckwheat, rye, and cornmeal with bread flour to help strengthen the structure of these breads. I also combine tougher bread flour with more tender all-purpose flour to make softer breads. One secret of making chocolate chip cookies with butter that don't spread when baked is to combine half cake flour and half bread flour.

Look for bread flour in the Fennel Egg Bread (page 86), Moroccan Sesame-Anise Bread (page 87), Greek Country Barley Bread (page 142), Ukrainian Buckwheat Rolls (page 185), Seeded Multi-Grain Sourdough Bread (page 186), Buckwheat Cinnamon-Raisin Bread (page 188), Greek Feta Cheese Bread (page 261), Danish Pastry Braid with Goat Cheese and Cardamom (page 273), Cornmeal Pizza Dough (page 392), Turkish Seeded Hazelnut Bread (page 502), Guinness Oatmeal Bread (page 574), Currant-Walnut baguette (page 761), Sauerkraut Rye Bread (page 784), and the California Walnut-Rosemary Bread (page 844).

The recipes for sweet yeast-raised doughs like the Sardinian Sebadas: Fried Stuffed Rounds with Ricotta Cheese (page 517), Hot Cross Buns with Currants (page 230), and Babàs al Limoncello Pansa (page 56) call for bread flour to help doughs heavy with eggs and sugar to rise. The Chocolate Caramel Éclairs (page 817) include bread flour so the éclairs rise better due to bread flour's elasticity. The tender dough for the Black Currant-Apple Linzer Torte (page 411) uses bread flour so a smaller amount of flour is needed to hold the rich hazelnut-based pastry together.

BROMATED FLOUR: This flour has had bromate or other ingredients, including phosphates, ascorbic acid, and malted barley, added to help the flour develop more gluten and to lighten its color. Commerical bakeries will use bromated flour to make bread that rises higher with strong, springy texture. Although it is banned in much of the world, because it is a potential carcinogen, bromated flour is sold in the United States. It must be labeled bromated flour. I don't use it.

CAKE FLOUR: For the lightest and most tender of cakes, bakers use brilliant white bleached cake flour, a soft, low-protein flour milled to an extra-fine consistency. Cake flour contains only 5 to 8 percent protein.

Cake flour is also bleached using chlorine, which helps starch granules to absorb water and swell more readily, producing a stronger structure that can hold more sugar without collapsing. However, bleached flour has a distinctive taste of its own and the chlorine accumulates in animal bodies. In the European Union and Great Britain, bleached flour is forbidden.

Because cakes made with bleached cake flour require less flour, American food manufacturers have been able to produce "high-ratio" cake mixes, in which the sugar outweighs the flour by as much as forty percent, making them extremely popular in this sugar-addicted country. I prefer not to use bleached flour, so I often combine unbleached all-purpose flour with potato starch for lighter cakes (page 722). To adapt your own cake recipe, substitute up to twenty percent of all-purpose flour with potato starch.

ITALIAN 00 FLOUR: In Italy, flour is classified either as 1, 0, or 00, which refer to how finely it has been ground and how much of the bran and germ have been removed. *Doppio zero* (double zero) is the most highly refined and is as soft as talcum powder. Many people mistakenly assume that this softness also means the flour is low in protein. However, flours of varying protein levels can be milled to the 00 category. Higher protein 00 flours that are suitable for making bread are labeled in Italy as *panifiable*, meaning "bread-ready." The most common doppio zero flour is equivalent to American all-purpose flour. Bakers in the United States sometimes substitute a mix of cake flour and all-purpose flour for the 00 flour called for in Italian recipes. Marcella Hazan, the American doyenne of classic Italian cooking, says she finds that all-purpose flour does the "most consistently satisfying job" in standing in for doppio zero. I use doppio zero to make the Italian Taralli (page 584), and it does seem to perform better, though unbleached all-purpose also works. Order 00 flour from Todaro Brothers, an Italian grocery in New York City (www.todarobros.com).

PASTRY FLOUR: This is a moderately low-protein flour that is used in making biscuits, cookies, pie crusts, and pastries. Pastry flour contains 8 to 9 percent protein, between the lightness of cake flour and the strength of all-purpose flour. I have never found pastry flour in the supermarket, but it can be ordered from King Arthur flour (www.bakerscatalogue.com). I have not used pastry flour in this book because it is not that common and can be approximated by mixing all-purpose with starch when I need a lighter flour.

WHEAT GERM: Wheat germ is sometimes added to recipes for its nutty flavor, soft, fibrous consistency, and nutritional benefits. It is high in protein—twenty percent by weight, ten percent oil, and thirteen percent fiber. I use wheat germ in the Florida Tangerine Kiss-Me Cake (page 602) and the Fig and Pine Nut Bread (page 674).

WHOLE WHEAT FLOUR: Whole wheat flour is produced by grinding or mashing the wheat's entire grain, including the bran, germ, and endosperm. With its brownish, speckled look, whole wheat flour is used to add flavor, texture, fiber, and body to baked goods, along with increased nutritional benefits, including naturally-occurring vitamins and minerals. Tannins and phenolic acid in the outer bran of whole wheat flour impart a strong, slightly bitter taste. On its own, whole wheat flour makes for heavy baked goods, so it is usually mixed with white flour.

To make lighter whole wheat breads, increase the water content of the dough because this type of flour absorbs more water. It is important to knead the dough for a long time to develop the gluten. Allow for a longer rising time so the heavier dough rises well. If possible, allow the dough to rise a second time to make it even lighter. Because of the higher oil content from the wheat germ, whole wheat flour tends to get rancid or buggy easily, so store it in the freezer.

WHITE WHOLE WHEAT FLOUR: I use white whole wheat flour made from a naturally occurring albino variety instead of the more common whole wheat flour ground from red wheat. White whole wheat flour has all the nutritional benefits of common whole wheat flour, but is milder in flavor. I combine white whole wheat flour with unbleached all-purpose flour in many of the recipes in this book, both for its more interesting, slightly nutty flavor and mealy texture, and its numerous nutritional benefits. You may adapt most recipes to include up to about twenty percent white whole wheat flour, but keep in mind that it will absorb more water than all-purpose flour. Purchase white whole wheat flour from King Arthur Flour (www.bakerscatalogue.com) or look for it in natural foods markets.

Aside from the recipes in the wheat chapter, look for white whole wheat flour in the following breads: Greek Country Barley Bread (page 142), Ukrainian Buckwheat Rolls (page 185), Seeded Multi-Grain Sourdough Bread (page 186), Fennel Egg Bread (page 86), Fig and Pine Nut Bread (page 674), Guinness Oatmeal Bread (page 574), Sauerkraut Rye Bread (page 784), and Le Bec-Fin's Fruited Walnut Bread (page 843).

I also use white whole wheat flour in the Slovenian Almond-Apricot Tea Bread (page 117), Banana-Pecan Roulade (page 132), Morning Glory Muffins (page 240), Greek Feta Cheese Bread (page 261), Braided Cheese Danish with Cardamom (page 273), Almond Cantucci Pratesi (page 289), Spiced Polvorones (page 349), Oatmeal-Pecan Fruities (page 425), Canadian Maple-Black Walnut Gingerbread (page 491), Savory Oatmeal-Cheddar Tart (page 573), Peanut Butter and Jelly Cake (page 629), Rum Pecan-Praline Sandies (page 652), Onion Poppy Seed Kichels (page 715), and the Bourbon-Spice Pumpkin Cake (page 742).

ANTICO MOLINO CAPUTO

Antico Molino Caputo, a flour mill in Naples near the birthplace of pizza, has the reputation in that city of producing the world's best pizza flour in a town that's tough to please. The flour is specially milled for pizza so the dough is extensible (easily stretchable) rather than elastic, which snaps back. The flour has no additives like extra bulk gluten. The mill's flour contains 11 to 12 percent protein, just right to make perfect Pizza Napolitana, which has a thin center and a raised rim that tends to balloon in the oven, forming nicely charred bubbles. Order Antico Molino pizza flour from Forno Bravo (www.fornobravo.com).

GIUSTO'S ARTISANAL BREAD FLOURS

In 1940, Matthew and Amelia Giusto established a flour milling business in San Francisco, specializing in organic and conventional flours for bread bakers. Giusto's (www.giustos.com) is now run by their two sons and has become a mecca for artisanal bread bakers and pastry chefs across the Western United States. The company contracts directly with American and Canadian farmers who produce organic and number 1 (top quality) conventionally grown grains. Samples of every lot are tested for protein and ash (mineral) content and to see how each particular strain of wheat or batch of flour performs in bread production. The grain is blown pneumatically to remove dust and by-products before being milled. Most of the grain is roller milled, stone ground, or hammer milled through an air-cooled system, so the flour is kept as cool as possible, preventing oxidation and preserving vitamins and minerals.

The four main types of wheat flour sold by Giusto's are:

ARTISAN UNBLEACHED BREAD FLOUR: This is an unbleached wheat flour, 11 to 11.5 protein that contains barley malt (page 139) for better browning. Their Bakers' Choice Unbleached Bread Flour is 100 percent organic.

HIGH PERFORMER HIGH-GLUTEN UNBLEACHED BREAD FLOUR: This wheat flour contains 13 to 13.5 percent protein and works well for certain types of chewy breads. Their Ultimate Performance High-Gluten Unbleached Bread Flour is the equivalent to their bread flour but organic.

GOLDEN CRESCENT PASTRY, CAKE, AND COOKIE FLOUR: This unbleached organic pastry flour has the light texture desirable for pastry, cakes, and cookies. They also make an equivalent non-organic pastry flour.

WHOLE WHEAT STONE GROUND HIGH-GLUTEN BREAD FLOUR (MEDIUM GRANULATION): This flour is 100 percent whole wheat flour, produced by the stone-ground milling method and contains 13 to 13.5 percent protein. They also mill an equivalent organic flour.

Woodfire Grill Pizza Dough

This classic pizza dough could be served in Naples, Italy, where the Vera Pizza Napoletana *(VPN, Real Neapolitan Pizza) movement promotes and protects the style of pizza and tradition that originated in Naples. In 2004, the VPN Association presented Pizza Napoletana to the European Union as a protected food product, similar to cheese, olive oil, or wine. According to the Neapolitan recipe, this dough is made from only yeast, water, flour, salt, and extra-virgin olive oil.*

YIELD: $1\frac{1}{2}$ POUNDS, 2 (14-OUNCE) DOUGH ROUNDS

1 ($\frac{1}{4}$-ounce) package ($2\frac{1}{2}$ teaspoons) active dry yeast
$1\frac{1}{4}$ cups lukewarm water
1 pound ($3\frac{3}{4}$ cups) unbleached all-purpose flour
1 tablespoon fine sea salt
$1\frac{1}{2}$ tablespoons extra-virgin olive oil, plus extra
 for brushing
Semolina, for sprinkling

Dissolve the yeast in the water.

In the bowl of a standing mixer fitted with the dough hook attachment, combine the flour and salt. Add the water-yeast mixture and mix on low speed. Slowly add the olive oil and continue to mix on low for 2 minutes. Turn the mixer to high speed and mix for 7 minutes, or until the dough forms a fairly tight ball around the dough hook. The finished pizza dough should be soft and slightly sticky: a finger pressed into the dough should be able to be pulled away cleanly after sticking briefly.

Transfer to a large, oiled bowl and turn around so that the dough is coated with the oil. Allow the dough to rise at warm room temperature until doubled in volume, about 1 hour.

Punch the dough down, divide into 2 portions and form into rounds.

Note that most pizza doughs don't freeze very well, although the dough may be made one day, allowed to partially rise, then refrigerated overnight for use the following day or even punched down again and kept chilled for use the second day. Allow the dough to come to room temperature before rolling or stretching into a circle or a tongue shape

---

VERA PIZZA NAPOLETANA

To be considered true Neapolitan pizza—as made in the home of pizza, Naples, Italy—a pizza must be baked in a wood-fired dome oven at about 800°F. The pizza must be made from all-natural, non-processed ingredients, including 00 flour, San Marzano tomatoes, fresh mozzarella called *fior-di-latte* (flower of the milk) or mozzarella di bufala, made from the milk of South Italy's water buffalos, fresh basil, salt, and yeast. The dough must be kneaded by hand or with a low-speed mixer, and it can't be shaped with a dough press or a rolling pin. The pizza, which should be no bigger than 14 inches in diameter, should be baked in less than one and a half minutes. Once out of the oven, the pizza must be soft and elastic, and easily foldable, not hard or brittle. In Naples, and now in the United States, many of the best pizzerias use the special pizza flour milled by Antico Molino Caputo (see page 857).

Woodfire Grill
Duck Confit Pizza

Several years ago, I planned to finally open my own restaurant and found a model in the Woodfire Grill restaurant in Atlanta (www.woodfiregrill.com). While I later reluctantly abandoned my plans in favor of concentrating on my writing, I had a chance to visit the restaurant while on a business trip to that city and had the pleasure of meeting the restaurant's chef/owner and now friend, Michael Tuohy, and sample his wonderful rustic woodfire cooking. When Starting with Ingredients *was published in 2006, the chef put together a special tasting dinner at his restaurant. Later, when I asked him for a favorite recipe to include in this book, he sent me his recipe for this hearty and sophisticated Franco-Italian pizza. As Chef Tuohy says, "If you have a wood-burning oven, you're way ahead of the game!" Duck confit can be purchased at a gourmet store or online at specialty food websites, or see the recipe in* Starting with Ingredients. *"Buon apetito!" from Chef Tuohy.*

YIELD: TWO 12-INCH PIZZAS, 4 TO 8 SERVINGS

½ pound (2 legs) duck confit, purchased or homemade
1½ pounds Woodfire Grill Pizza Dough (page 858), at
   room temperature
Semolina, for sprinkling

Extra-virgin olive oil, for brushing

1/4 pound Fontina Val d'Aosta cheese, trimmed of rind, frozen until firm, then shredded

1 cup Caramelized Sweet Onions (see page 860)

1/4 pound Gorgonzola Dolce cheese, cut into bits

2 tablespoons finely chopped fresh rosemary

1/2 cup pine nuts

8- or 12-year-old aged balsamic vinegar, for drizzling

Preheat the oven to 500°F preferably with a baking/pizza stone inside.

Place the duck legs in a microwaveable bowl and microwave on high power for 1 to 2 minutes to melt the fat. Pull off the meat from the legs, discarding the skin, fat, and connective tissue. Pull the meat apart into bite-size chunks.

Roll or stretch out the pizza dough by hand (preferred) and transfer it to a 12-inch pizza pan sprinkled with semolina. Repeat for the second pizza. Brush both rounds of dough with olive oil, especially on the edges. Leaving a half-inch border all around, sprinkle each round with half the Fontina cheese. Spoon on an even layer of caramelized onions. Cover with the shredded duck confit, dot with the Gorgonzola, and sprinkle with rosemary and pine nuts.

Bake the pizzas until bubbling and well-browned, about 8 minutes, switching their positions if you bake them in a single oven. Brush the outer edges of the crust again with extra-virgin olive oil and serve immediately drizzled with the best balsamic vinegar you can afford. If you have any pizza leftover, wrap in foil and reheat at 375°F for about 20 minutes, uncovering for the last 5 minutes of baking time to crisp the top.

Caramelized Sweet Onions

Because the onions cook here into a thick, deep, golden brown concentrated jam, it's best to make them in larger batches, using at least three pounds of onions. Use Georgia Vidalias or other seasonal, locally-grown sweet onions, such as Pennsylvania Simply Sweets, Empire Sweets, or Walla Walla onions. Once the onions have been caramelized, they will keep quite well for several weeks in the refrigerator. Just be sure to cover them tightly. Try spreading these caramelized onions on the Herbed Focaccia with Goat Cheese, Red Onion, and Black Olives (page 725) instead of the red onions.

YIELD: 3 CUPS

3 pounds sweet onions, thinly sliced

2 ounces (1/2 stick) unsalted butter

Fine sea salt and freshly ground black pepper

Optional flavorings

2 bay leaves and/or 1 tablespoon chopped fresh thyme (or 1 teaspoon dried thyme)

1/2 teaspoon ground cloves or 1 teaspoon ground allspice

1/2 cup dry white wine or 1/4 cup brandy

In a large, heavy Dutch oven, cook the onions in the butter, covered, at moderate heat until the juices are released, about 15 minutes. Add salt and pepper to taste and any or all of the optional flavorings. Uncover the pot and keep cooking, stirring occasionally, until the onions are deep-golden brown, about 30 minutes.

Cool to room temperature. The onions will keep for at least 2 weeks, covered and refrigerated.

Torta Rustica

This hearty, rustic tart is baked in an olive oil–enriched yeast-raised pastry shell. The torta is well known in southern Italy and is a specialty of the Puglia region on the Adriatic side and the Campania region on the Mediterranean side. The filling may contain anything from artichokes, porcini mushrooms, roasted peppers, zucchini, and escarole, to capicola ham, dry-cured salami, ricotta cheese, mozzarella, and provolone cheeses. Here, I combine spinach, whole-milk ricotta, grated Parmigiano-Reggiano and Romano cheese, Genoa-style salami, and oven-roasted tomatoes. Serve the torta for brunch or lunch; it's a perfect buffet dish and can successfully be reheated.

YIELD: ONE 10-INCH TART,
10 TO 12 SERVINGS

Dough

1 ($\frac{1}{4}$-ounce) package (2$\frac{1}{2}$ teaspoons) active dry yeast

1 cup lukewarm water

1 teaspoon fine sea salt

1 tablespoon honey

$\frac{3}{4}$ pound (2$\frac{3}{4}$ cups plus 1 tablespoon) unbleached all-purpose flour

2 tablespoons olive oil, plus extra for the pan

Filling

12 ounces fresh spinach, cooked briefly, drained, and excess water squeezed out, coarsely chopped

1 (15 ounce) container whole-milk ricotta

2 ounces ($\frac{1}{2}$ cup) grated Parmigiano-Reggiano or Grana Padano cheese

2 large eggs

3 to 4 large sprigs fresh basil, finely shredded (about 1 cup)

Fine sea salt and freshly ground black pepper

Freshly grated nutmeg

$\frac{1}{4}$ pound Genoa salami, cut into small dice

2 ounces ($\frac{1}{2}$ cup) grated Romano cheese

$\frac{1}{4}$ pound (1 cup) fresh mozzarella cheese, cut into small dice

$\frac{1}{4}$ pound (1 cup) Oven-Roasted Plum Tomatoes, homemade (page 888) or purchased, diced

2 tablespoons olive oil (or oil drained from tomatoes), for brushing

Make the dough: In the bowl of a standing mixer fitted with the paddle attachment, combine the yeast, water, salt, honey, and 1 cup of the flour, and let stand for 15 minutes until bubbly.

Beat in the remaining flour, continuing to beat until the dough is shiny and elastic and it mostly comes away cleanly from the sides of the bowl. Transfer to a lightly oiled bowl and turn the dough so it is oiled all over. Cover with plastic wrap, place in a warm spot and allow the dough to rise until doubled in bulk, about 1$\frac{1}{2}$ hours.

Make the filling: In a medium bowl, combine the spinach, ricotta, Parmigiano-Reggiano cheese, eggs, basil, salt and pepper to taste, and nutmeg to taste, and mix well.

Brush a 10-inch removable-bottom tart pan or a spring-form cake pan at least 2-inches high with olive oil.

Punch down the dough and divide it into two sections: one-third for the lattice top and the remaining two-thirds for the crust.

On a floured surface, roll out the larger portion of dough to a 13-inch round. Drape the round over a rolling pin and transfer it to the prepared pan (the dough will drape over the edges of the pan). Trim the overhanging edge evenly with a pair of scissors to about 1 inch beyond the edge. Sprinkle the salami over the dough. Evenly spoon the ricotta mixture over the salami, then sprinkle with Romano cheese, mozzarella, and tomatoes.

Divide the remaining dough into 12 equal pieces. Roll each piece into a 10-inch rope. Arrange the ropes across the filling in both directions to make a lattice: Lay half of the ropes, evenly spaced, on top of the filling. Fold alternate dough ropes back halfway, then lay a rope crosswise on the center of the torta. Unfold the pastry strips, then alternate folding back the remaining rope. Lay another rope crosswise, about 1 inch away. Fold back half the ropes, lay another rope crosswise about 1 inch away and repeat the weaving until the lattice covers the filling.

Fold the edge of the dough up over the lattice top and crimp or roll under to make a raised edge similar to a pie edge. The torta should be about 2 inches high in the pan. Brush the lattice and the edge of the dough with the remaining olive oil. Allow the torta to rest and rise at warm room temperature until light and puffy, about 45 minutes.

Preheat the oven to 375°F. Bake the torta for 30 minutes or until well-browned. Cool in the pan on a wire rack for 10 minutes. Remove the side of the pan and carefully slide the torta off the pan onto rack. Serve slightly warm or at room temperature.

Store covered and refrigerated up to 3 days. Wrap in foil and reheat for 20 minutes in a 350°F oven, uncovering for the last 5 minutes of baking time to crisp.

Savory Spiced Whole Wheat Pastry

Use this hearty, yet tender and flaky pastry made with white whole wheat flour for the French Roquefort, Apple, and Leek Tart (page 103) or the Radicchio and Fontina Torta (page 260). The pastry's nutty flavor and full-bodied texture will complement any other savory vegetable, egg, and cheese tart such as Quiche Lorraine. It also freezes quite well up to three months, but label it clearly so that you don't end up using it for a sweet pastry.

YIELD: 1¼ POUNDS DOUGH, ENOUGH FOR
1 LARGE AND 1 SMALL TART

½ pound (2 cups minus 2 tablespoons) unbleached
    all-purpose flour

¼ pound (1 cup plus 2 tablespoons) white
    whole wheat flour

1 teaspoon ground coriander seed

¼ teaspoon mace

¼ teaspoon cayenne pepper

1 teaspoon fine sea salt

½ pound (2 sticks) unsalted butter, chilled

and cut into bits

1/4 cup ice water

In the bowl of a standing mixer, fitted with the paddle attachment, combine the dry ingredients: flour, whole wheat flour, coriander seed, mace, cayenne pepper, and salt. Add the butter and place the mixing bowl in the freezer for about 30 minutes.

Beat the chilled flour mixture until it resembles oatmeal. While the mixer is beating, pour in the ice water and beat only long enough for the dough to come together into a ball. Transfer the dough to a plastic bag and shape it into a flattened rectangle. Chill in the refrigerator for 1 hour or in the freezer for 30 minutes until firm but still malleable before rolling out, or freeze for up to 3 months, defrosting in the refrigerator before using.

Sweet White Whole Wheat Tart Pastry

This pastry dough works well for boldly-flavored fillings for sweet pastries, such as the Butterscotch-Ginger Pear Tart (page 641) and the Persimmon Meringue Torte (page 662). It is also well-suited to tarts with custard fillings, like the Greek Blueberry-Yogurt Tart with Ouzo (page 165), because the eggs in the pastry keep it from getting soggy. Baking powder makes the pastry light, while sugar makes it tender and sweet, and a bit of cinnamon gives it a comforting, homey smell as it bakes.

YIELD: 1 1/2 POUNDS DOUGH,
ENOUGH FOR TWO 10-INCH TARTS

1/2 pound (2 cups minus 2 tablespoons) unbleached
    all-purpose flour
1/4 pound (1 cup plus 2 tablespoons) white
    whole wheat flour
1 teaspoon baking powder
1/2 teaspoon ground cinnamon
1/2 teaspoon fine sea salt
1/2 pound (2 sticks) unsalted butter, softened
1/2 cup sugar
2 egg yolks
1 large egg

In a bowl, whisk together the dry ingredients: both flours, the baking powder, cinnamon, and salt.

In the bowl of a standing mixer fitted with the paddle attachment, cream the butter and sugar until light and fluffy, 5 to 6 minutes. Beat in the egg yolks, then the egg. Add the dry ingredients and beat only long enough for the dough to form large, moist clumps. Remove the dough from the mixer and knead briefly and lightly until the dough is smooth.

Transfer the dough to a plastic bag and shape it into a flattened rectangle. Chill in the refrigerator for 1 hour or in the freezer for 30 minutes until firm but still malleable before rolling out, or freeze for up to 3 months, defrosting in the refrigerator before using.

Tunisian Semolina Griddle Bread

This quickly-made golden semolina flatbread, is served in North Africa to welcome guests. In the mountainous region of Tabarka in Tunisia, it is traditionally cooked on top of a domed terra cotta cooker fired from underneath with wood or charcoal. Elsewhere in Tunisia, a flat clay cooker called a ghanay *is used. A more modern way to make this bread is to cook in on a flat-ribbed aluminum griddle, also fired from underneath. I use a cast-iron griddle that I heat on my stove; an electric griddle would also work well. The bread is formed the same way mozzarella cheese is made: using the action of dividing the dough-like kneaded curd without using a knife in a process called mozzare).When the dough is filled with the vegetable ragout called* chakchouka, *it is called* mtakba *(meaning "folded bread") or* mellaoui *(meaning "turned bread"). The dough may also be spread with spicy Harissa Sauce (page 866), formed into a spiral then flattened and baked. This recipe calls for instant yeast, which is preferred for this quick-rising bread.*

YIELD: ABOUT 12 BREADS

1½ pounds (4 cups minus 1 tablespoon) fine semolina

2 teaspoons fine sea salt

1 (¼-ounce) package (2¼ teaspoons) instant yeast

Olive oil

Harissa sauce, purchased or homemade (page 866), or Chakchouka (page 865)

In the bowl of a standing mixer fitted with the paddle attachment, combine the semolina, salt, and yeast and briefly beat with to combine. Add 2 cups lukewarm water and beat until the dough is shiny and elastic and mostly comes away from the sides of the bowl, 6 to 8 minutes. The dough will be soft enough to gush through your fingers, but still firm enough to hold together.

Cover and allow the dough to rest at room temperature for 15 minutes to relax the gluten.

Coat a large baking pan with olive oil. Preheat the griddle until medium hot and brush with oil.

Grab a 2- to 3-ounce portion of the dough in your hand, close your hand tightly, and squeeze out a small handful of dough through the opening at the top of your fist, then twist it off. Using your fingertips, spread the portion of dough out onto the prepared the pan as thinly as possible, without breaking it (one or two holes are okay). Brush the dough with oil, then fold in the sides all around to make a rough square.

Using both hands, lift up the dough square and quickly place it on the hot griddle, stretching it out as thin as possible to the edges of the griddle. It will stick at first, but when it cooks, the dough will release from the griddle. Cook until the dough is well-browned on the bottom, about 2 minutes. Flip the dough over and cook on the second side until browned, about 2 minutes.

Meanwhile, continue making more dough squares, repeating the directions above. As soon as you remove the first bread, add the second bread to the griddle. Continue cooking and stacking the cooked breads until all the dough has been used.

Store the bread at room temperature in a plastic bag for up to 2 days or refrigerate for up to 4 days. The breads are best eaten hot. They can be reheated by wrapping in aluminum foil and heating in a 350°F oven for about 15 minutes, or until steaming hot, uncovering for the last 5 minutes of baking.

Baker's note: Instant yeast, which is mixed directly into the flour without the need for proofing in warm water, is called for here. You may substitute active dry yeast, but warm the water to 120°F to 130°F (warm to the touch) to activate the yeast.

HARISSA GRIDDLE BREAD VARIATION, spread the dough square with a very thin layer (about 1 teaspoon) of harissa sauce, then fold over the dough along two long sides to make a long strip with the harissa enclosed. Roll up the dough the long way to make a spiral. Place the dough with the spiral up and flatten with your fist into a flattened spiraled circle, then bake on the griddle.

CHAKCHOUKA GRIDDLE BREAD, spread the dough square with a thin layer (about 2 tablespoons) of chakchouka (plus 1 teaspoon harissa, if desired for spicy flavor). Fold in the sides all around to make a rough square with the sauce in the middle, then fold in half to make a triangle, then bake on the griddle.

Chakchouka (Tunisian Vegetable Stew)

Chakchouka is a vegetable ragout made from tomatoes, sweet and hot peppers, and spices, all cooked on a low flame. While Chakchouka is of Berber origin from Tunisia, it is also popular in Sephardic cooking and has made its way to Israel, where it is known as shakshukah, *which has come to mean "shaking it all up." Often, the dish is topped with egg then cooked in the oven until the egg has set and is eaten with pita. So, use any extra chakchouka left from making the chakchouka griddle bread to make this delicious dish, usually eaten for lunch, adding bits of browned merguez (spicy North African lamb sausage), if desired.*

YIELD: 3 CUPS

¼ cup extra-virgin olive oil

6 large garlic cloves, thinly sliced

1 teaspoon ground caraway seed, substitute ground cumin

6 plum tomatoes, peeled, cored, and cut into thin wedges

3 red, yellow, and/or orange bell peppers, cored, seeded, and cut into thin strips

1 poblano pepper, cored, seeded, and cut into wedges

1 tablespoon tomato paste, preferably Italian or other high-quality

2 teaspoons paprika

2 teaspoons Harissa Sauce, purchased or homemade (page 866), optional

2 teaspoons chopped fresh thyme

1 teaspoon fine sea salt

Heat the olive oil in a large skillet over moderate heat. Add the garlic and cook until it sizzles and is aromatic, about 2 minutes, stirring often. Add the caraway and stir to combine. Add the tomatoes, bell peppers, poblano pepper, tomato paste, paprika, harissa, thyme, and salt, and cook for about 20 minutes, or until thickened. Store covered and refrigerated up to 1 week. Use to fill the Semolina Griddle Bread above. Or, reheat in an ovenproof skillet until bubbling and top with 1 or 2 eggs for each serving. Broil about 5 minutes or until the whites of the egg have set and the yolks are still liquid.

Spicy Harissa Sauce

Harissa is Tunisia's basic seasoning paste, made of sundried sweet and hot peppers boldly flavored with garlic and ground caraway. Concentrated and hot in flavor, harissa is spread judiciously on sandwiches and is also delicious on flatbread which has first been spread with hummus. Prepared harissa may be found in tubes or cans; the best comes from Tunisia. Slightly bitter, faintly numbing ground caraway is essential to the flavor of the harissa, though it may be hard to find. Use about 1½ tablespoons of whole caraway seeds ground in a clean coffee grinder or finely crushed using a mortar and pestle. In a pinch, use ground cumin.

YIELD: 3 CUPS

³⁄4 pound (2 to 3 medium) red bell peppers,
    roasted and peeled

2 ounces (2 to 3 small) red hot chile peppers, such as
    red Serrano, jalapeño, or Holland red peppers,
    roasted and peeled
¹⁄2 cup sweet Spanish paprika
¹⁄4 cup extra-virgin olive oil
4 large garlic cloves, crushed
2 tablespoons ground caraway seed
1 tablespoon fine sea salt

Combine all of the ingredients in the bowl of a food processor and purée to a fine paste. The layer of olive oil that rises to the top helps prevent the sauce from getting moldy, so add more olive oil, if necessary. Store, tightly covered, in the refrigerator for up to 2 months.

Lahmacun (Armenian Lamb Flatbread)

Lahmacun is popular throughout Turkey as inexpensive street food. On my first visit to Istanbul, I lived on freshly baked lahmacun and ate well, despite my extremely limited funds. I would visit the special lahmacun bakery that made it fresh all day long, buy a thin round, sprinkle it with lemon, roll it up and eat it while it was still deliciously soft and hot. I had to wait 30 years to learn how to make this delicious pizza-like dish from a baker in the seaside town of Çesme. The tomatoes were fresh, the lamb topping thin and delicate, the dough light and chewy, but best of all, the lahmacun was baked in a wood-burning oven, giving it that inimitable smokiness that I adore. Although most of us don't have a wood-

burning oven, lahmacun is still well worth making.

YIELD: 8 FLATBREADS

1 pound fresh beefsteak tomatoes or 1 (15-ounce) can
  chopped plum tomatoes

2 large shallots, finely chopped ($^1/_2$ cup)

2 garlic cloves, minced

1 pound ground lamb or beef

2 tablespoons pomegranate molasses

1 teaspoon Aleppo pepper, substitute 1 teaspoon
  paprika plus $^1/_4$ teaspoon cayenne pepper

1 teaspoon ground cinnamon

1 tablespoon finely chopped fresh mint, preferably
  spearmint

Fine sea salt and freshly ground black pepper

1$^1/_4$ pounds Pide Dough (page 900)

Olive oil, for brushing

2 ounces ($^1/_4$ cup) pine nuts

1 lemon, cut into wedges, for garnish

Cut the tomatoes in half through the "equator." Using the large-holed side of a box grater, grate the tomato halves with the flesh side toward the grater until only the skins are left. You should have about 2 cups of grated tomato. (Discard the skins or save them to add to a stock pot later.)

In a large bowl, combine the tomatoes, shallots, garlic, lamb, pomegranate molasses, $^1/_4$ cup water, Aleppo pepper, cinnamon, mint, and a generous amount of salt and pepper. Using your hands, mash the ingredients together. The mixture should be loose and soft but not watery.

Preheat the oven to 450°F. Brush two 18 x 13-inch half-sheet pans (or other large baking pans) with olive oil.

On a floured surface, cut the dough into eight 5-ounce pieces, then roll each piece into a smooth ball. Cover the balls with a damp towel and allow them to rest for 15 minutes to relax the gluten.

Lightly flour your palms and use them to flatten out one piece of the dough at a time, keeping the rest of the dough covered. With a rolling pin, roll out each piece (or with your hands, stretch it out) to an 8- to 9-inch circle about the thickness of a tortilla. Transfer to the prepared baking pans, placing two rounds on each pan.

Brush the top of the dough rounds lightly with olive oil and spread $^1/_2$ cup of the meat mixture in a thin, even layer, almost to the edge. Sprinkle each round with a few pine nuts. Bake the lahmacun, one sheet at a time on the top shelf of the oven, until lightly browned, about 8 minutes, or until fully cooked and lightly colored, but still soft and pliable. Serve immediately rolled up into cones with a wedge of lemon to squeeze over top. Continue until all the lahmacun have been baked. Store wrapped and refrigerated up to 2 days. Reheat by wrapping in aluminum foil then heating in a 350°F oven for about 15 minutes.

IS LAHMACUN TURKISH OR ARMENIAN?

There is controversy about whether this dish is Turkish or Armenian in origin, though it seems as though it originated in Armenia and was brought to Istanbul by Armenian immigrants. In Turkey, *lahmacun salonu* specialize in this street food; in Armenia, it is prepared at *lahmacuanots*. In the Turkish city of Urfa, they add onions to lahmacun; in Gaziantep, they add garlic. In Syria, the same flatbreads are known as *lahamajene* and are flavored with tamarind, or *temerhindy*. *Lahtnajun* and *lahmajeen* are other spellings of basically the same phrase: *lahma bi ajun*, which means "meat with bread" in Arabic.

ALEPPO PEPPER

The earthy and robust Aleppo pepper originated in the Syrian culinary capital of Aleppo. This gritty, coarsely ground red pepper is dark red in color and mildly hot yet rich and fruity in flavor. It may be purchased from specialty spice stores such as Penzey's (www.penzeys.com) and Middle Eastern markets such as Kalustyan's (www.kalustyans.com).

ABOUT TAMARIND

Tamarind is the bumpy, brown, hard-shelled fruit pod that comes from the *Tamarindus indica* tree, native to tropical Africa. By prehistoric times, the tree had spread to India, and today grows throughout the tropical and subtropical regions of the world. The flesh of the fruit is mashed and strained into thick, deep-brown pulp that is tart, with hints of prune and orange. It is used in hot regions much like lemon and vinegar. Tamarind gets its name from the Arabic *tamar hindi*, which means "Indian date" because its pulp reminded Arabs, who imported

tamarind from India, of the more familiar date. Spanish and Portuguese explorers brought the tamarind to the New World, where it is incredibly popular, especially when it is thinned out and served as a refreshing juice, in frozen fruit pops, or to lend acidic balance to all sorts of recipes.

TO PREPARE TAMARIND

Tamarind pulp is commonly sold in rectangular blocks called "wet tamarind" that keep indefinitely. To use this form of tamarind, you must first soak it in hot water to cover for about 30 minutes, or until the dense, stringy pulp has softened. Break up the pulp with your hands to speed the process. Rub the tamarind with its liquid through a sieve or food mill, discarding the fibers and large seeds. The resulting thick brown pulp is ready to use, and will keep for at least one month in the refrigerator, or it can be frozen for up to six months. Frozen tamarind purée is sold in Asian and Latino supermarkets; small plastic cans of salted tamarind concentrate are sold in Indian markets, though not as desirable, because its flavor is harsher. If you use this type of tamarind in a recipe, cut down on the amount of salt.

Turkish Semolina Sponge Cookies (Sekerpare)

I learned how to make these delicious, soft, and syrupy semolina sponge cookies accented with hazelnuts at a relaxed day-long cooking class in Istanbul. If you're planning a trip to Istanbul, I recommend taking one of the classes given by Cooking a la Turka (www.cooking alaturka.com). Sekerpare translates to "sugary pieces," an apt description for these moist, light sugar syrup soaked cookies. If you can get peeled green pistachios, process them until finely ground for a lovely and traditional garnish. (Order Sicilian peeled green pistachios from Albert Ulster Imports, www.auiswiss.com, where they are listed as Savoir Fare Premium Pistachios.)

YIELD: 36 TO 40 COOKIES

Dough

$3/4$ pound ($2^3/4$ cups plus 1 tablespoon) unbleached all-purpose flour

$1/4$ pound (1 cup minus 2 tablespoons) fine semolina

2 teaspoons baking powder

1 teaspoon fine sea salt

10 ounces ($2^1/2$ sticks) unsalted butter, softened

$1/4$ pound ($3/4$ cup minus 1 tablespoon) confectioners' sugar

2 teaspoons vanilla extract

2 large eggs

1 egg white

40 whole hazelnuts

1 egg yolk, lightly beaten

Syrup and Garnish

2 cups sugar

Juice and grated zest of 1 lemon (3 tablespoons juice, 1 tablespoon zest)

2 ounces ($1/2$ cup) pistachios, optional

Make the dough: Rub two 18 x 13-inch half-sheet pans (or other large baking pans) with softened butter. Note: DO NOT preheat the oven. If possible, set each baking pan inside a second pan so the cookie bottoms bake evenly without burning on the bottom.

Whisk together the dry ingredients: flour, semolina, baking powder, and salt.

In the bowl of a standing mixer fitted with the paddle attachment, combine the butter, confectioners' sugar, vanilla, eggs, and egg white, and beat until light and fluffy, 5 to 6 minutes, scraping down the sides once or twice. Add the flour mixture and beat again, just long enough for the dough to come together.

Dust your hands with flour and form the dough into one or two long, thin logs, about 1 inch in diameter. Cut the logs into 1-inch sections, and shape each section into walnut-sized balls. Toss the balls lightly but vigorously onto the baking pans so they stick to the pan and flatten slightly. Rearrange if necessary so the balls are evenly spaced on the pans.

Press one hazelnut, with the pointy side facing up, into the center of each dough ball, so the tip of the hazelnut is at the same level as the cookie. Brush the cookies lightly but evenly with egg yolk, making sure that excess egg yolk doesn't pool into the center.

Place the trays in the oven, and set the oven temperature to 400°F. Bake the cookies for 25 to 30 minutes or until the tops of the cookies are light golden and crackled.

Make the syrup: The syrup must be ready when the cookies come out of the oven. Combine 3 cups water and the sugar in a medium heavy-bottomed pot. Bring to a boil over medium heat then simmer for 2 minutes or until the syrup is completely clear. Remove from the heat and combine with the lemon juice.

As soon as the cookies come out of the oven, pour all the hot syrup over them, making sure that all the cookies are evenly drenched in the syrup. There should be about $1/2$ inch of syrup in the pans, which will be absorbed by the cookies as they cool.

Make the garnish: bring a small pot of water to a boil. Add the pistachios and boil for 1 minute. Drain, then rub off skins and spread the pistachios out on paper towels to dry. Place them into the bowl of a food processor and process to a fine green powder. Or, simply process green pistachios to a fine green powder. Cool the cookies to room temperature, then sprinkle with the pistachios before serving. Store covered and at room temperature for up to three days.

TURKISH PASTRIES FROM GAZIANTEP TO CONEY ISLAND

Güllüoglu Baklava Bakery in New York's Coney Island is the first American branch of a venerable Turkish chain which dates from 1871. The bakery and café imports all its offerings from Gaziantep, the pistachio capital of Turkey, which is also known for its excellent cuisine. The bakery uses the world famous emerald-green Boz pistachios from Barak, Turkey, extra-rich and flavorful pure goat's milk, sheep's milk butter, and Turkish-grown durum wheat flour. So, if you have a taste for Turkish treats and don't want to make your own (or you want to compare your own with the benchmark), order from Güllüoglu at www.gulluoglubaklava.com.

YEAST

Making Sourdough Starter ... 875

Working with Yeast ... 875

Types of Yeast ... 876

High–Altitude Baking ... 877

Bread Dough Tips ... 877

Temperature and Humidity When Rising Bread ... 878

Salt and Yeast ... 878

Sugar and Yeast ... 879

Kneading Dough ... 879

Keeping Dough Moist when Rising ... 880

Thermapen Instant Read Thermometer ... 880

SOURDOUGH BREAD STARTER ... 880

How to Tell When Bread is Done ... 881

SPANISH TUNA EMPANADAS WITH SOFRITO ... 881

SPANISH SOFRITO ... 882

Sofrito ... 883

SARDENAIRA (RIVIERA-STYLE OLIVE AND ANCHOVY PIZZA) ... 883

Peeling Fresh Plum Tomatoes ... 884

Niçoise Olives ... 884

Salt–Pack Anchovies ... 884

GARLIC-SESAME GRISSINI ... 885

NEW HAVEN-STYLE WHITE CLAM PIZZA ... 886

Using a Wooden Pizza Peel ... 887

ARUGULA AND ROASTED TOMATO PIZZA ... 888

OVEN-ROASTED PLUM TOMATOES ... 888

BLACK OLIVE-HERB BREAD ... 889

EGYPTIAN FLATBREAD WITH DUKKAH SPRINKLE ... 890

PAN DUSHI (ARUBAN SWEET BREAD WITH ANISE) ... 891

YEAST

All the many sweet and savory breads in this book rely on yeast for their lightness. Yeast is alive: it is made up of the microscopic single-celled fungus (an organism related to mushrooms), *Saccharomyces cerevisiae*. When activated by a warm liquid (like water or milk) and fed with sugar or starch, yeast gives off tiny bubbles of carbon dioxide gas. This gas, trapped in the network of stretchy gluten molecules formed by kneading the dough, is what makes bread rise and achieve its light texture and chewy character. One pound of yeast contains 3,200 billion yeast cells, which multiply rapidly when combined with sugar in a moist, warm environment.

Yeast thrives on starch, which it converts to glucose, a simple sugar. This process ferments the sugar, which converts to alcohol and carbon dioxide. You can smell the alcohol when you punch down any fully-risen bread dough. The minimal amount of alcohol burns off during the baking process, and the yeast also dies with the heat. The carbon dioxide gas given off by the fermenting yeast expands inside bubbles created by developing the gluten present in the flour. The higher the gluten (or protein) content of the bread, the more bubbles it can hold. Yeast is also essential to fer-

menting beer (really a kind of liquid bread), wine, and other alcoholic beverages (page 48).

The history of bread-baking began with Neolithic cooks and developed through time according to ingredient availability, technological advances, economic conditions, cultural influences, legal rights (medieval guilds), and evolving taste. The earliest breads were unleavened and baked directly on hot stones. In many parts of the world, especially the Middle East with pita, Turkey with pide, Lebanon with manaqish (za'atar coated pita), Iran with laffa, Central Asia and India with naan, Tunisia with m'lawi, and Morocco with breads like the Sesame-Anise Bread (page 87). Yeast was used by the Egyptians by about 4000 BCE, both for leavening bread and brewing beer. Evidence from a Mesopotamian trading outpost called Godin Tepe in present-day Iran shows that barley was being fermented there around 3500 BCE.

Most sources agree that the powers of yeast were discovered by accident. Fermentation, which takes place naturally, must have happened countless times before humans began to control the process. It seems that the discovery of ale was stimulated by the process of bread-making. At some stage in the

Neolithic era, people learned that if, instead of using ordinary grain, they used grain that had been sprouted and then dried, they were able to make bread that kept quite well. The Egyptian process was to sprout the grain, dry it, crush it, mix it into a dough, and partially bake it. The loaves were then broken up and put to soak in water, where they were allowed to ferment for about a day before the liquor was strained off and considered ready for drinking. So the Egyptians first made their bread and then converted it into beer.

Leavening was perhaps discovered when airborne yeast spores, which would have been plentiful in a bakery/brewery, drifted onto a mass of dough set aside before baking. Once the yeast had a chance to act on the dough, it would have risen enough to make a lighter bread. The brewing of beer may well have occurred soon after the production of cereal crops, and no doubt for a long time, beer was home-produced and in the hands of housewives responsible for preparing the gruel or bread. The first production of beer may be reasonably considered an accidental discovery resulting from the malting of grain for other purposes.

Sourdough, the oldest type of leavened bread, most likely originated in Egypt about 1500 BCE and was the most common form of leavening in Europe until medieval times. It was first replaced by *barm*, an old English word for yeast, referring to the yeast-rich foam formed on top of beer during the fermenting process. Following the work of French scientist Louis Pasteur, methods of culturing pure strains of yeast developed, making modern commercial yeast possible.

A sourdough starter is a symbiotic culture of bacteria and yeast present in a mixture of flour and water that will cause a kneaded wheat-based dough to develop the gluten present in the flour to retain gas, enabling it to rise. Always use unbleached flour for a starter, as it contains more microorganisms than highly processed flours. Getting a full rise with a sourdough starter is more difficult than with packaged yeast because the bacteria almost always outnumber the yeast, and the acidity of the bacteria prevents the yeast from producing leavening gas. The acidic conditions, along with the fact that the bacteria also produce enzymes which break down proteins, result in weaker gluten and a denser finished product. Because of this, I usually combine the starter and yeast for insurance and lighter bread. Breads made with sourdough will also be firmer and chewier, a quality that I enjoy.

Sourdough was the main bread made in Northern California during the California Gold Rush, and it remains a part of San Francisco culture today, partly because the humidity of the air (due to San Francisco's abundant fog) helps the sourdough rise and gives it a more distinct "sour" taste. *Sourdough* became a nickname for gold prospectors. Some San Francisco bakeries can trace the origins of their starter back to this time. The yeast in San Francisco breads is of a slightly different breed, *Saccaromyces esigus*, and multiplies at a much lower rate than standard baker's yeast. The resulting bread is more compact and dense and more acidic in flavor because this yeast cannot digest maltose sugar, so the indigenous San Francisco bacteria takes over. The by-product of the bacteria is highly acidic, giving the bread its characteristic sour flavor. Italian Biga and French Pouliche or Poolish impart sourdough-like flavors to breads by slowly fermenting small amounts of starter made with commercial yeast. In general, the slower the rise, the more highly developed the flavor of the final product. However, making sourdough starters and breads is a complex subject with many opinions on the best way to proceed.

From the beginning of the twentieth century until World War II, perishable but reliable cake yeast was developed and was the main type sold. During World War II, the Fleischmann's Company developed granulated active dry yeast for the armed forces. Unlike the compressed yeast common at the time, granulated active dry yeast didn't require refrigeration and had a longer shelf life and better temperature tolerance than fresh yeast. The French company Lesaffre, under the name SAF, created instant yeast in the 1970s, which has become quite popular, especially for use in bread machines. I use instant yeast in the Tunisian Semolina Bread (page 864), which requires a quick rise and the Grape, Gorgonzola, and Walnut Focaccia (page 788), because this highly active yeast produces desirable large bubbles in the dough.

In this chapter, I use yeast to rise the dough for the hearty and flavorful Spanish Tuna Empanadas with Sofrito (page 881), the Sardenaira, Riviera Style Olive and Anchovy Pizza (page 883), the Garlic-Sesame Grissini from Torino, Italy (page 885), the New Haven Style White Clam Pizza (page 886), the Arugula and Roasted Tomato Pizza (page 888), the Black Olive-Herb Bread on (page 889), the Egyptian flatbread with Dukkah Sprinkle (page 890), and the Pan Dushi (Aruban Sweet Bread with Anise) (page 891).

Elsewhere in the book, look for these savory yeast-raised breads and breadsticks: Currant-Walnut baguette (page 761), Ukrainian Buckwheat Rolls (page 185), Greek Cornmeal Raisin Bread (page 762), Sauerkraut Rye Bread (page 784), Turkish Sesame-Coated Bread Rings (page 798), California Walnut-Rosemary Bread (page 844), Grilled Indian Naan Bread with Nigella Seeds (page 902), Cucuzzara (Durum Wheat Bread with Squash, Tomatoes, Onions, and Peppers) (page 736), and Buckwheat-Cinnamon Bread (page 188). Other yeast-raised doughs in this book include Rye and Rosemary Breadsticks with Lemon (page 783), Garlic-Sesame Grissini (page 885), Potato-Rye Pizza Dough (page 786), Calas (New Orleans Rice Fritters) (page 773), Turkish Pide Dough (page 900), Grape, Gorgonzola, and Walnut Focaccia (page 788), Woodfire Grill Pizza Dough (page 858), Greek Black Barley Rings (page 140), and Cornmeal Pizza Dough (page 392). Sweet yeast-raised doughs include Le Bec-Fin's Fruited Walnut Bread (page 843), Potica (Slovenian Honey-Walnut Ring) (page 845), Hot Cross Buns with Currants (page 230), Braided Cheese Danish with Cardamom (page 273), German Butter Cake (page 216), and Babàs al Limoncello Pansa (page 56).

MAKING SOURDOUGH STARTER

A fresh sourdough culture begins with a mixture of flour and water. Fresh flour naturally contains a wide variety of yeast and bacteria spores as does the air around us. When wheat flour comes into contact with water, naturally-occurring amylase enzymes break down the starch into complex sugars (sucrose and maltose); maltase converts the sugars into glucose and fructose that yeast can metabolize. The lactobacteria feed mostly on the metabolism products from the yeast. The mixture develops a balanced, symbiotic culture of yeast and bacteria after repeated feedings. Two yeasts, *Candida milleri* and *Saccharomyces exiguus*, act symbiotically with the bacteria *Lactobacillus sanfranciscensi* (named for its discovery in San Francisco) in making a sourdough starter.

The potato starter I use (page 880) is only one of many types. Many people begin their starter using crushed organic grapes, which contain many yeasts. In Greece, I learned from Aglaia Kremezi to make a starter using fermented (spoiled) tomatoes. Depending on climate and the type of bread being made, the starter can be either a more liquid batter or a stiffer dough; as a general rule, the more liquid in the starter, the more sour the bread. You can buy sourdough starter from King Arthur Flour (www.bakerscatalogue.com) and from Sourdough Breads (www.sourdoughbreads.com).

WORKING WITH YEAST

The action of yeast will slow down if the liquid is cold and the yeast itself begins to die at 120°F. Allow your dough to rise in a spot where the temperature is between 80 to 95°F, which I call warm room temperature in this book. Under ideal conditions, a quarter ounce of yeast (one $2\frac{1}{4}$-teaspoon package) will raise one pound of dough in $1\frac{1}{2}$ to 2 hours. To make sure your yeast is still active, proof it by mixing it with lukewarm water and a small amount of sugar or honey. The mixture should begin to bubble and ferment within 10 minutes. If it doesn't, the yeast is dead and should be discarded.

I have tested all the recipes in this book (except the Tunisian Semolina Bread, page 864 and the Grape, Gorgonzola, and Walnut Focaccia) using active dry yeast sold in $\frac{1}{4}$-ounce packets and in 4-ounce glass jars. I actually went through an entire pound of active dry yeast! If you prefer to use fresh (or compressed) yeast, substitute a 1-ounce cake for a $\frac{1}{4}$-ounce ($2\frac{1}{4}$ teaspoons) packet of active dry yeast. It is not necessary to refrigerate yeast in single-serving packets. Because I've been buying yeast in jars, I do store it in the refrigerator, making sure to keep it covered and dry, and allowing it to come to room temperature before use.

If you run out of time when rising dough, allow the dough to rise, then punch it down, cover it with plastic wrap, and refrigerate it overnight, a process that bakers call "retarding the dough." The next day, allow the dough to come to room temperature, then shape it and rise it again before baking. Many bread bakers use this method to make it easier to bake fresh bread as needed. Dough that has been retarded will develop characteristic small blisters on the crust when baked.

TYPES OF YEAST

ACTIVE DRY YEAST: Active dry yeast consists of brownish-colored, coarse-textured, oblong-shaped granules of yeast, with live yeast cells enclosed in a thick jacket of dry, dead cells with some growth medium, a substance that supports the growth of these microorganisms. Although it keeps quite well, this type of yeast is more sensitive than other forms to thermal shock when used in recipes, so it is important to dissolve it in lukewarm water, between 100 to 110°F, adding a little sugar or honey to jump-start the growth of the yeast. If yeast grows too quickly, it will produce large bubble pockets in the baked product, desirable in certain types of breads like Italian ciabatta, but not for any of the recipes in this book.

FRESH YEAST: The small blocks of soft, beige-colored, fresh, compressed yeast contain 70 percent moisture. Commercial bakers use fresh yeast because it is more tolerant of low temperature and is more active and easier to control than dry yeast so that it works well with automated bakery equipment. Store fresh yeast in the refrigerator up to two weeks, after which it will start to lose its vitality. Fresh yeast may be stored in the freezer. Defrost to room temperature, then use immediately.

INSTANT YEAST: Instant yeast is more perishable than active dry yeast, has granules about half the size, and a much higher percentage of live cells. Compared to active dry yeast, instant yeast speeds up rising times by about fifty percent because the proofing stage is eliminated and the yeast grows much faster. It is designed to mix directly with the dry ingredients using liquid at 120 to 130°F. Instant yeast generally has a small amount of ascorbic acid (Vitamin C) added as a preservative. Note, however, that liquid that is too hot will destroy the yeast. It is best to use a thermometer to measure the water temperature when using instant yeast. I use this type of yeast to make the Grape, Gorgonzola, and Walnut Focaccia (page 788), and the Tunisian Semolina Bread (page 864) as recommended by the baker who shared these recipes.

RAPID-RISE YEAST: Rapid-rise yeast is a type of instant yeast designed to provide greater carbon dioxide output allow faster rising at the expense of shortened fermentation times. This type of yeast is used in bread machines but most baking experts believe it reduces the flavor of the finished product. I don't use it in this book.

BREWER'S YEAST: This type of yeast, used in brewing of beer, has no leavening properties but is added to products for its nutritional benefits; it is rich in B vitamins.

HIGH-ALTITUDE BAKING

General Tips: Flour tends to be drier at high elevation and will absorb more liquid, so increase the amount of liquid by 2 to 3 tablespoons for each cup of flour at 5,000 feet, and by 3 to 4 tablespoons at 7,000 ft. Because flour strengthens the structure of baked goods, increase the flour by 1 to 2 ounces at 5,000 feet, more for higher altitudes.

Rapid evaporation at high altitude concentrates sugars, especially where humidity is low, affecting the texture of baked goods. Reduce sugar and other sweeteners by about 1 tablespoon per cup at 3,000 feet, more at higher altitudes.

For cakes, cookies, and quick breads, raise the oven temperature by 15°F to 25°F to set the batter before the leavening gases expand too much, causing the produce to fall. Decrease the baking time accordingly, by about 5 to 10 minutes.

Because eggs add liquid and structure to baked goods, it is a good idea to use extra-large eggs instead of the large eggs I call for in this book, or simply add one extra egg.

Yeast-Raised Breads: Because yeast breads tend to rise more quickly at high altitudes, they don't have a chance to develop complex flavor. Use flour with high gluten content (at least 12 grams per cup, listed on the nutritional label). Decrease the amount of yeast by 1/4 teaspoon to help slow down the rise and avoid using instant yeast. Watch that the dough doesn't overexpand to more than double in size, or it will tend to collapse in the oven. Increase the amount of salt to slow down the action of the yeast.

Rising the dough at cooler temperatures will also slow down the yeast action.

Chemically Leavened Baked Goods: At high altitudes, lower air pressure and generally lower humidity cause liquids to evaporate more rapidly, so that baked goods rise more quickly and dry out easily. Decrease the amount of baking powder or soda in your recipes by 15% at 5,000 feet, and by 25% at 7,000 feet. Because the structure of baked good batters is weaker at higher altitude, reduce the fat content by 2 to 4 tablespoons for muffins and quick breads to compensate.

Cakes: Carefully balanced cake batters are most easily affected by altitude changes. For cakes leavened by beaten egg whites, beat only to a soft-peak consistency so the bubbles don't overexpand and collapse in the oven. You may need to increase the size of a cake pan to allow for the extra expansion of baked goods at high altitude. It's best to fill the pan less than two-thirds full. If appropriate, bake in a Bundt or tube pan. (See *Pie in the Sky* by Susan Purdy for detailed information about baking at higher altitudes.)

BREAD DOUGH TIPS

Save the water you use to cook potatoes and use it as the liquid in making yeast-risen doughs for lighter results.

If your bread falls or wrinkles on top, too much liquid was used or the dough was allowed to rise too much. If it doesn't rise enough, there are a number of possibilities: the yeast was old, the water temperature was too high and it killed the yeast, the dough wasn't kneaded enough to develop the gluten and distribute the yeast, or the temperature when rising the dough was too low.

If your bread tastes flat, you probably forgot the salt.

TEMPERATURE AND HUMIDITY WHEN RISING BREAD

Bread doughs rise best in a warm and humid environment. A hot, sticky day is actually the best day to make bread (although it is the worst day to make anything crispy like meringue shells or brandy snap cookies). Professional bakers calculate the temperature of the room and the temperature of the flour and adjust the water temperature as needed. If the day is cold, you'll have to compensate by making the liquid a bit warmer than usual; on a hot day, the water can be cooler. Setting up a humidifier in the room will also help you get a good rise out of your dough, while spritzing the inside of the oven with water or even throwing a few ice cubes into the oven will keep the crust moist and flexible so it can continue rising. (Once the crust is hard, it can't rise further.)

In summer, with hot and humid weather, yeast-risen dough may be left to rise at room temperature. In winter, with cold and dry weather, I have several suggestions for helping dough rise that have worked well for me.

One: Place the bread dough (covered) in an elec-

tric oven near the light (which must be on) or in a gas oven with pilot lit.

Two: Place the bread dough (covered) on top of a running dryer. (I love this double use of the dryer and try to plan my washing and drying days to coincide with bread baking.)

Three: Fill a large, wide pot about halfway with water and bring it to a boil. Reduce the heat to the lowest possible setting. Cover the pot with a half-sheet pan or other large, solid baking pan, or the pot's lid, upside-down. Place several layers of kitchen towels or pot-holders onto the pan or lid to insulate the bottom from too much heat. Place the bread dough (covered) on the towels and let it rise.

Four: Place the dough in front of a sunny window.

SALT AND YEAST

Salt inhibits the growth of yeast, so don't mix yeast with salted water for proofing. Because most tap water is filtered with a process that uses salt, dedicated bread makers prefer distilled or filtered water for baking. I use tap water filtered through a Brita system. In hot weather, when the yeast tends to grow too quickly, add a little extra salt to slow it down and use cooler water. Once the yeast has been proofed and mixed into the dough, it is important to add salt to give a firmer crust, a finer crumb, and better flavor.

Traditionally, Tuscan bread was made with no salt, because of the high taxes on salt in medieval times. People in the region have become accustomed

SUGAR AND YEAST

Sugar is not essential to leavened baked goods, but it does make the product tenderer by allowing the dough or batter to rise to a greater volume before setting into shape and adds more flavor to sweet yeast doughs. Doughs that contain a large amount of sugar will need a larger amount of yeast and a longer rising time to lift up the heavier dough. Even for sweet breads, it is important to add a small amount of salt to balance the sweetness and to control the growth of the yeast.

KNEADING DOUGH

Yeast and kneading go together. Once yeast has been proofed and incorporated into the dough, it must be kneaded to distribute the yeast cells evenly throughout the dough, so it will rise evenly. Kneading also helps develop the gluten present in the flour, providing a firm and elastic structure to hold the carbon dioxide-filled bubbles that make the bread dough rise.

When kneading dough, think of it as a ball you've got to keep round. Using the heel of your hands, push the dough away from you using a rolling motion without breaking the dough and destroying the gluten strands. Then pull the dough back in to make it round again and turn the mass a quarter turn. Continue kneading until the dough is smooth, satiny-looking, and stretchy. When you poke the dough, it should spring back and you should be able to stretch it into a thin sheet without it breaking.

In most of these recipes, I knead the dough almost all the way using the paddle attachment to a standing mixer, then the dough hook. Most doughs should be firm enough to pull away cleanly from the sides of the bowl. If your mixer isn't large or powerful enough to knead a full batch of dough, divide it in half and knead it in two batches, kneading both halves together by hand.

Some sweet doughs, like the Orange Blossom Brioches (page 470) and the Alsatian Kugelhopf (page 717), focaccia, and breads made with rye and barley flours, such as the Greek Country Barley Bread (page 142) and the Sauerkraut Rye Bread (page 784), will be sticky, and specialty dough will be sticky even when fully kneaded. I have indicated this in the particular recipes.

To check whether the dough has fully risen, press your fingertips lightly and quickly about $1/2$ inch into the dough. The impression should stay in place; if it springs back, the dough needs to rise further.

Sourdough Bread Starter

A giant of American cuisine, James Beard, said in his book, James Beard on Bread, *that sourdough bread "is much overrated and is difficult to perfect at home" and that he was "not sure it is worth the trouble." It's a good thing America's hundreds of artisan bakers didn't listen to him in this case. The recipe below is an easy way to make your own sourdough bread starters. Just remember to feed the starter regularly and it will stay happy and potent for years.*

YIELD: 1 QUART STARTER

$1/2$ pound Idaho potato, peeled and cut into chunks

$1 1/4$ pounds (5 cups) bread flour, must be unbleached

In a medium pot, place the potato chunks in cold water to cover. Cover the pot and bring to a boil. Reduce the heat and cook the potatoes until soft, about 12 minutes. Remove from the heat and drain the potatoes, reserving the cooking liquid. Purée or rice the potatoes. In a large bowl, combine the purée with 2 cups of the cooking liquid and allow the mixture to cool to room temperature.

Add 1 pound of the flour to the potatoes and whisk to combine well. Leave the mixture to proof at room temperature or 48 hours (tightly covered). Stir it down, add $1/2$ cup lukewarm water and $1/4$ pound flour to refresh the starter and let it sit for 48 hours longer at room temperature.

Once a week, add 2 ounces ($1/2$ cup) of unbleached bread flour and $1/4$ cup warm water to refresh the starter, stirring to combine well. Remove as much starter as needed to create a new recipe and replace with an equal amount of the flour/water mix. Store refrigerated indefinitely.

called sofrito. Make these easy-to-transport hand-held empanadas for a summer picnic.

called sofrito. *Make these easy-to-transport hand-held empanadas for a summer picnic.*

YIELD: 16 EMPANADAS

HOW TO TELL WHEN BREAD IS DONE

An easy way to check whether bread is fully cooked inside is to use an instant read thermometer inserted into the thickest part of the bread, preferably through the bottom, so you don't make a hole in the top crust. The internal temperature should be between 190° and 205°F, depending on how crusty you like the surface. The most common recommendation is to to tap the middle of the bottom of the bread. (If it's baking in a pan, you'll need to turn it out, check it, and then put it back in the pan. The dough should make a hollow sound when it's tapped.

Spanish Tuna Empanadas with Sofrito

Empanadas originated in the Spanish region of Galicia though today endless types of empanadas, or stuffed bread turnovers, are made in Spain and in Spanish-influenced Latin America, especially Argentina. (See the unusual 'mpanatigghi Siciliano on page 331 for another variation). In this traditional recipe the filling is made from olive oil–packed canned tuna mixed with hard-cooked eggs, salty, tangy capers, and moistened and flavored with the Spanish basic seasoning mixture

Dough

1 pound (4 cups) unbleached bread flour

2 teaspoons Spanish sweet paprika

1 teaspoon fine sea salt

1 ($\frac{1}{4}$-ounce) package ($2\frac{1}{2}$ teaspoons) active dry yeast

$\frac{1}{2}$ cup lukewarm water

$\frac{1}{2}$ cup lukewarm milk

$\frac{3}{4}$ cup extra-virgin olive oil

2 large egg whites ($\frac{1}{4}$ cup) mixed with 2 tablespoons water, for egg wash

Filling

4 (6-ounce) cans light tuna packed in oil, drained

4 hard-cooked eggs, with a soft undercooked center, peeled and chopped

$\frac{1}{4}$ cup capers, drained

1 cup sofrito (page 883)

$\frac{1}{4}$ cup chopped flat-leaf parsley

$\frac{1}{4}$ cup chopped cilantro

Make the dough: Whisk together the dry ingredients: flour, paprika, and salt in a medium bowl.

In the bowl of a standing mixer fitted with the paddle attachment, dissolve the yeast in the water and milk. Stir in about 1 cup of the flour mixture and allow the mixture to proof in a warm place for about 20 minutes, or until bubbling and puffy.

Beat in the olive oil, and then beat in the remaining

flour mixture. Continue beating until the dough is smooth and elastic and comes away cleanly from the bowl, about 5 minutes. Transfer the dough to a large oiled bowl and turn it around so the dough is oiled all over; cover with plastic wrap or a damp cloth and allow the dough to rise until doubled in bulk, about 2 hours, at warm room temperature.

Make the filling: Place the tuna in a mixing bowl and flake it with a fork. Add the eggs, capers, sofrito, parsley, and cilantro, and combine well.

Preheat the oven to 375°F. On a lightly floured board, roll the dough out about $3/8$-inch thick. Cut out 5-inch circles, using a small plate or bowl as a guide. Place about 2 tablespoons of the tuna mixture into the center of the circle, leaving a $1/2$-inch border all around. Brush the border with the egg wash and then fold the dough over to enclose the filling. Seal the edges by crimping with a fork. Brush the tops of the empanadas with more egg wash. Cut several small slits in each empanada to allow steam to escape.

Arrange the empanadas on one or two baking pans lined with parchment paper or a silicone mat. Bake for 20 minutes or until lightly browned and the filling is bubbling, switching the positions and directions of the pans halfway through baking so they brown evenly. (If using two pans, allow 5 minutes longer baking time.)

To freeze empanadas: If you want to prepare empanadas ahead of time, place the filled and unbaked empanadas in a single layer without touching each other on a wax paper-lined baking pan and freeze until firm. Transfer to a large container or zipper lock bag and store frozen up to 1 month. To bake them, remove them from the freezer, separate and arrange on parchment paper or silicone mat-lined baking pans and allow them to defrost for about 1 hour at room temperature, or until no longer cold to the touch. Bake 35 minutes at 350°F or until lightly browned and the filling is bubbling.

Spanish Sofrito

The word sofrito *refers to a concentrated, slow-cooked fragrant and flavorful sauce and is related to the Italian verb,* soffrigere, *meaning "to cook by browning lightly." In Spanish cuisine, sofrito consists of garlic, onions, and tomatoes cooked in olive oil or pork fat with many variations in Cuban, Puerto Rican, Sephardic, and Italian cooking. The sofrito is used as a base for flavoring and moistening other ingredients, including the tuna and egg filling for the empanadas above.*

YIELD: 3 CUPS

$1/4$ cup extra-virgin olive oil

1 yellow onion, chopped

1 long, green, mildly hot pepper, such as cubanelle or Anaheim, seeded and diced

2 large garlic cloves, thinly sliced

1 (15-ounce) can diced tomatoes

2 teaspoons Spanish sweet paprika

Fine sea salt and freshly ground black pepper to taste

2 tablespoons chopped flat-leafed parsley

2 tablespoons chopped cilantro

Heat the olive oil in a large heavy skillet, preferably

cast-iron. Add the onions and sauté until they are transparent about 5 minutes, reducing the heat if necessary to keep them from burning. Add the pepper and continue to cook for 5 minutes, or until the pepper is softened. Add the garlic and sauté for 1 minute, or until fragrant. Add the tomatoes, paprika, salt and pepper and combine well. Continue to cook at moderate heat for 10 to 15 minutes or until the mixture is thick enough for the oil to rise to the top, stirring often to prevent sticking and burning. Remove from the heat, stir in the parsley and/or cilantro and cool to room temperature, chilling over a bowl of ice water to speed things up. Store the sofrito covered and refrigerated up to 2 weeks.

SOFRITO

In the Caribbean and Latin America, *sofrito* is a combination of tomatoes, roasted peppers, garlic, onions and herbs like cilantro or culantro (saw-toothed cilantro). In Cuba, bacon and ham are sometimes added and the sofrito may be seasoned with cumin, oregano, bay leaf, cilantro, and culantro. In Puerto Rico, *recao* (another name for culantro) and *ají dulce*, or sweet chile peppers are used along with salted pork, cured ham, and lard. In Eastern Mediterranean Sephardic Jewish cooking, sofrito is made with stock, lemon juice, turmeric, garlic, and cardamom. In Italian cuisine, sofrito is a mixture of onions, celery, carrots, and herbs, equivalent to the French *mirepoix* (chopped carrots, onions, and celery used as a sauce or stock base flavoring). In Greece on the island of Corfu, influenced by many years of Italian control, sofrito is made from white wine, garlic, and herbs.

Sardenaira (Riviera–Style Olive and Anchovy Pizza)

This type of pizza is made in the Italian Riviera towns of Ventimiglia and Bordighera between Genoa and the French border. Sometimes the filling is made without cooked onions, while the thinnest of slices of raw onion are laid underneath. Elsewhere, oregano or capers are added. It seems that the inventor of this dish was none other than the great Genovese Admiral Andrea Doria. At first it was called pizza di Andrea *which became* pizzalandrea *or* pissadella *in the Italian Riviera, where it is made using the local anchovy paste called* macchetto. *In nearby France, it is known as* pissaladière *and is made without tomatoes and plenty of onions instead (see my book* Starting with Ingredients *for a recipe). This recipe is dairy-free.*

YIELD: TWO 12-INCH PIZZAS, 4 TO 8 SERVINGS

¼ cup extra-virgin olive oil, plus more for brushing

1 medium red onion, thinly sliced

2 pounds plum tomatoes, peeled, seeded, and diced (see Peeling Fresh Plum Tomatoes (page 884))

2 or 3 sprigs of fresh basil

¼ pound whole salt-packed anchovies, cleaned, rinsed, and chopped

1½ pounds Woodfire Grill Pizza Dough (page 858)

4 large garlic cloves, thinly sliced

½ cup Niçoise olives, pitted or not, substitute pitted and halved Kalamata or Gaeta olives

Heat the olive oil in a large heavy-bottomed skillet over moderate heat. Add the onion and cook until it is wilted and just beginning to brown. Add the tomatoes and basil and cook for about 15 minutes or until the oil floats to the top. Remove from the heat and stir in the anchovies.

Preheat the oven to 500°F. Divide the dough in half. Coat 2 12-inch pizza pans with olive oil.

Roll each half of the dough into a 5- to 6-inch circle. Stretch it out, preferably by hand, and transfer it to the prepared pan. Divide the tomato sauce (minus the basil sprigs) evenly among the pizzas, leaving a $\frac{1}{2}$-inch border. Sprinkle with the garlic and olives. Bake for about 8 minutes or until the dough is brown on the edges and the filling is bubbling, switching positions in the oven halfway through baking. Cut each pizza into 8 wedges and serve immediately.

PEELING FRESH PLUM TOMATOES

While I don't bother peeling thinner-skinned round or beefsteak tomatoes, plum tomatoes have thick, indigestible skin that should be removed. The skins will easily slip off of fully ripened tomatoes. To skin them, bring a pot of water to a boil and have a bowl of ice mixed with water ready. Drop the tomatoes in the boiling water and allow them to cook only long enough for the skin to move easily against the flesh, about 1 minute. Immediately scoop the tomatoes from the pot (dumping them out will crush them) and drop into the ice water.

When cool enough to handle, slip off the skins. Cut out the core, using a tomato shark, small paring knife, or a small melon baller. If you care to remove the seeds, cut in half "through the equator" and lightly squeeze the seeds out of the exposed seed pockets. Strain the delicious liquid from the seeds if desired, then dice the tomatoes and add the strained juice.

NIÇOISE OLIVES

These petite French black olives come from the region of Provence near the city of Nice. They are harvested when fully ripe and have a nutty, mellow flavor and a high pit-to-meat ratio. They are often packed stems intact in brine with local herbs. Because they are so small, these olives are often served complete with pits. You may, however, pit them if desired.

SALT-PACK ANCHOVIES

The salt-pack anchovies called for in the Sardenaira (page 883) come from Sicily and are packed whole (minus their heads but including innards) in large tins layered with sea salt and covered with a wooden board to keep them submerged in salt. To prepare them, rinse the anchovies under tepid water, discarding the bones and innards. Surpris-ingly, these anchovies are quite mild and firm in texture, much more so than the standard oil-packed anchovies. The best alternative is the oil-and-vinegar-packed white anchovies, commonly found as *boquerones*, imported from Spain. Ordinary anchovy fillets are the third-best choice; it you do use them, drain their oil and rinse them under tepid water and pat dry.

Anchovies are a small, warm-water fish related to the herring of Northern Europe. Like herring, anchovies are salt-packed to preserve these highly perishable, oil-rich fish. In Italy, whole salt-packed anchovies are preferred for their meatier flavor and firm texture rather than the filleted oil-packed anchovies commonly found in the United States. Excellent-quality salted anchovies from Agostino Recca of Sicily are imported to America and can be found in Italian delis and from online specialty food suppliers. Store all canned anchovies in the refrigerator, because even though they are canned, anchovies can still deteriorate in a warm environment. Once the can is opened, keep the contents tightly covered and refrigerated up to six months.

Garlic–Sesame Grissini

I've been making these tasty, crisp breadsticks since about 1980, when I developed the recipe for Ristorante DiLullo, the influential Northern Italian restaurant where I cheffed from 1979 to 1985. They were a big hit with the customers as I'm sure they will be in your house. Grissini are pencil-thick, long sticks of crispy, dry bread that originated in Turin and the nearby region of Piedmont around the fourteenth century. In Italy, grissini Torinese (Turin-style breadsticks) are thicker, longer, often twisted, and always hand-made. The less-interesting grissini in glassine envelopes served in many Italian restaurants are called grissino stirato *(straight), and are machine-made. Roll thinly-sliced prosciutto or other Italian cured meats, like Genoa salami, bresaola,*

or spicy capicola ham, around the grissini for a quick, typically Italian bocconcino *(small bite) to serve with drinks or a glass of wine.*

YIELD: 36 (1-FOOT) BREADSTICKS

2 (1/4-ounce) packages (5 teaspoons) active dry yeast

1 tablespoon honey

1 cup lukewarm water

1 3/4 pounds (7 cups) unbleached bread flour

4 teaspoons fine sea salt

1 tablespoon granulated garlic

1 1/2 tablespoons dried oregano

1 tablespoon ground fennel seed

2 teaspoons freshly ground black pepper

1 1/2 teaspoons hot red pepper flakes

1/4 cup sesame seeds

1/2 cup extra-virgin olive oil

1 cup heavy cream

1 large egg, lightly beaten with 2 tablespoons water, for the egg wash

Line two 18 x 13-inch half-sheet pans (or other large baking pans) with parchment paper or silicone baking mats.

In the bowl of a standing mixer fitted with the paddle attachment, dissolve the yeast and honey in the lukewarm water. Allow the mixture to proof in a warm place for about 15 minutes, or until bubbling and puffy.

Beat in about half the flour, then beat in the seasonings: salt, garlic, oregano, fennel seed, black pepper, chile pepper, and sesame seeds. Beat in the olive oil and cream, then beat in the remaining flour. Continue beating for about 5 minutes or until the dough is smooth and elastic and comes away cleanly from the sides of the bowl. Transfer the dough to a large oiled bowl and turn it around so the dough is oiled all over; cover with plastic wrap or a damp cloth and allow the dough to rise at warm room temperature until doubled in size, about 2 hours.

Preheat the oven to 350°F.

Punch down the dough and divide it into 36 portions. Using a rolling pin, roll each portion into a long oval shape. Roll the dough up the short way, to make a log shape, then, using your hands in a back-and-forth motion, roll into 12-inch long sticks, about the thickness of your forefinger. Arrange the breadsticks on baking trays and allow them to rise again until almost doubled, about 30 minutes.

Bake for 20 minutes or until the breadsticks are firm on the outside but still light-colored. Remove from the oven, brush with egg wash, and place back in the oven. Bake for 10 minutes longer or until browned on the outside and crispy inside. Cool and then store wrapped in heavy-duty aluminum foil up to 5 days.

New Haven–Style White Clam Pizza

The unpretentious pizzeria, Frank Pepe's Pizzeria Napoletana in New Haven, was founded in 1925 by Frank Pepe, an Italian immigrant. Pepe's originated New Haven-style, thin-crust called apizza (closely related to the original Neapolitan pizza) baked in a huge coal-fired brick oven. It is well known for a regional specialty: white pizza topped with fresh clams. The nearby Sally's Apizza, founded in 1938 by Pepe's nephew Sal Consiglio, has a long-standing rivalry. (Sally's was closed when I visited, so I haven't had a chance to compare the two.) People wait for a seat outside of Pepe's for hours, as I've done several times. It is well worth the wait. At Pepe's, I saw just how long a wooden peel can be. Supported on special hooks hanging from the ceiling, the peels are used to deposit and retrieve the delicious, thin-crust pizzas with the charred bubbles created in the hot coal oven that hasn't been turned off since 1948. Go to www.pepespizzeria.com for more information and don't miss a visit when in New Haven. While this is not a completely traditional clam pizza (it's more like Clams Casino on a pizza), I was inspired to make it by my visits to Pepe's.

YIELD: TWO 12-INCH PIZZAS, 4 TO 8 SERVINGS

12 little neck clams or 24 cockles or Manila clams,
    scrubbed clean

$1/2$ cup dry white wine

3 tablespoons extra-virgin olive oil

2 ounces pancetta, thinly sliced and diced,
    substitute bacon

3 large garlic cloves, finely chopped

Large pinch red pepper flakes

Grated zest of 1 lemon (1 tablespoon)

1 tablespoon chopped fresh oregano,
    or 1 teaspoon dried oregano

2 tablespoons chopped flat-leaf parsley

$1^{1}/_{2}$ pounds Woodfire Grill Pizza Dough (page 858)

Cornmeal or semolina, for dusting

Combine the clams and wine in a large pot, cover, and cook over high heat to steam the clams open, shaking the pan several times, about 6 minutes. Remove the clams from the pot and allow them to cool, discarding any clams that stubbornly refuse to open. Strain the liquid from the pan through a dampened paper towel set in a sieve to catch any sand. Remove the clams from their shells, discarding the shells. Chop the clams roughly and reserve.

In a large skillet, heat 2 tablespoons of the olive oil, add the pancetta and sauté until the pancetta starts to brown and get crisp, about 4 minutes. Add about two-thirds of the garlic and the red pepper flakes and sauté until sizzling, about 1 minute. Add the strained clam broth and cook down until the liquid is syrupy about 5 minutes, then remove from the heat and stir in the chopped clams, lemon zest, oregano, and parsley.

Preheat the oven to 500°F, with a pizza stone in the oven if possible.

Stretch out the pizza rounds to the size of wooden peel (see Using a Wooden Pizza Peel on this page) sprinkled with cornmeal. Alternatively, roll out the pizzas and transfer them to 12-inch pizza pans that have been dusted with cornmeal. Mix the remaining tablespoon of olive oil and the garlic and use to brush the round especially on the edges.

Spread the clam topping onto the pizzas and bake for 8 minutes or until the edges are well-browned. Cut each pizza into 8 wedges and serve immediately.

USING A WOODEN PIZZA PEEL

A peel is a long-handled wooden board that is used to transfer pizza and bread dough to and from a hearth-oven or onto a pizza stone. It takes a bit of skill and the willingness to try a few times to use the peel, but this way you can bake the pizza directly on a pizza stone in your oven, coming as close as possible to the way the pros bake their pizzas. To use the peel, sprinkle it lightly and evenly with cornmeal or fine semolina. Stretch out the pizza round to the size of the wooden peel. This is easier if you first roll the dough out into a 5- to 6-inch circle and then continue stretching it out by hand. The dough should be slightly thicker at the edges.

Top the pizza as desired, without being tempted to overdo the toppings. If the pizza is too heavy and juicy, it will be difficult, if not impossible, to shake off the peel. Give the pizza a couple of shakes to make sure it will come free from the peel, lifting off any stuck portions and sprinkling underneath with cornmeal. Transfer the unbaked pizza to the pizza stone by placing the peel at a low angle to the stone and giving it a fast, vigorous thrust forward and then back, so the pizza jumps right onto the stone. Once the pizza has baked, use the peel to remove it from the stone. (It may take a few tries to get that pizza to jump.)

Arugula and Roasted Tomato Pizza

This is a modern pizza, although made with traditional Italian ingredients like arugula (la rucola in Italian), fresh mozzarella (poetically called fior di latte, or "flower of the milk" in Italian), extra-virgin olive oil, and roasted plum tomatoes. I've added Kalamata olive halves and tangy white goat cheese, which contrast in flavor and texture, with the other ingredients, making for a colorful California Mediterranean–style pizza. Use the Cornmeal Pizza Dough for a crunchier pizza; use the Woodfire Pizza Dough for a chewier, softer pizza.

YIELD: 1 (12-INCH) PIZZA, 2 TO 4 SERVINGS

2 tablespoons extra-virgin olive oil

2 cups baby arugula or washed and drained
   field-grown arugula

³/₄ pound Cornmeal Pizza Dough (page 392) or
   Woodfire Grill Pizza Dough (page 858)

2 garlic cloves, finely chopped

¹/₂ cup Oven-Roasted Plum Tomatoes (page 888),
   cut into thin strips

2 tablespoons pitted Kalamata olive halves

2 ounces (¹/₄ cup) thinly sliced fresh mozzarella

2 ounces (¹/₂ cup) crumbled mild goat cheese,
   crumbled

Preheat the oven to 500°F, with a pizza stone in the oven if possible.

Heat 1 tablespoon of the olive oil in a large skillet, add the arugula and cook until just wilted, about 2 min-utes. Remove the pan from the heat and cool the arugula to room temperature (this may be done 1 to 2 days ahead).

Roll or stretch out the pizza dough and transfer it to a 12-inch pizza pan dusted with cornmeal. Alternatively, follow the instructions on page 887 for using a wooden pizza peel. Mix the remaining tablespoon of olive oil and the garlic and use the mixture to brush the round, especially on the edges. Arrange small mounds of the arugula on the pizza, then sprinkle with the tomato strips and olives. Arrange the mozzarella and goat cheese over top.

Bake until bubbling and well-browned, about 8 min-utes. Cool slightly, then cut into 8 wedges.

Oven-Roasted Plum Tomatoes

Make these wonderful tomatoes when large, ripe plum tomatoes are plentiful. It's really not worth making in quantities of less than five pounds, because the toma-toes shrink so much when baked. They are excellent on pizzas and in pasta sauces, but must be kept refriger-ated up to two weeks. If you remove some of the tomatoes, be sure to keep the remainder covered with olive oil. When they are all used, strain the olive oil and reserve it in the refrigerator to use for pasta sauces, to spread on sliced Italian bread to bake for crostini, or to make vinaigrette dressings.

YIELD: ABOUT 6 CUPS

5 pounds ripe plum tomatoes, cored and halved
lengthwise

3 tablespoons kosher salt

$3/4$ cup extra-virgin olive oil

$1/4$ cup chopped fresh oregano (about $1/2$ bunch)

$1/4$ cup chopped fresh rosemary (about $1/4$ bunch)

$1/4$ cup chopped fresh thyme (about $1/2$ bunch)

6 to 8 cloves garlic, (about $1/4$ cup chopped)

2 teaspoons freshly ground black pepper

Preheat the oven to 225°F.

In a large bowl, combine all of the ingredients. Arrange the tomatoes in a single layer on 2 large metal baking pans with their cut sides up and slowly roast for 4 hours. The tomatoes should be dried and wrinkly-looking, but still plump.

Remove the tomatoes from the oven and cool to room temperature. Transfer to a covered container and refrigerate up to 2 weeks.

Black Olive–Herb Bread

This tasty bread is studded with bits of intense, oil-cured black olives and redolent with fragrant, resinous herbs. It comes out of the oven deep brown, big, and puffy, and it makes outstanding sandwiches. Use it to make sandwiches filled with tuna salad, preferably dressed with vinaigrette rather than mayonnaise or roasted vegetables and goat cheese. Toast slices of the bread and serve with hearty vegetable and bean soups with extra-virgin olive oil for dipping. The bread also freezes beautifully.

YIELD: ONE $2^1/2$-POUND LOAF

$3/4$ pound ($2^3/4$ cups plus 1 tablespoon) unbleached all-purpose flour

$1/2$ pound (2 cups) unbleached bread flour

$1/4$ pound (1 cup minus 1 tablespoon) buckwheat flour

2 teaspoons fine sea salt

1 ($1/4$-ounce) package ($2^1/2$ teaspoons) active dry yeast

$1^3/4$ cups lukewarm water

1 tablespoon honey

$1/4$ cup extra-virgin olive oil

2 tablespoons finely chopped fresh thyme, oregano, and/or rosemary

1 cup pitted, oil-cured black olives, chopped

2 tablespoons Shiny Cornstarch Glaze (page 393)

In a medium bowl, whisk together the dry ingredients: flour, bread flour, buckwheat flour, and salt.

In the bowl of a standing mixer fitted with the paddle attachment, dissolve the yeast in $3/4$ cup of the water. Stir in the honey and about 1 cup of the flour mix. Allow the mixture to proof at warm room temperature for about 30 minutes, or until bubbling and puffy.

Beat about half the remaining flour mix into the yeast mixture, then beat in the olive oil, herbs, and olives. Beat in the remaining flour mixture. If the dough is too large for your mixer, knead in the remaining flour mix by hand. Switch to the dough hook and beat (or knead by hand) until the dough is smooth (except for the lumpy olives) and elastic and comes away from the sides of the bowl. Transfer the dough to a large oiled bowl and turn it around so the dough is oiled all over; cover with plastic wrap or a damp cloth and allow the dough to rise at warm room temperature until doubled in bulk, about 2 hours.

Punch down the dough and roll it out into a rectangle about ³⁄₄-inch thick and fold in thirds, like a letter. Fold over the top portion then fold over the bottom portion to meet it. Fold the dough in the middle where the two portions meet to make a thick rectangular block. Press down the edges to seal. Place the loaf seam-side down on a baking pan lined with parchment paper or a silicone baking mat. Brush the loaf with the Shiny Cornstarch Glaze. Using a French baker's lame, a single-edged razor, or a box cutter, cut 5 or 6 shallow diagonal slashes across the loaf. Cover with oiled plastic wrap and allow the loaf to rise at warm room temperature until almost doubled in bulk, about 1¹⁄₂ hours.

Preheat the oven to 375°F.

Bake the bread for 45 minutes or until it sounds hollow when tapped on the bottom and a thermometer inserted in the center reads 190 to 205°F. Cool completely before slicing.

Egyptian Flatbread with Dukkah Sprinkle

In Egypt and much of the Middle East and North Africa, flatbreads like this one are the norm. Here, a simple dough made with all-purpose flour mixed with white whole wheat flour is stretched out into a large, thin rectangle and sprinkled with dukkah, a typical Egyptian mixture of herbs, nuts, and spices. Alternatively, bake the breads in rounds and dip them into fruity extra-virgin olive oil and then into the dukkah at the table. Extra dukkah can be sprinkled on salads or vegetables or combined with breadcrumbs and used to bread chicken, fish, seafood, or vegetables, especially cauliflower, which is very common in Egyptian cooking. Dukkah is related to za'atar (page 798), a similar Levantine mixture popular in Israel, Palestine, Syria, and Lebanon.

YIELD: 4 (10-OUNCE) FLATBREADS, 2 CUPS DUKKAH

Dough

2 tablespoons honey

1 (¹⁄₄-ounce) package (2¹⁄₂ teaspoons) active dry yeast

1¹⁄₄ cups lukewarm water

³⁄₄ pound (2³⁄₄ cups plus 1 tablespoon) unbleached all-purpose flour

¹⁄₄ pound (1 cup plus 2 tablespoons) white whole wheat flour

2 teaspoons fine sea salt

2 tablespoons extra-virgin olive oil

Dukkah

6 tablespoons natural or white sesame seeds

2 ounces (¹⁄₂ cup) skin-on hazelnuts, lightly toasted, skinned, and chopped

2 ounces (¹⁄₂ cup) pistachio nuts, chopped

¹⁄₄ cup crushed coriander seed

3 tablespoons crushed cumin seed

1 tablespoon chopped thyme, or 1 teaspoon dried thyme, crumbled

Fine sea salt and freshly ground black pepper

¹⁄₄ cup extra-virgin olive oil

Make the dough: In the bowl of a standing mixer fitted with the whisk attachment, combine the honey and yeast, then whisk in 1¼ cups lukewarm water, mixing until the yeast is dissolved. Allow the mixture to become foamy, about 10 minutes.

Attach the dough hook to the mixer and beat in both kinds of flour, the salt and oil, continuing to beat until the dough is smooth, elastic, and comes away from the sides of the bowl cleanly, about 5 minutes. When pressed with your fingers, it should stick briefly then come away. Transfer the dough to a large oiled bowl and turn it around so the dough is oiled all over; cover with plastic wrap. Allow the dough to rise in a warm, draft-free place until doubled in bulk, about 2 hours.

Punch down the dough and transfer it to a lightly floured surface. Divide the dough into 4 pieces and form each piece into a ball. Allow the dough balls to rest, covered with plastic wrap for about 15 minutes, to relax the gluten.

Make the dukkah: Lightly toast the sesame seeds in a dry skillet (with no oil), shaking often until the seeds are aromatic and light brown, about 3 minutes. Cool to room temperature and then combine with the hazelnuts, pistachios, coriander seed, cumin, thyme, and salt and pepper to taste.

Line two 18 x 13-inch half-sheet pans (or other large baking pans) with parchment paper or silicone baking mats.

Roll out a piece of dough about ¼-inch thick into a rectangle large enough to fill a pan. Transfer the dough to one of the pans. (Repair any tears in the dough by pinching it together.) Repeat with a second piece of dough, transferring it to the second baking pan. Brush the dough with olive oil and sprinkle one quarter of the dukkah over each rectangle. Allow the flatbreads to rest at warm room temperature for 45 minutes or until light and puffy. Repeat with the remaining two rounds of dough or freeze up to one month. Defrost and allow the dough to come to room temperature before rolling out.

Preheat the oven to 425°F. Bake the flatbreads, switching the position of the pans and rotating them halfway through baking, until golden, about 20 minutes. Cool the bread in the pans on wire racks for 5 minutes, then transfer them to a cutting board and cut each into pieces with a sharp heavy knife. Serve immediately.

Pan Dushi (Aruban Sweet Bread with Anise)

Dushi is the word for "sweet" in Papiamento, the language spoken in the former Dutch Antilles islands of the Caribbean: Aruba, Bonaire, and Curaçao. These raisin-studded sweet breads get their special flavor from small, licorice-flavored aniseeds and brown sugar. Pan dushi is typically served with coffee for breakfast or as an afternoon pick-me-up with tea. Leftover pan dushi makes incredible French toast or bread pudding, such as the Papiamento Bread Pudding (see recipe page 562) and is also excellent toasted and buttered.

YIELD: 2 1½-POUND LOAVES OF BREADS

3 (¼-ounce) packages (6¾ teaspoons) active dry yeast

½ cup lukewarm water

¾ pounds (7 cups) unbleached bread flour

1 tablespoon baking powder

1 tablespoon aniseeds, lightly crushed

1 1/2 teaspoons fine sea salt

4 large eggs

2 cups dark brown sugar

1/2 cup milk

1/4 pound (1 stick) unsalted butter, melted and cooled

1 cup raisins, soaked in 1/4 cup water until plump
   and drained

1 tablespoon vanilla extract

1 tablespoon almond extract

Spray two 9-inch cake pans with nonstick baker's coating or rub with butter and dust with flour, shaking off the excess.

In the bowl of a standing mixer fitted with the flat paddle attachment, dissolve the yeast in the lukewarm water. Stir in 2 ounces (1/2 cup) of the flour and allow the mixture to proof about 15 minutes, or until bubbling and puffy.

In a bowl, whisk together the dry ingredients: the remaining flour, baking powder, aniseeds, and salt, and reserve.

Add the eggs, 1 1/2 cups of the brown sugar, the milk,

butter, raisins, vanilla, and almond extract to the yeast mixture. Switch to the dough hook and beat in the flour mixture. Continue beating for 5 to 10 minutes or until the dough is smooth and elastic, though still a bit sticky. Transfer the dough to a large oiled bowl and turn it around so the dough is oiled all over; cover with plastic wrap or a damp cloth and allow the dough to rise until doubled in size, about 2 hours, at warm room temperature. Punch down the dough and divide it in half. Roll each half into a smooth ball, then flatten it so that it fills the bottom of the pan. Allow the dough to rise again until light and puffy, about 1 hour.

Preheat the oven to 350°F. Bake both breads for 30 minutes, or until golden brown. Combine the remaining 1/2 cup brown sugar with 1/4 cup lukewarm water in a small bowl, whisking until the sugar dissolves. Remove the breads from the oven and brush with the brown sugar mixture. Cool about 5 minutes and then remove from pans. Cool completely on a wire rack before cutting with a serrated knife. Store the breads in opened plastic bags or brown paper bags and at room temperature for up to three days. This bread freezes well up to 2 months.

YOGURT

American Water Buffalo and
Goat's and Sheep's Milk Yogurt . . . 896

Yogurt Cures the French King . . . 896

Making Yogurt . . . 897

Types of Yogurt . . . 897

TURKISH BAKED CHEESE
TURNOVERS (PUAÇA) . . . 8989

Nigella Seeds . . . 899

TURKISH PIDE DOUGH . . . 900

FETA CHEESE AND EGG PIDE . . . 900

TAHINI AND GRAPE MOLASSES PIDE . . . 901

GRILLED INDIAN NAAN BREAD
WITH NIGELLA SEEDS . . . 902

GREEK HONEY-WALNUT CAKE
WITH YOGURT (KARYTHOPITA) . . . 903

GREEK YOGURT-CURRANT
RING CAKE (YIAOURTOPITA) . . . 904

YOGURT

Eating yogurt is a way of life in the region stretching from Bulgaria to Greece, Turkey, Syria, Lebanon, Iran, and into India and Russia. Every morning in Greece, I enjoyed scoops of incredibly rich yogurt, complete with a thick layer of light gold cream at the top. The tangy yogurt drizzled with superb Greek thyme–blossom honey made the perfect breakfast. Serve yogurt topped with honey accompanied by the crunchy Greek Black Barley Rings (Mavrokoulouria) (page 140). Yogurt (also spelled yogourt or yoghurt) is a semi–solid fermented milk product that developed into its present form centuries ago in Bulgaria, which is still noted for the excellent quality of its yogurt. Milk of various animals can be used to make yogurt. The incredibly rich and smooth yogurt made from water buffalo milk that I enjoyed at Caseificio Vannullo (Vannullo Cheese-making) near Paestum in Campania, Italy, is the best yogurt I've ever had the pleasure of eating so far.

Yogurt is one of the oldest foods known to man. Most food historians agree that it, and related fermented milk products, were discovered accidentally by Neolithic peoples living in Central Asia.

These foods occurred naturally due to local climate and primitive storage methods. Although there is little proof, it is believed that yogurt was almost certainly used in Mesopotamia and Palestine, and possibly Egypt. Ancient Greek doctors, like the famous Galen, were familiar with the health properties of yogurt, and there are references to it by the Greek historian Herodotus, who lived in the fifth century. Yogurt was well known to the Romans, including the scholar and natural scientist Pliny, who lived in the first century CE and wrote about how "barbarian" tribes produced yogurt. Yogurt was also widely respected in the Arab world in the Middle Ages, and a book that appeared in Damascus in 633 praised its therapeutic properties.

Yogurt is traditionally believed to be an invention of the Bulgars from Central Asia, who lived about 4,500 years ago. They were the earliest Turkic–speaking people to migrate to Europe, starting in the second century CE. By the end of the seventh century, they had settled in the Balkans. Yogurt, like other fermented foods, such as bread, beer, and wine, was probably first fermented spontaneously, perhaps as a result of wild bacteria residing inside goatskin bags the Bulgars used for transportation. The word "yogurt" derives from a Turkish word meaning "to blend," a reference to how yogurt is made.

Yogurt is basically a form of curdled milk, much like sour cream and crème fraîche. Bacteria in milk ferment and coagulate to thicken the milk to a creamy texture, adding a tangy, slightly astringent flavor. In commercial manufacturing, the friendly bacteria is added, but heat fresh milk and keep it at about 100°F for a few hours, it will naturally turn to yogurt. Koumis, a dairy product closely related to yogurt, is made from fermented mare's milk and originated in Central Asia where horses were plentiful but other milk-producing animals were not.

Yogurt remained a food of the East until the 1900s, when Ilya Ilyich Mechnikov, a Russian biologist and Director of the Pasteur Institute in Paris, theorized that a diet rich in yogurt was responsible for the unusually long life spans of Bulgarian peasants. Mechnikov, who was known for his pioneering research into the human immune system, worked to popularize yogurt throughout Europe and received the Nobel Prize in 1908. However yogurt arrived in Western Europe, it was little-known there until the 1920s.

In America, yogurt was propagated widely after the First World War by Greek immigrants who made yogurt and served it in their many restaurants. In 1919, a Spanish entrepreneur named Isaac Carasso started the first commercial yogurt plant in Barcelona, naming the business Danone

after his son. Today, the company is known as Dannon in the United States. Yogurt with fruit preserves was invented and patented in 1933 in Prague, in an effort to get yogurt to keep longer. The first commercially produced yogurt sold in the United States was in 1929, by two Armenian immigrants, Rose and Sarkis Colombosian, whose family business later became Colombo Yogurt.

Yogurt didn't become a mainstay in the United States until the latter part of the nineteenth century. The Dannon company achieved some minor success in 1947 when it first mixed strawberry preserves into yogurt and offered it as a sweetened dessert. However, it was health guru Gayelord Hauser who pushed yogurt into the limelight when he proclaimed it a wonder food in his book *Look Younger, Live Longer*, published in 1950. Sales of yogurt skyrocketed, increasing production 500% by 1968. Although no miracle health benefits, other than the standard nutritional benefits of milk products, have been proven to date, yogurt does have some beneficial cooking applications. (In 1962, the FDA ruled that yogurt manufacturers could not make any specific health claims.) It is certainly tasty enough on its own and works well in conjunction with other ingredients.

While traveling, cooking, and baking in Greece and especially Turkey, I learned how to make all sorts of doughs using yogurt. Its acidity tenderizes dough and makes a moist product. Every dough I've made with yogurt is absolutely delicious. I hope you'll find the same to be true. In this chapter, yogurt goes into the dough for the Greek Feta

Cheese Bread (page 261), the Turkish Savory Corn-bread (page 388), and the Turkish Sesame-Coated Bread Rings (page 798). It also goes into the doughs for the savory Turkish Baked Cheese Turnovers (page 898), Turkish Pide (page 900), Grilled Indian Naan Bread with Nigella Seeds (page 902), the sweet Greek Honey-Walnut Cake with Yogurt (page 903), and Greek Yogurt-Currant Ring Cake (page 904). I also use yogurt to make the filling for the French Apricot Tart Scented with Cloves (page 120), the topping for the Austrian Apricot Dumplings (page 122), the dough for the Cretan Kalitsounia (page 276), and the batter for the Brandied Prune Pound Cake (page 710).

AMERICAN WATER BUFFALO AND GOAT'S AND SHEEP'S MILK YOGURT

Water buffalo yogurt is now being made in the United States by the Woodstock Water Buffalo Company in Vermont and sold at Trader Joe's. My favorite yogurt of the moment is imported from Greece under the Fage name and is made from sheep's and goat's milk and sold at Whole Foods. (Trader Joe's carries other yogurts by this company, but not the top-of-the-line sheep- and goat's-milk type.) There are other small producers of goat's- and sheep's-milk yogurt in the United States, including Seven Stars Farm in Chester County, Pennsylvania, who makes a biodynamic yogurt that I used in the kitchen in my restaurant days.

YOGURT CURES THE FRENCH KING

Yogurt became known in France in 1542 when King Francois I was suffering from what would now be diagnosed as severe depression. The doctors could do nothing for his listlessness and neurasthenia until the Ambassador to the Sublime Porte disclosed that there was an Armenian and/or Jewish doctor in Constantinople who made a brew of fermented sheep's milk of which people spoke in glowing terms, even at the Sultan's court. The king sent for the doctor, who refused to travel except on foot; he walked through the whole of southern Europe, followed by his flock. He started the king on a regimen of several weeks of sheep's milk yogurt, ultimately curing the king. The sheep, however, didn't recover from their long walk and caught cold in the air of Paris. Every last one of them died, and the doctor left again, refusing to stay despite the king's offers. He went home, taking the secret of his brew with him and the secret of yogurt was forgotten in France for nearly four centuries.

MAKING YOGURT

Yogurt-making involves the introduction of specific "friendly" bacteria into preferably unpasteurized, unhomogenized milk in order to maintain the healthy balance of bacteria and enzymes of milk in its unprocessed state under very carefully controlled temperature and environmental conditions. The bacteria ingest the natural milk sugars and release lactic acid as a waste product; the increased acidity, in turn, causes the milk proteins to tangle into a solid mass, forming a denatured protein called curd. The increased acidity also prevents other potentially harmful bacteria from growing.

Yogurt cultures generally include two or more different bacteria for more complete fermentation, most commonly a form of streptococcus and lactobacillus such as acidophilus and bulgaricus. Depending on the particular culture, the milk can turn into yogurt, buttermilk, or sour cream. Other strains of bacteria transform milk into French crème fraîche, Italian mascarpone, and Devonshire clotted cream.

If yogurt is not heated to kill the bacteria after fermentation, it is sold as containing "live active cultures," which some believe to be nutritionally superior and helpful to digestion. Because live yogurt culture contains enzymes that break down lactose, some individuals who are lactose intolerant find that they can enjoy yogurt without ill effects.

If the fruit is already stirred into the yogurt, it is often called Swiss-style. Most yogurt in the United States has pectin or gelatin added to make it firmer. Greek yogurt and some full-fat specialty American yogurts have a layer of thick cream at the top. Wheat berries and cooked rice are added to yogurt in Italy, and in America, it may be flavored with chocolate, coffee, lemon, vanilla, and various fruit jams.

TYPES OF YOGURT

AYRAN: This cooling drink, popular in Turkey, is made of yogurt and water with salt, and sometimes black pepper. It usually accompanies kebabs and meat pastries. In Turkey, even McDonald's serves ayran. In rural areas of Turkey, ayran is always offered to guests, and in Syria and Lebanon, it is available in all restaurants as well as fast food shops. A similar drink, *doogh*, is found in Iran and is called *tan* in Armenia. It differs from ayran in that mint and other herbs are usually added, and it is carbonated, usually with seltzer water.

BULGARIAN YOGURT: Bulgarian yogurt is often considered the finest type of yogurt, and it certainly has one of the oldest traditions. It is prized for its taste, aroma, and quality, and is usually eaten plain. Bulgarian yogurt producers are currently taking steps to legally protect the trademark of Bulgarian yogurt on the European market and distinguish it from other product types that do not contain live bacteria. Bulgarian yogurt is often strained by hanging it in a cloth for a few hours to reduce its water content. The resulting yogurt is creamier, richer, and milder in taste because of increased fat content, similar to cream cheese.

GREEK YOGURT: Greek "full" yogurt is made from milk that has been blended with cream to a fat content of exactly ten percent. Standard yogurt at five percent fat, low-fat at two percent, and non-fat versions are also made. Greek yogurt is often served with honey, walnuts, or the soupy Greek fruit preserves known as "spoon fruit" as a dessert.

KEFIR: Kefir is a sour, carbonated, slightly alcoholic drink with a consistency like thin yogurt. Kefir originated in the Caucasus. A related Central Asian-Mongolian drink made from mare's milk is called *kumis* or, in Mongolia, *airag*. It is made by mixing cow's or goat's milk with the grains—a combination of beneficial bacteria and yeasts—from previous kefir batches. Most commercially available American "kefir" is neither carbonated nor contains any alcohol, but is rather thinned yogurt. In Chile, this beverage is called *Yogurt de Pajaritos*. Due to the slight amount of alcohol in kefir, Russians often use it as a hangover cure. *Kephir, kewra, talai, mudu kekiya, matsoun, matsoni, waterkefir,* and *milkkefir* are other names for this drink.

LASSI YOGURT: Lassi is a yogurt-based beverage, originally from India, where it is made in two versions: salty and sweet. Salty lassi is usually flavored with roasted cumin and chile peppers; the sweet kind contains rosewater and/or lemon, mango, or other fruit juices.

MATSONI OR CASPIAN SEA YOGURT: In Japan, Caspian Sea yogurt is a very popular homemade yogurt believed to have been introduced into the country by a sample brought from the Caucasus region of Georgia in 1986. This Georgian yogurt has a viscous, honey-like texture and is milder in taste than many other yogurts. It is easy to make at home and, in Japan, freeze-dried starter is sold, but many people obtain some yogurt from a friend to use as a starter.

Turkish Baked Cheese Turnovers (Puaça)

These small, turnovers are made with yogurt in the dough, which makes it tender due to its acidity. They are filled simply with feta cheese and sprinkled with slightly bitter, but flavorful black nigella seeds. According to Senay Ornek, a wonderful Turkish cook who taught me to make the turnovers, the dough should be as "soft as your earlobe," an evocative description found in many Turkish recipes. In her home near Izmir, we made the turnovers by hand from start to finish. Turkish feta is tangier but milder than the more familiar Greek type. Rinse the feta under cold water to cut down on the saltiness or combine half feta and half mild goat cheese or labne (yogurt cheese).

YIELD: 36 SMALL TURNOVERS

1¼ pounds (4¾ cups minus 1 tablespoon) unbleached
   all-purpose flour

2 teaspoons baking powder

1 teaspoon fine sea salt

1 cup whole milk plain yogurt, preferably Greek-style

2 eggs

½ cup canola oil

1 pound feta cheese, crumbled

2 tablespoons nigella seeds, substitute sesame seeds

Line two 18 x 13-inch half-sheet pans (or other large baking pans) with parchment paper or silicone baking mats, or rub with softened butter.

Whisk together the dry ingredients: flour, baking powder, and salt.

In the bowl of a standing mixer fitted with the paddle attachment, combine the yogurt, 1 egg, and the oil. Beat lightly then reduce the speed to low and beat in the flour mixture. Beat only long enough for the dough to come together and form a soft ball.

Separate the remaining egg and combine the yolk with the feta.

Lightly beat the egg white with 1 tablespoon of water and reserve for the egg wash.

Divide the dough into 36 small balls about the size of a golf ball. Flatten each ball in the palm of your hand to a circle about 2½ inches in diameter and about ³/₈-inch thick. Place about 2 teaspoons of the feta mixture in the center then bring two halves of the dough together to seal in the feta, pressing well to seal.

Preheat the oven to 400°F. Arrange the turnovers equidistant from each other, about 2 inches apart, on the pans. Brush them with the egg wash and sprinkle with nigella seeds. Bake for 25 minutes or until well-puffed and golden brown. Note that some of the cheese filling inevitably leaks out. Store covered and refrigerated for up to three days. Wrap in foil and reheat at 350°F for about 20 minutes, uncovering for the last 5 minutes of baking.

NIGELLA SEEDS

Nigella (*Nigella sativa*) seeds are small, dense, black, hard, pyramid-shaped seeds used for their intense flavor, sharp resinous aroma, and striking color. Nigella is cultivated from Egypt to India and is popular all places in between. You may have tasted the hauntingly fragrant, acrid, smoky-tasting, slightly bitter nigella in Armenian string cheese, or in Indian naan bread (see the Grilled Indian Naan Bread with Nigella Seeds, page 902). It is thought that the black cumin mentioned in the Old Testament is actually nigella, which has been found in the Giza pyramid and King Tutankhamen's tomb in Egypt. Nigella is known by many names, including onion (or wild onion) seed, because of their similarity in appearance, although the two are unrelated. Nigella may also be called black cumin (though also unrelated), which is actually called *kala jeera* in India.

Nigella is known as *charnushka* in Russia, where it tops black bread and white cheese; *kalonji* in India, where it tops naan bread and chutneys. When lightly toasted, the seeds flavor Turkish pide and cornbread (see the Turkish Savory Cornbread (Misir Ekmegi, page 388), as well as Lebanese, Iranian, and Indian baked vegetables, salads, flatbreads, pickles and chutneys. Find nigella seeds at Middle Eastern or Russian markets or order online from Penzey's Spices (www.penzeys.com) or Kalustyan's in New York City (www.kalustyans.com).

Turkish Pide Dough

I learned how to make this supple, soft dough enriched with yogurt and olive oil from my Turkish friend and fellow food fiend, Didem Ornek Ertan and her energetic and talented mother-in-law, Sadiye Ertan, at their home in the Turkish Aegean coastal town of Çesme, Turkey. After making the dough, we took it down the street to their friend's pide restaurant where I learned how to stretch it out by hand into the proper elliptical shape, then pinch up the sides and point the ends to make the traditional plump canoe-like shape. Of course, baking the pide in their wood-fired dome oven yielded pide with wonderful wood-smoke flavor, but I've since had much success in baking it in my own standard electric oven.

YIELD: 1¼-POUNDS DOUGH, 6 PIDE

10 ounces (2½ cups minus 2½ tablespoons) unbleached all-purpose flour

2 ounces (½ cup plus 1 tablespoon) white whole wheat flour

1½ teaspoons fine sea salt

1 (¼-ounce) packet (2¼ teaspoons) active dry yeast

1 tablespoon honey

6 tablespoons lukewarm water

½ cup plain, thick yogurt, not non-fat

2 tablespoons extra-virgin olive oil

In a medium bowl, whisk together the dry ingredients: flour, white whole wheat flour, and salt.

In the bowl of a standing mixer fitted with the paddle attachment, dissolve the yeast and honey in the water. Stir in about ½ cup of the flour mixture and allow the mixture to proof in a warm place for about 15 minutes, or until bubbling and puffy.

Beat in the remaining flour mixture, the yogurt, and the olive oil. Continue to beat until the dough is shiny and elastic and comes away from the sides of the bowl, 5 to 6 minutes. Shape the dough into a ball and transfer to a lightly oiled bowl. Cover with plastic film and allow the dough to rise for 1½ hours, or until the dough has doubled in size.

Punch down the dough before using it for the Tahini and Grape Molasses Pide (page 901), the Feta Cheese and Egg Pide (page 900), or the Lahmacun (page 866).

Feta Cheese and Egg Pide

In Turkey, pide is a type of pita bread that is soft and chewy in texture. Confusingly there are two Turkish breads called pide. The first is shaped sort of like a large pizza—biggish and round and flattish (though not completely flat)—crisp on the outside, and soft on the inside, similar to Arab pita bread. The second is the stuffed canoe-shaped bread in this recipe. Here, I fill it with feta cheese, dill, and cracked egg. The lamb filling for the Lahmacun (page 866) may also be used to make canoe-shaped pide.

YIELD: 8 PIDE

1¼ pounds Turkish Pide Dough (page 900)
Cornstarch, for rolling
½ pound (1½ cups) feta cheese, crumbled
6 ounces (¾ cup) whole milk ricotta cheese
½ cup thinly sliced scallions
2 tablespoons chopped dill
2 large eggs
Freshly ground black pepper

Preheat the oven to 450°F, with a pizza stone in the oven if possible. Line two 18 x 13-inch half sheet pans (or other large baking pans) with silicone baking mats and brush with oil (or just brush the pans with oil with no mats).

Divide the dough into 8 pieces. Dust the work surface and the dough with cornstarch. Roll each piece into a tongue-shaped oval, about 10 x 5 inches, and arrange them, two at a time, on the pans. Alternatively, form the pides two at a time on a baker's wooden peel sprinkled with semolina or cornmeal.

In a medium bowl, combine the feta, ricotta, scallions, dill, the 2 eggs, and black pepper. Spread each pide with about 6 tablespoons of the mixture, leaving a ½-inch border all around. Fold over the edges. Use your fingertips to press the border down every inch or so. Form the pide into a fat canoe shape by firmly pinching the ends together into points.

If you are using a pizza stone, use a wooden peel to transfer the pides to the stone. Bake for about 8 minutes, or until the edges of the pides are nicely browned. Use the peel to remove them from the oven and repeat with the remaining pide.

Alternatively, form the pide on the pans and bake 5 minutes, then slide the pide directly onto the oven rack and continue baking for about 5 minutes longer or until the edges are nicely browned.

Serve the pide warm. Store up to 3 days covered and refrigerated. Reheat by wrapping in aluminum foil and then baking in a 350°F oven for about 15 minutes.

Optionally, crack one egg for every two pide, preferably into a lipped measure to make it easier to pour. Break the egg up lightly with a fork, so that the yolk is broken but not combined with the white. Once the pide have been transferred to the oven, pour half the egg over the cheese filling onto each pide, without allowing it to spill over the sides and allow the pide to finish baking.

Tahini and Grape Molasses Pide

My food-loving Turkish friend, Didem Ornek Ertan, showed me how to make this unusual, layered, sweet pide at her parents' lovely home near Izmir with the help of her father, Rahmi Ornek. We spread the soft dough with tahini and folded it over to make flaky layers. Next, we spread it with thick, dark grape molasses. We baked the breads in her father's prize wood-burning outdoor oven set in the middle of a lush, green garden with a swimming pool in the center—an experience to remember! I have since made the pide spread with Greek, Turkish, or Middle Eastern fig preserves. Turkish quince preserves would also work well as would the date and orange filling for the Anise-Scented Date-Orange Spirals (page 423).

YIELD: 6 TO 8 PIDE

1¼ pounds Turkish Pide Dough (page 900)

½ cup tahini

½ cup grape molasses or honey

¼ cup light brown sugar (if using the grape molasses)

¼ cup sesame seeds

Cornstarch for rolling

Preheat the oven to 425°F, with a pizza stone in the oven if possible. Line two 18 x 13-inch half-sheet pans (or other large baking pans) with silicone baking mats, then brush them with oil for easy clean-up (or just brush the pans with oil).

Divide the pide dough into 6 pieces. Dust the work surface and the dough with cornstarch. Roll each piece into an long, oval tongue-shape, about 10 x 5 inches and about ³⁄₈th-inch thick. Working with one piece of dough at a time, spread each piece with 1 tablespoon tahini, then fold in threes like a letter. Roll the dough out to an oval, then fold it in three again and roll it out again into a long oval to make a flaky layered dough. Brush again with 1 tablespoon tahini, then drizzle with 2 teaspoons grape molasses (or drizzle with 1 tablespoon honey). Sprinkle with 1 tablespoon brown sugar if using, then with sesame seeds. Continue with the remaining pieces of dough and fillings.

If you have a pizza stone in the oven, bake the pides on the pans for 8 minutes, then slide them off onto the stone and continue baking for about 6 minutes longer or until the breads are puffy and golden. If you don't have a pizza stone, continue baking the pides in the pans for 14 minutes total. Serve warm. Store up to 2 days covered and refrigerated. Reheat by wrapping in aluminum foil and then baking in a 350°F oven for about 15 minutes.

Grilled Indian Naan Bread with Nigella Seeds

Naan is a teardrop-shaped flatbread that is baked directly on the inside walls of a tandoor oven and is found in Iran, Afghanistan, Pakistan, India, and other surrounding countries. Naan is served for dipping or is stuffed with a variety of meats and vegetables. It is like pita, yet softer and, most of the time, larger. The baked naan can be frozen in freezer bags for up to 30 days. Wrap in foil and reheat at 400°F for about 25 minutes. The naan dough is moistened with the flavorful liquid in which acrid black negilla seeds have been soaked. The seeds themselves are also mixed into the dough.

YIELD: ABOUT 12 NAAN BREADS

1 tablespoon nigella seeds

½ cup cold water

1 (¼-ounce) package (2½ teaspoons) active dry yeast

1 cup plain yogurt

1 pound (3³⁄₄ cups) unbleached all-purpose flour

2 teaspoons fine sea salt

¹⁄₂ cup Clarified Butter (page 202), melted

Vegetable Oil for brushing the grill

Line two 18 x 13-inch half-sheet pans (or other large baking pans) with parchment paper or silicone baking mats.

In a small pot over high heat, combine the nigella seeds and the water and bring to a boil. Remove from the heat and transfer the mixture to the bowl of a standing mixer, and allow to cool until lukewarm.

Sprinkle in the yeast, add the yogurt, and mix well using the paddle attachment. Add about half the flour and beat until well-combined. Cover and leave in a warm place until partially risen and puffy, about 30 minutes.

Beat in the salt, half of the butter, and the remaining flour, then switch to the dough hook and continue beating until the dough is smooth and elastic but still rather sticky. Cover again and proof until the dough has doubled in size, about 2 hours at warm room temperature.

Dust the work surface and the dough with cornstarch. Divide the dough into 12 pieces and form each one into a round. Preheat an electric grill to high (or heat an outdoor charcoal grill). Working one at a time, roll each ball of dough out into a thin circle. Lightly oil the grill. Brush the round of dough lightly with clarified butter. Place one end of the dough on the grill, pulling the other end to make a teardrop shape, then let it drop onto the grill. Cook for 2 to 3 minutes, or until puffy and lightly browned. Brush the uncooked side lightly with more butter. Turn over and cook until the dough is covered with nicely browned bubbles, 2 to 3 minutes. Remove from grill, and continue the process

until all the naan has been prepared.

Keep the cooked naan warm in a 200°F oven while preparing the remaining breads. Serve hot. Store any extra naan well-wrapped and refrigerated for up to 2 days. Wrap in aluminum foil and reheat in a 350°F oven for about 15 minutes. Wrap the naan well and freeze, if desired, up to 2 months.

Greek Honey–Walnut Cake with Yogurt (Karythopita)

This easy cake from Greece is scented with lemon zest, cinnamon, and cloves. After it comes out of the oven, the cake is drenched in a honey and lemon syrup. However, the cake is not overly sweet because tangy yogurt and faintly tannic walnuts help balance the sweetness. The cake keeps well for several days at room temperature. Like most Turkish and Arabic-influenced baked goods, this cakes tastes best at room temperature.

YIELD: 12 TO 14 SQUARES

Cake

¹⁄₂ pound (2 cups minus 2 tablespoons) unbleached
    all-purpose flour

2 teaspoons baking power

¹⁄₂ teaspoon baking soda

1 teaspoon fine sea salt

1 teaspoon ground cinnamon

Pinch ground cloves

¹⁄₂ pound (2 sticks) unsalted butter, softened

1 cup sugar

6 large eggs

Grated zest of 1 lemon (1 tablespoon)

1 cup plain whole milk yogurt

$^{1}/_{2}$ pound (2 cups) walnuts, lightly toasted
   and finely chopped

Syrup

1 cup sugar

$^{1}/_{2}$ cup honey

Grated zest of 1 lemon (1 tablespoon)

Juice of 1 lemon (3 tablespoons)

Make the cake: Preheat the oven to 350°F. Spray a 9 x 9-inch baking pan with nonstick baker's coating or line with parchment or waxed paper cut to fit the pan.

In large bowl, whisk together dry ingredients: flour, baking powder, baking soda, salt, cinnamon and cloves.

In the bowl of a standing mixer fitted with the paddle attachment, cream the butter and sugar until light and fluffy, 5 to 6 minutes. Add the eggs, one at a time, beating well after each addition. Beat in the lemon zest. Reduce the mixer speed to low, then add the flour mixture alternately with yogurt, beginning and ending with the flour mixture. Fold in the walnuts.

Spoon the batter into the prepared pan and smooth the top. Bake for 35 to 40 minutes, or until the cake starts to come away from the sides of the pan and a toothpick or skewer stuck in the center comes out clean. Cool in the pan on a wire rack.

Make the syrup: In 1-quart saucepan, stir together sugar, honey, $^{3}/_{4}$ cup water, and the lemon zest. Bring to a boil over medium heat, stirring occasionally and

skimming off the white foam, until the syrup is completely clear, about 4 minutes. Stir in the lemon juice and cool to room temperature.

Poke holes in the cake with a toothpick or skewer and spoon the lukewarm syrup over the cake, which will absorb the syrup completely. Slice into 12 or 16 squares. Store the cake covered and at room temperature for up to 3 days.

Greek Yogurt–Currant Ring Cake (Yiaourtopita)

Make this moist and tender cake, studded with tiny currants and bits of walnuts, and no one will guess how easy it is to make. The currants work well because they're so small, you don't get an overly large bite of sweetness at any time. The cake stays moist because of the yogurt it contains, which also makes for tenderness. Lemon zest, cinnamon, nutmeg, and vanilla impart their subtle flavors along with a hint of cloves (be sure to use only a pinch).

YIELD: ONE 9-INCH RING CAKE,
10 TO 12 SERVINGS

$^{3}/_{4}$ pound ($2^{3}/_{4}$ cups plus 1 tablespoon) unbleached
   all-purpose flour

$1^{1}/_{2}$ teaspoons baking powder

1 teaspoon baking soda

1 teaspoon fine sea salt

6 ounces ($1^{1}/_{2}$ sticks) unsalted butter, softened

1½ cups sugar

5 large eggs

1½ cups plain yogurt, not non-fat

Grated zest of 2 lemons (2 tablespoons)

2 teaspoons vanilla extract

5 ounces (1 cup) Zante currants

¼ pound (1 cup) walnuts, chopped

1 teaspoon ground cinnamon

½ teaspoon freshly grated nutmeg

Pinch ground cloves

Preheat the oven to 350°F. Spray a 9-inch ring cake pan with nonstick baker's coating or rub with butter and dust with flour, shaking off the excess.

Whisk together the dry ingredients: flour, baking powder, baking soda, and salt.

In the bowl of a standing mixer fitted with the pad-dle attachment, cream the butter and sugar together until light and fluffy, 5 to 6 minutes. Beat in the eggs, one at a time, beating well after each addition. Beat in the yogurt a few tablespoons at a time, along with the lemon zest and vanilla. Fold in the flour mixture.

In a small bowl, mix together the currants, walnuts, cinnamon, nutmeg, and cloves.

Spoon half the batter into the prepared pan. Sprinkle half the currant mixture evenly over it. Spoon the remaining batter evenly over top and sprinkle with the remaining currant mixture, pressing lightly so the mix-ture adheres to the top.

Bake for 35 minutes or until the cake is golden brown on top and a skewer stuck in the center comes out clean. Cool to room temperature on a wire rack. Store the cake, covered and at room temperature, for up to 4 days.

INDEX

A

Alcohols, 47–64
    Andalusian Bittersweet Chocolate–Sherry
        Cake with Sherry Custard Sauce, 55–56
    apricot brandy, about, 124
    Aruban Ponche Crema Liqueur, 63
    Babàs al Limoncello Pansa, 56–67
    common flavored alcohols, 64
    Danish Rum Raisin Cupcakes, 764
    distilled spirits and base ingredients, 50
    eau de vie, about, 49
    Florentine Chocolate Nut Zuccotto,
        58–60
    general information, 48–49
    German Apple and Rum-Raisin
        Custard Torte, 54–55
    grappa and marc, about, 49–50
    Homemade Limoncello, 537–538
    kümmel liqueur, about, 89
    Lemon-Blackberry Bavarese with
        Limoncello, 481–482
    limoncello, about, 58
    Madeira wine, about, 52
    Pasta Frolla, 62–63
    percentage of alcohol retained after cook-
        ing, 51
    Pineapple-Coconut Flan with Dark Rum,
        684–685
    Pineapple Rum-Pecan Bars, 685
    rum, about, 53
    Rum Pecan-Praline Sandies, 652–653
    Rum-Vanilla Custard Sauce, 61
    Scotch whisky, about, 52
    sherry and port, about, 53
    Sherry Custard Sauce, 61–62
    sherry varieties, 53–54
    slivovitz (plum brandy), 711–712
    Zaleti: Venetian Cornmeal Cookies with
        Grappa Raisins, 60
Aleppo pepper, about, 868
Aliza's Wedding Cake, 227–228
Almonds, 65–79
    Almond Cantucci Pratesi, 289–290
    Almond-Crusted Blackberry-Tangerine Pie,
        161–162
    Almond-Lime Bars, 545
    almond milk (Almond Breeze), buying, 71
    Almond Milk and Chocolate Malt Cake,
        146–148
    almond paste, about, 70
    Almond–Sour Cherry Torte with Brown
        Butter and Sour Cherry Sauce, 303–304
    almond varieties, 68
    Baci de Dama with Nutella

    (Lady's Kisses), 335
    blancmange made from, 72
    B'stilla of Chicken, 436–437
    buying, in various forms, 68
    choosing and storing, 71
    Cranberry-Semolina Ktefa, 401–402
    Crostata di Riso: Italian Rice Tart, 776–777
    A Date in a Blanket, 421–422
    Dutch Almond-Filled Spice Tart, 74–75
    Dutch Speculaas with Rye, 789–790
    Financiers, 215–216
    Florentine Chocolate Nut Zuccotto,
        58–60
    French Puff Pastry Peach Galette, 618–619
    freshly shelled almonds on ice, 71
    general information, 66–68
    German Bee-Sting Cake: Bienenstich, 523–
        524
    German Muerbeteig Dough (Mellow
        Dough), 444–445
    green almonds, about, 70
    ground almonds, buying and storing, 68
    Hot Apple-Cranberry Crisp with
        Oatmeal-Almond Topping, 403
    Kourambiedes with Olive Oil, 586–587
    macaroon paste, about, 70
    Majorcan Lemon-Almond Cake, 77
    Maltese Kwaresimal Cookies, 603–604
    marzipan, about, 70
    Mexican Spiced Cocoa Meringues,
        352–353
    M'hancha: The Serpent, 695–696
    'mpanatigghi Siciliano, 331–332
    orgeat made from, 72
    Rustic Fresh Fig Galette, 454–455
    Savory Eggplant and Spiced Almond Tart,
        72–73
    Siennese Panforte, 232–233
    Slovenian Almond-Apricot Tea Bread,
        117–118
    Spiced Almond Pastry, 74
    Spiced Honey–Almond Rings with
        Brandied Persimmon Bits, 665–666
    Tangerine Semolina Torta, 605
    Torta Caprese: Bittersweet Chocolate–
        Almond Cake, 336–337
    Torta Sbrisolona alla Lombarda
        (Lombardian Crumbly Cake), 390–391
    Velia's White Chocolate–Lemon Torta
        Caprese, 78
    Venetian Cornmeal and Cherry Crostata,
        305
    weight and volume equivalents, 42
    Zach's Almond Macaroon Cake, 76
Alpine Mushroom Pizza with Potato-Rye

    Dough, 787
Alsatian Plum Muerbeteig, 710
Amaretti
    Bonèt Piemontese: Chocolate-Amaretti
        Baked Custard, 439–440
    notes about, 440–441
Amish Black Walnut Oatmeal Pie, 575–576
Amish Peanut Butter Cream Pie, 626–627
Anchovies
    salt-packed, about, 884–885
    Sardenaira (Riviera-Style Olive and An-
        chovy Pizza), 883–884
Andalusian Bittersweet Chocolate–Sherry Cake
    with Sherry Custard Sauce, 55–56
Animal fats. *See* Fats, animal
Anise, fennel, & caraway, 81–93
    anise and anise extract, buying and
        storing, 83
    aniseed, about, 82–83
    Anise-Scented Date-Orange Spirals,
        423–424
    caraway seed, about, 84–85
    Caraway Seed Bundt Cake, 88–89
    caraway seedcakes and harvest feasts, 90
    Fennel Egg Bread, 86–87
    fennel pollen, about, 92
    fennel seed, about, 84
    general information, 82–85
    kümmel liqueur made from, 89
    Moroccan Sesame-Anise Bread, 87–88
    Mrs. Beeton's original seed cake
        recipe, 89
    Pan Dushi (Aruban Sweet Bread with Anise),
        891–892
    Pizzelle "of the Angels" with Fennel Pollen,
        91–92
    Sambuca and Candied Orange Tozzetti,
        90–91
    Spanish Sesame-Anise Cookies, 799–800
Annatto coloring, 206
Apples, 95–111
    Apple-Apricot Strudel, 121–122
    Apple-Blueberry Crumb Pie with
        Cardamom, 163–164
    Apple-Date Buckwheat Muffins, 188
    best varieties, for baking, 98–103
    Black Currant–Apple Linzer Torte, 411–413
    Brown Bread Apple Charlotte with Rum-
        Vanilla Custard Sauce, 108–109
    Candied Walnut Apple Pie, 109–110
    French Roquefort, Apple, and Leek Tart,
        103–104
    Fuji Apple Cake, 105
    general information, 96–98
    German Apple and Rum-Raisin Custard

Torte, 54–55
Hot Apple-Cranberry Crisp with
    Oatmeal-Almond Topping, 403
least suited to baking, 98
Oatmeal-Apple-Upside-Down Tart, 577–
    578
Spanish Apple Torte, 105–107
Stark Brothers Nursery and Orchards, 98
storing, 98
weight and volume equivalents, 42
Apricots, 113–124
    Apple-Apricot Strudel, 121–122
    apricot brandy, about, 124
    Apricot Brandy Sauce, 123–124
    Austrian Apricot Dumplings, 122–123
    Baked Quince with Pine Nuts and Dried
        Fruit, 754
    California Apricot Cheesecake, 118–120
    dried, choosing, 115–116
    dried, substituting, for fresh apricots, 117
    dried California, about, 116
    French Apricot Tart Scented with Cloves,
        120–121
    fresh, blanching and skinning, 117
    fresh, choosing and storing, 117
    fresh, substitutes for, 117
    fresh California, varieties of, 116
    general information, 114–115
    Le Bec-Fin's Fruited Walnut Bread,
        843–844
    Peach and Apricot Tarte Tatin, 616–617
    Sesame Honey Cones with Ricotta Filling,
        800–802
    Slovenian Almond-Apricot Tea Bread,
        117–118
    Torta di Zucca (Squash Cake with Pine Nuts
        and Apricots), 741–742
    weight and volume equivalents, 42
    White Bean, Chestnut, and Apricot Cake
        alla Povera, 316–217
Argentinean Alfajores Cookies, 563–564
Aruban Cashew Cake, 178–179
Aruban Ponche Crema Liqueur, 63
Arugula and Roasted Tomato Pizza, 888
Asian Pears, Carrots, and Ginger, Morning Glory
    Muffins with, 240–241
Australian Pavlova with Lemon Filling and
    Tropical Fruits, 442–444
Austrian Apricot Dumplings, 122–123

B

Babàs al Limoncello Pansa, 56–67
Baci di Dama with Nutella (Lady's Kisses), 335
Baharat spice blend, about, 146
Baked Quince with Pine Nuts and Dried Fruit,
    754
Baker's ammonia
    as baking powder substitute, 281
    buying and storing, 281–282
    Chocolate-Glazed Praline Profiteroles,
        287–289
    general information, 280–281, 291
"Baker's dozen," etymology of, 361–362

Baking powder
    Almond Cantucci Pratesi, 289–290
    aluminum in, 285
    double-acting, about, 284
    general information, 291
    Iced Malted Milk Cookies, 285–286
    Indian Pudding Cake, 286–287
    ingredients in, 285
    quantity of, for recipes, 284–285
    Rumford's Baking Powder, for recipes, 285
    single-acting, about, 283
    single-acting, homemade, 284
    substitutes for, 281, 283
    testing freshness of, 284
Baking soda
    as baking powder substitute, 283
    general information, 282–283, 291
    Iced Malted Milk Cookies, 285–286
    Indian Pudding Cake, 286–287
    mixing with cream of tartar, 283
    putting out kitchen fires with, 283
    testing freshness of, 283
Bananas & plantains, 125–134
    Baby Banana Cream Pie in Coconut-
        Cashew Crust, 131–132
    banana-growing countries, 128
    Banana-Pecan Roulade, 132–133
    banana plants, about, 128
    banana varieties, 128–129
    general information, 126–127
    Plantain Empanadas with Black Bean and
        Añejo Cheese Filling, 129–130
    plantains, notes about, 127–128
    Red Banana–Brown Butter Bars, 133–134
    sweet or yellow banana varieties, 127
    weight and volume equivalents, 42
Banneton bread baskets, 187
Bar cookies
    Almond-Lime Bars, 545
    Canadian Date-Oatmeal Squares, 576
    English Millionaire's Shortbread, 769–771
    Peanut-Chocolate Bars with Espresso, 627–
        628
    Pineapple Coconut Shortbread Bars with
        Macadamia Nuts, 687–688
    Pineapple Rum-Pecan Bars, 685
    Red Banana–Brown Butter Bars, 133–134
    Spiced Fuyu Persimmon Bars, 664
    Turtle Brownies with Caramel and Pecans,
        653–654
Barley & malt, 135–148
    Almond Milk and Chocolate Malt Cake,
        146–148
    barley, storing, 138
    barley flour, baking with, 138
    barley flour, weight and volume
        equivalents, 40
    barley stick candy, 138–139
    general information, 136–138
    Greek Black Barley Rings, 140–141
    Greek Country Barley Bread, 142–143
    Iced Malted Milk Cookies, 285–286
    Kea Stuffed Griddle Bread, 144–145

    malted barley, about, 139
    malted milk, about, 139–140
    malted milk powder, buying, 140
    paximadi (barley biscuits), about, 141
Bavarese, Lemon-Blackberry, with Limoncello,
    481–482
Beans
    Plantain Empanadas with Black Bean and
        Añejo Cheese Filling, 129–130
    White Bean, Chestnut, and Apricot Cake
        alla Povera, 316–217
Beef
    Kea Stuffed Griddle Bread, 144–145
    Steak, Guinness, and Mushroom Pie,
        213–215
Berries, 149–169. See also Blackberries;
    Blueberries; Cranberries; Raspberries;
    Strawberries
    general information, 150–153
    lingonberries, about, 165
Biscochitos, 218–219
Biscotti
    Biscotti Rococò, 536–537
    Chocolate-Cherry Biscotti with Cocoa
        Nibs, 305–306
    Lemon Poppy Seed Biscotti, 719–720
    One-Bowl Hazelnut Cornmeal Biscotti,
        503–504
Bitter Chocolate–Hazelnut Torta with
    Pears, 645
Blackberries
    Almond-Crusted Blackberry-Tangerine Pie,
        161–162
    Blackberry–White Chocolate Tart,
        483–484
    choosing and storing, 155
    English Summer Fruit Pudding with Lemon
        and Mint, 415–416
    general information, 150, 154–155
    hybrid cousins, 155–156
    July 4th Cheesecake, 833–835
    Lemon-Blackberry Bavarese with
        Limoncello, 481–482
Black Currant–Apple Linzer Torte, 411–413
Black Kugelhopf, 717–718
Black Olive–Herb Bread, 889–890
Black walnuts. See Walnuts & black walnuts
Blancmange, about, 72
Blueberries
    Apple-Blueberry Crumb Pie with
        Cardamom, 163–164
    Blueberry-Walnut Streusel Muffins, 164
    choosing and storing, 153
    English Summer Fruit Pudding with Lemon
        and Mint, 415–416
    freezing, 154
    frozen, adding to batter, 154
    general information, 150–153
    Greek Blueberry-Yogurt Tart with Ouzo,
        165–166
    July 4th Cheesecake, 833–835
    low-bush blueberries, names for, 153
    wild bears' affinity for, 153

Wyman's wild blueberries, 166
Bonèt Piemontese: Chocolate-Amaretti Baked
    Custard, 439–440
Borek, bourekas, brik, and boureki, 798
Borekas, Cigari, with Moroccan Spiced Lamb,
    212–213
Bourbon-Spice Pumpkin Cake, 742–743
Brandied Prune Pound Cake, 710–711
Brazil nuts
    Brazil-Nut and Guava Sandwich Cookies,
        175–176
    Brazil Nut Cake with Espresso, 373–374
    "Brazil Nut Effect" expression, 173
    general information, 172–173
    Ruby Grapefruit–Orange Brazil Nut
        Torte, 174–175
Bread-based recipes
    Brown Bread Apple Charlotte with Rum-
        Vanilla Custard Sauce, 108–109
    English Summer Fruit Pudding with Lemon
        and Mint, 415–416
    Papiamento Bread Pudding with Ponche
        Crema, 562
    Québécoise Maple Bread Pudding,
        554–555
Bread baskets, banneton, 187
Bread dough
    adding sugar to, 879
    beating, 30
    cutting slashes in, 32
    kneading, 879
    proofing, in unsalted water, 878–879
    rising, 37, 875, 877–878, 880
    rolling into bread sticks, 37
    scoring, with lame, 264
    shaping into loaf form, 38
    Sourdough Bread Starter, 880–881
    sourdough starters, 875
    Turkish Pide Dough, 900
Bread flour
    about, 854–855
    artisanal, buying, 857–858
    weight and volume equivalents, 40
Breads. See also Bread dough; Muffins; Pizza
    Black Olive–Herb Bread, 889–890
    Buckwheat Cinnamon-Raisin Bread,
        188–189
    Buttermilk-Sourdough White Sandwich
        Bread, 726–727
    California Walnut Rosemary-Bread,
        844–845
    Catalan coques, about, 673
    Catalan Flatbread with Spinach, Onion,
        and Pine Nut Topping, 672–673
    Chestnut Cornbread, 318–319
    Chestnut-Currant Scones, 313–314
    Corsican Chestnut Rolls, 317–318
    Crisp Swedish Coconut "Dream"
        Cookies, 361
    Currant-Walnut Baguette, 761–762
    Dilled Potato-Onion Rolls, 727–728
    Durum Wheat Bread with Squash, Toma-
        toes, Onions, and Peppers, 736–737

Fennel Egg Bread, 86–87
Feta Cheese and Egg Pide, 900–901
Fig and Pine Nut Bread, 674
Garlic-Sesame Grissini, 885–885
Ginger Fig Scones, 491
Grape, Gorgonzola, and Walnut Focaccia,
    788–789
Greek Black Barley Rings, 140–141
Greek Cornmeal Raisin Bread, 762–764
Greek Country Barley Bread, 142–143
Greek Feta Cheese Bread, 261–262
Grilled Indian Naan Bread with Nigella
    Seeds, 902–903
Guinness Oatmeal Bread, 574–575
Herbed Focaccia with Goat Cheese, Red
    Onion, and Black Olives, 725–726
and high-altitude baking, 877
Honduran Coconut Bread, 360–361
Hot Cross Buns with Currants, 230–231
Kea Stuffed Griddle Bread, 144–145
Lahmacun: Armenian Lamb Flatbread,
    866–867
loaf bread pans, buying, 23
Le Bec-Fin's Fruited Walnut Bread, 843–844
Moroccan Sesame-Anise Bread, 87–88
Onion Poppy Seed Kichels, 715–716
Orange Blossom Brioches, 470–471
Pan Dushi (Aruban Sweet Bread with Anise),
    891–892
Persimmon–Black Walnut Bread, 666
Potica (Slovenian Honey-Walnut Ring),
    845–847
Rye and Rosemary Breadsticks with
    Lemon, 783–784
Sardinian Potato Torta, 728–729
Sauerkraut Rye Bread, 784–786
Seeded Multi-Grain Sourdough Bread,
    186–187
Slovenian Almond-Apricot Tea Bread,
    117–118
Stilton Scones, 269–270
Sweet Fig Focaccia, 455–456
Tahini and Grape Molasses Pide, 901–902
Taralli: Boiled and Baked "Pretzels" from
    Puglia, 584–585
testing for doneness, 29, 881
Tunisian Semolina Griddle Bread, 864–865
Turkish Savory Cornbread, 388–389
Turkish Seeded Hazelnut Bread, 502–503
Turkish Sesame-Coated Bread Rings:
    Susamli Simit, 798–799
Ukrainian Buckwheat Rolls, 185
Brik pastry leaves, about, 402
Brioches, Orange Blossom, 470–471
Broccoli Rabe, White Pizza with, 266–267
Bromated flour, about, 855
Brown Bread Apple Charlotte with Rum-Vanilla
    Custard Sauce, 108–109
Brownies, Turtle, with Caramel and Pecans,
    653–654
Brown sugar
    Brown Sugar–Pecan Sweet Dream
        Cookies, 821–822

measuring, 22
types of, 812
Brushes, natural bristle, 26
Brustengolo (Umbrian Cornmeal, Pear,
    Raisin, and Nut Cake), 389–390
B'stilla of Chicken, 436–437
Buckwheat, 181–189
    Apple-Date Buckwheat Muffins, 188
    Buckwheat Cinnamon-Raisin Bread,
        188–189
    buckwheat flour, weight and volume
        equivalents, 40
    general information, 182–183
    Kasha-Mushroom Knishes, 183–184
    Seeded Multi-Grain Sourdough Bread,
        186–187
    Turkish Seeded Hazelnut Bread, 502–503
    Ukrainian Buckwheat Rolls, 185
    Wolff's Kasha, about, 183
Bundt pans, cast-aluminum, 23, 473
Butane torch, 23, 663
Butter, 191–219. See also Puff pastry
    baking with, notes about, 196, 197, 203
    Biscochitos, 218–219
    "bog butter," about, 194
    Brown Butter, 202
    brown butter, about, 193–194
    butter-based pastry dough, handling, 201
    Butter Pie Pastry, 203–204
    buying, in stick form, 196
    Cigari Borekas with Moroccan Spiced
        Lamb, 212–213
    Clarified Butter, 202
    compared with shortening, 196
    creaming with sugar, 19, 31–32, 203
    cutting in, for pastry dough, 19, 32, 203
    European-style, 198
    Financiers, 215–216
    freezing and thawing, 203
    general information, 192–194
    German Butter Cake, 216–217
    handling, in hot weather, 197
    historical notes, 195–196
    mixing with animal fats, 201
    Québécoise Tourtière with Mushrooms,
        210–211
    role of, in baked goods, 194
    Savory Tart Pastry, 206
    smen (butter-based cooking fat), about, 194
    storing, 196, 203
    Tarte Tatin Pastry, 206–207
    unsalted, for recipes, 19, 201
Buttercream
    rewarming, 336
    White Chocolate Buttercream, 336
Buttermilk
    Buttermilk-Sourdough White Sandwich
        Bread, 726–727
    Buttermilk Tart Pastry, 565
    general information, 561
Butterscotch-Ginger Pear Tart, 641–643

C

Cake flour
    about, 855
    sifting, note about, 338
Cakes. *See also* Cheesecakes
    Aliza's Wedding Cake, 227–228
    Almond Milk and Chocolate Malt Cake, 146–148
    Almond–Sour Cherry Torte with Brown Butter and Sour Cherry Sauce, 303–304
    Andalusian Bittersweet Chocolate–Sherry Cake with Sherry Custard Sauce, 55–56
    angel food, preparing, 468
    Aruban Cashew Cake, 178–179
    Banana-Pecan Roulade, 132–133
    Bitter Chocolate–Hazelnut Torta with Pears, 645
    Black Kugelhopf, 717–718
    Bourbon-Spice Pumpkin Cake, 742–743
    Brandied Prune Pound Cake, 710–711
    Brazil Nut Cake with Espresso, 373–374
    Brustengolo (Umbrian Cornmeal, Pear, Raisin, and Nut Cake), 389–390
    Bundt pans for, 23
    cake pans for, 25
    Canadian Maple–Black Walnut Gingerbread, 491–492
    Caraway Seed Bundt Cake, 88–89
    cardboard cake circles for, 316
    carrot cake, history of, 239
    Chocolate Sponge Cake, 339
    Chocolate Torte with Orange and Pistachio, 697–698
    Cocoa Nib and Pecan Praline Chocolate Roulade, 340–341
    Cornmeal and Rosewater Pound Cake, 469
    Cranberry-Ginger Upside-Down Cake, 399–400
    Cranberry-Walnut Pound Cake, 400–401
    Danish Rum Raisin Cupcakes, 764
    Financiers, 215–216
    Florida Tangerine Kiss-Me Cake, 602–603
    Frangelico Mousse Cake with Gianduia-Rice Crunch, 771–773
    Fuji Apple Cake, 105
    German Apple and Rum-Raisin Custard Torte, 54–55
    German Bee-Sting Cake: Bienenstich, 523–524
    German Butter Cake, 216–217
    gooey, slicing, 36
    Greek Honey-Walnut Cake with Yogurt, 903–904
    Greek Tahini Cake, 802
    Greek Yogurt-Currant Ring Cake, 904–905
    Hazelnut–Brown Butter Cakes with Bosc Pears, 505–506
    and high-altitude baking, 877
    Honey Glazed Lavender-Lemon Cake, 472–473
    Hungarian Red Currant–Hazelnut Torte, 413–414

Indian Pudding Cake, 286–287
Indian-Spiced Carrot Cake with White Chocolate–Kewra Icing, 237–239
Italian Bittersweet Chocolate–Orange Torta, 331
Italian Walnut Cake with Candied Fruit, 226–227
kugelhopf, history of, 719
Lady Baltimore Cake, 452–454
Majorcan Lemon-Almond Cake, 77
Melting Caramel Cake: Caramel Coulant, 820–821
Mexican Chocolate Tequila Soufflé Cake, 729–730
Meyer Lemon Bundt Cake, 533–534
Mrs. Beeton's original seed cake recipe, 89
Pan di Spagna, 441
Peanut Butter and Jelly Cake, 629–630
Pear and Toasted Pecan Bundt Cake with Brown Sugar Glaze, 644–645
Pecan-Ginger Cake with Caramel Icing, 494–495
Piedmontese Mocha-Chestnut Torta, 314–315
Pilar's Tres Leches Cake, 564
pound cake, history of, 470
Red Plum Streusel Cake, 708–709
Rigo Jancsi, 333–334
ring or tube pans for, 26
Rose-Scented Angel Food Cake, 467–468
Ruby Grapefruit–Orange Brazil Nut Torte, 174–175
Siennese Panforte, 232–233
slicing into layers, 38
soaking, with sugar syrup, 38
Spanish Apple Torte, 105–107
Spanish Orange and Olive Oil Cake, 599–600
Strawberry Devil's Food Cake, 166–168
Swiss Carrot-Semolina Torte, 239–240
Tangerine Semolina Torta, 605
testing for doneness, 28–29
tiered wedding cake, preparing, 229
Torta Boscaiola (Italian Chestnut Flour and Hazelnut Cake), 319–320
Torta Caprese: Bittersweet Chocolate–Almond Cake, 336–337
Torta di Miele (Italian Jewish Honey Cake), 522–523
Torta di Savoia with Candied Citron, 535–536
Torta di Zabaglione, 480
Torta di Zucca (Squash Cake with Pine Nuts and Apricots), 741–742
Torta Gianduia, 506–508
Torta Sbrisolona alla Lombarda (Lombardian Crumbly Cake), 390–391
Velia's White Chocolate–Lemon Torta Caprese, 78
White Bean, Chestnut, and Apricot Cake alla Povera, 316–217
Zach's Almond Macaroon Cake, 76
Calas (New Orleans Rice Fritters), 773–774

California Apricot Cheesecake, 118–120
California Walnut Rosemary-Bread, 844–845
Canadian Date-Oatmeal Squares, 576
Canadian Maple–Black Walnut Gingerbread, 491–492
Candied Citrus Peel, 225–226
Candied fruit, 221–233
    Aliza's Wedding Cake, 227–228
    candied angelica, about, 229
    Candied Citrus Peel, 225–226
    general information, 222–223
    from Genoa, Italy, 224
    high-quality, where to buy, 223
    Hot Cross Buns with Currants, 230–231
    ingredients in, 223
    Italian Walnut Cake with Candied Fruit, 226–227
    Siennese Cavalluci, 224–225
    Siennese Panforte, 232–233
Candied Walnut Apple Pie, 109–110
Candied Walnuts, 847
Caramel
    Chocolate Caramel Éclairs, 817–819
    general information, 814
    Making Hard Caramel, 832
    Melting Caramel Cake: Caramel Coulant, 820–821
    preparing, 34–35, 815
    Vanilla Caramel Sauce, 822
Caramelized Nectarine and Ginger Shortcakes with Sour Cream, 617–618
Caramelized Sweet Onions, 860–861
Caraway seeds
    Caraway Seed Bundt Cake, 88–89
    caraway seedcakes and harvest feasts, 90
    general information, 84–85
Carrots, 235–242
    carrot cake, history of, 239
    choosing, storing, and preparing, 237
    general information, 236–237
    Indian-Spiced Carrot Cake with White Chocolate–Kewra Icing, 237–239
    Morning Glory Muffins with Carrots, Asian Pears, and Ginger, 240–241
    Swiss Carrot-Semolina Torte, 239–240
    Turkish Carrot Pastry Rolls, 241–242
    weight and volume equivalents, 42
Cashews
    Aruban Cashew Cake, 178–179
    Baby Banana Cream Pie in Coconut-Cashew Crust, 131–132
    choosing and storing, 174
    fresh cashews in India, 179
    general information, 173–174
    Sephardic Stuffed Monkey, 176–177
    weight and volume equivalents, 42
Cast-aluminum Bundt pans, 23, 473
Cast-iron skillet, 23
Catalan Flatbread with Spinach, Onion, and Pine Nut Topping, 672–673
Chakchouka Griddle Bread (variation), 865
Chakchouka (Tunisian Vegetable Stew), 865–866
Charlotte, Brown Bread Apple, with Rum-Vanilla

Custard Sauce, 108–109
Cheese, 243–277. *See also* Cheese recipes;
    Cream cheese
    aged, general information about, 254–257
    for baking, 257–259
    buying, at Beecher's, 269
    buying and storing, 259–260
    cheddar-type cheeses, 257
    "cheesy," origin of expression, 257
    cotija, about, 250
    cottage cheese, about, 252
    dry Jack, about, 266
    etymology of, 259
    farmer cheese, about, 252
    feta, Greek-made, about, 264
    feta cheese, about, 259
    fresh, general information about, 245–248
    fresh American cheeses, 252–253
    fresh French cheeses, 249–250
    fresh German and Eastern European
        cheeses, 251–252
    fresh Greek cheeses, 277
    fresh Indian cheeses, 251
    fresh Italian cheeses, 248–249
    fresh Latin American cheeses, 250
    fresh Middle Eastern cheeses, 251
    fresh ricotta, about, 248
    fresh ricotta, buying, 249
    fromage blanc, about, 249
    gaymera, about, 251
    goat cheese, about, 258–259
    Halloumi, about, 251
    kaymak, about, 251
    made by Vermont Butter and Cheese
        Company, 253
    mascarpone, about, 248–249
    Mastelo, about, 277
    Monterey Jack, about, 266
    myzithra, about, 277
    Neufchâtel, about, 250
    panir, about, 251
    pasta filata (pulled string), about, 258
    pecorino Romano from Fulvi, 73
    Petit-Suisse, about, 249–250
    prescinseua, about, 439
    pre-shredded, note about, 269
    quark, about, 251
    queso añejo, about, 250
    queso blanco, about, 250
    queso fresco, about, 250
    requesón, about, 250
    Roquefort, choosing and storing, 104
    Stilton, choosing and storing, 270–271
Cheesecakes
    California Apricot Cheesecake, 118–120
    Coconut Mango Cheesecake, 482–483
    July 4th Cheesecake, 833–835
    Pineapple Cheesecake with Ginger-
        Macadamia Crust, 682
Cheese recipes
    Alpine Mushroom Pizza with Potato-Rye
        Dough, 787
    Arugula and Roasted Tomato Pizza, 888

Cheddar and Chive Gougères, 268
Chicken-Cheese Empanadas, 264–266
Country-Style Greek Greens Pie, 262–263
Cretan Kalitsounia (Sweet Cheese Pastries),
    276–277
Crostata della Nonna: Grandma's Ricotta–
    Pine Nut Tart, 676–677
Danish Pastry Braid with Goat Cheese and
    Cardamom (and Variations), 273–275
A Date in a Blanket, 421–422
Feta Cheese and Egg Pide, 900–901
French Roquefort, Apple, and Leek Tart,
    103–104
Grape, Gorgonzola, and Walnut Focaccia,
    788–789
Greek Eggplant and Walnut Phyllo Rolls,
    842–843
Greek Feta Cheese Bread, 261–262
Guava and Cheese Empanadas, 271–272
Herbed Focaccia with Goat Cheese, Red
    Onion, and Black Olives, 725–726
Kea Stuffed Griddle Bread, 144–145
Plantain Empanadas with Black Bean and
    Añejo Cheese Filling, 129–130
Radicchio and Fontina Torta, 260–261
Sardinian Potato Torta, 728–729
Sardinian Sebadas: Fried Stuffed Rounds
    with Ricotta Cheese, 517–518
Savory Oatmeal-Cheddar Tart, 573–574
Sesame Honey Cones with Ricotta Filling,
    800–802
Sicilian Pan Pizza with Zucca, 737–738
Stilton Scones, 269–270
Strawberry-Vanilla Coeur à la Crème Tart
    with Goat Cheese, 832–833
Torta Pasqualina Genovese, 438–439
Torta Rustica, 861–862
Turkish Baked Cheese Turnovers, 898–899
Turkish Ricotta Cookies, 272–273
Turkish Savory Cornbread, 388–389
White Pizza with Broccoli Rabe, 266–267
Woodfire Grill Duck Confit Pizza, 859–860
Chef's knife, 26–27
Chemical leaveners, 279–291. *See also* Baking
    powder; Baking soda
    Almond Cantucci Pratesi, 289–290
    baker's ammonia, notes about, 280–281, 291
    Chocolate-Glazed Praline Profiteroles,
        287–289
    general information, 280–283, 291
    Iced Malted Milk Cookies, 285–286
    Indian Pudding Cake, 286–287
    pearlash (potassium carbonate), 282
    saleratus (aerated salt), 282
Cherries, 293–308
    alcohol made from, 301
    Almond–Sour Cherry Torte with Brown
        Butter and Sour Cherry Sauce, 303–304
    Baked Quince with Pine Nuts and Dried
        Fruit, 754
    candied, in fruit cakes, 298
    Cherry-Maraschino Cream Pie, 306–307
    Chocolate-Cherry Biscotti with Cocoa

Nibs, 305–306
    choosing and storing, 303
    etymology, 298
    general information, 294–298
    Le Bec-Fin's Fruited Walnut Bread, 843–844
    maraschino cherries, about, 301
    Michigan-grown, 300
    Montmorencys, 300
    morello cherries, 300
    Oatmeal Pear Crisp with Dried Cherries,
        643–644
    Quince and Sour Cherry Strudel, 751–752
    removing pits from, 301
    Sour Cherry Sauce, 304
    sour cherry varieties, 299–300
    sweet cherry varieties, 298–299
    sweet-sour cherry varieties, 300
    Tart Cherry Clafouti, 307–308
    Venetian Cornmeal and Cherry
        Crostata, 305
    weight and volume equivalents, 42
Chestnuts, 309–320
    buying, 312
    Chestnut Cornbread, 318–319
    Chestnut-Currant Scones, 313–314
    chestnut flour, weight and volume
        equivalents, 40
    from Corsica, about, 318
    Corsican Chestnut Rolls, 317–318
    general information, 310–311
    Pennsylvania-grown, 320
    Piedmontese Mocha-Chestnut Torta,
        314–315
    preparing and cooking, 312–313
    Torta Boscaiola (Italian Chestnut Flour
        and Hazelnut Cake), 319–320
    from Tuscany, about, 315
    weight and volume equivalents, 43
    White Bean, Chestnut, and Apricot Cake
        alla Povera, 316–217
Chicago Metallic loaf and muffin tins, 23
Chicken
    B'stilla of Chicken, 436–437
    Chicken-Cheese Empanadas, 264–266
Chlorophyll (Natural Green Coloring), 699–700
Chocolate, 321–341. *See also* Chocolate recipes;
    White chocolate
    bloom formed on, 326
    buying, 19, 325
    cacao products, 325
    cacao varieties, 327–328
    chocolate bean varieties, 327–328
    chocolate blends, 329
    chocolate nibs, about, 329
    cocoa, for recipes, 19
    cocoa, notes about, 325
    cocoa, sifting, 338
    conching process, 325
    general information, 322–325
    high-quality, baking with, 19, 326, 330
    melting, 35
    recommended baking chocolates, 330
    single-origin chocolates, 329

storing, 325
tempering, 326–327
Tuscan, buying, 338
types of, 328–329
Chocolate recipes
Almond Milk and Chocolate Malt Cake, 146–148
Andalusian Bittersweet Chocolate–Sherry Cake with Sherry Custard Sauce, 55–56
Baci de Dama with Nutella (Lady's Kisses), 335
Bitter Chocolate–Hazelnut Torta with Pears, 645
Black Kugelhopf, 717–718
Bonèt Piemontese: Chocolate-Amaretti Baked Custard, 439–440
Chocolate Caramel Éclairs, 817–819
Chocolate-Cherry Biscotti with Cocoa Nibs, 305–306
Chocolate-Dipped Coconut Macaroons, 364
Chocolate-Glazed Praline Profiteroles, 287–289
Chocolate-Kahlúa Silk Pie, 374–376
Chocolate Sponge Cake, 339
Chocolate Torte with Orange and Pistachio, 697–698
Cocoa Nib and Pecan Praline, 340
Cocoa Nib and Pecan Praline Chocolate Roulade, 340–341
English Millionaire's Shortbread, 769–771
Florentine Chocolate Nut Zuccotto, 58–60
Frangelico Mousse Cake with Gianduia-Rice Crunch, 771–773
Homemade Gianduia, 508
Italian Bittersweet Chocolate–Orange Torta, 331
Mexican Chocolate Tequila Soufflé Cake, 729–730
Mexican Spiced Cocoa Meringues, 352–353
Milk Chocolate and Pistachio Cookies, 696–697
Mochaccino Swirl Cookies, 376–377
'mpanatigghi Siciliano, 331–332
Peanut-Chocolate Bars with Espresso, 627–628
Peanut Meringue with Spiced Bittersweet Chocolate Pudding, 63–631
Piedmontese Mocha-Chestnut Torta, 314–315
Rigo Jancsi, 333–334
Shiny Chocolate-Mocha Glaze, 334–335
Strawberry Devil's Food Cake, 166–168
Torta Caprese: Bittersweet Chocolate–Almond Cake, 336–337
Torta Gianduia, 506–508
Turtle Brownies with Caramel and Pecans, 653–654
Choux paste, about, 289
Cicerchiata or Teiglach, 587–588
Cigari Borekas with Moroccan Spiced Lamb, 212–213
Cinnamon, 343–353

cassia, compared with cinnamon, 349
cassia, types of, 346–348
cassia sticks, about, 349
cassia sticks, crushing, 348
cinnamon quills, about, 349
cinnamon quills, crushing, 348
Crispy Lemon-Cinnamon Cookies, 351–352
general information, 344–345
Hazelnut-Cinnamon Thumbprint Cookies with Red Currant Jam, 350–351
Mexican Spiced Cocoa Meringues, 352–353
Speculaas Spices, 353
Spiced Polvorones, 349–350
varieties of, 346–348
Citrons
Biscotti Rococò, 536–537
French Candied Citron and Lemon Cookies, 534–535
general information, 531–532
Torta di Savoia with Candied Citron, 535–536
Citrus zesters, 179
Clafouti, Tart Cherry, 307–308
Clam Pizza, New Haven–Style White, 886–887
Clarified Butter, 202
Cocoa Nib and Pecan Praline, 340
Cocoa Nib and Pecan Praline Chocolate Roulade, 340–341
Cocoa powder
notes about, 325
for recipes, 19
sifting, 338
Coconut, 355–364
Baby Banana Cream Pie in Coconut-Cashew Crust, 131–132
Chocolate-Dipped Coconut Macaroons, 364
choosing and storing, 358
Coconut Cream–Filled Cookie Turnovers, 362–363
Coconut Mango Cheesecake, 482–483
Crisp Swedish Coconut "Dream" Cookies, 361
general information, 356–357
growth stages, 357–358
Honduran Coconut Bread, 360–361
Key Lime Cheesecake Pie in Coconut-Pecan Crust, 548
opening and grating, 359
Pineapple-Coconut Flan with Dark Rum, 684–685
Pineapple Coconut Shortbread Bars with Macadamia Nuts, 687–688
Southern Million-Dollar Pie, 685–687
unsweetened grated, buying, 359
weight and volume equivalents, 43
Coffee, 365–379
from arabica beans, 370
blending and roasting, 370
Brazil Nut Cake with Espresso, 373–374
Chocolate-Kahlúa Silk Pie, 374–376
coffee roast bean varieties, 373
decaffeinated, notes about, 372

espresso, notes about, 371–372
general information, 366–369
grown at high altitudes, 369
instant and freeze-dried, 372
Mochaccino Swirl Cookies, 376–377
Peanut-Chocolate Bars with Espresso, 627–628
preparing, tips for, 372–373
from robusta beans, 370
Shiny Chocolate-Mocha Glaze, 334–335
storing, 370
White Chocolate, Hazelnut, and Espresso Dacquoise, 377–379
Confectioners' sugar
about, 810
confectioners' granite sugar, about, 809
measuring, 22
Cookbooks
Lowney's Cookbook (Howard), 109
Mrs. Beeton's Book of Household Management (Mayson), 89
World Hazelnut Tastes, 242
Cookies. See also Bar cookies
Almond Cantucci Pratesi, 289–290
Anise-Scented Date-Orange Spirals, 423–424
Argentinean Alfajores Cookies, 563–564
arranging, on baking trays, 176
Baci de Dama with Nutella (Lady's Kisses), 335
Biscochitos, 218–219
Biscotti Rococò, 536–537
Brazil-Nut and Guava Sandwich Cookies, 175–176
Brown Sugar–Pecan Sweet Dream Cookies, 821–822
Chocolate-Cherry Biscotti with Cocoa Nibs, 305–306
Chocolate-Dipped Coconut Macaroons, 364
Coconut Cream–Filled Cookie Turnovers, 362–363
cookie cutters for, 24, 363–364
Crisp Swedish Coconut "Dream" Cookies, 361
Crispy Lemon-Cinnamon Cookies, 351–352
Crunchy Macadamia-Ginger Quaresemali, 489–490
Cuccidati (Sicilian Fig Cookies), 457–458
Dutch Speculaas with Rye, 789–790
French Candied Citron and Lemon Cookies, 534–535
gooey, slicing, 36
Greek Honey-Nut Cookies with Mastic, 518–519
Hazelnut-Cinnamon Thumbprint Cookies with Red Currant Jam, 350–351
and high-altitude baking, 877
Honey–Poppy Seed Hamantaschen, 716–717
Iced Malted Milk Cookies, 285–286
Kourambiedes with Olive Oil, 586–587
Lemon Poppy Seed Biscotti, 719–720

Lime Cornmeal Cookies, 547
Mahmoul (Syrian Pistachio-Stuffed
 Semolina Cookies with Rosewater),
 466–467
Makroud (Tunisian Semolina Cookies
 Stuffed with Dates), 422–423
Maltese Kwaresimal Cookies, 603–604
Mexican Spiced Cocoa Meringues, 352–353
Milk Chocolate and Pistachio Cookies,
 696–697
Mochaccino Swirl Cookies, 376–377
Molasses-Ginger Brandy Snaps, 819–820
Oatmeal-Pecan Fruities, 425
One-Bowl Hazelnut Cornmeal Biscotti,
 503–504
Pizzelle "of the Angels" with Fennel Pollen,
 91–92
Rum Pecan-Praline Sandies, 652–653
Sambuca and Candied Orange Tozzetti,
 90–91
Sephardic Pan Levi Cookies, 442
Siennese Cavalluci, 224–225
Speculaas, history of, 791
Spiced Honey–Almond Rings with
 Brandied Persimmon Bits, 665–666
Spiced Polvorones, 349–350
Spiced Quince and Walnut Thumbprint
 Cookies, 750–751
Swedish Ginger-Spice Cookies:
 Pepparkakor, 493
Turkish Hazelnut Macaroons, 504
Turkish Ricotta Cookies, 272–273
Turkish Semolina Sponge Cookies,
 869–870
Zaleti: Venetian Cornmeal Cookies with
 Grappa Raisins, 60
Cooling racks, wire, 28
Corn, 381–393. See also Cornmeal
 cornstarch, about, 384–385
 cornstarch, weight and volume
 equivalents, 41
 corn syrup, notes about, 386
 general information, 382–383
 nixtamalization process, 385
 Pennsylvania Dutch Corn Pie, 387–388
 Shiny Cornstarch Glaze, 393
 types of, 383–384
Cornbread
 Chestnut Cornbread, 318–319
 "eating the cornbread" expression, 387
 Turkish Savory Cornbread, 388–389
Cornmeal, 381–393
 Brustengolo (Umbrian Cornmeal, Pear,
 Raisin, and Nut Cake), 389–390
 Chestnut Cornbread, 318–319
 Cornmeal and Rosewater Pound Cake, 469
 Cornmeal Pizza Dough, 392
 general information, 384
 Greek Cornmeal Raisin Bread, 762–764
 Guinness Oatmeal Bread, 574–575
 Indian Pudding Cake, 286–287
 Lime Cornmeal Cookies, 547
 Maple Cornmeal Muffins with Pine Nuts

 and Currants, 553–554
 One-Bowl Hazelnut Cornmeal Biscotti,
 503–504
 Torta Sbrisolona alla Lombarda
 (Lombardian Crumbly Cake), 390–391
 Turkish Savory Cornbread, 388–389
 types of, 384–385
 Venetian Cornmeal and Cherry
 Crostata, 305
 Venetian Cornmeal Tart Dough, 391–392
 weight and volume equivalents, 40
 Zaleti: Venetian Cornmeal Cookies with
 Grappa Raisins, 60
Cornstarch
 about, 384–385
 Shiny Cornstarch Glaze, 393
 weight and volume equivalents, 41
Corsican Chestnut Rolls, 317–318
Country-Style Greek Greens Pie, 262–263
Cranberries, 395–403
 choosing and storing, 398
 cooking tips, 398
 Cranberry-Caramel Pecan Tart, 654–655
 Cranberry-Ginger Upside-Down Cake,
 399–400
 Cranberry-Semolina Ktefa, 401–402
 Cranberry-Walnut Pound Cake, 400–401
 general information, 396–398
 heirloom varieties, 399
 Hot Apple-Cranberry Crisp with Oatmeal-
 Almond Topping, 403
 New England Cranberry-Maple-Raisin Pie,
 552–553
 Quince-Cranberry Tarte Tatin, 753
 weight and volume equivalents, 43
Cream. See Milk, cream, & buttermilk
Cream cheese
 Banana-Pecan Roulade, 132–133
 beating, for cheeseckae, 29
 California Apricot Cheesecake, 118–120
 Coconut Mango Cheesecake, 482–483
 Cream Cheese Pastry Dough, 565–566
 Guava and Cheese Empanadas, 271–272
 Indian-Spiced Carrot Cake with White
 Chocolate–Kewra Icing, 237–239
 July 4th Cheesecake, 833–835
 Key Lime Cheesecake Pie in Coconut-
 Pecan Crust, 548
 notes about, 252–253
 Pineapple Cheesecake with Ginger-
 Macadamia Crust, 682
 Strawberry-Vanilla Coeur à la Crème Tart
 with Goat Cheese, 832–833
Crème Anglaise (English Vanilla Custard
 Sauce), 835
Creole Pecan Pralines, 650
Cretan Kalitsounia (Sweet Cheese Pastries),
 276–277
Crisp Swedish Coconut "Dream" Cookies, 361
Crispy Lemon-Cinnamon Cookies, 351–352
Crostata della Nonna: Grandma's Ricotta–Pine
 Nut Tart, 676–677
Crostata di Riso: Italian Rice Tart, 776–777

Crumb crusts, making, 33–34
Crunchy Macadamia-Ginger Quaresemali, 489–
 490
Cuccidati (Sicilian Fig Cookies), 457–458
Culinary butane torch, 23, 663
Cupcakes, Danish Rum Raisin, 764
Currants, dried
 Chestnut-Currant Scones, 313–314
 Currant-Walnut Baguette, 761–762
 general information, 757
 Greek Yogurt-Currant Ring Cake, 904–905
 Hot Cross Buns with Currants, 230–231
 Maple Cornmeal Muffins with Pine Nuts
 and Currants, 553–554
 Spiced Fuyu Persimmon Bars, 664
 Zante currants, about, 759
Currants, fresh, 405–416
 Bar-le-Duc seedless currant jelly, 409
 Black Currant–Apple Linzer Torte, 411–413
 buying, 410
 English Summer Fruit Pudding with Lemon
 and Mint, 415–416
 general information, 406, 408–409
 Hungarian Red Currant–Hazelnut Torte,
 413–414
 seasonality of, 410
Cuscurols, Maria's, 588–589
Custards
 Bonèt Piemontese: Chocolate-Amaretti
 Baked Custard, 439–440
 cooking, 31
 preventing curdling of, 62
Custard Sauce, Sherry, 61–62

D
Dacquoise, White Chocolate, Hazelnut,
 and Espresso, 377–379
Dairy-free recipes
 Biscochitos, 218–219
 Candied Citrus Peel, 225–226
 Cigari Borekas with Moroccan Spiced
 Lamb, 212–213
 Corsican Chestnut Rolls, 317–318
 Cuccidati (Sicilian Fig Cookies), 457–458
 Greek Black Barley Rings, 140–141
 Greek Tahini Cake, 802
 Italian Meringue Twists and Cake
 Decorations, 836
 Italian Walnut Cake with Candied Fruit,
 226–227
 Kourambiedes with Olive Oil, 586–587
 Lemon Poppy Seed Biscotti, 719–720
 Majorcan Lemon-Almond Cake, 77
 Maltese Kwaresimal Cookies, 603–604
 Maria's Cuscurols, 588–589
 Mexican Spiced Cocoa Meringues, 352–353
 'mpanatigghi Siciliano, 331–332
 One-Bowl Hazelnut Cornmeal Biscotti,
 503–504
 Pan di Spagna, 441
 Raspberry Salzburger Nockerln, 160–161
 Rose-Scented Angel Food Cake, 467–468
 Ruby Grapefruit–Orange Brazil Nut Torte,

174–175

Sambuca and Candied Orange Tozzetti,
90–91

Sardenaira (Riviera-Style Olive and
Anchovy Pizza), 883–884

Seeded Multi-Grain Sourdough Bread,
186–187

Sephardic Pan Levi Cookies, 442

Siennese Cavalluci, 224–225

Spanish Honey-Dipped Spiral Pastries
(Hojuelas), 585–586

Spanish Sesame-Anise Cookies, 799–800

Taralli: Boiled and Baked "Pretzels" from
Puglia, 584–585

Teiglach or Cicerchiata, 587–588

Torta Boscaiola (Italian Chestnut Flour and
Hazelnut Cake), 319–320

Torta di Miele (Italian Jewish Honey Cake),
522–523

Torta di Savoia with Candied Citron,
535–536

Torta di Zucca (Squash Cake with Pine Nuts
and Apricots), 741–742

Torta Sbrisolona alla Lombarda
(Lombardian Crumbly Cake), 390–391

Turkish Seeded Hazelnut Bread, 502–503

White Bean, Chestnut, and Apricot Cake
alla Povera, 316–217

Danish Pastry Braid with Goat Cheese and
Cardamom (and Variations), 273–275

Danish Rum Raisin Cupcakes, 764

Dates, 417–425

Anise-Scented Date-Orange Spirals,
423–424

Apple-Date Buckwheat Muffins, 188

Canadian Date-Oatmeal Squares, 576

A Date in a Blanket, 421–422

date varieties, 420–421

general information, 418–420

Makroud (Tunisian Semolina Cookies
Stuffed with Dates), 422–423

Oatmeal-Pecan Fruities, 425

weight and volume equivalents, 43

Deep-frying techniques, 32–33

Dilled Potato-Onion Rolls, 727–728

Disher or ice cream scoop, 23

Disposable pastry bags, 24

Duck Confit Pizza, Woodfire Grill, 859–860

Dufour Brand, 207

Dukkah, 890–891

Dulce de leche

Dulce de Leche, 566

English Millionaire's Shortbread, 769–771

history of, 567

versions of, 567

Dumplings, Austrian Apricot, 122–123

Durum wheat

about, 853

Durum Wheat Bread with Squash, Tomatoes, Onions, and Peppers, 736–737

weight and volume equivalents, 40

Dutch Almond-Filled Spice Tart, 74–75

Dutch oven, enameled cast-iron, 24

Dutch Speculaas with Rye, 789–790

E

Eau de vie, about, 49

Éclairs, Chocolate Caramel, 817–819

Eggplant

Greek Eggplant and Walnut Phyllo Rolls,
842–843

Kea Stuffed Griddle Bread, 144–145

Savory Eggplant and Spiced Almond Tart,
72–73

Eggs, 427–445. See also Meringue

Australian Pavlova with Lemon Filling and
Tropical Fruits, 442–444

beating into batters, 29–30

beating with sugar, 30

blood spots in, 433

Bonèt Piemontese: Chocolate-Amaretti
Baked Custard, 439–440

B'stilla of Chicken, 436–437

buying, for recipes, 19, 434

egg whites, beating, 30, 432–433

egg whites, freezing and thawing, 19

egg whites, notes about, 432

egg yolks, notes about, 431–432

egg yolks and whites, separating, 35–36, 431

expansion properties, 434

Feta Cheese and Egg Pide, 900–901

general information, 428–430

German Muerbeteig Dough (Mellow
Dough), 444–445

grades and sizes, 430

hard-cooked, preparing, 388

Pan di Spagna, 441

parts of the egg, 430

Sephardic Pan Levi Cookies, 442

size and volume equivalents, 44

Smoked Salmon and Spinach Quiche,
434–435

storing, 434

testing freshness of, 433

Torta Pasqualina Genovese, 438–439

Egyptian Flatbread with Dukkah Sprinkle,
890–891

Empanada Dough, Savory, 205

Empanadas

Chicken-Cheese Empanadas, 264–266

forming and baking, 33

Guava and Cheese Empanadas, 271–272

historical notes, 130

Plantain Empanadas with Black Bean and
Añejo Cheese Filling, 129–130

Spanish Tuna Emapanadas with Sofrito,
881–882

Enameled cast-iron Dutch oven, 24

English Millionaire's Shortbread, 769–771

English Summer Fruit Pudding with Lemon and
Mint, 415–416

Equipment

cast-aluminum Bundt pans, 23, 473

cast-iron skillet, 23

Chicago Metallic loaf and muffin tins, 23

cookware information on internet, 28

culinary butane torch, 23, 663

disher or ice cream scoop, 23

disposable pastry bags, 24

enameled cast-iron Dutch oven, 24

Escali scales, 22

Fante's Cookware, 28, 93

Foley food mill, 24

food processor, 24

French composite plastic cutters,
24, 363–364

half-sheet pans, 25

immersion blender, 24–25

KitchenAid mixer, 25

kitchen scissors, 25

knife sharpener, 25

Magic Line cake pans, 25

microplane zester, 26, 179

natural bristle brushes, 26

parchment and wax paper, 26

ring or tube pan, 26

rolling pin, 26

Roul-Pat, 26

sharp chef's knife, 26–27

silicone spatulas, 27

Silpat silicone mats, 27

stainless steel bowls, 27

Thermapen instant-read thermometer,
27, 880

whisks, 27–28

wire cooling racks, 28

Escalivada, preparing, 673

Exotic Mushroom Puff Pastry Pillows, 207–208

F

Fante's Cookware, 28, 93

Fats, animal. See also Butter

Biscochitos, 218–219

lard, notes about, 198–199

Lard Pie Dough, 204

leaf lard, about, 200

mixing with butter, 201

in pastry dough, notes about, 201

poultry fats, 200–201

Savory Empanada Dough, 205

Steak, Guinness, and Mushroom Pie,
213–215

suet, notes about, 199, 200–201

Suet Meat Pie Dough, 204–205

Fennel

about, 84

Fennel Egg Bread, 86–87

fennel pollen, about, 92

Pizzelle "of the Angels" with Fennel Pollen,
91–92

Figs, 447–458

Cuccidati (Sicilian Fig Cookies), 457–458

dried, choosing and storing, 451

Fig and Pine Nut Bread, 674

Fig Newton cookies, origin of, 451

fig varieties, 451–452

fresh, choosing and storing, 450

general information, 448–450

Ginger Fig Scones, 491

Lady Baltimore Cake, 452–454
Le Bec-Fin's Fruited Walnut Bread, 843–844
Rustic Fresh Fig Galette, 454–455
seasonality of, 450
Sweet Fig Focaccia, 455–456
weight and volume equivalents, 43
Financiers, 215–216
Flan, Pineapple-Coconut, with Dark Rum, 684–685
Florentine Chocolate Nut Zuccotto, 58–60
Florida Tangerine Kiss-Me Cake, 602–603
Flour, 849–870. See also Semolina; specific types of flour
    buying, for recipes, 19–20
    general information, 850–852
    and high-altitude baking, 877
    Lahmacun: Armenian Lamb Flatbread, 866–867
    measuring, on scale, 22
    for pizza, buying, 857
    Savory Spiced Whole Wheat Pastry, 862–863
    Sourdough Bread Starter, 880–881
    storing, 20
    Sweet White Whole Wheat Tart Pastry, 863
    Torta Rustica, 861–862
    types of, 853–857
    weight and volume equivalents, 40–41
    Woodfire Grill Duck Confit Pizza, 859–860
    Woodfire Grill Pizza Dough, 858–859
Flowers, 459–473
    candied, buying, 466
    candied, preparing, 464
    candied and fresh, garnishing ideas, 464
    Cornmeal and Rosewater Pound Cake, 469
    edible flowers, buying, 466
    edible flowers, common types of, 465–466
    Florida Tangerine Kiss-Me Cake, 602–603
    flower waters, adding to recipes, 464
    flower waters, buying, 466
    general information, 460–464
    Honey Glazed Lavender-Lemon Cake, 472–473
    kewra water, about, 463
    lavender, about, 464
    lavender-infused simple syrup, preparing, 464
    Mahmoul (Syrian Pistachio-Stuffed Semolina Cookies with Rosewater), 466–467
    Maltese Kwaresimal Cookies, 603–604
    Orange Blossom Brioches, 470–471
    Orange Blossom Glaze, 471
    orange blossom water, about, 463
    rose petals and rosebuds, 462
    Rose-Scented Angel Food Cake, 467–468
    Rose-Scented Raspberry Sauce, 161
    rose syrup, about, 462
    rose syrup, buying, 466
    rosewater, about, 461–462
Focaccia
    Grape, Gorgonzola, and Walnut Focaccia, 788–789

Herbed Focaccia with Goat Cheese, Red Onion, and Black Olives, 725–726
    Sweet Fig Focaccia, 455–456
Foley food mill, 24
Food processor, 24
Frangelico Mousse Cake with Gianduia-Rice Crunch, 771–773
French Apricot Tart Scented with Cloves, 120–121
French Candied Citron and Lemon Cookies, 534–535
French Caramel Puff Pastry Fruit Tart, 830–832
French composite plastic cutters, 24, 363–364
French Puff Pastry Peach Galette, 618–619
French Roquefort, Apple, and Leek Tart, 103–104
Fresh Strawberry Coulis, 168
Fritters, New Orleans Rice (Calas), 773–774
Frosting. See Buttercream
Fruits. See also Candied fruit; specific fruits
    Australian Pavlova with Lemon Filling and Tropical Fruits, 442–444
    fan-shaped, cutting, 32
    French Caramel Puff Pastry Fruit Tart, 830–832
    weight and volume equivalents, 42–44
Fuji Apple Cake, 105

G

Garlic-Sesame Grissini, 885–885
Gelatin, 475–484
    Blackberry–White Chocolate Tart, 483–484
    Coconut Mango Cheesecake, 482–483
    effect of fruit enzymes on, 479
    European sheet gelatin, working with, 478
    general information, 476–478
    Lemon-Blackberry Bavarese with Limoncello, 481–482
    preparing, 35
    Torta di Zabaglione, 480
    weight and volume equivalents, 44
    working with, 479
Gelato, Pistachio, 698–699
German Apple and Rum-Raisin Custard Torte, 54–55
German Bee-Sting Cake: Bienenstich, 523–524
German Butter Cake, 216–217
German Muerbeteig Dough (Mellow Dough), 444–445
Gianduia
    Frangelico Mousse Cake with Gianduia-Rice Crunch, 771–773
    historical note about, 508
    Homemade Gianduia, 508
    Torta Gianduia, 506–508
Ginger, 485–495
    Butterscotch-Ginger Pear Tart, 641–643
    Canadian Maple–Black Walnut Gingerbread, 491–492
    Caramelized Nectarine and Ginger Shortcakes with Sour Cream, 617–618
    Cranberry-Ginger Upside-Down Cake, 399–400

Crunchy Macadamia-Ginger Quaresemali, 489–490
    crystallized, about, 489
    fresh, buying, storing, and preparing, 488
    general information, 486–487
    Ginger Fig Scones, 491
    ground (powdered), about, 489
    Hawaiian, about, 488
    mature, about, 488
    Molasses-Ginger Brandy Snaps, 819–820
    Pecan-Ginger Cake with Caramel Icing, 494–495
    Pineapple Cheesecake with Ginger-Macadamia Crust, 682
    preserved, about, 489
    Swedish Ginger-Spice Cookies: Pepparkakor, 493
    young (spring), about, 488
Glazes
    Orange Blossom Glaze, 471
    Shiny Chocolate-Mocha Glaze, 334–335
    Shiny Cornstarch Glaze, 393
Gluten-free recipes
    Andalusian Bittersweet Chocolate–Sherry Cake with Sherry Custard Sauce, 55–56
    Bonèt Piemontese: Chocolate-Amaretti Baked Custard, 439–440
    Candied Walnuts, 847
    Chocolate-Dipped Coconut Macaroons, 364
    Frangelico Mousse Cake with Gianduia-Rice Crunch, 771–773
    Italian Bittersweet Chocolate–Orange Torta, 331
    Italian Meringue Twists and Cake Decorations, 836
    Majorcan Lemon-Almond Cake, 77
    Mexican Chocolate Tequila Soufflé Cake, 729–730
    Mexican Spiced Cocoa Meringues, 352–353
    notes about, 723–724
    Piedmontese Mocha-Chestnut Torta, 314–315
    Raspberry Salzburger Nockerln, 160–161
    Ruby Grapefruit–Orange Brazil Nut Torte, 174–175
    Torta Boscaiola (Italian Chestnut Flour and Hazelnut Cake), 319–320
    Torta Caprese: Bittersweet Chocolate–Almond Cake, 336–337
    Turkish Goat's Milk Rice Pudding, 774–775
    Turkish Hazelnut Macaroons, 504
    Velia's White Chocolate–Lemon Torta Caprese, 78
    White Bean, Chestnut, and Apricot Cake alla Povera, 316–217
    White Chocolate, Hazelnut, and Espresso Dacquoise, 377–379
Goodfellow, Elizabeth, 469–470
Gooseberries, 405–416
    buying, 410
    English Summer Fruit Pudding with Lemon and Mint, 415–416

general information, 406–407
Gooseberry Cobbler with Walnut Crunch, 410–411
seasonality of, 410
Gougères, Cheddar and Chive, 268
Graham crackers, size and volume equivalents, 45
Grains. *See also* Flour; *specific grains*
weight and volume equivalents, 40–41
Grapefruit, Ruby, –Orange Brazil Nut Torte, 174–175
Grapes
Grape, Gorgonzola, and Walnut Focaccia, 788–789
Tahini and Grape Molasses Pide, 901–902
Grappa and marc
notes about, 49–50
Zaleti: Venetian Cornmeal Cookies with Grappa Raisins, 60
Greek Black Barley Rings, 140–141
Greek Blueberry-Yogurt Tart with Ouzo, 165–166
Greek Cornmeal Raisin Bread, 762–764
Greek Country Barley Bread, 142–143
Greek Eggplant and Walnut Phyllo Rolls, 842–843
Greek Feta Cheese Bread, 261–262
Greek Honey-Nut Cookies with Mastic, 518–519
Greek Honey-Walnut Cake with Yogurt, 903–904
Greek Phyllo Pumpkin Pie: Kolokythopita, 739–740
Greek Tahini Cake, 802
Greek Yogurt-Currant Ring Cake, 904–905
Greens. *See also* Spinach
Arugula and Roasted Tomato Pizza, 888
Country-Style Greek Greens Pie, 262–263
Radicchio and Fontina Torta, 260–261
Torta Pasqualina Genovese, 438–439
wild, types of, 264
Grilled Indian Naan Bread with Nigella Seeds, 902–903
Guarapo (sugar cane juice), about, 808
Guava
Brazil-Nut and Guava Sandwich Cookies, 175–176
Guava and Cheese Empanadas, 271–272
Guinness Oatmeal Bread, 574–575

H

Half-sheet pans, 25
Hamantaschen, Honey–Poppy Seed, 716–717
Harissa Griddle Bread (variation), 865
Harissa Sauce, Spicy, 866
Hazelnuts, 497–509
Bitter Chocolate–Hazelnut Torta with Pears, 645
Chocolate-Cherry Biscotti with Cocoa Nibs, 305–306
cookbook about, 242
Dukkah, 890–891
Florentine Chocolate Nut Zuccotto, 58–60
Frangelico Mousse Cake with Gianduia-Rice Crunch, 771–773

general information, 498–502
Hazelnut–Brown Butter Cakes with Bosc Pears, 505–506
Hazelnut-Cinnamon Thumbprint Cookies with Red Currant Jam, 350–351
Hazelnut Praline, 509
Homemade Gianduia, 508
Hungarian Red Currant–Hazelnut Torte, 413–414
July 4th Cheesecake, 833–835
One-Bowl Hazelnut Cornmeal Biscotti, 503–504
Siennese Panforte, 232–233
Swiss Carrot-Semolina Torte, 239–240
Teiglach or Cicerchiata, 587–588
Torta Boscaiola (Italian Chestnut Flour and Hazelnut Cake), 319–320
Torta Gianduia, 506–508
from Turkey, historical note about, 505
Turkish Carrot Pastry Rolls, 241–242
Turkish Hazelnut Macaroons, 504
Turkish Seeded Hazelnut Bread, 502–503
Turkish Semolina Sponge Cookies, 869–870
weight and volume equivalents, 43
White Chocolate, Hazelnut, and Espresso Dacquoise, 377–379
Heirloom Sweet Potato–Praline Pie, 651–652
Herbed Focaccia with Goat Cheese, Red Onion, and Black Olives, 725–726
Hickory nuts, notes about, 649
High-altitude baking, 877
Homemade Limoncello, 537–538
Homemade Pumpkin Spice Mix, 733
Honduran Coconut Bread, 360–361
Honey, 511–524
etymology, 517
general information, 512–516
German Bee-Sting Cake: Bienenstich, 523–524
Greek Honey-Nut Cookies with Mastic, 518–519
Greek Honey-Walnut Cake with Yogurt, 903–904
Honey Glazed Lavender-Lemon Cake, 472–473
Honey–Poppy Seed Hamantaschen, 716–717
measuring, tip for, 517
Potica (Slovenian Honey-Walnut Ring), 845–847
Sardinian bitter honey, 517
Sardinian Sebadas: Fried Stuffed Rounds with Ricotta Cheese, 517–518
Sesame Honey Cones with Ricotta Filling, 800–802
Sfratti di Pitigliano, 520–522
Spanish Honey-Dipped Spiral Pastries (Hojuelas), 585–586
Spiced Honey–Almond Rings with Brandied Persimmon Bits, 665–666
Teiglach or Cicerchiata, 587–588
top American varieties, 517

Torta di Miele (Italian Jewish Honey Cake), 522–523
Hot Apple-Cranberry Crisp with Oatmeal-Almond Topping, 403
Hot Cross Buns with Currants, 230–231
Huckleberries, notes about, 152–153
Hungarian Red Currant–Hazelnut Torte, 413–414

I

Ice cream scoop, 23
Iced Malted Milk Cookies, 285–286
Immersion blender, 24–25
Indian Pudding Cake, 286–287
Indian-Spiced Carrot Cake with White Chocolate–Kewra Icing, 237–239
Ingredients
ingredient standards for recipes, 19–21
liquid and dry, alternating, 28
measuring, 21–22
Italian Bittersweet Chocolate–Orange Torta, 331
Italian 00 flour, about, 583–584, 855–856
Italian Hachiya Persimmon Meringue Torte, 662–663
Italian Meringue Twists and Cake Decorations, 836
Italian shops and establishments
Antico Molino Caputo flour mill, 857
Guastini Hotel and Restaurant, 522
La Champagneria bar and caffè, 79
La Molina Tuscan chocolates, 338
Le Solane farm, 315
Locali Storici d'Italia, 58
Pasticceria Pansa in Amalfi, 57–58
Pietro Romanengo fu Stefano, 224
Slow Food Ark of Taste, 748
Italian Walnut Cake with Candied Fruit, 226–227

J

Jam, Spiced Quince, 749–750
July 4th Cheesecake, 833–835

K

Kadayif pastry, notes about, 695
Kasha, buckwheat. *See* Buckwheat
Kea Stuffed Griddle Bread, 144–145
Kewra water, about, 463
Kewra water, buying, 466
Key Lime Cheesecake Pie in Coconut-Pecan Crust, 548
Kichels, Onion Poppy Seed, 715–716
Kippered salmon, about, 435
KitchenAid mixer, 25
Kitchen scales, from Escali Company, 22
Kitchen scissors, 25
Knife, chef's, 26–27
Knife sharpener, 25
Knishes, Kasha-Mushroom, 183–184
Kourambiedes with Olive Oil, 586–587
Ktefa, Cranberry-Semolina, 401–402
Kugelhopf, Black, 717–718
Kugelhopf, history of, 719
Kümmel liqueur, about, 89

L

Lady Baltimore Cake, 452–454
Lahmacun: Armenian Lamb Flatbread, 866–867
Lamb
    Cigari Borekas with Moroccan Spiced
        Lamb, 212–213
    Lahmacun: Armenian Lamb Flatbread, 866–
        867
Lard
    Biscochitos, 218–219
    Lard Pie Dough, 204
    leaf lard, about, 200
    notes about, 198–199
    Savory Empanada Dough, 205
    Steak, Guinness, and Mushroom Pie,
        213–215
Lavender
    general information, 464
    Honey Glazed Lavender-Lemon Cake,
        472–473
    lavender-infused simple syrup, preparing,
        464
Le Bec-Fin's Fruited Walnut Bread, 843–844
Lemons & citrons, 525–539
    Australian Pavlova with Lemon Filling and
        Tropical Fruits, 442–444
    Biscotti Rococò, 536–537
    citrons, about, 531–532
    Crispy Lemon-Cinnamon Cookies, 351–352
    French Candied Citron and Lemon
        Cookies, 534–535
    Fresh Lemon Sauce, 539
    general information, 526–529
    Homemade Limoncello, 537–538
    Honey Glazed Lavender-Lemon Cake,
        472–473
    Lemon-Blackberry Bavarese with
        Limoncello, 481–482
    Lemon Galataboureko, 532–533
    Lemon–Pine Nut Tart, 675–676
    Lemon Poppy Seed Biscotti, 719–720
    lemon varieties, 530–531
    Light Lemon Pastry Cream, 538
    Majorcan Lemon-Almond Cake, 77
    Meyer Lemon Bundt Cake, 533–534
    Rye and Rosemary Breadsticks with Lemon,
        783–784
    Torta di Savoia with Candied Citron,
        535–536
    Velia's White Chocolate–Lemon Torta
        Caprese, 78
    weight and volume equivalents, 43
Leslie, Eliza, 470
Light Lemon Pastry Cream, 538
Limes, 541–548
    Almond-Lime Bars, 545
    choosing and storing, 544–545
    general information, 542–544
    Key Lime Cheesecake Pie in Coconut-Pecan
        Crust, 548
    Lime Cornmeal Cookies, 547
    Mexican Lime and Tequila Tart with Mango

    Topping, 546
    weight and volume equivalents, 43
Limoncello
    Homemade Limoncello, 537–538
    Lemon-Blackberry Bavarese with
        Limoncello, 481–482
Lingonberries, about, 165
Linzer Torte, Black Currant–Apple, 411–413
Loaf pans, Chicago Metallic, 23
Loukum, rose-scented, about, 462
Lox, about, 435

M

Macadamia nuts
    Crunchy Macadamia-Ginger Quaresemali,
        489–490
    general information, 490
    Pineapple Cheesecake with Ginger-
        Macadamia Crust, 682
    Pineapple Coconut Shortbread Bars with
        Macadamia Nuts, 687–688
    storing, 491
Macaroon paste, about, 70
Macaroons
    amaretti, about, 440–441
    Chocolate-Dipped Coconut Macaroons,
        364
    Turkish Hazelnut Macaroons, 504
Magic Line cake pans, 25
Mahlab kernels, about, 143
Mahmoul (Syrian Pistachio-Stuffed Semolina
    Cookies with Rosewater), 466–467
Majorcan Lemon-Almond Cake, 77
Makroud (Tunisian Semolina Cookies Stuffed
    with Dates), 422–423
Malted barley, about, 139
Malted milk
    about, 139–140
    Almond Milk and Chocolate Malt Cake,
        146–148
    Iced Malted Milk Cookies, 285–286
    powder, buying, 140
Maltese Kwaresimal Cookies, 603–604
Mangoes
    Coconut Mango Cheesecake, 482–483
    English Summer Fruit Pudding with Lemon
        and Mint, 415–416
    Mexican Lime and Tequila Tart with
        Mango Topping, 546
Maple syrup, 549–555
    buying and storing, 551–552
    Canadian Maple–Black Walnut Ginger-
        bread, 491–492
    general information, 550–551
    maple-based products, 552
    Maple Cornmeal Muffins with Pine Nuts
        and Currants, 553–554
    Maple Syrup Pie with Walnuts: Tarte au
        Sirop d'Erable, 555
    New England Cranberry-Maple-Raisin Pie,
        552–553
    Québécoise Maple Bread Pudding, 554–555
Marc and grappa, about, 49–50

Maria's Cuscurols, 588–589
Marzipan, about, 70
Mastic, about, 519–520
Meat
    Cigari Borekas with Moroccan Spiced
        Lamb, 212–213
    Kea Stuffed Griddle Bread, 144–145
    Lahmacun: Armenian Lamb Flatbread,
        866–867
    'mpanatigghi Siciliano, 331–332
    Québécoise Tourtière with Mushrooms,
        210–211
    Steak, Guinness, and Mushroom Pie, 213–
        215
Melting Caramel Cake: Caramel Coulant,
    820–821
Meringue
    Australian Pavlova with Lemon Filling and
        Tropical Fruits, 442–444
    Italian Hachiya Persimmon Meringue Torte,
        662–663
    Italian Meringue Twists and Cake
        Decorations, 836
    Mexican Spiced Cocoa Meringues, 352–353
    Peanut Meringue with Spiced Bittersweet
        Chocolate Pudding, 63–-631
    White Chocolate, Hazelnut, and Espresso
        Dacquoise, 377–379
Mexican Chocolate Tequila Soufflé Cake, 729–
    730
Mexican Lime and Tequila Tart with Mango
    Topping, 546
Mexican Spiced Cocoa Meringues, 352–353
M'hancha: The Serpent, 695–696
Microplane zester, 26, 179
Milk, cream, & buttermilk, 557–567
    Argentinean Alfajores Cookies, 563–564
    buttermilk, about, 561
    Buttermilk-Sourdough White Sandwich
        Bread, 726–727
    Buttermilk Tart Pastry, 565
    clabber, notes about, 560
    cream, notes about, 559–560
    Cream Cheese Pastry Dough, 565–566
    Dulce de Leche, 566
    dulce de leche, history of, 567
    dulce de leche, versions of, 567
    evaporated milk, about, 560
    general information, 558–559
    heavy cream, whipping, 38
    Papiamento Bread Pudding with Ponche
        Crema, 562
    Pilar's Tres Leches Cake, 564
    sour cream, notes about, 560
    sweetened condensed milk, about, 561
Milk Chocolate and Pistachio Cookies, 696–697
Minneola Orange Tart, 600–601
Mistrà liqueur, about, 390
Mixing bowls, stainless steel, 27
Mochaccino Swirl Cookies, 376–377
Molasses
    general information, 816
    Indian Pudding Cake, 286–287

Molasses-Ginger Brandy Snaps, 819–820
recommended brands, for recipes, 20
Tahini and Grape Molasses Pide, 901–902
types of, 817
Morning Glory Muffins with Carrots, Asian
Pears, and Ginger, 240–241
Moroccan Sesame-Anise Bread, 87–88
'mpanatigghi Siciliano, 331–332
Muffins
Apple-Date Buckwheat Muffins, 188
Blueberry-Walnut Streusel Muffins, 164
Maple Cornmeal Muffins with Pine Nuts
and Currants, 553–554
Morning Glory Muffins with Carrots, Asian
Pears, and Ginger, 240–241
muffin tins for, 23
Muffin tins, Chicago Metallic, 23
Mushrooms
Alpine Mushroom Pizza with Potato-
Rye Dough, 787
Exotic Mushroom Puff Pastry Pillows,
207–208
Kasha-Mushroom Knishes, 183–184
Québécoise Tourtière with Mushrooms,
210–211
Steak, Guinness, and Mushroom Pie,
213–215
Myer's Dark Rum, 864

N

Natural bristle brushes, 26
Nectarines
Caramelized Nectarine and Ginger Shortcakes with Sour Cream, 617–618
choosing and ripening, 614
general information, 612
removing pits from, 615
white nectarines, about, 613
New England Cranberry-Maple-Raisin Pie, 552–
553
New Haven–Style White Clam Pizza, 886–887
Nigella seeds
about, 899–900
Grilled Indian Naan Bread with Nigella
Seeds, 902–903
Nova lox, about, 435
Nuts. See also specific nuts
buying, for recipes, 20
grinding, note about, 374
storing, 20
weight and volume equivalents, 42–44

O

Oats, 569–578
Amish Black Walnut Oatmeal Pie, 575–576
Canadian Date-Oatmeal Squares, 576
general information, 570–572
Guinness Oatmeal Bread, 574–575
Hot Apple-Cranberry Crisp with Oatmeal-
Almond Topping, 403
oat flour, weight and volume equivalents,
40
Oatmeal-Apple-Upside-Down Tart,

577–578
Oatmeal Pear Crisp with Dried Cherries,
643–644
Oatmeal-Pecan Fruities, 425
Savory Oatmeal-Cheddar Tart, 573–574
weight and volume equivalents, 40
Oils, 579–589
baking with oil, 580–581
frying with oil, 581–583
Kourambiedes with Olive Oil, 586–587
Maria's Cuscurols, 588–589
pine nut oil, about, 672
Spanish Honey-Dipped Spiral Pastries
(Hojuelas), 585–586
Taralli: Boiled and Baked "Pretzels" from
Puglia, 584–585
Teiglach or Cicerchiata, 587–588
Olives
Black Olive–Herb Bread, 889–890
Herbed Focaccia with Goat Cheese, Red
Onion, and Black Olives, 725–726
Niçoise, about, 884
Sardenaira (Riviera-Style Olive and
Anchovy Pizza), 883–884
Turkish Savory Cornbread, 388–389
One-Bowl Hazelnut Cornmeal Biscotti, 503–504
Onions
Caramelized Sweet Onions, 860–861
Catalan Flatbread with Spinach, Onion, and
Pine Nut Topping, 672–673
Dilled Potato-Onion Rolls, 727–728
Durum Wheat Bread with Squash, Toma-
toes, Onions, and Peppers, 736–737
Onion Poppy Seed Kichels, 715–716
Spanish Sofrito, 882–883
Woodfire Grill Duck Confit Pizza, 859–860
Orange blossom water
buying, 466
Florida Tangerine Kiss-Me Cake, 602–603
general information, 463
Maltese Kwaresimal Cookies, 603–604
Orange Blossom Brioches, 470–471
Orange Blossom Glaze, 471
Oranges, 591–605. See also Tangerines
Anise-Scented Date-Orange Spirals,
423–424
blood oranges, from Malta, 604
buying and storing, 597
Chocolate Torte with Orange and
Pistachio, 697–698
cutting into slices or sections, 597
general information, 592–594
Italian Bittersweet Chocolate–Orange
Torta, 331
Maltese Kwaresimal Cookies, 603–604
Minneola Orange Tart, 600–601
Orange or Tangerine Caramel Sauce,
601–602
orange varieties, 594–596
Ruby Grapefruit–Orange Brazil Nut Torte,
174–175
Sambuca and Candied Orange Tozzetti,
90–91

Sephardic Stuffed Monkey, 176–177
Spanish Orange and Olive Oil Cake,
599–600
Oven-Roasted Plum Tomatoes, 888–889

P

Pan di Spagna, 441
Pan Dushi (Aruban Sweet Bread with Anise),
891–892
Pans
cast-aluminum Bundt pans, 23, 473
Chicago Metallic loaf and muffin tins, 23
half-sheet pans, 25
Magic Line cake pans, 25
pan size measurements, 38–39
pan sizes, substituting, 39
ring or tube pan, 26
Papiamento Bread Pudding with Ponche
Crema, 562
Parchment and wax paper, 26
Pastechi (Aruban Stuffed Pastry Turnovers),
760–761
Pastries
Apple-Apricot Strudel, 121–122
arranging, on baking trays, 176
borek, bourekas, brik, and boureki, 798
B'stilla of Chicken, 436–437
Chocolate Caramel Éclairs, 817–819
Cigari Borekas with Moroccan Spiced
Lamb, 212–213
Cretan Kalitsounia (Sweet Cheese Pastries),
276–277
Danish Pastry Braid with Goat Cheese and
Cardamom (and Variations), 273–275
A Date in a Blanket, 421–422
Exotic Mushroom Puff Pastry Pillows, 207–
208
Greek Phyllo Pumpkin Pie: Kolokythopita,
739–740
Lemon Galataboureko, 532–533
made by convent nuns, 333
M'hancha: The Serpent, 695–696
'mpanatigghi Siciliano, 331–332
Pastechi (Aruban Stuffed Pastry Turnovers),
760–761
Pistachio Bird's Nest Pastries, 693–694
Quince and Sour Cherry Strudel, 751–752
Rigo Jancsi, 333–334
Sardinian Sebadas: Fried Stuffed Rounds
with Ricotta Cheese, 517–518
Sephardic Stuffed Monkey, 176–177
Sesame Honey Cones with Ricotta Filling,
800–802
Sesame Spinach Borekas, 796–797
Sfratti di Pitigliano, 520–522
soaking, with sugar syrup, 38
Spanish Honey-Dipped Spiral Pastries: Ho-
juelas, 585–586
stuffed, forming and baking, 33
Turkish, from Güllüoglu Baklava Bakery, 870
Turkish Carrot Pastry Rolls, 241–242
Pastry bags, 24
Pastry cream

Light Lemon Pastry Cream, 538
lumpy, remedy for, 484
White Chocolate Pastry Cream, 484
Pastry dough
  blind-baking, 30–31, 107
  Buttermilk Tart Pastry, 565
  butter or animal fat–based, handling, 201
  Butter Pie Pastry, 203–204
  choux paste, about, 289
  Cream Cheese Pastry Dough, 565–566
  cutting in butter for, 19, 32, 203
  etymology of, 107
  German Muerbeteig Dough (Mellow
    Dough), 444–445
  kadayif, notes about, 695
  Lard Pie Dough, 204
  Pasta Frolla, 62–63
  rolling out, for tarts, 37
  Savory Empanada Dough, 205
  Savory Spiced Whole Wheat Pastry,
    862–863
  Savory Tart Pastry, 206
  Spiced Almond Pastry, 74
  Suet Meat Pie Dough, 204–205
  Sugar Pastry, 823
  Sweet Walnut Pastry, 848
  Sweet White Whole Wheat Tart Pastry, 863
  Tarte Tatin Pastry, 206–207
  Venetian Cornmeal Tart Dough, 391–392
  yufka dough, about, 213
Pastry flour, about, 856
Pavlova, Australian, with Lemon Filling and
  Tropical Fruits, 442–444
Paximadi (barley biscuits), about, 141
Peaches, 607–620. See also Nectarines
  choosing and ripening, 614
  clingstone peaches, about, 613
  donut peaches, about, 614
  English Summer Fruit Pudding with Lemon
    and Mint, 415–416
  freestone peaches, about, 613
  French Puff Pastry Peach Galette, 618–619
  general information, 608–612
  Peach and Apricot Tarte Tatin, 616–617
  removing pits from, 615
  Tarte aux Pêches (French Baked Peach Tart),
    619–620
  White Peach and Sour Cream Pie, 615–616
  white peaches, about, 613
Peanut butter
  Amish Peanut Butter Cream Pie, 626–627
  buying and storing, 626
  Peanut Butter and Jelly Cake, 629–630
  Peanut-Chocolate Bars with Espresso,
    627–628
Peanuts, 621–631. See also Peanut butter
  Amish Peanut Butter Cream Pie, 626–627
  buying and storing, 625–626
  general information, 622–624
  Peanut Butter and Jelly Cake, 629–630
  Peanut-Chocolate Bars with Espresso,
    627–628
  Peanut Meringues with Spiced Bittersweet

Chocolate Puddings, 630–631
  peanut varieties, 625
  Planter's Peanut Company mascot, 625
Pearlash (potassium carbonate), 282
Pears, 633–645
  antique pear varieties, 641
  Bitter Chocolate–Hazelnut Torta with
    Pears, 645
  Brustengolo (Umbrian Cornmeal, Pear,
    Raisin, and Nut Cake), 389–390
  Butterscotch-Ginger Pear Tart, 641–643
  choosing, storing, and ripening, 637–638
  general information, 634–637
  Harry and David's "Royal Riviera" pears, 640
  Hazelnut–Brown Butter Cakes with Bosc
    Pears, 505–506
  modern Italian pear varieties, 641
  Morning Glory Muffins with Carrots, Asian
    Pears, and Ginger, 240–241
  Oatmeal Pear Crisp with Dried Cherries,
    643–644
  Pear and Toasted Pecan Bundt Cake with
    Brown Sugar Glaze, 644–645
  poaching, 643
  summer pear varieties, 639–640
  winter pear varieties, 638
Pecans, 647–655
  Banana-Pecan Roulade, 132–133
  Brown Sugar–Pecan Sweet Dream Cookies,
    821–822
  buying and storing, 649
  Chocolate-Kahlúa Silk Pie, 374–376
  Cocoa Nib and Pecan Praline, 340
  Cocoa Nib and Pecan Praline Chocolate
    Roulade, 340–341
  Cranberry-Caramel Pecan Tart, 654–655
  Creole Pecan Pralines, 650
  Florida Tangerine Kiss-Me Cake, 602–603
  general information, 648–649
  Heirloom Sweet Potato–Praline Pie,
    651–652
  Key Lime Cheesecake Pie in Coconut-Pecan
    Crust, 548
  Oatmeal-Pecan Fruities, 425
  Pear and Toasted Pecan Bundt Cake with
    Brown Sugar Glaze, 644–645
  Pecan-Ginger Cake with Caramel Icing,
    494–495
  Pineapple Rum-Pecan Bars, 685
  Rum Pecan-Praline Sandies, 652–653
  Southern Million-Dollar Pie, 685–687
  substituting, with hickory nuts, 649
  Turtle Brownies with Caramel and Pecans,
    653–654
  weight and volume equivalents, 43
Pennsylvania Dutch Corn Pie, 387–388
Peppers
  Chakchouka (Tunisian Vegetable Stew),
    865–866
  Durum Wheat Bread with Squash, Toma-
    toes, Onions, and Peppers, 736–737
  Spanish Sofrito, 882–883
  Spicy Harissa Sauce, 866

Persimmons, 657–666
  choosing, ripening, and storing, 662
  general information, 658–660
  Italian Hachiya Persimmon Meringue Torte,
    662–663
  Persimmon–Black Walnut Bread, 666
  persimmon varieties, 660–661
  Spiced Fuyu Persimmon Bars, 664
  Spiced Honey–Almond Rings with
    Brandied Persimmon Bits, 665–666
Phyllo dough
  Apple-Apricot Strudel, 121–122
  buying, 742
  Country-Style Greek Greens Pie, 262–263
  Greek Eggplant and Walnut Phyllo Rolls,
    842–843
  Greek Phyllo Pumpkin Pie: Kolokythopita,
    739–740
  Lemon Galataboureko, 532–533
  M'hancha: The Serpent, 695–696
  Quince and Sour Cherry Strudel, 751–752
  scoring, 37
  Turkish Carrot Pastry Rolls, 241–242
  working with, 740
Pide
  Feta Cheese and Egg Pide, 900–901
  Tahini and Grape Molasses Pide, 901–902
  Turkish Pide Dough, 900
Piedmontese Mocha-Chestnut Torta, 314–315
Pies. See also Tarts
  about Pumpkin Pie, 743
  Almond-Crusted Blackberry-Tangerine Pie,
    161–162
  Amish Black Walnut Oatmeal Pie, 575–576
  Amish Peanut Butter Cream Pie, 626–627
  Apple-Blueberry Crumb Pie with Car-
    damom, 163–164
  Baby Banana Cream Pie in Coconut-
    Cashew Crust, 131–132
  Candied Walnut Apple Pie, 109–110
  Cherry-Maraschino Cream Pie, 306–307
  Country-Style Greek Greens Pie, 262–263
  edges, preventing darkening of, 37
  etymology of, 107
  Heirloom Sweet Potato–Praline Pie, 651–
    652
  historical notes, 107–108
  Key Lime Cheesecake Pie in Coconut-
    Pecan Crust, 548
  lattice top crust for, preparing, 34
  Maple Syrup Pie with Walnuts: Tarte au
    Sirop d'Erable, 555
  New England Cranberry-Maple-Raisin Pie,
    552–553
  Pennsylvania Dutch Corn Pie, 387–388
  Québécoise Tourtière with Mushrooms,
    210–211
  Southern Million-Dollar Pie, 685–687
  Steak, Guinness, and Mushroom Pie,
    213–215
  Torta Pasqualina Genovese, 438–439
  tourtière, about, 211
  White Peach and Sour Cream Pie, 615–616

Pilar's Tres Leches Cake, 564
Pineapple, 679–688
    choosing, ripening, and storing, 682
    general information, 680–681
    Pineapple Cheesecake with Ginger-
        Macadamia Crust, 682
    Pineapple-Coconut Flan with Dark Rum,
        684–685
    Pineapple Coconut Shortbread Bars with
        Macadamia Nuts, 687–688
    Pineapple Rum-Pecan Bars, 685
    pineapple varieties, 681–682
    Southern Million-Dollar Pie, 685–687
Pine nuts, 667–677
    Baked Quince with Pine Nuts and Dried
        Fruit, 754
    Brustengolo (Umbrian Cornmeal, Pear,
        Raisin, and Nut Cake), 389–390
    buying and storing, 670
    Catalan Flatbread with Spinach, Onion, and
        Pine Nut Topping, 672–673
    Crostata della Nonna: Grandma's Ricotta–
        Pine Nut Tart, 676–677
    Fig and Pine Nut Bread, 674
    general information, 668–670
    Lemon–Pine Nut Tart, 675–676
    Maple Cornmeal Muffins with Pine Nuts
        and Currants, 553–554
    pine nut oil, about, 672
    toasting, 671
    Torta di Zucca (Squash Cake with Pine Nuts
        and Apricots), 741–742
    traditional harvesting of, 671
Pistachios, 689–700
    Chocolate Torte with Orange and
        Pistachio, 697–698
    Dukkah, 890–891
    general information, 690–693
    Le Bec-Fin's Fruited Walnut Bread, 843–844
    Mahmoul (Syrian Pistachio-Stuffed
        Semolina Cookies with Rosewater), 466–
        467
    M'hancha: The Serpent, 695–696
    Milk Chocolate and Pistachio Cookies,
        696–697
    Pistachio Bird's Nest Pastries, 693–694
    Pistachio Custard Sauce or Pistachio
        Gelato, 698–699
    Sicilian pistachios, 691
    from Zenobia Nuts, 693
Pizza
    Alpine Mushroom Pizza with Potato-Rye
        Dough, 787
    Arugula and Roasted Tomato Pizza, 888
    best flour for, 857
    Cornmeal Pizza Dough, 392
    etymology, 267
    Neapolitan pizza, standards for, 859
    New Haven–Style White Clam Pizza,
        886–887
    Potato-Rye Pizza Dough, 786
    Sardenaira (Riviera-Style Olive and
        Anchovy Pizza), 883–884

Sicilian Pan Pizza with Zucca, 737–738
    White Pizza with Broccoli Rabe, 266–267
    wooden pizza peels, using, 267, 887
    Woodfire Grill Duck Confit Pizza, 859–860
    Woodfire Grill Pizza Dough, 858–859
Pizzelle "of the Angels" with Fennel Pollen,
    91–92
Plantains
    general information, 127–128
    Plantain Empanadas with Black Bean and
        Añejo Cheese Filling, 129–130
Plums, 701–712. See also Prunes
    Alsatian Plum Muerbeteig, 710
    choosing, ripening, and storing, 705–706
    general information, 702–705
    Plum Gingersnap Brown Betty, 708
    plum varieties, 706–707
    Red Plum Streusel Cake, 708–709
    slivovitz (plum brandy), about, 711–712
    weight and volume equivalents, 43
Poppy seeds, 713–720
    Black Kugelhopf, 717–718
    choosing and storing, 715
    general information, 714
    Honey–Poppy Seed Hamantaschen,
        716–717
    Lemon Poppy Seed Biscotti, 719–720
    Onion Poppy Seed Kichels, 715–716
Pork
    Québécoise Tourtière with Mushrooms,
        210–211
Port, notes about, 53
Potatoes, 721–730
    Buttermilk-Sourdough White Sandwich
        Bread, 726–727
    Dilled Potato-Onion Rolls, 727–728
    general information, 722–723
    Heirloom Sweet Potato–Praline Pie, 651–
        652
    Herbed Focaccia with Goat Cheese, Red
        Onion, and Black Olives, 725–726
    Mexican Chocolate Tequila Soufflé Cake,
        729–730
    Potato-Rye Pizza Dough, 786
    potato starch, weight and volume equiva-
        lents, 41
    potato types, 724–725
    Québécoise Tourtière with Mushrooms,
        210–211
    Sardinian Potato Torta, 728–729
    Sourdough Bread Starter, 880–881
Potica (Slovenian Honey-Walnut Ring), 845–847
Praline
    Cocoa Nib and Pecan Praline, 340
    Hazelnut Praline, 509
Pralines
    Creole Pecan Pralines, 650
    history of, in Louisiana, 651
"Pretzels," Boiled and Baked, from Puglia
    (Taralli), 584–585
Profiteroles, Chocolate-Glazed Praline, 287–289
Prunes
    Brandied Prune Pound Cake, 710–711

general information, 703–704
    weight and volume equivalents, 43
Puddings
    best type of rice for, 775
    English Summer Fruit Pudding with Lemon
        and Mint, 415–416
    Florentine Chocolate Nut Zuccotto, 58–60
    Papiamento Bread Pudding with Ponche
        Crema, 562
    Peanut Meringue with Spiced Bittersweet
        Chocolate Pudding, 630–631
    Plum Gingersnap Brown Betty, 708
    Québécoise Maple Bread Pudding, 554–555
    Turkish Goat's Milk Rice Pudding, 774–775
Puff pastry
    Exotic Mushroom Puff Pastry Pillows, 207–
        208
    French Caramel Puff Pastry Fruit Tart, 830–
        832
    French Puff Pastry Peach Galette, 618–619
    notes about, 208–209
    working with, 209
Pumpkin, 731–743
    about Pumpkin Pie, 743
    best, for baking, 735–736
    Bourbon-Spice Pumpkin Cake, 742–743
    general information, 732
    Greek Phyllo Pumpkin Pie: Kolokythopita,
        739–740
    Homemade Pumpkin Spice Mix, 733

Q

Québécoise Maple Bread Pudding, 554–555
Québécoise Tourtière with Mushrooms, 210–211
Quiche
    baking tips, 436
    Smoked Salmon and Spinach Quiche,
        434–435
Quince, 745–754
    Baked Quince with Pine Nuts and Dried
        Fruit, 754
    choosing, ripening, and storing, 749
    general information, 746–748
    peeling and cutting up, 749
    Quince and Sour Cherry Strudel, 751–752
    Quince-Cranberry Tarte Tatin, 753
    quince varieties, 748
    Spiced Quince and Walnut Thumbprint
        Cookies, 750–751
    Spiced Quince Jam, 749–750

R

Radicchio and Fontina Torta, 260–261
Raisins, 755–764. See also Currants, dried
    Baked Quince with Pine Nuts and
        Dried Fruit, 754
    Brustengolo (Umbrian Cornmeal, Pear,
        Raisin, and Nut Cake), 389–390
    Buckwheat Cinnamon-Raisin Bread,
        188–189
    Crostata della Nonna: Grandma's Ricotta–
        Pine Nut Tart, 676–677
    Danish Rum Raisin Cupcakes, 764

drying process, 758, 760
Florida Tangerine Kiss-Me Cake, 602–603
general information, 756–758
Greek Cornmeal Raisin Bread, 762–764
Greek Tahini Cake, 802
Honey–Poppy Seed Hamantaschen, 716–717
New England Cranberry-Maple-Raisin Pie, 552–553
Pan Dushi (Aruban Sweet Bread with Anise), 891–892
Pastechi (Aruban Stuffed Pastry Turnovers), 760–761
raisin varieties, 759
seeded, note about, 758
seedless, note about, 758
Sephardic Stuffed Monkey, 176–177
Torta di Miele (Italian Jewish Honey Cake), 522–523
weight and volume equivalents, 44
in wintertime parlor game (snapdragon), 759
Zaleti: Venetian Cornmeal Cookies with Grappa Raisins, 60
Ras el hanout spice blend, about, 146
Raspberries
choosing and storing, 159
general information, 150–151, 158–159
July 4th Cheesecake, 833–835
Raspberry Salzburger Nockerln, 160–161
Rose-Scented Raspberry Sauce, 161
types of, 159–160
Red Plum Streusel Cake, 708–709
Rhubarb
general information, 170
Strawberry-Rhubarb Tart with Walnut Sweet Pastry, 169
Rice, 765–777
best type, for rice pudding, 775
Calas (New Orleans Rice Fritters), 773–774
Crostata di Riso: Italian Rice Tart, 776–777
English Millionaire's Shortbread, 769–771
Frangelico Mousse Cake with Gianduia-Rice Crunch, 771–773
general information, 766–768
puffed rice, about, 769
rice flakes, about, 769
rice flour, about, 769
rice flour, weight and volume equivalents, 41
rice milk, about, 769
rice starch, about, 769
Turkish Baldo rice, about, 775
Turkish Goat's Milk Rice Pudding, 774–775
Rigo Jancsi, 333–334
Ring or tube pan, 26
Rolling pin, 26
Rose petals and rosebuds, 462, 466
Rose syrup, about, 462
Rose syrup, buying, 466
Rosewater
buying, 466
Cornmeal and Rosewater Pound Cake, 469

general information, 461–462
Mahmoul (Syrian Pistachio-Stuffed Semolina Cookies with Rosewater), 466–467
Rose-Scented Angel Food Cake, 467–468
Rose-Scented Raspberry Sauce, 161
Roul-Pat, 26
Ruby Grapefruit–Orange Brazil Nut Torte, 174–175
Rum, 53
Danish Rum Raisin Cupcakes, 764
German Apple and Rum-Raisin Custard Torte, 54–55
Myer's Dark Rum, 864
Pineapple-Coconut Flan with Dark Rum, 684–685
Pineapple Rum-Pecan Bars, 685
Rum Pecan-Praline Sandies, 652–653
Rum-Vanilla Custard Sauce, 61
Rustic Fresh Fig Galette, 454–455
Rye, 779–791
Alpine Mushroom Pizza with Potato-Rye Dough, 787
Dutch Speculaas with Rye, 789–790
and ergot poisoning (St. Anthony's Fire), 783
general information, 780–782
Grape, Gorgonzola, and Walnut Focaccia, 788–789
in maslin bread, 782
in Pain Bouilli, 782
Potato-Rye Pizza Dough, 786
Rye and Rosemary Breadsticks with Lemon, 783–784
rye flour, storing, 783
rye flour, weight and volume equivalents, 41
rye flour, working with, 783
Sauerkraut Rye Bread, 784–786

S

Saleratus (aerated salt), 282
Salmon
cold-smoked, 435
hot-smoked, 435
Smoked Salmon and Spinach Quiche, 434–435
Salt, for recipes, 20
Salt-packed anchovies, about, 884–885
Salzburger Nockerln, Raspberry, 160–161
Sambuca and Candied Orange Tozzetti, 90–91
Sardenaira (Riviera-Style Olive and Anchovy Pizza), 883–884
Sardinian bitter honey, 517
Sardinian Potato Torta, 728–729
Sardinian Sebadas: Fried Stuffed Rounds with Ricotta Cheese, 517–518
Sauces
Apricot Brandy Sauce, 123–124
Aruban Ponche Crema Liqueur, 63
Crème Anglaise (English Vanilla Custard Sauce), 835
Dulce de Leche, 566

Fresh Lemon Sauce, 539
Fresh Strawberry Coulis, 168
Orange or Tangerine Caramel Sauce, 601–602
Pistachio Custard Sauce or Pistachio Gelato, 698–699
preventing curdling of, 62
Rose-Scented Raspberry Sauce, 161
Rum-Vanilla Custard Sauce, 61
Sherry Custard Sauce, 61–62
Sour Cherry Sauce, 304
Spicy Harissa Sauce, 866
Vanilla Caramel Sauce, 822
Sauerkraut Rye Bread, 784–786
Savory Eggplant and Spiced Almond Tart, 72–73
Savory Empanada Dough, 205
Savory Oatmeal-Cheddar Tart, 573–574
Savory Spiced Whole Wheat Pastry, 862–863
Savory Tart Pastry, 206
Scones
Chestnut-Currant Scones, 313–314
Ginger Fig Scones, 491
note about, 270
Stilton Scones, 269–270
Scotch whisky, about, 52
Seafood
New Haven–Style White Clam Pizza, 886–887
salmon, types of, 435
salt-packed anchovies, about, 884–885
Sardenaira (Riviera-Style Olive and Anchovy Pizza), 883–884
Smoked Salmon and Spinach Quiche, 434–435
Spanish Tuna Emapanadas with Sofrito, 881–882
Sebadas, Sardinian: Fried Stuffed Rounds with Ricotta Cheese, 517–518
Seeds. See also Anise, fennel, & caraway; Poppy seeds; Sesame seeds
buying, for breads, 187
Grilled Indian Naan Bread with Nigella Seeds, 902–903
Moroccan Sesame-Anise Bread, 87–88
nigella seeds, about, 899–900
Seeded Multi-Grain Sourdough Bread, 186–187
Spanish Honey-Dipped Spiral Pastries (Hojuelas), 585–586
Turkish Seeded Hazelnut Bread, 502–503
Semolina
Cranberry-Semolina Ktefa, 401–402
general information, 853–854
Mahmoul (Syrian Pistachio-Stuffed Semolina Cookies with Rosewater), 466–467
Makroud (Tunisian Semolina Cookies Stuffed with Dates), 422–423
Swiss Carrot-Semolina Torte, 239–240
Tangerine Semolina Torta, 605
Tunisian Semolina Griddle Bread, 864–865
Turkish Semolina Sponge Cookies, 869–870

weight and volume equivalents, 41
Sephardic Pan Levi Cookies, 442
Sephardic Stuffed Monkey, 176–177
Sesame seeds, 793–802
    choosing and storing, 796
    Dukkah, 890–891
    Garlic-Sesame Grissini, 885–885
    general information, 794–795
    Greek Tahini Cake, 802
    Moroccan Sesame-Anise Bread, 87–88
    Sesame Honey Cones with Ricotta Filling,
      800–802
    sesame oil, about, 796
    Sesame Spinach Borekas, 796–797
    Spanish Honey-Dipped Spiral Pastries: Ho-
      juelas, 585–586
    Spanish Sesame-Anise Cookies, 799–800
    Tahini and Grape Molasses Pide, 901–902
    tahini (sesame paste), about, 796
    toasting, 796
    Turkish Seeded Hazelnut Bread, 502–503
    Turkish Sesame-Coated Bread Rings:
      Susamli Simit, 798–799
    in za'atar spice mix, 798
Sfratti di Pitigliano, 520–522
Sherry
    notes about, 53
    Sherry Custard Sauce, 61–62
    sherry varieties, 53–54
Shiny Chocolate-Mocha Glaze, 334–335
Shortbread, English Millionaire's, 769–771
Shortbread Bars, Pineapple Coconut, with
    Macadamia Nuts, 687–688
Shortcakes, Caramelized Nectarine and Ginger,
    with Sour Cream, 617–618
Sicilian Pan Pizza with Zucca, 737–738
Sicilian pistachios, 691
Siennese Cavalluci, 224–225
Siennese Panforte, 232–233
Silicone spatulas, 27
Silpat silicone mats, 27
Simple syrup, preparing, 36
Skillet, cast-iron, 23
Slivovitz (plum brandy), about, 711–712
Slovenian Almond-Apricot Tea Bread, 117–118
Smoked Salmon and Spinach Quiche, 434–435
Sofrito, Spanish, 882–883
Sofrito, versions of, 883
Sourdough Bread, Seeded Multi-Grain, 186–187
Sourdough Bread Starter, 880–881
Sourdough starters, about, 875
Southern Million-Dollar Pie, 685–687
Spanish Apple Torte, 105–107
Spanish Honey-Dipped Spiral Pastries (Hojue-
    las), 585–586
Spanish Orange and Olive Oil Cake, 599–600
Spanish Sesame-Anise Cookies, 799–800
Spanish Sofrito, 882–883
Spanish Tuna Emapanadas with Sofrito, 881–882
Spatulas, silicone, 27
Speculaas
    Dutch Speculaas with Rye, 789–790
    history of, 791

Speculaas Spices, 353
Spelt, about, 854
Spiced Almond Pastry, 74
Spiced Fuyu Persimmon Bars, 664
Spiced Honey–Almond Rings with Brandied
    Persimmon Bits, 665–666
Spiced Quince and Walnut Thumbprint
    Cookies, 750–751
Spiced Quince Jam, 749–750
Spice Mix, Homemade Pumpkin, 733
Spices, Speculaas, 353
Spicy Harissa Sauce, 866
Spinach
    Catalan Flatbread with Spinach, Onion,
      and Pine Nut Topping, 672–673
    Chlorophyll (Natural Green Coloring),
      699–700
    Sesame Spinach Borekas, 796–797
    Sicilian Pan Pizza with Zucca, 737–738
    Smoked Salmon and Spinach Quiche,
      434–435
    Torta Rustica, 861–862
Squash, 731–743. See also Pumpkin
    butternut, choosing and storing, 733
    butternut, preparing, 734
    cooking in microwave, 733
    cucuzza squash, about, 737
    Durum Wheat Bread with Squash, Toma-
      toes, Onions, and Peppers, 736–737
    general information, 732
    Greek Phyllo Pumpkin Pie: Kolokythopita,
      739–740
    roasting, 733
    Sicilian Pan Pizza with Zucca, 737–738
    steaming, 733
    Torta di Zucca (Squash Cake with Pine Nuts
      and Apricots), 741–742
    winter squashes for baking, 734–736
Stainless steel bowls, 27
Steak, Guinness, and Mushroom Pie, 213–215
Stein, Neil, 111
Stilton Scones, 269–270
Strawberries
    choosing and storing, 157
    Fresh Strawberry Coulis, 168
    general information, 150–151, 156–157
    July 4th Cheesecake, 833–835
    Southern Million-Dollar Pie, 685–687
    Strawberry Devil's Food Cake, 166–168
    Strawberry-Rhubarb Tart with Sweet
      Walnut Pastry, 168
    Strawberry-Vanilla Coeur à la Crème Tart
      with Goat Cheese, 832–833
    washing and trimming, 157
Strudels
    Apple-Apricot Strudel, 121–122
    Quince and Sour Cherry Strudel, 751–752
Suet
    buying, 200
    notes about, 199, 200–201
    rendering, 200
    Steak, Guinness, and Mushroom Pie,
      213–215

Suet Meat Pie Dough, 204–205
Sugar, caramel, & molasses, 803–823. See also
    Sugar syrup
    beet sugar, about, 20–21, 813
    brown sugar, measuring, 22
    brown sugar, types of, 812
    Brown Sugar–Pecan Sweet Dream Cookies,
      821–822
    cane sugar, about, 20–21, 813, 815
    caramel, cooking tips, 815
    caramel, general information, 814
    Chocolate Caramel Éclairs, 817–819
    C&H pure cane sugar, about, 815
    confectioners' granite sugar, about, 809
    confectioners' sugar, about, 810
    confectioners' sugar, measuring, 22
    general information, 804–808
    guarapo (sugar cane juice), about, 808
    Indian Pudding Cake, 286–287
    measuring, 22
    Melting Caramel Cake: Caramel Coulant,
      820–821
    molasses, buying, for recipes, 20
    molasses, general information, 816
    molasses, types of, 817
    Molasses-Ginger Brandy Snaps, 819–820
    Steen's cane syrup, about, 813
    sugar, beating, with eggs, 30
    sugar, buying, for recipes, 20–21
    sugar, creaming with butter, 31–32
    sugar, measuring, 22
    sugarcane sticks, about, 808
    Sugar Pastry, 823
    sugar refining, old-fashioned, 809
    sugar weight and volume equivalents, 45
    Tahini and Grape Molasses Pide, 901–902
    Vanilla Caramel Sauce, 822
    white sugar, types of, 809–811
Sugar syrup
    drizzling onto baked goods, 740
    firm ball stage, 36
    preparing, 36, 809
    soaking cakes and pastries with, 38
    soaking with sugar syrup, 811
    soft ball stage, 36
Swedish Ginger-Spice Cookies: Pepparkakor, 493
Sweet Fig Focaccia, 455–456
Sweet Potato–Praline Pie, Heirloom, 651–652
Sweet Walnut Pastry, 848
Sweet White Whole Wheat Tart Pastry, 863
Swiss Carrot-Semolina Torte, 239–240

T

Tahini
    about, 796
    Greek Tahini Cake, 802
    Tahini and Grape Molasses Pide, 901–902
Tamarind, about, 868
Tamarind pulp, working with, 868
Tangerines, 591–605
    Almond-Crusted Blackberry-Tangerine
      Pie, 161–162
    buying and storing, 599

Florida Tangerine Kiss-Me Cake, 602–603
general information, 597–598
Maltese Kwaresimal Cookies, 603–604
Orange or Tangerine Caramel Sauce, 601–602
peeling, 598
removing seeds from, 598
Tangerine Semolina Torta, 605
Tapioca starch, about, 162
Taralli: Boiled and Baked "Pretzels" from Puglia, 584–585
Tarte Tatin Pastry, 206–207
Tarts
Alsatian Plum Muerbeteig, 710
baking, tips for, 107
Blackberry–White Chocolate Tart, 483–484
Black Currant–Apple Linzer Torte, 411–413
Butterscotch-Ginger Pear Tart, 641–643
Chocolate-Kahlúa Silk Pie, 374–376
Cranberry-Caramel Pecan Tart, 654–655
Crostata della Nonna: Grandma's Ricotta–Pine Nut Tart, 676–677
Crostata di Riso: Italian Rice Tart, 776–777
Dutch Almond-Filled Spice Tart, 74–75
French Apricot Tart Scented with Cloves, 120–121
French Caramel Puff Pastry Fruit Tart, 830–832
French Puff Pastry Peach Galette, 618–619
French Roquefort, Apple, and Leek Tart, 103–104
Greek Blueberry-Yogurt Tart with Ouzo, 165–166
Italian Hachiya Persimmon Meringue Torte, 662–663
Lemon–Pine Nut Tart, 675–676
Mexican Lime and Tequila Tart with Mango Topping, 546
Minneola Orange Tart, 600–601
Oatmeal-Apple-Upside-Down Tart, 577–578
Peach and Apricot Tarte Tatin, 616–617
Quince-Cranberry Tarte Tatin, 753
Radicchio and Fontina Torta, 260–261
rolling out pastry for, 37
Rustic Fresh Fig Galette, 454–455
Savory Eggplant and Spiced Almond Tart, 72–73
Savory Oatmeal-Cheddar Tart, 573–574
Strawberry-Rhubarb Tart with Walnut Sweet Pastry, 169
Strawberry-Vanilla Coeur à la Crème Tart with Goat Cheese, 832–833
Torta Rustica, 861–862
Venetian Cornmeal and Cherry Crostata, 305
Techniques
alternating liquid and dry ingredients, 28
baking bread until done, 29
baking cake until done, 28–29
baking in a water bath, 29
beating bread dough, 30

beating cream cheese, 29
beating eggs and sugar, 30
beating egg whites, 30
beating whole eggs and yolks, 29–30
blind baking a pastry crust, 30–31
chilling over ice water, 31
cooking a custard, 31
creaming butter and sugar, 31–32
cutting fan-shaped fruits, 32
cutting in butter for pastry dough, 32
cutting slashes in bread dough, 32
deep-frying, 32–33
forming and baking empanadas, 33
making a crumb crust, 33–34
making a lattice top crust pie, 34
making caramel, 34–35
melting chocolate, 35
preparing gelatin, 35
preparing simple syrup, 36
preparing sugar syrup, 36
proofing yeast, 37
protecting edges of a pie, 37
rising yeast dough, 37
rolling bread sticks, 37
rolling out tart pastry, 37
scoring phyllo dough, 37
separating eggs, 35–36
shaping a loaf of bread, 38
slicing a layer cake into layers, 38
slicing gooey cakes and cookies, 36
soaking cakes and pastries with sugar syrup, 38
whipping heavy cream, 38
Teiglach or Cicerchiata, 587–588
Thermapen instant-read thermometer, 27, 880
Tomatoes
Arugula and Roasted Tomato Pizza, 888
Chakchouka (Tunisian Vegetable Stew), 865–866
Durum Wheat Bread with Squash, Tomatoes, Onions, and Peppers, 736–737
Kea Stuffed Griddle Bread, 144–145
Oven-Roasted Plum Tomatoes, 888–889
plum, peeling skin from, 884
Sardenaira (Riviera-Style Olive and Anchovy Pizza), 883–884
Spanish Sofrito, 882–883
Torta Rustica, 861–862
Torta Boscaiola (Italian Chestnut Flour and Hazelnut Cake), 319–320
Torta Caprese: Bittersweet Chocolate–Almond Cake, 336–337
Torta di Miele (Italian Jewish Honey Cake), 522–523
Torta di Savoia with Candied Citron, 535–536
Torta di Zabaglione, 480
Torta di Zucca (Squash Cake with Pine Nuts and Apricots), 741–742
Torta Gianduia, 506–508
Torta Pasqualina Genovese, 438–439
Torta Rustica, 861–862
Torta Sbrisolona alla Lombarda (Lombardian Crumbly Cake), 390–391

Tourtière, Québécoise, with Mushrooms, 210–211
Tres Leches Cake, Pilar's, 564
Tube pan, 26
Tuna Empanadas, Spanish, with Sofrito, 881–882
Tunisian Semolina Griddle Bread, 864–865
Turkish Baked Cheese Turnovers, 898–899
Turkish Carrot Pastry Rolls, 241–242
Turkish Goat's Milk Rice Pudding, 774–775
Turkish Hazelnut Macaroons, 504
Turkish Pide Dough, 900
Turkish Ricotta Cookies, 272–273
Turkish Savory Cornbread, 388–389
Turkish Seeded Hazelnut Bread, 502–503
Turkish Semolina Sponge Cookies, 869–870
Turkish Sesame-Coated Bread Rings: Susamli Simit, 798–799
Turnovers
Pastechi (Aruban Stuffed Pastry Turnovers), 760–761
Turkish Baked Cheese Turnovers, 898–899
Turtle Brownies with Caramel and Pecans, 653–654

U

Ukrainian Buckwheat Rolls, 185

V

Vanilla beans, 825–836
Crème Anglaise (English Vanilla Custard Sauce), 835
Crunchy Vanilla Pods, 830
curing process, 828
fold vanillas, about, 828
French Caramel Puff Pastry Fruit Tart, 830–832
general information, 826–827
Italian Meringue Twists and Cake Decorations, 836
July 4th Cheesecake, 833–835
Strawberry-Vanilla Coeur à la Crème Tart with Goat Cheese, 832–833
vanilla beans, buying, 832
vanilla beans, for recipes, 829
vanilla beans, preserving, 830
vanilla bean varieties, 829
Vanilla Caramel Sauce, 822
vanilla extract, for recipes, 21, 829
vanilla extract, labeling of, 828
Veal
'mpanatigghi Siciliano, 331–332
Vegetable Stew, Tunisian (Chakchouka), 865–866
Velia's White Chocolate–Lemon Torta Caprese, 78
Venetian Cornmeal and Cherry Crostata, 305
Venetian Cornmeal Tart Dough, 391–392

W

Wafer paper, about, 233
Walnuts & black walnuts, 837–848
Amish Black Walnut Oatmeal Pie, 575–576
black walnuts, about, 840–841

black walnuts, sold by Hammons, 841
Blueberry-Walnut Streusel Muffins, 164
Brustengolo (Umbrian Cornmeal, Pear, Raisin, and Nut Cake), 389–390
California Walnut Rosemary-Bread, 844–845
Canadian Date-Oatmeal Squares, 576
Canadian Maple–Black Walnut Gingerbread, 491–492
Candied Walnut Apple Pie, 109–110
Candied Walnuts, 847
choosing and storing, 841–842
Cranberry-Walnut Pound Cake, 400–401
Currant-Walnut Baguette, 761–762
general information, 838–840
Gooseberry Cobbler with Walnut Crunch, 410–411
Grape, Gorgonzola, and Walnut Focaccia, 788–789
Greek Eggplant and Walnut Phyllo Rolls, 842–843
Greek Honey-Nut Cookies with Mastic, 518–519
Greek Honey-Walnut Cake with Yogurt, 903–904
Greek Phyllo Pumpkin Pie: Kolokythopita, 739–740
Greek Tahini Cake, 802
Greek Yogurt-Currant Ring Cake, 904–905
Honey–Poppy Seed Hamantaschen, 716–717
Italian Walnut Cake with Candied Fruit, 226–227
Le Bec-Fin's Fruited Walnut Bread, 843–844
Maple Syrup Pie with Walnuts: Tarte au Sirop d'Erable, 555
Persimmon–Black Walnut Bread, 666
Potica (Slovenian Honey-Walnut Ring), 845–847
Sfratti di Pitigliano, 520–522
Siennese Cavalluci, 224–225
Spiced Fuyu Persimmon Bars, 664
Spiced Quince and Walnut Thumbprint Cookies, 750–751
Sweet Fig Focaccia, 455–456
Sweet Walnut Pastry, 848
Torta di Miele (Italian Jewish Honey Cake), 522–523
weight and volume equivalents, 44
Water, chilling mixtures over, 31
Water, filtered or spring, for recipes, 21
Water bath, baking in, 29
Wax paper and parchment, 26
Wheat. See also Flour
general information, 850–852
types of, 853–854
Wheat berries, about, 854
Wheat germ, about, 856
Whisks, 27–28
White Bean, Chestnut, and Apricot Cake alla Povera, 316–217
White chocolate
Blackberry–White Chocolate Tart, 483–484
Indian-Spiced Carrot Cake with White Chocolate–Kewra Icing, 237–239
White Chocolate Pastry Cream, 484
Velia's White Chocolate–Lemon Torta Caprese, 78
White Chocolate, Hazelnut, and Espresso Dacquoise, 377–379
White Chocolate Buttercream, 336
White Peach and Sour Cream Pie, 615–616
White Pizza with Broccoli Rabe, 266–267
White whole wheat flour
about, 856–857
weight and volume equivalents, 41
Whole wheat flour, about, 856
Wire cooling racks, 28
Woodfire Grill Duck Confit Pizza, 859–860
Woodfire Grill Pizza Dough, 858–859

Yeast, 871–892
Arugula and Roasted Tomato Pizza, 888
Black Olive–Herb Bread, 889–890
bread dough, kneading, 879
bread dough, rising, 37, 875, 877–878, 880
buying and storing, 875
Egyptian Flatbread with Dukkah Sprinkle, 890–891
Garlic-Sesame Grissini, 885–885
general information, 872–874
and high-altitude baking, 877
New Haven–Style White Clam Pizza, 886–887
Pan Dushi (Aruban Sweet Bread with Anise), 891–892
proofing, 37, 875, 878–879
salt and, 878–879
Sardenaira (Riviera-Style Olive and Anchovy Pizza), 883–884
Sourdough Bread Starter, 880–881
in sourdough starter, 875
Spanish Tuna Emapanadas with Sofrito, 881–882
sugar and, 879
testing for freshness, 37, 875
types of, 876
weight and volume equivalents, 45
working with, 875–876
Yogurt, 893–905
Feta Cheese and Egg Pide, 900–901
general information, 894–896
goat's and sheep's milk yogurt, 896
Greek Blueberry-Yogurt Tart with Ouzo, 165–166
Greek Honey-Walnut Cake with Yogurt, 903–904
Greek Yogurt-Currant Ring Cake, 904–905
Grilled Indian Naan Bread with Nigella Seeds, 902–903
in sixteenth century France, 896
Tahini and Grape Molasses Pide, 901–902
Turkish Baked Cheese Turnovers, 898–899
Turkish Pide Dough, 900

types of, 897–898
water buffalo yogurt, 896
yogurt-making process, 897
Yufka dough, about, 213

Z

Za'atar spice mixture, about, 798
Zach's Almond Macaroon Cake, 76
Zaleti: Venetian Cornmeal Cookies with Grappa Raisins, 60

NOTES